ABNORMAL, CLINICAL AND FORENSIC PSYCHOLOGY

Visit the Companion Website for *Abnormal, Clinical and Forensic Psychology*, 1st edition, at **www.pearsoned.co.uk/davidholmes** to find valuable **student** learning material including:

- A bank of over 100 videos including interviews with real patients, day-in-the-life documentaries that chart their experiences and news stories exploring the issues and debates that shape the subject

- Multiple choice questions, with feedback, to reinforce your learning

- Flashcards to test your understanding of key terms

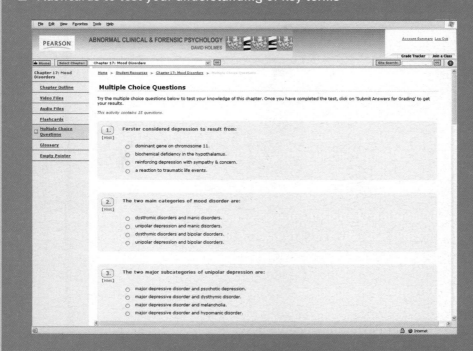

ABNORMAL, CLINICAL AND FORENSIC PSYCHOLOGY

"A very promising and welcome textbook which integrates the related areas of abnormal, clinical, and forensic psychology . . . This book will go a long way in meeting student's needs and yet it has sufficient depth of material to keep the more advanced student engaged. For the course I teach it would be great advantage to have a book that integrates all three areas in one fell swoop. I personally found the textbook sections to be of great interest and demonstrable scholarship. I would certainly use this text as my main text book. I look forward to it being published . . . The material is well written, engaging and has a pronounced contemporary feel to it. The author has adopted a style of writing and reference which will be familiar to British and Irish students – it does not have a North American bias. I believe readers will see this text as being comprehensive, contemporaneous and clinically orientated . . . (Would I consider it as my course text?) Without a doubt – I impatiently await publication of this text! I can see it being the sole text for my course. The material is superior to other textbooks I have reviewed or used. There is an extra depth of material I would consider relevant"

John Bogue, National University of Ireland, Galway

"Well written . . . it gives a broad overview of clinical psychopathology"

Leonore de Wit, Vrije University Amsterdam

"The author goes beyond what is usually covered in this type of textbook and makes a real effort to present the picture of a disorder in the context of the wider society"

Phil Tyson, University of Gloucestershire

"An authoritative description of some mental disorders with links to applied psychology fields. It is both informative and educative . . . I found the material interesting and the case studies very appealing"

Jose Prados, University of Leicester

"Clearly written, interesting and engaging"

Val Tuck, Newcastle University

"Overall I am very impressed with the quality of the writing and the content"

Ronan O'Carroll, University of Stirling

ABNORMAL, CLINICAL AND FORENSIC PSYCHOLOGY

DAVID A. HOLMES

Prentice Hall
is an imprint of

PEARSON

Harlow, England • London • New York • Boston • San Francisco • Toronto
Sydney • Tokyo • Singapore • Hong Kong • Seoul • Taipei • New Delhi
Cape Town • Madrid • Mexico City • Amsterdam • Munich • Paris • Milan

Pearson Education Limited
Edinburgh Gate
Harlow
Essex CM20 2JE
England

and Associated Companies throughout the world

Visit us on the World Wide Web at:
www.pearsoned.co.uk

First published 2010

© Pearson Education Limited 2010

ISBN: 978-0-13-197536-1

British Library Cataloguing-in-Publication Data
A catalogue record for this book is available from the British Library

Library of Congress Cataloging-in-Publication Data
Holmes, David A.
   Abnormal, clinical, and forensic psychology / David Holmes.
      p. cm.
   Includes bibliographical references and index.
   ISBN 978-0-13-197536-1
   1. Psychology, Pathological.   2. Clinical psychology.   3. Forensic psychology.   I. Title.
   RC454.H616 2010
   616.89—dc22

                                                                  2010010266

10 9 8 7 6 5 4 3 2 1
13 12 11 10

Typeset in 9.5/12pt Minion by 35
Printed and bound by Graficas Estella, Navarra, Spain

Brief contents

Contents

Part One Fundamentals of Abnormal, Clinical and Forensic Psychology

Chapter 1 Introduction to abnormal, clinical and forensic psychology 2

Chapter 2 Critical issues in abnormal, clinical and forensic psychology 24

Chapter 3 Paradigm approaches to causes and treatments 42

Chapter 4 The assessment, diagnosis and formulation of clients 102

Chapter 5 Research methods used in clinical and forensic psychology 124

Supporting resources

Visit the Companion Website for *Abnormal, Clinical and Forensic Psychology*, 1st edition, at
www.pearsoned.co.uk/davidholmes to find valuable online resources:

Companion Website for students
- A bank of over 100 videos including interviews with real patients, day-in-the-life documentaries that chart their experiences and news stories exploring the issues and debates that shape the subject
- Multiple choice questions, with feedback, to reinforce your learning
- Flashcards to test your understanding of key terms

For instructors
- An Instructor's Manual including author guidance on using the video material, essay and seminar questions exclusive to the web and outline essay answers
- PowerPoint slides of all figures and self-test questions from the book
- An extensive Testbank of question material
- Access to the extensive video bank

Also: The Companion Website provides the following features:

- Search tool to help locate specific items of content
- E-mail results and profile tools to send results of quizzes to instructors
- Online help and support to assist with website usage and troubleshooting

For more information please contact your local Pearson Education sales representative or visit
www.pearsoned.co.uk/davidholmes

Preface

By inviting me to create this text, my publishers presented an excellent opportunity to reify a vision developed over my years of teaching and researching the areas of abnormal, clinical and forensic psychology as well as my involvement in the practical application of these overlapping domains. Being relatively new disciplines, there are few texts on clinical or forensic psychology that are internationally based, rarely any covering clinical forensic psychology, and I have not found one that encompasses all of these with the full coverage of abnormal psychology. I thus intended *Abnormal, Clinical and Forensic Psychology* to be unique amongst textbooks in psychology. It combines the traditional breadth of coverage found in large abnormal psychology texts with thorough and integrated coverage of both clinical psychology and forensic psychology, as well as the hybrid clinical forensic psychology. As these areas increasingly cross paths, this text should provide students of any one, or all of these areas with both substantial support and critical challenge, extending to both academic and professional contexts.

In representing a more international perspective, this text is more empirically based, critical and evaluative, whilst being accessible and incorporating areas of current interest. Abnormal, clinical and forensic psychology are primarily US disciplines, in that they had their origins in the States, where the largest groups of related professionals are based. In the UK and Europe, forensic and clinical psychology differ from their US counterparts in terms of health, training, legal and penal systems. Thus, this text reflects the differing professional contexts.

Undergraduate students whose courses relate to the areas of abnormal, clinical or forensic psychology should find this text indispensable during each year of their degree. It will support first-year students with a critical coverage of neuropsychology, individual differences and other foundation areas through to higher-degree students taking forensic psychology and clinical psychology doctorates, who will appreciate the extensive critical coverage and integration of their disciplines. Students of other areas will also be surprised at content integrating areas as diverse as health psychology, probation and prison, research, risk assessment, stress management, media psychology, psychiatry, law, health policy, sociology, criminology, social work, crime scene analysis, educational psychology and parapsychology, to mention a few.

Certain topics within the clinical and forensic areas receive disproportionate student interest, such as stalking, eating disorders, offender profiling, Münchausen's syndrome by proxy and autism, and are consequently featured in more detail. Although the book is primarily for students, it is appropriate for police, politicians and any member of the public who wishes full and correct information about areas that are a constant focus for media attention as well as a source of much controversy and misguided opinion.

This full-colour text spanning 19 chapters has colour illustrations, diagrams and a glossary of highlighted novel or salient terms from the text. Each chapter features headed contents, European-based case studies, self-test questions, essay topics, critical evaluation sections, chapter summaries as well as focus, international and research boxes. There is a full reference section for the entire book with key references for further reading for each chapter. The title 'Abnormal, Clinical and Forensic Psychology' was finally arrived at after lengthy discussion amongst all involved. As the first book of its genre, it was felt that the comprehensive breadth of the text was best represented by reference to the long history of Abnormal Psychology texts but also to establish that the Clinical and Forensic aspects were also comprehensively represented and not merely 'bolted on'.

David A. Holmes

About the authors

Dr David A. Holmes

© Sam Furlong.

Senior Lecturer in Psychology at the Department of Psychology and Director of the Forensic Research Group at Manchester Metropolitan University

Dr Holmes began his academic career in 1982 at Manchester Polytechnic, and started lecturing in 1985 at every level from GCSE to MSc in the UK and Hong Kong. He gained his doctorate in 1994 and then specialised in psychopathology, clinical and forensic psychology. Dr Holmes founded the Forensic Research Group as long ago as 1998 at Manchester Metropolitan University. This organisation has grown to international recognition and membership, producing publications, newsletters and annual conferences. He has published many academic books and papers in clinical and forensic areas from autism to stalking, in addition to gracing the pages of the serious and popular press. He has explained complex aspects of psychology in terms that the public can assimilate on hundreds of international television and radio broadcasts.

Dr John Stirling, author of Chapter 18: Schizophrenia

Reader in Psychology at the Department of Psychology, Manchester Metropolitan University, and senior visiting research fellow to the Neurosciences and Psychiatry Unit at the University of Manchester

John Stirling has worked as a lecturer, senior lecturer and reader in psychology at MMU since 1976, having graduated from London University and then from the University of York. This period of work has been interrupted only by a year-long visiting professorship to California State University (Sacramento) in 1992/3 and a research secondment to the University of Manchester from 2002 to 2005. He has also taught short courses in the USA, Belgium, Germany, Holland and Hong Kong. His teaching has encompassed biopsychology, neuropsychology, psychopathology, statistics and research methods. He has published over 30 journal articles and is the author of three books, the most recent of which (*Introducing Neuropsychology*, co-written with Rebecca Elliott) appeared as a fully revised second edition in June 2008.

Dr Emma Barkus, author of Chapter 5: Research Methods used in Clinical and Forensic Psychology

Psychologist and lecturer at the School of Psychology, University of Wollongong, New South Wales, Australia

Emma completed her undergraduate degree and PhD at Manchester Metropolitan University before working at the University of Manchester and the Institute of Psychiatry, London. Her research interests are within the field of risk factors for psychosis, where she makes use of psychological, cognitive and biological measures to determine what leaves people vulnerable to experiencing psychotic symptoms.

Author's acknowledgements

I would like to thank John Stirling and Emma Barkus both for their specialist contributions and for sharing at least some the daunting task of producing this book. Thanks also to Rohan Morris whose hard work on the test materials made the final deadline possible. I thank all those involved at Pearson Publishing for having the faith, determination and professionalism to make this text so much more than just another publication. From Morton Fuglevand's initial proposal through Janey Webb's stoicism to the kind but firm diplomacy of Sarah Busby in getting me over the line, and also the professionals I did not see but learned to appreciate with time. I thank each and every one of my reviewers on the editorial board for helping me to craft this text with their useful and constructive insights.

Texts of this size come at a personal cost, some of which has been shared by those around me. Thanks to all my family and colleagues for tolerating rather one-dimensional conversations. Friends have not only provided moral support, but have given sound advice, encouragement and practical assistance; Al, Andy, Anne, Don, Frances, Gill, Noel, Piers, Pip and Sara have stood the test of time amongst many others who have suffered for their loyalty. A special thanks to Jane Glaister for setting the example that led me to believe I could accomplish this task and whose immortal words 'What else would you be doing?' haunted me during the years of confinement.

The author and publishers would like to thank the editorial board who kindly offered their time, effort and academic expertise which proved an invaluable contribution to the shaping of the first edition:

Christine Mohr, University of Bristol
Tamar Pincus, Royal Holloway, University of London
Joy Mitra, University of Warwick
Val Tuck, Newcastle University
John Bogue, National University of Ireland, Galway
Ingunn Skre, University of Tromsø
Ronan O'Carroll, University of Stirling
Ron Roberts, Kingston University
Sieglinde McGee, Trinity College Dublin
Phil Tyson, University of Gloucestershire
Gavin D. Phillips, University of York
Jose Prados, University of Leicester
Leonore De Wit, Vrije University Amsterdam
John McCartney, London Metropolitan University
Jakob Smári, University of Iceland

Publisher's acknowledgements

We are grateful to the following for permission to reproduce copyright material:

Figures

Figure 3.1a from *Psychology*, Allyn and Bacon (Carlsson, N. R. 1992), reproduced by permission of Pearson Education Ltd, Inc.; Figure 3.1b from *Abnormal Psychology*, 6th edn, John Wiley & Sons, Inc. (Davison, J. and Neale, J. M. 1994), reproduced with permission of John Wiley & Sons, Inc.; Figures 3.2 and 3.3a from *Psychology*, Allyn and Bacon (Carlson, A. 2000), reproduced by permission of Pearson Education Ltd, Inc.; Figure 3.3b from *Psychology*, Allyn and Bacon (Carlsson, A. 1997), reproduced by permission of Pearson Education Ltd, Inc.; Figures 3.4 and 10.1 from *Psychology*, Allyn and Bacon (Carlsson, A. 1992), reproduced by permission of Pearson Education Ltd, Inc.; Figure 18.4 from *The Schizophrenic Disorders: Long-term patient and family studies*, Yale University Press (Bleuler, M. 1972/1978); Figure 18.9 from 'A PET study of voluntary movement in schizophrenic patients experiencing passivity phenomena (delusions of alien control)', *Brain*, 120, 1997–2011 (Spence, S. A., Brooks, D. J., Hirsch, S. R., Liddle, P. F., Meehan, J. and Grasby, P. M. 1997), by permission of Oxford University Press.

Table

Table 16.1 from 'The Social Readjustment Rating Scale', *Journal of Psychosomatic Research*, 11(2), 213–18 (Holmes, T. H. and Rahe, R. H. 1967), Elsevier.

Photographs

(Key: b-bottom; c-centre; l-left; r-right; t-top)

Alamy Images: Photos 12 p. 398, Stock Connection Distribution p. 206, Julie Woodhouse p. 346; Archives of the History of American Psychology/The University of Akron: University of Akron p. 80; Corbis: Dominique Aubert/ Sygma p. 421, Lester V. Bergman p. 483, Bettmann pp. 78 and 392, Rune Hellestad p. 500, Karen Kasmauski p. 517, John Lund/Sam Diephuis/Blend Images p. 179, Matthew Polak/Sygma p. 410, Reuters p. 526, Jeffery Allan Salter p. 24, Mo-Spector/Kipa p. 270; Getty Images: pp. 12, 32 and 42, FilmMagic p. 364, Chris Gleave/AFP p. 443, Time & Life Pictures pp. 259 and 383, Wireimage p. 453; David Holmes: 29, 94, 143, 145, 186, 330, 336, 380, Brandi Grooms Photography 396, Roger Moody 476; Pearson Education Ltd: 7, 26, 33, 44, 68, 71, 76, 88, 103, 193, 194, 288, 289, 291, 296, 298, 301, 302, 312, 313, 316, 321, 322, 325, 327, 328, 332, 340, 350, 356, 359, 361, 362, 368, 370, 374, 424, 479, 486, 487, 510, 519, 520, 572, 580, 585; The University of Pennsylvania: 513; Press Association Images: David Duprey 112, Gerald Herbert 587, Courtesy of the Merseyside Police 426; Science & Society Picture Library: Science Museum 9; Science Photo Library Ltd: 582; John Sterling: 547, 548t, 548b, 549, 550; tbc: tr/8.1, bl/8.1, br/8.1, /10.1; Telegraph Media Group: tl/8.1.

In some instances we have been unable to trace the owners of copyright material, and we would appreciate any information that would enable us to do so.

Guided tour

Each chapter opens with a list of topics covered, an overview and a **vignette** offering a topical and thought-provoking discussion of current issues. It tackles debates such as how genes dictate our behaviour, whether there's a link between mood disorder and creative success, and the portrayal of disordered individuals in the media.

Case studies also start each chapter and appear throughout the book, bringing the concepts to life through personal experience and providing an intimate portrait of living with a disorder. Some also explore provocative issues such as the tension between science and belief.

International Perspective puts the spotlight on cross-cultural issues and perspectives such as cultural relativism and how psychological disorder in one society may be traditional behaviour in another.

The **Focus** feature highlights the most interesting debates and examples in more depth, from nature vs. nurture and the mad *or* bad debate, to obesity as food addiction.

Guided tour (continued)

In *The Blind Watchmaker* (Dawkins, 1986) critically addresses a second layer of creationist argument, **intelligent design theory** (see Scott, 1997). 'Intelligent design' explains complex information by acts of intelligence and, in the case of life, a Divine being, rather than by evolution. For Dawkins (1986) this argument is countered by the errors of evolution during natural selection.

Such arguments are irresolvable when belief can be its own evidence and can be backed by force, as in the power struggle between science and the Church in the Middle Ages. The scientific argument for evolution is not proof of all aspects of **evolutionary theory**, but is certain proof that creationist 'theory' is wrong. The fact that counter-arguments survive this and gain legal backing does provide some support for James Randi's fears of an imminent intellectual dark age.

Belief confounding education, politics and law exists on the fundamentalist fringe of some established religions. The punishment for apostasy or unrepentantly leaving ('turning their back on') the Islamic faith is death, as it is for 'moral' crimes such as adultery or even being in the company of an unrelated man, which are not recognised as criminal acts elsewhere. These executions along with amputations for theft are considered to be religious occasions and, until mobile phone technology, were rarely witnessed by the non-initiated. It is also worth considering the extreme suffering inflicted by belief in an afterlife enabling **suicide bombers**. The escalating place of belief across the globe coincides with and relates to abnormal, clinical and forensic psychology being vulnerable to losing their way as sciences, which is examined further in the next section.

Research

Lunar effects – belief or science?

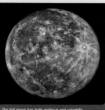

The full moon has both mythical and scientific effects on people.
Source: Pearson Online Database.

The term 'lunatic' comes from the Latin *luna*, pertaining to the moon and its apparent cycles or phases. Luna, the Roman goddess of the moon, perhaps represents an association between the moon and feminine issues.

The association between the moon and behaviour mixes historical mythical belief with some known empirical effects of the moon. One of the most learned societies of the 1700s was the Lunar Society founded in 1766. On this basis, members were referred to as lunatics, the derogatory implications worsened by considering the effects of the medicinal herb **Digitalis** (Foxglove). However, the name resulted from these empirical scientists meeting around the time of the full moon for safety, as extra light assisted their journeys on poor roads with highwaymen.

The lunar beliefs

Mystical properties have been attributed to the full moon. In Bedlam, inmates were chained, tied up and flogged at the full moon to prevent anticipated aggression and violence (McG. Kelley, 1942). A widespread perceived association existed between mental derangement, crime and violence, with supernatural forces invoked by the moon's luminescence still prevalent today, especially amongst mental health workers (Wilson and Tobacyk, 1990). In 1843, the *Lancet* reported a popular belief at the time that the moon was responsible for episodes of epilepsy and insanity (White, 1914). Implications of this belief include psychiatric administrators employing more staff during a full moon in anticipation of increased workload, creating superstition-based resource implications.

The **Research** feature explores how psychological studies have shaped psychopathology; for example Fischer's twin studies on the genetic underpinnings of schizophrenia.

Short self-test questions at the end of each section test your factual knowledge and understanding and **suggested essay questions** at the end of each chapter encourage more nuanced and critical discussion of the issues.

These distinctions and areas of overlap between the disorders within this chapter, as well as the similarities and differences between these and disorders from other chapters, have implications for clinical treatment. This is especially the case where they co-occur in the same individual, in that each disorder needs to be addressed and assessed independently. Thus, although these differing classifications share some interventions and there is an overall similarity in appropriate treatment types, there are clear variations in outcome from these interventions and a general worsening of pathology as well as a poor prognosis in individuals who are comorbid (e.g. Fernandez-Aranda et al., 2006).

It may be assumed that other C–I disorders will soon be on the clinical horizon as well as C–I shopping; that is, C–I skin picking, C–I sexual behaviours and C–I internet usage. However, these proposed disorders have been recognised and researched for a number of years already. For example, Young (1996) modified the criteria for pathological gambling in order to produce a diagnostic questionnaire for internet addiction. Even in the early days of Internet use, this revealed substantial differences in internet usage in those identified as Internet addicted and a very short period of use being required to form this addiction or dependency. More recent studies have confirmed that the number of individuals remains a significant proportion of a much larger user-base but most published research still refers to internet addiction as a 'new disorder' (e.g. Murali and George, 2007).

Self-test questions

- What are the possible evolutionary origins of compulsive buying?
- How does obsessive–compulsive disorder relate to compulsive hoarding?
- In what ways does culture influence levels of compulsive buying?
- What is the Diogenes syndrome and how does it relate to hoarding?
- What are the treatment options for compulsive buying and hoarding?
- What are the compulsive–impulsive disorders proposed for *DSM-V*?

Chapter summary

Disorders covered in this chapter involve the loss of control over eating behaviour or an impulse to carry out an action that is dysfunctional in itself or in its consequences. The eating disorders **anorexia** and **bulimia nervosa** involve the overcontrol of body weight by diet, exercise and purging, which reduces body mass dangerously in anorexia and is maintained in bulimia. Other eating conditions such as **binge eating disorder** and **obesity** are increasingly recognised as having psychological components and, in the latter case, as posing a serious risk to the health of a substantial proportion of the world's population. **Body image dissatisfaction** is common in most of the eating conditions and can be a factor fuelled by celebrity-driven culture in increasing eating disorder levels in developed countries.

Impulse control disorders share features such as arousal prior to a relieving and pleasure-giving act, such as anger displays in **intermittent explosive disorder**, **pathological gambling**, fire setting in **pyromania**, hair pulling in **trichotillomania**, and shoplifting in **kleptomania**. Many of these acts are also criminal activities and individuals with these disorders may need to receive treatment within the criminal justice system. **Compulsive buying** will probably appear in *DSM-V* as **C–I shopping**, and the disorder is only slowly being recognised as a distressing and destructive disorder with an alarmingly high prevalence. Along with **compulsive hoarding**, this behaviour is also extensive and problematic at subclinical levels in market economy countries. There are forensic issues involving corporate responsibility for some control-based disorders, particularly obesity.

Suggested essay titles

- Discuss the distinctions between the eating disorders anorexia and bulimia nervosa.
- Evaluate the implications of compulsive buying and hoarding for the individual.
- Discuss the forensic implications of compulsive gambling and pyromania.

Visit **www.pearsoned.co.ul/holmes** for access to over 100 **videos** including one-to-one interviews with real disorder sufferers, "day in the life" documentaries that capture the challenges they face, and news stories that explore the relevant issues and debates that shape the subject.

Multiple choice questions and **a flashcard glossary** for each chapter offer a quick solution to revision.

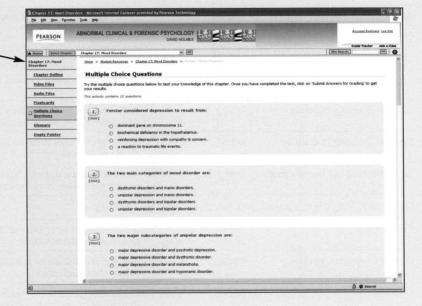

Lecturer's resources

- An **instructor's manual** with author guidance on each chapter, essay questions and seminar questions exclusive to the manual, sample essay outlines and guidance on using the video content
- A **test bank** of over 400 multiple choice questions
- **PowerPoint** slides of every illustration and diagram in the text
- Access to a **bank of over 100 videos** of clinical interviews with patients, day-in-the-life documentaries and news stories exploring the relevant issues

Video matrix

Video Title	Length in minutes	Brief description
Chapter 1: Introduction to Abnormal, Clinical and Forensic Psychology		
Asylum	03:30	A history of mental institutions in America
Historical explanations	01:40	Historical explanations of abnormal behaviour and mental illness
Gun control	04:48	Exploring the controversial stance in the US regarding gun control
Trends in treatment	02:14	Sue Mineka gives a short overview of recent trends in treatment
How much do you know about Psychology?	03:53	College students are quizzed on their general knowledge in psychology
Chapter 2: Critical Issues in Abnormal, Clinical and Forensic Psychology		
Going 'crazy'	02:08	Exploration of myths and misconceptions about mental disorders
Carlos	04:17	False belief detective, James Randi, and friend, Jose, create spiritualist character Carlos to see who they can fool
Cold Reading	03:35	An examination of mediums claiming to communicate with deceased relatives including popular heaven medium James Van Praagh
Magical Thinking in adults	02:52	ABC explores how adults are prone to superstitious and unsupported beliefs or 'magical thinking'
Magical Thinking in children	02:47	ABC explores how children are prone to suggested fictional beliefs or 'magical thinking'
'Straightening out homosexuals'	04:57	ABC explore the dubious 'treatments' for being gay proposed by ex-gay groups such as Exodus
Chapter 3: Paradigm approaches to causes and treatments		
B. F. Skinner	02:56	A biography of B. F. Skinner, the 20th century's leading proponent of behaviour modification
Current Diagnostic models	03:06	Sue Mineka discusses paradigm approaches to treatment and the biopsychosocial model
Junk DNA	01:30	The human genome project is revealing that DNA previously thought to be inconsequential or 'Junk DNA' may be very important in the common needs of many creatures
C. J. Jung	01:18	C. J. Jung answers questions about the unconscious
Synaptic transmission	00:43	Animation and explanation of Synaptic Transmission
Studying Squid	01:47	How the giant neurones of the squid are used for research into the human nervous system and may provide clues to disorders such as Alzheimer's and Parkinson's
Brain pain	01:42	Exploring the benefits of virtual reality games used to distract burns victims from the pain of therapy
Humour and brains	01:37	Exploring the neurophysiology of humour as treatment
How the human genome map affects you	01:21	A geneticist discusses how the human genome map will eventually provide personalised medical treatments

Video Title	Length in minutes	Brief description
Chapter 4: The assessment, diagnosis and formulation of clients		
Cultural Influence on intelligence	02:31	Robert Sternberg discusses the influence of culture on measures of intelligence
Are intelligence tests valid?	01:50	Robert Guthrie discusses come of the many questions surrounding the validity of tests of intelligence
Cultural limitations on psychometric testing	04:46	Robert Guthrie discusses the cultural limitations of psychometric tests
Inside a Cognitive Neuroscience laboratory	04:40	Dr Handy demonstrates the inside workings of his cognitive neuroscience laboratory which uses fMRI and ERP technologies
Chapter 5: Research methods used in clinical and forensic psychology		
Why we use research	04:57	A discussion of why we use research
Fear of public speaking	02:01	Explores the fear of public speaking, one of the most common fears, utilised for research into anxiety
Twin studies	01:02	Looking at twin studies, exploring the effects of environment and genetic cognitive skills on ability, or nature vs. nurture
Twins separated at birth	05:52	Following the story of twins, separated at birth and reunited in adulthood, who provide the opportunity for research into their similarities and differences
MKM and brain scans	03:08	How brain scans using the MKM system can provide more precise neuro-imaging required for neurosurgery and insight into migraines
Naturalist observation techniques	01:07	Explores Naturalistic Observation, the method of observing behaviour in its natural context
Research methods in sexuality	00:47	Michael Bailey discusses ethics and prejudice in research funding and the difficulty in getting support for more controversial studies on sexuality
Unethical studies from history	02:59	Robert Guthrie discusses historical cases of unethical studies
Chapter 6: Clinical Psychology		
Medicating Children	01:33	A discussion of the issue of Ritalin use for ADHD
Skinner and the pigeons	00:35	Classic footage of Skinner's study of behaviour modification – teaching pigeons to play 'table tennis'
Clinical Approaches	01:35	A brief historical overview of clinical approaches
The effect of touch	01:03	The powerful effects of touch
How emotion boosts memory	01:40	Research which shows how emotion affects recall, which is useful for clinicians dealing with emotionally charged experiences
Chapter 7: Forensic psychology		
Attempting the Milgram obedience study	09:43	A replication of the Milgram study giving the subjects the option of not proceeding
The original Milgram study	02:28	Original footage of the Stanley Milgram study of obedience
Reflecting on the Stanford prison experiment	05:18	Philip Zimbardo discusses the classic prison scenario that he created to study the influence of nature and nurture on behaviour
The original Stanford prison	08:10	Footage of the original Stanford Prison Experiment experiment
Detecting lies	01:27	Explanation of how thermal imaging technology can detect lying
Artificial intelligence	02:07	A company attempting to develop artificial intelligence in a computer, HAL, based on the approaches suggested by Alan Turing
Moral Dilemma test	02:07	The Heinz dilemma test of moral development is illustrated with four children giving their opinions

Video Title	Length in minutes	Brief description
Chapter 8: Clinical forensic psychology		
Child sexual abuse	06:22	The effects of sexual abuse in childhood reported by a victim
Television violence	03:59	Discussing the pathology of learning violence
Bandura's Bobo doll experiment	01:49	A demonstration of Bandura's Bobo doll experiment, the classic study of violence
Temperament uninhibited		Early uninhibited behaviour
Sexual coercion: Coya: Rape crisis coordinator	02:15	Coya, rape crisis counsellor, discusses the psychological effects of rape
Commercial sex: Silvia, transsexual escort	02:19	Silvia reflects on her success and popularity as a transsexual escort
Chapter 9: Disorders usually first diagnosed in infancy and childhood		
Asperger's Syndrome, interview with David	08:38	A clinical interview with David, who suffers from Asperger's, and his parents – Susan and Howard
Asperger's Syndrome, 'a day in the life' with David	08:36	A 'day in the life' documentary following David who suffers from Asperger's Syndrome
Theory of mind	01:15	Children of different ages take part in tasks to demonstrate their theory of mind and the ability deficient in Autism
Autism, interview with Xavier	03:13	An interview with Xavier and his mother who talks about how she discovered his autism, his behaviour and the impact it has on his functioning
ADHD, interview with Jimmy	03:34	An interview with Jimmy and his mother who discuss his ADHD and the effect it has had on him and his family
Dr Raun Melmed on ADHD	01:23	Developmental paediatrician, Dr Raun Melmed, discusses the subtypes of ADHD
Dr Kathy Pratt on Autism	03:37	Dr Kathy Pratt discusses the causes of Autism
Chapter 10: Disorders of control and addiction part I: Eating and impulse control disorders		
Impulse Control Disorder, interview with Ed	08:56	An interview with Ed, pathological gambler, who suffers with this impulse control disorder
Impulse Control Disorder, 'a day in the life' with Ed	08:29	A 'day in the life' documentary following Ed who has an impulse control disorder
Eating disorders	01:20	An exploration of the causes and symptoms of eating disorders
Anorexia Nervosa, interview with Natasha	09:45	An interview with Natasha, who suffers from Anorexia Nervosa
Anorexia Nervosa, 'a day in the life' with Natasha	06:48	A 'day in the life' documentary following Natasha who suffers from Anorexia Nervosa
Anorexia Nervosa, interview with Jessica	13:55 and 15:32	A two part interview with Jessica who suffers from Anorexia Nervosa (binge-eating and purging type)
Addiction to video games	02:41	Study of addictive behaviour and video games – one that may feature in future classification systems
Your brain on food	01:41	Exploring the neurochemistry of overeating and how food can become a 'drug'

Video Title	Length in minutes	Brief description
Chapter 11: Disorders of control and addiction part II: Substance-related disorders		
Alcoholism, interview with Chris	23:53	An interview with Chris who discusses how his alcoholism progressed and the impact it has had
Alcoholism	01:22	Exploring predicting factors for alcoholism
Alcohol withdrawal	01:44	How the brain's adaptation to alcohol creates anxiety problems
Drug addiction and the Law	02:06	A discussion of the issue of legality in drug use and its impact on drug addiction
Substance Abuse, interview with Kathy	01:58	An interview with Kathy who explains how her problems with substance abuse developed through her life
Substance abuse: Therapist Louise Roberts	04:40	Therapist and ex-drug user, Louise Roberts, talks about how her substance disorder evolved
Teen drinking		Health effects on young drinkers
Cocaine	01:06	Explaining the effects of cocaine
Teen alcoholism	01:07	A study that explores the characteristics predicting teen drinkers and perhaps even alcoholism
Is the Sun a drug?	01:33	Research into how people can become addicted to UV light and sun beds
Chapter 12: Anxiety disorders		
PTSD, interview with Bonnie	09:25	An interview with Bonnie who has suffered with Post Traumatic Stress Disorder since her experience of 9/11
PTSD, 'a day in the life' with Bonnie	07:25	A 'day in the life' documentary following Bonnie, who suffers from Post Traumatic Stress Disorder
Panic Disorder	01:33	Talking to artist Judy Niosi about living with panic disorder and its causes
Phobias	01:32	Talking to Ken about his experience of agoraphobia and its treatment
Social Anxiety Disorder, interview with Steve	10:41	An interview with Steve who discusses his social phobia and how it impacts on his life
Obsessive Compulsive Disorder, interview with Dave	10:12	An interview with Dave who discusses the positive and negative effects of living with Obsessive Compulsive Disorder
Obsessive compulsive disorder, interview with Margo	01:41	An interview with Margo who suffers from Obsessive Compulsive Disorder
PTSD and 9/11	01:44	Examples of sufferers from the 9/11 incident
PTSD, interview with Sara	16:39	An interview with Sara who discusses her Post Traumatic Stress Disorder which developed from an abusive relationship
Panic Disorder, interview with Larry	00:54	The account of a 58 year old sufferer's experiences of panic attacks
Panic disorder, interview with Donald	02:04	Interview with Donald, a panic disorder sufferer

Video Title	Length in minutes	Brief description
Chapter 13: Sexual disorders		
Atypical Sexual Behaviour: Dominatrix Jade	02:00	Jade, a Dominatrix, discusses what her role entails and how it can provide 'therapy' for her clients
Sexual Dysfunctions; Dr Stephenie Kielb	01:39	Urologist, Dr Stephenie Kielb, discusses sexual dysfunction in men
Sex & sexual dysfunction	01:12	The effects of sexual dysfunction on men and their ability to seek help
Paedophilia		
Paedophilia, interview	01:49	An interview with an anonymous paedophile
Gender Identity Disorder: Denise	05:33	Denise speaks about coming to terms with Gender Identity Denise Disorder
Cognitive behavioural therapy	01:43	How Cognitive Behavioural Therapy can be used for drug-resistant Schizophrenia
Chapter 14: Personality disorders		
Borderline Personality Disorder, interview with Liz	18:04	An interview with Liz who discusses living with Borderline Personality Disorder
Borderline personality disorder, interview with Janna	02:05	Interview with Janna about living with bipolar disorder
Chapter 15: Somatoform, dissociative and factitious disorders		
Hypochondriasis, interview with Henry	16:36	An interview with Henry who suffers from Hypochondriasis
Dissociative Identity Disorder: Dr. Holiday Milby	07:16	Psychologist Dr. Holiday Milby describes the signs and symptoms of Dissociative Identity Disorder
Dissociative Identity Disorder: The Three faces of Eve	04:39	Classic footage of Dr Thigpen interviewing the 'original' patient suffering from Dissociative Identity Disorder in her three states; Eve White, Eve Black and Jane
Chronic Fatigue Syndrome, interview with Elizabeth	02:02	An interview with Elizabeth who explains what it is like living with Chronic Fatigue Syndrome
Chapter 16: Psychophysiological disorders		
Adjustment Disorders, interview with Julia	18:49	An interview with Julia who discusses her life before and after contracting HIV and problems with adjustment
Rude atmosphere in the workplace	02:35	The effect of stress from encounters in the workplace
Optimism and resilience	01:51	Exploring how an optimistic outlook can lead to survival of life events
Applying Positive Psychology	01:30	Martin Seligman and other authors introduce positive psychology
Stress and Wellness	00:55	A discussion of the concept of prevention in health psychology
Socialising and stress	01:33	A study of worms outlines genetic reasons for eating when stressed

Video Title	Length in minutes	Brief description
Chapter 17: Mood disorders		
Bipolar Disorder, interview with Feliziano	08:39	An interview with Feliziano who discusses living with Bipolar Disorder
Bipolar Disorder, 'a day in the life' with Feliziano	06:37	A 'day in the life' documentary following Feliziano, who suffers from Bipolar Disorder
Major Depression, interview with Everett	23:36	An interview with Everett who discusses living with Depression since childhood
Depression and self-harm, interview with Sarah	15:37	An interview with Sarah who discusses her early onset depression and deliberate self-harm
Explaining Bipolar Disorder	02:38	Looking at the symptoms of and treatments for bipolar disorder
Bipolar Mood Disorder with psychotic features, interview with Anne	16:44	An interview with Anne who discusses her Bipolar Disorder with psychotic features and its affect on her life
Amish community studies	01:36	Genetic studies of mood in isolated Amish communities
Chapter 18: Schizophrenia		
Schizophrenia, interview with Larry	16:54	An interview with Larry who discusses living with paranoid Schizophrenia and its impact on his functioning
Cognitive Behavioural Therapy	01:43	A discussion of how CBT can help sufferers interpret their symptoms realistically
Schizophrenia, interview with Georgina	03:04	An interview with Georgina, who suffers from Schizophrenia, about the early stages of the disorder
Schizophrenia, interview with Rodney	02:13	An interview with Rodney about the development of his Schizophrenia
Genetic schizophrenia	01:37	Studies that are isolating genes that produce schizophrenic symptoms
Schizoaffective disorder, interview with Josh	20:23	An interview with Josh, who suffers from the hybrid Schizoaffective disorder, describing his symptoms
Chapter 19: Neurological and age-related disorders		
Dementia, interview with Alvin Paige	11:10	An interview with Alvin Paige, writer and sculptor, who talks about living with Alzheimer's disease
Dementia, 'a day in the life' with Alvin Paige	07:55	A 'day in the life' documentary with Alvin Paige who suffers from Alzheimer's disease
What happens with Alzheimers?	02:16	Explanation of a biological diagnosis of Alzheimer's disease
Alzheimers and Dementia	01:48	An overview of Alzheimer's disease
Alzheimer's disease: the case of Wilburn	04:36	The family of Wilburn Johnson discuss the real life problems of coping with Alzheimer's disease
Aging Well: A longitudinal study	04:25	Discussing some of the factors contributing to health in old age
Genetic time clock	01:46	Scientists explore the effect of the gene Sir2 gene on ageing and lifespan
Centenarian	02:57	A centenarian discusses her experience of being 102 years old
Death and dying	00:37	Discussing the practical reality of death

List of figures

List of photographs

List of tables

FUNDAMENTALS OF ABNORMAL, CLINICAL AND FORENSIC PSYCHOLOGY

The areas of abnormal, clinical and forensic psychology encompass the most popular aspects of psychology for undergraduate students and lead to the premier career choices for psychology graduates. However, this interest in the subject does not apply only to students of psychology: the most consistently successful film genre at the box office and the most popular TV series (e.g. *CSI*) are also drawn directly from this area. Within these pages are the theories, findings and basic facts that have frequently propelled psychologists on to the pages of popular magazines, into headline news stories and on to almost every reality TV show. It is also the foundation for real world professional psychologists at the front line helping those suffering psychological distress and assessing those committing the most heinous of crimes.

This section contains the basic background and generic principles of abnormal psychology as applied to clinical and forensic contexts. The first chapter defines the terminology and historical background to abnormal behaviour, making explicit both the essence of its constitution and its disciplinary context. This is followed in Chapter 2 by a critical discussion of the continuing need for an empirical scientific approach when dealing with the mental health of real people and how this has to be differentiated from more philosophical approaches that promote academic debate and ethical insights, but have less direct value to the behaviourally disordered. The paradigms in Chapter 3 reflect the current status of differing conceptual approaches within abnormal, clinical and forensic psychology, and are structured with some reference to the debates on empiricism in Chapter 2. Causes and treatment approaches for abnormal behaviour are covered within the framework of each paradigm. Chapter 4 examines the assessment and diagnostic process and Chapter 5 provides a critical overview of research methods and analyses pertinent to clinical and forensic areas.

Chapters in this section

1 Introduction to abnormal, clinical and forensic psychology

Discover historical explanations of mental disorder. This is one of several videos that explore issues and disorders relevant to this chapter at **www.pearsoned.co.uk/davidholmes**

2 Critical issues in abnormal, clinical and forensic psychology

Hear about the myths surrounding mental illness. This is one of several videos that explore issues and disorders relevant to this chapter at **www.pearsoned.co.uk/davidholmes**

3 Paradigm approaches to causes and treatments

Discover the concept of humour as treatment. This is one of several videos that explore issues and disorders relevant to this chapter at **www.pearsoned.co.uk/davidholmes**

4 The assessment, diagnosis and formulation of clients

See the inside workings of a cognitive neuroscience laboratory. This is one of several videos that explore issues and discorders relevant to this chapter at **www.pearsoned.co.uk/davidholmes**

5 Research methods used in clinical and forensic psychology

Hear about unethical studies from history. This is one of several videos that explore issues and disorders relevant to this chapter at **www.pearsoned.co.uk/davidholmes**

CHAPTER 1 Introduction to abnormal, clinical and forensic psychology

 Discover historical explanations of mental disorder. This is one of several videos that explore issues and disorders relevant to this chapter at **www.pearsoned.co.uk/davidholmes**.

Organised approaches to abnormal behaviour

The dramatic approach portrayed by the US FBI-style profilers tends to translate into more mundane but realistic paperwork in the hands of UK profilers who are usually psychologists.
Source: David A. Holmes.

Popular crime films and novels such as *Silence of the Lambs* (Demme, 1991) often feature the **Behavioural Science Unit** (now changed to **Investigative Support Unit**) at Quantico in the USA. Founded by the **Federal Bureau of Investigation (FBI)**, this unit was the first to offer objective training in the psychological detection and 'profiling' of serious crimes and criminals.

In Europe, **Professor David Canter** established the **Centre for Investigative Psychology** in 1994 at the University of Liverpool both to teach and to research specialist aspects of psychological investigation. Former pupils of the present author were trained at this centre and subsequently joined the UK version of the FBI, the **National Crime Squad**, before the establishment of the **Serious Organised Crime Agency** in 2004. This chapter will examine the accelerating progress in organised approaches to addressing abnormal behaviour in clinical and forensic areas during the twentieth century as well as their origins further back in history.

As an introductory chapter, this chapter will define terms used in abnormal, clinical and forensic psychology, and introduce the role of concepts such as normatology in delineating that which is abnormal. Origins of the debates and distinctions in these areas of psychology can be seen in their history from ancient times into the last century as well as witnessing vast change in therapeutic effectiveness. Within this, empirical science emerged in both clinical and forensic areas in the midst of less helpful beliefs and misguided thinking (see Shorter, 1997). Contemporary issues in this area still reflect some of the problems of the past and in particular the credibility of psychology as a science. There are a number of professions awaiting students of abnormal, clinical and forensic psychology, which are described in the final section of this chapter along with professions allied to the area.

Case study

Marten from the woods

Estonia, 1620. Marten had little to do with other adolescents. He was a loner and would spend much of his time walking at the edge of the wood at night or curled asleep by the fire. Mostly shunned by other children as he grew up because of his pale, hairy, ulcerated skin, he was still without friends as an adult. During the hours of darkness, he rubbed his dry eyes and set out to hunt with a hound he had befriended from the local village. As Marten grew older, some of the land workers would chase him from their fields nicknaming him 'the beast' and occasionally throwing stones at him. He would not retaliate; only stare at them with his hollow eyes.

In the following year a young girl vanished from her home and was found dead in the woods a week later. She had been assaulted and left for dead by her uncle, an innocent-looking herdsman, who often took children to help with his work. The local justice's men thought the girl's death to be of little consequence, but the villagers began to gossip about Marten despite his being far from the girl's home. Late that evening a hunting party sent to the woods found the youth hunting by moonlight. They killed his hound and struck him to the ground, calling him a beast and a werewolf. Marten was beaten to death, his skull smashed, and his heart staked and cut from his body to prevent his return from the dead.

Superstitious fear is quick to fill the gaps in our knowledge and in earlier centuries fear of devils and demons led to individuals with an odd appearance or behaviour being persecuted for the ills of the community. They were also blamed for the crimes of others, who were more innocent looking (and in this case a relative), as serial killing or paedophilic crimes were assumed to be the province of beasts. Primitive thinking believed that men could transform into animals (**zoomorphism**) and in Europe the belief in lycanthropy, where a man would turn into a wolf (werewolf), was rife. Individuals such as Marten, suffering from porphyria (which gave him his pale, ulcerated skin and dry, hollow eyes), or those with animal-like deformities were vulnerable to accusation and were tried and killed in a ritualistic manner. **Clinical lycanthropy** is the delusional belief that one is or can become a werewolf or other animal, and is thus distinct from the case of Marten (see Fahy, 1989).

Definitions and terminology

The terminology of abnormal psychology can be described from a myriad of perspectives, changing contexts and usage over many volumes, but only the more pertinent arguments will be dealt with here. Hopefully, this text will strike a balance between purely academic material and content that both has practical value in the effective relief of suffering for the client as end user and also improves the efficacy of professionals in abnormal, clinical and forensic psychology.

Abnormal, clinical and forensic psychology

The very broad discipline of abnormal psychology is the study of abnormal behaviour, thinking and feeling, and the relevant biological processes that predict and parallel them. These maladaptive processes may be labelled broadly as mental illness or criminal behaviour, the latter being largely ignored by almost all current abnormal psychology texts. The high levels of mental illness found in prison populations serve to illustrate a degree of overlap between these labelled behaviours. Within the scope of abnormal, clinical and forensic psychology there are major areas of more specialist focus, which are defined below.

- Clinical psychology can be interpreted literally as 'bedside psychology' (from the Greek *klinik*). It is the applied approach to studying abnormal behaviour from a psychological perspective and uses psychological techniques to change or moderate such behaviour in affected individuals, adopting the scientist-practitioner role.

- Criminology is the theoretical approach to crime and its management. Causes of criminal behaviour, the penal and justice systems of particular countries and more sociological explanations of deviant behaviour are critically analysed in this discipline.

- Forensic psychology, a term derived from the Greek *forensis* or forum, refers to the use of psychology and psychologists in the criminal courts. This definition has broadened considerably as many forensic psychologists now work in prisons and with police Behavioural Units. For Gudjonsson and Haward (1998) this area of psychology must involve the consideration of individual cases.

- Clinical forensic psychology sits at the interface between the law and clinical psychology, involving the assessment and treatment of individuals with forensic involvement. A more narrow definition would be the collection, examination and presentation of clinical evidence for judicial purposes. There is an increasing need in many countries for professionals qualified in both clinical and forensic psychology, though as yet a combined qualification is not widely available.

Focus

Further related disciplines in abnormal, clinical and forensic psychology

In addition to the main disciplines in these areas, other specialist subdisciplines are commonly involved. The most salient of these in terms of current thinking and professional expertise are as follows.

Educational psychology: assessment and management of children within and surrounding the school or other learning context.

Neuropsychology: the relationship between neuroanatomy and neurochemistry (including endocrinology), and behaviour, thinking and feeling.

Evolutionary psychology: the study of how adaptive (and maladaptive) behaviour, thinking and feeling have evolved through natural selection.

Occupational psychology and stress management: how abnormal behaviour affects, and is affected by, working and the workplace, with emphasis on occupational stress.

Parapsychology: how and why individuals and groups come to believe in entities, concepts and experiences beyond those of common experience and empirical evidence.

Probation: the area of prevention and rehabilitation whereby probation officers supervise the efforts of offenders towards self-improvement and away from criminal activity.

Counselling: problem-focused guidance and support, usually for normal clients with problems of living (a non-clinical intervention, unless given by a clinical professional or counselling psychologist rather than a counsellor).

Professions less directly associated but commonly in contact with psychologists include nurses as well as police and prison officers.

- **Psychiatry** is the medical approach to abnormal behaviour. In this approach, psychological deviance is more often viewed in biomedical terms with consequently biological explanations and medical interventions (it is in this respect that psychiatry differs from clinical psychology).

- **Psychopathology** is the scientific study of abnormal behaviour (Stirling and Hellewell, 1999), with the aim of understanding the nature and origins of this behaviour. Psychopathology tends to lie at the interface of medical and psychological science.

Definitions of abnormal behaviour

Throughout evolution, abnormal or deviant individuals have been driven from the various groups of humans and other creatures. Such ostracism would isolate the individual and prevent them from breeding with the group, and may even have resulted in physical attack or death. This crude defence is a double-edged process in excluding overtly abnormal genetic and environmental influences from the group as well as rejecting the affected individuals themselves. Humanity is not alone among the species in having limits to its accepted 'normality', but is alone in trying to define and justify it.

The study of abnormal behaviour is vital to our understanding of the detail of normal functioning, as when mechanisms break down their functions are often revealed. If this divide between abnormality and normality is so central to the development of psychological science, then a definition of these terms is an essential requirement. Views of abnormality are further confounded by philosophical arguments regarding the differing perspectives of individuals using variant or even contradictory criteria for normality. Offer and Sabshin (1991) present a detailed examination of **normatology**, the study of normality, and have outlined some of the difficulties of defining normality and abnormality.

Various approaches to such a definition have been proposed and all have their limitations, as in the following examples (for more detail, see Offer and Sabshin, 1991).

- **The statistical model** assumes the average to be normal and deviations from the average to be progressively more abnormal (Offer and Sabshin, 1991). Although this makes logical sense, it is not practical in terms of abnormal psychology. Being schizophrenic or even being a serial killer may be a statistically infrequent occurrence, but so is being able to run a mile in four minutes. Clearly, the exceptional is not average but such athleticism does not fit our concept of abnormality.

- **The psychometric approach** is related to the above, in that the psychological measurements taken are said to be abnormal when they deviate sufficiently from the average (Offer and Sabshin, 1991). An example would be a measure of a client's Intelligence Quotient (IQ), where this single score is compared with the average for various age groups to determine his or her '**mental age**'. This 'mental age' may be *abnormally* low according to a predetermined criterion (e.g. an IQ of less than 70 would be in the abnormal range). Such rating instruments (often questionnaires) are used to measure individuals along dimensions such as neuroticism or impulsivity, but these traits have to be decided in advance and, as with the statistical model, place abnormality at *either* scoring extreme. Thus an IQ score of 150 may be outside the normal range, but is it abnormal? As frequent participants in studies, many psychology students have produced 'abnormal' scores on 'neuroticism' and continue to function well and are (or at least seem) clinically normal. Psychometric approaches often assume one **index construct** whereas many factors may be involved.

- **The surprisingness or difference model** pertains to behaviour which is significantly out of character for that individual. Thus in contrast to statistical or psychometric models, the behaviour may be within the normal range, but deviating from what is expected of that individual. For example, a quiet, shy, retiring person becomes animated, confident and loud – but this has to also exclude individuals enthusiastically celebrating or supporting a team at sport.

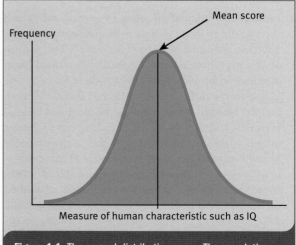

Figure 1.1 The normal distribution curve. The population frequency distribution of most human variables tends towards this 'bell-shaped curve' – called the normal distribution curve.

- **The Utopia model** identifies a minority of individuals who are in perfect mental health as being normal (Offer and Sabshin, 1991). In this, the rest of us mere mortals fall short of the ideal and could thus be seen as abnormal. To some degree, Rogers (1951) assumes this in his therapeutic approach, encouraging clients towards self-actualisation to realise their full, somewhat 'utopian' potential, although not necessarily labelling those who fail 'abnormal'.

- **The absence of pathology, deviant or bizarre behaviour approaches** relies on clearly differentiated behaviour or symptoms to identify the abnormal individual (Offer and Sabshin, 1991). It is obvious that what is deviant varies between social groups – what is termed cultural relativism. For example, levels of drug taking and provocative dress in the youth culture would cause alarm among more rigidly 'respectable' social groups. Unfortunately, this approach does not clearly distinguish eccentricity from pathology, leaving a large grey area, including non-conformists such as 'new-age travellers', open to the label 'deviant'.

- **The systems model** sees normal functioning as a set of systems, which interact in harmony and adapt well. Freudian psychopathology is an example of this, where harmony or conflict between the systems of the id, ego and superego determines normality and abnormality respectively. This approach recognises the interplay between such independent but interacting systems as biological, occupational and emotional adaptive functioning (Offer and Sabshin, 1991). Although this model accounts for maladaptive functioning, it is less useful in determining what is normal or abnormal.

- **Evolutionary adaptation** refers to normal individuals successfully evolving to deal with their environments, inferring abnormality to be faulty adaptation. A form of this hypothetical approach has been termed **harm dysfunction** by Wakefield (1999), where harm can be judged by the cultural context. Here Wakefield assumes that the harmful dysfunction can be identified by professionals and also that the dysfunction can be readily judged as maladaptive. Although this is an admirable ultimate explanation, there is no empirical consensus as to what is adaptive in evolutionary terms (Lloyd, 1999). Indeed, the very success of natural selection is based on the almost infinite diversity of adaptive phylogenetic development (i.e. change which occurs during evolutionary development across vast numbers of lifetimes).

- **Cultural-relativist views** state that what is abnormal from one cultural perspective may be seen as normal in another. Thus what may be seen as pathological and labelled schizophrenia by one culture may be labelled as visionary or prophetic in another. However, this tends to be based on a rather dated, quaint view of other cultures in which fictional caricatures are projected on to less advanced groups by well-intentioned observers, in the manner of **Margaret Mead**'s early studies. This normatological nihilism occurs less in the twenty-first century, where what is defined as a serious disability or crime in one group is rarely considered differently across cultures.

The definition of abnormality is also hampered by its subject matter being mostly in the mental, rather than physical plane. The mind could be referred to as a hypothetical construct squashed between biology and the environment, which is how many of the critics of the medical approach to abnormal psychology (psychiatry) would like it to stay. Szasz (1960) has played devil's advocate in this debate to great effect, reminding us that the 'mind' is not an organ of the body and therefore cannot be diseased as such (see Chapter 2). However, modern technology is beginning to overtake this position when it distinguishes between the problems of computer hardware and software. When we observe that sophisticated computer software programs break down due to computer 'viruses', we may recognise a crude analogy for the diseased mind. However, it is dangerous to use this analogy literally in abnormal psychology, with such breakdowns being hypothesised to result from a fault in either the computer software ('mind') or hardware ('brain'). In the case of the brain, there is no clear dichotomy as neural software and hardware are one and the same.

A further complication in defining abnormality is the variation over **time** and **space** in what is thought to be 'abnormal'.

What has been considered abnormal has also varied over time. Throughout history, many of the acts celebrated during wartime were subsequently condemned as crimes during times of peace.

Producing an acceptable theoretical definition of abnormality would seem to be an imprecise endeavour built on the shifting sands of time and place. However, a more practical definition used in abnormal psychology holds that abnormal behaviour has the following features.

- It causes significant discomfort and distress to the individual concerned.

- It causes significant disruption, harm or distress to other people (e.g. personality disorder).

- It causes significant impairment of their occupational or social functioning.

- It demands the attention of medical, legal or community authorities.

These are the criteria used in practice and indicate some form of intervention. However, in some countries,

International perspective

Culture and abnormal behaviour

The Inuit landscape, a cold and unwelcome place to be old and infirm.
Source: Pearson Online Database.

Cultural relativism refers to how behaviour that may be considered normal in one culture or social grouping may seem quite alien or abnormal to another. These differences may be socially generated (e.g. religious beliefs) or simply a result of geography.

An example of how one culture's practices can seem at odds with another can be found in old Inuit tradition. In this, a 'party' was held for an elderly, infirm relative. At the height of this occasion, the unfortunate elder would be hanged, with a favoured younger relative placing the first hand on the rope. This would seem a barbaric crime in another culture or country, but the Inuit landscape was a brutal unforgiving environment for the old and infirm. Leaving a relative to flounder in sub-zero temperatures and freeze to death would have seemed equally cruel in the old Inuit culture.

However, some abnormal behaviour seems to be **transcultural** and is considered abnormal regardless of culture or era. Depression, schizophrenia and acts of homicide are examples of these.

individuals have been designated insane as a result of holding particular political views (particularly under authoritarian regimes), or sometimes as an alternative to prison, providing permanent rather than temporary incarceration (see Chapter 2). In England during the early part of the twentieth century, young women were still being pressured into asylums by relatives for having illegitimate children, thus relieving these relatives of this 'moral embarrassment'. These misuses of incarceration are often overemphasised by many authors to the extent that students are left with the erroneous impression that the unfortunates in question comprised the majority of inmates, which is far from the reality in which many seriously ill patients filled these institutions. Despite such abuses, this working definition of abnormality provides for some flexibility in making clinical judgements.

Important concepts in abnormal, clinical and forensic psychology

Some terms used in abnormal psychology and psychiatry have survived both time and deliberate attempts to end their use. This is because the concepts that they represent are valuable to both the student and clinician, even though some of the terms themselves may be seen as dated. Some examples of these are described below.

- The organic–functional distinction refers to whether the potential causes of a disorder are biological in origin, or a product of function (psychological). This division is similar to the nature–nurture debate in developmental psychology, in producing rather polarised views. The medical model assumes that mental disorders are similar to physical disorders in having a biological basis. Hunter (1973) believed that all functional disorders were actually organic disorders for which the physical basis had yet to be discovered. History supports this view, as although schizophrenia was listed as a functional disorder, its current aetiological status is biological (e.g. Cutting, 1985). However, current thinking has also somewhat overemphasised the importance of psychological factors in precipitating episodes of schizophrenia (see Chapter 18). Thus, the organic–functional division still provides much debate in abnormal psychology.

- The diathesis–stress approach (Goldman, 1992; see Chapter 3) to the aetiology of a disorder is one rationalisation of the above organic–functional debate. In the diathesis–stress explanation, there is a genetic or biological predisposition to the disorder and the disorder is then precipitated by some form of environmental stress (see Chapter 3). The diathesis–stress approach may provide a basis for the sudden violence when individuals with congenitally low levels (or even high levels, in some studies) of the neurotransmitter serotonin are environmentally frustrated.

- The reactive–endogenous distinction is a dated concept that was applied to depressive disorders. It was thought that some forms of the disorder emerged from within the body due to physical or biochemical change in the brain (i.e. endogenous type), and other forms were a reaction to external events (i.e. reactive type). However, there is no clear cut-off point between these influences.

- The neurotic–psychotic distinction involves the old term 'neurotic' (referring to 'weak nerves'), which was reserved for less severe psychological disorders such as those discussed in Freud's case studies. The term 'psychotic' was reserved for severe disorders such as schizophrenia. A glib way of illustrating this distinction was to refer to neurotic clients building castles in the air, while psychotic individuals tried to live in them. Later the division was reinforced by the fact that neurotic patients mostly attended as outpatients at psychological medicine units, whereas psychotic patients were admitted to psychiatric hospitals. The current classificatory system, DSM-IV TR (see Chapter 4), has eliminated the term 'neurotic' entirely. Many professionals still frequently use these terms, but with more specific meanings. Describing an individual as neurotic indicates a persistent susceptibility to anxiety disorders. The label 'psychotic' is now reserved for individuals who display hallucinations, delusions and severe thought disturbance.

- The personality trait–episode distinction is an old controversial concept in psychology, making the difficult distinction between enduring, lifelong ways of behaving or personality traits, and non-permanent episodes of behaviour disturbance. Both can affect the same individual at one time (i.e. they are comorbid) and this difficulty is acknowledged by the DSM-IV system of disorder classification, which requires the user to rate clients separately on different axes (dimensions of diagnosis) for current disorders and long-standing personality disorder. This is an important distinction, as being diagnosed with a psychopathic personality in the USA may make the death penalty more likely due to the condition being resistant to change.

- Mad–bad distinction. This can be a very fine judgement that sometimes has to be made in diagnosis or at courtroom sentencing. It is the decision as to whether an individual is suffering from a mental disorder and as a consequence their judgement of right and wrong is impaired (i.e. they are 'mad'), or whether their condition is such that they have clear judgement in their abnormal behaviour (i.e. they are 'bad'). This distinction can be influenced by gender, in that females tend to be judged more 'mad' and males more often 'bad', and by culture, as in some countries many more people may be designated 'mad' than 'bad'. The sum total of 'mad' and 'bad' is roughly equal in each population and varies only in terms of where the mad–bad distinction is drawn for political or practical reasons.

Self-test questions

- How are criminology and forensic psychology distinguished?
- Why is abnormal behaviour difficult to define?
- What criteria are used to differentiate abnormal behaviour in practice?
- What are the advantages and disadvantages of the stress–diathesis and eclectic approaches?

A history of abnormal, clinical and forensic psychology

Pre-history to ancient China

Abnormal behaviour seems to have existed as far back as our means to detect it can determine. As with the rest of science, the further we go back in history, the greater the dependence on *belief* rather than *knowledge* in explaining abnormal behaviour. Superstition and imagination rapidly fill the gaps in what is known and sometimes continue to compete against scientific evidence. Twenty thousand-year-old skeletal remains, from the **Palaeolithic period**, show signs of trephination where circular holes about 2 inches in diameter had been cut into the skulls of living individuals with a primitive instrument, a trephine. Bone growth around the holes indicates that at least half of them survived their 'operation'. There are two competing explanations for this procedure. The first supposes that the hole was cut to relieve pressure following **head injury** and attributes these early 'surgeons' with rather advanced neural knowledge. The second proposes that the recipients were disturbed and the hole was cut to release the '**evil demon**' believed to cause their disturbed behaviour. Demonic possession is the earliest known and by far the longest-surviving explanation for abnormal behaviour, having survived even through to the twenty-first century. Exorcisms still take place to cast out 'demons' (e.g. Ferracuti, Sacco and Lazzari, 1996). This primitive thinking may lie behind our dismissal of those committing horrific criminal acts as being 'evil' rather than coming to terms with any possible underlying pathology.

The Greek and Roman scientific enlightenment

The rise of the **Greek and Roman civilisations** marked an important step forward for the treatment of abnormal behaviour (Davidson, 2006). Greek philosopher **Plato** (427–347 BC) attributed much mental disorder to morality

International perspective

Early origins of abnormal, clinical and forensic areas

Trephinated skull. The trephine tool was used to cut holes in the skull to allow demonic spirits to escape. Bone growth suggests that half of these individuals survived the process.
Source: Science and Society Picture Library.

Evidence of possession by evil spirits as an explanation for abnormal behaviour has been found among the remains of cultures as diverse as the Incas, Chinese, Greeks and Egyptians, often with the introduction of a religious element. Some of these spiritual approaches in **ancient China** were relatively humane, including caring for the disturbed in institutions, over 2000 years before such care was available in other parts of the world.

As an early forensic tool, the use of fingerprints for identification purposes was also first established in ancient China. Fingerprints have also been found on pre-civilisation cave paintings, which might have been signatures, but this is conjecture. In the Roman courts around AD 88, palm prints left in blood were supposedly used to accuse a blind civilian of his mother's murder by a legal representative named **Marcus Fabius Quintilianus** (AD 35–95). The use of the Greek and Roman courts as forums for debate provided the origins of the term 'forensic'.

As communities across the world moved from rural environments to those of early villages, the mentally ill and criminals became too salient and numerous to be ignored by emergent authorities. Other means of dealing with them were developed, varying from ancient Chinese and Roman open areas to European asylums.

or intervention by the gods. However, Hippocrates (460–377 BC), 'the father of modern medicine', had earlier rejected such demonic explanations of abnormal behaviour and instead believed in natural causes and the importance of physiological processes. Hippocrates was also the first to separate psychological causes (psychogenesis) from physiological ones (somatogenesis). Although Hippocrates has come to be revered as a strategic figure in medical history, he was largely ignored in his own time, as science was always on fragile ground in a sea of religious governance. Practical medical knowledge in this era was limited, perhaps due to religious limitations on uncovering bodily organs. For example, at this time the disorder termed hysteria involved the concept of the 'wandering uterus', where the organ was thought to wander within the bodies of females (usually virgins or widows), causing ailments relative to the place where it was newly attached – a belief that persisted for several hundred years. Thus, limitations were also evident in the ideas of Hippocrates, who held that differing mental states resulted from the imbalance of four '**bodily humours**' (fluids): blood, phlegm, and yellow and black bile (Davidson, 2006). He described three abnormal states – **mania**, melancholia and **phrenitis** (brain fever) – which Hippocrates related to an excess of the key bodily humours. He also gave detailed descriptions of personality types that resulted from the relative dominance of one of the four bodily humours (see Table 1.1).

The terms and concepts introduced by Hippocrates persisted in the thinking of his successor **Galen**, who added to the bodily humour typology of Hippocrates. This can still be found in relatively recent twentieth-century texts such as Hans Eysenck's (1916–1997) use of the character descriptions of Hippocrates and Galen, when applying his personality theory to criminal behaviour (see Eysenck, 1964). Some Eastern communities also practised on the basis of Galen's initial writings for many centuries: for example, an Arab called **Avicenna** (AD 980–1037) continued the scientific approach independently with **humoral theory**, whilst such insights declined and were lost to much of the world.

Alexander the Great (356–323 BC) founded a number of institutions, '**sanatoriums**', with regimes of exercise and occupation, which were used for the recovery of the insane. This practice continued until the decline of the Greek and Roman empires, under pressure from barbarian invasion and the rise of Christianity. Other parts of the world also witnessed more enlightened early approaches to abnormal behaviour. Possibly the first book on **forensic medicine** was published in China in 1248 with the title *Hsi duan yu* (the washing away of wrongs). This detailed how to differentiate the medical consequences of crimes; remarkably, a second edition was not published until 1980.

From the Dark Ages through the Middle Ages

In Europe, the Dark Ages (AD 400–900) followed the decline of these civilisations, as religious superstition grew across Europe and other parts of the world. Christian monasticism provided some care for the sick, but the knowledge from previous civilisations was left unread in the monasteries, and many of the insane were left to wander as vagabonds.

Religious superstition guided the treatment of those among the insane who were kept in monasteries, including the concept of driving out the 'evil' influence with rituals such as purging and all-night vigils. Criminal behaviour and psychological disturbance were not differentiated and both were approached from a moral–spiritual, rather than medical or behavioural standpoint. During this period, disease was widespread in Europe and elsewhere, this being a consequence of belief replacing science. Thus rather than looking for causes in unsanitary conditions and armies spreading disease across countries, such events were seen as the work of evil forces such as 'the Devil' – a resurgence of demonology. By 1300, fear of the Devil and a belief in **witchcraft** were widespread and those suffering from mental disorders were easily portrayed as witches, providing scapegoats for the ills of society. Symptoms such as being withdrawn or eccentric, hearing voices or holding strange beliefs could be seen to characterise possession by the Devil. Religious leaders supported such views and 'treatment', usually some form of **exorcism**, was also within the jurisdiction of the Church.

During the fifteenth and sixteenth centuries, scientific advances began to contradict the teachings of the Church. The Church reacted to this threat with force, persecuting

Table 1.1 The early Greek view of bodily humours and their believed consequences

Humour	Consequences
Black bile	Domination by black bile led to a *melancholic* individual with depressive symptoms, which would be severe if in excess.
Blood	The dominance of blood produced an optimistic, fearless and jovial or *sanguine* personality, which in excess would lead to mania.
Yellow bile	The personality resulting from a dominance of yellow bile, or a *choleric* personality, was short-tempered and impulsive, and in extreme quantities would suffer *phrenitis* or brain fever.
Phlegm	The *phlegmatic* personality was cold, sluggish and unemotional, and became indifferent to others in excessive states.

its critics and heavily sanctioning the pursuit of witches. In 1484, **Pope 'Innocent' VIII** issued a papal bull to pursue witches. Following the Pope's orders, two Dominican monks, **Henry Kraemer** and **James Sprenger** of the Order of Preachers, published Malleus Maleficarum (the witches' hammer). This became a widely accepted manual for dealing with unnatural phenomena, giving 'signs', 'tests' and 'treatments' for witches and ungodly activity. For example:

■ **Signs** of witchery included loss of reason, red spots on the skin and insensitive skin areas. These signs could also be present in individuals suffering from somatoform disorders (see Chapter 15), delusions or cognitive disorders.

■ **Treatments** for witchery usually consisted of life imprisonment if the victim confessed during torture. However, they faced burning at the stake, beheading or hanging if they did not confess, or failed 'tests' such as immersion in water. In the immersion test, if you drowned you were innocent, but if you survived you were deemed guilty and killed.

Zilboorg and Henry (1941) have estimated that amongst others, thousands of insane individuals, mostly females, were killed as witches during this time as scapegoats for plagues, religious wars and other problems. Some individuals took advantage of the Zeitgeist (spirit of the times) to falsely accuse others, even relatives, to gain property or simply to rid themselves of those they disliked. In such cases, deception was often used to reveal 'signs' of witchery, taking advantage of victims who were confused as a result of torture ('loss of reason') or using retractable needles to 'reveal' insensitivity to pain. These corrupt, overzealous purges by the Church have found their way into popular media with horror films such as *Witchfinder General* (Michael Reeves, 1968) and *The Devils* (Ken Russell, 1971) based on the book *The Devils of Loudon* by Aldous Huxley.

Those who objected to the witch trials were condemned as collaborators. Now thought of as the founder of modern psychopathology, **Johann Weyer** (1515–1588) produced a book in 1563 in Germany claiming that the 'witches' were insane or disturbed ordinary individuals. He was fortunate in only having his books burned; some other 'collaborators' were burned at the stake themselves. During the Renaissance period, **humanitarianism** began to spread, with increasing numbers of people in power opposing the charge of witchcraft. In most parts of Europe the practice died out during the fifteenth and sixteenth centuries with the English law against witchcraft ending in 1736 and the last legal execution being carried out in Switzerland in 1782 (Trevor-Roper, 1967). However, in remote areas of Britain such trials continued into the nineteenth century.

Not all disordered individuals were accused of witchcraft during this period, and some question the accuracy of such accounts of the mentally ill being victims of religious persecution (Phillips, 2002). Most were left to wander as **beggars**, though a few were taken into early asylums. These institutions were converted from **leprosaria** when leprosy declined from around 1200, as wars in the East ended and armies no longer spread the infection. Unlike those of earlier civilisations, these institutions provided very poor conditions and were overrun with beggars, being essentially workhouses.

One of the first purpose-built hospitals was the Priory of St Mary of Bethlehem, which was founded in 1243 and came to house a handful of mentally ill individuals over the following two centuries. It was used exclusively for the mentally ill from 1547, run by the London authority to clear some of the disordered individuals from their streets. Care fell far short of clinical; many institutions were **tourist attractions** for the paying public, who gave one or two pence to watch chained inmates strewn with their excrement. 'Bedlam', as the early institution came to be known, now means a place of chaos. The 'patients' were self-funding and when their funds were at an end they were given an 'official' badge to beg outside for their keep. Although our view of Bedlam tends to be somewhat negative, some sophistication began to emerge beyond its primarily custodial function. By 1820 Bedlam had developed beyond its custodial function and inmates were examined to determine whether their ailment was an inherited disorder.

Insane relatives of the wealthy were often locked in remote rooms of the household and referred to as 'eccentric', or not referred to at all. Alternatively, the unfortunate relative could be placed in private accommodation, usually some distance away. The need for relatives to distance themselves from mentally ill family members reflected the shame they felt this brought on the family as well as the possible inconvenience. Examples of such shame can still be seen today in Chinese and other communities. Less well-off families with a disordered relative at home often restrained them by chaining them to a corner of the room. The 'coal-house' was commonly used for this practice, which was still prevalent in the mid-nineteenth century, and remnants of shackles can still be found. The disordered relatives of the very poor were usually left to beg or, if they were fortunate, entered an institution such as Bedlam.

The Renaissance and the humanitarian movement

Mental institutions were little different from penal institutions until the nineteenth century. Prisoners were incarcerated in solitary confinement and given a Bible in order to discover the moral error of their ways. However,

The brutal reality of supposed witches being burned at the stake in Germany is a grim reminder of the dangers of allowing belief to override logic.
Source: Getty Images.

very few could read and almost all suffered mental degeneration due to confinement and lack of stimulation. Small signs of reform also showed early indications of a clinical forensic science to come, such as the testing for pregnancy of women sentenced to be hanged at a time when it was deemed immoral to hang the innocent foetus. As early as the fifteenth century a shrine in Gheel, Belgium turned into a 'caring' colony for the mentally disordered. Around 1800, the **humanitarian** movement that had developed during

the Renaissance period produced reformers with an interest in the treatment of both incarcerated prisoners and the mentally ill. One of the active pioneers of this movement in Europe was **William Tuke** (see the Focus box).

For many authors (e.g. Reisman, 1966), Philippe Pinel (1745–1826) represented the liberal Zeitgeist, and his ordering the removal of chains from patients came to illustrate the movement symbolically. However, Pinel embraced medicine and was considered the 'father of scientific psychiatry'

Focus

William Tuke (1732–1822)

William Tuke was a Quaker in the York Society of Friends whilst working in the family tea and coffee merchandise. His interest in mental disorder began with a group of Quaker friends coming to him regarding a colleague, Hannah Mills, who was kept in the Lunatick Asylum near York. They had been refused entry when trying to visit her and afterwards were told that she had died. Their suspicions about malpractice prompted Tuke to visit the asylum. He was so appalled at the conditions to which the inmates were subjected that he dedicated the remaining 30 years of his retirement to improving treatment of the mentally ill.

In 1792 Tuke launched an appeal before the Society of Friends and in 1796 he opened the **'York Retreat'** in England with his religious colleagues. Quakers rejected the term 'asylum' and Tuke's wife supplied the more acceptable 'retreat'. The organisation was founded on religious principles and placed great emphasis on nutrition, respect, freedom and medical treatment. Restraints and confinement were minimised and partly replaced by the rigours of occupational tasks. However, drug treatment with alcohol, opium and cannabis was also included within this regime. In its rural setting, the York Retreat appeared more like a farm than the prison layout of previous asylums. With more space, the mentally ill tended farm animals as part of their daily 'chores' – an early example of the deliberate therapeutic use of animals with patients (Perelle and Granville, 1991). Seen as a success by visiting Quakers, further retreats were built in the USA.

The term 'moral treatment' was used by Tuke's grandson, Samuel, in his 1813 text *Description of the Retreat*. Descendants of Tuke continued his work, producing texts including Daniel Hack Tuke's co-authored *Manual of Psychological Medicine* in 1858. With little communication between authors, the moral approach seems to be a case of **Zeitgeist**, rather than being against the tide of contemporary opinion, or Ortgeist.

Like others using 'moral treatment', Tuke found he could only cater for 30 patients, which made little impact on the mental health needs of the district. Nor could moral treatment cope with the seriously disordered, who did not respond and remained resident for life. These limitations made it impractical for future mental health provision and the 'moral therapy' era only spanned a century. However, the York Retreat is still in operation and inspired other units with liberal conditions for less seriously ill patients, such as the Tavistock Centre in London. Some myths have grown up to replace the realities of the York Retreat and a critical account of the events over a major part of the retreat's history can be found in Digby (1985).

The 'moral motive' in Tuke's philanthropic work followed from Quakers having been persecuted and misunderstood for over a century and being able to empathise with the mistreated patients. The assumption that the mentally ill were closer to beasts angered Quakers, who believed in an element of 'God in every person', regardless of their mental state. Thus the good work by the Tuke dynasty could also be seen to propagate their faith. It is ironic that in 1975 Harold Shipman was admitted to the retreat for his pethidine addiction. Over the next 25 years he went on to become one of the world's most prolific serial killers.

as well as being a defender of liberalism and the poor. A tragedy in which a friend suffering from bipolar disorder (see Chapter 17) was killed by wolves motivated Pinel to understand the insane. He researched manic conditions and was encouraged to write by a colleague, **Joseph Daquin** (1733–1815).

Pinel viewed the insane as suffering human beings rather than depraved animals, and during the period of post-revolutionary French liberalism he was appointed director of **Bicêtre Asylum** in 1793. Bicêtre was an old prison that had been used as an asylum since 1660. Contrary to his historical image, Pinel did not strike the chains from inmates but progressively had his employees – former patients – implement humane conditions. Pinel initially waited for permission from the authorities to free a handful of inmates, one of whom saved Pinel from being hanged by a mob enraged by his freeing of the insane. He only dispensed humanitarianism to more able patients, retaining straitjackets and other restraints for lower-class patients. Pinel's success in reducing the mortality rate at Bicêtre led in 1795 to his appointment to, and transformation of, Salpêtriére, then the largest asylum in Europe (see Shorter, 1997).

Moral treatment and improvements to diet and hygiene spread beyond France, helped by the practical advantage of patients becoming more manageable with humane treatment. **Dorothea Dix** (1802–1887) in the USA raised money to modernise mental hospitals by persistent campaigning. Paradoxically, Dix spread both hospitals and the harsh physical treatments she opposed, as the physicians employed could not cope using humanitarian regimes alone.

Moral treatment failed to cope with seriously disordered individuals for whom institutionalisation was the only intervention. Open conditions with few beds, such as York Retreat, could not cater for the increase in mentally ill individuals as science advanced. At the same time, prejudice against the mentally ill rose amongst the public, who became less sympathetic to individual suffering. Thus, conditions in the many large institutions built in the wake of this period were less than ideal, having to house larger numbers.

Acceptance of natural selection after Charles Darwin (1809–1882) led to countries across the world passing laws prohibiting criminals, the 'feeble minded' and those with milder mental illness from having children, and even led to them imposing compulsory sterilisation. This form of eugenics or 'unnatural selection' was a clear misuse of Darwinian thinking (see Chapter 3). Counter to popular belief, Nazi Germany was one of the last countries to pass such laws, although it clearly distinguished itself by adding extermination to sterilisation.

Despite reforms in the 1800s, the management of patients and prisoners has always remained a compromise between humane and secure treatment. This compromise is paralleled in contemporary penal institutions, where rehabilitation is also seen to be at odds with security and order. In both contexts, overcrowding and a need for security undermine attempts to provide humane treatment. The parallel between mental state and criminal culpability has long been evident in the concept of insanity as mitigation at trial. Following an assassination attempt on King George III in 1800, James Hadfield's defence counsel successfully presented a head injury from the Anglo-French war as evidence that he failed to demonstrate 'clarity of mind' in his crime.

Previously, an insanity defence was allowed only if the insane offender conformed to the wild beast test in acting more animal than human, and was thus totally out of contact with reality. The Hadfield case 'rationalised' the forensic definition of insanity to evidence that could be scientifically demonstrated, but also led to the Criminal Lunatics Act 1800 for detaining the criminally insane. In the wake of Darwin's work, the view of criminals as evolutionary throwbacks was to re-emerge in the work of Cesare Lombroso's (1835–1909) flawed study (Lombroso, 1876), identifying primitive 'atavistic' physical features (i.e. features belonging to remote ancestors) in prisoners. In 1885, Lombroso was also one of the first to use blood pressure to indicate deception in a forensic context.

Empiricism and the scientific approach

Ignorance of the aetiology of abnormal behaviour limited treatment to physical forms of calming and restraint, such as purging, bleeding, spinning, immersion in water, pressing and chaining. These procedures mostly kept order, paralleling the restraint of criminals, but by trial and error some methods were found to have beneficial effects on behaviour and were retained as advances in science brought new treatments during the nineteenth century, and as religious superstition abated.

In the seventeenth century, Thomas Sydenham had called for an empirical approach to insanity, and for Griesinger (1845) mental illnesses were unambiguously diseases of the brain. Despite primitive scientific methods, there was a gradual association of physical illness with disturbed mental states, as in the case of general paresis (see the Research box), and this assumed biological basis characterised the emergent discipline of psychiatry. Reynolds (1855) divided mental disorders into 'organic' or of known underlying pathology, and those due to high or low functionality, termed 'functional', with unknown pathology. For Hunter (1973), all functional disorders were of organic origin yet to be discovered.

Emil Kraepelin (1856–1926) produced a biologically based, coherent classificatory system, *A Textbook of Psychiatry* (Kraepelin, 1885). Wilhelm Wundt (1832–1920) inspired Kraepelin's scientific methodological approach, but also considered psychology to be a fledgling science with little future! Kraepelin pioneered drug effects and surgical procedures as clinical investigations, which due to the clinical authority of Kraepelin's work led to their premature and rapid adoption.

Kraepelin identified the clinical syndrome as a group of symptoms tending to occur together and suggested two broad syndromes in mental disorder, 'Dementia Praecox' (schizophrenia) and 'manic depressive disorders', at the Burghoelzli in Zurich. Kraepelin identified and differentiated many disorders in the absence of exact causes and, along with Eugen Bleuler, laid the foundations for psychiatry in the twentieth century.

Although the psychological paradigm and biological paradigm should complement and confirm one another, their historical origins reveal areas of conflict.

From pseudopsychology to Freud

In a possible example of Ortgeist, Austrian physician Franz Anton Mesmer (1734–1815) claimed that patients with hysteria suffered an imbalance in 'bodily magnetic fluid' that could be corrected using magnetic rods used in a theatrical manner like a magician's wand. He also used mesmerism, producing a sleep-like suggestible state related to hypnotism. The resultant dramatic show and claims of success attracted some criticism and a committee eventually discredited him as a fraud in 1784. Although

Research

General paresis of the insane (neurosyphilis)

The history of 'general paresis' illustrates how links between disordered thinking and physical damage or disease were slowly forged as scientific research progressed.

In 1798, John Haslam described the co-occurrence of distinctive progressive dementia, paralysis and delusions. Termed 'general paresis' in 1825, this syndrome was widespread across Europe and empiricists such as Griesinger searched for physical causes for these slowly emerging symptoms. By 1857, it was established that sufferers had contracted syphilis years before the onset of their paresis symptoms. The work of **Louis Pasteur** soon revealed **germ theory**, or how organisms invade the body and remain to cause damage. In 1897, **Richard von Krafft-Ebing** (1840–1902) introduced matter from syphilitic eruptions into the bloodstream of the paresis patients, who did not develop the disease and thus must have already contracted it. This link between the physical disease and the mental disorder was made explicit in 1905 when **Fritz Schaudinn** identified the syphilitic organism responsible, **Treponema pallida**. Now termed **neurosyphilis** (tertiary syphilis), it is rare due to this pioneering research. Many famous individuals were infected: Friedrich Nietzsche, Franz Schubert, Abraham Lincoln and possibly Adolf Hitler suffered the symptoms and primitive interventions such as the Mercury treatment (Hayden, 2003).

Although this was a biomedical scientific success, such advances were rare until the accidental discovery of effective pharmacotherapy in the 1950s.

---

the legacy of Mesmer's theatrical performances with a 'magic wand' did little to further the credibility of psychogenesis, there was value in the trance produced. In 1841, **James Braid** used the term **neurohypnotism** and emphasised suggestibility in this process. The effects of suggestibility would later have profound implications for false memory syndrome and the forensic investigation of suggestibility in eyewitness testimony.

French neurosurgeon Jean-Martin Charcot (1825–1893) used hypnotism following work at the **Nancy school** in cases of hysteria. Two of the Nancy school, **Ambroise-Auguste Liébeault** (1823–1904) and **Hippolite-Marie Bernheim** (1840–1919), both treated and *generated* hysteria with hypnosis in suggestible individuals. They considered hysteria as a form of **self-hypnosis**, which has merit today (see Chapter 15; Spanos, 1996). Individual differences in suggestibility and suggestible patients improving if they believed in the effectiveness of therapy led to the serious consideration of psychogenic causes. The work of Josef Breuer (a colleague of Charcot) and **Freud** followed, forming the basis of the **psychoanalytic paradigm** (see Chapter 3).

The twentieth century and the emergence of clinical and forensic psychology

Cesare de Baccaria had already considered the cost–benefit approach to punishment in focusing on deterrence not punishment, but it was the slow intrusion of medicine and other scientific expertise into courtrooms that brought in psychology. Symbolised by the backward-looking face of Janus, the law relies on precedent and is resistant to allowing in new authorities such as psychology. However, in 1843 the insanity defence set its legal precedent when Daniel McNaughton killed UK Prime Minister Robert Peel's secretary in reaction to paranoid ideation (believing he was persecuted). His unprecedented defence of four barristers and nine expert medical witnesses led to a not-guilty verdict by reason of insanity. The **McNaughten rule** defining legal insanity became established by the House of Lords.

At this time, forensic evidence was the preserve of the medically qualified, including psychiatrists. As psychology divorced from philosophy, it took a scientific approach, mostly using laboratory-based work, following the first psychology laboratory in Leipzig established by Wundt in 1875. Clinical work on memory by **William Stern** (1871–1938) identified the way witness testimony could be distorted by leading questions or interrogation, and this was followed later by Loftus's (1979) account of the suggestibility of memory. **James McKeen Cattell** (1860–1944) produced complex work on testimony accuracy, and with **Alfred Binet** (1857–1911) supported Stern in its use in court. Possibly the first **forensic psychologist, Albert von Schrenk-Notzing**, pointed to the confusion when witnesses were exposed to pre-trial media reports in Munich in 1896.

Coinciding with forensic applications of memory studies and shortly after Freud had pointed out the value of psychology to Austrian judges, Hugo Munsterberg (1863–1916) published *On the Witness Stand* (Munsterberg, 1908). Munsterberg promoted the application of psychology to justice and courtroom, but the legal profession predictably rejected this and Wigmore (1909) even ridiculed his work. For Munsterberg the fierce resistance from lawyers combined with being on the wrong side in the First World War to lower his credibility with the rest of Europe and the USA. At the turn of the twentieth century, the status of forensic psychology was low, even though the **Federal Bureau of Investigation** (1905) was being founded in the USA by Roosevelt, and Lightner Witmer (1867–1956), founder of the world's first psychological clinic at the University of Pennsylvania in 1896, was actually running courses in criminal behaviour.

Early contributions to the courtroom were based on extensive experimental work in the form of psychometrics or psychological tests (Gudjonsson and Haward, 1998). This was when many scientists were applying their expertise to legal issues, such as **John Larson** completing the first prototype of the polygraph in 1921 (see Chapter 7). Also in 1921, a court rejected an expert's assertion that a witness was unreliable as a result of his use of a psychological test, the reliability of which had not been established by research. This opened the way for psychologists to establish forensic and clinical psychometric testing as a reliable science. The Second World War accelerated the establishment of psychometric tests and led to the psychological testing commercial industry by the end of the twentieth century.

In the early twentieth century, psychiatrists asserted their medical authority and administrative superiority over that of psychologists in court. As late as 1962, US psychologists were not allowed as experts in court with regard to mental illness. However, psychometric testing and the interpretation of assessment results rapidly created a specialist field that required formal training. In 1958, a psychiatrist's re-reporting of the work of psychologist L. R. C. Haward failed

Table 1.2 Specialist roles of psychologists in courtrooms

- The actuarial role is where the probability of an event happening needs to be established and presented to a court (e.g. how common are suicides in teenagers?).

- The experimental role involves producing test data to support statements in court.

- The advisory role is a controversial role in which a psychologist may give an opinion of another professional's evidence.

- The clinical role is where clinical forensic psychologists present clinical assessment data in court.

to impress a court when he could not fully understand the psychological detail and his evidence was ruled as 'hearsay' (i.e. not first-hand evidence). This led to the 'hearsay rule' in 1973, which gave recognition to the psychologist's expert role in court, ending the psychiatrist's monopoly (see Gudjonsson and Haward, 1998). Clinical and forensic roles of psychologists began to overlap considerably from 1970. The psychologist's courtroom work began to fractionate into specialist roles as in Table 1.2.

The **Behavioural Science Unit** at Quantico in the USA by the **Federal Bureau of Investigation** (FBI) employed detectives but began to use psychologists and their work in this training (Canter, 1994). In Europe and elsewhere, psychologists, initially mostly clinical psychologists, began to advise police in crime investigations, interrogations and negotiations (see Chapter 8).

Clinical psychology was dominated by Freudian influences into the early twentieth century, undermining the development of clinical psychology as serious applied science, partly as psychoanalysis was greatly supported by psychiatry. Although psychoanalysis was little dented

International perspective

Establishing clinical psychology

In the USA, clinical psychology was established early, with the psychological clinic and journal founded by Witmer at the beginning of the twentieth century. In Europe and the USA, psychometric testing during the Second World War increased the number of psychologists in employment. The establishment of the UK National Health Service in 1948 provided an employment structure for fledgling clinical psychology practitioners, as most were still based in laboratories and not practising as therapists. By the 1970s and 1980s, these laboratory-based scientists had evolved

into the current role of the clinical psychologist as scientist-practitioner.

The British Psychological Society (BPS) formed the **Division of Clinical Psychology** in 1966, giving academic focus, authorised recognition and a network structure for clinical psychologists in the UK. Most countries have an equivalent support organisation, such as the Berrufsverband deutscher Psychologen in Germany and American Psychological Association in the USA. This has enabled international agreement over qualification standards and practice guidelines.

by **John B. Watson**'s empirical behaviourism at the beginning of the twentieth century (see Chapter 3), his legacy resurfaced with Joseph Wolpe in 1958 and eventually led to a clinical psychology relatively free from psychoanalysis by 1970. Aaron Beck was so disillusioned with his Freudian training during the 1950s that he developed his own **cognitive therapy**, which proved more effective and became an established treatment in clinical psychology in the 1970s. Combined with the behavioural approaches of Joseph Wolpe and **B. F. Skinner**, cognitive behavioural therapy became the major treatment approach in clinical psychology in the twenty-first century and has developed to be more disorder specific.

Self-test questions

- In what ways were the early Greek and Roman approaches to abnormal behaviour considered enlightened?
- Why was the behaviourist movement so important to clinical psychology?
- Discuss the development of the mental institution.
- How did professional psychologists enter courtrooms?

Stability and change in abnormal, clinical and forensic psychology

The hypothesis that mental illness and deviance are products of modern living and were less prevalent before civilisation has been stated even more strongly – as abnormal behaviour being purely defined by, and a product of, society. Claims that serious disorders such as **schizophrenia** are recently developed products of modern living conditions have reached almost mythical proportions amongst supporters of **anti-psychiatry**. However, these disorders date beyond the earliest records can be traced and are found not only in geographical locations remote from modern influence, but also at remarkably similar frequencies in developed and less developed cultures (Jablensky, 1995).

One such argument focuses on modern life creating unremitting stress, leading to higher levels of mental disorders. Although the modern world is densely populated, actual levels of daily stress are probably less in modern society than in previous eras. Could modern living be more stressful than when children worked all daylight hours up soot-filled chimneys, slaves died building pyramids or hunting for food was a lethal occupation? Psychological stress viewed as replacing physical stressors in modern times ignores the extreme psychological stress of life-threatening primitive occupations. The psychophysiological effects of occupational stress will be explored in Chapter 16.

Factors that do contribute to new forms of disorder and their apparent prevalence include increased public awareness of abnormal behaviour. As fewer sufferers are institutionalised, there is greater public contact with a wide range of disorders and disabilities. Public and media acceptability means that individuals are no longer hidden from public gaze in many cultures. The informed acceptance of Mohammed Ali or Pope John Paul II speaking in public during the advanced stages of **parkinsonism** may be one milestone in the progressive erosion of inherent prejudice.

Public awareness of criminal behaviour has similarly been increased by the popular media exploiting public fascination with violent crime. However, disproportionate reporting of violent and bizarre crimes involving disordered perpetrators has led to public fears of a plague of such crime. Thus artificial media amplification of bizarre crime may have led to perceptions of increased levels of abnormal behaviour (Jewkes, 2004).

More subtly, the media exploit public voyeurism, with documentaries disseminating more factual information but also raising awareness in professionals such as hospital staff and police as well as amongst the public. Fictional media have attempted more realistic and more detailed portrayals, such as the late twentieth century films *Rain Man*, focusing on a detailed case of autism, and *Hannibal*, portraying a psychopathic serial killer as coldly manipulative rather than the crude 'crazy' and 'most dangerous' of earlier films. However, 'Hollywood facts' will always be over-amplified; thus not all autistic individuals have savant abilities and few psychopaths are intelligently versed in the classics. Heightened awareness of forensic and clinical issues has led to more disordered and deviant individuals being identified and managed rather than overlooked, which adds to the illusion of increasing levels of disorder and crime. For example, rates of diagnosis of **autism** (see Chapter 9) have multiplied in recent years as public and professional awareness has grown (Frith, 2003).

Professional interest in certain disorders can affect prevalence, such as the over-diagnosis of **attention-deficit hyperactivity disorder** (ADHD) in the USA (see Chapter 9), perhaps labelling disruptive schoolchildren who do not fully meet ADHD criteria. A remarkable one thousand-fold increase in the diagnosis of **dissociative identity disorder**

(Chapter 15) over the last few decades in the USA defies most orthodox explanations (Putnam, 1989). An epidemic outbreak of these disorders specific to certain locations and diagnosed by only a few clinicians is improbable (Simpson, 1989; Spanos, 1996). Economic and political pressures to pathologise unruly children and media publicity with cult-like networks of therapists have had a profound effect on reported levels of these disorders, and over-diagnosis creates a false impression of increasing abnormal behaviour over time. In this way, publicity for a particular disorder or crime can influence the allocation of police or health resources, which in turn may reveal more cases, such as in the paedophilia scares in the mid-1990s (Thomas, 2000).

Behaviour labelled 'abnormal' can decrease or disappear over time, producing the impression of change. Homosexuality has been labelled as both a mental illness and a criminal activity, but the number of such 'cases' logically dropped to zero as soon as its nosological (study of classification) and criminal status was changed. Again, there have been no overall changes in the incidence of the phenomenon; only change in how it is viewed or categorised.

Another reason for change is illustrated by humans enjoying longer life expectancies over time. In populations living to a greater age, disorders beginning in later life increase in incidence. Paradoxically, dementias (see Chapter 19) are diagnosed more frequently as the health of and facilities for the elderly both improve. In the UK, the levels of dementias in the elderly will increase beyond the capacity of current health systems to offer dignified provision. This area needs to be a priority for research and resources, as it is likely to be *the* major ethical and financial challenge in the twenty-first century.

Living longer as a species allows the expression of new abnormal behavioural phenotypes (see Chapter 3) or genetically based disorders not expressed till later in life. In addition, children are being born to older parents, particularly fathers, increasing the chances of genetic mutations and chromosomal abnormalities (Chapter 3) in offspring, such as is the case in **Down's syndrome** (see Chapter 9).

Genetic mutation progresses rapidly amongst viruses and bacteria, enabling disorders to move between species, including humans. Often there is little evolutionary opportunity to gain any immunity or even develop vaccines as first cases arise. Acquired immunodeficiency syndrome (AIDS) provides one example of how disorders can develop drug-resistant strains in a short period of time. The ability to mutate rapidly and jump species has turned common bacteria and viruses, such as the flu virus, into lethal new organisms, such as the **H5N1** variation of avian flu, with the ability to wipe out large percentages of animal species, including humans, in pandemics.

Increasing environmental pollution can have a profound effect on the occurrence of abnormal behaviour. Pollution is changing in an unpredictable and apparently uncontrolled way with both complex inorganic and increasingly organic pollutants. Metal pollutants have led to clinical and forensic problems in children. For example, lead has been progressively eliminated from fuels and paint as a result of its neurotoxic effects.

Abnormal psychology is not an exact science and as such is susceptible to **paradigm** changes. Demonology could serve as a crude but illustrative example of a paradigm in abnormal psychology, in which aberrant behaviour confirms possession by a demon whilst other explanations would be suppressed. Thomas Kuhn (1922–1996) described how paradigms change over time (Kuhn, 1996). Thus, in our example, influential groups would support this view until anomalies appeared along with a competing explanation. Thus if the medical approach explained anomalies in the 'witchcraft paradigm', there could be a **paradigm shift** to the medical paradigm. Paradoxically, demonology and its supposed remedies have survived from pre-civilisation to modern times (Ferracuti, Sacco and Lazzari, 1996; Davis, 1980), making it the longest surviving paradigm in mental science. Kuhn was a physicist and tended to refer to the 'hard sciences', but psychology is considered to be at a **preparadigmatic stage**, with many rival camps competing to become the next paradigm (Staats, 1981). Thus behavioural, cognitive, evolutionary and other explanations of abnormal behaviour coexist without agreed dominance by any one coherent view (see Chapter 3).

Kuhn's view is limited, as in abnormal psychology a number of paradigms have coexisted for much of its history. Steady advances in some areas would seem irrefutable, regardless of competing paradigms; thus, in genetics it is unlikely that the human genome data could change according to the current paradigm. Additionally, refuted views such as demonology continue to defy extinction. Thus, a tolerance for eclecticism is a long-standing feature of psychology, creating an illusion of instability and change as competing explanations are presented sequentially or even simultaneously.

The current context of abnormal, clinical and forensic psychology

Mental health services around the world are facing new challenges as well as dealing with legacies from earlier eras. Coping with the reactions of sufferers and the public to

AIDS made demands on psychologists during the decade following its identification. Its relentless spread on the African continent still presents a challenge to psychologists and health educators in combating widespread basic prejudice, poor education and counter-propaganda. Increased awareness of **post-traumatic stress disorder** (PTSD) has led therapists to cope with adult effects of childhood sexual abuse as well as meeting growing demands from the emergency and military services at public expense. A daunting challenge is the increasing number of people with **chronic** and **age-related disorders**, which is exacerbated by the rising proportion of older people and economic prosperity being concentrated amongst few people, leaving larger numbers of dependent individuals with insufficient resources. This is evident in dealing with disorders such as chronic **schizophrenia** and **Alzheimer's disease**, in which resource-limited care provision can be tragically inadequate.

The current environment for clinical psychologists reflects this stretching of economic resources and changes in the aims of mental health care provision. Changes include the move from patients being seen in large mental hospitals to service delivery in the community. These are fine theoretical aims, but practice in a cash-limited context is not satisfactory. In addition, mental health care has had a 'bad press' in many countries, encouraging a NIMBY (Not In My Back-Yard) reaction to community care from the public. Cash-limited care has also produced many disordered homeless on the streets of *both* poor and affluent capital cities (Pilling, 1991).

In much of Europe, health care is increasingly run along business lines, placing an additional administrative burden on clinicians. The cumulative effect translates into greater workloads and stress for the clinician, in addition to less public respect. The practicalities of the current environment are met by increasing use of 'economic therapy'. One-to-one therapy sessions are viewed as a luxury and restricted to brief therapy, with greater use of **group therapy** (see Chapter 3) and pre-therapy screening (see Carr and McNulty, 2006). Economic pressure also favours short-term **pharmacotherapy** in place of longer-term psychological therapy in terms of initial cost, despite the benefits of combining them. Although these therapies have many merits, economic choices will inevitably prevail with limited resources. Paradoxically, with predominantly private health provision in the USA, expensive extended therapies are offered for converse financial reasons.

The current abnormal psychology context includes an increased focus on **ethics** and **litigation**. **Informed choice** for patients and participants in clinical research is a current key topic. Should patients have the right to treatment, to refuse treatment, or even to choose whether or not to be a patient? Choice would confound a therapist's attempts to select the best treatment. Where **double-blind** research depends on patients participating without knowledge of procedures, should rights be subservient to the benefit of future patients? This can undermine the clinician's role as **scientist-practitioner**: that is, someone bringing specialist knowledge from one aspect of their work to resolve practical problems in the other (Cheshire and Pilgrim, 2004).

The current **Zeitgeist** tends to confirm the rights of the patient or prisoner over research needs, coinciding with more aggrieved patients taking **legal action**. This was once considered a US phenomenon, but is now common practice globally. Clearly a balance is needed to avoid most health care funding being paid to lawyers. This issue also prevails in forensic settings, with individuals passing through the various justice systems gaining more perceived legal/ethical status and protection than victims. It also impedes research, treatment and rehabilitation, in that such rights include the right not to participate. Another focal moral dilemma is **compulsory treatment** and hospitalisation, which has become redefined in the twenty-first century and backed by new legislation, including a revision of the Mental Health Act in the UK (see Chapter 6).

The **compulsory detention** of those personality-disordered individuals seen as a threat to the safety of others is an exceptional case (see Chapters 7 and 14). The term **psychopath** was applied to individuals detained until safe to release under mental health laws, even though this diagnosis was unlikely to be changed by intervention or remit (Cleckley, 1976). In the twenty-first century, the concept of **preventative detention** could include those who have not offended. In the UK, the term dangerous and severe personality disorder (DSPD) represents those potential offenders held in custody prior to offending (see Chapter 14; Bowers, 2002). The European Court of Human Rights makes prophylactic detention less likely to be implemented in Europe as compared with the USA. The moral dilemma posed by this concept in 2000 in the UK was exacerbated up to 2009 by the use of detention without trial following terrorist attacks, particularly those under the banner of Al Qaeda. Psychologists have played a prominent role in solving issues generated by these significant changes in legal status (Kinderman, 2002).

The USA leads in more than litigation by dominating many aspects of **abnormal, clinical and forensic psychology**, including most texts in the areas. This can confuse students, as there are differences in clinical and forensic psychology training, practice and the health service and justice system structures in the USA compared with many European countries. For example, in the USA, clinical psychologists work mostly in private practice, but in the UK it is usually within the National Health Service, as in other European countries with the NHS model. This leads to financing of costly therapies such as psychoanalysis in the USA that are rare in Europe. Although much of the framework for abnormal, clinical and forensic psychology is still USA led, differences have diminished as European countries have moved closer to the dominant American system, raising the status of clinical psychologists and training to doctorate level. To some degree there has also been a move towards the US *DSM* classificatory system from the European *ICD* (see Chapter 4).

Qualification to treat is a clinical issue, with individuals offering psychological services with the minimum of training. Regulatory and professional bodies such as the **British Psychological Society**, the **European Association of Counselling** and the **American Psychological Association** have attempted to regulate client services and training. However, a public trend towards 'value added' treatments that are non-interventive, natural or 'alternative', such as herbal and diet treatments, or a cosmetic makeover for offenders, has undermined regulation of therapy and support. The danger of belief undermining science and blurring the boundary between professional and enthusiastic amateur is a reason for identifying and examining the recognised professional roles that address abnormal behaviour (see Chapter 2).

Some of these professions from a broad range of disciplines are career choices for psychology graduates but others emanate from different domains, as described in the next section. Professional symbiosis is the goal of each differing role, but not without some friction between a few.

Professional roles in abnormal, clinical and forensic psychology

Psychologists in the UK have their professional status recognised by the **British Psychological Society** (BPS) in two parts, an accredited first degree in psychology (Part I) followed by an accredited postgraduate professional qualification and a subsequent supervised period of work (Part II) to gain **chartership**. In Europe, standards are maintained by equivalent bodies but much professional training takes place at undergraduate level (i.e. Part I). The brief descriptions below outline the main professional roles associated with abnormal, clinical and forensic psychology, many of which do overlap with one another.

- **Clinical psychologist.** The clinical psychologist's work applies psychology to area of mental health (see Chapter 6). Clinical psychologists begin as psychology graduates and gain sufficient experience (as nursing assistants through to assistant psychologists) to enter a **clinical psychology doctorate** programme (3 years). In the USA, academic training is separate from and precedes clinical training, which normally begins as part-time clinical practicum rotations in year 2 of the 5-year programme. Fortunate trainees take up internships in their final year, with greater opportunity to specialise in specific areas of clinical psychology than in other countries. In the UK, this training is funded by the **National Health Service** (NHS) and places are very limited, leading to a shortage of qualified professionals. To address this and improve the experience of psychology graduates the creation of Associate Clinical Psychologists (Management Advisory Service, 2003) has been proposed. In some European countries such as the Netherlands, Germany and Norway, clinical training is incorporated seamlessly into the first degree with more trained clinical psychologists as a result. The **BPS** confers **chartered psychologist** status on psychology professionals, including clinical psychologists, who have sufficient supervised post-qualification experience. Chartered status is also offered to clinical psychologists who have qualified elsewhere in the world by application to the **BPS Committee for the Scrutiny of Individual Qualifications in Clinical Psychology**, which identifies further training needs. Chartered status can reinforce the public credibility of professional psychologists. The clinical psychologist's major activities are psychological assessment and therapy as well as research and routine evaluations of assessment and intervention methods. Clients are referred by family doctors to clinical psychology outpatient departments, or clinical psychologists within community mental health teams, as well as inpatients referred by consultant psychiatrists. Clinical psychologists are not medically qualified and cannot prescribe medical treatments, though this is changing in the USA.

- **Forensic psychologist.** Forensic psychologists work in various roles in relation to offending under the various national legal systems. Many work in prisons but they also report and assess for courts or work with the police. Graduates in psychology with sufficient forensic work experience will complete a 1-year professionally accredited Forensic Psychology MSc programme and then work under supervision for a minimum number of years to gain chartered forensic psychologist status. Forensic psychologists are sometimes also qualified clinical psychologists involved in assessing and treating offenders.

■ **Psychiatrist.** Psychiatrists begin as graduates of medicine and then specialise in psychiatry for about three years, usually gaining recognition of the body governing the profession for that country, such as the Royal College of Psychiatrists in England. They then work towards a consultant psychiatrist post. Being medically qualified, psychiatrists can prescribe medical treatments, including drug therapy, but can also give psychotherapy. Psychiatrists have more responsibility than other professionals and although an inpatient may be seen by a variety of therapists, they remain the responsibility of a particular psychiatrist. Psychiatrists also carry out assessments and, in addition, they will formally **diagnose** a patient's disorder.

■ **General practitioner (family doctor).** General practitioners (GPs) are fully qualified medical doctors who have 'specialised' in general practice. They have a central role in **community health care teams** and are the main primary care service delivery agents. GPs are usually the first port of call for individuals suffering a mental disorder. Being on the 'front line' of patient contact, GPs have to be skilled in diverse areas of intervention from emergency medication to effective counselling of patients. Normally, GPs utilise their training to detect signs of mental disorder and refer clients to the appropriate specialist. Goldberg and Huxley (1980) call this the 'filter model' of family doctor referrals.

■ **Psychiatric nurse.** The largest group of health care professionals with greatest level of patient contact, nurses cater to the daily needs of mentally ill inpatients, including safety, security and restraint, diet, hygiene, behavioural schedules and medication. Their training is now usually by 3 years of professional psychiatric nursing training, often to degree standard. Further training can change the career to **community psychiatric nurse**, with emphasis on outreach work. Along with families, nurses bear the brunt of disturbed behaviour and there is need for psychological support for the stress inherent in the job.

■ **Psychiatric (or special/approved) social worker.** Graduates (mostly sociology or social administration) undergo 2 years of professional training, including specialisation in psychiatric work. The psychiatric social worker focuses on their patient's social support, involving contact with the patient, their family and welfare agencies. Further training can give **approved social worker** status for work involving compulsory admissions.

■ **Educational psychologist.** Beginning with their first degree in psychology, educational psychologists were usually qualified teachers with a master's in educational psychology. However, this has moved towards a 3-year doctorate in educational psychology. Their work includes assessing and addressing the problems of school age children that are challenging the regular teacher's professional capacity, such as hyperactivity, truancy or educational underachievement.

■ **Occupational psychologist and stress management.** These professionals enter 1-year occupational psychology master's courses from their undergraduate psychology degrees. Professional careers will often involve psychological testing, improving job performance and job satisfaction. Those specialising in stress in the workplace may work in forensic settings, such as prison or the police amongst others, providing assessment and intervention strategies.

■ **Counselling psychologist.** Counselling psychologists begin as psychology graduates and must then undergo the BPS 3-year diploma in counselling psychology (or equivalent). They are qualified to take responsibility for clients referred to health services, and to provide more in-depth advice if needed. This differs from the training of counsellors, who can undergo a relatively short training period.

■ **Counsellor.** Counsellors were once regarded as **semi-professional** due to the briefer training required without a degree, but can now undergo an extended period of training. Helping to found the **European Association for Counselling**, the **British Association for Counselling** is the overseeing body in the UK and approves a certificate (3 months), diploma (1 year) and even a master's in counselling. Counsellors see normal individuals on a one-to-one basis, talking through their problems and giving support, enabling clients to deal with their difficulties.

■ **Health psychologist.** Health psychologists help patients and their relatives cope with all types of illness and, alongside health educators, promote healthy lifestyles, focusing on prevention. As with many professional psychologists, a degree in psychology is followed by an accredited master's degree in health psychology prior to supervised work in the field for 2 years.

■ **Health educator.** These often have a psychology background and are selected for their specialist knowledge and ability to communicate and generate public interest. Their campaigns include promoting good mental health and raising public awareness of mental health issues.

■ **Paramedic and ancillary worker.** These terms cover a range of workers such as **occupational therapists** and physiotherapists, who deal with the rehabilitation and support of patients. Their training is highly specific to the task and contains many practical elements.

- **Therapist.** Therapists vary widely, from highly trained psychologists or psychiatrists who are dedicated to a particular form of therapy, to individuals with minimal training in obscure therapeutic approaches. Studies have discovered well over 300 ostensibly different therapies, though probably with minor variations. There is a need to regulate therapists in most countries, particularly those with minimal or self-approved training.

- **Paraprofessional and self-help groups.** Some untrained ex-patients may form self-help groups to help relatively new patients and others with the same ongoing problem. Such roles are also found in forensic settings. For example, experienced prison inmates may provide support for first-time inmates at risk of self-harm. Some former offenders tour schools to dissuade youngsters from criminal careers, drawing from their experiences.

- **Researcher.** Ethics panels containing patients, offenders and victims may come into contact with undergraduate psychology students researching for their dissertations, or post-doctorate research fellows coordinating large-scale studies. Although this does not always involve therapy or other interventions, patients often find the attention given therapeutic.

A comprehensive list of those involved would be endless: for example, the **police** are involved in initial patient contact and casualty nurses routinely treat offenders. An important current issue concerns the coordination of the differing services and professionals working in teams. Organisation and communication are often found lacking when failures of care result in tragedy.

Self-test questions

- What factors contribute to the illusion of increasing abnormal behaviour?
- What are the consequences of the US domination of abnormal, clinical and forensic psychology?
- What are the consequences of increased patient litigation?
- Discuss how the roles of a psychiatrist and a clinical psychologist differ.
- What is the difference between counselling and therapy?
- Describe the means to qualify as a clinical psychologist.

Chapter summary

Normatology considers **models of normality**, but the working definition adopted involves the suffering of individuals or contacts, and violation of cultural or legal rules. Important concepts in the area focus on separating **biological** and **psychological** influences on behaviour, which form irresolvable debates with compromises such as the **stress–diathesis** concept. Reasons for public scepticism over psychology can be found in history: for example, **Mesmer**'s theatrical displays of 'therapy'. Developments over the last hundred years dwarf what went before, although they have not been translated into improved care for the modern patient. Current issues in the area include: the eclectic view of mental illness, the strong **US influence**, psychology's public credibility, the changing environment

in terms of **community care**, the prominence of ethics, political aims and use of litigation. The **professions** in mental health care are varied and expanding as more areas find they have expertise to offer to the management of abnormal behaviour.

Suggested essay questions

- Critically evaluate the definition of abnormal behaviour in clinical and forensic contexts.
- Critically discuss the development of penal and psychiatric institutions.
- Discuss the establishment of clinical and forensic psychology as scientific disciplines.

Further reading

Overview texts

Gudjonsson, G., and Haward, L. R. (1998) *Forensic psychology: A guide to practice.* London: Routledge.

Hergenhahn, B. (2005) *An introduction to the history of psychology* (5th edn). Belmont: Wadsworth Thompson.

Maguire, M., Morgan, R., and Reiner, R. (2007) *The Oxford handbook of criminology* (4th edn). Oxford: Oxford University Press.

Manzillier, J., and Hall, J. (1999) *What is clinical psychology?* (3rd edn). Oxford: Oxford University Press.

Micale, M., and Porter, R. (1994) *Discovering the history of psychiatry.* Oxford: Oxford University Press.

Offer, D., and Sabshin, M. (1991) *The diversity of normal behaviour.* US: HarperCollins.

Palmer, S., Dainlow, S., and Milner, P. (1996) *Counselling: The BAC counselling reader.* London: Sage.

Shorter, E. (1997) *A history of psychiatry: From the era of the asylum to the age of prozac.* Chichester: John Wiley.

Specific and more critical texts

Berlim, M. T., Fleck, M. P., and Shorter, E. (2003) Notes on antipsychiatry. *European Archives of Psychiatry and Clinical Neuroscience,* **253**, 61–7.

Brigham, J. (1999) What is forensic psychology, anyway? *Law and Human Behaviour,* **233**, 273–98.

Freeman, H. (1998) Mental health policy and practice in the NHS: 1948–1979. *Journal of Mental Health,* 7(3), 225–39.

Jewkes, Y. (2004) *Media and Crime.* London: Sage.

Jones, K. (1993) *Asylums and After.* London: Athlone.

Pilgrim, D., and Rogers, A. (1993) *A sociology of mental health and illness.* Buckingham: Open University Press.

Visit **www.pearsoned.co.uk/davidholmes** for a range of resources to support study. Test yourself with multiple choice questions and access a bank of over 100 videos that will bring the topics to life. Video coverage for this chapter includes a history of mental institutions in America, historical explanations of mental illness, and recent trends in psychological treatment.

CHAPTER 2 Critical issues in abnormal, clinical and forensic psychology

- Overview
- Case study
- Science versus belief
- What is science?

- The scientific status of abnormal psychology
- A new dark age
- Anti-psychiatry and abnormal, clinical and forensic psychology

- A critical balance
- Chapter summary

 Hear about the myths surrounding mental illness. This is one of several videos that explore issues and disorders relevant to this chapter at www.pearsoned.co.uk/davidholmes.

Belief and the media

In many countries across the world, there is an increasing media market for mystical belief, whether this is books and magazines on spiritual or 'alternative' treatments or health regimes, or TV programmes about psychic detection or chasing ghosts, such as ITV's *Most Haunted* in the UK. This dramatic public thirst for the paranormal has motivated supporters of scientific rationality such as **Ciaran O'Keeffe**, who has criticised the *Most Haunted* series 'medium' Derek Acorah for deceiving by pretence, showmanship and dramatics, as well as for obtaining information about locations prior to filming. However, the intent of *Most Haunted* is entertainment and honest enquiry, which inevitably may conflict with the methods of popular personalities demanded by the public.

The **James Randi Educational Foundation** offers a $1 million prize to anyone who can show, under proper observing conditions, evidence of any paranormal, supernatural, or occult power or event, and as yet has had no takers. This chapter will examine the serious issue of unfounded or mystical beliefs when they are applied to clinical and forensic areas as if they were factual (see Wheen, 2004).

James Randi, magician and false belief detective, offers $1 million of his own money to anyone who can demonstrate paranormal phenomena. The cash is still in the bank.
Source: Corbis/Jeffrey Allan Salter.

Overview

This chapter is intended as a critical reflection on a pivotal issue in and beyond abnormal, clinical and forensic psychology, and one that is historically and disciplinarily pervasive. In taking both a critical and a client-supportive position, this author will be expressing his personal opinion in this chapter, both to aid coherence and also to present challenging views for the student. The divide between scientific empiricism and belief should have dissolved with the advances of science but it has widened and hardened. There are signs of a rift opening beneath the discipline with little middle ground. This chapter will attempt to make this debate more transparent and at the same time to steer a stormy path towards the practical needs of the clients and public served by clinical and forensic professionals. This discipline is best placed to examine the issue of belief where it controls politics, law or education, borders on to delusion and is destructive to individuals and society.

Case study

Edmund: pathology or possession?

Edmund had worked for his uncle the miller since he was a child, in a small sixteenth-century German village. He had never been a well boy; he had twitches as he walked and could often be heard talking aloud to himself. By his late teens his behaviour had become erratic and he would often arrive at the mill injured. By his thirties he had no wife and still worked for his uncle. Edmund had also taken to repetitious behaviour such as might be seen in a caged animal and spent much time in conversation with himself. He would occasionally shout loudly as if in pain and frequently behaved as if others meant to harm him or were maliciously talking about him.

The miller had thought of him as family but could no longer keep him on, not even for grain. In the eyes of his father, Edmund was of little practical use in the home, but he was helped by his frail but stubborn mother. However, other people nearby were fearful of Edmund and his behaviour. They met in groups after church and eventually made forceful representations to the church leaders. Some 12 months later, visiting representatives of the church demanded that Edmund have his peculiarities examined, as they considered that he might be possessed by the Devil. Edmund was held for safety with five others from the district, who also appeared to be 'driven from within' to behave with poor reasoning.

Edmund's father became concerned that his son's further examination was being referred to as a 'test' and 'trial' by an inquisitor empowered by the Church and State. He was horrified to see his son publicly denounced to a restless crowd and given tests with needles as well as having his flesh examined for marks. Edmund did not understand the demands that he publicly renounce the Devil. Three of those 'possessed', including Edmund, failed to 'show reason' and were rapidly taken and hanged, as they were said to be possessed by the Devil. Edmond's family felt great loss, but also shame and fear.

In the twenty-first century, we view such primitive superstition as having no place in modern psychiatry. However, this chapter will critically discuss eras when superstitious belief subverted the rigours of science, and conclude that this may no longer be entirely confined to the past.

Science versus belief

Psychology in general is very vulnerable to criticism when compared to disciplines seen as objective or 'hard' sciences, such as physics or chemistry. The description of psychology as a 'subjective science' does not mean that psychological methods lack objectivity but that the data studied are mostly subjective. Students will meet the divide between psychologists favouring **quantitative** or science-supportive methods and those preferring **qualitative** methods, the latter tending to attract those supportive of belief-based psychology, or who are uncomfortable with empiricism (see Chapter 5). This section will examine the detail behind these conflicts as well as the potential dangers of an overcritical and abstract approach to abnormal psychology as a science.

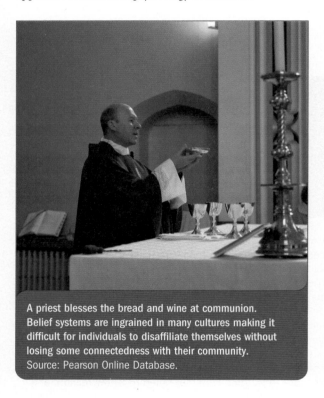

A priest blesses the bread and wine at communion. Belief systems are ingrained in many cultures making it difficult for individuals to disaffiliate themselves without losing some connectedness with their community.
Source: Pearson Online Database.

What is science?

Psychology being offered in the UK as both a science degree (BSc), requiring certain empirical components, and a less scientific arts degree (BA), would indicate some conflict over its scientific status. It may never fully meet the criteria of science due to its inherent subjectivity (Bell, 2002). The following section will examine the criteria for science and if they are met by psychological approaches.

The scientific method

Science is a means of knowing our universe and causal relationships within it (Bell, 2002). This approach assumes determinism, with all events having non-mystical antecedent causes. The scientific method is **empirical observation**, or categorising and organising observations validated by sensory experience. Karl Popper (1902–1996) demonstrated one limitation of this approach by asking his students to note what they observed. They were quick to ask what they were supposed to observe, illustrating that we are selective in what we examine and how we record and interpret observations. This selectivity can be aligned with the inconsistent views of the world within differing **scientific paradigms** observed by Kuhn (1996).

Empirical observations have principles such as logic applied to them and scientific theories inferred from these analyses of observations. Emergent theories should comprise confirmable propositions, which when tested establish robust **scientific laws**. Such laws are recognised and respected within that scientific discipline but should also be credible to the public. Historically, failure to be accepted by the public has harmed research and occasionally jeopardised scientists' lives, as in the case of Galileo.

Karl Popper also critically analysed component parts of theories (Popper, 2002). Critical appraisal was important to Popper, so theories had to be falsifiable (i.e. able to be tested and disproved) to be scientific, but theories should also be useful and have risk in their prediction. Thus, there is little risk or value in theorising that Mount Everest will be in the Higher Himalaya in 100 years. For Popper (2002) theories fail these criteria by being: of no value; vague; tautological (self-validating); or reliant on post-diction (post-hoc confirmation). For example, crystal ball predictions are vague, cannot be empirically tested, and suffer post-diction in that any subsequent event is reinterpreted as confirmation. There is less support for Popper's belief that all theories will be disconfirmed in time and that the highest scientific status of any theory is that it is not yet disconfirmed.

Empiricism and the philosophical inheritance

William of Occam (1285–1349) emphasised the need for parsimony and empiricism in scientific endeavour, but part of intelligence associates factors that appear to relate, confounding the true principles operating (Guthrie, 1942). Thus, Occam's view requires the pruning of all but that causing the outcome observed. There is an important distinction between **correlational** (see Chapter 5) and causal laws; thus a developing child's shoe size correlates with language ability, but neither of these causes the other. Both are products of a third factor, physical and behavioural development. This third factor reveals the true causal law – an example of **determinism** (Bell, 2002).

Given the strict scientific criteria, researchers developing testing laws in the 'hard' sciences are familiar with the frustration of having theories disproved and criticised. However, those pursuing pseudoscientific methods such as the 'crystal ball' example may be used to their ideas being confirmed unconditionally and could be viewed as the 'spoilt children of academia'. Perhaps the mundane reality and formidable detail involved in investigating testable laws, such as testing the effectiveness of a drug on the 1000th sample of brain tissue, is less inspiring when compared with the mystery and adventure that may accompany less empirical approaches, such as reading someone's 'aura' on a breakfast TV show.

Philosophy: antecedent of psychology

For **Ebbinghaus** (1897), psychology had a short history as a discipline but a long past, in that its core issues reach deep into history in the territory of philosophy (Hergenhahn, 2005). Students need to separate the entanglement of psychology and philosophy that can confound contemporary approaches to disordered behaviour. The abstracted supposition of philosophy supplied interim answers until questions were answered by empirical experimentation, just as belief fills the voids in our knowledge until they are sealed by scientific facts.

Hegel (1770–1831) aimed towards a philosophically based single integrated knowledge system, joining all knowledge into a coherent whole. This evaporated as scientific endeavour separated into increasingly diverse subdisciplines (Hergenhahn, 2005). René Descartes (1596–1650) thought that science branched from the tree of philosophy, which may reflect historical origins but not the superiority of philosophy as he intended. As each scientific discipline gained support from empirical inquiry, they distanced themselves from any roots in philosophy. Left behind by its connections to the 'real world', philosophy became a sanctuary for moral, religious and political values. As its subject matter became more abstract, philosophy became intellectually discredited by those disciplines embracing scientific principles (Hergenhan, 2005). Psychology had more difficulty breaking its philosophical apron strings, as it shared historical dilemmas with philosophy.

Mind, brain and free will

Philosophical dilemmas relevant to abnormal psychology could in essence be conceptualised as a single issue viewed from differing perspectives. The main forms of this issue are:

- the mind–body distinction: are mental events and brain function separate entities or two ways of viewing the same thing?

- the **nature–nurture** issue, or the effects of genetic and biological determinism versus those of environmental experience on behaviour

- free will versus determinism, i.e. do we decide what we do or are we are passive observers of the processes of our brains?

- can the apparent continuity of **mental experience** be explained in terms of the machinery of the brain and senses?

The common assumption is the idea that mental experience is somehow distinct from the brain, accentuated by the continuous nature of conscious experience seeming separate from brain activity. However, if the brain is damaged, the mental experience of the owner is curtailed. There are no mental events that occur without corresponding brain activity. Thus, earlier thinkers failed to appreciate the remarkable potential of the brain, despite its unimpressive visual appearance.

Although some follow an interactionist view, such dilemmas are simply irresolvable 'non-arguments', a phrase **Michael Rutter** uses for the nature–nurture dilemma, and are often made redundant in the light of modern neuroscience. Research has progressively established the primary role of the brain in the mind–brain argument and that other philosophical dilemmas are resolved by brain function.

The brain's greater role in higher thought has been illustrated by the remarkable functions of single cells, such as that found to respond only to the concept of 'two', whether this is two eyes, two trees or making two cups of coffee. Quiroga et al. (2005) have monitored single neurons that respond exclusively to one identity, whether it is a picture, line drawing or their name. For example, one subject's neuron would respond to a photo or drawing of film star **Halle Berry** or even the letters of her name presented separately. Non-monitored cells may also respond, but this does not detract from the remarkable differentiating power of the single cell. Brain damage reveals how much of the philosophical 'mind' is routine brain processing. Stone and Young (1997) found brain injury to alter beliefs and emphasised the known role of the left temporal lobe in belief systems, including 'religious experiences'. The brain is not a passive vehicle for mental events but the active agent that creates them.

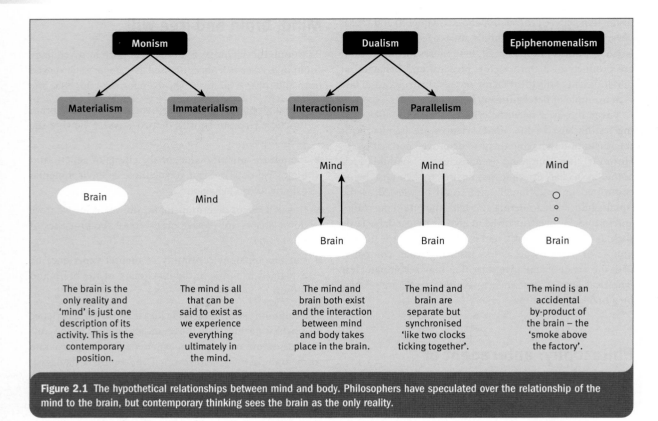

Figure 2.1 The hypothetical relationships between mind and body. Philosophers have speculated over the relationship of the mind to the brain, but contemporary thinking sees the brain as the only reality.

Mental events leave a trace in the brain and repeatedly recalled memories become permanent in the structure of the brain. This suggests the brain's structure is influenced by its function, often experienced as mental free will. However, it is *the brain* doing this thinking, and opponents of determinism may be less comfortable with this lump of grey matter having free will. At this point, most texts bring in an analogy for the relationship of brain structure to mental experience. Although there is no true analogy for this unique relationship, it is still useful to consider the function of a simple loudspeaker converting electrical impulses into air movement in the form of sound. If you shout into a loudspeaker, it can act as a weak microphone producing a small electrical current, reversing its normal function. Thus, the repeated mental events that parallel transitory **electrochemical events** in the brain will alter the brain's permanent structure, or the reverse of the process may happen, whereby the brain's established structure produces characteristic mental events (Carlson, 2004). This means of manipulating mental events and characteristic brain responses is used in **cognitive therapy** (see Chapter 3) and can lead to permanent change in abnormal behaviour (Wells, 2009).

There is widespread criticism of the importance of genetic inheritance in the development of abnormal behaviour. In the absence of certain environmental factors, some genetically predisposed behaviour will not develop, but in the absence of this genetic predisposition, no amount of environmental influence will precipitate the behaviour. More blatantly, in the absence of a tiny percentage of genetic code there would simply be no organism. This brief empirical view would not satisfy the more vociferous critics (e.g. Kamin, Rose and Lewontin, 1984) and these perceived weaknesses in psychology as an empirical science have allowed historical philosophical arguments to remain within the remit of the subject.

The 'crystal ball' example may seem divorced from current methods in abnormal, clinical and forensic psychology and closer to **parapsychology** (the study of paranormal belief, literally 'the beyond'). However, psychology has struggled with equally dubious theories lacking in empiricism. **Franz Joseph Gall** (1758–1828) considered that the brain dictated personality, but his method of measurement supposed that the skull's shape reflected personality aspects of the brain. This theory of phrenology was a scientific cul-de-sac, undermining psychological science and producing the pseudoscientific legacy of a relationship between physique and criminality that spanned **Lombroso** (1876) and **Sheldon** (1942). However, recent work has established stature as a factor in crime but with a clear causal path (Raine et al., 1998). The longevity of the pseudoscience of phrenology is greater than psychology as a discipline and hampered psychology in gaining acceptance as a 'hard science'.

The scientific status of abnormal psychology

Associated disciplines

Persistent philosophical associations and inherent subjectivity have weakened the scientific standing of psychology. The **positivist** approach pursues objectivity and minimises subjective experience, paralleling the traditional approach of psychiatry. Psychiatry emphasises a medical view but does not exclude psychological approaches; but just as a book on **psychotherapy** would not emphasise medical treatments, so a psychiatric text primarily considers physical well-being. The medical prerequisites for psychiatry have always given it authority over psychology in a clinical context. Whilst professional bodies such as the British Association of Behavioural and Cognitive-Behavioural Psychotherapies battle to establish worldwide standards, some therapeutic

approaches are seen by the public to limit scientific acceptability. For example, 'clown therapy' sessions (clown role play for anxiety and depression) may have good intentions, but they feed the stereotype of professional psychologists being as eccentric as their patients.

Paradigms within psychology tend to be studied in an unbiased, eclectic manner and students are not encouraged to discriminate on the basis of practical value to the patient or offender. Abnormal, clinical and forensic psychology has become a diverse, popular and fast-growing subject domain. However, popularity is no substitute for scientific credibility, whilst diversity and familiarity may undermine its status.

Role confusion

The increasing need for clinical and forensic psychologists, which constantly outstrips supply, would suggest that professional psychology is a secure career providing its credibility as a science is at least maintained. Psychology is a popular lay science, featured extensively in newspapers and magazines. The media, including the internet, now eclipse more traditional sources of information for the public (Devereux, 2003). '**Media psychologists**' have transcended their role as experts disseminating the psychological viewpoint and are now placed as entertainers, indistinguishable from the presenters on programmes such as reality TV shows in the *Big Brother* tradition. This has contributed to

David A. Holmes being interviewed on TV. Bringing psychology within the realm of public understanding via the media can also undermine the credibility of professional psychologists.
Source: David A. Holmes.

the view that anyone can apply psychology to abnormal behaviour. Thus, the public feel they have some 'expertise' in psychology, which they would never claim to have in surgical medicine.

Other professionals such as nurses or counsellors, taking a similar role to professional psychologists, can also undermine status. A greater threat is posed by 'therapists' who operate in the manner of **religious cults**. They are minimally qualified, prey on vulnerable or suggestible clients, and may inflict further harm. **False memory syndrome** is where zealous therapists induce 'memories' of childhood abuse in suggestible individuals (see Chapter 15), which are often impossible to verify (Spanos, 1996). This dilemma is more common in the USA, which embraces more psychogenic (psychological causes) approaches, particularly psychodynamic views, than Europe, where more somatogenic (biological cause) explanations are established.

Imprecise terminology

Abnormal, clinical and forensic psychologists have some media authority in correcting misconceptions, such as referring to schizophrenia as 'split personality', although the correctly attributed split in dissociative identity disorder is also disputed (see Chapter 15; Spanos, 1996). The media also refer to the mentally ill with the phrase 'should be sent for counselling'. Such individuals would never be sent to a counsellor, only a trained therapist or psychiatrist, as counsellors support individuals with problems, not first-episode psychiatric patients.

There is misuse of terminology within the profession as well. For example, the term **psychotherapy** encompasses all psychological therapies, including behavioural and cognitive therapies. However, the term is adopted for psychoanalytic and humanist approaches, appearing to exclude other paradigms. Thus, a narrow range of psychoanalytically based therapies are associated with 'psychotherapy', tending to exclude the major therapy in clinical psychology of cognitive behavioural therapy. The term 'individual therapy' has also been interpreted both narrowly and broadly with similar outcomes. Inaccurate use of their own terminology does not help the image of professionals amongst other disciplines and the public. The media keep abreast of current thinking where fashion and celebrity are concerned, but they perpetuate the archaic and erroneous belief that clinical psychology and psychiatry involve patients lying on couches talking about their childhood.

Paradoxically, the credibility of abnormal, clinical and forensic psychology is under greater threat as demand increases. Thus, practitioners of psychology may need to be 'marketed' to improve public confidence in their work. It is of concern that an academic discipline should reinvent itself every few years like an ageing celebrity. The next section will examine the possible Achilles heel of psychology. This dilemma reaches beyond psychology but may be best addressed by abnormal, clinical and forensic psychology.

A new dark age

Belief systems persist in abnormal psychology that are in opposition to the methods, theories and laws established by scientific means (Wheen, 2004). These are **non-determinist** approaches or assumptions devoid of scientific causality. For magician and psychic-sceptic James Randi, non-scientific belief systems are proliferating to the degree that he considers the world to be entering a new dark age where scientific proof is sidestepped in favour of belief-based views. At a point where scientific achievement is well integrated into our lives, regressing over a millennium to where science began a long battle against superstition would be dangerous, as the original solution of scientific proof is already available (Roberts and Groome, 2001). Across all disciplines, public interest in and study of belief-based information has escalated (Randi, 1995), including established religions and cult-like counterparts, paranormal phenomena and numerous alternative therapies of varying credibility.

Science undermined

Some factors encouraging the rejection of science and the need to embrace belief-based systems are as follows.

- **Complex technology.** A steam engine is finely engineered but its function is explicit in its structure. However, computerised devices appear closer to magic than science, as the means by which they function is not intuitively obvious. Inaccessibility due to complexity is true of the human brain, and neuroscience has to be 'translated' for the untrained to gain insight. The public are suspicious of this complexity and suggestible to more accessible alternative views of the world: for example, the simplistic belief that having mental illness or being the victim of a crime such as rape is punishment for not adhering to a belief system or its rituals (see Dawkins, 2006; Pfeifer, 1994).

- **Scientific complexity.** As complex and specialist subdisciplines diverge and become abstracted, the chances of their conclusions coming into conflict increases. Further to this, where science does not yet have sufficient data to produce coherent answers, the resultant changing hypotheses (and conflict between disciplines) can portray the efforts of science as being no more 'scientific' than the ready and consistent answers supplied by belief systems such as religion (Dawkins, 2006).

- **Sound bite psychology.** The 'dumbing-down' of professional psychology in the media makes it difficult to distinguish professional expertise from showmanship (Roberts and Groome, 2001). Thus, claims of **psychics** may be equated with the trained judgement of forensic psychologists when it comes to identifying criminals (see Chapter 8). This confusion can become a clear bias when scientific explanations seem inaccessible and lacklustre in comparison with the more exotic views of pseudo-psychological practice (Dawkins, 2006). Simple myths have always been more attractive and 'media friendly' than complex truths. Financially rewarding media careers can encourage the well-trained showman to create audiences of believers. **Uri Geller** has enjoyed a long career based on his ability to mix trickery with psychology and showmanship (Randi, 1995).

- **Charisma and cults.** The aggressive manipulation of large numbers of the public by charismatic leaders of belief systems can produce the formation of cult-like cohesion amongst followers (Randi, 1995). Insularity, suggestibility and dominant individuals abusing their leadership role can lead to situations such as the mass suicide (or homicide) by burning in Kanungu, Uganda of members of the Restoration of the Ten Commandments cult under the leadership of **Joseph Kibweteere** in March 2000. Organisations may camouflage their cult image by promoting themselves as official religions: for example, the Unification Church has also been known as the Moonies. In the UK, pro-foxhunting groups have used The Free Church of Country Sports to gain protection from anti-hunting laws.

- **Anti-science.** Disaffected professionals who are hyper-critical of scientific explanations and perceive an allegiance between contemporary science and politics will support belief-based approaches as a means of retaliation. Disordered individuals are suggestible and easily recruited to belief explanations, especially when part of that belief is a denial that they are really disordered. Patients suffering auditory hallucinations formed the self-help group 'The Hearing Voices Network' with professionals, in which they cope with the symptom unmedicated with varying success. However, this is exaggerated by some to a belief that no sufferer has schizophrenia (see Chapter 18).

- **A sense of history.** Much of the history and pre-history of abnormal psychology has been dominated by non-scientific approaches and this legacy provides a basis for arguing the legitimacy of belief-based approaches (Prins, 1990).

- **Superstition and suggestion.** Certain functional and individual factors, such as **suggestibility** and **schizotypy** (see Chapter 14), increase proneness to non-scientific beliefs (Holmes, 1998). **B. F. Skinner** (1904–1990) frequently demonstrated superstitious behaviour in pigeons by administering non-contingent rewards. The pigeons developed eccentric behaviour patterns as they tried hopelessly to match their behaviour to random rewards. This behaviour is also seen in humans as futile ritual intended to bring good fortune, such as 'lucky' lottery numbers or a rabbit's foot.

- **Adaptive functions of belief systems.** Some beliefs are so persistent that it may be that they have some evolutionary component or function (Cartwright, 2008). Activity in certain locations in the brain such as the **left temporal lobe** (see Chapter 18) appears to produce heightened belief experiences (Carlson, 2004). Further evidence that belief is part of our **phylogenetic** development arises from belief about death and the dead being consistent throughout civilisation and even amongst animals such as elephants and apes (Morris, 1990). Belief in afterlife may have the function of helping comfort the elderly or terminally ill facing their final days.

Belief versus science

Belief systems that overextend their remit not only undermine science but become a danger when enmeshed with education, politics and law. A clear illustration is the conflict between established evolutionary theory and the 'creationist' viewpoint that God created the world, based on the Old Testament in the Christian Bible. In 1925 Tennessee became the first US state to outlaw evolutionary teaching due to conflict with religious explanations (Larson, 1989). In countries with fundamentalist Christian movements, there are attempts to have **creationist theory** taught as fact. This resurgence of activity by creationist proponents is seen as a sign of a twenty-first century dark age. Political capital can be gained by supporting popular belief over science in the USA and elsewhere. Moves to outlaw teaching Darwin's theory by Serbia's Orthodox Church were taken seriously by the Serbian Minister for Education in 2004. In the UK, **Richard Dawkins** has condemned a Gateshead college for teaching children that evolution was wrong.

International perspective

Popular culture and public belief

Richard Dawkins has transcended his role as biologist to become an international spokesperson for evolutionary rationality.
Source: Getty Images.

Primitive belief has always been associated with 'underdeveloped' countries, but such thinking now appears to be advancing rather than receding in most countries across the world. Although some folk beliefs are more in line with medicine than the supernatural, public beliefs about the causes of mental illness have always had a non-scientific component (Jorm, 2000) both in emergent and in Western civilisations. Surprisingly, up to a third of many Western religious populations still consider that these disorders may be self-inflicted because the sufferers strayed from the righteous path – a belief that is even more common amongst patients

themselves (Pfeifer, 1994). Primitive demonological explanations are still surprisingly common internationally and the practice of **exorcism** still survives in many advanced countries. For example, Ferracuti, Sacco and Lazzari (1996) report on a case in Italy in the 1990s.

The media took advantage of increased superstitious tendencies in the wake of the 1970s film *The Exorcist* from the USA, which produced a sudden rise in the number of self-proclaimed exorcists and exorcisms. This complemented existing cult belief systems such as in Japan (e.g. Davis, 1980) and had a disturbing influence on suggestible groups of patients (Whitwell and Barker, 1980). The very theatrical acting out of the exorcism process influenced the impressionable, leading to proliferation of so-called **possessions** in most countries of the world, including the UK (Fountain, 2000). In 2005, Channel 4 in the UK screened a 'live exorcism' of a supposedly possessed volunteer whilst monitoring his brain patterns. This was widely criticised by many people, including European Church leaders wishing to distance themselves from it, as well as psychologists and psychiatrists who feared that a wave of patients may discard their diagnoses and medication in favour of a demonic explanation.

The US TV series *The X-files* portrayed supernatural events purported to be based on true accounts but marginalising the more factual mundane explanation (e.g. having hallucinations). At the turn of the millennium, media fiction became confounded with fact to the extent that figures such as Richard Dawkins took issue with programme makers for this unclear distinction and the public for following this masquerade. This confounding of science with popular fiction has influenced other belief systems, such as religious claims of creationism, which are supported in parts of the USA and the Middle East, and are now more plausible to wider audiences in Europe.

This century, skilled UK magician **Derren Brown** staged a media séance and was surprised himself by the degree of suggestibility and conviction shown by the immediate audience and public. Fed on a diet of fictional characters such as 'psychic counsellors from Venus', the public frequently see professional psychologists as being associated with supernatural abilities. This is ultimately unhelpful to their international public image or academic standing.

In *The Blind Watchmaker* (Dawkins, 1986) critically addresses a second layer of creationist argument, **intelligent design theory** (see Scott, 1997). 'Intelligent design' explains complex information by acts of intelligence and, in the case of life, a Divine being, rather than by evolution. For Dawkins (1986) this argument is countered by the errors of evolution during natural selection.

Such arguments are irresolvable when belief can be its own evidence and can be backed by force, as in the power struggle between science and the Church in the Middle Ages. The scientific argument for evolution is not proof of all aspects of **evolutionary theory**, but is certain proof that creationist 'theory' is wrong. The fact that counter-arguments survive this and gain legal backing does provide some support for James Randi's fears of an imminent intellectual dark age.

Belief confounding education, politics and law exists on the fundamentalist fringe of some established religions. The punishment for apostasy or unrepentantly leaving ('turning their back on') the Islamic faith is death, as it is for 'moral' crimes such as adultery or even being in the company of an unrelated man, which are not recognised as criminal acts elsewhere. These executions along with amputations for theft are considered to be religious occasions and, until mobile phone technology, were rarely witnessed by the non-initiated. It is also worth considering the extreme suffering inflicted by belief in an afterlife enabling **suicide bombers**. The escalating place of belief across the globe coincides with and relates to abnormal, clinical and forensic psychology being vulnerable to losing their way as sciences, which is examined further in the next section.

Research

Lunar effects – belief or science?

The full moon has both mythical and scientific effects on people.
Source: Pearson Online Database.

The term 'lunatic' comes from the Latin *luna*, pertaining to the moon and its apparent cycles or phases. Luna, the Roman goddess of the moon, perhaps represents an association between the moon and feminine issues.

The association between the moon and behaviour mixes historical mythical belief with some known empirical effects of the moon. One of the most learned societies of the 1700s was the Lunar Society founded in 1766. On this basis, members were referred to as lunatics, the derogatory implications worsened by considering the effects of the medicinal herb **Digitalis** (Foxglove). However, the name resulted from these empirical scientists meeting around the time of the full moon for safety, as extra light assisted their journeys on poor roads with highwaymen.

The lunar beliefs

Mystical properties have been attributed to the full moon. In Bedlam, inmates were chained, tied up and flogged at the full moon to prevent anticipated aggression and violence (McG. Kelley, 1942). A widespread perceived association existed between mental derangement, crime and violence, with supernatural forces invoked by the moon's luminescence still prevalent today, especially amongst mental health workers (Wilson and Tobacyk, 1990). In 1843, the *Lancet* reported a popular belief at the time that the moon was responsible for episodes of epilepsy and insanity (White, 1914). Implications of this belief include psychiatric administrators employing more staff during a full moon in anticipation of increased workload, creating superstition-based resource implications.

Research continued

Myth and legend have drawn the moon into a seductively sexual role in addition to its role as a romantic symbol in song and fiction. In fictional **lycanthropy** (see case study), susceptible individuals become werewolves at full moon and moonlight has played a dramatic role in many tales of the supernatural. This created belief in the moon's power over sexual libido.

The lunar science

Observable effects of the moon's movements include the moon freeing itself from the earth's shadow, producing an increase in light reflected from the sun and turning night into a dim version of day. The moon also exerts a strong and changing gravitational effect on the earth, causing the rising and falling tides across the planet. Both of these empirical effects of the moon may alter the expectations of individuals regarding 'moon-related' events.

Increased lunar light levels at night are less noticeable in modern city lighting but more marked in the past, with individuals having sleep disrupted around the full moon and light facilitating more night-time activity in general. A full moon reflects enough light to read by, 12 times brighter than the half-moon. This can disrupt sleep, which can have an effect on temporal lobe epilepsy, a condition very sensitive to even slight sleep deprivation (Rajna and Veres, 1993). Sleep deprivation has been employed in treating depression

and inducing mild hypomania (see Chapter 17) in both mood-disordered and normal individuals (Wright, 1993). This effect is short-lived, creating the impression of mild insanity at the time of the full moon.

Evidence of violence and psychiatric violence at the time of the full moon is inconsistent. Leiber (1978) found an increase in psychiatric admissions and assaults, but Owen et al. (1998) found no relationship with violent behaviour. Similarly equivocal findings exist for recorded incidents of animals biting humans, in that Bhattacharjee et al. (2000) found a relationship with the moon's cycle, but Chapman and Morrell (2000) found no such correlation.

Although the moon's gravity affects the tides, it is unlikely to act on human bodily fluids such as hormones, neurotransmitters or amniotic fluid. However, gynaecological studies reveal consistent relationships with the moon's cycles. Ghiandoni et al. (1998) uncovered lunar cycles relating to the frequency of full-term deliveries of children, and Law (1986) found that female menstruation coincides with the full moon. However, the gravitational effects of the moon on human behaviour have to cope with complex tidal fluctuations, which do not clearly coincide with the moon's phases (Myers, 1995), indicating that such studies may need further analysis.

Thus, despite the bizarre nature of myths surrounding the lunar cycles, from 250,000 miles away the moon has effects felt on earth (for further reading, see Rotton and Kelly, 1985).

Self-test questions

- Why is the credibility of psychological approaches to abnormal behaviour vulnerable to criticism?

- Discuss the role of the media and education in relation to empirical and belief-based information dissemination.

- Discuss the survival of belief systems in the context of advancing science.

- What are the arguments against 'intelligent design theory'?

- Can the moon's cycles affect mental states?

Anti-psychiatry and abnormal, clinical and forensic psychology

The primary historical critics of the scientific approach originated from the established religious authorities (Hergenhahn, 2005). In the Middle Ages, the Church defended its control of the population against the threat to belief posed by rational scientific thought. As science gained ground in some disciplines, abnormal behaviour remained a soft target for criticism. The elusive mechanisms of mental illness and grossly ineffective treatments left psychiatric science vulnerable to attack by the newly emerging critics in the humanitarian and reform movement. Until the 1950s, treatment of the mentally ill, particularly involuntary admissions, was little different to that of prisoners (Hergenhahn, 2005). This provided a comparison for humanitarian critics, which was more poignantly illustrated by the case of the mentally ill offender in prison and the patient who offends in a secure unit (Mason and Mercer, 1999).

Paradoxically, in a decade when major scientific treatments were implemented, literature was published forming the building blocks of the anti-psychiatry movement (e.g. Laing, 1960; Kesey, 1962). When psychiatrists were effective in bringing calm and rationality to patients, they were under attack from sociologists and from within their own profession. This apparent inconsistency may result from how the humanitarian movement was accommodated within psychiatry.

The religious idealism of many in this humanitarian movement, such as Tuke, was frustrated by a return to restraint and confinement during the 1800s. During this period, a belief system with a religious cult-like structure began to establish itself within psychiatry. The psychoanalytic movement capitalised on the failures of biological science in treating mental illness (Shorter, 1997). Psychoanalysis, involving prolonged individual interaction with patients and a non-scientific belief system, appealed to those humanitarian psychiatrists stranded between limited humane treatment on the one hand, and incarceration and restraint on the other. Ironically, many of the 'successful' cases reported by psychoanalysts were probable neurological disorders and were never 'cured' (Webster, 2004). In 2009, the UK government proposed the state regulation of 'talking therapies' under the **Health Professions Council**. The requirements include specified outcomes for therapy and this is vociferously opposed by many psychoanalytic therapists.

Scientific approaches to abnormal behaviour were limited during the period dominated by **psychoanalysis**, apart from the effective but mistrusted **behaviourist school** (see Chapter 3). Also a psychological approach, **behaviourism** was critically attacked by the psychoanalytic school as, unlike psychoanalysis, behavioural treatment was scientific and highly effective. In the 1950s, the crude medical approaches to mental illness were revolutionised by effective drug treatments (Shorter, 1997). This posed a serious challenge to psychoanalysis in psychiatry, with claims to *any* effectiveness questioned by critics such as **Hans J. Eysenck** (Eysenck, 1952). With their credibility challenged, those aligned with the non-empirical psychoanalytic and humanist approaches attacked this newly effective medical psychiatry with surprising venom (see Shorter, 1997). Thus, most of those leading the anti-psychiatry movement of the 1960s and 1970s supported the **psychodynamic** school of thought.

Anti-psychiatry

The **anti-psychiatry movement** did not only result from conflicting disciplines. Effective medical interventions diminished the interpersonal role of the psychiatrist, leaving them rushing from patient to patient prescribing and monitoring medications. To staff and patients the psychiatrist became a powerful figure and could personally hold the legal right of a patient's freedom (Shorter, 1997). In mental illness, the ability to make rational, informed decisions is the very ability that is disabled. Just as a patient with broken arms would not be expected to carry heavy bags, so a patient who has lost rationality should not be making important decisions. The psychiatrist effectively become the patient's informed advocate, apparently disempowering patients and provoking the wrath of humanists, sociologists and other politicised groups. Psychiatrists needed to be emotionally aloof to cope with the daily cycle of tragically disordered individuals. Some found it useful to hide behind this 'intellectualisation', which did not endear them to critics challenging their apparent power over patients (Clare, 1980).

Early in the 1950s the Church of Scientology campaigned against perceived psychiatric abuses and 'survivors of psychiatry' formed a union for patients' rights in the UK. Scientology had proponents such as Thomas Szasz, but by the twenty-first century it included celebrities such as **Tom Cruise** and **John Travolta**. In the 1960s, sociologists had also become relentless critics of psychiatry (Roth, 1973). They already had a history of criticising prisons and the justice system in many countries (see Williams, 2001) and levelled similar arguments at the treatment of the mentally ill. **Foucault** (1980) noted the involvement of sociologists in social medicine and medical epidemiology, perhaps leading to their involvement with anti-psychiatry. Sociologists posed as 'moral guardians' of the mentally ill or criminal against a scientific establishment lacking in humanitarianism. Sociologists restate the nature–nurture argument and assume that established psychiatry opposes social factors in the cause of mental illness. However, it is more precise to assume that the sociological view denies any involvement of biological determinants or 'nature'.

The academic Zeitgeist during the 1960s was that of rebellion, with students protesting as in the anti-Vietnam war movement. The factors fuelling anti-psychiatry predated this period, but in the 1960s critical changes saw psychiatry shaken from its apparent complacency (see Nolan and Hopper, 1997). A coherent group of individuals questioned the medical model and privileged legal status of psychiatrists. Termed 'anti-psychiatry' by psychoanalyst Cooper (1967), this label was used by history but not by anti-psychiatrists.

A central focus was the status of schizophrenia and the labelling of schizophrenic individuals. Critical issues specific to schizophrenia will be returned to in Chapter 18. Anti-psychiatry portrayed biological psychiatrists as uncaring robots, at a point when they were most effective (Shorter, 1997).

At this time, the vulnerability of psychiatric patients and disordered offenders provoked sympathy amongst a public fed on the 'love revolution' of the 1960s and 1970s. Reformers and politicised groups seeking modern demons seized on psychiatric power over the disturbed, '**chemical straitjackets**' and ECT (see Chapter 3). Stories of patients falling though the mental health care net were presented by anti-psychiatry as indicating widespread professional abuse, and psychiatry was urged to account for its lack of humanity and consider the individual behind the label 'patient' (Shorter, 1997). The film and the book *One Flew Over the Cuckoo's Nest* (Kesey, 1962) was a *fictional* account, but a rebellious generation treated it as a documentary source with graphic, emotionally charged accounts of ECT and psychosurgery to punish patients for rebellious acts. Anti-psychiatry needed a charismatic focal leader to pose as a defender of humanity at its most vulnerable.

Focus

Ronald David Laing – psychiatrist or guru?

R. D. Laing (1927–1989) symbolised anti-psychiatry from his initial publication in 1960 through to his worldwide cult-like status of 'psychiatrist as prophet', launching an assault on Western psychiatry. His posthumous influence today perhaps rests more on Laing the inspirational humanitarian than on his achievements on behalf of anti-psychiatry, a label that Laing himself rejected.

Laing was an existential psychiatrist and, in common with so many of the anti-psychiatry movement, grounded in the psychodynamic and psychoanalytical. When he left his hometown of Glasgow and subsequent medical training for the army in 1951, Laing discovered a rapport with the mentally disordered soldiers he saw as a psychiatrist. He saw rapport as more important than the crude treatments he had witnessed, such as lobotomies, and believed that schizophrenia was a sane reaction to bizarre circumstances.

Laing shifted emphasis three times as a leader of psychiatric rebellion. In the first phase he described the disturbed as playing at being mad to avoid responsibility. Taking responsibility was fundamental to the existentialist school, as was 'ontological insecurity' or awareness of one's place in the world and the precarious nature of existence. Near the end of his first book, *The Divided Self*, Laing focuses on the family context. In his second phase he de-emphasised the individual patient and adopted Gregory Bateson's 'double bind' hypothesis (Bateson et al., 1956), seeing schizophrenic behaviour as normal in the context of 'disturbed families'. **Gregory Bateson** was head of the Palo Alto school of schizophrenia research, which was influential for Laing and acknowledged the pathological family structures described by **Theodore Lidz** (Lidz et al., 1957).

In his third phase, Laing denied that schizophrenia was a disorder but considered the diagnostic process a type of disorder he termed '**psychiatrosis**'. He saw madness as personal development, a divine transformation producing psychedelic signs of an expanding creativity, which allowed transformation into superior mental beings. Laing and colleagues founded therapeutic communities such as Kingsley Hall in 1965 as a supportive environment for patients on this journey of self-realisation. Running as a 'sanctuary' blurred the distinction between staff and inmates, counter to psychiatric training in which clear boundaries are drawn between patient and psychiatrist. Kingsley Hall was closed by the Department of Health due to high rates of suicide, sexual assault and pregnancy (Kotowicz, 1997). In Kandubodda Ceylon (now Sri Lanka), Laing learned and practised Theravada Buddhist meditation.

Laing's involvement with his work took its toll on his personal life: his first marriage floundered and his drinking habits became salient. Laing never recovered emotionally from his second wife's affair and alcoholic behaviour led to his resigning from the General Medical Council in 1987. In his final and unfinished book, *The Lies of Love*, Laing refers to his devastation at the age of 5 that Father Christmas did not exist and was impersonated by his parents. This indicates the importance of belief for Laing and why he placed faith in his own ideals rather than psychiatric science. In retrospect, Laing was both loved and hated by his own profession: some saw him as a clever, witty humanitarian, and others only as an alcoholic who fell from grace whilst clinging to popularity. He died of a heart attack in 1989 whilst playing tennis in France. The Society for Laingian Studies has extensive descriptive information on R. D. Laing.

R. D. Laing

UK psychiatrist **R. D. Laing** rode high upon this tide of rebellion with his **existentialist** but essentially psycho-dynamic approach (see Chapter 3) to understanding the patient's experience of their illness (see the Focus box). Laing explained the infinite regress of the psychiatrist's reaction to their experience of the patient's reaction to their experience of the psychiatrist's reaction to them, and so on. This raised awareness of the patient's subjective experience. However, Laing erroneously considered the patient a normal person reacting to this interactional confusion pro-duced by families and authorised by psychiatrists, rather than the patient as cause of such reactions. Laing was delighted that visitors to his Kingsley Hall therapeutic community could not distinguish patients from therapists. His guru status and occasional accusations of unprofessional activity further distanced him from orthodox psychiatry. A vinyl album of Laing's sonnets bought by his cult-like following symbolised the fading professional credibility attributed to Laing by the scientific community.

Szasz and mental illness

Thomas Szasz (born 1920), professor of psychiatry, self-proclaimed radical-libertarian in the USA and trained psychoanalyst, published *The Myth of Mental Illness* (Szasz, 1960), attacking the term 'mental illness'. For Szasz, what is mental cannot be physical, failing his **pathoanatomical criteria** for being susceptible to disease. He saw psychi-atrists as disempowering patients under the false pretence that the mind could be diseased. However, the mind and brain are only separate semantically; in practical terms they are indistinguishable, confining Szasz's argument to definition of terms rather than psychiatric realities. As Clare (1980) points out, if you refer to a different diction-ary to that used by Szasz, his argument loses substance. The terms 'mentally ill' or 'mental illness' probably derive from Tuke's wife applying them to inmates of the York Retreat in preference to the more derogatory 'lunatic' or 'mad', without consideration of inherent conceptual weaknesses.

Szasz saw compulsory detention and treatment as state control, with psychiatrists perpetrating mythical disorders and therapy. Szasz criticised Laing for lack of rigour but had a surprisingly similar background and shared existential views of patients being responsible for their behaviour. Both Szasz and Laing saw abnormal behaviour as rational and acted out in the family, and both objected to the term 'anti-psychiatry'. Unlike Laing, Szasz never tested his views in the real world of patients.

Although his work was of little practical value, Szasz made a substantial academic contribution to the relation-ship between legal and psychiatric responsibility. Few would agree that schizophrenic patients are legally responsible for their behaviour, but many would agree with Szasz that individuals escaping justice on grounds of mild and irrelevant 'mental disorder' are culpable. Szasz asserted that psychiatry was not a science (Szasz, 2001) and drew atten-tion to its loose terminology, a criticism that may benefit the discipline in time (for more, see Wyatt, 2004).

Kendell (2001) has attempted to clarify the distinction and areas of contention between mental and physical illness. Kendall explains that all physical illnesses have psycho-logical symptoms: for example, pain is a psychological experience and psychological factors such as worry can impact on physical illnesses such as asthma (see Chapter 16). As many psychiatric disorders have physical symptoms, such as in anorexia, the robust distinction made by Szasz is less convincing, even on his own terms. In Kendell's (2001) view, it is the degree to which the disorder affects the nervous system that dictates whether the disorder is quantifiably mental or physical.

The cult-like adherents of anti-psychiatry tended to inhabit an intellectual fringe but provided useful crit-ical monitoring of clinical and forensic practice. Fading enlightenment in the twenty-first century is assisted by popular media not differentiating empirically established fact from anti-psychiatric opinion. An article in the UK *Guardian* in 2005 (James, 2005) asserts that mental illness stems from parental mistreatment and not from biological causes, which is very much in line with the early anti-psychiatry movement. This assumes that disturbances in early childhood caused the illness rather than the dis-turbances being a result of the disorder in combination with abnormal genes in the family.

Critical psychiatry and postmodernism

Critical psychiatry and psychology

The anti-psychiatry movement waned in the 1980s as the psychotherapeutic communities met the same limitations as their counterparts at the turn of the nineteenth century. Even radical anti-psychiatry movements with large-scale implementation policies, such as the deinstitutionalisation movement of **Franco Basaglia** (Basaglia, 1968) in Italy, fell short of their patient-centred ideals. Implementation of care in the community initiatives and revised patients' rights removed much of the ammunition from the humanitarian critics and, for many, led to anti-psychiatry being con-signed to history (Tantam, 1991). A philosophical and academic counterpart remained and at the turn of the twenty-first century there was an upsurge in more academ-ically astute professionals subscribing to '**critical psychiatry**' or critical psychology. Enduring weaknesses inherent in psychiatry preserved its critics and these vulnerabilities were not reflected in other medical disciplines, illustrated by the lack of rebellious groups such as 'anti-oncology' or 'anti-haematology' (Bracken and Thomas, 2001).

Critical psychiatry was quick to distance itself from anti-psychiatry (as were those leading the anti-psychiatry movement). Organisations such as the Critical Psychiatry Network view science as a source of problems not solutions for the mentally ill (see Leudar and Thomas, 2000; Bracken and Thomas, 2001). These critics politicise mental health issues, introducing a limiting ethical perspective and chal-lenging **clinical neuroscience**, when neuroscience made salient gains. Similar to Laing, critical psychiatry placed the expertise of patients above that of psychiatrists. Patient views have contributed helpful insights into the shortcomings of their treatments (e.g. Boyle, 1993). Boyle (1993) has also identified the vested interests of drug companies amongst others in the genetic–medical explanation of mental illness. Bentall (2003) has questioned this genetic–medical focus in the case of schizophrenia as distracting from the breadth of psychotic experiences in the population and many other contributing factors diluting the concept of 'patient'.

Postmodernism

This critical movement adopted the existing term **post-modernism** to represent their challenge to psychiatry and other professional areas (Pilgrim and Rodgers, 1993).

Postmodernism in the modern context has been referred to as 'contemporary intellectual fashion' by **Charles Murray** and is associated with assumptions of **social constructionism** and critical approaches such as **deconstructionism**. The original postmodernist movement famously attacked the scientific enlightenment movement. As with the ancient Sophists, postmodernists and humanist movements believe that truth is relative to cultural, group and personal per-spectives. This 'tail wagging the dog' view of reality was sometimes termed **radical relativism** (Smith, 1994). Some extend the meaning of postmodernism to include post-science, as if empirical science was a passing fashion of the twentieth century and would eventually disappear, in the way that Greek and Roman medical enlightenment passed into the first Dark Age. Those anticipating a new dark age may agree with this view.

Foucault became a reference point in the latter post-modernist movement with his focus on the shared thought and talk of experts, groups and cultures rather than the subjective reality of patients revered by anti-psychiatry and critical psychiatry. This **Wittgenstein**-inspired con-centration on the use of language and 'language games' to create localised realities focused on the use of language or discourse analysis as a method of 'deconstructing' psychiatry. The abstraction of the language of psychiatry from its real world context and its placing into a political and philosophical context was certain to lead to conclu-sions divorced from clinical reality. Where the empirical approach is rejected completely and replaced by politic-ally based manipulation of language (which is inherently ambiguous part of its versatility), outcome will often be determined by an initial agenda – in a sea of ambiguity, you will find whatever it is you are looking for.

Research

The dangers of abstract reasoning

The earlier consideration of philosophy, becoming distanced from empirical science, provided a historical model of how a discipline can become dangerously abstracted from reality. However, there are systemic perils of abstracting reasoning from reality.

These caveats can be illustrated in pure mathematics. By logical manipulation of abstract formulae without any application to the real world, it is possible to have 2 being equal to 1 within a few short steps in a **simultaneous equation**. When real world parameters are applied to this equation, it becomes clear that multiplication or division by zero has occurred.

The inherent danger of engaging in purely abstract thinking is that of an illogical conclusion only sustain-able in the absence of real world grounding. At this level, much of the postmodernist critique of psychiatry, as with philosophy before it, becomes an impressive academic exercise with little application to the real clinical world. Postmodernism rejects the scientific approach, which unfortunately means its beliefs will not be subject to scientific testing and thus neither refutable nor accepted as valid by the scientific com-munity (Smith, 1994).

These arguments are not intended to underestimate the academic worth of deconstructing our notions of mental illness and crime, in which the exhaustive literature is both academically challenging and culturally inclusive (see Parker et al., 1995; Parker, 1999). There is a vast distance between the genuine intentions, complex insights and highly intelligent argument of the contemporary postmodernist and the duplicitous nature of other proponents of belief-based approaches described earlier in this chapter.

On criticising the critical

Patient autonomy

Some of this argument may seem a little harsh towards the good intentions of the possible intellectual descendants of the humanitarian movement, but there are tragic risks in reapplying manipulated logic to clinical reality. When such logic merges with the premise derived from Foucault, in seeing a conspiracy to control society behind expert discourses in psychiatry, there may no longer be benefit for the patient. Humanitarian advances have given patients much greater autonomy and risky decisions have become more probable. But these independent, but still psychiatrically disordered individuals are no less suggestible or vulnerable, or in the case of a disordered offender, no less a danger to others. Self-advocacy could be problematic with regard to treatment choice for the mentally ill. If a non-psychiatric medical patient were given the choice between a surgical procedure and a rather pleasant **alternative therapy**, issues of immediate discomfort and fear would cloud their judgement. A mentally ill patient given similar choices would be far more susceptible to making this self-defeating decision.

A vulnerable patient could accept the critical school view literally, that their medication is toxic and that medical support be rejected. Seriously disordered patients suffering medication side-effects are very vulnerable to such influences and suggestions of conspiracies fit well with delusional ideation. The mentally ill in this position have often caused serious harm to themselves or others whilst disordered and unmedicated. Though this may not be the intention of those wishing reform, it can be the unintentional outcome. This is not to demonise the well-intentioned critical school; Freud had a reputation amongst his colleagues for having his suggestible patients say just about anything (Webster, 2004; Shorter, 1997). Unlike the anti-psychiatrists before them, the postmodernist critics do not accept medically defined illness. However, the prospect of appealing to oncology patients to give up their medical treatment may pose a more serious threat to the health of the critic than this particular patient.

Limited resources

A further negative outcome of the proliferation of critical or belief schools is the diversion of resources. Exacerbated by increasingly stringent ethical guidelines (Hearnshaw, 2004), funding for empirical medical research is being diverted to non-invasive studies with theoretical outcomes. Such inhibition of empirical research due to ethics is itself unethical (Gilbertson, 1999). Thus it becomes far easier to gain ethical clearance and funding to ask patients about their feelings towards their illness than to test a potentially life-saving but ethically challenging medical procedure. These and similar pressures result in only one-third of research funding being used to identify medical causes of abnormal behaviour, whereas half of available funding is used to examine social issues surrounding these disorders. Some social issue research is valuable, such as Brown and Harris (1978) on depression, but not at the absolute expense of more ethically challenging work. Many studies, including Brown and Harris (1978) often ignore the primacy of the endogenous disorder *producing* social and environmental events.

If this balance shifts further towards reducing empirical research, the situation could be illustrated by the anecdote utilised by Ornstein (1975) regarding a man losing his house key. A friend found the man searching the road outside his home and, in order to help, the friend asked where the man thought he last had his key. The man affirmed that it was definitely in the house and that was where he probably lost it. The friend inquired as to why the man was searching outside if the key was lost inside the house. 'Why, because there is more light outside and I can see what I am doing.' The easiest route to researching mental illness is not always in the patient's long-term interest.

A critical balance

As with the anti-psychiatry movement before them, there are positive outcomes from the critical psychiatry and postmodernist movements. There is a greater focus on the patient as a human being rather than as a collection of brain abnormalities and unbalanced **neurotransmitters**. Treating the person rather than the symptoms would clearly be a step too far; however, treating both ensures a better outcome regardless of the success in direct reduction of symptoms. This said, it is central to the training of skilled psychiatrists (Goldberg, Benjamin and Creed, 1994) that they never lose sight of the patient as human being amidst the chaos surrounding disordered behaviour. In the aftermath of critical assaults on these professionals, some have bridged the divide between science-based orthodox psychiatry and postmodernist beliefs in presenting a pragmatic approach (e.g. Fishman, 1999). Farber (1990) has aligned the psychiatric medical model with the psychoanalytic approach, describing the latter as assuming inflexible biological mental structures formed in childhood. Farber does criticise both for assuming that the disordered individual will not change over time without their particular intervention.

In the past, humanitarian movements have acted as the conscience of practitioners and administrators in clinical and forensic settings. However, it would be redundant for the hypercritical descendants of such movements to berate current clinical practitioners, as they are painfully aware of shortcomings. Current care limitations are not the remit of pressured psychologists but within the realms of politics, resourcing and a public with a little tolerance for the disordered and criminal. Any resurgence of belief systems in the context of a stressed scientific profession can only ultimately worsen the plight of the vulnerable disordered individual. Such a retreat from scientific enlightenment would also suggest a less than optimistic future for those pragmatic professionals who would rather eradicate than celebrate disorder.

In the forensic domain, serious disordered offenders could have their condition redefined as 'within the normal spectrum' and released without treatment, with consequent danger to others, including any well-meaning humanitarian advocate. However, in clinical and forensic settings, the error rate for the prediction of dangerousness errs on the side of caution, with only one person actually causing harm to self or others for every three individuals detained as being a risk. This has been reduced over the last 30 years for clinical patients but remains high for offenders (see Prins, 1999). Thus, there is a place for critical movements in the twenty-first century, though their focus should be less on the amplification of idealistic belief and more on inaccuracies and complacency in dealing with abnormal behaviour.

Self-test questions

- What is meant by a 'new dark age'?
- What was Szasz's contribution to anti-psychiatry?
- Why can belief systems be problematic in clinical practice?
- In what ways does social constructionism differ from the humanitarian movement that emerged around 1800?
- What is the relationship between anti-psychiatry and critical psychiatry?
- What are the positive outcomes of humanitarian pressure on psychiatry?

Chapter summary

The history of abnormal psychology reveals a battle between a very slowly developing empirical **science** and **superstition**, the latter having been supported in the past by corrupt religious power. The historical emergence of abnormal, clinical and forensic psychology reveals some of the reasons for public scepticism of it. The legacy of the adversarial relationship between belief and empirical science from the past would seem to be re-emerging in the twenty-first century to the extent that this era has been referred to as a **new dark age**. Critics include **anti-psychiatry** and **critical psychiatry**, which have made a detailed attack on orthodox psychiatry. Abnormal, clinical and forensic psychology seem to be more of a focal area for this conflict than other disciplines, and psychiatry remains a target for those, such as postmodernist schools, opposed to scientific approaches in this area.

Suggested essay questions

- Evaluate the degree to which belief systems compete with empirical science.
- Is psychology a science? Discuss.
- Critically discuss the place of psychoanalysis in the anti-psychiatry movement.

Further reading

Overview texts

Bentall, R. P. (2003) *Madness explained: Psychosis and human nature*. London: Penguin.

Clare, A. (1980) *Psychiatry in dissent* (2nd edn). London: Tavistock.

Cooper, D. (1967) *Psychiatry and antipsychiatry*. London: Tavistock.

Dawkins, R. (1986) *The blind watchmaker*. London: Penguin.

Dawkins, R. (1998) *Unweaving the rainbow*. London: Penguin.

Dawkins, R. (2006) *The God delusion*. London: Bantam.

Eysenck, H. J. (1985) *Decline and fall of the Freudian empire*. Harmondsworth: Penguin.

Jones, K. (1993) *Asylums and After*. London: Athlone.

Prins, H. (1987) Understanding insanity: Some glimpses into historical fact and fiction. *British Journal of Social Work*, 17, 91–8.

Shorter, E. (1997) *A history of psychiatry: From the era of the asylum to the age of prozac*. Chichester: John Wiley.

Specific and more critical texts

Berlim, M. T., Fleck, M. P., and Shorter, E. (2003) Notes on antipsychiatry. *European Archives of Psychiatry and Clinical Neuroscience*, 253, 61–7.

Bracken, P., and Thomas, P. (2001) Postpsychiatry: a new direction for mental health. *British Medical Journal*, 332, 724–7.

Freeman, H. (1998) Mental health policy and practice in the NHS: 1948–1979. *Journal of Mental Health*, 7(3), 225–39.

Kotowicz, Z. (1997) *R. D. Laing and paths of anti-psychiatry*. London: Routledge.

Persaud, R. D. (1992) A comparison of symptoms recorded from the same patients by an asylum doctor and 'a constant observer' in 1923: The implications for theories about psychiatric illness in history. *History of Psychiatry*, 3, 79–94.

Prins, H. (1999) *Will they do it again? Risk assessment and management in criminal justice and psychiatry*. London: Routledge.

Rotton, J., and Kelly, I. W. (1985) Much ado about the full moon: A meta-analysis of lunar-lunacy research. *Psychological Bulletin*, 97, 286–306.

Webster, R. (1995) *Why Freud was wrong: Of sin science and psychoanalysis*. London: HarperCollins.

Wyatt, R. C. (2004) Thomas Szasz: Liberty and the practice of psychotherapy. *Journal of Humanistic Psychology*, 44, 71–85.

Visit **www.pearsoned.co.uk/davidholmes** for a range of resources to support study. Test yourself with multiple choice questions and access a bank of over 100 videos that will bring the topics to life. Video for this chapter includes myths about mental disorders, the work of false belief detective, James Randi, and an exploration of 'magical thinking' in children and adults.

CHAPTER 3 Paradigm approaches to aetiology and treatment

- Overview
- Case study

Part 1: Biological approaches
- The neuropsychological approach
- The evolutionary approach

Part 2: Psychological approaches
- The behavioural approach
- The cognitive and cognitive behavioural approaches
- Non-empirical approaches

Part 3: Social and eclectic approaches
- Group, cultural and family aspects of therapy
- Beyond paradigms: diathesis–stress and eclectic approaches
- Chapter summary

 Discover the concept of humour as treatment. This is one of several videos that explore issues and disorders relevant to this chapter at www.pearsoned.co.uk/davidholmes.

Natural born killers?

Some fiction and much public belief or popular psychology subscribes to the idea that 'animal instincts' are to blame in serial murder and other serious crime. Society is quick to distance itself in this way from such disturbing crimes such as that of UK serial killer **Fred West** or US child abductor **Philip Garrido**. This belief in such crimes as being rooted in primitive instincts is historically present in legal definitions such as the **'wild beast test'** (1724), which assumed the amoral animal reflexes of criminals being closer to animals and **Lombroso**'s view of their being evolutionary throwbacks. It is also enshrined in folklore by 'animal possession', such as in the mythical werewolf.

In this chapter we will uncover that the biological underpinnings of homicide are related to disinhibition of more primitive brain areas rather than to any animal instincts. In fact, the section on **comparative psychology** will reveal that the animal equivalent of homicide or killing one's own species is exceedingly rare in other animals. However, it is very common in humans, who consider themselves an 'advanced' species.

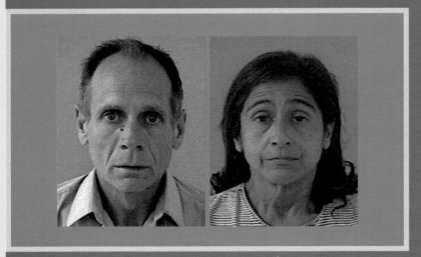

Disturbing crimes, like those committed by Philip Garrido, are often blamed by the public on primitive, animalistic behaviour.
Source: Getty Images.

Overview

Each of the various historical approaches to psychological disorder discussed in Chapter 1 was based on particular conceptual frameworks – what Thomas Kuhn refers to as **paradigms**. These approaches tend to compete to explain abnormal behaviour and, as Kuhn (1996) notes, these paradigms tend to evolve naturally and sometimes collapse. Each makes its own assumptions about the underlying cause or **aetiology** of disorders, consequent **therapies**, the aims of the approach, and evaluation of the outcome for the client. One limitation of the single paradigm approach is that it can be a self-fulfilling prophecy. A behavioural paradigm intervention targets behaviour, but the outcome is also measured in terms of behaviour. If the outcome were measured in terms of the client's feelings or thought patterns, it might seem less successful. Thus there are limitations of one-dimensional approaches. However, staying within a paradigm can lead to a higher level of specialist expertise.

In covering the major paradigms in psychology, this necessarily extensive chapter is divided into three sections, though some overlap is inevitable. The **biological approach** has been given more emphasis, as it took a commanding role in clinical and forensic areas in the latter half of the twentieth century, making it essential for psychologists in the area to have a working knowledge of these principles and practices. Genetic endowment would appear to predispose much behaviour and, along with the structure and chemistry of the brain, explains much of what we see as abnormal behaviour (Bazzett, 2008). Biological treatments have advanced from the days of restraint and crude surgery to include genetic manipulation during the lifetime. **Evolutionary psychology** now provides explanations for clinical and forensic cases by placing them in a **phylogenetic** context. This growing but theoretical approach sheds light on some behaviour that has been difficult to conceptualise.

In the second part of this chapter, the interrelated **behavioural and cognitive paradigms** are linked to evolution via **comparative psychology**. These are the major paradigms used in practice by clinical and forensic psychologists in addressing abnormal behaviour, now normally combined as **cognitive behavioural therapy** (CBT). Treatment by CBT has developed in the twenty-first century to be more disorder specific, though much of the founding work of **Aaron T. Beck** and others is still evident.

The final part of this chapter has two elements. One has been titled 'non-empirical approaches' and includes older methods mostly based on Freudian theories, which did not produce objective evidence of effectiveness and for many lack any therapeutic value (Eysenck, 1952; Eysenck, 1985; Piper, 2000; Shorter, 1997; Webster, 1995; Webster, 2004). More recent techniques have been evaluated, but little evidence of their effectiveness can be attributed to the original paradigm, although early branches such as the **humanistic school** have value in counselling techniques. Finally, there are additional approaches of **group**, **family system**, **cultural**, **eclectic**, and **diathesis–stress approaches**, which may be applicable to many of the other paradigms. Some, such as the cultural approach, need to be considered regardless of the paradigm adopted for assessment and treatment.

Case study

Ian

Jean's pregnancy with Ian was unexpected and precipitated a rushed engagement and marriage to Tom. Tom was less than enthusiastic about commitment, which Jean thought was related to his father's suicide when Tom was only 5 years old. When Tom missed Ian's fourth birthday party, Jean was shocked to find Tom at her friend's house having the *second* affair of their marriage. Tom pleaded with Jean but left home abruptly and Jean was left to bring Ian up on her own. Help from her mother enabled her to attempt a university degree, but she dropped out during a bout of depression following a brief relationship. Ian did well at school but had problems concentrating and attending. He had a girlfriend, Teresa, at this time, but the relationship ended abruptly after a public argument. Teresa was rapidly replaced by a succession of girlfriends.

Ian's behaviour became erratic, not finishing jobs he had enthusiastically started, and he had problems sleeping. He disappeared for 2 days and his mother suspected that Ian was involved with drugs. His girlfriend Ann claimed that Ian had never taken anything, although many of his musician friends had. Ian reappeared, agitated, exhausted and dishevelled, claiming he needed money for something very important. Jean called the police to save her son from what she thought might be a 'drug ring'. The community police officer came to the house but after a few minutes asked if Ian was seeing a 'doctor'. Two hours later, Ian was referred by the GP to the department of psychiatry as a psychiatric emergency.

Ian was admitted for assessment as at 'risk of suicide'. Ian's assessment revealed periods of disorganised 'driven' behaviour as well as increasing periods of inactivity. When Jean finally collected Ian, the dread of a son following too closely in his grandfather's footsteps led her to remove anything she saw as an aid to suicide from the house. Ian accused her of 'over-mothering' him. Jean blamed this behaviour on Ian's tranquilising medication but then reflected on his medication being used for self-harm.

Ian was put on Lithium treatment but insisted the medication was 'killing his inner self'. Jean did not realise that Ian had already stopped his treatment. Her life had been overshadowed by the behaviour of three generations of men, but this led to her being somewhat cold and indifferent to the chaos that surrounded her. One day Ian became very agitated and stormed out of the house to confront his ex-girlfriend Ann. Ian walked straight in to find Ann with her new boyfriend and attacked both of them in succession. In the fracas Ann's boyfriend struck Ian on the back of the head. This resulted in Ian being in a coma and Ann and Peter being held by the police. From being so involved with Ian's manic episodes, these events hardly registered on Jean. Her view of Ian was now aligned with how she regarded his father and grandfather; 'it's something in the blood,' she said to her neighbour.

(This case will be briefly examined at the end of each section of this chapter from the differing perspectives covered.)

Part 1: Biological approaches

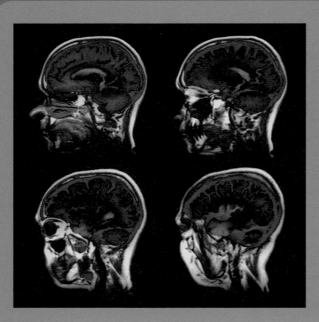

The biological approach to psychopathology looks at the relationship between brain, body and behaviour, using evidence such as MRI scans to study the brain.
Source: Pearson Online Database

The neuropsychological approach

In Chapter 1 the beginnings of the neuropsychological paradigm were traced from early Greeks such as **Hippocrates** and **Galen**, with their limited understanding of the relationship between brain, body and behaviour, to **Kraepelin**'s view of brain pathology causing a range of distinguishable disorder categories. It was established that physical illness can produce psychological abnormality, or **somatogenesis** (literally, 'bodily caused'), when tracing the cause of 'general paresis' or neurosyphilis. Awareness of the true complexity of the nervous system has developed slowly by relying on the relationship between damage to the brain and its effect on physical or mental functioning. For example, the case of Phineas Gage (see the Focus box on p. 53) illustrates clearly how brain damage affects personality and morality. Many socially orientated professionals reject this causal link, fearing that this portrays humans as programmed biological machines like automatons. This fear is ill founded as the sophistication and interactive nature of human **neurochemistry** (the functioning of the nervous system) and neurophysiology (the structure of the nervous system) far outstrips the decision-making activities experienced by human consciousness, let alone the crude approximations of machines. If this seems hard to accept, consider the millions of decisions made by a computer to represent this single sentence on its screen, and yet how many of the vast number of decisions made by your brain whilst reading it are you aware of?

In the following sections, sources of biological influence will be described and considered in terms of the associated biological therapies. Four major sources can be considered to contribute to the neuropsychological paradigm, each of which is complex and interacts with the others.

- Genetics and neurodevelopment
- Neuroanatomy
- Neurochemistry
- Neuroendocrinology

Genetics and neurodevelopment

Although the genetic–neurodevelopmental approach and the **evolutionary** approach are categorised within separate paradigms, they are clearly micro and macro aspects of the same process. As such, these sections should be considered in combination not in isolation.

The basis of genetic–neurodevelopmental influence is the gene, its **expression** (the activation of its potential) and the mediating interaction with the environment as development progresses. Thus the genotype, or trait information carried by the gene, will often differ from the **phenotype**, or actual trait expressed in the developing organism. Genes are chemical structures linked together in groups called chromosomes and this information is carried in the nucleus of cells. The basic laws of genetic inheritance were identified by empirical observation of pea plants in the nineteenth century by Gregor Mendel (1822–1884), in his short monograph *Experiments with Plant Hybrids* in 1865. His laws have proven to be less than strict but show the general principles of inheritance at the gene level. Simplified, each parent contributes half the genes towards their offspring. Genes that code for varying traits are in opposing forms or **alleles**, which are **dominant** over each other or **recessive**, i.e. subservient. These opposing forms are at the same relative location, one on each of the pairs of chromosomes, and can combine in four ways in the offspring, allowing for the expression of either opposing trait on a probability basis. Thus dominant traits only dominate when opposed by a recessive trait. If the opposing alleles code for the same form of the trait, the individual is said to be homozygous for that trait; they are heterozygous in the case of differing alleles.

In this manner, the normal human foetus begins as a single cell or **zygote** with 23 *pairs* of chromosomes. One set of 23 chromosomes comes from each parent as **gametes** (ova or sperm) and these 'half-cells' are produced by **meiosis**. The many genes on each chromosome carry 'survival blueprints' in the form of deoxyribonucleic acid (DNA) from previous generations about how to construct and organise a human being. The information in DNA itself is in the form of differing sequences of the four **bases**, **adenine**, **thymine**, **guanine** and **cytocine** (or cytosine), which are held in place by the structural strands of sugar and phosphates forming the famous '**double-helix**' structure of DNA.

The DNA code of an individual is like a 'genetic fingerprint' and is used in **forensic science** to link a crime suspect to a crime scene. DNA is in every cell in the body and can be analysed quickly for its main distinguishing features, producing a rough **DNA profile**. With improved technology, smaller numbers of cells can be replicated then analysed: for example, saliva on a cigarette is sufficient. This is particularly useful in identifying a suspect by their sperm in rape cases where conviction rates are traditionally very low. **DNA kits** are produced for the fast retrieval of evidence and, with an error rate (i.e. two people with the same profile) of around 1 in 8 million, matched suspects are unlikely to contest this in court (see Evett and Weir, 1998).

Genes pass DNA information on by three basic processes: self-replication (**mitosis**), the less common **meiosis** and releasing the information by **transcription**. In transcription, the bases on one strand of DNA code for matching bases on **ribonucleic acid** (RNA) or, more specifically, **messenger RNA** (mRNA), producing a kind of 'negative copy' of the DNA. The sequence of bases on mRNA is then expressed utilising another form of RNA called **transfer RNA** (tRNA), each segment of which matches its own specific set of three bases to the corresponding group of three bases on the mRNA sequence or **codon**. Each differently coded tRNA also has one of 20 **amino acids** attached. As the tRNA segments are lined up in a sequence dictated by mRNA, so the attached amino acids are correspondingly sequenced into **proteins**. The production of proteins by tRNA from the mRNA sequence is a process called **translation**: the code derived from mRNA is translated into a protein, which will contain hundreds of the 20 available amino acids in sequence. Proteins are very important for the structure and function of the living organism, and errors in production make a major contribution to abnormal behaviour. Identifying problems in the production of proteins and their actions can link disrupted genes and disordered behaviour.

It is essential for the success of these processes that the **environment** of the developing human being bears a reasonable resemblance to that of previous generations, i.e. that planned for by the 'genetic blueprint'. For example, if the world were suddenly plunged into darkness, structures of the eye, such as the retina, would fail to develop due to lack of light stimulation, causing a failure in the expression of the relevant genes. Thus abnormal interaction between genes and the environment can lead to various disorders. However, past environmental change has made gene expression a robust procedure, enabling humans to adapt to fairly poor environments (see the evolutionary paradigm). Genetic influence can directly cause deviant neurodevelopment, which can be minimised by a developmental environment that suppresses the expression of abnormal traits.

Non-inherited genetic problems include faults in the formation and division of cells. Once in about 1500 births, a fault of division results in three chromosomes instead of the usual two at the twenty-first pair (**trisomy**). The expression of this chromosome abnormality is termed **Down's syndrome**, with characteristic facial features, slower mental development and shortened life expectancy. Other disorders may be the consequence of maladaptive gene mutation. Mutation occurs in genes as a result of errors in meiosis (the production of sperm or ova) or environmental toxins, particularly radiation. Mutations can be adaptive or maladaptive, and being adaptive increases the chances of their evolutionary survival as a result of conferring advantages on those inheriting them. However,

some maladaptive mutations survive, leading to genes in the human gene pool being destructive, either singly or in combination. These are not always expressed in everyone and symptomless **carriers** may pass the genes on.

Disorders carried by females but expressed in males are often sex-linked characteristics, partly due to the twenty-third pair of chromosomes, which in females approximate in shape to XX and in males to XY. Each parent supplies one of the pair, determining the **genetic sex** of the offspring. A second X chromosome dictates a female by default, which can only be opposed by the male Y chromosome. The 'missing arm' of the Y chromosome leads to unopposed traits being expressed on the paired X chromosome. In female offspring, all alleles are opposed (XX) and the trait tends to be carried but not expressed. Haemophilia is only expressed in males, but females act as carriers with no phenotypical signs of the disorder. Disorders where these sex-chromosomes are themselves abnormal include males with an extra Y chromosome or XYY, labelled 'supermale' and considered criminally inclined. XYY males have physical and learning difficulties, but media-publicity-generated 'criminality' (see Chapter 7). Table 3.1 shows the very rare sex-chromosome disorders, although some surveys claim higher incidences (Nielsen and Wohlert, 1991).

In overview, abnormality may begin with damaged, destructive or deviant genetics, predisposing for a disorder, which may be susceptible to events early in life (e.g. birth trauma) with consequent neurodevelopmental abnormalities in brain structure or function. Later environmental factors, such as infection or stress, may compound this early damage, producing pronounced psychopathology. Thus neurodevelopmental mental disorders cannot be treated as an acute (recently developed) disorder may be. Over time, secondary effects of psychopathology lead to aberrant functions being reinforced at the expense of normal function, leading to the disorder becoming chronic (Faraone, Tsuang and Tsuang, 1999).

Genetic treatments were historically limited due to the inability to alter genetic information during the lifetime and because irreversible neurodevelopment had already taken place. Late in the twentieth century, there was a dramatic increase in genetic engineering research altering actual genes, or **targeted mutations** with mutated material from mouse embryos (Mayford and Kandel, 1999). Progress enabled these procedures to transfer to human subjects, often targeting a specific gene, which is 'knocked out' by deleting that part of the DNA sequence responsible for initiating the replication of that gene.

Altering genes during the lifetime, or **ontological genetic engineering**, is now a therapeutic science and it is possible to use retroviruses to insert new gene sequences in human

Table 3.1 Sex-chromosome disorders

23rd Chromosomes	Consequences
XYY	Males with an extra Y chromosome or **Jacobs syndrome** are taller and suffer significant learning difficulties, skin problems and behavioural problems in adolescence (1 in 1000 males).
XXY	Males with an extra X chromosome or **Klinefelter syndrome** have mild learning difficulties that affect speech and academic performance. There is low testosterone 'feminising' development, i.e. breast growth, infertility, etc., controllable by hormone treatment (1 in 1000 males).
X (or XO)	Females with only one X chromosome or **Turner syndrome** miscarry in all but 1 per cent of cases. Survivors have infertility problems, are physically short, have lower IQ and do not mature through puberty without hormone intervention (1 in 2500 females).
XXX	Females with **Triple-X syndrome** can seem normal but more often have significant learning difficulties, infertility problems and smaller head circumference (1 in 1000).
XXXX and XXXXX	**Tetrasomy-X** and **Pentasomy-X** females have very similar features to Triple-X females (1 in 1000).

beings. Genes crucial for developing disorders are 'knocked out' or new sequences added, which are replicated locally at the point of infection or throughout the organism if more widely replicated (e.g. blood borne). This process of recombinant DNA technology uses **enzymes** to cut out a gene sequence from isolated DNA, insert it into the **vector** of a **bacterium** and then replicate this gene within rapidly multiplying bacteria. Genes can be deactivated or transferred and inserted from one organism or even species to another, but they cannot yet be created from the basic DNA components.

Risks and ethical problems pervade genetic therapy at the molecular level. Germ line therapy involving pre-embryonic treatment can be unpredictable in terms of phenotypic outcomes. Many gene therapies can produce rare, potentially fatal, unexpected immune responses. Cause of death in such cases is unclear and easily attributed to the disease process treated. One ethical concern often raised by critics of genetic research is the deterministic view of disorders being simply genetic or non-genetic, whereas those working in genetic research only consider the *proportion* of genetics and environment involved (Faraone, Tsuang and Tsuang, 1999).

Genetic counselling applies when a sufferer or carrier of a genetically influenced disorder considers offspring. Problem gene(s) are identified by family history or genetic screening, and impartial factual advice allows an informed choice based on the probability of transmitting the gene(s). However, the **autosomal dominant gene** ('soma' meaning one of 22 'body' chromosomes) causing **Huntington's disease** expresses late in life, after carriers have children. With no cure (Tyler, Ball and Crawford, 1992), early testing invokes the ethical dilemma of psychological harm in discovering that the future is bleak (see Chapter 19). For this reason, genetic screening for such disorders is

not advised unless an effective intervention is available (Plomin et al., 2001). However, it is also necessary to consider the rights of relatives and the wider population regarding the risks and responsibilities imposed on them (Plomin et al., 2001). The sufferer may have their information used by life insurance firms or health insurance providers to raise premiums or refuse cover.

As screening becomes possible for more disorders, this issue may become critical. Those who choose to smoke should pay higher insurance for willingly incurring increased health risk, but we do not choose to be born with certain genes. Including such factors needs to be banned as it eliminates all risk, and this undermines the fundamental principle of insurance, which is to share risk.

Genetic screening has advanced from implying risk from a parent having the gene to using genetic **markers** for the disorder gene. A marker is an easily detected genetic trait, which is inherited along with the disorder gene due to linkage, or the tendency for genes located closely to be passed on together. More markers are being found for single-gene disorders such as Huntington's disease, **phenylketonuria** (PKU) and **fragile-X disorder** (see Chapter 8). **Linkage analysis** is a much slower process for disorders involving many genes, such as schizophrenia. Linkage analysis can identify other causal factors for a disorder co-occurring with its markers.

Where gene expression is not inevitable, such as in **diathesis–stress** cases (see pp. 97–8), awareness can help reduce or prevent phenotypical effects of the disorder, such as by avoiding severe stress in schizophrenia, or in the controversial case of using a regulated diet to avert the symptoms of a specific form of autism (see Chapter 9). Plant research has revealed a non-Mendelian form of inheritance (i.e. one that does not follow Gregor Mendel's laws of inheritance) which may allow generations to side-step the effects of destructive genes. Genes from previous (healthy) generations are 'archived' in RNA and accessed to overcome the destructive mutations that have developed subsequently (Pennisi, 2005).

Family or pedigree studies examine the disorder's frequency amongst different relatives within families, showing the degree of heritability. Smaller families, increases in people living alone and single-parent families in the West limit the number of family studies, but this is partly compensated by better record systems. Twin studies compare identical or monozygotic twins (from the separation of one fertilised ovum) with non-identical or dizygotic twins (from separate ova), where one of each pair (the **proband** or index case) has the disorder, to apportion the relative influences of environment and genetics. Ideally, identical twins reared apart with the same genetic endowment but arguably different environment (differences due to environment) are compared with non-identical twins reared together with differing genetic influence but same environment (differences due to genes). Thus, the greater the **concordance** of the identical twins (i.e. both develop it) for the disorder, the greater the genetic influence, and the greater the concordance among non-identical twins, the greater the effect of the environment.

Early twin studies poorly distinguished monozygotic and dizygotic twins until **karyotyping** was available. In karyotyping, stained extracted chromosomes are organised and photographed, and use of fluorescent dyes that bind to specific regions of chromosomes have improved this process (Schröck et al., 1996). The karyotypes from twins make identification a routine empirical process, but cost and inaccessibility of expertise means that research reverts to the earlier crude method of visually estimating physical similarity, which has around 90 per cent of the accuracy of karyotyping (Chen et al., 1999).

Twin studies are confounded by environments of separated twins being similar, and all twins share an identical environment for 9 months in the womb. Many such difficulties are avoided in adoption studies, especially where the *father* is the known carrier, or half-sibling adoption studies. Genetic influence is examined without any environmental contact, including the prenatal environment. However, with effective contraception fewer people now have unplanned pregnancies, and illegitimacy is less stigmatised, resulting in fewer adoptions and reduced samples for adoption studies.

There are caveats involved in preventing genetic disorders by controlling reproduction, as this method was abused during the Third Reich in wartime Germany, culminating in **genocide**. Gene combinations producing disorders can also be responsible for positive traits, particularly in different permutations (e.g. Jamison, 1992). For example, in bipolar disorder (see Chapter 17), productivity and creativity occur amongst relatives, and sometimes in the same individual. Thus the genetic predisposition leading to a disabling mood disorder also produces controlled rapid thought, and eradicating the disorder may also eradicate the beneficial trait. This illustrates the trial and error process of **natural selection**.

Genetic and neurodevelopmental applications are accelerating steadily, and the initial mapping of the **human genome** at the turn of the century brings us closer to the molecular origins of most disorders. Although advances in gene-based disorders and gene therapy appear fast and frequent, the size of the human genome, with DNA containing billions of pairs of the chemical bases, necessitates an immense task in comparing the expected structure with disordered variations. There are also variations in the molecular origins of many disorders. For example, a hundred different mutations of the same gene lead to the disorder PKU (Guldberg et al., 1998) and each mutation may require a different marker to be identified in separate linkage analyses. With a myriad of research outcomes constantly poised for publication, any textbook in this area, including this one, is destined rapidly to become out of date – a caveat applying to most areas in neuropsychology.

Neuroanatomy

The human nervous system is the most complex computational system on the planet and orchestrates our behaviour. Neuroanatomy is the study of the 'hardware' of the nervous system based on the group action of fundamental units called **neurons** or nerve cells. As its functioning is biochemical, the neuron is examined in the neurochemistry section below (pp. 56–61). **Nerves** are long chains of variable-sized neurons that reach microscopic distances or stretch across the length of the body.

The nervous system has three functional components, which are as follows.

- The central nervous system (CNS) includes the brain and spinal cord.

- The peripheral nervous system (PNS) comprises the spinal nerves, cranial nerves and the **somatic nervous system**. The somatic nervous system comprises nerves that control muscles or **efferent pathways** as they **effect** responses. Nerves referring sensation to the brain, facilitating **affect**, are termed **afferent pathways**.

- The autonomic nervous system (ANS) specifically controls the opposing responses for alarm and recuperation (see below).

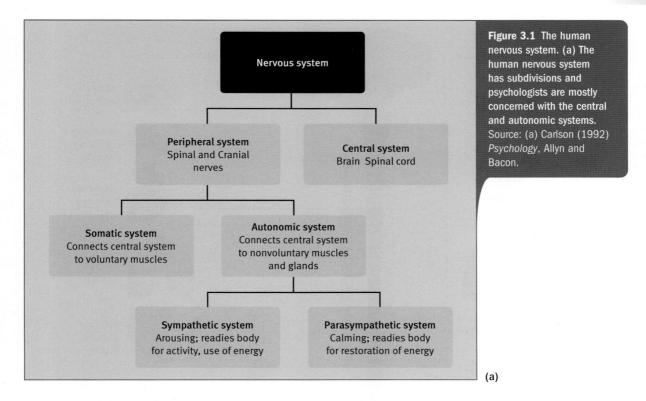

Figure 3.1 The human nervous system. (a) The human nervous system has subdivisions and psychologists are mostly concerned with the central and autonomic systems. Source: (a) Carlson (1992) *Psychology*, Allyn and Bacon.

(a)

The ANS has two opposing subsystems: the **sympathetic** division prepares the body for activity and expenditure of resources, and the parasympathetic division stimulates organs to relax and recuperate. Demands of the environment trigger the different divisions. Faced with danger, the sympathetic division prepares the body for combat or escape, leading to Cannon's (1927) term, **'fight or flight' response**, with increasing heart rate, decreasing digestion, etc. Perspiration is increased to keep the active body at a steady temperature. This is an example of homeostasis, by which the brain maintains variable bodily subsystems at optimum levels. Perspiration moistening the skin when we are aroused has been utilised in lie detection (see Chapter 7). This is achieved by a machine measuring galvanic skin response (GSR), as the moistening of the skin increases its electrical conductivity, inferring that the person is unduly aroused due to lying. In the absence of danger, the parasympathetic system dominates, aiding recovery, digestion and repair. See Table 3.2 for the specific actions of each ANS division.

In the modern world, this primitive function is confounded and triggered in the absence of anything to be confronted or escaped, eventually resulting in stress damage to the body (see Chapter 16). Adrenaline released by the sympathetic division persists in the system for some time after the event, which can lead to criminally aggressive acts that appear out of character. For example,

Table 3.2 The effects of activating opposing divisions of the ANS

Sympathetic activation	Parasympathetic activation
Dilation of the eye pupil	Constriction of eye pupil
Inhibits salivation	Stimulates salivation
Relaxes bronchi	Constricts bronchi
Speeds up heartbeat	Slows heartbeat
Inhibits digestion	Stimulates digestion
Liver releases glucose	Stimulates gall bladder
Relaxes bladder	Contracts bladder
Arousal of sex organs	Relaxes sex organs
Releases adrenaline and noradrenaline	Ejaculation in male
Perspiration	Perspiration inhibited

after an arousing confrontation you may drive a car in an uncharacteristically aggressive manner. In **anxiety states**, the sympathetic division is strongly stimulated in inappropriate circumstances with no trigger. The autonomic system may be overly sensitive due to genetic inheritance or, physical damage, or sensitised as a result of experience. Most biological treatments for anxiety (e.g. drugs) reduce the effects of the sympathetic division of the ANS.

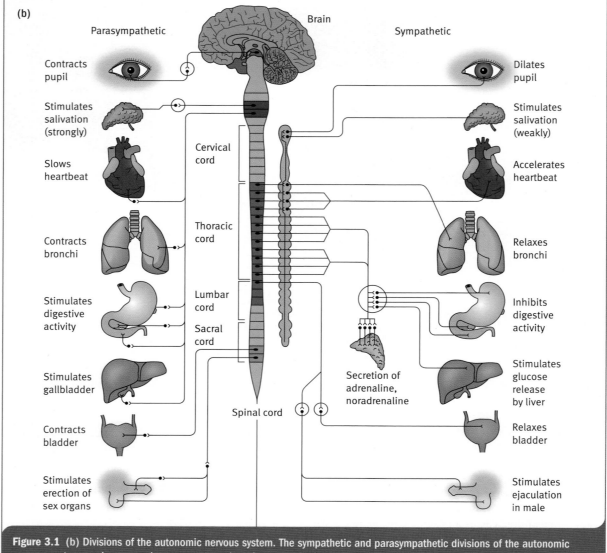

Figure 3.1 (b) Divisions of the autonomic nervous system. The sympathetic and parasympathetic divisions of the autonomic nervous system produce opposing responses and are important in the understanding of psychological phenomena.
Source: (b) Davison and Neale (1994) *Abnormal Psychology*, 6th edition. Wiley.

Within the **central nervous system** (CNS), the different structures or subsystems of the **brain** are interconnected (see Carlson, 2004). These structures develop specialist functions; thus, the **hypothalamus** controls the autonomic nervous system, whereas the cerebral cortex is subdivided to govern functions from the planning of actions to the experience of sight. As it comprises an irregular-shaped mass and not tidy, organised boxes, describing the brain's structure in terms of differentiated functions is difficult. However, despite this interconnectedness, the independent modularity of its substructures producing highly developed behaviour makes it essential to differentiate these component elements. General damage to the brain produces a variety of psychological problems, including epileptic fits. This is important in forensic approaches, such as blows to the head from childhood abuse or even in professional boxing leading to moral disinhibition, impulsivity and diminished conscientious behaviour. More specific damage to substructures in the brain can reliably predict any of a vast range of characteristic conditions.

Brain structures are described in order of **phylogenetic development** (how they evolved) and/or ontogenetic development (development within the lifespan). The major components of the brain are the **forebrain, midbrain**

Table 3.3 The main brain areas and the structures within them

Main area	Structures	Main functions
Hindbrain	Medulla (oblongata) Pons Cerebellum	Laterality of function Signal integration Complex movement
Midbrain	Tectum Tegmentum (reticular formation)	Auditory and visual processing Arousal and attention
Forebrain	Hypothalamus Thalamus Limbic system Basal ganglia Cerebral cortex	Homeostasis Relaying sensory information Emotional integration Movement regulation Control and planning

and **hindbrain**, formed from the upper **neural tube** during foetal development. The forebrain is more recently evolved and the hindbrain contains the more primitive structures. Table 3.3 shows the functional substructures in these areas; even those that are physically very small have profound effect on behaviour.

The spinal cord connects the brain and the PNS but can make 'automatic decisions'. These 'decisions' are made in a reflex arc or short-circuit in the spinal cord, where a large afferent sensation (e.g. a burned hand) entering via **sensory neurons** automatically triggers an efferent response (hand withdrawal) via **motor neurons** without reference to the brain, but through **interneurons** in the spinal cord. This involuntary reflex can be forensically significant, as any harm it may cause cannot be considered a conscious criminal act. The spinal cord is the most primitive part of the CNS, followed by vital function structures developed directly from it.

Structures in the hindbrain

The **brain stem** at the top of the spinal chord includes the **medulla (oblongata)**, **pons** and cerebellum. The medulla is the initial left and right hemisphere contralateral (opposite side) crossover point for the forebrain, containing the lower **reticular formation** (literally 'net': a tangle of nuclei mostly located in the midbrain) concerned with vital ANS functions such as heart rate and respiration. The cerebellum ('little brain', as it resembles the cerebrum) coordinates sensory information with fine muscle control, producing balance and fluid movement from the myriad of command and feedback signals. It also remembers complex sequences of movements, such as playing a musical instrument. Without the cerebellum, a performer such as **Vanessa Mae**

would be unable to lift her violin into position, let alone play it. The pons ('bridge') also has elements of the reticular formation and continuing integrating signals to the contralateral hemispheres of the brain, as well as playing a part in attention, sleep, breathing and alertness.

Structures in the midbrain

The midbrain is visibly indistinct, containing the **tectum** and below that the **tegmentum**. The tectum has roles in both auditory and visual reflexes. The tegmentum includes the areas **red nucleus**, **substantia nigra** and **periaquaductal grey matter**, as well as a section controlling eye movement and much of the reticular formation. The substantia nigra and red nucleus help control movement, and cell death in the substantia nigra produces symptoms of **Parkinson's disorder** (see Chapter 19). Pain regulation, ritualised mating and combat behaviour relate to the periaquaductal grey matter. The reticular formation occupies the centre of the brain stem from the bottom hindbrain to the upper midbrain. It is important in arousal, attention, sleep and other essential reflexes. Eysenck (1970; 1990) refers to the lowered activity of the reticular formation in the underpinnings of his personality dimension of **extraversion**, which is applied in clinical and forensic settings.

Structures in the forebrain

The forebrain structures are lateralised in symmetrical left- and right-hand structures. These include the thalamus, the **hypothalamus**, the structures comprising the **limbic system**, the **basal ganglia**, and the two hemispheres of the **cerebrum** (and the **corpus callosum** that connects them).

The thalamus relays sensory information to the **cerebral cortex** and has a role in its stimulation as well as in wakefulness and attention. The hypothalamus is located below the thalamus and both thalami are 'sensory relay stations'. The hypothalamus also regulates the four 'Fs' – fighting, fleeing, feeding and reproduction – and has a close relationship with the function of the pituitary gland, controlling all hormone levels throughout the body (see the **endocrinology** section, pp. 63–5). Hypothalamic control over the ANS maintains **homeostasis**, i.e. keeps variables such as temperature at the optimum required.

The limbic system consists of the **limbic cortex**, the **hippocampus**, the **amygdala** and shared structures such as the **mammillary bodies** and fornix. Emotional processes are primarily located in the limbic cortex and amygdala (see Chapter 17), whereas the hippocampus is central to learning and memory. The **basal ganglia** include

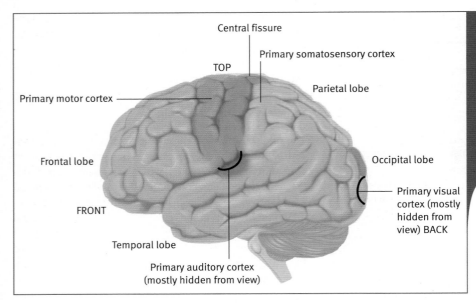

Central fissure

Primary somatosensory cortex

TOP

Parietal lobe

Primary motor cortex

Frontal lobe

Occipital lobe

FRONT

Primary visual cortex (mostly hidden from view) BACK

Temporal lobe

Primary auditory cortex (mostly hidden from view)

Figure 3.2 The area and structures of the brain. Although the brain appears as an amorphous mass, it is important to be able to map out brain areas, as each tends to have specialist functions. Source: Carlson (2000) *Psychology*, Allyn and Bacon.

the **putamen**, the **globus pallidus** and the **caudate nucleus**, which are involved in movement. Cell death in the substantia nigra produces Parkinson's symptoms realised in the basal ganglia, controlling such movements.

Three-quarters of neurons are in the **cerebrum** and its size differentiates species in terms of phylogenetic development. Its shape results from evolving a large surface area folded to fit inside the skull. The crumpled appearance comprises 'hills' or **gyri**, 'valleys' or **sulci** on its surface, and deeper 'valleys' termed **fissures**. A 3-millimetre layer of cells on its surface, called the **cerebral cortex**, controls both conscious functions and higher processes of the brain, and cortical damage shows immediate, specific loss of functioning.

The cerebral hemispheres can be subdivided into the four naturally occurring protrusions or **cerebral lobes** (see Figure 3.2), or can be mapped by the functions linked to these areas (see Table 3.3). Cerebral lobes are named by their positions under the divided bones of the skull.

The frontal lobe (front)

This comprises the front sections of the cerebral hemispheres back to the central sulcus just including the **primary motor cortex**. The motor cortex is a strip of gyri transversing both hemispheres, which controls the body muscles in a logical order. This can be mapped across its surface, with the left hemisphere controlling the right side of the body and vice versa. Within the frontal lobe is the **motor association** area, close to the primary motor cortex and speech production areas; also known as Broca's area, it is named after **Paul Broca** (1824–1880), who in 1861

noticed that left cortical area damage impaired speech articulation in a Bicêtre patient. This had already been revealed in 1825 by **Jean-Babtiste Bouillurd** (1796–1881) but was confounded with phrenology. The frontal lobes contain executive function areas with widely dispersed connections, including that for planning behaviour. Damage results in irresponsible and even criminally reckless behaviour, particularly damage to the area just behind the forehead referred to as the **pre-frontal cortex**.

The consequences of subtle and specific damage to the frontal lobe area are of particular clinical forensic interest. It is sensitive to frontal head impact or repeated blows bringing soft brain tissue forcibly against the hard inside of the forehead. Damage to the **medial pre-frontal cortex** reduces emotional sensitivity to actions with unpleasant outcomes, as this area integrates our planned actions with emotional associations in the limbic system. Thus being hit or surviving a head-on collision may reduce revulsion at carrying out a violent or gruesome act, as was possibly the case with UK serial killer **Fred West**.

The orbitofrontal cortex also plays a role in regulating emotional responses, and damage can result in a dangerous lack of restraint, leading to anti-social acts (Zeld and Rauch, 2006). It is located above the eyes behind the eyebrow area, and repeated blows such as punches to the eye could lead to **lesions** in this and other frontal lobe regions. Thus, change in moral judgement or even aspects of personality may slowly emerge in the wake of being hit in contact sports, street and domestic violence, or during physical abuse in childhood. It frequently occurs with specific and severe injury (see the Focus box).

Focus

The case of Phineas Gage

In 1848 whilst leading a Vermont crew of railway construction workers, 25-year-old Phineas Gage forced explosive into a hole using a steel rod 6 millimetres in diameter, which ignited the charge and blasted the rod with assumed lethal impact at Gage's head. It entered his left cheek, passed through his brain and exited through the top of his left forehead. Astonishingly, he not only survived but remained conscious and started writing in his record book, appearing to retain his intellectual faculties. Following 2 days of relative normality, he succumbed to infection and, on recovery, showed no major signs of memory or other cognitive defects.

However, Gage's brain damage had led to a change in his personality as well as his behaviour. Gage had been a conscientious and industrious railway worker until the accident, after which his level of responsibility was reduced to that of a child and his ability to plan forward to account for the outcomes of his actions

was lost. He used child-like reasoning in decisions that reflected transient whims. The change in his personality convinced former associates that he was no longer Phineas Gage.

The rod passed through vital planning areas of Gage's frontal lobes, damaging his pre-frontal cortex and destroying the functioning of his orbitofrontal cortex, which removed the emotional restraints on planned actions that inhibited rash and dangerously impulsive decisions. His ability to integrate 'feelings' consequent on his behaviour with his immediate planned activities had been severed by the steel rod. His case is a vital landmark in neurological history and a reference point for the effects of prefrontal lobe damage.

Gage resorted to displaying himself as a curiosity in Barnum's Circus and then worked in livery stables. In 1861, he died of epilepsy, another effect of his injury and a common by-product of brain trauma (see Damasio et al., 1994).

The parietal lobe (wall)

Under the skull's rear upper wall, behind the central sulcus, is the parietal lobe containing the **primary somatosensory cortex**, which is the afferent complement and adjacent to the primary motor cortex of the frontal lobe. The processing of touch sensation in the primary somatosensory cortex is in proportion to the nerve impulses from the body area. Thus the tiny tongue will have more processing space than a leg. The rest of the parietal lobe relates to the primary sensory cortex function in initiating movement, object manipulation, the integration of senses and visual attention.

Damage to the parietal lobe disrupts the integration of labelling information with actions and thus can result in **anomia** (the inability to name objects) and dilemmas such as not being able to distinguish right from left. Literary and mathematical skill can also be disrupted as can co-ordination of hand and eye (**Balint's syndrome**).

The occipital lobe (back)

The smallest cerebral lobe, the occipital lobe is at the back of the brain and, like the frontal lobes, is vulnerable to head impact. The primary function of the occipital lobe is vision and sudden (usually temporary) loss of visual function follows a blow to the back of the head. Logically, damage to the left and right halves of the occipital lobe will

affect vision in the **contralateral** field of vision. Recognition disorders or agnosia may result from lesions in this region, such as movement agnosia or the failure to recognise the movement of an object.

The temporal lobe (temple)

The left and right temporal lobes are on either side of the brain just above the ears. These have diverse functions, including hearing and memory acquisition, some visual perception and object categorisation. In the temporal region of the dominant cerebral hemisphere is Wernicke's area, named after **Carl Wernicke** (1848–1905), which is essential for the comprehension of speech. Damage results in failure to understand speech or **Wernicke's** aphasia. Non-dominant temporal lobe damage can induce incessant talking behaviour and musical deficits. The **parahippocampal gyrus** on the medial surface of the temporal lobe connects to the hippocampus itself and lesions here will interfere with memory, mimicking **Korsakoff's syndrome** (see Chapter 11). Temporal lobe injury can decrease sexual behaviour or increase aggression.

Temporal lobe epilepsy can result in **visual hallucinations** and to a lesser extent smell or taste hallucinations and a disruption of experiences and memories. Sufferers of temporal lobe fits report sudden heightened comprehension or déjà vu, which combined with hallucinations produce religious or **paranormal** experiences. Thus, temporal lobe function may be important to the understanding of psychoses and in the study of **parapsychology**.

Left and right cerebral hemispheres

The brain is divided into two similar halves and many component parts have left and right versions, such as the two hippocampi, though we refer to *the* hippocampus to avoid confusion. The two hemispheres communicate with each other via the **corpus callosum**, which connects the **association cortex** of each hemisphere via a complex network of neuronal **axons** (the extended arm of a neuron, often referred to as a 'nerve'). This connection means that any component of the left cerebral cortex is informed of what is happening in the corresponding right component. In the 1960s **Roger Sperry** (see Sperry, 1982) severed the corpus callosum to stop the escalation of neural activity between hemispheres in severe **epileptic** patients. These 'split-brain' procedures produced an apparent separation of thought processes and competition between the hemispheres over volition and even consciousness (see Springer and Deutsch, 1997).

Some important brain functions have become **lateralised** or specialised more in one hemisphere, such as the speech function (**Broca's area**) in the left frontal lobe only, and these are illustrated in 'split-brain' patients. Illustration utilises images presented briefly to the left eye of a split-brain individual, which are received by the right hemisphere but not transferred to the left hemisphere due to a severed corpus callosum. The patient is unable to utilise Broca's area immediately and cannot verbally name the image, even though they recognise it. Much can be learned from such opportunist situations, which could never be ethically justified for this purpose but lack experimental control.

There seem to be global differences in left and right hemisphere processing, in that the left hemisphere *tends* to specialise in the **analysis** of serial events, such as language in reading, speech and writing. The right hemisphere involves more Gestalt processing or the **synthesis** of component parts to realise the whole, such as considering the spatial relationships in maps or three-dimensional drug design. Ornstein (1975) considers the implications of these hemispheric specialisations in more detail. In individuals who are to a greater extent left-handed, hemispheric lateralisation is progressively less pronounced. Thus handedness can be important when making assumptions about brain asymmetry, which is influenced by sex-type and can be graded using the **Annett Handedness Questionnaire** (Annett, 1970).

The brain has evolved from its stem outwards in the manner of a flower blooming. Thus, 'higher' intellectual functions are located in the outer structures such as the cortex, and more basic functions closer to the stem, and it may be useful to consider the 'higher' functions as **selectively inhibiting** the instinctive demands of the 'lower' structures. For example, alcohol is thought of as 'stimulating' by the lay public, but it is initially inhibiting the inhibitive effect of the cortex, releasing the primitive activity of the lower brain. Thus intoxicated individuals indulge in increasingly risky and self-gratifying behaviour (see Chapter 11).

Neuroanatomical interventions

The terms used to navigate the three-dimensional structure of the brain can form parts of brain area names and are easier to understand in non-human species, due to the human brain changing orientation to the spinal cord as we stood erect. Evolution placed a curve in the rostral (anterior or 'towards the beak') to caudal (posterior or 'towards the tail') dimension, the line from the front of the brain through the brain-stem down the spinal cord to the 'tail'. The other dimension runs from the dorsal (back) or top of the brain to the ventral (front) or out through the limbic system.

Lateral means away from and **medial** towards the midline of the body. Ipsilateral indicates 'same side' and **contralateral** 'opposite side' of the body: for example, left and right hemispheres of the brain control the contralateral sides of the body. In cross-sectional views of the brain, 'slices' dividing front and back are in the **coronal or transverse plane**, those separating top and bottom are in the **horizontal plane** and cross-sections separating left and right brain are in the **sagittal plane**. The sagittal plane at the corpus callosum is the **midsagittal plane**.

Abnormal behaviour can result from genetic predisposition, abnormal development, injury, insult or infection of the CNS, particularly the brain. Genetic structural errors and dysfunctions become compounded as abnormal neurodevelopment deviates and becomes progressively impossible to reverse. **Injury** can be a blow to the head, intrusion into the brain or events such as a stroke; insult is damage from toxins such as drugs; and many **infections** also damage brain function. The point where damage stops neural information is a **lesion**. Injury, infection and insult can mimic disorders and need eliminating for accurate diagnosis.

Neuroanatomical treatments permanently alter brain structure and are a last resort. Experimental ablation of animal brains by **Pierre Flourens** (1794–1867), followed by **Paul Broca**, helped relate brain areas to behavioural dysfunction. Primitive early brain surgery resulted in much 'peripheral' or 'collateral' damage. Jacobson et al. (1935)

removed the frontal lobes of an excitable chimpanzee, calming without apparent change in intellect or other behaviour. Neuropsychiatrist **Egas Moniz** (1874–1955) received the Nobel Prize for transferring this principle to humans, overseeing around a hundred pre-frontal leucotomies, which is Greek for cutting the 'leuco' or 'white-matter' of the pre-frontal lobes with a 'tome' (knife). **Walter Freeman** (1895–1972), a neurologist without formal surgical training, pioneered an alarmingly convenient procedure in 1946, which could be performed in the physician's office in 10 minutes. A **transorbital leucotome** inserted under the upper eyelid was driven through the orbital bone with a mallet into the brain and then moved back and forth to cut the white matter of the frontal lobes. The procedure being simple, quick and very economical, thousands of patients had anxiety and obsessions treated in this way and still performed well on intellectual ability tests. In time, however, signs of prefrontal lobe damage appeared, such as irresponsibility, childishness and poor planned behaviour, leading to discontinuation of the procedure.

Early accounts support alarmist views of neurosurgery as a form of punitive butchery. The reckless overconfidence in early experimentation illustrates ignorance of sophisticated brain function in the early days of experimentation. However, the profound suffering of the pre-operative patient that frequently ended in suicide tends to be overlooked. Modern neurosurgery is rarely if ever carried out where physical brain damage is absent, and is reassuringly cautious and precise in targeted brain areas, with detailed neural knowledge and computer-aided accuracy for creating lesions.

Accurate brain imaging was beyond **radiography** (X-rays), as it did not detect brain matter, and even **pneumoencephalograms** (replacing the **cerebrospinal fluid** with air) or **angiograms** (X-ray absorbing fluid injected into the blood stream) were poor at revealing brain structure or function. However, computer-aided X-ray technology produces detailed 'slices' along the coronal, horizontal or sagittal axes. These CAT scans (computerised axial tomography) use high levels of X-ray radiation. NMR (nuclear magnetic resonance imaging) is safer, using a magnetic field rather than x-rays (see Chapter 4).

With clearer detailed images of brain structure, common reference points can be generalised across individuals to locate specific brain areas. Stereotaxis utilises neural reference points common across individuals by firmly clamping the skull and calculating neural targets in three-dimensional space by reference to a **stereotaxic atlas**. A **cannula** (hollow probe) can then be inserted safely, enabling accurate computer-guided cutting procedures monitored by NMR. Stereotaxis also calculates the entry point in the skull, avoiding unnecessary surgical damage.

In contrast to Moniz, modern techniques minimise lesions and consequent collateral damage. By pumping super-cooled liquid through a **cryoloop**, temporary 'lesions' are made, enabling the effects to be checked prior to any permanent intervention. Local anaesthetic has been used in a similar manner. Permanent lesions are conservative in extent, allowing for subsequent increases after affective and behavioural consequences have been assessed.

Modern lesion creation has been achieved on the surface of the cortex by aspirating tissue through a fine vacuum nozzle, and more recently by computer-controlled non-thermal **laser technology**. Subcortical lesions are rare and were made to reduce the symptoms of Parkinson's disease as they had been for depression, targeting the limbic system (Kelly, 1985). Neurotoxic chemicals can be introduced accurately via tiny nozzles and are specifically taken up by certain cells, leaving adjacent ones untouched. Subcortically, cells can be destroyed by implanted, limited-life, locally acting radioactive implants, usually **yittrium seeds**. This procedure was associated with **stereotactic subcaudate tractotomy** for intractable depression, which is no longer carried out in the UK, although it may be available elsewhere in Europe.

One of the two main twenty-first-century lesioning methods is **radio frequency thermo-coagulation**, which involves passing a radio frequency across fine steel electrodes to kill cells at that precise location by heat. The other is the gamma-knife method introduced by **Lars Leksell** in 1972, which uses converging cobalt gamma rays to destroy the target cells without surgery. These are used in **anterior capsulotomy** and **anterior cingulotomy** procedures (see Christmas et al., 2004).

Neurosurgery is very rare for long-term, treatment-resistant mental disorders and barely reaches double figures per annum in the UK, with only two neurosurgical units offering such procedures. These involve exceptional **mood disorder** and **obsessive–compulsive disorder** (OCD) cases that are protracted and treatment resistant (see Royal College of Psychiatrists, 2000). These disorders share common brain circuitry, and surgery has relieved symptoms that have been unremitting for decades. Despite suffering, patients have to reach stringent criteria before a specialist panel will sanction surgery. Non-OCD anxiety disorders were treated at the **Geoffrey Knight Unit** in London prior to its closure and were recently available at the **Stockholm Karolinska Institute**.

In some US states and Germany, neurosurgery for these conditions is banned. In many countries, other procedures have ceased or been banned, such as **bilateral amygdalotomy** for aggressive behaviour in criminal populations. The debate as to whether all remaining procedures should be allowed to die out is ongoing (e.g. Persaud, Crossley and Freeman, 2003). Arguments such as patient suicide due to surgery not being effective are countered by such patients being at very high risk for suicide anyway, with continuation of surgery seen as an effort to restore some hope in essentially hopeless situations. Most studies find improvement at follow-up for those few patients receiving treatment (e.g. Dougherty et al., 2002), although controlled trials would be unethical.

Another factor in preserving neurosurgery concerns the techniques and allied skills that will fall into disuse. These will be increasingly needed for neural implants of **stem cells** and prosthetic devices in a move from lesion-based surgery to non-destructive interventions. Other non-destructive techniques include deep-brain stimulation by stereotactically implanted electrodes, positioned by MRI and powered by subcutaneous programmable generators, and **vagus nerve stimulation**, where a subcutaneous pulse generator alters central brain circuits from outside the brain via the vagus nerve (Christmas et al., 2004). Non-destructive approaches rely on developing existing neurosurgical skills.

Thus far, the **macro** view of the brain has been considered, but at the **micro** level we have the **neurons** (nerve cells; also spelt 'neurones'). Internal and external neuron function is based on biochemical communication and this neurochemistry is also very important in interventions.

Neurochemistry

The neuron is an example of evolution, rather than design, creating a very indirect means of communication that allows more flexibility and sophistication in processing. A worm may manage its life with 23 brain cells whereas humans have billions of neurons, but no one has counted the number of neurons in an individual; thus estimates vary by *ten-fold* between 100 billion and 1000 billion (Carlson, 2004). The neural processes below are important, as each provides a point of chemical intervention to alter thought, affect and behaviour – an area referred to as psychoneuropharmacology.

Types of neuron

Varieties of neuron have three different basic shapes and roles, as follows, but their component parts and modes of functioning are very similar.

Some **sensory neurons** can receive stimulation from light, sound, taste and smell (**bipolar neurons**) and other sensory neurons receive stimulation from **somatosensory** sources such as touch, balance and pain (**unipolar neurons**).

The 'receiving' end of an individual sensory neuron is adapted to respond to physical stimuli, passing stimulation via **afferent pathways** to the sensory areas of the CNS.

Motor neurons receive stimulation from the movement areas of the brain and pass this stimulation via **efferent pathways** to the **neuromuscular junction** (**motor end plate**), initiating the flexing of the respective muscles. The efferent and afferent pathways in the peripheral nervous system consist of bundles of long axons (some called **dendrons**) encased in tough tissue. These axon projections (white matter) may reach great distances and such nerves in the CNS are called **tracts**.

Interneurons receive and pass on signals between other neurons in the CNS and connect motor and sensory neurons, as in the reflex arc in the spinal cord, where response to pain bypasses the brain.

Neuron 'support cells', called glial cells, form the bulk of CNS growth during development and vastly outnumber neurons. The many types of glia hold neurons in place, feeding them nutrients and raw materials, insulating them from each other and clearing away dead neurons.

Communication within the neuron: the action potential

The neuron 'receiving end' is a tree-like formation of **dendrites**, and on these **post-synaptic membranes** are signal receptors. Receptors can also be on the **soma** or 'body' of the neuron, containing the nucleus of the neuron, within which are the chromosomes, protein synthesis components and other nucleus components, including mitochondria. Mitochondria provide energy in the form of **adenosine triphosphate** and are believed to be an invading parasite that evolved to coexist within our cells; as such they have their own DNA. The many inhibitory and excitatory signals coming into the neuron are added together by a process of summation, and if the biochemical threshold of stimulation within the cell is reached, the neuron 'fires'.

When the neuron 'fires', its own signal passes down its axon, which is a protruding tube from the soma that can be tiny or reach a metre away as bundles of axons or nerves. The fluid inside the axon is normally negatively polarised to −70 millivolts, partly by **protein pumps** (pumping sodium out and lesser amounts of potassium in) and other selective channels in its semi-permeable membrane. The slightly higher proportion of positively charged sodium ions being pushed out of the cell and the fact that large negatively charged anions are trapped inside produces this dynamic disequilibrium across the axon wall. This is the resting potential or electrical gradient around the membrane which, like a dam holding back water, has the potential for sudden release.

At the critical threshold of stimulation, an action potential (a newly generated signal) passes down the axon by electrochemical **depolarisation**, moving across the axon wall to the axon tip. **Ion-dependent voltage channels** open in the axon membrane, allowing sodium ions into the cell interior or **axoplasm**, which rapidly depolarises until it 'overshoots' to +40 millivolts. This action is self-propagating as local depolarisation stimulates the adjacent area to depolarise. Depolarisation travels to the axon tip, stimulating the terminal button(s). During **repolarisation** the potential of the membrane to fire again is initially impossible (this is termed the **absolute refractory period**), and as repolarisation nears completion (the **relative refractory period**), only a strong signal would produce an action potential. If the initial depolarisation is insufficient, the local effect does not propagate at all, such that the neuron obeys the all or none law, i.e. it fires or does not fire. The **rate law** means that action potentials are exactly the same size, and the importance of the signal lies in the rate of 'firing' or frequency coding, aided by depolarisation being rapid at around 2 milliseconds and localised around the axon wall.

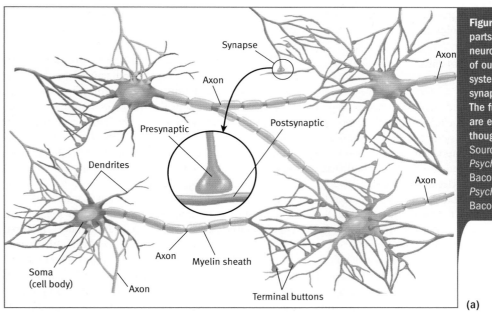

Figure 3.3 (a) Component parts of a neuron. The neuron is the building block of our brain and nervous system. (b) Detail of the synapse and its functions. The functions at the synapse are essential to every thought, feeling and action. Source: (a) Carlson (2000) *Psychology*, Allyn and Bacon; (b) Carlson (1992) *Psychology*, Allyn and Bacon.

(a)

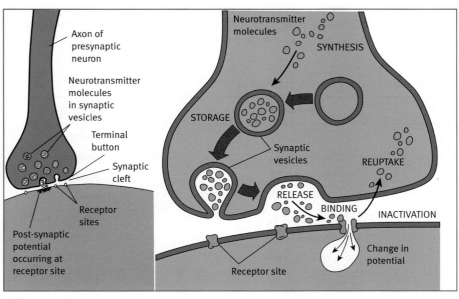

(b)

The progress of depolarisation accelerates in **myelinated** axons, where **oligodendroglia** in the CNS and **Schwann cells** in the PNS lay myelin in segments along axons, which provides insulation against signals in other axons. Myelin segments have gaps called **nodes of ranvier**, just far enough apart for the local effect of depolarisation to 'jump' from gap to gap. This speeds up the action potential in wider, fast axons, which are 100 times faster than thin, unmyelinated, 'slow' axons. In the autoimmune disorder multiple sclerosis, the body erroneously identifies myelin as an invading body and attacks it, resulting in axons becoming dysfunctional and widespread neurological symptoms such as loss of balance. Thus, signals within a neuron are important, but passing the signal between neurons provides a valuable point of intervention.

Communication between neurons: neurotransmitters and the synapse

Many neurons produce and use substances called **neurotransmitters**, which 'transmit' stimulation between neurons across tiny gaps called synapses. Each neuron may have 1000 or even 10,000 synaptic connections and there are more potential connection combinations in a brain than the estimated number of particles in the known Universe! In 1920 **Otto Loewi** demonstrated neurotransmission by using a frog's heart muscle to show the effect of the neurotransmitter **acetylecholine**. Motor neurons terminate at neuromuscular junctions or **motor end plates**, where muscular activity is initiated by the release of acetylcholine.

When the action potential reaches the axon **terminal button**(s), electrochemical stimulation opens calcium channels in the membrane. Incoming calcium ions enable **vesicles** or sacs of neurotransmitter substance to fuse with the terminal button membrane. This process, called **exocytosis**, allows the vesicle to spill its contents of neurotransmitter into the synaptic cleft and across to the **post-synaptic membrane** on the next neuron. Unused transmitter is cleared by various means, including reuptake by **transporter** proteins in the membrane or on **astrocytes** (a glial cell) outside the neuron. Transmitter substances not contained by vesicles are broken down by an enzyme such as **monoamine oxidase** for the **catecholamines** group of transmitters. In this way the effect of transmitter released into the synapse is finite.

Autoreceptors monitor how much of a transmitter substance is around, influencing its release and manufacture. Neurotransmitters are mostly manufactured from **precursors** in the axon terminals, though the precursor can be another neurotransmitter such as noradrenaline synthesised from dopamine. They are stored in vesicles ready for transport to the synapse.

Of the 100 substances acting as neurotransmitters, some are **neuromodulators** manufactured in the soma and moderate the action of 'classical neurotransmitters'. In Table 3.4 the last three transmitters are considered neuromodulators, as they do not conform to the exact criteria for neurotransmitters. Nitrous oxide and carbon monoxide act as atypical neurotransmitters. Being gases, they pass through membranes and cannot be stored in vesicles, but stimulate calcium ion levels influencing the release of the main neurotransmitter at that terminal.

The most common neurotransmitter in the CNS is γ-aminobutyric acid (**GABA**), which is inhibitory, followed by **glutamate**, which is excitatory in its effect. Other transmitters modulate the effects of GABA and glutamate by affecting groups of neurons, often in specific pathways in the brain. For example, noradrenalin primes brain areas promoting readiness for activity. Peptide neuromodulators and hormones (many neurons have hormone receptors) are dispersed over a wider range and are less neuron specific, producing a prolonged effect.

Table 3.4 A sample of neurotransmitter and neuromodulator substances

Substance	Chemical grouping	Implicated in
GABA (γ-aminobutyric acid)	Amino acid	Anxiety
Glutamate (L-glutamic acid)	Amino acid	Dementia
Dopamine	Monoamine	Parkinson's disease
Noradrenalin (norapinephrin)	Monoamine	Mania
Serotonin	Monoamine	Aggression control
Acetylcholine	Acetylcholine	Alzheimer's disease
Endorphins	Neuropeptides	Pain and reward
Anandamide	Lipid	Cannabis effects

Transmitter substances cross the synapse then attach to molecules called **receptors** in the surface of the post-synaptic membrane of the receiving neuron. The receptor's reaction contributes to an action potential in the receiving neuron. Slow-acting **metabotrophic** receptors are single proteins that activate **G-proteins** in response to binding with a transmitter molecule. G-proteins influence the opening of ion channels in the membrane (usually inhibitory) or activate post-synaptic enzymes that break down the **second messenger** molecules, which initiates the complex process of **phosphorylation**. **Ionotrophic receptors** are fast-acting clusters of molecules with a channel to admit ions when a transmitter molecule binds to the receptor. Various types of ionotrophic receptor admit differing ions and can determine if transmission is excitatory or inhibitory. Admitted calcium ions can also act as a second messenger, instigating a cascade of processes.

Synaptic connections and transmitters involved may be **excitatory**, increasing the chance of the next neuron 'firing', or **inhibitory**, reducing the chance of passing the signal on. This simple relationship conceals a myriad of processes evolved to allow a complex balance, as in the following examples.

- Neurotransmitters may be inhibitory or excitatory. Serotonin is mostly inhibitory in its effect and inhibits impulsive activity. Multiple neurotransmitters may create complex interaction between two neurons.

- Some receptors may inhibit the stimulation of the receiving cell, moderating primary neurotransmitter effects.

- If an inhibitory transmitter is used to inhibit a neuron, which itself is having an inhibitory effect, the overall effect will be excitatory.

- Subprocesses such as neurotransmitter production can be facilitated or inhibited by moderating mechanisms.

- Some excitatory synapses create an overall inhibitory effect by producing a subthreshold depolarisation, making it very difficult for the second neuron to fire when fully stimulated. Examples are **axo-axonic synapses**, where the axon terminal button of one neuron synapses on to the axon of another neuron.

- Axo-axonic synapses are also excitatory if stimulation of the second axon *adds* to its action potential.

- The summation effect is crucial, as neurons may receive as much inhibition as excitation. This simple outcome can be the culmination of a multitude of finely balanced processes. The behavioural outcome could mean that a person does not commit a criminal act of violence.

Some of the many processes at the molecular level that affect excitation and inhibition will be examined in the effects of drug intervention at the synapse below. In summary, if the overall stimulation is excitatory in one neuron, the transmission and summation process begins over again in each neuron receiving this stimulation.

The many concurrent processes taking place within a neuron equate to a large industrial country rather than a simple factory. Textbook diagrams are essential to visualise the basic principles but fall far short of a veridical view of neuronal activity: for example, there are many billions of sodium channels in the area of axon membrane shown in the average illustration.

Psychopharmacology

Synaptic processes are complex, highly interactive and readily altered by small biochemical changes or the psychological state of the individual and the interaction of the two. Psychoneuropharmacology or **psychopharmacology** is the main biological treatment approach and is largely dependent on influencing synaptic events. Drugs are described as agonists or **antagonists**, depending on whether they increase or decrease transmission respectively at their target synapses. Neuron interaction is highly complex and the reader is directed to the further reading at the end of the chapter.

The following examples illustrate how synaptic mechanisms can be altered pharmacologically.

- **Neurotransmitter precursors.** Drugs can increase or decrease the availability of precursors, and may be the raw material themselves, thus controlling levels of the neurotransmitter. The brain protects itself from unknown chemicals through the 'blood-brain barrier' and psychoactive drugs either are or mimic the structure of brain chemicals. **L-Dopa** is the precursor for **dopamine**, administered to increase the low levels of dopamine in **Parkinson's disease**.

- **Neurotransmitter vesicles.** Drugs such as **resepine** cause vesicles to leak their contents. Thus when the vesicle is triggered, there is nothing to release into the synapse.

- **Triggering neurotransmitter release.** Black widow spider venom releases acetylcholine, which initiates actions and may lethally overstimulate vital muscles. Conversely, **Botulinium toxin** reduces acetylcholine, leading to understimulation.

- **Neurotransmitter breakdown.** Monoamine oxidase (MAO) is the enzyme that breaks down excess monoamine neurotransmitter substances. MAO inhibitors (MAOI) have an agonistic effect in increasing the amine transmitter available. **Tranylcypromine** (**Parnate**) increases noradrenaline, countering the effects of depression.

■ **Neurotransmitter reuptake inhibition.** Preventing uptake into the cell body produces the agonistic effect of greater quantities in the synaptic cleft. **Fluoxetine (Prozac)** is an **SSRI** (selective serotonin reuptake inhibitor). These are controversial anti-depressant drugs that increase **serotonin** levels, or **5-hydroxytriptamine** (5HT). The older trycyclic anti-depressants such as **amitriptyline** inhibit the reuptake of serotonin but have side-effects, as they also prevent reuptake of noradrenaline.

■ **Neurotransmitter reuptake increase.** Lithium carbonate moderates mood swings in **bipolar mood disorder** (see Chapter 17). Lithium increases reuptake of noradrenaline and slows its release in an antagonist effect. The drug is also a serotonin agonist and interferes with second-messenger processes.

■ **Autoreceptors.** Autoreceptors monitor synaptic neurotransmitters, to maintain levels by adjusting production. Thus, increasing a neurotransmitter may lead to its depletion in the long term, as production is reduced. Drugs take advantage of autoreceptors by 'impersonating' the neurotransmitter to reduce production. **Apomorphine** acts thus to reduce **dopamine.**

■ **Post-synaptic receptors.** Drugs may stimulate these receptors, increasing signal transmission. Alternatively, drugs can block the receptor by mimicking the part of the transmitter that 'matches' the receptor molecule but does not activate it. The net result is antagonistic to transmission. Some **anti-schizophrenic** drugs block certain dopamine receptors, reducing receptor activity and schizophrenic symptoms.

■ **Transmitter modulation.** Some drugs show cross-tolerance, indicating a common mechanism. **Alcohol** and **benzodiazepines** such as **Valium** bind to the modulatory sites of GABA receptors, producing an agonist effect on this inhibitory neurotransmitter.

Psychoactive drugs act on nerve transmission in many other ways (see Meyer and Quenzer, 2005). These micro-level activities are realised by the patient in terms of their psychological state. There are three important limitations on the effectiveness of drug therapy.

Side-effects

It is currently impossible to target the *exact* neural connections responsible for a specific abnormality of behaviour. Given the number of possible synaptic combinations, such a project would dwarf that of inter-galactic travel. For example, a drug intended to counter depression would inevitably affect other related areas of brain function. Bennett (2006) illustrates this: a woman treated with **SSRIs** for depression had her sexual interest restored but suffered the side-effect of not being able to orgasm. Having *all* the expected effects of medication explained can avoid misinterpretation and possible panic confounding drug effects. Patients may also believe that their symptoms have worsened or draw other disturbing conclusions as a result of side-effects.

Although the 'taking a sledgehammer to crack a nut' analogy is currently less applicable, the general effects of drugs intended for specific purposes are unavoidable. Side-effects can be worse for long-term users and drive patients to abandon medication with tragic results, such as suicide, accidents or even homicide. Modern drugs are more specific in the functions they target, and although drug therapy is viewed critically as 'damage limitation', for some disorders it is the *only* relief from intolerable distress.

Tolerance and withdrawal

The body is not a machine; it is organic and adapts to situations by changing, sometimes structurally, to compensate for biochemical change. The brain tolerates the presence of the drug in returning to its former equilibrium, producing two counterproductive effects. Higher doses are needed to maintain the therapeutic effect and discontinuation of the drug may result in **withdrawal** with worse symptoms than prior to medication. This **adaptation** varies with the type of medication and the brain system targeted. Thus, not only illicit drugs result in addiction. Barbiturates were at one time over-prescribed to elderly people with agitation and insomnia in the belief that they were safe for long-term use, but they proved very addictive and withdrawal was worse than that for **heroin**, sometimes resulting in death (see Chapter 11).

Commercial concerns

Combining economic profit and drug production does not benefit the patient: as with most drug dealing, profit takes precedence. As mentioned above, **lithium carbonate** has been the treatment of choice for bipolar disorder and is an unpatented salt available in its **generic** (unbranded) form. Due to its low profitability, its benefits were not promoted and its use was restricted by poor availability and lack of information. Drug development is extremely expensive and, as with other areas of health, is best conducted as a national service not a commercial enterprise.

For Kraepelin, only nine types of drug were used for abnormal behaviour: alcohol, opium, bromides, morphine, scopolamine, barbiturates, chloroform, chloral hydrate and hashish. Until very recently, psychopharmacological treatments came about by accident or whilst

Table 3.5 Drugs commonly used in therapy

Drug type	Examples	Applications
Anti-psychotics		
Phenothiazines	Chlorpromazine	Schizophrenia, mania
Butyrophenones	Haloperidol	Schizophrenia, mania
Dibenzodiazepines	Clozapine	Schizophrenia
Anti-depressants		
Trycyclics	Imipramine	Depression, anxiety
MAOIs	Tranylcypromine	Depression, panic disorder
SSRIs	Sertraline, fluoxetine	Depression, OCD
Anxiolytics		
Barbiturates	Pentobarbital	Anxious insomnia
Benzodiazepines	Diazepam (Valium)	Anxiety, insomnia
Hypnotics	Flurezepam	Anxiety, insomnia
Newer anxiolytics	Buspirone	Anxiety, panic, OCD
Beta-blockers	Propranolol	Panic, hypertension
Mood stabilisers		
Anti-manic agents	Lithium carbonate	Bipolar disorder
Anti-convulsants	Carbamazapine	Bipolar disorder, hypertension

developing treatments for other disorders, as with most other effective therapies in psychiatry. Amongst the many 'fortunate accidents', neuroleptic drugs as effective dopamine antagonists reducing schizophrenic symptoms were first considered by **Henri Laborit** when in use as a **pre-medication** to calm patients before surgery. This tranquillising effect was originally a side-effect of the neuroleptic's initial use as an **anti-histamine** (anti-allergy drug). When **Jean Delay** and **Pierre Deniker** finally used them on psychotic patients in 1952, the effect changed the course of psychiatry.

The anti-depressant effects of MAOIs were noticed during their initial use for tuberculosis. Many other effective treatments in psychiatry were stumbled upon by accident, such as electroconvulsive therapy.

Electroconvulsive therapy (ECT)

The use of ECT for severe depression has a similar history to that of neuroleptics; however, developed across Europe, ECT provoked greater controversy (see the International Perspective box). Modern ECT involves the patient having **atropine** (to reduce salivary and bronchial secretions), a short-term anaesthetic, a modern muscle relaxant (such as **succinylcholine**) and pre-oxygenation of the brain. An electrical current is then administered at about 70–130 volts through one or both hemispheres of the brain, whilst oxygen is also administered. A small but detectable **seizure** must be induced, identified by sensitive seizure-monitoring equipment. The therapeutic effect of ECT seems proportional to the seizure magnitude, which in turn depends on the current and whether it is passed through one (**unilateral** – the non-language hemisphere) or both (**bilateral**) hemispheres.

Unfortunately, side-effects of memory loss, confusion and occasional mania are *also* proportional to the current, added to the risks of anaesthesia. However, ECT is dramatically effective in severe, catatonic or drug-resistant depression, as well as catatonic schizophrenic states. It appears to alter serotonin (increasing post-synaptic receptors), dopamine and noradrenaline transmission by three treatments a week until improvement is noted. This will involve 6–12 treatments if the voltage is unilateral and moderate. ECT works faster than anti-depressant drugs and some cases only respond to ECT. Baldessarini (1977) pointed out that ECT saves lives that would otherwise be lost through suicide.

Biochemical brain activity can be monitored in vivo (in a living brain) using positron emission tomography (PET). The patient is injected with any radioactive substance that emits positrons and then placed in a scanner, which pinpoints the particle emissions. Using radioactive sugar, a 'slice' image of the areas of greatest sugar demand or activity is produced. Neurotransmitter precursor could be used to highlight activity in the neurotransmitter producing neurons. **Nuclear magnetic resonance** (NMR) is less invasive for viewing brain activity in real time utilising natural emissions. Functional magnetic resonance imaging (FMRI), detects relative activity in different brain areas as tasks are carried out. Magnetoencephalography (MEG) is a hybrid technique that combines technologies producing high image and temporal resolution.

International perspective

ECT across Europe: benefit or barbarism?

The therapeutic use of electrical charges across the brain dates back hundreds of years. In 1792 in England, **John Birch** reported using six electric shocks on a melancholic (depressed) patient, who rapidly recovered and remained well for a number of years. In the early twentieth century, mental patients with high fever showed improvement. In 1917, **Julius Wagner-Jauregg** in Vienna noted neurosyphilis remitting following typhoid or malaria, and even Hippocrates believed that malaria-induced convulsions helped the insane. Thus, it seemed useful to induce epileptic-like seizures in confused and depressed patients by ingesting camphor or **insulin shock therapy**. In Berlin around 1927, **Manfred Sakel** treated schizophrenia by insulin-induced coma and convulsions, 'Sakel's technique', later using other substances. There was widespread interest in producing convulsions and analysing why they produced such calm, added to a mistaken belief that epilepsy countered schizophrenia. Around 1934 in Budapest, **Ladislaus von Meduna** used pentylenetetrazol or **metrazol** in place of insulin, as it was more powerful, more reliable (dose dependent), cheaper and easier to use, though less controllable or reversible. Before metrazol-induced therapy was discontinued around 1940, **A. E. Bennett** added **curare** (muscle relaxant) and **scopolamine** (sedative) to reduce side-effects of seizures, pre-empting the ECT procedure.

The work of Italian physicians **Ugo Cerletti** and **Lucio Bini** (along with a German, **L. Kalinowski**) led directly to ECT today. Cerletti observed and experimented with seizures and unconsciousness when 'calming' slaughterhouse animals with electric shocks. He thought using insulin and metrazol too dangerous. Bini produced a versatile 'electric-shock box' sufficiently controllable for use on humans. Once Cerletti was convinced that the voltage needed to create a seizure was not lethal, he used a human patient.

In 1938 Cerletti used a **catatonic schizophrenic**, who was confused, incoherent and unidentified. He began with a low-voltage shock, producing a mild spasm, and then a higher voltage, which met resistance from colleagues and an impassioned plea from the patient, who seemed no longer confused but fearing for his life. Cerletti delivered the increased shock and produced the first electroconvulsive seizure. He subsequently found that a series of 10–20 shocks on alternate days produced an improvement in acute schizophrenia. This limited success was superseded by a dramatic benefit in depressed patients. Cerletti found the side-effect of anterograde amnesia (loss of past events) to be a *benefit*, as patients did not remember to fear or resist the therapy. Other methods of inducing convulsions, such as metrazol, insulin and radio magnetic microwaves, were abandoned in favour of ECT.

Since Cerletti's work, much progress has been made in ECT technique but less in revealing its therapeutic mechanism. Unfortunately, the trial-and-error route to improvement produced undermining reports of memory loss and patients so confused that they did not know which side of a bus stop to stand, as well as burns from the electrodes, bitten tongues, and bones broken during seizures. This created an image of torture and drew comparisons with the electric chair. The portrayal of ECT as a punishment for disruptive American patients in the influential US film *One Flew over the Cuckoo's Nest*, based on the book by Kesey (1962), exacerbated already antagonistic professional and public attitudes, blurring the boundary between fact and fiction. Dies (1969) even argues that this is how ECT has its effect, by punishing depressive behaviour. Thomas Szasz was an influential member of a committee set up by the **Scientology movement** to utilise the publicity generated by Kesey's work to ban ECT.

In contrast, modern ECT's refined techniques, technology and sophisticated pre-shock medication has ended these earlier injuries. To be fair to ECT, graphic descriptions of modern surgery, or even dental surgery, would terrify prospective patients and make early descriptions of ECT seem very mild. Despite its image and acute effects on memory, the main advocates for ECT around the world are still the patients themselves, many of whom feel that the immediacy of its therapeutic effects averted their suicidal inclinations.

Evaluation of the effects of ECT is controversial, especially the use of a true control group, i.e. an equivalent group of patients who undergo the same procedure but do not receive real ECT. Although fraught with ethical problems, 'real' ECT is found more effective than the 'simulated' placebo condition. Nowadays, there is focus on economics and overstretched resources, with the concern that ECT is seen as a 'cheap alternative' and administered with inadequate precautions due to time and resource pressures. In the UK, the **Royal College of Psychiatrists'** guidelines on using ECT provide some means of reducing such problems.

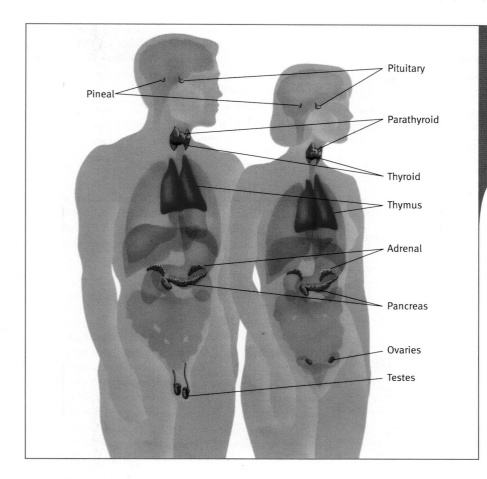

Figure 3.4 Position of the endocrine glands in the human body. The endocrine system has a profound and sustained effect on behaviour via glands around the body.
Source: Carlson (1992) *Psychology*, Allyn and Bacon.

Labels: Pineal, Pituitary, Parathyroid, Thyroid, Thymus, Adrenal, Pancreas, Ovaries, Testes

Neuroendocrinology

Neuroendocrinology involves endocrine substances or **hormones**, which overlap and interact with neurotransmitter systems; some substances, such as noradrenaline, are both hormones and neurotransmitters. Hormones are often stored and excreted into the body using **vesicles**, as neurotransmitters are emptied into synapses. They are produced by **endocrine glands** and travel in the extracellular fluid and bloodstream to stimulate receptors at various sites in the body. Although endocrine glands have specialist functions, they may produce more than one hormone.

The pituitary gland and hypothalamus

The pituitary or 'master gland' sends out specific 'hormone stimulating hormones' that stimulate hormone release from other glands, particularly the hypothalamus. Hypothalamic hormones affect ANS 'fight or flight' behaviours via adrenaline, specific feeding and sexual and other reproductive behaviours.

The combination of pituitary and hypothalamus also maintains homeostasis. For example, low fluid levels detected by the hypothalamus create thirst via the cortex, and the pituitary provides an **anti-diuretic hormone** that leads to more fluid being absorbed into the blood and less being excreted. Other major pituitary hormones are as follows:

■ **Human Growth Hormone** (HGH, also termed **somatotropin**) stimulates growth agents in the body, especially during development, and may be supplemented to avoid restricted height and development.

■ **Prolactin** adapts the breast for milk production in pregnancy. **Hyperprolactinaemia** produces lack of female sexuality and fertility, and emotional problems. In males the disorder produces breast growth. Treatments are unsatisfactory as they are indirect – they promote dopamine, which inhibits prolactin but causes mood changes and other psychological side-effects.

- Oxytocin prepares the female for birth but also facilitates bonding with the child. This also generalises to assist bonding between male and female partners and even increases the level of trust one has in others.
- **Thyroid stimulating hormone** is one of the pituitary/hypothalamic hormones that stimulate other endocrine glands, some of which are described below. Deficiencies or overproduction often results from failure at this 'executive level' rather than with the hormone-producing gland.

Pineal gland

The pineal gland produces **melatonin** in response to lack of light, aiding sleep. Levels also change with circadian rhythms (daily cycles) regardless of light levels. Melatonin supplement regulates sleep in the blind or those on long aircraft journeys across time zones.

Thyroid gland

This gland secretes **calcitonin**, which governs distribution of calcium. More importantly, **thyroxine** is produced which increases metabolism such as heart rate. Hyperthyroidism or thyrotoxicosis, an excess of thyroxine, can mimic anxiety and panic disorders, whereas the reverse, hypothyroidism, has symptoms of lethargy and depression, and is dangerous in childhood.

Adrenal glands

These have two components, **adrenal cortex** and **adrenal medulla**. **Adrenaline** and **noradrenaline** are released from the adrenal medulla in reaction to threat, danger or other need to prepare for action by activating the sympathetic ANS 'fight or flight response' (see the Focus box on p. 66).

Glucocorticoids released by the adrenal cortex raise blood-sugar levels and can reduce the immune response, helping control inflammation and over-reactivity such as asthma. The main hormone in this group is cortisol or the 'stress hormone' (also termed **hydrocortisone**), which adapts the body's resources under stress. Prolonged stress and consequent high cortisol levels can lead to serious physical damage and even death. Wilkinson (2005) provides an epidemiological illustration of this. He points out that the reason for life expectancy in Harlem in the USA being on a par with that in Bangaladesh is not violence or poor living conditions per se, but heart disease resulting from raised cortisol, due to the constant stress of being at the bottom of the US rich–poor divide.

These glands are also a low-level source of androgens, which are barely noticeable in males but have a profound effect on females where this is the only source. Alcohol and other factors can greatly multiply the levels of testosterone in females, making them more sexual and aggressive, whereas males have adapted to these levels. In females the androgen **androstenedione** helps the growth of pubic and other hair.

Pancreas

The pancreas produces **insulin** to break down complex sugars. **Diabetes** is the excess production of urine, which is associated with unpleasant physical and mental effects, including sexual disorders. **Insulin-dependent (type-1) diabetes** is due to a lack of insulin production and is treated by insulin injection.

Ovaries

Estriadol is the principal **estrogen** that produces female characteristics in development, even inhibiting bone growth and helping females to be shorter than males. Estrogen has become a pollutant in the food and water of many countries, as a result of its feminising effects increasing the commercial value of livestock and farm products. This will have effects across the population, such as breast growth in males and uterine growths and excess bleeding in females. Production of estrogen is stimulated by **follicle stimulating hormone** and indirectly by the **hypothalamic gonadotropin releasing hormone**.

Progesterone is important for maintaining the lining of the uterus and can be antagonistic to the effects of estrogen. Progesterone production is stimulated by **luteinising hormone** and indirectly stimulated by the **hypothalamic gonadotropin releasing hormone**. The synthetic steroid **RU-486** is a progesterone antagonist used to induce **abortion** in unwanted pregnancy.

Testes

These produce most androgens in males, the principal amongst these being testosterone. At a critical period in **gestation**, androgens will dictate whether a foetus develops into a male or remains female by default. In cases of androgen insensitivity, a genetic male may develop into a normal-looking and behaving (but infertile) female, demonstrating the power of hormones to determine behaviour.

At puberty a surge of androgens, mainly testosterone, promote male characteristics such as muscle and beard growth, but also increase levels of aggression (see the

Focus box on p. 66) and competitiveness. Levels of androgens in gestation will usually dictate later sensitivity to these hormones, and a physical marker for testosterone sensitivity is the amount by which the ring finger exceeds the length of the index finger (Manning, 2002). This ratio can predict testosterone-related characteristics such as physical performance and competitiveness. **Synthetic androgens** (**anabolic steroids**) were used in sports for performance, but this 'chemical advantage' and the damaging side-effects of high steroid levels have led to a progressive ban.

As an example of the hidden complexity of neurobiology, a range of substances, including pollutants such as pesticides, can masculinise the foetal brain – not just testosterone. Testosterone is mostly converted into estriadol in the receiving cells during the masculinisation period. Consequently, estriadol is more effective than testosterone in masculinising male brains (see Kandel, Schwartz and Jessell, 1995). This may seem confusing to psychology students, as the physiological landscape they work with is greatly simplified. To fully learn the infinite complexities of neuroscience would leave little time for other aspects of abnormal, clinical and forensic psychology.

Gut

Amongst the gut hormones is secretin, which is of interest in the treatment of a certain form of **autism**. A lack of secretin leads to excess endorphins being absorbed, producing classic symptoms of autism (see Chapter 9).

Other hormone-producing glands are found in the liver, kidney, skin and heart, but they are currently of less interest to students of abnormal, clinical and forensic psychology.

Endocrinology as a neglected science

Because the effects of hormones are widespread, they have traditionally provided an imprecise treatment, limiting their use in rectifying simple deficits in hormonal action. For example, some women suffer severe mood swings when approaching the **menopause**. Hormone replacement therapy (HRT) can help to alleviate this and the cardiovascular problems caused by low oestrogen. However, others taking HRT may suffer side-effects worse than menopausal symptoms, illustrating the widespread effects and complexity of hormone balance.

The perceived problematic complexities of hormonal actions and interventions has limited research and expertise relative to other biological approaches. This is a serious area of concern as the relative significance of substances that can change our apparent gender, shape and physical performance is being realised. More importantly for this text, hormonal disturbance is associated with personality and mood changes as well as behaviour of forensic interest, such as aggression (see the Focus box).

Viral agents

Viral infections can cause abnormal behaviour and change as they interact with other organisms, and in turn will change their host at the intracellular level. Produced by a **prion**-type virus, **Creutzfeldt–Jakob disease** (CJD) creates insidious mental and physical symptoms. Disorders such as schizophrenia and obsessive–compulsive anxiety disorder have been subject to virus-based research into their aetiology (e.g. Brown et al., 2005), although evidence for this type of infection has been found lacking when reviewed (e.g. Kirch, 1993).

Evaluation of the neuropsychological approach

Critics of the neuropsychological model are rare, but tend to be vociferous, especially if biologists enter a controversial area. For example, stem cell implants for degenerative disorders provoked a moral and ethical outcry that science would create a Frankenstein monster. Sadly, there is no moral or ethical outcry about the horrific plight of once brilliant human beings left to degenerate and atrophy due to such cruel disorders. Nor is there protest when highly trained researchers in such disorders are diverted from effective interventions by a few politically active groups.

Inferring from animal research to humans is problematic due to species-specific biological mechanisms and this, combined with ethical restraints, limits a complete picture of human neuropsychology. However, research is greatly facilitated by advances in imaging, **nanotechnology** and computer-based modelling, which are bringing advances in knowledge without unethical interventions.

Despite increasing sophistication, the impact of biological techniques on abnormal behaviour remains limited and crude due to side-effects and dependence on natural organic processes. However, by working with nature, it may be unnecessary to operate at the fine-grained level of microbiology. Such a symbiosis between science and nature is important, as there is a financial limit to what society is prepared to pay for the management of abnormal behaviour. In addition, the commercial viability of any intervention will ultimately dictate the boundaries of its practical implementation.

Focus

The neurochemistry of aggression

Aggression in non-human species relies greatly on instinctive, stereotyped behaviour patterns. One pattern is **threat** behaviour, in which the aroused animal displays species-specific aggressive acts or postures. These are recognised by the reproductively competing male, who will respond either with a pattern of **defensive** behaviours that escalates aggression or with **submissive** behaviours and postures, which will stop the aggression. In **predatory** aggression the prey is usually another species and the act is efficient and cold-blooded, involving much lower arousal than threat or defence.

Instinct-based behaviour is still evident in humans, but predatory aggression is also conducted against other humans, with ourselves and chimpanzees being the only species where groups of males hunt and kill rivals from their own species. Displacement of threat behaviour with predation has probably been facilitated by weapons that distance the aggressor emotionally from the victim. As Morris (1990) observes, blood letting amongst most animals is rare, as the ritualised aggressive–defensive cues prevent unnecessary harm – a system corrupted by humans and their nearest relatives. Contemporary threat behaviour in humans over resources or partners is found in more socially acceptable **dominance behaviour**, i.e. deceit, assertion or the abuse of authority, power and wealth.

An animal's perceptual system scans the environment for threat information; this is passed to the limbic system, triggering aggressive or defensive responses in the brain stem. The **amygdala** and **hypothalamus** mediate this process, stimulating the **peri-aquaductal grey** (PAG) matter, which differentiates between predatory behaviour via the ventral PAG and defence behaviour via the dorsal PAG. In human aggression, Blair (1995) proposed a **violence inhibition mechanism** (VIM) based on Lorenz's (1966) submission cues that stopped an aggressing animal. Role-taking in humans allows an attacking individual to empathise with a victim's distress, stopping aggression. Blair considers the VIM to be biologically or developmentally absent in **psychopathic** individuals, who *understand* the pain they inflict but *feel* no empathy (see Blair, Mitchell and Blair, 2005). This does not increase aggression; there are just no restraints to stop it.

Other biological intervening inhibitory processes in humans involve the **prefrontal cortex** and the **orbitofrontal cortex** (see the previous section). Aggressive acts are chemically facilitated by **adrenaline** and **noradrenaline,** and their sustained effect can lead to forensically violent consequences. For example, a heated argument will precipitate hormonal preparedness for aggression, although no violence occurs. Later this individual may drive more aggressively and any altercation is far more likely to escalate into assault.

In humans, the level of and sensitivity to testosterone governs the likelihood and intensity of aggression (e.g. Dolan, Anderson and Deakin, 2001). Foetal exposure to androgens makes brain circuits sensitive to future stimulation by these hormones. However, with low testosterone sensitivity, aggressive responses can be elicited by injecting testosterone, which is consistent with the lowered aggression found in early uncontrolled studies of **castration**, reducing testosterone production. Synthetic androgens became common amongst bodybuilders 1980s, but these anabolic steroids also increased violent behaviour. However, increased testosterone is also a *consequence* of aggression and levels are raised in those successful in competition.

The depression of higher brain activity as a result of alcohol disinhibiting lower brain activity results in high levels of assault and affray in Western city centres at night. Groups of males in close proximity competing over females provide environmental triggers for aggression, and alcohol also stimulates higher levels of testosterone in both males and females, further fuelling aggressive reactions in both sexes. Less accustomed to the effects of androgens, females are increasingly involved in street violence, particularly those females sensitised to androgens by sharing the prenatal period with a male sibling.

Serotonin inhibits the human aggressive response, particularly in the forebrain (Coccaro et al., 1997), and aggression towards the self in the form of suicide (Lidberg et al., 2000). This offers a means of intervention for individuals with low serotonin, as aggression is reduced if levels are raised by SSRI fluoxetine (Coccaro, Kavoussi and Hauger, 1997). However, Dolan, Anderson and Deakin (2000) emphasise that impulsivity and risk-taking behaviour are influenced much more by low serotonin than by aggression alone.

Much research into aggression utilises forensic populations (prisoners), but biological factors also correlate with aggressiveness in the wider population, suggesting that for individuals most at risk, gathering in predatory groups and drinking alcohol is not the best form of recreation.

The almost infinite complexity of neuroscience can be problematic. An individual in lifelong specialist research cannot grasp the overall dynamics of abnormal behaviour relating to its biological underpinnings. Nor could one author draw together the myriad of influences at all levels into a coherent series of volumes and maintain access to specialist detail when needed. The internet has provided the potential for a flexible and factual web resource maintained by experts, but implementation will require resources and agreement between those institutes that currently attempt small-scale versions in economic competition. As Harrington (2006: 13) states, 'your role as scientist is to be sceptical and question everything'. Thus the questions as to who decides what is entered or edited in a single resource and at what point research is sufficiently established to be entered may prove insurmountable. Published neuroscience will always be more than one step behind current awareness.

Although the area of social and environmental interaction with biology has been shrinking in the face of greater neurological explanation, it cannot be entirely dismissed in accounting for the totality of behaviour. Thus wherever the boundary between nature and nurture emerges, the interplay of these factors has to be acknowledged.

The neuropsychological approach applied to the case study of Ian

From a genetic point of view, Ian's moody, unstable behaviour reflects his father's philandering and eventual suicide, indicating a shared genetic predisposition to bipolar mood disorder and possibly personality disorder (see Chapters 14 and 17). Ian's father will have had lower levels of serotonin, contributing to mood disturbance, promoting impulsive, even aggressive behaviour, and facilitating his sexual psychopathy. These traits were also evident in Ian. His mother appeared over-tolerant of both father and son, and seemed prone to unipolar depression.

These factors may have produced more mood disturbance in Ian than in his parents. Fluctuating levels of noradrenaline, dopamine and serotonin could have been moderated earlier by lithium pharmacotherapy, avoiding the worst excesses of his behaviour. It would have helped to instruct family members as to the importance of Ian's adherence to his medication. Such intervention can avoid the escalation of chaotic behaviour into the forensic domain, in families that are frequently caught up in tragedy when clear warning signs are simply tolerated or not understood.

Self-test questions

- What is meant by genetic linkage?
- What is the importance of the autonomic nervous system in explaining abnormal behaviour?
- What are the costs and benefits of neurosurgery?
- Why are events at the synapse important for drug treatments?
- Why is ECT still a viable treatment?
- How can aggression be precipitated biochemically?

The evolutionary approach

Although deficient in literature, the evolutionary paradigm may eclipse other approaches as it places abnormal behaviour in its true context. However, this section should be read in conjunction with the related section on genetics and neurodevelopment (pp. 45–8) as well as the section on the behavioural approach, with its shared study of animal behaviour (pp. 77–83).

The origins of a paradigm

Towards the end of the twentieth century, the evolutionary perspective developed from a small sub-section of genetics and animal behaviour into a major explanation of behaviour in its own right. Although founded on the nineteenth-century work of **Charles Darwin** (1809–1882), only in the last two decades has this paradigm been seen as relevant to abnormal behaviour. In 2000, Abed reported that there were still no evolutionary approaches in the training curriculum for psychiatrists. This would have been different if psychologists at the time of Darwin, or even subsequently, had understood Darwin's conclusions and their implications, and evolutionary psychology would be a paradigm in psychology's theoretical establishment.

The Origin of the Species (Darwin, 1859) and other literature began treating humans as just another species and, controversially in this era, as descending from the same ancestry. Darwin was a functionalist in that he believed inherited characteristics survived to the degree that they were functional. He also attempted to identify how various species originate and assumed certain fundamental principles:

- All living species originate from less varied ancestors by a process of **evolution**.

- Species evolved their characteristics by **natural selection**.

- Natural selection is based on the **adaptive value** of characteristics.

Darwin referred to *characteristics* being inherited as he was not aware of the work of Gregor Mendel (see the previous section) and the existence of genetic processes, making it difficult to conceive of behaviour patterns being inherited. Thus, in neodarwinism we refer to inheriting genes rather than physical characteristics. When published in 1865, Mendel's work also provided Darwin's theory with a mechanism for inheriting many characteristics but only expressing some, i.e. opposing gene traits.

Referring to humans as just another species with ancestors common to other animals brought Darwin into conflict with religious authorities, whose manufactured accounts of human origins were far removed from the facts Darwin had uncovered. Darwinian theory and the evolutionary approach had sceptical support from the scientific world but serious and powerful enemies in various religions. This battle of belief versus science continues in the twenty-first century (see Chapter 2). Opposed by religious leaders and the popular press, Darwin's methods were also criticised by contemporaries such as **Wilhelm Wundt** (1832–1920) as being anecdotal. However, his evolutionary theory became established and various disciplines developed from studying humans as any other species. See the Research box for detail on Darwin.

Research

Charles Darwin: origin of a paradigm

The tribute to Charles Darwin and his beloved pigeons on London's fourth plinth in 2009 clearly reflects the eternal influence of his evolutionary theory.
Source: David A. Holmes.

In 1809 Charles Robert Darwin was born in Shropshire into an age dented but not penetrated by science. Religious teaching supplied explanations for the origin of humans, but for many, this would change within Darwin's lifetime as a result of his radical research. Darwin's dedication to research spanned most of his life and provided the basis for an entire scientific paradigm, as well as bringing about historic enlightenment regarding the origins of all species.

His mother died when Darwin was 8 and he went on to be enamoured by science in a makeshift chemistry lab in the shed with his brother. Disappointed with his academic performance, his father withdrew him from school. Darwin went on to fail at medicine and theology (almost), and to lose his girlfriend to his passion for entomology, which stemmed from John Edmonstone (a freed slave from Guyana) teaching him taxidermy. Ironically, Darwin's early study of nature had a theological framework and was conducted under the shadow of **Jean Baptiste Lamarck** (1744–1829), both of which he later undermined.

After further career struggles with his father, Darwin secured the job of naturalist on *HMS Beagle*'s survey of South America, leaving Plymouth in December 1831. Amid sea-sickness, Darwin noted geological evidence of the earth being very old, in accord with **Charles Lyell**, and he collected many specimens, mostly his beloved beetles. He progressed to larger fossils and found more evidence of the earth being too old for theological accounts, emphasised by an earthquake in Valdivia. After visiting Africa, Australia and many islands, he arrived back in England in October 1836. Whilst struggling with many crates of specimens, Darwin was made fellow of the Royal Geological Society and began to piece together his ideas of species mutation and extinction. In 1837, his research on the remains of ancient apes suggested that mankind had ape ancestors – an idea he suppressed for fear of being labelled a heretic. However, he kept the now familiar tree-like drawing of the descent of species along with his thoughts on the laws that he considered applied universally across species.

Darwin married in 1839 but continued to devote his time and health to research solving the 'transmutation' of species problem. He even considered the Lamarckist idea that animal traits disappeared due to lack of use during a creature's lifetime. His health further declined as his circle of friends and colleagues evolved into the intellectual elite of the period. Darwin contemplated the extreme age of the earth and the artificial breeding of domestic animals alongside the non-functional vestigial organs and limbs he had found in his specimens. By 1842, Darwin had a rough draft of his theory and still considered that his laws were created by a divine being, but he did not publish for fear of religious opposition and ridicule. He concentrated on personal domestic and health issues, which Darwin thought might overtake his life's work.

Darwin struggled over geographical divergence until real-world observations confirmed that species had indeed crossed oceans. He found some support amongst a few intellectuals, when in 1858 he received the second draft of **Alfred Russel Wallace**'s paper (Wallace, 1858) containing many of the concepts that had been Darwin's life for 20 years. Wallace's ideas were idealistic and polluted with morality, and Darwin battled ill health, which had been fatally shared by some of his children, to complete his work. Powerful friends arranged extracts of Darwin's and Wallace's work to be presented to the Linnean Society in June 1858. The following year, Darwin completed his rather large book and retired to Ilkley Hydropathic Hotel to regain health and hide from the outrage that he was certain his work would provoke. Predictably, the Church rejected his work, but many, such as **Thomas Huxley**, championed it and even coined the term **Darwinism**. Public opposition to Darwin's assumptions seem odd, as **artificial selection** had been used to breed characteristics into working and domesticated animals and this had already been applied to 'unsuccessful' human populations.

Darwin produced further work on plants and domestic animals as his writing was increasingly accepted. In 1866, **Herbert Spencer** used the phrase 'survival of the fittest', which largely replaced 'natural selection'. Darwin also preferred the new phrase; he privately held firm to the non-theological version of his theory and felt the phrase 'natural selection' implied that something divine might be doing the selecting. This was also reflected in Darwin's dim view of Wallace's later defection to theological explanations. In 1871, Darwin published part of his sex-selection work as *Descent of Man*, though this contained concessions to the Church, and in 1872 he published *Expression of the Emotions in Man and Animals*. He produced more works on plants until his death in April 1882.

Darwin worked with cumulative evidence to produce a hypothesis, which he could not test. However, across the entire history of science and academic thought, the importance of the concept of evolution by natural selection as presented by Darwin is unsurpassed and will probably always remain so.

Other areas of study overlap with the evolutionary approach or simply try relabelling its concepts. All share the view of mankind as just another animal species with common ancestry (for more detail, see Cartwright, 2000). Those to be briefly mentioned are comparative psychology, ethology, behavioural ecology and sociobiology.

Comparative psychology

From the assumption that humans are related to other animals, the systematic study of animal behaviour should provide insight into human behaviour. In comparing humans with other species, new insights can be gained into behaviours habitually accepted as 'normal human behaviour', which are more clearly seen as instinctive or inherited in animals. We tend to be 'instinct-blind' in psychology and social science. Comparative psychology also emphasises how both humans and animals similarly develop behaviour patterns in response to environmental stimuli, requiring a detached scientific view of all species, focusing on common behaviours.

Darwin (1872) provided support to comparative psychological views in his publication *The Expression of the Emotions in Man and Animals*, directly comparing humans as just another species. Despite his pivotal importance, Darwin's anecdotal methods left a vacuum in comparative psychology, partly filled by Wundt and **Conwy Lloyd Morgan** (1852–1936) in the USA with his 1894 text, *An Introduction to Comparative Psychology*. Morgan's legacy was the conservative empirical method illustrated by 'Occam's razor' (see Chapter 1), accepting the simplest, unembellished explanations. Morgan's version or 'Morgan's cannon' avoided blurring the boundaries between man and animals with errors such as **anthropomorphism**, highlighting the dangers of attributing specifically human aspects to animals and vice versa.

This facilitated the empirical approach of **behaviourism** (see below). The work of **Pavlov** and **J. B. Watson** examined animal learning experimentally in the laboratory, isolated from other factors such as their natural environment, and thus became labelled **empiricism**. This eventually led to the work of comparative psychologists separating from that of ethologists.

Ethology

Literally the study of habits or characteristics, ethology examines the naturalistic behaviour patterns of animals in evolutionary terms; Lamarck is considered an early ethologist. These patterns are usually the specific behaviours that characterise a species, such as revealed in the work on bee communication by **Karl von Frisch** (1886–1982). The German ethologist Konrad Lorenz (1903–1989) observed **imprinting** behaviour in geese and considered whether this also occurred in humans, providing evidence for the maternal deprivation studies of Bowlby (1944; see Chapter 9).

Lorenz's work was continued in the UK by his student **Nikolas Tinbergen**, who made more direct cross-species references between animal and human behaviour and refined Lorenz's methods. Whilst staying with Tinbergen's PhD student in Oxford, the present author was impressed by the ethologist's need to study animals in their natural context, despite the methodological difficulties entailed, in contrast with the relative methodological ease of comparative psychologists studying 'animals in cages'.

Comparing across species raises the issue of which behaviours can be learned in a number of animals and which are instinctive or species specific. Ethologists disagree with comparative psychologists or **behaviourists** over the line drawn, and undermined the behaviourist assumption that animals are born with a mental tabula rasa (scraped slate) and that all is learned. Instinctual drift was found, where instinctive patterns override learned behaviour, showing species-specific **preparedness**. Thus it would seem that not all behaviour is simply learned and that genetic **preparedness** plays a role. This has progressively led to the conclusion that most stable behaviour patterns or personality traits in humans are genetically inherited (Penke, Denissen and Miller, 2007; Plomin et al., 2001). More ethologist evidence came from the inherent **language acquisition device** of Noam Chomsky, providing better explanation than the behaviourist view of language acquisition as entirely learned (Chomsky, 1957). However, the language acquisition device only provided a generic system, with the specific language being learned in the same manner as stereotyped birdsong being inherited, but individual variations being a result of early contextual learning.

Lorenz identified instinctive behaviours or fixed action patterns, which are resistant to change, are species specific, need no learning, and are often triggered by innate releasing mechanisms, such as the features of a baby's face releasing protective behaviour in human adults. Tinbergen considered cascading fixed action patterns, where one pattern provides the trigger for another, creating complex behaviour; this resembles the chaining of behaviour used by behaviourists in behaviour modification (see below). Eventually, assumptions of inherited behaviour associated ethologists with eugenic concepts, with criticism directed at Lorenz. The issue of findings being abused should not, however, lead to denial of evolutionary facts established by ethologists.

Eugenics, anthropologists, behavioural ecology and sociobiology

The legacy of **Herbert Spencer** (1820–1903) went beyond the phrase 'survival of the fittest', used more by the critics of evolution than its supporters. Examining the evolution of human behaviour was termed **social Darwinism** and utilised by Darwin's cousin, **Francis Galton** (1822–1911), who coined the term 'eugenics'. The basic premise of the eugenics movement was that 'successful' individuals should breed more and that the 'unsuccessful' should breed less. This led to the implementation of policies of sterilisation of those considered genetically inferior in the USA and Europe, escalating to the extremes of mass killings under the Third Reich (see Chapter 1).

The religious and political powers, once opposed to Darwinism, joined forces to improve the 'good' in the human species by eliminating the 'bad', based on human artificial selection. Modern genetic counselling utilises similar principles to eliminate the gene for **Huntington's disease**, but traits targeted by eugenic purges were crudely or morally defined and polygenic. Eugenic methods were not just unethical but would eliminate many good traits with the 'bad'. Lessons were not learned from animal breeding, where defective traits are exaggerated in pedigree animals. This entire episode reflected very little of true evolutionary theory, but was subsequently used to tarnish and repress its study and is still referred to by misinformed critics today.

Anthropologist **Franz Boas** (1858–1942) moved from supporter of natural selection to critic of eugenics and the 'unfairness' of natural selection creating differences within the human species, pointing to history and culture as creating these differences. With early sociologists, Boas adopted what Cosmides and Tooby (1992) termed the **standard social science model** of behaviour, that all humans are born equal and learn their differences from culture

A naïve view of inheritance and prejudiced intolerance led to the brutal abuse of eugenic principles under the Third Reich. Source: Pearson Online Database.

and society rather than through instinctive reactions. This perhaps culminated in the work of Boas' student **Margaret Mead** (1901–1978), who concluded from flawed studies of Samoans that sex roles were not biologically defined and could be socially reversed. Such ideological moral thinking seemed so divorced from reality that its academic impact is astonishing. However, during the heyday of sociology from the 1930s to the 1970s, the anti-evolution camp was thirsty for evidence of any type, rapidly adopting 'nice' explanations of behaviour regardless of their factual basis. Paradoxically, the assumption of behaviour being entirely learned was aligned with behaviourism, which was also rejected due to its perceived mechanistic assumptions.

During the years when evolutionary theory was out of favour, scientific advancements substantiated this approach and undermined sociological as well as the enmeshed spiritual/humanitarian assumptions. As the spectre of the eugenics movement faded, evolutionary theory became acceptable and revitalised by new enthusiasm and terminology.

Behavioural ecology considers the ecological and evolutionary foundations of behaviour and its adaptive value, emerging from ethology when Tinbergen distinguished between proximate and ultimate explanations of behaviour. These proximate and ultimate explanations correspond to the immediate (proximate) influences, such as genetics or biology, and the longer-term evolutionary (ultimate) reasons for that behaviour existing in the first place. Tinbergen opened the door to a flood of ultimate explanations, some competing and others being anecdotal with little weight to their argument. A cost–benefit method of examining the value of behaviours developed in behavioural ecology, with complex trade-offs being argued between intrinsic (e.g. need to sleep) and extrinsic (e.g. predator avoidance) demands on behaviour, which change with time and environments. These arguments produced creative invention, as more than one adaptive behavioural solution to a situation is possible (Buss, 1999).

Wilson (1975) coined the term sociobiology to replace behavioural ecology, though for Hinde (1982) the new term added little. The sociobiologists' position was perceived as extreme in explaining social behaviour in evolutionary, genetic and biological terms. Heated debate in the 1980s (see Cartwright, 2000) served to place evolutionary theory prominently on the academic landscape. Reactions to personal appearances by Edward Wilson bordered on physical violence, and resistance to biological explanations tend to keep evolutionary psychologists involved in debate rather than research. However, the cumulative work of ethologists and comparative psychologists made the biological view of behaviour more credible for sociobiologists, behavioural ecologists and **neuroethologists** to utilise. In the twenty-first century the umbrella term 'evolutionary psychology' is again a major paradigm, although it still subsumes a number of disciplines.

The evolutionary process

For half of the 3 billion years of life on earth, we were single-celled organisms. Fifty million years ago our ape ancestors emerged, but homo sapiens have been in their current form for only 200,000 years. Mass extinctions occur, such as the meteorite in Mexico 65 million years ago, radically changing the evolutionary pecking order for succeeding generations (see Buss, 1999). Evolution's pace remains steady, but the complexity of organisms has increased, giving the illusion of evolutionary acceleration. Humans share 98.8 per cent of their DNA with their nearest relative, the chimpanzee. This illustrates the immense power that a few genes can exert over development and behaviour, which needs consideration in the behavioural implications of genes in evolution.

Various factors, such as sunlight radiation, produce genetic mutations (see above). Offspring with these mutations are mostly aborted or die young, though some survive, usually with damaging traits. In a small percentage, the characteristic confers a selective advantage to the individual, and the chances of this mutated gene being passed on is increased by natural selection. Some mutations are relatively benign in terms of advantaging or disadvantaging the individual and provide the variation found within species, such as eye colour in humans.

Brain structure and neurodevelopment also evolve and this modifies behaviour in addition to inherited behaviour patterns. Early evolutionary developments such as the eye are clearly linked to inherited specialist brain areas – a principle applied to cognitive processes. Fodor (1983a) described inheritable mental **modules** for specialist functions or problem solving, evolved through natural selection. Cognitive psychological approaches have relied on the concept of modularity, and modular specialism now explains functions where general-purpose brain architecture had been assumed.

Evolution is also a means of changing the frequency of each gene in a gene pool, which are interbreeding groups of a species. Gene pools may be separated geographically or simply do not or cannot interbreed. Subgroups within a pool may form and speciation may take place when subgroups no longer interbreed and become separate gene pools. Certain genes may become excluded from each pool. Contact between geographically separated but reproductively compatible pools may allow gene **immigration** and **emigration**. Important to evolutionary psychology are the processes of natural selection and **random drift** in the gene pool, the latter not considered by Darwin due to his being unaware of **gene alleles**. One form of random drift occurs in small populations with limited offspring. However, not all gene alleles can be carried through to succeeding generations by random fluctuations assisting speciation. Tooby and Cosmides (1992) describe the environment of evolutionary adaptedness (EEA) as the statistical composite of selection pressures that occurred during the period of evolution of an adaptation (e.g. erect

stature), attempting to account for all factors responsible for developed adaptations.

Natural selection equates to the reproductive survival value of genetic traits in combination or individually. Most surviving genes produce traits that enable carriers to remain healthy, feed and avoid predators in accord with Darwin's concept of naturally selected adaptive traits. However, many genes confer reproductive advantage, in that we are attracted to healthy, strong providers of children or security and protection (Buss, 1999). Not all features that increase reproductive success are functionally adaptive in Darwin's concept. A controversial example is the healthy human female breast not having evolved its shape for feeding offspring, as it would be of a very different structure. It has evolved to project an image of sexual reproductive health to attract a prospective mate, hence the use of cosmetic surgery to exaggerate these features. Thus it can be seen that natural selection on the basis of adaptive success can be at odds with sexual selection in terms of competitive success.

Salient, reproductively attractive features in many species are clearly maladaptive by other criteria, such as the attractive plumage of the peacock seriously impeding its ability to flee or fly. In humans, some females find cruel, anti-social, rebellious males sexually attractive, but these males make poor providers, are unfaithful and can be a danger to themselves and offspring. However, this attraction and feckless approach to mating may allow them to reproduce more frequently (Mealey, 1995). Similarly, males may be attracted to unhealthy, thin, vulnerable females, who may be poor providers and carers of children. Thus, reproductive potential and provider potential can be very separate routes to gene survival, as illustrated by opportunist paternity data: UK DNA testing by Cellmark Diagnostics revealed that in one in seven cases the presumed father did not match the child's DNA (*The Times*, 23 January 2000). A healthy, strong but unattractive male often acts as cuckold carer for offspring of an unhealthy but sexually attractive male neighbour. Paternity uncertainty may contribute to males showing less unconditional regard to children than females, and also accounts for the significantly high number of statements regarding the supposed father's resemblance to a newborn child by mothers (see Buss, 1999).

This form of reproductive strategy enables females to select one mate as provider and parent, but another for sexual satisfaction and genetic material. Baker (1996) presented this as one of many strategies in 'Sperm-wars', as well as males countering female selectivity by evolving sperm that battles with that of a competitor. These strategies are not uniquely human and are also found in the rest of the animal world. Dawkins (1989) has been associated with the strategy whereby males will often drive out or kill the offspring of former partners and suspected offspring of cuckolding to ensure survival of their own genes. This was supported by research on some human populations (e.g. Daly and Wilson, 1989), though not by others (Temrin, Buchmayer and Enquist, 2000). Dawkins' (1989) 'selfish gene' approach portrays humans as survival machines for their genes and has been critically linked to sociobiology (Hayes, 1994) in its overprediction of hostility to strangers and the deceptive use of language to gain advantage in 'selfish' gene survival.

In this genetic battleground, there seems little need for the cohesiveness of society or altruistic behaviour. However, for one individual's genes to survive, other genetically related individuals who also carry and protect these genes must survive, as it is ultimately fruitless if one's offspring do not reproduce. Hamilton (1964) termed this inclusive fitness, in that we protect our genes being carried by relatives to the degree of that relatedness. Thus sacrifice to preserve other carriers will increase as reproductive ability declines with advancing age, and nepotism perhaps has an evolutionary basis.

Ultimate explanations of abnormal behaviour examine the social and physical environment in which our immediate ancestors evolved, as these circumstances may be different from those of the twenty-first century. Orians (1986) claims that it was the African savanna-type habitat where humans spent most their hunter-gatherer existence. However, coherent arguments regarding bipedalism (essential in shallow water), loss of body hair (common in shore-dwellers), body fat (for buoyancy) and vocal speech (as non-verbal is of less use in water) is evidence for humans having adapted to living in shallow water on coastlines (Morgan, 1997). Groups of humans during this period were thought to number 40–50 with around 20 females, 10 males and 20 children in each grouping. Inclusive fitness will have been a cohesive factor in bonding these individuals, who will have had shared responsibilities.

Many factors require protective groups of humans or **inclusive fitness** to be maintained, such as the size of the human brain. The female birth canal has not evolved to accommodate a larger infant skull, restricting the size of the brain at birth. This leaves more post-natal brain development, leading to neotony, or a greatly extended childhood as a vulnerable infant requiring feeding and protection (Buss, 1999). This provides a long learning period, but places a burden on the resources of parents, eased in these early groups by sharing child care with older relatives. However, in modern society extended child development periods could be reflected in 'overprotective', pathologically extended parenting or even neglect where parents reject this commitment.

Evolution and abnormal behaviour

Diverse theories try to map evolutionary explanations on to abnormal behaviour in clinical and forensic fields. Explanations tend to be unverifiable hypotheses that are anecdotally convincing but better judged by their usefulness in understanding the ultimate origins of behaviour and how it may be changed. For example, many millennia spent as hunter-gatherers provides an intuitive explanation for the compulsive 'shopaholic' behaviour seen in modern urban settings. However, this may have a more parsimonious explanation in avoidance and reward producing addictive compulsion without recourse to longer-term evolutionary origins.

Tinbergen's conceptual division into proximate and ultimate explanations for behaviour can enlighten approaches to abnormal behaviour in evolutionary terms. For example, higher levels of testosterone are a proximate explanation for more aggressive acts amongst males, but the ultimate explanation for testosterone and aggression differences lies in the usefulness of these factors in mating, fathering or protecting offspring (Cartwright, 2000). Some disorders only have proximate causes, such as head injury leading to criminal irresponsibility. Analysis of abnormal behaviour at the right level ensures that ultimate causes are not overlooked by overly focusing on proximate biology, and also that spurious evolutionary effects are not proposed, missing obvious proximate causes.

Distressing symptoms such as pain and vomiting, can have a clear evolutionary basis, but without these adaptations most creatures would probably not have survived. In the same way that these mechanisms keep us away from sources of danger, we experience aversive anxiety in dangerous situations, also seen as a symptom of abnormal behaviour. Confidence in making links between adaptive mechanisms and maladaptive symptoms can lead to taking a specific disorder and searching for an evolutionary explanation to fit. In such cases, enthusiasm for phylogenetic explanations can give evolutionary psychology a bad reputation.

General conclusions relating evolution to abnormal behaviour are less speculative. Extreme and rapid environmental change provides the greatest challenge to the adaptive abilities of species both in the short term, in surviving the initial change, and in the long term, through survival of the species by adaptive mutation. Failure to adapt may result in **extinction**. The evolutionary approach assumes that abnormal behaviour results from a failure of an individual to adapt to their current environment, or that the adaptive mechanism is dysfunctional in the current context (Buss, 1999). A verifiable non-human example may illustrate this most clearly. The hedgehog developed spines and curling into a ball as a very successful defence, but this evolutionary development did not deal with motor vehicles, for which this defence is fatally maladaptive.

Thus, formally adaptive behaviour could manifest itself as abnormal behaviour in a new context where it is maladaptive. An inherent fear of heights kept our ancestors away from dangerous cliffs and crevasses by the aversive mechanism anxiety, but in a modern landscape avoidance of such situations can become a debilitating phobia (acrophobia; see Chapter 12). The reverse of this process can explain the survival of abnormal behaviour mutations, which in a modern context could have adaptive potential (Cartwright, 2000). Thus, the maladaptive trait of **psychopathy** could have adaptive aspects in a new environment. In small hunter-gatherer groups, the selfish and uncaring traits may have alienated such individuals. However, a densely populated modern society provides an endless supply of victims, where psychopathic individuals can engage in short-term parasitic activity and avoid facing long-term consequences by moving social and geographical locations. Mealey (1995) has provided a detailed model of how this disorder is adaptive in terms of its reproductive strategy (see the Focus box).

An abnormal trait may have other adaptive traits that are genetically linked to it, particularly with polygenetic disorders. Bipolar mood disorder is associated with creativity and industriousness as well as being a devastating illness (Jamison, 1992). Relatives of bipolar sufferers often

Focus

Are disorders and crimes evolutionary adaptations?

Some evolutionary theories take the view that criminal or psychiatric behaviours such as psychopathy or bipolar mood disorder are not disorders but adaptive traits, which have reproductive or survival value. McGuire et al. (1994) considered the selfishness of **anti-social personality disorder** and the attention seeking of **histrionic personality disorder** (see Chapter 14) to facilitate manipulation of others to obtain resources. McGuire and Troisi (1997) argued that the modern environment is not so different from that of our evolutionary past and should not be dismissed as pathogenic, conflicting with our evolved behaviour, though this has been disputed (Stevens and Price, 1996).

Cantor (2005) detailed an evolutionary explanation of **post-traumatic stress disorder** (PTSD; see Chapter 12), conceptualised as a product of neurologically evolved defences with symptoms tied to defensive origins. This demonstrates the usefulness of evolutionary analysis, reducing criticisms that it is merely speculative by dealing thoroughly with detail of the disorder and its explanation.

Evolutionary approaches have thrown light on overly common and destructive behaviours. Where mothers with **post-partum depression** (see Chapter 17) tend to reject rather than bond with a newborn, this perhaps relates to a cost–benefit approach to investing resources differentially in offspring. Thus the disorder is considered an evolutionary adaptation, where a child is seen as a poor investment of the considerable resources needed because of human extended childhoods (Richman, Raskin and Gaines, 1991), in accord with parental investment theory (Chisholm, 1993). Thus related factors, such as being a single parent and the parent or child being ill, correlate with post-partum depression, which is also seen in fathers (Atkinson and Rickel, 1984). Others have produced data contradicting these extrapolations (O'Hara, Rehm and Campbell, 1982). Similarly, Daly and Wilson (1989) associate these same evolutionary investment factors, alongside having too many offspring and parental uncertainty (fear of cuckolding), with crimes such as **infanticide** and injury to children; Canadian stepchildren suffered 100 times more fatal abuse than those living with genetic parents (Daly and Wilson, 1988). However, Temrin, Buchmayer and Enquist (2000) failed to find this in a Swedish population.

Sexual disorders are considered seriously in evolutionary terms, as they directly affect reproductive ability, but they are less frequently researched than other disorders. The crime of rape can be explained in terms of its advantage to the perpetrator's inclusive fitness, and analysis of crime demographic data can undermine other assumed motives. Stevens and Price (1996) consider reproductive disorders and even include an evolutionary consideration of sadomasochism. However, their interpretation utilises older psychodynamic approaches, confounding clear interpretation. Original Freudian theory contains evolutionary thinking in considering instinctive behaviour and unconscious processes, but it adds unnecessary layers of assumption and invention, which are confusingly burdensome in an evolutionary context where empirical parsimony is essential.

inherit the genes promoting optimistic energetic behaviour without the extreme moods of individuals with a full compliment of disordered genes. Thus successful relatives will propagate the disordered genes along with more adaptive traits.

Abnormal behaviour can involve the breakdown of an evolved adaptive mechanism, such as the fixed action patterns of Lorenz seen in schizophrenic **perseverance**, where a pattern of behaviour continues when no longer purposeful (see McKenna, 1997). This resembles animals continuing fixed actions when redundant, such as a bird continuing the action of rolling a stray egg back into the nest with its bill when the egg is removed. This supports considerations of disrupted habituated behaviour in schizophrenia. A biological proximate cause disrupting an evolved mechanism, such as a pituitary tumour disrupting hormonal control, is a more explicit explanation for abnormal behaviour. Disturbed hormonal control can lead to diverse malfunctions in adaptive activity, from obsessive maternal behaviour and cleaning rituals to anger outbursts, violence and homicide. A maladaptive environment can also precipitate adaptive behaviour dysfunction. However, differentiating a maladaptive environment from adaptable change in environment is a moot point.

Evaluation of the evolutionary approach

Treatment approaches based on the evolutionary paradigm are lacking, but it does have therapeutic value in taking the 'long view'. Environmental interventions can limit or prevent the expression of evolved abnormal behaviour, just as shade can prevent freckles being expressed. Vulnerability to psychopathic manipulation can be limited by raising the forensic awareness of potential victims via education. In examining behaviour management from an evolutionary standpoint, we can also avoid proximate interventions, which may be at odds with, or could exacerbate, underlying ultimate causes.

Modularity (Fodor, 1983a) has been criticised as a false premise by Seigert and Ward (2002), particularly cognitive modules proposed by evolutionary theorists. These authors also point to the lack of supporting evidence for many accounts of adaptations. The more tenuous evolutionary explanations of behaviour have been labelled 'just so' explanations. 'Just so' explanations earn their title from Rudyard Kipling's *Just So Stories*, where exaggerated Lamarkian stories are used to explain animal characteristics, such as the leopard's spots being the fingermarks of an Ethiopian bushman. Although evolutionary assumptions

regarding anxiety disorders are more difficult to contest than defend, more speculative accounts invite criticism. Gibson (1999) pointed to 'just so' explanations being testable at the non-mammalian level by gene manipulation, rightly placing the Kipling analogy back in 1902.

True controlled experiments in human evolution would span thousands of generations and hundreds of thousands of years, beyond the most generous research grant. Historical science is detailed over the 5000 years since agriculture began, but this is too short a time period for much evolutionary change. Future predictions may be confounded by humans making ontogenetic and environmental changes that vastly outpace the process of evolution. Mankind is also engaged with a form of biotechnology that may even disrupt the evolutionary process for the human species (see Chapter 19).

Not only have evolutionary assumptions regarding human behaviour development been criticised as being unverifiable, but the foundations of evolutionary psychology have been likened to a leap of faith rather than evidence-based science (Cartwright, 2000). This is partly a misunderstanding, as the EEA of human behaviour can mostly be verified, at least to the extent that theory is built upon it (Buss, 1999) and it is unlikely that events were so bizarrely different from that estimated, such as having no predators or not forming groups.

Evolutionary approaches have been criticised as genetically determinist and as arguing that natural selection leads to perfection by removing that least functional. These are myths attributed to this paradigm (for detail, see Buss, 1999). Evolutionary theory is interactionist in considering both the genes evolved and their relative success in differing environments. The outcomes of this interaction would be a 'biological design nightmare'; as Dawkins (1989) points out, useful adaptations tend to be the exception not the rule, due to the many bizarre routes to reproductive success in sexual selection. In addition to these ill-founded criticisms of evolutionary approaches, Buss (1999) identifies the misconception that gene proliferation is an obsessive conscious agenda for all creatures. Clearly, this is an implicit not explicit process because, if gene proliferation were left to conscious motivation, we would have missed the evolutionary bus as we do so many of the four-wheeled variety.

The evolutionary approach applied to the case study of Ian

Although genetic traits such as the bipolar genes in Ian's family may not be adaptive for survival, they may lead to reproductive success in making the individual sexually attractive. Thus Jean may have been attracted to the 'bad guy' image of Ian's father, particularly in manic moments of optimism and dynamism. Jean's dependency on others may be her own strategy for ensuring inclusive fitness with regard to her offspring.

Ian perhaps followed his father's reproductive strategy, assisted by the adaptive aspects of his mood traits. This strategy may include his apparent irrational jealousy in protecting the exclusivity of his 'mating' rights to his ex-girlfriend, despite this being socially unacceptable. Such jealousy over sexual fidelity is greater in males than females as a result of being part of a reproductive strategy (Buunk et al., 1996), with Ian's girlfriend being more concerned with emotional fidelity.

Self-test questions

- Why did evolutionary theory take over 100 years to gain acceptance?
- Contrast the approaches of Darwin and Lamarck with an example.
- How do comparative psychology and ethology contribute to the evolutionary paradigm?
- What are meant by proximate and ultimate explanations of behaviour?
- Describe an example of a disorder explained as an evolutionary adaptation.

Part 2: Psychological approaches

Sky diving is something that the average person would fear, but many people have phobias of everyday things, like buttons, that make living a normal life very difficult. Psychological approaches to psychopathology suggest that this phobia could be a learned sensitivity.
Source: Pearson Online Database.

The behavioural approach

During the nineteenth century, comparative psychologists focused on animals isolated from their natural environments and looked for replicable principles of behaviour that could be generalised across species, culminating in the work of Ivan Pavlov (1849–1936) and **Edward Thorndike** (1874–1949). Psychology had previously mostly used **introspection**, considering mental processes in a subjective way. Some comparative psychologists only considered observable behaviour of animals, rejecting subjective speculation as not only unscientific but valueless. This became known as **behaviourism** or **empiricism**. A major proponent, John Broadhurst Watson (1878–1958) claimed that scientific psychology should stick to the observable aspects of objective experiments. Watson was a figurehead for behaviourism, even practising it in his own family, and despite much criticism, probably made the greatest contribution to psychology of his era. This revolt against introspective techniques marked a clearly delineated behavioural (or learning) paradigm in psychology and led to the more extreme movement, radical behaviourism.

The radical behaviourist movement's rejection of mental processes as irrelevant to the prediction of behaviour led to a damaging backlash from less empirical approaches, such as the psychodynamic school, along with criticism of 'mechanical' views of behaviour relating to events during the Second World War, as well as the rise of cognitive psychology. However, its principles have survived well, as they have genuine practical value and due to the industrious career of Burrhus Frederic Skinner (1904–1990). Skinner carried the banner of behaviourism through the challenges of the twentieth century. The principles derived from the behavioural approach have been the most useful that pure psychology has offered in addressing abnormal behaviour.

Types of conditioning

There are two **elemental** forms of learning, **habituation** and **sensitisation**. Habituation is where an organism ceases to respond to a stimulus such as a passing car, when the stimulus has no significant consequences. However, if a passing car should mount the kerb and hit a pedestrian, you may then become sensitised to approaching cars and overreact to them. Thus, significant consequences lead to sensitisation to that stimulus, as demonstrated by **Eric Kandel** using the large neural structure of the sea mollusc Aplysia (Kupfermann et al., 1970). Elemental types of conditioning form the basic reflexes utilised in other learning.

There are two types of **associative learning** as well as passive learning.

- Classical conditioning (also termed **respondent** or **Pavlovian** conditioning) involves **involuntary** responses (reflexes) and is related in principle to sensitisation. The reinforcer precedes the response.
- Operant conditioning (also termed **instrumental** or **Skinnerian** conditioning) involves **voluntary** responses and the response precedes the reinforcer.
- Vicarious learning **or modelling** is where one is influenced by seeing another creature being punished or rewarded for a behaviour, or simply providing an example of behaviour to be imitated.

Classical conditioning

Conditioning of behaviour by association, or classical conditioning, was established by the work of Pavlov at the end of the nineteenth century. In 1904 he received the Nobel Prize for his work on the dog's digestive system. He measured a dog's salivation in response to stimuli such as meat powder and noticed that the dog salivated before the food arrived, sometimes on seeing the inedible food bowl. Pavlov experimentally tested the association between the food and other stimuli in the dog.

Pavlov considered the food the unconditioned stimulus (UCS), as this needed no conditioning to produce an instinctive unconditioned response (UCR), food being a 'natural reinforcer'. He introduced a bell as a conditioned stimulus (CS), which although the dog would notice it, had no reinforcing value. Pavlov sounded the bell briefly about half a second before the arrival of the food. He repeated this many times, and found that sounding the bell without the food resulted in salivation or the conditioned response (CR). This procedure is sometimes written as in Table 3.6.

For Pavlov the CS substituted the UCS, producing the dog's involuntary response. If the test trial is repeated without the UCS, the CR will reduce, termed **extinction**. The learned response is not lost but is superimposed by learning not to respond; this is demonstrated by presenting a novel stimulus such as a loud noise or leaving the animal out of the experiment for some time, which produces **spontaneous recovery** of the response. The CS is

Table 3.6 The production of a conditioned response

Initial responses:	CS	results in no response
	UCS	already produces a UCR
Trials 1–100:	CS + UCS	produces the UCR
Test trial:	CS	produces the CR

generalised to similar stimuli, and less similar stimuli produce a weaker response. **Discrimination** is conditioned by reinforcing one stimulus (e.g. small bell) but not another (e.g. medium bell), countering the effects of generalisation. A secondary reinforcer is a strong CS which is used as if it were a primary reinforcer, even though it has no intrinsic value to the organism (e.g. money). These are powerful principles applied to abnormal behaviour.

Operant conditioning

Although some argue that classical and operant conditioning differ only in terminology, classical deals with involuntary responses and operant with voluntary actions followed by a reinforcer (see Mackintosh, 1995).

Operant conditioning experiments began with Edward Thorndike examining the effect of a single behaviour on its future occurrence. Thorndike studied the link between sensation (stimulus) and future action (response), or **connectionism**. He formulated a **law of readiness** to perform an action and the strengthening of connections by repetition and weakening by disuse in his **law of exercise**.

Thorndike trapped roaming cats in cages, finding they produced a range of behaviours in their efforts to escape and eventually accidentally released the cage door. Placed back in the cage, escape became less random and faster. These behaviours died out if they did not escape and increased in frequency if they escaped, termed the law of effect by Thorndike. Thus, behaviour followed by punishment will decrease in frequency and that followed by reward will increase in frequency. Although this seems tautological, rewards could be used outside of the causal 'loop' (Meehl, 1950).

B. F. Skinner reformulated the 'law of effect', emphasising reinforcing consequences rather than the value-laden 'reward'. Skinner supported Thorndike's views that mere repetition of responses increased their probability and that punishment was less effective than reward – a position that strengthened in the course of his career. He introduced the concept of the discriminative stimulus, such as a light signalling that behaviour is only reinforced when it is on. Skinner produced a specially designed 'Skinner box' for conditioning rats and pigeons. By a process of shaping, he reinforced simple or partial behaviours until more complex ones occurred, then by differentially reinforcing these and not the simple movements, shaped highly complex behaviour patterns. Critics have tried to argue that this is not effective in changing behaviour. However, Skinner produced staggering demonstrations of the power of conditioning, such as training pigeons to play table tennis!

Skinner claimed that all behaviours such as speech are learned. He recognised other factors, but considered them

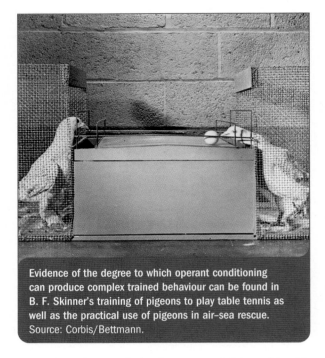

Evidence of the degree to which operant conditioning can produce complex trained behaviour can be found in B. F. Skinner's training of pigeons to play table tennis as well as the practical use of pigeons in air–sea rescue.
Source: Corbis/Bettmann.

unnecessary for speech development, publicly pushing his learning explanation beyond its capacity, and he lost ground to modular and instinctive theories such as Chomsky's. He widened behaviourism to explain the problems of humanity in terms of reinforcing bad or maladaptive behaviour (Skinner, 1986). His principles are still very important when applied to abnormal psychology.

Generalisation, discrimination and extinction also apply to operant conditioning but, in contrast to classical conditioning, the qualities of the reinforcer (see Table 3.7) and economies of reinforcement are important.

Table 3.7 The four basic forms of reinforcement in operant conditioning

- **Reward** is a positive reinforcer such as food (though rewards can be diverse with humans) to increase preceding behaviour.

- **Punishment** decreases preceding behaviour (e.g. squirting lemon juice into the mouth of a biting child). What is a punisher depends on circumstances (one person's punishment may be another's reward).

- Negative reinforcement increases preceding behaviour by the *removal* of a punisher (e.g. allowing a well-behaved child to watch TV following a ban for disruptive behaviour).

- Omission decreases preceding behaviour by the removal of a positive reinforcer. This is *badly* applied in most families, such as parents threatening to ban TV watching if bad behaviour continues, then giving in for (short-term) peace. Firmly applied removal of TV privileges would be omission.

Economies of reinforcement by partial or intermittent reinforcement can strengthen learning in operant conditioning. These are termed schedules of reinforcement (Ferster and Skinner, 1957) and comprise the following.

- **Continuous reinforcement.** A reinforcing reward is delivered for each response (1:1), usually the start-point when training begins. This is a weak form of conditioning, with rapid steady responding that extinguishes quickly on removing the reinforcer or satiation (which is rapid).

- **Fixed ratio schedule.** Reinforcement is after a specific number of responses, such as FR10, or reinforcement every 10 responses. Responses following the reinforcer are slower than those preceding it and extinction is slower than in continuous reinforcement but still rapid. Pigeons have been shaped up to an FR8000!

- **Variable ratio schedule.** A reward is delivered after varying numbers of responses per trial, totalling a fixed average across trials. A VR8 means an average of 8 responses across trials. This is slower to extinguish than a fixed ratio and produces the highest response rate. It is similar to the addictive arcade gambling machines (which can have their VR adjusted).

- **Fixed interval schedule.** Here reinforcement only occurs at the end of a given time period, during which at least one response must be made (e.g. FI-8 sec). Extinction is fairly rapid and responses speed up towards the end of the schedule, but are very slow, and eventually absent, at the start. The animal learns that only one response is required and becomes remarkably efficient at delivering this just before the interval end, similar to student essay deadlines, which are ignored for months and the essay hastily written a day before the deadline.

- **Variable interval schedule.** A VI-20 sec indicates that the time period in which a response has to be made is on average 20 seconds, but the time varies on individual trials. This produces a very steady response rate and is very slow to extinguish, creating a great deal of uncertainty in the animal.

Secondary reinforcers are also used in operant conditioning and can be combined with schedules to delay access to primary reinforcement. These are useful in clinical situations where behaviour change needs to be sustained in the absence of a primary reinforcer. Skinner also identified **superstitious behaviour**, which is produced by randomly delivering a reward irrespective of the animal's behaviour, or **non-contingent reinforcement**. This causes the animal to associate arbitrary behaviours with reinforcement, often producing peculiar mannerisms, which are paralleled in humans by 'lucky' behaviours or artefacts associated with success (e.g. a 'lucky' National Lottery pen).

Social learning

Vicarious reinforcement is increasing a specific behaviour by watching another individual being rewarded for it, enjoying it or simply performing it without fear. Julian Rotter (born 1916) established this as social learning, although it had previously been noticed by Thorndike. Albert Bandura (1925–) linked social learning to violence in his study, in which children were shown acts of violence and then observed in their tendency to perform them (Bandura, 1965). Bandura found that learning took place whether the 'actor' was punished or rewarded, but if punished, performance was suppressed.

Behaviour therapy

Behaviour therapy is the therapeutic use of classical conditioning, such as the removal of irrational fear by exposure. The central principle of reciprocal inhibition refers to certain physiological states being mutually exclusive, such as being relaxed reciprocally inhibiting anxiety due to the antagonistic functions of the **sympathetic** and **parasympathetic** divisions of the **autonomic nervous system**. Intended to confront or escape danger, the sympathetic response sustained as fear becomes debilitating and aversive. This is a moot point in evolutionary terms, as 'freezing' with fear can avoid some predators but provide easy prey for others. Aversive fear also leads to avoidance of the feared stimulus, which is helpful in avoiding danger but can escalate phobic responses to harmless stimuli. Thus evolutionary adaptations are involved in anxiety disorders.

After conditioning a phobia in Albert, J. B. Watson found a child with an existing phobia to test **counterconditioning**, or conditioning a new response to counter a previous one. Watson and **Mary Cover Jones** (1896–1987) initially used vicarious learning by showing 'Peter' (a 3-year-old frightened of rats and rabbits) children fearlessly playing with animals. Peter improved but relapsed following illness. Jones then used reciprocal inhibition to reduce a child's fear of animals (Jones, 1924). She had the child eat a meal, encouraging a parasympathetic response, whilst keeping a caged rabbit, which would normally produce a sympathetic response (fear), at a 'safe' distance of 40 feet away. At succeeding meals she brought the animal gradually closer until the child was able to touch the rabbit whilst eating without undue fear. Here, the relaxed parasympathetic response has replaced the fear response.

Research

Applying conditioning to abnormal behaviour

Although now seen as unethical, Watson and Rayner's (1921) training of a phobia in 'little Albert' led the way to the major treatment for such disorders.
Source: Archives of the History of American Psychology/The University of Akron.

In 1920, **J. B. Watson** and **Rosalie Rayner** (later Rosalie Rayner-Watson) reported an unethical, but highly influential series of classical conditioning trials (Watson and Rayner, 1920). 'Albert' was less than a year old and had no fear; in fact, he was quite interested in the white rat that the researchers presented to him. However, he was instinctively alarmed by the loud noise they made behind his head whenever he approached the rat. After a number of trials in which the loud noise (UCS) was paired with the rat (CS), producing fear (UCR), Albert showed fear (CR) when presented with the rat (CS) alone. This demonstrates that an irrational fear of a specific object or situation, or **phobia** (see Chapter 12), can be created by classical conditioning. **Edwin Ray Guthrie** (1886–1959) also pointed out the importance

of the first exposure to the stimulus and the fact that **one-trial learning** can take place, producing a phobic response (Guthrie, 1942).

Watson and Rayner's study was carried out at a time when psychoanalytic explanations of anxiety problems such as phobias were widespread. By demonstrating a simple behavioural cause for these states, Watson provided a strong argument against complex psychoanalytic explanations that involved early childhood relationships. Further to this, if a phobia can be classically induced, then **extinction** by behavioural means should be possible for all phobias. And this behavioural intervention could be carried out without taking a childhood history or even knowing how the fear came about in the first place.

However, extinction tends not to occur naturally and phobic fears, once established, seem to worsen over time. The neurotic paradox refers to the fact that irrational anxiety tends to worsen in the absence of the feared stimulus or further learning. Thus if a child is trapped in a small dark cupboard with a cat and the intense fear produces a fear of cat fur (a case of one-trial learning), why does the 'cat fur fear' worsen in the absence of the cupboard situation (the UCS)? The main explanation is in terms of negative reinforcement from operant conditioning. The child is reinforced (relief) for **escaping or avoiding** the feared stimuli (CS), and therefore avoids **exposure** and extinction. Thus any exposure is brief, reinforced with fear and escaped from before fear can subside. Avoidance behaviour is therefore targeted by behaviour therapy.

The basic principles derived from this ethically challenging early research by Watson and others provided the basis for behaviour therapy, which was to be the foundation for effective **clinical psychology**.

Although clearly effective, behaviour therapy did not impact on clinical practice for 30 years, partly as there was more focus on theoretical issues. There was also criticism from other approaches that it was 'dehumanising and mechanical,' hinting at links with Nazism, and some professional jealousy from approaches whose methods proved ineffective in comparison to behaviourism. Psychoanalysts criticised behaviour therapy for creating symptom substitution, removing the symptoms of the disorder and leaving the 'underlying disorder' to re-emerge as a different set of symptoms. For the behaviourists, the symptoms were the disorder, with no evidence of symptom substitution ever being established. Attempting to bridge the divide, Dollard

and Miller (1950) translated psychoanalytic concepts into behavioural terms. During the 1950s, however, **Hans J. Eysenck** made scathing attacks on the psychoanalytic approach and advocated behaviour therapy.

In 1958, the year J. B. Watson died, **Joseph Wolpe** published an influential book outlining basic procedures for behaviour therapy. There were three major approaches based on classical conditioning, which Wolpe greatly helped to promote.

■ Systematic desensitisation is based on reciprocal inhibition and counterconditioning – the gradual replacement of fear with a relaxed response during exposure.

- Flooding **and implosion** are dependent on the exhaustion of the fear response in continuous exposure.
- Aversion therapy is where the target stimulus is associated with an unconditioned stimulus, which is unpleasant.

In **systematic desensitisation**, the therapist first trains the client in an activity that reciprocally inhibits the fear (sympathetic) response, usually relaxation in the form of **deep muscle relaxation**, or even meditation techniques. Although less common, alternatives to relaxation are used, such as eating or **self-assertion training**, in which the client gains an additional skill. Next, a hierarchy of about ten feared situations is constructed from mild scenarios to the most feared situation. This is a SUD scale (subjective unit of discomfort) and serves two purposes: a reference scale for the client to indicate their subjective level of fear, and a series of situations for the client to work through whilst remaining calm. Trying to carry on with escalating fear is counterproductive, as the process takes a number of sessions and cannot really be rushed. Systematic desensitisation utilises the principle of stimulus generalisation by using stimuli similar to the phobic target that produce a weaker fear response, such as a drawing of a spider rather than a live one. This enables the therapist to approach the target situation from the lower end of the SUD scale, at a level of fear the client can work with.

Systematic desensitisation can use imaginary or **in vivo** (in real life) stimuli. Although for practical considerations in vivo exposure can be restricted to checking that gains have generalised to real life, it is more effective than imaginary stimuli (Tryon, 2005). The client must be able to image and checks need to be made that they are not indulging in cognitive avoidance by imagining something else. Virtual desensitisation is becoming more common in clinical psychology, as the relative cost of **virtual reality** (VR) technology is low. In VR, imaging ability is not needed and there are no complications of using live animals, with the computer interface providing vivid and infinitely variable interaction with three-dimensional images from a vast library. Studies have found exposure therapy for acrophobia (fear of heights) using VR to be as effective as in vivo exposure for some measures (Emmelkamp et al., 2002).

In **flooding** the client is confronted with the most fear-provoking situation first. **Enforced confrontation** is maintained until the fear subsides, as the client enters a resolution period (which can be accompanied by euphoria) whilst imagining (or in) the feared situation without fear. This paradoxical situation comes about because the sympathetic division of the nervous system is designed for short-term use and after about 20–30 minutes at full response the effect dissipates, preventing permanent damage or depletion of the organism's resources. A few

sessions can bring long-term relief from irrational fear and, being more time-efficient than systematic desensitisation, flooding proves popular in times of restricted resources (Tryon, 2005). However, the ordeal can be challenging for the client, who has to be both able and motivated to withstand it.

Motivation is important, to maintain high levels of fear during flooding. Clients 'taking a break' may recover sufficiently to prolong the therapy procedure greatly. Wolpe took about 4 hours of driving an **agoraphobic** girl (with fear of open spaces) around in a car to achieve resolution. **Implosion** involves using exaggerated imagery, often with the therapist adding to the descriptions, beyond what can be experienced in vivo. However, implosion therapy is less effective than flooding and is likely to be replaced with a VR system. Regardless of the technique, the key element in behaviour therapy is actual exposure to the feared stimulus (Tryon, 2005).

In **aversion therapy**, an unpleasant UCS is used, such as an emetic, noxious smell or unpleasant imagery. The choice is limited by any potential harm and accurate timing of effect. This is paired with the unwanted stimulus, such as **alcohol** or an inappropriate sexual stimulus (e.g. picture of sexual violence), and over a number of trials the CS, say alcohol, presented alone produces noxious feelings. This should lead to the increasing avoidance of the alcohol, in the manner of the **neurotic paradox**. However, this needs the voluntary cooperation of the client, who may be in a **special hospital** or an out-patient of an alcohol treatment unit, and who is likely to see compliance as a means to gain freedoms; hence treatment needs to be sustained outside the clinical environment. The unwanted stimulus is not benign: alcohol is strongly reinforcing, difficult to avoid and socially sanctioned, with aversion therapy for alcoholism having a low rate of success. With paedophilic responses, recidivism is high and the response needs to be replaced with a legally acceptable one. The use of aversion in forensic settings and with sexual disorders involves other issues (see Chapter 13).

Behaviour modification

Behaviour modification applies **operant conditioning** to change behaviour by observing and manipulating its **contingent reinforcers**. This has been criticised for treating people as performing circus animals, with the same process being involved. However, behaviour modification has produced humane results in situations where there was only hopelessness (see the Research box).

There are problems in administering the techniques described in the Research box, with slow progress and simple

Research

Shaping of speech in autism

In Chapter 9 the disorder of **autism** will be described as a very stubborn disorder to treat, and one for which there is no cure. Half of the individuals with the disorder grow up without speech, and many of those who do speak, do so as a result of behaviour modification methods. **Shaping** speech in autism is a very slow process, as sufferers do not respond well to reinforcers, sometimes only basic ones such as foods. This was termed **behavioural intervention by** Lovaas (1987), who used these techniques in discrete trials grouped into progressive stages. In each trial, **continuous reinforcement** was utilised with basic reinforcers such as food. The stages are as follows.

- Initially rewarding the child for **looking** at the therapist, as giving attention to the other person is a prerequisite for speech.

- Reward is then contingent on making **vocalisations** *whilst* attending.

- Vocalisations, which approximate to **words** in response to the therapist's initiations, are then the only reinforced items.

- The process of then differentially reinforcing longer **phrases and sentences** will depend on the responsiveness of the autistic individual.

Although appearing simplistic, the shaping of behaviour in this way has been extensively and successfully used in **learning disability.** Prior to applying behaviour modification, individuals with **profound mental handicap** had been dismissed as incompetent and beyond therapy. Behaviour modification was not a miracle cure, but replaced hopelessness with hope and improvement. Sometimes the behaviours established were simple, such as lever pulling, but success was also achieved with toileting, interpersonal communication and basic social skills. Learned helplessness (see Seligman, 1992; Chapter 17) was widespread amongst the mentally handicapped prior to these interventions. Lever pulling may not impress a student, but if it is a lifetime achievement, this simple act can produce a sense of control and self-respect.

schedules (often continuous reinforcement). In **spontaneous extinction**, the client suddenly stops responding and the schedule has to be abandoned. Reinforcers are often difficult to establish (as in autism) and will benefit from prior testing: for example, grading reinforcers for **approachability**, which is a good predictor of their effectiveness for the specific client. When complex sequences of behaviour are being shaped, **chaining** of behaviour 'units' may be possible. In chaining, the completion of one behaviour unit (putting on a jacket) can act as both a **discriminative stimulus** (a cue or sign) for the following unit (buttoning the jacket) and a reinforcer (i.e. sense of accomplishment) for the preceding unit (holding the jacket).

Challenging behaviour presents a challenge for the clinician or carer, including **self-stimulatory behaviour** (SSB), such as rocking or rubbing, and self-injurious behaviour (SIB), such as biting or head-banging. Behavioural techniques meet this 'challenge' as follows.

- **Punishment**. This obvious but rarely used option, such as squirting lemon juice into the mouth when screaming or biting, is highly effective when other methods have failed. However, in SIB it is difficult to establish what constitutes a punisher.

- Differential reinforcement of incompatible behaviour (DRI). In DRI, behaviour is encouraged which makes the unwanted behaviour impossible. For example, rewarding 'standing behaviour' would make it impossible for the individual to bang their head on the floor.

- Differential reinforcement of other behaviour (DRO). DRO is the rewarding of any behaviour other than the unwanted behaviour.

- **Removing the sensory consequences**. Preventing the sensory reinforcement of the unwanted behaviour can sometimes eliminate it. For example, being placed on a soft surface can discourage a patient from repeatedly banging an object (or even their body) on the floor, by removing the sensory feedback that may be maintaining the behaviour.

The reinforcement of desirable behaviour is applied to inpatients on psychiatric wards in the form of token economies. Ayllon and Azrin (1968) reported using tokens as secondary reinforcers to encourage self-care behaviours among withdrawn and apathetic 'institutionalised' patients. The tokens are exchanged for primary reinforcers such as food or cigarettes. The token reinforcers should be replaced with social reinforcement and eventually a sense of achievement, as reliance on tokens means that productive behaviour is not always maintained after the patient is discharged. Links to occupational support can help to sustain productive activity.

The initial analysis of problem behaviour is an important stage in applying behavioural techniques. Although its application has widened, the term applied behaviour analysis is used when examining the way the environment reinforces problem behaviour. Therapists observe behaviour in its **natural environment**, unobtrusively noting the triggers (discriminative stimuli) and consequences, such as observing that a scolding from her mother always followed a child's clinging and disruptive behaviour. It would seem that the child's good behaviour was ignored but bad behaviour gained attention (scolding), which was therefore reinforcing. In a functional analysis, the functional purpose of the unwanted behaviour to the client is identified and can be utilised in any intervention, such as a child engaging in SIB to avoid a task rather than attention seeking; the latter is often presumed in the absence of functional analysis (see Leslie, 2002).

Biofeedback combines classical and operant techniques with modern technology. Small portable devices can now monitor multiple autonomic functions, such as heart rate, blood pressure, peripheral temperature and galvanic skin response (rate of perspiration measured by skin conductance). When this information about their involuntary responses is fed back, the client can modify their voluntary behaviour to change the responses indirectly. This is used in health psychology as a **stress intervention**, such as lowering blood pressure in individuals prone to heart attacks.

Social learning approaches based on vicarious learning include the clinical use of **modelling** behaviour. The client observes the clinician carry out a type of behaviour without making abnormal responses, changing the client's reactions having seen someone else do it without adverse consequences. For example, a child fearing cats may watch the therapist enjoying playing with cats without fear and the child may be encouraged to join in. Thus, mental preparation precedes actual exposure, which borders on to cognitive behavioural approaches.

Behavioural approaches have continued to develop independently during the years since their incorporation into cognitive behavioural therapy (see the next section). **Contextual** variants of modern behavioural psychology have included examples such as **relational frame theory**, developed by Steven Hayes and Dermot Barnes-Holmes. This form of functional contextualism explains how language is developed by learning and environmental interactions, perhaps placing the debate over language acquisition into a more pragmatic context (see Hayes, Barnes-Holmes and Roche, 2001).

The cognitive and cognitive behavioural approaches

The term 'cognitive behavioural therapy' (CBT) has greatly superseded 'behaviour therapy'. This may be due to the need of professionals to distance themselves from the 'mechanistic' and other criticisms of behaviourism, but it creates the illusion that the behavioural component may be of lesser importance. This would be an error, as the behavioural component tends to be more therapeutically effective than the cognitive in most evaluations (Kazdin and Wilson, 1978) and almost equal to full CBT (Dobson et al., 2008), an exception being with social phobia. However, in a modern clinical context, engaging a client in behaviour therapy must include a cognitive component and cognitive therapy almost always contains a behavioural component, either implicitly or explicitly. Given that the training of clinical psychologists contains a substantial component of CBT, it would be odd not to deliver these therapies under the shared banner (see Scott, 2009). The origins of cognitive therapy are also closely tied to the behavioural approach.

Cognitive therapy

Although early behaviourist views diminished the importance of cognitive events, cognitive approaches emerged from the behavioural paradigm to form the hybrid CBT. Behavioural psychologists considered mental events similar to behavioural ones, assuming they can be changed in the same way. Following reciprocal inhibition, or mutually exclusive autonomic states, the concepts of mutually incompatible affective and cognitive states were considered by **neo-behaviourists** such as Dickinson and Dearing (1979). Social learning theorist Bandura considered cognitive change to result from vicarious learning, distinguishing him from the radical behaviourists. This is closer to a **cognitive behavioural** view of therapy, suggesting a continuum of therapies with radical behaviourism at one end and cognitive approaches at the other, under the banner of CBT.

The original cognitive therapies borrow little from **cognitive psychology**, which views human thought in terms of **information processing**. Cognitive therapy concentrates on the preconceptions, biases in thinking and limitations placed on responding that colour human cognition and distinguish it from the information processing of a computer. Humans approach situations with **expectations**, a mental framework or schema, into which they fit information, which is useful but can be maladaptive and resistant to change (Hawton et al., 1989).

The central aim of cognitive therapy is to change maladaptive perceptions and thought patterns, or **cognitive restructuring**, often in *addition* to changing behaviour, or as a precursor by assuming that behavioural shift will follow cognitive change. Cognitive therapists deal with the here and now, rather than examining presumed historical causes (Scott, 2009). Although individual therapists share the same overall aim, their approaches differ sufficiently to consider a few of the leading therapies.

Albert Ellis and rational emotive behavioural therapy (REBT)

Ellis proposed that people are anxious or maladaptive because incorrect, negative and unproductive thoughts or attitudes prevent them from responding usefully. His clients blamed their own inadequacies or the situations. Ellis instructed his clients to think logically about their negative beliefs, to seek out their **illogical basis** and then to substitute more **realistic expectations** of themselves. Table 3.8 shows how the client addresses the **self-fulfilling prophecy** of negative expectations leading to failure.

The client works through the negative cognitions and in Ellis's view, exposes their basis in nonsense. Substituting realistic expectations reduces anxiety and the negative attitude that precipitates failure. Positive action and self-belief then produce positive experiences, increasing the expectation of success.

Ellis identified three groups of ideas rigidly held by disturbed individuals.

- 'I must achieve and win the approval of my peers, failure means I am incompetent'

Table 3.8 An example of a maladaptive approach in three stages

Ordinary situation:	Asking someone for a dance at a nightclub
Negative cognitions:	Fear of doing something accidentally foolish Fear of being rejected Fear of embarrassment
Negative outcomes:	Failing to ask them 'Freezing' in public Precipitating rejection by a nervous, negative approach

- 'Other people must always be fair and kind to me, they are worthless if they do not'

- 'I cannot tolerate a world of disorder, where I cannot have the things I need immediately'

These irrational beliefs set absolute impossible standards and, in Ellis's reasoning, lead to negative and **'musturbatory thinking'**, i.e. thinking based on 'musts'.

Donald Meichenbaum and self-instructional therapy

Donald Meichenbaum noted how anxious and unsuccessful people make excuses for themselves and engage in self-defeating thoughts. Meichenbaum had his clients identify where this occurred and produce **scripts** of positive instructions that put the responsibility for success on their own actions. Thus, an alcoholic thinking 'I have had a bad day, I deserve a drink, I will be anxious if I do not' would be given 'self-talk' such as 'I feel well, I do not want to feel ill with drink, I am proud of myself as a sober successful individual'. Self-instruction can be very specific, emphasising a **coping strategy** approach, and can even reduce psychotic speech. Meichenbaum admits that self-instruction needs a high level of repetition and must be habitual to be effective.

In Meichenbaum's (1986) **stress inoculation training** (SIT) clients use their coping strategies to deal with artificially induced stressors, such as gruesome films, in a successful way. This can then be generalised to future situations.

Aaron Beck's cognitive therapy

Aaron Beck's approach also assumes that maladaptive thought patterns cause difficulties. However, Beck questions the validity of the assumptions on which negative expectations are based, such as lacking self-worth, despite evidence to the contrary. Beck is credited with greatly advancing cognitive therapy and with its becoming a major approach in the management of depression and in his later work on anxiety.

For Beck, a depressed individual has an unrealistically pessimistic view of the world – a cognitive triad, involving a negative view of themselves, their personal future and their current experiences. In this there are **cognitive errors of distortion**, such as personalisation, overgeneralisation and selective abstraction. These errors of information processing magnify negative events and overgeneralise negative outcomes, such as, when a relationship fails, 'no one will ever want me'. Like Ellis, Beck also identified impossible goals such as 'I must be liked by everybody', though he saw these as originating in childhood.

Beck has a highly structured approach to therapy, setting agendas and time limits, although his interaction with the client is warm and enthusiastic. The client identifies habitual automatic thoughts by keeping a daily record. These are tested as hypotheses, questioning their evidence and looking for alternative views. Beck uses this **Socratic method** of questioning the client's assumptions, rather than arguing or telling the client they are wrong. Beck uses both behavioural and cognitive techniques, employing **behavioural approaches** if the client is not responsive to cognitive activity.

Cognitive behavioural therapy

Cognitive focus on how situations and mental states are interpreted, anticipated and labelled, combined with changing behavioural actions and interactions, produces a formidable therapeutic intervention. Thus CBT is a rapidly expanding approach and is the therapeutic foundation of clinical and clinical–forensic psychology practice (Department of Health (UK), 2001), applied to many problems from sex offending to psychotic disorders in Europe and more widely in the USA. Although normal functioning can be expected with anxiety disorders and maladaptive behaviour, reduction of and self-control over symptoms are the aims with biologically based disorders such as schizophrenia and treatment-resistant behaviours such as psychopathy or stalking.

Essentially, there are three dimensions to dealing with a situation or state: behaviour, cognition and emotion. For example, following assault one will be behaviourally less adventurous and avoid similar situations, will cognitively anticipate conflict and frequently think about the event, and will suffer physical arousal and a low mood. The latter emotional and physical states are biologically based and not directly addressed by CBT. However, change in cognition and behaviour will indirectly change physical and emotional states, just as behavioural change alters thinking to fit, and change in thinking can also change behaviour (Scott, 2009).

CBT therapists see clients individually or in groups for around 45 minutes per week, for as few as 5 or, exceptionally, over 20 sessions, usually in a hospital clinical psychology department. In a prison setting, an inmate will be seen more frequently and the programme of therapy may be more proscribed. Following assessment, suggested change to maladaptive thinking and behaviour will be discussed and agreed with the client, and 'homework' will

be given, as well as working through new behaviour in a practice session (especially for institutionalised clients) or the modelling of adaptive behaviour by the therapist (Hawton et al., 1989). The feedback at subsequent sessions checks that change is evident across cognitive, behavioural, emotional and physiological dimensions, helped by keeping diaries and notes. The therapeutic relationship is important and clients are encouraged by the therapist to feel good about achieving beneficial change.

In CBT a trusting relationship with the client is essential and all aspects of the process are explicit, helping the client comply with challenging suggestions. It has the immeasurable bonus of giving clients the skills to maintain gains and identify relapses after therapy. This reduces patient dependency, encouraging them to take responsibility for themselves rather than rely on the therapist as 'expert'. This major advantage of CBT over other therapies is dependent on the honest, open 'here and now' CBT therapist–client relationship (Scott, 2009). Over time, CBT approaches have become more disorder specific and, by a process of empirical testing, validated models have evolved such as Salkovskis and Warwick's model of hypochondriasis. Recent focus on the process of thought has produced a 'third wave' of CBT therapies, such as mindfulness therapy in addressing the client's relationship with their thoughts.

Other therapy approaches rely on the success of CBT but invoke unnecessary complexity. An example is cognitive analytic therapy, which merges the dissimilar camps of psychoanalysis and CBT. This hybrid is reviewed positively by its proponents (see Ryle and Kerr, 2002), but results fall short of the effective directness of CBT. More insidiously, others have tried to introduce excessive psychoanalytic terminology and explanation into CBT. The message here is to be explicit, as with cognitive analytic therapy, and not masquerade as CBT. Most new clients are referred to qualified clinical or clinical forensic psychologists, but other individuals offer 'therapy' under similar or even exotic titles that mislead naïve clients. The increasing need for stricter guidelines to make this practice explicit to the public led the UK **Health Professions Council** to impose regulation in 2009.

CBT can be beneficially delivered to suitable clients in groups such as patients with social phobia, where peer support is combined with exposure to the anxiety trigger. Individual CBT is oversubscribed in most countries, with consequent waiting lists resulting in interim self-help measures appearing, often web based. **Computerised cognitive behavioural therapy** has proven remarkably effective under controlled conditions (Proudfoot et al., 2004) and may reduce waiting lists for suitable cases.

Evaluation of behavioural and cognitive behavioural approaches

Behavioural and cognitive behavioural approaches have received criticism from their earliest incarnations, and it may be useful to review both myths and genuine limitations of these approaches (see Scott, 2009).

Watson and Rayner (1920) inadvertently illustrated the ethical dangers of behavioural manipulation with 'little Albert', as his mother unfortunately removed him before the experimental fear could be countered. This has been overgeneralised to condemn all behavioural therapy and even CBT as unethical. A colleague of the author had his behaviour modified without his permission by a class of students, who used interest and lack of interest to control where he stood during a lecture. He found it interesting that the 'experiment' had worked, but rather disconcerting that he had no awareness of being manipulated (he had previously explained that this was the case for animals in such studies). In this way, behavioural psychology also challenges our notion of free will. This rings alarm bells for more humanistic therapists, who make accusations of CBT being mechanistically cold and creating 'artificial' behaviour, in that human nature is somehow being replaced with robotic commands. In some cases this cannot be denied, but it erroneously assumes that normal behaviour is not conditioned, biological or instinctive, and appears blind to the possibility that 'free will' may be underpinned by these factors.

Behavioural therapies alone have around an 80 per cent success rate, which is often sustained in the long term (Kazdin and Wilson, 1978), but the criticism remains of behavioural approaches failing to sustain change without reinforcers outside the learning environment. Modern CBT involves clients in the process and sustains change outside the clinical environment to the extent that it is used to improve compliance with other therapies, such as medication. CBT has been compared to teaching a starving man how to fish and feed himself, whereas other therapies are analogous to simply supplying fish. Thus, part of the transparent approach of CBT allows the client to learn skills to sustain their recovery when therapy ends (Scott, 2009).

CBT being criticised for limited effectiveness for some disorders may be a reaction to its vastly broadened remit towards the end of the twentieth century, where CBT was established as useful in disorders such as schizophrenia (Jones et al., 2004). This is especially the case with biological disorders where the abnormality is irreversible and CBT techniques are the only means of improvement, as in the case of **autism** or **profound mental handicap**. However, some disorders are highly resistant to therapy, including CBT, such as some **personality disorders**, particularly **psychopathic disorder**, although the therapy in these difficult cases is CBT (see Chapters 8 and 14). There are differences in delivering CBT in forensic settings with limited real-world practice and client–therapist relations.

The psychodynamic school claims that CBT addresses the symptoms, not the 'underlying disorder', and that symptom substitution takes place. CBT takes the approach that the symptoms are the disorder and that other symptoms do not substitute those treated, as no study has shown evidence of symptom substitution. Further to this, analysts consider that CBT leaves the client without insight into their problem, in contrast to the intensive 'bedside manner' of psychoanalysis. This is not supported by the reality of analysts remaining aloof to the client, whilst CBT therapists are open and explain the process, offering the additional reassurance that there is no 'serious underlying disorder' or 'emotional conflict from their past' to concern clients.

Evaluations of cognitive therapy by its exponents are predictably good, with professionals such as Ellis claiming over 70 per cent success rate. Independent studies have not been as favourable, especially in comparison with behavioural therapies. Studies tend to find that cognitive and behavioural therapies fit together well in clinical practice, but this combination does not seem to produce any measurable benefit over and above the use of behavioural therapies alone (Kazdin and Wilson, 1978). Last, Barlow, O'Brien and Last (1984) consider thought patterns not important for change in behaviour, suggesting that change must be *acted out* in the real world (in vivo) for long-term change. However, it is unlikely that behavioural therapy could be delivered without *some* cognitive component and it would seem irresponsible to remove the cognitive from CBT, given that it adds little to cost and time and certainly enhances the process by making therapy itself reinforcing.

There are inherent difficulties in studies that evaluate therapeutic approaches including CBT. Almost all studies are favourable and large-scale **mega-studies** (where original data are combined, not just the *results* of analysis) again support this outcome. However, studies in this area are subject to limitations, two of which are described below.

In analogue studies, participants are not clinical patients, but are 'prepared' by therapy for stressful situations and their abilities to cope compared. This limits generalisation to clinical populations (see Kazdin and Wilson, 1978; Kazdin, 1999). Carefully matched clinical trials are more difficult to carry out due to conflict between **ethical constraints** and experimental rigour, as the latter may require genuine clients to believe they are receiving therapy when they are not. Thus, methodological demands may understandably give way to ethical objections.

When comparing therapies that operate on different areas of human functioning, any effects may be rather specific to that area of function alone. In Lang's (1968) three systems model of fear, he examined the independence of three levels of therapy and assessment.

- **Cognitive:** anticipation and verbal accounts of fear.
- **Behavioural:** resisting escape and avoidance from the feared situation.
- **Physiological:** does the feared situation produce autonomic arousal?

Lang (1968) considered a client confronting a feared situation (behaviour), but continuing to show a marked emotional and bodily response (physiological), and verbally labelling themselves as fearful (cognitive). Other outcomes can produce similar disparities at these three levels. If Lang is correct in the independence of these areas of functioning, studies comparing, say, cognitive with behavioural therapy should not evaluate their results in terms of behavioural change only. Although this model has been criticised for difficulties of definition (see Hugdahl, 1981), it still makes a strong point in favour of combined therapy approaches, CBT being one example.

Behavioural and cognitive behavioural approaches to the case of Ian

Ian, his father Tom and his grandfather had little insight into their mood disorders or how to manage erratic behaviour and maladaptive attitudes in relationships. Ian's automatic response of blaming others and his inability to sustain relationships would provide target behaviours for therapy. CBT would encourage improved interactions in close relationships and move from self-serving short-term goals to long-term achievements. CBT could be effective for the depression and inactivity in Ian's mood disorder episodes.

The lack of control that Jean felt would indicate **learned helplessness**, the feeling that she had no influence on important events in her life. CBT could promote learned effectiveness (Seligman, 1992) and encourage Jean not to make Ian dependent on her, relating to him as an adult. Forensic aspects are apparent, such as the **differential association** (Sutherland, 1939; Sutherland and Cressey, 1970) evident in Ian's friends, as he associated with individuals prone to **borderline personality** traits, although it was Ian's reactivity that precipitated the unpleasant conclusion. Clearly, Skinner (1953) would have pointed

to the reinforcement of chaotic womanising behaviour in the three generations of men.

Self-test questions

- How do the therapies derived from classical and operant conditioning differ?
- What is meant by reciprocal inhibition?
- Why is CBT the standard therapy in clinical and forensic settings?
- What is social learning?
- What did Beck mean by 'automatic thoughts'?
- What are the 'three systems' in Lang's (1968) model of fear?

Non-empirical approaches

The term 'non-empirical' is used for paradigms very reliant on theoretical assumptions and lacking in objective verification of therapeutic effectiveness. It is useful to understand these approaches, as their legacy of assumptions and terminology has become inextricably woven into the fabric of contemporary therapeutic approaches.

The psychodynamic approach

Freudian psychodynamic theory is still interesting in historical and academic terms as the first accepted psychological approach. Freud made sound observations, such as unconscious processing and limited conscious control. In common with major contemporaries, he noted the importance of sexuality and survival instincts throughout human behaviour and motivation, paralleling the sexual selection and natural selection of Darwinism. However, Freud did not link with evolutionary theory and drifted further from factually based strands as his theory became more speculative and tautological.

Freud also highlighted the importance of relationships, particularly formative ones in childhood. He recognised the place and participation of the patient in the therapeutic process, the patient's insight into their condition and the emotional state of the patient themselves. However, Freud's own approach was more aloof and authoritative than supportive and, for some, was even predatory (Shorter, 1997;

Webster, 1995; 2004). Some aspects have been adopted and developed by other succeeding paradigms.

Freudian theory and the development of psychoanalysis

Although its precursors can be traced back to **Franz Anton Mesmer** (1734–1815) and the hard work of **Josef Breuer** (1842–1925), psychodynamic approaches truly began with **Sigmund Freud** (1856–1939). Freud formulated psychodynamic personality theory based on clinical experiences, initially using **hypnosis** to access the early experiences of his neurotic patients, as his colleague Breuer had done previously. However, Freud was not satisfied that hypnosis produced the best therapeutic effect and believed the client should find their own way to their past in normal consciousness. He used free association, the basis of **Freudian psychoanalysis**, and Freud's followers developed their own variations on his approach, becoming known

Sigmund Freud was a great thinker of his time, but his legacy of psychoanalysis proved more of a hindrance to the advancement of psychiatry.
Source: Pearson Online Database.

sequentially as **post-Freudians** and **neo-Freudians**. The aim of Freudian psychoanalysis is for the client to gain an **insight** into their emotional past, as unresolved emotional conflicts are thought to produce **unconscious conflicts** resulting in symptoms. Thus, psychoanalysis is described as an **insight therapy**.

Developing his **theory of personality** from clinical experience, Freud used this theory to explain his clients' problems in a characteristic tautological manner. He introduced new concepts to the scientific and lay world, such as **unconscious motivation** and **infantile sexuality**, which were not always well received.

The term 'psychodynamic' refers to the active nature of the three mental structures that form the basis of Freud's theory, which are thought to develop from one another in the early childhood years.

- The **id** ('it') is the home of **Eros**, one source of the psychic energy or **libido** thought to build up and require release by gratification of the id's instinctive impulses. These impulses are inherited primitive biological needs, present at birth and represented by the id. Immediate gratification of these drives is termed primary process thinking, governed by the **pleasure principle**. Following the cold brutality of war, Freud later considered **Thanatos** to be an additional, destructive source of psychic energy. This destructive force, along with regression to id states, provided some basis for a forensic–dynamic approach to criminal acts.

- The **ego** ('I') is formed when the primary processing of the id is thwarted and gratification is delayed. This gratification is secondary process thinking and is balanced against the demands of reality, under the **reality principle**. Part of the ego is the conscious self and negotiating between the id's and outside world's demands.

- The **superego** develops when the id and ego have to take on board the accumulated moral rules of adults and society. Part of the unconscious, the superego acts as a 'conscience' putting moral demands on the ego, in contrast to the id's primitive demands. Forensic interpretations of behaviour relate to the superego failing to develop.

These three hypothetical structures should be in approximate harmony, balancing their needs. If they are in conflict, or one is overly dominant or underdeveloped, the individual suffers proportionate degrees of disorder. Freud also believed that a mentally healthy individual successfully passes through five **psychosexual stages**, during which the id, ego and superego are formed. Distortions of personality occur if an individual is over- or under-satisfied at each stage, or fails to progress and is fixated at that stage. The characteristics of distortions are determined by the specific stage and whether the individual is under- or over-gratified.

- **The oral stage** (0–1 year) is governed by the id. The child uses its mouth to explore the world, beginning with reflexes for the breast and generalising the oral gratification to substitutes such as dummies, thumbs and food. Thus the child gains oral gratification, channelling libidinal energy via the mouth, Freud considering this a form of sexual energy finding its release. Conflict occurs over feeding, and fixation at this stage is associated with overeating, smoking or verbal excess amongst others.

- In **the anal stage**, focus moves from mouth to the **anus**. A child gains comfort from bowel movements and may develop a less than welcome (to the parents) interest in them. Reality then demands **potty training** and conflict over this leads to the formation of the ego. Fixation at this stage is associated with untidiness and aggression, termed the **anal-expulsive personality**, or meanness and acquisitiveness, termed the **anal-retentive personality**.

- **The phallic stage** contains the important **Oedipal** or **Electra** conflict areas, as a result of which the superego is formed. The focus for libidinal energy is the penis or clitoris. The child is 4 or 5 years old and, being sexual but naive, has problems adjusting to the acceptability of attraction to their own genitalia. Fixation at this stage can result in inferiority at one extreme and forensic levels of promiscuity and narcissism at the other.

   The Freudian way children adopt moral codes governing male and female sexual behaviour and develop a superego has many critics, partly due to their refusal to accept **infantile sexual desires**, but also due to the unscientific nature of Freud's speculations. Freud would consider that the critics were **repressing** their infant sexuality – another example of Freud's tautological reasoning. For Freud, males undergo Oedipal conflict, desiring their mother sexually and seeing their father as a (large) competitor, wishing him dead (as Oedipus). Believing that these thoughts are open to his parents and that the father will punish the child with castration, the child resolves the dilemma by **identifying** with the father. This is not just a matter of imitation; the child considers himself to *be* the father and no longer needing to compete with, or fear, 'himself'. In this way the child adopts both sex-specific behaviour and the values of his parent in the form of the superego. Freud's female equivalent, the Electra complex, is vague and received more criticism. In this the girl envies the father's penis (**penis envy**), and wishes to possess the father sexually as compensation. Her conflicting emotions

towards her mother are resolved by identification with the mother.

- **The latency stage** refers to *latent* sexual development when the sexual turmoil of previous stages dissipates and the child turns outward to develop other life skills.

- **The genital stage** begins in adolescence, where the focus of sexual energy is the genitalia of the desired sex. **Unresolved conflicts** from the earlier stages may re-emerge to create problems during this stage, which lasts through maturity.

For Freud, early-stage conflicts distort personalities. These are further disturbed by threats from the real world creating **realistic anxiety**, conflict between id and ego in controlling urges (**neurotic anxiety**), and **moral anxiety** from fear of violating demands of the superego. The ego defends itself against anxieties with strategies termed **ego defence mechanisms**. Some defence mechanisms are more adaptive, although all can be maladaptive if used excessively. Examples of more successful strategies are as follows.

- **Sublimation** is the channelling of repressed, usually sexual desires into acceptable outlets, such as sport, art or religion.

- **Identification** with significant others (real or not) can lead to higher achievement, if in moderation.

Less adaptive defence mechanisms offer short-term solutions and longer-term problems. The main process is **repression**. Repression of anxiety provokes conflict in the unconscious, requiring one of the following ego defences to provide a distorted outlet.

- **Projection** is the projecting of one's undesirable urges on to others, preventing the recognition of one's own problems.

- **Rationalisation** provides a justification for one's desires or fears, in terms that camouflage and deny true feelings.

- **Reaction formation** is overcompensation; urges are repressed and expressed in their opposite form, as in the terrorist who fights for peace, but really enjoys the process of war.

- **Regression** is reverting to an earlier stage of development to evade anxiety, 'seeking the comfort of childhood', or to evade responsibility through child-like responses.

When the ego defences fail or break down, there is a disintegration of the personality or decompensation. Freud considered neurotic, or even psychotic, conditions treatable by **psychoanalysis** (though he personally had reservations about psychotic states).

Psychoanalysis

Freudian psychoanalysis requires clients to be able to afford the treatment, which can take many hours a week for 3 or more years. Freud considered older clients (45+) too fixed in their ways to benefit from treatment, and clients also needed to be reasonably intelligent to engage in the verbal process. Giving the clients insight into the source of their distress does not remove it, but enables them to deal with it in a more realistic way, replacing their neurotic misery with common unhappiness.

Analysis typically has the client relaxed on a couch, with the analyst out of view behind them. With little prompting, the client engages in **free association**, allowing their verbalised thoughts to drift back in time, with the associated material being slowly drawn closer to the source of the repression, but meeting unconscious defences to thwart this progress. Slowly, clients reveal clues about the repressed material.

As the source of the repression is approached, defences and symptoms increase. As repressed material is brought into consciousness, there should be a **cathartic** release of repressed feelings. At this point the client's unconscious **resistance** may result in 'sudden cure' or some other ploy to subvert therapy. Repressed feelings may be **projected** on to the analyst instead of the individual from the past experience, in a process termed transference. The analyst may have unresolved conflicts, which may be projected on to the client, and this is termed **countertransference**. Thus, the psychodynamic school see their own analysis as essential in analyst training. Freud also used **interpretations of dreams** in his analytic process.

Followers of Freud were critical of him and altered his process or emphasis, producing their own form of psychoanalysis. Subsequent forms of analysis can be selected from a variety of techniques, most of which are briefer and subject to more guidance or 'leading' by the therapist. Post-Freudians and later neo-Freudians still propagated psychoanalysis, but unlike the disciples of a religious movement, they altered the original text (see the International Perspective box).

The psychoanalytic movement has altered in its methods during its history and has led to other therapeutic approaches that also have insight as a therapeutic goal.

International perspective

Post- and neo-Freudians

Post-Freudians and the neo-Freudians who followed spread the cult-like psychoanalytic methods of therapy around the world during the early twentieth century.

- Carl Gustav Jung (1875–1961) was a Swiss psychiatrist who opposed Freud's emphasis on sex, giving prominence to philosophical and religious aspects in his **analytical psychology**. For Jung, personality extended beyond the personal to inherited archetypes, formless predispositions awaiting realisation that reside in the **collective unconscious**, the product of common inheritance that connects individuals. He suggested hidden or repressed sides of our personalities with archetypal concepts such as the **shadow**, animus and anima (the female and male aspects of individuals), and **persona** (public face or 'mask'). He described psychological types as being along continua: **extravert** or **introvert**; **thinking** or **feeling**; **sensing** or **intuiting**; **rational** or **irrational**. Jung was criticised as being pseudo-philosophical, and even *less* scientific than Freud. He travelled widely, drawing a great deal from experiences of Australia, north Africa and India.
- Alfred Adler (1870–1939) was an Austrian physician and core member of the **Vienna Psychoanalytic Society** and also later worked in the USA and UK. He founded **individual psychology**, emphasising the struggle to overcome feelings of **inferiority**. He was less concerned with early experience than with conscious strivings and any **overcompensation** (e.g. a deaf musician), or **retreat into illness**. He overlapped with behaviourists in thinking that individuals should face the consequences of their actions.
- **Harry Stack Sullivan** (1892–1949) promoted psychoanalysis in the USA during his industrious career. He used psychoanalysis with schizophrenic patients, which despite his claims had limited therapeutic success. Sullivan's non-confrontational style still survives among many analysts in the USA.
- Melanie Klein (1882–1960) promoted psychoanalysis in the UK, examining early childhood relations and focusing on first encounters with 'objects', the primary 'object' being the breast. Her object relations view of an infant adjusting to the good and bad aspects of the same object, involved mental processes such as **splitting** good and bad aspects, **projecting** bad aspects out, and **introjecting** good aspects inside.

Humanistic, existential and Gestalt approaches

Each of these approaches views the client as a **whole person**, with the same potential for growth as anyone else. Abnormal behaviour is attributed to failure in the client's past, restricted self-development or failure to face up to life's challenges. Each therapy gives clients insight into the dynamics of their problem and enables them to cope with and rise above their difficulties. These therapies have similarities to cognitive approaches and are often adopted by counsellors; thus they tend not to be used with more disturbed individuals.

The humanistic approach

Many of the approaches described so far tend to ignore free will, considering behaviour to have biological, conditioned or unconscious determinants. Humanistic approaches emphasise that people *have* choices, and that constraints on their free will are self-imposed rather than determined for them.

The main humanistic proponents are **Abraham Maslow** and **Carl Rogers**. Rogers' influence on therapy has been substantial, to the extent that his client-centred therapy is referred to as **Rogerian therapy**.

- Abraham Maslow (1908–1970) described a **hierarchy of needs**, which all human beings strive to work through. Individuals begin by satisfying the lower physical needs in order eventually to achieve their 'highest' need, that of **self-actualisation**. Influenced by concepts traced back to Carl Jung, he also based some of this on studies of self-actualised individuals such as **Albert Einstein**. For Maslow, people have mental distress when influences such as the family block their progress towards self-actualisation. Helping the person to understand how these influences block their needs, Maslow hopes their personalities will strengthen in realising the potential to satisfy all their needs.

- Carl Rogers (1902–1987) produced a theory of personality in 1959, which assumes humanity to be basically good and motivated toward improvement. This was based on his **client-centred** approach, described in *Client-centred Therapy* (Rogers, 1951). He aims to **actualise** clients' potential, and by **self-actualisation** develop the characteristics of the **healthy personality**. He considered that the need to enhance the 'self' was genetically programmed and more important than basic needs. Rogers believes that society imposes conditions

of worth, transmitted by **conditional positive regard** as the standards by which individuals are judged. Disharmony results from great disparity between the self-value imposed by significant others in society and that individual's potential. He uses **unconditional positive regard** to develop positive 'selves' in therapy, believing the attitude and style of the therapist to be more important than specific techniques. Client-centred therapy has since become **person-centred therapy**, to aid the client's self-worth by referring to them as a person rather than 'client' or 'patient'. Roger's supportive approach is extensively used non-therapeutically in counselling.

The existential approach

The existential approach also emphasises individuals' positive attributes, which are inhibited or distorted by the environment. However, the existential approach is less optimistic than the humanistic approach, seeing the modern world as **alienating** and de-humanising. In existential therapy, the client is encouraged to face up to the realities and **responsibilities** of life, and self-fulfilment is insufficient in recognising their responsibilities to others. There are three principles in existentialism.

- **Being.** Humans are aware of their existence and have to take responsibility for it. They have freedom of choice and should not make excuses to evade this.

- **Non-being.** Humans are aware that they will cease to exist at some point in time and this creates existential anxiety. If an individual cannot accept being and non-being as applying to them, their choices become restricted and the self-actualisation process becomes distorted.

- **Being in the world.** Disorder can result from alienation – a feeling that they have lost 'their world'. Such individuals feel estranged from other human beings or isolated from the natural world.

Existentialism encourages the client to face up to the inevitabilities of existence, life, accidents and death, at the same time as taking the responsibility for their own role. They are also taught to face up to an existence that leaves them essentially **alone in the world**, but are encouraged to relate to others in an unpretentious, direct way. Though seemingly depressing in its outlook, the existential view is more realistic than that of the humanistic school. The existential therapist attempts to see the world as the client sees it, in order to understand their distortions. The client is made aware of their potential for growth and finding meaning in the world. With support and encouragement, the client takes responsibility for making choices, aware of living with the lifelong consequences. As with humanistic therapy, the attitude of the therapist takes precedence over therapeutic techniques. **R. May** and **R. D. Laing** provide just two examples of a variety of existential views.

- **Rollo May** (1905–1994) studied under Alfred Adler as a psychoanalyst, and moved into humanistic therapy before popularising existential therapy in the USA. May perceived a threat to the individual posed by rapid growth in **science and technology** and reliance on science to solve all our ills. He quotes from existentialist literature (e.g. May, 1983) and refers to novels and films depicting the dehumanising technology. He saw six characteristics of therapy referring to ways of relating to patients and their potential insights. For May, the client is responsible for writing the script for his or her own existence at that moment.

- Ronald D. Laing (1927–1989) was much revered in the 1960s as an **anti-psychiatrist** and 'psychic guru' (see Chapter 2). As a psychiatrist, Laing utilised existential or phenomenological philosophy to address disorders such as **schizophrenia**. Mildly psychotic individuals were treated as sane and their view of the world was examined for what sense they made of their experiences. In the context of the 1960s this seemed admirable, and Laing and his colleagues seemed proud of the fact that visitors had difficulty differentiating the patients from the therapists. Such experimental **therapeutic communities** are viewed far more critically in retrospect.

The Gestalt approach

Gestalt psychology focuses on perceiving the whole above the detail of which it is comprised. Thus we perceive a song rather than a collection of individual notes, regardless of the key it is played in or the instrument it is played on. **Gestalt therapy** aims to integrate the whole person, including aspects of their personality and feelings that may have been denied.

Frederich Perls (1893–1970) developed the Gestalt approach to therapy after he disagreed with analyst colleagues over their assumptions. As with the humanistic view, Perls saw his clients as potentially good, claiming that they should be aware of, and accept responsibility for their needs and fears, as in existentialism. There are a number of techniques in Gestalt therapy involving role-play, such as the examples below. Again, the resulting attitude of the client is of primary importance.

- The **empty chair** helps the client address their true feelings. The client imagines they are confronting an individual or an object in the chair opposite, talking directly to the representation of the feeling rather than *about* it.

- **Reversal** requires clients to role-play the *opposite* of the way they feel. In a Jungian sense they perceive the 'other side' of themselves to confront repressed feelings.

- **Use of metaphor** involves role-playing or symbolising a situation analogous to the problem preventing the client confronting a feeling. If the parallel situation evokes the same feeling, the client may recognise the barrier.

Humanistic, existential and Gestalt approaches all emphasise attitudes in therapy and give the patient insight and ability to cope with difficulties. Differences are in emphasis and style of interaction between therapist and client.

Evaluation of Freud and psychoanalysis

Derived from Freudian origins, the paradigms in this section tend to lack objective evidence of therapeutic effectiveness, although psychoanalysis provided a basis for good relationships with clients (Webster, 1995). Client support and encouragement is characteristic of the humanistic approach, but offers little beyond the good support offered by counsellors and falls short of CBT in effectiveness. Part of CBT as an evidence-based therapy is continuous empirical evaluation of therapeutic effectiveness.

Despite unremitting support from a few therapists, psychoanalysis was not a peak in the history of interventions but more an interruption in the development of effective therapy (see Shorter, 1997). Paralleling the expansion of cognitive approaches, psychoanalytically based therapies peaked and declined during the twentieth century. Decline was more marked in Europe, while in Russia they have survived and in the USA there is still a flourishing market for psychoanalysis and related therapies, possibly due to the private health care system. In the twenty-first century, Freud's legacy is unlikely to survive due to lack of empirical support and the inherent ineffectiveness of its treatment approaches when evaluated (see Eysenck, 1952; 1985; Piper, 2000; Shorter, 1997; Webster, 1995; 2004).

Freud's methods were unscientific, relying on **case studies**, without any testing of hypotheses or other experimental procedures (see Wolpe, 1982). He generalised from a small group of (mostly) middle-class, neurotic, female patients, to the wider population. He kept no empirical record of his data (patient verbalisations) and used **introspection** or subjective speculation to fill gaps and organise his work. His theories were tautological, and thus not falsifiable (testable), and psychoanalysis was labelled as an **art-form** rather than a scientific therapy, and therefore was difficult to research. According to Popper (2002), any theory that is not falsifiable is not scientific. The Freudian psychoanalytic movement is closer to a **religious cult** than a scientific movement (see Webster, 1995). However, more contemporary studies have attempted to test therapies based on this approach with some reported success (e.g. Westen, Novotny and Thompson-Brenner, 2004).

Freud's explanations of patients' cases have been challenged, such as the 'little Hans' case, in which a child's fear of horses was related to a castration complex from fearing his father, symbolised by the horse's teeth. Joseph Wolpe's explanation in terms of classical conditioned fear due to frightening experiences with horses seemed more plausible (see Wolpe, 1982). Freud himself had limited faith in the effectiveness of psychoanalysis in improving people and tended to publish those fewer cases that appeared successful.

Many critics thought Freud too preoccupied with **sex** in his theories, and that this reflected his personal obsessions. His pursuit of the sexual underpinnings of behaviour led him to being suggestive and even abusive towards his middle-class female patients (Shorter, 1997), ironically lacking insight into his own motives. Sexual obsession is a potential reason for dubious collaborations with 'fringe theorists' such as Wilhelm Fliess and his 'nasal–genital response' explanation of disorder, which borders on fetishism (see Masson, 1985). Freud caused professional embarrassment amongst colleagues at the Society of Physicians by his public admiration of Charcot (Shorter, 1997).

Freud is an easy target for criticism, particularly where personal failings overlapped with his professional lack of empiricism, but his pioneering contribution to the psychologist as therapist needs recognition. His work and limitations need placing into historical context, as he was working in an era when little was known of neurological function and belief was often accepted as fact. However, those perpetuating his errors in the current scientific context have no such excuse.

Evaluation of other non-empirical approaches

Non-empirical approaches including psychoanalysis claim improvement in how their clients feel post-therapy. However, this rarely refers to improvement in the disorder and relies on boosting the esteem of the patient or having them come to terms with accepting the symptoms.

Carl Rogers relied almost entirely on a 'feel-good factor' in his clients, claiming the resources were in the client not the therapist. Although Rogers' 1951 text led large numbers of psychologists into the psychiatric arena, his shunning of systematic therapy labelled followers as using all 'bedside manner' and no therapy. For this, he was critically attacked by psychiatrists, who also tried to close his clinic.

Some interventions have actually proven harmful to patients (Lieberman, Yalom and Miles, 1973). Acknowledging this, blame has been placed on the client's attitude (Mohr, 1995). Grunebaum (1986) followed up a number of clients (who were also therapists) who complained about personal therapeutic experiences that they viewed as harmful. Some of these were described as distant and cold, but others were characterised by intense emotional and/or sexual involvement.

In most cases of non-empirical therapy the same improvement can be obtained by non-therapeutic attention and interaction with an untrained individual (Eysenck, 1952). This **control condition** is used in evaluating therapies and termed **placebo control**, though placebo effects have been considered therapy (Frank, 1989). Patients often experience spontaneous remission of symptoms over time in the absence of any intervention and these time periods are similar to the (rather lengthy) duration of non-empirical therapy. For Eysenck (1952; 1985) this equated with having no objective therapeutic effect; he asserted that behaviour therapy was the only form of psychological treatment worth consideration (Eysenck, 1960). Non-empirical therapists cite the few attempts to evaluate such therapies objectively (e.g. Westen, Novotny and Thompson-Brenner, 2004) and also argue that objective evaluation is not appropriate where subjectivity and interaction are a focus. However, most clients would be outraged at defending random effectiveness in this way. It would be reasonable for prospective clients to have wider access to less subjective evaluations that invariably place BT and CBT ahead of non-empirical therapies, which tend to equate to chance recovery (see Kazdin and Wilson, 1978; Shapiro and Shapiro, 1982).

Application of non-empirical approaches to the case of Ian

In Freudian terms, Ian's father Tom would be fixated at the phallic stage due to the loss of his own father around the age of 5. This was repeated in the following generation with Ian being disrupted at the same stage, resulting in his promiscuous and narcissistic behaviour. Disrupted Oedipal conflict producing sex-role confusion and insecurity exacerbated difficulties in Ian's psychosexual development. These factors contributed to Ian's inability to commit to a relationship due to underlying insecurities as a result of his father leaving.

Rogerian therapy could help Jean see her own self-worth beyond her family's needs. Existential and Gestalt views of Jean's predicament would also have her reflect on her place in the world and encourage her to be at one without living her life through others and the subsequent disappointments. Ian would benefit from facing up to responsibility for events in his life and gain insight into his sense of isolation being a result of his own way of viewing himself in his world.

Self-test questions

- What clinical significance did Freud's psycho-sexual stages have?
- What is the aim of psychoanalysis?
- What is the 'empty chair' technique?
- Can we usefully distinguish humanistic, existential and Gestalt therapies?
- Is psychoanalysis scientific?
- How effective are non-empirical therapies?

Part 3: Social and eclectic approaches

The social paradigm reminds us to take note of the social and economic context of sufferers, as this can have a profound impact in terms of cause and treatment. The social divide in health provision can be quite stark, as in this case in Hong Kong. Source: David A. Holmes.

Group, cultural and family aspects of therapy

Although group, cultural and family aspects of therapy fall short of being actual paradigms, they are important factors to be considered in therapy, and the increasing research into cultural effects can be usefully combined with the evolutionary approach. Some interventions acknowledge that the client is not acting in isolation and their **social context** may adversely influence their behaviour. If the social context of the individual can affect their behaviour negatively, then that context could be used in therapy. Those close, especially family, are the most influential aspect of this context, though all may be collectively influenced by their **cultural context** or heritage. Therapists are increasingly recognising these influences on abnormal behaviour and, as far as possible, utilising them in their therapeutic approaches. However, it must be emphasised that just because factors have an effect on abnormal behaviour, this *does not* mean they have a causal role in that behaviour.

Group therapy

Although there were some positive reasons, the origins of group therapy were economic. It is at times of economic pressure on health resources of a particular country that the use of group therapy increases. In the current economic climate, there is pressure on the health service and, at the same time, clinically and forensically precipitated conditions, such as the **adult effects of child sexual abuse** and **post-traumatic stress disorder**, are being revealed as more prevalent than previously thought. Such conditions benefit from group therapy settings at some stage, although individual therapy will also be needed. However, the use of group settings will often be driven by the need to help a large number of clients with limited therapist time.

There are many varieties of group therapy, and therapy approaches described so far have versions for multiple participants. Groups are around 12 participants, often directed by a single therapist, though others are as small as five members or consist of only clients interacting, perhaps with minimal prior instruction. They can be heterogeneous groups of sufferers gathered to gain useful generic skills and motivation, or focused around a particular topic or behaviour. Time-limited groups meet for eight or ten sessions, though some may be ongoing, which may often be the case in a forensic context. As well as groups for sufferers, victims and perpetrators, it is also the case that relatives, colleagues and friends benefit. Groups create the opportunity for **role-play** or other exercises, and even physical contact as in **encounter groups**. Group therapies can be broadly divided into three types.

- **Groups led in therapy.** These are extensions of individual therapies with the additional advantages (and disadvantages) of the group setting. They use cognitive, behavioural or other approaches, led by the therapist(s) giving suggestions or comments and encouraging input from the client group. The entire group may undergo desensitisation therapy together or share a single member's achievements. Participants are given 'homework' as in individual therapy.

- **Self-help groups.** These are clients with similar problems, who organise their own meetings in informal or

health care settings. One or more clients with experience of both the disorder and its therapy often initiate this activity. Experienced clients encourage the others to cope, see therapy through or simply admit they have a problem. To their credit, highly trained professionals sometimes admit the limitations imposed by not having first-hand experience of the disorder. For example, self-help groups are valuable in coming to terms with child sexual abuse.

- **Activity-based groups** have a variety of names, often specifying the activity used. Professionals and public often view these with scepticism, sometimes with justification on the (usually rare) occasions when clients suffer adverse effects (e.g. Lieberman, Yalom and Miles, 1973). Skills can be learned, such as social skills, self-assertion or the educational function of the long-established **sensitivity training** or **T-groups**. More dramatic or confrontational activities include the emotional and physical interactions characteristic of ethically questionable **encounter groups**.

Some clients are less well adapted to group therapy, but such individuals can be helped to benefit by **pre-group training** on how to act in the group setting and gain from it. The internet is used to provide group therapy using closed (password-protected) 'chat-rooms' and virtual conferencing facilities. Barak (1999) found that chat-room group therapy offers advantages in terms of considered replies, more confidentiality and greater disclosure, as well as time and place being unrestricted.

Evaluation of group therapy

Group therapy can provide a great deal of support and reassurance not available from individual therapy with lesser power dynamics between professional and client. Other clients can reassure individuals they are not alone in their condition, and peer support helps clients persist with therapy in difficult circumstances, such as substance abstinence. Motivation of an individual by the group goes beyond verbal encouragement; they become public witnesses to one's commitment to change and 'prove oneself'.

Group-based interventions are particularly useful in forensic settings, where peers can more easily challenge denial or lack of insight in crimes such as sex offending, than therapists, who may be perceived as 'outsiders'. Thus the group provides a consensus that can directly dispute the irrational thinking of an individual member. Just being in the group may provide social facilitation for some, as well as other members' attitudes and achievements providing vicarious learning experiences when peers model changed behaviour.

There are disorders for which group therapy may be inappropriate and occasions when it has proved harmful (Lieberman, Yalom and Miles, 1973). Some may thrive in group settings, but others do not and need individual therapy. However, the group context can directly help those who have difficulty relating to others and desensitise clients to communicating about their problem, allowing more sociable attitudes and useful coping strategies to develop.

Roback (2000) examined adverse and iatrogenic (disorder resulting from therapy) aspects of group therapy, such as poor leadership and client characteristics, but pointed to the importance of the interaction of such factors producing poor outcomes. There are confidentiality, consent and ethical issues involved, which may not be apparent until it is too late in the process to prevent unwanted disclosures. Just as helpful experiences may be shared, so clients may be exposed to unhelpful events or corrupting individuals even in supervised groups. Self-help groups by definition lack qualified professional input and the risk of adverse experiences and misinformation is increased despite safeguards.

Cultural considerations

Culture is not the same as ethnicity. Ethnic minorities within a population may undergo acculturation on contact with the surrounding culture and become assimilated into it; then their children may undergo **enculturation** directly into the new culture. A distinct culture requires a differing set of beliefs, lifestyle practices, values and behaviour patterns. Tseng (2003) presented a detailed evaluation of how culture interacts with abnormal behaviour in terms of aetiology, conceptualisation, presentation and management. Three major sources of influence relating cultural factors to abnormal behaviour are **cultural relativism**, so called **culture-bound syndromes** and **culture conflict**.

Cultural relativism

The way abnormal behaviour is interpreted or expressed differently can depend on the cultural context, and some behaviour may not even be considered disordered or criminal. For example, interpretation of schizophrenic symptoms has historically been influenced by the cultural context. Although it is diagnosed in every culture, symptoms such as hearing voices are associated with religious experience in some cultures and seen as a 'gift' rather than disability. Thus rates of diagnosis may vary, even though the same diagnostic criteria are available, with 'revered' sufferers never entering the health care system. Equally, European individuals may find themselves arrested on very serious charges in Middle Eastern cultures where modes of dress and substance-use behaviour may not be tolerated and are a serious focus for forensic attention.

Culture-bound syndromes

The effects of culture can influence the occurrence of disorder, or shape the type of disorder found. These are usually related to strong beliefs within the particular culture, such as suicide in Japanese culture being associated with public disgrace or financial failure rather than depression and hopelessness, and can involve **family suicide**. In the Chinese culture, the delusion **Koro** (Shook Yang) represents the cultural emphasis on conservation of spermatic fluids (Prins, 1990), preserving balance between yin and yang. In this delusion, men believe their penis is retracting into the body or shrinking. The West is not immune to such influence: **anorexia nervosa** has been primarily a Western disorder, related to the media pressure on young Western females to be slim.

Culture conflict

This occurs when individuals from one culture live in contact with another, whilst maintaining their cultural identity. In individuals emigrating geographically to a new culture, this is confounded by a sense of alienation and the stress of adjusting to another environment. Culture-induced pressures add to the stress of relocation, compounding the problems, and can pressure such individuals into cultural assimilation. Immigrant cultures suffer greater levels of mental illness, though this varies with the degree of alienation experienced. Difficulties of interpretation are magnified in this situation, as culturally specific ways of expressing abnormal behaviour may appear more alien in a different cultural context. Further difficulties arise when clinician and client are from different cultures. A patient or inmate acting in their own culturally sanctioned way might have these actions misinterpreted by a professional unfamiliar with other cultures.

Culture conflict is inevitable with subcultures where a culture is deliberately maintained as separate from the host culture. Some ethnic minorities in various countries maintain their own culture and reject their host culture, leading to conflict in legal, educational and other areas, such as family systems. Rastafarian subcultures maintained their cannabis smoking tradition against the legal framework of many cultures in the twentieth century. Criminal subcultures and criminal gangs maintain their own illegal cultural practices in direct conflict with host cultures across the world (Huff, 2002). Social groups within what would ostensibly seem to be the same culture may in fact turn out to have very different social practices. Just as a Haitian may experience cultural conflict when settling in Berlin, so an individual from a farming community in Sicily may show some difficulties of adjusting to life in inner-city Milan. Clinicians need to be aware of these potential effects, which can colour their client's perceptions, or even their own expectations.

Cultural effects have been eroded by migration and political invasion following wars. However, the resultant acculturation has not been as great as expected. Clearly evident with twenty-first century global media, especially the internet, the exchange of information from differing cultures alone does not necessarily alter cultural boundaries. This may be less so with international media icons, who penetrate most cultures around the world.

Family therapy

Family therapy differs from group therapy, as the dynamics of the family 'group' have been established prior to meeting for therapy; indeed, it is often the purpose of therapy to change these fixed patterns, or the *culture* of interaction. Family therapy has a great deal of overlap with **couples therapy** and **marital therapy**, especially if involving children.

A level of conflict in families is sometimes inevitable, especially with children, such as weaning children from dependency on the family to adult independence. In Western countries there has been a rapid shift from living as couples to being single individuals or single parents. This has on average reduced the child's contact with both male and female role models and the level of parental control over behaviour. These factors increase the frequency and severity of family conflict, despite a greater level of public knowledge regarding family dynamics.

In the family systems approach, the family is addressed as a system of complex interrelationships. Family therapy is engaged in for two basic reasons.

- **Extreme conflict.** This is where the dynamics of the family have become so distorted, or conflict so intense, that one or more members present with stress-related disorders. The disorder is sustained by the current family dynamics and intervention will involve the whole family meeting together, or in combinations, with a therapist.

- **Abnormal behaviour in the family.** Where a member of the family is exhibiting abnormal behaviour, this may not be caused by the family dynamics, but may be adversely affected by them. The effects of expressed emotion within the family of a schizophrenic individual would affect the sufferer's relapse rate (Chapter 18). Addressing the family interactions can help stabilise the family member who has the problem.

Problems of misunderstanding or lack of communication can quite rapidly be addressed by having the family communicate honestly and directly with an experienced therapist. Analysis of the contingencies supporting conflict and disparities between verbal statements and behaviour can uncover factors that can be manipulated to beneficial effect. Other situations can only be managed rather than resolved, such as a death or serious rift in the family.

In the early twentieth century, family therapy was the province of non-empirical therapists. However, behavioural and CBT interventions have replaced these older approaches and become the subject of a number of TV shows such as *The House of Tiny Tearaways* (BBC3 UK), which, although clearly voyeuristic, were highly instructive for many parents and highlighted the lack of parenting skills instruction in contemporary societies.

Beyond paradigms: diathesis–stress and eclectic approaches

Many closely related to schizophrenic individuals do not develop the disorder, perhaps even as a twin with the same genetic predispositions. Others have survived emotional turmoil and severe illness in childhood, or have been in an earthquake as an adult, witnessing horror and carnage, and still have no signs and symptoms of mental disorder. Adopting a single paradigm, such as purely viewing clients from a biological or environmental point of view, is very limiting. Thus a cognitive therapist may only be aware of, and treating, part of the problem, and if abnormal behaviour is sustained by biological factors, cognitive treatment has only an ameliorative role.

However, paradigms such as the biological approach progressively explain much more abnormal behaviour and other approaches consequently lose that proportion of their intellectual domain. Consequently, critical attacks by retreating disciplines concentrate on the expanding paradigm, illustrating the process of paradigm shift (Kuhn, 1996). There is a need to consider the interactions between paradigms and the factors they propose and rather than any intellectual apartheid or allowing a dominant paradigm to gain an effective monopoly. Debates on the politics of paradigm conflict are thus seen as enlightening rather than restrictive in the practical application of theoretical approaches (Masters, 2001).

The diathesis–stress approach

First proposed by Meehl (1962), the diathesis–stress approach assumes a **predisposition** to a disorder (diathesis) and a **precipitating stressor** (stress) to develop the disorder. In practice, the diathesis is almost always biological or genetic and the stressor environmental (for the **expression** of the predisposition). This is not the case with biological disorders such as Down's syndrome or Huntington's disease, where the environment cannot prevent expression. Only some disorders can be prevented or significantly limited by environmental factors.

In rare cases it has been argued that an individual carrying a biological predisposition for schizophrenia who meets little stress may escape developing the disorder fully. However, if the individual is subject to great stress but lacks the biological predisposition, they cannot develop schizophrenia (see Chapter 18). The diathesis–stress approach is associated with **behavioural medicine**, where behavioural and biological therapies are adopted to cope with stress and related physical illness, which is closely linked to **health psychology** and **stress management**.

Individuals with the diathesis for a disorder could thus be advised to avoid precipitating stressful events, although these tend to be subjectively scaled and difficult to specify across individuals. Increasingly, people have information on their genetic predisposition to various disorders but can be inhibited in such prophylactic strategies due to fear of becoming an insurance risk or hampering their career following availability of their genetic status.

The eclectic approach

This involves the use of each therapeutic approach to the extent that it is useful to the individual patient, rather than adhering to one paradigm. This integrated approach is not always easy to achieve in practice, as therapists develop bias in their training and there is often antagonism between some approaches, especially the analytic and behavioural approaches. There is criticism of those few therapists who abuse the eclectic label, when their approach would better be described as unsystematic and random. In contrast, some professionals have developed well-defined eclectic approaches, such as Lazarus's (1984) description of **multimodal behaviour therapy**, addressing behaviour, cognition and affect. Other existing therapies illustrate how opposing approaches appear to become less distinct in actual practice, such as cognitive analytic therapy.

Multiple or eclectic approaches militate against the aims of the specialist, who can offer in-depth skills and knowledge beyond that of the therapist with an eclectic approach. However, this view tends to assume that one single-therapy approach can be superior to another. As mentioned above, behavioural approaches tend to do better in evaluations, but usually incorporate cognitive or even elements of humanistic approaches as part of their 'bedside manner'. However, the therapist being versed in all therapies, but master of none, may not be in the client's best interest in terms of a complete recovery. Therapy is about treating the client, not the therapist's ego.

Self-test questions

- What are the advantages of using group formats in therapy?
- What effects do differing cultural backgrounds have on the processes of diagnosis and treatment?
- What are the disadvantages of the eclectic approach?

Chapter summary

There are theoretical viewpoints within abnormal clinical and forensic psychology that represent the disciplines on its borders, such as biology. These **paradigms** consider the causes of disorders in their own terms, producing therapies that act on these assumptions and are guided by the theoretical principles of that paradigm.

The **neuropsychological approach** considers the contribution of **genetics** to disorders, and although genetic codes are not easily changed, **genetic counselling** is available to limit the passing on of detectable, destructive gene information. Errors and damage can occur in the **neurochemistry** and **neuroanatomy** of the brain, and in the **endocrine system**, resulting in abnormalities of behaviour, thinking and emotion. Although their actions are still relatively crude, **drugs, psychosurgery, electroconvulsive therapy** and **hormone therapy** have provided welcome relief from the symptoms of some of the most stubborn disorders.

The **evolutionary** approach is relatively new, developed from **Darwin**'s recognition of the **law of natural selection**. Following research on animals by **comparative psychologists** and **ethologists**, the adaptations found have been applied to human behaviour by **behavioural ecologists** and **sociobiologists**. From this the **evolutionary paradigm** became recognised as providing **ultimate** as opposed to **proximate** explanations of abnormal behaviour in terms of adaptation to life in small groups in savannah environments, transposed to contemporary social and physical environments.

The **behavioural approach** relies on the principles of **classical** and **operant conditioning**, which provide **behaviour therapy** and **behaviour modification** respectively. In behaviour therapy, methods such as **systematic desensitisation** and **flooding** expose clients to feared situations, reducing the anxious response, or as in **aversion therapy**, associate an undesirable situation with a noxious stimulus. In behaviour modification, the basics of desired behaviour are **reinforced**, from which more complex behaviours can be **shaped**. Similarly, undesirable behaviour is not reinforced, or is punished if necessary. These learning approaches can be combined

in **biofeedback**, where a client learns to control their blood pressure and other internal functions. Learning can also take place **vicariously** and clients can learn appropriate behaviour by observing others – the process of **modelling**. Behavioural methods prove both effective and efficient in comparisons of therapies.

Cognitive and **cognitive behavioural approaches** developed from behavioural ones and, as such, attempt to change maladaptive thinking patterns to be more productive. In rational emotive therapy, clients have their irrational beliefs about their behaviour questioned and substituted by more realistic expectations. Self-instructional therapy makes use of the client's **self-talk**, giving them corrective phrases to use in this process. The cognitive therapy of **Beck** has mostly been applied to depression. In this, negative **automatic thoughts** are identified and undermined by a **Socratic method** of questioning.

Non-empirical approaches are those paradigms that are difficult to evaluate objectively or that are reluctant to be analysed in this way. These include the **psychodynamic, humanistic, existential** and **Gestalt** approaches. **Psychodynamic** approaches stem from the work of **Freud**, who produced his own theory of personality and the associated therapy of **psychoanalysis**. His personality theory proposes stages of **psychosexual development**, during which the mental structures of the **id, ego and superego** are formed. In this, abnormality results from **conflict** between these structures as a result of early emotional experiences, which have become **repressed**. Psychoanalysis claims that **free association** allows the client to access these early experiences and release the repression. Freud's followers often disagreed with some aspect of his explanations, but maintained the same **insight**-oriented approach in producing their own versions of his therapy. Psychoanalysis has been criticised as being unscientific and its followers accused of practising an art-form rather than an empirical therapy.

Other insight-based therapies include the **humanistic, existential** and **Gestalt approaches**. The humanistic approach of **Rogers**, or **client-centred therapy**, involves helping clients to **actualise** their

Chapter summary continued

potential and achieve a **healthy personality**. In existential and Gestalt therapy, clients are encouraged to take responsibility for the choices they make in life and to realise the potential for improvement these choices can bring.

Multiple person therapies such as **group** and **family therapies** can provide for **economy** in therapeutic practice. In addition, group methods usefully introduce practical support, shared experience and peer pressure into the therapeutic environment. In **family systems approaches**, the dynamics of the whole family are considered in therapy, with the members in attendance. Interactions in the family can then be considered in terms of their influence on the client. **Cultural factors** are now considered when assessing clients from different cultures, especially where the clinician is from another culture or the client has moved into a culturally alien environment.

Adopting a single paradigm approach can deny a client the benefits of an **eclectic approach**: that is, selecting from a variety of approaches those which are most useful to the individual case. Some approaches

assume more than one causal agent, such as the **diathesis–stress approach**. This assumes a **predisposition** to some disorders, but also requires **environmental stressors** finally to precipitate an episode. Although most modern therapeutic approaches are useful, cognitive behavioural approaches have more evidence of effectiveness.

Suggested essay questions

- Discuss the ways in which genetic influences may be responsible for abnormal behaviour.
- Critically discuss the idea that some abnormal behaviour may have been adaptive behaviour in our evolutionary past.
- Evaluate the contribution made by behavioural and cognitive approaches to therapy during the twentieth century.
- Critically discuss the contribution made by Freud and psychoanalysis to contemporary therapy.

Further reading

Overview texts

Beck, A. T. (2005) The current state of cognitive therapy. *Archives of General Psychiatry*, **62**, 953–9.

Buss, D. (1999) *Evolutionary psychology: The new science of the mind.* Boston: Allyn and Bacon.

Carlson, N. (2004) *The physiology of behaviour* (8th edn). London: Allyn and Bacon.

Carr, A., and McNulty, M. (2006) *The handbook of adult clinical psychology: An evidence-based practice approach.* Hove: Routledge.

Cartwright, J. (2000) *Evolution and human behaviour.* London: Macmillan.

Dryden, W. (2008) *Rational emotive behaviour therapy.* London: Routledge.

Faraone, S., Tsuang, M., and Tsuang, D. (1999) *Genetics of mental disorders.* London: Guilford Press.

Martin, G., and Pear, J. (2007) *Behaviour modification* (8th edn). New Jersey: Prentice Hall.

Meyer, J., and Quenzer, L. (2005) *Psychopharmacology.* Sunderland MA: Sinauer Associates Inc.

Specific and more critical texts

Bazzett, T. (2008) *An introduction to behaviour genetics.* Sunderland, Mass: Sinaur Associates.

Cantor, C. (2005) *Evolution and posttraumatic stress: Disorders of vigilance and defence.* London: Routledge.

Christmas, D., Morrison, C., Eljamel, M., and Mathews, K. (2004) Neurosurgery for mental disorder. *Advances in Psychiatric Treatment*, **10**, 189–99.

Cosmides, L., and Tooby, J. (1992) *The adapted mind.* Oxford: Oxford University Press.

Dawkins, R. (1998) *Unweaving the rainbow.* London: Penguin.

Dolan, M., Anderson, I., and Deakin, J. F. (2000) Relationship between 5-HT function and impulsivity in male offenders with personality disorders. *British Journal of Psychiatry*, 178, 352–9.

Farber, B., Brink, C., and Raskin, P. (1996) *The psychotherapy of Carl Rogers*. England: Guilford Press.

Hodgins, S., and Müller-Isberner, R. (eds) (2000) *Violence, crime and mentally disordered offenders: Concepts and methods for effective treatment and prevention*. Chichester: Wiley.

Leach, M., and Aten, J. (2010) *Culture and the therapeutic process*. New York: Routledge.

Leonard, (1997) *Fundamentals of psychopharmacology* (2nd edn). London: Wiley.

Leslie, J. (2002) *Essential behaviour analysis*. London: Arnold.

Moorey, S. (1996) Cognitive-behavioural therapy for whom? *Advances in Psychiatric Treatment*, 2, 17–23.

O'Mahoney, G., and Lucey, J. (1998) *Understanding psychiatric treatment: Therapy for serious mental disorder in adults*. Chichester: Wiley.

Plomin, R., DeFries, J., McLearn, G., and McGuffin, P. (2001) *Behavioural genetics*. New York: Worth.

Scott, A. (1994) Contemporary practice of electroconvulsive therapy. *British Journal of Hospital Medicine*, 51, 334–9.

Scott, M. (2009) *Simply effective cognitive behavioural therapy: A practitioner's guide*. London: Routledge.

Shorter, E. (1997) *A history of psychiatry: From the era of the asylum to the age of prozac*. Chichester: Wiley.

Tseng, W. S. (2003) *Clinician's guide to cultural psychiatry*. San Diego: Academic Press.

Wettstein, R. (1998) *Treatment of offenders with mental disorders*. New York: Guilford Press.

Visit **www.pearsoned.co.uk/davidholmes** for a range of resources to support study. Test yourself with multiple choice questions and access a bank of over 100 videos that will bring the topics to life. Video coverage for this chapter includes a discussion of paradigm approaches to treatment, Jung and the unconscious, and how the human genome map may help create personalised treatments.

CHAPTER 4 The assessment, diagnosis and formulation of clients

- Overview
- Case study
- Assessment, diagnosis and formulation
- Reliability and validity in diagnosis and assessment
- The development of a systematic approach and associated historical problems
- The assessment process
- Diagnosis: *DSM* and *ICD* systems
- The importance of the individual: the formulation
- Critical evaluation
- Chapter summary

 See the inside workings of a cognitive neuroscience laboratory. This is one of several videos that explore issues and disorders relevant to this chapter at **www.pearsoned.co.uk/davidholmes**.

Pharmaceutical companies and the DSM

A 2009 BBC Radio 4 documentary in the UK investigated the possibility that the production of new mental disorders in succeeding versions of the influential **Diagnostic and Statistical Manual** (*DSM*) by the **American Psychiatric Association** (APA) in the USA may be influenced by the pharmaceutical industry. The programme explained that when a new disorder is created, these drug companies are able to target it with new or existing products, inevitably increasing sales. *DSM* panel members usually vote on these new inclusions and the majority of the panel members have financial links to pharmaceutical companies. Some of these conflicts of interest cannot be made transparent by the APA due to confidentiality of disclosure restrictions.

There has been criticism of the **not otherwise specified** (NOS) category included for each disorder as providing a catch-all diagnosis for milder cases, again providing more sales opportunities. This has been examined in the planning of *DSM-V* (estimated publication 2012) with a view to changing criteria so that NOS cases are given a specific diagnosis, but clearly increasing the sales of mainstream drug treatments. Eminent UK psychiatrist **David Goldberg** is helping with *DSM-V* but wants to reduce the number of disorders and introduce dimensions of severity, which may moderate any anticipated benefits to pharmaceutical companies. This chapter will detail this diagnostic process and discuss the suggestion of dimensional approaches for future diagnostic systems.

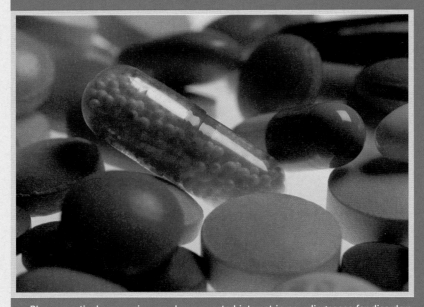

Pharmaceutical companies may have a vested interest in new diagnoses for disorders.
Source: Pearson Online Database.

Assessment, diagnosis and formulation are the stages that clinical or forensic clients will go through prior to treatment by a qualified psychologist or psychiatrist. This chapter will show that there is a need for reliability and validity in the methods of assessing and diagnosing a patient or offender, and that a methodical and universal approach is necessary for international consistency in diagnosis and the sharing of research information. A pedantic and lengthy assessment process, guided by a structured approach, is needed for the benefit of clients and health care providers. This chapter will also examine diagnosis, giving an insight into the major classificatory systems in use across the world in the twentieth and twenty-first centuries. This leads to the formulation of a more tailored and personal approach to the clinical management of individuals exhibiting abnormal behaviour. The critical approach is paramount to exploring the limitations of given ways of identifying and recording abnormal behaviour, and this will be discussed along with alternative approaches in the final section of this chapter.

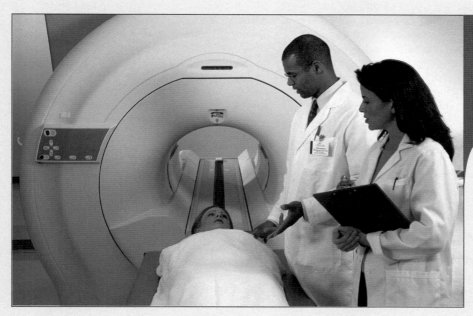

MRI is a very safe option for assessing neurological and other problems, but does require the patient to tolerate cramped, enclosed conditions.
Source: Pearson Online Database.

Case study
A case of reformulation

John had been a regular visitor to Simon, the only clinical forensic psychologist in the prison. Although he had been seen by three clinical psychologists and a forensic psychiatrist from a regional secure unit, Simon was the only professional left where there was any degree of mutual tolerance. During his life John had spent more time in institutions than Simon, whose job had always been within the prison context. Simon asked, 'Why did you strangle that girl, John? You could just as easily have run for it. She was unconscious for heaven's sake', to which John replied, 'I was doing her a favour, sir. You wouldn't want her to wake up and find out what happened, would you, sir?' It was an uncomfortable reply, but a little less manipulative than when John had first been assessed as having a dangerous personality disorder.

Following the brutal murder of his ex-girlfriend and her daughter, John had been arrested whilst trying to convince an elderly lady that it would

CASE STUDY CONTINUED

be a good idea to loan him her car to visit his dying son. As John was wondering how much petrol was in the car, the insightful lady rang the police and not her insurance company, as she had led him to believe. At interview, John protested innocence, even when confronted with two witness statements placing him at the scene of the crime. When told that his fingerprints had been found on the chisel used for the murder, and that traces of blood from his shoes were being analysed, John fell silent. He collapsed forward, then, lurching back, stared at one of the officers, exclaiming, 'Who are you?' in an odd but prominent Australian accent. 'Come on, John. That sort of thing doesn't work. Just be honest for once in your life,' the officer calmly told him, but he was taken aback by the alien and intense stare from John, who bellowed, 'I know John. That loser will die in prison.' After another 10 minutes of such utterances and disturbingly uncharacteristic behaviour from the interviewee, who now referred to himself as Pete, the process was terminated.

The psychiatrist assessing John looked down at her notes. 'You say you have had these blackouts for many years, but there is nothing on any of your prison medical records,' she said. John slowly replied, 'I didn't want to look weak in there you know. Anyway, I must have done things OK when I was blacked out because no one noticed.' When the psychiatrist said that she would like more detail from his childhood, John smiled briefly. Her professional (and personal private) experience of abusive childhoods was nothing on the scale that John related. He claimed it had never been on record because he had had a friend to help him, who took charge and 'sorted any scary things out'. Further revelations of waking up to find new clothes and smoked cigars or half-drunk wine when he did not touch either, led the psychiatrist to see John as a victim of abuse. As John revealed further symptoms, the psychiatrist consulted a colleague in the USA and became increasingly convinced that this was

the very first case of **dissociative identity disorder** (DID; see Chapter 15) that she had seen in practice. Every one of the diagnostic criteria for the disorder had been met by John, and after one rather overly dramatic transformation from 'innocent' John to 'guilty' Pete, the psychiatrist felt she needed further opinions, not least because a murder trial outcome might depend on verifying this rare disorder.

John was seen individually by five professionals, including a psychiatrist specialising in DID, who was rapidly convinced of the authenticity of his condition. Simon stood alone against the professionals, but in agreement with the prison officers, in considering John's condition suspicious. Simon arranged to see John in the presence of two psychiatrists and suggested to him that he could be faking, as there had never been a case of DID with only two identities, and that perhaps there were more in there. Simon was amazed at the speed at which two more personalities emerged over the space of only 40 minutes. During John's 'possession' by the identity of a rather unconvincing small girl called Clare, Simon suddenly called out, 'John!' to which John spun round and replied 'What!' John rolled his eyes and attempted to look disoriented, but the act had become a farce. Over the next 2 years, Simon received no cooperation or truth from John and he eventually accepted that there was no hope of a therapeutic relationship.

This very rare case illustrates the possibility that even professionals can be mistaken, as had occurred in the original case of Kenneth Bianchi, one of the two 'Hillside Stranglers' in the USA. Bianchi was exposed in a similar manner to 'John' by psychologist **Martin Orne** using demand characteristics (see Chapter 5). Thus a structured approach to cautious assessment and diagnosis is essential, whether this be for a vulnerable client with anxiety or indeed an offender facing serious criminal charges.

Assessment, diagnosis and formulation

Whether a client arrives at outpatients, is referred by a court or is admitted to hospital as a result of psychological problems, what follows is a three-stage process. When you are first seen in these contexts or even at a visit to your GP, your condition will be assessed. This assessment may only consist of a few questions and a discreet glance at some physical ailment in the case of a GP visit. The GP will then make an initial diagnosis, or a hypothesis as to what is the cause, condition and appropriate treatment. The GP may subsequently hand over a prescription for your treatment and add this information to your medical records, with a means of monitoring the condition in the future, crudely equivalent to a formulation. In the case of an individual with a serious mental condition or who has been referred by a court of law, the stages of this process are more complex, discreet and detailed.

Because identifying a mental state with any certainty is more difficult than identifying a cold sore, the procedures involved are lengthy and include gathering more information about the client as a person. This also applies to choosing treatment options as well as the overall management of the client. Thus **formal assessment** of a client consists of taking in sufficient information for a **formal diagnosis**, identifying their condition from an exhaustive classificatory system, or at least narrowing this judgement to closely related conditions, where one of these may subsequently be eliminated by differential diagnosis. Information regarding the assessment data, diagnosis, treatment and other factors including prognosis (a judgement as to the future outcome for the client) will form part of the **formulation** for that client. The following sections will examine the development, process and limitations of these three aspects of client management in detail.

Reliability and validity in diagnosis and assessment

As recently as 1980, Anthony Clare regarded a diagnosis of a mental disorder as a hypothesis to be tested and refined, such is its inherently imprecise nature. A useful assessment and diagnosis of abnormal behaviour depends on a valid classificatory system of disorders, a reliable method of assessment and diagnosis, and a consensus among the professionals about their reliable use. The two concepts of reliability and **validity** are important in the clinical and forensic approaches to disorders.

Reliability

Reliability is where the same judgement, rating or test result occurs on different occasions, perhaps using different raters or judges (**inter-rater reliability**). Thus, a reliable psychological test should produce a very similar score when assessing the same client on different occasions (**test–retest reliability**), even if the assessment is administered by different psychologists. It is more difficult for two psychiatrists to diagnose the same disorder reliably in different clients in different countries, and achieving this level of reliability is one aim of the current classificatory systems such as DSM.

Validity

Validity refers to something genuinely representing what it claims to be. Thus, an assessment test of memory should give a measure of memory ability and not simply reflect general intelligence or some other ability. Validity of a diagnosis assumes that the disorder to be diagnosed represents a valid construct (i.e. the *constructed* measure), termed **construct validity**, which is far more difficult to ascertain than reliability. For example, to apply the label 'schizophrenia' correctly, there has to be a set of signs and symptoms reliably recognised across individuals, clinicians and cultures, but also the underlying disorder labelled 'schizophrenia' must be a valid construct distinguished from other disorders, which is an assumption that has often been challenged for this particular disorder (see Chapter 18).

Testing validity is difficult and will often require an alternative measure of the same construct to be available. An alternative measure is another instrument that purports to measure the same thing but by a different approach. Unfortunately, the alternative measure in this particular case could make the same correct or erroneous assumptions in reaching agreement. Thus the initial use of statistical procedures such as **discriminant function analysis** to identify consistent interrelationships between symptoms of abnormal behaviour tends to be greatly relied upon. If these interrelationships can then be related to other parameters of the construct, such as aetiology, treatment and outcome, the validity of the construct is strengthened but may never be certain (Gill, 2007).

There is an **asymmetrical relationship** between reliability and validity, in that you can have reliability without validity, but not validity without reliability. Thus a 'height test' that consists of weighing a client may produce repeatable results without ever being a valid measure of height. These two concepts have not always been the strongest features of the clinical approach to mental disorders, as these are weakly defined in objective terms. The author's own research has found **clinical judgement** of behaviour to be at odds with **systematic observation** of the same phenomena: for example, a clinician may consider a client to be avoiding eye contact, whereas direct observation from a video may reveal eye contact to be normal (Holmes, 1994). It would be rash to assume that either was the more valid approach, though both may prove to be reliable.

The development of a systematic approach and associated historical problems

Whilst the causes of death records were being formalised (see the International Perspective box), attempts were being made to classify mental disorders. Before the Munich psychiatrist **Emil Kraepelin** (1856–1926) produced a comprehensive classificatory system of mental conditions in 1898, there were numerous descriptions of disorders, but these were not well organised. They tended to be closely related to the historical concepts of mental disorder, such as **melancholia** (depression), **mania**, **hysteria**, **dementia** and an increasing number of **neurological disorders**. At this time, many professionals still considered some of these to be stages of the *same* disorder: that is, a depression followed by mania and resulting in dementia, conditions which had been treated by letting blood, as had been the historical method for most illnesses. Earlier in the nineteenth century, **Morel** identified the criteria for classifying disorders as being symptoms, course and outcome, but also included the aetiology of the disorder. The latter inclusion later became a source of professional conflict and, according to Jaspers (1959), eventually divided classificatory approaches into those inferring a cause and those maintaining a more descriptive approach, or **analysers versus describers**. Many would see this conflict as not in the client's best interest and a middle way as preferable (Clare, 1980). Thus, the history of psychiatric diagnosis was one of error and confusion until the turn of the nineteenth century, but during the twentieth century there was slowly emerging objectivity and reliability, owing much to the work of Kraepelin.

Although less popular classificatory systems were produced earlier in France and England, such as those that attempted to place all mental disorders under the categories of 'intellectual', 'emotional' and 'volitional', Kraepelin devised the most widely used and durable system. By 1913, Kraepelin's systematic description of mental disorders had been adopted in a number of countries. However, this was not universal and the use of different systems has caused a persistent lack of agreement between clinicians and

International perspective

Origins of diagnostic systems

Classificatory systems for medical conditions began with the statistical analysis of causes of death, such as the study of child mortality in London UK by **John Graunt** (1620–1674). **François Bossier de Lacroix** (1706–1777), also known as **Sauvages,** is thought to have produced the first systematic classification of diseases, **Nosologia methodica**, in Paris. This was superseded by **Synopsis nosologiae methodicae**, produced in 1785 in Glasgow by **William Cullen** (1710–1790). These systems were dependent on the limited medical knowledge of the time and evolved as the understanding of disease and disorder advanced.

The need for an internationally accepted system was fulfilled to a great degree, as there were always reluctant participants, by London medical statistician **William Farr** (1807–1883), later realised as the **International List of Causes of Death**, much of the credit for the development of which went to the Paris-based statistician **Jaques Bertillon** (1851–1922), possibly due to his position as Chief of Statistical Services of the City of Paris. The succeeding revisions of the International List of Causes of Death incorporated the causes of illness from 1938. Shortly after, under the responsibility of the Geneva-based World Health Organisation (WHO), the sixth revision in 1948, renamed the **International Statistical Classification of Diseases and Related Health Problems** (ICD), finally included mental disorders.

Thus the classificatory history of abnormal behaviour paralleled that of physical disease but received less organised international focus.

confounded research into mental health. Thus Kraepelin placed emphasis on the 'form' of abnormal behaviour, or objective description, and he was directly criticised for this, particularly by Laing (1965), who placed the emphasis on the 'content' of abnormal behaviour, or what is being communicated by the client. However, a focus on objective form led the way to more successful and standardised approaches to assessment, diagnosis and treatment.

Diagnostic and treatment decisions can only be as accurate as the information on which they are based. Thus the more thorough and accurate the data-gathering process, the greater the confidence in any categorisation or formulation for the individual case. Given the economic and temporal practicalities of professional contact with clients and specialist resource use, the assessment process that precedes any final diagnostic decision is a compromise between desired comprehensiveness and tolerated resource limitations.

Table 4.1 Areas covered in the assessment of a new client

- Physical examination
- History taking
- Mental state examination or standardised interview
- Clinical psychology report
- Social work report
- Probation report
- Forensic assessment

procedures are implemented to different degrees and give differing weightings to subjective judgement and objective tests. This aside, an assessment of a new client with pronounced symptoms should ideally include the procedures in Table 4.1.

The last two items in Table 4.1 are not always available but are viewed as increasingly important, as the use of DSM style checklists spreads, requiring **life stress** and **global functioning** information. The clinical psychology report or forensic assessment report may be the only inputs from psychologists. History and mental state are more often assessed by a **psychiatrist**, who will be responsible for the eventual diagnosis, but may also carry out routine items of the physical examination. However restricted the role of the clinical psychologist is in diagnosis, they should be aware of all aspects of assessment. Thus, each component of the assessment will be examined.

Self-test questions

- What is the relationship between assessment, diagnosis and formulation?
- Why are each of these necessary?
- What is the relationship between reliability and validity in tests?
- How can each be ascertained for a specific procedure?
- What were the difficulties faced in the past when making a psychiatric diagnosis?
- Why was a systematic approach to classification needed?

The assessment process

The historical difficulties in making an accurate and reliable diagnosis mean this decision must be supported by as much information as possible. The assessment process is where information is systematically gathered, and it tends to be more extensive than for physical illness due to the difficulties of psychiatric diagnosis in dealing with phenomena that are inferred from behaviour rather than seen. The breadth of the assessment will depend on whether the client has been seen before and the seriousness of their complaint. Although many texts present a **standardised assessment procedure**, in practice these guidelines and

Physical examination

The extent of the physical examination will depend on the client's age and apparent health, as these factors will carry their own symptoms, which may obscure those under examination. However, physical factors can be deceptively influential and it is better to err on the side of caution. Routine blood and urine tests may reveal physical disorders contributing to the client's current state, but also provide a check on **alcohol** and **drug intake**. Specific tests are carried out for known physical disorders that mimic psychiatric symptoms, such as **hyperthyroidism**, which mimics anxiety symptoms, in order to prevent misdiagnosis. **Autonomic nervous system measures**, such as blood pressure, will indicate arousal levels and point to psychologically influenced physical conditions such as **hypertension**. Assessment of general physical state and the presence of disease is important not only for their influence on the client's current psychological state, but also for judging their ability to withstand some treatments, such as ECT.

Research

Neurological assessment

Neurological investigations are divided into looking at the **hardware,** the actual physical parts of the brain, and the **software** or **soft signs** of brain function, i.e. inferring neurological problems from psychological and behavioural tests. Soft signs will be described under the clinical psychology report. **CAT scans** (see Chapter 3 for more detail of the scans in this paragraph) are used quite widely, as the equipment is based on multiple x-rays.

Although **NMR** (nuclear magnetic resonance) is safer in being non-invasive, it is more expensive. Along with the imaging of brain **activity** in techniques such as **PET scans** as well as **f-MRI,** NMR has only relatively recently become routinely used for the screening of clients. In another technological advance, **single photon emission tomography (SPET** or **SPECT)** is cheaper than PET and, despite lower-quality image production, has become commonly used in the clinical context. Some scans can reveal anatomical abnormalities and others poor or abnormal metabolism, which can impair cognitive function or even produce psychotic-type symptoms in otherwise normally functioning individuals.

The **electroencephalogram (EEG)** produces a graphical record of electrical activity near the surface of the brain, which can be detected at various points *on* the scalp. Patterns of activity characterise different mental states, and abnormalities can be used to *infer* neurological problems or detect disorders where electrical activity is disturbed, as in **epilepsy** where it makes the vital differentiation between **temporal lobe epilepsy** and psychosis. Some inherited traits, such as a susceptibility to alcohol tolerance, have been associated with abnormal **evoked potentials** (specific areas of electrical activity in response to external stimuli, such as movement across their area of vision).

An important part of the physical assessment is the **neurological examination**, which is essential in cases where neurological function may be implicated (see the Research box).

History taking

A full history needs to be taken when a client is first seen, and updated on subsequent occasions. Some of the client's history can be taken at the **psychiatric interview**, which has grown to be a very important part of the assessment process and as such has been more formally structured. During the interview, aspects of the client's **manner, presentation and attitude** may be noted, in addition to the actual answers to questions. The interview is intended to be exploratory, not simply to confirm initial presumptions about the client's disorder. Other details may more reliably be gained from relatives, documented records or other professionals, such as their **GP** or **social worker**. In each case, doubts about the credibility of the source are recorded at the time. This information can be vital in determining what may be causing or maintaining the client's symptoms. The areas of the client's history usually fall under the following headings.

- **History of the current illness.** Whilst establishing the duration, symptoms, effects and management of the disorder to date, the client is encouraged to disclose as much information as possible: for example, 'are there things that make the condition worse?'

- **Medical and psychiatric history.** Although medical records may supplement this history, it is helpful to get the client's account even if the illness or its treatment seems to have no bearing on the current disorder.

- **Family history** (e.g. parents and siblings). In addition to identifying family membership, deaths and disorders among members, the client's feelings and interactions with members are also explored.

- **Personal history.** This has various components that help to build a social and psychological picture of the client's life, with the following typical components.

  - **Childhood** – social and developmental problems in infant and childhood stages.

  - **School and education** – relations with teachers and peers as well as attainment.

  - **Occupation** – again, relations at work may be as important as success.

  - **Sex and marriage** – the ability to form and sustain relationships, including sexual ones.

  - **Forensic** – any criminal activity and what action resulted from this, as well as incidents that were not officially dealt with.

Additional personal information also includes resources, interests, activities and drug/alcohol intake.

- **Pre-morbid personality.** The client's social and personal functioning prior to the illness is sometimes difficult to assess and can bring into question the true point of onset. It is important to establish the *rate* of onset of a disorder as well as the change it produced.

- **Current living circumstances.** Ascertaining whom they live with, in what type of accommodation and whether there is friction, can help to build a cross-sectional snapshot of the client's current circumstances.

This information will inform other aspects of the assessment and there will also be areas of overlapping information. However, *conflict* between information sources could be important and worth pursuing, as one or other source may be based on misinformation.

The mental state examination

This is the main component of the **psychiatric interview** and can take up to an hour. As when taking a history, aspects of the client's behaviour during the interview are being observed and noted. These aspects observed by the clinician are **signs** of disorder (e.g. agitation), in contrast to **symptoms**, which are complaints that the client mentions (e.g. hearing voices). The clinician needs to take account of factors that may confound these observations, such as age, ethnic background or subcultural affiliations (e.g. member of a teenage gang). All such factors need to be separated from the effects of the disorder and the clinician needs to provide a full account and not brief comments in the notes taken. The content of the examination is grouped under the following headings and an absence of such activity is also noted.

- **General information.** This concerns the general appearance of the client, appropriateness of dress, grooming, movement and how they react to the interviewer.

- **Speech.** The quantity, continuity and speed of speech are noted, with special note for these being abnormal. There may be abnormal features of speech, such as rhyme or sudden change of topic; it may be incoherent or disconnected.

- **Thought.** This has to be inferred from speech. Abnormalities of thinking include loss of boundaries with others' thoughts (thoughts being 'shared', 'broadcast' or interfered with), disconnected thinking or thinking that returns obsessively to the same topic. Thoughts may be unduly pessimistic or wildly optimistic. **Delusions** (i.e. unshakeable irrational beliefs) may be presented.

- **Perception.** Abnormalities of perception may be reported, such as **hallucinations** – perceptual experiences that have no basis in reality. These should be distinguished from illusions, or misinterpretations of reality.

- **Mood.** Extremes of mood for the situation, inappropriate mood or sudden changes of mood are important signs. Abnormal autonomic nervous system activity may be inferred from anxious behaviour, sweating or evidence of obsessive–compulsive activity.

- **Cognitive (intellectual) function** is examined in these areas.

  - **Memory.** Short-term memory can be checked by **digit span tests** (testing recall for two 9-digit numbers). Long-term memory can be checked using their history information. Other graded tests can move from easy (who is the leader of your country?) to hard (name six scientists from your country).

  - **Attention and concentration.** Counting backwards in threes or fives usually reveals distraction.

  - **Orientation.** Establishing the client's awareness of where they are can be judged by graded questions, from 'what is the current time and what is the name of the place you are in?' to 'is it day or night?'

  - **Overall intelligence.** This is an estimate by the clinician, perhaps supported by the result of a formal IQ test.

  - **Abstract ability.** The ability to deal in abstract thought can be tested by asking the meaning of proverbs or poetic phrases.

- **Insight.** This is basically to establish that the client knows why they are being assessed, that they may be suffering from a disorder and that their symptoms are part of that disorder. Each of these can be directly questioned and the client's level of judgement rated by degree.

It is important to record the clinician's reaction to the client, a type of **reflexive analysis**, as this could consequently influence the client's attitude throughout the interview. There may be justification for the clinician's reaction to be noted and in forensic settings the clinician may be aware of, or overly sensitive to, threat or manipulation by the client.

Standardised interviews

Rather than relying on the clinician to question and observe the client in an unstructured way, an increasing number of structured questionnaires have been produced and tested for use when making these assessments. These assessment **instruments** have questions for both signs and symptoms, and usually require the clinician to rate each item on a scale of severity. In this way, the interview is standardised and a preliminary diagnosis can be derived by referring to a manual that suggests which specific items indicate the disorder in question. Well-established instruments, such as the Present State Examination (PSE), have long been analysed by use of computers. Computerised versions or assisted procedures of most assessment methods are available and many assessments and diagnostic instruments are currently developed only in computerised form, greatly speeding up many aspects of the process, especially the processing of ratings. The General Health Questionnaire (GHQ) has been developed for general medical patients to fill in themselves, and this enables the detection of psychiatric disorders. The major diagnostic and classificatory system, DSM-IV, has its own structured interview, the Structured Clinical Interview for DSM-IV (SCID).

These structured interviews aim to achieve a general screening of clients. Where a specific disorder is suspected, questionnaires have been devised which are dedicated to the symptoms of that disorder, and which are intended to measure the severity of the disorder. For example, **psychopathy** may be screened for, particularly in forensic settings for which the PCL (Psychopathy Checklist) has been reliably used by trained raters over a number of years and revisions (e.g. Hare, 2003). These instruments can be self-report questionnaires, such as the Beck Depression Inventory (BDI), or may require a clinician with training to carry out the ratings, as with the **Scale for the Assessment of Negative Symptoms (SANS)**. Standardised interviews and questionnaires have been used mostly for research, where high levels of reliability are necessary to produce controlled conditions between comparison groups, and these instruments have since spread to clinical practice and been used routinely as tools of the clinical psychologist's trade.

Clinical psychology report

Some minor complaints, such as a specific phobia, which are referred to a **clinical psychologist** (by a GP) may not warrant a full psychiatric assessment, which is a lengthy process. The assessment by the psychologist in this case would be specific to the complaint and lead to psychological treatment by a clinical psychologist as a hospital outpatient or by visits to a health centre. In the case of more serious or less easily identified disorders, the psychologist's assessment will be just one part of the assessment process.

The clinical psychologist has been historically associated with administering tests, and although they are now mostly involved in other procedures, testing is still a major area of expertise. Psychiatrists and neurologists may also administer such tests, but the clinical psychologist usually has more **psychometric** knowledge. This is partly because **psychological testing** is a specialist

area of psychology dealing with the construction, validation, correct administration and interpretation of tests. The standardised administration of tests and questionnaires is also a major part of the psychological assessment process, giving the psychologist greater experience of this process and the tests themselves.

The clinical psychologist's report (see Chapter 6) will contain the results of standardised tests, such as intelligence and personality tests, which can be **norm referenced**. Thus, the average scores will be available for groups of normal (the 'norm') and disturbed individuals to enable comparisons. There may also be data from observation of the client during interview or other information on their cognitive functioning. A clinical psychologist usually assesses the following aspects.

Intelligence

General intellectual functioning is represented by the **intelligence quotient** (**IQ**), an estimate based on a comparison with one's age group and which can be weighted for (i.e. can account for) other factors. The 'norm' is represented by a value of 100, so a score of 110 is above and one of 85 below the 'average intelligence' value represented by the norm. However, as many psychologists have struggled with the definition of 'intelligence', from Spearman (1904) to Gottfredson (1998), its definition usually falls back on the pragmatic but tautological definition of 'that which is sampled by an IQ test'. Some widely used tests, such as the Wechsler Adult Intelligence Scale (e.g. WAIS-III) (Wechsler, 1997a; 1997b) have been accused of being culturally biased, as they are in the language of the West and based on Western cultural symbols. Raven's Progressive Matrices claim to be a culture-free test of IQ as they are relatively language and symbolism free, using only pattern matching.

Personality

These tests have been divided into **projective** and **objective** types.

Projective tests assume that internal conflicts will be 'projected' into benign situations and are clearly dependent on the psychodynamic approach. The Rorschach ink blot test has been made famous through popular fiction and consists of a number of ambiguous 'ink blot' designs first produced by **Herman Rorschach** in 1912. The client's interpretations of these patterns are subject to complex analysis requiring dedicated training (Exner and Erdberg, 2005). The Thematic Apperception Test (TAT) is used in a similar manner, but consists of a series of pictures involving people interacting in various settings, for which there is no single clear interpretation. Established by **Murray** in 1935, the TAT interpretation is also subject to complex analysis (e.g. Weertman et al., 2006). Projective tests are poor in terms of reliability and validity, and as a consequence are infrequently used nowadays. They are often difficult to evaluate by research, requiring complex analyses that are subject to copyright, and they have outputs that are difficult to validate against other tests. Such techniques have sometimes been employed in a forensic setting when exploring the personalities of suspected serious offenders. However, their lack of objectivity and reliance on psychodynamic principles undermine their value in practice, although their image is disproportionately popular as a result of media representations of clinical and forensic examinations.

Objective personality tests are so called because they are subject to objective psychometric criteria in their construction, testing and subsequent use, and consequently have good reliability and validity values associated with them. However, it should be remembered that the tests themselves are usually self-report questionnaires and as such they cannot be truly objective in a scientific sense, as clients may give biased or false answers (though will not usually). The 90 or so question items in the Eysenck Personality Questionnaire (EPQ) provide measures along three dimensions of personality, described by **Hans Jürgen Eysenck** as **extraversion, neuroticism** and **psychoticism** (Eysenck and Eysenck, 1975), with the addition of a 'lie scale' to detect false self-reporting. More factors are assumed in the **16PF Questionnaire** by **Cattell** (Cattell, 1956), and as with Eysenck's scale, there are score ranges, which can be associated with abnormal functioning. The US-based **MMPI-2** (Minnesota Multiphasic Personality Inventory) is intended for clinical use, but *despite* its numerous subscales, it tends to indicate a general level of disturbance in clients rather than helping to identify specific disorders.

The unimaginatively titled '**Big Five**' approach (Goldberg, 1990) or the **five-factor model** (McCrae and Costa, 1999) has five traits derived from previous personality measures (neuroticism, extraversion, openness to experience, agreeableness and conscientiousness) and has grown rapidly in popularity since its inception. The questionnaire used for this model is the **NEO-PI** Five Factor Inventory (Costa and McCrae, 1992). **Personality disorders** can be detected by some of the above tests (e.g. the Big Five), but these usually require more specific tests for each personality disorder and a lengthy interview (2 hours) for diagnosis (see Chapter 14).

Specific area tests

The above personality and intelligence tests identify general areas of poor or abnormal function, whereas other tests target specific dysfunctions and abnormalities.

Observation methods

These involve the non-intrusive observation of the client's behaviour, usually in interaction with others. In practice, a specially designed room with a **two-way mirror** is used, behind which the observers (usually psychologists) sit with video and other recording equipment. Discussion and assessment may occur at the time, or standardised procedures may be used so that recordings can be systematically analysed later and perhaps compared with those of other individuals. These techniques are important in difficult cases, such as disturbed parents being assessed for their ability to care safely for their children. They may be routine in forensic cases where offenders may be observed in a variety of situations or even whilst being interviewed.

Research

Tests of specific functions

One specific area test is the **Maudsley Obsessional–Compulsive Inventory,** which assesses obsessive–compulsive behaviour and has sub-scales for such activities as checking or washing/cleaning. There are a large number of such questionnaires or checklist-based assessment instruments available for most disorders and even individual symptoms. For a critical review of a selection of these, see Peck and Shapiro (1990) in the suggested reading for this chapter.

Other specific area tests are used by psychologists to assess **soft signs** of neurological malfunction. In this, the psychological effects of neurological problems are measured and used to *infer* specific defects in the neurological 'hardware', such as damage to the hippocampus in memory function. Such neurological tests are often assembled into **test batteries** designed to screen for any existing and potential brain abnormality. The **Halstead–Reitan** and **Luria–Nebraska** test batteries are common examples of such instruments. Increasing numbers of clinical psychologists are employed in the area of **clinical neuropsychology,** some to limit the trauma and assist in the recovery of head-injured patients, but many to assess the functioning of clients in **old age psychiatry** units (see cognitive function tests above).

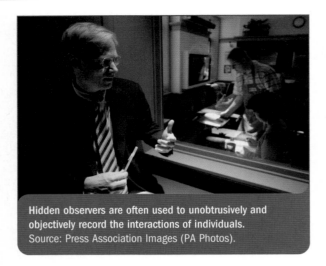

Hidden observers are often used to unobtrusively and objectively record the interactions of individuals.
Source: Press Association Images (PA Photos).

Cognitive assessments

These refer to assessments of the thinking styles of clients and should be distinguished from the current use of the term 'cognitive disorder' to refer to neurological dysfunction. The cognitive assessments carried out by clinical psychologists are usually linked to the use of cognitive therapy.

The clinical psychology report (see Chapter 6 and website) will summarise these assessments together with other test information such as memory function, which can provide more detail for the mental state examination.

The social work report

Social workers (usually **psychiatric social workers**) can assess the client's financial and other circumstances. In addition to a home assessment, the client's family may be interviewed to ascertain both their effect on the client and the client's effect on them. Social support is important when considering the client's ability to live at home. Social work reports are more important when a client is being assessed for discharge from inpatient care than at first admission.

Probation report

Probation officers or their equivalents in many countries originated as suitable persons to take over the supervision of minor and younger offenders discharged or diverted from prison. Over a number of reforms, this developed into a case-based therapeutic relationship as part of the

penal–welfare system to change the individual offender and avoid further offending (see Maguire, Morgan and Reiner, 2002, ch. 31). Probationers are often at the interface between prison and the outside world when offenders face financial occupational and domestic adjustment on release – factors that can precipitate **recidivism** (see Ward, Scott and Lacey, 2002). Probation officers assigned to an existing offender or disordered offender will contribute information such as lack of offending, educational support engagement, compliance with orders and occupational progress. This input is seen as important in assessing 'risk' in individuals (see below).

Forensic assessment

Forensic assessments often resemble and contain the same elements as clinical assessments and may be conducted by psychologists trained in clinical and/or forensic psychology, or forensic psychiatrists. They may be supplemented by information from or intervention by probation, police or agencies such as **Multi-Agency Public Protection Panels** (MAPPPs; see Chapter 8). Computer software has also been employed successfully to assist forensic assessment, as it has in other areas where decision making is based on a large number of variables. Specialist computerised assessments also open up the possibility for routine assessments to be carried out by officers without extensive professional training.

It is important to deal appropriately with disordered offenders or patients who offend, in order to avoid subverting their treatment at the expense of rehabilitation, or vice versa. This is not always a simple issue to resolve (Kiernan and Bailey, 1999) and the change of status between offender and patient can invoke differing laws and regulations in most countries. For example, should an individual in sheltered accommodation with mental impairment who has committed a minor offence have their condition taken as mitigation and not be prosecuted, or should they be treated as any other offender in order to maintain their progressive adjustment to the real world and not encourage dependency on their disability status? These are delicate issues and require individual case decisions rather than blanket guidelines.

In assessing offenders for release prior to completion of their sentence (i.e. on **parole**), or in the case of dangerous offenders (Walker, 1996) and mentally disordered offenders (Webb and Harris, 1999) prior to their release at any time, consideration has to be given to the likelihood of their re-offending or harming themselves and/or others. This assessment of the risk that an individual poses is an important part of forensic assessment.

Risk assessment

Humans tend to avoid uncertainty and will invent overly cautious practices to control risky possibilities such as sealed residential estates, even when that risk may be manufactured from unwarranted fears (Prins, 1999). This may be evident in dealing with the potentially dangerous behaviour of offenders, particularly mentally disordered offenders where a tendency towards overprotective responses is often fuelled by media amplification of danger as a result of excessive focus on sensational and fear-provoking crime (Smith, 1984). For example, the public fear being a homicide victim, which has only a 1/100,000 risk, but not catching flu, where the risk of death is greater at 1/5000. This media distortion of the public's inherently poor understanding of risk can in itself produce dangerous behaviour, as in the outbreaks of vigilantism in the UK in the 1990s directed against mis-identified 'paedophiles' (Thomas, 2000). The professional prediction of actual risk presented by an offender to others is termed risk assessment.

An over-cautious public will add to the pressure on those professionals who have the job of assessing the risk of danger to others presented by releasing an offender, particularly when the case may be complicated by psychiatric considerations. The decision as to whether an offender is safe to release is linked to the use of indeterminate sentences for offences that place the well-being of others at risk. These more recent indeterminate sentences (similar to the previous discretionary life sentences) for non-homicide, sexual and violent offences have similarities to and provide an alternative to the clinical psychiatric route used under mental health legislation (see the next section), in that the offender may be detained until they present no risk, inferring something paralleling 'treatment'.

Techniques employed to reduce risk in offenders are referred to as forms of **risk management**. Those factors associated with future risk can be divided into **predictors** and **causes** (Howitt, 2009). Predictors are non-causal correlates such as age or offending history, whereas causes are those factors that independently increase the risk of being a danger, such as genetic predisposition to impulsiveness or criminal peer groups. Some causal elements can be managed to reduce risk, but others, such as genetics, can currently only be moderated indirectly (e.g. impulsive behaviour training). A number of methods of risk management have been established as immediately useful but not changing the client's long-term behaviour, such as pharmacological control or controlled environments (e.g. video surveillance). Other interventions, such as anger management training, may reduce long-term risk in individuals.

Those individuals still perceived as presenting some level of danger on release or who have not been institutionalised may be placed on a **register**, either as a general risk or for a specific risk (e.g. sex offenders). This invokes the problem of stigma and also public opposition of the NIMBY (not in my back yard) or even vigilante forms. However, it eases administration of offenders in the community and provides responsible professionals with some form of protection should there be reoffending (Prins, 1999). This can lead to overenthusiastic registration of potential offenders in order to cover one's 'professional back', creating an illusion that the problem of risk is being addressed. However, such form-filling exercises per se cannot address the realities of posing a danger to others, but can become an exercise in 'being seen to address the problem' (Inch, Rowlands and Solomon, 1995). Some professionals emphasise the importance of preventative interventions during the early life of the offender to reduce later risk, particularly where predictive risk factors have been identified by epidemiological studies (Bailey, 1999).

As already referred to, offenders who are deemed a danger to the public and have a psychiatric diagnosis can be diverted to mental health provision, which can change the regulations governing their keep and progressive discharge. As Prins (2005) points out, this diversion process has frequently failed in the past, resulting in many disordered offenders being inappropriately held in penal institutions who should never have entered the prison system in the first place. It can also change the status of the person detained in a significant manner: for example, the diagnosis of the 1960s UK 'moors murderer' Ian Brady as psychopathic placed him within mental health care regulations, preventing him from starving himself to death, which would not have been the case had he been under routine prison regulations at the time.

Thus risk assessment is not confined to offenders or mentally disordered offenders; non-offending patients with mental disorder may still pose a risk to themselves or others and are likely to be dealt with under mental health legislation. Most countries in the world have some form of legislation and provision to compel institutionalisation and treatment of those patients thought to be a danger to themselves and/or others. The following sections describe the example of UK (primarily England and Wales) legislation that has been used during the twentieth century and its recent controversial revision.

Patients and risk: the UK Mental Health Acts

One tragic consequence of mental disorder occurs when a patient loses **insight** into his or her own condition. This usually indicates a **psychotic state** (see Chapter 18), in which the patient has lost contact with reality, but it may simply indicate that they do not recognise their own behaviour as being abnormal or harmful. Other individuals may have disorders that make them likely to be a danger to others, such as some paraphilias (see Chapter 13) or **personality disorders** (see Chapter 14), particularly the current category of DSPD or **dangerous and severe personality disorder** (see Bowers, 2002). When such individuals can be a danger to themselves or others and refuse to be voluntarily admitted or treated, most countries have laws to enforce these procedures. In the first half of the twentieth century, most patients were 'involuntarily committed', but due to various advances in treatment and education, fewer than 10 per cent of psychiatric patients are currently held under legal orders.

As such legal restraint only applies to mental and not physical illness, moral issues tend to be raised as well as legal difficulties. To illustrate this moral dilemma, consider a fictitious but comparable situation. What would be the reaction to a 'compulsory surgery order', where someone at risk of heart problems is taken into hospital under legal restraint and operated on 'in their own interest'? Outrage is a probable reaction, and such a patient would be unlikely to tolerate the conditions in which psychiatric

patients often find themselves. This differential treatment may be a legacy from the past, but it may equally reflect the very different behaviour and attitudes that are experienced by the two groups of patients. Legal difficulties arise from the rigid nature of legislation and the infinite variability of human behaviour. This mismatch is generally resolved by relying on the expertise of professionals such as psychiatrists, increasingly on approved (psychiatric) social workers and in many countries on specially appointed panels or tribunals. The shift in responsibility from a few individuals has partly been fuelled by accusations of abuse of such powers over a patient's liberty (see the Focus box).

In England and Wales the **1983 Mental Health Act** and its subsequent revisions, such as the 2006 Mental Health Bill, provided for involuntary commitment and treatment in the case of **mental illness**, **levels of mental impairment**, **psychopathic disorder** or DSPD (see Chapter 8). In the case of alcohol or drugs, intoxication was insufficient: there had to be additional mental disturbance as a consequence of use (e.g. amphetamine psychosis). The disorder had to be of a nature that requires inpatient treatment, and in the case of less severe or longer-term disorders (e.g. psychopathy or DSPD), treatment was expected to alleviate or prevent deterioration of the condition, though this was a

Focus

Roles involved in applying the 1983 Mental Health Act

Some of the individuals involved in the process of implementing sections of the Mental Health Act are as follows.

- **Relatives** can initiate the process of **compulsory admission** and can qualify to sign the necessary forms. It is the nearest relative (in familial terms) who usually carries this responsibility.

- **Psychiatrists** qualify as having approved status as doctors and their signatures are usually needed for assessment and treatment orders. They are increasingly being required to assess **risk** (of harm to self or others).

- **General practitioners (GPs)** often provide the second doctor's signature (though other medical doctors can do this). The GP is often involved, as they are usually the 'first port of call' for patients or their relatives.

- **The police** are increasingly being involved in supporting psychiatrists and social workers in the compulsory admission process. In England and Wales they have their own powers of detainment under section 136 of the **Mental Health Act (MHA)** (see below).

- **Approved social workers (ASW)** have specific powers of assessing whether an individual should or should not be admitted, for which they have special training.

- **A registered psychiatric nurse** has some powers of restraint over voluntary inpatients under section 5(4) of the MHA.

- **The** Mental Health Review Tribunal is a case reviewing body consisting of a legal professional, an independent psychiatrist and a lay individual. A detained patient may appeal to the tribunal within a specified time period to have their detention reviewed. The tribunal may discharge the patient if it agrees their detention is no longer necessary, sometimes with **conditions** (e.g. outpatient attendance) and if the patient is a prisoner they may be discharged back to prison. Wood (1993) has critically reviewed the effectiveness of the tribunal system and it has been subsequently modified but remains in place under current mental health provision.

moot point in the 2008 revision of the UK Mental Health Act. The various powers and the circumstances for their use were detailed in specific **sections** of the 1983 Act. Reference to these sections of the Act resulted in the common use of the term **sectioning**, meaning involuntary detention. Some of the 1983 sections that referred to commitment and treatment are listed below.

- **Section 2.** This is an **assessment order** allowing detention in a suitable place for up to 28 days. It requires the signatures of two doctors (one of these must be approved under section 12 of the Act) and the nearest relative (who also has the right to oppose an order) or an approved social worker (ASW), who will normally have made the initial application.

- **Section 3.** This section is a **treatment order** also requiring the signatures of one approved and one other doctor and supported by the nearest relative or ASW. This order can last for 6 months in the first instance (renewable), allowing the patient to be both detained in an appropriate place and treated.

- **Section 4.** This is used as an **emergency admission order** allowing detention for 72 hours without right of appeal. It is applied for by the nearest relative or social worker and requires the signature of just one doctor who has recently seen the patient. This section is rarely used independently but is usually an interim measure while waiting for a section 2 order.

- **Section 5(2)** is an **admission order** signed by the doctor in charge of the patient within a hospital to retain them for 72 hours.

- **Section 5(4)** is a **holding order** that can be signed by a psychiatric nurse to retain a hospitalised patient for 6 hours.

- **Section 37** is a **hospital order** that normally requires the signatures of two doctors and magistrates or Crown Court sanction. This is a 6-month order that will often require secure confinement.

- **Section 41** is a **restriction order** allowing an indefinite detention and must be signed by a Crown Court judge.

- **Section 136** allows a **police officer** to detain a disordered individual found in a public place for 72 hours.

All aspects of this Act and its replacement are under supervision by the **Mental Health Act Commission**.

UK Mental Health Act revision 2008

Many countries struggle with the compromises involved in both protecting the public and maintaining the human rights and fair treatment of those patients and offenders who may pose a threat (see Prins, 2005). In the UK, a revision of the above 1983 Mental Health Act began with a green paper in the form of the **2006 Mental Health Bill**, following the highly controversial draft Mental Health Bill of 2002 (Zigmond, 2004). Although some health professionals have supported the principles included within the Act, many have voiced reservations with regard to the relative ease with which an individual could be detained without committing any offence but merely by being a potential threat (Zigmond, 2004). This hints at prophylactic detention: that is, incarceration in order to prevent an offence prior to it being committed, a moral dilemma illustrated in the film *Minority Report* (Spielberg, 2002). During the period of controversy over the UK bill, the Mental Health (Care and Treatment) (Scotland) Act 2003 was passed, which was seen as a better reform due to its not being used as a vehicle for government departments overly concerned with locking up dangerous offenders at the expense of mental health care (Darjee and Crichton, 2004). This approach to the management of dangerous offenders and patients has been referred to as a new culture of control (Easton and Piper, 2005).

Further arguments were provoked by the loose definition of 'treatment' in drafts of the bill and how such treatment could be administered by what is very broadly defined as an acceptable professional (Kinderman, 2002). This provoked speculation that if a non-medical professional such as a life coach could be thought to treat the offender, the process could be sanctioned by bodies that no longer had the inclusion of medical membership as a requirement. The removal of specifics and limitations also caused unease, with a broadening of what could be considered a mental disorder, which no longer had to impair judgement or decision making, and treatment that no longer had to be in the best interest of the client. The rights of relatives and approved social workers in the treatment order process were reduced or removed and yet almost anyone was allowed to request a compulsion order (Zigmond, 2004). During the development of the revision to the Mental Health Act, many of these points were opposed and arguments put forward as to how such apparently unrestricted abilities to restrain individuals distanced the UK from other European countries.

The Mental Health Bill 2006 came into force in 2008 as a revision of the 1983 Mental Health Act in modified form. Some of the more controversial aspects had been further considered but others remain, albeit in latent form, and the concept of prophylactic detention is amongst these. The diagnosis of certain disorders such as DSPD can have even greater forensic implications for the individual than under previous legislation, in terms of preventative detention. Thus in addition to specific forensic assessment instruments (e.g. the Psychopathy Checklist Revised; (**PCL-R**) Hare, 2003), the precision of classificatory systems has now become an important forensic as well as clinical consideration. See Chapter 8 for discussion of the UK mental health revision in a clinical forensic context.

Self-test questions

- What are the main features of the assessment process?
- Why is the concept of risk important to forensic assessment?
- Why is assessment so lengthy and detailed?
- What issues confound mental health legislation?

Diagnosis: *DSM* and *ICD* systems

The development of the current classificatory systems

In 1948, the Geneva-based WHO published an edition of its International Classification of Diseases (*ICD*) (see above how this was originally titled in full: *International Statistical Classification of Diseases, Injuries and Causes of Death*), containing a complete listing of mental disorders. This listing still retained many of Kraepelin's categories. Shortly after in the USA, the **American Psychiatric Association** produced the first edition of the Diagnostic and Statistical Manual (*DSM*) in 1952. There have since been many revisions and new editions of both systems, the *DSM* being in its fourth edition and the *ICD* in its tenth. Statistical procedures such as **cluster analysis** are used to refine symptom groupings and determine the boundaries of disorders. At each revision some efforts have been made to bring what are by far the most widely accepted systems in line with one another. However, the *ICD* has tended to be a listing of disorders with some inference as to causes, with the *DSM* aiming more towards detailed, somewhat pedantic descriptions of symptom criteria. The development of these instruments did not end the difficulties of diagnosis, even though clinicians may have been using the same listings or even working in the same hospital.

For Feinstein (1967), clinical judgement depended on 'patient knowledge' not classificatory systems, which highlights the clinician's reliance on their own subjective judgement in the diagnostic process. Such variable judgements led to a difference in the diagnosis of schizophrenia *within the same hospital* of between 22 and 60 per cent (Passamanick, Dinitz and Lefton, 1959). In 1973, **Rosenhan** published a report in which he and seven others presented themselves at 12 mental hospitals in the USA. They each complained of one symptom, hearing voices, and most were admitted for an average of 19 days with a preliminary diagnosis of schizophrenia. However, their 'voices' were not of the type found in schizophrenia and following admission they behaved normally (e.g. those who were researchers took notes), these activities being recorded as 'behavioural signs' by hospital staff. Rosenhan used this to argue that if schizophrenia cannot be reliably diagnosed, then perhaps the category is invalid (see Chapter 18). It could also be argued that the hospitals were being correctly cautious in making the type one (i.e. false positive) error of admitting 'fakes' rather than turning potentially genuine patients away, or type two error (false negative). Would their scheme have worked in England? As Clare (1980) points out, the rate of diagnosis of schizophrenia at the time was about three times greater in the USA than in England. Despite the counter-arguments, diagnostic agreement was not one of psychiatry's strengths before the 1980s.

Syndromes such as schizophrenia achieved notoriety during the 1960s and 1970s due to the different forms of the disorder and varying symptoms in individual cases. This was also a time when studies critical of the diagnostic process were being publicised (e.g. Rosenhan, 1973; Passamanick, Dinitz and Lefton, 1959). If disorders were not consistent, how can diagnosis be consistent? These discrepancies became a focus for the anti-psychiatry movement (see Chapter 2), which used such weaknesses to discredit the medical approach in psychiatry, including the *ICD* and *DSM* classificatory approaches. The *DSM* approach was deliberately descriptive and, as with Kraepelin's view, avoided the subjective experience of the client. This was seen as a weakness by opponents of the medical model, in reducing the world of the client to one of description or form without regard for content or meaning, the latter being of most concern to the client.

Avoiding such criticism required the standard and consistency of diagnosis to improve. To achieve this, the *DSM* incorporated even *more* detailed description, devoid of inferred aetiology. These descriptive diagnostic criteria have been supplemented in literature by more illustrative descriptions of psychopathology, such as Mayer-Gross,

Slater and Roth (1969). Although not perfect, the wider use of the *ICD* and *DSM* improved agreement between professionals and encouraged collaborative research, even between countries. In 1960 Kessel reduced the number of potential psychiatric cases from 520 to 50 from a sample of 1000 presenting patients by applying the *ICD* system. However, such discrimination between cases could also indicate that *validity* is partly being sacrificed for *reliability* and that this may have inadvertently been the way forward for diagnosis and classification towards the end of the twentieth century.

The limitations of the current classificatory systems

The rather lengthy assessment process described earlier is far more extensive than would be considered for physical illness. Despite the extra information, a psychiatric diagnosis is still less certain than that made in general medicine. The problems of past diagnostic procedures described earlier have illustrated some of the difficulties involved. However, some difficulties are inherent in the nature of psychiatric disorders and the limitations of the human judgements made. The inconsistency of symptoms presented in schizophrenia has been mentioned, but even more 'programmed' disorders such as the genetically based **Huntington's chorea** occasionally present widely varying symptoms. Most psychiatric departments keep training videos, showing clients with various disorders or illustrating individual symptoms. Even with training, these examples present a challenge to professionals, and for the student of abnormal, clinical and forensic psychology they could clearly demonstrate the difficulty of translating textbook descriptions of symptoms into the continuous and variable behaviour of disordered individuals.

The diagnostic process is one of pushing ideopathic (i.e. individualistic) behaviour into nomothetic (i.e. law giving across individuals) categories: that is, assigning individual behaviour patterns to fixed classifications of behaviour common to all in that category. Even if the causes of a disorder were the same in each case, the physical and psychological differences between individuals can produce unique reactions to those same causes. In addition, many psychiatric disorders are syndromes in having a range of possible symptoms, a selection of which may be presented by an individual client, but none of which occurs in every case. The boundaries between disorders can also overlap considerably (see personality disorders for an example of this), requiring a **differential diagnosis** to examine on which side of the boundary the particular case lies.

There are other factors that can confound the diagnostic procedure. The effects of medication or self-medication (i.e. alcohol or other drugs) distort behaviour, as do the long-term effects of institutionalisation or impoverished environments.

With all these difficulties, making an accurate diagnosis requires skilled training and knowledge of clients, and is dependent on the extensive information gained from client assessment. Further implications when making a diagnosis placing pressure on the psychiatrist are as follows.

- Labelling refers to the effects of attaching a label such as 'schizophrenic' to an individual. The stigma that some diagnoses can bring depends on the unsympathetic reaction of others in seeing the label as a reason for prejudice and discrimination. The sociological view has also described secondary labelling, where the labelled individual accepts the label and associated discrimination and begins to act in accord with these expectations. For these reasons alone, a diagnosis is given only if the psychiatrist is reasonably certain of their judgement.

- **Legal and financial** implications of a diagnosis also place pressure on the clinician. In the USA and some other countries, health insurance payments may be appropriate for one diagnosis but not another. A particular diagnosis may also make the difference between a severe prison sentence (or the death penalty) and treatment in a secure hospital for a person on trial for a serious offence. A psychiatrist needs to be able to recognise the very real pressures placed on them to make a diagnosis for other than sound clinical reasons.

- **Treatment** implications often follow a diagnosis. The treatment for some disorders may be inappropriate or even damaging if applied to another disorder in the case of an incorrect diagnosis. For the same reason, necessary treatment may not be given.

- **Prognosis** (i.e. expected future outcome) tends to vary greatly depending on the disorder present. A client's reaction to a bleak prognosis may be understandably negative and it may affect their progress or even result in suicide. With such serious implications, some diagnoses are not made lightly.

- **Professional agreement and research.** Without close agreement between professionals over the criteria for diagnosing different disorders, professional communication between them would be confounded by their terminology having a different interpretation, especially between cultures. The situation for research is more crucial as the agreement needed is more exacting. For this reason, more stringent standardised criteria may be used, such as the **Research Diagnostic Criteria** (Spitzer, Endicott and Robins, 1978) when making diagnoses for experimental comparisons.

Thus the combined pressures on psychiatrists to produce a reliable and valid diagnosis lead them to seek all possible assistance and support. In addition to assessment information, extensively researched classificatory systems are available to the clinician.

As described earlier, the major diagnostic and classificatory systems for mental disorders are the US-based *Diagnostic and Statistical Manual*, currently in its fourth text revised edition or *DSM-IV-TR* (American Psychiatric Association, 2000), and the Geneva-based *International Classification of Diseases*, currently in its tenth edition or *ICD-10* (World Health Organisation, 1992). These are both geared towards providing a comprehensive set of disorder classifications with unambiguous criteria for their diagnosis.

The *ICD* system

The fifth chapter of the *ICD-10* contains a listing of 458 types of mental disorder, some of which are discrete disorders and others sub-types of more major psychiatric disorders. As with the DSM, it is a multi-axial system (see below). The ICD is sometimes referred to as the 'F' scale, simply due to this letter being the prefix for the numbering of the disorders. There are ten major categories of disorders as follows.

- **Organic, including symptomatic, mental disorders** – types of dementia and delirium.

- **Mental and behavioural disorders due to psychoactive substance use** – alcohol and other substance use, and associated disorders.

- **Schizophrenia, schizotypal and delusional disorders** – types of schizophrenia and disorders with similar symptoms.

- **Mood disorders** – types of depression and mania, and mixtures of these.

- **Neurotic, stress-related and somatoform disorders** – types of phobias (fears), anxiety problems and maladaptive reactions to stress, such as physical complaints or psychological attempts to escape.

- **Behavioural syndromes associated with physiological disturbances and physical factors** – disorders of natural functions, such as eating, sleeping and sex, of psychological origin.

- **Abnormalities of adult personality and behaviour** – distortions of personality, and impulse control disorders, sexual identity and preference problems.

- **Mental retardation** – degrees of learning disability.

- **Disorders of psychological development** – difficulties with language and scholastic skills, and pervasive developmental disorders (e.g. autism).

- **Behavioural and emotional disorders with onset usually occurring in childhood and adolescence** – behavioural disturbances, problems with early relationships and social functioning, and forms of tic disorders, stammering and bedwetting/soiling.

Both *ICD* and *DSM* systems have **unspecified** or **not otherwise specified** classifications at the end of each listing for cases that do not conform to specified categories but have the general characteristics of that grouping. Some see these as a great weakness in the exhaustiveness of the systems. Others view them as necessary to help prevent clinicians 'forcing' such cases into the existing categories.

The *ICD* system is descriptive but retains some inference as to the **aetiology** (or causes) of the disorders. For example, the term **neurotic** has been retained although it has vanished from the *DSM* system. There have been many studies researching and checking the validity of both *ICD* and *DSM* systems. The *ICD* system is the major system in the UK and much of Europe. However, the *DSM* system is more prevalent in the (mostly US) literature, and thus may be more familiar to the reader, as mentioned in Chapter 1. In large-scale research, Sartorius et al. (1995) found a high degree of agreement between *DSM-IV* and the *Diagnostic Criteria for Research* for the current ICD system, *ICD-10-DCR*.

Diagnostic systems such as the *ICD* are translated for use across the world, such as the German edition of *ICD-10* translated by the Deutsches Institut für medizinische Dokumentation und Information in 1994. The wide international distribution of classificatory systems increases global standardisation, which aids a universal language in research and treatment criteria. However, this is at the cost of local specialist requirements and population variations in the presentation of abnormal behaviour (Graubner and Brenner, 1999). The *ICD* system is also adapted for use in the USA with additional morbidity data by the National Center for Health Statistics. This is referred to as *ICD* 'clinical modification' or *ICD-CM*, the latest version of which is *ICD-10-CM*.

The *DSM* system

The *DSM* system differs from the *ICD* system in that greater effort has been made to remove inference of aetiology, leaving a highly descriptive set of **operational criteria** for diagnosis. For Compton and Guze (1995) the current revisions of both systems represent a welcome move away from **psychodynamic** terms and inferences that no longer hold credibility in mainstream psychiatry, towards a more phenomenological description reminiscent of **Kraepelin**. In short, they have become more descriptive, though this process is more pronounced with the *DSM-IV* and *DSM-IV-TR* (i.e. *DSM-IV* 'text revision') (American Psychiatric Association, 2000). The *DSM* system has tended to acknowledge new disorders quickly and provides an extensive list seeming to cover every eventuality in diagnosis. Preskorn (1995) has criticised such an approach for 'creating' new illness categories before current ones are fully understood.

The *DSM-IV-TR* is a **multi-axial** system with five 'axes'. Each client is rated on each of these separate axes (independent scales or dimensions) in order to give a full picture of the individual's pathology and functioning in different areas. This encourages the clinician to consider the possibility of comorbidity, which is the presence of more than one disorder in the same individual at one time. Comorbidity usually takes the form of one diagnosed disorder against a background of an enduring state such as a pervasive developmental disorder or personality disorder. The five axes of the DSM-IV-TR are described in Table 4.2.

Despite the efforts of many professionals to produce the fourth edition of the *DSM*, some critics such as

Follette and Houts (1996) claim that little has fundamentally changed beyond clarification of terms and that early problems with reliability of earlier *DSM*-derived diagnoses remain. Lewis (1994) has criticised both systems for retaining the 'organic disorders' division, implying that all other disorders are 'non-organic', which is far from the case and therefore misleading. In producing the latest editions of the *DSM* and *ICD* systems, deliberate efforts have been made to bring them into line with one another to aid diagnostic agreement.

Future editions of the *DSM* are intended to bring *ICD* and *DSM* closer still, particularly if *ICD10-CM* is considered as part this comparison. The anticipated period between *DSM-IV* and *DSM-V* has been so long (*DSM-V* is anticipated around 2010) that *DSM-IV-TR* was produced in 2000. This text revision simply bridges this gap by updating the *DSM* with more recent research and correcting errors, but updating the *DSM-IV* may reinforce this older structure and may inhibit radical change. Thus, although the gap between *DSM-IV* and *DSM-V* was sufficient to allow a great deal of *DSM* and *ICD* convergence, the lack of radical interim change in *DSM-IV-TR* may have inhibited this potential. However, the degree of criteria from one system being used to support another system or 'crosswalk' (Lehmann, 2004), mostly between *DSM-IV* and *ICD-10-CM* (in brief, see Bertelsen, 2004), may be an increasing tendency and could be taken as an indicator of greater uniformity and acceptance of system interdependence in the future. The possibility of a future common international system may still be some time away and, in the opinion of this author, is somewhat inhibited by the many bodies and individuals with a vested interest in the continued existence of individual systems.

Table 4.2 The axes of the *DSM-IV-TR*

- **Axis I** is a listing of most of the clinical syndromes with their diagnostic criteria, disorders such as schizophrenia and anxiety disorders.

- **Axis II** contains those conditions which are considered permanent states, mainly personality disorders and mental retardation.

- **Axis III** provides a list of general medical conditions that may co-occur with and influence mental disorders.

- **Axis IV** is a checklist of environmental and psychosocial stressors, which are considered in order of severity of effect.

- **Axis V** is a rating scale called the **Global Assessment of Functioning scale (GAF scale),** giving the client's current ability to function and cope with life. The range extends from superior ability to imminent danger to self and others.

The importance of the individual: the formulation

The formulation is a method of integrating the comprehensive data required to treat a particular individual and predict the outcome for the case. Clearly there must be *sufficient* data to provide appropriate treatment and a realistic prognosis. The term 'nomothetic' is used to describe the diagnostic process involved in 'pigeonholing' a client in a particular classificatory category by which the client conforms to the general 'laws' of that classification. The formulation has a more ideographic approach in providing a fuller prescriptive description of the unique case in hand (see the Focus box).

Focus

Example formulation format

A possible format for the formulation may be given by the following headings (see Goldberg, Benjamin and Creed, 1994).

- **Demographic data** includes such information as marital status, age and employment.

- **Descriptive formulation** contains a description of the client's admission and examination, including the salient features, and the circumstances surrounding it.

- **Differential diagnosis** will cover the possible alternative diagnoses that could account for the signs and symptoms present, with some evaluation of their relative appropriateness. Consideration can be given to overlapping disorders and comorbidity.

- **Aetiology.** Different aspects of possible causation can be examined here. Factors **predisposing** the individual to the condition can be considered, such

as family inheritance. **Precipitating** factors, such as significant events during the premorbid period (the period before the onset of symptoms), can add to this picture. It is also important to explore the possibility that there may be factors **maintaining** the condition, such as substance use or stress.

- **Investigations.** These include relevant information from various sources, such as medical reports and observation of behaviour as an in-patient or reports from relatives and friends.

- **Treatment.** An important part of the formulation is the recommended type and approach to treatment. Physical and psychological approaches can be considered separately.

- **Prognosis.** This is another important section, which should examine the factors pointing to good and poor outcomes for this particular client.

As can be seen from the Focus box, the formulation is not simply a case history or diagnosis; it contains information and recommendations that are helpful to those professionals involved with the management of the individual case.

Critical evaluation

The origins and incarnations of assessment, classification and diagnosis methods have been driven by necessity. They are essential for any organised and systematic approach to effectively managing and researching abnormal behaviour. Research and technical advances have improved both the instruments and methods of assessment as well as the process and implementation of diagnostic classificatory systems. The progressive process of establishing greater commonality between the major classificatory systems (i.e. the *ICD* and *DSM*) has enabled greater validation of the more closely shared disorder concepts and pooling of reliability and other research data.

Few outside of the anti-psychiatry school would argue with the need for the existence of classificatory and assessment tools, but many criticise the methods, criteria and even conceptual approaches used (Cooper, 2004; Jablensky, 2005). Meehl (1999) describes the statistical procedure for determining whether relationships among observables reflect the existence of a latent taxon (e.g. a disorder category),

which is termed **taxometrics**. It is useful having a mathematical rationale for determining what critics think of as some form of arbitrary psychiatric judgement. Such procedures help where commonsense methods of distinguishing disorders from one another fail. Such taxa in general medicine are rarely the subject of argument (i.e. a tumour is unquestionably distinct from a bacterial infection), but in psychiatry, groups such as the anti-psychiatry and critical psychiatry movements rather nihilistically oppose *any* form of taxonomy. Others oppose the categorical system but with a less philosophical and rather more practical argument. Despite the indecision over treatment implications that abandoning the categorical boundaries may imply, a further approach to the quantification of disorders could be implemented: that of the **dimensional approach** (Meehl, 1999).

Categorical versus dimensional approaches to classification and diagnosis

The implied existence of boundaries in the conceptualisation and classification of mental disorders is a subject of heated contemporary debate (Jablensky, 2005). This centres on there being a fixed dividing line between disorders as well as between disorder and normality. Many support the dichotomous view of the border between normality and abnormality as being indeterminate. These approaches are often based on latent anti-psychiatry assumptions that undermine the entire medical labelling approach. Bennett (2006) uses auditory hallucinations as an example of a symptom that occurs in the normal population without a diagnosis of schizophrenia. In the present author's experience, cases of persistent pronounced hallucinations do warrant a diagnosis, despite the ability of some individuals to cope and evade the criterion of 'suffering of self' in defining abnormality. However, the humanitarian argument of treating the person as an individual (as formulations attempt in a standardised way) rather than 'treating the specific diagnosis' is also relevant to this debate. Thus the assumed boundaries between different disorders as well as that distinguishing abnormality are also open to argument.

Fundamentally, current classificatory systems are based on this assumption of discrete disorder categories and focus their criteria on making the judgement as to the absence or presence and type of disorder. Although *DSM-IV-TR* states in its introduction that these criteria are to be used not in a 'cookbook' manner but in conjunction with professional clinical judgement, it also goes on to state that this flexibility should not be so loose as to undermine the criteria for classification (American Psychiatric Association, 2000: p. xxxii). Thus these artificial 'boundary' lines have been reinforced and agreed by an assumed consensus in order to make reliable diagnoses and apply valid treatments. Without this standardised approach and assumptions of disorder types, the resources required for treating individuals would be astronomical, unregulated and lacking in research.

This process of 'carving nature at the joints' (Cooper, 2004; Meehl, 1999) for the sake of standardisation of disorders and treatment may bring into question whether the artificial boundaries thus created also create 'artificial disorders', as many clients present with symptoms that fulfil several disorder criteria simultaneously (Goldberg, 1996; Cooper, 2004). Gill (2007) points out that within the *DSM* and *ICD* systems there are 'crossover' categories, such as schizoaffective disorder, and 'default classifications', such as *DSM*'s 'disorder not otherwise specified', indicating some admission of unclear boundaries between disorders. In countries with private health care systems backed by insurers (e.g. the USA), such a default diagnosis may invalidate the client's funding for care.

Goldberg (1996; 2000) proposed a dimensional system with symptoms rated separately. Such a profile would be more useful than the categorical approach, particularly in relating anxiety to depression. Thus, in a **categorical system** you would have either anxiety disorder *or* depression, but in a dimensional system you could have a profile with a high score on anxiety symptoms, yet also have a high score on depressive symptoms in the same diagnosis. In practice, dimensional systems have limitations that in order for the client to receive a specific treatment a specified set of criteria need to be in place, which will still be identical conceptually to a category, even if derived from dimensional scores. However, in statistical terms a dimensional profile would contain far more specific information on an individual, which would mostly be lost if merely used to decide between two categories. This was to some degree found in practice when using multidimensional criteria for the diagnosis of depression (Angst and Merikangas, 2001).

Jablensky (2005) has argued that a further diagnostic boundary (i.e. that between categorical and dimensional approaches) is also spurious and that research should be directed towards resolving a merging of the conceptual approaches rather than somewhat limited arguments for an either-or approach. Cooper (2004) argues that categorical disorders and conditions in the *DSM* system do not clearly distinguish themselves from factors outside of the *DSM* system (e.g. poverty). Further critical approaches argue for the abandonment of these ultimately construct-based approaches and propose a piecemeal 'problem-based' approach to treatment rather than the more conceptual 'disease-based' approach (Barraclough and Gill, 1996).

The approaches to the assessment and diagnosis of abnormal behaviour are clearly subject to argument and ongoing professional debate. However, radical change amongst the sheer number of professionals, clients, and professional and legislative bodies involved, provokes the analogy of an ocean liner trying to turn around on a coin. Clearly, universal dependency and continuity of care will mean that change as a result of professional critical concern will take many years of progressive reform to implement.

Self-test questions

- How do the *ICD* and *DSM* systems compare?
- What is meant by a dimensional system?
- Why is international agreement for classification so important?
- How does the formulation differ from other case information?
- What is a prognosis?
- What would be the attributes of a successful dimensional system for mental disorders?
- What is meant by the metaphor 'carving nature at the joints' and why do some critics oppose this?

Chapter summary

Key concepts in assessment are **reliability** and **validity**, the repeatable and genuine measurement of human attributes. The history of psychiatric diagnosis and assessment is one where reliability and validity have been poor, even after the errors in **Kraepelin**'s comprehensive classification of mental disorders have been revealed by studies. As classificatory and diagnostic systems (such as *DSM* and *ICD*) were developed during the latter half of the twentieth century, diagnostic reliability and validity has improved. The **assessment process** for first episode psychiatric patients is lengthy and pedantic and can cover: **physical examination; history taking; a mental state examination** (which may use a **standardised interview**); **a clinical psychology report**; **a forensic psychology report**; and **a social work report**. The extensive nature of the assessment is justified by the difficulties faced in making an accurate **diagnosis**, such as the variable nature of these disorders as **syndromes**, the **individual differences** between clients and the fallibility of **clinical judgements**. There may also be legal, financial, **labelling**, treatment and research implications that follow a diagnostic judgement. The European-based *ICD* diagnostic system can aid this judgement by providing explicit criteria for diagnosis. The system is descriptive but retains some inference of **aetiology**. Its US counterpart, the *DSM* system, has removed more of such inferences, giving strict **operational criteria** for diagnosis in a **multi-axial** structure. Diagnostic and assessment information is integrated with other information in the **formulation**, giving the appropriate **treatment** and **prognosis** for the individual client. These systems are not without limitations and, aside from criticisms of the medical approach applied to mental illness, conceptual criticisms propose replacing categorisation with continua or dimensions of symptoms.

Suggested essay questions

- Critically evaluate the concepts of reliability and validity applied to the diagnosis of mental illnesses.
- Critically discuss the application of risk assessment in clinical and forensic contexts.
- Evaluate the usefulness of the formulation.

Further reading

Overview texts

American Psychiatric Association (2000) *Diagnostic and statistical manual of mental disorders, DSM-IV-TR*. Washington DC.

Easton, S., and Piper, C. (2005) *Sentencing and punishment*. Oxford: Oxford University Press.

Gill, D. (2007) *Hughes' outline of modern psychiatry* (5th edn). London: Wiley.

Goldberg, D., Benjamin, S., and Creed, F. (1994) *Psychiatry in medical practice* (2nd edn). London: Routledge.

World Health Organisation (1992) *The ICD-10 classification of mental and behavioural disorders: description and diagnostic guidelines*. Geneva: World Health Organisation.

Walker, N. (1996) *Dangerous people*. London: Blackstone Press.

Specific and more critical texts

Cooper, R. (2004) What is wrong with the DSM? *History of Psychiatry*, **15**(1), 5–25.

Gregory, R. J. (2004) *Psychological Testing: History, principles and applications*. New York: Pearson.

Harding, L., and Beech, J. (1995) *Assessment in neuropsychology*. London: Routledge.

Morrison, J. (1995) *The first interview*. New York: Guilford Press.

Peck, D., and Shapiro, C. (1990) *Measuring human problems*. Chichester: Wiley.

Pilgrim, D., and Rogers, A. (1993) *A sociology of mental health and illness*. Buckingham: Open University Press.

Prins, H. (1999) *Will they do it again? Risk assessment and management in criminal justice and psychiatry.* London: Routledge.

Sartorius, N., Kaeber, C., Cooper, J. et al. (1993) Progress towards achieving a common language in psychiatry. *Archives of General Psychiatry,* **50**, 115–24.

Towl, G. J., and Crighton, D. A. (1996) *The handbook of psychology for forensic practitioners.* London: Routledge.

Ward, D., Scott, J., and Lacey, M. (2002) *Probation: Working for justice.* Oxford: Oxford University Press.

Webb, D., and Harris, R. (1999) *Mentally disordered offenders: Managing people nobody owns.* London: Routledge.

Visit **www.pearsoned.co.uk/davidholmes** for a range of resources to support study. Test yourself with multiple choice questions and access a bank of over 100 videos that will bring the topics to life. Video coverage for this chapter includes a tour inside a cognitive neuroscience laboratory, a discussion about the validity of intelligence tests and the effect of culture on measures of intelligence.

CHAPTER 5 Research methods used in clinical and forensic psychology

Hear about unethical studies from history. This is one of several videos that explore issues and disorders relevant to this chapter at **www.pearsoned.co.uk/davidholmes**.

Do our genes dictate our behaviour?

Advances in technological platforms for extracting DNA have made the process sufficiently cheap that genetics are becoming a commonplace component of studies of behaviour. Determining the genes that underpin psychological and psychiatric conditions may have some utility in identification of novel targets for new pharmacological interventions. However, genetic research is being taken one step further and researchers are now interested in how our genetic make-up is related to more everyday behaviour.

For example, in 2009, researchers from the University of Oregon (Mendle et al., 2009) reported that genes helped to determine the age at which people first have sex. This research suggests that children who come from homes where their father was absent are more likely to have sex at a younger age than children from homes with a resident father. Using data from the 1,382 cousins from the American National Longitudinal Survey of Youth, they reported that genes contributed towards the age at which children first had sex, regardless of whether their father was present or absent. This research has many implications and interpretations, which people can use to their own ends. The authors of the paper suggest that the genetic contribution may be related to personality traits or other risk behaviours (such as substance use) which are also associated with a younger age of first sexual intercourse. However, such research can lead other people to feel that too many aspects of our everyday behaviour are becoming almost predetermined by our genes, reducing the degree of responsibility and control that we feel we have over our lives. Responsible use of research methods as well as using them to address relevant and ethical questions is central to psychological research.

Increasingly, clinical forensic research is looking to our genes for both causes and interventions.
Source: Pearson Online Database.

Overview

Throughout the chapters in this book you will have read descriptions of many clinical and forensic disorders which highlight the complexity of human behaviour. In order to effectively treat and understand clinical and forensic patients, systematic research is required to determine the factors (both biological and environmental) which cause these disorders. It is only through understanding the causes of the disorders in this book that it is possible to determine effective treatments and management strategies. This chapter aims to highlight the diversity of the methods and techniques available, give an overview of their uses and provide a few examples of where they have been used. Even if the reader is not aiming to have a

career in research within the areas of clinical and forensic psychology, a sound understanding of research techniques ensures that reading other people's research becomes more accessible and allows for a critical eye.

There are a wide variety of approaches and techniques available at the fingertips of any keen researcher. The chapter will cover many of the areas traditionally found in research method chapters, including the different approaches to research, an overview of quantitative and qualitative methods, how to develop a psychometrically sound instrument for your own research, and some of the ethical issues involved in conducting responsible research. Advances in technology have made available and cost effective a number of methods, such as genetics and neuroimaging, which were previously inaccessible. Therefore, an overview of neuroimaging techniques, genetics and using the internet in research will also be offered.

Case study

Task development

Rachel graduated from her BSc (Hons) Psychology course with a 2:1. After applying for a number of research assistant vacancies she obtained a post examining cognitive processes in children with hearing and visual impairments. As part of her new role she was asked to develop a task which measured intelligence in this specialised group of participants. She remembered from her undergraduate degree the individual difference course on which she learnt about all the different types of intelligence (such as verbal and non-verbal) and that there are many tests available to measure intelligence in both adults and children. Rachel's first question was to ask her supervisors what aspect of intelligence they wished to measure, although initially she reviewed the existing literature for both verbal and non-verbal intelligence so that she had a broad knowledge to inform the devising of her task. Her supervisors pointed out that measuring verbal intelligence in children who are deaf may be difficult given

the verbal impairments that may be induced by their disability.

After considering this Rachel realised she needed to take into account the capabilities of her participants when devising the tasks. Therefore she decided the best start would be to write a list of what her participants would be able to do, both physically and verbally. She found that existing tests which comprised both verbal and non-verbal measures of intelligence were not suitable for her participants, so she set about devising a test which would be.

Rachel focused on a measure of non-verbal intelligence, since this may be more readily tapped into in children (given their educational limits), plus a task could be devised which could be completed by both hearing and visually impaired children. She developed highly standardised written instructions for her participants and wrote them in simple language so that a child could understand what they needed to do. Rachel had them printed on to a card for the hearing-impaired children, but also learnt how to explain the instructions in sign language so that she could connect better with her participants and establish a rapport. For the visually impaired children she ensured the instructions were written in large print, that they could be read out to participants, and that a version was made in Braille.

Rachel realised that a task where participants had to sort bricks into a given shape would be easy for children of all ages to complete. She developed a series of different patterns with increasing complexities in their design, in an attempt to produce different levels of difficulty in the task. The blocks were large to ensure that children's small hands and limited motor skills did not affect how quickly they could complete the task. She had the patterns printed on to laminated card and raised so that the visually impaired children could feel the pattern they needed to make. Her supervisors were impressed with the creativity and insight shown in her task development. However, they suggested that she initially pilot the task in healthy children to generate some normative data and also to establish how well her task correlated with an already established measure of verbal intelligence.

Rachel had not realised there was so much work involved in developing a new task! She gained access to a class of school children after asking the head of the school, the children's parents and the teacher whether she could complete the tasks with their children. She explained the tasks to the children with their teacher there to ensure that someone who had the child's best interests in mind was present when taking informed consent. After generating data from 100 children of different ages and showing that her task was highly correlated with an existing measure of verbal intelligence, she was finally able to begin testing using children with visual and hearing impairments.

Approaches to research

Key concepts

Before launching into a description of the research methods available, an overview of some of the key concepts will be given which will be useful to keep in mind throughout the reading of this chapter.

Regardless of the type of research being performed and the method being used, most research investigates either the **relationship** between variables or **differences** between sub-groups in the sample that has been collected. When investigating relationships, investigators are concerned with whether scores on behavioural measures or questionnaires vary together in a manner that suggests they may be related. When a researcher is concerned with differences between groups in their data, participants will often have been selected on the basis of a characteristic of interest, such as gender. The researcher will use their study to determine whether the two groups differ or score higher or lower than one another on scores in behavioural tests or questionnaires. Statistical analyses are performed to determine whether the relationships between variables or the differences between groups are statistically significant and occur to a degree more than would be expected by chance.

In an experiment or study, the researcher usually starts with a research question that is based on previously published research, but some studies extend work already done (otherwise there would be no point in doing yet another study). The research question usually presents the 'big picture': that is, it reflects how the smaller study's goals fit into the wider body of research. Based on previous studies and the researcher's knowledge, hypotheses are made which make a statement about the differences or relationship expected. The hypotheses are usually tested by any statistical analysis. The hypotheses are specific to the study and, although they may be informed by the bigger picture, they refer specifically to the contents (measures, groups, sample) being used in the study for which they are designed. A **hypothesis** is a statement of what researchers are expecting to find. A hypothesis can be one-tailed, in which case the researcher predicts the direction of a difference: for example, that patients with schizophrenia will make more errors on a working memory task than healthy volunteers. Alternatively, a hypothesis can be two-tailed, where the direction of the difference is not predicted and the researcher simply states, for example, that there will be a difference between the groups in the study without any prior assumption concerning whether one group will perform better than another.

There are at two types of **variable** in any experiment:

- An independent variable is the variable that defines groups of participants. These groups can be either central to the research question, such as the groups in an experiment, or grouping variables over which the experimenter has no control, such as gender. The independent variable is thought to have some effect or influence on the dependent variable.

- A dependent variable is expected to be altered or be affected by the independent variable. For example, reaction time would be a dependent variable in an experimental design comparing highly impulsive to non-impulsive individuals.

The participants in an experiment can take part in all groups in the study, which is called a repeated measures or within subjects design. Alternatively, each group in the study can comprise a different group of participants – an independent or between subjects design.

Case study

A case study is detailed information gathered about one or two individuals. Case studies provide the researcher with the opportunity to gain a large amount of information about a single individual. Case studies are useful for:

- Describing unusual, exceptional or rare conditions, or uses of techniques in great detail. It was through case study reports such as **Phineas Gage** that scientists realised the importance of the prefrontal cortex in inhibiting anti-social behaviour (see Chapters 3 and 14).

- Countering widely held beliefs by demonstrating that there are exceptions to theoretical propositions.

- Generating hypotheses about an individual's behaviour and responses to a situation. In understanding their responses to a situation, the factors which led to their behaviour can be teased apart. For instance, a case study of a man with anti-social personality disorder (see Chapter 14) may reveal how he was abused by a foster father and then only remained with foster families for brief periods of time afterwards. From this case study, one might hypothesize that anti-social behaviour in adults is caused by childhood abuse and instability in family life.

The information in a case study can focus on all aspects of the individual's past and current situation. Many of **Sigmund Freud**'s theories were formed on the basis of a series of case studies. His case studies were detailed descriptions of his patients and their responses during psychoanalytic sessions. It was through these case studies that Freud and other psychoanalytic therapists thought that childhood experiences might be important in understanding the origins of normal and abnormal adult behaviour. As well as containing a description of individuals' lives in words, case studies may also include biological factors, such as genetic liability or family history of disorders. However, although case studies allow for detailed evidence to be gathered, they cannot test hypotheses. No matter how detailed the information gathered, it is still only describing the experiences of one person and cannot be generalised to other individuals.

In conclusion, case studies provide rich, detailed information about single individuals, which may help to inform therapy (see the Focus box), and theory, refute widely held assumptions and generate hypotheses. However, large-scale studies are required to test hypotheses, whether or not they have been generated through case studies. In large-scale studies, there are many individuals included. The large sample size will allow for any hypotheses to be tested in a statistical manner: for example, are negative childhood experiences associated with adult anti-social behaviour at a rate greater than chance? They will contain individuals who have and have not had the experiences of interest, and it will be possible to determine whether, for example, negative childhood experiences go with adult anti-social behaviour more often than not.

Focus

Cognitive behavioural therapy formulation

A case study approach is often used during cognitive behaviour therapy to explore the factors that lead to the development of symptoms and beliefs. Past experiences as well as more recent events will be explored in order to determine the impact that they may have had upon the individual's beliefs about themselves and the world. Cognitive behaviour therapy has been developed on the principles of emotional cognitions outlined by **Aaron Beck** (see Chapter 3). The case study approach is used in order to explore how early experiences may have led to the development of dysfunctional beliefs. An example of a case study formulation can be seen in Figure 5.1.

The left-hand side of the model can be applied to all disorders described in this book and may allow for all the factors which contribute to the development and maintenance (continued experiencing) of a disorder. Often in a therapeutic situation, rather than focusing on disorders as a whole (e.g. schizophrenia), particular symptoms (e.g. paranoia or auditory hallucinations) can be targeted in an attempt to reduce the distress associated with them, or to reduce their frequency. The idea is to explore the content of symptoms rather than directly challenging them. Then behavioural experiments are devised to challenge automatic thoughts and beliefs about the self and the world. For example, someone

Focus continued

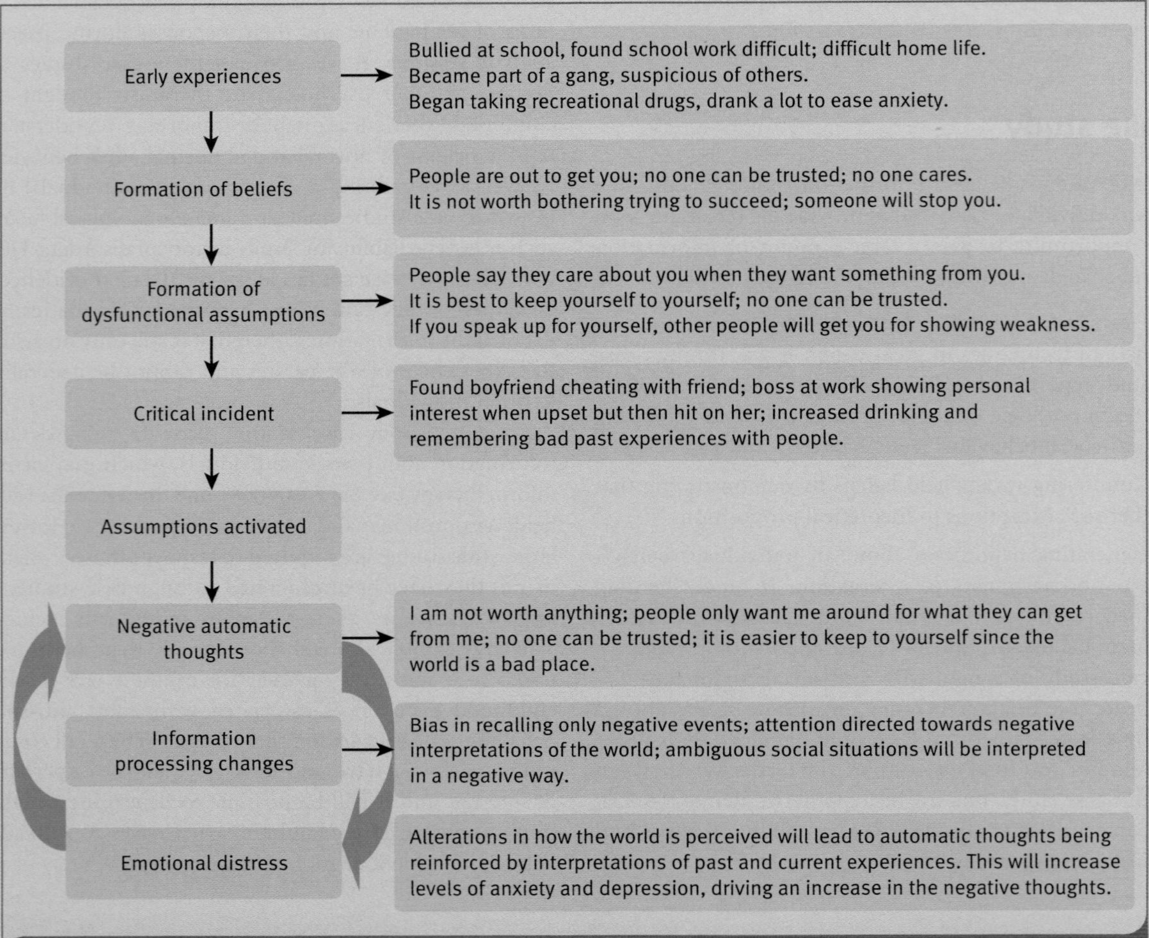

Early experiences	Bullied at school, found school work difficult; difficult home life. Became part of a gang, suspicious of others. Began taking recreational drugs, drank a lot to ease anxiety.
Formation of beliefs	People are out to get you; no one can be trusted; no one cares. It is not worth bothering trying to succeed; someone will stop you.
Formation of dysfunctional assumptions	People say they care about you when they want something from you. It is best to keep yourself to yourself; no one can be trusted. If you speak up for yourself, other people will get you for showing weakness.
Critical incident	Found boyfriend cheating with friend; boss at work showing personal interest when upset but then hit on her; increased drinking and remembering bad past experiences with people.
Assumptions activated	
Negative automatic thoughts	I am not worth anything; people only want me around for what they can get from me; no one can be trusted; it is easier to keep to yourself since the world is a bad place.
Information processing changes	Bias in recalling only negative events; attention directed towards negative interpretations of the world; ambiguous social situations will be interpreted in a negative way.
Emotional distress	Alterations in how the world is perceived will lead to automatic thoughts being reinforced by interpretations of past and current experiences. This will increase levels of anxiety and depression, driving an increase in the negative thoughts.

Figure 5.1 An example of how the case study approach informs cognitive behavioural therapy based on Beck's model of emotional disorders.

who automatically perceives people they do not know to be against them may be challenged to go out with a friend and talk to some people they do not directly know. When their experiences of talking to new people are positive, friendly and not as hostile as they might have supposed, their belief that all new people will dislike them will have been challenged. Cognitive behavioural therapies (in most psychological disorders) are considered an adjunctive treatment alongside pharmacological interventions. They offer a way of teaching coping mechanisms for symptoms, which may not be successfully treated by drugs.

Epidemiological research

Epidemiological research involves large numbers of individuals – sometimes thousands of participants – usually from the same geographical area. Epidemiological studies are a contrast to case studies in that they tend to gather limited (although often surprisingly detailed) information on a large group of people. Epidemiological research is used because most clinical and forensic disorders occur relatively infrequently in the general population. Additionally, most of the factors that predispose individuals to these disorders also occur infrequently in the general population.

Epidemiological research looks for relationships between different variables.

Broadly speaking, epidemiological research focuses on three aspects of any disease:

- **Prevalence** – the number, proportion or percentage of a given population who have an illness at a given time point.

- **Incidence** – since epidemiological studies collect data across different time points in the same individuals, they allow for the number of new cases over a period of time (usually a year) to be calculated. Such research may help to indicate whether there are particular periods of risk for the development of a disorder.

- **Risk factors** – the identification of variables or factors that leave individuals at risk or prone to the development of a disorder. The identification of risk factors is the most important contribution which epidemiological studies make. Many risk factors in psychiatric disease occur infrequently and account for only a small amount of variance. Put another way, each risk factor confers only a small amount of risk for a disorder. As such, it is difficult to detect new risk factors in smaller studies, and where it is possible there is not sufficient **power** to identify variables that have a small effect. Some examples of risk factors are: cannabis use in early adolescence predicting the onset of schizophrenia (e.g. van Os et al., 2002); being female and unmarried and having a family history predicting adult obsessive–compulsive disorder (e.g. Fontenelle and Hasler, 2008). Risk factors are identified in order to determine what predicts the onset of a disease in the hope that, first, vulnerable groups of individuals can be identified for monitoring; and secondly, the risk factors may allow for education or an intervention to be developed which prevents the onset of a disorder. Unfortunately, in clinical and forensic psychology the risk factors identified occur too frequently without leading to any adverse outcomes to use any one risk factor as an indicator of proneness to a disorder. Therefore, the current epidemiology research in clinical and forensic psychology is focused on identifying groups of risk factors and how they seem to confer proneness to different disorders in different people.

Epidemiology studies also allow for the lifetime prevalence rates of disorders to be calculated. The lifetime prevalence rate is the percentage or proportion of a population who, over their lifetime, may develop a particular condition. This measure is similar to the prevalence rates often reported in epidemiological studies, with the added bonus that it takes into account the age of the sample, since individuals may not yet have reached the age at which the disorder is most likely to have its onset: it gives an indication of risk across the life span, not just at a given point in time. The lifetime prevalence rate allows for comparison across different groups of people or populations to determine how risk factors such as drug use, childhood neglect, trauma or abuse, living in a city and moving to another country (migration) increase or decrease the lifetime risk of developing a particular disorder.

Epidemiological research may identify the risk factors that leave individuals prone to a disorder. However, due to the nature of the data collected in epidemiological research, it is not possible to determine what underpins the risk factor. Or put another way, we cannot tell from an epidemiological study the mechanisms which explain how risk factors confer proneness to a disorder. The data collected in epidemiological research tell the 'big picture' of what personality traits, demographic factors, environmental factors or experiences leave individuals prone to a disorder. Epidemiological studies give researchers clues to the areas of behaviour, biology, personality or the environment which need to be investigated in more detail using smaller, more intense studies. For example, an epidemiology study may identify childhood exposure to violence as a risk factor for anti-social personality disorder. However, further smaller studies would need to be performed to determine whether childhood exposure to violence is a risk factor because violence becomes an accepted solution for problem solving in social situations. The change in attitude towards violence would be the mechanism which underpins the relationship between childhood exposure to violence and adult anti-social personality disorder.

For a study to be considered truly epidemiological, it needs to have recruited a representative sample from the wider population. For example, an epidemiological survey that recruits participants from a geographical area would need to recruit enough participants from each ethnic and socioeconomic group to ensure that all **demographic** groups from an area are appropriately represented in the final sample. Initially, this may mean that focus is placed on recruiting groups which are generally under-represented in research studies (usually the socially disenfranchised or isolated), to ensure the final sample is appropriately stratified. Stratification of a sample is just a scientific way of referring to the different demographic groups within a sample. Sometimes researchers will aim to separate out particular groups within their sample because they think risk factors may have a different effect on different groups of individuals. For example, gang membership during adolescence may be predictive of more adverse consequences (violence, excessive drinking, risk taking) in boys from homes with a single parent than in boys who live with both parents, or in girls. In this example the researcher would stratify their sample on the basis of gender and parents' marital status. When particular groups of individuals need to be recruited for an epidemiological study, either to ensure it is representative or to identify particular groups of individuals, particular consideration needs to be given to how to recruit and encourage such groups to take part in research studies.

Recruiting participants from a particular geographical area is one approach to gaining a sample suitable for epidemiological research. Another is the recruitment of a birth cohort. Participants (or their parents) are recruited into studies from a young age, often at birth, and followed up over a number of years to determine whether developmental milestones or other outcome variables (variables of interest) are achieved. This approach has particularly been used to examine risk factors for disorders such as schizophrenia, which are thought to have neurodevelopmental origins that may be detectable in childhood. For example, Izumoto, Inoue and Yasuda (1999) reported data from a Japanese birth cohort demonstrating that, if mothers were exposed to the influenza virus when pregnant, there was increased likelihood of schizophrenia in females, but not males. The exposure to the influenza virus also seemed to need to take place before the third trimester for it to have an effect.

One of the major strengths of epidemiology studies is that the same individuals are followed up over a number of time points. This means that each person will act as their own control, since data will be available for the same person before and after they develop a disorder or are exposed to an environmental risk factor. The number of follow-up time points in these studies as well as the huge sample sizes involved are what give epidemiology studies their statistical power and advantage in identifying risk factors for disorders.

Correlational approach

A correlational approach is used when the researchers are interested in the relationship between variables. It allows the researcher to determine whether two scores increase or decrease together; or whether, as one score increases, another decreases. To use a more scientifically and statistically correct turn of phrase, correlational methods examine the degree to which variables co-vary together. When correlations are being used in research, the relationship between the two variables is often displayed graphically using scatterplots. An example of the three possible outcomes from a scatterplot of two variables is displayed in Figure 5.2.

International perspective

The Swedish conscript studies

One of the important factors in epidemiology research is access to a representative sample of the population being studied. In the United Kingdom there are not many national databases which the majority of the population are found in. Additionally, existing databases of information are not currently linked, so information from one database, such as details of your birth, cannot be linked, for example, to ongoing health. In other European countries, more detailed records are available which permit such analysis.

One such country is Sweden. The Swedish National Board of Health and Welfare maintains a register of births which contains 99 per cent of those born since 1973. This database is regularly validated and contains details on the mother, and complications pre, during and postnatal. Each person born in Sweden is given an identification number which then follows them throughout their lives and is used across any other databases that they enter. An additional factor which ensures that many epidemiological studies emerge out of Sweden is that compulsory conscription for military service still exists for all males between 18 and 24 years. Only approximately 2.4 per cent of the population per birth cohort who have disabilities which mean they are unfit for military service do not appear in the Swedish Conscript Register. At conscription, males are given a detailed physical and psychiatric assessment as well as receiving measures of intelligence. Additionally, given that all conscripts are exposed to the stressful life event of military service, it is possible to examine the interactions between biological and environmental factors in these individuals.

To date there have been a number of papers which have resulted from these databases. They have contributed to research on patterns of alcohol use (Rossow and Romelsjö, 2006), cannabis use and psychosis (Andréasson et al., 1987; Zammit et al., 2002), mortality and cannabis use (Andréasson and Allebeck, 1990), whether low IQ increases risk for the development of psychiatric disorders (David et al., 2008) and the relationship between foetal growth and stress tolerability (Nilsson, Nyberg and Ostergren, 2001).

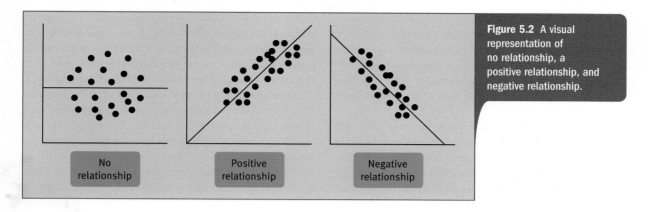

Figure 5.2 A visual representation of no relationship, a positive relationship, and negative relationship.

In scatterplots, each dot or data point represents the relationship between the two variables for each participant. Therefore it is the shape of the data points on the graph which indicates the nature of the relationship between the two variables. A line of best fit is added through the data points. This line, as its name suggests, is placed so it explains the largest number of data points or variance in the data. The gradient or slope of the line indicates the strength of the correlation between the two variables. In Figure 5.2 the far left-hand graph demonstrates a scatterplot where no relationship exists between the two variables. The data points are randomly distributed in no given pattern and the line of best fit is flat. The middle scatterplot represents a positive correlation. The data points are distributed in an oval shape with scores on one variable increasing with scores on the other. This is a positive correlation and the line of best fit goes from the bottom left of the graph to the top right. Finally, the scatterplot on the far right represents a negative correlation, with the same oval-shape distribution of data points and the same angle on the line of best fit as seen in the positive correlation, but in the opposite direction. In a negative correlation, the scores on one variable decrease as the scores on the other variable increase.

Correlations are often used in epidemiological studies, since more often than not the variables are measured in their natural form. Or phrased another way, the variables tend to measure aspects of behaviour in everyday life without any inference from the researcher. This is in contrast to experimental approaches (see below), where the experimenter manipulates the variables of interest. A hypothetical study is displayed in Figure 5.3 in order to demonstrate the differences between the correlation and experimental approaches. The study is concerned with the relationship between alcohol use and aggressive behaviour. If a correlational approach were taken, participants would be asked about their behaviour on occasions when they have been drinking and the amount of alcohol they have consumed. Either an interview or questionnaires would be used to record the types of behaviour participants report after drinking as well as the amount they generally drink. For each participant, the researcher would have a score indicating their degree of aggressive behaviour when drinking and the number of units of alcohol they drink on average. These measures would be taken retrospectively: that is, they would be based on the participants' recollection of their past behaviour in their normal life.

However, if the relationship between alcohol used and aggression were being examined with an experimental approach, a more strict and artificial environment would be created where many factors could be controlled. Participants might be asked to come to a behavioural lab for a full morning of testing. They would be asked to have a normal breakfast before arriving, and not to drink alcohol 24 hours before attending; the researcher might also only want to

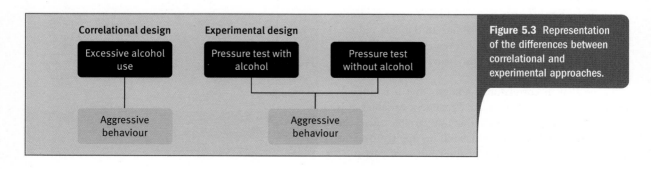

Figure 5.3 Representation of the differences between correlational and experimental approaches.

have non-smokers taking part in the study. The participants would be screened to rule out any current or past psychiatric or substance abuse/dependence problems, and family history of such disorders would also be recorded. Participants would then be exposed to the same amount of alcohol while completing a pressure test and their levels of aggression objectively rated.

You can see the stark differences between these two approaches in terms of the number of variables taken into consideration and the degree of control which the researcher can exert over the possible factors that may influence aggressive responses from alcohol use. Both of these approaches have their merits and the most appropriate approach would be determined by the questions that the researcher was trying to address while performing the research.

There are, however, two problems with correlational approaches. A correlation tells you that two variables are related to one another: as scores on one variable increase, scores on another variable also seem to increase in a manner which suggests they are related. However, from using a correlation it is not possible to determine which of the two variables is the dependent or the independent variable. This problem is known as the problem of directionality. Put another way, correlations do not allow you to determine the direction of causality between two variables, only the positive or negative relationship between the scores. It is possible from a scientific point of view to postulate which of the two variables in the correlation is the independent variable; it just cannot be tested statistically. This problem is also related to determining the cause and effect relationship between two variables.

The problem associated with determining whether one variable causes another applies to a certain extent to all the approaches described in this chapter. However, it is most relevant when using a correlational approach. Refer back to Figure 5.2, displaying the lines of best fit for positive and negative correlations. The proximity of the data points to the line of best fit reflects how well the line explains the data. These diagrams are somewhat idealised correlations between two variables, where the data points cluster nice and tightly around the lines of best fit. However, in real-world research in clinical and forensic psychology, the relationship between two variables is never perfectly explained. The amount of variability in the data reduces the strength of the correlation between two variables and may indicate that another unmeasured variable would better explain the relationship.

Given that in correlational analysis that it is difficult to identify the independent and dependent variables, it is very difficult to determine whether one variable causes the other. Again the discussion which follows applies to all the approaches described in this chapter but is of particular

relevance to correlational approaches. Generally, the determination of whether one variable causes another is open to scientific debate and replication until a body of irrefutable evidence emerges – a state which has not been achieved in the debates that exist in clinical and forensic psychology.

As an example of the problem of determining causality in research, let us consider the possible explanations for a relationship between life-events and depression. There is a positive relationship between life-events and depression or depressive relapse (Figure 5.4(a)). Thus, with an increase in the number of events in your life, you are more likely to suffer from depression or a depressive relapse if you have had depression previously. One may conclude that increasing life-events *cause* depression or a depressive relapse. However, another unmeasured variable may cause both the depression and life-events. For example, increased levels of anxiety may lead to normal everyday occurrences and benign stresses perceived as serious life events, and higher levels of anxiety may lead to the development of depression (Figure 5.4(b)). Alternatively, there may be an intermediate variable between life-events and depression, such as background levels of stress, which would significantly contribute to the relationship (Figure 5.4(c)).

All of these variables (life events, depression, anxiety and stress) would be positively correlated with one another. It is the problem of the researcher to determine, using knowledge of the wider literature, which variables may cause or mediate one another. As previously mentioned, any discussion of causality needs to be highlighted as speculation only until such time that a large body of literature has been established which can support the pathways involved. However, one of the advantages of the correlational approach is that given measures tend to be measured in the real world rather than in an artificial experimental setting. Thus, the results will have ecological validity and be directly relevant to everyday experiences of the participants taking part in the research.

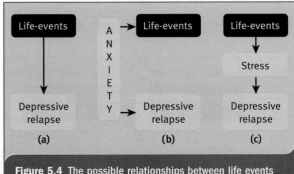

Figure 5.4 The possible relationships between life events and depressive relapse.

Experimental approach

Unlike the measurement of variables in correlational and epidemiological studies, experimental approaches are carefully designed to test a specifically targeted hypothesis. An experimental approach is where the researcher 'tests' the participant usually using a combination of questionnaire and behavioural measures. In an experiment, at least two conditions or groups will be used. The groups will differ in a predefined (independent) variable. Thus, the researcher usually has full control over the factor that defines the groups in a study. For example, groups in an experiment may differ in terms of their exposure to a drug (drug or no drug), or whether they receive a psychological intervention or a control, or whether they receive one version of a behavioural test or another (recall of words with and without distracting background noise). Since all groups in an experiment are the same except for the variable manipulated by the researcher, it will be possible to determine the effect of the manipulated (or independent) variable on performance in the tasks used to assess behaviour. The groups in an experiment are compared using statistical analysis to determine whether they differ from each other sufficiently for the difference not to have occurred by chance. If the results from statistical analysis are significant, it means that the independent variable is causing a change in performance on the measures used, over and above what you would expect to find by chance testing of many participants.

Let us consider a published example of the use of an experimental approach. Howard and Menkes (2007) were interested in determining the degree to which the acute effects of cannabis alter electro-cortical (EEG) measures of affective impulsivity. Their research question was 'what brain mechanism mediates the disinhibiting effects of cannabis on emotional behaviour?' (p. 114). They were interested in this research question since there have been an increasing number of reports that use of cannabis recreationally can lead to violent behaviour in humans. More often than not, violence occurs under conditions when the normal inhibition of behaviour is reduced or removed. Cannabis may be a substance that makes people disinhibited and its use may lead to aggression and violence in some people as well as general relaxing and increasing of creativity in others.

A graphical representation of Howard and Menkes' experimental design can be seen in Figure 5.5. Participants completed the Go/No Go paradigm. During this paradigm, participants are asked to respond by pressing a button every time a letter comes up on a screen in front of them. However, when the letter 'V' appears, the participants are told not to press the button. The idea is that participants become

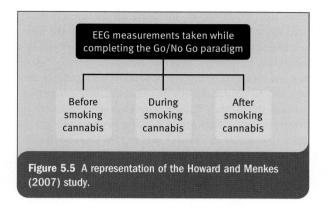

Figure 5.5 A representation of the Howard and Menkes (2007) study.

used to pressing the button every time the screen changes (known as behavioural habituation), but when the 'V' appears on the screen they have to inhibit the response they have been used to giving (the button pressing). EEG recordings were taken from the participants' brains during the completion of the task, before, during and after they smoked cannabis with a controlled amount of Δ-9-tetrahydrocannabinol (the psychoactive ingredient in cannabis) in each 'joint'. The authors demonstrated alterations in the EEG readings only after cannabis had been smoked, when the levels of intoxication will have peaked.

In an experiment, the same participants take part in all conditions in the study, as in the Howard and Menkes' study described above. If the same participants take part in all groups, this is known as a related or within subjects design, since all groups are related to one another because they contain the same participants. This design has the advantage that fewer participants need to be recruited, since one group will complete all aspects of the study. Additionally, each participant can act as their own control, so there will be no differences between the groups in terms of age, gender, socioeconomic status, exposure to recreational drug use or any other extraneous variable attached to the participants in a study which may or may not influence performance on the tasks being used. In a related design, individual differences in the participants' ability to performance the tasks will have less effect on the results, since within all groups in the experiment the same group of participants will express the same level of individual variance in their performance. However, there are disadvantages to related designs, such as practice and order effects (see below). It can also be difficult to get participants to come back time after time to take part in an experiment, leading to increased rates of dropouts in the study.

The opposite design to a related design is an **independent or between subjects design**, where different participants take part in each session or stage of the study. There are generally fewer participants dropping out in independent study designs. However, the participants in each group need to be closely matched to ensure that only the independent variable will be influencing performance and not individual differences between the participants. Taking baseline measures of intelligence and/or performance may be a way to reduce the effects of having different participants in the groups. These relevant variables can then be controlled for, if they prove to differ between the groups when statistically analysed. Assuming the tasks being used are not affected by practice effects, the change in baseline performance to experimental condition performance can be used as a compromise between the within subjects and between subjects designs.

There are occasions when the order in which participants complete different parts of the study may be important. There are a number of reasons why participants should complete aspects of a study in a different order.

- To remove any chance that alterations in performance on tasks are not due to practice effects. Completing the same task (even a different version of the same task) may lead to improvements in performance unrelated to the effects of the independent variable manipulated by the researcher.
- If the independent variable is an intervention, either psychological or pharmacological, you would want to show that it is effective regardless of whether it is given before or after a placebo (non-active) condition or before or after an active control (which would be another drug or psychological intervention).
- The order in which which participants complete tasks in a study may also need to be varied to ensure that previously completed tasks in the same session do not influence one another, or that fatigue will not skew the performance on tasks completed later in the session.

To control for any effects of the order in which a study design is given, it can be counterbalanced so that half the participants complete one part of the study first and another second. Counterbalancing can also be used to remove any effects of completing tasks in a particular order within an experimental condition. In clinical trials, a crossover design is often used to counter any effect of giving drugs in a particular order. All participants receive the same drugs, but in a different order (generally with a washout period in between, if this is ethically viable and the research is not on a clinically acute sample). From an ethical point of view, it is difficult to justify not allowing participants from a clinical sample access to a pharmacological intervention that may help their condition. A **crossover design** bypasses this problem: half the participants in a trial would be started on the drug, while half would receive a placebo for a period of, say, 2 weeks. All participants would then experience a washout period for 2 weeks (to remove the drug from the central nervous system of the participants who received the active drug). Then participants would receive either drug or placebo for 2 weeks according to whichever they had in the previous condition. The washout period becomes important to show that changes in presentation are due to the introduction or withdrawal of the active drug.

More often than not, it is important for the participants not to be aware of which experimental condition they are experiencing. This is referred to as participants being **blind** to their condition. If a particularly helpful participant is recruited, they may try to produce the results that they think the researcher is hoping for. Alternatively, a malicious participant may aim to thwart the study by trying to produce results they think the researcher does not want. Either way, these types of participant will skew the data in a counterproductive manner when it comes to trying to analyse the results. Ensuring that participants are unsure what is expected of them will ensure that they do not know in which direction to be helpful or hindering.

When behavioural ratings are being used, it is often important for the experimenter or rater to be blind to the condition in the experiment, as well as the participants. This is referred to as **double blind**, since neither the participant nor the experimenter knows whether the participant is receiving the drug or placebo. As with the helpful participant, a non-blind rater may try to bias the results in a particular direction if they know the status of the participants in the experiment and the aim of the study. It is easy for both the participant and experimenter to be blind during a pharmacological study. However, when a psychological intervention or experiment is being conducted, it becomes more difficult to 'disguise' whether a participant is receiving an active or inactive compound or intervention. It is also more difficult (often impossible) for experimenters to remain blind to which is the experimental group.

Self-test questions

- Does the study hypothesis reflect the wider literature in which the research study fits?
- What is an independent variable?
- What is the difference between prevalence and incidence?
- What does a positive correlation reveal about the data being explored?
- What is an extraneous variable?

Research methods

Regardless of the approach taken to investigate a research question, a method of analysis is used to determine whether the data support the research question. There are broadly two approaches to analysing data: **qualitative** and **quantitative** methods. Qualitative methods are primarily concerned with words, while quantitative methods, the focus of much of the previous discussion, are concerned with numbers.

Qualitative methods

Qualitative methods are concerned with spoken or written words and examine the way language is used. They offer the opportunity to collect a large amount of information in written or spoken form in a small number of participants. Qualitative methods are frequently used in their own right to investigate research questions, but they can also be used to validate quantitative methods (for example, a detailed interview developed to validate participants' scores on a new questionnaire), or support quantitative methods by providing more detailed information on a subset of participants who could be selected on the basis of a questionnaire or quantitative measure. Qualitative methods are often used in case studies (see above) and the detailed information that they provide on unusual cases or cases of interest can then be used to generate hypotheses which can subsequently be tested using quantitative methods in larger samples.

The data gathered for qualitative methods are often collected using interviews. Interviews may be **structured**, where all participants are asked the same questions without any variation from a set script. Alternatively, interviews can be semi-structured, where interviewers are able to digress from an agreed set of questions in order to elicit further information. Often the amount of information that can be obtained will depend upon the individual being interviewed and how responsive they are. This seems obvious, but depending on the personal nature of the interview topic, people may be very willing to volunteer information and therefore using a structured interview may be too restrictive. Referring back to information that interviewees have previously provided, using their terminology and language as well as using small-talk, all helps to build a rapport and encourages people to talk freely. Additionally, designing questions in an open-ended way, perhaps with prompts, will mean that people cannot respond by only giving yes or no responses. This is important regardless of whether a structured or semi-structured interview is used.

As well as using interviews to gather data for qualitative methods, any written or verbal material can be used. For example, a researcher may be interested in the way in which women are presented in the media. Media by most definitions would encompass adverts on the internet, adverts on the television and the words used in broadsheet and tabloid newspapers and magazines. The information which this would yield would be a combination of scripted material from adverts, written material from newspapers and magazines, and possibly slogans used in advertising.

Three qualitative methods are used: **content analysis**, **thematic analysis** and **discourse analysis**.

Content analysis

Content analysis is the least purely qualitative method. Usually content analysis is applied to interviews or the written word, where it is the frequency of phrases or particular words that are of significance to the researcher: for example, going back to the researcher interested in women's portrayal in the media, the number of times words like 'home', 'children', 'image' and 'husbands' or 'partners' appear in articles directed at women. Content analysis does not just count frequencies; enough information can sometimes be produced to lead to comparative statistical methods. For example, when interviewing prisoners about their experiences of violent situations, a researcher may have reason to believe that anxiety, substance use and dissociative symptoms may precede outbursts of violence (see Chapter 15). A researcher would have a **structured interview schedule** (list of questions) which would be applied to both offenders who had a history of violent outbursts and those who use violence in an instrumental and less impulsive manner. After completing the interviews, the researcher would examine whether those with a violent history characterised by impulsive acts more frequently described using substances, experiencing anxiety and feeling separate from themselves and reality. The transcripts for the interviews would be read and each time a phrase which fitted into the categories of interest appeared, it would be counted. Categories or phrases that could be of interest include descriptions of being either 'high' or drunk, feeling like someone else is doing your actions, feeling controlled by some outside force, and feeling fluttering or uncomfortableness in your stomach or chest. When the rates of the phrases of interest have been counted, they may be compared in those prone to instrumental and impulsive violence, either using descriptive statistics or using the more formal methods described below. We would assume that those who use violence in an instrumental manner would report lower rates of anxiety and substance use, since instrumental violence requires some plan or manipulation of other individuals or the environment. However, those who use violence in an instrumental manner may still have similar levels of dissociative symptoms (like feeling separate from reality, or looking down on themselves from above) to those prisoners whose violence is characterised as impulsive.

Thematic analysis

Thematic analysis is more exploratory than content analysis. As in content analysis, categories are constructed when using thematic analysis; however, the categories in thematic analysis are not preconceived and are generated from the data. Often the categories will be based on evidence from previous literature or generated from the research question of interest. Interviews used when the researcher is intending to use thematic analysis are also based on the topic central to the research question. They are designed with multiple questions, which may aim to address different aspects of the same experience. Other information may emerge which is unexpected and this will form a separate category or theme. The themes will reflect the data generated by the interviews and will be supported by previous literature in the area. Thematic analysis may generate hypotheses that can be tested at a later date using quantitative methods, or may be used to validate the construction of a new questionnaire in order to meet a gap in the literature.

Discourse analysis

Discourse analysis is the most complex of the qualitative methods, and is also most influenced by politics. Discourse analysis is concerned with language, how it is used, how it influences the dynamics and status of individuals, and what language says about the individuals using it. In its simplest form, consider how a student of English would approach deciphering a Shakespearean play. First of all, the student would consider what the words used reflect about the person using them and about their position in relation to the other characters in the play. The language of an Elizabethan noble would have been very different from that used by a peasant, for example. Such contrasts do not exist in modern-day language, but clues to a person's standing are still reflected in the words they use. Consider the different words used to describe bread rolls depending on local dialect, such as barm-cakes, cobs, bread cakes and so on.

Another example is the use of language with implicit assumptions in tabloids as compared to broadsheet newspapers. It is the use of language in this way which discourse analysis teases apart. Discourse analysis is concerned with analysing how language is used in a 'loaded' manner and what this bias in language means or indicates. The words used by a psychiatrist to describe depression or psychosis may be very different from those used by the patient who is experiencing the symptoms. Most researchers who practice discourse analysis feel that language has the power to immobilise and empower the individual, and that our identities are constructed by the language used by us and by other people when interacting with us. Many people who use discourse analysis are part of the anti-psychiatry movement (see Chapter 2) and feel that the labels applied to individuals, whether they are diagnostic or not, have detrimental effects. Given that such researchers mostly adopt this viewpoint, it is very rare that discourse analysis is used in a more constructive manner in the fields of forensic and clinical psychology.

One of the suggested strengths of qualitative methods is the presence of a reflexive analysis. In this the researcher outlines what they take to the research situation, their perceptions of the research process and what they have learnt as part of the research process. Since a significant proportion of qualitative methods require subjective interpretation of the material, it is vital that the initial standpoint of the researcher be openly declared, since their 'biases' will have influenced the analysis process. However, even though the researcher may acknowledge their opinions, they still allow them to feed into their interpretations of the data. This could not happen in quantitative methods where objective analysis methods are applied, which cannot be legitimately biased to the same extent qualitative methods can. Statistical findings can also be manipulated. A good example of this comes from general medicine: when reporting survival times for cancer patients, the median survival time is reported because this makes it appear that patients in general live longer.

Quantitative methods

Quantitative methods simply refer to methods that make use of numbers: each participant will have a value on a questionnaire or behavioural measure. Quantitative methods are used when the researcher is interested in testing a relationship between two variables or whether there is a significant difference between two or more groups. In contrast to qualitative methods, quantitative methods tend to include a large number of participants with specific hypotheses being tested. Quantitative methods allow you to generalise from the sample which you have tested to the larger population from which your study sample was drawn. The measures used in quantitative methods tend to be structured and measure a narrowly defined variable of interest. There are some basic terms which it is useful to understand before considering the quantitative methods that are applied to clinical and forensic psychology.

The first and most basic concept is concerned with the different types of data or measurement which can be used. There are essentially three types of quantitative (numerical) data:

- **Continuous.** These are statistically referred to as **interval data**, if there are equal increments in value between each number, such as height in centimetres.

- Discrete. An example of a discrete variable would be response to a question from a questionnaire on a Likert scale such as 1 = rarely or never, 2 = from time to time, 3 = sometimes, 4 = more often than not, 5 = almost always. The numbers used represent increments on a scale to which the researcher attributes their own value. If the scale represents increasing values of (theoretically) equal distance, discrete data can generally be treated like interval data. Quantitative methods are usually applied to subscales for questionnaires rather than to the individual questions themselves.

- Dichotomous. Both discrete and dichotomous data are statistically referred to as categorical or **nominal data**. Dichotomous data reflect a value that the researcher attributes to them: for example, Yes/No or Male/Female. Generally, dichotomous variables reflect two opposites.

Quantitative techniques are split into parametric and **non-parametric** methods. Within these subgroups of statistical tests, there are tests which examine differences between groups and, relationships between variables, and both sets of tests can deal with all the types of data outlined above. However, parametric tests are more flexible and powerful, and there are a larger number of statistical tests available which are parametric, giving researchers greater choice in what they can do with their data. See Figure 5.6 for a summary of some of these statistical tests.

Parametric tests have criteria that must be met by the data before they can be used (see below). If data do not conform to these requirements exactly, the parametric analysis will still be reliable; however, extreme violations mean that non-parametric analysis will need to be used. Non-parametric tests can be used under any circumstances and may be more appropriate under circumstances where a small sample size is being used. Non-parametric techniques make no assumptions about the nature of the relationship between the dependent and independent variables, and are considered **distribution free** (i.e. the dependent variables do not have to be continuous or normally distributed).

All statistical tests can be divided broadly into **tests of difference** or **relationship**. An outline of what these statistical tests can tell us and how they feed into the different approaches to research in clinical and forensic psychology is given below. The focus of the discussion will be on parametric analyses, since these are the most frequently used. However examples of the non-parametric equivalents are given in Figure 5.6.

Focus

Parametric requirements

The requirements which need to be met for data to be considered parametric are:

- that data are continuous, are with even value increments between each data point

- that they approximate to a normal distribution, or are drawn from a sample where the variable would be normally distributed

- that homogeneity of variance exists between groups of participants.

The **dependent variables** used in parametric analyses must approximate to a **normal distribution**. If data are normally distributed, they should approximate to a 'bell curve' with the peak of the curve in the middle of the x-axis and 'tails' of equal distance from the peak on either side.

Homogeneity of variance is an assumption about the amount of variance in each group in the study. The **variance** (or difference in individual participants' scores from the group mean) found within groups of volunteers is thought to express individual differences or general variation that you might expect in the general population. As a researcher, it is necessary to assume that the groups of participants that you have are representative of the population they have been drawn from. Therefore the amount of individual differences expressed in each group of participants should be the same. This assumption is considered more relevant to studies where there are different participants in each group (**independent or parallel groups**).

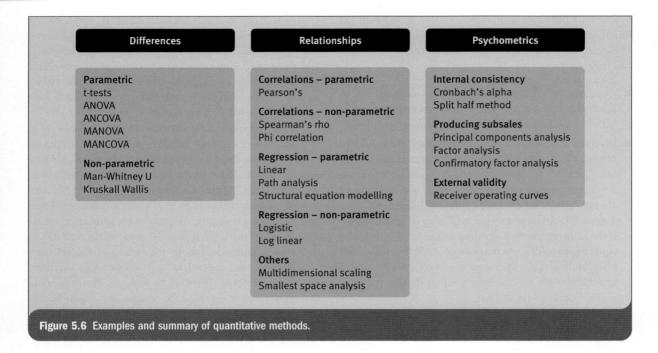

Figure 5.6 Examples and summary of quantitative methods.

Tests of difference

Tests of difference are generally used in experimental approaches when researchers want to compare one group to another. They tell a researcher whether one group scores significantly higher or lower than another. When there are two groups to be compared, **t-tests** are used. T-tests examine whether the means from two subsets of data are significantly different from one another.

When there are three or more groups being compared to one another, **ANOVAs** or analysis (AN) of (O) variance (VA) models are used. Unlike t-tests, ANOVAs examine **variance** rather than mean difference. The ANOVAs compare whether the variance *within* groups in an analysis is significantly smaller than the variance (or difference) between the groups. Thus, for the results from an ANOVA to be considered statistically significant, there needs to be a larger difference between the groups in the analysis than the variation in scores expressed within each group. The variance within a group of participants is thought to be due to individual difference (i.e. the amount scores of any measure would differ by in any given population) and error. Differences between the groups in an ANOVA will be attributed to the effect of the independent variable. This could be three or more treatment groups (e.g. anti-depressant, cognitive behavioural therapy and placebo), three or more groups of participants defined by a measure determined by the experimenter (patients with schizophrenia, high psychosis-prone individuals,

relatives of patients with schizophrenia and controls), or three or more groups of data collected from the same individual (attitudes towards drug taking measured at baseline, before starting a motivational interviewing intervention, during the intervention, a week after completing the intervention and 6 months after completing the intervention).

One important difference between ANOVAs and t-tests is that ANOVAs take into account a measurement error. This includes errors in the measurement of variables included and the effect of variables that you have not measured but which may have an effect on the results (confounding variables). MANOVAs are like ANOVAs but allow you to include multiple dependent variables which are 'lumped' together to determine what effect the independent variables have upon them. MANOVAs are useful when you are using a large number of variables assumed to measure the same underlying trait or cognitive domain (the M stands for 'multivariate').

ANCOVAs and MANCOVAs are the same as ANOVAs and MANOVAs except they allow for variables to be included as covariates, which means the analysis will take into account any effect that the covariate has on the relationship between the independent and dependent variables. The covariates may be either continuous or discrete variables. This is a useful way to account for differences between groups at baseline, or to take into account variables that you have measured which are known to influence the dependent variables.

Tests of relationship

In naturalistic and epidemiological studies, the statistical analysis is generally concerned with relationships between variables. The parametric tests of relationship assume that the relationship between variables is linear: that is, the relationship can be explained by a line of best fit which is straight. Initially a correlation can be used to determine whether there is any relationship between two variables (see Figure 5.2). Correlation values vary between −1 and +1, representing a perfect negative and positive relationship respectively. However, it is more usual that the correlations reported in research in clinical and forensic psychology are much less than +/−1, with at least some variance between two variables being explained by other, unmeasured variables. A correlation only tells the researcher the direction and degree of strength of the relationship between two variables. In order to determine whether one variable predicts another, it is necessary to use a statistical method known as **regression**.

Regression is used when researchers are interested in determining whether one variable predicts another. As with correlations, it is assumed that the relationship between the variables is linear. It is possible to use regression to determine which combination of variables, or which variable on its own, best predicts the outcome measure. Alternatively, blocks of variables can be combined to predict another variable. Regression is used when the variables being predicted and the predictors are continuous. **Logistic** and **loglinear** analysis are regression methods used with categorical data or a combination of categorical and continuous data. Parks and Bard (2006) were interested in seeing which variables predicted reoffending in adolescent sex offenders. The variables they used to predict recidivism were taken from two measures and included sexual drive, impulsive anti-social behaviour, community stability and four aspects of psychopathy (interpersonal, affective, behavioural and anti-social). From these variables they found that impulsive and anti-social behaviour, and the interpersonal aspects of psychopathy predicted reoffending. Only 6.4 per cent of their sample re-offended with a sexual crime, while 30.1 per cent reoffended with a non-sexual crime. The authors highlighted that the rates of reoffending were similar to those found in adult populations and that the results suggested that impulsive and interpersonal psychopathy in adolescent offenders would be good targets for intervention to reduce reoffending rates.

Path analysis and **structural equation modelling** are an extension of regression models. You would use path analysis or structural equation modelling when a large number of variables have been measured and you are interested in the relationships between the variables. They allow you to predict variables, but also allow for the relationship between to be characterised in more detail. For example, the direction of the relationship between variables can be tested (remember the problem of directionality highlighted in the correlational approach section?). The researcher will initially have to make assumptions about the direction of the relationship between variables, but once formally tested, the direction of the relationship between two variables can be corrected if necessary. Path analysis and structural equation modelling permit the testing of multiple combinations of variables, and how groups of variables are related to one another.

Such analyses are largely used in epidemiological research when there are large numbers of participants in the data set and the variables of interest often occur infrequently. For example, the rates of schizophrenia in the general population are approximately 1 in every 100. Consider the example in Figure 5.7. Psychosis proneness is a **normally distributed** trait in the general population, which means a small (but significant) number of individuals score particularly high on this trait. However, psychotic symptoms such as hallucinations and delusions are not normally distributed and occur infrequently in the general population, but are thought to be related to psychosis proneness. Therefore it is hypothesised that those who are psychosis prone may require an additional trigger before they will experience psychotic symptoms: in other words, psychosis proneness and psychotic symptoms correlate and overlap with one another. In this you are interested in determining what 'pushes' an individual from being psychosis prone into experiencing psychotic symptoms. Such a trigger may be life events. However, is it the life events themselves, the stress from the life events or an interaction between these and background levels of stress which lead to psychotic symptoms in those who are

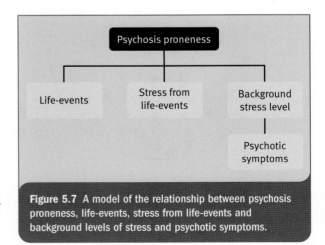

Figure 5.7 A model of the relationship between psychosis proneness, life-events, stress from life-events and background levels of stress and psychotic symptoms.

psychosis prone? These research questions can be answered to a certain extent using path analysis and explicitly tested using structural equation modelling.

Rather than relationships between continuous variables, researchers may be interested in the relationship between questionnaire items or distances between cities or types of crime. In order to examine these relationships, statistical tests other than regression have to be used. Two alternative methods which can handle such non-parametric variables are multidimensional scaling and **smallest space analysis**. Multidimensional scaling (MDS) and smallest space analysis (SSA) use variance, but in slightly different ways: rather than examining the degree to which scores vary together, as correlations do, MDS and SSA determine the distance between different variables in a mathematically theoretical space or from a set point in this space. MDS produces similar results to factor analysis (see below) when looking at how items from a questionnaire cluster together. It has most frequently been applied in the field of forensic psychology. It is used to examine data which are frequencies. Although the statistics around MDS and SSA are statistically quite complex, consider these methods as very visual ways of displaying data and the way in which they work can be understood in a relatively simple way.

Since SSA is the technique most frequently used in forensic psychology, an example from this field will be used. In Figure 5.8 the variables from Canter et al. (2003) are represented. In all SSA the variables are arranged in

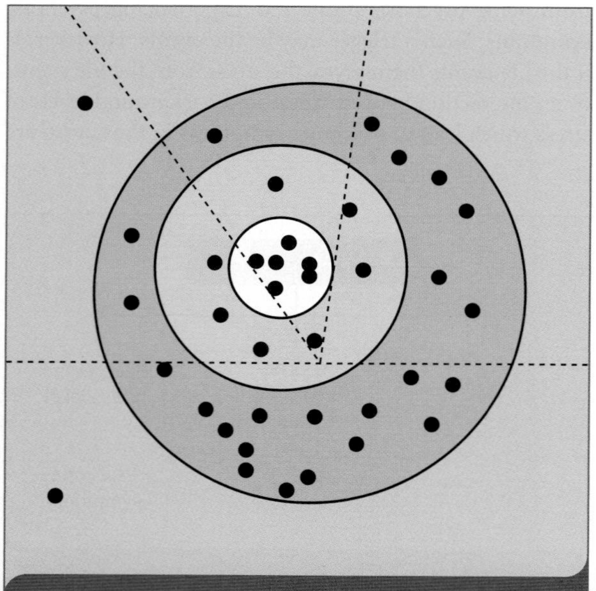

Figure 5.8 A schematic representation of the type of image which can be produced using smallest space analysis.

a diagram like the one shown in Figure 5.8. A point in the diagram is considered the significant point; the distance of all other variables from this point is an indicator of how closely related the variables are to one another. Additionally, as in MDS, the way in which variables cluster together regardless of the significant point can also tell you something about the variables. Canter et al. (2003) applied smallest space analysis to examine the characteristics of stranger rape and which behaviours were most likely to co-occur. They wanted to use the SSA to determine the most useful way of summarising a large number of variables. Using SSA, these summary variables can be revealed in two ways. First, the variables which are closely grouped towards the centre of the space are most strongly associated with one another. This is like the strength in a correlation; the closer to the centre of the space, the stronger the relationship or common ground between the variables. Secondly, regardless of their proximity to the centre, the way in which the variables are grouped together will reveal which variables may be summarised by an overarching title.

Canter et al. (2003) reported data which were explained by two dimensions, so the data would have looked similar to the schematic. The two dimensions also suggested that the data points could be explained by two different ways of grouping the data points. Canter et al. (2003) reported that the points moving out from the centre of the space were summarised by the levels of violation which the perpetrator inflicted on the victim (personal, physical and sexual). The way in which the variables were grouped, regardless of their proximity to the centre, was explained by the varieties of violation inflicted upon victims (involvement, hostility, theft and control). Summarising the data from 112 rapes in this way allowed the authors to produce a classification of rape types and to determine which characteristics were unique to individual rapists (these would be far from the centre of the diagram) and which behaviours were more likely to co-occur.

As with classification of psychiatric disorders, approaching criminal behaviour in this way may help to reveal something of the underlying difficulties leading to such behaviours. Additionally, determining patterns of behaviour may aid in the capture of rapists, and also help to determine whether victims are one in a series or whether rapes have been committed by different offenders. Canter et al. (2003) used smallest space analysis on data which were collected during interviews and this is another example of how qualitative data can be quantified and analysed in a useful manner. For another example of the application of this technique, Fritzon, Canter and Wilton (2001) have used smallest space analysis to examine the behaviours reported during arson and terrorist offences.

Self-test questions

- Does content analysis focus on the meaning of the words used?
- Why is discourse analysis so inherently bound within the social context in which the research is taking place?
- What are the assumptions behind parametric data?
- When would you use a statistical test of difference?
- What is a confounding variable?

Developing psychometrically sound measures for abnormal, clinical and forensic psychology

In Figure 5.6 the statistical methods specific to developing **psychometric tools** are highlighted on the far right. Psychologists are often called upon to produce tools, either interviews or questionnaires. These may be to meet a gap in the literature not previously considered, or an adaptation of an existing measure to test a specific hypothesis. Either of these will require knowledge of the psychometric properties of a scale and how to determine whether a scale is **valid** and **reliable**. For a measure to be useful, it must be both reliable and valid. Reliability means that the test is able to produce the same results time after time in the same set of people. Validity is whether the test actually measures what it claims. A test can be reliable without being valid, but it cannot be valid without being reliable. It has to be designed to record what it claims to record, time and time again before a test or measure can be considered useful. An example of a measure recently produced by a psychologist is the **Cannabis Experiences Questionnaire** (Barkus et al., 2006). The questionnaire was produced to measure people's experiences when they have smoked cannabis. They produced a scale to measure the immediate effects and the after-effects from cannabis. In the previous literature, the experiences that people had were only recorded in an anecdotal fashion rather than systematically. The researchers were interested in how a proneness to psychosis was related to having psychosis-like experiences when using cannabis. Using this systematic measure, the authors confirmed that there was

a correlation between psychopathological experiences in response to cannabis and psychosis proneness.

When producing a measure, a number of aspects of the items and the measure need to be considered. These will be briefly outlined.

Face validity

One of the aspects of validity considered in test selection is face validity. Simply put, face validity indicates that a questionnaire can be seen to measure the **construct** it was designed for from the impression the items give. Under some circumstances, it may actually be disadvantageous for the area that the questionnaire is targeting to be readily identifiable simply by looking at the items on the questionnaire. For example, if you were developing a measure of psychopathy, it would be necessary to disguise what the questionnaire was targeting, since those who score highly on psychopathy are likely to lie in order to give the answers that they feel the researcher wants. This can also be a problem when using measures in the general population, since there are always individuals who are interested in biasing the results of a study, or indeed trying to please the experimenter, leading to error. Often questionnaires use filler items as well as the questions of interest in order to disguise the purpose of the questionnaire. However, the filler items need to be considered carefully, since these will influence what the questionnaire appears to measure at face value.

External criterion validity

Face validity only reflects the viewer's perception that the questionnaire items measure what they appear to. In order for a questionnaire to be useful, it needs to measure what it claims to measure at least as well as an existing tool. This is referred to as external criterion validity. It is the ability of a new tool to produce measures of a trait or behaviour which are highly related to another measure that has already had its reliability and validity previously established. This is usually achieved by looking at the correlations between a new scale and an existing and well-established measure. Alternatively, a questionnaire could be compared to an interview measure, with the obvious advantage that a questionnaire would be considerably less time consuming than an interview, assuming it proved to be equally valid.

Item reliability

The first and perhaps the most important parts of any questionnaire are the items which are written to comprise it. Item reliability is where each item contributes to the sub-scale of a questionnaire on which it appears, and has some underlying feature in common with the other items on this subscale. In order for this type of reliability to be achieved, the questionnaire items need to be selected on the basis of a particular theory which informs the overall goal of the questionnaire. It would be difficult to explain any results produced by a questionnaire if items were not selected on the basis of a logic with its roots in the ideas that led to the initial production of the questionnaire.

Test–retest reliability

Test–retest reliability is the degree to which a measure produces the same results over multiple time points when used on the same people. Usually, when establishing test–retest reliability a week is left between one test occasion and the next. However, if a questionnaire measures a trait which is thought to be a particularly stable trait, it should remain approximately the same over time periods as long as a year. There are traits such as schizotypy or extraversion that are thought to decrease as people age. Therefore leaving long periods of time between retesting on these traits may not produce results that are stable.

Internal reliability

As well as showing consistency over time, it is necessary for a useful questionnaire to produce subscales with items that seem to measure the same thing consistently. Internal reliability is when the items on a subscale all measure the trait or construct for which the subscale is designed. In examining internal reliability, the subscale items can be compared one against the other, or one-half of the sub-scale can be compared to the other half. This is **split-half** testing.

Factor and principal components analyses

In order to determine the statistically valid subscales for a new questionnaire, either factor analysis (FA) or principal components analysis (PCA) is used. These two measures are very similar to one another and deal with the degree to which items vary in relation to one another – or, put another way, how responding to one item may determine how you respond to others. FA and PCA are a way of summarising a large number of items in a way which is statistically meaningful and representative of what the questionnaire

items have in common with one another. PCA and FA are used to produce subscales for questionnaires, since they group questionnaire items in a way that reflects participants' responses to them and therefore highlights and enables the grouping of items that appear to have something in common. Although these statistical methods group the questionnaire items, it is the researcher's job to determine how meaningful the results are in the wider context of the aims of the questionnaire and the literature from which the questionnaire items have been drawn. The labels are given to the questionnaire subscales by the psychometrics researcher and are more dependent on their knowledge and understanding of the research area than the way in which the statistical methods group the questionnaire items.

Self-test questions

- What is the difference between reliability and validity?
- What is external criterion validity?
- How would you determine whether a questionnaire measured a stable trait over time?

Research tools

With advances in technology, research tools such as neuroimaging and genetics, which were once too costly for researchers, have become more accessible. It is difficult to consider human behaviour without investigating how the brain works and what parts of the brain are associated with particular behaviours. It is thought that, by understanding the biological mechanisms using imaging technologies and genetics, the predispositions to behaving in a particular manner can be better understood. Additionally, both genetics and neuroimaging of behaviour may highlight new targets for treatments and other interventions for forensic and clinical disorders. Below is a brief outline of the imaging tools available and what they are able to demonstrate, which is followed by a summary of the types of genetic research used today.

Structural imaging methods

Structural imaging techniques are of interest to clinical and forensic psychologists because alterations in brain structure may offer clues to the causes of illnesses and may give some indication of disease progression if these alterations are detectable over time. We know genes are involved in the development of the brain prenatally, and as our knowledge of the role of specific genes develops, it may be possible to use the information about structural changes associated with diseases to develop pharmacological interventions more closely targeted at the biological processes.

Computerised tomography

Computerised tomography (CT) is considered a relatively old technique and is similar to the X-rays performed on other parts of the body. CT uses X-ray technology to produce images of the structure of the brain. It was one of the first methods developed to investigate the structure of the brain and has now been surpassed by other technologies in the quality of the images produced. CT is no longer generally used in research in clinical and forensic psychology. It is more frequently used for diagnostic purposes in physical disorders such as strokes and tumours, where its relatively low cost, its exposure to radiation and its (relatively) crude results are both justifiable and viable as a first port of call.

Magnetic resonance imaging

Magnetic resonance imaging is currently more frequently used in research in the fields of clinical and forensic psychology. **Structural MRI** is a technique used to examine the structure of the brain by detecting changes in the signal produced by the varying relaxing rates of hydrogen in water molecules caused by local variation in tissue type. The nuclei or centre of water molecules move about or 'spin' all of the time. The amount of space and the density of the tissue in which they are located will affect the degree to which they can move about or spin. MRI takes advantage of these factors. A large magnet is used to make the spin of the nuclei of the water molecules point in the same direction. A radio frequency is applied at right angles to the magnetic field. The radio frequency changes the direction of alignment of some of the hydrogen in the water molecules. This hydrogen then enters a high energy state when the radio frequency is applied, meaning they will be moving about a lot and moving away from their initial alignment with the magnet. When the radio frequency is turned off, the hydrogen nuclei slowly return to their original alignment with the magnet and their energy is scattered into their surroundings. The water molecules in different substances (such as blood or tissue) lose their energy (or move about) at different rates; this process is known as **relaxation**. This difference in relaxation rate is the

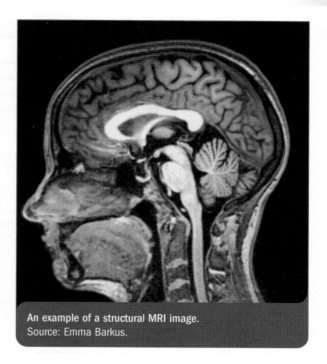

An example of a structural MRI image.
Source: Emma Barkus.

basis of structural MRI and produces a contrast which allows for the grey matter (the 'thinking part') and white matter (the support material) of the brain to be clearly shown as different from one another on an image. The grey areas of the brain are where the electrochemical neuronal processing takes place, while the white areas comprise the tracts of the axons which then end (or terminate in synapses) in the grey areas to produce the electrical currents that constitute brain activity.

Functional imaging techniques

A number of methods are used to examine the functioning (as opposed to the structure) of the brain, including magneto-encephalography (MEG), electroencephalography (EEG) and event-provoked potentials (EPPs). The focus of this chapter, however, will be on three functional imaging techniques: positron emission tomography (PET), single photon emission computerised tomography (SPECT) and functional magnetic resonance imaging (fMRI). In Table 5.1 the quality of these different techniques is directly compared. Functional imaging techniques offer a clue to which receptors and/or brain areas are involved while completing cognitive tasks. The key to obtaining successful results from functional imaging methods is to develop tasks which specifically tap into the cognitive domain or function of interest.

Table 5.1 Comparison of PET, SPECT and fMRI imaging techniques

	PET	**SPECT**	**fMRI**
Temporal resolution	Poor resolution	Very poor resolution	Good resolution
Possible time of study	Restricted by time to decay of isotope	Restricted by time to decay of isotope	Restricted by quality of software in the computer (delayed reconstruction of the functional images permits the use of longer paradigms)
Possible analysis	Receptor location, levels of neurotransmitters, glucose consumption, oxygen flow; however, only block design	Receptor location, ligands; however, only block design	Metabolites, blood-oxygen flow, movement of water, event-related and block designs possible
Invasiveness	Radioactive isotope required	Radioactive isotope required. Long half-lives of isotopes used make repetition difficult	Non-invasive
Image acquisition	Relatively slow	Slow	A trade-off between the quality of the images produced and the number required
Directness of measurement	Receptor location good, functional techniques adequate	Very indirect measure of function	BOLD currently viewed as a correlate of functioning, spectroscopy limited by location (bone interference) and quality of scanner

Single photon emission computerised tomography

Single photon emission computerised tomography (SPECT) looks at cerebral blood flow or brain metabolism using **radioactive isotopes** or **ligands**. The radioactive isotopes or ligands make the blood flow or **neurotransmitters** 'light up' so they can be seen using the SPECT camera. It is the **gamma ray photons** of energy produced by the isotope as it decays (or breaks down) which are detected by the camera. The length of time it is possible to scan using SPECT is determined by the time taken for the isotopes to break down, since without the isotope binding the receptor or oxygen molecules it is not possible for the camera to detect it. A SPECT scanner contains a **collimator** made up of parallel channels placed on sodium iodide (NaI) crystal. A collimator is a filter that will detect signals running parallel to one another and in the same direction. This allows for the background noise to be filtered out from the actual signal. The gamma rays pass through the collimator and hit the NaI crystals to produce light. Behind the NaI crystals there is a grid of photosensitive tubes, which capture the light produced by the crystals. It is this configuration of lights which is used to produce the SPECT image.

Positron emission tomography

Positron emission tomography (PET), like SPECT, can be used to examine the activation of different substances or the location of particular receptors in the brain. Radioactive ligands or isotopes are developed which bind to the substance or receptors of interest. The isotopes are usually given intravenously (through a vein, often the carotid artery in the neck, which is the quickest external route to getting something into the brain). The isotopes decay in the brain and lead to a releasing of energy which is detected by the PET camera as the energy is dispersed in both directions from the point of origin. The PET camera only detects the dispersal of energy when it is dispersed in two opposite directions, so the signal can be detected against a backdrop of noisy energy being released by other processes. The PET scanner acquires the brain images in slices (or segments which cut across the brain either up and down or back to front of the head) and can acquire more than one slice at once.

The half-life of the isotopes that have been developed for PET varies between 2 minutes and 120 minutes. The exposure to radiation, the relatively reduced quality of the images and the length of time which the isotopes last for restrict the design of the studies that can be performed using PET studies. PET can be used to determine the flow of blood in the brain. However, it can also be used to examine more physiological research questions, such as the effect of dopamine uptake in a particular task or condition.

Functional magnetic resonance imaging (fMRI)

The quality of the images and the length of time for which participants can be scanned is superior using **functional**

magnetic resonance imaging (fMRI) compared to both PET and SPECT. Additionally, since the technique does not involve exposure to any radiation, it is considered less harmful to participants and is therefore seen as more 'participant friendly' by ethics committees.

Functional magnetic resonance imaging (fMRI) is a non-invasive process that has been developed to examine changing neuronal activation. It is assumed that when a particular brain area is being used to complete a task, this area of the brain will give off a signal indicating that it is 'active'. fMRI can be used to examine a number of functional aspects of brain activity as follows:

- **Blood oxygen dependent level (BOLD)** measures changes in oxygenation of blood around regions in the brain.
- **Perfusion fMRI** measures the regional changes in cerebral blood flow.
- **Diffusion-weighted fMRI** measures the movement of water molecules through the brain.
- **MR spectroscopy** measures the changes in a number of metabolites in the brain.

BOLD does not measure blood flow directly, but is considered a correlate of it (i.e. is closely related to it). In the human body there are certain metal elements that have a high magnetic susceptibility relative to water or air: that is, they are more likely to align to a magnetic field. One such metal is the iron contained in **blood haemoglobin** (this is what gives blood the red pigmentation). Oxygenated blood contains oxygenated haemoglobin, which is not magnetic and therefore does not align to the magnet field of the fMRI scanner. However, the deoxygenatation of haemoglobin produces relatively more iron that is magnetic and consequently aligns to the magnetic field. It is the fluctuation in the presence of oxygenated relative to deoxygenated blood in a given area which produces changes in signal during brain activation that are detected by the fMRI scanner. Initially, when a brain area becomes active there is a slight decrease in the amount of oxygen available as the neurons take up the available oxygen. In 3 to 6 seconds an oxygen-rich supply of blood reaches the area to maintain the activation. There will be far more oxygen available than is actually required by the neurons. The excess oxygen-rich blood will fill the surrounding area close to the part of the brain that is activated. The increase in the levels of oxygenated blood increases the amount of signal detected by the fMRI scanner, relative to the surrounding deoxygenated tissue. The changes in signal during periods of activity are typically in the region of 1–10 per cent relative to the rest state, although this may vary.

Since fMRI has greater temporal and spatial resolution than PET or SPECT, there is greater flexibility in the tasks

and areas of cognition that can be investigated using this technique. However, the participant's head must remain still during tasks, since fMRI is highly sensitive to movement artefacts. Additionally, any equipment (or participant) used in the fMRI scanner needs to be non-metallic, since metallic objects create MRI artefacts and are also a safety hazard. It is generally recommended that fMRI paradigms contain 'rest' periods in order to randomise when the 'slices' are taken, as well as providing a basis for comparison in the experimentally active periods. The tasks used in fMRI

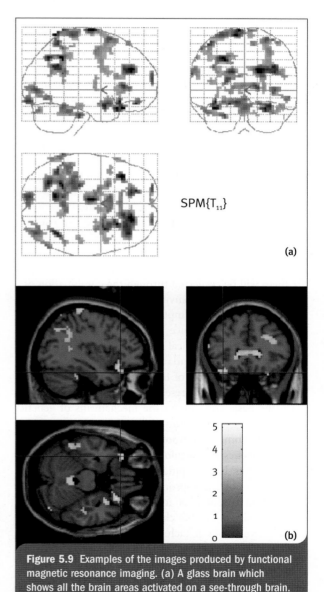

Figure 5.9 Examples of the images produced by functional magnetic resonance imaging. (a) A glass brain which shows all the brain areas activated on a see-through brain. (b) Three orientations of the brain showing areas activated by decision making.
Source: David A. Holmes.

can be either block (or 'on–off') designs, like those used in PET and SPECT scanners, or they can be event related, where specific time points throughout the scanning time are identified and placed in the analysis. A particular aspect of the experience of being in an fMRI scanner that needs to be highlighted, especially in auditory paradigms, is the noise that the magnets make as they vibrate in the scanner. This can be uncomfortable for some participants, although most seem to tolerate the conditions well.

Genetics

The use of genetics in research has had a long and controversial past. However, given the current ethical and technological infrastructure for researchers, genetic analysis has now become a sound and financially realistic addition to most projects.

The same caveat relating to correlation and epidemiological studies applies to genetic studies: a relationship between a particular gene and a group of patients or a particular pattern of behaviour does not imply direct causation. Not until the mechanism of a gene has been established as relevant from a biological and behavioural perspective can a gene be implicated in the causal pathway for proneness to a behaviour or disorder. Unfortunately for researchers in the fields of clinical and forensic psychology, the disorders of interest are complex and risk for them will be conferred through the combination of a large number of genes, environment and life experiences. Genes are, however, an important cog in the machine that produces behaviour, since they may indicate biological targets for pharmacological intervention.

Some review of fundamental principles is needed before a brief overview of the research approaches taken in clinical and forensic research is given. It is difficult to grasp the basic concepts of the mechanisms of genetics because we are talking about things that are impossible to see without complex technology. The technologies underpinning genetics are ingenious and complex. Most cells in human beings' bodies contain 23 pairs of **chromosomes**. The 23 pairs of chromosomes contain all the necessary information to allow a cell to divide multiple times to produce an embryo. On the chromosomes are many **genes**; we have two copies of each gene, one inherited from our mother, one from our father, which is why we have pairs of chromosomes. The genes contain instructions for every aspect of existence from the development of the foetus in the womb, to what colour our hair and eyes are. Each gene comprises a sequence of **bases**, which we have in pairs. Bases are usually 'read' from left to right (much like a book), although this is not always the case. The bases are

the information that the genes follow when they complete their effects upon our bodies.

The changes that occur to leave individuals prone to psychiatric disorders occur at the level of the bases or the information for the genes to follow. These changes are referred to as single nucleotide polymorphisms (or SNPs). Other changes that take place in the bases are insertion/deletions, where another base may be added, or a base may be missing altogether, or a particular sequence of bases may be repeated. These changes may alter the functioning of what a particular gene controls the production of; however, the effects of many changes associated with clinical and forensic disorders are not known as yet. It is difficult to appreciate how changes that take place on something so small can alter human behaviour. However, when you consider the subtle variation of human behaviour, and how infrequently this behaviour alters to produce psychiatric problems, it is easy to appreciate how it requires a large number of very small changes to lead to clinical and forensic disorders.

Association studies

Association studies are population-based studies where the frequency of particular SNPs is compared in two different populations or groups of individuals. These groups can be patients versus the general population, or they can be people who express a particular trait compared to ones who do not. A representation of the design of association studies can be seen in Figure 5.10. There are two large samples, one clinical and one drawn from the non-clinical population. Each small circle represents a variation in a base located on a gene. The individuals who have the 'risk' variation in the base, or risk SNP, are represented by small shaded circles, while those who have the normal non-risk SNP are represented by clear circles. Association studies compare the frequencies of the risk SNPs in two groups of participants to determine whether the SNP is significantly associated with a clinical disorder or type of behaviour.

For example, Haberstick et al. (2006) were interested in extending the literature on aggression and the role of the **serotonin** (5HT) system. Serotonin is a neurotransmitter that has been implicated in the modulation of mood, impulsivity and aggression. The neurotransmitter is taken from one area of the brain to another using a vessel called a **transporter**. It is an SNP on the gene which contains the information for producing the transporter that has previously been associated with a number of mood modulating factors, such as life event. Haberstick et al. (2006) suggested that, since a relationship between serotonin and aggression has been previously reported, it is possible that it is the transporter rather than the serotonin itself which contains

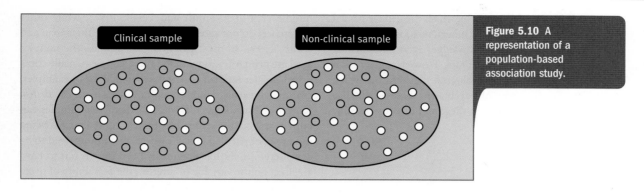

Figure 5.10 A representation of a population-based association study.

the change that leads to aggressive behaviour. They were particularly interested in aggressive behaviour in children. They got family and teacher ratings of aggressive behaviour in children at multiple time points and looked for a relationship between these ratings and the SNP change on the 5HT transporter gene. Across the time points they found the strongest association existed at aged 9 years, where those who had the ss alleles (or bases) on the 5HT transporter gene SNP had the highest scores on the aggression questionnaire.

Linkage

Linkage studies are often completed prior to tests of association. In a linkage study, rather than the emphasis being placed on particular SNPs, the degree to which sections of chromosomes are passed from one affected relative to another is examined. For an example, consider Figure 5.11. The squares represent males and the circles females; the circles and squares which are shaded express a particular disease, such as bipolar disorder. Within this family we can see that in each generation at least one relative expresses the disorder, although they were not

always born to parents who expressed the disorder (the latter would be referred to as **carriers**, since they carry the genetic liability for a disease but have not expressed it). Examining which sections of chromosomes in this family (or pedigree) are common to those who express the disease compared to those who do not may help to identify biological pathways involved in the development of a disease. This approach has been used in many physical diseases; however, it has not been so effective in psychiatric and behavioural disorders. There are a number of reasons why this might be the case. First, the incidence of most psychiatric disorders is relatively low in the general population and it is not particularly often that the disease seems to segregate in families with a pattern of inheritance which is easy to determine. Often isolated genetic communities are used for linkage studies, since there is less background variation in their genotype. An example would be the higher rates of bipolar disorders in Mormons in the USA. An additional complication in linkage studies in psychiatric diseases is that they are caused by a combination of biological and environmental factors that combine to lead to an underlying vulnerability being expressed in the development of a disorder. Furthermore, all the analysis methods for linkage

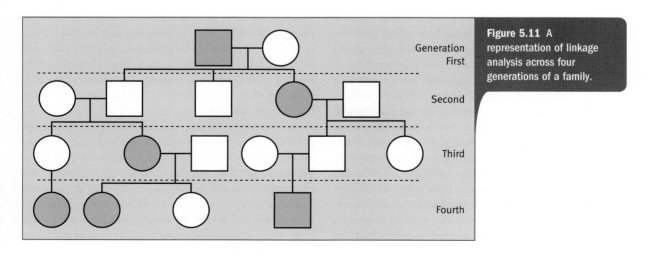

Figure 5.11 A representation of linkage analysis across four generations of a family.

studies require that the means by which the gene is passed from parent to child (mode of inheritance) is known.

At the current state of knowledge, even an educated estimate may be rather inaccurate. However, given that there are some clues to the biological mechanisms which lead to the development of psychiatric diseases, linkage studies can be used to confirm these and identify possible new areas of interest.

Using the internet as a research and therapy tool

Since the development of the internet in 1984, its use has drastically changed the amount of information to which people have access. It has also meant that electronic communication has become the norm in business and educational backgrounds. This has opened up new territory for researchers and therapists alike. The internet can be used as either a primary or secondary research tool. When the internet is used to recruit participants or collect data, it is referred to as primary research; while use of the internet to search for information (using search engines) to inform research is called secondary use of the internet for research. This section will focus on the use of the internet for data collection and recruitment. It is not possible to do complete justice to the use of the internet as a research tool, but some of the most important issues will be highlighted in brief. Additionally, with the focus on clinical research in this book, some discussion about the use of the internet as a therapeutic tool will also take place.

Recruitment

Many issues of concern with recruiting from the internet are an extension of those concerning recruiting from the general or student populations. Some authors have suggested that those who use the internet are not representative of the general public, since it requires they have access to a computer and dial up or broadband as well as the skills to use the technology. However, within the last two decades of the internet becoming more widely available for use by the general public (rather than private agencies), it has become an integral part of education and the workplace. With approximately 500 million users estimated to log on, it is difficult to see how such a large potential resource of participants cannot be considered representative. Some authors have suggested that those who respond to internet recruitment are more likely to be male, well educated and

middle class (e.g. Smith and Leigh, 1997), while other researchers do not agree with this claim (e.g. Buchanan and Smith, 1999). In most psychological studies, the samples used are primarily students and these samples usually comprise a greater number of females than males. For examples, examine the articles published in most issues of the *British Journal of Psychology*. It is possible that these samples can both be used in the same study to help combat any skewing in the sex of participants. However, two points need to be considered. If sex has previously been shown not to have an effect on the variable of interest, the possibility of over-representation of either males or females is not of concern. Additionally, if a large enough sample is recruited, it has a much greater chance of being representative and will also allow the detection of small effects of any differences caused by such demographic variables. Internet recruitment is more likely to lead to a larger sample of participants being collected.

As with non-internet recruitment, in order to recruit a representative sample it is necessary to advertise the study appropriately. Participants can be recruited using the internet by placing advertisements on relevant chatrooms, website banners or pop-ups, and websites that advertise psychological studies, such as the American Psychological Society's Psychological Research on the Net: www.psych.hanover. edu/APS/exponent.html. Websites can also be registered with search engines, and when key terms are entered, the web page for your study will come up as a result. There are also websites that will list links for free. The content of websites on which you advertise your studies will determine the type of sample you will encourage to complete your study. For example, if you were interested in the degree to which characteristics of schizotypal personality disorder (see Chapter 14) are present in the general population, you would want to advertise on spiritually related websites (odd beliefs within society are shared by people who express schizotypal trait). If you also advertised on an anti-psychiatry or hearing voices website, you would obtain a different pool of potential participants. These concerns are not specific to web-based research and should be familiar to the discerning researcher. However, when reading journal articles it is worth considering where they recruited their sample from to highlight any underlying biases in the sample.

An alternative method of recruitment would be to email potential participants to highlight your web page. Sending unsolicited emails or spam may have the same effect as pop-up banners on websites, in that very few people will pay attention. In the case of banners, it has been suggested that less than 1 per cent of people who view pop-up banners on websites will follow the links (Birnbaum, 2004); it is likely spam emails will receive a similar level of attention.

An alternative is to send an email via a source which legitimises your status as a scientist, such as via the host for online organisations or one which has access to university or college students. Many educational institutions now have weekly newsletters which are delivered via email, and studies can legitimately be advertised in these.

Surveys and questionnaires

Birnbaum (2004) reported that the internet allows for a large sample to be accumulated in a short period of time. This makes it a useful way of recruiting a large number of respondents in a relatively short period of time and using relatively cheap methods. Using the web, it is possible to recruit more heterogeneous samples than the student samples used in most psychological survey studies (e.g. Hertel et al., 2002; Mueller, Jacobsen and Schwarzer, 2000). It has also been reported that collecting data for longer questionnaires using the internet produces fewer errors (without producing different response styles) than using traditional pen-and-paper methods (Pettit, 2002).

There are a number of psychological mechanisms associated with internet research which may ensure that individuals' responses are more indicative of themselves than face-to-face data collection:

- Internet responses are thought to be less socially desirable (Kiesler and Sproull, 1986).

- Communications over the internet are thought to increase self-awareness (Matheson and Zanna, 1988), which in turn is thought to lead to greater self-focus (Lea and Spears, 1991).

- Perceptions of anonymity may encourage honesty in those completing surveys on the internet (Prentice-Dunn and Rogers, 1982).

The internet may be a useful tool for piloting new questionnaires that have been developed to meet a gap within a body of literature. However, the issues concerned with recruitment methods need to be kept in mind in order to ensure that the most appropriate individuals are approached to participate. If the topic is of a particularly sensitive and personal nature, using remote data collection, as in the internet, may be an opportunistic method of obtaining data that are unbiased by social conformity or other interview-related demands. However, remote data collection may lead to the validity and reliability of the responses being questioned by non-initiates to web-based research. Much less control can be exercised over the state and sincerity of respondents to web-based surveys. Efforts such as including lie scales may be one method of reducing these problems. However, some care needs to be taken with lie scales, since some personality traits lead some people to respond in a manner that may be consistent with lying even though they are actually being honest.

Lie scales contain a list of questions to which all people should respond in a highly predictable manner. For example, individuals with a particularly strong moral sense are likely to endorse the question 'I have never stolen or taken any object, however small, from someone else without permission', which is a standard question on many lie scales. Another approach would be to look at the internal consistency (see the section on psychometrics, pp. 141–2) of the items to ensure that participants are responding consistently across items which are known to be measuring similar traits or subscales. The concern of insincere responding is not restricted to internet-based research and to a certain extent all that can be done is to assume respondents are engaging in the research in a genuine manner.

Ethical issues

Research is considered both a process and a product that informs practice (Smith and Rodgers, 2000) and that needs to consider the participants' vulnerability within the experimental situation. Excellent standards of research are only the preliminary position from which ethical research can develop (Roberts, 1999). For the true value of research to be fully assessed, it is necessary for the ethical issues raised within the research to be openly discussed (Miller, Pickar and Rosenstein, 1999).

An ethical consideration that influences all stages of research is informed consent. It is considered central to protecting the rights and welfare of the participants (Carpenter and Conley, 1999). Roberts and Roberts (1999) have developed a model of informed consent which can be applied in most settings. They define informed consent as follows: 'Informed consent requires that individuals truly understand and freely undertake the decision to participate in any kind of experimental or clinical care' (Roberts and Roberts, 1999: p. 1028). Informed consent is the product of three constitutional elements, information, decisional capacity and autonomy, plus two further aspects relating to the research situation, professional relationship and context. When using participants from the general population, they have the capacity to make decisions for themselves provided the information is presented in accessible language. However, when performing research with patients, prisoners or people under 18 years old, their capacity to make a decision may be questionable and it may require a surrogate or guardian to sign for them.

In some studies, sensitive information may be collected, such as information about drug use. Potential participants who may disclose a type of lifestyle which might not be within legal limits will be fully protected by the confidentiality within research. Under these circumstances, breaches of confidentiality, which are damaging either emotionally or financially, are covered within the English legal system under 'tort' law and are considered admissible in court (Dickens and Cook, 2000). Confidentiality can only be breached if participants reveal activities that are potentially harmful to themselves or other people. Additionally, the cultural norms of the groups being studied need to be taken into consideration. For example, a student or patient population may engage in greater risk-taking activities (such as illegal drug use or excessive drinking), which may be normal within the subcultural group they belong to.

Self-test questions

- What information would a computerised tomography image supply?
- What is the difference between positron emission tomography and functional magnetic resonance imaging?
- What would you be interested in if you made use of functional magnetic resonance imaging while a participant was completing a working memory task?
- What is an SNP?
- What genetic analysis method is usually used in family studies?

Chapter summary

Four different approaches can be used to address research questions: case studies, **epidemiological research**, and experimental and correlational approaches. These differ in terms of the number of participants and the degree of detailed information that is obtained from the participants. The type of data which can be collected is either quantitative or qualitative, which differ in that they are concerned with numerical data or the language used by participants. **Quantitative methods** examine either the degree to which scores vary together (correlational) or whether groups of participants differ from one another (test of difference).

When developing a measure or **questionnaire** to be used in a study, a number of aspects of the tool need to considered: whether the questionnaire appears to measure what the researcher intends it to (face validity), whether each item contributes to the questionnaire and measures a similar construct (**item validity** and **internal reliability**), whether the measure produces consistent results in the same people on successive occasions (**test–retest reliability**), and whether scores correspond to already existing measures (**external criterion validity**). Statistical methods called **principal components** and **factor analysis** are available to help reduce the items on questionnaires to produce subscales and also to highlight any items which may be redundant in the measure.

With swift changes in technology, biological methods such as imaging techniques and genetics are increasingly becoming part of the palette of tools at the disposal of researchers. Existing measures permit the exploration of the structure of the brain (**CT**, **MRI**), functional activity of neurotransmitter levels, glucose and oxygen using radioactive ligands (**SPET**, **PET**) and the levels of oxygen in blood (**fMRI**). Genetic studies can inform researchers about the small genetic changes (**polymorphisms**) associated with a particular illness, while family studies highlight which areas of a gene are passed from one affected relative to another within a family pedigree (**linkage**).

As a greater percentage of the general population become engaged in the use of email and the **internet**, this opens up a new tool for recruitment and delivery of therapy to vulnerable groups. The use of remote methods to recruit participants allows for access to a large number of participants in a relative short space of time with targeted and appropriate advertising. Additionally, with software developments it is possible to collect survey and behavioural data on the internet which can be stored in a secure but readily accessible location. Developing and validating self-help or therapeutic interventions for delivery over the internet leads to low overheads, while increasing the ability to access vulnerable patients with restricted mobility.

Ethical considerations are essential to good-quality research, since they aim to protect both the participant and the researcher. The process of informed consent and considerations around the storage of data are paramount in all research, regardless of the approach being taken.

Suggested essay questions

- What are the advantages of quantitative methods when compared to qualitative research methods?
- Discuss the statement: 'case studies have little place in modern-day psychological research'.
- Evaluate the merits of epidemiological research when compared to experimental studies.
- Discuss the degree to which current ethical procedures for research are a straitjacket which restricts the progress of psychiatric research.
- Do you agree that validity is more important when developing a psychometric tool than reliability?
- With advances in functional magnetic resonance imaging methods, has the use of radio ligand imaging methods (e.g. positron emission tomography) become redundant?
- What are the ethical issues to consider when using the internet to deliver a therapeutic intervention?

Further reading

Overview texts

Banister, E. W. (1997) *Qualitative methods in psychology: A research guide.* Buckingham: Open University Press.

Bartol, C., Bartol, A., Davies, M., and Croall, H. (2007) Criminal behaviour: A psychosocial approach: WITH Criminal justice, an introduction to the criminal justice system in England and Wales AND Research methods in criminal justice and criminology. London: Prentice Hall.

Coolican, H. (2004) *Research methods and statistics in psychology.* London: Hodder Arnold.

Howitt, D., and Cramer, D. (2004) *Introduction to statistics in psychology.* London: Prentice Hall.

Howitt, D., and Cramer, D. (2005) *Introduction to research methods in psychology.* London: Prentice Hall.

Specific and more critical texts

Brown, G. G., and Eyler, L. T. (2006) Methodological and conceptual issues in functional magnetic resonance imaging: applications to schizophrenia research. *Annual Review of Clinical Psychology*, **2**, 51–81.

Foster, J., Barkus, E., and Yavorsky, C. (2006) *Understanding and using advanced statistics.* London: Sage.

Hewson, C., Yule, P., Laurent, D., and Vogel, C. (2003) Internet research methods: *A practical guide for the social and behavioural sciences.* London: Sage.

Pearlson, G. D., and Calhoun, V. (2007) Structural and functional magnetic resonance imaging in psychiatric disorders. *Canadian Journal of Psychiatry*, **52**(3), 158–66.

Visit **www.pearsoned.co.uk/davidholmes** for a range of resources to support study. Test yourself with multiple choice questions and access a bank of over 100 videos that will bring the topics to life. Video coverage for this chapter includes a discussion of why we use research, the uses of twin studies and a snapshot of unethical studies from history.

PART TWO

CLINICAL AND FORENSIC PSYCHOLOGY

This section will introduce the professional and applied approaches to abnormal behaviour. Chapter 6 gives an overview of clinical psychology and its place as a discipline as well as what is involved in applying the subject in its professional context. However, much of this entails clinical practice: that is, assessing or treating clients, and interventions associated with specific disorders, which can be found in those respective chapters elsewhere in this book. Chapter 7 provides a similar overview of forensic psychology as well as an insight into areas of practice not subsumed under other sections of the text, including major contributions such as prison-based work and how evidence is obtained by the police and presented in court. Further contemporary concerns will be examined in the wake of the relentless advance of technology, as exemplified by criminal use of computers and the spectre of contemporary lie detection actually realising the potential raised by accounts from fiction. The hybrid profession of clinical-forensic psychology is covered in Chapter 8 with examples of its value to the contemporary student, such as criminal profiling, as well as examples of challenging abnormal offenders, including sex offenders, the various types of stalkers, and psychopathic or dangerous and severe personality-disordered offenders.

Chapters in this section

6 Clinical psychology

Watch classic footage of Skinner's study of behaviour modification with pigeons.
This is one of several videos that explore issues and disorders relevant to this chapter at
www.pearsoned.co.uk/davidholmes

7 Forensic psychology

Discover how thermal imaging technology can detect lying. This is one of several videos that explore issues and disorders relevant to this chapter at www.pearsoned.co.uk/davidholmes

8 Clinical forensic psychology

Discover the pathology of learning violence. This is one of several videos that explore issues and disorders relevant to this chapter at www.pearsoned.co.uk/davidholmes

CHAPTER 6 Clinical psychology

- Overview
- Case study
- Historical development of clinical psychology
- What is contemporary clinical psychology?
- Clinical psychology in practice
- How to become a clinical psychologist
- Chapter summary

Watch classic footage of Skinner's study of behaviour modification with pigeons. This is one of several videos that explore issues and disorders relevant to this chapter at www.pearsoned.co.uk/davidholmes.

Public misconceptions

The media stereotype of modern clinical psychologists or psychiatrists still portray couches and Rorschach tests, which belong to a bygone era of psychoanalysis. Source: Pearson Online Database.

Media call for mentally disordered individuals to be 'sent for counselling' is an error that incorrectly portrays the roles of counsellors, clinical psychologists and psychiatrists. Counsellors are not qualified to administer treatment to such clients, but apply skills in support and guidance where treatment is not an issue, such as in bereavement (see Chapter 1). This misconception often co-occurs with treatment for the mentally ill being portrayed as a patient 'on the couch' receiving psychoanalysis, which is archaic. These media-amplified errors unfortunately influence the public, who are then rather surprised to receive cognitive behavioural treatment face-to-face with a clinical psychologist.

The public are also confused as to the differences between a clinical psychologist and a psychiatrist. As covered in the text so far, the psychiatrist is medically qualified and is able to prescribe medication or administer other medical procedures. This is not a requirement for clinical psychologists, but although they cannot prescribe drugs, their normal treatment approach of CBT can be superior to medication, particularly in the long term.

The opening case study is not typical of cases seen, but its rare nature illustrates some of the professional and practice issues in clinical psychology addressed in this chapter. The historical development of clinical psychology draws from diverse aspects of psychology and psychiatry, but a thread of empiricism can be traced from its early formative years through its professional expansion later in the twentieth century.

In Europe, the historical relationship between clinical psychology and health service providers, particularly the National Health Service in the UK, has been important in defining the diverse roles of the contemporary clinical psychologist and the nature of this discipline. This tenuous relationship with the NHS as provider was tested in the twenty-first century and the competing model of provision in place in the USA, parts of Europe and elsewhere in the world may provide the UK's future, as described in the section 'Clinical psychology in practice'. Here the diverse contexts and specialist areas of need for this relatively new and expanding profession are described and their role as scientist-practitioner implementing evidence-based practice is evaluated. Embedded in these roles are issues involving work experience, training and supervision for those psychologists developing their careers. In the final section, international variations in the practice and training of clinical psychologists are considered in the light of a need for standardisation and regulation between professional bodies throughout the world.

Case study
A case of mistreatment

When John married Maria it was a delight for their parents but a journey into the wilderness for the young couple. They were inexperienced sexually and in relationships. They had met on holiday in Spain and their accompanying parents had thrust them together, hoping their shy, retiring offspring might start a new life, away from home. Three years later, what had been a perfect parental match was beginning to become a local scandal. Maria was still a virgin but John had an affair with his employer's somewhat predatory daughter, who was anything but discreet.

This initially caused a rift in parental relations with accusations that there was something wrong with John for which Maria's mother had discovered the word satyriasis (excessive, uncontrollable sexual desire). All parents agreed that something had to be done and an appointment was made with a private marriage counsellor in the nearby town, who seemed eminent and rather expensive. John and Maria attempted to explain their problems together and then individually. The counsellor, who also ran a private detective agency, was more puzzled by the reasons why the couple were together than where their difficulties lay. After a third unproductive appointment in which John had offered the observation that Maria and he were sexually incompatible, the counsellor advised them to see a friend of his who offered relationship analysis and therapy.

The counsellor and his friend's lack of affiliation to any professional body was obscured by a mass of odd qualifications, but these inexperienced families just wanted to pay to have the problem 'fixed'. John and Maria entered a practice offering exotic treatments for everything from work stress to baldness. The 'therapist', Forrester, spotted that the couple had little prior knowledge of each other, or of relationships, but his eventual suggestion that John had not entirely left his relationship with his mother, and that Maria was too pure for John, who should get in touch with his childhood emotions, simply scared John, who restated that they were sexually incompatible.

Unbeknown to either of the parents, John visited his family doctor and after several embarrassing moments told the story so far. 'I could make an appointment for you at the sexual health clinic we have,' the doctor finally surmised, 'but I have a colleague, a clinical psychologist, with a lot of experience with couples like yourselves'. Dr Trainor is very discreet, but you must go as a couple to see her.' Dr Trainor was far removed from the image of the relationship analyst; she was like a friendly, cheerful aunt and did not hide behind a desk but rather managed to put both Maria and John at ease and encouraged them to explain how they saw their relationship. A few gentle, guiding questions began to uncover parental pressure, insecurity, severe anxiety and very little sexual knowledge.

Necessarily, Dr Trainor saw John and Maria separately and from John's limited explanation of 'sexual incompatibility' and the 'compatibility' of his affair, she had an idea of how to approach the painfully shy Maria. Dr Trainor's preliminary hypothesis proved remarkably accurate. A combination of John's inexperienced clumsiness and Maria's anxiety was causing vaginismus or an involuntary muscle spasm at the entrance to the vagina. 'I am not a medical doctor but all my experience tells me this is not a permanent condition but is entirely due to your anxiety, your fears about sex and John's limited approach to sex.'

Dr Trainor taught Maria how to use Kegel's exercises and her own fingers progressively to reverse the problem, but also had two sessions with John on basic sexual technique with a few sensate focus exercises for the couple to practise, which were to be instigated by John himself. The results were slow but spectacular in terms of both the couple's relationship and their individual confidence. Dr Trainor reflected how far this was from her original training and how she would like to have given the parents some training in reduction of obsessive control. However, she felt satisfied that the combined abilities developed during her extended placement as psychologist at the sexual health centre had enabled her to make a difference in this odd and mostly hidden area of people's lives.

Not all clinical psychologists work with a predictable client group. Many professionals in the twenty-first century work in more specialist areas and bridge gaps that patients such as Maria and John would otherwise fall through. Being a qualified and properly trained professional is also an issue in days when a confusing array of therapies and advice are available from diverse approaches. Its is good to have diversity but safer in the long run if diverse interests and specialisms follow well-regulated professional training, which for a psychologist should begin with a **clinical psychology doctorate**. The following chapter will explain what clinical psychology is and how it developed into the main area of professional employment for psychologists.

Historical development of clinical psychology

In Chapter 1 it was made clear that clinical psychology is central to the study of abnormal psychology, in that it is the practical application of psychological knowledge and principles to reduce the problems of individuals in a clinical context. The main activities of clinical psychologists are psychological assessment and therapy, though they are also expected to carry out research and routine evaluations of assessment and intervention methods. In this chapter, a more detailed examination of these roles will be discussed in the light of the many guiding principles that have evolved during the historical development of the profession, such as the **scientist-practitioner** model.

As outlined in Chapter 1, contemporary clinical psychology methods evolved from the early work of behaviourists such as **John B. Watson** against a relatively ineffective backdrop of psychoanalysis. Paradoxically, the psychoanalytic mystique tended to be the domain of psychiatry, whose 'ownership' was defended as stoically as their professional authority over the emergent clinical psychologists. Thus the credibility of psychoanalytic forms of therapy tended to rely on their being a major part of the psychiatric establishment rather than on any empirical success in treating patients. The acceptable use of psychoanalytic intervention was greatly enhanced by its application with First World War casualties suffering psychosomatic complaints and the effects of 'shell-shock'. However, much of this work was therapeutically ineffective and, in addition, a major proportion of the involvement of psychologists in the First World War was intended to prevent the 'tainting of the gene pool' in order to avoid using troops who would break down in the trenches. This was the impoverished state of clinical psychological knowledge in the UK and

Europe at this time. Despite the pioneering work of **Lightner Witmer** in establishing the world's first psychological clinic in the USA in 1896, psychoanalysis and crude psychiatric treatments predominated until the 1950s.

In the UK, the Ministry of Defence recruited psychologists to assist with the psychometric selection of troops for the impending Second World War. The intensive development of psychological tests and testing techniques during the war period up to 1945 built up some occupational momentum for those clinical psychologists who had been employed. As Cheshire and Pilgrim (2004) point out, the 'old school' dominance of psychoanalysis was not left behind entirely during the war, as the development of tests in this period tended to be headed by psychoanalytically oriented clinical psychologists such as **J. R. Lees**, the ex-director of the Tavistock clinic, a centre for psychoanalysis in London. After the war, one of the first clinical psychology courses ran at the formative psychology department headed by the highly influential empirical psychologist **Hans J. Eysenck**. This was housed at the London Institute of Psychiatry and mostly focused on psychometric assessment. Others were at the Tavistock clinic and the **Crichton Royal Hospital** in Scotland.

The financial and structural occupational support of the NHS for clinical psychologists from 1948, following shortly after the widespread need for psychometric instruments for testing troops in the Second World War, gave the profession secure employment. However, in practical terms, it was behavioural pioneer Joseph Wolpe's (1958) relaunch of the highly effective behaviour therapy that would truly propel psychological treatments into mainstream therapy, severely denting the assertive dominance of both psychiatry and psychoanalysis. Simultaneously, there was the emergence of the first effective treatment for schizophrenia in the form of neuroleptic medication, which also undermined the assumptions of psychoanalysis and those psychiatrists with this orientation (Shorter, 1997).

Even at this early juncture, the fact that clinical psychology did (and still does) not truly own its own knowledge base (or, to a great extent, its own history) was still evident as it was often viewed as a mere accessory of psychiatry and allied professions. However, it was from this point that the profession began to develop its own clinical expertise (Cheshire and Pilgrim, 2004). This intensified the pressure on clinical psychology either to compete or to cooperate with other health care professions, particularly psychiatry. It may be necessary to consider the historical rise of the 'professional' in society to understand why such a complex struggle for status can arise in health care, where the general public tend to consider all professionals to be working towards the common good of the client/patient.

Cheshire and Pilgrim (2004) consider a sociological view of how the professions slowly developed their relationships with other structures in society, including the general public. In this view, professionals gain status by their professional dominance over clients, intellectual superiority over the public (and most in public office), and social closure: that is, excluding 'outsiders' and vetting their own ranks to maintain the unique status of their expertise. The inherent weaknesses of early psychology as a science and the lack of clear boundaries between clinical psychology and other professionals (e.g. psychiatric nurses, psychiatrists) made the attainment of status that much more difficult. As a consequence of having to justify its existence continuously throughout its history, clinical psychology has become more adept than other professions at maintaining its public professional integrity, defending its boundaries and validating its methods. During the postwar period, advances were made in terms of psychological theory as well as techniques arising from clinical practice, which enabled clinical psychology to become a distinct profession with its own expertise and more exclusive approaches to intervention.

Apart from cognitive and behavioural contributions, other aspects of directly applicable psychological research have made inroads into the territory of clinical practice. For example, Martin Seligman proposed the **learned helplessness** model for some forms of depression (Seligman, 1975) and the accompanying suicidal behaviour based on behaviourist studies, which demonstrated that the inability to control significant events can be generalised to other situations, resulting in behavioural apathy and depression. In addition to providing a fundamental approach to explaining the development of depressive states, this approach also led to the therapeutic approaches of **learned optimism** and **learned effectiveness** (Seligman, 1992). These approaches have in turn become institutionalised as the twenty-first-century discipline of positive psychology (Seligman and Csikszentmihalyi, 2000), with its clinical application combining the outcomes of studies on the origins of happiness with Seligman's earlier principles.

Early clinical psychologists hardly deserved the label 'practitioner', as actual therapeutic practice was very rare, even in the heartland of clinical psychology, the USA. The majority of qualified clinical psychologists were based in laboratories for many years, working in the routine manner of the experimental scientist. In the UK, the BPS Division of Clinical Psychology was formed in 1966. This not only gave an academic focus but also authorised professional recognition and a professional structure for clinical psychologists in the UK. It also enabled a network of clinical psychologists to reinforce their unique position in health care by drawing up their own working practices

Focus

Cognitive behavioural therapy and clinical psychology

The emergence of cognitive therapy during the 1970s, following the application of behavioural principles to thinking patterns, added to the growing platform from which the profession of clinical psychology could directly change the behaviour and thinking of clients. Clinical practice benefited from **Aaron Beck's** disillusionment with psychoanalysis, leading to his formulating a form of cognitive therapy that proved far more effective. Combining cognitive therapy with behavioural therapy and behaviour modification approaches, clinical psychology gained a therapeutic model that provided a serious alternative to the medically based approach. **Cognitive behavioural therapy** (CBT) not only proved effective, but could also provide transferable skills to maintain improvement for the clients themselves and thus became staple therapy of clinical psychology.

An analogy often used by the Oxford-based proponent of CBT David Clark illustrated this advantage well. His illustration likens pharmacological treatment to supplying a starving man with fish to eat in that he will simply starve once the supply is stopped. Passing the skills and insights of CBT approaches to a client is likened to teaching the starving man to fish for himself, providing self-sufficiency rather than dependence on the clinician. This aspect of the therapy provided a further challenge to the assumed superiority of the medical interventions of psychiatry and carried none of the dangers and side-effects of physical treatments, whilst producing direct and measurable change in behaviour, cognition and affect.

Around the end of the twentieth century, CBT seemed suddenly to appear as an intervention used in more serious disorders such as schizophrenia and bipolar disorder, giving clinical psychologists a major role in serious psychiatric disorder. However, it was recognised within bodies such as the British Association of Behavioural and Cognitive-Behavioural Psychotherapies (BABCP) that evaluations of CBT use in more severe disorders had been ongoing for many years, but that many outcomes from these studies were being published over a short time span.

and guidelines. In the UK this included a carefully negotiated relationship with the National Health Service, aided by reports such as the Trethowan report (Department of Health and Social Security, 1977). This relationship came under pressure in 2006 due to government restrictions on funding that placed pressure on training throughout the NHS. From the 1970s onwards, clinical psychologists had evolved from laboratory-based scientists into the enduring role of the **scientist-practitioner** (see below).

What is contemporary clinical psychology?

Clinical psychology can be currently thought of as the applied aspect of abnormal psychology, with clinical psychologists being one of the few professions trained to assess and treat abnormal behaviour. They apply psychological principles and theory in a clinical context to effect change in the client's behaviour, thinking and consequent physical and emotional state. In the main, clinical psychologists are not qualified and in most countries they are not legally authorised to apply physical or medical treatments such as prescribing drugs, the use of surgery or ECT (electroconvulsive therapy; see Chapter 3), which can only be administered by a professional qualified in medicine. This is one of the distinctions between a clinical psychologist and a **psychiatrist**, with only the latter being allowed to use medical interventions, produce a psychiatric diagnosis or order the detention of clients for inpatient treatment. This distinction has been challenged by US clinical psychologists, who see their role as closer to that of psychiatrists in that context.

As mentioned at the start of this chapter, the public, media and sometimes the legal professions are often unclear as to how clinical psychologists, psychiatrists and psychotherapists are distinguished from each other. A psychiatrist will have qualified as a medical doctor and then specialised in psychiatry for 3 years, qualifying for membership of bodies such as the **Royal College of Psychiatrists** in the UK. Although psychiatrists and clinical psychologists may use various forms of psychotherapy (in its broad sense covering all psychological therapies, including behavioural and cognitive behavioural interventions), a psychotherapist may have had no professional background and have only attended a specific course of therapy training, which may have had a duration of only weeks, though some courses can last years. Registration of therapists is now routine by psychology governing bodies such as the **British Psychological Society** (BPS) in the UK or more specialist societies such as the **British Association of Behavioural and Cognitive-Behavioural Psychotherapies** (BABCP). However, *regulation* of the ability to practise is far less easily achieved, with a few psychotherapists having levels of training in mainstream therapies (e.g. cognitive behavioural therapy) equivalent to that of qualified professionals, but others having had minimal training in obscure and sometimes poorly validated treatment.

As a psychology graduate, a clinical psychologist will also have been trained in psychological therapies, mainly cognitive behavioural approaches, but as only part of their formal 3-year postgraduate professional training to doctorate level. However, in some countries training is still only 2 years to master's level, though this is becoming a rarity. This training will cover not only therapy, but assessment, clinical placements, evaluation and administration (this is discussed further below).

However, as Huey and Britton (2002) point out, there are many other duties beyond the concise treatment-oriented definition that can be essential to the role. Huey and Britton (2002) refer to some of these as: teaching and supervision of clinical trainees and new graduates; service planning; clinical research (as well as evaluation of practice); ambassador roles; and the organisation, management, administration and staffing duties of any professional organisation. They go on to point out that hardly any of these roles are specific to clinical psychology, which leaves the question 'how do clinical psychologists distinguish their profession?' somewhat unanswered, except in the application of the term 'psychology' to each of the previously mentioned roles.

In 1988, Derek Mowbray helped to identify the key skills of clinical psychologists for a Manpower Advisory Group report (also known as the Mowbray report) and focused on what distinguished these professionals from those adjacent in the field (MPAG, 1990). The levels at which these skills are applied can be seen in Table 6.1 below and served to reinforce further the role of the clinical psychologist as scientist-practitioner (see the next section).

The MPAG report identified the flexible application of **nomothetic** (i.e. rules drawn from generalisable principles) psychological knowledge to **idiopathic** (i.e. a novel, individual presentation) case details as being the skill unique to clinical psychologists. Thus the routine application of this adaptable problem-solving skill is seen as central to

Table 6.1 Skill levels for clinical psychologists derived from the MPAG report

Level 1	Those skills in gaining and maintaining rapport that can facilitate simple treatment and support, such as stress management or counselling skills.
Level 2	Skills involved in the delivery of established interventions defined by existing protocols that are more complex than the above.
Level 3	The skill of drawing on complex and multiple psychological theories and principles, applying these in a flexible way to devise individually tailored strategies to address complex idiopathic presenting problems.

Focus

Defining the clinical psychologist

Definitions of clinical psychologists tend to reflect their aims, activities and responsibilities. One of the simplest of these is 'the application of psychology to health and community care' (British Psychological Society, 2001). Thus, many of the day-to-day duties of clinical psychologists involve the assessment and treatment of patients. These activities have already been outlined in general terms in Chapters 3 and 4. However, clinical psychologists are also expected to carry out routine evaluations of the assessment and intervention methods used. Nietzel, Bernstein and Mirlich (1998) consider further attributes of clinical psychologists as:

- having an interest in behaviour and mental processes
- conducting research into understanding human functioning
- the use of measurement to verify observations of individuals
- helping the psychologically distressed.

However, most definitions tend to focus on the duty of clinical psychologists, as an extension of the latter point, to relieve suffering and help individuals excel in their daily lives.

the definition of what clinical psychologists are and how they are distinguished from those in allied professions.

Thus clinical psychologists are distinct in their clinical attitude, a flexible integration of inductive and deductive skills to provide a critically variable approach to intervention and its constant evaluation: that is, the idea of science in action rather than fixed prescriptive responses. Described as open-minded scepticism by Huey and Britton (2002) and as the role of the reflective practitioner by Schön (1983), this process of critically applying psychology to improve practice underpins the scientist-practitioner role of the clinical psychologist.

The scientist-practitioner role of clinical psychologists

Many clinicians simply train until qualified, then engage in practice with their clients. Although this is true of most health care professionals such as psychiatrists, the clinical psychologist is expected to take on the dual role of both clinical practitioner, assessing and treating clients, and investigative and evaluative scientist, applying the scientific method to inform and evaluate their practice. The historical role of the clinical psychologist as experimental laboratory scientist and the somewhat insecure nature of psychology as a science have made the term 'scientist-practitioner' an important part of the definition of a contemporary clinical psychologist. Thus the reflective role of the scientist-practitioner should ensure that treatment approaches are constructed and modified on the basis of available empirical evidence of their value as well as implementing ongoing evaluations of their efficacy in a particular clinical context. The role is considered to be 'reflective', in that the clinical psychologist is expected to be aware of their own work in context and to adapt readily to novel contexts and feedback from their research and routine evaluations.

The laboratory-based empirical work originating with Wilhelm Wunt and William James was operationalised by Lightner Witmer. This feeding of clinical practice by psychological research and theory as a continuous process was made explicit at a highly significant 1949 postgraduate education conference at Boulder, Colorado, which recommended the scientist-practitioner model for training all professionals but had its most direct impact on clinical psychologists (Huey and Britton, 2002). Following this, the scientist-practitioner model was also known as the Boulder model both in the USA and elsewhere. Specific recommendations emerged from this conference regarding training, including that clinical psychologists should be university trained; be psychologists first and clinicians

second; serve a clinical internship; be competent in assessment, therapy and research; and complete an original research PhD (Trull and Phares, 2001). These criteria were not just implemented in the USA, but many appeared in training courses in Europe and elsewhere. It is often seen by other academics as surprising that many qualified clinical psychologists in the UK, having completed a practitioner doctorate, will then also complete a PhD thesis by research in order to be fully research qualified, emphasising the importance of research in the scientist-practitioner role.

As leader of clinical psychology for the UK, Eysenck pushed for research and testing in place of clinical practice, placing the clinical psychologist in the supporting role for other professionals. However, this was based as much on his reservations regarding psychoanalysis as an intervention as on any consideration of the professional remit for clinical psychologists (Cheshire and Pilgrim, 2004). Whilst not directly treating patients, clinical psychologists during this period played a somewhat marginalised role by advising psychiatrists in their interventions and were often seen as an unnecessary impediment by many in the psychiatric profession. This scientific appraisal of interventions was eventually to produce an empirical psychological approach to treatment that could be systematically applied by clinical psychologists in a manner pioneered by **Monte Shapiro**. In 1958, the year Joseph Wolpe published his strategic text on the approach (Wolpe, 1958), Eysenck approved and introduced behaviour therapy as an intervention that should be the preserve of clinical psychologists. This demarcated the remit of clinical psychologists, in that they would manage more behaviourally based disorders, such as anxiety disorders, leaving psychiatrists to treat those disease-based disorders that warranted a medical intervention. Here Eysenck was redefining the boundaries of the clinical psychology profession, so-called 'boundary work', whilst maintaining the scientist-practitioner ethos. 'Boundary work' is the process by which a profession defends the territory of its expertise and excludes other workers from gaining entry, hence establishing and maintaining the 'boundaries' of the profession (also see Abbott, 1988).

This demarcation of the territories of psychiatry and clinical psychology continued for a period, with clinical psychology tending to be responsible for the treatment of the 'walking wounded' in outpatient units, whilst psychiatry monopolised inpatients with organic disorders and psychoses, with mutual respect attained by both adhering to the scientist-practitioner approach. However, the anti-psychiatry movement, which was gaining strength towards the 1970s, also targeted the scientist-practitioner approach as being inflexible and inhuman as part of the movement's general attack on the scientific method (see

Chapter 2). Psychologists who also preferred differing non-empirical methods reinforced this challenge to the Boulder approach and the compromise term 'scientific humanism' (Pilgrim and Treacher, 1992) evolved in the wake of the establishment of the Psychology and Psychotherapy Association in 1973 (Cheshire and Pilgrim, 2004). This resulted in more diverse theoretical orientations in the clinical training courses during the 1980s. This supposed 'eclectism' resulted in fewer clinical psychologists being regularly engaged in research, if at all, further undermining the scientist-practitioner model.

In the twenty-first century, the majority of clinical psychologists are now trained in both the scientist and the clinical practitioner role, and regardless of the nature of their professional post will be expected to apply scientific practice to their clinical role. However, some clinical psychology posts do demand higher levels of theory and research applied to clinical practice. In teaching hospitals that are allied to universities, many clinical psychologists have their time divided equally between teaching on the clinical training courses and seeing their clients. In this type of post, the demands for the application and refinement of academic psychological theory as well as research to improve methods of assessment and intervention are high, as these departments not only strive for clinical excellence but also compete for extra funding on the basis of research and teaching quality. Thus in addition to teaching and client duties, clinical psychologists will be encouraged to initiate projects, attract funding for and publish research, and undertake associated administrative and consultancy roles (see the next section).

As in other areas of academia, those qualified clinical psychologists already engaged in research and bids for funding tend to form a minority of highly research-active individuals, although often carrying out studies that can be highly specific and often experimentally weak (Spellman and Ross, 1987). Other clinical psychologists with high caseloads, administrative pressures and little experience of research funding tend to view research as a luxury they can ill afford. This weakens the generalised assumption of the clinical psychologist as scientist-practitioner constantly evaluating good practice Beutler et al. (1995) found in a US national survey that practitioners make efforts to understand research findings, but that specialist researchers are less likely to understand the day-to-day problems of practitioners. Thus although Beutler et al. (1995) consider the reasons for keeping scientist and practitioner roles separate, the combined role may be the only way to produce operationally useful research.

Evidence-based practice and clinical governance

The level 3 skill (MPAG, 1990) referred to above, whereby clinical psychologists apply generic specialist psychology knowledge to idiosyncratic patient data, is dependent on the principles of **evidence-based practice**. Evidence-based practice is clinical practice that is both informed and improved by objective data from ongoing innovative research and the routine evaluation of current applications. Thus, this is a process rather than a goal or achievement.

Research

Practice-based evidence

The converse term to **evidence-based practice** is practice-based evidence. This refers to the use of clinical practice in the field for research, which is similar to the routine evaluation of current applications above but involves **inductive** reasoning (i.e. the testing of pre-formulated research aims) as well. Thus the **naturalistic setting** of the clinical psychology unit provides **external validity** (see Chapter 5) for generating study evidence that can then be utilised in future clinical practice as part of the process of evidence-based practice (Newman, Kellett and Beail, 2003).

An example of this would be a series of clients receiving cognitive behavioural therapy for social anxiety, who may be asked to rate the duration of their sessions on the basis of their degree of anxiety towards the end of their treatment. Thus no experimental change has been made to their clinical session, but feedback may help to judge whether progressively longer sessions may help future clients adjust to their intervention programme more comfortably.

Due to the convenience of administration, most of this type of practice-based evidential research involves the use of questionnaires, which places limits on the validity of the results (see Chapter 5). However, this initial evaluation may then be followed up by a study, which experimentally manipulates the variable of session duration.

In the UK, the government introduced clinical governance in a 1998 White Paper (Department of Health, 1998) in order to ensure that 'excellence in clinical care will flourish' (Murray et al., 2004). This refers to a framework by which the NHS intended to make it compulsory for NHS organisations to continuously improve the quality of their service and its delivery in all departments, and particularly at the point of contact with the client. For all clinical units there was an appointed lead person for the implementation of clinical governance, but staff at all levels were expected to implement the process. This requires good staff attitude towards quality improvement (usually by time-consuming research into evidence-based practice issues) rather than a tick-box approach representing minimal compliance. Murray et al. (2004) outlined the areas in which there was a statutory requirement to improve quality, the so-called 'seven pillars' of clinical governance: the clinical audit; risk management; service user experience; professional development via training; education and life-long learning; research and effectiveness; clinical information and staffing (including staff management).

Implementation of clinical governance required all services to have structures in place to monitor and evaluate the quality of patient care. Most pertinent in the case of clinical psychology is the 'pillar' of research and effectiveness, in the form of the process and outcome of therapy and its flexibility in the face of variable presentations and contexts. Clinical psychologists are already familiar with the scientific evaluation of the effects of intervention in different dimensions of a specific case problem, and in situations that will inevitably be coloured by the particular setting and client group, and even the theoretical orientation of the therapist's training (Boyle and Whitely, 2003). Thus the contemporary clinical psychologist tends to fit into the framework of clinical governance very easily and has already developed the prerequisite skills to continuously evaluate and improve the service they deliver.

As can be seen in the processes of practice-based evidence and evidence-based practice, the essential higher-order aim of clinical psychologists is the focus of the level 3 skill, that of clinical problem solving. In the light of this, Huey (2001) evaluated the benefits of introducing problem-based learning (i.e. the practical development of problem-solving skills in the manner of 'discovery learning') into clinical psychology training. The conclusion that problem-based learning trains future practitioners *how* to think about their approaches to clinical issues, rather than simplistically *what* to think in approaching a problem, further emphasises the importance of the flexible scientist-practitioner role in training as well as qualified practice (Huey, 2001).

In a modern context, it is not surprising to find the jargon of monitoring and evaluating clinical practice appearing to take the focus away from the client as patient and towards the patient as source of research data. Parry, Cape and Pilling (2003), in a review of the (international) guidelines for evidence-based practice that relate to clinical psychology, concluded that they needed to be supplemented with a means of monitoring what is actually done in practice. Thus the processes of evidence-based practice and practice-based evidence within a clinical governance structure should not be seen as an end in themselves but as a means to improve the well-being of the client efficiently. This goal may also require clinical psychologists to adapt to new or more effective applications from theory or to new theories as a basis for their work (Marzillier and Hall, 1999), even though this may mean fundamental change to the approaches they have been familiar with for many years. This very flexibility in their approach, practice and evaluation is often what distinguishes clinical psychologists from their professional colleagues.

Self-test questions

- Discuss why US clinical psychology has been important in the development of the profession throughout the world.
- Why were psychological tests useful in expanding the profession of clinical psychology?
- What are the reasons for behavioural therapeutic approaches taking over 50 years to be accepted?
- In what ways is a clinical psychologist distinct from a psychiatrist?
- What is meant by the term 'scientist-practitioner'?
- Why is evidence-based practice important in the day-to-day work of a clinical psychologist?

Clinical psychology in practice

Clinical psychology employs the largest number of professional psychologists of any profession. Thus apart from psychologists in the media, the face of psychology that the public sees most frequently tends to be that of the clinical psychologist. However, clinical psychologists tend to differ from other health professionals in the wide variety of settings within which they work and the diverse roles they play within these contexts. Although all should have

Focus

The settings and clients of clinical psychologists

The clientele of clinical psychologists are also remarkably varied. Many are routinely referred by family doctors to clinical psychologists in various settings, such as outpatient departments, community mental health teams, specialist university departments and high street private practices. Within these settings the clinical psychologist will often be working in a team under a principal team psychologist, or even within a team of non-psychologist professionals as the sole clinical psychology representative, often in a general medicine context.

Others may see private clients as 'paying customers' on an individual basis in their private practices. Some clinical psychologists may have very little if any contact with clients, as they may mainly focus on training or consultancy work with other professionals. In the USA, the majority of clinical psychologists work in private practices and patients tend to have health insurance (Trull and Phares, 2001).

received the same standard of postgraduate training, each trainee will differ in their more specialist area of interest, which will usually become focused in the topic for their practitioner thesis and may also have been evident during their clinical placements. Thus, not only do the final destinations of graduates vary, but also the specialist interests and orientations of the qualified clinical psychologists entering them. It will only be possible to discuss a sample of these roles and settings in this section, as well as examining the additional duties that tend to be common to most qualified clinical psychologists.

The roles and activities of clinical psychologists

As stated above, the daily activities of clinical psychologists around the world can vary greatly and few will engage in all the possible roles and responsibilities. However, most will have had contact with the activities briefly described below.

Assessment and intervention

These are the primary roles guiding the training of clinical psychologists and as their primary expectation on taking up their first post. Although Chapters 3 and 4 deal with these activities in detail, it is worth considering how varied these generic activities can be in practice. Differing settings and client groups will present specialist demands on clinical psychologists, who may have to assess and manage patients with neurological damage, child clients who have been abused or even drug users in forensic settings. The most common disorders treated by clinical psychologists tend to be anxiety disorders, states of depression, somatoform disorders and substance disorders.

Clinical teaching and training

Many clinical psychologists either teach on clinical psychology courses as part of a dual contract (differing days allocated to teaching or clinical caseloads) or are brought in from clinical practice to teach specific units. Some teaching staff on clinical psychology courses in the UK may be purely academic psychologists with no clinical contact. It is often the latter lecturers who are responsible for the administrative duties on clinical courses, though the heads of courses are more usually senior clinical psychologists. In addition to training those on clinical doctorate courses, other professionals and NHS staff such as nurses may also receive psychological training. In the UK, training has traditionally been funded by the NHS but this is not the case elsewhere and may change in the UK in the future.

Development

Self-development for qualified clinical psychologists may take a number of forms. Routinely, such professionals will be subject to evaluation by senior staff, feedback from those acting as supervisors and perhaps wider career advice from line management. However, most clinical psychologists will pursue specialist interests, which may require further in-house or external training (e.g. newer or more specialist therapy courses). For some, such as those wishing to work as both chartered clinical *and* forensic psychologists, this may require substantial training and further qualifications.

Supervision

This term could refer to the one-to-one supervision received by a trainee during clinical training, when a tutor supervises their practitioner thesis. However, it is more commonly interpreted as the supervision of clinical practice by a senior clinical psychologist. Clinical supervision for a period of years by a senior is a normal part of post-qualification training for a newly qualified clinical psychologist, though this may be seen as something of an extra burden in many countries, such as the USA. However, casework supervision of colleagues is one of the expectations of good practice in clinical psychology departments throughout the world. This is not always found in practice, with the majority of qualified clinical psychologists being dissatisfied with their supervision and around a quarter not receiving any at all in a UK sample (Gabbay, Keimle and Maguire, 1999).

Consultancy

The consultancy role for clinical psychologists can be routinely exercised within their circle of colleagues to provide specialised advice on a particular case or in an ongoing consultant role for a department or area for a particular specialism (e.g. neuropsychology). Some clinical psychologists also act as consultants to non-psychology professionals. For example, they may be consulted about the psychological complications of changing appearance or even body dysmorphic disorder (see Chapter 15) by a plastic surgeon. Increasingly, clinical psychologists are providing consultancy services for the police and courts in forensic settings (see Chapter 8).

Administration and management

Most working clinical psychologists engage in some form of administrative duties, whether it is simply clinical record keeping as a basic-grade clinical psychologist, or acting as the clinical director of an NHS Trust with managerial responsibility for multiple departments and a myriad of professionals. Thus, although very few clinical psychologists have their clinical work entirely replaced by managerial duties, many, such as heads of department, have substantial administrative roles; but none escape administration entirely. The following are a few examples of the many components in the expected administrative and managerial role of clinical psychologists.

■ **Communication and coordinator role.** In settings where a clinical psychologist works with others, particularly multidisciplinary teams, the role of coordinator communicating and facilitating cooperation between team members is not only important for the smooth running and effective delivery of services, but may also be inspirational in steering the unit to new areas of specialism and efficacy.

■ **Representation and policy development.** Clinical psychologists will often attend a number of routine committees, such as departmental or research committees. However, others may take on more substantial contributions and attend specialist meetings to establish departmental policy and changes to current practice. As an 'insecure science', clinical psychology tends to be over-concerned with guidelines, which often leads to a relative surfeit of such policy-making groups and meetings.

■ **Collective decision making.** This usually involves being appointed, though sometimes volunteering to make collective judgements or decisions: for example, serving on research ethics committees or recruitment and appointments committees.

■ **Record keeping.** Even at the most basic level, accurate record keeping is an essential daily feature of clinical work. Although there are many fledgling centralised computer systems in use across the world, it is in the individual clinician's interest to ensure they have accurate client and intervention records that are durable, detailed and accessible. These records not only inform future decisions, assessments and evaluations, but may also be needed in cases where problems arise or potential litigation may be an issue.

Evaluation

Evaluation is an essential part of clinical governance and is most often achieved by evaluation studies in the form of client surveys. Thus, clients' ratings of various aspects of the service they receive, from appointments systems through to the perceived efficacy of a new specialist therapy, can be gathered and statistically analysed. These data are then used to implement and test changes that may ultimately refine and improve interventions as well as other aspects of practice. Another element of evaluation is the feedback given to clinical psychologists as part of their peer supervision, which is intended to 'maintain the quality of performance and to extend the psychologist's range of skills' (Division of Clinical Psychology, 1995).

Research

Given the framework of the scientist-practitioner model as a basis for clinical psychology, there is the expectation that all qualified clinical psychologists should engage in research as part of their professional commitment. In practice, many do not contribute, ostensibly due to weighty clinical commitments, though they may keep up to date with current research literature and findings. Perhaps as a result of the 'publish or perish' pressures of research-based funding (e.g. Research Assessment Exercises in the UK), psychologists in clinical teaching departments are far more likely to engage in research than their counterparts in purely clinical settings. This may change as a result of clinical governance directives but it is still unlikely that the two settings will be equivalent in their research output. Producing successful research proposals for funding and subsequent project (including project team) management have become much-prised skills amongst professionals. These are often highly correlated with another measure of professional status: the number of research papers published. Funding potential, project management, publications and higher management experience are often the criteria for securing more senior positions in the profession of clinical psychology.

Ethics and ethical governance

As clinical psychologists deal exclusively with people, much research will inevitably involve clients. Thus, ethical procedures and guidelines for practice and research have become a major consideration and part of daily practice within the profession, emanating from its origins after the Second World War in the internationally agreed Nuremburg Code of 1947. In the UK there has been formation and regulation of Research Ethics Committees. Although bodies such as the UK Ethics Committee Authority, formed in 2004, primarily focus on the testing of medicines, the regulations governing the use of any human subject (including staff) in the NHS for research have become very strict (Parliamentary Office of Science and Technology, 2005). European requirements have begun to extend many of the guidelines to operate outside of the NHS (or its equivalent in other countries). The requirement to have an organised, structured approach to implementing ethical screening is represented by the term ethical governance. Each time errors occur, resulting in publicised harm to human subjects, there is pressure to impose even more strict and complex ethical limitations, which now seriously impact on research for clinical theses and even undergraduate psychology projects. Barry (2006) has argued strongly that the current overuse of ethics has inhibited research to the extent that patients (and thus study participants) are themselves opposed to it, as they consider they are being denied effective interventions as a consequence.

These aspects of the work of clinical psychologists are by no means exhaustive and many are common to other health professions. However, they should paint a more complex picture of the work of a clinical psychologist than the stereotyped bearded male eternally talking to patients on a couch all day. Real clinical psychologists do a lot more than assess and treat clients sitting face to face, and nowadays most clinical graduates are female. Although the above activities are commonly found across many different working situations, these elements appear very different when seen in the very varied settings in which clinical psychologists may find themselves.

The clinical psychologist: examples of settings

Even within a fairly standard hospital clinical psychology department setting, the methods of dealing with clients can vary. As discussed in Chapter 3, one-to-one client appointments may be supplemented by inviting the client's partner or significant family member in order to gain more information for assessment and better support for treatment. This client environment can be formalised into a more established intervention of this nature, such as couple or family therapy. Group therapy has a different format and agenda, as discussed in Chapter 3. However, many clinical psychologists work outside of the standard settings and are widely dispersed within and to some extent outside the NHS or its equivalent. Thus with the current shortage of qualified clinical psychologists, in countries such as the UK newly qualified professionals can choose from a wide variety of settings in which to work, patient groups to work with, and even approach methods and the paradigms to adopt.

Most clinical psychologists are still located in adult primary care within the NHS (or equivalent), although such services for children and older adults are increasing (Cheshire and Pilgrim, 2004). Some work in multidisciplinary teams in inpatient and day-care hospital settings, where the primary problems of the patients may be medical rather than psychological (e.g. an oncology unit). In such settings, clinical psychologists may be involved in helping patients and their families come to terms with terminal illness, or in pain management and various approaches to the patient's quality of life. Clinical psychologists may initiate and develop new services within these diverse settings, such as setting up self-assertion classes within a domestic violence unit. With such a range of functions for clinical psychologists, examples of settings become remarkably numerous as more diverse roles are considered. As can be seen from the following brief examples, setting specific issues and duties can make adaptive demands on newly employed clinical psychologists.

Older clients

One of the settings that places clinical psychologists adjacent to other specialists and presents unique challenges is that of clinical services for older adult people. This group will have higher levels of anxiety and depression, which will become compounded with other life events such as accidents or being a victim of crime. These disorders are also logically exacerbated by any loss of control over the client's life due to retirement or infirmity and the consequent effects of learned helplessness (Seligman, 1975) as well as the fragility of their mortality being highlighted by peer deaths. These disorders have an explicit psychological component that adds to any endogenous origins, and all interact further with the most prevalent psychiatric disorders of older adults, the organic dementias such as Alzheimer's disorder, vascular dementias and dementia with Lewy bodies (see Chapter 19). In the UK this clinical area has its own specific funding in recognition of the difficulties in coping with such chronic and increasing clinical challenges, as longevity and the proportion of elderly in the population both increase.

One contribution made by psychology to this setting has been to identify and challenge ageism within the many systems involved, from assessment and treatment assumptions to the many interactions with these patients throughout their clinical experience. It is difficult as many professionals will tend to classify clients broadly and it can take something of a change in culture to perceive the individual with a problem, rather than treating them as primarily an 'old person' with the associated stereotyped expectations. This is particularly an issue in the case of those inpatients with prominent disabilities. Legislation to combat ageism, although primarily for occupational contexts, came into force in the UK in 2006 and will assist efforts to reduce the extent of this clinically damaging tendency as the effects of such legislation broaden. Ideally, the experience of those aged over 65 should be a smooth transition from that of younger age groups. However, the reality is that a few older adults present particular challenges, often referred to as 'thick case-note patients' and the attitude towards them becomes generalised.

Byrne (2000) has examined the broader issue of the stigma of mental illness and detailed the factors involved. Clearly, the risk of prejudicial treatment if you are both elderly and suffering from such disorders provides scope for change, particularly for a psychologist working in this setting. Burns, Dening and Baldwin (2001) argue

that, although there are obvious limitations to services and evidence of ageism, the future conditions of elderly people with mental health problems in the UK are likely to improve. The Mental Capacity Act (2005) in the UK includes statutory provision of advocacy for those with limited ability to make health decisions. This has also given considerable support to clinical psychologists engaged in countering ageism in the treatment of those older patients with mental health problems.

Services for older adults include the input of clinical neuropsychologists (usually within neurology and neuropsychiatry units). Neurological determinants are now seen as primary in the explanation of cognitive, emotional and behavioural dysfunction in the twenty-first century. Neuropsychology involves the assessment and management of brain damage and dysfunction. This can be the result of injury, insult (usually drug damage), tumours or infections, which can occur at any age, and strokes, progressive disease (e.g. Parkinson's disorder) and the dementias that primarily affect the elderly. As already stated, anxiety disorders and depression are also more common in the older client, and although clinical psychologists are able to treat these two disorder groups directly, differentiating the effects of dementia from those of depression can present a more difficult challenge. Neuropsychologists have an important role here in using their historical expertise in psychological testing (see Chapter 4) or **psychometrics**, not only for differential diagnosis, but importantly to infer specific brain dysfunction from the results of psychometric tests of such abilities as cognitive, manipulation or memory function, to support data from more direct assessment such as NMR scans. These **soft signs** of dysfunction are very important in establishing the extent and risk of progression of a dysfunction, as they may be regularly administered compared with the 'hard' evidence from scans, which may not.

In being able to detect minor neurological problems prior to any observable change from routine brain scans, the clinical neuropsychologist has an important role in the early detection of progressive conditions such as dementia, allowing for valuable early interventions. There are now many specific tests of function inferring neurological impairment (see Goldstein and McNeil, 2004; Peck and Shapiro, 1990); however, the **Wechsler Adult Intelligence Scale** (WAIS-III; Wechsler, 1997b) and its many sub-scales are still the commonest instruments in such assessments.

Goldstein and McNeil (2004) give an illustration of how psychometric subtleties can solve logical difficulties in detecting problematic neurological change. Cognitive function decline in an elderly client is difficult to reveal by **normative tests** (i.e. where values are judged by comparison with population averages), as individual differences can be so great. Thus it is important to have some measure of premorbid functioning (i.e. prior to onset of illness) with which to compare current measures. For situations of this type, the National Adult Reading Test or **NART** (Nelson and Willison, 1991) will give a measure of ability but place minimal demand on current cognitive function, as the test is somewhat passive in nature (involving the reading out loud of single words). Thus, this allows current function to be compared with a reliable estimate of premorbid functioning. In such situations, the historical legacy of the clinical psychologist as expert in psychometrics is being usefully applied in more contexts over time.

Clinical neuropsychologists and other clinical psychologists working with the elderly will carefully document the pattern of effects that cognitive decline has on many aspects of the client's life and behaviour. These observations can be indicators of specific neurological decline and guide the clinician in selecting further assessment procedures. However, the effects on the client's behaviour also provide scope and detail for interventions based on countering the very behavioural effects observed.

In settings that deal with older adults, it is evident that far from playing a secondary role to medical staff, clinical psychologists both initiate and lead many of the services delivered. In the past, routes to clinical neuropsychology would rely on simply choosing posts in that setting as well as being oriented in that direction during training placements and in choice of thesis. However, in the UK the BPS has developed accredited training courses in clinical neuropsychology within the BPS Division of Neuropsychology.

Teaching hospital settings

This is a very common setting for clinical psychologists to take up posts, as there are clinical psychology departments in many universities across the world, and in the UK, as in some other countries, the number of accredited clinical psychology courses is increasing to help meet the demand for these professionals. Often new recruits will be seeking to enhance their career in this setting by taking advantage of increased opportunities for publication and funded research. There is often more impetus to network with other professionals across the world via conferences, collaboration and professional organisations, which tend to centre on teaching hospitals and university-linked departments. There are also links and consequent opportunities with outside units providing placements for students, which can be some distance from the university hospital department itself. Teaching staff will also be frequently engaged in consultancy work with a wide variety of contacts on specific issues related to their expertise (see Marzillier and Hall, 1999).

In addition to running clinical psychology courses, staff in teaching departments are expected to take on a normal caseload of patients (in proportion to their teaching load), often with the additional expectation that such departments are viewed as 'centres of excellence' or that they have some specialist area of clinical expertise (e.g. intervention in psychoses). Much of this reputation is based on the idea of recruiting higher levels of academic and research expertise in order to teach undergraduates, but also on having sufficient academic and clinical attainment to be accredited to run a clinical course in the first instance. Conversely, high expectations of staff in teaching units may reflect the need to maintain this reputation in terms of attracting research funding and meeting their annual quota of published output. It has been assumed that under this pressure, such staff may prioritise their research role over their clinical caseload, but the reverse seems to be the case, in that staff may become even more engaged in their work and their clients as a result of their academic activity, particularly where research and practice are integrated in the manner of evidence-based practice (Cheshire and Pilgrim, 2004).

A clinical psychologist in a teaching department is likely to have their week split into teaching days and days when they receive clients. Teaching duties can vary from simply delivering and assessing part of a teaching unit (e.g. the module 'Contact with the client') to having major administrative roles on the course, such as being the clinical tutor (placement organisation) or even head of course. Supervising clinical theses can enable staff to merge their teaching with their research specialism and they may also encourage students to publish from their theses. As with clinical practice, academic teaching has to be evaluated, updated and developed, requiring time to be devoted periodically to course revision and continuously to course development and evaluation. A major part of clinical training courses is spent on clinical placement, which usually increases during the final year of training. This requires supervision and substantially adds to the workload and responsibilities of senior staff working in teaching units.

Professional bodies related to clinical psychology tend to base activities in teaching units. This means clinical staff will be responsible for organising meetings, conferences and regular seminars that are open to the interested public. Although audiences tend to comprise mainly of clinical course students, outside staff and even clients will attend open seminars, as well as the events acting as an excellent recruitment tool by attracting undergraduate psychology students. The **British Association of Behavioural and Cognitive-Behavioural Psychotherapies** (BABCP) operates in this way in the UK.

Clinical psychologists in teaching departments usually play major roles in organisations such as BABCP and national guiding bodies such as the **Division of Clinical Psychology** of the BPS in the UK. These duties add to the daily communication and administrative workload, and for those playing a senior external organisational role they may require the devolution of some tasks to staff interested in developing this aspect of their academic or clinical career. For example, an aspiring member of staff may be given the responsibility for organising a national conference – an extensive task that would often be over and above their existing academic, clinical and research duties. Involvement in the running of national organisations or the major funding bodies for clinical psychology, such as the government or NHS in the UK, will usually mean involvement in shaping national policies and other roles in the national development of the profession and discipline. An example of this could be the creation of nationally established client liaison groups for clinical psychology in the UK to parallel the existing service user groups in other medical professions (Cheshire and Pilgrim, 2004).

Thus a clinical psychologist working in a teaching department will expect to have extensive demands placed on their time by multiple and varied roles in clinical, teaching, research and administrative duties. In addition, they may be expected to take on the further responsibility for shaping and developing national issues in clinical psychology. They will also have the satisfaction of not only implementing such changes in their clinical practice, but also integrating them into the clinical teaching course content.

One of the rapidly expanding areas of employment and consultancy for clinical psychologists are the many **forensic settings** that will be outlined in the following two chapters. Here clinical psychologists will work alongside prison staff and police and for the courts, as well as with **forensic psychologists** (see Chapter 7), who have been trained for this context but will lack clinical skills. An increasing number of psychologists working in the forensic context are qualified in both clinical and forensic psychology, which is a skill combination of particular value in both prison and courtroom settings.

Although the contexts may vary greatly for clinical psychologists around the world, certain generic skills and activities tend to be found in every area of practice. Assessment and treatment tend to be common to most settings, as is the distinguishing ability to apply psychological principles to clinical situations.

Clinical psychology reports

Report writing will be described in more detail in Chapter 8 when dealing with both clinical and forensic aspects of a case or incident. A clinical psychology report is normally a document giving a clinician's preliminary opinion as well as other client-relevant information and their problem, as well as any action taken.

Clinical psychology report writing is a routine activity undertaken as part of practice, but it may also be requested in order to gain a second opinion or even be requested by a professional or team outside of clinical psychology: for example, a solicitor wanting a report for court purposes. Although some professional bodies (e.g. the BPS in the UK) and even individual departments provide guidelines for professional reports, there is no fixed or ideal format (Trull and Phares, 2001). Increasingly, however, reports to be presented to specific bodies have highly defined formats, such as those submitted to Mental Health Review Tribunals in the UK. In preparing a report for such a purpose, it may be expedient to check for proformas or templates from relevant websites.

The lay public tend to think of reports as documents by professionals for professionals, and not really interpretable by those outside of the discipline. However, many reports are not submitted to someone belonging to the same discipline or even the same level of educational standing. As a result of this, aspects such as subject-specific jargon or complex grammar need to be minimised and target-specific accessibility emphasised. However, a real danger in applying such principles is that the document succumbs to the 'Barnum effect' (Trull and Phares, 2001). Barnum was a circus owner attributed with coining the phrase 'there's one born every minute' and associated with descriptions so general that they could apply to anyone or anything, which are used by 'fortune tellers' and others, and are part of the study of **parapsychology**. Thus, in an effort to make the report readable by anyone, it should not be written in such general terms that it becomes meaningless in terms of its purpose and could apply to any client. It must also take full account of the receiving audience and their information needs, and be coherent in communicating without loss of important detail or depth where appropriate. It may be expedient to stay within the same familiar framework or paradigm as the recipient.

Although background information can set the context, particularly to an idiopathic case, a good report should focally address the referral question for which it has been requested and not deviate substantially from this or simply provide unstructured information. Exhaustive detail is no substitute for relevance to the referral remit; nor will

Focus

Clinical psychology report content

A generic format for a clinical psychologist's report may follow these subheadings.

- **Basic client (and author) information.** As one would expect, this should include the client's name, age and other demographic detail as well as the name, position and location of the author.

- **Report remit.** This is the reason for the report being requested and should be succinct and able to be addressed within the scope of the document. It should be unambiguous both in statement and in how it is answered within the report.

- **The context to the referral.** This is a brief history and background to the problem, which should logically conclude with the reason for the referral.

- **Psychometric procedures and other assessments.** This should give the names (in full) of tests and procedures carried out and their immediate results.

- **A summary of the assessment outcomes.** This should give a picture of the client's functioning and limitations in areas such as: cognitive functioning; emotional stability; social and interpersonal functioning; general behaviour.

- **Preliminary diagnosis.** Depending on the remit of the report, this could be a short conclusion with justification criteria, or more extensive, including prognosis and other features of a formulation for the client (see Chapter 4).

- **Recommendations and directions.** In essence, this should address the report remit but make additional suggestions if aspects are uncovered that were not foreseen in the original recommendation for referral.

- **Further comments.** This section should include information and observations thought useful to the case but either not directly relevant to the referral remit or thought important to the welfare of the client if tangential to the inquiry.

---

it provide an 'intellectual smokescreen' in place of valid, client-specific valid data. All this said, producing a report should not be an intimidating process for a newly qualified clinical psychologist if the above caveats are considered and an appropriate format is followed (see the website for a sample report).

As accountability increases throughout the professions, the need to produce concise and focused clinical psychologist reports will become routine in clinical practice. This task should be regarded as a valuable opportunity by newly qualified staff as part of their normal professional development, and full advantage should be taken during supervisory periods to gain context-specific guidance from their mentor.

Future considerations

Although clinical psychology seems to have stabilised during its development in the twentieth century, progress in the twenty-first century is far from static. If anything, the rate of progress and change in this relatively new profession would seem to be accelerating. The adaptation to new practice and technology places demands on the modern clinical psychologist, as do the aim to reach all potential clients and the further establishment of the clinical psychologist's professional status. These areas of future concern will be part of daily routine in very few years, in what is still seen as a fledgling profession.

Statutory registration of clinical psychologists may simultaneously address the problems of regulating and controlling individuals, who are underqualified or are guilty of professional misconduct. Although a step towards this in the UK has been mentioned above in the form of the Register of Psychologists, full statutory registration would seem inevitable in the near future. As with most advances in health care, this will be dependent on sufficient funds being available for implementation, monitoring and maintenance.

The use of technology has revolutionised many aspects of health care delivery internationally. In clinical psychology, these advances tended to affect only administration and research, with clinical delivery remaining largely in the interpersonal domain. However, the use of computer-assisted assessment, formulation and prognosis in the form of databases, statistical modelling and probabilistic prediction is becoming more common. Despite the need for human contact, judgement in, and the idiopathic nature of, much clinical work, speed and accuracy cannot be simply dismissed.

Somewhat reinforcing the need to accept at least the parallel use of more mechanised means, White et al. (2006) in a large meta-analysis (see Chapter 5) of mental health clinical predictions made by practitioners, as compared with those derived from statistical predictions, found that statistical predictions were more accurate across the situations included. Although this has implications for the reliance on clinical judgement alone, it also has greater implications for the training of clinicians including clinical psychologists, in that they will need to be increasingly statistically literate and familiar with relevant developing technologies.

The technological competence required of clinical psychologists in training will also extend to more specialist areas. The use of artificial intelligence in the modelling and diagnosis of disorders, as developed in general medicine, has now spread to the area of mental health (see Chapter 4). The use of virtual reality technology in the treatment of phobias has become much more common over the last decade as more powerful technology has become cheaper and more widely available, and again the outcomes compare favourably with normal exposure techniques (Emmelkamp et al., 2002). Virtual reality has numerous advantages in being much closer to in vivo exposure than, say, imagined feared stimuli or two-dimensional images, as well as supporting exaggerated stimuli (e.g. spiders the size of a horse for arachnophobics). In addition, there have been numerous computer packages available for the controlled delivery of CBT in a clinical context (Proudfoot et al., 2004). Such packages can support and assist in a structured and logical delivery, and may enable 'therapy by computer' within limits. These advances may provide welcome challenges to time-consuming orthodox approaches, but they also provide a challenge for the providers of clinical training, in that rapidly advancing and highly specialist training is going to be required in the immediate future.

For Llewelyn (2003) the future of clinical psychology is clouded by the successes of the past. The ubiquitous penetration of health care delivery by psychology evident over the last 40 years has been a success story of critical science reflexively applied to clinical practice. To sustain the successes of the past, Llewelyn (2003) suggests that clinical psychology penetrates the dark area of suffering: those people with mental health issues who never attend a clinic and those in general health care provision whose psychological suffering is bypassed in favour of addressing their immediate medical needs. Thus even in the absence of new advances in psychological treatment, there is a wide population of those in psychological distress who could be brought into the net covered by future clinical psychological services.

Casting a wider client net may involve changing the demographic profile of the clinical psychology practitioner by building a more diverse population of clinicians beyond the androcentric and Eurocentric bias currently representing the profession (Boyle and Whitely, 2003). For example, one case of an Asian mother with severe anxiety problems remained virtually untreated due to her evasive nature with well-intentioned and skilled clinical psychologists. The case was eventually addressed by a (relatively new) graduate who understood the mother's background and the nature of her cultural defences, and by chance spoke Hindi. At this point the lady in question became compliant with assessment and treatment. This example may seem simplistic in its resolution, but without diverse demographic resources being in existence, the case might have remained in stasis.

Self-test questions

- What are the main treatments used by clinical psychologists?
- What roles might a clinical psychologist be expected to perform?
- What is meant by the term 'scientist-practitioner'?
- Why is evidence-based practice important to contemporary clinical psychology?

How to become a clinical psychologist

In practice there are four stages to becoming a qualified chartered clinical psychologist: a psychology degree; clinical work experience; postgraduate training; and supervised clinical psychology practice. All clinical psychologists begin their careers with a first degree in psychology. In the twenty-first century it is expected that they will graduate with a minimum of a 2:1 in a psychology degree that has accreditation from the governing body for that country, such as the BPS in the UK, the BDP in Germany or the APA in the USA. This accreditation is important for a graduate to be accepted into postgraduate training. Exceptions to this pattern are not impossible but tend to be unusual (see Knight, 2002). For example, a candidate with a 2:2 degree may be accepted due to extensive work experience or other compensatory attribute.

Case study
Anyla – clinical psychologist

versity, she found there was a National Autistic Society unit not far from her university accommodation and her experience to date made her a very welcome part of their team, albeit still on a voluntary basis.

In choosing psychology for her first degree, Anyla had already decided that her career should involve working with people and helping ease the kind of problems she had witnessed first hand in her own family, as her younger brother Imran had been diagnosed with autism at the age of 3. This happened when Anyla was 10 years old, at which point she was young enough to be very much involved with Imran, yet old enough to comprehend that his difficulties were due to an ongoing mental condition. Whilst still studying for her A-levels, Anyla had been helping at a school for children with a mixed level of special needs. When she moved to uni-

In choosing Abnormal Psychology as one of her options in her second year as a psychology undergraduate, Anyla learned what comprised the work of a clinical psychologist. She spoke to her tutor at length regarding her ambition to work with children with pervasive developmental disorders and whether this fitted in with the work of a clinical psychologist. Her tutor confirmed that, in order to have professional standing for the kind of work she wanted to do, clinical psychology would clearly be her best option, and that following training she could specialise in the area of child disorders. He supplied Anyla with a list of contacts in clinical psychology departments and one in an old age psychiatry unit. She queried the relevance of the latter contact and her tutor explained how those assessing clinical psychology applicants judge clinical

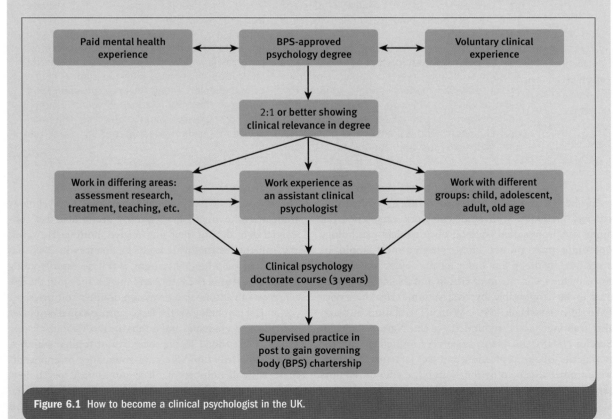

Figure 6.1 How to become a clinical psychologist in the UK.

work experience. 'Not only do they expect you to have worked at differing levels and proximity to clients', he said; 'they will expect you to have experience of differing client groups, child, adolescent, adult and older adult, not just the child group you are interested in personally.'

Anyla was somewhat daunted by the prospect of working with the elderly, having set her sights on work with children, but she rapidly settled in to working with dementia patients. She discovered not only the importance of the neurological basis to disorders in the elderly, but also the neurological underpinnings of pervasive developmental disorders. Anyla's half-day in the dementia unit spawned a new ambition: that of working in neuropsychological research into autism. Not yet in her final degree year, Anyla had begun to expand her career options and even suggested following a research route by applying for neuropsychological projects for a PhD. Having become her final year dissertation supervisor, her Abnormal Psychology tutor recommended that she persisted with expanding her experience towards clinical training and kept her neuropsychological ambitions as a second option.

At graduation, in addition to a good 2:1 grade, Anyla had accumulated a remarkable portfolio of clinical work experience and in addition had been angered to discover retrospectively how limited the management of her brother's condition had been. With a great deal of persistence and eight arduous applications for assistant psychologist posts, she was interviewed for a post working alongside a clinical child psychologist. After the interview Anyla was distraught as the topic of resource targeting had come up and she had overreacted in the light of Imran's treatment. However, the interview panel viewed her concern and more particularly her detailed knowledge in a very positive light. She accepted the offer of the post and proudly informed her former tutor, who advised her to make the most of all learning opportunities within and beyond the job remit.

Some 6 months later the two principal clinical psychologists at the unit were giving Anyla a very tough time. She did not mind this, as they had kindly offered to provide her with mock clinical course interview experience following her first application through the clearing-house system. Anyla was delighted then to be offered an interview for the Leeds course, but was initially devastated at her rejection. Following a mournful email from Anyla, her former tutor encouraged her to see the rejection objectively – yes, she had the experience and attitude, but had this come over in the interview? Following a further research assistant post in an accident and emergency neuropsychology unit, Anyla made her second and successful clinical application, joining the clinical course at Manchester. Today Anyla is the main fund-holder for an MRC (Medical Research Council) funded neuropsychology project into the hemispherical asymmetries in autistic spectrum disorder.

In the UK and many other countries, accredited psychology graduates with sufficient work experience can apply for professional training on a **clinical psychology doctorate** programme. These programmes should be accredited by the BPS in order for the course to be recognised by the Department of Health and thus for its graduates to be employable by the National Health Service (Marzillier and Hall, 1999). With accreditation in place, this training has been funded by the **National Health Service** (NHS) and places were very limited due to the popularity of the profession and the fact that not only were trainee fees paid by the NHS but a substantial bursary had been paid to support trainees. Such funding stands in contrast with other postgraduate training courses where the student receives no financial living support and in addition has to pay his or her own fees.

This was a particularly salient factor for UK psychology graduates who might have already accumulated a substantial debt during their first-degree training. However, government restructuring of NHS finances in 2006 has shown that such funded training is not necessarily going to be supported in the future and the UK may join the less generous but sustainable provision of other countries.

Clinical psychology is the largest professional employer of psychology graduates and is thus the most popular career choice. This, added to the incentive of funded training, has led to a situation where an abundance of applicants chase a small number of places on clinical psychology courses. On the other side of the equation, there has been a chronic shortage of qualified clinical psychologists. This 'bottleneck' in the training system has substantially added to this constant shortage of clinical graduates. During the

1990s, there were an increased number of places for clinical training, which were funded by reducing the bursary paid to trainees. As mentioned in Chapter 1, another way of addressing this shortfall and improving the experience of suitable psychology graduates is via the creation of **associate clinical psychologists** (Management Advisory Service,

2003). This new UK NHS post is open to more able and qualified assistant psychologists but below the grade of qualified clinical psychologist.

The BPS in the UK confers **chartered clinical psychologist** status upon a qualified graduate clinical psychologist who has gained sufficient supervised post-qualification

International perspective

Variations in clinical psychology

Across the globe, the USA still dominates clinical psychology due to the early establishment of clinical psychology in that country and it is the main producer of journals in the area, partly aided by the dominance of the English language. However, this US lead has not aided international standardisation within the discipline, but has discouraged some professionals from becoming familiar with work from countries other than their own and the dominant US material. This can seriously impede progress in the area when valuable research functionally remains within its country of origin, although allowing free access to material on the world wide web may counter this. In Europe there is some conflict between academic and practitioner interests, which again becomes explicit in terms of control over journal content. Thus the international picture of clinical psychology may seem less harmonious than would be expected from a caring profession. However, efforts to network and standardise are very salient with the **International Society of Clinical Psychologists** and its journal *International Clinical Psychologist* aiming to bring these somewhat ethnocentric elements together.

Most countries have an equivalent psychological body to the BPS in the UK. For example, the **Berrufsverband Deutscher Psychologen** in Germany and the **American Psychological Association** in the USA accredit courses, clinical training and professional status. The networking and agreements between these professional bodies as well as the acceptance of hierarchical structures (i.e. European bodies over those of individual European countries) may assist international standardisation. Lundt (1998) reported on the attempt to standardise professional practice in 28 European psychology associations by the **European Federation of Professional Psychologists Associations** in the form of **Optimal Standards for Professional Training**. Chartered clinical psychologist status can also be offered to clinical psychologists who have qualified elsewhere in the world by application to the BPS Committee for the Scrutiny of Individual Qualifications in Clinical Psychology in the UK, which will identify any further training needs.

International differences are evident in the varied courses on clinical psychology, which may still be to MSc rather than doctorate level, although the doctorate programme has been standard throughout the UK since 1995. McGuire (1999) reported resistance to the move towards a doctorate award in Australia, even though the doctorate is standard in nearby New Zealand. In many European countries, such as the Netherlands, Germany and Norway, clinical training is incorporated seamlessly into the first degree and leads to a larger number of trained clinical psychologists as a result. In the 1980s some UK universities, such as Hull, began to offer similar clinical training following directly on from their undergraduate programme, with all aspects being fully accredited, in this case by the BPS. However, most UK courses are not structured in this way. There is much greater variation across Europe and the rest of the world, including in their approaches to training, methods and even admission systems (McGuire, 1999; Lundt, 1998).

In the USA, academic trainees have a greater opportunity to specialise in specific areas of clinical psychology than in other countries, as they take up 1-year full-time internships as trainees in an independently financed system. This contrasts with UK training where supervised clinical experience in the field tends to be for a few days a week alternating with study and the approach is more generic to provide the publicly funded NHS with broadly skilled individual clinicians. The UK approach has been criticised for separating academic and clinical aspects instead of integrating them (Marzillier and Hall, 1999).

Thus the international picture of clinical psychology appears to be moving relentlessly towards greater standardisation of professional practice and training, although this process has been predicted for many years (e.g. McPherson, 1992). However, many obstacles to this universal ideal remain, not least of which are the fundamental disagreements over theoretical orientations, the rapid spread of clinical psychology across the globe and the historical bias towards US-based material.

experience. Chartered status provides some regulation of professional training and standing, though persistent individual differences in the effectiveness of clinical psychologists would indicate some limitations within this system. However, this final stage of the qualifying process is often beyond the horizon for the aspiring clinical psychologist because undue focus tends to be placed on the entry to the clinical doctorate course, and because of the vagaries and difficulties in gaining the prerequisite work experience.

There will of necessity be a large number of rejections from clinical course entry, so superstitious behaviour and accusations of bias and unfairness in the selection criteria and process abound. Often arising from gossip and rumour, such perceived unfairness can produce 'urban myths', which should be ignored by prospective candidates and replaced with commonsense advice (see Knight, 2002). These added anxieties for candidates are unnecessary and both the assessment of applications and the decisions at interviews have been found to be fair and consistent when evaluated (Knight, 2002). In the UK, applications are made through a clearing-house system on a form that has a fairly open format in comparison to other professional courses. Useful generic practical advice on applications and interviews is often ignored by candidates, as are good dedicated texts on the specific process of becoming a clinical psychologist (e.g. Knight, 2002). This may mean that sound advice, such as relating interview questions to one's work experience or academic knowledge, or demonstrating the logic of one's career path, is pushed aside in favour of a belief that one needs an indefinable mythical quality. This may cultivate a negative attitude that anticipates and to some degree precipitates failure.

The process of gaining sufficient work experience to make a course application can be daunting, as this may be considered as important as academic attainment, if not more so. Work experience serves a dual purpose, in that it not only gives the candidate a great deal of prior learning but will also help them to test whether or not they are suited or even able to be a clinical psychologist. Ideally, an **assistant psychologist** post will have been held for 6 months to a year prior to application, in which the candidate will have carried out many of the duties of a qualified clinical psychologist under close supervision. However, as one psychology graduate complained, 'the catch 22 is they want you to have experience before they will give you experience'. Often the most difficult stage is gaining that first entry into the clinical work experience world. As Knight (2002) points out in detail, there are many entry points for this first step, such as being a paid nursing assistant (mental health), care work and many diverse voluntary posts and possibilities.

In gaining work experience, it is important to try and work with different disorders, settings and client age groups. Whilst working in a different capacity, for example as a care worker, progressively use your work contacts to gain the attention of a clinical psychologist who may work in the same building or visit regularly. All qualified clinical psychologists are well aware that potential candidates need experience and, despite their hectic schedules, will help if they can. The closer the work experience is to that of a clinical psychologist, the more weight will be given to it on application. Hence the emphasis placed on assistant psychologist posts, **research assistant** or even the new **associate psychologist** posts in clinical psychology. Although not all such posts deliver quality or varied experience, most successful applicants will have held these posts. Many successful candidates may spend 2 or even 3 years gaining paid and voluntary experience. It is thus essential that individuals considering this career begin gaining and documenting vocational experience as early as possible, at least by the second year of their undergraduate degree.

In addition to clinical work experience, other factors can help an application. Research experience is useful, as this is an important part of being a scientist-practitioner, and publications will also count because such skills are going to be valuable during research training and predict an increased chance of further publication upon qualification. Teaching experience in clinically related areas can be seen as an asset, as is the related skill of communicating complex ideas via various media. Having a mature attitude to the prospective role and towards clients also needs to be demonstrated as well as an appreciation of the demands of being a clinical psychologist and the level of work involved in training. Recent graduates will have chosen units related to clinical psychology, such as abnormal psychology, during their first degree and a clinically related area for their final dissertation. Persistence and the ability to recognise and change deficits will succeed in the long term.

Upon being accepted for the doctorate training, new recruits tend to be daunted by the busy schedule of teaching days and placement days, but they will find a great deal of support and advice from peers, tutors and existing clinical students. After chasing a place on the course for a number of years, finally securing a place can seem an anti-climax, but genuine enthusiasm will soon handle this sudden shift from aspiration to industry. Consideration should be given as early as possible to the choice of clinical thesis and the most suitable supervisor, as this may facilitate any specialist interest that the candidate has and make it explicit to future employers. Upon qualification, supervision of clinical work will continue for a number of years (the number has varied over time) until chartered status is allowed by the BPS in the UK.

Self-test questions

- What training is required before a clinical psychologist can practise professionally?

- How can a psychology graduate gain useful clinical psychology work experience?

- What factors are involved in the need for clinical psychologists constantly outstripping their supply?

- Why is international standardisation within clinical psychology an important issue?

- Itemise and address the problems involved in changing clinical psychology training and regulation across countries with different health care systems.

Chapter summary

This chapter has charted the historical origins and development of clinical psychology from its roots in empirical behaviourist schools of **J. B. Watson** through the Second World War development of **psychometrics** as a tool 'owned' by psychologists. In the UK the support for clinical psychology within the **NHS** led to the establishment of the discipline with its own division of the **BPS** in 1966. **Cognitive behavioural therapy**, combined with psychometric expertise, enabled clinical psychologists to gain independence from their domination by psychiatrists towards the end of the twentieth century. The question of what constitutes clinical psychology was then addressed by delineating its role from that of other allied professions and summarising its unique attributes. These have been represented by the **Mowbray report** on skill levels in clinical psychology. The origins of the scientist-practitioner role in the USA under Lightner Witmer were then traced through the **Boulder model** to current practice, research and training. The place of evidence-based practice and practice-based evidence as the foundation stones for the UK government-backed requirement of clinical governance in clinical establishments was related to the role of the clinical psychologist as **scientist-practitioner**.

Clinical psychology in everyday practice was analysed for generic features. Practice in the real world was examined by reference to the daily work carried out in older-adult units, with particular attention to the expanding role of the clinical neuropsychologist. The example of a busy multi-tasking teaching department also provided an illustration of the many daily roles expected of clinical psychologists in practice. These were clearly only two examples representing a seemingly infinite need for these professionals at every level within and outside of national health care systems around the world. The clinical psychology report and its function were then explained with an example of possible structure and content. Future issues in clinical psychology were briefly considered, including furthering the establishment of the profession and the incorporation of new technology. The process of becoming a clinical psychologist was then addressed with some supportive and practical advice for aspiring trainees. International variations in clinical psychology and its training completed this chapter.

Suggested essay questions

- Discuss the strategic points in the historical development of clinical psychology.
- Discuss the differing roles played by a contemporary clinical psychologist.
- Select a case study of interest from the rest of this textbook and attempt to create a clinical report from this, using the suggested headings in this chapter.

Further reading

Overview texts

Beinart, H., Kennedy, P., and Llewelyn, S. (2009) *Clinical psychology in practice.* Chichester: Wiley.

Boyle, M., and Whitely, C. (2003) Clinical psychology. In R. Bayne and I. Horton (eds), *Applied psychology.* London: Sage.

Carr, A., and McNulty, M. (2006) *The handbook of adult clinical psychology: An evidence-based practice approach.* Hove: Routledge.

Davey, G. (2008) *Clinical psychology.* London: Hodder.

Knight, A. (2002) *How to become a clinical psychologist: Getting a foot in the door.* Hove: Brunner-Routledge.

Llewelyn, S. (2003) Clinical psychology: New directions in applied psychology. In R. Bayne and I. Horton (eds), *Applied psychology.* London: Sage.

Trull, T., and Phares, E. J. (2001) *Clinical psychology.* Belmont, CA: Wadsworth.

Specific and more critical texts

British Psychological Society: Division of Clinical Psychology (1995) *Professional practice guidelines.* Leicester: British Psychological Society.

British Psychological Society: Division of Clinical Psychology (2001) *Core purpose and philosophy of the profession.* Leicester: British Psychological Society.

Cheshire, K., and Pilgrim, D. (2004) *A short introduction to clinical psychology.* London: Sage.

Hawton, K., Salkovskis, P. M., Kirk, J., and Clark, D. M. (1989) *Cognitive behaviour therapy for psychiatric problems.* Oxford: Oxford University Press.

Hersen, M., and Gross, A. M. (2010) *Handbook of clinical psychology (vols. 1 and 2).* Chichester: Wiley.

Huey, D., and Britton, P. (2002) A portrait of clinical psychology. *Journal of Interprofessional Care,* 16(1), 69–78.

Marzillier, J., and Hall, J. (1999) *What is clinical psychology? (3rd edn).* Oxford: Oxford University Press.

Milne, D. (2009) *Evidence-based clinical supervision.* Chichester: Wiley.

Parry, G., Cape, J., and Pilling, S. (2003) Clinical practice guidelines in clinical psychology and psychotherapy. *Clinical Psychology and Psychotherapy,* 10, 337–51.

Visit **www.pearsoned.co.uk/davidholmes** for a range of resources to support study. Test yourself with multiple choice questions and access a bank of over 100 videos that will bring the topics to life. Video coverage for this chapter includes classic footage of Skinner's study of hehaviour modification using pigeons, an exploration of how emotion boosts memory and an historical overview of clinical approaches.

CHAPTER 7 Forensic psychology

- Overview
- Case study
- Historical development of forensic psychology

- What is forensic psychology?
- The forensic psychology practitioner
- Other areas related to forensic psychology

- How to become a forensic psychologist
- Chapter summary

 Discover how thermal imaging technology can detect lying. This is one of several videos that explore issues and disorders relevant to this chapter at **www.pearsoned.co.uk/davidholmes**.

Crime in the media

The TV series *CSI* is at this time the most popular TV series in the world. Most TV and film producers are aware of the pulling power of crime with the public. The Crime Channel along with less dedicated channels as well as film producers have seen this situation intensify in the twenty-first century, especially focusing on the **forensic psychologist**. Even unrealistic, if well-acted, dramas from the 1990s, such as the UK's *Cracker* (Jimmy McGovern), have been remade for the US market. Such portrayals can mislead the public into thinking that **forensic psychologists** chase and apprehend criminals, whereas the reality is less dramatic but arguably more intriguing.

Other TV depictions attempt technical realism, such as the glossy *CSI*, or directly inform in documentaries such as **David Canter**'s *Mapping Murder*, and have the effect of increasing **forensic awareness** in criminals. Such viewers become less likely to leave the featured physical or psychological clues and are more aware of techniques used in **interrogative interviews**. However, these intriguing programmes have also increased the intake on psychology degrees and of those wishing to continue on to postgraduate forensic psychology courses.

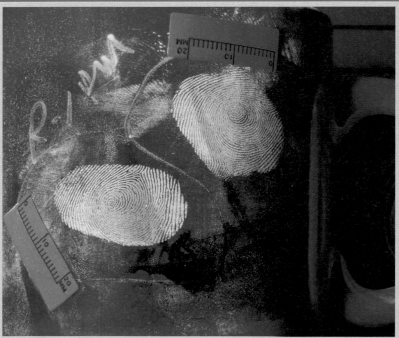

Forensic psychologists attempt to read the psychology of crime scenes as being unique as the fingerpoints left behind.
Source: Pearson Online Database.

This chapter will open with a case study that relates to aspects of forensic psychology covered in later sections and will also indicate how this chapter will lead towards Chapter 8, covering clinical forensic psychology. The historical development of forensic psychology will then be explained in more detail than the general coverage of this area given in Chapter 1. The following section on what forensic psychology is will attempt the very difficult task of delineating the boundaries of the discipline and defining its professional and academic remit. The professional working areas of practising forensic psychologists begin with prison the major employer, and the defining context of the courtroom. The established areas of eyewitness testimony and forensic interviews will be discussed in relation to both research and their application to practice. The construction of reports for forensic psychology purposes will be described and differentiated from those covered in the previous chapter for clinical purposes. The growing contemporary areas of cybercrime and the related aim of lie detection are then discussed as specific focal areas where forensic psychology has a stake. The requirements that need to be met to qualify as a forensic psychologist end the chapter, with the UK model providing a template that can be related to this profession throughout the world.

Many factors influence eyewitnesses and even selection from an identity parade can produce errors.
Source: David A. Holmes.

Case study
A case of identification

Heinz had always worked night shifts at the electronics warehouse on the edge of the city, arriving home at around 5 a.m. On this particular Friday morning, two men in rather wet overcoats waiting outside his front door interrupted his almost ritualistic routine. He was approached by name and asked questions about his whereabouts earlier in the week. Heinz replied honestly and was astonished when he was asked to accompany the police officers to a police station in the city centre. Desperate to show he was not only innocent of any crime but also honest and ready to help in any way he could, he readily agreed. After only an hour, Heinz was formally arrested and led to a police cell in shock – the charge was rape.

For Heinz the long night in the cell seemed like a nightmare that would last forever, broken only by a visit from a duty solicitor. When the police offered him one phone call, Heinz had no one he could call apart from his employer, and Heinz valued his rather routine job very highly. The following morning a terrified Heinz began ritually checking his buttoned-up shirt in front of his interrogating officers and asking for his tie to be returned. The officers made a note of this behaviour as well as his averted gaze during questioning. Heinz was asked if he would take part in an identity parade. Needless to say he agreed to this, assuming his innocence would be verified. This was not to be and a very agitated and confused Heinz was charged with rape. He appeared at the magistrates' court and was refused bail. His solicitor explained that this was not to try him but to refer him to a crown court due to the serious nature of the offence. Heinz's reactions led his solicitor to call a psychologist as well as a barrister.

The newly qualified forensic psychologist was asked to assess and report on Heinz as being fit to plead at the initial court appearance and any further information that might help the defence case. After a brief interview, the psychologist immediately reported back to the defence solicitor that the case should be passed to her supervisor, a more senior **clinical forensic psychologist**, in the interests of the client. Somewhat worried about spiralling costs, the solicitor requested clarification and was informed that his client might have Asperger disorder in addition to being the victim of misidentification. The psychologist added that her former supervisor's specialisms included these areas. Following an initial assessment of Heinz, the clinical forensic psychologist hypothesised what may have transpired in a meeting with Heinz's newly appointed barrister.

Heinz had survived independently after his devoted mother had died some 5 years earlier, having lived at home all of his 47 years. His rigid adherence to the routine of his monotonous warehouse job and his frugal home existence had enabled Heinz to evade the attention of both psychiatric and social services. Indeed, he had slipped through life unnoticed by anyone but the strangers he passed in the early hours of the morning and his employer, who enjoyed having a reliable employee who worked so hard for a basic wage. However, it was some of those strangers who found Heinz's face familiar in the context of the shadowy street and who gave his description to the police on the night of the rape, and who selected him in the police line-up due to his familiarity. His evasive and aloof manner had made him seem suspicious in retrospect and at the time of police questioning.

Sara, the clinical-forensic psychologist, was unequivocal in declaring that Heinz could not have carried out the sexual attack, as he did not have the sexual experience, competence or inclination to match the reported details of the offence. For the barrister, being convinced of this reality did not equate to Heinz being innocent in the eyes of the law. It would be a difficult battle if the **Crown Prosecution Service** (CPS) presented eyewitnesses and clinical or forensic psychologists to testify that, in general, some Asperger individuals are sexually active. However, Heinz had the good fortune that the assigned CPS barrister appreciated the validity of the clinical forensic report and recommended that the case be dropped. This view that was reinforced by the subsequent apprehension of the actual offender when attempting a further assault.

Although justice might have been done in this instance, the psychological aspects tightly woven into such cases can remain invisible without outside expertise to identify and explain them. Thus the place of the forensic and clinical forensic psychologist in the many justice systems around the world can be vital, and consequently demand for these professionals is growing in the twenty-first century. This has not always been the case, and the history of forensic psychology has been as much about the acceptance of the discipline as about the progress of its scientific development.

Historical development of forensic psychology

Early application of forensic psychology

In Chapter 1 the historical development of forensic psychology as a discipline and practice was integrated into the history of abnormal and clinical psychology. It would be useful at this point to isolate and review this development in terms of forensic psychology alone. In the previous chapter we found that clinical psychology had a relatively brief professional history, but the past of forensic psychology as an independent discipline has been arguably shorter. The use of psychology in relation to law has been traced back before the discipline truly emerged with Wundt's laboratory in the nineteenth century, in terms its antecedent of philosophy. However, much of this history overlaps greatly with that of the medical profession's intervention in law, which for some authors tends to be equated with the initial legal involvement of psychology. Paralleling and supporting the advent of forensic psychology, Cesare Lombroso (1876) took a **sociological-evolutionary approach** to the individual causes of crime and founded a somewhat flawed 'science of the criminal' (Maguire, Morgan and Reiner, 2002) but at the same time establishing

the first criminological methodology. It would be the turn of the twentieth century before the presence of forensic psychology was evident in courts and even later, in 1906, that Freud himself advised the Austrian judiciary of the value of psychology, albeit regarding psychoanalysis. Freud saw parallels between the truth-revealing remit of the therapist and that element in the role of the magistrate in a court of law (Brigham, 1999).

At the time of the insanity plea (see the Focus box), psychology began its inroads into the preserve of medicine and psychiatry in the legal forum. In addition, as shown in Chapter 1, the memory work of Cattell, Binet and Stern was seen to be applied in the courtroom in terms of witness testimony being distorted by leading questions or interrogation. This psychology-laboratory research enabled the actual forensic psychologist role to be pioneered in court by **Albert von Schrenk-Notzing**, in identifying retroactive memory falsification due to the effects of pre-trial media reports on witnesses in 1896 (see Gudjonsson and Haward, 1998). Stern himself established the first journal that dealt with forensic psychology issues, *Betrage zur Psychologie der Aussage*.

The standing of forensic psychology was greatly furthered by the work of **Hugo Munsterberg**, particularly his experimental work on presented evidence, having travelled to the USA in 1892 and set up a psychology laboratory at Harvard. His book on the use of psychology in the courtroom, *On the Witness Stand* (Munsterberg, 1908), was not

Focus

Daniel McNaughton and the insanity plea

It has been considered that psychology initially entered the courtroom in support of medical science in identifying a sufficiently weakened mental state that fell short of the legal requirement for guilt of *mens rea* (clarity of mind). As noted in Chapter 1, the mitigation of a head injury in the trial of James Hadfield for homicide during his attempted assassination of King George III successfully placed limits on culpability. This explicitly removed the non-psychological vagaries of the earlier **wild beast test** (1724), which assumed amoral animal reflexes, and replaced it with the more objectively scientific approach of **not guilty by reason of insanity**.

Also termed the **McNaughten rule**, the insanity plea was established as a definition of legal insanity by the UK House of Lords after the 1843 trial of Daniel McNaughton for homicide, in which paranoid ideation (delusions of persecution) was used as mitigation.

(Note: McNaughton misspelled his own name many times, and some of these spellings are used in different texts, hence the legitimate variation in spelling.) McNaughton believed the 'Tories in my native city' were persecuting him and purchased a pair of pistols with which he shot the secretary of the prime minister, Sir Robert Peel, in the back thinking it was the prime minister himself.

The insanity plea was based on the persecutory delusions leading McNaughton not to be responsible for his actions, and this was presented in court by Alexander Cockburn, a very powerful counsel at the time (see Prins, 2005). However, although this case set a precedent, Brigham (1999) makes it clear that it was probably the political focus and legal strength of McNaughton's defence team that made this case significant, rather than the validity of the disturbance of his mental state (see Moran, 1981).

universally welcomed; in particular, it was shunned by many in the legal profession and even attacked by Wigmore (1909). Brigham (1999) adds that Munsterberg's promotion of psychology was somewhat overzealous, even arrogant, often denigrating lawyers for ignoring psychology. Munsterberg was critical of would-be allies, dispensing with Freud's unconscious motivation hypothesis thus: 'The story of the unconscious mind can be told in three words, there is none' (Munsterberg, 1909). Much of Munsterberg's remarkably dedicated effort to secure a place for psychology in the forensic context was also confounded by the adversarial legal system in the UK and USA, which made it difficult for such evidence to penetrate these systems, as opposed to the inquisitorial system used in parts of Europe, which allowed a wider spectrum of evidence in court (Gudjonsson and Haward, 1998). The inquisitorial legal system focuses on uncovering, analysing and considering the facts of a case, whereas the adversarial system has defence and prosecution counsel and witnesses in opposition in court, trading legal blows in a battle to establish the truth. Politically and by nationality, Munsterberg was on the German side in the First World War, which tended to sever any professional connections with the UK and its allies. Stern (1903) was sceptical of Munsterberg's approach and was less certain of psychology's place in court until sufficient laboratory work had been done (Brigham, 1999). A student of Munsterberg, William Marston used the experimental method to develop a form of lie detection (see pp. 205–8).

Psychological testing and the establishment of forensic psychology

One of the products of extensive psychological laboratory work was the development of psychological tests. In 1898, **Alfred Binet** worked at the first psychological laboratory in France, developing his interest both in eyewitness testimony and in the psychometric tests that would carry his name, as well as earning the title of 'father of French experimental psychology'. Early tests of IQ (Intelligence Quotient) were applied to police recruits in the USA around the turn of the twentieth century (Rees, 1995). The Stanford–Binet test of ability (Binet and Simon, 1911) was updated by Terman and Merrill (1937) and formed the basis of the tests that proliferated around the subsequent world war. This constant development of psychometrics (psychological testing) directly benefited clinical psychology; however, much of the credibility of forensic psychologists in court would also come to depend on this area of expertise.

Following research fuelled by the vast demand for psychometric testing of personnel in the Second World War, forensic psychology should have found a permanent role in the justice system once these tests established their credibility and validity for courtroom use.

Notwithstanding psychologists' efforts to master **psychometric instruments** (questionnaires to measure psychological traits), however, the medical authority of psychiatrists still dominated the role of courtroom expert for many years, and they were not willing simply to allow another profession to usurp their position. The legal profession also defended their boundaries, as in their own view they were the only true forensic profession. Lawyers resented all such intruding forensic experts, especially newcomers such as forensic psychologists. However, the increasing specialist knowledge required for the application and particularly the interpretation of psychometric instruments led directly to an elevation of the status of the psychologist in court.

This forensic reappraisal of psychologists arose from a psychiatrist's interpretation of a psychologist's (in this case L. R. C. Haward's) test results being declared **hearsay**, as it was not considered to be first-hand evidence and thus was inadmissible in court. A psychiatrist may present evidence from the point of view of a haematologist, as this is a legitimate part of their medical training, but they are not trained in psychometric interpretation and thus are not qualified to present such data first-hand (Gudjonsson and Haward, 1998). Thus in addition to psychological laboratory experimental work, this hearsay ruling meant that from 1973 psychologists should present their own test results in court – a decision that would be both defended and contested fiercely over time.

For Gudjonsson and Haward (1998), the position of psychologists under the hearsay rule was strengthened by the Best Evidence Rule (where copies were deemed inferior to original evidence) and the Multiple Admissibility Rule (where evidence should be used for its original purpose only and not submitted for another). However, these authors also point out that the 'hearsay rule' protection for psychologists giving evidence had been undermined in civil law by the greater discretion given to judges and a relaxed attitude to evidence in this area. Later, the **1995 Civil Evidence Act** effectively made the 'hearsay rule' void in the majority of civil cases. Most forensic psychologists suspect that, despite the Best Evidence Rule and the Multiple Admissibility Rule, the erosion of the hearsay rule in civil cases may spread to the area of criminal law (Gudjonsson and Haward, 1998). In the USA, a similar predicament faced psychologists in courtrooms due to their inheriting the UK adversarial system and its limitations for these professionals.

Independence for forensic psychology as a profession

In the UK the establishment of the National Health Service provided support not only for clinical psychologist services to the medical profession, but also for those psychologists involved in forensic contexts. In 1977 the **Legal and Criminological Division of the British Psychological Society** (BPS) was established in the UK. This provided support and an organisational framework for those working in the area of forensic psychology and was thus aptly renamed the **Division of Forensic Psychology** in 1999. As with its counterparts in the rest of the world, this division provides a hub structure for a wide variety of psychologists working in the more broadly defined area that is forensic psychology in the UK. Similar organisations have evolved in the USA, Europe and elsewhere.

In 1959 the UK Obscenity Act paved the way for psychologists to be able to testify as to what would be for 'the public good' and thus not legally obscene. This placed the psychologist in the somewhat precarious but appropriate role of guardian of the public's psychological health. The role was demonstrated in the somewhat exaggerated defence in the Anderson case in 1971, in which the largest number of psychologists testified that the publication *Oz Magazine* was not obscene in legal terms. *Oz Magazine* was an 'underground' publication in the 1960s, which attempted to push the boundaries of good taste in text and graphics whilst pursuing its somewhat tongue-in-cheek anti-establishment stance. It is worth noting that, historically, obscenity was not a legal issue until the nineteenth century and was thus a relatively new crime with new expertise.

A few years later, the work of Elizabeth Loftus brought many decades of study of eyewitness testimony into sharp focus in a series of experiments that undermined the assumptions of eyewitness validity that were so often firmly held by non-psychologists in court (Loftus, 1979). The mistaken assumption that an eyewitness records events in the manner of a DVD recorder will be addressed later in this chapter. In later years, Loftus also campaigned against the uncritical acceptance of **repressed memory** (usually of childhood sexual abuse) based on experimentation (Loftus, 1993). This became a highly contentious issue, particularly in the USA where many families had been divided by an overzealous acceptance of 'recovered repressed memories' of child abuse. This practice was further confounded by the application of hypnosis in such forensic contexts (see Chapter 15).

In 1956 forensic psychology was to gain a great deal of (possibly unwarranted) publicity as a result of the psychological and physical description of George Metsky, the 'Mad Bomber' of New York, by James H. Brussel (see Jackson and Bekerian, 1997). This reasonably accurate 'psychological profile', although not the first attempt at offender profiling, led to developments in the 1970s at the **Federal Bureau of Investigation** (FBI, founded 1905). Although the FBI used detectives for what was essentially specialist police work, in 1973 its **Behavioural Science Unit** at Quantico was established and eventually began to use psychologists in training its detectives and to assist in some investigations (see Chapter 8). With the advent of popular films such as *Manhunter* (Michael Mann, 1986), based on the work of fictional 'forensic psychologists' working as FBI agents, the student intake to psychology degrees across the world increased for what more serious-minded professionals consider to be the wrong reasons, and this continues in the USA with CBS TV series *Criminal Minds*. In the UK a similar effect followed the 1980s ITV series *Cracker*, in which a charismatic Robbie Coltrane misrepresented the work of police psychologists as pursuing criminals rather than simply advising the police (see Grover and Soothill, 1996). Although most modern forensic psychologists are quick to distance themselves from these fictional portrayals, when asked the simple question as to what exactly comprises forensic psychology, most provided inconsistent answers and some did not provide any answer at all (Brigham, 1999).

As the work of forensic psychologists has become more diverse in the twenty-first century, prisons have become the major employers of forensic psychologists. In 2001 the amalgamation of the newly formed National Probation Service with the Prisons Psychology Service to provide continuous support and monitoring has led to forensic psychologists being actively recruited into this dual service (Clifford, 2003). Prior to this, psychologists were employed on an ad hoc basis and did not have anything remotely equivalent to the employment vacuum in clinical psychology that put newly qualified clinical psychologists in such demand. In the UK, growth of the membership of the BPS Division of Forensic Psychology has been logarithmic (i.e. growing at an accelerating rate) rather than linear, and this trend looks set to continue in this century, boosted by the 'What works' approach to interventions in prison. It may be fuelled still further by a growing need for the dual qualification of clinical forensic psychologists. Contemporary forensic psychologists are now involved at the stages of crime causation, prevention, detection, judgement, punishment and the consequences of criminal acts. This diversity within the profession has led to many arguments surrounding the definition of forensic psychology. The next section will attempt to make the role of the contemporary forensic psychologist more explicit.

What is forensic psychology?

Forensic psychology is the interface between psychology and the legal, criminal and justice systems. As mentioned in Chapter 1, the term 'forensic' comes from the Latin *forensis*, referring to the Roman forum, and thus relates directly to the role of the psychologist in the courtroom.

Thus it is the *context* in which a forensic psychologist works, rather than the actual work done, that earns the label 'forensic'. Gudjonsson and Haward (1998) amongst others favour a narrow definition of forensic psychology, focusing on the collection, examination and presentation of evidence for judicial purposes (Haward, 1981). Similarly, Blackburn (1996) maintains the legal focus in his description of forensic psychology as 'the provision of

Focus

Roles of the forensic psychologist

Some of the (overlapping) individual roles of the forensic psychologist may be found in the following areas.

- **Prison duties.** Psychologists have carried out assessments of prison inmates for many years. Increasingly, clinical psychologists are being involved in psychological treatment in prison medical units and modifying the behaviour of offenders who present a risk to others and themselves.

- **Expert witness**. Expert witnesses are called upon to give opinions in court based on their area of expertise, not as individuals having witnessed criminal acts. For the psychologist, this can draw on a number of areas of psychology, some of which are listed below.

- **Eyewitness testimony.** Two areas of psychology have a function here. One concerns the factors that affect the honest, accurate acquisition, recall and presentation of eyewitness testimony. The other involves the degree of impact that statements can have on the court, especially jurors and their collective decisions.

- **Ability to testify in court.** Psychologists may be requested to assess the mental state of the defendant or a witness in order to ascertain their ability to give testimony in court. The status of psychologists in these judgements varies between countries.

- **Offender profiling.** A few forensic psychologists are contracted to work with the police to help describe or identify offenders who are often disordered. In Europe, a significant number of these forensic psychologists are also clinical psychologists (see Chapter 8).

- **Police psychology.** Some psychologists work full time in police behavioural units, creating systems and researching this and other aspects of crime detection. This data gathering has helped to produce computerised investigative systems. Some police officers study and qualify in psychology in order to extend their role within the police force (see Mathias, 2003).

- **Police occupational psychology.** Psychologists have been involved with police recruitment for some time (Rees, 1995) and this became more specific and focused following failures attributed to firearms officers (Brown, 1998). Psychologists also began to work with the police to help with the effects of occupational stress in the wake of major disasters, such as the Bradford City football stadium fire. This also overlaps with the occupational role below.

- **Risk assessment.** An increasingly important forensic area is to estimate the risk of an offender reoffending, or of a mentally disordered patient causing harm to self or others if discharged. Prediction has been generally poor in the past, with only one-third of those 'at risk' proving to be a real danger. These risk assessments are improving with research, but the context is also changing with increasingly overcrowded institutions. Forensic psychologists are applying risk assessment and management to more areas as the profession has moved into the twenty-first century (see the following sections).

- **Criminology.** Some forensic psychologists focus on the theoretical aspects of crime as well as research into or teaching these areas, and thus their work overlaps considerably with that of the criminologist. One of these aspects is the abnormal offender.

- **Victimology**. A specialist area is victimology, which has traditionally been studied by criminologists (see Walklate, 1989), but forensic psychologists have been increasingly involved in support for victims in the wake of a crime, who may also have to attend court. What factors affect the likelihood of becoming a victim of crime is also an area of research, as are the issues of policy and gender (see Goodey, 2005).

- **Occupational forensic psychology**. Growing specialisms, particularly in the USA, are legal issues around employment and business. Examples tend to cover diverse problems such as integrity in the workplace, stress compensation claims and corporate crime.

psychological information for the purposes of facilitating a legal decision'. A survey by McGuire (1996) revealed that terms used in Europe, such as *Rechtpsychologie* (Germany) or *psicologia legal* (Portugal), are interpreted as having this narrow definition in line with Gudjonsson and Haward (1998) or Blackburn (1996).

A broader definition of forensic psychology may necessary for the twenty-first century, given that most forensic psychologists who are qualified by training subsequently work outside of the courtroom context, often in prisons. In McGuire's (1996) European survey, a broader set of criteria applied to the Spanish term *psicologia juridica*. However, Brown (1998) identifies that the Spanish term is also hierarchical and subsumes a number of specific subdivisions referring to work with police, prisons and juveniles etc., thus providing a compromise between the broader and narrower schools of thought. This said, broader definitions could endanger the integrity of the profession, as forensic psychology may then overlap considerably with criminal psychology, criminology and the work of the many psychologists of varying specialism, whose activities make some contact with crime and criminals.

The expanding job description for forensic psychologists has also begun to confound the boundaries between their discipline and those of criminal psychologists or criminologists amongst other professionals in the area of crime and justice. Although criminal psychologists tend to focus on the individual criminals and their crimes, and criminologists on societal or individual influences on them, as opposed to the forensic psychologist's orientation towards the courtroom, there has clearly always been a great deal of overlap in the subject matter of each. This overlap is increasing with time, and in practice their activities can on occasion be very similar (Howitt, 2009). However, the methodological approaches underpinning these disciplines differ historically, with criminology emerging from sociological and critical sociological assumptions (see Taylor, Walton and Young, 1973), in contrast with forensic psychology's reliance on experimental psychology.

As mentioned earlier, the duties of the modern forensic psychologist have extended beyond advising or appearing in law courts, and the extent of this diversity is greater than that for forensic psychiatrists and those working in forensic medicine. Although some of the distinctions between psychiatrists and psychologists remain, in the forensic field these have been eroded to some degree, with forensic psychologists providing assessments of prisoners and contributing to judgements as to whether individuals are mentally fit to appear in court. Thus much of the historical remit of the forensic psychologist has expanded from the pre-existing overlap between medicine, psychiatry and law. For Brigham (1999) in the US context, examining the medical–legal dimension suggests that there are now two emerging forensic

psychologies, a focused clinical forensic psychology and a broad legal psychology branch of forensic psychology. The increasingly important hybrid profession of **clinical forensic psychology** will be fully covered in Chapter 8.

Some of the roles described in the Focus box can often be carried out by the same forensic psychologist, who may also be qualified as a clinical psychologist. However, most practising forensic psychologists are specialised, with very few individuals carrying out a broad range of duties in different contexts. Brigham (1999: p. 273) reports that there are many psychologists working in a wide variety of roles in the forensic domain, who if individually asked, would not be able to say if they were forensic psychologists or not. Thus a parsimonious (i.e. economical) definition of a forensic psychologist may arise from the dilemma of these diverse roles, in that those individuals who have completed postgraduate training in forensic psychology and remained working in the field beyond their subsequent supervisory period have earned the professional title and others must apply for it. A narrowing of the definition would clearly help to protect the professional boundaries of the **chartered forensic psychologist**. Since the late 1980s in the UK, fully qualified psychologists in various professional roles could apply for chartered status from the relevant BPS division, in this case the Division of Forensic Psychology, allowing regulation and some control over professional practice (see pp. 208–10 on how to become a forensic psychologist).

Thus a definition of forensic psychology has grown more complex as the roles within the profession have diversified. The forensic psychology practitioner now works in many contexts, and the next section will illustrate some of the context-specific activities included in the broader role played by the contemporary forensic psychologist.

Self-test questions

- How has development of forensic psychology related to the historical use of medical expertise in court?
- Why was the insanity rule important to the development of forensic psychology?
- Why was Hugo Munsterberg a key figure in the development of the discipline?
- Why is the job description for a forensic psychologist so hard to define?
- What are the difficulties involved in moving between countries for a forensic psychologist?
- Name five of the areas in which the forensic psychologist plays a role.

International perspective

Legal systems and forensic psychology

Forensic psychologists work in most countries across the world, and although training and local needs may vary, the activities are internationally similar. However, forensic psychologists working close to Gudjonsson and Haward's (1998) view of the profession as closely pertaining to judicial processes suffer the same limitation as the legal profession itself. This is that legal systems and related processes such as policing and penal systems vary considerably between countries and even between states within them.

For example, there are similarities between the UK and the USA, such as that, both have adversarial legal systems, but there are also important differences, such as the death penalty persisting in some US states but not in the UK. There are countries that have inherited or adopted the same legal systems, but as with legal professionals, forensic psychologists need considerable adaptive skills to travel. Thus the training of forensic psychologists tends to be in the country in which they will eventually practise, even within the European community. This is less the case with clinical psychologists, who may move across Europe relatively easily.

The psychological approaches to crime also vary internationally and the advert on a Hong Kong bus may not be seen as effective in other countries.
Source: David A. Holmes.

The forensic psychology practitioner

The diversity of forensic psychology as a twenty-first-century discipline in its broadest sense defies definitions and now incorporates areas traditionally attributed to criminology, cognitive psychology and clinical psychology, amongst many others. However, this range is a little more focused when considering the actual work of forensic psychology practitioners, if only in terms of the contexts in which the majority are found. In this section, the main employer of forensic psychologists, the prison service, will be examined as well as the court services . In addition, the contribution made by research to court and police procedure in the important areas of eyewitness testimony and interviewing will be summarised along with a review of report writing oriented towards forensic context.

The prison context

Penal institutions and their functions were a focus for research and theoretical debate amongst psychologists and criminologists long before forensic psychologists had a regular role within the prison context (see Jewkes, 2007). Issues such as whether prisons and custodial sentences met the aims attributed to them by the justice system as well as the difficult balance between secure containment and rehabilitation have been a focus for many forensic disciplines (see Bottoms, Rex and Robinson, 2004). Public order, or the protection of the offender from public vigilantism, has been a continuing issue with notorious offenders such as 'moors murderer' Myra Hindley spending the rest of their lives in prison to protect them from public reaction as well as consideration of their risk to others. This case also illustrates the aim of maintaining public confidence in the prison system, in that retaining infamous offenders has also been a result of political sensitivity to public opinion. Aims such as being a deterrent to potential offenders, punishing offending behaviour and reducing reoffending have been critically appraised by psychological research and examined in relation to theory (see Cavadino and Dignan, 2002; Easton and Piper, 2005).

Offenders tend not to be deterred by prison, as they do not consider they will be caught when committing crimes and are thus little concerned by the type or degree of punishment. In behavioural terms, an effective punishment would invariably follow an act swiftly, and be unpleasant and of a short duration. However, reinforcement of behaviour by punishment is considered a weaker means of changing behaviour than rewarding alternative or good behaviour (Skinner, 1953). Prison clearly fails on all of these criteria in being delayed by the justice system, lengthy, made ethically palatable and far from inevitable with up to 98 per cent of those committing crimes not being convicted or punished (Maguire, 1997; Easton and Piper, 2005). These difficulties are compounded by the prison environment, which also acts as a breeding ground for criminal allegiances and as a 'crime school' that educates the more naïve offender in prison. These factors led in the 1970s to a significant shift in politically driven policy away from the aim of offender *rehabilitation* towards the aim of protecting the public by secure containment. Such a sudden move away from attempting to reform offenders, under the general principle of 'nothing works', was partly fuelled by an overstatement of the conclusions of an analysis of 231 studies by Martinson (1974). This meta-analysis reported that no rehabilitation programme had been found consistently to reduce recidivism. The cost-cutting approach of 'humane containment' that followed was rationalised by unsubstantiated economic arguments that rehabilitation would not be maintained on release, that it had no effect on those not apprehended and that any reformed individuals would be rapidly replaced in the 'criminal job market' (see Blackburn, 1993; Hollin, 2002). In this approach, reward

and punishment were still present in the form of the 1967 **parole system**, allowing early release for 'good conduct', which is only loosely tied to low reoffending rates.

Prisons in most countries now have psychologists working within them and the prison service is the largest employer of forensic psychologists. In the UK, the presence of psychologists in prisons can be traced back to 1946 (McMurren and Shapland, 1989) and in the twenty-first century they work in many aspects of prison function, usually from psychology units within the institutions. Somewhat counter to public expectations, forensic psychologists in prison tend to be younger than other prison staff and over 80 per cent are female (Needs and Towl, 2004). This may be a consequence of the prison service taking on many younger trainee forensic psychologists, who remain in post when they have finished their supervisory period following training. This placement training of forensic psychologists has helped to elevate general levels of continuing professional development in prisons (Needs and Towl, 2004).

England and Wales are divided into 12 areas, within which prison psychology services are coordinated by area psychologists, who now are also well placed to integrate services with the Probation Service. In addition to the 12 prison service areas, there are two specific functional divisions: namely, prison services for females and high-security prisons. High-security and remaining special hospital prisons may have their own area psychologist, as their inmate populations require more intensive and varied psychological input. Partly a legacy of the design of old psychiatric institutions, special hospitals were and (despite opposition) still are large mental hospitals with prison security. These institutions, such as **Broadmoor**, **Rampton** and **Ashworth** in the UK (see the Focus box), were designed to detain and treat dangerous, mentally disordered or mentally disabled offenders.

Despite name changes, the concept of a concentration of psychological and psychiatric services in a secure environment, remote from the general population, has remained and provided forensic psychologists with focal points for the study of dangerous and disordered offenders. However, reports such as the **Blom-Cooper** and **Fallon Inquiries** and the Tilt Review in 2000, in addressing security and other problems, have recommended that at least some of the larger patient groups in these institutions be relocated in smaller units. In addition to these public inquiries, broader criticism of the principles of such institutions have recurred over many years (e.g. Pilgrim and Eisenberg, 1985).

Regional secure units (RSUs) were intended to provide secure places in the locality and expand the provision for disturbed offenders, leaving some places in the remote

Focus

Therapeutic intervention versus containment

The somewhat negative attitude to preventing reoffending has been partly reversed in the twenty-first century, and much of this refocusing on rehabilitation can be attributed to the growing number of psychology professionals working in prisons. There has been a historical legacy of prisons as **therapeutic communities,** which was illustrated by the establishment of Grendon Underwood psychiatric prison in 1962. Grendon and a few other prisons considered treatment and reform above mere containment. An important component of the concept of prison being therapeutic rather than punitive is that the former requires a therapeutic alliance or collaboration between inmates and staff (Needs and Towl, 2004), whereas the latter suggests a more confrontational interaction.

This collaboration between service users or inmate-patients and service providers could be seen to transcend the containment philosophy, but only to the extent that the two elements have common aims. The 'stronger in partnership' scheme (Welsh Assembly Government, 2004) is a good example of a policy framework for this in a forensic psychiatric setting, which is supported by both service users and providers (see C. Robert, 2006). This approach contains an essential element for avoiding reoffending, which is that of offender compliance.

Support for this important shift of emphasis has come from broader public service reform in the UK (Office of Public Services Reform, 2002), which has embraced a 'stakeholder' approach to priorities, making the needs of those involved in the prison system a focus rather than the needs of prison function (Needs and Towl, 2004). With the launch of the **National Probation Service** in 2001, prison and probation were interlinked to provide a more seamless service for users and staff (Towl, 2002). This 'joining up' of services means that a short-term prisoner discharged before completing a therapeutic intervention programme can have this continued and completed in the community, which would also enable short-term prisoners to begin therapy that would otherwise be denied them due to the brevity of their stay. Liaison between these services also allows better awareness of the work of each group of professionals by those in other groups.

special hospitals free for more dangerous patients. RSUs offer a medium level of secure confinement with psychiatric facilities and may be used to house more specialist populations (e.g. adolescent RSUs). Inquiries and reviews of special hospital provision have been consistently critical, as can be seen in the Focus box. However, in addition to this opposition to large special hospitals, the alternative provision of regional secure units has also been subject to criticism.

Most of the work of forensic and other psychologists in the prison setting falls broadly into the areas of treatment or **behavioural programmes**, risk (see Chapter 4), personnel and management.

Behavioural programmes

Reduction of offending in those released from prison not only addresses the public protection agenda but also directly meets a major aim of the penal system and is thus viewed as a vital role for psychologists, but subject to critical appraisal. Most of these behavioural programmes are subject to the **What Works** criteria and are thus subject to meta-analysis (see Chapter 5) in order to establish their effectiveness empirically (see Blud et al., 2003). Many

forensic psychology projects can be involved in providing input to larger studies which evaluate the change resulting from particular interventions that are then compared with other approaches. This process leads to psychologists justifying their work before formal hearings, following the theme of evidence-based practice (see Chapter 6). The Correctional Services Accreditation Panel (CSAP) independently accredits offender behaviour programmes (Blud et al., 2003; Towl, 2002).

Accredited behaviour programmes can be specific to offender sub-groups such as the different types of **Sex Offender Treatment Programme**: for example, those for low-risk offenders (general rolling programme) and medium to high-risk offenders (core programme). Ray Novaco (e.g. 1994) developed an **anger management** programme, and although early interventions were not fully utilised on prison populations, variants of this approach have since been implemented with offenders and disordered offenders prone to violence in the UK, the USA and Europe (see Novaco, 1997). Other treatment approaches raise broader issues within prisons, such as addressing illicit drug use, as these substances are often available on the prison 'black market', confounding assessments and client progress. Many programmes are geared to long-term

Focus

Ashworth special hospital

Ashworth began its existence as a hospital in 1872 following the purchase of a former private family home by Liverpool Select Vestry. As 'Moss Side House' it was a convalescent home for children before being used for minor cases of 'lunacy' until it was expanded with new buildings and purchased by the Lunacy Board of Control at the start of the First World War. As a consequence of this timing, the new hospital was used for wartime casualties with psychological problems, such as shell-shock. With the advent of the National Health Service in 1948 there were four major hospitals in the UK securely housing the mentally ill and the 'mentally deficient': namely, **Broadmoor, Rampton, Moss Side** and **Carstairs** (in Scotland). The 1959 Mental Health Act identified a need for 'special hospitals' for the secure detainment of the dangerously mentally ill, which also included the criminally insane, including the psychopathic offender.

As one of the four major special hospitals, Moss Side became a site for expansion and major building. In 1984 the then named **Park Lane Hospital** was completed adjacent to Moss Side. Having been recently furbished, it had the facilities and appearance of a modern approach to mental health, in contrast with the imposing older Victorian institutions. At this time the 1983 Mental Health Act gave all patients more rights, including access to a review process formally carried out before Mental Health Review Tribunals. Changes to the management of special hospitals took place at this time and again later in 1995. Moss Side and Park Lane were amalgamated under the single name Ashworth Hospital in 1990.

During the 1990s, Ashworth seemed to receive more than its fair share of public attention. A televised documentary in 1991 attracted official attention and precipitated the 1992 **Blom-Cooper** public inquiry into allegations of inmate mistreatment. Radical changes to the regime at Ashworth were in place by the time the special hospitals in England were made independent authorities in 1996, enabling them to tailor their individual regimes to suit the differing client groups. However, only a year later the personality disorder unit at Ashworth became a focus of public and government attention with tabloid-reported incidents such as patients indulging in drug and pornography dealing (to the extent of around £14,000 in a 10-month period) and the ambiguous story of a 7-year-old girl being groomed for paedophile purposes during regular visits to patients (Warden, 1999). The ensuing **Fallon** public inquiry made 58 recommendations in 1999, mostly directly pertinent to Ashworth. Serious understaffing was identified in terms of quantity and more particularly quality, due to poor recruitment, with less than half of the professional staffing required for the personality disorder unit. The inquiry blamed the liberal system at Ashworth rather than individual staff for allowing control to slip dangerously towards the side of the patients rather than staff, and it threatened the unit with closure. In a unit housing psychopathic patients, it was not difficult for a small group of inmates to orchestrate illicit activity where there was no firm leadership.

Government opposition to closure allowed the hospital to produce an action plan to address all the relevant Fallon recommendations. The plan was sufficiently wide ranging to mark a way forward for the hospital. Amongst the general recommendations Fallon made was the somewhat cosmetic renaming of 'psychopathic disorder' as the euphemistically generic 'personality disorder', later to become 'Dangerous and Severe Personality Disorder', with some form of reviewable detention for these patients. This paved the way for some of the suggestions for the recently revised Mental Health Act (which were, however, not fully implemented). Other suggestions were to break up large patient groups into smaller units and to develop new regional special units.

A further recommendation of the Fallon inquiry into Ashworth was that a review of security at special hospitals should take place. This **Tilt** Review was published in 2000 and called for increased security measures and more intensive therapeutic interventions at the same time as suppressing the counterculture that tends to become established by the patient population. The main thrust of the Fallon and Tilt outcomes fed into the running of Ashworth and informed system overviews at Rampton and Broadmoor hospitals. In 2002 Ashworth joined its sister institutions in forming partnerships with adjacent authorities, in this case Mersey Care NHS Trust. In the years since being the target for public inquiries, Ashworth has become a focal point for research into personality disorder and related interventions, and is regularly used as the meeting place for a number of national organisations, such as the Royal College of Psychiatrists, and local specialist groups, such as the North West Forensic Academic Network.

prisoners, and life sentence prisoners may often have their own assigned psychologist who may implement a more structured approach to reducing the risk of reoffending, including harm to self or others (see Towl and Crighton, 1996). Another issue with this particular inmate group is the hidden area of palliative care in prison and the philosophical dilemma that, for some, the outcome of some treatment programmes may only be realised within prison.

Sometimes the cognitive behavioural treatment approaches in these interventions are termed 'cognitive skills programmes' as a result of the focus on changing the fixed and erroneous thinking patterns of many offender groups. Effective principles of these cognitive skills programmes can be identified by meta-analytic studies and usefully transferred between programmes from different countries (Friendship et al., 2003). These generic elements can be found across a variety of accredited interventions. Many of these treatments are 'manual led', meaning that once established as effective, they are delivered in a reliably prescriptive way from pre-structured manuals that ensure not only that the offenders receive the same treatment but also that evaluative data from studies comparing programme outcomes are thus controlled for variations in programme delivery. However, treatment 'by the book' can be limiting for a trainee psychologist seeking varied and challenging work experience. Forensic psychologists may deliver treatment programmes as groupwork or in individual interventions with longer-term prisoners. Successful programmes to reduce reoffending often have certain common characteristics, such as challenging the attitudes, values and beliefs that support offending behaviour and high programme integrity (Vennard and Hedderman, 1998).

Risk assessment and management

Risk of re-offending is not just based on intervention outcomes, as there are static as well as dynamic factors involved. Factors such as biological predispositions and childhood experiences (see pp. 223–6) are more difficult to modify by treatment programmes but will be taken into account in any risk assessment in relation to reoffending. Thus in any risk assessment there will be an analysis of a broad range of factors that predict reoffending (usually violence or sexual offences are the key offences to be minimised), as well as identifying any available and potentially effective interventions available for that individual.

Risk of harm to self or **suicide** has become a high priority for psychologists in assessing prisoners, due to a rise in such occurrences in the twenty-first century. Targeting those most at risk, such as new arrivals at the prison or those with HIV infection (see Casale, 1995),

existing depressive illness or self-harm indications, amongst other factors, can contribute to more efficient monitoring and intervention for suicidal prisoners. Prison populations are at greater risk of suicide than those who have not experienced prison (Towl and Crighton, 1996) and simple interventions such as changing prison staff attitudes to those at risk can be effective. Thus risk assessment by forensic psychologists using criteria derived from research can also identify those needing more specialist help from suicide prevention teams. In Australia, the **Real Understanding of Self-Help** (RUSH) scheme has been successful with very high-risk groups of prisoners with borderline personality disorder (Eccleston and Sorbello, 2002). In the UK the Listeners network has been very well received in some prisons. This dual-purpose scheme uses volunteer prisoners trained by the Samaritans to support their peers identified as high risk (Coackley and Richman, 2003), thus producing benefit for both recipient and 'listener'. Risk of suicide often continues after a prisoner is released and will thus benefit from continuity of monitoring with psychologists in the Probation Service.

Risk of **bullying** in prison has also risen in recent years, or at least has been more accurately reported. Ireland (2002) clarifies that fear of, and as a result of, bullying refers not only to that between prisoners but also between staff and inmates, between staff and prison management and between members of staff themselves. She further distinguishes between prisoner–prisoner bullying that is symmetrical, where both prisoners are aggressors and victims, and that which is asymmetrical, where one stays in the aggressive role and the other is the victim. In order to address the dearth of research into bullying in the prison context, Ireland had to develop her own measures, such as the self-report DIPC (Direct and Indirect Prisoner behaviour Checklist; Ireland, 1998). Bullying in prison is extensive and very damaging in increasing the risk of suicide, promoting the climate of fear and reinforcing the prison subculture that is so toxic to rehabilitation.

Risk assessments of hostage taking in prisons and other dangerous prison incidents have been a focus for forensic psychologists, who have contributed substantially to the efficient resolution of these dangerous situations whilst minimising risk (Evans and Henson, 1999). Successful approaches to incident management have wider implications, such as improving public confidence in the prison system and adding to the smooth running of prisons as well as staff safety (Towl, 2002).

Prison personnel and management

Forensic psychologists may be involved in the occupational role within the prison context. This may be a specialist approach to staff recruitment criteria and adding to training methods and courses. Stress management interventions and screening for prison staff have important implications for both quality and continuity of service, particularly for the growing number of female staff who will be working in a male-dominated environment, which has become an issue throughout the justice systems of many countries (see Hurst and Hurst, 1997). The real risk of attempted intimidation, being taken hostage or even involvement in riots requires more specialist stress management interventions than non-forensic occupational approaches. Thus routine attrition due to stress in the prison context is more likely to progress to 'stress burnout' or chronic stress due to a range of factors, such as work pressure or conflict with management and inmates in continuous close contact (see Brown, 2004). Stress interventions can be directed at the individual, including avoidance of conflict and techniques of stress reduction, or directed at the level of the organisational structure, including improving management infrastructure, environment and human resource management (Schaufeli and Peeters, 2000). Post-traumatic stress reactions following incidents need additional interventions from psychologists.

Psychologists are increasingly taking on project management roles, often as a result of their extensive training in research methods both as undergraduate and postgraduate psychologists. Postgraduate trainee input to the prison research base is a growing valuable resource but one that has a cost in terms of quality supervision. Although some of this input may be somewhat routine research prearranged by the supervisor, the introduction of fresh trainees into the environment will inevitably lead to innovation and progress. Evidence-based practice has been a part of professional psychology for many years and is now making a difference within prison function and staff training.

Prison policy tends to be politically led rather than developing from grassroots feedback. This opens up management consultancy needs for forensic psychologists to secure a more balanced compromise over policy generation, with the needs of all parties considered in the light of current evidence-based practice on 'what works'. Psychologists tend to generalise principles whereas the legal system has a more ad hoc approach based on individual cases (Clifford, 2003). This has also been true of prisons, where a psychologist in the job of coordinating across many sources of evidence generation will be in a position to produce generalisable policy and guidelines from an empirical perspective. The prioritisation of performance management in prison has also resulted in the psychologist's role within it being better integrated with the needs of the prison. These developments at managerial level for forensic psychologists will be reinforced by the pivotal role of area psychologists in helping to coordinate psychological services between prison and probation. The development of a broad understanding of what organisational skills are required in these functions has opened up the role of management consultant for experienced forensic psychologists.

The courtroom context

In most countries during the latter half of the twentieth century, it became accepted that any psychologist from any area of expertise could be requested to fulfil the role of **expert witness** in a court unless there are ethical grounds for not so doing. Appearing in court can demand special skills for which training and support is available from specialist groups in most countries (see the Focus box).

As briefly mentioned in Chapter 1, the narrowly defined work of the forensic psychologist in relation to the judicial context has become diversified into now established specialist roles (Gudjonsson and Haward, 1998), including the following.

The actuarial role

This is where probabilities are established that give the court baselines by which to judge those occurrences presented to the court. For example, a defendant may claim that they have no memory for an event due to a subsequent minor, non-physical, traumatising event. An actuarial psychologist may present the (controversial) data that such minor psychological traumas almost never result in memory loss and that claims such as this are improbable.

The experimental role

This reverts back to the early laboratory role of forensic psychologists, in producing experimental data for presentation in court. This may often be a specific requirement very much in the manner of forensic science (see James and Nordby, 2005) or, as in early cases of the rejection of psychometric data in court, the validation of instruments used to generate evidence.

The advisory role

This can be a very contentious area in which one psychologist may give an opinion of another professional's evidence. Clearly this clashing of professionals of potentially

Focus

Courtroom experience

Courtroom experience itself can be taken as giving greater expertise than qualifications for psychologists in court, as is often the case for other legal professionals. Memon, Vrij and Bull (2003: ch. 9) provide a good overview of the limitations of the role of expert witnesses in court.

Forensically inexperienced psychologists appearing in court for the first time can be a liability to their employers as a result of naivety in respect of the legal process. Ignorance of court procedure may lead to basic mistakes, in that psychologists may make a hearsay error or fail to distinguish opinion from fact. They must also consider the general effect their statements have on the court and the consequences for sentencing, and learn to present evidence in a clear, concise way without jargon. As with any expert, the factual value of a psychologist's contribution to a case in court should outweigh any prejudicial effects on a jury.

In BPS surveys carried out by Gudjonsson (1996) into court and tribunal work of psychologists, good experts in court put their evidence into context and admitted the limitations of their contributions. For example, if a client had a personality disorder, it would be helpful to add that such disorders may affect over 10 per cent of the population and are therefore common.

Even trained forensic psychologists need to be fully aware of the changing complexities of the legal process should they need to enter the court. However, many of the psychologist roles in the courtroom do not specify that they have to be carried out by a qualified forensic psychologist.

equal status can be destructive to the credibility of the court process and requires diplomacy, professionalism and professional respect by all parties.

The clinical role

This can be a diverse role, in addressing the court's concerns regarding the mental health of parties in court. In this, clinical psychologists may take also on the dual role of **clinical–forensic psychologist** to present clinical assessment data in court. This may involve general limitations placed on witnesses (i.e. in the case of children or those with psychological disorder) or the form of evidence given (e.g. limitations on testimony; see pp. 193–201). Particularly in the USA, forensic psychologists are only allowed to advise courts on these general aspects of a witness or defendant's ability to give testimony and not to state whether a particular witness is reliable in their specific judgement. If a witness has a disability, then the general effects on evidence production of such a disability may be presented that have been drawn from research. However, such a presentation could be used to *imply* that a witness had a disability because the evidence would not have to be specific to that witness.

Psychologists are most often involved in assessing the defendant (accused offender) for different purposes, depending on the stage of the legal process. For each of these, they may be requested to produce a **court report** to be considered in evidence. The crucial stages are as follows.

- **At the time of offence.** In order to be convicted under English criminal law, the defendant must conform to two criteria: actus reus, to have committed the act; and **mens rea**, to have guilty intent as their state of mind. In order to support a plea of insanity (as in the McNaughten rule, mentioned above) and establish the client as not being responsible for their actions at the time of an offence due to unsound mind, they would have to be assessed by a psychiatrist or a psychologist acting in the clinical role. This judgement may on occasion have to be made retrospectively and conform to the legally accepted definitions of mental disorder. There are degrees of mitigation: guilty but insane, where the defendant may be diverted from the penal system into psychiatric care (until fit); and diminished responsibility, where the sentence is reduced to reflect the contribution of a disorder to the criminal act.

- **Competence to stand trial.** This is independent of the above and usually requires only a minimum level of competence, i.e. to understand the charge and court proceedings. The defendant will often be held in custody until fit for trial.

- **Competence to be sentenced.** Similarly, the defendant must be able to understand the implications of the sentence passed and be mentally fit to serve it in prison if that is the case.

These roles for the forensic psychologist are by no means exhaustive and many psychologists providing services to the courts will work outside of this framework.

Psychologists in court and ethics

Although integrity is a part of the professional code for lawyers, remuneration more clearly plays a secondary role to ethics for the psychologist in court when compared with the lawyers who employ them, particularly in the USA where lawyers tend to be fee driven. In 1997 the BPS Division of Criminological and Legal Psychology issued ethical guidelines for its members and those working in forensic contexts. These guidelines borrowed heavily from those of the American Psychological Association and attempted to address current ethical challenges, such as diversity in the workplace, and improve critical awareness of ethical issues. Issues such as the boundary between coercion and consent have always been in need of critical examination within forensic practice (Needs and Towl, 2004).

The expertise of psychologists could place them in the role of judging the motivation of an offender: that is, whether they intended to commit the offence or not. This could also be extended to having a psychologist ascertain if a defendant or witness testimony is truthful or not. In many countries, such judgements would be seen to undermine the entire court system and justice as a transparent process that is 'seen to be done', and thus such judgements by psychologists are not allowed in this direct sense. This dilemma will be returned to in the section on lie detection (pp. 205–8).

There are now many courts in which forensic psychologists may find themselves giving expert opinion.
Source: Pearson Online Database.

Eyewitness testimony

Fictional recreations of courtroom procedure in popular film and television programmes will often focus unduly on part of the oath sworn by witnesses, i.e. 'to tell the truth, the whole truth and nothing but the truth'. Regardless of the expectations of justice, the rather exacting phrase 'nothing but the truth' may actually be untenable in court if human memory or perception is relied upon for this evidence. Yet this phrase remains, despite evidence from the earliest work by forensic psychologists of the 'treachery of human memory' (Munsterberg, 1909). However, it took many years before the rather theoretical empirical research approach of cognitive psychology (see Baddeley, 1990; Neisser, 1967) and the highly applied requirements of forensic psychology in the courtroom had their combined representation in the critical study of eyewitness testimony. **Ulrich Neisser** recognised the limitations of the traditional approach of cognitive psychology to memory research, in that it did not address the everyday problems of memory (see Neisser, 1982). For Neisser, adherence to rigour in cognitive psychology had led to a

situation in which any subject that was socially significant or simply interesting would be ignored for research purposes, as it would be seen as pandering to the sensational at the expense of experimental empiricism and rigour. However, the renewed approach to applied cognitive psychology that began to develop in the latter half of the twentieth century would impact on many areas of everyday life, including the basis for giving evidence in court, eyewitness testimony.

Despite progress in the psychology of memory and perception, the dichotomy between the cognitive psychologist's explanation of human recall as a constructive process and the legal profession's view of testimony as objective still fails to be adequately bridged. Most forensic psychologists would not be surprised at the fact that, internationally, there have been many miscarriages of justice in which the recollections or perceptions of a witness have been pivotal in the conviction of innocent defendants. However, these errors in the judgements of

Research

DNA and testimony

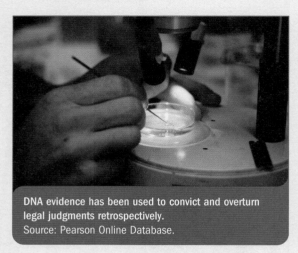

DNA evidence has been used to convict and overturn legal judgments retrospectively.
Source: Pearson Online Database.

Advances in DNA (deoxyribonucleic acid) technology have enabled accurate retrospective DNA fingerprinting of convicted individuals that in many cases have resulted in their being released as innocent of the crime for which they had been tried and convicted (Howitt, 2009). The majority of wrongful convictions in the USA were a result of eyewitness error. Thus objective scientific evidence has provided absolute proof that eyewitness testimony cannot be taken to represent 'nothing but the truth', and that believing what you say in court may be honest, but this 'evidence' may still not be sufficiently accurate to rightly convict a defendant.

Concern was shown about the further retrospective use of DNA to apprehend newly identified offenders from cold cases in a debate in the UK House of Lords in 2003. The idea that the long arm of the law could stretch decades into the past was thought to unduly disturb the innocent as well as the guilty. However, the public's approval of offenders such as Bryan Keen being brought to justice by DNA 11 years after his crime soon provided evidence that the careful use of DNA in this manner was justified. The UK BBC TV drama series *Waking the Dead* is based on cold cases (closed cases of unsolved crimes) bringing forensic anthropology to life!

witnesses tend to be rather reluctantly accepted by the legal profession and judiciary, who rely so heavily on these testimonies when presenting cases to jurors.

Human memory is considered to be analogous to the operation of a DVD recorder by the lay public and much of the legal profession. In this version of reality, a witness simply observes a sequence of events and then plays them back at will in a slightly foggy version but exactly the same detail. From very early memory research in psychology, such as Ebbinghaus (1897), it was clear that human memory could be facilitated by the coherence of data and inhibited by contradictory information. Memory errors can occur at the stage of encoding information, which can then be confounded by new information and finally confused or biased at the point of recall. When humans perceive new information, it is recognised and stored by both **bottom-up** and **top-down** processes, which are far removed from the digital camera or recorder analogy.

'Bottom-up' refers to lower-level sensory information (i.e. from the eye and ear receptors etc.) being filtered up through the nervous system and reaching the sensory cortex of the brain. Using the example of the visual system, a great deal of interpretation of this incoming visual information occurs via a vast array of simple, complex, hypercomplex and other specialist cells that respond to specific details in the visual field (see Frisby (1979) for a clearly illustrated overview). To a great extent, these specialist parts of the sensory system are 'hard wired' and automatically reconstruct a version of reality in the brain that is most useful to us, but not necessarily one that is veridical. When using this example of the rather bizarre human visual system, which has its wiring *in front* of its sensors, its picture upside down and all colour 'added' on the basis of light frequencies, it is clear that the enhancement of the impoverished 'bottom-up' signals in the system has to be considerable and involve more than mere enhancement of the original sensory signal. Thus, in addition, 'top-down' processes further organise this information on the basis of preconceived expectations in the brain. These 'top-down' expectations take into account a wide range of influences, such as the context or surprisingness of the information based on experience and pre-existing stereotypes or even prejudices. Thus Gregory and Coleman (1995) thought of the 'intelligence of perception' as a process of problem solving for the brain and closer to continuous guesswork than digital recording.

Allport and Postman (1947) used a 'Chinese whispers' technique in the manner of Bartlett (1932) to demonstrate prejudice intervening into memory errors in a forensically relevant example. When a picture of a white man holding a knife and sitting opposite an unarmed black man was described from subject to subject in this study, the details became corrupted in a manner that conformed to contemporary prejudices: that is, the knife was held by the black man in the end versions of these descriptions. Social influences affecting existing memories were referred to by Schrenk-Nortzing in his 1896 appearance in court as 'retroactive memory falsification'. A witness to a crime may not only 'fill in the blanks' in their memories of events, but may also have already incorporated a great deal of their own expectations and assumptions into how they perceived the event at the time. For example, a child running and the sound of a breaking window may be unrelated events, but they can be linked in the brain of a witness to form one coherent act based on expectation.

Even the use of machines for evidence or the identification of suspects cannot be fully relied upon, as the same sources of human error described above will intervene in the process. Poor and ambiguous information from **CCTV** cameras or computerised police facial composites ('photofit' sketches) are limited by the human judgements made on the images obtained. In the case of **E-FIT** (Electronic Facial Identification Technique) facial composites, the errors are doubled as these likenesses are created with errors incorporated by one individual witness and often identified by the judgements of another person's fallible recognition and memory processes.

Research by **Elizabeth Loftus** and her colleagues began to isolate some of the influences on eyewitness testimony in a number of frequently quoted studies. The most salient of these demonstrated how the precise language used in questioning 'witnesses' could bias recall of events. After they had viewed film of a crash, asking subjects how fast cars were travelling when they '*smashed* into each other' produced higher speed estimates than when the question was phrased as '*bumped* into each other'. Thus not only can errors occur as a result of memory and perceptual processes, but also deliberate bias can be induced by questioning styles used by police and in court (see the next section). Most research in this area has been accused of lacking ecological or external validity (see Chapter 5), in that these are artificially generated events mostly utilising college students (Yuille and Cutshall, 1986) and lacking in the trauma or threat of real-world crimes (Ainsworth, 1998). However, ethical limitations dictate that much has to be inferred from this type of empirical research for progress in the field of eyewitness validity.

It is sadly true that 'an eyewitness report, confidently delivered, has swayed many a jury' (Leippe, 1994: p. 385).

It has also been found that the majority of UK police believe that witnesses were invariably accurate (Kebbell and Milne, 1998). Thus an entire case and the freedom or otherwise of a defendant may depend on a single witness statement, which is why the limitations of such testimony need to be precisely defined by forensic psychologists. Leippe (1994) refers to confidence in testimony delivery, which can be interpreted by the court as certainty over recall, but which in fact has no significant relationship to the validity of testimony. There are aspects of individuals that are better recalled, situational factors pertaining to the event and individual differences in witnesses in addition to the pressures placed on witnesses that can influence final testimony.

Data from Van Koppen and Lochun (1997) indicate that witnesses tend to be very accurate in reporting the gender of a target individual as well as eye shape, and have a good recall of hair colour. However, the height of an individual is less accurately reported, as is their race, whereas vocal accents and facial hair (beards etc.) are subject to very poor recall. Witnesses tend to be better with races and ages more similar to their own as a result of familiarity, which can be altered by training. The speed at which a witness recognises a suspect, for example in a police identification parade, is a good predictor of accuracy and has been referred to as the 10–12-second rule (Dunning and Perretta, 2002), this being the optimum time for making an accurate decision (see Howitt, 2009). The reverse is true of the duration of the original event, where a longer exposure time predicts a greater subsequent frequency of correctly recognised faces (positive 'hits'). Although some studies also found an increase in incorrect identifications (e.g. Shapiro and Penrod, 1986), others such as Memon et al. (2002) have found a decrease in errors with exposure time. Clearly, the exposure time to an event does not always indicate the time the witness spent looking at a particular face (Memon et al., 2002) and some events are always very brief, such as road traffic accidents, although witnesses greatly over-estimate the duration of these experiences (Ainsworth, 1998).

The effect of a weapon on witnesses tends to lower accuracy of identification by drawing attention from faces; this is termed weapon focus. However, this effect could also be explained by over-arousal due to fear disturbing attention and memory efficiency, in line with the Yerkes–Dodson Law of optimum arousal producing the best performance (Ainsworth, 1998). The results of Maass and Köhnken (1989) suggest that it is weapon focus rather than arousal that lowers accuracy as descriptions of hand cues increased if they held a weapon (in this case, a syringe). The surprisingness of the weapon context appears to govern the degree of distraction; thus a policeman with a gun draws less attention than a religious figure with the same weapon (Pickel, 1999). The personalised nature of the threat can also change attentional focus, in that the eyes of an aggressor become indicators of their intended actions in a dynamic situation.

Novel events attract attention, but witnesses to more horrific events will often avert their gaze and thus become less accurate in reporting details of more serious crimes. Thus **crime seriousness** is also a factor in eyewitness accuracy, and as ethical considerations prohibit realistic recreations, inference from **analogue studies** (see Chapter 5) has to be made cautiously (Ainsworth, 1998). Most such studies find the seriousness of crimes in terms of violence against individuals to lower accuracy of recall of the event details (e.g. Clifford and Hollin, 1981). Although it is assumed that the serious crime may be more distracting, it also has to be considered that recall of events can be state or mood dependent: that is, being in the same mental state at recall as at the time of the event enhances memory (see Williams et al., 1988; Eich, Macauley and Ryan, 1994). Brain scan research has indicated that memory recall may be a case of *recreating* the brain activity state at the point of encoding (Polyn et al., 2005). Clearly the experience of a victim of crime will differ from that of a bystander witness in arousal levels and proximity as well as other factors (Ainsworth, 1998). These factors when combined seem to reduce differences between victims and bystanders, although a victim's memory for events tends to be more durable over time.

A victim of crime may feel obligated to select a suspect on the basis that they *should* know who attacked them, as it would be embarrassing not to know in front of concerned officers who have spent time over the issue. They may also feel that the defendant has to be there for a reason and thus should be selected. These social pressures on witnesses, particularly victims, can lead to an identification based on the 'next best fit', where the person in a line-up or picture nearest in appearance to the perpetrator may become a defendant in court. Context-free familiarity can also lead to false identification of an individual. Thus if a witness is presented with the same photograph twice in a sequence, they may select it the second time on the basis that it seems familiar and erroneously attribute this familiarity to the person in the photograph being the perpetrator (Köhnken, Malpass and Wogalter, 1996). This is illustrated in the case of Heinz at the start of this chapter, who was selected as he appeared familiar.

There are individual differences in terms of witnesses' memory abilities, which are often exaggerated by police into the categories of 'good' and 'bad' witnesses. These differences in ability are not consistent, in that one person may recall times and events well, but not faces, and another may demonstrate yet further differing proportions of

ability. Other witness variables, such as age, gender and personality, have also been examined in relation to accuracy of recall. Although there can be a slight decline in ability with age, these factors do not produce clear differences in the ability to be a reliable witness.

One individual variable that has been a focus of research in relation to testimony and defendant statements is **suggestibility**. Sidis (1898) considered humans to be the 'suggestible animal' and defined suggestibility as a peculiar state of mind that is favourable to suggestion. Eysenck, Arnold and Meili (1975) referred to an individual's degree of susceptibility to influence by suggestion and hypnosis. This link between the degree to which an individual is influenced by suggestion and the degree to which an individual is hypnotisable (Schumaker, 1991) is important in the context of using hypnosis to 'enhance' recall and will be returned to in the next section. Some individuals, such as children and those with learning disabilities, may be more prone to suggestion due to naïveté and the power relationship in being questioned by an experienced adult. In terms of eyewitness testimony, a witness or defendant who is highly suggestible is likely to be more easily led to identify an innocent individual or even falsely confess to a crime they have not committed.

Clearly the legal profession's reliance on eyewitness testimony as a valid record of events is not supported by the work of forensic psychologists. However, in many cases the police and courts may have little else other than a witness to bring about a prosecution; thus the eyewitness can be viewed as a fallible necessity rather than a preferred route to justice. This section has presented some of the limitations of eyewitness testimony identified by psychologists and is linked to many of the issues in the following section on interviewing witnesses and defendants.

Forensic interviews and questioning

Police interviews

Most forensic interviews are part of police procedure and have been a focal part of police work throughout their history when dealing with more serious crimes. Some issues raised by these interviews also apply to witness or defendant questioning in court and are clearly closely related to the problems of eyewitness testimony discussed in the previous section. A particular focus for research in the area of forensic interviewing is where the subject is vulnerable due to suggestibility or a mental condition, or in the case of a child witness. Even where vulnerability is negligible, the power relationship in a forensic interview, with the officer in charge of the agenda, timing and other aspects of the process, requires similar factors to be

Research

Interrogative suggestibility

The form of suggestibility that is pertinent to police and courtroom questioning is termed interrogative suggestibility. This is the degree to which an individual may be coerced into a particular answer by the style of questioning. In a theoretical model, Gudjonnsson and Clark (1986) viewed interrogative suggestibility, rather wordily, as the extent to which, within a closed social interaction, people come to accept messages communicated during formal questioning as the result of which their subsequent behavioural response is affected. Interrogative suggestibility differs from the suggestibility associated with hypnosis (Gudjonsson, 1987).

A psychometric instrument for measuring interrogative suggestibility was initially developed by Gudjonsson (1984). This is in the form of text that the subject learns and is subsequently questioned about

in a manner that is intended to bias answers away from the original material. This produces a **yield** score representing incorrect statements agreed with. It also produces a **shift** score for replies that the subject changes when prompted by the tester falsely suggesting to the subject that previous replies had been incorrect (Gudjonsson, 2003). The shift score has a dual role, in that it accounts for a different dimension of suggestibility from the yield score and acts as an indicator of someone attempting to fake high suggestibility in order to appear vulnerable (Howitt, 2009).

Although the Gudjonsson Suggestibility Scale (Gudjonsson, 1984) is somewhat lengthy to administer, the instrument can be valuable in the case of those individuals who may falsely confess to crimes or have brought about serious charges due to suggestion from a third party (see the following section).

---

recognised in all routine 'interrogations' of non-vulnerable suspects. Along with the work on eyewitness testimony, the study of forensic interviews is extensive and the reader is guided to further reading for greater detail (e.g. Milne and Bull, 1999; Ainsworth, 1998).

The fictional image of the **police interview**, with a detective hovering over a suspect under a spotlight, blowing smoke in their eyes whilst verbally assaulting them with accusations and contradictions, may not represent the true picture of a police interview, but it may represent traditional police attitudes to questioning suspects.

Until the 1980s in the UK, police interviewing techniques contained many coercive, manipulative and intimidatory approaches. The police interviewer would confront the witness, or more commonly the accused, with allegations of lying, inflate the seriousness of the crime to intimidate them, or conversely by trivialising the event encourage confession. Although public opinion would often sympathise with the police in trying to convict a dangerous criminal on minimal evidence, the situation from a forensic psychologist's point of view was one of prioritising a 'confession' above the truth or facts of the matter.

Focus

The Police and Criminal Evidence Act

The Police and Criminal Evidence Act of 1984 (PACE) revised the traditional priorities for interviewing witnesses in order to focus on obtaining the facts of a crime rather than on securing a prosecution. Thus a balanced approach was prescribed that did not assume guilt or innocence and explicitly had to recognise any special needs of the interviewee. This led to a significant change for the better in the approach of many police officers, carrying out interviews with more engagement skills and far less coercion or threat. However, the culture of 'extracting a confession' by whatever means necessary that prevails in many

countries, including the USA, still persisted in the UK after the introduction of PACE.

Although confessions obtained in police interviews tended to have limited respect in UK courts, Pearce and Gudjonsson (1999) revealed that in the majority of cases courts had allowed confessions obtained by forceful questioning, and many past studies reveal widespread acceptance of physical threat in gaining confessions as justified amongst police officers (see Milne and Bull, 1999). The cost and repercussions of miscarriages of justice have helped progressively to promote adherence to the more ethical practices brought in with PACE.

The cognitive interview

The need for better interviewing practices suggested in PACE and the inherent difficulties in recalling critical information from fallible human memories was met to some extent by the cognitive interview developed by US psychologists **Ed Geiselman** and **Ron Fisher** (Geiselman and Fisher, 1985; Geiselman et al., 1984; Geiselman, 1987). This series of interview techniques was a product of cognitive psychology research refined for use in police interviews and has been used in police training since the 1990s. Independent evaluation of the cognitive interview has found that it produces significantly more accurate information than previous interview methods (Aschermann, Mantwill and Köhnken, 1991). The technique aims to maximise the amount and accuracy of information recalled by a witness in interview, but it is not recommended for all potential interviewees. For example, it would exclude uncooperative individuals such as the more obvious suspect intent on covering his or her tracks, but also witnesses resentful of being involved or resentful of incriminating acquaintances.

The cognitive interview attempts to recreate the state of mind, thoughts and feelings at the time of the event, and to this end the recall environment may be manipulated to replicate the original context. Cognitive research had already established the importance of context to recall (e.g. Tulving, 1974) and more recently confirmed the need to recreate the same brain state as that of encoding to retrieve information (Polyn et al., 2005). Differing strategies and viewpoints are adopted by the interviewee to access fragmented information, and they are instructed to report all detail, no matter how trivial it may seem, as irrelevant information may allow links to more vital aspects. Timings and sequences of recall are varied to increase the amount retrieved, requiring the interviewer to keep the elicited information organised and correctly sequenced (Howitt, 2009).

The stages of the cognitive interview reflect the above principles, and police officers trained in this follow the same sequence (see Fisher, Brennan and McCauley, 2002). Initial introductions should set up a trusting rapport with the interviewee and explain the importance of their producing as much information as possible without holding anything back, regardless of questions, relevance or sequence. The next stage is exploratory, allowing the witness to produce an information framework by placing him or herself back at the scene with the use of imagery and extended description. The third stage of the interview involves more focus on important aspects of the event by drawing on the techniques identified by Geiselman and Fisher, such as imagining the crime scene from different perspectives. Care has to be taken in this not to imply that, in taking on a role (e.g. describing the scene *as if* they were a burglar), the witness should *create* information appropriate to this role; they should simply review the sequence from the different perspective (see Milne and Bull, 1999). The next stage is to feed the information back to the witness, perhaps prompting more recollection and checking for errors. The final stage is to end the interview in such a manner as to make it very easy for the witness subsequently to add more detail that may come to mind, by establishing how welcome this would be and making communication explicit and uncomplicated.

Geiselman and Fisher saw scope for improving the cognitive interview, especially for the purposes of interviewing anxious, vulnerable individuals or those with poor communication skills. The **enhanced cognitive interview** (see Fisher and Geiselman, 1992) provides a more structured order for the questions in the original interview. There is also a greater focus on establishing personal trust, engagement and rapport with the witness by both verbal and non-verbal techniques, so that consequent dialogue is relaxed and free rather than tense and sparse. The interviewer also makes it clear to the witness that they are in control of the interview and that they can take as long as needed to answer each question. To this end, the interview questions should be clear and productive with the minimum of interruptions from the interviewer.

Forensic hypnosis and recovered memories

The use of **hypnosis** to enhance recall of information, or **forensic hypnosis**, is controversial and to some extent this also applies to the clinical use of hypnosis. There is little evidence for a unique 'hypnotic state', but much evidence for the same kind of relaxed suggestible mood being obtained reliably by other means (see Spanos, 1996). An obvious danger in the forensic use of hypnosis is that suggestibility is increased both by the process and by the fact that the traits of hypnotisability and suggestibility tend to co-occur in the same individuals. Heightened suggestibility in forensic hypnosis is problematic (Wagstaff, 1993), often leading to the 'recollection' of false memories and the conviction of innocent suspects (Orne, 1979). Rather than facilitating memory, forensic hypnosis seems to make witnesses more readily 'recall' information of which they are uncertain, leading to more errors (Spanos, 1996). In addition to producing false convictions of others, the use of hypnosis in suggestible individuals can also increase levels of **false confessions**. Although it is assumed that false confessions are rare, analogue studies have revealed levels as high as 82 per cent in those who are falsely accused without hypnosis (Horselenberg, Merckelbach and Josephs, 2003).

A rather more dangerous outcome from the use of hypnosis emerged as a serious issue in the 1990s, that of so-called recovered memories. This highly controversial technique will be returned to in Chapter 15 in relation to **dissociative disorders**. In essence, there were increasing reports of memories of childhood sexual abuse being 'recovered' during psychoanalytic forms of psychotherapy, particularly with the additional use of hypnosis and suggestive interview techniques. Some if not all of these 'memories' were very likely to be false, having been imagined or suggested during 'therapy'. Loftus (1997) identifies some of these as 'impossible memories', in which memories of events shortly after birth are claimed. Loftus points out that at this age development of the hippocampus in the brain is incomplete, preventing memory creation. Further claims of events recalled from below the age of 3 years again run counter to established data on the inaccessibility of such memories (see Milne and Bull, 1999). Freudian 'repression' is used to explain the latent recovery of these memories even though there is no empirical evidence for repressed memories and most researchers in the area prefer the term 'suppression' (Spanos, 1996; Loftus, 1993; Milne and Bull, 1999).

Case study
Childhood reinvented

Carol visited her friend Ann whenever her husband Tim had to stay late at work, 'and who is he working on tonight Carol?' Ann would say on almost every occasion. Carol would laugh this off, but there was a tension and a driven aspect to Ann that could be uncomfortable and her constant questioning could prove unnerving. However, Ann did provide a useful distraction from Carol's tendency to worry about everything in her life. Then, one evening Ann surpassed her usual probing nature when she announced, 'I think a lot of your problems with Tim stem from abuse as a child. I was abused you know, but I have therapy for it.' Carol stared ahead, not wanting to look at Ann and tried to change the subject. Ann returned to the theme a number of times during the night, and as she left, found herself coerced into a coffee evening with a group of Ann's friends.

The next week Carol was introduced to the group of six ladies, who were instantly and intensely polite to her. A very strident lady in her mid-fifties introduced herself as Fiona and proceeded to engage Carol in questions about her feelings towards men, her husband, and why she had no children, and pushed the level of disclosure to a point where Carol fell silent and was clearly uneasy. 'You don't feel comfortable talking about feelings and relationships, do you?' Carol momentarily reflected on this, and considered that perhaps it might be true. 'Look,' Fiona said, 'why don't you come and see me at my rooms for a chat? You're a friend of Ann's, so I wouldn't charge you.' She added, 'Come tomorrow morning to this address. You must – it will make such a difference to your life, I am certain.' Yet again, Carol showed how she could be pushed into things despite her mounting suspicion over exactly what the coffee morning was really about.

Carol was shown to a very comfortable chair and the session began. After questions about Carol's relationship history, Fiona moved on to her childhood and seemed to become obsessed with Carol's admission that her dad used to play with her at bathtime. She asked about exactly where he may have touched her and who took off her clothes, but Carol kept thinking what a loving home it had been and how she had felt cared for and safe. Fiona could see her expression and calmly but firmly said, 'But most women have been sexually abused as children and there is evidence for at least half of them experiencing this in the books on the subject. I'll lend you a copy of one by my colleague.' Over the next few weeks, Carol began to doubt many of her own memories, and following hypnotherapy with a colleague of Fiona's she began to have some rather disturbing thoughts of what had gone on in her family home. Fiona was extremely happy with Carol's 'progress', but suggested they should actually do something about what had clearly happened to her as a child.

Before Carol could truly comprehend what was going on, there seemed to be an army of supporters, who referred to her and each other as 'survivors' and wanted Carol to 'go public' about her condition. Others suggested she join them and write about her memories, but at the point when they were talking about lawyers who were colleagues she felt faint and excused herself to visit the bathroom. Carol headed straight for the door to the street and hailed a taxicab home, where she sat in silence in front of Tim. 'Just tell me what has been going on', he said softly. Carol proceeded to tell her husband the whole story. As she finished he rose and said, 'Right, I have heard of this before and Mike who works for our legal firm has been involved in this sort of thing. Would you let him speak to you, Carol?'

Mike was a forensic psychologist and was quick to oblige. 'I take this very seriously, Fiona,' he said, 'and I have had to deal with some of the people you name before in a similar case. It always seems to be the same group and they all know each other.' Mike explained how a family had been torn apart by these accusations. 'It's not as if child sexual abuse does not exist, but it is usually remembered only too well and often documented at the time,' he said. 'It's when there has been no sign whatsoever of

abuse until the person is in therapy, and usually one of the same group of therapists who are often former patients themselves.' Mike's assured tone and obvious experience began to bring Carol back from scenes that she thought were real to the warm, familiar world inhabited by Tim and also her parents, who were blissfully unaware of their daughter's trauma and what could have transpired.

Spanos (1996) and Piper (1997) amongst others have identified the dangers of pursuing memories for events that have left no trace or effects, and although there may be value in retrieving fragmented memories, accounts that have been recovered entirely during therapy, especially hypnotherapy, should be treated with suspicion. Clearly Carol was suggestible and may have been led to believe distortions of memory generated by the therapist, which could happen accidentally or by design. **False memory syndrome** has wreaked havoc on families in the USA (Goldstein and Farmer, 1992) and can make it very difficult for genuine cases of abuse to be treated sympathetically.

The sudden rise in **false memory syndrome** in the USA (see the case study) led to many families being devastated by unfounded accusations; even if these accusations are dropped, the integrity of the affected family may never be restored. In less fortunate cases, individuals may be convicted of child abuse and imprisoned, with uncertainty always overshadowing the crucial testimony for forensic psychologists (Spanos, 1996). Rosenthal (2002) advocates that suggestion-induced accusations of child abuse are excluded from evidence in court, in the same manner as suggestion-induced identifications in the USA. Proponents of techniques such as hypnotic regression tend to be zealous in their use, and opponents equally motivated in their condemnation (see Brigham, 1999). These techniques are less often used in the UK, where the cognitive interview is part of police procedure. Similar concerns that the cognitive interview may encourage imaginative and suggestible individuals to produce false information so far seem to be unfounded (see Milne and Bull, 1999).

Courtroom interviewing

Many of the above factors affecting the recall of eyewitnesses during interviews also apply in the context of a witness undergoing **courtroom questioning**. However,

although much research has been carried out in relation to police questioning, the validity of witness statements in court, particularly under the pressure of cross-examination, has received very little research attention (Wheatcroft, Wagstaff and Kebbell, 2004) and is difficult to research except under simulated circumstances. In a UK court, witnesses will be subjected to **examination in chief**, in which the counsel calling them to appear will allow the witness to recall events in their own way without pressure or guiding questions. They may on occasion be subject to **re-examination** and also be questioned by the judge. For a witness, the most difficult form of courtroom questioning is that of **cross-examination** by the opposing counsel. In a cross-examination it is often seen as the duty of the opposing counsel to undermine the statements and credibility of the witness, in order ostensibly to test their truthfulness, but clearly this will also help the solicitor or barrister win the case in an adversarial court system.

The methods adopted for the cross-examination of witnesses have been thought to undermine the accuracy of their statements (Kebbell and Giles, 2000) and have been referred to as 'lawyerese', a verbal style of questioning that may manipulate the content of an answer. This style of interviewing a witness may produce 'results' but not necessarily the truth (Milne and Bull, 1999) and in addition may be intended to undermine the credibility of the individual witness from the point of view of the jury (Wheatcroft, Wagstaff and Kebbell, 2004). The court will tolerate suggestive, suppositional and leading questions, providing the aims are seen as relevant to the case and justice. Suggestive questions may also restrict the scope of the answer by providing both the preferred answer and a forced choice for the reply: for example, 'Do you agree that the defendant used a threatening manner?' Negative feedback regarding a witness's reply, such as 'Could you please consider the accuracy of your last statement?' may undermine the confidence of a witness and can lead to alternative replies, particularly in the case of suggestible or vulnerable individuals. Wheatcroft, Wagstaff and Kebbell (2004) found that witness accuracy was lowered by negative feedback in questioning, but only when the questions were complex or difficult to answer.

Forensic interviewing will always be necessary as long as human beings are relied on as witnesses or as interpreters of mechanically gathered evidence. Improvements initiated by PACE and implemented in the form of the cognitive interview have greatly improved the quality of witness statements obtained from police interviews. However, courtroom interviewing still has potential for inaccuracy due to traditional 'lawyerese' questioning styles, and would benefit from more feedback from forensic psychological research that limits this courtroom practice.

Forensic reports

In Chapter 6, the structure and process of preparation for reports by clinical psychologists was described in some detail, and much of the structure and layout will also apply to forensic psychology reports. In the section on clinical psychology reports, specific emphasis was placed on orienting the document content to the reader, and this tends to be an even greater issue when writing reports for a solicitor (lawyer) or court. As referred to earlier in this chapter, the viewpoints of psychologists and lawyers differ in a number of ways, and it is this divide that most often needs to be bridged by a forensic psychologist's report. For example, psychologists tend to give graded judgements along a continuum such as a personality dimension, whereas the legal profession deal daily in dichotomous judgements such as guilty or not guilty, or whether an individual is a risk to others or not, with less tolerance for any 'grey area'. As a consequence, they may expect psychologists to fall on one side or the other in their expert opinion (Clifford, 2003).

Because there may be many diverse psychological aspects of relevance in giving expert advice in report form, a forensic psychologist may have to recall facts and theory from beyond the forensic domain. These could include the application of developmental psychology when reporting on family conflicts, or even cognitive psychology when considering the limits of perception in the case of an offence at dusk. However, most courtroom personnel and those in the legal profession are not normally conversant with psychology and its concepts, and a forensic report may include these less familiar psychological concepts drawn from the full spectrum of a psychologist's training. Thus, constructing a report for a solicitor may require more than a mere mention of psychological concepts, as even the most basic psychological terms may need clarification, especially where these may then need to be referred to by a barrister before a judge and jury.

Reports may vary between those within the sphere of civil law, which may involve compensation claims or guardianship issues, and those aimed primarily at criminal cases, which often require opinion on the ability to stand trial or pre-sentencing reports to inform disposal choices (see Allnutt and Chaplow, 2000). In addition to lawyers, the recipients of forensic reports can be judges or the defendants themselves, and legal counsel may be acting for the defence or prosecution, which should not alter the factual nature of the report but needless to say will change the focus to a degree. With regard to the adversarial system, it is a necessity for a report to identify issues that may confer advantage on opposing counsel in order that the recipient may prepare for this line of questioning. For example, in the prosecution of an elderly man accused of rape, it is advantageous to claim poor memory of events due to the age factor, but it is also necessary to warn that possible declining sexual desire and competence may advantage the defence.

With a report for court purposes, it is important to submit information (e.g. psychometric test results) that is drawn from sources that are acceptable in a courtroom if the data are to stand alone as evidence. In the same way, expert opinion must be clearly identified as graded opinion, as this may be presented to a court as a dichotomous decision – for example, that the defendant has dementia rather than that the defendant could be suffering early dementia. The unambiguous nature of a good report should be supported by readability, conciseness, simplicity of language and, as with clinical reports, the avoidance of jargon or obscure terminology. Sub-sectioning and the use of bullet points can enhance the accessibility of a forensic report for a busy legal recipient, who may read it on the way to court. It can also be advantageous to clearly separate the outcome of assessments and tests from any final opinion based on these outcomes. In avoiding unnecessary psychology jargon, a forensic psychologist should not feel obliged to incorporate legal jargon, regardless of the context for which the report is to be used. This may prove just as confusing and even embarrassing as the misuse of complex psychology jargon by a lawyer in court.

Objectivity, lack of bias and professional integrity in producing reports and giving preliminary opinion can help to protect the forensic psychologist from any sense of having prejudiced a case in retrospect. Judicial judgments are usually independent of individual expert opinion, but overzealous emphasis of a psychological point that may be the product of a personal issue may be a source of regret if subject to the cold analysis of legal debate, and is best omitted from professional reports. Ethical issues and conflicting ethical standpoints between psychology and law are often relevant to the construction of reports and may be best addressed by following the codes of one's own profession, which can then be subject to further ethical guidelines by the legal representative receiving the report (see Allnutt and Chaplow, 2000).

Forensic psychology reports will be expected from any forensic psychologist, but will frequently be produced by those directly employed by courtroom personnel. Most governing psychology societies produce guidelines for these, but the reports themselves inevitably vary with the writer, recipient and purpose. However, those paying for the report universally appreciate the basic requirements of conciseness, accuracy, accessibility and clarity.

Self-test questions

- What contexts do forensic psychologists work in?
- What is a special hospital?
- Why might an eyewitness be unreliable?
- Can questioning style change the accuracy of the answers obtained?

Other areas related to forensic psychology

Much of this chapter has emphasised the diversity of forensic psychology as an expanding profession, and it is clear that an exhaustive coverage of all the contributions made by psychology to the explanation and management of crime and its consequences is beyond the scope of a single text. This is even more apparent if the other areas covered by

forensic or criminal psychology as well as criminology are included (e.g. see Howitt, 2009; Jones, 2006).

The psychology involved in **jury decision making** has been a focus of studies and forensic psychology advice to court reaching back to the work of Munsterberg and Albert von Schrenk-Notzing's assertions in 1898. Although not all countries use juries and they are only involved in a tiny proportion of cases, the assumptions of a fair trial rely heavily on a psychologically flawed jury system, but one with no clearly acceptable alternative. Size and selection of juries have been studied as well as the interpersonal dynamics during decision making, which may be influenced by whether a majority decision is allowed (see Lloyd-Bostock, 1996; Howitt, 2009). The study of victims of crime or **victimology** has its origins in examining the relationship between victim and offender in understanding how a crime occurs (Walklate, 1998). Controversial areas, such as some victims being seen as contributing to the crime and the rights of victims over offenders, are studied alongside support for victims, the effects of **fear of crime** and restorative justice, the latter two being major areas of study and practice in their own right. Restorative justice is where offenders have controlled meetings with the victims of their crimes and, where possible, help deal with the aftermath of the event (see Goodey, 2005).

Two expanding areas of forensic science that have had a considerable input from forensic psychology are **cybercrime** and the forensic use of **lie detection**.

Cybercrime and psychology

Cybercrimes: new versions of old crimes?

The modern computer originated from the need to create and decode encrypted messages, evolving from the vital importance of military secrecy in the Second World War. This purpose remains an aspect of forensic interest today, though it is unclear which side of the law benefits most from hidden messages and their decoding, as fraudsters can capitalise on the confidence that thinking your data are safely encrypted may engender (Newman and Clarke, 2003). The progress and ubiquitous nature of computer technology during the latter half of the twentieth century has had an irreversible effect on our daily lives and an insidiously progressive effect on human–machine dependency (see Bocij, 2006). This dependency has been exploited by the modern cybercriminal, who has been inadvertently assisted by a public that tends to be both trusting of technology and either unaware of the dangers of leaking their information (e.g. keeping their **personal identification number** (PIN) with their credit cards), or too lazy to

Focus

Crime statistics

Crime statistics tend to be flawed for a number of reasons: for example, the way an offence is reported can change the seriousness of the actual crime recorded. The police have discretion much of the time as to how an offence is recorded or whether a suspected offender will be charged with an offence, cautioned or simply released. In terms of official statistics, police have been accused of recording more crime to gain greater resources or less crime to appear to be more efficient at prevention, and similarly influencing arrest and prosecution figures, which have led to changes in the way statistics are gathered (Maguire, 2002).

For some time now, victim report studies have provided data supplemented by the '**dark figure**' of crime: that is, the inclusion of crimes not officially recorded. **Race** and **gender** are issues that enter into most levels of the statistical analysis of crime from a forensic psychology perspective, whether this involves racist or sexist crimes or prejudice within the criminal justice system (Phillips and Bowling, 2002; Walklate, 1998). Thus female crime is low partly because females are less likely to be processed at all points in the justice system, and for similar reasons black male crime may appear higher (Phillips and Bowling, 2002).

protect the integrity of personal information: for example, not cross-shredding old bills and bank statements (see Jewkes, 2003).

Much cybercrime takes place on the **internet**, which offers at least as many (and exponentially expanding) opportunities for cybercrime as facilities for criminal detection (Thomas and Loader, 2000). Examples of internet-based crime vary from the ostensibly innocuous 'hobby' of hacking into an individual's information with varied motives (Liebert, 2003), to large-scale electronic embezzlement, paedophilic networking and identity theft (see Finch, 2003). The rapid spread of identity theft may be a product of the fact that it only takes three or four items of personal information to create a virtual replica of you for financial purposes. The first hint that something is wrong may be long after the value of a small home has been removed from accounts in your name and it is only when the debt collectors call round that you realise a complete stranger has declared you bankrupt. Thus low-integrity information such as an old electricity bill can be used to construct a very high-integrity identity (Finch, 2003). Identity theft is beginning to represent twenty-first-century crime and is being used to commit more than fraud, as terrorist networks have identities as one of their resources to avoid early detection (see Finch and Fafinski, 2007).

Of particular interest to forensic psychology and criminology is the debate as to whether the permutations of cybercrime form an entirely new genre of criminal activity, requiring new forms of management, or whether these are fundamentally traditional crimes in new contexts. An example that will be dealt with in the next chapter is that of the distinction between stalking behaviour as a crime and its virtual equivalent of cyberstalking (see Bocij, 2004).

One test of whether these differences are indeed fundamental is the degree to which resources required by law enforcement authorities to detect, arrest and punish offenders differ from those prior to cybertechnology. These do appear to be qualitatively different, as specialist police units and trained personnel are proving essential for dealing effectively with cybercrime (see Jewkes, 2003).

Cyberforensics: a new response to a new threat

These new cybercrimes or computerised versions of real-world crimes have prompted a response in terms of cyber-detection and new means of prosecution by the police and courts, as well as increasing investment in data security by banks and other commercial bodies. New specialist police units, such as the National Hi-Tech Crime Unit, are dedicated to the detection and prosecution of computer-related crime. Ironically, a valuable resource in tackling cybercrime are the cybercriminals themselves, who may be subsequently employed in detection of, and protection from, the very crimes they perpetrated.

Traditional use of computing technology for forensic purposes has become more sophisticated, such as new data sets for the Police National Computer (PNC) and the use of smaller, more specialist databases. Other forms of cyber-detection and monitoring technology, especially that utilising **artificial intelligence** (AI) have matured into cyberforensic tools that need careful evaluation in terms of their use, interpretation and interaction with both operators and their targets (Jewkes, 2003). Databases of crimes, criminals and their characteristics have been of increasing value to law enforcers in the last decade. Almost half of all police communications involve the accessing of information on computer databases. These programs are so fast and sophisticated that they are now proactive in offender detection rather than simply having an archival or reference role.

Databases of crimes and criminals are only as good as the integrity of the data that humans enter into them (see Aitken et al., 1995). However, the sheer volume of paperwork involved in the Yorkshire Ripper enquiry actually made the cross-referencing of Peter Sutcliffe's data physically impossible, which led to the original criminal detection computer database with the acronym HOLMES (Home Office Large Major Enquiry System). Following this (see Chapter 8) Derbyshire's CATCHEM (Centralised Analytical Team Collating Homicide Expertise and Management) has proven so successful as a rapid resource for monitoring sex offenders and identifying offenders from crime details (see Stevens, 1997), that it is being integrated with the PNC in the UK and has been copied in style in the USA. However, it can be argued that these systems are merely super-efficient versions of traditional cross-referenced police pencil and paper records, implying that the difference is merely quantitative not qualitative.

Keppens and Zeleznikow (2003) report on an AI system for serious **crime scene analysis**. The possible (and impossible) causes of death for murders, as well as the events that can (or cannot) lead up to this particular crime, are fed into the program's database. This 'knowledgebase' can assimilate all kinds of evidence, such as eyewitness accounts. The program then produces a probability scale of all *possible* causes of death (e.g. even if most factors point to suicide, the program will still offer murder as a low probability because it has not been excluded). The software cross-references each strand of evidence to check for logical impossibilities. This 'knowledgebase' requires extensive data entry in order

for the AI program to 'learn', but it is ultimately worth while due to long-term savings in police time (Holmes, 2003b). The ability to produce a number of predicted scenarios from a few variable elements also makes this system efficient in practice (Keppens and Schafer, 2006).

In applying AI software to multiple cases of burglary, Oatley and Ewart (2003) found that probabilistic data can be produced that give potential geographic locations of future crimes. Such programs combine forensic psychology theory with statistical techniques (e.g. **multidimensional scaling**; see Chapter 5). Another example of **crime mapping** software is the **Crimestat** program, which includes journey to crime modelling (see Levine, 2006). Velastin, Lo and Sun (2004) have reported a further application that would otherwise require expensive and demanding vigilant observation. In this project, an AI-backed CCTV (computer-controlled TV cameras for observing public places) program identifies odd or criminal behaviour by calculating automatically what would be unusual changes in the normal patterns of behaviour derived from CCTV images and other sensors. Given the name Intelligent Pedestrian Surveillance system (IPS), it has been tested on UK and French underground train stations and other locations with some level of success.

A variation on the use of enhancing existing technology with intelligent software, designed to identify motor vehicles rapidly, is used by most police forces in the UK. This **Automatic Number Plate Recognition** software identifies the registration number of each vehicle passing and automatically checks for unlicensed vehicles, the name of the legal owner and whether the vehicle is insured, and it records the location of the vehicle for later tracking. Here the greatest source of error is not in the recognition and tracking of registration plates but in the poor updating

Focus

Artificial intelligence (AI)

For many years, computers have been able to transcend their role as the 'fast calculator' and carry out, rather than mimic, intelligent decision making. **Artificial intelligence** has tended to be the research preserve of cognitive psychology and computer science, and has been overly concerned with passing the (Alan) Turing test: whether a computer can convince a person that it is human rather than machine. Passing the Turing test would pass off a machine as human intelligence.

AI programs can now perform complex tasks responsively; they learn as they process by mimicking

the human brain with artificial neural networks: in other words, they become more efficient with use, hence the 'intelligence' parallel with the human ability to learn. AI applications in the forensic field have been limited, partly due to the processing power needed, but domestic computers now operate fast enough to run AI programs for complex purposes, including forensic applications (see below). In short, the machine can now come to the task rather than having to take the task to the machine (Holmes and Gross, 2004).

of information on the main computer system, particularly updating by outside agencies such as motor insurance companies. The problems of cyberforensic tools all too often lie in the area of the human–machine interface, or how users interact with the software, and the errors that occur when inputting the data as well as in the interpretation of the output of the program.

Protection from identity theft is far more difficult than would first be supposed, as few individuals take enough precautions to protect their key items of information. Trust becomes necessary in many commercial exchanges where the employee of a store or bank will have access to coherent identity data: that is, multiple pieces of information on a single person (see Newman and Clarke, 2003; Finch, 2003). Biometric data, such as fingerprints, retinal images or DNA information, can be encoded and verified against the living version. This could theoretically make identity verification foolproof, but most transactions, particularly those on the internet, involve you not being present and current versions of the hardware needed to read these remotely are rare, let alone universal. Thus the initial purpose of computers in wartime, data encryption, remains one of its current challenges.

This section has given a brief insight into the issues that have drawn forensic psychology into the realm of cybertechnology. A further area of applying science to humans that predates the computer in its formal inception is that of lie detection, which is examined in terms of the contributions from forensic psychology in the next section.

Lie detection

Lying is more important to the smooth running of our lives than we may care to admit, with 'white lies' saving the feelings of others and embellishments by sales personnel an accepted tool of business. However, in the area of crime, lying provides a difficult challenge to establishing culpability and administering justice fairly. Thus, lie detection could be seen as the ultimate forensic tool, as being able to ascertain the honesty of statements by suspects, eyewitnesses or offenders being assessed for risk would eliminate the need for much of forensic science and the legal system. Even with a perfect lie detection system, however, only dishonest answers would be detected, whereas factually incorrect statements by witnesses who are genuinely mistaken would not involve lying and thus would not be detected. This is often why a mistaken but honest eyewitness can frequently convince a jury. A perfect detection system is beyond current psychology and technology, and it is for this reason that the forensic use of lie detection is limited to police investigations and only admissible in a few courts, such as those in some states in the USA.

The history of lie detection can be traced back to ancient Greek and Roman civilisation, and some Babylonian writings where myths regarding non-verbal behaviour, such as gaze avoidance, may have been initiated. More recently, deception has tended to be inferred from physiological measures of anxiety or stress. In 1885 Lombroso used blood pressure to estimate deception in a forensic context – an approach much refined by Marston in the following century (Marston, 1917). By 1914 science had also provided the pneumograph, which measures changes in breathing, and the galvanic skin response apparatus (GSR) that indicates arousal from increased perspiration as measures of 'guilt'. Although Larson's prototype emerged in 1921, it was not until later that Keeler, working under Larson, combined these mechanised measures with blood pressure and heart rate under the now familiar title **polygraph** (Keeler, 1933; Larson, 1932).

Other instruments supplemented the original polygraph measures, such as the electroencephalogram (EEG), which records electrical brain activity via detectors on the scalp. The use of physiological measures to detect arousal is only one aspect of this particular lie detection procedure. The fear of detection when faced by the complex wiring of the EEG, GSR, etc. often prompts the guilty suspect to confess, but unfortunately this also coerces innocent parties into confessing falsely. The building of rapport and the use of challenging questions (i.e. to suggest that statements are not true) have therefore developed, along with the use of differing questions that are directly related or unrelated to the crime in question (see Howitt, 2009). Thus in the **control question** polygraph procedure, responses to emotive control questions are compared with responses to questions relevant to the crime, with the guilty responding more to relevant questions and the innocent more to control questions. In the **guilty knowledge** procedure, crime-relevant items known only to the guilty party will be responded to more by the guilty than the innocent when presented amongst other items of no specific relevance to the crime. In these and other polygraph procedures, such as the relevant–irrelevant question test and the directed lie test, the construction of the questions is both difficult and crucial to the outcome of the test.

The polygraph is one of four approaches to lie detection identified by Memon, Vrij and Bull (2003). The others are brain matching and mapping, verbal content of dishonest statements and non-verbal indicators of deception. These will be briefly discussed below.

Detection equipment has utilised functional magnetic resonance imagery to spot differentially activated brain areas during lying, as exemplified by the studies of O'Craven

Research

Limitations of the polygraph

The polygraph in use with a subject, who may be more persuaded to tell the truth by its intimidatory technical nature than by the data it produces.
Source: Alamy Images/Stock Connection Distribution.

A focal area of current research into cyberforensics is lie detection, the 'holy grail' of forensic psychology. Manufacturers of the modern polygraph assure prospective users that the cost of the machine and training are offset by accuracy in detecting deception by multiple physiological measures backed by almost a century of research. As the polygraph fundamentally detects arousal, however, from which it *infers* deception, there have always been reliability and validity problems (Harrelson, 1998; Lykken, 1998).

Increased arousal during questioning may be due to factors other than lying, and questions may also be relevant for reasons other than guilt. The decision over truth is dependent on the subjective interpretation of the responses in the context of the question by the examiner, who is neither impartial nor blind as to the relevance of the question or the status of the suspect. In addition, as each measure is arousal based, people can be trained to defeat this response, particularly during the control questions when baseline arousal measures are established (Lykken, 1998).

In the main, the polygraph is good at detecting the guilty but poor at spotting the innocent (Patrick and Iacono, 1991), although the guilty knowledge procedure is better at establishing innocence than guilt. The antique nature of the polygraph is emphasised in its highly intrusive requirement of having the subject 'wired up' to the various components of the apparatus, even though current versions have more compact recording units. Although this serves the purpose of intimidating suspects, it is cumbersome and cannot be used covertly.

The critics of the polygraph still admit that it has some value, and it has been considered sufficiently useful as to be introduced into the management of sex offenders in the UK.

(see O'Craven and Kanwisher, 2000). Magnetic resonance technology, however, is not conducive to portability or affordability at this point in the twenty-first century. Farwell has used brain activity measures to focus on 'memory matching' by presenting stimuli specific to a crime and checking for recognition in the subject, in a manner similar to the guilty knowledge test polygraph procedure (see Farwell and Smith, 2001). In both these cases, validity depends on brain activity not being elicited by non-deception and intrusive methods using costly equipment.

Voice stress analysis (VSA) is a means of detecting anxiety and arousal in vocal signals, which can be applied to telephone recordings. This approach has been successful in both dissuading deception and detecting it in applications such as false insurance claims in a number of countries. As with the psychologically intimidating effect that the presence of the polygraph has on the guilty, when individuals making insurance claims are told that their call will be subject to VSA, they very often decide not to continue or simply hang up. However, being intimidated by lie detection equipment is not always a sign of guilt and people failing to make claims for whatever reason cuts outgoings for the insurance company.

Another verbal content approach to lie detection is **statement validity analysis** (Undeutsch, 1992), which is mostly used for checking the accounts given by victims in cases of childhood abuse, but has also been used for adult rape accounts. This is based on the identifiable differences between descriptions of real events that have been experienced and fictitious or false accounts. There are two components to statement validity analysis. One is the **validity checklist**, which assesses the suggestibility, plausibility and motives of the victim subject to the analysis. The other is the actual analysis of the content of the statement, or **criterion-based content analysis**, where 19 specific criteria are identified in the suspect statement transcript. These criteria appear more frequently in experienced event descriptions than fictitious ones and can provide a probabilistic judgement as to whether fabrication is present when used in conjunction with the outcome of the validity checklist (Memon, Vrij and Bull, 2003). Overall evidence suggests that statement validity analysis provides a valid judgement of accounts in most cases (Howitt, 2009).

Psychologists have long known that deception alters our **non-verbal behaviour** (see Vrij, 2000). The importance and consistency of non-verbal behaviour have long been recognised as an indicator of intentions and emotions, and the reading of these non-verbal communications pre-dates language development by many millions of years (Holmes, 1994). As a consequence of this, humans have an overwhelming reliance on non-verbal aspects of a message as compared with its verbal content. Thus in terms of lie detection, words deceive but behaviour 'leaks' this deception, and as humans we have come to 'sense' this, usually by automatic parallel processing. This 'feeling that something is wrong' is difficult to translate into objective non-verbal criteria for detecting lies. Further to this, there are no single reliable non-verbal indicators of deception (DePaulo et al., 2003), although there are a number of aspects of behaviour that indicate that deception is more likely (see Table 7.1).

It is often the combination of many small facial and other non-verbal changes that is interpreted by our reading of non-verbal behaviours as deception. These specific short-lived movements or channels of non-verbal behaviour,

Table 7.1 Clues to deception: a selection of hits and myths

Clues to deception

■ **False expressions** – these are indicators of deception but can also be indicators of nervousness, such as the false smile, which tends not to involve the eye muscles and uses a differing set of nerves to instigate it.

■ **Lack of movement or gesture** – this is usually a result of over-control of movements and concentration on what is being said.

■ **Longer pauses, slowing and errors in speech** – again, greater concentration on the dual content when lying and thinking time to manufacture content detract from smooth flow.

■ **Raised pitch and louder speech** – these are a result of angry or anxious emotional states.

■ **Lack of detail in verbal content** – liars tend to be conservative with detail, as there is no reference in memory to consult and detail makes contradiction more likely.

■ **Perspiration, swallowing, breathing and complexion changes** – all indicate increased arousal and likely deception but also nervousness.

Misleading clues

■ **Gaze aversion** – there is little relationship between gaze and deception.

■ **Inconsistency of statements in lies** – truthful statements tend to vary more over time.

■ **Increased fidgeting and body movement** – these tend to decrease with deception, as above.

■ **Lack of confidence** – accomplished liars tend to be very confident.

■ **Attractive, middle-class individuals are honest** – this is an inherent error in most human judgements that 'what is good is beautiful'.

such as the tensing of an eyebrow corner muscle, have been termed **microbehaviours** or **microexpressions** (Rothwell et al., 2006; Ekman, 1992; 1997). Detection of micro-expressions originally required the laborious frame-by-frame analysis of film for behaviour changes (Efron, 1941); however, cyberforensic technology has been applied to this task. Rothwell et al. (2006) combined the information from microexpressions with AI architecture to detect and analyse the presence of deception. They named this AI software Silent Talker, as part of a generic system using covert camera, microcomputer and software termed Adaptive Psychological Profiling (APP), which has been partly paralleled by Paul Ekman in the USA.

The Silent Talker system is almost unique, in that it can be used covertly, but in contrast to the Pavlidis, Eberhardt and Levine (2002) system of remotely detecting thermal change around the eyes to infer deception, Silent Talker does not work on the principle of inferring deceit from arousal and thus avoids this particular source of unreliability (Memon, Vrij and Bull, 2003). By analysing many channels of microbehaviours, Silent Talker 'learns' which changes indicate deception using artificial neural networks, and the program can then be 'trained' to focus on the most revealing behaviours *and* ignore individual differences or context. It has the advantages of portability and not being reliant on potentially biased subjective human judgement. It is also difficult to defeat a system that analyses many involuntary movements simultaneously, and actors may fool the right-brain 'feel' for honesty (Pease, 1994) of human observers, but the Silent Talker format can differentiate acting from honesty. However, it is necessary to 'trust' the AI program from experimental evidence that has to be accepted by courts, and specific databases for populations need to be created for the program to reference.

Clearly, any successful lie detection system will not be popular amongst wrongdoers, but it may also fail to find favour amongst those whose jobs may become less essential with the rise of cyberforensic technologies. However, the potential sweeping changes to society resulting from the use of readily available, reliable lie detection, particularly for purposes beyond forensic applications, such as infidelity and the diplomacy of politicians, may make the applications of such a device subject to limitation. Such technological reforms of society are also framed in the context of police officers convinced of their lie detection abilities, which actually are little better than chance (Vrij and Mann, 2001), unless trained in the cues indicating deception (Vrij et al., 2006). Intriguingly, prisoners tend to be better informed with respect to lie detection than other populations (Granhag et al., 2004).

How to become a forensic psychologist

Although some forensic psychologists work in contexts such as police behavioural units or courtrooms (under internationally differing legal systems), most work in prisons. Those working in prisons are under the salary and conditions of the civil service and those in special hospitals are under NHS structures in the UK (Clifford, 2003). Unlike other professional psychologists, forensic psychologists may be judged more by their experience than by their qualifications (in line with other legal professionals, such as barristers). However, forensic psychology posts are normally filled by psychology graduates who have gained a relevant postgraduate degree in forensic psychology from an accredited psychology society (i.e. the BPS in the UK or the APA in the USA). They will have also preferably completed their initial supervised 2-year work placement and registered as **chartered forensic psychologists** in the UK (Clifford, 2003). Failing to gain chartered status (or its equivalent in other countries) will severely restrict employment opportunities. This somewhat parallels the training of clinical psychologists prior to the introduction of the doctorate programme.

Graduates in psychology, normally 2:1 and above from degrees that carry BPS **Graduate Basis for Registration** (GBR), and with some evidence of interest in forensic psychology and related disciplines, will also be expected to gain a substantial amount of work experience as close to that of a forensic psychologist working in the field as possible (e.g. a minimum of 50 hours). Forensic psychology work experience is frequently gained in a prison setting, although this presents security difficulties if the student is not employed as a psychology or research assistant because prisons are difficult to navigate without official key access. Most police station inquiry desks will not recognise the relevance of a psychologist wanting work experience, but many now have behavioural and crime analysis units where work experience can be gained performing mundane tasks such as data entry or shadowing psychologists involved in occupational roles; it may even be possible to help forensic psychologists attached to serious crime units.

Since the merging of resources between prison and probation, there has been more scope for recognised work experience relevant to forensic psychology applications with the Probation Service. Work with the Probation Service can be varied and, as with prisons, there is often the opportunity to help with research projects, such as those evaluating probation drop-out rates or other aspects of the service (see Ward, Scott and Lacey, 2002). Work experience can be gained in the area of courtroom services and many legal firms will employ psychology graduates in legally related activities, but it is always worth enquiring with postgraduate admissions whether a specific post will count as valid work experience towards their entry requirements, as not all do so.

Quality experience is fast becoming an essential element of gaining a place on the few forensic psychology courses in the UK. There is a shortage of forensic psychologists prepared to teach on these courses, partly due to the better salary and job structure in prison or other areas of practice, although some forensic psychologists teaching on postgraduate courses work externally in a consultancy role. This shortage has made it difficult to expand the number of courses and places available, creating a 'bottleneck' between graduating psychologists and postgraduate admissions. This situation has been familiar to those aiming for a clinical psychology career and creates the same 'catch 22' dilemma for students who cannot gain work due to a lack of qualifications and cannot gain qualifications due to lack of work experience (Clifford, 2003). This may worsen, as it has with the clinical route, to the situation where students are not being accepted for work experience without prior work experience!

As mentioned above, a successful applicant will then complete a professionally accredited forensic psychology master's programme, many of which may soon expand to become doctorate programmes. They will then work under supervision of a **chartered forensic psychologist** in a forensic setting for a minimum number of years (currently 2) and complete stage 2 of the **BPS diploma in forensic psychology**. The qualified individual may then apply for chartered forensic psychologist status. Very often, forensic psychologists are also qualified clinical psychologists involved in assessing and treating offenders, usually in a prison context.

This dual role is currently accomplished by psychologists qualifying separately and serially, but may be better addressed by new hybrid courses offering dual qualification which are being considered by national governing societies such as the BPS and APA. This important area of clinical forensic psychology will be examined in the next chapter.

Self-test questions

- Why is identity theft so common?
- Is accurate lie detection possible?
- Is cybercrime any different from its terrestrial counterpart?
- What is a chartered forensic psychologist?
- What qualifies as good work experience for this area?

Case study

Anna

Anna had worked as a nurse for almost 12 years before returning to education in an attempt to find a new career path. It was not that she did not enjoy her job, but she needed a challenge and was interested in psychology and sociology, both of which she had studied at school before her nursing training. As Anna had not studied for a number of years, the admissions tutor thought it would be better for Anna to complete an evening class or join the foundation year leading into the university's combined honours degree.

Completing the foundation year was a personal challenge for Anna. Having decided to continue working shifts as a nurse, her relationship with her long-term partner broke down and, although there were no children to support, the financial strain and stress almost made her give up the course. Beginning a joint degree in psychology and sociology seemed like a dream come true and the debts this incurred began to matter less, as she was surrounded by younger colleagues who seemed unconcerned about far greater financial deficits, and after all, Anna always had nursing to fall back on. Anna majored in psychology but also studied two criminology units in the sociology department in her final year. Her psychology department maintained a good academic profile, with specialist staff publishing in diverse research areas, but offered little guidance when it came to career building or channelling students into appropriate career paths during their undergraduate studies. When nursing colleagues asked her what she was doing her degree for, Anna's reply was almost always, 'I am now a nurse and I am going to become a psychologist!'

Upon graduating with a 2:1 (narrowly missing a first-class degree), Anna was surprised to discover that it was far too late to apply for most professional postgraduate courses, and in a moment of panic over mounting debts she found herself back on the wards as a nurse. Although she dearly loved the profession, this was not the way her career was supposed to develop. It was a chance remark by a fellow nurse that finally motivated Anna towards an alternative career. Following yet another violent incident in the accident and emergency department, her friend Amy remarked that, being a psychologist, Anna should be able to study what could be done about these criminal acts that seemed to be tolerated by hard-working staff. This stopped Anna in her tracks, as she recalled one of her lecturers telling her that she seemed to be an ideal candidate for forensic psychology.

An appointment with her former lecturer proved more fruitful than previous generic career counselling, and armed with addresses of the main BPS-accredited postgraduate forensic psychology courses, Anna applied to work at a local **regional secure unit** as a mental health nurse. To gain more relevant prerequisite experience for her chosen forensic course, she would have to put in extra hours directly helping a forensic

psychologist at the unit, but this was far from a chore; in fact, Anna found this to be the most intriguing part of her new work. Unfortunately, the assessment of adolescents with conduct problems proved so absorbing that Anna missed the deadline for her MSc in forensic psychology application. This mistake did not happen the following year, by which time she was working as an **assistant psychologist** in a special hospital and had not only sufficient work experience, but also sufficient contacts and resources to help with her MSc thesis and work placements for the course. Anna now works as a forensic psychologist for the UK police within the National Crime Faculty, and will soon take up a senior position in a new national police serious crime initiative.

Chapter summary

A case study involving misidentification and undiagnosed autistic spectrum disorder introduces some of the needs for **forensic psychologists**. The history of forensic psychology follows the development of the **insanity defence** and work on **eyewitness testimony** led by **Hugo Munsterberg** to the establishment of psychologists as recognised experts in courts around the world. Paralleling this courtroom progress, forensic psychology established itself in other areas, such as **offender profiling** and work in **prisons** with offenders. Definitions of the work of forensic psychologists have broadened over time from only pertaining to the courtroom to **probation research**, **police occupational psychology** and many other functions. Work in prisons includes **risk assessment** and **management**, and **programmes of therapy** in contexts such as **prison psychology departments**, **special hospitals** and **regional secure units**. Work in courtrooms can involve roles such as presenting experimental and actuarial evidence, advising on the evidence of another, or giving opinion on the mental state of offenders in terms of their ability to undergo aspects of the justice process.

The validity and vulnerability of **eyewitness testimony** has been the subject of research and professional opinion for forensic psychologists, as has the **forensic interview** process. Factors such as **interrogative suggestibility** and **false confession** rates

have led to the **cognitive interview** being adopted by police, although courtroom **cross-examination** is still an area criticised by forensic psychologists. Professional forensic psychologists will be required to produce **forensic psychology reports**, which will have to be easily and rapidly understood by those with a legal rather than psychological background. Other areas of involvement by forensic psychologists are whether the advent of **cybercrime** is a new form of offending requiring specialist **cyberdetection** methods and a special focus on the development of **lie detection** techniques. The route to qualifying as a forensic psychologist has become more formalised in the twenty-first century, and candidates wishing to qualify as **chartered forensic psychologists** in the UK are increasingly required to gain work experience, as has been the case for those pursuing clinical careers for many years.

Suggested essay questions

- Discuss the historical difficulties of establishing psychologists as professionals in courtrooms.
- Evaluate the difficulties in accepting eyewitness statements in court.
- Critically discuss the assumption that cybercrime is distinct from ordinary terrestrial crime.

Further reading

Overview texts

Alder, J. R. (ed.) (2004) *Forensic psychology: Concepts, debates and practice.* Uffculme, Devon: Willan.

Bartol, C., and Bartol, A. (2004) *Introduction to forensic psychology.* Thousand Oaks, CA: Sage.

Blackburn, R. (1993) *The psychology of criminal conduct.* Chichester: Wiley.

Bocij, P. (2006) *The dark side of the internet.* London: Praeger.

Davies, G., Hollin, C., and Bull, R. (2008) *Forensic psychology.* Chichester: Wiley.

Jones, S. (2006) *Criminology* (3rd edn). Oxford: Oxford University Press.

Maguire, M., Morgan, R., and Reiner, R. (2007) *The Oxford handbook of criminology* (4th edn). Oxford: Oxford University Press.

Wrightsman, L. (2001) *Forensic psychology.* Toronto: Wadsworth.

Specific and more critical texts

Ainsworth, P. B. (1998) *Psychology, law and eyewitness testimony.* Chichester: Wiley.

Ainsworth, P. B. (2000) *Psychology and crime: Myths and reality.* Harlow: Pearson.

Brigham, J. (1999) What is forensic psychology, anyway? *Law and Human Behaviour,* **233**, 273–98.

Gudjonsson, G., and Haward, L. R. (1997) *Forensic psychology: A guide to practice.* London: Routledge.

Howitt, D. (2009) *Introduction to forensic and criminal psychology* (3rd edn). Harlow: Pearson.

Memon, A., Vrij, A., and Bull, R. (2003) *Psychology and law* (2nd edn). London: Wiley.

Milne, R., and Bull, R. (1999) *Investigative interviewing: Psychology and practice.* Chichester: Wiley.

Prins, H. (1999) *Will they do it again? Risk assessment and management in criminal justice and psychiatry.* London: Routledge.

Ward, D., Scott, J., and Lacey, M. (2002) *Probation: Working for justice.* Oxford: Oxford University Press.

Warden, J. (1999) Ashworth report confirms problems with special hospitals. *British Medical Journal,* **318**, 211.

Visit **www.pearsoned.co.uk/davidholmes** for a range of resources to support study. Test yourself with multiple choice questions and access a bank of over 100 videos that will bring the topics to life. Video coverage for this chapter includes original footage of the Milgram study of obedience and the Stanford Prison Experiment as well as a report on thermal imaging technology that can detect lying.

CHAPTER 8 Clinical forensic psychology

- Overview
- Case study
- Clinical forensic psychology
- The abnormal offender

- Clinical correlates of crime: constitutional and psychological factors

- Criminal profiling
- Challenging issues in forensic psychopathology
- Chapter summary

 Discover the pathology of learning violence. This is one of several videos that explore issues and disorders relevant to this chapter at **www.pearsoned.co.uk/davidholmes**.

Plagues of disorder and crime

Society has to decide whether placing the mentally ill who offend in prison produces the best outcome.
Source: Pearson Online Database.

Headlines in newspapers often utilise statistics to fuel the public's fear of crime, such as 'a wave of violent crime' or 'burglaries up by 30 per cent'. A lesser story may also be 'mental illness on the increase!' Behind these overly sensational headlines are many factors, such as increased detection rates, a need for more resources (which can be gained by recording more cases), increases in police and clinicians, greater public awareness (leading to greater reporting) or, in the case of mental illness, having better diagnostic and assessment systems. Arguably more attention grabbing is the combination of crime and pathology in headlines such as 'disturbed woman stalks the Beckhams' or 'released mental patient stabs man in street'. Even some professionals in the area can be unsure of the true, delicate relationship between various mental disorders and criminal acts. Thus, such incidents involving both factors tend to be much more intriguing to a badly informed public. This chapter will examine the merging of clinical and forensic skills to form a hybrid discipline in order to address the overlap between mental disorder and crime.

The case study presents elements of clinical forensic psychology that will be returned to throughout the chapter, particularly in the section on stalking. A central aspect of this hybrid discipline, covered in the next section, is the *abnormal offender*, in which clinical and forensic issues become inseparable. The study of clinical causes of crime has traditionally been the preserve of criminology, but as more modern approaches have been adopted, this area has become a focus for clinical forensic psychology. In the following section we learn that abnormal offenders are far more amenable to *criminal profiling* than those offenders with fewer detectable distinctions. In the final section, three groups of offenders who present a particular challenge for professionals in clinical forensic psychology are discussed. Those individuals who stalk or harass others present similar difficulties to sex offenders in terms of being recidivists who are resistant to treatment. Ending this section is that group of offenders clinically referred to as psychopathic but who may be 'rebranded' as dangerous and severe personality disordered, and who are often considered to be untreatable and consequently difficult to detain or release.

Case study
Anonymous missives

In terms of crimes of harassment or stalking behaviour, anonymous missives are usually unwanted letters repeatedly sent by an individual, who withholds their identity, to a particular recipient.

Professor King had been head of medical science at the university for over 10 years. When his secretary handed him a note amongst the usual bundle of committee notes and memos, he paused to allow the contents to refocus. What had struck Professor King was not the content of the letter, which seemed to ramble from Nazi Germany via the Holocaust to the after-effects of the bombing of Hiroshima. It was the intricate and obscure construction of the note as it unfolded. Although it was no more than two sides of A5 paper, there were intricate and almost pointless extended sections folded in on themselves with most of the surfaces covered in carefully pasted cuttings, pictures and text, which had been sporadically but intricately underlined in red pen. He tossed it into the bin, annoyed at its convoluted content.

Professor King was not in the least disturbed by the note, but he was intrigued by the apparent time and effort someone had taken to construct it. The next 'note' arrived about a week later and, although it resembled a large wallpapered scrapbook, the authorship was unmistakeable. Again the folded inserts and carefully cut and pasted pictures and text, but now the theme was clearer. Despite the apparently unconnected medical report and social services inserts, the majority of the vignettes in collage form condemned medical science and proposed a creationist backlash against 'the abominations of science'. Professor King still felt no sense of threat but was just perplexed why someone would take probably weeks to construct this, simply to send it to him.

Ten years passed and although there had been months when no letters arrived, they had still averaged one a fortnight, unsigned to the same address with the same UK postmark. The message remained constant: medical science was evil and religion would 'witness the demise of the puny efforts of scientific men'. 'Those letters don't worry me, but I might actually worry if they suddenly stopped,' Professor King quipped to a colleague. His colleague asked if he had done anything about the missives and mentioned that her friend Dr Watson was a clinical forensic psychologist; perhaps Professor King could send the letters to be examined or analysed. He collected what letters he could and added new arrivals to deliver to Dr Watson.

'Being anonymous missives, they are a rare form of stalking letter. Could you send me some copies?' enquired a forensic colleague of Dr Watson, who pondered over the pile of

CASE STUDY CONTINUED

letters before him. 'But they are so difficult to photocopy' Dr Watson thought. Over the next month Dr Watson's researcher Michelle had begun to carry out a **content analysis** on the letters and to sketch a preliminary profile of the sender, as well as undertaking the laborious task of photocopying the letters for herself and further copies for Dr Watson's colleague. One morning Michelle burst into Dr Watson's office to announce that she did not need to copy the latest letter as it had arrived in triplicate, each copy complete with added sections and underline. It would appear that the letter sender somehow knew how many readers he or she had. 'Quite scary!' said Dr Watson, trying to sympathise with his assistant. 'Not as scary as finding something in the last letter the stalker could only know if he had been in the library at the same time as me, and very close to me!' said Michelle, without a smile. Dr Watson looked up. 'Michelle, I want you to stop dealing with these letters, just write up what you have so far, please.' The letters to Professor King continued to arrive, improved by technology, but still using current news to make the same point over and over again, to this day, some 20 years later.

The anonymous missives were unsuccessfully checked for fingerprints and none of the addresses or names from documents pasted in the earliest letters could be traced to persons living or dead. Analysis for recurring themes and threat content revealed low personal threat but higher implied threat of revenge against scientists as well as a sketchy profile of the sender. The sender seemed to be a male son of a middle-European father, who may have been mentally ill and perhaps unsuccessfully treated before passing away, perhaps precipitating a deep distrust of medical science. The pronounced creationist opinions hinted at a religious fundamentalist stance, which was not simply at odds with science but had more pointed criticism bordering on threat towards medical science. However, after such a long time without contact or escalation, it appeared the letters themselves constituted the full extent of the stalking and were ultimately benign, if annoying. This is not always the case with missives, which may not contain threat but can sometimes predict actual physical harm (see Dietz et al., 1991).

Clinical forensic psychology

The hybrid area of clinical forensic psychology has become increasingly important. As clinical psychology and forensic psychology have advanced as separate professions, the area of overlap between them has increased. Having both forensic training and the clinical skills needed to assess and treat clearly facilitates dealing with criminal offenders who are also disordered, often in prison contexts. Specialist clinical knowledge can be vital in cases where the absence of informed judgement may condemn an individual to fall through the gaps in the justice system. The forensic implications of impulsive disorders are unlikely to be understood by a magistrates' court regarding a shoplifting offence, but an expert in this field with forensic training can place the offence in its pathological context and arrive at the appropriate degree of mitigation. The above case of anonymous missives provides another example of a case that is better addressed by the services of a clinical forensic psychologist than either of the component professions. Much of the work for these hybrid professionals may be focused on the **abnormal offender**, a hybrid offender who provides many challenges for health and justice systems which assume clients that are singly disordered or offenders. The variable forms of the abnormal offender will be examined further in the next section.

The abnormal offender

Within clinical forensic psychology and criminology there is a strong connection between criminal deviance and mental abnormality, sometimes referred to as the mad–bad debate. There is an area of overlap between these two forms of deviance and the interpretation of behaviour into one or other category can vary. For example, males are more frequently seen as 'bad' and females as 'mad', though their actual behaviour may be the same, and some countries may hospitalise more abnormal individuals whereas others tend to imprison more. However, it is difficult to identify why it is that these different labels can be interchangeably applied in practice, and many factors play a part in the labelling decision which may or may not be indicators of criminality or pathology (Jones, 2006).

If a proportion of crime can be attributed to mental abnormality, then an examination of mentally disordered populations should reveal a higher rate of crime. Studies carried out early in this century tended to find that rates of crime were similar in mentally disordered populations (usually in institutions) to that in the general population (e.g. Brennan, 1964). However, the general population are not in institutions, where detection is easier and living conditions different from outside. Later studies reveal apparently increasing levels of some crimes (but not others) among the psychiatric population (e.g. Grunberg, Klinger and Grumet, 1977). The reason for this may lie in the progression towards only having the most dangerous, criminally recidivist or unstable patients admitted to hospital (and therefore the disordered sample), with those less at risk and therefore less likely to offend being supported in the community (Gunn, 1996). According to Hollin (1989), an exact estimate of the relative crime rates is difficult to ascertain, as the factors of crime, mental illness and being in institutions interact to confound any attempt to isolate one of them.

The types of disorder associated with serious crimes are more easily identified, as these are the disorders most readily accepted as mitigation in court. The hallucinations, delusions and paranoid ideation in schizophrenia (see Chapter 19) have led sufferers to harm others, though self-harm is also a frequent outcome. Schizophrenic individuals form 1 per cent of the population but are responsible for about 5 per cent of homicides. Patients often act on instructions from hallucinatory 'voices' or from false beliefs that others mean them harm. In mood disorders (see Chapter 18), symptoms of depression can lead to one-sided suicide pacts, in which the sufferer sees only a bleak future in a threatening world for those close to them, their way out being to kill their loved ones then themselves. In the bipolar form of the disorder, symptoms of mania can lead to reckless acts of irresponsibility or even paranoid reactions, as in schizophrenia. However unpalatable to a politically correct view of the world it may be, the association between psychosis (usually schizophrenia) and serious violence is real (Gunn, 1996) and not confined to tabloid headlines. This situation has been recognised by the UK government in producing a bill to compel patients in the community to take their medication or face enforced institutionalisation, and allowing the detention of patients even if there is no effective treatment for them (including the category of psychopathy). This coincided with results of a UK Department of Health study headed by Louis Appleby, which reported that in 8 years over 400 people had been killed in the UK by patients with mental health problems, who were mostly unmonitored or unmedicated.

Substance abuse (see Chapter 11) has a close association with petty crime. In the case of alcohol, although violence and serious motor offences are also associated with its use in the 'non-alcoholic' population, rates of crime among alcoholics are very high, varying between 40 and 80 per cent (across a number of different studies). Mental retardation is associated with crime, in that many in the criminal population tend to be below average in their IQ, especially those acting as accomplices. However, when retardation is more profound, a similar approach to that of the child offender is adopted regarding criminal responsibility. Although rare, the lack of empathy and 'people-reading skills' in autism and Asperger syndrome (see Chapter 9) can lead to callous acts by sufferers, who do not always react to the distress of others (see Mawson, Grounds and Tantam, 1985). Thus, mental illness has a definite but inconsistent relationship with crime, which is specifically evident but may be masked if generalised across both crimes and disorders.

Theoretical links between crime and abnormality are also pertinent to the mad–bad debate identified above. Simply stated, if criminality is determined by a disorder, then this would favour the label 'mad', with the attendant possibility of an insanity plea. However, if the offender were acting under his or her unimpaired **free will**, then the verdict would be 'bad', with no such claim to insanity as mitigation. This principle underlies the *mens rea* ('clear mind') criterion for guilt in UK and other courts. The very serious issue here is that, if acts shown to be caused by antecedent conditions (i.e. insanity) are not punished by law, then as the science of psychiatric aetiology expands, criminal liability may disappear altogether (Wilson and Herrnstein, 1985).

Here the interface between clinical forensic psychology and law is vitally important, as rational views of culpability in the mentally ill population must incorporate the fact that, in most cases, mentally ill individuals can distinguish right from wrong. This is exemplified by the twinkie defence argument, in which Dan White claimed he shot the mayor of San Francisco due to hyperglycaemia as a result of eating too many sweet confectioneries. In the UK, Richard Blackwell had his plea of diminished responsibility accepted when sentenced for killing his own parents, reducing his charge from murder to manslaughter. This was on the basis of a diagnosis of **narcissistic personality disorder**, a very rare disorder in which judgements of right and wrong are not lost. Courts tend to have to follow the advice of clinical forensic expert witnesses in such cases and it may transpire that the common sense of the court's discretion is lost as mental disorder has the potential to outweigh *mens rea*.

A number of psychological approaches to crime assume that some abnormality *predisposes* individuals to crime in the first place. A selection of putative factors will be examined in the next section, as they have historically developed into clinical explanations of criminality. These include factors such as: a personality type based on physiological differences (Eysenck, 1964); the XYY sex-chromosome abnormality (see Hollin, 1989); genetic predispositions to crime (Mednick, Gabrielli and Hutchings, 1984); maternal deprivation (Bowlby, 1944); abnormalities of brain structure and function (Raine, 1993); and disorders such as attention deficit hyperactivity disorder, linked to crime due to stimulus seeking and disruption of education (Satterfield et al., 1994).

Clinical correlates of crime: constitutional and psychological factors

Theoretical approaches to explaining the causes of criminal behaviour in individuals have traditionally been produced under the heading of criminology or criminal psychology, supplemented by consideration of criminogenic environmental factors and societal forces from the various sociological schools of thought (see Downes and Rock, 1998). However, forensic psychologists have increasingly carried out research on prison populations, and grand theories of criminality have tended to give way to a more pragmatic approach in which the forensic psychologist play a prominent role. This section will briefly outline the more simplistic traditional approaches to explaining what underpins an individual's propensity for crime, and consider how this is currently conceptualised. This section will briefly outline the more simplistic approaches to explaining what underpins an individual's propensity for crime and consider how this is currently conceptualised, identifying the substantial use of abnormal psychology to explain criminality.

There are assumptions regarding the individual causes of crime built into the legal system. For example, in the UK the 1969 Children and Young Persons' Act assumes that young criminals are victims rather than inherently 'bad' and that delinquency is a cry for help. It is difficult for society to accept that persons of sound mind offend willingly and uninfluenced, as *anyone* could then be criminal. The public's collective sense of security is better supported by the notion that criminals are in some way distinct from the rest of the population. This need for forensic self-validation finds some satisfaction in accepting constitutional theories of crime causation, even in their most primitive incarnations.

Biological causes of crime: the enigma of the constitutional criminal

Most species have a means of ritually defending the integrity of their species against individuals who deviate from accepted norms, by excluding them physically or genetically, or even killing the deviant individual. Humans also carry this process out, though in more recent times this has been in the form of institutionalisation. This primitive approach to identifying crime as emanating from the deviant individual has popular and economic appeal, as it is easier to label an individual as constitutionally 'bad' than consider complex and expensive changes to society, such as reducing the differential between rich and poor or alcohol use. This 'mark of Cain' approach to crime causation is termed biological positivism, as it focuses on only objective empirical evidence in the biological sphere.

Trends in biological positivism tend to parallel contemporary scientific trends, beginning with nineteenth-century Darwinism and passing through the discovery of genes and aspects of the nervous system to detail from brain scans towards the end of the twentieth century. In its earliest incarnations, biological positivism appealed to middle-class prejudices, as it offered the view that the criminal classes may be a 'breed apart', distancing them from non-criminals. It is relatively easy to see weaknesses in older biological positivist theories and approaches, and as such they became easy targets for criticism by sociologically based criminologists in the latter half of the twentieth century (see Hollin, 1989; Williams, 2001).

Older biological approaches to crime

Cesare Lombroso (1835–1909) was one of the first to apply anything approaching a scientific method to the study of criminality in a move away from religious and philosophical argument, and consequently gained the label 'father of modern criminology'. His focus on physical features linked him to the dubious school of phrenology founded by **Gall** (1758–1828), a pseudoscience that inferred traits from the shape and size of the skull. He was very much influenced by the physical anthropology of **Paul Broca** and also incorporated some of **Darwin**'s evolutionary theory into his explanation of the causes of criminality. Lombroso studied and categorised racial types, bringing him uncomfortably close to the **racial anthropology** movement with its social policy influences (Garland, 2002). This association also muddied the positivist aim of impartial scientific objectivity (see Taylor, Walton and Young, 1973). Drawing on a pre-existing view of criminals as degenerates, Lombroso (1876) compared the heads of prisoners with non-prisoners (army recruits) and found his criminal population to have more atavistic or evolutionarily primitive features than his controls. Thus for Lombroso criminals were not fully phylogenetically developed and had 5 or more of the 18 physical features or 'stigmata' that he identified as distinguishing them. Following clashes with more sociologically based theories from France at international congresses, Lombroso later added other factors to his anthropometric approach, such as contact with 'degenerates' and poor education, revising his earlier premise to that of only one-third of criminals being 'born bad' (Hollin, 1989).

Goring (1913) criticised Lombroso's statistical analysis and failed to replicate his results in a large English study of around 3000 convicts. He did not subscribe to Lombroso's view that criminality was consequent upon physical features but believed that criminals had exaggerated versions of traits found in non-criminals. However, he subjectively assessed intelligence by interview and thought that criminals had subnormal intelligence and small stature, underpinned by genetic factors, and he advocated that such individuals should not be allowed to procreate. Hooton (1939) criticised Lombroso's methodology in that within his study of racial types there were also systematic racial differences in his criminal and non-criminal populations. Lombroso's prisoner population mostly consisted of poor immigrants and the controls were drawn from the indigenous Italian population; he was thus comparing different races, which would inevitably uncover consistent biological differences. Hooton still supported genetic explanations of criminality, however, describing criminals as 'biologically inferior'. Although he was as rigorous as Lombroso in applying his methods, they still contained unscientific value judgements (Sutherland and Cressey, 1970).

Kretschmere (1921) introduced the concept of body build indicating personality types. Sheldon (1942) applied this approach to crime by considering the basic three somatypes (see Table 8.1) in terms of temperament, then extrapolating this to criminality.

Table 8.1 Three somatypes from Sheldon (1942)

- The ectomorph was thin and frail, and being a quiet introvert was thus not predisposed to crime.

- The endomorph shape implied a soft, rotund body and a relaxed, sociable personality, who would be less likely to turn criminal.

- The mesomorph refers to an athletic and muscular body build and was considered by Sheldon the most likely of the somatypes to be criminal.

Sheldon could reasonably assume that body type was largely a product of genetic inheritance and that the body type could be linked to criminality via personality. Sheldon (1949) claimed he could spot these features as early as 6 years of age, which he believed made this an ideal screening tool. Sutherland and Cressey (1960; 1970) identified some of the many weaknesses in Sheldon's work, in that: he relied on subjective scoring and assessment; he left very large overlaps between categories; and his theory predicted far more criminals than were found – the 'embarrassment of riches error' (Matza, 1964). Glueck and Glueck (1950; 1956) attempted to support the criminality of the mesomorph, but their initial findings did not stand up to further scrutiny; however, they added psychological and situational factors, which did weaken the criticism of overprediction of mesomorphic criminals. Amongst others, Feldman (1977) considered that the mesomorph would be more frequently asked to participate in crime and be successful due to physical ability. The suspect mesomorph would be more likely to attract police attention and heavier sentences, in part, because they fit the criminal stereotype (Bull, 1982). Thus early biological positivist approaches tended to pioneer the scientific method in crime research but were remarkably weak in establishing cause and effect relations with the factors on which they focused.

Chromosomal abnormalities are usually non-inherited abnormalities in the structures containing the DNA sequences that form genes. The twenty-third pair of chromosomes are sex influencing and their approximate shape indicates the sex typing of the individual, with 'XY' designating a male and 'XX' a female. There are a number of abnormal formations of the sex chromosomes, most of which are non-viable (will not survive). One viable abnormality is the XYY male resulting from non-disjunction (i.e. the chromosome pairs divide unevenly during meiosis) with a prevalence of around 1 in 1000 births. Sandberg et al. (1961) found XYY males in their patient population in 1961. Having an extra Y or 'male' chromosome led to such individuals gaining the tabloid-friendly title of 'supermale'. This presumption made the acceptance of the XYY male as a criminal type far easier and such speculation led to research on prison populations. Jacobs, Brunton and Melville (1965) found an estimated 36 times more XYY males in Carstairs maximum security prison than the expected rate in the general population. This led to the assumption that the XYY male was more aggressive, more criminal and thus overrepresented in prisons (Jarvic, Klodin and Matsuyama, 1973).

The main established characteristics associated with the XYY abnormality were tallness, mental retardation or immaturity (including sexual) and mild acne. Mental

Research

Evidence for inherited criminality

Some evidence for criminality being partly biologically determined comes from genetic research, particularly studies of twins. Twin studies attempt to show that the concordance rates for criminality (i.e. if one of a pair is criminal, so is the other) in **monozygotic twins** (identical twins and genes) are greater than for **dizygotic twins** (fraternal twins sharing about 50 per cent of genetic material). Early studies such as Lange (1929) were poorly controlled, with methods of testing **zygosity** that simply relied on twins looking similar to be monozygotic. However, this error had the tendency to underestimate genetic influences on criminality by overestimating the number of monozygotic twins (Williams, 2001). Later studies were more aware of sources of error and often took advantage of official Danish twin registers for their sources of data.

Christiansen (1968) found the concordance for dizygotic twins to be around a third that of monozygotic twins, indicating a substantial genetic component, which was found to be even greater for more serious crime (Christiansen, 1974). Dalgaard and Kringlen (1976) also provided similar evidence but were somewhat overly critical of their study limitations in emphasising the psychological closeness of monozygotic twins as a source of mutual influence in addition to genetics. These findings and limitations were re-examined by Cloniger and Gottesman (1987) and assumptions regarding psychological closeness were not in evidence. The conclusion drawn from these and later studies (e.g. Rowe, 1990) is that there is no evidence that all criminality is genetic but some imprecise evidence that there is some level of significant genetic basis for criminality. This genetic influence will in itself impact on an individual's environment, in that those with the same genotype will seek similar environments and close company (Rowe, 1990).

Adoption studies remove many of the confounding variables of twin studies, such as shared home environment and social closeness as sources of criminal influence. In these studies, comparisons are made between characteristics of the biological parents and those of the adopting parents with the children concerned. Characteristics that are consistently similar between the biological parents and children will be due to genetics and little else, whereas characteristics across the adoptive relationship will be a result of environmental effects.

A paternal adoption study found genetic influence on criminality to be greater than that found for environmental influences, and in a study using both parents, the weaker relationship between criminality and genetics was still significant (Mednick, Gabrielli and Hutchings, 1984). However, although this overall significance has been questioned (Williams, 2001), close scrutiny of genetic data tends to confirm that the criminality–genetics relationship is still significant, if small (Walters, 1992). In a meta-analysis across both adoption and twin studies, Rhee and Waldman (2002) found a moderate genetic and environmental effect on anti-social behaviour.

Despite a degree of professional prejudice against the concept of inherited factors in crime, due to early associations with eugenics, it remains as dangerous to deny the genetic factor now as it was for early biological positivists to deny any environmental influences (Brennan and Raine, 1997). Jones (2006) uses the environmental influence example of a rose thriving in fertile soil and emaciated by desert conditions; similarly, without sun freckles may never appear, but it has to be understood that without the gene for freckles, no amount of sun will produce them.

retardation rather than aggression would account for a higher proportion of them ending up in institutions. It has been speculated that their tallness and other features may make them more likely to be accused, charged and sentenced, due to perceived threat or 'difference' in appearance. It is important to bear in mind that humans are inherently prejudiced in judging the culpability of others in terms of their appearance. A series of studies by Dion revealed that attractive children were judged less malicious than those rated less attractive (see Dion, 1972) and the same judgements were subsequently made by young children themselves, suggesting that this bias may not be simply learned. This bias may relate to the rejection of that which is different by other species mentioned at the beginning of this section. Thus, as with other targets for biological positivism who are 'different' in appearance, the XYY may be differentially treated by the justice system.

Owen (1972) identified limitations of both the research and assumptions surrounding the XYY male, in that poor karyotyping of chromosomes and crude assumptions of aggression and violence very much weakened any argument for criminality. In a large study, Witkin et al. (1976) concluded that the XYY was not related to violence against others and only slightly to opportunist property crime, probably as a result of levels of mental retardation. Mechanisms for the expression of the XYY syndrome have included genetically altered monoamine oxidase activity (see Chapter 3) and its consequent effect on neurotransmitters (Jones, 2006). Rutter and Giller (1983) echoed an overall conclusion made at an earlier 1969 Cambridge symposium on the topic, which was that this research involved undue focus on a tiny minority of criminals, ignoring the vast majority of XY males who are criminal.

Other biological positivists have looked at lead pollution, lack of vitamins or food additives, etc. as environmental agents that may have a criminogenic influence via biology, with mixed results (Hollin, 1989). The very important action of hormones in the area of crime has tended to focus on the finding of higher levels of testosterone in violent offenders (Rada et al., 1983). The complexity of multiple hormone action and interaction, let alone the cascade effect on the rest of human neurochemistry, has dissuaded many from broadening this line of research, which may hold the key to many clinical and forensic issues.

Eysenck: personality and crime

One of the major figures in the area of biological positivism was **Hans Eysenck**, who re-oriented his 1947 trait theory of personality towards a biologically based theory of the criminal personality (e.g. Eysenck, 1964). Eysenck's approach to crime causation places his work in at least three camps: that of biological positivism, a personality-based psychological approach and also **control theory** (see below). The latter approach theorises that everyone could be a criminal but some factor restrains (i.e. controls) the majority; in the case of Eysenck, this factor is socialisation or the development of a conscience, and those failing to develop this restraint are more likely to become criminal. He also used learning theory in his approach, and later in the development of his explanation of crime he incorporated many approaches (e.g. Eysenck and Gudjonsson, 1989). Using factor analytic data (see Chapter 5), Eysenck initially produced two dimensions of personality but later added a third, with all individuals being located at some point along each of these orthogonal (i.e. independent or uncorrelated) continua. Eysenck designed the Eysenck Personality Inventory (EPI; Eysenck and Eysenck, 1964), a questionnaire measuring the two dimensions of extraversion and neuroticism, and later the Eysenck Personality Questionnaire (EPQ; Eysenck and Eysenck, 1975) to include psychoticism. Both scales include a lie scale to indicate responses contrived to 'look good'.

Before presenting the dimension of psychoticism, Eysenck considered two dimensions sufficient to describe an individual's personality, and much of the data produced from prison, institutionalised and other population scores was mapped on to the axes formed by the extraversion and neuroticism dimensions, as depicted in Table 8.2.

Focus

Eysenck's personality dimensions

Eysenck (1964) described the three independent dimensions of personality thus:

- **Extraversion–introversion.** This dimension is similar to that of Jung (1921) but with Eysenck's version having an explicit biological basis. At the introvert end of the continuum, an individual is highly aroused cortically via the ascending reticular system stimulating the frontal cortex more than average. Introverts, being highly stimulated internally, seek less external stimulation: for example, they are non-smoking and engage in quiet activities such as book reading to attain optimal cortical functioning. Conversely, the high-scoring extravert is under-stimulated internally and needs more external stimulation: that is, they are more outgoing and stimulus seeking, etc.

- **Neuroticism–stability.** Individuals scoring high on neuroticism tend to be anxious or 'nervous' types due to an unstable and over-reactive ANS (autonomic nervous system; see Chapter 3). According to Eysenck, more neurotic individuals would admit to having regular headaches than non-neurotic individuals, even though both groups actually have the same number of headaches.

- **Psychoticism–normality.** Eysenck and Eysenck (1968) added this third dimension, which H. J. Eysenck claimed was independent of extraversion and neuroticism. Again this was initially claimed to be biologically based, this time on levels of circulating androgens (hormones associated with masculinity) and frontal lobe function. The majority of people score very low on this dimension, but high scorers are claimed by Eysenck to be criminal, psychopathic, alcoholic or schizophrenic.

Table 8.2 Eysenck's criminal and non-criminal personality types

- **Neurotic introvert.** A 'melancholic' or moody and anxious type, prone to mental disorders.

- **Neurotic extravert.** A 'choleric' or restless and aggressive type, prone to criminality.

- **Stable introvert.** A 'phlegmatic' or peaceful, controlled and reliable type.

- **Stable extravert.** A 'sanguine' or optimistic, outgoing and responsive type.

Eysenck also included Galen's four personality 'types' in the relevant quadrants, adding a rather anachronistic historical credibility to his theory. In summary, he posited four basic types who scored at the extremes of his two dimensional continua with the neurotic extravert being the 'criminal type'.

Eysenck explained that his high-scoring unstable extraverts failed to be socialised as a result of poor learning in the development of a conscience. He also cited studies such as Franks (1956; 1957), in which extraverts trained more slowly than introverts in eye-blink classical response training. Eysenck draws the conclusion that extraverts would also be poor at learning more complex forms of behaviour, although studies have subsequently cast doubt on socialisation based on classical conditioning (Raine and Venables, 1981). By requiring more stimulation in an attempt to maintain optimum arousal levels in accord with the **Yerkes–Dodson** principle, extraverts may not find punishment aversive, and may find that aggression provides needed stimulation. Thus anti-social behaviour may not be inhibited by fear of punishment. Eysenck develops this argument further to include such 'anti-socialisation' influences as biosocial interaction between parents and poor learning mechanisms (see Brennan and Raine, 1997).

Eysenck claims that the overreactive ANS of individuals scoring high on neuroticism leads to learning being disrupted in anxiety-producing formal learning situations. Thus the neurotic individual tends to learn irrelevant things outside of this situation rather than important aspects that lead to legitimate success and inhibition of anti-social behaviour. For Eysenck, the combination of extraversion with neuroticism makes an individual difficult to socialise, and consequently more liable to anti-social and thus criminal behaviour.

Eysenck modified this approach by dividing extraversion into the components of impulsiveness and sociability, with impulsiveness identifying the criminal trait. He also fractionated criminal activity, relating different personality variations to different crimes. Before his death in 1997, Eysenck had also incorporated data from brain scan tech-

nology into his early approaches. Eysenck evaded many critics by accepting some environmental influence, limiting his criminal predictions to anti-social individuals, and although he asserted that crime was genetically determined, he recommended behavioural treatment. However, he maintained his position as a frequently cited psychologist by being the focus of criticism that is often as much directed at biological positivists in general as at Eysenck himself.

Eysenck cited unpublished studies or those that were methodologically weak (e.g. Sheldon, 1942; Lange, 1929) and at the same time failed to mention those that did not support him (e.g. Banister et al., 1973), or contradicted his work (e.g. Hoghughi and Forrest, 1970). Eysenck's studies relied on correlations, which reveal relationships but not causal direction – a lesson that Eysenck himself was quick to point out regarding the correlational studies linking smoking to lung cancer in the 1950s. In addition there is evidence that prisoners tend to become neurotic as a *result* of prison (Goffman, 1968). Eysenck's questionnaires have a substantial subjective element, in contrast with the empiricism expected of positivist research. Psychoticism appears to be tautological, as it is defined by the same criteria as criminality, which it purports to measure, and is poorly developed in contrast to the other dimensions.

Eysenck's theory depends on a consistent personality that is, individuals acting the same way in different situations – and does not acknowledge situationalist arguments that personality may change with context. Eysenck makes no allowance for the **labelling** of an individual having an effect on the likelihood of reconviction, or the idea that a person's manner or appearance can influence judgements and reactions of others (e.g. Dion, 1972). As with many biological positivist theories, Eysenck's overpredicts criminality, and using male prisoners for his studies limits their validity to caught male criminals. However, in Eysenck's favour is the fact that crime is male biased and vastly underreported. He also assumes a consensus in society accepting the definition of criminality, which has often been contested (e.g. Taylor, Walton and Young, 1973). One truism that kept the public interested in early biological positivist approaches is the sad fact that simple myths are often more popular than complex realities.

Other psychological approaches to crime

Early psychodynamic approaches to crime

Early psychological theorists employed the historical psychodynamic approach, relying substantially on Freud's psychosexual stages of development. Thus Aichhorn

(1925) focused on genetics and early emotional relationships in explaining 'latent delinquency'. Here a lack of socialisation due to a failure of the reality principle results in a weak superego, leaving a latent form of the pleasure principle guiding behaviour. Similarly Alexander and Healy (1935) thought criminals unable to postpone gratification, which again indicates a failure of the reality principle. Johnson and Szurek (1952) considered a weak superego reinforced by unconscious parental permissiveness that tacitly approves delinquent behaviour (for a review of early psychodynamic approaches, see Marshall, 1983). The main criminogenic theory to emanate from the psychodynamic school of thought was John Bowlby's concept of **maternal deprivation**, which also relied heavily on ethology and evolutionary psychology. This theory of disrupted emotional attachment and development can be found in Chapter 9 and is summarised here in terms of its contribution to explaining delinquency.

Bowlby (1944) found that a greater proportion of delinquents at a child guidance clinic had been separated for more than 6 months in the first 5 years of life from their primary carer (their mother). Thus, this maternal deprivation was thought to lead to delinquency. Bowlby described the majority as having an 'affectionless character', also referred to as affectionless psychopathy, and in addition to having a criminal inclination they were unable to form close personal relationships. The link between maternal deprivation and crime has received moderate support from studies such as Little (1965), where more maternal deprivation was found to relate to a lower age of first appearance in court. However, Bowlby tended to gather many critics, partly due to his outspoken approach

to the topic, but also as a result of his work being overstated by others (Rutter, 1972). For example, Clarke and Clarke (1976) suggested that the whole family and not just the mother should be considered, but Bowlby did not actually specify that deprivation just involved mothers, only that it was *usually* the mother bond that was broken.

There are factors that can offset or counter the effects of maternal deprivation, such as an initial secure relationship, the child being prepared for a predictable separation (e.g. hospitalisation), or the use of substitute parents (Wooton, 1959; 1962). It is also more important to have the key parent emotionally rather than physically present, placing emphasis on the quality rather than quantity of the family relationship (Rutter, 1972; 1979; 1991; Wooton, 1959; 1962). There has been little proof of irreversibility of maternal deprivation or its prevalence in the general population (i.e. it may be very common without leading to delinquency). Also, there is the argument (Wooton, 1959; 1962) that if only 17 of the 44 'thieves' in Bowlby's study were maternally deprived, what of the majority (27) of 'thieves' who were not separated?

Rutter (1972; 1979; 1991) considered that the long-term consequences from the early animal studies resulted from maternal privation rather than deprivation, drawing attention to this distinction. He also emphasised the other characteristics of good parenting: that is, a loving relationship and stimulating interaction as well as secure attachment and an unbroken relationship. This draws attention to the distinction between physical separation and deprivation of a secure emotional base. In addition, Rutter (1972) argues that maternal deprivation is just one factor and a child also needs food, care, protection, play and discipline. Bowlby's

Focus

Differential association theory

Sutherland (1939) proposed differential association theory, in which crime is learned by association with other criminally inclined people in close personal groups. In such relationships, the techniques, attitudes and motives for crime are learned in place of other means of earning a living; thus crime may be seen as acceptable means to live and law enforcement as an undesirable enemy. The balance between the criminal path and the legitimate may be a product of which methods are learned (Hollin, 1989). Learning from close personal others such as parents or peers is not necessarily explicit (e.g. overt theft) but may be implicit in daily behaviour (e.g. not paying a train fare

or falsely claiming benefit). Thus, differential associations vary between individuals, producing a variable criminal outcome across populations.

Although crime is learned in the same way as other behaviour, reward and punishment alone cannot explain crime, as the methods and motives are also learned. Sutherland and Cressey (1970) claim that this theory is just a framework and that further research was needed for a more comprehensive explanation. However, sociologists have utilised the original approach of Sutherland in order to explain crime (see Blackburn, 1993).

work influenced the 1969 Children and Young Person's Act, initiating the need to keep a family together in adverse circumstances, which is not now seen as quite so desirable. Maternal deprivation as a cause of criminality tended to fade from the literature during the latter half of the twentieth century. However, studies of the factors influencing the development of criminality have lent some support to the idea of separation from mothers leading to delinquency (Juby and Farrington, 2001) and maternal rejection interacting with biological factors predicting later violence (Raine, Brennan and Mednick, 1997).

Learning and criminality

Learning theory is a major source of explanation for behaviour but has had relatively little impact on explaining criminality and, until recently, applied only weakly to modifying such behaviour.

Drawing on **operant conditioning**, Skinner (1938; 1974; 1986) considered that behaviour 'operates' in an environment to produce 'criminal' change, which is reinforcing to that particular individual. Such reinforcement can be: material, as in the outcomes of theft; avoidance, as in avoiding heroin withdrawal; or increasingly in the form of social esteem or status (Short, 1968). Punishment can suppress behaviour, although the methods are still acquired as with differential association theory (see the Focus box). The balance of the consequences for criminal acts in terms of punishment and reinforcement for each activity explains the individual criminal's predisposition for certain acts in a hybrid approach by Jeffrey (1965). He incorporated operant conditioning principles into a differential association theory framework, with a focus on the learning of the individual across contexts.

Rotter (1954) initiated the concept of **social learning**, which was applied experimentally by **Albert Bandura** as vicarious learning, or learning by observing the consequences of other's behaviour. This is basically a cognitive form of operant conditioning and has been applied to the lengthy debate over whether media violence is copied and subsequently enacted by observers. For Bandura (1976), social learning occurs in the family, in the subculture and via cultural symbols such as TV or magazines. Social learning theory has been combined with **control theory** in explaining why some people commit crimes and not others. Bandura (1986) considered how social learning takes place over criminal acts, but emulation may be inhibited by internalised moral self-sanctioning – again a cognitive process.

Later study data have failed to support differential association and the premise that criminal activity is passed between peers (e.g. Farrington, 1982). Neitzel (1979) has proposed a number of shortcomings of learning and social learning approaches to crime, including the comment that, although many are exposed to vicarious effects, only a few seem to commit crimes. This may be met by both Bandura's (1986) application of the control factor and also by the counter-argument that many may commit acts but very few are caught. Rutter and Giller (1983) further point out that behaviourists ignore individual factors such as sex, race and age, which are predictive factors in criminal activity.

Cognitive explanations of crime have examined the 'thinking styles' of criminals, often identifying these as being more impulsive and concrete (i.e. material rather than flexibly abstract) in their patterns (Glueck and Glueck, 1950). Frequently quoted in this area are the studies of Yochelson and Samenow (1976) which identified over 50 criminal thinking patterns by interviewing an unusual sample of offenders with mental health problems. The somewhat fanciful aim to 'fractionate the criminal mind and then synthesise it' fell short of scientific rigour given the sample, the lack of a control group and poor control and reliability over the interview procedure. Nevertheless, Ross and Fabiano (1985) reported on 52 of these thinking styles and cognitive errors in criminals, such as empathy failure and irresponsible decision making (see Hollin, 1989).

Control theories of crime

The assumptions of control theories of crime are that everyone has the potential to be criminal but that the factor identifying a particular control theory approach is what restrains the majority who do not commit crimes. The main approaches considered from a psychological viewpoint concern moral development and morality restraining criminal inclinations. Jean Piaget's three stages of moral development – pre-moral; authoritarian; and negotiability and consensus – were not specifically applied to crime, but a similar structure by Kohlberg (1964) has been applied to criminal behaviour. In this, a lack of moral control disinhibits criminal behaviour progressively as moral development continues from childhood through adolescence.

As with most stage theories, Kohlberg's stages were considered to be linear and fixed in order of development, with each stage being a prerequisite for its successor. Kohlberg developed moral dilemmas with a range of solutions that related to the reasoning behind each of his stages of moral development, which were considered culturally universal. These were selected by respondents to ascertain their level of moral functioning. Kohlberg's three levels and six stages of moral development are shown in Table 8.3.

Table 8.3 Kohlberg's stages of moral development

Preconventional Level 1 (before entering society)

Stage 1 Punishment and obedience (size equates authority)

Stage 2 Hedonistic relativism (what is good for me is good)

Conventional Level 2 (societal viewpoint)

Stage 3 Good and bad (meaning well is equated with being good)

Stage 4 Law and order (maintaining social structure)

Postconventional Level 3 (beyond society)

Stage 5 Social contract (societal view challenged by democratic means)

Stage 6 Universal ethical principles (principles beyond society's democratic process)

The three basic levels pass through the reasoning of the school playground into the regulations of society and then beyond society to more universal ethical principles. This approach had limitations, one of which was the tendency for some of those at stage 4 to regress to stage 2, undermining the basic principle of stage theories. There were also limitations with regard to the differing ways in which some societies express such principles and, although Kohlberg recognised some sex differences in reasoning, others such as Gilligan (1982) saw this as a potentially overriding factor. However, a fundamental error in the use of the dilemma identified by Ross and Fabiano (1985) was that individuals evidence little dissonance in expounding one set of moral codes if tested, but tended actually to live by more hedonistic rules. Perspectives from evolutionary psychology and biology have supported this conclusion, in that humans have inherited the systems represented by Kohlberg's earlier stages, but fail to match the cooperative systems implicit in his higher stages, and instead make moral decisions that favour their direct adaptive interests (Krebs, 2000). It is also clear from many studies of compliance and obedience (e.g. Asch, 1952; Milgram, 1963) that individuals will behave in ways they know to be wrong.

Twenty-first-century approaches to crime causation: biological positivism revisited

The modern biological positivist engages in far less speculation from behind the traditional critic-proof 'cloak of scientific impenetrability' that earlier theorists were accused of using as an intellectual shield. Contemporary proponents of the role of biology in crime are often at pains to explain the complexity of rapidly advancing areas such as neuroscience to their critics, and readily admit the limitations of a purely biological criminogenic component (e.g. Raine, 2002; 1993). Raine (1997) makes the point that, just as social variables can protect those who are biologically vulnerable to crime, so those socially vulnerable to crime may escape due to protective biological variables. This consideration of both biological and social-environmental factors in the explanation of individual differences in the propensity for crime not only differentiates modern biological theorists from their more biased predecessors but also coincides with a sharp acceleration in the accuracy and detailed knowledge of crime-related biological processes. Thus the lines of study that are based on later biological approaches do capitalise on the remarkable logarithmic progress in biopsychology and neuroscience over the last two decades, but have also developed a modesty commensurate with this heightened insight into the processes underpinning criminal behaviour. Paradoxically, the unavoidable complexity of current bioscience does make this work somewhat difficult for the scientifically naïve critic – those from a sociological background, for example – to evaluate with any realistic degree of detailed insight. Research in the areas of early developmental correlates of crime have begun to be focal in this area, as they have greater potential for intervention as compared with the study of personality disorders (see Chapter 14).

Attention deficit hyperactivity disorder (ADHD)

In a series of longitudinal studies (e.g. Satterfield et al., 1994; Satterfield, Satterfield and Cantwell, 1981), hyperactive children, who would now be diagnosed with **attention deficit hyperactivity disorder** (see Chapter 9), were later found to be involved in more anti-social and criminal activity than non-hyperactive children. The ADHD group went on to commit 6 times more serious offences and 28 times more 'multiple offences', and would prove to be 25 times more likely to be institutionalised in these studies. Delinquency and substance abuse are common features of ADHD across studies, and although linked to **conduct disorder** in adolescence, there are physiological distinctions between these disorders (Beauchaine et al., 2001). ADHD has subtypes for diagnosis (see Chapter 9) and it is often those who are predominantly impulsive that are linked with later criminality. Further subtypes of ADHD have been suggested that may differentiate those with anti-social tendencies (Banaschewski et al., 2003), particularly where ADHD is comorbid with conduct disorder.

The primary deficits in many cases of ADHD, such as **frontostriatal** networks dysfunction and **catecholamine** dyregulation, are the neuropsychological substrates underpinning aberrant behaviour patterns that have genetic origins (Tannock, 1998). **Magnetic resonance imaging** (MRI) has also revealed other subtle abnormalities in the caudate nucleus and corpus callosum, and reduced frontal lobes (Castellanos et al., 1996). The behavioural consequences of these dysfunctions and particular deficits such as poor verbal IQ conspire to limit educational attainment and thus thwart normal means of achievement and occupation. Poor verbal IQ is evident before reading age and could provide a marker for later risk and early intervention.

Treatment for ADHD has been controversial, as it often involves the use of maintenance medication with stimulants such as methylphenidate (Ritalin). Other pharmaceutical approaches than stimulants have been used in ADHD, including tricyclic anti-depressants, monoamine oxidase inhibitors, selective serotonin reuptake inhibitors and more recently, noradrenaline reuptake inhibitors such as **atomoxetine** (Biederman, Spencer and Wilens, 2004). Interventions can be implemented from 2–9 years of age and the combination of parent and child behavioural training along with medication can reduce problem behaviour by at least 50 per cent, in which, however, medication tends to prove more effective than behavioural treatment (MTA Cooperative Group, 1999). In addition, medication has not only been found to reduce the core impairments in ADHD, but also to improve self-esteem, cognition and social functioning (Biederman, Spencer and Wilens, 2004). Early intervention has the effect of reducing symptoms and improving functioning, and may lead to fewer educational difficulties, while also avoiding anti-social activity with its associated career path to crime. There has been less focus on ADHD in adults, as some behaviours subside after childhood and there has been an erroneous assumption that children 'grow out' of ADHD. The 10 per cent or so of adults who still have ADHD symptoms have also been effectively helped with maintenance medication (Biederman, Spencer and Wilens, 2004).

Brain area function and criminality

Raine, Buchsbaum and La Casse (1997), using positron emission tomography (PET), reported that impulsive murders of strangers showed low activity in brain areas controlling planning, strategies, impulsive behaviour, reading and mathematics. Raine and Yang (2006) summarise the brain areas structurally or functionally impaired in anti-social or criminal behaviour as including dorsal and ventral regions of the prefrontal cortex, amygdala, hippocampus, angular gyrus and anterior. This particular subgroup of the population have been linked to the small proportion of juvenile offenders who commit a high proportion of serious crimes and become adult career criminals, which is pathologically linked to those receiving diagnoses of conduct disorder leading to adult diagnosis of anti-social personality disorder. Raine et al. (2000) consider these biological underpinnings to concurrent anti-social behaviour to be a greater predictor of criminal potential than social factors. Many studies around the turn of the twenty-first century have added considerably to the biological risk factors for violence and anti-social behaviour (e.g. Susman and Finkelstein, 2001; Raine, 2002) and all types of studies have revealed genetic influences on anti-social behaviour (Rutter, 1997; Rowe, 2001). As noted above, these influences can also be protective against the outcomes of anti-social or violent behaviour. However, genes do need certain environments in order to be expressed and the nature of this interaction

Research

Limitations of ADHD research

Inevitably, it is problematic that the pharmaceutical companies themselves fund some of the research evaluating the use of long-term medication for disorders such as ADHD. Ostensibly, independent research teams tend to be appointed to carry this research out.

Contention in the ADHD area is not limited to medication, but the assumption that the disorder may be a cause of criminality has also drawn criticism, particularly the work of Satterfield. Earll and Licamele (1995) have suggested that other comorbid disorders confound the implication of a direct causal link from ADHD to later criminality. However, this point was argued on behalf of Satterfield (Weiss Cohen et al., 1995) and the overwhelming weight of evidence currently available confirms the latent forensic effects of the disorder (e.g. Banaschewski et al., 2003; Barkley et al., 2004).

The criminogenic effects of disorders such as ADHD may contribute to the stable individual differences found across populations, showing a continuity of criminal behaviour from childhood to adulthood identified by Nagin and Farrington (1992).

between biology and the environment has been an important consideration for Raine (1997; 2002).

The interaction effect on anti-social outcomes is as much as double that of the sum of the component influences of biology and environment (Cloninger and Gottesman, 1987). Thus it is important to understand the means by which the varieties of these influences interact, which may not be easily observed or understood and for which putative hypotheses will be inevitable. There are factors that may further confound these attempts to make the aetiology of crime and violence explicit. For example, the biological offspring of anti-social parents can elicit negative parenting responses from normal adopting parents (Raine, 2002). The social-environmental causes of crime may mask the biological contribution from an individual, and this biological contribution may thus be more salient in the anti-social behaviour of children from socially benign backgrounds (Raine, 2002). An example of the latter would be **low heart rate,** which can indicate a lack of fear response and stimulus seeking, and by these means is associated with violent crime. Low heart rate is found to be more evident in anti-social individuals from a high social class background (Farrington, 1997).

Brennan et al. (1997) found high **autonomic arousal** in individuals to be a factor that is protective against criminality if they have an anti-social home environment. Conversely, low autonomic arousal can predispose an individual to anti-social behaviour and is associated with reduced prefrontal lobe brain activity (Raine et al., 1998). For Raine (1997; 2002), damage to the frontal lobes may lead to other factors such as reduced autonomic arousal and attention deficits, which in turn predispose such individuals to more violent behaviour. Raine et al. (2001) used neuroimaging to establish that reduced right hemisphere functioning in the context of childhood abuse can lead to serious violence in later life.

Raine (2002) speculates that a child with neurophysiological deficits in crucial areas of the brain such as those above may pass through early adolescence within the confines of a highly structured environment, which places little demand on these areas of the brain. In late adolescence, however, social autonomy places sudden and extensive demands on the executive and planning aspects of brain function. Unable to cope with these demands, the individual with poor executive brain function will turn to violence and anti-social behaviour. For Raine (2002), it is no coincidence that violence and anti-social behaviour also reach their peak at about the same age.

Bio-environmental factors that occur around birth have been linked to violent but not non-violent criminal acts, especially when they co-occur and are mixed with poor family environments. Birth complications such as damage from forceps delivery have been found to interact with adverse family environments to produce later lifelong persistent violent offending (Moffitt and Caspi, 2001). In vitro nicotine exposure has also been linked to later violence, but this risk increases fivefold if combined with damage from birth complications (Brennan, Grekin and Mednick, 1999). Genetic factors and disorders in early pregnancy result in minor physical abnormalities such as low-seated ears, which can act as markers for concomitant neural abnormalities and later violent behaviour (Raine, 2002). This birth state interacts with unstable home environments to become a greater risk factor (Brennan, Mednick and Raine, 1997); however, minor physical abnormalities in themselves are associated with later violent behaviour independent of any poor family environment (Arseneault et al., 2000).

It can be seen that those working on the biological correlates of crime in the twenty-first century may be heading in the direction of accurate prediction of forensic risk based on identifiable biological factors and the degree to which that risk increases in the context of social-environmental adversity. This does potentially lead to the moral dilemma of **prophylactic detention** or even compulsory treatment based on biological assessment for criminal risk, as portrayed in the BBC TV documentary-drama *If . . .* (BBC 2, 2004). An attempt to justify the application of interventions for crimes that have not yet been committed is inevitably contentious. However, interventions are already used for many disorders with early onset in order to avert later disabling effects and there would seem little difference in terms of later anti-social behaviour. This anomaly in political and public opinion would seem to offer greater protection for the right of an individual to be criminal but not to be mentally or physically ill. This crucial issue in clinical forensic psychology will be returned to later in this chapter.

Explanations for the origins of criminal behaviour can be seen to range from the scientifically limited work of Lombroso to the relative sophistication of controlled longitudinal studies utilising brain-imaging technology. In the majority of these approaches, abnormal and clinical psychology forms the foundation for explaining crime on an individual basis. Thus, the importance of the combination of abnormal, clinical and forensic psychology to the explanation and potential management of deviant behaviour needs to be recognised, particularly in the context of the abnormal offender. Buried in the examination of the role of clinical factors in criminality is the question of what causes criminality, but another approach is to consider what kind of person committed a specific crime. The following section addresses the latter question and again it is in the context of offences committed by abnormal offenders that this question is more easily answered.

Focus

Evolutionary explanations of criminality

Evolutionary theory has begun to play a role in the explanation of criminal behaviour in offering **ultimate explanations** (i.e. the adaptive value of criminal behaviour) rather than relying on the more **proximate explanations** (i.e. the more immediate causes of crime, such as genetic, constitutional, environmental or social factors).

For example, Quinsey (2002) has applied this reasoning in the cases of: age and sex as factors in crime; the inverse relationship between kinship and homicide; paedophilia; persistent anti-social behaviour; and sexual coercion. In each case, the ultimate explanations (e.g. ensuring the selective survival of one's genetic material) combined with the proximate explanations (e.g. predisposition to violence and

infidelity in a spouse) provide more complete insights into the origins of these criminal behaviours than either approach individually.

A further example can be found in Wrangham and Wilson (2004). They point out that the social status motivations for individual violence in human youths leading to group violence tend to be context specific, as opposed to the more universal use in chimpanzee groups. They also make other comparisons that help to shed light on the use of violence in gangs. Although some authors have interpreted evolutionary theory narrowly to support their own views (e.g. Miles, 2000), others have utilised the approach to explain the known shortcomings of other theoretical approaches to crime (e.g. Krebs, 2000).

Self-test questions

- How have the biological positivist explanations of crime changed between the nineteenth and twenty-first centuries?
- Why has Eysenck's 'criminal personality' proved so enduring?
- How is maternal deprivation used to explain latent criminality?
- How can the child with ADHD be diverted from potential criminality in adulthood?
- In what ways has the advent of neurological science advanced our understanding of crime?

Criminal profiling

The pathological nature of the crimes committed by disordered, psychopathic and sexual offenders, and the tendency to repeat them, have made such offenders special targets for the police and other specialist agencies such as the **National Crime Squad** in the UK, the **National Police Agency** in Holland and the **FBI** in the USA. Public outrage at such crimes has also placed great pressure on these agencies to use all possible resources to catch the

perpetrators. One increasingly used resource is that of the psychologist, especially the clinical forensic psychologist in the role of **psychological profiler** or **criminal profiler** or, as introduced by Kocsis in Australia, **crime action profiler** (Palermo and Kocsis, 2005). Of the differing approaches adopted by those carrying out the role of 'profiler', that of the **clinical forensic profiler** tends to be a marginally more successful approach, as a result of most of the cases amenable to profiling involving disordered offenders (Pinizzotto and Finkel, 1990; Copson, 1995).

Offender profiling has come to supplement the work of **crime scene analysis** (see the Focus box) and investigating officers. In addition to the search for physical evidence and clues such as fingerprinting and **DNA analysis**, the psychological aspects of a crime scene, such as the choice of location, type of victim, style of assault, time of day and the way the offender spoke and related to the victim, can also be skilfully used to infer characteristics of the offender. Offenders are increasingly more **forensically aware**, particularly if they plan their crimes and are thus less likely to leave physical evidence such as DNA. Such factors place more police reliance and consequent pressure on the profiler, as psychological aspects of a crime scene are less obvious to the untrained offender. As a result of this pressure, the psychologist may be faced with producing a report based on very limited evidence to meet the almost impossible expectations of investigating officers. Thus profiling has been described as 'an educated attempt to provide investigative agencies with specific information as to the type of individual who would have committed a

Focus

Public images of profiling

The media have glamorised and popularised the work of this branch of clinical forensic psychology, with dramatic pursuits of psychopathic sexual serial killers in films such as *The Silence of the Lambs* (Jonathan Demme, 1991) and to a lesser extent *Hannibal* (Ridley Scott, 2001), often with the collaboration of established profilers such as Robert Ressler of the FBI. The concept of the detective who produces the characteristics or a *profile* of the offender from the characteristics of the offence and crime scene has been around in fiction as far back as the tales of Sherlock Holmes.

Real-life profiling also has a longer history than would first be assumed, with one of the first documented profiles being made of the original Whitechapel 'Jack the Ripper'. This was by Dr Thomas Bond (who autopsied the last victim of the ripper, Mary Kelly) in 1888, at a time when it was common for established medical professionals to offer opinions on offender characteristics based on their clinical and forensic experience (Canter, 1994: p. 6). A profile of **Adolf Hitler** was also attempted during the Second World War to assist allied strategies.

certain crime' (Geberth, 1996: p. 710), which more than hints at this process being an art rather than a science (Ainsworth, 2001). This is a muted criticism that has less substance in the twenty-first century as offender profiling has built on past experience and statistical data to become a useful investigative tool in its own right when carried out by experienced professionals (Holmes and Holmes, 2002).

Overview: USA to Europe

The dramatic tracing of **Metsky**, the 'mad bomber of New York', started a serious interest in the use of profiling in the USA. Psychiatrist James Brussel described the offender by personal characteristics and probable residence, and proved remarkably accurate in terms of background and residence, down to his reputedly wearing a double-breasted suit buttoned up, on arrest. However, in retrospect most men wore such suits at this time and Brussel himself contradicts this almost mythical story in claiming Metsky was actually wearing faded pyjamas on arrest (Brussel, 1968: p. 69). In 1974 the FBI caught **David Meierhofer** by predicting he would telephone his victim and used the term **criminal personality profiling**. Based on these successes, the **FBI** later initiated fact-finding interviews with 36 murderers at the then **Behavioural Science Unit (BSU)** (Ressler, Burgess and Douglas, 1985a), which has since changed its title to the **Investigative Support Unit (ISU)**. They focused on sexual and serial murderers, and discovered that there were characteristic *types* of murders and murderers, especially sexual homicide, which is the killing of a person in the context of power, sexuality and brutality (Ressler, Burgess and Douglas, 1988).

One of the distinctions made by the FBI that has been supported over time is that of the **organised** versus **disorganised murder** (Ressler, Burgess and Douglas, 1985b). From previous crimes, the organised and disorganised crime scenes can be linked to the differing characteristics of organised and disorganised murder suspects, and these can then be used to focus the police inquiry. At a later date, the FBI also arrived at a typology of rapists by interviewing 41 convicted serial rapists (see the section on sex offenders, pp. 241–6). Thus, using these characteristics provided by profilers, investigating officers could cut down the search area and number of suspects for a specific crime dramatically. Profiling has also been useful in cases of serious assault, hostage taking, letter-threats, abduction of children and violent offences that show characteristics of psychopathology in the perpetrator (see Jackson and Bekerian, 1997).

Although the FBI had dedicated significant resources to the work of the BSU, the use of profiling in other countries did not start till much later. One FBI agent, Robert Ressler, offered BSU services to police in the UK during the 'Yorkshire Ripper' case, but this offer was not taken up. The first use of a profiler in the UK was geographical and statistical **investigative psychologist David Canter**'s contribution in the pursuit of John Duffy, the 'railway rapist', in 1986. Although useful, this was not considered a successful profile, but a later one for a different case by clinical psychologist **Paul Britton** was deemed a success in bringing about an arrest. Britton is a clinical profiler, who has since worked on very many cases, being more a 'profiling practitioner' than an academic or researcher (see Britton, 1997; 2000). In the UK, it is usually **statistical**, **clinical** or **forensic psychologists** who are asked to produce profiles, not investigative agents (as is the case in the

Table 8.4 Characteristics of organised and disorganised homicide crime scenes and murderers

Organised crime scene	Disorganised crime scene
Offence planned	Spontaneous act
Victim is a stranger	Victim known
Personalises victim	Location known
Controlled conversation	Depersonalises victim
Crime scene controlled	Minimal conversation
Submissive victim	Crime scene random
Restraints used	Sudden violence to victim
Aggression pre-death	Minimal restraints
Body hidden	Sex-acts after death
Weapon or evidence absent	Body left in view
Moves body	Evidence left
	Body left at scene

Organised murderer	Disorganised murderer
Good intelligence	Average intelligence
Socially competent	Socially immature
Skilled work	Not well employed
Sexually competent	Sexually incompetent
Father in stable work	Father's work unstable
Inconsistent discipline	Harsh discipline
Controlled mood	Anxious during crime
Use of alcohol in crime	Minimal use of alcohol
Precipitating stress factor	Minimal stress at time
Live with partner	Live alone
Mobile and has a car	Lives near crime scene
Follows media coverage	Little media interest
Change of job or home	No change in lifestyle

USA). These psychologists tend to use a **theoretical** rather than practical approach, and although similar criticisms pass in both directions across the Atlantic, FBI agents and their psychologist counterparts in Europe have been accused of reinforcing their almost fictional images by overemphasising their individual abilities.

The somewhat mystical image of the psychological profiler may have led to some of the police regarding profiling as equivalent to spiritualism or astrology, as the methods were not accessible to them. This lack of under-standing may have led the Association of Chief Police Officers (ACPO) in the UK to form a subcommittee to examine the practical aspects of profiling. Paul Britton was commissioned by ACPO to review offender profiling in the UK and in 1994 the **Police Research Group** developed the **Offender Profiling Research Program**. Less 'intuitive' profiling methods have also been developed in the UK. In Derbyshire a computerised statistical database known by the acronym **CATCHEM** (standing for Central Analytical Team Collating Homicide Expertise Management) has been set up and used with some success. Crime details can be input to the program and the computer will output likely offender details. Perhaps it is the *empiricism* of this approach that has led the FBI to set up similar databases

in the USA. The FBI has also incorporated crime analysis into this use of computer assistance with programs such as **VICAP** (Violent Criminal Apprehension Programme).

Although much criticised, the FBI approach has formed the basis for profiling in many countries, perhaps as a result of its willingness to spread its methods and the fact that the FBI is far more open about the exact techniques employed than some psychologists (e.g. see Ressler et al., 1992). One example has been the creation of an Offender Profiling Unit in the National Criminal Intelligence Division of the National Police Agency in Holland (Ainsworth, 2001). The Dutch approach to profiling tends to be one of teamwork rather than having the process led by a specific profiler, and they are also keen on evaluating their work and publishing outcomes.

The profiling process

The FBI considered the process of profiling a crime to be the four-stage process, as outlined in the Focus box (Jackson and Bekerian, 1997).

UK profilers tend to add two more important stages to the list in the Focus box: that of police investigation leading to the apprehension of a suspect; and also the interviewing and successful prosecution of the offender, in which clinical forensic psychologists will advise on interview techniques and appear as expert witnesses. The Police Research Group's Offender Profiling Research Programme (1994) also includes the establishment of whether the crime is part of a series and the development of an inquiry management plan (including managing media coverage) as important stages in the process.

As mentioned above, one basic means of allocating crimes to types emanating from the work of the FBI is by classifying a crime scene as **organised** or **disorganised**. The organised murder has characteristics such as evidence of planning, control, use of restraint and removal or hiding of any evidence (including the body), whilst the disorganised murder scene is where evidence and victim may be left at the somewhat random primary scene with signs of impulsiveness and sudden violence. From this classification of the crime scene, corresponding offender types can be inferred based on past probabilities. An *organised* murderer would be expected to be of good IQ, be socially, sexually and occupationally competent, live with a partner, have transport, follow crime coverage and take steps to evade discovery, whereas the *disorganised* murderer should show the reverse of these characteristics: living alone, being less competent and often living near the crime scene without transport. Some of these factors may cut down the search for a suspect, such as likely

Focus

The FBI four-stage process of profiling crime

1 **Data assimilation** involves the collection and collation of as much *relevant* information as possible. Too much data would simply imply moving the crime scene to the office, swamping the profiler and obscuring any emerging traces of the offender. This would include police reports, photographs, statements, autopsy reports, logging timelines, etc.

2 **Crime classification** is the decision making process of classifying the crime from types, such as the organised–disorganised distinction, and consequently the possible type of offender involved.

3 **Crime reconstruction** is now a routine process in police investigation and involves examining the detail and sequence of events from various viewpoints in order to establish how the victim and offender interacted at each stage, and therefore to establish the overall **modus operandi** or method and sequence of events.

4 **Profile generation** follows by assimilating all of the above information into a series of hypotheses about the perpetrator's probable physical, behavioural, demographic and geographic details, and more specific sexual, psychological and pathological deviations. The profile may need to be further oriented towards the needs and understanding of the police in not using jargon and separating characteristics into those more useful in preliminary police inquiries and those more useful at interview.

residence or car ownership, but others would be difficult to check on the doorstep, such as inconsistent discipline as a child or sexual competence. Although the FBI claims that this division is reliable and reliably identified (Ressler, Burgess and Douglas, 1985a), lower reliability figures that have been obtained, such as 74 per cent would suggest that the classification may not be as intuitively obvious as the FBI suggests (Risinger and Loop, 2002).

David Canter in the UK came from an environmental psychology background to a position of authority in the area of offender profiling, which he prefers to term investigative psychology. He has translated his environmental background into expertise in **geographical profiling**, which has developed into a discipline of its own (see Canter, 2003). He has focused on a number of aspects of offender behaviour, amongst which are the following.

■ Interpersonal narratives are the ways in which the offender interacts with other factors, including their relationship with the victim. In this there is interpersonal coherence, in that the relationship with the victim tends to reflect the offender's relationships in the rest of their life.

■ Spatial patterns refer to the areas within which an offender feels safe, usually because they are familiar. These can be seen in the pattern of the locations of linked offences. This may also relate to successful **journey-to-crime** methods of prioritising suspects, similarly based on residence and crime locations (see Snook et al., 2006).

■ Crime careers develop as an offender refines their behaviour over a number of repeat offences, in which they may become more confident or less liable to leave evidence. This can change aspects of the crimes, confounding the certainty of a crime series.

■ **Forensic awareness** is where an offender learns to cover up evidence and discovers what enables them to evade capture or conviction, usually as a result of contact with the justice system or a narrow escape during a crime.

Canter has attempted to introduce empiricism and the experimental method into the area of profiling and has popularised one particular statistical technique, which makes crime scene data and other relationships in crime analysis more intuitively accessible. He has adapted **facet theory** (Canter, 1985) and a form of **multidimensional scaling** called **smallest space analysis** to the explanation of the interrelationships between aspects of various crimes. Although these are complex statistical techniques, one graphic output from the analysis can draw together many variables into the same two-dimensional space. This can simultaneously illustrate both the importance (nearness to the centre of the space) and degree of relatedness between the elements (proximity of the elements to each other), which allows the grouping of factors likely to co-occur with a particular individual. This is something of an oversimplification, but the technique is a popular way of explaining such an analysis to individuals with minimal statistical expertise (see Howitt, 2009: pp. 229–33).

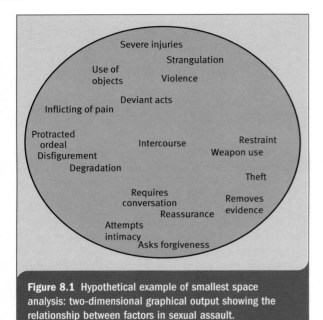

Figure 8.1 Hypothetical example of smallest space analysis: two-dimensional graphical output showing the relationship between factors in sexual assault.

A critical evaluation of profiling

The disagreements and arguments within psychology as a discipline (see Chapter 2) are also evident amongst profilers in the UK and mainland Europe. Some would not accept the accusation that profiling was an art-form not a science whilst pursuing a more empirical-clinical, behavioural or statistical approach themselves, and others of a more analytic or qualitative orientation would welcome being classed as art rather than empirical science. This said, there is less merit in remaining academically aloof from the day-to-day practice of profiling in order to be critical and maintain a 'pure' theoretical approach than there is in being involved in many varied cases and producing practical guidelines based on hard earned experience (see Ainsworth, 2001; Canter and Allison, 1999b).

The successfulness of offender profiling is usually thought of in terms of their work leading directly to the capture of the actual offender. The successes of the early BSU agents were limited, but as the FBI tend to promote their successes and are quiet regarding failures their

Focus

Crime scene investigation and analysis

Around the turn of the twenty-first century, the most popular TV series worldwide was *CSI* or 'crime scene investigation', in which glamorised characters brought to bear psychological and scientific expertise to solve crimes and even confront and arrest offenders. This attempted to replicate the reality of a white-suited SOCO (Scene of Crime Officer) in the UK picking their way through the contents of a dustbin. However, it then diverged from reality as the real-life SOCO would not personally uncover the offender, meet them face-to-face or interview them.

However, the varied work of crime scene analysts draws on the limits of scientific and psychological knowledge, skills and technology in a manner that excites both public and professional. Its united purpose is to identify the what, how, why and who of a primary crime scene (i.e. the site of the offence or location of the victim) or secondary crime scene (i.e. the homes or possessions of suspects or victims). The interest in the rather mundane detail of real-world crime scenes was illustrated by the lengthy news coverage of the serial murder of five prostitutes around Ipswich, Sussex, in 2006. In static tent-covered scenes depicted for hours on end, police had the daunting task of searching multi-occupancy premises and

body recovery sites where much evidence had been destroyed or polluted by many individuals passing through.

Central to this inquiry was the search for **DNA** in order to establish who amongst the suspects and victims had been where and at what stage of the homicides. Between the twentieth and twenty-first centuries, the quantity of DNA required to produce an identifiable sample dropped dramatically, allowing very small samples to identify individuals with probabilities approaching certainty. However, this is dependent on the **integrity** of the DNA and its documented location, which may be contaminated at the crime scene or at any stage in the collection and processing. Even tiny contaminants will be amplified in the process of replicating the DNA, usually by polymerase chain reaction (PCR) to produce an adequate sample for final analysis (see James and Nordby, 2005). Most DNA testing involves material from the nucleus of cells or **nucleic DNA,** but in old samples the cell nuclei may be damaged, so **mitochondrial DNA** is often recovered from the cell as the mitochondria are more robust. Being able to use tiny samples of DNA also means that contaminated DNA can be divided up into its integral parts for analysis.

During the 2006 Sussex murder inquiry, forensic and clinical forensic psychologists will have been consulted to deduce the characteristics of the potential offender from what was known of the crimes and their sequence. Examples of potential offender profiles for these crimes were published in both broadsheet and tabloid newspapers at the time, demonstrating the level of interest that the public has come to have in all aspects of crime scene analysis and psychological profiling (see Geberth, 1996). Generic profiles for this type of offender drew on probable characteristics from statistics on previous offenders. For example, the offender would be older (over 35), possess a reliable vehicle and possibly work within the victim's environment (to abduct yet not be 'noticed'). Clearly, the investigating officers did not release this type of information, as it would also have informed the offender as well as potential witnesses.

Clinical forensic psychologists and others employed as offender profilers tend to work from photographs and reports. They may visit the crime scene but only after each member of the crime scene investigation has completed their systematic search. This search tends to follow a fixed pattern, though there are variations in this. Once a crime has been detected, the perimeter of the extent of the crime scene will be established and a boundary set up to keep others out. With a single or small number of SOCOs or crime scene investigators (CSIs), spiral pattern searches are possible, either working from the perimeter to the centre or in an outward spiral. Parallel or grid searches tend to involve a number of SOCOs crossing the scene a short distance apart in straight lines. As any item of evidence is found, it may be photographed in place then carefully placed in a bag with its precise location and time found – details that may be vital, should it prove significant in the enquiry.

The modern CSI has highly sophisticated technology at their disposal to investigate and record the crime scene, such as improved 'kits' for and techniques of fingerprinting, DNA recovery and taking shoe prints. Ballistics experts can now not only identify firearms and bullets but also use a **laser trajectory kit** to help work out the exact position of the victim and the gun when it was fired. Recovering evidence from computers is now a specialist task and most police divisions have dedicated officers for this purpose. One computerised technique that may prove useful in the future for difficult or important crimes is to recreate the crime scene in virtual reality, complete with evidence for officers, profilers and other experts to walk through as often as they want and to view from any angle or level of detail. Future virtual modelling will also allow crime re-enactment to take place within the computerised version for analysis. However, sufficient specific detail will need to be input to the program if it is not simply to default to a generic sequence of preset scenarios.

Good teamwork and working relationships between SOCOs, investigating officers and other experts such as offender profilers can help to merge the psychological, physical and logical pictures with traditional investigative experience to produce outstanding results from relatively barren crime scenes.

---

general claim of a 40 per cent success rate and some individual claims up to 80 per cent (Ressler and Shachtman, 1992) were objectively difficult to verify. An FBI survey produced rates of being 'helpful in identifying the offender' in around 7.8 per cent of cases (see Holmes and Holmes, 2002). Representative estimates for the usefulness of the FBI agents and other profilers around the world are inherently difficult to ascertain with any degree of fairness. Profilers are all too often required in cases where there is public demand either to stop a serial killer or to catch the perpetrator of a particularly horrific crime. Such crimes are often committed by more experienced criminals where evidence and clues are covered up or absent. Thus, many cases are only given to profilers when there is little or no useful evidence for the police to work with and they have no leads to follow. Thus these cases are often the most difficult to solve and it would be somewhat miraculous if profilers could produce a high success rate if this is to be measured in terms of information leading to capture.

However, another means of evaluating the usefulness of profiling is just to consider the accuracy of the profile against the characteristics of the convicted offender.

Pinizzotto and Finkel (1990) compared professional profilers and detectives with novices in a 'profiling test', finding that the profilers did demonstrate some superiority against detectives, psychologists and students, but only for the crime of rape. Holmes and Holmes (2002), among many others, have pointed out that success in profiling is greater when the degree of psychological disturbance in the offender is high and in cases of sexual crimes. Copson (1995), in a review of profiling use in the UK, found that clinical approaches were the most useful form of profiling but that profiling only led to the identification of the offender in 3 per cent of the cases in which it was used. However, profiling was deemed to be 'useful' in around 16 per cent of such cases and a substantial number of UK police forces thought having a profiler involved to be of value in various ways, such as introducing new ways of examining crimes (Copson, 1995; Copson and Holloway, 2003; Gudjonsson and Copson, 1997). Kocsis et al. (2000) found that the police thought they themselves would benefit from psychology training, but they also produced study data that gave professional profilers no significant advantage against comparison groups. Although the outcomes of studies and surveys of profiling are less than encouraging, these evaluations and analogue studies suffer methodological limitations, such as studies being necessarily divorced from real-world investigations or surveys only involving difficult cases. From a Dutch study of 20 cases, in none of the six suitable cases for profiling did the process lead to arrest (Jackson, van Koppen and Herbrink, 1993).

UK psychologist-profilers have been accused by their FBI counterparts in the USA of lacking empiricism in their methods. The UK psychologists' apparently '**intuitive**' way of analysing crime scenes and use of psychological methods have given the more famous UK profilers a guru-like image. This criticism is perhaps more appropriately directed at the original FBI agent-profilers, who based much of their research on qualitative interviews and actively encouraged their own 'investigative guru' status in promoting their individual publications and media output (Canter, 1989; 1994), such as somewhat sensationalised published memoirs (e.g. Douglas and Olshaker, 1995). One danger of using a prestigious 'expert' in the context of a crime inquiry is that the 'ordinary investigator' may give too much weight to a single profile and an offender who falls just outside of this profile may be eliminated as a suspect in error. Profiles are probable portraits coloured by individual insights and experience, and can on occasion be simply wrong.

Although profiling failures are less newsworthy, some cases have made headlines and perhaps tarnished the image of profiling in the UK. Paul Britton's suspect in the **Wimbledon Common** case was released when **Judge Ognall** refused to allow the evidence that Britton had gained using an undercover policewoman, and made disparaging remarks about psychological profiling in general (Ormerod, 1999; Ainsworth, 2001). Britton had been so convinced by his *theory* as to the suspect's identity that he used coercive tactics deemed unfair by the judge in attempting to extract a confession. The way that the UK profiler's theory had overridden procedure meant that *other evidence* could not be heard. Many years later another individual was convicted of the crime casting a shadow over Paul Britton's confidence in identifying the original suspect.

Clearly, the work of the forensic psychologist and the legal systems they work with are not always in harmony with one another. As profilers and other forensic psychologists become more experienced with the workings of the legal system and gain more understanding and respect from the police, as well as respecting the experience of other professionals, their evidence may carry greater weight (see Canter and Alison, 1999a). However, the police have a great deal of experience with courtroom procedure and can still find *themselves* at odds with it.

Offender profiling has certainly generated more money in fiction than in reality, as most profilers carry out their analyses for nominal if any remuneration. Thus the glamour attributed to the activity really does have little grounding in real life. However, the satisfaction gained in helping to end a series of horrific crimes using one's clinical forensic, intuitive or statistical skills cannot be measured merely in monetary terms. The targets of profilers are often those difficult offenders who pose considerable risk to the public and the greatest challenge to police and the justice system. Some of these difficult, dangerous and disordered offending populations are discussed in the next section.

Self-test questions

- How do offender profilers help to catch criminals?
- How has the development of profiling differed in the USA and the UK?
- What is meant by organised and disorganised crime scenes?

Challenging issues in forensic psychopathology

Some forms of criminal activity and groups of offenders lie within the overlap between clinical and forensic psychology. These are rarely new forms of crime, but they often share the common feature that they have proven increasingly challenging for all agencies to deal with as research and its residual knowledge base advances with time. In other words, the more we know about these criminals, the more we realise how difficult they are to deal with in the given legal and medical frameworks at our disposal. The following examples of stalking, sex offenders and psychopathic or DSPD offenders may seem to be discrete categories of criminals, but there are overlaps between each and all of these. The sexual predator type of stalker (see Mullen, Pathe and Purcell, 2000) may thankfully be a rare form of offender in comparison to crimes such as obsessive psychosexual stalking behaviour (see Boon and Sheridan, 2002) and the psychopathic sexual assailant (see Prins, 2005), but each of the following clusters of deviant behaviours are not as exclusive as their category labels may imply. They can be understood in context by referring across numerous case examples, such as can be found in Mullen, Pathe and Purcell (2000) for stalking, Eskapa (1989) for sex offences and Hare (1993) for psychopathy.

Stalking

Stalking in a clinical forensic context refers to a pattern of behaviour that involves the repeated significant harassment of one individual by one or more other people. Counter to public perceptions, the majority of stalkers do not kill or seriously injure their victims. However, Hickey (1998) reminds us that most serious serial crimes begin with stalking behaviour and that many stalking victims would prefer to be assaulted than suffer the unremitting threats and consequent fear this generates, which has been referred to as 'psychological terrorism' or 'psychological bullying'. Stalkers are primary examples of systems abusers in that they break the rules that victims and others abide by giving them a functional advantage. Stalking is both common and under reported, Budd and Mattinson (2000) recorded 2.9 per cent of the population covered by the British Crime Survey, i.e. some 900,000 victims, had been stalked in a single year (Prins, 2005). Stalking has been used as the basis for Hollywood films such as *Fatal Attraction* (Adrian Lyne, 1987) and *Play Misty for me* (Clint Eastwood, 1971), in which the relentless pursuit has fascinated and horrified audiences but often left little in the way of realistic clinical forensic explanation for the behaviour.

Victims of stalking are greatly stressed by the continuous nature of the unwanted surveillance and intrusion.
Source: Pearson Online Database.

Definitions of stalking

Although thought of as a 'new crime', stalking behaviour has been traced as far back as ancient Roman law (Sheridan and Davies, 2004). Although the behaviour pattern can also be traced through literature and indeed across recorded crimes over many years, it was not until a series of high-profile cases came to public attention in the 1990s that legislation directed at this behaviour began to appear around the world. Often rushed and based on little research, anti-stalking legislation rarely mentioned the word 'stalking' when struggling with the precise definition of this behaviour, whilst also delineating legitimate activities that might otherwise be accidentally criminalised. Sheridan, Davies and Boon (2001) identified a number of subgroups of 'non-stalking behaviours' that were

Focus

Stalking definitions

A widely accepted definition of stalking focuses on 'the wilful, malicious and repeated following and harassing of another person that threatens his or her safety' (Meloy and Gothard, 1995: p. 258), but this and many other definitions may not fulfil the distinctions required of legal/forensic and clinical approaches. Although clinicians focus on the actual behaviours rather than the consequences, most legal views require four elements to be explicit:

- unwanted and intrusive behaviours
- these behaviours are repeated

- some form of threat to the victim
- fear in the victim as a result of the above.

The last two elements are often criminal acts independent of their being part of the stalking constellation; the first can be interpreted widely, but the second element could be considered to be a key element of stalking behaviour – that it is persistently repeated (Sheridan and Davies, 2004). Mullen, Pathe and Purcell (2000) have placed the temporal threshold for stalking behaviour at around 2 weeks, below which the behaviour seems to dissipate and above which it tends to persist.

confounded with harassment, such as activities they labelled 'courtship behaviours'.

Public views of stalkers tend to assume they are lonely people, who are hopelessly in love with a prospective partner, refusing to put out the candle in the window. In reality, stalkers are very controlling, emotionally abusive and usually have psychiatric and/or criminal histories. They are manipulative serial bullies, motivated by anger and control rather than sex or love, to inflict psychiatric injury on their victims. Around 79 per cent of stalkers are male (Spitzberg, 2002), who are on average more intelligent and older than other criminals (Sheridan, Blaauw and Davies, 2003). The predominance of males has been explained in a variety of ways, such as relating stalking to the evolutionary role of males as hunters stalking prey, or that males, being less socially skilled, would be less able to engage others by non-stalking approaches. However, the gender ratio in stalking is similar to that of other crimes and may have similar explanations, including the concept of females committing the same acts being underreported – a view supported by the large proportion of male victims stalked by male perpetrators (Tjaden and Thoennes, 1998). Canter (1994) refers to the **consistency of interactional style** of those who offend against others, and this is true of stalkers who, although single, will often have a history of failed and disturbed relationships (e.g. Meloy, 1999). The average stalker is also underemployed, giving them a temporal advantage over their (usually) busy victim. Around 50 per cent of stalkers have been found to have existing criminal records (Blaauw and Winkel, 2002).

Types of stalker

Having a typology for stalkers can lead to more effective interventions to prevent harm without wasting resources. Early typologies tended to be limited in this respect (see the Focus box).

Other typologies have been proposed, such as Mohandie et al. (2006) with their **RECON** typology. A proven, functionally useful typology in terms of case management is that of Mullen, Pathe and Purcell (2000), who identified the five types of stalker listed below.

■ Rejected stalker. The rejected stalker is the most common type. In this case, the victim is an ex-intimate and the stalker purports to seek reconciliation, though this may turn to revenge over their rejection. They deny the relationship has ended whilst seeking a perpetuation of what has usually been a poor relationship. The rejected type is often sane but angry, showing dependent characteristics, poor social skills and interpersonal inadequacy. They are normally responsive to treatment and legal sanction, but may resort to physical attack more often than the other types of stalker with the exception of the predatory type. Violence can be easily provoked if they encounter the victim with an acquaintance and is exacerbated by the rejected type's strong sense of entitlement, self-righteousness and jealousy (Mullen, 1997).

■ Intimacy seeker. The intimacy seeker is often deluded or otherwise disordered, but even if pathology is not

---

Focus

An early typology of stalkers

Zona, Sharma and Lane (1993) found three groups of stalkers emerging from a sample of cases that had come to the attention of the police.

- **The love obsessional subtype** only knows his or her victim through the media. They believe that the victim loves them despite contradiction, but also tend to suffer delusions in other areas of their lives against a backdrop of other psychiatric symptoms.

- **Simple obsessional subtypes** are the commonest stalkers, having previous knowledge of the victim, and tend to seek retribution as a result of their distortion of the prior relationship and consequent resentment over perceived abuse.

- **The erotomanic subtype** is a rare subtype congruent with de Clérambault's (1942) description of 'pure'

erotomania. Such individuals are usually female, with the specific delusion that the victim, normally of a higher status, is in love with them and initiated the 'relationship'. Despite clear rejection by the victim, the delusion extends to the belief that the victim secretly stays in contact and wants no other relationship, and that this 'relationship' has universal support. Although such individuals are rare, their delusional state makes them difficult to deal with in legal terms; however, they sometimes respond well to anti-psychotic medication (e.g. Chiu, 1994).

Zona, Sharma and Lane's (1993) categorisation of perpetrators had limitations in terms of its usefulness in clinical and forensic terms for case handling and treatment, as well as providing rather few classifications.

apparent, they will still engage in a one-sided fictional relationship with a particular stranger. Their solitary real lives are usually lonely and devoid of intimacy, and as a result their understanding of intimacy may be drawn from fiction and lack reality testing (Mullen, Pathe and Purcell, 2000). This category will include the historical erotomanic or de Clérambault type (see above) and, although rare, may gain disproportionate publicity and sometimes infamy as 'celebrity stalkers'. Celebrities and the famous have more fantasy value to fuel the illusion of intimacy built by the intimacy seeker. They interpret rejection or almost any response from the victim as affirmation of mutual affection. The media may enhance this fantasy, giving the stalker a sense of identity that may prove dangerous if they walk into the real lives of their victim, particularly if they engage in one-sided suicide acts to be with the victim in an 'afterlife' or simply to be 'together' in the consequent publicity. The intimacy seeker tends to be 'faithful' to one victim, but their fictional relationship may not always be of the romantic type and could be parental (Mullen, Pathe and Purcell, 2000). If the delusion is responsive to medication, the behaviour may diminish, leaving the intimacy seeker more amenable to skills training.

■ Incompetent suitors. The incompetent suitor is deficient in interpersonal skills and particularly in 'courtship skills', but still wants a relationship or at least some approximation to their understanding of a relationship. They may vary from the socially isolated with schizoid or autistic-like traits to the arrogant, insensitive and over-confident, but all will lack effective intimacy skills and be indifferent to the preferences of their victim (e.g. Lindsay et al., 1998). The incompetent suitor's pursuit tends to be very brief and they are easily dissuaded from this by sanctions. However, they are serial stalkers and rapid recidivists, moving on to a new victim with the minimum of respite. Their poor skills provide a target for intervention, and training can be a successful treatment approach for their stalking behaviour.

■ Resentful stalker. This group deliberately frighten their victims, exerting power and control by utilising more extreme tactics such as sending wreaths or some form of offensive material to their victim's address, and may involve the victim's work colleagues, family or friends. Tactics such as emailing pornographic material to the victim's work colleagues on behalf of the victim broadens the effect of the stalking activity and increases the psychological stress on the victim dramatically. This is often in supposed retribution for the victim having failed the stalker in some capacity, often as professionals

who have 'let them down' or as representatives of an organisation that has done this. The resentful types are often resentful against authority in general and tend to see themselves as victims rather than perpetrators (Mullen, Pathe and Purcell, 2000). They are suspicious of therapy, but it is useful in addressing their paranoid traits and sometimes comorbid disorders such as depression and substance abuse.

■ Predatory stalker. This is the most dangerous but fortunately a rare form of stalker in Mullen, Pathe and Purcell's (2000) typology. The predatory stalker pursues in preparation for attack, usually sexual assault or even homicide, without alerting their victim. These are stranger stalkers driven by power and control, who derive pleasure from the secretive, voyeuristic observation and planning of their assault. They are dangerous, almost always male, and their sexual intent is deviant and predatory. Their victims may be female, male or children and, in common with many sex offenders, they are usually lacking in sexual skills, confidence and experience (Mullen, Pathe and Purcell, 2000). Predatory stalkers may have specific paraphilic needs that may be evident in their approach to the victims, such as scatologia or telephonicophilia (arousal from making sexually explicit phone calls); see Mullen, Pathe and Purcell (2000) for a case example.

These five types of stalker require differing approaches to policing, management, skills training and treatment in the case of those with disorders. These classifications are not entirely exhaustive or exclusive, but they provide a very useful set of self-evident labels that are helpful to those front-line services dealing with stalking cases.

Victims of stalking

Media coverage tends to focus on the stalking of famous personalities, and many public figures consider minor acts of stalking an occupational hazard. Stalkers of the famous may seek (and achieve) fame or, more often, infamy for themselves. However, the vast majority of victims are ordinary people, who rapidly find their lives dominated by pathological pursuit, suffering privately without the public interest given to their celebrity counterparts. There are evident risk factors for becoming a victim of stalking such as being female, professional, educated, single and in the age group 18–30 (Sheridan and Davies, 2004). There are victims who are outside of all of these risk factors, but they are simply less probable. There is also a close association between stalking and domestic violence, in that stalking victims are likely to have a prior history of reported domestic violence, which may outlive the relationship

(Mechanic, Weaver and Resick, 2000). A sense of involvement, 'ownership' and entitlement tends to exacerbate interpersonal violence between ex-intimates. As with homicide in general, serious outcomes of stalking tend to be more common amongst ex-intimates: for example, McFarlane et al. (1999) found 76 per cent of women killed by their partners to have been stalked.

Overall, 75 per cent of known victims of stalking are female (Spitzberg, 2002) and in a sample described by Pathe and Mullen (1997), 84 per cent of victims had some form of prior contact with their stalkers. As with many crimes, only half of the incidents of stalking are ever reported to the police and thus even extensive research is likely to underestimate the true prevalence. Figures for the rates of physical assault on victims also vary greatly between studies. For example, Zona, Sharma and Lane (1993) found a rate of 2.7 per cent compared with Pathe and Mullen's (1997) figure of up to 31 per cent of victims assaulted. Violence is found to be greater for female victims and in cases where there has been a prior relationship with the victim (Pathe and Mullen, 1997). However, most victims find the persistent threats and intrusive behaviour of their stalkers far more damaging to their health, occupation, and social and personal relationships than physical assault. Fear before an assault is brief and recovery can be short, but the continuous fear from threat can slowly destroy an individual's inner and outer functioning. The scope for clinical forensic psychologists being involved with victims of stalking is extensive, as their treatment and support can be complex (Spence-Diehl, 2004). Victims of stalking are a diverse group and their management requires an understanding of the specific effects of protracted stalking and its clinical forensic issues as well as the associated disorders (see Pathe, Mullen and Purcell, 2001).

The impact of stalking on the victim cannot be overemphasised. Pathe and Mullen (1997) note that almost all victims in their sample reported significant changes in their lifestyle, such as taking security measures (including acquiring weapons) and severely curtailing outings, to the point of losing friends and even family ties. The erosion of social capital at a point when it is most needed leaves the victim even more vulnerable psychologically, socially and physically. The measures taken to avoid stalkers reflect the fact that victims live with the expectation that *anything* can happen, at *any* time, without warning. As a result of this psychological attrition, most of Pathe and Mullen's (1997) victims suffered high levels of anxiety, insomnia and other such symptoms with over a third having met the criteria for **post-traumatic stress disorder** (Kamphuis and Emmelkamp, 2000). A quarter had contemplated suicide, and most had been prescribed

medications such as sleeping pills by 'sympathetic' general practitioners. In the UK, the charge of grievous mental harm was established in 1996 during the well-documented harassment of Tracy Morgan by Anthony Burstow, which marked a real legal step forward in establishing that physical injury was not the only way to evidence harm to a victim. Victims change address, sell and move home, and change jobs and even careers in expensive and often futile attempts to escape. Escape is not really an option in the case of a highly motivated stalker with time on their hands. It is essential that legal and clinical intervention into cases of stalking takes place as early in the process as possible.

Stalking of professionals

Professionals prone to being victims of stalking can be anyone in public eye, but those in one-to-one contact with clients are more at risk: for example, GPs, psychiatrists, counsellors, lawyers, therapists and even dentists are all at an increased risk from all types of stalkers (Mullen, Pathe and Purcell, 2000). This vulnerability also applies to those in the media where pseudo-intimate relationships occur, as they become a familiar face that appears to speak directly to those prone to stalk, such as intimacy seekers. An example of a pseudo-intimate would be a local TV newsreader, who may appear to speak directly and personally to the viewer on a daily basis. Stalkers of professionals will mistake attention or concern for affection, perceive the professional relationships as personal and treat professional duty as a form of interpersonal commitment (Mullen, Pathe and Purcell, 2000). Resentful stalkers in this position will feel professionally let down, either due to some minor lack of satisfaction with service (Mullen, Pathe and Purcell, 2000) or more often because the professional 'relationship' does not conform to their expectations of personal support and intimacy.

The clients regularly encountered by therapists and counsellors are, by definition, people with problems, often lonely, who may also be disordered. Their client population is more likely to contain deluded, obsessional and personality-disordered individuals, who are clearly more predisposed to stalking behaviour than the general population (Mullen, Pathe and Purcell, 2000). Not all stalkers of professionals are clients or former clients, as some professionals such as nurses seem vulnerable to non-client stranger stalkers (Ashmore et al., 2006). Brown et al. (1996) found some clinicians were subject to multiple stalking episodes and that they were often over-tolerant of disturbed behaviour, failing to spot early warning signs such as professional boundary violations. Stalking is seen as 'professional failure' by such victims, who tend to receive gifts, letters and phone calls rather than being subject to surveillance (Mullen, Pathe and Purcell, 2000). Their professional colleagues or managers can be more suspicious than supportive due to the apparent 'lapse of boundaries' and, in addition, this lack of support or belief from colleagues can isolate and make the victim more vulnerable (Mullen, Pathe and Purcell, 2000).

Most clinicians (counsellors, in particular) will have broached the subject of ethical issues surrounding the relationship with their client during their training. In fact, guidelines, complaint procedures and overseeing professional organisations have grown to be a major factor in the clinician's day-to-day practice. However, most procedures were evolved at a time when the client was seen as the only vulnerable party in the professional relationship. Thus they are designed to protect the *client* from abuse or incompetence. This provides a near-perfect context for a stalker, particularly if such a situation has never been addressed in a clinician's training, which could identify those factors that indicate stalking behaviour. Clients who stalk will readily use complaints procedures, professional bodies and litigation, but these professional systems seem to work against the therapist victim (Holmes, Taylor and Saeed, 2000).

Forms of contact

Forms of contact by stalkers vary from daily letters and perhaps 200 phone calls a day (and night), to receiving a mutilated animal by post or having pornographic material delivered to the victim's work colleagues. Some stalkers frequently confront their victims, and will break into their home to achieve this. The victim may routinely find their stalker waiting outside home or work, as well as following their movements (Pathe and Mullen, 1997). Property damage is common and persistent, cars being a frequent target. A victim's sense of control of the situation is greatly challenged when the stalker involves their spouse, family, friends and employer by fabricating information, or by direct threats to these key people in the victim's life. Physical injury tends to be frequent in rejected stalker cases where it overlaps with domestic violence.

Stalking by letter is common, but anonymous letters are rare in stalking. Stalkers who send letters are generally less likely to have physical contact with the victim, but a high level of threat in such letters is associated with *less* risk of actual physical attack (Dietz et al., 1991), and implicit threat is associated with more violence than explicit threat (Zona, Lane and Palaria, 1997). The case study at the beginning of this chapter illustrates a resentful type of letter writer, who has a general grudge or paranoia, which has been directed at one individual. However, this case is unusual in that it has little impact on the victim and in legal terms becomes borderline stalking as it fails to create fear and a sense of threat in the victim.

Cyberstalking

As communication media contour themselves into our most private personal spaces, the phenomenon of stalking seems set to intensify along with these increased forms of contact, and what has been labelled **cyberstalking** may

Research

Studies of the stalking of professionals

Holmes, Taylor and Saeed (2000) identified a high level of underreporting of stalking incidents by therapist victims, arising from their feeling particularly vulnerable to accusations of malpractice as a consequence of being party to a disturbed professional 'relationship', even though they were in the role of the victim. In a US sample of counselling staff, Romans, Hays and White (1996) found only a 5.6 per cent incidence of reported stalking, although 63 per cent reported some form of harassment. Thus a stalking episode could be seen as some kind of failure on the part of a professional as victim (Romans, Hays and White, 1996).

The training and support available to clinicians and other professionals with regard to stalking were also found lacking in the late 1990s (Holmes, Taylor and Saeed, 2000) and still deficient in the following decade (Ashmore et al., 2006). Romans, Hays and White (1996) found such training lacking in 60 per cent of their sample. Contemporary advice to professionals tends to identify the types of indicative behaviour relevant to that client group. They are also recommended to keep within office working hours, be strict over time allocated to clients and not to give out a home number or contact out of work. This is in addition to more generic advice, such as calling the police as soon as warranted, as well as documenting and keeping evidence of harassment.

Focus

Stalking by proxy

The use of third parties to pursue the stalker's activities is termed stalking by proxy (Mullen, Pathe and Purcell, 2000). This one aspect of stalking seriously undermines the victim's psychological health, as it creates the illusion that the world is against them, there is nowhere to hide, and there is no one they can trust or rely on. Victims of stalking often come to depend on a diminished social network of family, friends and colleagues to provide stability and security in the chaos of stalking. Having one's spouse or employer influenced by a stalker and doubting the victim can be emotionally or financially devastating in itself.

Stalkers may coerce a range of others to assist in their pursuit of a victim, such as lawyers, undertakers, clergy, radio disc jockeys, home delivery firms and their own acquaintances. Mullen, Pathe and Purcell (2000) give the example of a stalker who persuaded his (non-English-speaking) family to join him outside his victim's home wearing T-shirts bearing the victim's photo and to help serenade the victim with 'romantic' ballads. Although this may seem quaint in comparison to the delivery of wreaths or offal, the experience was unpleasant and the persistence sufficient to drive the victim from her home.

---

prove to be a further legal and behavioural category of crime distinct from 'terrestrial stalking' (see Bocij, 2004). Victims are particularly disturbed by having detail of their daily movements related back to them by their stalker via constant emails, SMS or instant messaging. Cyberstalkers use computer technology to stalk and the activity has become so prevalent that many organisations such as **CyberAngels** have sites on the internet offering help and information on avoiding cyberstalking. The internet has become a playground for cyberstalking, as those skilled in its use can track victims, enter their records and even meddle with their personal computer's hard disk (Holmes and Gross, 2004). Internet technology has fought back with protection such as active firewalls (Goncalves, 1998), to shield internet sites from such interference. However, most victims are new to the technology and just coming to understand their computer's basic functions, let alone protective technology. There is the ever-present threat of cyberstalkers going 'off line' and pursuing or assaulting their victims, and with more than one cyberstalker per 1000 internet users, the potential number of cyberstalkers that may be online at one time is formidable (see Bocij, 2004). The gender ratio of stalking victims is similar to that of terrestrial stalking with it affecting around 4–5 times more women than men (McFarlane and Bocij, 2003).

Most of us are familiar with the fact that what is written in a text or email can be far less inhibited than a face-to-face communication, and the anonymity offered by the internet for *both* stalker and victim can dehumanise the victim sufficiently to facilitate virtual sadism and callousness. The internet and electronic communication allow

vengeful activity by resentful stalkers online on a scale not possible in a terrestrial situation, and this assault and humiliation may be witnessed worldwide rather than locally (see Bocij, 2004). Thus victims of cyberstalking can be subject to intense psychological stress and public denigration that cannot be simply dismissed as less harmful or even equivalent to **terrestrial stalking**, as in many cases the effects can be much worse (Bocij and McFarlane, 2003).

Cyberstalking is difficult to define as it has so many potential behaviours and contexts, and due to the nature of the technology, tends to evolve faster than any definition (Bocij and McFarlane, 2002). Activities often referred to as **cyberaggression**, such as flaming, mail bombing or spamming, and ultimately **identity theft**, have become the tools of cyberstalkers. Terrestrial stalking victims may attempt to move home and job in often futile attempts to escape, but it is the same internet and world wide web everywhere and many people's jobs and hobbies depend on their being connected and active in this domain. Legislation is a difficult issue in terrestrial stalking (see below), but legal protection in cyberspace relies on the goodwill of **internet service providers** (ISPs) and the cooperation of many governments. Worldwide legislation is as unlikely as world peace, and although a great deal of agreement has been reached on an international basis, there are a number of countries that are outside such agreements. If an offender is within a country that has similar legislation to the country of their victim, there are some legal frameworks that can be used, but a cyberstalker operating from a remote international location will always provide a legal challenge that may not be met (see Bocij, 2004).

Help for victims: stalking legislation

Advice to those who think they may be stalked was scarce prior to 1997, and until police stalking expert Hamish Brown produced a booklet for the specific purpose, practical guidance for police officers dealing with incidents was also scarce. General advice to potential victims tends to oppose their natural reactions, including bringing in the police as soon as viable to avert future stalking, keeping all evidence of harassment (including phone messages, texts and emails) and documenting incidents. Victims tend to suffer in silence and destroy evidence that would be valuable for prosecution in a similar way to rape victims, to rid themselves of reminders, which makes prosecution difficult if not impossible. In an effort to appease or be reasonable, victims also respond to stalkers, which unfortunately means that if, for example, they responded after 100 stalking phone calls, the stalker will try 101 or more times in the future.

Victims of stalking most frequently turn to family and friends for help, and tend only to involve the police where crimes are overt (e.g. damage to their car). The police are increasingly more sympathetic and less suspicious of complaints of harassment and may rapidly give a verbal warning to the other party, which can be effective in many milder cases. Until 1997, however, unless the criteria for crimes were met and evidence kept, legal action had been limited until specific legislation was put in place. The first relatively contemporary anti-stalking legislation was passed in California in 1990, and in the UK this finally emerged as the Protection from Harassment Act (s.3[9]) 1997. The UK Act has two levels of seriousness with the summary offence of harassment carrying a 6-month sentence but the indictable offence of 'putting in fear of violence' carrying a 5-year jail term. As with prior legislation utilised for stalking (e.g. the Telecommunications Act 1984 for phone calls), there is a tendency to focus on individual acts rather than considering the 'behavioural career' of the stalker, thus emphasising punishment as opposed to prevention (Addison, 1996). In the past, it had been difficult to establish that harm had been sustained by a victim who showed no physical signs of assault. The establishment of grievous mental harm as a recognised legal term in 1996 gave impetus to the 1997 law, as prior to this police had difficulty in charging a perpetrator with harming another by psychological means rather than physical assault.

Anti-stalking legislation is thought more effective in some countries, such as the 'peace bond' in Canada, which is backed by criminal not civil law and treats the innocent party as a *victim*, not a 'party to litigation' as often occurs in the USA, and also in the UK under the Protection from Harassment Act (Addison, 1996). The police, the Crown Prosecution Service and the courts have been accused of applying the Act inconsistently (Petch, 2002). However, there have been over 4000 prosecutions per annum in Britain under the 1997 Act, which is more than had been anticipated at its inception (Harris, 2000), and the first Police Anti-stalking Unit came into operation in the UK in 2000. There have been abuses of the UK Act whereby some parties to domestic disputes will use the term 'harassment' in order to have the police intervene as a high priority, which can make the police suspicious of a genuine victim's complaints of stalking. There is a great

Focus

Perpetrator use of legal processes

Paradoxically, legal processes can inadvertently further the stalker's aims rather than restricting them. Stalkers will fight litigation, ignore and violate restriction orders and readily counter-sue their victims. Long drawn-out legal proceedings will stress and even bankrupt the victim, whereas for the stalker the process simply extends and strengthens the 'relationship' with the victim by maintaining contact and making this 'relationship' public.

The singer Madonna had the indignity of being served a warrant and compelled to attend court to face her stalker as part of the judicial process in the USA. With this imbalance, it is not surprising that stalkers become adept at the use of litigation, complaints procedures, professional organisations and even the victim's own employers and unions to further their aims, and may even pre-empt the victim's efforts in this direction. Stalkers have even attempted to use anti-stalking legislation against their victims, claiming the harassment was in the opposite direction.

Thus individuals in careers that involve regular contact with the public may find that the professional rules that surround them make them *more* vulnerable as stalking victims (see above). The use of legal procedures to further the aims of the stalker in this way again illustrates **stalking by proxy,** in that the law furthers the aims of the stalker.

deal of overlap between domestic violence and harassment by rejected types of stalker that could be very usefully re-examined in terms of the detail of the law (see Roberts, 2005). Legal sanction is relatively ineffective with some stalkers, such as the erotomanic subtype and other more seriously disordered stalkers, who may not realise these laws refer to them or that they are doing anything wrong (McGuire and Wraith, 2000).

Clinical aspects of stalkers and their management

As with other areas of crime, many stalkers also have *DSM-IV-TR* (American Psychiatric Association, 2000) personality disorders (Mullen Pathe and Purcell, 2000). In particular, **cluster 'B' personality disorders**, including anti-social personality disorder and psychopathic person-alities, are associated with predatory stalking. Narcissistic personality disorder is rare, but more common in stalkers who pursue famous or high-standing victims, and schizoid personality or autistic spectrum traits can characterise some of the 'incompetent suitor' types of stalker, who have poor social skills and may display an indifference to the feelings of their victims. Other personality disorders are also found in this population, such as paranoid per-sonality disorder, reinforced by Mullen, Pathe and Purcell (2000) noting the prevalence of consistent paranoid thinking in a number of stalking subgroups, particularly the resentful type. Morbid jealousy often co-occurs with paranoid personality and is also a feature shared with a number of stalkers, particularly rejected ex-intimates. Dependent personality disorder is common amongst rejected stalkers, but it can also occur amongst some long-suffering victims, who may be over-tolerant of harassment. Although fewer stalkers than may be assumed have clinical levels of obsessive disorders (Mullen, Pathe and Purcell, 2000), many resentful stalkers also show the rigidity of behaviour and imposing self-righteousness associated with obsessive–compulsive personality disorder.

Although a minority of stalkers clearly suffer from delusional disorders and could be termed erotomanic, Mullen, Pathe and Purcell (2000) found 42 per cent of their sample of stalkers to qualify for a *DSM* axis-1 psy-chiatric diagnosis, which in the main was for delusional disorders. Hypomanic states are also found amongst mood-disordered stalkers, greatly exacerbating the scale and intensity of stalking behaviours, in that ambition, confidence and proactive intrusion become more extreme. Treating mood disorders amongst stalkers can reduce their harassing behaviour and improve their receptiveness to further interventions.

Many authors are quick to point out that not all stalkers qualify for a diagnosis of a mental disorder (McGuire and

Wraith, 2000), taking the 'perceptual approach' in viewing these behaviours as emanating from an aberration of relational processes (see Spitzberg, 2002). Some, such as Thomas Szasz, consider the attribution of such behaviour to mental disorders to be pathologising criminals in order to excuse them of their crimes (see Szasz, 1987; 1993). Approaches to the initial management of stalkers tend to reflect this view, in that the emphasis is on dissuasion at the various stages of the law enforcement process, from front-line warnings by police officers through restraining orders to full-term imprisonment.

Clinical approaches to stalkers will often take place during detention in prison with a strong emphasis on risk assessment and careful evaluation of the outcomes of interventions, as stalking is an extremely persistent behaviour (Sheridan and Davies, 2004). Medication has been used successfully to reduce stalking behaviour in some individuals. This may be a result of treating mental conditions that contribute to the behaviour, such as low-level anti-psychotic treatment for delusional disorders, although erotomanic delusions are less responsive to this approach (Mullen, Pathe and Purcell, 2001). **Selective serotonin reuptake inhibitors** (SSRIs) can be used with a number of stalkers, as this class of medication can address symptoms of depression and sexual or aggressive impulse disorders (Mullen, Pathe and Purcell, 2000). SSRIs are also of value in obsessive behaviour, and thus are more generally effective for obsessive stalking behaviour.

For the clinical forensic psychologist, the use of **cognitive behavioural therapy** (CBT) is an important intervention that can erode aspects in the thinking and behaviour of stalkers that precipitate and sustain their behaviour. For many perpetrators, it is useful for them to realise the impact they have on the victim and reduce denial that what they do causes real harm. Encouraging victim empathy helps in most cases but is less useful in the case of resentful or predatory stalkers, who see harm as a goal (Mullen, Pathe and Purcell, 2001). As psychological bullies, stalkers need their victims – these victims are their only source of self-worth and this chain would have to be broken to avoid their being *dependent* on their victims. CBT can be used in this way to appeal to the selfish motives of a stalker in getting them to admit that stalking is functionally a substitute for a proper relationship and to consider evaluating their 'lost investment' of feelings and effort. Thus they may begin to see that stalking ruins two lives, not just that of the victim, which may help the stalker to have a more 'dignified exit' from their behaviour and be less prone to recidivism (Mullen, Pathe and Purcell, 2000). Improvements in social skills and the consequent improvement in social networks can also keep these indi-viduals from returning to prison.

Paradoxically, it is often not until the stalker is imprisoned that clinical assessment and treatment is possible. This creates difficulties for the treatment and assessment processes. It is very difficult to evaluate treatment and assess risk in the isolation of the prison context, as practising skills and improved attitudes cannot be reality tested in everyday life. Although there is no specific register for stalkers, they can be registered as dangerous offenders and monitored post-release by **Multi-Agency Public Protection Panels** (see p. 249). The management of stalkers has similar caveats and complications to that of sex offenders, which will be discussed in the next section.

Sex offenders

Sexual offences tend to fall into three overlapping areas: rape and sexual assault; paedophilic offences; and other paraphilic offences. The clinical approaches to the paraphilias are covered in Chapter 13 but will be referred to here in a clinical forensic context. This is a moot point, as it is rare for paraphilic behaviour not to be simultaneously both of clinical and forensic concern, as almost all cases of paraphilic activity can also be defined as criminal acts by legal systems. There is a great deal of variation in acceptable sexual practice over time, between cultures and thus in terms of what is allowed by law between countries. In English law, homosexuality was no longer a crime from 1967 but male rape became a criminal offence in 1994, making the same act criminal one day but legally benign the next, and vice versa. A similar situation can arise between countries, where what is a crime in one is seen as acceptable in another. This variation has been illustrated between the USA and UK and to some extent *within* the same culture and country by rock and roll legend **Jerry Lee Lewis**, who found his marriage to his young cousin viewed very differently in Europe and even between some states in the USA.

Sex offenders in general and paedophilic offenders in particular are often considered distinct from other criminals by the justice system, and are demonised by both media and public (Thomas, 2000). The particular public venom reserved for sex offenders is an important issue, in that it impacts adversely on the detection, management and treatment of this group of offenders. This also links with the issue of treatment and punishment being somewhat antagonistic in their aims, reflecting one of the difficulties of separating the clinical and forensic domains. A logical consequence of releasing untreated sex offenders who have 'served their time' is the issue of risk in relation to reoffending. In clinical terms, the paraphilias are a subgroup of the sexual disorders (see Chapter 13), and although they may be distinct in legal terms, the disorder groups are related in terms of therapy and ultimately risk assessment. In reoffending terms, it may be as important to encourage acceptable sexual desire and skills as it is to reduce paraphilic or offending behaviour.

Prevalence of sexual offending is very difficult to ascertain due to victims' reluctance or embarrassment in reporting it and the skill of most offenders in covering up their crimes. The undetected, unreported or **dark figure** proportion of sexual offences is probably greater than that in most other areas. This not only means that the majority of offenders go unpunished, but also that victims suffer in silence; in addition, the offender never receives treatment, and in many cases never even recognises the wrongfulness of their actions (see Hollin and Howells, 1991). To the lay observer this would seem an intolerable situation; however, many attempts by justice systems around the world have only marginally improved this situation, due to the requirements of the legal process and difficulties inherent in the sexual offences themselves.

Sexual offences

A central issue in defining offences is that of **consent**, or the extent to which the intentions and actions of the perpetrator are unwanted and unsolicited by the victim. Consent is assumed to be absent in the case of children below the age of consent set by a particular country, and often in the case of those whose mental judgement is considered insufficient to reasonably give informed consent on their own behalf. The issue of consent also introduces a grey area into what is often thought of as a black and white issue by the media and public. The traditional difficulty of establishing consent in a legal context is one of the issues that maintain the high levels of unreported and untreated sexual offending. Thus, in the case of **rape** within a pre-existing relationship it would be very difficult actually to prove that consent was absent or denied, and even with a change in the law requiring the offender to prove that consent was given, the absence of material evidence and corroboration can lead cases to fail at many points before conclusion. It has been suggested that consent should not be part of the definition of sexual offences, in order to avoid focus on the victim's contribution to a case and to concentrate on the offender (see Elliott and Quinn, 2000). However, the UK 2003 Sexual Offences Act provided a definition of consent in order to assist the judicial process and, in particular, make the legal position transparent for jurors in rape cases.

Rape is the non-consenting penetration of vagina, anus or mouth, or in the case of **statutory rape**, penetration of a child under the age of consent. Rape tends to stigmatise both offender and victim, which is often used to dissuade victims from pursuing their case and can intimidate those who are accused but innocent. The clinical picture of those committing rape is varied, although there are a number of ways of classifying rapists and rapes that have been developed based on the implied motives of the offender. The 'relationship' between victim and offender is important in some typologies, such as the degree of attempted intimacy with the victim or so-called 'unselfishness', which some authors prefer to term 'pseudo-unselfishness' (e.g. Ainsworth, 2001). Hazelwood (1987) considered the distinction between the more violent and aggressive disregard for the victim of the selfish rapist, on the one hand, and the attempts to provoke intimacy and lack of overt force of the less confident, pseudo-unselfish rapist, on the other, to be useful to investigations in its implications for the personality of the offender.

Some rapists show a lack of self-esteem and a need to assert their dominance via sexual assault and have often limited sexual skills or the ability to relate to females as a route to sexual experience. Such a deficit in skills and esteem can be addressed by cognitive behavioural therapy

Focus

A typology of rapists

Groth, Burgess and Holmstrom (1977) put forward distinctions in motivation between rapists, such as those based on hostility or control. Groth et al. (1977) also produced a classification of rapists, which was utilised and elaborated by Hazelwood, and four types have emerged, which are listed below.

- **The power reassurance type** requires affirmation of their masculinity and sexual ability, and as a sign of their lack of confidence, they may carry a weapon but not use it. As a pseudo-unselfish type, they will try to establish some kind of relationship with the victim, which may even extend to asking to be forgiven or making contact after the assault. Lacking violence or aggression, the rape is viewed as a relationship by the offender to the extent of keeping trophies and other records of his victims. For the offender, reassurance is usually temporary and they tend to be serial offenders.

- **The power-assertive type** is confident in their sexual prowess and is skilled at enticing a victim into a situation where their ability to charm and persuade will dissolve into aggression and violence in a confident and well-hidden attack. Actual harm to the victim and her clothing is common, and this may intimidate and distress the victim into delaying reporting the crime. This 'selfish' type of rapist is skilled and intelligent, making them difficult to prosecute, having coerced the victim into a compromising situation of their own free will before the offender's sudden switch in character.

- **The anger-retaliatory type** uses victims to vent their anger, usually anger at another person, who may share characteristics with the victim. A rapid and very violent 'blitz attack' ends when the anger is spent, until it builds again and the crime is repeated. The anger-retaliatory rapist has a 'selfish' approach to rape, involving an emotional outlet of extreme aggression.

- **The anger-excitement type** of rapist receives positive feedback from the degree of fear produced in, and suffering of, the victim, which encourages the offender to escalate the assault. Although the attacks are brutal and violent, leading to homicide, they are usually meticulously planned to avoid errors or evidence. This rare, selfish type of rapist will use a weapon and remove evidence from the crime scene.

In each of these cases a different motivation will be evident in the crime scene and victim's report that may link rapes as being by the same offender and, if it were a series, the probability of any future assault and likely **cooling-off period** (time between attacks). Examining the relationship between offender and victim from victim statements, Canter et al. (2003) produced a typology of rapes, summarising distinctions in the essential process unfolding in the crimes. In line with other similar studies, they found rapes characterised by: **hostility** associated with violent assault, threats and penetration; **control** where there are factors such as the use of restraints or weapons and other attempts to control the process; **involvement** where the offender tries to endear the victim, trying to establish a relationship; and **theft** where valuables would be taken or demanded. These differing crime scenes show obvious parallels with Hazelwood's (1987) typology of rapists. Although offenders who rape are less often seen as a disordered group in the manner of paraphilic offenders, there are clear pathological traits in many that would warrant a clinical forensic focus.

and training, as can the tendency for some rapists to attribute their offending to factors beyond their control rather than themselves, or **external** locus of control (Rotter, 1966). MacCulloch et al. (1983) examined the role of fantasy in motivating sexual assault and rape, particularly where the fantasy builds for a period and involves violent and sadistic imagery. Cognitive training of offenders to control their fantasies and reduce these patterns of thinking can be implemented by clinical forensic psychologists to reduce the risk of offending. Evolutionary theories of rape enter the murky waters of establishing adaptive reproductive advantages for rape as a strategy, which may provide an ultimate explanation for any genetic contribution to rape behaviour, but for some authors this approach is of less value in revealing proximate approaches to its reduction (see Howitt, 2009).

Police units have made more specialist provision for the victims of rape in the UK, with specifically trained officers, availability of equipment such as DNA kits and less imposing surroundings for those in distress. Clinical forensic resources are increasingly being made available to victims by health services, where local funding is both available and sustainable. In addition to specialist expertise, sexual assault referral centres (SARCs) provide a range of services, such as emergency contraception, management of unwanted pregnancy and dealing with sexually transmitted diseases, as well as forensic support, procedures and advice. Trained staff will not only be able to reduce the impact of the trauma and subsequent examination on the victim but also have training in specific areas such as the legal requirements for statements and preserving the integrity of forensic findings in the chain of evidence (McLean, 2003). All of these resources are immensely useful in avoiding long-term complications for the victim, whether physical or psychological, and can help to increase the chances of a rapist being identified or prosecuted. Thus measures directed at victims may prevent future sexual crimes in terms of that specific offender and increase the ongoing deterrent effect of assailants being more frequently and successfully prosecuted.

The paraphilias are described in Chapter 13 and most are reflected in legal systems as sex offences: for example, degrees of exhibitionism are criminalised in most countries as forms of indecent exposure. However, many paraphilias have traditionally had to be 'translated' into existing categories of offences in order to be brought to court, which can obscure the motivation and clinical aetiology of the behaviour. As West (2000) states, men and women engaging in consensual sadomasochistic practices for mutual enjoyment can be prosecuted along with those undertaking a wide range of activities that would be thought of as legal by a clinical psychologist without forensic training.

Many paraphilic acts are only prosecuted in certain circumstances, such as bondage if injury occurs, transvestism if it involves deception, and fetishistic collection of underwear when it involves theft or children (West, 2000). This piecemeal way of criminalising component acts of the paraphilic pattern of behaviour is reminiscent of the way stalking was dealt with in law prior to the 1997 Harassment Act discussed in the previous section. Overlapping paraphilic diagnoses can also add to this confusion, as if the clinical picture is unclear (Lee et al., 2001), it provides little for the law to follow. One of the inherent difficulties in the area of clinical forensic psychology is the tendency for the law to focus on individual acts rather than considering the risk posed by long-standing psychopathological traits, but legislation revisions have attempted to address this for some offender groups including sex offenders.

Although the UK Sex Offenders Act 1997 clarified some aspects of sexual offending, especially in relation to child victims, the Sexual Offences Act 2003 removed many of the grey areas that had made the definition and prosecution of sexual offences problematic. As mentioned above, the Act clarified what was meant by consent for the purposes of the law, and specified that children under 13 years of age cannot legally give consent. Under this legislation, consent has to be active not passively assumed, which many interpret as shifting the burden of proof from the victim to the accused. The 2003 Act made it illegal to use communications technology for sexual messages to children or to 'groom' children for future sexual purposes. **Multi-agency public protection arrangements** (MAPPA; see the next section) were also strengthened in their ability to track previous sexual offenders, and legal protection from forms of sexual coercion was specified for those with mental health problems. In the twenty-first century, revision of sexual offending legislation in many countries has focused a great deal on offences against children, including offending within the family.

In clinical terms, paedophilia is a form of paraphilia in which the inappropriate target for sexual gratification is a sexually immature child, and in contrast to the context-specific prosecution of other paraphilias, paedophilic acts tend to be universally criminalised. When paedophilia is translated into terms that are legally enforced, the victim is designated as a person below the age of consent. For some authors (e.g. McConaghy, 1999), this legal aspect confounds a clinical approach to the offence, as the assumed clear legal distinction between sexual partners aged 15 and 16 has less meaning in clinical terms where attraction to pre-pubescent children indicates a distinct disorder. The UK 2003 Sexual Offences Act's specific references to sexual offences against children under the age of 13 years are more compatible with a clinical view of paedophilic activity. However, the Act also includes offences involving indecent photographs of individuals aged 17 years, which may be less intuitively obvious in clinical terms (especially given the historical legal emphasis on children under 16). One less desirable by-product of more specific legislation is that more detailed prescriptive limits leave less room for discretion by the court.

Paedophilic offences are most commonly non-contact offences involving child pornography, exposure or paedophilic voyeurism. Paedophilic penile penetration is relatively infrequent and paedophilic offences by strangers are far less frequent than offences within families, which is often counter to public perceptions (Thomas, 2000). Lowenstein (2006) highlights the high proportion of sexual offences against children by adolescent offenders, which again is in contradiction to the public stereotype of the older offender who is also a stranger. One of the reasons for the poor detection and prosecution rate regarding paedophilic crimes and sex crimes in general is that the public assume offenders to resemble the media stereotype of the eccentric older stranger. Thus many of the more common offenders, who may be younger and well known or related to the victim, tend to go undetected and therefore untreated.

Issues in the management of sex offenders

The management of sex offenders involves their initial assessment, treatment, risk assessment and subsequent monitoring in the community. The UK 1983 Mental Health Act attempted to separate clinical psychology and psychiatry from sex offenders and some other offenders on the basis that their training with the vulnerable mentally ill would be inadequate to prepare them for the challenge of this forensic group (see Thomas, 2000). However, in the twenty-first century the major treatment approaches of cognitive behavioural therapy tend to be delivered by forensic or clinical psychologists and increasingly clinical forensic psychologists. In a similar shift, assessments of offenders both for diagnosis and for risk used to involve physical phallometric means in the form of plethysmography (see

---

Focus

Treatment approaches for sex offenders

Walker (1996) identifies three basic treatment approaches for sex offenders.

- Cognitive programmes aim to educate and alter the thinking styles of offenders, encouraging empathy and challenging their denial of wrongdoing as well as addressing other patterns of thought that support their offending.

- Behavioural techniques and physical measures can assess the specifics of an offender's deviant responses, which can then be reoriented to more acceptable outlets by behavioural treatments (see Chapter 3).

- Medical interventions can be used to reduce hormone levels and the physical responsiveness of offenders or 'chemical castration'.

Although cost-effective, these interventions tend to fall short of being an overall success and cannot guarantee the kind of risk assessment outcomes needed to release treated offenders confidently. In the case of the latter approach, they will also repress legitimate sexual activity (Quinsey et al., 1993).

Sex offender treatment began to integrate behavioural, skills and cognitive approaches in the 1970s and more comprehensive sex offender treatment programmes (SOTP) primarily based on cognitive behavioural approaches were developed in the 1990s (Brooks-Gordon, Bilby and Wells, 2006). Meta-analyses of sex offender treatment approaches tend to find cognitive behavioural approaches superior to behavioural, psychosocial and hormone treatments (Gallagher et al., 1999).

Custody-based cognitive behavioural programmes can target victim empathy and insight into wrongful acts with some selective success, even with challenging offender groups (Keeling, Rose and Beech, 2006). Although the overall effects of treatment have not been high, the fact that many offenders have multiple victims means that even small treatment effects will be cost-effective in reducing future victimisation (Hanson, 2000). Cognitive behavioural treatment has been found effective in reducing reoffending after 1 year but less effective after 10 years (Brooks-Gordon, Bilby and Wells, 2006).

In the twenty-first century there have been innovations increasing the apparent effectiveness of sex offender treatment programmes, but accompanying research, replication and fine adjustment to programmes as a result of research outcomes are necessary for reliable and sustainable progress in reducing recidivism (Mann, 2004).

Chapter 13) and clinical judgements. However, assessments now tend to use actuarial instruments (psychometrics), which are seen as more cognitively orientated than phallometry (Marshall, 1996) and which outperform clinical judgement, especially if dynamic risk factors are incorporated with them (Craig et al., 2006).

Irrespective of treatment outcome, all convicted sex offenders in many countries are placed on **sex offender registers**, from which police have access to information such as home address and what offence has been committed, and they also enable police to monitor how many offenders are in their area. The UK register is given the acronym **ViSOR** (Violent and Sex Offenders Register) and will register all sex offenders, even those who have only been cautioned, for a period of time governed by the seriousness of their conviction. For example, an offender receiving a caution will remain on the register for 7 years, whereas those receiving a sentence greater than 30 months may remain on it for life. Offenders must register with the police within 3 days or face a possible jail term and compliance in the UK has been around 97 per cent. However, the register is only as accurate as the information fed into it, and errors as well as the failure of offenders or administrators to update information can limit its usefulness (Tewksbury, 2006). Inaccuracies in the register can also lead to offenders not complying for fear of errors or not being removed. In the UK, increased levels of information gained from offenders by the use of **lie detection tests**, in the form of the polygraph for most cases, has led to their adoption for the monitoring of offender behaviour, their adherence to register requirements and assessing reoffending risk (see Madsen, Parsons and Grubin, 2004).

Although treatment should theoretically be a top priority for this group of disordered offenders, public protection from offending risk tends to take priority. There is inevitably an antagonistic relationship between these two aims and in most countries the uncertain outcome of treatment in terms of risk, combined with the costs involved in those released reoffending, pushes policy towards a pragmatic approach. Emphasis on control of offenders within the community by the use of registers and multi-agency and Probation Service monitoring tends to follow the realistic approach to management in the tradition of 'what works' from the last chapter (Webb and Harris, 1999). SORMA or the Sex Offender Risk Management Approach (see Grant, 1999) is an example of this management by practical surveillance and multi-agency intelligence exchange. However, the potential for more effective treatment should not be ignored and the possibility of a policy shift away from 'community containment' not abandoned (Walker, 1996). Craig et al. (2006) have found the reoffending risk of sex offenders to be more in line with that of general offenders and identify violent offenders as being a higher risk and having greater psychopathology than sex offenders. It may be that public pressure over potential risk to children has led to a disproportionate focus on the sex offender as being at greatest risk of reoffending, despite research evidence to the contrary.

Sex offenders, the media and public

In clinical and etymological terms, paedophilia infers the behaviour of a lover and not an abuser of children (West, 2000). The zealous demonisation of paedophiles as an assumed homogeneous mass by the tabloid press and their readership in the UK, and by their US counterparts, may reflect an aggressive defence against an obvious widespread latent interest in immature children often displayed within the same individuals and publications that portray sex offenders as modern folk devils. This depiction may fall short of actual paedophilia but is expressed in the use of children in suggestive dress and poses (Kincaid, 1998), which still bears many of the hallmarks of child pornographers. The widespread use of very young girls as fashion models emaciated to the point of prepubescent body shapes perhaps broadens the number of those exhibiting this hypocritical standpoint. The evolutionary fact that all adults are orientated towards child sign stimuli in order to protect them probably provides both the foundation for the dilemma facing those who like child pictures but simultaneously vilify paedophiles and a probable genetic basis for the direction of the deviant sexuality of the paedophiles themselves.

Awareness of this dubious aspect to the use of the attractiveness of the child-like image has even prompted the twenty-first-century international fashion industry to set limits to the use of overly youthful and 'size 0' models for its major brands. The bizarre double standard where the same members of the public demanding that sex offenders be treated as subhuman simultaneously indulge in child pageants or consume child 'cute-fashion' media respectively impacts a great deal on the monitoring and treatment of sex offenders in general (see Thomas, 2000).

The simple use of children in newspaper stories increases sales, as does the addition of sex, and although it is commercially risky, stories combining the two with a demonic offender have been successfully resorted to by tabloid papers in the UK, which is unusual in having a number of papers competing at national level. These stories led to campaigns to 'name and shame' sex offenders, using the readership of these newspapers (see Thomas, 2000). The degree of publicity drawn by one of these campaigns exerted political pressure to instate a 'Sarah's law' (after

Despite a move to not use young underweight models in fashion, the demands of the market still produce influential images.
Source: Pearson Online Database.

victim Sarah Payne), which would allow the public access to local sex offender names and addresses, in a similar manner to 'Megan's law' in the USA (Dean, 2000). Police and probation representatives opposed public access to such information when the sex offender register was instated in the UK in 1997. Dean (2000) notes that the validity of the police stance on this issue was demonstrated when the Sunday newspaper itself published the photographs, names and addresses of known child sex offenders in 2000, precipitating vigilante attacks on both innocent citizens and treated sex offenders. The cumulative damage caused by this and other campaigns led to large-scale damage to property, serious injury and even death, affecting innocent families of offenders, police and even a paediatrician, whose profession was mistaken for 'paedophile' by the ignorance of the vigilante mob. The same Sunday newspaper claimed a further 'success' in 2006 when child sex offenders were removed from hostels considered to be near schools following another campaign. Internet websites have also posted details of sex offenders online, such as the Child Exploitation and Online Protection (CEOP) website, although these tended to be offenders evading the sex offender register.

The naming and shaming approach has even been considered as a policy strategy (e.g. Pawson, 2002).

In addition to the injury, damage and immense cost in police time, campaigns such as these have a direct effect on the management of sex offenders. Some in fear for their safety fail to register, effectively disappearing not only from police monitoring, but also from therapy sessions (Thomas, 2000). More seriously, in these circumstances, offenders will commit very serious offences in order to destroy evidence, including killing their victims. Vigilantes tend to equate accused offenders who are innocent of sex offences with convicted offenders and potential witnesses to sex crimes, and some professionals in the field tend to withdraw their services for fear of involvement with indiscriminate vigilantism. Hostels and other institutions would refuse to house sex offenders in the wake of such attacks. The loss of supervision, surveillance and treatment inevitably leads to increases in attacks and abuse both in the short and long term (Thomas, 2000). Paradoxically, this may co-occur with a drop in officially reported sex offences, due to a vast increase in unreported incidents and a proportionate decrease in reported offences.

Moral dilemmas such as those brought about by the use of sex offenders to boost media audience figures are issues that may in the future be addressed by clinical forensic psychologists. These professionals have both the knowledge of the clinical and practical realities of sex offending and offenders and also insight into the psychology of group dynamics, persuasion and attitude management. Issues of balancing public protection with the clinical requirements of offenders have also been debated at length regarding another group of offenders, those with personality disorders considered dangerous from a forensic standpoint.

Psychopathy, DSPD and public protection

This section will outline the place of **psychopathic disorder**, as well as its later categorisation under the heading of **dangerous and severe personality disorder** (DSPD), in the clinical forensic field and by what means the public are protected from these offenders. Clinical and abnormal psychology detail on these disorders can be found in Chapter 14. In contrast to most disorders that may be used as mitigation in court, **cluster 'B' personality disorders** are often seen as aggravating rather than mitigating in a defendant, and are considered more important in a forensic than a clinical setting. Some personality disorders have their symptoms defined in almost the same terms as criminal behaviour. Primarily, this refers to **anti-social personality disorder**, but arguably **psychopathy** belongs with this nosological grouping. However, the psychopathic person-ality is not listed in the current *DSM* and *ICD* classificatory systems as a personality disorder, though there is a reference to a 'sociopathic' manifestation of personality in *ICD-9* (Wong, 2000). The problems posed by the psychopathic offender and those now described as having DSPD could be considered the heartland of clinical forensic psy-chology. These individuals have an enigmatic presence in the study of both psychopathology and crime, being close to an irresolvable problem for both disciplines as well as posing something of a dilemma for the governments of most countries.

Psychopathy and its relationship to DSPD

All psychopathic individuals can also be diagnosed with anti-social personality disorder (APD; also referred to as **dissocial personality disorder** in *ICD-10*) but less than an estimated third of APD individuals could be classified as **psychopathic** (Müller-Ishberner and Hodgins, 2000). APD criteria include persistent behaviours that are adult versions of conduct disorder, such as offending, impul-siveness and disregard for others, the truth, finances or future plans. A *DSM* diagnosis of APD usually requires conduct disorder to be diagnosed before the age of 15. About half of adolescents with conduct disorder go on to be diagnosed as APD, with most of the others shedding such behaviour with maturity. Around 80 per cent of convicted criminals could be diagnosed as APD, given that the behavioural criteria include offending behaviours (see Chapter 14). Whereas APD is defined in terms of anti-social behaviours (e.g. running up debts), psychopathy tends to include more psychological descriptions (e.g. lacking in emotion). See Chapter 14 for more clinical detail on APD.

The psychopath differs from the ordinary offender or most individuals with APD, in their greater *potential* for harm. As Cleckley (1976) identified, psychopaths offend without apparent purpose, show no remorse, are loyal to no one, and frequently indulge in perverse sexual and harmful behaviour, and these traits permeate all areas of their lives. Over 90 per cent of sexual and serial killers are diagnosed as psychopaths; however, in the USA there are around 150 serial killers but over 3 million psychopaths, as most will devastate the lives and finances of those around them without resorting to homicide. Psychopathic individuals have a lack of empathy or conscience that often makes them *more able* in such areas as business, the military or politics, though they are usually less than suc-cessful due to recklessness (Hare, 1993). Individuals with APD commit most crimes, but psychopaths account for a disproportionate excess of these crimes due to their life-time traits and consequent recidivism. In the case of some

psychopathic individuals, a relentless tendency to exploit others without conscience or limits has provided the back-ground for notorious and highly dangerous criminal acts such as those of **Fred West** in the UK.

The fact that those individuals with psychopathic dis-order commit half of all serious crime (Hare, 1993) would suggest that treating the disorder should be a very high priority for society as a whole. However, psychopathy is controversial as a disorder, as the 'sufferer' rarely suffers, only those near to them, and although they have good contact with reality, they have little insight into the con-cept that there is something wrong with them or their behaviour. Pritchard (1835) aptly described psychopaths as showing 'moral insanity', with the term 'moral' refer-ring to emotion and psychology rather than any religious connotation (see Prins, 1999). They do not wish to change their behaviour and gain pleasure from exploiting and manipulating. Thus, psychopathic individuals are not simply resistant to therapy; they will also manipulate the therapeutic relationship to their advantage and even sub-vert the treatment programmes of fellow inmates (Müller-Ishberner and Hodgins, 2000). Susceptibility to treatment is a fundamental issue when considering the disposal and management of psychopathic individuals. Psychopaths were often confined on the basis that they could be treated: for example, under the old UK 1983 Mental Health Act. However, Cleckley (1976) among others believes the con-dition is *virtually untreatable*, as one of the prominent traits of psychopaths is that they 'do not learn from experience' (see Wong, 2000). One of the most difficult distinctions to make is that between the psychopathic offender and the non-psychopathic but dangerous offender, as both have similar characteristics. Oddly enough, given Cleckley's assertions, this distinction has in the past been made on the basis that psychopathy is a *treatable* condition disorder and dangerousness is not. Thus a dangerous individual would be incarcerated in prison, but a diagnosed psycho-path could be held under mental health legislation as a patient in a special hospital or secure unit.

Reliable criteria for identifying psychopathy are very important in determining the outcome and level of risk for individuals identified as showing persistent offending behaviour. Hare (1986) revised his own version of Cleckley's (1976) psychopathy checklist, which has been developed by Robert Hare into versions such as the *PCL-R* (psycho-pathy checklist revised version), now in its second edition (Hare, 2003). A further version of the revised psychopathy checklist, frequently used in both forensic and non-forensic contexts for efficiency, is the *PCL-SV* or psychopathy checklist – screening version (Hart, Cox and Hare, 1995). These checklists have included items such as superficial charm, emotional immaturity, inability to profit from experience, pathological lying and an inability to maintain relationships. Although studies such as O'Kane, Fawcett and Blackburn (1996) have compared psychopathy checklists and some have favoured alternatives (e.g. Buffington-Vollum et al., 2002), the *PCL-R* and *PCL-SV* have become accepted as the instruments of choice for identifying threshold psychopathy and have proven very useful in determining risk of offending or violence in a range of offenders (e.g. Dolan and Doyle, 2000).

At the end of the twentieth century, the term DSPD was adopted in the UK to represent not only those individuals in high-security or special hospitals but also those serious offenders with personality disorders in prison (Bowers, 2002). This followed public pressure over incidents such as that of Michael Stone, who committed homicide after he was dismissed by psychiatrists due to his personality disorder being considered 'untreatable'. The government proposed provision in between prison and hospital for those with personality disorders who posed a risk to others (Bowers, 2002). This covered any individual who could be assessed as dangerous as a result of their personality problems. DSPD is not a true diagnosis but more a result of government policy (Home Office and Department of Health, 1999) and to some extent was intended to displace the term 'psychopathy' (see Bell et al., 2003). More than half of those known to be DSPD are in prison, with the remaining figure to be found in similar numbers in special hospitals or living in the community (Home Office and Department of Health, 1999). The legal position and liberty of these individuals was an issue of heated and prolonged debate in the early twenty-first century during the revision of the 1983 Mental Health Act, focusing on the issue of detention for the protection of the public.

Risk and public protection

One job of the clinical forensic psychologist is to predict the reoffending risk or dangerousness of offenders with psychopathy or DSPD, as risk assessment needs to be carried out for anyone with persistent mental health or offending problems due for discharge or resettlement into the community (see Prins, 1999). With well-publicised accounts of both patients and offenders being released with tragic consequences, assessment of disordered offenders tends to err on the side of caution, with many who would pose no threat being detained. With an increasing shortage of secure unit and prison places, there has in the past been pressure on those making risk assessments to be *less cautious*. However, psychopathic disorder is mentioned in the UK Mental Health Acts up to 1983 as one of the disorders for which compulsory detention was almost always specified, although many such as Robertson (1992) have argued against this automatic diversion. Thus a situation regarding psychopathy and DSPD parallels Scull's dilemma (referring to psychiatric discharge), i.e. that 'you cannot let them out but you cannot keep them in' (also see Scull, 1999), in that letting these individuals out poses an unacceptable risk to the public, but their being untreatable and not having committed an offence makes detention problematic. Thus, where treatment and rehabilitation are limited but their condition raises their risk to others, detention becomes a purely preventative measure and the primary aim of reform gives way to public protection.

The reform of the UK **1983 Mental Health Act** began at the end of the twentieth century (see Department of Health, 2000). Following a series of draft Mental Health Bills, an amending bill was published in 2006. This 2006 Green Paper was expected to be put before Parliament in its final form in 2007/8. Earlier proposals contained controversial plans to resolve the dilemma posed by psychopathy and DSPD by preventative detention to protect the public, even if no offence had been committed, and with a vague open reference to any form of treatment that may benefit, which critics commented could be superficial and delivered by paraprofessionals (Kinderman, 2002; Edwards, 2002). This led to a compromise between the demands of human rights and liberty groups and the intentions of government to remove the 'treatability' loophole from mental health legislation, which was formulated into a lengthy draft Mental Health Bill in 2004. The published **2006 Mental Health Bill** still contained contentious elements, such as compelling individuals to maintain their treatment in the community or be detained and treated. Issues such as this have been approached in some countries by outreach work for a number of years, such as the community-based forensic treatment programmes in the USA (Heilbrun and Griffin, 1998). Mohan and Fahy (2006) have put the case for **community forensic mental health services** in the UK and Europe reducing monitoring the risk of forensic patients outside of institutional care.

The 2006 bill was criticised for eroding the rights of patients to quell public fears over safety following well-publicised homicides by dangerous patients, such as that of John Barrett, who was only given an hour's leave from a UK secure unit, or more globally, the tragic murder of US psychiatrist Wayne Fenton by a patient in his office (Rosack, 2006). Although a higher proportion of homicides are accounted for by someone with, rather than without, mental illness, the number of stranger homicides by those requiring psychiatric care has not varied greatly during a time period when the total number of stranger homicides has almost doubled (Shaw et al., 2004). Further secondary legislation for the 2006 bill was debated in 2007, again centring on supervision of treatment in the community, as well as preventative detention and the idea that this would dissuade personality disordered individuals from coming forward for treatment for fear of detention. The 2006 Mental Health Bill also addressed the question of risk and the roles of those with the responsibility for monitoring and managing these risks in institutions and the community.

Amendments to the 1983 Mental Health Act have broadened the roles of **approved social workers** and **responsible medical officers** to involve other professionals, and new role titles have been designated as **approved mental health professional** and **clinical supervisor** respectively. Although the encroachment of other professionals into these roles confirms the suspicions of some critics (e.g. Kinderman, 2002), the UK Home Office and Department of Health aim is to provide a wider range of support for all forensic patients seen to be a risk (Department of Health, 2006). This will include DSPD individuals, who will be included in a wider range of treatment possibilities rather than excluded as they were under the old 'treatability test' (i.e. that treatment was not effective, thus they could not be detained). **Mental Health Review Tribunals** continued to oversee the risk of forensic and other patients' release, but would also monitor risk and treatment compliance in the community.

Risk assessment and management is not an exact science, but certainty is unfortunately what the public and politicians tend to expect where public safety is concerned. It is a graded response that tries to balance public protection with the rights of offenders and forensic patients (see Prins, 1999). Clinical forensic psychology is one of the few disciplines that has the knowledge base and skills that apply to most aspects of dealing with dangerous disordered offenders, but it also has its basis in professional psychology, which has often been called upon in matters that balance moral and ethical issues on behalf of the public.

Self-test questions

- How does a typology of stalkers help in their management?
- How does cyberstalking differ from its terrestrial counterpart?
- Why is the crime of rape seldom prosecuted?
- To what extent are the public and media responsible for difficulties in the management of sex offenders?
- What is DSPD and how is it to be managed?
- What are the functions of MAPPA in the twenty-first century?

Focus

Multi-agency public protection arrangements

Many of the publicised incidents involving harm to the public have been attributed to a failure to ensure treatment, but almost all have led to criticism over communication breakdown between the official agencies involved (see Grant, 1999). As a consequence and in addition to the Department of Health provision previously mentioned and the schemes for the registration of violent, dangerous and sexual offenders, a further system of **multi-agency public protection arrangements** (MAPPA) was set up in 2001 in the UK following their legal establishment under the 2000 Criminal Justice and Court Services Act.

MAPPA delivers a statutory framework to enable inter-agency cooperation and coordination directed at the assessment, monitoring and management of violent and sex offenders in England and Wales. Thus in addition to coordinating those directly responsible such as prison, police and probation, other agencies, including less obvious ones such as housing departments, can help in the communication chain by providing information that ensures much closer supervision of dangerous offenders.

MAPPA was reinforced by the 2003 Criminal Justice Act introducing a 'duty to cooperate' for the agencies involved, but also made the process subject to public scrutiny. Around 1 in 20 of the offenders covered by MAPPA were considered high risk and subject to more intensive scrutiny by a **Multi-Agency Public Protection Panel** (MAPPP), which consists of representatives from the agencies for that area (see Wood, 2006). The level of risk can vary between identifiable groups of these high-risk offenders, and similarly, not all members of the public are at the same level of risk from this offender population (Wood, 2006).

Chapter summary

The case example of **anonymous missives** illustrates the often unusual behaviour studied in the hybrid discipline of **clinical forensic psychology**. A focal part of this area is the abnormal offender and the relationship between crime and mental disorder, often termed the **mad–bad debate**. Research in this area has considered the idea of psychological differences or disorders leading to crime. These approaches have often been the basis for theories of crime causation. These theories consider biological and psychological causes, from basic physical features put forward by **Lombroso** in the nineteenth century, through to abnormalities of brain structure and function discovered by **Adrian Raine**. Other approaches to criminality have examined **body build, genetics, personality theory** applied to crime, the **XYY** sex-chromosome abnormality, Bowlby's **maternal deprivation, moral development, differential association theory** of learned criminality and, more recently, **neural abnormalities, evolution** and disorders such as **attention deficit hyperactivity disorder, conduct disorder** and **psychopathy**.

Psychological profilers produce the psychological characteristics of offenders from the characteristics of the crime in the hope of limiting the search for suspects. Originating in the USA with the **FBI**, profiling has spread to the UK in a more psychologically based form, and although it claims some successes there are many failures, much controversy and a lack of empirical evaluation. Profilers are part of a team of crime scene analysts, and some **crime scene investigators** will specialise in other sciences, such as the analysis of **DNA** or **ballistics**. Some offenders lie closer to the remit of clinical forensic psychologists and present a challenge to societies and their health and justice systems worldwide. These include stalkers, sex offenders and psychopathic or DSPD (dangerous and severe personality disorder) individuals.

Stalking or harassing behaviour is difficult to define as a crime and has only recently been legislated against in many countries. Types of stalker defined by **Paul Mullen** have helped to clarify differing approaches to the crime, and research has revealed the extreme suffering of victims of stalking, some of whom may be further stressed by their own professional rules. **Cyberstalking** has extended the frequency and scope of stalking, and can be distinguished from its terrestrial counterpart in a number of ways. **Sex offenders** such as rapists, and paraphilic offenders, including those who offend against children, tend to be viewed as a homogeneous group by the public and media, who vilify this difficult offender group, confounding attempts at sex offender management. **Psychopathy** is an enigmatic disorder which does not conform to the usual view of mental disorder and has been described as **moral insanity**, with only the arguable 'treatability' of the disorder distinguishing the psychopath from any **dangerous offender**. The term **DSPD** has been introduced to represent the majority of offenders seen as a constant danger to others due to personality distortions. Current mental health legislation in the UK continues to struggle with constitutionally disordered individuals who pose a risk to others, but who may not have committed an offence that would warrant continuous detention. As the areas of clinical and forensic psychology overlap considerably, the relatively new discipline of clinical forensic psychology has yet to delineate its boundaries clearly, and much of the material allocated elsewhere in this text could be added to this chapter.

Suggested essay questions

- Discuss the similarities and distinctions between early and more recent biological positivist approaches to criminality.
- Critically assess the usefulness of criminal profiling to serial crime investigation.
- Critically discuss the practical value of typologies of stalkers.

Further reading

Overview texts

Boon, J., and Sheridan, L. (2002) *Stalking and psychosexual obsession: Psychological perspectives for prevention, policing and treatment.* Chichester: Wiley.

Gallagher, R. (2001) *I'll be watching you: True stories of stalkers and their victims.* London: Virgin.

Jackson, J. L., and Bekerian, D. A. (1997) *Offender profiling: Theory, research and practice.* Chichester: Wiley.

Mullen, P. E., Pathe, M., and Purcell, R. (2000) *Stalkers and their victims.* Cambridge: Cambridge University Press.

Thomas, T. (2000) *Sex crime, sex offending and society.* Cullompton, Devon: Willan.

Walker, N. (1996) *Dangerous people.* London: Blackstone.

Specific and more critical texts

Ainsworth, P. B. (2001) *Offender profiling and crime analysis.* Cullompton, Devon: Willan.

Blair, J., Mitchell, D., and Blair, K. (2005) *The psychopath: Emotion and the brain.* Oxford: Blackwell.

Department of Health (2006) *Plans to amend the Mental Health Act 1983.* London: HMSO.

Prins, H. (1999) *Will they do it again? Risk assessment and management in criminal justice and psychiatry.* London: Routledge.

Prins, H. (2005) *Offenders, deviants or patients?* (3rd edn). London: Routledge.

Raine, A. (2002) Biosocial studies of antisocial and violent behaviour in children and adults: A review. *Journal of Abnormal Child Psychology*, **30**(4), 311–26.

Warden, J. (1999) Ashworth report confirms problems with special hospitals. *British Medical Journal*, **318**, 211.

Webb, D., and Harris, R. (1999) *Mentally disordered offenders: Managing people nobody owns.* London: Routledge.

Visit **www.pearsoned.co.uk/davidholmes** for a range of resources to support study. Test yourself with multiple choice questions and access a bank of over 100 videos that will bring the topics to life. Video coverage for this chapter includes a discussion of the pathology of learning violence and a demonstration of the classic Bandura Bobo doll experiment.

DISORDERS BEGINNING EARLIER IN LIFE

Part 3 of this textbook will examine those disorders that tend to have their onset earlier in life and may persist into adulthood. This cannot be an absolute rule as there are many exceptions, such as some phobic disorders that have their onset in adulthood (although predisposing autonomic sensitivity may have been present since childhood).

Logically, this part is headed by Chapter 9 on specifically childhood disorders, featuring those disorders that present in these early years, such as autism, or are confined to childhood by diagnostic criteria, as in the case of conduct disorder. Disorders where there is an impulsive or addictive element are divided between Chapter 10, exploring impulsive and compulsive behavioural disorders, and the area of substance disorders and addiction in Chapter 11. A wide range of anxiety disorders include post-traumatic stress disorder, which has been a particular focus for clinical psychology in the last 20 years, and one of the most intractable psychiatric disorders, obsessive–compulsive disorder.

Sexual disorders in Chapter 13 have their origins in childhood but tend to become more evident in adolescence and early adulthood. Included in these disorders are dysfunctions, which affect a high percentage of the population at some time in their lives and the paraphilias. The latter are mostly considered as forensic issues and include the predilection towards sexual crimes. There is also forensic interest in some of those individuals with personality disorders covered in Chapter 14, especially the 'cluster B' disorders and the allied construct of psychopathy. Personality disorders are common, with a collective prevalence of more than 10 per cent of the population, and are difficult to treat. Chapter 15 covers somatoform and dissociative disorder, which have historical links to the psychoanalytic paradigm. There are reasons to question the validity of some of the cases within these *DSM* disorders, particularly their means of diagnosis. Chapter 15 also includes factitious disorders, including Munchausen syndrome by proxy, in which forensic procedures are normally essential.

Chapters in this section

9   Disorders usually first diagnosed in infancy and childhood

Follow a 'day in the life' of David who suffers from Asperger's. This is one of explore videos that explore issues and disorders relevant to this chapter at **www.pearsoned.co.uk/davidholmes**

10   Disorders of control and addiction Part I: Eating and impulse disorders

Watch this interview with Jessica, who suffers from anorexia nervosa. This is one of several videos that explore issues and disorders relevant to this chapter at **www.pearsoned.co.uk/davidholmes**

11   Disorders of control and addiction Part II: Substance-related disorders

Hear about the physical and psychological effects of cocaine. This is one of several videos that explore issues and disorders relevant to this chapter at **www.pearsoned.co.uk/davidholmes**

12   Anxiety disorders

Watch Bonnie discuss the impact of post traumatic stress disorder. This is one of several videos that explore issues and disorders relevant to this chapter at **www.pearsoned.co.uk/davidholmes**

13   Sexual disorders

Hear Jade discuss her role as a dominatrix. This is one of several videos that explore issues and disorders relevant to this chapter at **www.pearsoned.co.uk/davidholmes**

14   Personality disorders

Watch this interview with Liz who suffers from borderline personality disorder. This is one of several videos that explore issues and disorders relevant to this chapter at **www.pearsoned.co.uk/davidholmes**

15   Somatoform, dissociative and factitious disorders

Watch this classic footage of 'Eve' in her three dissociative states. This is one of several videos that explore issues and disorders relevant to this chapter at **www.pearsoned.co.uk/davidholmes**

CHAPTER 9 Disorders usually first diagnosed in infancy and childhood

- Overview
- Case study
- Development and disorder
- Pervasive developmental disorders: the autistic spectrum
- Attention-deficit and disruptive behaviour disorders
- Other disorders beginning in childhood
- Clinical and forensic issues
- Chapter summary

Follow a 'day in the life' of David who suffers from Asperger's. This is one of explore videos that explore issues and disorders relevant to this chapter at www.pearsoned.co.uk/davidholmes.

Autism and Asperger's syndrome

When **Dustin Hoffman** portrayed the part of the adult **autistic savant** called 'Raymond', corrupted to 'Rain man', in the film *Rain Man* (Levinson, 1988), many of the viewing public had their interest in this enigmatic disorder amplified. Although they were left with the correct impression of obsessive inflexibility, many assumed that all autistic individuals had **savant** abilities and could defeat Las Vegas card tables! However, the film did convey the inevitability of autistic children becoming adults with the same traits. A similarly endearing effect was produced by the novel *The Curious Incident of the Dog in the Night-time* (Haddon, 2003), which showed mechanical introspection or 'geek-like behaviour', such as obsession with mathematical puzzles, as endearing features of an autistic boy. The story is told from the point of view of the boy, Christopher, as he tries to understand the alien world of non-autistic adults. In the twenty-first century, the geek-like behaviour of males involved in computer technology may be seen as showing an autistic trait (Baron-Cohen, 2002). However, in the world of computers mild aspects of such traits can be highly successful, such as in **Bill Gates**' highly successful work, as was the full disorder in the notorious abilities of the Asperger's hacker **Gary McKinnon**.

Many **high-functioning** real-world autistic or Asperger individuals have fascinated the public, such as **Temple Grandin** or the singer-songwriter **Gary Numan**, as their approach to their world seems intriguingly different, yet emphasises a relentlessly inquisitive and impersonal trait within us all. In this chapter the enigma of autism or Asperger's disorder is explained as a lifelong biological disorder producing a different way of conceptualising the world (also see Tantam, 2009). A curious footnote to media interest in the autistic spectrum is that the individual on which Dustin Hoffman's part in *Rain Man* was based, **Kim Peek**, was rediagnosed in 2008 as having an X-chromosome abnormality (Opitz, Smith and Santoro, 2008), not autism.

Autism is still a mysterious disorder that attracts more research than other, more common, disorders.
Source: Pearson Online Database.

Overview

This chapter will consider aspects of development that can lead to disorders and further factors that can confound diagnosis, including the older work on **attachment** and **maternal deprivation**. In **autistic spectrum disorders**, the focus is mostly on autism – a relatively rare disorder that is common in the literature and with an as yet unclear **aetiology**. It is also difficult to treat, especially in severe cases but the challenge of autism has shed light on traits in the general population, such as certain traits of 'maleness' (Baron-Cohen, 2002). Other **pervasive developmental disorders** in the autistic spectrum range include **Asperger's disorder**, a less disabling disorder related to autism.

Attention-deficit hyperactivity disorder (ADHD) is controversial in terms of its prevalence, and challenging for carers and clinician. Clinical and forensic psychologists have a role to play in this disorder in terms of making home and education manageable, as well as averting a tendency to engage in criminal behaviour (Satterfield et al., 1994). These forensic implications apply to children with **conduct disorder**, which is defined by antisocial acts and as such is seen as a precursor to **anti-social personality disorder** (see Chapter 14). A number of other childhood diagnoses are covered in this chapter, including learning disabilities, feeding and tic disorders, all of which have a substantial psychological component to their expression or treatment. Clinically common disorders such as **depression** and **anxiety** in childhood have been omitted, as there are chapters dedicated to these disorders in adults. However, these disorders are important to be aware of in children and may show some differences in expression or treatment. A number of childhood disorders have forensic implications, which are very important in preventing the development of long-term adult criminality.

Case study
Charles, a good baby

Charles was a very 'good' baby as he very rarely cried and did not demand attention. His mother thought this and his reluctance to be cuddled might have been some sort of compensation for the painful and complicated birth that heralded his arrival. As Charles grew, his apparent indifference to others became a source of worry to his mother, though his father thought this was just his 'personality', as the father's own brother had been unsociable as a child, and quite isolated and eccentric as an adult. By the time her friends' babies had been putting two-word phrases together, Charles had not shown any interest in speaking or in his mother's numerous attempts at creating some rapport. This upset his mother, who began to feel rejected by the child and tried to shun thoughts of serious illness in her child. Despite having had his hearing tested at a clinic, his mother returned to her GP twice claiming that Charles must be deaf, whilst secretly fearing he might be brain damaged. Her GP explained that Charles did not react normally to sound but was not deaf. The experienced family doctor became concerned that Charles might be developmentally delayed and that the cause might be neurological, but did not reveal this to the mother, trying to allay her worries.

Working on his experience of similar problems, the GP made an appointment with a psychiatrist known for his research into infant disorders. Charles's mother was at last satisfied that 'something was being done', but had reservations about attending a psychiatric outpatients unit, feeling that her son was not mentally ill. After a few follow-up appointments, the decision was made that Charles was autistic and his mother and father were given information on what the disorder was, what to expect and how to cope in practical terms. Charles's father was a little uneasy with some of the symptoms listed for autism, as they paralleled his own behaviour, particularly his habit of working alone in his study at home as a software analyst for most of the day. They were put in touch with a number of organisations offering support and advice, and Charles was also placed on a (rather long) waiting list to attend a special day school.

CASE STUDY CONTINUED

Charles was a very attractive boy with a strange aloofness, always seeming 'distant' when in company. This 'distance' could be literal when they had guests; Charles would enter the room and sit by the door watching the seconds hand of the clock (as he often did) and never making eye contact. His mother was thankful that Charles was an exceptional case of autism in not being notably retarded and having gained the use of one or two words by the time he was 5 years old. He rarely used these words, one of which was entirely his own. For Charles, 'golead' was the family dog and was probably a contraction of his father's words in addressing the dog with 'go get your lead!' Charles would stare at his hands for long periods of time but still showed little interest in other children, or others in general. He was never sociable unless he wanted something and then would stare fixedly at the object without speaking or looking at his mother.

For about a year, life became very difficult for Charles's mother as a result of sudden tantrums in public (for reasons known only to Charles), a similar reaction to any change in routine, and a number of odd mannerisms and embarrassing 'comfort motions', as his mother called them. At one point his mother felt she was a prisoner within her own home and his father began to 'work away' more often. A clinical psychologist introduced a number of behavioural measures to moderate this behaviour, which over time became reasonably successful in changing the rather stubborn behaviour. However, Charles's mother felt that ignoring her son's demands and tantrums went against her 'instincts', and she occasionally subverted the treatments. When Charles finally entered special school his tantrums at home worsened, but they almost disappeared when his mother complied fully with the school professional's suggestions.

As he matured, Charles did not lose some of his less sociable habits of stimulating himself, but these became more inhibited outside the home due to the strict regimes in place at school. He had subtle peculiarities of behaviour that other neighbourhood children found fascinating, such as rubbing the corners of books with his fingers and ritually sniffing them. Charles's sense of smell seemed very important in his exploration of the world. He also memorised all of the types of bird's eggs found in his area and would collect live specimens, much to his parents' disapproval. Charles also had a fascination with the internal components of electrical appliances, which littered his room in a bizarrely organised series of boxes. Charles's outstanding talent was related to his habitual need to visit post offices in nearby villages and walk around the adjoining streets in an obsessive manner. On returning home he drew remarkably well-scaled maps of the areas he had visited, but always with a 2B pencil on his mother's letter paper.

Charles did not have much interest in girls as a teenager and never had a girlfriend as such. However, he did develop an obsession for a few months, in which he noted down his estimate of bra sizes of girls he saw and kept these records carefully with girth and cup size but no other detail, seeming to use the numbers to identify girls he thought 'important'. The 'hobby' came to an abrupt end when Charles made a sudden attempt to physically check his estimate. Charles's other hobby of taking old transistor radios apart and putting the components into different cardboard boxes offered a much safer, though even less sociable alternative hobby to his numerical approach to females. Since his mother has been ill, Charles has lived in a hostel and supplements his keep by putting junk mail in envelopes. He slowly folds each pamphlet into its envelope and carefully stacks them into neat piles of exactly 11 envelopes.

Actual cases of **autism** vary greatly in severity and can be difficult to differentiate from other problem behaviours early in life without expertise. The case of Charles illustrates many of the facets of this intriguing disorder and how these features require insight into autism not to be misinterpreted or mismanaged.

Development and disorder

Covering the period from birth to 16 years of age by most diagnostic criteria (American Psychiatric Association, 2000), childhood disorders are not always detected at the time of their onset for a number of reasons, such as the following.

- Children do not possess the same degree of insight that adults have into their own mental functioning.

- Children lack the ability to communicate effectively about these states and rely on carers (mainly parents) to be their **advocates** in seeking help.

- There may be reluctance on the part of a carer to admit that a child has a mental disorder, as the carer may feel it reflects on their parenting skills.

- Additionally, professionals may be reluctant to place a damning label on one so young until they are absolutely certain of their judgement.

Although there is no clear division between the types of disorder affecting children and adults, there are **confounding factors** to be considered when the onset is early in life. Children do not arrive complete with an instruction manual, and few parents are fully trained prior to a child's birth. The areas of parenting and other important life skills are an embarrassing omission in the education systems of many countries. It is difficult to consider a very young child's behaviour in isolation from their immediate carer due to the close interaction between them (Sameroff and Emde, 1989). A child and its carer adjust to one another's behaviour and any sudden *change* in the child's behaviour may alert the carer to the possibility that there is something wrong. However, normal children's behaviour can be quite aberrant at times; they may wet the bed or have a tantrum without having developed a disorder. Children are often more self-centred or egocentric than adults and thus more prone to behaviour that infringes the rights of others or that may be labelled criminal in an adult. These behaviour problems are often transient or intermittent rather than increasing or persistent (Kendall, 2000). Thus, we should be cautious about bringing children into the forensic or clinical domain prematurely, but this does not mean carers should tolerate such behaviour.

Amongst others, Krueger et al. (1998) refer to externalising disorders where behaviour is outward affecting others (e.g. **conduct disorder**), and **internalising disorders**, such as depression, where behaviour is thought to be directed inward towards the self. This conceptual division works well in examining the *effects* of childhood behaviour and as such is used routinely by behaviourally oriented clinicians. However, it tends to imply an unsupported Freudian aetiology for each type of abnormal behaviour and as a consequence will not be referred to in this text. However, it is recognised that some abnormal behaviour causes more suffering to others, with important forensic implications, and that other behaviour leads to greater distress in the sufferer, with important clinical implications. These are not mutually exclusive, as a child who is abusive to others will ultimately suffer alienation, conflict and reduced opportunity itself, and a depressed child will produce distress in those close to them.

Parents and professionals will also anticipate some behavioural and biological **milestones** as part of normal **maturation**. For example, if a child fails to talk by a certain age, the carer will become increasingly anxious about such an indicator of abnormal development and the child may also be disturbed by the carer's anxious state. Thus the interaction between child and carer can amplify (or moderate) the problems of either. Parenting styles will directly affect a child's behaviour and may encourage abnormal behaviour, but they cannot cause biologically based disorders such as **childhood schizophrenia**. Clearly, parenting at extremes of care, such as **neglect** or hypochondriasis by proxy (respectively, lack of concern and over-concern with a child's welfare), will result in aberrant behaviour. However, less extreme parenting can also result in abnormal behaviour, such as a child's behaviour being disturbed by significant events in their life, such as a family bereavement, moving home or inevitable hurdles like starting school. Although most children exhibit adverse reactions to these events, it is prolonged or profound reactions that indicate underlying problems (Rutter, 1991).

The process of maturation is an interaction between **genetic expectation** and **environmental conditions**, and disturbance in early childhood can have its effect magnified by disrupting or retarding normal development, making the longer-term effects of disorder more profound than onset in adulthood. However, human development is a resilient and adaptive process designed to survive in adversity with contingency genetic programming, which has a way of guiding development back on course. In addition and because there is more potential for change during development, abnormal behaviour that is resistant to change in an adult may be altered during the relative plasticity of childhood.

The paradigms in abnormal psychology described in Chapter 3 apply to both adult and childhood onset disorders, but they are arguably more influential in childhood. Some examples may illustrate this view.

- **Biological** changes that take place during childhood are far more rapid and profound than those that occur in adult life. Children have to adapt to a changing body-image, hormonal turmoil and neural development, which constantly alter their relationship with the world in which they live. Thus, abnormal behaviour needs to be interpreted with reference to this biological instability, particularly in adolescence when hormonal influences can have a pronounced effect on behaviour and emotion in the absence of much outwardly obvious physical change.

■ **Behavioural** learning is at its peak in childhood and much maladaptive behaviour is inadvertently encouraged and fears created. The parent who responds to a child's tantrum with attention and giving in to the child's demands should also accept the blame when tantrums become a way of life for the child as it becomes older (and larger). An adult carer with a debilitating fear of spiders should seek professional help *before* their child picks up on the fear and develops the phobia itself. There is no period of life when a greater impression can be made on behaviour and being a responsible parent means taking responsibility for this process.

■ **Genetic-evolutionary** influences on behaviour are often 'invisible' to parents and professionals in the course of normal development, as we are habituated to them as unquestioned 'normal behaviour'. However, these familiar patterns seem all the more alien when abnormality disrupts them. Genetic disruption of frontal lobe development can produce an apparently bright child but with serious moral and behavioural deficits, perhaps leading to cruel acts and criminal behaviour. Even in the absence of genetic abnormality, early evolutionarily adaptive bonding with a close carer may be disrupted with effects on the child's future ability to form relationships as will be described below.

Attachment theory and maternal deprivation

John Bowlby's (1908–1990) theory of attachment in humans (Bowlby, 1951) was grounded in the psychodynamic paradigm (see Chapter 3) but drew heavily on the more empirical findings of ethologists such as Konrad Lorenz. Lorenz amongst others had demonstrated **imprinting** in geese and other animals. The newborn chick imprints, or forms a remembered image, of the first moving object it senses and stays in close proximity to what normally turns out to be its carer (usually the mother); more controversially, it may use this imprinted image as a template for a mate in later life. Lorenz assumed this process would have a human parallel. Bowlby also recognised that humans have a very long childhood and are ill-prepared for survival at birth, in contrast with those species that

are born independent. Mary Ainsworth's studies of close reciprocating interactions between a mother and her young child have demonstrated how this selective bond provides a template for much of the growing infant's social behaviour. As a close colleague, Ainsworth has related her work to support Bowlby's theories of attachment (see Ainsworth, 1989).

In a primitive environment, Bowlby considered that this secure physical and emotional attachment in the early years would be vital to the survival of an infant human. Even within contemporary civilisation, he considered that such a bond would be essential for psychological health. He combined this thinking with studies of apes as near relatives of humans. In a series of studies, Harlow (1959) raised rhesus monkeys with artificial surrogate 'mothers' (made of wire or towelling), or an empty cage. In what would be viewed today as cruel experiments, Harlow revealed the damage caused by **maternal privation** (the animals never had a real mother in order to experience deprivation). These monkeys did not develop affectionate relations with others and became poor mothers themselves in later life. Bowlby found parallels in his own study of '44 juvenile thieves' (Bowlby, 1944), where 17 of his 'thieves' had been separated from their carers in comparison with only 2 controls from the same London child guidance clinic (see Dixon, 2003). Thus most children with a history of separation were described as delinquents with the forensic and clinical implications of an '**affectionless character**', which Bowlby has compared with the effects seen in Harlow's experimental monkeys.

Bowlby extrapolated that this disruption of the bond with the primary carer, normally the mother, was profoundly damaging to a human child – a syndrome he labelled **maternal deprivation**. His emphasis on the importance of a secure and unbroken bond between child and its nearest carer led to changes in hospitals and prisons in keeping mother and young child together. For Bowlby (1951; 1980), maternal deprivation in the early years (from 6 months to 6 years of age) leads to greater levels of mental disorder and criminal behaviour in later life, as exemplified by the 'affectionless character'. Bowlby's work is not without its critics (e.g. Rutter, 1991), although even these authors accept that early bonds are important and continue to produce evidence of the effects of early deprivation (e.g. O'Connor et al., 2000). Animal studies have produced some hormonal underpinnings for the effects of maternal deprivation in the activity of corticotrophin releasing systems, which are related to stress reactions (Ladd, Owens and Nemeroff, 1996). The disruption of attachment described by Bowlby has been aligned with **reactive attachment disorder**, although the latter term encompasses more diverse causes and outcomes (Zeanah, 2000). In addition to not

Early, unethical, experiments with rhesus monkeys established the damaging effects of maternal privation.
Source: Getty Images/Time and Life Pictures.

making affectionate bonds, such children are also prone to inappropriate relationships and overdependency as they mature. Preparation before separation and a supportive post-separation environment can ameliorate the effects of maternal deprivation and symptoms of reactive attachment disorder (Rutter, 1979; 1991).

Other problems of attachment concern the overuse of this parent–child bond, usually due to a parent's over-dependency on the child and a refusal to allow the growing individual sufficient independence to become a secure adult (see Rutter, 1997). As referred to in the next subsection, there is a tendency for parents to make children over-dependent on them, creating young adults who are unable to leave the parental home and who may not only become dependent on parental support but also pathologically bonded emotionally. The parent's emotional dependence on the child can lead to relationship problems for both generations.

As a species we tend to be overly protective of our children, viewing them as vulnerable, innocent individuals surrounded by predatory adults. This view often leads to the child being brought up with little experience of dealing with the real world and perhaps suffering as a consequence. This move to overprotection almost always involves children least at risk, with those at greatest risk receiving least protection. In recent times this protective approach has been incorporated into a **child-centred** policy for dealing with families across most welfare, health and justice systems, which can produce tyrannical, self-indulgent children and lead to some families being governed by a child's inexperience and lack of responsibility rather than being led by a responsible, experienced adult. On the other side of this failure to empower children effectively, there

Focus

Family systems theory

This approach sees the family as a dynamic and functional unit, which is self-regulating with its own rules and individual characteristics (see Chapter 2). Change in a relationship within the family affects all members, and the family unit may remain upset until normal interactional forces return it to a state of equilibrium. According to this approach, a child within a dysfunctional family suffers due to the *inflexibility* of its dynamics, unequal power relationships within it and the family's inability to adapt to changing demands of its membership.

Other family approaches are those that consider **family communications theory**, looking at the style of communication between members, and **family structural theory**, examining dysfunctional family structures, such as members 'ganging up' on other individuals in the family. There are also helpful aspects to interactions in families and factors such as shared positive experiences and the way experiences are propagated within and outside the family (e.g. Rutter, 1999). Families are also seen as therapeutic in providing a social support group, which is often lacking in many isolated disordered individuals (Mawson, Grounds and Tantam, 1985).

are the increased numbers of reports of **abuse** of children who are bullied into silence.

Thus, the background to mental disorders beginning in childhood is somewhat chaotic, confounded by developmental factors and centred on a time of conflict between dependency and the process of becoming independent. In the following sections, the current classifications of childhood disorders will be examined in brief and illustrated by a detailed focus on the **pervasive developmental disorders** of **autism** and **Asperger's disorder**, and **attention deficit hyperactivity disorder**.

Pervasive developmental disorders: the autistic spectrum

The symptoms of pervasive developmental disorders (PDDs) pervade most aspects of the affected individual's life, persisting into later life. **Communication** and **social functioning** are most affected in PDDs, with the addition of stereotyped behaviour and restricted interests. Autism has come to characterise the pervasive developmental disorders, possibly as a result of there being more literature on and public interest in this disorder, such as film *Rain Man* (Levinson, 1988) and the novel *The Curious Incident of the Dog in the Night-time* (Haddon, 2003).

Autism

Phenomenology, diagnosis and prognosis of autism

Wolf-Schein (1996) notes that, although rare, autism is one of the most discussed and researched developmental disorders, which raises the issue: why is such a rare condition the focus of so much academic attention? The answer probably lies in the intrigue that autistic symptoms create for non-autistic people: the selectivity of disrupted function in a child who outwardly appears to be so normal. The aloof, enigmatic, often physically attractive child that withdraws from social interaction and inhabits its own idiosyncratic, mechanical, wordless world has fascinated professionals and public.

The term 'autism' was used by Bleuler (1911) when referring to the withdrawn behaviour in some cases of schizophrenia, what we would now term **negative syndrome schizophrenia** (see Chapter 18). **Leo Kanner** (1943)

adopted the term to describe a group of children who 'have come into the world with innate inability to form the usual, biologically provided affective contact with people' (Kanner, 1943: p. 250). Kanner initially used his own name to label what he saw as an undiscovered disorder as **Kanner's syndrome**, substituting **early infant autism** the following year. The confusion caused by name changes and the use of the term beyond Bleuler's original application was exacerbated by autism being labelled as a '**childhood psychosis**' (as some authors still do) and it not being differentiated from **childhood schizophrenia** in early classificatory systems. Thus, some early publications have erroneously referred to autism as 'childhood schizophrenia', whereas the two disorders are different: for example, there are no hallucinations or delusions in autism and onset is earlier.

In 1980 autism was finally recognised as a distinct disorder in *DSM-III* and it is listed in *DSM-IV-TR* and *ICD-10* as a **pervasive developmental disorder** (PDD), along with the very similar **Asperger's disorder**. Szatmari (1992) has considered the evidence for an '**autistic spectrum disorder**' to cover *non-autistic* diagnoses that are within the pervasive developmental disorder category. In the UK, parents of children with autism and related conditions prefer to refer to their children as being in the 'autistic spectrum' rather than having a PDD (Wing, 1996). This has encouraged the widespread use of this term in Europe, which has led to some initial confusion over diagnostic boundaries, in the same manner as the euphemistic extension of the term **learning disability** in practice to incorporate **mental retardation**, again initiated in the UK, created conflict with established diagnostic categories. Tantam (2009) has examined the use of the term 'autistic spectrum' in detail.

Wing and Potter (2002) have examined the rate of autism in the general population and considered the apparent rise in its prevalence from the time it was first described by Kanner in 1943. At that time the prevalence of the disorder was estimated at 2–4 cases per 10,000 individuals, although subsequent studies have produced rates of around 60 cases per 10,000. However, Wing and Potter (2002) have made it clear that the apparent change in prevalence is not due to a sudden increase in incidence of the disorder itself. They attribute the rising figure to factors such as increased awareness of the autistic spectrum, better diagnostic criteria and changes in referral practices since 1970, before which many cases of autism were not differentiated from other learning disabled children. However, Wing (1996) acknowledged that an increased risk of certain inter-uterine viral factors associated with autism may have been facilitated by increased migration across Europe.

Research

Autism as an extreme male trait

Autism affects 4–5 times more males than females (Volkmar, Szatmari and Sparrow, 1993), which has drawn attention to the 'maleness' of some characteristics of autism, such as fascination with inanimate objects and lack of social interaction. In researching the disorder from this perspective, Baron-Cohen (2002) has referred to the 'extreme male brain' of autistic individuals, in that they are more interested in mechanical objects than the average male and far more than females in general, based on evidence from studies of the non-autistic relatives of autistic individuals.

Autistic traits include a fascination with numbers and an acute ability to spot mathematical regularities, such as that if 1 April is a Tuesday so is 1 July. These traits and abilities are often found in mild forms in the relatives of autistic individuals, which is one adaptive evolutionary reason for the survival of the genes that lead to the disorder. Baron-Cohen et al., (1998) found autism to be more commonly reported in families of professional engineers, mathematicians and physicists, to some degree confirming the presence of these genetic traits in the relatives of autistic children in whom they are extreme. These professions of relatives are considered to be 'male' characteristics and are increasingly adaptive in the cybertechnological world of the twenty-first century.

The neurology of this 'male' characteristic (see the Research box) is probably responsible for the so-called **autistic savant** (once referred to as 'idiot savant'), which is an autistic individual who displays one or more 'special abilities' that seem out of keeping with the level of functioning of the sufferer. Contrary to popular belief, these abilities are only notable in about 10 per cent of individuals as a 'by-product' of autism and relate to the mechanical, impersonal and obsessive interests mentioned above. Examples of these significant abilities are: exceptional mathematical abilities; musical performances; meticulous reproduction of complex geometric shapes as artwork; and the ability to memorise large lists (e.g. dates, names or numbers). The repetitive nature and lack of creativity or emotional content can be evident in complex musical performances by savants, which are often delivered with the same lack of emotional involvement as computer-generated music. It has been suggested that specialist areas of the brain that fail to be fully developed for language are utilised for such interests, to some degree accounting for the trade-off between social and mechanical abilities.

Autism is usually diagnosed at 2–3 years of age, although the child has often seemed 'odd' from birth (Rutter, 1974). For a diagnosis, onset should be before 3 years of age, which may need to be a retrospective diagnosis due to the difficulties in making such a serious decision about one so young. Family doctors are usually the first point of contact for an autistic child, and as a consequence need to be aware of the current criteria for preliminary identification of the disorder and its differentiation from other childhood conditions (Blake 2005).

Wing and Gould (1979) identified the **autistic triad** of impairments characterising autism, which are the major areas used for diagnosis. The child will show deficits in the areas of social interaction, communication and flexible thought.

Social interaction

The autistic child withdraws from social contact and fails to form relationships even in the absence of mental retardation, which is **comorbid** with autism in 80 per cent of cases (scoring less than 70 on IQ tests), i.e. is not part of its diagnosis. The autistic infant does not 'engage' when being held, avoiding eye contact, and does not seek attention (Holmes, 1994). They often form attachments to inanimate objects, which are far removed from the 'cuddly toys' of normal children. Instead items such as bricks and mechanical parts become their 'attachment objects'. The autistic child tends to engage in repetitive activity with these objects in place of the increasingly symbolic play of normally developing children. Kanner observed an '**extreme autistic aloneness**' in these children, an isolation that extends into adulthood. As Tantam (1988) observed, however, when the older autistic individual *does* show any interest in others, they drastically lack the cumulative social skills needed to maintain relatedness. In place of social skills they have often developed displacement behaviours, which are socially undesirable. Fluent social interaction does not come naturally to the autistic child. When social exchanges are possible, they are often consciously constructed from 'rules' used to synthesise a 'mathematical copy' of the way others relate, often utilising the autistic individual's excellent rote memory. This can lead to very idiosyncratic behaviour, which is only explicable when one is aware of this 'socialising by numbers' process.

Autistic individuals tend to be object orientated but socially or people avoidant, and are usually happiest when alone. Thus they tend to relate to 'people as objects' rather than as human beings, in what have been called 'cat-like' attachments as opposed to the 'dog-like' attachments of non-autistic people (see Hobson, 1986). Cats tend to be as friendly to a chair leg as they are to human touch, whereas dogs tend to be more 'personable' in relating to humans. Thus, an autistic child tends to be indifferent to other people, perceiving them as unpredictable objects in their obsessively predictable world. Even with more able autistic adults, social encounters are started and ended abruptly with little social use of gaze, which tends to be used instrumentally to obtain things. These deficits can lead to forensic involvement due to autistic indifference to the emotional states and non-verbal signals of other people (see the section on forensic issues, pp. 279–81). This indifference can be exacerbated by communication difficulties.

Communication

Mutual attention is a basic requirement for communication. The autistic infant avoids eye-contact and shared attention, and usually shows severe deficits in verbal and non-verbal communication development. Pre-speech utterances are more infrequent and less related to the communication of information in autistic infants (Ricks, 1972). Only half of autistic people learn to speak, and those who achieve language use often fail actually to use it, or use it abnormally. Clearly if the child lacks any interest in others, they also lack any interest in communicating with them. The development of some speech by the age of 5 years signifies a good prognosis in terms of autism. Conversational speech in autism may be dependent on memorising phrases and may simply stop abruptly when the conversation is expected to progress. The language they do develop often has distinctive features.

- Echolalia is the phonologically accurate repeating of sounds, usually speech. This provides a key to other language peculiarities in autism, as the form of echolalia resembles 'digital sampling' of sound. Autistic individuals repeat words and phrases parrot fashion rather than constructing them, and use the same intonation and phrasing. This can sometimes precipitate misunderstanding if the recipient does not realise the phrase is 'copied'; they may be offended or misjudge the intellectual level of the sufferer. Thus autistic individuals make good mimics but very poor impersonators. In delayed echolalia the repetition may occur hours or weeks after the original sound. Autistic individuals also tend to use non-echolalic speech repetitively, particularly intrusive questioning, which can greatly annoy or distract carers (Howlin, 1997a). Condon (1975) observed a delayed multiple response to sound in children with autistic symptoms, which may indicate a neural underpinning to their obsession with echo-like repetition.

- Pronoun reversal is where the autistic individual will refer to himself or herself as 'he', 'she' or 'you' instead of 'I' or 'me'. This is probably a product of echolalia: in other words, they refer to themselves in the exactly the same way they hear others talk to them. Thus an autistic child hearing a mother ask, 'where is Peter?' is likely to reply, 'Peter is here.'

- Neologisms are 'new words' or words with a novel application. In autism this again is related to echolalia, in that the new words are often repeated verbatim or synthesised from others' speech when referring to the thing they have now come to represent, as with 'golead' in the case study above. Thus an autistic individual's speech comes to be littered with idiosyncratic associations, forming their own personal variations on language.

- **Non-verbal deficits** are evident in their verbalisations as well as their movements, which are fewer and confounded by mannerisms. Speech may be monotone and repetitive, and will often form a monologue, ignoring the attempts of others to interrupt. They are poor at understanding and responding to the non-verbal communications of others (Holmes, 1994; Tantam et al., 1989).

Flexible thinking

This is restricted in autism, especially in childhood at the time when it is well developed in normal children. This is very evident in play, which requires second order thinking (see Frith, Morton and Leslie, 1991), such as the use of pretence (e.g. pretending a plate is a hat; for the autistic child it will always be a plate). In the same way, the autistic child does not understand complex jokes, which require flexible imaginative thought and the use of metaphor. Although they do have a sense of humour, it tends to be limited to less subtle jokes (Howlin, 1997a). They tend to understand things in very literal terms: for example, the autistic reply to 'take a seat' may be 'take it where?' This inflexibility combined with obsessive traits makes it difficult to share accommodation with autistic individuals.

Leslie (1990) has related a lack of true flexible thinking to what he terms a lack of a **theory of mind** in autism, meaning the autistic child lacks a theory as to what is in another person's mind, which has become a major explanatory approach in autism (see below).

In addition to these three major areas of deficit, there are other features that are common in autism.

- **Obsessive ritualistic behaviour.** The autistic child is likely to react with distress and tantrums to disruption of their ritualistic behaviour, sudden noise, or a change in their environment or daily routine. They often have a rigid insistence on sameness, which pervades most aspects of their behaviour: for example, eating the same foods, at the same time and in the same setting every day. This rigidity affects the autistic child's play, often creating repeated patterns or endless lines of objects such as building bricks, and is also reflected in the rigidity of his or her thinking. These rituals can overlap with savant abilities such as the routine memorising of timetables or complex lists. If parents do not confront the insistence on sameness, they may find themselves party to the rituals, such as the parent who had to rise at 6 a.m. every day to make her daughter her breakfast porridge, including Christmas day.

- **Mannerisms.** Examples of mannerisms such as hand-flapping or walking on their tip-toes are common, as are stereotypies, or self-stimulatory behaviour and self-injurious behaviour. These activities, which are socially limiting and can stigmatise the autistic child in public, seem to serve three functions: to increase social avoidance; to provide immediate self-comfort; and to compensation for rigid controlled behaviour and lack of social reward. Thus the social void in the autistic individual's world tends to be filled with mannerisms and self-directed behaviour.

- **Objectification.** The autistic individual avoids people and emotion, and may gravitate towards a more mechanical view of the world. Autistic children can make very fine distinctions in the characteristics of objects but lack the interest in differentiating between people. They often reduce human characteristics to objective ones, such as describing people in terms of height or weight instead of more personal aspects such as 'sensitivity' or 'friendliness'.

- **Emotional deficits.** These have been mentioned, but some professionals see the autistic individual's inability to recognise or relate to emotion as more fundamental to autism and its symptoms (see Hobson, 1990). Autistic children tend to have a constant placid expression regardless of changing emotional circumstances, appearing to be indifferent to the emotional states of others. Although an autistic individual may be able to explain emotion and empathy in factual terms, they have little insight into the experience of these qualities.

The aetiology of autism

Neurodevelopmental theories

The modern view of autism is one of a biologically based disorder, although any specific and consistent biological mechanism is elusive. Clearly, the problem occurs too early in life to be a result of life events, and is closely associated with mental retardation, which occurs in the majority of cases. Autism is associated with **perinatal complications** (problematic births) (see Gillberg and Gillberg, 1983), which often result in neurological damage, and nervous system disorders such as **encephalitis** can result in autistic-like symptoms. Some prenatal disorders such as **rubella** are associated with higher rates of autism. As with many neurologically based conditions, as many as a third of autistic individuals suffer epilepsy by the time they are adult. All of these factors suggest that autism results from some form of neurological abnormality, which interferes with normal infant development.

Genetics and neurodevelopment

Abnormalities of **neurodevelopment** are likely to be a product of early neural damage or genetically based neural abnormality. The evidence for a genetic contribution to the aetiology of autism is strong, despite the difficulty in determining this in a rare disorder that results in sufferers hardly ever marrying or having children. There is about a 4 per cent risk of having a second child that also has autism, as compared with around a 0.0003 per cent risk for births in the general population. Evidence from **twin studies** is also convincing. Steffenberg et al. (1989) found concordance rates of 91 per cent for monozygotic (identical) twins, as against 0 per cent for dizygotic (non-identical) twins, which is evidence that genetics plays a large part in the aetiology of autism. As the occurrence in identical twins is not 100 per cent, there must be other factors intervening in the neurodevelopmental process, but as mentioned above, there may be different causal mechanisms producing different forms of the disorder. Further along these lines, it has been suggested that different genetic disorders (i.e. genetic heterogeneity) contribute to varying forms of autism. Unfortunately, the diversity of the genetic and other factors clearly implicated in autism does not predict a simple neurogenetic intervention. Indeed, the prospect of ever reversing such

Research

Autism and the neuropeptide secretin

Research is continuing to examine if one inherited biochemical feature of a subset of autistic children may be amenable to direct treatment. Although, based on original investigations by Panksepp in 1978, much of the research into treatment was initiated by **Stephen Dealer** and **Paul Shattock** in the 1990s. Those autistic infants with bowel problems appeared to have a deficiency in the neuropeptide **secretin** (Reichelt et al., 1994). This 'leaky gut' syndrome found in autism allows opioid peptides from food products such as milk to be absorbed by the gut, which can be detected in urine. These opiate-like substances have been hypothesised to cause the aloof and anhedonic symptoms seen in autistic individuals, which are reduced by avoiding the food products (Whiteley et al., 1999).

Anecdotal cases of 'overnight cures for autism' have fuelled research in this area, and further support for this set of assumptions has come from studies of the effects of opiate antagonists on children with autism (Campbell et al., 1988).

Initially, this explanation of autism seemed to offer a complete biological explanation of the disorder with treatments that directly addressed the aetiology (see below). However, success with this neuropeptide approach appears to be limited to a small subset of cases of autism, with inconsistent success within this population, in keeping with the concept of heterogeneity in autism. This has become an area of research controversy in which the original assumptions have been questioned.

---

inconsistent neurodevelopmental abnormalities is daunting for the most optimistic professional.

In 1991, Smalley suggested an autosomal recessive inheritance (a recessive gene on the 'body' or non-sex chromosomes) for autism. However, completion of the initial stages of the **human genome project** has provided a foundation for moving towards identifying the heterogenetic basis of disorders such as autism, although its inconsistent presentation still impedes this progress (Spence, 2001). This approach has already implicated multiple loci for autism (e.g. 17q11.2 and 19p13) using linkage analysis (McCauley et al., 2005).

Biochemistry and neurodevelopment

Other biochemical differences have been found that seem to distinguish autistic individuals, such as the level of the neurotransmitter **serotonin**, which has been found to be high in autism (Freeman and Ritvo, 1984). High levels of serotonin can parallel the effects attributed to opioids described above in accounting for symptoms of autism, but reduction of serotonin does not have the profound effect attributed to opioid reduction in anecdotal studies and this would imply a limited role for serotonin in autism. Richdale and Prior (1995) consider the severe sleep problems found in younger autistic children a result of social cues to synchronise sleep; however, it is clear that such abnormalities are also likely to have neurochemical or other biological correlates. This may warrant further investigation in terms of candidate biochemical substances.

Many children are vaccinated against measles, mumps and rubella using a single injection of the combined MMR vaccine. This is usually given at about the same age as autism is first detected or diagnosed in those few children with the disorder. This unfortunate co-occurrence led many parents of children to associate the two events in a causal way, believing that the vaccine might have caused or perhaps precipitated the autism. Superstitious behaviour is often the result of the false association of pleasant or unpleasant outcomes with salient random events that seem to precede them. Thus the parent's behaviour could be explained in **parapsychological** terms as a selective focus on non-contingent events. However, some poorly sampled studies drew the conclusion that the MMR vaccine produced **lymphoid hyperplasia** or an inflammation of the gut in susceptible children and that this led to an excess intake of opioids from food in a similar manner to the 'leaky gut' syndrome above. In order to prevent a vaccine scare, studies were gathered to identify if there was a genuine link between autism and MMR (e.g. Taylor et al., 1999) and the results from these studies strongly suggested that there was no such link. However, continuing superstition led to children not being inoculated, putting the lives of many children at risk from these avoidable diseases.

Neurophysiology and neurodevelopment

Evidence for neurological abnormalities in autism has involved a number of brain areas. Bauman and Kemper (1985), amongst some of the early studies, have found differences in the cerebellum in autism, whereas, Jacobsen et al. (1988) identified increased third ventricle size, implying a reduced brain mass (in that region) in autism. Sokol and Edwards-Brown (2004) produced evidence of abnormalities in brain areas such as the **frontal lobes**, the **corpus callosum**, the limbic system and the cerebellum that are frequently but inconsistently found amongst individuals in the autistic spectrum. Areas of brain growth were also seen to accelerate at about the time when autistic symptoms are first noticed, i.e. 1–2 years of age. Carper and Courchesne (2000) revealed an inverse relationship between the size of frontal lobe and cerebellar abnormalities in those children showing either abnormality. The autistic deficit in extracting social information from faces is similar to that displayed by individuals with damage to the amygdala (Adolphs, Sears and Piven, 2001). This assumption has been supported by fMRI studies showing lack of amygdala use in high-functioning autistic (Asperger) individuals when processing social information (e.g. Baron-Cohen et al., 1999). Although Rojas et al. (2004) found amygdala differences to be inconsistent, they did find abnormal growth of the hippocampus in both adult autistic individuals and the parents of children with autism. This would indicate a genetic basis for neurodevelopmental abnormalities in this part of the limbic system.

As far back as 1987, Prior considered that the evidence for a neurological basis to autism was very strong, but that most findings were diverse and inconsistent. This would suggest that different abnormalities may be involved in combining to produce different forms of the disorder. Sokol and Edwards-Brown (2004) confirm that this position has not substantially changed despite better brain imaging techniques and more precise control over comparison procedures. These authors further propose that, although these diverse abnormalities can be more precisely identified, they are not sufficiently consistent to use neuroimaging as a screening tool for autism. However, the biologically based movement abnormalities that can be evident from birth in autistic infants would provide a very early screening tool for autism by the use of videodisk analysis (Teitelbaum et al., 1998). Baranek (2002) has evaluated sensory and motor interventions based on these detectable abnormalities, which Wing and Shah (2000) have referred to as mild catatonic symptoms (see Chapter 18).

In an early review of the evidence for a biological basis to autism, Bailey (1993) drew attention to studies showing involvement of the frontal cortex. The importance of this brain area in an overall biological explanation of autism is that it may link biological explanations with the cognitive explanations of how the symptoms may arise from such neurological abnormalities. One of these cognitive explanations that became established towards the end of the twentieth century is that of 'theory of mind' (Leslie, 1990).

Theory of mind and other neurocognitive explanations of autism

The major cognitive explanation of autism is the theory of mind approach of Frith, Morton and Leslie (1991) mentioned above. These authors suggested that this cognitive explanation is neurologically based but did not specify a location. Research has subsequently implicated parts of the frontal lobes in theory of mind function (Rowe et al., 2001), with a differing approach activating the anterior cingulate cortex and left temporopolar cortex (Vogeley et al., 2001). Povinelli and Preuss (1995) propose that theory of mind results from evolutionary changes in the prefrontal cortex and that this may be one of the more subtle aspects of social cognition that distinguish human children from their ape relatives. In lacking this ability to judge the mental states of others, or in many cases differentiate them from their own mental state, autistic individuals are very poor at reading people. This cognitive aspect of empathy is fundamental to social relatedness. Baron-Cohen (1995) referred to this as 'mindblindness' and considered a number of standardised tests of hidden exchanges or acts of deception in its detection (see the Research box).

Frith, Morton and Leslie (1991) see a lack of a theory of mind as the basis for most of the characteristic features of autism, though some have argued with this (e.g. Tantam, 1992; Hobson, 1990). Tantam (1992) does not dispute the assumed organic basis, but does take issue with the primacy of the lack of 'theory of mind'. In normal children this ability does not develop until after the age when some of the social deficits of autism have become evident (see Tantam, Holmes and Cordess, 1993). Tantam (1992) proposes that a failure to develop the social gaze response is a more fundamental disability leading on to the other deficits, including that of 'theory of mind'. He interprets 'social gaze response' to mean the inherent tendency to focus gaze on social cues and learn to follow the gaze of others, which can develop into the social use of gaze and attention.

It may be possible that an even more fundamental deficit in figure–ground perception may precipitate the failures of both 'social gaze response' and 'theory of mind' (see Holmes, 1994). The figure–ground distinction is the ability to distinguish a central 'figure' against a background or 'ground', and it is one of the earliest cognitive abilities to develop. This possible weakness in development would make it difficult for the autistic infant to distinguish what was important in the general and social environment. It is possible that this is what Frith (2003) is considering in

Research

The 'Sally-Anne scenario' test for theory of mind

Baron-Cohen, Leslie and Frith (1985) adopted a test for the presence of theory of mind from Wimmer and Perner (1983). In the 'Sally-Anne scenario', autistic children demonstrated deficits in comprehending that the understanding of another may differ from their own, when compared with mental-age matched controls. In this scenario, the Sally doll places a marble in a basket and leaves the situation whilst a second Anne doll moves the marble to a box. Unaware of this transfer, the Sally doll returns and the question to the testee is 'where will Sally doll look for the marble?'

The autistic child tended to choose the new location, as they were unaware that the mental view of the Sally doll differed from their own. Mental age-matched Down's children and much younger non-autistic children were found to choose the original location, as they were aware of the Sally doll's false belief. This inability to take the role of the other is thought to undermine the social abilities of the autistic individual, making many social exchanges seem alien to them. This makes pretence play or humour based on role-play difficult to understand, with most such events being taken literally or at face value. Thus pretending a banana is a mobile phone may fail with an autistic child, for whom it will still be just a banana.

describing a deficit in finding '**central coherence**', which she has supported by showing that autistic children are less distracted by 'central coherence' in performing on an embedded figure test (Shah and Frith, 1983) (i.e. finding geometric shapes hidden in complex figures), a measure of field-dependence. A failure of the figure–ground ability is almost certain to be neurogenetically based, as this is one of the few cognitive abilities thought to be present at or near birth. Again, this is an explanation of autism based in the area of cognitive neuroscience.

Early psychogenic theories

Early views of autism could not equate the appearance of these children with their social deficits, so **psychogenic** causes were popular – the child was assumed to be normal at birth and disturbed by some environmental experience. Parents, particularly mothers, were thought to be 'cold' and 'unresponsive' to the child's needs, as a result of which the child withdraws into what Bettelheim (1967) called 'an empty fortress', based on the observation of children in wartime prison camps. However, research has not supported this (e.g. Rutter, 1983), finding that autistic symptoms cannot simply result from social withdrawal and that the parents of autistic individuals do not significantly differ from parents of non-autistic children. It would seem that any parental 'coldness' must result from bringing up an unresponsive child and that such theories simply add blame to the worries of already stressed parents. However, this approach still has modern adherents such as proponents of **holding therapy** (see below).

Another psychogenic approach was that of Ferster (1961), who considered that lack of parental attention made the parents 'poor reinforcers' (i.e. a behavioural explanation), leading to the behavioural and communication problems in autism. Such an explanation would be limited by the same research undermining Bettelheim's explanation.

Treatments of autism

Biological treatments

Other factors that may lead to autistic symptoms have been examined and some have led to experimental treatments. Levels of the neurotransmitter **serotonin** have been found to be high in autism (Freeman and Ritvo, 1984). This has led to attempts to reduce these levels using **fenfluramine**, with some resulting improvement in behaviour and intelligence quotient (IQ) scores, but these were complicated by the side-effects of the drug. This was also the case when using **neuroleptic** drugs intended simply to calm the autistic child. **Megavitamin** treatment resulted in very limited and inconsistent improvement, and although studies have persisted in using vitamin B6 and the mineral magnesium, results are equivocal (Rimland, 1998).

The amino acid peptide secretin has been used intravenously to counter the inherent deficit thought to lead to autism in those children with 'leaky gut' syndrome (see above). Many doses have been used for varying periods of up to 12 months, with a large number of claims of success in reducing symptoms (Kamińska et al., 2002). Some of these anecdotal reports have given the impression that secretin is a miraculous biochemical key unlocking the prison of autism with instant results. However, when carefully controlled studies are used to evaluate secretin use, the results are not positive enough to support its widespread implementation in autism (e.g. Owley et al., 1999).

Behavioural and educational treatments

As with irreversible conditions such as mental retardation (comorbid with autism), behaviour modification techniques simply target problem behaviours and try to change them. The fact that this practical and pragmatic approach is the most successful in autism leads to paradoxical asymmetry with its aetiology: that is, a behavioural treatment for a biologically based disorder.

Autism presents unique difficulties for the behavioural approach. Normal individuals respond to basic reinforcers (see Chapter 2) such as food, but are then 'weaned' on to social reinforcers (e.g. praise) and eventually will perform required acts for the sense of achievement alone (i.e. self-supporting behaviours). This is not the case with autistic individuals, who do not find people or social rewards reinforcing. They also tend not to initiate action themselves and are overselective in their focus of attention. Learning can be very specific to the context in autism; thus if the child learns to ask for a cup, they may only do this with the one person or only with cups and nothing else. It is not uncommon for this whole process to seem unrewarding and demotivating for the therapist involved. A tragic example of this is the progressive conditioning of speech production using basic reinforcers to shape attention, sounds, words and then phrases, only to find that the autistic individual has no interest in developing, or even using, their acquired language skill.

Behaviour modification methods in the form of applied behaviour analysis are useful in reducing **challenging behaviour**, such as **self-stimulatory or self-injurious behaviour** in autism, by identifying and manipulating reinforcers. Occasionally punishment, such as squirting of lemon juice into the mouth, may be required in the case of biting or screaming (part of tantrum behaviour) if other methods fail. Blake (2005) has examined aspects of behavioural treatment for autism and notes the need to target specific behaviour areas for this resource-intensive treatment. In order to avoid the autistic child having their deficits being amplified by expecting spontaneously initiated exchanges, focal structured communication such as role-play or board games can be employed to ease them into communication. Charlop-Christy et al. (2002) have demonstrated the value of PECS (picture exchange communication system) for

pre-speech assessment and training of autistic individuals. This allows those with no basic elements of speech to use pictures on cards to obtain related reinforcement and thus gain a foundation for communication as well as being introduced to the basic concept of reinforcement for behaviour. Blake (2005) points out that the targeting of behavioural problems and deficits can be greatly helped by the application of **functional analysis/assessment** of that behaviour. By analysing the function that the behaviour serves for the autistic child, the reinforcing aspect of the environment that supports the behaviour can be identified and addressed (Repp and Horner, 1999). Thus reinforcers such as parental attention can be removed from a particular unwanted behaviour, or in the case of a stimulus such as supermarket noise leading to tantrums, the stimulus can be masked by music from a personal music player.

The best outcomes tend to result from behavioural programmes that are intensive and sustained, and which extend the learning environment to the home, school and every aspect of the child's life. Involvement of parents is particularly effective and has been more effective than formal treatment situations when delivering the same training. The most successful intervention carries the name of its originator and this **Lovaas programme** continues to be widely used in many countries in the twenty-first century. This programme is a strict behavioural regime that involves controlling the child's entire environment, including the reinforcing behaviour of their parents. Lovaas (1987) reported remarkable global improvements in applying one of the most scientifically designed schemes for 40 hours a week for over 2 years. In this well-controlled evaluation, Lovaas used terms such as **normalisation** to describe the outcome. The goal of 'mainstreaming' the children so they could gain further benefit from a normal social and educational environment was mostly achieved: 47 per cent of the children gained entry to mainstream education and IQ gains of 25–30 points separated the treatment group from controls. These figures remained the same at follow-up, even in long-term follow-up studies a number of years later (McEachlin, Smith and Lovaas, 1993). However, this success was *not* a cure and the autistic children chosen for the scheme did not include 'low functioning' cases.

Another intensive comprehensive educational treatment is that of the Higashi approach originating from Japan. This involves group-oriented instruction and centres on learning by imitation or modelling utilising music, movement and art. The routine activities are highly structured and involve rigorous physical exercise, which combine to reduce stereotyped behaviour and mannerisms. Quill, Gurry and Larkin (1989) have positively evaluated this daily life therapy (DLT) approach at the Boston Higashi School.

Ozonoff and Cathcart (1998) noted measurable gains when applying daily TEACCH or TEACHC (treatment and education of autistic children and communication handicapped children) home sessions in addition to the existing educational programme. Educational and behavioural approaches have also been adapted into computer-assisted learning packages, some of which have incorporated **virtual learning environments** such as the **AS Interactive Project** (Parsons et al., 2000). These computerised interventions enable more control over the environment, restricting the level of distraction for an autistic child. Rogers (1998) acknowledges the successes of broad-based treatment schemes such as those using Lovaas techniques and the TEACCH programme. However, she sees a need to identify the successful elements in these varied comprehensive programmes rather than being overly involved in their differing philosophies.

Cognitive and behavioural training has been used successfully in assisting the learning of theory of mind strategies. The use of cartoon-style 'thought bubbles' can convey the differences in what other individuals may be aware of during situations of deception and other forms of second-order thinking. This helps to educate the autistic child in alternative routes to understanding the independent thoughts of others (Wellman et al., 2002). Rajendran and Mitchell (2000) have evaluated this approach adapted for computerised delivery, the 'Bubble Dialogue' program, to improve executive function but with limited improvements in theory of mind.

Other treatment approaches

Focus

Holding therapy treatment or abuse?

In the USA, **Martha Welch** has used the term 'cure' in relation to her holding therapy for autism, although there is no empirical evidence of the efficacy of this treatment and certainly no support for extravagant claims of curing autism (Howlin, 1997b). 'Holding' involves the parent holding the autistic child to enforce eye-to-eye contact, regardless of the child's (often violent) protests. The emotional drama is intense and often frightening to witness, eventually reaching a **'resolution'** when the child will sometimes accept comfort and seem less emotionally distant. There is little empirical research on this approach and it is omitted from most literature. This may be because Welsh claims that 'holding' repairs the (psychodynamically) damaged bond between the autistic child and its immediate carer and, through them, other people (see Welch, 1989). This psychodynamic 'neo-Bettelheim' explanation tends to blame the parent and is subject to the same criticisms as the original theory by Bettelheim. In examining the process of holding, it could be viewed as parents abusing their children emotionally (and to some degree physically) in order to gain some brief semblance of normal interaction with their child. Welch has changed the descriptions of her approach to 'the Welch method of regulatory bonding', which she recommends for 'dysregulated children' with everything from autism to **post-traumatic stress disorder**. She now refers to her therapy sessions as 'direct synchronous bonding sequences'.

Artificial 'hugging machines' have been adopted in eastern Europe to desensitise children to physical contact, though without the ambitious claims of holding therapy. However, the holding procedure is identical to the behavioural technique of **flooding**, where enforced exposure to a feared stimulus (in this case, human social and emotional contact) results in a 'resolution period' when these fears subside. The exhaustion of the child's ANS response may be augmented by **endorphins** released due to the confrontation involved, which could make the child more passive and less resistant to contact. However, this could exacerbate the symptoms of autism in those autistic children with secretin deficits, as it would add to their high levels of endogenous opioids.

Regardless of the underlying mechanism or the aetiological claims of the proponents of holding, if it is effective in some cases of autism, then holding is worthy of immediate empirical research. Some treatment methods may seem ill-founded or even bizarre, but this can simply reflect the level of dedication of parents wanting their child to enjoy normal feelings and expression. Education towards a reasonable level of expectation can be useful in avoiding tragedies such as the UK child who died undergoing heavy metal detoxification due to exaggerated suspicions of mild mercury poisoning, which arose from a somewhat spurious and random association with the mode of delivery of MMR vaccine.

Concluding autism

At the time when autism was first identified, the prognosis for these children was bleak. As the twenty-first century progresses, the improved differential diagnosis of the disorder since 1980 and the subsequent targeting of more effective interventions should be making the prognosis for future autistic adults far more optimistic. Autism is both a fascinating and tragic disorder, and almost all aspects could be considered special issues. It is true of many disorders that we can understand some of the traits in the normal population by studying these extreme forms. Perhaps our disproportionate interest in autism reflects some recognition of the changing human condition in this increasingly impersonal, mechanical and unemotional world.

Asperger's syndrome (Asperger's disorder)

Around the time when Kanner (1943) was describing autism, **Hans Asperger** (1944) wrote a description of a group of children who had many of the social deficits of autism but differed in significant ways. Many professionals like to think of the pervasive developmental disorder of Asperger's syndrome as a 'pure form of autism', lacking the severe retardation and language complications, or even 'mild autism' (Wing, 1981). Klin et al. (1995) have carried out a neurological assessment of both Asperger's individuals and a sample with 'higher-functioning autism', finding distinctions on some tests. Some have argued whether the separate Asperger's category should exist at all, claiming overlap with autism and **schizoid personality disorder** (see Kay and Kolvin, 1987). Others conclude that there are reasons for Asperger's syndrome as an independent classification (see Tantam, Holmes and Cordess, 1993). For Asperger (1979) the differences between autism and his syndrome were substantial. In order to avoid repetition of the above description of autism, the following will deal only in the similarities and differences between the two disorders (for more detail, see Frith, 1991).

The similarities between the disorders include the following.

■ They use language in an inflexible pedantic way, not reciprocating but engaging in monologues, both showing the speech peculiarities described for autism (e.g. pronoun reversal). They have poor non-verbal skills, but tend to 'mimic' well.

■ Flexibility of thought and imaginative play is lacking and both are obsessive in wanting sameness in the environment, displaying stereotyped behaviour and perhaps

being very sensitive to sound, smell, etc. They show rigid, mechanical, impersonal, interests (e.g. astronomy or archaeology), and may have specially developed abilities in their chosen interests. They are withdrawn and socially isolated, regarding people as objects, and may be indifferent to the emotions of others (see Tantam et al., 1989).

■ Both disorders show a male bias, physical clumsiness and aggressive, restless behaviour.

Asperger's syndrome differs from autism in the following ways.

■ Those with Asperger's syndrome develop language early, in contrast to the delay or absence in autism. Although language use is abnormal, they sometimes seem in advance of normal children in terms of 'adult-type' speech. Asperger's syndrome is thought to have a later onset, is diagnosed later and has a better prognosis than autism.

■ They rarely show the mental retardation evident in most cases of autism but have an awkward, 'eccentric' or poorly presented appearance, whereas autistic individuals are sometimes attributed with having 'inherent attractiveness'.

■ They more frequently have special interests and develop these, providing they do not involve human intimacy. This applies to the development of motor skills: for example, if they 'take to' walking at an early age, they overtake others in this ability; otherwise it may be delayed in development.

■ Although they have some of the indifference to others seen in autism, Asperger's individuals are more aware of the presence of other people. As they mature, Asperger individuals more often show interest in other people, but their symptoms become very apparent when they attempt to socialise. They tend to be over-eager and have inappropriate non-verbal and verbal behaviour, which is lacking in pragmatic language use (i.e. is inflexible and does not adapt to the context) (Volkmar and Klin, 2000). Their pedantic and straightforward honesty in exchanges tends to make the Asperger's child a vulnerable target for sarcasm the jokes of other children (Tantam, 2000).

Although Asperger's individuals have better developed language and other abilities, the causes are thought to be similar to those of autism and treatment approaches share many of the same limitations. Public and professional interest in autism seems to have been transferred to Asperger's syndrome, as the term has become more familiar. Many personal accounts have been published

Dan Ackroyd acknowledged having traits of Asperger syndrome, and is a case where the characteristic traits may have added to career success.
Source: Corbis/Mo-Spector/Kipa.

that have helped to further educate, enlighten and open the minds of non-professionals to the differing experience of the Asperger's mind (e.g. Hadcroft, 2005).

Rett's disorder

There are similarities in the deficits of autism and Rett's disorder with stereotyped hand movements, expressive and receptive language deficits, poor coordination and a lack of interest in social activity, as well as psychomotor retardation. A major difference lies in the fact that, in Rett's disorder, development is normal for the first 5 months of life, following which head growth decelerates and the symptoms, usually including mental retardation, begin to appear over the following years. It is less common than autism at a rate of about 1 in 10,000 births and appears only to affect females. As with other PDD, the cause is probably biological and there is no cure as such, making it a diagnosis that indicates a poor prognosis.

Childhood disintegrative disorder

Whereas the period of normal development in Rett's disorder is 5 months, in childhood disintegrative disorder this period of normal growth is about 2–4 years. At some point in the years after this (up to 10 years), there is a *loss of the already acquired skills*, resulting in severe deficits in the areas of language, adaptive behaviour and motor skills. The disorder is very rare, about 1 in 100,000 births, and is more frequent in males than females. There is no cure for the apparently biologically based progress of childhood disintegrative disorder, with treatment consisting of behaviourally retraining some of the lost skills. It was once termed **Heller's syndrome** after **Theodore Heller**, who described the disorder at the beginning of the twentieth century.

Self-test questions

- What did Bowlby propose were the effects of maternal deprivation?
- Why is the concept of attachment forensically important in childhood disorders?
- Why are pervasive developmental disorders so prevalent in the literature?
- How can conduct disorder and oppositional defiant disorder be distinguished?
- What is the autistic triad of symptoms?
- What is meant by theory of mind?
- How is secretin thought to relate to autistic behaviour?
- Name three areas of evidence pointing to autism as a biological disorder.
- How is Asperger's disorder differentiated from autism?

Attention-deficit and disruptive behaviour disorders

Each of these disorders is marked by a degree of behaviour, which is disruptive for those around them and detrimental to the sufferer's adaptive and academic abilities. These disorders can be strong indicators of later **personality disorders** and **criminal activity**, but this is not inevitable.

Attention deficit and disruptive behaviour disorders are more common in males than females, though as with criminal activity itself, this bias is subject to criticism (see Hollin, 1989). Thus there are important implications in terms of educational, forensic and clinical forensic psychology for the identification and management of children with these disorders.

Attention-deficit hyperactivity disorder (ADHD)

Phenomenology, diagnosis and prognosis of ADHD

ADHD is characterised by persistent inattention and impulsive hyperactive behaviour. The child will usually shift from one activity to another without completing tasks, exhibiting enormous energy and enthusiasm. Adult carers are rapidly exhausted by the task of monitoring their child's activity and may find themselves in constant conflict whilst trying to moderate their demands and behaviour levels. This can be made worse by similar traits being present in the close genetic relatives, exacerbating conflict escalation in family exchanges. The conflict, damage to property and occasional injuries resulting from this behaviour would imply maliciousness and vandalism, but this is not usually the case. The child is often surprised by the damage and hurt that can result from their actions. Many normal children are very active, curious and energetic, but can inhibit this behaviour if instructed or if the situation demands it. In ADHD, this inhibitory ability seems weak or absent and the extreme activity and inattention is persistent with little or no respite.

Although the majority of children with ADHD are normal in most other respects including intelligence, school work is disrupted by their inattention and classroom order is threatened by their hyperactivity. About a quarter of affected children have *additional* learning disabilities, which are considered as **comorbid** rather than as part of the same disorder. ADHD also often co-occurs with **conduct disorder**, which can cause some problems in differential diagnosis and identifying the origins of these disorders (Faraone et al., 1997).

As the case study demonstrates, the prognosis for many sufferers of ADHD can be poor with links to later **anti-social personality disorder** and **criminal recidivism** (see Young, 2007; Satterfield et al., 1994). However, not all those diagnosed with the disorder follow this course and nowadays many are trained to utilise their active nature very usefully.

A diagnosis of ADHD must establish that inattention and hyperactivity-impulsivity pervade different aspects of the child's life (e.g. school and home). A number of these styles of behaviour, such as fidgeting, not listening and impulsive speech, should also persist over time and not be a reaction to a single event (see Fitzgerald, Bellgrove and Gill, 2007). There are three forms of ADHD that may be diagnosed based on the levels of each symptom group present.

- **ADHD predominantly inattentive type.** This is where the full (six) criteria for attention problems are present but fewer than six symptoms of hyperactivity.

- **ADHD predominantly hyperactive-impulsive type.** With six of the symptoms of hyperactivity but fewer symptoms of inattention present, this subtype is diagnosed.

Focus

Epidemiology of ADHD: a Western epidemic?

ADHD appears to be becoming more widespread with levels of diagnosis during the school years having moved from around 4 per cent to an incidence of 5–9 per cent of children and more in the twenty-first century (Swanson et al., 1998). *DSM IV-TR* gives more conservative rates of 3–7 per cent (American Psychiatric Association, 2000). This apparent increase is possibly due to greater awareness of the condition and a readiness to include children on the borders of diagnosis in Western countries, notably the USA.

This 'apparent epidemic' has led to accusations that the label is overused to pathologise children who provide any challenge to their parents or a school's performance record. These arguments have been used as a vehicle to undermine the science behind the diagnostic category and even to suggest that ADHD is a cultural construct (e.g. Timmi and Taylor, 2004) in the manner of anti-psychiatry. However, the reality of genuine cases distinguish the ADHD child very clearly from those children who are poorly trained or badly socialised. It is much more prevalent in males than females, which may indicate potential gender-based neurogenetic factors in its aetiology or again bias in readiness to diagnose.

Case study
Attention-deficit hyperactivity disorder

Jason was the product of a normal birth, but became a very demanding infant, often seeming unwell, crying frequently and sleeping poorly. This placed a strain on his mother, who was left to cope with Jason on her own much of the time. Possibly as a result of the stress, she managed to find a secretarial post when Jason was 3 years old. By this time, the child's incessant questions and boisterous behaviour were notably excessive. After the first 3 weeks, his first child minder claimed that Jason's 'personality' did not fit with the other children in her care and refused to take him in again, but then admitted that he was simply disruptive and upset the other children.

After he had been similarly rejected from two nurseries, his mother's GP referred Jason to a neurologist to eliminate the possibility of brain damage, although this referral was also a result of his (now unemployed) mother's distress, concern and fears that Jason might have a progressive condition. No obvious neurological defect was apparent, though some of Jason's brain activity had been judged low when he was given a PET scan as part of a research project. His lack of impulse control and inattentiveness was evident during further testing, at which his general IQ was judged normal. His mother was given dietary advice for Jason, which had little effect on his behaviour, though she was not very thorough in its implementation. During this time, the strained relations between Jason's parents had led to divorce. Arguments had often centred around his mother's extreme concern for Jason's health and, in his father's view, being 'soft on him'.

In the home, Jason's driven behaviour began to dominate the family and fewer friends or guests of any kind visited, or if they did, their stay was brief. Jason's older brother and sister had been told he was ill and that they needed to make allowances for him, but this was not the way they saw their little brother. His sister Katherine tried to avoid being in the same room as Jason and made a point of slamming doors behind her to discourage his chasing after her. Jason's brother John would confront and shout at him, but persistent aggressive argument into the early hours of the morning would take its toll on John. The constant conflict ended when John ran away from home at 14 and refused to return until 'something was done' with Jason. John moved to live with his father, which placed greater stress on Katherine and her mother. Jason's only babysitter lasted just 2 hours.

During Jason's second year of school, complaints by the parents of other children made it clear that something would have to be done about his disruptive behaviour. By this time his mother was having a relationship with a younger man, who viewed Jason's behaviour as endlessly amusing. The educational psychologist involved with the school arranged for Jason and his mother to be seen by a team of professionals who dealt with child behaviour problems. He was a professional who recognised Jason as having ADHD, but he did not want to have Jason diagnosed by a psychiatrist and possibly medicated with Ritalin if enough progress could be made by behaviour modification. A functional analysis was carried out, making careful record of his disruptive behaviour in the home and at school as well as the reactions of his mother, sister and teachers. From this, a system of rewards were devised for not being disruptive, as well as negative consequences such as being confined to the stair-well (time out).

After a shaky start, Jason's behavioural treatment began to show reductions in the target behaviours, which encouraged his mother to stick to the programme. Jason's behaviour improved greatly in more general terms, but the disruptive behaviour never disappeared altogether. Jason is now in his late teens and has just been convicted for stealing cars (for the third time) and given a short jail sentence, although this unfortunate outcome is becoming less common with better interventions.

- **ADHD combined type.** This subtype requires six symptoms of each of hyperactivity and inattention to fulfil its criteria. This is the commonest form of the disorder.

Aetiology and treatment of ADHD

Feingold (1973) considered the biochemical effects of diet and specifically the action of **food additives** on a child's behaviour. Although such research has shown the effectiveness of removing additives from the diet, this only seems to apply in a small proportion of cases and subsequent studies have failed to uphold links between the condition and food additives. Environmental lead poisoning and smoking during pregnancy have been hypothesised as leading to ADHD; however, evidence only supports the latter factor. Nicotine exposure in the womb is thought to affect the developing **dopamine** system of the foetus, and smoking during pregnancy has a significant but not absolute association with ADHD (Chabrol and Peresson, 1997). However, the association may also be with genetic factors in mothers that led them to risk smoking heavily during pregnancy, and which are shared with children, predisposing them to ADHD.

Genetic approaches

Dopamine abnormalities in the pathology of ADHD have become an established area of research. However, rather than being due to maternal smoking, studies are beginning to identify gene locations for these abnormalities, which indicate a polygenetic aetiology for this aspect of the disorder (Kirley et al., 2002). In ADHD the gene for the D4 dopamine receptor (i.e. the seventh repeat of the DRD4 allele) is thought to lead to subsensitivity of the D4 receptor or other abnormal effects on dopamine action (Swanson et al., 2000). Although there is evidence of dopamine involvement, there are few research studies of ADHD on the effects of neuroleptics, which block dopamine receptors (Gillberg, 2000). However, it is probably counterintuitive to examine the effects of dopamine receptor blockers in a disorder where dopamine agonists dominate treatment. Twin studies have confirmed a substantial overall genetic component to ADHD with a monozygotic concordance of 58–83 per cent against 31–47 per cent for dizygotic twins (Wender, Wolf and Wasserman, 2001).

As mentioned above, there is a great deal of comorbidity in ADHD. Almost half the cases of the condition are comorbid with at least one other disorder, producing possible clues to the underlying aetiology of ADHD. Genetic studies have found evidence for an unspecified and probably multifactorial inherited characteristic that predisposes

individuals to ADHD (e.g. Faraone and Biederman, 1994). Faraone et al. (1997) have cautiously proposed two genetically distinct subtypes: an anti-social ADHD, which is often seen as comorbid with conduct disorder, and one which is less associated with forensic outcomes. This proposal to some degree validates the retention of **hyperkinetic conduct disorder** in the *ICD-10* classificatory system. There is also consistent evidence for a genetic overlap between ADHD and low IQ, conditions which co-occur frequently (Kuntsi et al., 2004). This would point to shared inherited characteristics underpinning aspects of both disorders. Conversely, Carlsson (2001) compared the opposing features of ADHD and **obsessive–compulsive disorder** in relation to the function of the transmitter **glutamate** in the prefrontal cortex, and identified the former to be hypoglutamatergic and the latter hyperglutamatergic, with implications for treatment. ADHD also co-occurs with other disorders such as depression and can lead to anti-social personality disorder diagnosis later in life.

Neurological approaches

Neurological investigations have been a focus of research, with some tentative success. The size of parts of the corpus collosum, which divides the hemispheres of the brain, has been found to differ in children with high levels of hyperactivity. Lower levels of brain function have been inferred from PET scans of levels of glucose metabolism in ADHD. As a centre for restraining behaviour and planning, the frontal lobes have been an obvious putative locus for the aetiology of ADHD. Evidence from imaging studies has implicated the fronto-striatal circuitry in this disorder, in line with behavioural disinhibition (Durston, 2003). However, imaging and anatomical studies have also implicated posterior areas such as abnormal size of the **cerebrum** and **cerebellum**, as well as differential use of brain areas in ADHD as compared to non-ADHD children. From the cumulative evidence so far, ADHD is certain to be a disorder with multiple factors in its aetiology (see Fitzgerald, Bellgrove and Gill, 2007).

Behavioural treatments

Treatments for ADHD tend to be biological and behavioural. Behavioural treatments involve moderating the child's behaviour by the selective reinforcement and non-reinforcement of 'good' and disruptive behaviours. A behavioural assessment will establish the basic level of unwanted behaviour, against which any improvement due to **behaviour modification** techniques can be compared. Inconsistency in the reward and non-reinforcement of the child's behaviour in the home, or an absence of differential reinforcement, can exacerbate the behavioural problems greatly (Fitzgerald, Bellgrove and Gill, 2007). ADHD children can intimidate and exhaust adults into submission, which quite simply leads to tyrannical domination by the child as it becomes older and larger. This can lead to a distortion of relations between family members and unremitting stress in the household (see the case study or p. 272).

One focus for behavioural intervention is the continued educational development of the child, as good educational attainment is associated with a better prognosis. Problems evident in the home are often repeated in the classroom, which can lead to exclusion for the benefit of other children, but clearly lead to a worse prognosis for the individual ADHD child. Thus keeping to strict behavioural contingencies in the child's early years may moderate later educational problems. However, even when behavioural contingencies are correctly in place (see the case study), there are sometimes still problems evident, which would indicate that some overriding biological mechanism is operating, which is only partly modified by behaviour treatments.

Biological treatments

A long-standing biological treatment for ADHD is the use of stimulants such as **methylphenidate** (Ritalin) and **dextroamphetamine** (Dexedrine). Paradoxically, these stimulants calm the behaviour of the (underactive) brain function of children with ADHD and improve their response to reward (see Fitzgerald, Bellgrove and Gill, 2007). This is because stimulants increase cortical activity and reduce the need for external stimulation. This treatment also adds weight to some aetiological research, as it involves both agonist action on dopaminergic pathways and the stimulation of the **frontal lobes**. In stimulating these pathways, methylphenidate improves both hyperactivity and attention problems, and can produce a dramatic improvement in educational capabilities, including cognitive flexibility and memory functioning (Coghill, 2004).

The problems of long-term use of stimulants, including their side-effects and the question of terminating their use, cannot be overlooked as this treatment increases in popularity. Tabloid headlines have often generated unwarranted fear in parents and some professionals that children are being made into drug-addled addicts. Used in the context of the disorder, these drugs are bringing brain function into line with that of other children, rather than producing rewarding effects in the normally functioning brain, as with the use of illicit amphetamines. In their use for over half a century, adverse effects are surprisingly rare with benefits outweighing them. Side-effects disappear on withdrawal and adverse problems tend to occur if these drugs are used with others (Coghill, 2004). However, some health care practices confound the effective use of this intervention, such as the administration of pharmacotherapy in the USA, where only half of the recipients meet the criteria for ADHD. The use of stimulant drugs for other disruptive children will justifiably produce emotive arguments as to the long-term outcome in this new population. Thus the dangers of stimulant treatment tend to result from inconsistent diagnosis and not from the drugs themselves.

The status of ADHD as a disorder has been attacked on the basis that it is unfair to put such a label on a child who may simply 'not fit' into the school system, or that poor school and home discipline is being ignored by pathologising the child. Cumulative biological evidence and the

Focus

Symptoms of conduct disorder

The four main symptom groupings for conduct disorder are as follows.

- **Aggressive behaviour** that could harm other people or animals, often initiating fights or bullying, being more likely to use a weapon, and stealing during violence (i.e. mugging), or further assault such as rape. They demonstrate cognitive distortions in initiating this aggression, in that they perceive random events and the acts of others as malicious or threatening towards them.

- **Damage to property or theft,** sometimes in the form of arson and more frequently as vandalism.

- **Deceitfulness** in the forms of lying, 'conning', petty theft and indifference to debt.

- **Rule breaking,** which may include playing truant, persistently breaking parental curfews, violating school regulations and running away from home.

Each of these relates to items of criminal conduct, but in combination they indicate the disorder.

pervasiveness of ADHD behaviour have to some degree countered these arguments and established effective behavioural and pharmacological approaches to intervention (see Fitzgerald, Bellgrove and Gill, 2007).

Conduct disorder

As mentioned in the previous section, **conduct disorder** often leads on to the adult **anti-social personality disorder**, for which it is a diagnostic criterion. Thus, the relationship between the two disorders is such that anti-social personality disorder always has conduct disorder as a precursor, but conduct disorder does not always lead to anti-social personality disorder. A key feature of both these disorders is an apparent disregard for the rights and feelings of others, including the rules and laws of society in general, which is evident in the criteria for the disorder shown in the Focus box.

The subgroups of behaviour in the Focus box manifest without any substantiated precipitating factor (e.g. former abuse). In conduct disorder, the child is purposefully anti-social in that they choose to hurt others and offend, rather than such behaviour being a consequence of a disorder, such as the tantrums in autism. This has important forensic implications, as most legal systems around the world require that an offender has clear intent to do wrong (in UK law, *mens rea*), and conduct disorder does not provide mitigation against this culpability. The context in which the child lives, or has recently lived, needs to be noted in making a diagnosis. For example, a child who has recently arrived from an area where civil conflict or gang warfare is part of daily life may have some aggressive behaviours that are adaptive or normal in that context. Males with conduct disorder tend to outnumber females by around 5:1, though this varies between studies. Females tend to engage in more promiscuous behaviour, lying and truancy, whilst males will commit more acts of stealing and fighting, but this may also be due to gender differences in detection and prosecution. A worse prognosis is associated with traits that originate in early childhood, have poor environmental support and show biological underpinnings: for example, high saliva **cortisol** indicating poor (serotonergic and noadrenergic) behavioural inhibition and lack of anxiety (Gray, 1992).

Subtypes of conduct disorder

DSM-IV recognises two subtypes: onset before the age of 10 years, or **childhood-onset type**; and onset after this age, or **adolescent-onset conduct disorder**. The latter type is less male biased, has fewer aggressive features and has a better prognosis: that is, the subtype is less likely to lead on to anti-social personality disorder in adulthood. Females with adolescent-onset tend to be more aggressive than their male equivalents, but this may be due to aggression being less overt in female children. Frick and Ellis (1999) have examined studies that further this distinction and additionally divide the childhood onset subtype. They distinguish a callous and unemotional group that can be aligned with the concept of the **fledgling psychopath**, who are unsociable even with their offender peers. The latter group are less likely to respond to treatment as adults (Hare, 1993).

Aetiology of conduct disorder

The term **equifinality** is often used in the context of the causes of conduct disorder, as it is felt that there multiple developmental routes and risk factors in its origins. There is little research into the aetiology of conduct disorder itself, though there are more studies into aggressive behaviour in general, which may not be specifically relevant to explaining the broader symptomatology associated with later-onset subtypes. Conduct disorder is more common in the offspring of biological parents with anti-social personality disorder, alcohol problems, mood disorders or schizophrenia, or who have had conduct disorder or ADHD themselves in earlier life (American Psychiatric Association, 2000). There is a definite genetic component involved here (Hudziak, 2001), though transgenerational transmission (non-genetic family influence) also has an effect. Cadoret et al. (1995) examined anti-social behaviour in adoptees and found that anti-social behaviour in both the biological and adopting parents was predictive of this behaviour in the adoptees. Kendall (2000) considers this a good illustration of the diathesis–stress approach to aetiology.

Antisocial behaviour in children can result from poor parenting styles of all types (e.g. permissive, anti-social or arbitrary discipline). However, this holds true for offspring who are not conduct disordered. Thus the abnormal behaviour that results from poor modelling and reinforcement in the home or school can muddy the waters of diagnosis in childhood disorders such as conduct disorder. It may be that within the multifactorial development of more serious child and adolescent behaviour, increasing genetic factors may identify the more serious subtypes that take their callous anti-social behaviour on into adulthood.

Management of conduct disorder

Early behavioural management of the child's behaviour can be effective, but it is often applied long after the behaviour

Children are often allowed to develop symptoms of conduct disorder by being unsupervised in gangs and given no alternative activity. Source: Pearson Online Database.

has become well established and in the worst cases not until adulthood. Interventions may be simple skills trained in the child: for example, older children may be taught to use the CBT strategy of self-talk to calm aggressive feelings. Poor parenting offers an obvious intervention strategy, which is being recognised by some justice systems in Europe and the USA. Behaviourally oriented parent-training schemes are effective (Southam-Gerow and Kendall, 1997) and have even become the focus for successful reality TV shows. Courts are beginning to order parent training as a means of addressing the offending behaviour of their children. Early clinical intervention in families prior to offending behaviour is preferable but requires greater education, awareness and vigilance on the part of parents, schools and all professionals likely to come into contact with a disruptive child.

Oppositional defiant disorder

Most children are defiant at some time or other, but to fulfil the criteria for this disorder behaviour such as defiance, hostility and disobedience must be persistent and well above the level expected for a child of the given age. It is found at a rate of about 6 per cent in children but this increases to around 15 per cent of adolescents. It affects around twice as many boys as girls, though this gender difference reduces in adolescence. The areas of behaviour that are of clinical interest are loss of temper, arguing with adults, non-compliance with adult rules or requests, deliberately annoying others, blaming others for their own errors, and being resentful, touchy and vindictive towards others.

Oppositional defiant disorder is often conceptualised as being allied to the milder end of the conduct disorder subtypes as they are often placed under the same heading, but this is misleading. Children with this disorder tend to lack the behaviours that *violate* the rights of others, which would qualify them as being conduct disordered. Oppositional defiant disorder is less serious than conduct disorder, is less likely to lead to adult offending and has an earlier onset than conduct disorder.

Self-test questions

- In the case study on p. 272, how did Jason's behaviour impact on his parents' lives?
- What are the possible causes of ADHD?
- Why is the prevalence of ADHD controversial?
- What treatments are available for ADHD?
- What are the criteria for defining conduct disorder?
- What is meant by the term 'equifinality' in relation to conduct disorder?

Other disorders beginning in childhood

In addition to pervasive developmental disorders and ADHD, the *DSM-IV-TR* and *ICD-10* list a number of other categories of childhood onset disorders. In this section we will focus on the remaining *DSM* disorders that are specifically related to childhood, though realising that many adult disorders begin at this time. Classificatory systems always include a final 'catch-all' category of **disorder not otherwise specified** for each disorder group. In order to avoid unnecessary redundancy, this category has not been included here but should be assumed for every classification of disorder.

Mental retardation

Where intellectual functioning is significantly below the average for a particular age group and there is impairment of adaptive functioning, mental retardation may be diagnosed. The basic criterion for retardation is an **IQ score** of less than 70, but values below this provide a scale of **mild, moderate, severe** and **profound mental retardation**. The term 'learning disability' has been used to cover this disorder and has become a loosely defined lay term applied to a range of child and adult disabilities.

Learning disorders

In these, academic functioning is *substantially* below age-appropriate performance. The subclassifications of learning disorders specify the area of academic difficulty: that is, **written expression, mathematics** and **reading disorder**.

Motor skills disorders

This is diagnosed when specified motor skills are *substantially* below their intellectual performance and that expected for their age. **Developmental coordination disorder** is the main disorder specified here.

Communication disorders

Specific difficulties with language or speech are **expressive language, mixed receptive-expressive language and phonological disorders**, and **stuttering**. Some forms of 'baby language' are common and may be maintained behaviourally by *carers* accommodating the deviant speech. Communication disorders are usually *more persistent* than 'baby language' deviations.

Feeding and eating disorders

Many children go through periods of conflict with adults over eating habits, perhaps overeating, refusing to eat, or eating 'junk' food. Persistent peculiarities of eating and general levels of eating that affect health are the areas of clinical concern. The adult disorders of **anorexia nervosa**, a failure or refusal to eat sufficiently, **bulimia nervosa**, bingeing and purging, and **obesity** or overeating, often have their onset in childhood and adolescence (see Chapter 8). *DSM-IV* has these disorders in a separate section and only lists **pica, rumination disorder** and the more general **feeding disorder of early childhood** among its childhood disorders.

- **Pica** is the persistent eating of substances with *no nutritional value* at an age when this would be inappropriate. Infants may chew on various materials, but in pica the infant ingests available substances such as plaster or cloth. The older child may eat stones, worms and soil or any of the possible non-nutritive substances. This is in addition to, not as a substitute for, normal food and not part of some religious or subcultural practice. In some cases the disorder is associated with **mental retardation**.

- **Rumination disorder** refers to the persistent regurgitation and rechewing of food, which is often reingested or sometimes ejected from the mouth. There is an absence of the nausea normally associated with such activity and the child has no digestive disorders, which would otherwise explain this behaviour. The disorder is very rare and affects more males than females, usually in infancy.

- **Feeding disorder of infancy or early childhood** broadly covers a significantly lower than average intake of food, resulting in a failure to gain weight or weight loss. Failure to gain weight is a fairly common reason for carers to bring children to a clinician, but about half of these can be explained by factors other than this disorder.

Tic disorders

Tics are sudden stereotyped movements or vocalisations, which can be simple as in blinks or grunts, or complex as in facial expressions or suddenly produced words. These occur many times a day but do not have a rhythmic pattern. Tics are quite common among children, though most disappear with maturity. Tics may seem involuntary and of a neurological origin, but they are characteristically modified by social contexts and psychological factors. For example, complex vocal tics often take the form of obscenities (coprolalia) and may increase in frequency in situations where they would be least appropriate. Tics in tic disorders need to be distinguished from abnormal movements found in other disorders such as **Huntington's chorea**. There are three types of tic disorder distinguished by duration and type of tic, motor or vocal.

- **Tourette's disorder** was reported by **Gilles de la Tourette** in 1885. It is more common in males and is distinguished from the other tic disorders by having both *vocal and motor tics* for over a year without remission. The sufferer has the task of learning to deal with the consequent social embarrassment and stigma as well as the tics themselves. There is evidence of a genetic basis for Tourette's disorder and a dominant gene(s) has been suggested by Bowman and Nurnberger (1993). Treatment with the dopamine receptor blocking neuro-leptic **haloperidol** has been effective in reducing the tics, and newer drugs such as **clonidine** are also effective, with fewer side-effects (see Chapter 2). Tourette's disorder is about as common as autism with around 4 cases out of 10,000 individuals.

- **Chronic motor or vocal tic disorder** is distinguished by having vocal *or* motor tics but *not* both. The 'chronic' distinction is defined by a duration of at least a year without remission. The disorder is less debilitating than Tourette's, though both disorders are found in the same families and must have similar genetic origins.

- **Transient tic disorder** is distinguished by its duration of more than 4 weeks but *less than 1 year*. Transient tic disorder can include *either* vocal or motor tics *or both* together.

Elimination disorders

These have two forms, each requiring the occurrences to be repeated over a 3-month period. A child should be at least *4 years old* for such a diagnosis to be made.

- **Encopresis** is the inappropriate passage of faeces, soil-ing cloths, bedding or floor, and affects about 3 per cent of children over 5 years of age. This can be involuntary or intentional and should not be a result of the use of laxatives or a medical condition.

- **Enuresis** is the inappropriate emptying of the bladder, which is *not* the result of drug action (diuretics) or organic disease, but may be sustained by parental atten-tion. This can be **nocturnal** (night-time bedwetting), **diurnal** (day-time wetting of clothes) or both. Urinary incontinence is quite common among children over 5 years, but only 7 per cent of males and 3 per cent of females persist to meet the criteria of enuresis without a medical condition. Children can be trained to extend the period of time between each urination in stages, or be classically conditioned to wake on urinating – an 'enuresis alarm' (a buzzer triggered by damp). Older children can be operantly rewarded for having dry nights.

Separation anxiety disorder

This is only diagnosed if excessive anxiety occurs when a child has to be separated from the home environment or the person to whom they are attached. The child may exhibit a range of anxiety-related symptoms, such as enuresis, nightmares and somatic (i.e. 'body') complaints including headaches, dizziness, stomach-aches and nausea prior to separation. Bedtime for the child is difficult and various 'ploys' will be adopted to avoid being left alone in bed, in addition to getting up in the night to join the parents. Early behavioural training (slowly extending the separation time) can avoid these problems with most chil-dren, but the 4 per cent or so of those in whom it persists can be diagnosed with separation anxiety disorder. The disorder is often associated with a fear of *losing* the person to whom they are attached.

Selective mutism

Formerly *elective* mutism, this is the voluntary and per-sistent failure to speak in specific (selected) situations in which being mute is *not* usual (e.g. school). They may use gestures or a distorted voice in place of normal speech. The child may be shy but should *not* be suffering from other communication disorders. There tend to be more females with the disorder, which affects less than 1 per cent of children brought to clinics.

Reactive attachment disorder

This disorder involves age-inappropriate ways of relating to others. This is a rare disorder, which is closely associated with **pathological care** (usually physical neglect or abuse). There are two subtypes reflecting the polar opposites of social relatedness behaviour.

- **The inhibited type** fails to initiate or respond in social interactions and may become an 'anxious observer' of the situation, rejecting comfort. This should not be confused with the symptoms of disorders such as autism.

■ **The disinhibited type** lacks any selectivity in attachments and is indiscriminate when relating to others in social situations. This indiscriminate social activity should *not* be a result of developmental delay or retardation.

Stereotypic movement disorder

Stereotypical movement disorder is characterised by repetitive, non-functional motor behaviour (**self-stimulatory behaviour**), which disrupts normal behaviour. This may also involve **self-injurous behaviour**, such as biting or head-banging. It is associated with **mental retardation** and can affect up to 25 per cent of those with profound mental handicap.

Other childhood-based disorders

There are a number of disorders that can start in childhood but which are usually regarded as adult disorders. For example, **mood, anxiety-related and personality disorders** are often detected in childhood, and the origins of **sexual abuse, dissociative** and **gender identity disorders** are *expected* to be found early in life. Thus, as stated at the start of this chapter, there is no clear cut-off point between the disorders of childhood and adulthood. However, to avoid repetition, the reader is directed to the relevant adult disorders for descriptions, which generally apply whether or not the onset was prior to 16 years.

Clinical and forensic issues

Clinical issues in childhood disorders

Clinical psychology has an important role in the area of child disorders, and clinical psychologists may specialise in assessing and treating children, often working in conjunction with **educational psychologists**, who may be linked to specific schools. The developmental period spanning childhood and adolescence provides greater scope for the effectiveness of psychological interventions and where medical interventions would be less desirable if they can be avoided. Early behavioural interventions can avert or at the very least modify abnormal behaviour before it becomes more difficult to change, as it would be in the mature adult (for more detail, see Herbert, 1998).

Intervention in families (not necessarily 'family therapy') can have both proximate effects on the immediate problem and a prophylactic effect on the family unit with regard to succeeding children and in averting future difficulties, where skills and experience can be usefully reapplied. Psychologists and educational psychologists are well trained and placed to advocate for children where parents may not have insight into a child's problem, or may even be its source.

Forensic implications of childhood disorders

The maternal deprivation theory of Bowlby (1951) has been utilised by criminologists as a causal factor for crime. In his 1944 study, 14 of the 17 separated delinquents displayed what Bowlby termed **affectionless psychopathy**, a term he applies to those with strong criminal inclinations and an inability to make normal emotional bonds. He received support for this in terms of maternal deprivation being related to age of first court appearance (Little, 1965) and length of prison sentence (Koller and Castanos, 1970). However, there are overtones of psychodynamic reasoning in this approach, which tend to ignore the countering effects of subsequent behavioural and emotional interventions, and other factors such as surrogate carers (Rutter, 1991). Children can be prepared for separations and, so long as they are psychologically secure, physical separation has far less effect. Clearly the majority of offenders in Bowlby's study were not maternally deprived and clearly not all maternally deprived children offend. Also, there is little known about the extent of maternal deprivation in the general population (Wooton, 1962).

Forensic learning disability is an awkward term used to refer to the assessment and management of individuals of all ages with a degree of diagnosed mental retardation in a forensic context. There are immediate issues of culpability, as any attempt at managing wrongdoing and encouraging 'normalisation' of responsible behaviour has to involve treating the learning disabled (LD) individual in the same manner as other offenders. There is no ready solution to this problem, as in community living the controls and considerations of institutional settings are not possible and the rights of others are protected under the existent legal system. Also, an LD individual has to demonstrate abnormal aggression or irresponsibility to be restrained under mental health legislation, not simply mental retardation. Amongst other issues, Holland, Clare and Mukhopadhyay (2002) have identified the resource implications of problems such as the reintroduction of LD offenders back into institutions as a result of offending, having just moved many from those other institutions where they were placed as a result of their learning disability.

Intelligent enforcement of normal forensic culpability is infinitely preferable to protecting LD people from forensic consequences, and does not lead to dependency or legal abuses. However, this aim is often confounded because in real-world settings LD individuals tend to fall foul of the law more frequently, due to lowered abilities, but are far less likely to be prosecuted (see Kearns, 2001). Prosecution is less likely for a number of reasons: it is assumed that offending is 'part of their disorder'; enforcement officers do not wish to be seen as victimising vulnerable offenders; they also perceive more difficulty in coping with disability in custody and consider the chances of prosecution being successful to be low; many consider such situations to be a health service issue not a police matter. The difficulties of giving a comparable response in the case of LD can be even more complex in relation to sex offending and issues of consent (Johnstone and Halstead, 2000).

The child within the autistic spectrum tends to be indifferent to others rather than shy, and *can* be dangerous in circumstances where they may be indifferent to the suffering of, or harm done to, another. They lack the empathic ability to recognise fear or pain in other's faces (see Tantam et al., 1989). Asperger's individuals tend to be studied from a forensic point of view due to their being more able than many autistic insividuals and more likely to come into contact with other people. Mawson, Grounds and Tantam (1985) have pointed out that violence in Asperger's disorder is more common than had been previously supposed, particularly in those individuals who have been in long-term institutional care. In one tragic case, an Asperger's boy killed an elderly lady and when asked why that victim had been chosen, he stated that 'she was old, so it would not matter'. It must be emphasised that although such occasions reveal the potential danger of autistic objectification of people, they rarely happen because Asperger individuals tend to be extremely law abiding due to their obsessive rule-governed behaviour. Asperger's children tend to be victimised and exploited as a result of their straightforward pedantic approach to relations with others (Tantam, 2000).

Murrie et al. (2002) identify a number of cases which illustrate those aspects of Asperger's behaviour that lead to offending. Obsessive preoccupations can lead to intrusion and unacceptable behaviour, as illustrated by the obsession with bra sizes in the case study at the start of this chapter. Frith (1991) considers that this obsessive focus can take the form of rumination over trivial events in the past and meticulous planning of vengeful actions out of proportion to these original events. Social naïveté can inadvertently lead to situations that precipitate offending, such as the Asperger's individual who would 'hang around' women waiting for sex to 'happen'. Sexual frustration can lead to offending due to their not having the social skills to gain intimate relationships. This frustration combined with their obsessive preoccupations makes the Asperger's adolescent more prone to persistent **paraphilias** (Murrie et al., 2002). Silva, Ferrari and Leong (2000) have carefully examined the case of the serial killer Jeffrey Dahmer in terms of him displaying features of Asperger's disorder that account for his necrophilia as an obsessive preoccupation with dead bodies and bones from being a child.

Focus

Crime and Asperger's disorder

The lack of theory of mind and empathy, where the hurt of others may not register, in Asperger's disorder can resemble aspects of **psychopathy** (see Chapter 14). However, in contrast to psychopathy, Asperger's individuals are not charming, manipulative or exploitative, but are painfully honest, instantly admitting to offences when challenged. UK psychiatrist **Bill Deakin** has anecdotally explained the neurology of the two disorders: in Asperger's there is a lack of feeling for (empathy) *and understanding* of the pain of others; the psychopath also feels nothing, but is acutely aware of the degree of pain or fear they cause in others.

Asperger's individuals can seem to be a risk for future offending in courtrooms, as they are not deluded and plan crimes with focused, if odd precision. However, they are responsive to skill training and other interventions, and as they are not motivated to crime, their future offending risk tends to be incidental rather than intentional. Their specific traits would warrant them being separated from other offenders, of whom they are likely to become victims due to their lack of cognitive flexibility. Palermo (2004) considers that forensic involvement in those with pervasive developmental disorders may result primarily from other comorbid conditions rather than the PDD itself.

Despite unequivocal evidence, there is still controversy over the link between some ADHD children and their later delinquent behaviour. Current research tends to support this link and future work may point to the mechanisms involved (Satterfield et al., 1994). In longitudinal studies, Satterfield and colleagues found ADHD children later in life were involved in 6-fold more serious offences, were 25 times more likely to be institutionalised and were likely to be involved in 28-fold more 'multiple offences' than controls. In these studies, hyperactivity in childhood was a greater predictor of later crime than the social background of the children. See Young (2007) for a recent review.

Other childhood disorders, such as conduct disorder and oppositional defiant disorder, have behaviours in common with attention deficit hyperactivity disorder, and these also have a close relationship with adult crime. Conduct disorder is a condition of childhood or adolescence in which there is *persistent* anti-social behaviour, such as truancy, lying, theft, absconding and damage to property. As a result, conduct disorder is very expensive to society, not just in terms of the disruption to the child's educational and career potential, but also in terms of the fear and criminal damage for which society pays in terms of resources and disruption.

Although teenagers are generally associated with rebellious behaviour, offending behaviour in conduct disorder is consistent and deliberate, shows a pervasive disregard for the rights of all others, including their family, and is closely associated with adult anti-social personality disorder. Around half of children with conduct disorder become adults with diagnosable anti-social personality disorder and are often persistent offenders. Children with both ADHD and conduct disorder tend to be the worst recidivist offenders in adolescence and as adults, with offending in multiple areas. Frick and Ellis (1999) align this more destructive, callous and unemotional subgroup of children with the concept of adult psychopathy. They are not only likely to grow into anti-social adults but are also going to add to the treatment-resistant core element of recidivist offenders. In a separate study, Christian et al. (1997) identified a similar subgroup and labelled the callous unemotional group as the 'psychopathic conduct cluster', which exceeded other groups in terms of conduct and oppositional symptoms, parental anti-social personalities, offending and police contact – in the latter case, almost 3-fold.

Self-test questions

- What behaviours underlie the disorder pica?
- How is Tourette's disorder differentiated from other tic disorders?
- What are the symptoms of separation anxiety disorder?
- How do educational psychologists come to be involved with childhood disorders?
- To what extent should those with learning disabilities be protected from criminal culpability?
- What features of children with Asperger's disorder or autism place them at risk of offending?

Chapter summary

Disorders of childhood are confounded by **developmental factors**, with biological and behavioural influences being greater. The child's position in the **family** is also important, as is the **bond** with its nearest carer, and it is better to consider all involved parties rather than just the child. Important disorders for clinical and forensic approaches are the **pervasive developmental disorders** of autism and **Asperger's disorder**, and **attention-deficit and disruptive behaviour disorders**, including **conduct** and **oppositional defiant disorders**.

Autism is a pervasive developmental disorder for which there is no cure, although **behaviour modification** has helped to manage the difficult behavioural features. Autistic individuals show severe deficits of **social interaction, communication** and **flexibility of thought**. The latter deficit has been linked to a failure to appreciate the different thinking of others, or to have a **theory of mind**. They also display **obsessive behaviour and mannerisms** and a **lack of emotion**, but sometimes have special abilities of a **mechanical** type. **Speech** only develops in 50 per cent of cases of autism and then it is abnormal. This feature distinguishes autism from the similar **Asperger's disorder**, in which language develops normally but is used in an abnormal way.

Attention-deficit hyperactivity disorder (ADHD) is highly disruptive and has been linked to later delinquent behaviour. ADHD responds to both behavioural and drug treatments, though the latter are controversial.

Childhood disorders also include: the PDDs **Rett's** and **childhood disintegrative mental retardation; learning, motor-skills and communication disorders; feeding and eating disorders**, including **pica, rumination disorder** and **child feeding disorder; tic disorders**, including **Tourette's, chronic motor or vocal tic** and **transient tic disorders**; the **elimination disorders** of encopresis and enuresis; **separation anxiety disorder; selective mutism; reactive attachment disorder**; and **stereotypic movement disorder**.

There are clinical and forensic issues involved in childhood disorders, which are all the more important due to the effects of development as well as the opportunities for altering the course of abnormal behaviour during this period of relative **plasticity**.

Suggested essay questions

- Critically discuss how the proposed aetiology of autism relates to its major treatments.
- Discuss the contention that ADHD is pathologising naughty children.
- Evaluate how childhood disorders relate to criminal behaviour in adulthood.

Further reading

Overview texts

Attwood, A. (2006) *The complete guide to Asperger's syndrome.* London: Jessica Kingsley.

Barkley, R. (1996) *Taking charge of ADHD.* New York: Guilford Press.

Fitzgerald, M., Bellgrove, M., and Gill, M. (2007) *Handbook of attention deficit hyperactivity disorder.* London: Wiley.

Frith, U. (ed). (1991) *Autism and Asperger syndrome.* Cambridge: Cambridge University Press.

Frith, U. (2003) *Autism: Explaining the enigma* (2nd edn). Oxford: Blackwell.

Gillberg, C. (1995) *Clinical child neuropsychiatry.* Cambridge: Cambridge University Press.

Herbert, M. (1998) *Clinical child psychology: Social learning, development and behaviour* (2nd edn). Chichester: Wiley.

Klin, A., Volkmar, F., and Sparrow, S. (eds) (2000) *Asperger's syndrome.* New York: Guilford.

Murray Parkes, C., and Stevenson-Hinde, J. (1993) *Attachment across the life cycle.* London: Routledge.

Murrie, D., Warren, J., Kristiansson, M., and Dietz, P. (2002) Asperger's syndrome in forensic settings. *International Journal of Forensic Mental Health*, 1(1), 59–70.

Rutter, M. (1995) *Psychosocial disturbances in young people.* Cambridge: Cambridge University Press.

Seigel, B. (1996) *The world of the autistic child.* New York: Oxford University Press.

Specific and more critical texts

Baron-Cohen, S. (2002) The extreme male brain theory of autism. *Trends in Cognitive Sciences,* **6**, 248–54.

Mandel, H. (1997) *Conduct disorder and underachievement.* New York: Wiley.

Tantam, D. (2009) *Can the world afford autistic spectrum disorder?* London: Jessica Kingsley.

Weiner, J. (ed.) (1996) *Diagnosis and psychopharmacology of childhood and adolescent disorders* (2nd edn). New York: Wiley.

Wolf-Schein, E. (1996) The autistic spectrum disorder: A current review. *Developmental Disabilities Bulletin,* **24**, 33–55.

Visit **www.pearsoned.co.uk/davidholmes** for a range of resources to support study. Test yourself with multiple choice questions and access a bank of over 100 videos that will bring the topics to life. Video coverage for this chapter includes interviews with children and adults suffering from ADHD, autism and Asperger's and footage showing the effect that autism has on children's 'theory of mind'.

- Overview
- Case study
- Eating disorders
- Impulse control disorders
- Compulsive buying and hoarding
- Critical and evaluative issues
- Forensic issues
- Clinical issues
- Chapter summary

Watch this interview with Jessica, who suffers from anorexia nervosa. This is one of several videos that explore issues and disorders relevant to this chapter at www.pearsoned.co.uk/davidholmes.

Shopping and internet addiction

In 2009, the film *Confessions of a Shopaholic* (Hogan, 2009) light-heartedly prodded the consciences of consumer society in portraying a compulsive shopper whose habits cause huge debts. Whilst the film made fun of the addictive behaviour of the 'shopaholic' played by Isla Fisher, many of the public secretly identified closely with her predicament, which reflects the extent of compulsive buying in the twenty-first century, with the associated problems of **hoarding** and debt. As discussed in this chapter, the extent of our evolutionary drive to hunt and gather for trophies or winter provision is dysfunctional in the context of food and other products being readily available. Thus we shop well beyond our needs and often to fulfil other needs not met by our modern culture, such as a sense of community. The widespread nature of our consumer culture may make impulsive–compulsive buying one of the commonest future disorders for *DSM-V*.

Compulsive internet use seems to have little to do with our evolutionary past except for the drive to process information constantly, but perhaps more reflects the virtual world of our future. Again, considered as a future compulsive–impulsive disorder for *DSM-V*, overuse of the internet and electronic communication is increasingly prevalent. Amongst a generation of **digital natives,** or those who have known the internet all their lives, there is increasing preference for 'facebook' virtual friendships or 'myspace' media business networking above seeking friends or live events in the real world. However, the dysfunctional overuse of the internet to the exclusion of normal interaction and activity will form the criteria for a new disorder.

These future disorders clearly have damaging symptoms, but may possibly be indicators that in evolutionary terms, we may be creating pathology for those individuals who fail to adapt to the new environmental contexts we have constructed for ourselves.

This graffitti advice is a pertinent reminder to shopaholics regarding their priorities in life.
Source: David A. Holmes.

This chapter will examine disorders and conditions where impulsive, addictive and controlling behaviours become exaggerated or dysfunctional. It is a complex area with inevitable overlap with other disorder areas, such as obsessive–compulsive, mood and sexual disorders. *DSM-IV-TR* has a fairly narrow focus in this area, excluding conditions such as obesity and compulsive buying, and clearly distinguishing the anhedonic compulsions in obsessive–compulsive disorder from those more pleasure-giving compulsive behaviours covered in this chapter (American Psychiatric Association, 2000).

The first case study introduces some of the factors to be discussed in the eating disorder sections of this chapter with an example of **anorexia nervosa**. The degree of overlap between anorexia and **bulimia nervosa** symptoms follows, whilst emphasising the simple distinctions such as weight loss or maintenance. The eating-related issues arising from the study of body image are focused on including self-esteem and sense of control, which are also associated with eating disorders. In the next section, the

DSM-proposed **binge eating disorder** and the mental and physical health issues of **obesity** are examined. Whilst the latter conditions are familiar as health issues, their mental health implications have been slower to gain recognition when compared with anorexia, possibly due to a traditional overconcern with malnutrition as societies have developed, particularly in the case of children. Despite relative success with bulimia nervosa, treatments for all eating conditions lack the consistent outcomes of other disorders – a situation that is leading to professional concern, given the high morbidity in anorexia nervosa and obesity.

The term 'impulse control disorder' is applied to the relative absence of control over specific hedonistic activities, such as gambling and theft. These activities are often illegal, such as fire setting in **pyromania** or aggression in **intermittent explosive disorder**, and cause suffering and distress to those carrying the acts out and to others involved. Compulsive shopping is a disorder that is likely to appear in *DSM-V* with other newly defined compulsive–impulsive disorders. Along with compulsive hoarding, compulsive buying has often been portrayed as trivial by media coverage but is an extensive and personally debilitating disorder. This is illustrated in the case study of a compulsive buyer and featured in the Research box on p. 307.

Case study

Healthy competition

Julia and her sister had always been competitive and incessantly sarcastic. Anne had often thought of her younger sister as a happy-go-lucky girl, always laughing and seldom serious. However, on occasions, if they fought or if Anne had intruded on Julia without warning, there was something in her overly serious and determined reaction that disturbed the older sibling, and this is something that had concerned her mother on a few occasions. Julia's moods had been a lot less buoyant as she had grown up and she had taken to long weeks of not speaking and spending much time alone in her room. In later years there had also been the 'battle of the bathroom', with Anne complaining that Julia spent hours in there not doing anything.

Julia had excelled at sports from early school days and had even been selected to represent the region in national gymnastic events, but she abruptly dropped out after an argument with her school about training, although Julia denied this. Her mother and father were very concerned at what they perceived as a deliberate failure on the part of their daughter, particularly as they had invested a lot of their own time and money on special diets and travelling to training sessions. However, Julia did spend a lot more time studying at school and developed an interest in nutrition and food preparation, which extended to her leisure hours and rather a lot of searching for information on the internet. Her mother heard her laughing one evening, but was a little surprised to find Julia alone and online, declaring that her online 'fashionable friends' in Spain and California were both an entire dress size larger than her. Her mother smiled at this, thinking that her daughter was at last returning to her fun-loving self.

Julia began to put some of her skills into practice by preparing a meal for the entire family twice a week, to the relief of her mother, but unfortunately disrupting her father's somewhat rigid eating habits. Julia's mother did wonder if her daughters might take after their father, who had recently taken to wearing surgical gloves when on his computer to 'reduce static', and had already made her mind up that, if there were any sign of progressive obsessions, she would *not* ignore and tolerate them as she had with her husband. Anne first noticed that Julia had distinctly lost weight and taunted Julia about trying to be a size '0' model. Their mother also noticed her daughter looking very drawn in the face, but Julia had taken to wearing layers of clothing to conceal her true shape. It was after one of Julia's meals that her mother followed her daughter into the kitchen to confront her. 'You did not actually eat any of the food you made, did you, Julia?' 'No, mother. You know I don't like meat and you used the meat spoon in all the dishes,' replied Julia aggressively. 'Regardless of what you say, I think you are getting too thin and if it continues I am taking you to the doctor's. You must be 2 stone less than Anne!' her mother shouted at Julia as she ran up the stairs. Julia often ran up the stairs; in fact, she did this exactly 49 times a day, as Anne had counted.

Anne complained to her mother about Julia rushing noisily up and down the stairs seven times and then stopping, only to continue later for another seven trips. Alarm bells had gone off in her mother's head at the mention of Julia doing things by numbers, as this was reminiscent of her father. Two weeks later, a very slim Julia and her mother entered their doctor's surgery. Julia refused to be weighed and then stormed out after her mother had produced part of her hidden collection of laxatives in front of the doctor. 'I think we really have to do something here, don't we, doctor. Is she going to be like her father?' Julia's mother said tearfully. 'Your daughter is very underweight for no clear physical reason, but I am not an expert in these problems, Mrs Simpson', the doctor replied. 'I would rather your daughter saw a clinical psychologist for an assessment as soon as possible. Do you think she will attend?'

Despite doubts, Julia did attend and had even allowed her mother to keep a record of her weight as the doctor suggested, although this would have been more informative without the bags of rice Julia hid under her clothes. Her mother was still surprised when Julia began almost to interrogate the psychologist and made side comments to her regarding the professional's 'lack of expertise'. Meanwhile, the psychologist continued to question Julia and her mother about any depression or anxiety symptoms as well as Julia's weight and eating habits. Her mother reflected on just how thin, frail and pale her daughter was and found out for the first time that Julia had not had a period for over a year. At the end of the session, the psychologist confided that she thought Julia had **anorexia nervosa** and gave her mother a self-help pack, but suggested that Julia might need to be admitted to an eating disorder unit. 'But she is not seriously ill, is she?' her mother said with a sense of panic, dating back to when Julia's father had been treated for obsessions. 'I am afraid that I do believe so, Mrs Simpson, and the medical information passed to me by your GP would suggest Julia needs help to restore her weight as soon as possible,' the psychologist said calmly but firmly.

Within a month Julia found herself facing a simple choice, either to give in to her mother and the psychologist by having the planned three meals a day, or to enter the eating disorder unit for the same regime. In each case, her privileges, even cooking or reading magazines, were dependent on compliance with this schedule of weight gain. To her mother's genuine surprise, Julia began to change her attitude despite the discomfort of eating and digesting real meals after so long. Much of this change could be attributed to Anne, who had spent a full session with the psychologist, becoming aware of the seriousness of her sister's disorder, and who had managed to communicate this to Julia. Anne now spent a great deal of time with her sister, no longer competing and arguing but encouraging, joking and monitoring genuine weight gains. Julia made a successful shift from obsessively controlling her weight to taking control of her life, no longer ridiculing those in size 16 dresses or relying on her body shape for her self-esteem. Some 15 years later, Julia had another episode of anorexia following the breakdown of her marriage and this time had to be hospitalised. She recovered on this occasion as well, although it is uncertain just how much this recovery was helped by regular visits from her sister and best friend, Anne.

Eating disorders

In Chapter 9 we covered disorders of feeding and eating that occur in infancy and early childhood, such as pica and early childhood and rumination disorder. However, eating disorders of adolescence and adulthood are less varied, primarily involve a significant disturbance of eating behaviour and may involve unhealthy overcontrol, or inability to control body weight. These disorders have become a popular topic in the media and for research amongst undergraduate psychology students, possibly due to the close identification with eating problems amongst that population. They are difficult disorders to treat, as sufferers may actively resist attempts to help them or simply not comply with treatment (Fairburn and Harrison, 2003). The aetiological factors contributing to these disorders are complex and may include genetic or biological abnormalities as well as environmental factors such as conflict or isolation. However, in addition to these causes there are evolutionary factors that exert pressure on all humans in modern societies with regard to eating behaviour.

Anorexia nervosa

Anorexia nervosa was first identified in the 1870s (e.g. Gull, 1874); however, the term 'anorexia' means loss of appetite and this is misleading as, although there is loss of weight, there is generally no loss of appetite amongst sufferers. The disorder has one of the highest mortality rates of any psychological disorder, as high as 21 per cent in some estimates, mostly as a result of starvation and suicide (Bennett, 2006). These grim statistics are important in countering a Western fashion culture that prizes an excessively underweight physique and where there have been websites dedicated to promoting anorexic images as an ideal body shape to be aimed for. Most of us assess ourselves in terms of our careers, relationships or sporting achievements, but anorexic (and also bulimic) individuals evaluate themselves almost exclusively in terms of body weight (Fairburn and Harrison, 2003).

Anorexia nervosa entails the refusal to maintain minimally normal body weight and a fear of gaining even a tiny amount of weight. There is also a severe disturbance of their own body image, in that they perceive themselves as larger than is objectively apparent. Post-menarcheal females tend to become amenorrheic: that is, they no longer menstruate due to reduced **follicle stimulating hormone** leading to low levels of **oestrogen** (American Psychiatric Association, 2000), and males tend to lose sexual appetite and ability. This self-induced loss of body weight is greater than 15 per cent below normal with a body-mass index (BMI; measured in weight in kilograms/(height in metres)^2) of 17.5 kg/m^2 or less (Goldberg, Benjamin and Creed, 1994). There is persistent use of mirrors to check areas of perceived 'overweight', which is generally focused on the abdomen, hips and thighs. Fairburn and Harrison (2003) consider the overevaluation of body weight and shape to be the core feature of anorexia nervosa, and all other aspects such as loss of weight to be secondary. Thus, the study of body image is important to the study of eating disorders (see the Focus box on p. 289).

Focus

Evolution and obesity

One evolutionary mechanism in conflict with modern society is that of motivation for food consumption. Humans are very efficient machines when it comes to fuel consumption and need very little calorie intake to live. Overabundance of cheap food available within modern societies enables overconsumption.

We also have 'calorie counters' within us as a legacy from our primitive past when food was scarce. These reward us with pleasurable satisfaction for a high calorie intake so that we can survive long periods between food sources. This mechanism is abused by the abundance of high-calorie, low-nutrition foods offered by food manufacturers and retailers, which needless to say encourages overconsumption of high-calorie foods, leading to intake being much higher than energy expenditure. This leads to overweight and obesity problems, which produce less activity, tiredness, ill health, boredom and consequent accelerating weight gain. Control over this mechanism and food intake can reverse these effects to some degree and provide reward in the sense of control and higher activity gains made.

Thus, evolutionary mechanisms that enabled us to survive are contributing to eating disorders in the modern context. These disorders can be ones of over-control leading to **anorexia** or **bulimia nervosa**, or under-control associated with **binge eating** and **obesity**.

There is a great deal of social pressure on young girls to compete with 'impossible' celebrity images to attain an underweight body shape. Source: Pearson Online Database.

There are clear physical complications in anorexia nervosa, which tend to worsen as body weight is reduced, as follows.

- **Acid erosion.** As with bulimia nervosa, purging causes severe dental erosion due to stomach acid damage to enamel, which will also cause visible damage to other areas of the hand, mouth and throat.

- **Cardiovascular complications** occur with heart arrhythmias and, more commonly, sinus bradycardia.

- **Lowered oestrogen** in females, along with lowered calcium intake, leads to osteoporosis, which requires early intervention to prevent serious bone loss (Zipfel et al., 2001). This bone mineral density loss leads to chronic anorexic individuals having 7 or more times the number of fractures of non-sufferers and more serious complications in later years (see Zipfel et al., 2001).

- **Lowered testosterone** in males, and other hormonal abnormalities, can reduce sexual function and produce levels similar to those in prepubertal individuals.

- Lanugo, or the development of fine downy hair on the trunk of the body, can occur in some sufferers, as weight is lost.

- **Body electrolytes.** Some of these physical complications are secondary to weight loss and dangerous to overall health; the consequent imbalance of **body electrolytes** can prove fatal.

Strategies for losing weight can include self-induced vomiting, exercise and the use of laxatives or diuretics, but weight loss may be achieved by the use of excessive exercise and dieting only (Fairburn and Harrison, 2003). Although food intake is restricted, there is often an obsession with food in anorexia. This food focus can take the form of thinking about food excessively or even hoarding it. Fears about eating in public are also common, and anorexia may also be linked to obsessive perfectionism, control over their environment and inflexible thinking (American Psychiatric Association, 2000). A differential diagnosis of **obsessive–compulsive disorder** is not usually the case unless other criteria for anorexia fail to be met, as obsessions increase in anorexia with lowered weight and in areas other than food. In both anorexia and bulimia nervosa, the overlap with obsessive–compulsive behaviour may be evident, as in the anorexic girl who would run up and down stairs exactly 7 times or the bulimic lady who ate exactly 24 bars of chocolate at a sitting, no more and no fewer (DeSilva and Rachman, 2004). Overall, anorexic individuals tend to be over-controlled, in contrast to the more impulsive behaviour of bulimic individuals.

There are two subtypes to anorexia in *DSM-IV-TR*, which are distinguished by the regular engagement of the sufferer in binge eating or purging activities during the current episode of the disorder (American Psychiatric Association, 2000).

- **Restricting type** of anorexia is where weight loss is achieved by dieting, abstaining from eating or excessive exercise and an absence of purging or accompanying binge eating. This subtype is associated with over-controlled behaviour and a lack of insight into their condition.

- **Binge-eating/purging type** of anorexia, as the name suggests, is where the patient has been regularly engaged in binge eating or purging and commonly both during the current episode. Although there is no given minimum frequency for these behaviours, it is assumed that they will occur at least weekly and involve self-induced vomiting or the use of laxatives, enemas or diuretics. This subtype is associated with impulse-control problems (see below), suicide attempts and borderline personality disorder (see Chapter 14).

The disorder mostly affects younger, white, middle-class females, with around 90 per cent of sufferers being female. The age of onset is usually 14–18 years of age, with a later onset being associated with a worse prognosis (American Psychiatric Association, 2000). Although subclinical problems of eating abound in adolescence, anorexia is not as common as media interest may infer, with lifetime prevalence rates amongst females of around 0.5 per cent. It is more common in industrialised countries where there is an abundance of food production. It is also common where there is a high level of media penetration into the population, carrying a culturally accepted message that exerts pressure on individuals to be of a thin body build.

Many young females have eating and body image problems that do not develop further into the criteria for eating disorders. Others progress into a disorder, but the prognosis for some is good as they remit early with, or sometimes without, intervention. In some cases anorexia becomes well established and requires sustained treatment, but in 10–20 per cent of sufferers the disorder is unremitting and requires careful management over the lifetime (Steinhausen, 2002). The latter group tend to have severe weight loss and use purging strategies as well has having a later onset (Steinhausen, 2002). Mortality for this group can be higher than the conservative figure of 10 per cent for anorexia overall, usually from starvation, electrolyte imbalance or suicide (Neilsen, 2001).

Focus

Body image and eating disorders

Although famous as a sex symbol, Marilyn Munroe's fuller figure would not fit the equivalent modern image.
Source: Pearson Online Database.

Many of us are dissatisfied with our image in the mirror and may be temporarily motivated to diet or exercise. Some are more seriously affected by pride in appearance and make a more fundamental alteration of food intake and use extensive exercise, body-building or even cosmetic surgery. We may be proud of or dissatisfied with the results or comments from others if the change is noticeable. However, **body image** is the mental image we have of our bodies and ourselves. It is the combination of our perceptual image, and the way we feel about what we see, or imagined body image. Thus, body image is a more subjective sense of ourselves than a simple objective photo or mirror image, and as such can become greatly distorted as in anorexia nervosa. Since the early work of **Paul Schilder** in the 1920s, the importance of body image to self-esteem, status and even sexuality amongst many other factors has been recognised as being increasingly influential in the twenty-first century.

An individual's body image is 'elastic' rather than veridical (reflecting the real world) and can be changed by internal mood and external information or comparisons (Grogan, 1999). Media images and particularly body image stereotypes have a profound influence on the images that individuals hold of themselves and their satisfaction with this view. We all make comparisons with these media images as well as those of our peers, family and particularly those whom we attach special significance to, or model ourselves on. Susceptibility to this influence varies but is particularly heightened in the teenage years when body shape is constantly changing and we are looking out into the world for our

Focus continued

sense of identity. At these times, we tend to attribute positive qualities to celebrities who dominate the media with carefully managed images and we often try to emulate them. The social comparison theory (Festinger, 1954) is used to support how exposure to images in the media influences the body image and self-esteem of an individual. The phrase 'What is beautiful is good' was empirically supported in terms of the positive judgements made about attractive individuals by the work of Dion, Berscheid and Walster (1972), and thus comparisons made between one's self-image and that of an image-managed celebrity go beyond comparing appearance to comparative judgements of one's worth. Therefore altering our body and body image can be seen as changing more than simply our appearance.

Attractiveness and its positive associations have become linked to a slender shape, and conversely being a larger build has been associated with being unattractive, lazy, unhappy and less confident (Tiggemann and Rothblum, 1988). The somewhat shallow preoccupation with physical attractiveness in Western populations corresponds very closely with a similar bias in TV, film and magazine representations and storylines. Even the average female characters across TV programmes are disproportionately slim compared with the general population (Silverstein, Peterson and Perdue, 1986). More extreme images of thinness began to appear towards the end of the twentieth century and adjectives such as 'waif-like' or 'emaciated' were seen as complimentary within fashion circles. Although the media also ran stories exposing the levels of eating disorders and the use of stimulant drugs amongst fashion models and celebrities (e.g. Frankel, 1998), enhanced pictures of the same models would still be used throughout the same publication to boost sales. The effect on the average teenager's body image of these extreme contrasts is that they create dissatisfaction and encourage eating problems in the vulnerable (Harrison and Cantor, 1997). In the twenty-first century, the almost mythical celebrity image became available to Western females in the form of 'size 0' clothes (UK size 4). This 'gold standard' of fashionable slimness had already been associated with multinational celebrities such as **Victoria Beckham**. Most females see this extreme standard of thinness as unattainable (Hausenblas et al., 2002). In many cases, the images

presented in the media of models and celebrities are in fact unattainable, as they are enhanced by computer graphic systems to present impossible proportions. However synthetic these images are, this media image of thinness has been found to be a causal factor in the rise of pathological eating conditions in the West (Grylli et al., 2005). In an effort to distance this factor from their brand name, Omega withdrew advertising from *Vogue* magazine as a result of the 'anorexic' appearance of the photos of models published (Grogan, 1999).

Kim and Lennon (2007) not only acknowledge a tendency for a large number of females (and some males) to turn to unhealthy eating behaviours as a result of body image dissatisfaction, but also indicate that some will resort to more invasive measures such as plastic surgery. Some individuals try to manipulate their body image with undue focus on certain body parts in a manner reminiscent of **body dysmorphic disorder** (see Chapter 15), and may resort to multiple operations to correct a 'fault' that is personally subjective rather than objective. Males are also increasingly experiencing body image dissatisfaction, sometimes as **muscle dysmorphia,** in relation to both the slim but muscular ideal of the catwalk and the more rugged very muscular bodies presented as ideals in popular sports, or those whose body-building achievements have made them eligible as successful movie stars, such as **Arnold Schwarzenegger** (Grogan, 1999). For males trying to reduce body image dissatisfaction and attain a comparable physique, the methods of their 'slim image seeking' counterparts are supplemented by the use of anabolic steroids to facilitate extreme levels of muscle resistance training and muscle growth, which is often how their mentors achieved their own physiques originally (Epperley, 1993). Although less common, female body builders will also use steroids to create an overly muscular body.

Much of the literature regarding body image focuses on societal and media influence and its negative effects in terms of dissatisfaction and consequent pathological behaviour. Little consideration is given to more positive factors in body image satisfaction, such as improved self-esteem, sense of control and self-efficacy. Raising the levels of these three factors by strategies such as assertiveness training may also have the effect of improving body image satisfaction (Grogan, 1999).

Bulimia nervosa

Russell (1979) originally described bulimia nervosa as a disorder distinguished from anorexia nervosa. However, in bulimia nervosa there are many features of anorexia including the core feature of a distorted body image, with an excessive focus on weight and shape as their primary means of self-evaluation. However, this focus on body shape and weight tends to result in a sustained body mass, which does not decline in the manner of anorexia nervosa. Binge eating and methods of preventing weight gain are also essential aspects of bulimia, although some bulimic types do not purge. The name bulimia nervosa is often translated as 'to eat as an ox due to nervousness' and there may be undue focus on the binge eating aspect of the disorder that sufferers often consider to be a source of embarrassment and shame. Sufferers consequently hide their eating behaviour and eat in private, making detection and diagnosis more difficult than with anorexic behaviour. However, bulimic individuals are also motivated towards treatment as a result of their embarrassment and shame over their eating behaviour, and are less likely to exhibit denial (Fairburn and Harrison, 2003).

A diagnosis of bulimia nervosa requires a frequency and level of binge eating of at least twice a week and in clearly excessive quantities at one sitting. What is excessive can vary and may exceed 5000 calories, but is usually in the region of 1000–2000 calories at a single meal (Fairburn and Harrison, 2003) rather than small snacks spread over more than 2 hours, and such binging is outside of special festive occasions where such eating is socially acceptable (American Psychiatric Association, 2000). There is a focus on high-calorie foods such as cake, but it is the quantity of food consumed that identifies bulimic behaviour. Consumption may be impulsive or an out-of-control **feeding frenzy**. This will continue to oversatiation – that is, until the sufferer is uncomfortably full – unless secrecy is disturbed by the presence of an individual (rather than an event). Paradoxically, those with bulimia may appear to eat low-calorie foods or diet between binging episodes. Bulimic individuals may have been overweight during their lifetime and often experience more intense hunger than anorexic individuals.

As with anorexia nervosa, bulimia nervosa also has two subtypes as follows.

- **The purging subtype** denotes individuals who during their current episode of bulimia regularly misuse laxatives, enemas or diuretics, or self-induce vomiting. They comprise the majority (80–90 per cent) of bulimic individuals.

- **The non-purging subtype** is where weight-reducing strategies such as excessive exercise or food intake restriction are used, but not forms of purging during their current episode of the disorder.

Bulimia nervosa is associated with unipolar mood disorders (see Chapter 18) and the depressive symptoms often precede the eating disorder, undermining the assumption of sufferers that depression results from their eating condition. There may also be comorbidity with anxiety symptoms, and substance abuse is prevalent in bulimia involving alcohol as well as diet-related stimulant abuse

Five thousand calories can be a formidable amount for one sitting and some individuals exceed this.
Source: Pearson Online Database.

(American Psychiatric Association, 2000). As with the purging subtype of anorexia, bulimia sufferers often have personality disorders and in particular **borderline personality disorder**. Although the physical complications associated with weight loss in anorexia are relatively rare in bulimic individuals, some suffer menstrual irregularity, and the heavy use of laxatives can lead to electrolyte imbalances and even heart arrhythmias. The purging subtype will also suffer considerable damage to teeth, mouth, throat and stomach due to vomiting, as with their anorexic counterpart.

The prevalence of bulimia nervosa is up to four times that of anorexia nervosa with rates between 1–2 per cent (Hoek and van Hoeken, 2003). However, this may represent differential rates of diagnosis rather than actual prevalence in the population, as bulimic individuals have more insight into their behaviour than their anorexic counterparts. Bulimia has a higher average age of onset than anorexia and prognosis is worse for the purging subtype of bulimia and those with lower self-esteem or personality problems (Fairburn and Harrison, 2003). The mortality rate in bulimia nervosa is considerably less than that for anorexia but still above that for the general population.

Aetiology and treatment of anorexia and bulimia nervosa

Aetiology

Both anorexia and bulimia nervosa have been researched for evidence of putative aetiological factors more than other eating conditions (Fairburn and Harrison, 2003). The genetic influence on both anorexia and bulimia nervosa is considerable, with 10- and 4-fold increases in first-degree relatives for these disorders respectively, and there also appears to be cross-transmission between these two disorders, as well as the atypical eating disorders discussed below (Strober et al., 2000). This latter point means that the offspring of individuals with one disorder may grow up to develop one of the other eating disorders. Twin studies reveal differences of concordance of 55 per cent for monozygotic twins, against 5 per cent for dizygotic pairs in anorexia, whilst a lesser figure of 35 per cent against 30 per cent respectively is found for bulimia (Treasure and Holland, 1989). One study attributed 80 per cent of the variance in bulimia nervosa vulnerability to genetics (Bulik, Sullivan and Kendler, 1998), but adoption studies are yet to be established for these disorders and thus other factors may be confounding these results. One **linkage study** of anorexia has implicated a location on chromosome 4 for a gene relating to the disorder and in the case of the restricting subtype of anorexia on chromosome 1 (Grice et al., 2002). However, a reanalysis of this work implicated other loci including a different location on chromosome 1 and also loci on chromosomes 2 and 13 (Fairburn and Harrison, 2003).

Some neurotransmitter abnormalities have been associated with anorexia and bulimia nervosa, especially **serotonin**, which may prove to be instrumental in eating disorders rather than a consequence of their physiological effects (Kaye and Strober, 1999). Dopamine is also implicated in motivation to see food as rewarding in picking up on the cues for food (e.g. smell) as well as control over behaviour, and high activity in the dorsal striatum tends to co-occur with eating restraint (see Carlson, 2004). However, the role of **dopamine** in both bulimia and anorexia is as yet not fully explicit. It is clear that many physiological factors in anorexia may be a consequence of the progress of the disorder, and each could return to normal when body mass is restored (Walsh and Devlin, 1998). This is probably the case with the abnormal levels of hormones in anorexia that are controlled by the **hypothalamus**, such as **cortisol**. Indeed, the function of the hypothalamus itself is central to appetite and eating, but again, malfunction of its hormone regulation is probably a consequence of weight loss rather than any a priori causal role in eating disorders.

Endogenous opioids are **neuropeptides**, which are large molecule neurotransmitters (see Chapter 3) that act on brain receptors. As a matter of clarification, the term 'opioid' refers to the chemical produced within the body and opiates to the exogenous opium-based drugs. Endogenous opioids such as the **endorphins** have powerful reinforcing characteristics (as well as pain relief and reduction of fear response effects), and levels of these neuropeptides can be related to starvation, food type and manipulation of intake. Both restricting the intake of food and binging can release these substances, as can excessive exercise, providing an endogenous reinforcement to complement any sense of achievement in controlling body shape and weight (also see Kring et al., 2007).

In addition to these influences, motivation towards anorexia nervosa can also be facilitated by psychological factors such as competitiveness, perfectionism, asceticism and self-directed hostility or low self-esteem and assertiveness (Williams et al., 1993). This is in addition to a number of potentially predisposing events, such as childhood sexual abuse or dieting habits in the family. Stein, Wooley and McPherson (1999) found a certain potential for **transgenerational transmission** of eating disorders, in that mothers with eating disorders had more conflict over feeding their infant children than those mothers without disorders.

Alcoholism or obesity in parents can be related to the development of bulimia nervosa in their offspring, and an early menarche in the sufferer is also associated with bulimia. Critical parenting, especially regarding body shape and weight, as well as conflict in the home are also associated with anorexia and bulimia nervosa (see Fairburn and Harrison, 2003). The sense of control experienced in restricting eating behaviour and weight can provide reinforcement for anorexic behaviour by somewhat countering a sense of helplessness elsewhere in their lives (see Seligman, 1992). This can be extended to bulimia nervosa, as individuals with both disorders would find control over their overvalued body shape reinforcing.

Fairburn et al. (1999) have presented a cognitive behavioural model of anorexia nervosa (see Field, 2003). In this, they relate some of the factors, such as perfectionism, lack of **self-efficacy** and low **self-esteem**, as motivating the individual towards an extreme need for self-control. The self-control is expressed in eating behaviour as a result of other influences mentioned, such as family attention to dietary control, delaying or preventing puberty and its effects on control, media messages on body shape and because control over eating does not require reliance on others to be successful. They also identify three feedback mechanisms that perpetuate the disordered behaviour and thinking: increased sense of control, which rewards further progress; acceleration of diet due to weight loss (easier to feel full) and further attempts to increase control to counter the disorganising and confusion inducing effects of low weight; and increased focus on weight and body shape fitting the media stereotype and fear of relapse and losing that successful control. Models like this rely on serial assumptions and interactions that are difficult to test, but they do provide intervention points where therapy can be focused.

Other cognitive approaches have examined **attentional bias** in processing body shape stimuli, which is seen as a central feature of both anorexia and bulimia nervosa (Faunce, 2002). Attentional bias in anorexia and bulimia means that sufferers will tend to maintain these eating disorders by distorting the way they perceive and interpret their experiences. Attentional bias towards words pertaining to diet, restraint or body shape has been evidenced by studies using a modified Stroop test (Cooper and Fairburn, 1992). In this experimental procedure, the distraction effect of words can be measured by the delay in naming the ink colour in which such words are printed, as compared with words neutral to diet or body shape (see Faunce, 2002). As a primary feature of the disorder, not only may faulty schemata relating to body shape and weight provide a means of intervention, but also by shifting this fundamental bias, other aspects of the disorder may also come under control.

Treatments

Many individuals with eating disorders, particularly anorexia nervosa, resist diagnosis and treatment, resulting in the involuntary detention of patients whose weight loss is becoming life threatening. Fairburn et al. (1996) found the proportion of individuals with eating disorders who are not in treatment to approach 90 per cent. Treatment as an outpatient is preferable for this client group (Palmer, 2006). Treatment should primarily address the patient's weight and their attitudes to eating and weight gain, and help to prevent the patient's use of body image and weight control to address other personal issues in their lives. There are varied interventions, such as educational approaches focusing on raising self-esteem (O'Dea and Abraham, 2000) and the more familiar CBT, which some consider essential in engaging clients in the therapeutic process (Fairburn and Harrison, 2003).

Medical approaches to anorexia nervosa in the past have often focused on increasing body weight directly and even against the will of the patient, rather than attempting to assess or change their motivation. This to some degree reflects the historical view that the mental disorder aspect of eating disorders was trivial and merely related to young girls and fashion, as opposed to the current view of them being serious and lethal disorders (Palmer, 2006). Anorexia nervosa sufferers are often very knowledgeable about the areas involved in their disorder and are very critical of, as well as resistant to, clinicians and therapists, especially if they lack specialist knowledge. To a great degree, engagement of anorexia patients could be seen to involve the dual assessment of clinician by patient and vice versa (Palmer, 2006). Engagement with eating disorder

blue   blue   blue   green   green   yellow   red   yellow
yellow   blue   red   green   yellow   yellow   green
yellow   yellow   red   yellow   green   blue   yellow
red   blue   green   green   blue   blue   green   green
yellow   yellow   blue   yellow   yellow   red   blue
yellow   red   blue   red   yellow   blue   red   blue   red

Figure 10.1 The Stroop test. In the Stroop test, participants naming the colour of the print are slowed by reading a conflicting word but facilitated if print colour and word are the same.
Source: Carlson (1992) *Psychology*, Allyn and Bacon.

Research

NICE guidelines for treatment evaluation studies

In 2004 the National Institute for Clinical Excellence (NICE) chose eating disorders as the first topic for the issue of treatment guidelines (Palmer, 2006; also see Wilson and Shafran, 2005). NICE graded treatment approaches in terms of their supportive evidence base and implemented three gradings for these recommendations as follows.

- **Grade A** treatment recommendations have strong empirical support from well-constructed randomised trials.

- **Grade B** treatment recommendations fall short of the above but have support from empirical trials.

- **Grade C** treatment recommendations tend to rely on expert opinion without the support of good empirical data.

When applied to approaches to eating disorders, recommendations regarding treatments rarely rose above grade C, implying that in the majority of cases support for their use was weak, particularly in the case of anorexia nervosa. The use of objective family interventions in anorexia directly targeting the eating disorder was given recommendations rated at grade B. However, for bulimia nervosa, recommendations for CBT were grade A, and grade B recommendations were given to drug treatments of the anti-depressant type and some self-help programmes (see Wilson and Shafran, 2005).

In detailing some of the treatment approaches to anorexia and bulimia nervosa, it is useful to bear these recommendations in mind, particularly in the case of anorexia, which has lacked both the level of research into bulimia and the more successful outcomes that treatments for bulimia have achieved.

---

patients can be crucial to success, particularly in the case of anorexia nervosa. It is partly for this reason that treatments such as drug therapies are often combined with **cognitive behavioural therapy** (CBT), as this not only is effective in itself but also provides the level of engagement with the client necessary to promote maintenance and compliance with other therapies (Fairburn and Harrison, 2003).

As acknowledged in the NICE guidelines, anti-depressant medications of the **selective serotonin reuptake inhibitor** (SSRI) type (e.g. **fluoxetine** (Prozac)) are important in the treatment of bulimia nervosa. This effectiveness may often extend beyond the fact that bulimia is often comorbid with **unipolar depression** (Bourke et al., 2006). In addition, SSRIs are also effective with obsessive disorders, which may play a part in the symptoms of eating disorder patients, particularly anorexia nervosa. Neuroleptic medications reduce anxiety and have the side-effect of increasing weight, and were thus also thought to be of use for anorexic individuals. Although some of these effects have been realised in anorexia nervosa using the neuroleptic **Olanzapine** (Bosanac, Burrows and Norman, 2004), it is probable that the other effects of these powerful antipsychotics could outweigh the therapeutic gains (Kring et al., 2007). It is also the case that overall effectiveness for anti-depressant or neuroleptic therapies in treating anorexia nervosa has not been evident in reviews of studies (Attia and Schroeder, 2005).

The pharmacological treatment of choice for bulimia nervosa remains the SSRI fluoxetine (given at a higher dose than for depression), although other anti-depressants have also been shown to have some measure of success, including tricyclic anti-depressants (Mitchell, Agras and Wonderlich, 2007). As with the treatment of opiate use, substances that block the receptors for endogenous opioids such as naloxone also have the potential to block the rewarding aspects of food intake control. This pharmacological approach has been used to try to undermine the hedonistic aspect to binge eating in bulimia nervosa (see Mitchell, Agras and Wonderlich, 2007).

For many, the treatment of choice for bulimia nervosa is CBT (Fairburn and Harrison, 2003), but its effectiveness in anorexia nervosa is less well supported, although this is the case for almost all other treatment approaches for the latter disorder (Palmer, 2006; Wilson and Shafran, 2005). However, CBT is useful in both disorders in maintaining longer-term freedom from eating problems beyond the shorter-term goal of returning to normal weight. Giving the eating disorder patient good insight into their condition and what maintains it, in addition to self-monitoring and the skills to address future problems, can make a great deal of difference to long-term prognosis. Fairburn (1997) believes that CBT can be successful in anorexia nervosa as well as bulimia nervosa if there is additional focus on using the therapeutic relationship to motivate the client to change and restore their weight to a reasonable minimum.

Family therapy can be effective in changing the dynamics of inter-family relations, which may be used by the sufferer as a reason for controlling body weight, but family approaches only tend to be effective in anorexia if there is objective focus on the eating disorder (Wilson and Shafran, 2005).

Binge eating disorder and obesity

Binge eating disorder and obesity are not listed as disorders in *DSM-IV-TR*, although the former is included as a diagnosis in need of further study and the latter is recognised as a medical diagnosis of serious and growing concern throughout the world. Binge eating disorder is listed in *DSM-IV-TR* as an eating disorder not otherwise specified, and in *ICD-10* as an atypical eating disorder. Whereas in anorexia nervosa there is excessive control and manipulation of body weight or food intake, and to some extent a more impulsive approach to eating but maintenance of normal weight in bulimia nervosa, there is in contrast a lack of overall control in eating and weight maintenance in binge eating disorder and other sources of obesity.

Binge eating disorder

Binge eating disorder has yet to attain full disorder status in either the *DSM* or *ICD* diagnostic systems, but it is increasingly being recognised in the research literature and clinical practice (see Dinglemans, Bruna and van Furth, 2002). Currently listed in appendix B of *DSM-IV-TR* (page 785) under the heading of 'criteria sets and axes provided for further study', binge eating disorder is characterised by secretively and rapidly consuming a large amount of food until uncomfortably full in an uncontrolled way, which causes distress, guilt and embarrassment. This eating behaviour occurs with or without hunger and is not followed by methods of compensation such as purging, which would be the case in bulimia nervosa (American Psychiatric Association, 2000). Individuals with binge eating disorder are usually in their forties when first assessed and up to 25 per cent are male, thus further differentiating them from the younger and more frequently female sufferers of anorexia or bulimia nervosa (Barry, Grilo and Masheb, 2002).

As with bulimia nervosa, binge eating disorder is also associated with mood disorders, mostly depression but also anxiety. In the broader population of binge eaters, the behaviour tends to occur late in the day after a period of food abstinence, and it has been found that the behaviour temporarily reduces feelings of **anxiety** and dysphoric

mood, which rise again after the binge eating stops. This negatively reinforces binging, as it produces brief respite from negative affect (Deaver et al., 2003). Such 'emotional eating' behaviour is thought to be common when low mood coincides with high levels of food cues, such as may usually occur when the individual is at home alone with ample food, but it may also be triggered in the context of a restaurant or fast-food outlet (see Timmerman, 2006). There are few studies into the aetiology of binge eating, although factors that increase the risk of psychiatric disorders in general and obesity are also associated with binge eating disorder (Fairburn et al., 1998).

A further similarity to bulimia nervosa is that binge eating disorder is reasonably responsive to interventions, particularly cognitive behavioural therapy and behavioural weight control (Carter and Fairburn, 1998). **Functional assessment** of binge eating is an examination of the antecedents and consequences of this behaviour that cue the behaviour and subsequently reinforce it, such as the aforementioned feelings of anxiety and depression and their reduction by binging. These analyses allow behavioural and cognitive behavioural interventions to alter these contingencies to reduce the binge eating (Lee and Miltenberger, 1997). Antecedent variables that could be targeted in binge eating are mood, anxiety, boredom, time of day and being alone. However, the manipulation of these variables has been questioned on practical and ethical grounds, as well as their assumed relationship to the behavioural function of the binging itself (Lee and Miltenberger, 1997). Carter and Fairburn (1998) have found a cognitive behavioural self-help programme to have a substantial and sustained effect in reducing binge eating. Anti-depressant medication has also been used with mixed effectiveness, with **SSRIs** such as fluoxetine tending to reduce calorie intake but not the frequency of binging, and fluvoxamine reducing binging (Dinglemans, Bruna and van Furth, 2002).

Although obesity is not one of the criteria for binge eating disorder, the disorders are very frequently comorbid, and while there are logical links between the conditions, they tend to be treated in different ways and often by practitioners with different specialities (Dinglemans, Bruna and van Furth, 2002). Binge-eating obese individuals are distinguished from their non-binging counterparts in having more body image problems, higher levels of anxiety, depression and lower self-esteem, as well as greater disturbance in their eating behaviour and attitudes (Hsu et al., 2002). Binge eating can be a predictor of obesity with a latency of onset of a year or two. Although obesity is not a *DSM* or *ICD* mental disorder, it does have a significant relationship to the other eating disorders, and as such, it will be examined next.

Being overweight or even obese is no longer a rarity but now a condition affecting an increasing proportion of society. Source: Pearson Online Database.

Obesity

Obesity is a medically dangerous state of overweight resulting from a prolonged excessive intake of calories over and above those used by the body in the same period (Zigman and Elmquist, 2003). It is classified in *ICD-10* as a general medical condition and tends to be thought of as disordered eating with biological causes rather than as an eating disorder with psychological implications (Tanofsky-Kraff and Yanvski, 2004). Obesity greatly increased around the turn of the twenty-first century across the world (James, Rigby and Leach, 2004). There are well over 1 billion overweight individuals in the world, with a quarter of those being defined as obese (Hill, 2007), and the UK has one of the highest percentages of obese adults in Europe. This rise of epidemic proportions is widely realised to be one of the most serious public health issues facing the world today and one for which preventative measures are not succeeding (Holt, 2005). Although the levels of obesity in the USA seem high, with 31 per cent being classified as obese and rising, the increasing proportion of children with this problem would suggest a very pessimistic picture for the health of this population in the future (Hedley et al., 2004).

Focus

Body mass index (BMI) and obesity

Obesity is defined in terms of **body mass index** (BMI), defined as a person's weight divided by the squared function of their height (in kilograms per squared metre). According to the World Health Organisation (1997), it becomes an issue for concern at the following levels.

- **Overweight** occurs at a BMI of over 25 kg/m², just above the healthier range of 20–25 kg/m².

- **Obesity** is confirmed by a BMI of over 30 kg/m² and marks a point where increases in associated illnesses such as coronary heart problems, some cancers, musculoskeletal disease and diabetes increase dramatically: for example, the risk of type 2 diabetes increases almost 100-fold in middle age females at a BMI of 35 kg/m² (see Holt, 2005).

- **Morbid obesity** is defined by a BMI of over 40 kg/m² and can be life threatening in itself with more severe associated illnesses than obesity.

The BMI is highly correlated with levels of adipose tissue (fat) in the body, but the BMI can overestimate fat levels in very muscular individuals (Grilo, 2006). Waist measurement is also an accurate predictor of the health risk to those who are overweight, as it directly estimates **centralised fat** and is less confounded by high levels of muscularity.

The separation of obesity from eating disorders has led to the former being researched and managed by medical and biological scientists and the latter in the main by psychologists and psychiatrists, with little crossover between the two domains. This has been detrimental to progress in understanding the psychology of obesity (Hill, 2007). The relationship between obesity and binge eating disorder as well as some degree of relatedness to bulimia in terms of uncontrolled eating has been outlined above. Although the public may see each of anorexia nervosa and obesity as solutions for one another, the view of both conditions being due to problematic eating behaviour and having an undue focus on food is far more accurate. Studies have shown that, far from being a polar opposite, obsession with dieting early in life can be associated with obesity in later life, though the exact nature of this association is unclear (Neumark-Sztainer, 2005). The relationship between binge eating and obesity is also that it is one of two factors of disordered eating that contributes to obesity. The other factor is night-time eating or eating after the main evening meal to the extent of disrupting sleep (Stunkard, Grace and Wolff, 1955). This can be exacerbated by stress and contributes greatly to the calorie intake-usage equation, as night eating is followed by inactivity.

The biology of obesity has been increasingly explicit during the twenty-first century with increased but incomplete understanding of the molecular and neural substrates that control body weight homeostasis. Zigman and Elmquist (2003) have drawn attention to the way hormones such as leptin and ghrelin interact with autonomic regulatory neural circuits to regulate both food intake and body weight correctly, and indicate that over- or under-stimulation of these pathways can cause obesity or anorexia. Such research may provide alternative medical interventions for obesity to the rather invasive traditional approaches, such as laparoscopic surgery to reduce stomach capacity with bands or gastric bypass, or mechanically preventing passage of solids into the mouth, which simply assume an absence of control by the patient themselves. Although the use of medication to suppress appetite also makes this assumption, it is considered less drastic than surgery, but it has been associated with problems of addiction in the middle of the twentieth century, when amphetamine compounds were primarily used. Modern pharmaceutical approaches can aim to: alter homeostasis in changing energy intake and expenditure; enhance satiety; inhibit nutrient absorption; and change metabolic rate, which is the traditional route (Wilding, 2007).

The obese individual's own control over eating is often subverted by evolutionary mechanisms intended to motivate us towards once scarce high-calorie foods by providing neural reward for their consumption, which is dangerously counterproductive in a contemporary context of abundant food in attractive, high-calorie forms that abuse this very mechanism. This is exacerbated further by enhancement of flavour and olfactory cues leading to habitual consumption (Wardle, 2007).

In the light of advancing medical approaches, it is unfortunate that psychological factors in obesity have tended to remain the subject of popular media speculation, leaving a relative vacuum in professional research. This shortfall may be hindering attempts to address the increase in obesity because, as is the case with many issues related to health psychology, psychological factors assisting prevention clearly lead to better outcomes than treatment once obese. The assumption that obesity is the patient's fault has led to the application of medical interventions without consideration of valuable personal support for them (see Wilding, 2007). Improving the patient's ability to control his or her own behaviour would seem to be a longer-term solution requiring a contribution from psychology. Maio, Haddock and Jarman (2007) have examined the role of psychological factors in changing attitudes to healthy eating behaviour and considered the social psychology approach of reducing or at least utilising ambivalence towards such eating.

It is known that obese individuals have high levels of body image dissatisfaction and low self-esteem in common with anorexic patients (Grilo, 2006). These factors provide targets for psychological interventions to raise self-esteem and improve body image disparity for obese individuals. Directly addressing the calorie intake (eating behaviour) and calorie reduction (activity levels) with behavioural regimes can give the patient sustainable methods of altering the fixed habits producing obesity. Such interventions, combined with lifestyle interventions, can enable the patient to regain both control over their condition and also improve their motivation to maintain higher activity and lower intake (Wilding, 2007). All treatment strategies for obesity are being intensively reviewed and evaluated in the light of the possibility that within a few years, at the current rate of increase, obesity will overtake tobacco- and alcohol-related risks as the primary health problem facing the world's population.

Critical and evaluative issues in eating-related conditions

The distinction between anorexia and bulimia may be less distinct than the separate headings infer. Individual sufferers of eating disorders tend not to remain on their discrete pathways with regard to their aberrant behaviour. Bulimic individuals may begin to lose weight and be better

Focus

Eating as addictive behaviour

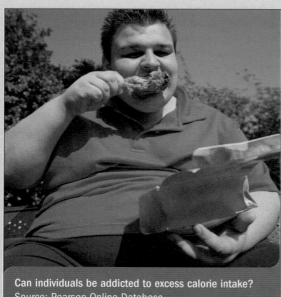

Can individuals be addicted to excess calorie intake?
Source: Pearson Online Database.

Obesity, binge eating, anorexia and bulimia nervosa are usually viewed from the perspective of their being eating disorders or conditions, but it can prove enlightening to consider the aberrant eating behaviours in this chapter as addictive forms of **food abuse**. In binge eating disorder and obesity, individuals are addicted to high levels of food intake, not just in order to feel physically 'full' and attain a biological sense of reward as a result of high calorie intake, but also to reduce anxiety or stress. In seeking psychological comfort from food, they may target simple carbohydrates, especially chocolate. The 'withdrawal' pain of feeling 'empty' and agitated, as well as having acquired habitual eating needs, makes it difficult to moderate intake or to diet, leaving a destructive cycle of increased inactivity and calorie intake. In anorexia and bulimia, control is exerted over the eating impulse and the reverse physical consequences to obesity occur, beginning a related but different behavioural, cognitive and physiological cycle. For anorexia nervosa this entails reduced food intake, increased activity and a sense of control over this important aspect of the sufferer's life, and in bulimia nervosa there is also a sense of control over significant events, which in both cases is addictive.

Theoretically at least, each of these conditions involves the abuse of food in psychologically and physiologically addictive behaviour cycles. Research has also established links between eating disorders and substance disorders (Grilo et al., 1995). The interrelationship between these disorders and the component behaviours of exercise and self-starvation may be partly explained by reference the **endogenous opioid reward system**. The effects of ß-endorphin release are mimicked by the use of addictive drugs in substance use disorders (see Chapter 11), and in the case of eating disorders, overeating and self-starvation, as well as exercise, will all stimulate the release of ß-endorphin. In conjunction with obsessive traits, this not only provides a link between these disorders, but also offers some explanation for the addictive and persistent nature of some of the weight-reducing strategies found in anorexia and bulimia nervosa (see Davis, Katzman and Kirsh, 1999). Davis and Claridge (1998) have proposed that an **addictive personality** (see Chapter 11) may underpin the frequent comorbidity of substance use disorder with eating disorders. Older psychobiological research has also presented evidence pointing to an opioid-based addiction model for eating disorders, and has proposed opiate-blocking medication as part of the therapeutic intervention for eating disorders (Marrazzi and Luby, 1986).

The neurotransmitter **dopamine** is associated with both control and a sense of control over activity and is involved in the reward pathways in the brain. Dopamine is specifically involved in the reward-based regulation of food intake (Schwartz et al., 2000). Dopamine D2 receptors have been found to be depleted in proportion to BMI in obese individuals (Schwartz et al., 2000). Thus those prone to obesity may not be gaining reward via this dopamine pathway and may be compensating for this by pathological eating behaviour. This would point to a possible intervention using dopamine **agonists** in reducing this type of compensatory eating in obese individuals (Schwartz et al., 2000). Higher levels of dopamine activity can thus be related to the over-control of body weight as seen in anorexia nervosa.

One advantage of conceptualising eating conditions and disorders within an addiction framework is that it may open up the possibility of further interventions, as illustrated by the psychobiological treatments above. Further to this, psychological approaches to addictive behaviour may also be available for application to the treatment of eating disorders where appropriate. An example would be the desensitisation of sufferers to the cued behaviours associated with eating conditions, such as learning not to respond to high-calorie food or very slim models (see Chapter 11 for such psychological applications to substance use disorders).

classified as anorexic; others may move between the eating disorders and obesity over their lifetime. In the first half of the twentieth century, obesity was assumed to have a psychological component, but this fell out of favour in later years as it became regarded as a biological disorder and was considered as disordered eating not an eating disorder (Tanofsky-Kraff and Yanvski, 2004). Not including obesity with the eating disorders anorexia and bulimia nervosa may just be keeping a piece of the explanatory jigsaw for eating disorders out of the research picture. This may also contribute to the relative success in managing bulimia nervosa and the comparative difficulty in interventions with both anorexia nervosa and obesity. Thus, one current critical issue for research in this area is to re-examine the psychological correlates of obesity and also to consider them in relation to anorexia and bulimia nervosa as well as binge eating disorder.

Self-test questions

- Obesity has been described as a 'modern epidemic'. Why is the disorder spreading so rapidly?
- How is bulimia nervosa distinguished from anorexia nervosa in the *DSM* system?
- Why is the treatment of anorexia limited in its effectiveness?
- What is the relationship between body image and eating disorders?
- How successful are pharmacological treatments in bulimia and anorexia nervosa?
- In what ways can conceptualising eating conditions as addictive disorders be advantageous?

Impulse control disorders

Each of the disorders in this section is characterised by the sufferer's inability to control or suppress an impulse, drive or temptation to carry out a specific type of behaviour. The acts carried out are harmful to the individual or others and are often preceded by mounting tension or arousal. This build-up of tension turns to relief, gratification or pleasure upon committing the act, which may or may not be accompanied by guilt or regret at having given in to the temptation to carry out the action. These three features – failure to resist harmful impulse; arousal prior to the act; and tension, release or pleasure in carrying out

the act – define and distinguish impulse control disorders (Dell'Osso et al., 2006).

Many of these behaviours correspond to criminal acts and thus involve clinical forensic issues in their detection and management. For example, kleptomania may first be detected as petty theft or shoplifting, but may subsequently be dealt with primarily by clinical intervention rather than a penal sentence. Instruments for detecting impulse control conditions can overlap with measures of obsessive–compulsive disorder with which they are still associated, such as the Schedule of Compulsions, Obsessions and Pathological Impulses (see Watson and Wu, 2005). The individual disorders are well distinguished by their characteristic feature, and problems of diagnosis tend to be in terms of the degree of behaviour reaching threshold criteria. Thus, the *DSM* and *ICD* systems are in agreement over these disorders, except for the absence of a distinct category of intermittent explosive disorder in *ICD-10*.

Intermittent explosive disorder

In intermittent explosive disorder there are discrete periods when there is a marked inability to resist aggressive impulses towards others or property. Assaults on people are intentional and may involve threatening, hitting or a full physical assault on another person. Attacks on property involve the deliberate destruction of or major damage to valuable property; minor or accidental damage falls short of the criteria for this disorder. Individuals with mood or anxiety disorders may also suffer rising arousal that is difficult to control, leading to aggression, but intermittent explosive disorder should not be diagnosed in these contexts. It is a rare disorder with widely varying prevalence estimates (see Dell'Osso et al., 2006) and may require a diagnostic interview to identify it and distinguish it from other conditions, such as substance abuse (Olvera, 2002). The culturally specific condition of **amok** has similarities to intermittent explosive disorder, but tends to involve a single episode of extreme aggression with dissociative features and is found predominantly in southeastern Asia (Prins, 1990).

The symptoms of intermittent explosive disorder lead rapidly to complications such as loss of job, relationship breakdown, accidents, counter-assaults and criminal proceedings. Onset of the disorder may become evident in forensic settings as a result of consequent assaults or vandalism, and sometimes during processes such as school expulsion or as a result of an earlier intervention by an **educational psychologist**. Adult sufferers may be found in penal institutions, where impulsive violence may be confounded with other motivation or form a contingent within other violent inmate pathology (see Mills and Kroner, 2003). Offenders apprehended for violence may malinger as having intermittent explosive disorder as mitigation for their offence or to be diverted from the standard penal system. Some sufferers have subthreshold violent impulses between episodes of the disorder, which may be suppressed or diverted into benign outbursts (Dell'Osso et al., 2006).

Intermittent explosive disorder is more common in males than females and there are signs that the disorder is inherited, as it is more common amongst first-degree relatives than in the general population (American Psychiatric Association, 2000). Neurological signs (letter reversal; reflex asymmetries) and abnormally slow **EEG** recordings (see Chapter 3) are also evident in this disorder, pointing to a neurobiological aetiology. As with other impulsive and compulsive disorders, low levels of serotonin have been inferred from low 5-hydroxy-indoleatic acid levels (American Psychiatric Association, 2000). This deficit has indicated pharmacological intervention using **SSRI** drugs such as fluoxetine or fluvoxamine (see Chapter 3) to raise serotonin levels. Other drug treatments have been used in intermittent explosive disorder, and **mood stabilisers** such as lithium, **beta-blockers** such as propranolol and atypical **anti-psychotic medications** such as risperidone have all shown some level of success in reducing symptoms (see Dell'Osso et al., 2006; Olvera, 2002). Cognitive behavioural therapy and also social skill training have been generally of use in reducing aggressive behaviour, and they have also been used to effect in intermittent explosive disorder (see Alpert and Spilman, 1997).

Kleptomania

In kleptomania there is a persistent inability to control an impulse to steal items of little or no personal use or value. As with other impulse control disorders, the act follows a build-up of tension and arousal and is accompanied by pleasure and gratification when carried out. Thus there is no clearly discernible motive for the theft (including delusional thinking) other than the relief from tension or gratification from the act itself. The similarity of the features of intrusive thoughts, tension and compulsion followed by relief have suggested to many that, as with other impulse control disorders, kleptomania may be better placed in the obsessive–compulsive spectrum of disorders (Durst et al., 2001), although this may be more appropriate with certain subtypes of kleptomania (Grant, 2006). There is also overlap with the symptoms of mood and substance disorders with which kleptomania (as well as other impulse control disorders) is often comorbid, to

the extent of being a secondary diagnosis to these disorders (Grant, 2006).

Prevalence of kleptomania is unclear with a few studies revealing relatively high levels of the disorder in psychiatric populations (Grant, Kim and McCabe, 2006). However, as a result of a reluctance to report due to shame and guilt over symptoms (Grant and Kim, 2005), kleptomania can be difficult to identify, in addition to problems in distinguishing it from other pathological states and similar behaviour emanating from non-pathological origins. To facilitate specific classification based on *DSM* criteria, Grant, Kim and McCabe (2006) developed and successfully tested the Structured Clinical Interview for Kleptomania (SCI-K), which proved to be sensitive as well as highly reliable and valid in their own results. Neurological tests of *DSM*-classified kleptomania sufferers have not revealed many deficits; however, the severity of symptoms has been related to poorer executive brain function (Grant, Odlaug and Wozniak, 2007). Sufferers very often fear apprehension and prosecution for their acts as well as guilt and shame over their inability to resist the impulse, and as a result have a significantly lowered quality of life (Grant and Kim, 2005).

Treatments for kleptomania have moved from psychological to psychopharmacological interventions over time (Durst et al., 2001). As with other impulse control disorders, SSRIs, mood stabilisers and opioid antagonists, in combination or individually, have all met with success in reducing the impulsive behaviour in kleptomania, but this has not yet been established in fully controlled trials (Dell'Osso et al., 2006). Anxiolytics such as the benzodiazapines have also provided minor evidence of usefulness, but overall SSRIs have been the most consistently successful pharmacological intervention (Durst et al., 2001). As with many of the impulse control disorders, forensic involvement in the process is almost inevitable. However, there is a common assumption amongst the public that shoplifting is a symptom of disorder rather than a crime, even though kleptomania accounts for less than 5 per cent of shoplifting (American Psychiatric Association, 2000).

Pyromania

As with other impulse control disorders, the criteria for pyromania include building tension and arousal prior to, and gratification or pleasure on carrying out, the focal act, which in this case is deliberate fire setting. The repeated fire setting seen in pyromania is not done for accidental, commercial or revenge reasons or as malicious behaviour, as happens in other conditions such as conduct disorder. In addition, there is a general fascination with fire and

Some of those with pyromania may start very destructive fires and then turn up with the fire-fighters to gain more satisfaction from the flames.
Source: Pearson Online Database.

associated activities or paraphernalia, such as emergency fire services (even joining them) and sufferers will attend both fires they have caused and others they have not (American Psychiatric Association, 2000). Very serious consequences involving property and human lives can result from such fires, but pyromania sufferers do not consider such outcomes, only the immediate relief from tension and the pleasure from the act.

Although fire setting is relatively common in those under 18, this is mostly associated with other disorders such as ADHD or conduct disorder (see Chapter 9), and fire setting due to pyromania in childhood and adolescence is rare. Pyromania is more common in males who are often lacking in social skills and academic ability, and can be related to neurochemistry and parental pathology (see Dell'Osso et al., 2006). Of all the impulse control disorders, pyromania is most likely to be underreported due to the act being always illegal and in many cases a very serious crime. It is also a cause of public concern that large-scale fires that destroy vast areas of forests, property and habitation appear to be human-caused and apparently motiveless (see Yang et al., 2007). Forensic interest in pyromania tends to be secondary to that of fire setting in the context of conduct disorder or anti-social personality disorder, especially as childhood fire setting is one of the triad of behaviours, along with bedwetting and animal cruelty, associated with later serial homicide (see Holmes and Holmes, 2002).

There is evidence for the successful use of CBT for fire setting but little evidence from controlled studies of pharmacological interventions (Dell'Osso et al., 2006).

However, SSRIs and mood stabilisers would seem likely candidates for evaluation. Difficulties in detection, compliance and availability of sufferers for research contribute substantially to the lack of pyromania-specific intervention data.

Pathological gambling

As the name implies, the behaviour that is preceded by tension and arousal and is accompanied by relief or pleasure in pathological gambling is recurrent and maladaptive gambling behaviour that significantly disrupts the sufferer's personal, occupational and social functioning. The prevalence of pathological gambling in adults from a US sample is around 2 per cent (Welte et al., 2001), although this may be much higher in some cultures. Rates of pathological gambling may be higher in adolescence, when onset of the disorder is most common (American Psychiatric Association, 2000). In the UK, socially acceptable recreational gambling has increased greatly in the last two decades with activities such as the National Lottery, large casinos as well as interactive-TV and internet gambling. Logically, it has unfortunately been found to be the case that as gambling in the general population has increased, so has the level of pathological gambling (Dell'Osso et al., 2006). However, this logic has been challenged by observing no increase in pathological gambling over time following the opening of a specific casino, and although this may involve commercial interest, it may be worth further research (see Arehart-Treichel, 2007).

Focus

Pathological and acceptable gambling

Some forms of gambling reach a very wide audience.
Source: Pearson Online Database.

Given that the vast majority of individuals in most countries now engage in some form of gambling behaviour, pathological gambling has to be clearly differentiated from its more benign counterpart.

Pathological gamblers are more concerned with maintaining their arousal levels by escalating gambling bets rather than with monetary gain.

Repeated failed attempts to reduce this behaviour are accompanied by restlessness and irritability, and the gambling continues despite great financial, personal and occupational loss as well as distress due to reliance on friends. Sufferers will also commit offences to support their gambling behaviour as well as eroding their social capital by borrowing or even stealing from their own family and acquaintances (American Psychiatric Association, 2000).

Pathological gamblers tend to be preoccupied or obsessed with associated aspects of gambling, such as reliving past experiences or planning future ventures, and focus on money as the source of and solution to all their problems (American Psychiatric Association, 2000). More acceptable levels of gambling tend to be context-specific behaviours and often social events shared with others, involving additional non-gambling activities.

The disorder is often comorbid with depression, bipolar disorder, obsessive–compulsive disorder and substance use disorders, with which it shares features such as addiction, suicidal behaviour and unrealistic optimism (Dell'Osso et al., 2006). Pathological gambling comorbid with substance abuse is more associated with some types of impulsivity where short-term gains are focused on (Petry, 2001). Pathological gambling sufferers often also tend to be workaholics and have scored highly on traits such as novelty seeking and immaturity, but low on self-directedness (Nordin and Nylander, 2007). Onset of problem gambling behaviour usually takes place in adolescence and it is presumed to be a chronic condition with a poor prognosis. However, there is some evidence that the behaviour fluctuates over time and also that a more insidious course for the disorder is associated with changes in patterns of gambling behaviour (Sartor et al., 2007).

Male pathological gamblers show some abnormalities of dopamine, noradrenaline, serotonin and platelet monoamine oxydase as well as other neurotransmitter and neuroendocrine systems (American Psychiatric Association, 2000). Genetic and family experience factors seem to account for 62 per cent or more of pathological

gambling behaviour (Eisen et al., 1998). Although gambling behaviour seems to be strongly environmentally influenced, there is a substantial inherited predisposition to the symptoms of pathological gambling as ascertained from follow-ups to Eisen et al.'s twin study. The close association with a number of comorbid disorders would tend to support this genetic aetiology and there is evidence for a shared genetic basis with major depression (Potenza et al., 2005).

Disorders such as major depression, bipolar disorder and substance use disorder that are frequently comorbid with pathological gambling help to define the treatments most suitable for this disorder. Pharmacological interventions such as SSRIs, mood stabilisers and opioid antagonists are common to many impulse control disorders, but are also pertinent to the treatment of the disorders comorbid with pathological gambling. Also in common with other impulse control disorders, there is strong evidence for the efficacy of SSRIs above other approaches (Dell'Osso et al., 2006). However, anti-depressants may interact with comorbid bipolar disorder with the risk of increasing the chance of manic episodes. Further caveats in evaluating gambling behaviour interventions have been considered by Westphal (2007) in order to avoid overestimating treatment effects, such as more care over blind aspects, greater equivalence of control groups and consideration of participant dropout rates in analysis.

Trichotillomania

In trichotillomania the impulse that the sufferer fails to resist is the recurrent pulling out of their own hair, resulting in noticeable loss. This causes significant distress and impaired functioning of the individual in their lives. There is brief momentary pleasure or gratification from pulling the hair out, which may occur during moments of distraction and is preceded either by mounting tension or by attempts to resist the urge. Hair may be pulled from any part of the body but mostly the scalp and around the eyes (American Psychiatric Association, 2000). Individuals with this disorder may also exhibit trichophagia by chewing or eating the hairs pulled and may also chew or bite fingernails. Trichotillomania is a covert disorder with sufferers being ashamed of the results, whilst denying and hiding the activity. Small sample surveys estimate a lifetime prevalence of around 0.6 per cent (Christenson, Pyle and Mitchell, 1991), with up to 10-fold more female than male sufferers.

There is a close relationship between trichotillomania and obsessive–compulsive disorder (see Chapter 12) with both disorders coexisting within the same families, suggesting some genetic overlap between the two conditions, which both have repetitive, ritualistic and compulsive features. However, there are no obsessive thoughts or intrusions but only tension in trichotillomania, and the behaviours are restricted to hair pulling, whereas in obsessive–compulsive disorder there may be a variety of actions such as cleaning or checking (Lochner et al., 2005). Further to this, trichotillomania has also been included in the spectrum of **self-injurious behaviours** (along with the proposed compulsive–impulsive disorder of skin picking) confounding the obsessive–compulsive association (Lochner et al., 2005; Dell'Osso et al., 2006).

Treatment of trichotillomania is similar to other impulse control disorders, but evaluation data based on controlled studies is less common. Cognitive behavioural therapy has been evaluated as very effective in reducing symptoms in controlled comparisons with pharmacological treatments (Dell'Osso et al., 2006). Controlled studies of SSRIs and mood-stabilising drugs tend to produce mixed results in comparison with the less ambiguous support for their use in other impulse control disorders, and results for trichotillomania are often confounded by relapse during the treatment period.

Self-test questions

- What treatments are consistently successful for impulse control disorders?
- Why are forensic considerations important in impulse control disorders?
- What diagnostic features are common to all impulse control disorders?
- Why would the comorbidity of pathological gambling with bipolar disorder complicate the use of SSRIs in treatment?

Compulsive buying and hoarding

A *DSM-V* taskforce has considered an obsessive–compulsive spectrum in which some impulse control disorders may be better amongst those currently listed under **impulse control disorders not otherwise specified**. This new spectrum of disorders termed the **compulsive–impulsive (C–I) disorders** will comprise at least four disorders (see below). Within this grouping, a new autonomous disorder of **C–I shopping** has been proposed (Dell'Osso et al., 2006). The current term for this condition within the literature is **compulsive buying**, although the label 'compulsive shopping' is also used as an alternative and within the popular media the term **shopaholics** is in common use when referring to individuals who enjoy binging on shopping behaviour (Black, 2007). Media interest in this disorder, such as the UK BBC 3 *Spendaholics* TV programme (BBC, 2007) tends to assume this is a modern phenomenon but both Kraepelin (1915) and Bleuler (1930) identified this clinical condition, referring to it as oniomania (buying mania). Black (2007) concisely summarised compulsive buying as 'excessive shopping cognitions and buying behaviour that leads to distress or impairment' (Black, 2007: p. 14).

Compulsive buying as a disorder has increased rapidly in the twenty-first century with significantly harmful psychological and financial consequences (Dittmar, 2005). The most conservative estimates for the prevalence of the condition are around 2 per cent but other surveys have produced figures as high as 16 per cent (see Black, 2007). Working with the modest 5.8 per cent from a large telephone survey in the USA (Koran et al., 2006) would place compulsive buying as having a very high prevalence. Most

Case study
Just a little retail therapy

Becky had a very caring home and three other older sisters, who may have bickered but generally supported one another and were close to their patient and tolerant parents. The last child to leave home, Becky had always had anxiety problems and had been obsessive about many aspects of her life since early adolescence. She would only eat certain foods and often in fairly fixed settings to avoid becoming anxious and unable to eat at all. In common with her mother, Becky became very sentimental about inanimate objects in her life, which involved not only a mountain of soft toys but also 'significant' train tickets, menus and cuttings from magazines. This emotional regard for the general detritus of life filled her bedroom at her parents' and spread along the upstairs landing to meet the piles of her mother's magazines and books spilling out in the opposite direction from the parental bedroom.

Becky had a great deal of difficulty in parting with even an old magazine without first scanning it thoroughly and cutting out important articles, which meant that she accumulated things at an almost infinitely greater rate than she was able to dispose of them. She confided to one of her friends at college about feeling very insecure and upset if any of her mounting possessions were lost or moved, but at the same time she felt ashamed that her bedroom carpet could not be seen and that she slept in a bed with clutter surrounding her on the duvet. She could not invite friends or boyfriends to her home, but delighted in staying over at other people's houses to be free of this bizarre security 'shell' at home.

Becky had one extreme pleasure and absolute escape from her obsessive home-life: she could shop for shoes, handbags, jewellery and clothes for longer and more intensely than anyone else she knew. Her knowledge of desirable items and even the boxes and bags they came in would have won her competitions on the subject. However, all these items complete with their bags, receipts

and boxes would eventually be packed into the same shrinking space in her bedroom, with some items never leaving their bags or wrapping. Becky was never happier than when rushing to the counter with a designer bargain, but she would cry at night, feeling helpless, depressed and surrounded by clutter that made her bedroom cold and damp. Becky had held down a weekend job since school and had earned the money for her manic shopping activities. However, having a credit card was beginning to take its toll and her debt was mounting.

Her parents were tolerant but complained each time she arrived home with yet more of those 'wonderful' shoes that would never see the light of day. After seeing the situation worsen, Becky's parents began to argue over what should be done. Her mother sympathised, having experienced difficulties with her own clutter all her life, but on finding insects living under Becky's clutter, she resolved that her daughter's life would not follow the same course. The family GP thought Becky had some problems facing life as an adult and said that he could prescribe some anti-depressants for her low mood, but he thought it might be worth Becky seeing the clinical psychologist attached to the community health centre.

From conversations with her mother, Becky expected to be reclining on a couch and felt a little disappointed when a smart young woman greeted her and her mother and very directly asked them what the problem was. The psychologist, or Kath as she insisted they called her, then saw Becky and her mother separately, giving Becky some tests to fill out during the latter interview. She then said, 'I want to be open with you about what I am doing with you. I had an idea from your GP's referral what the problems may be, and from what I have gathered so far, that seems to be the case.' Kath proposed that Becky needed some help with depression, which she had tried to fight with shopping sprees. However, Becky also showed increasing signs of serious obsessive behaviour that might be making the depression worse and had led to the hoarding and difficulties in moving on in her life.

As Kath continued, Becky's mother began to realise the problem she shared with her daughter and found herself interrupting: 'Is the obsession inherited?' Kath looked both of them in the eye and clearly stated, 'Partly, yes it is, but often specific behaviour can be learned from one

CASE STUDY CONTINUED

generation to the next.' Not wishing to compromise the mother–daughter relationship, Kath quickly moved on. 'I want to directly start changing a lot of Becky's behaviour patterns and thinking, and please stick with me because the obsessions are very hard to change but the results may transform your lives.' Kath arranged for a series of sessions and made a note of a colleague's name at the local hospital's obsessions unit. She would have to have a word with the GP anyway regarding Becky's mother, but hoped she would not need to refer Becky on.

Two years later, Becky had left home and moved in with her new boyfriend, which in Kath's opinion was a clear sign of improvement. During those years the entire family became familiar with the meaning of cognitive behavioural therapy, desensitisation and resisting impulses. Becky knew things might never be perfect, but she was much happier, her mother now read books and then takes them to the charity shop, and the family home was now a place to live rather than an obsessive emotional warehouse.

In this case, underlying obsessive–compulsive tendencies seem to have been passed from mother to daughter and might have helped provide the foundation for Becky's shopping and hoarding compulsions.

surveys and research use the Compulsive Buying Scale (Faber and O'Guinn, 1992), which may not exactly match the criteria for the future *DSM* disorder of C–I shopping. Surveys tend to find that the vast majority of sufferers are female (e.g. Bradshaw, 2007). It may be that males underreport such behaviour or label it differently: for example, as 'collecting' rather than 'shopping' (see Black, 2007).

Given the high incidence of pathological shopping behaviour, there is a distinct lack of research on the condition. This may be a result of the trivialisation of the area as a result of media portrayals, which may only scratch the surface of the degree of suffering and chaos brought to those individuals with this condition (Boulton, 2007). What evolutionary psychologists would see as contemporary 'gathering' in the form of shopping has become a major form of entertainment during the last century. Goods and provisions are easily obtained in modern society, leaving a frustrated urge to shop beyond our needs. Thus, provision for shopping accompanies almost every area of our lives from purpose-built shopping malls, to art gallery shops, airports and even holiday beaches. Unfortunately, susceptible individuals have difficulty resisting the impulse to maintain this behaviour at pathological levels.

Other problem behaviour often accompanies compulsive buying, magnifying the impact on the individual and those close to them. Hoarding, clutter, financial diversion and debt are closely related to compulsive buying and, once established, may require independent clinical attention in addition to any intervention for the compulsive buying behaviour (Bradshaw, 2007). A great deal of a sufferer's time is taken up by their focus on and occupation with shopping behaviour, which may be seen as a reward or escape from personal difficulty or depression. Relationships with others are put under strain by financial pressure and the sheer quantity of bought items in a shared household. Pathological shopping is often a solo activity, further undermining real relationships with others and avoiding having the behaviour challenged by close friends. Park and Lennon (2004) also found increased impulsive buying due to the effects of TV shopping and parasocial interaction with the media. Parasocial interaction is a synthetic illusory 'relationship' that is induced by interacting with the media: for example, a regular presenter on TV can be seen as a real acquaintance and the TV experience may substitute for a genuine personal relationship. TV or internet buying may further socially isolate the compulsive shopper, increasing the need to buy to compensate for lost intimacy.

Compulsive buying begins a destructive cycle of escalating debt and mounting clutter, from which further escape is sought through shopping and buying. Spending binges beyond the means of the compulsive buyer lead rapidly to mounting financial problems, which tend to be facilitated by credit card and multiple store-card use and may result in legal action or bankruptcy (Dittmar, 2005; Hartston and Koran, 2002). Some compulsive buyers are well aware of their financial jeopardy and will attempt to control the spiralling debt by destroying cards or returning goods. However, the urge to shop usually outweighs such attempts to avoid serious financial consequences. Behaviours related to and very often accompanying compulsive buying are **hoarding** behaviour and the accumulation of **clutter**.

Hoarding and clutter

Clutter in physical terms refers to having too many unused and unsorted possessions within a living space (Kay, 2005). Hoarding has similar definitions – for example, the excessive collection and failure to discard poorly useable objects – and has been referred to as a disorder in its own right: **compulsive hoarding** (Frost and Hartl, 1996). There is evidence from animal studies to accept hoarding as a further distortion of the evolutionary development of hunter-gatherer behaviour referred to above, in that hoarding supplies provided security and a temporary sense of resting place. Thus, studies of rodents hoarding food have provided not only the term 'hoarding' but also a motivation for non-pathological hoarding, which may also be labelled 'collecting'. Non-pathological hoarding is a widespread problem during the twenty-first century in commercially advanced countries, where clutter tends to fill garages, lofts and spare rooms, and unused or dated clothing is crammed into wardrobes instead of being recycled. Much living space is thus devoted to storage on the basis that items may prove useful in the distant future.

This instinct becomes compulsive hoarding when this instinct cannot be resisted and the individual is unable to part with objects at all. This inability to part with objects can be a result of investing emotion in them instead of people, or simply over-sentimentalising objects that should be discarded (e.g. keeping old carrier bags used on a certain occasion as well as old birthday cards etc.). In explaining this, reference has been made to the higher emotional attainments in Maslow's (1943) hierarchy of needs being invested in objects rather than people, and in turn the objects being treated as a somewhat unfulfilling personal relationship (Kay, 2005). This misapplication of emotion may also be accompanied by obsessive fears of loss or change. Thus, there are two fundamental components to compulsive hoarding: acquiring or collecting non-useful objects and a failure to discard these. A third component often co-occurs in hoarding in the form of self-neglect and neglect of living space, which is more common in old age and in some cases of schizophrenia (see Maier, 2004). This may also involve the hoarding of rubbish as well as neglect or syllogomania – a syndrome that has been labelled the Diogenes syndrome by Clark, Mankikar and Gray (1975), after the Greek philosopher who lived in a barrel. There is much symptom overlap and comorbidity between compulsive hoarding and obsessive–compulsive disorder and the combination is much more difficult to treat than obsessive–compulsive disorder alone (Black et al., 1998).

Aetiology and treatment of compulsive buying and hoarding

Evolutionary views of compulsive buying, and also the seemingly epidemic levels of non-pathological shopping behaviour seen throughout the modern world, interpret this behaviour into a framework based on innate drives from our **hunter-gatherer** past (see Buss, 1999; Cartwright, 2000). Having spent hundreds of millennia engaged in gathering food and useful items for most of our waking lives, this behaviour became abruptly redundant in the contemporary commercial context, where produce is available instantly and in excess. Thus, frustrated hunter-gatherer behaviour and the ubiquitous shopping provision that capitalises on this urge will provide a fertile context for compulsive buying behaviour to develop. Some confirmation of this can be drawn from compulsive buying and hoarding being concentrated in developed countries that have a market-based culture and very rare in poor cultures, other than amongst the few wealthy individuals, as with the shoe collection of Imelda Marcos (Black, 2007).

Differential brain area activity detected by fMRI can indicate both anticipatory shopping gains (nucleus accumbens) and losses (mesial prefrontal cortex), and provide a better indicator of the decision to purchase the self-report measures (Knutson et al., 2007). Such links to the reward mechanisms and the part played by dopamine have suggested a behavioural addiction explanation for compulsive shopping behaviour (see Holden, 2001). The use of opiate antagonists as a treatment has produced successful outcomes, but no data from controlled trials support this (Black, 2007). The frequent comorbidity of compulsive buying and hoarding with both depression and obsessive–compulsive disorder (Maier, 2004) implies some similarities in causal mechanisms and, in particular, the serotonergic system. This has led to the use of antidepressants, mood stabilisers and particularly SSRIs as a pharmacological treatment that can address all of these disorders. However, controlled trials with SSRIs have produced mixed results (Black, 2007).

Cognitive behavioural therapy has been used on an individual and group basis, with the latter producing good sustainable outcomes (Benson and Gengler, 2004), which again parallels the delivery of treatments for addictive disorders (see Coombs, 2004). Media interest in the concept of 'shopaholic' behaviour has led to the appearance of self-help publications of varying quality. More comprehensive self-help programmes have been designed and implemented using paper- and computer-based formats, with good feedback on their usefulness (see Black, 2007). Cognitive behavioural approaches used for obsessive–compulsive disorder can help to address compulsive hoarding and clients will gain skills applicable to compulsive buying behaviour. Debt counselling and interventions to manage spending also supplement behavioural interventions. Raising public awareness of the extent and seriousness consequences of compulsive buying behaviour is also an important issue, as the commercial and cultural context places increasing

Research

The Compulsive Buying Scale and correlational surveys

Much survey research is of a correlational type of design. That is, two or more measures of different traits are taken from the same population sample of participants. These measures are commonly in the form of **self-report questionnaires**.

In the case of compulsive buying research, studies have often included a form of the **Compulsive Buying Scale** (CBS) produced by Faber and O'Guinn (1992). This contains items such as:

Statement	Very often	Often	Sometimes	Rarely	Never
Bought things even though I couldn't afford them	____	____	____	____	____
Bought myself something to make me feel better	____	____	____	____	____

These are scored by the participant along the Likert-type scale, which is based on a subjective judgement of the degree to which the given statement applies to them or is in agreement with their own attitudes. In the work of Bradshaw (2007) and Boulton (2007), a number of other questionnaires were issued to the same participants based on associations raised by previous research with factors such as hoarding, obsessive–compulsive behaviour, self-esteem and depression (see Chapter 17). In addition to these **correlational variables**, data were also collected that would form **independent variables** which would allow these correlational measures to be used as **dependent variables** in a separate analysis **independent groups** comparison. For example, asking for the gender of respondents would allow gender differences in compulsive buying scores to be ascertained.

Depressive thoughts, feelings and behaviour were measured by incorporating a self-report scale (Goldberg et al., 2006) into the final questionnaire. This scale also included items scored on a Likert-type scale such as:

Statement	Strongly agree	Agree	Neutral	Disagree	Strongly disagree
I often feel blue	____	____	____	____	____
I feel that my life lacks direction	____	____	____	____	____

Amongst many other outcomes from these studies, the relationship between depression scores and compulsive buying was found to be statistically significant using the Pearson product moment correlation statistic. The Maudsley Obsessive–Compulsive Inventory (MOCI; see Hodgson and Rachman, 1977) was incorporated as the measure of obsessive–compulsive behaviour with **dichotomously** scored items such as:

Statement	True	False
I take rather a long time to complete my washing in the morning	____	____
I spend a lot of time every day checking things over and over	____	____

However, the correlation between the CBS and MOCI was not found to be statistically significant, even though previous studies had found a relationship between these factors (e.g. Koran, 1999). Significant relationships with other factors such as impulsive thrill seeking, as well as significant group differences, were also found in these studies. An intuition-confirming example of the latter set of findings was that females scored higher on compulsive shopping than males.

The research area of shopping behaviour has appeal in that it is both dealing with an interesting facet of contemporary society and also of clinical and forensic value in providing information on a serious behavioural problem that leads to suffering and legal complications. Studies of clinical problems often raise a number of ethical issues. An example of this in the above studies would be the need to avoid implying that high-scoring participants have a disorder in the absence of formal diagnosis, but yet to provide guidance and further information regarding clinical help should this be appropriate or requested.

pressure on the public to purchase without purpose or acquire celebrity-endorsed goods promoted by glossy magazines to fill what are emotional needs.

Critical and evaluative issues

The *DSM-V* taskforce-backed obsessive–compulsive spectrum of the compulsive–impulsive (C–I) disorders will include C–I shopping, C–I skin picking, C–I sexual behaviours and C–I internet usage. The specific definition and criteria for C–I shopping in its *DSM-V* form may differ from that currently used for compulsive buying, which appeared in *DSM-III* (under 'impulse control disorders not otherwise specified') but not *DSM-IV*. This updating of the diagnostic criteria may impact on the already established research outcomes in this area, in that new data may vary for no other reason than these possibly minor changes. Although this may be seen by some as a rapid increase in impulse control disorders that unnecessarily pathologises any behaviour problems (see Lee and Mysyk, 2004), these aberrant behaviours in their clinical form are profoundly disabling and damaging to both the individuals themselves and those in contact with them. Despite the similarities in aetiology and treatment, there are clear differences between these disorder areas, as well as very different forensic and other consequences for others and society at large. This said, the number of subtypes for C–I disorders could extend further and bring into question the limits of *DSM* or *ICD* breadth in encompassing behaviour that is problematic for society rather than pathological in its nature.

In response to Koran et al.'s (2006) work on the prevalence of compulsive buying disorder, Hollander and Allen (2006) consider the status of this disorder and whether it truly qualifies as belonging with other obsessive–compulsive-related disorders, or if compulsive buying fits more closely with behavioural and substance addictions. The latter category could also accommodate the other new C–I categories, substance disorder and other current compulsive disorders. This would align symptoms such as arousal in anticipation and pleasure in carrying out the behaviour as well as possible tolerance of and withdrawal from the behaviour with the symptoms of substance disorders. This association needs also to be considered in the light of the comorbidity of impulse control disorders and substance dependence, such as the strong association of alcohol dependence with pathological gambling (Lejoyeux et al., 1999). Hollander and Allen (2006) also consider whether compulsive buying should be classified

as a disorder, given that is has received challenges similar to those levelled at **attention-deficit hyperactivity disorder** (see Chapter 9). These authors address this same issue of pathologising the normal spectrum of behaviour by reference to the lack of concern over having depression as a classification, even though almost everyone experiences some degree of depression during their lifetime.

Forensic issues

In this chapter, reference has been made to food potentially overtaking tobacco as the most clinically harmful substance of abuse, whilst obesity and its consequences threaten more lives in developed countries than the diminishing consumption of tobacco. At the end of the twentieth century, tobacco companies found themselves the focus of legal battles that held them corporately responsible for the death and ill health of many smokers. In the twenty-first century there are increasing moves to attribute corporate blame for obesity to fast-food chains, the sugar industry, advertisers or even supermarkets for misleading consumers (e.g. by substituting carbohydrates for fat to reduce the stated fat content on food packaging).

This has even been brought to the public's attention via feature films such as *Super Size Me* (Morgan Spurlock, 2004). Although media obsessions such as dieting and 'size 0' in popular magazines have received criticism in relation to anorexia and bulimia nervosa, the real-world potential for large-scale litigation and consequent legal monitoring and guidelines is more likely to focus on the rising tide of obesity. Such a global movement will require a substantial psychological input to counter the 'free will' argument often utilised by industry with regard to the choice of vulnerable consumers simply not to purchase. This and many other issues regarding food as a potentially dangerous substance of abuse will be on the agenda for some senior clinical forensic psychologists.

All impulse control disorders as well as some potential C–I disorders have forensic consequences due to the specific behaviour involved being a criminal act. For example, pyromania has no legitimate outlets other than the peripheral interest in fire fighting and can lead to major disasters such as forest-fires with widespread damage and loss of life. Most impulse control sufferers feel guilt and regret over their behaviour, which can be seen both as part of the clinical criteria and as forensic mitigation. Further forensic complications arise in diverting individuals charged with related crimes and also suspected of having these disorders to areas of the justice system, where clinical intervention is possible and preferably the main component of disposal. The credibility of these forensically confounded disorders may be brought into question in this process, as well as the validity of any screening instruments and clear operational criteria for diagnosis. Familiarity and expertise in these conditions can be a scarce resource amongst the majority of forensic psychologists and psychiatrists, but it may be necessary to combat courtroom scepticism over a disorder that appears to compel an individual to commit offences.

Pathological gambling and compulsive buying (or C–I shopping), and to a lesser extent other compulsive disorders, involve the sufferer in real crimes, which may be deemed independent of the compulsion itself. For example, credit card misuse, forgery, theft and fraud may be resorted to in order to fund shopping or gambling binges. Sufferers of these disorders will frequently default on outstanding debts and, as a result of failure to pay bills or resorting to illicit means of finding immediate cash, face criminal charges for which their disorder only provides indirect or very limited mitigation. Contemporary use of virtual payment can also make serious crime in this area tempting to those whose need to spend and gamble is pathological, with credit card theft and even identity theft offering seemingly unlimited, if illegal resources. This may be more likely in those who resort to internet gambling. However, most compulsive shoppers only tend to exceed their credit limit.

Some eating disorder sufferers may also commit crimes as a result of their condition. Amphetamine use (see Chapter 11) is a very effective means of managing one's appetite and originally one of the medical applications of this type of drug. Some anorexic or bulimic individuals may abuse amphetamine as part of their disorder (Nagata et al., 2002). This may involve the individual in dealing in amphetamines and even the theft of supplies from medical stores as well as problems of addiction or substance-induced disorders.

Clinical issues

Eating disorders have been addressed in clinical psychology departments for many years, with specialist units being established in the UK and many other countries. Obesity has traditionally been subject to medical intervention but will increasingly need to be added to the caseloads of clinical psychologists in the future if the 'obesity epidemic' continues apace. This will have implications for clinical training as well as the knowledge and skill base of existing clinical psychologists. Further to this, greater contact between medical clinicians and psychologists will be part of the progress towards implementing the outcomes of research focused on combining the successful interventions from each field. Further research on the value of psychology in preventing or treating overweight issues and maintaining weight loss in those most vulnerable will also be an urgent priority as the twenty-first century progresses.

There are clear similarities between each of the impulse control disorders (and the proposed C–I disorders), and comparisons have also been drawn with the addictive disorders featured in the following chapter. In addition, a number of studies have examined associations across all the main categories of disorder in the current chapter, with links between eating disorders and impulse control disorders having been established for some time (e.g. Lacey, 1993). Individuals with bulimia nervosa and various impulse control disorders tend to present with more severe pathology and extreme traits than those with only the eating disorder (Fernandez-Aranda et al., 2006). The proposed C–I disorders also have a history of comorbidity with eating conditions. In the last century, Farber et al. (1995) examined the interrelationship between two such disorders that may fully feature for the first time in *DSM-V*. They found that compulsive buying was more common in women with binge eating disorder, and in a separate study that eating disorder was more often found in compulsive shoppers as well as having more of the symptoms of both binge eating and bulimia nervosa. These associations tend to confound clinical assessment and may require care and the wider use of specialised assessment instruments regardless of the initial presentation.

It is problematic in establishing just how to relate the classifications of impulse-control disorders and obsessive–compulsive disorder. In this chapter a close relationship and degree of overlap has been implied between these disorders (and to some extent eating disorders), yet there is clear nosological distance between them in that obsessive–compulsive disorder is grouped amongst the anxiety disorders. Both groups share repeated compulsions over which they have little control shortly after arousal or anxiety, from which they then gain some degree of perceived relief. Sufferers feel guilt and regret over their behaviour in both conditions, but the compulsions in impulsive and C–I disorders are often considered to be gratifying a pleasure-seeking impulse, whereas in obsessive–compulsive disorder the compulsive action is seen as ego dystonic (American Psychiatric Association, 2000). Ettelt et al. (2007) examined the relationship between the two disorder classifications and found impulsiveness not to characterise those with obsessive–compulsive disorder. They emphasise that the anxiety that is widespread in obsessive–compulsive disorder and relatively absent in impulse control disorders also forms a clear distinction between these disorder groups.

These distinctions and areas of overlap between the disorders within this chapter, as well as the similarities and differences between these and disorders from other chapters, have implications for clinical treatment. This is especially the case where they co-occur in the same individual, in that each disorder needs to be addressed and assessed independently. Thus, although these differing classifications share some interventions and there is an overall similarity in appropriate treatment types, there are clear variations in outcome from these interventions and a general worsening of pathology as well as a poor prognosis in individuals who are comorbid (e.g. Fernandez-Aranda et al., 2006).

It may be assumed that other C–I disorders will soon be on the clinical horizon as well as C–I shopping: that is, C–I skin picking, C–I sexual behaviours and C–I internet usage. However, these proposed disorders have been recognised and researched for a number of years already. For example, Young (1996) modified the criteria for pathological gambling in order to produce a diagnostic questionnaire for internet addiction. Even in the early days of Internet use, this revealed substantial differences in internet usage in those identified as Internet addicted and a very short period of use being required to form this addiction or dependency. More recent studies have confirmed that the number of individuals remains a significant proportion of a much larger user-base but most published research still refers to internet addiction as a 'new disorder' (e.g. Murali and George, 2007).

Self-test questions

- What are the possible evolutionary origins of compulsive buying?
- How does obsessive–compulsive disorder relate to compulsive hoarding?
- In what ways does culture influence levels of compulsive buying?
- What is the Diogenes syndrome and how does it relate to hoarding?
- What are the treatment options for compulsive buying and hoarding?
- What are the compulsive–impulsive disorders proposed for *DSM-V*?

Chapter summary

Disorders covered in this chapter involve the loss of control over eating behaviour or an impulse to carry out an action that is dysfunctional in itself or in its consequences. The eating disorders **anorexia** and **bulimia nervosa** involve the overcontrol of body weight by diet, exercise and purging, which reduces body mass dangerously in anorexia and is maintained in bulimia. Other eating conditions such as **binge eating disorder** and **obesity** are increasingly recognised as having psychological components and, in the latter case, as posing a serious risk to the health of a substantial proportion of the world's population. **Body image dissatisfaction** is common in most of the eating conditions and can be a factor fuelled by celebrity-driven culture in increasing eating disorder levels in developed countries.

Impulse control disorders share features such as arousal prior to a relieving and pleasure-giving act, such as anger displays in **intermittent explosive disorder**, **pathological gambling**, fire setting in **pyromania**, hair pulling in **trichotillomania**, and shoplifting in kleptomania. Many of these acts are also criminal activities and individuals with these disorders may need to receive treatment within the criminal justice system. **Compulsive buying** will probably appear in *DSM-V* as **C–I shopping**, and the disorder is only slowly being recognised as a distressing and destructive disorder with an alarmingly high prevalence. Along with **compulsive hoarding**, this behaviour is also extensive and problematic at subclinical levels in market economy countries. There are forensic issues involving corporate responsibility for some control-based disorders, particularly obesity.

Suggested essay titles

- **Discuss the distinctions between the eating disorders anorexia and bulimia nervosa.**
- **Evaluate the implications of compulsive buying and hoarding for the individual.**
- **Discuss the forensic implications of compulsive gambling and pyromania.**

Further reading

Overview texts

American Psychiatric Association (2000) *Diagnostic and statistical manual of mental disorders fourth revision, text revision (DSM-IV-TR)*. Arlington, VA: American Psychiatric Association.

Baker, A. (ed.) (2000) *Serious shopping: Essays in psychotherapy and consumerism*. London: Free Association Books.

Coombs, R. H. (2004) *Handbook of addictive disorders: A practical guide to diagnosis and treatment*. New York: Wiley.

Norring, C., and Palmer, B. (2005) *Eating disorders not otherwise specified*. London: Routledge.

Smith, G. (2003) *Anorexia and bulimia in the family: One parent's practical guide to recovery*. London: Wiley.

Specific and more critical texts

Black, D. W. (2007) A review of compulsive buying disorder. *World Psychiatry*, **6**, 14–18.

Dell'Osso, B., Altamura, A. C., Allen, A., Marazziti, D., and Hollander, E. (2006) Epidemiologic and clinical updates on impulse control disorders: A critical review. *European Archives of Psychiatry Clinical Neuroscience*, **256**, 464–75.

Fairburn, C., and Brownell, K. D. (2001) *Eating disorders and obesity: A comprehensive handbook* (2nd edn). Hove: Guilford Press.

Gordon, R. A. (1990) *Anorexia and bulimia: Anatomy of a social epidemic*. Oxford: Blackwell.

Grilo, C. M. (2006) *Eating and weight disorders*. Hove: Psychology Press.

Grogan, S. (1999) *Body image: Understanding body dissatisfaction in men, women and children*. London: Routledge.

Ladouceur, R., Sylvian, C., Boutin, C., and Doucet, C. (2002) *Understanding and treating the pathological gambler*. Ontario: Wiley.

Wadden, T. A., and Stunkard, A. J. (2002) *Handbook of obesity treatment*. Hove: Guilford Press.

Visit **www.pearsoned.co.uk/davidholmes** for a range of resources to support study. Test yourself with multiple choice questions and access a bank of over 100 videos that will bring the topics to life. Video coverage for this chapter includes interviews with patients suffering from anorexia nervosa and pathological gambling, and an exploration of video game addiction.

- Overview
- Case study
- General issues in substance-related disorders
- Classification and categorisation of substance-related disorders
- Depressants
- Stimulants
- Hallucinogens
- Further issues in the aetiology and treatment of substance-related disorders
- Clinical issues
- Forensic issues
- Critical evaluation
- Chapter summary

Hear about the physical and psychological effects of cocaine. This is one of several videos that explore issues and disorders relevant to this chapter at www.pearsoned.co.uk/davidholmes.

Hippies, alcopops and Trainspotting

The term **old hippies** has been applied to those participants of the psychedelic drug movement of the 1960s, and the description 'old' suggests that some survived this lifestyle in the manner of the iconic **Keith Richards** of the **Rolling Stones**. However, this is not the case for the '**Trainspotting generation**,' whose lifestyle shows strong parallels with the film *Trainspotting* (Boyle, 1996) based on the book by Irvine Welsh. The film portrays life based around heroin use in Scotland which, 100 years ago, was the main manufacturer of heroin in the world. Sadly, the current Scots generation trapped in, or choosing, this lifestyle provided a 26 per cent increase in drug-related deaths in the year 2006–7 (Edemariam and Scott, 2009). Ironically, the most memorable line from the film, which became a song lyric, was 'choose life'.

However, this level of heroin fatalities is tiny in comparison to the number of deaths directly or indirectly due to alcohol, a legal drug. The '**alcopops generation**' (alcopops are strong alcoholic drinks that resemble soft drinks) of young people who regularly binge in city centres or holiday resorts in Europe cast a grim shadow over the future fatality figures, due to this most popular and destructive substance of abuse. This paradox of legal drugs being more medically dangerous than illegal substances is a constant source of criticism of government policies in many countries.

As with most addictions, if children are never exposed to alcohol, the habit cannot develop.
Source: Pearson Online Database.

Overview

From Roman times, Addictus could not pay his debts and the courts dictated that he should be a slave to his creditors, forming a parallel to the contemporary use of the term **addiction** as a form of slavery to a substance. Research into alcohol or other drug use, abuse and addiction only began on a wide scale in the 1970s, and findings tended to remain within the scientific or academic communities, who had access to published journals in most countries, including those in Europe (Sánchez-Carbonell et al., 2005). This information was not always available to the public, who had a tendency to believe political rhetoric and media sensationalism. Substances of addiction and abuse are very varied in their effects, medical dangers and potential for dependency, which often has little bearing on their legal status or classification.

Drugs that depress the central nervous system (CNS) include alcohol and many prescription medications. Each has a high potential for dependence and addiction, though within CNS depressants specific effects vary considerably. CNS stimulants range widely, from the caffeine in tea or coffee to intravenous amphetamines, and have a high potential for abuse and rapid tolerance. Some stimulants, such as cocaine, share pain reduction effects with the depressants and illustrate the difficulties in establishing any precise means of classifying substances. Hallucinogens often have stimulant properties, but some tend to lack tolerance effects or the ability to stimulate areas of the brain associated with reward and the consequent levels of addiction associated with this pathway. These drugs tend not to be part of the drug repertoire of addicted individuals and users indulge sporadically, making the monitoring of long-term effects in humans difficult.

Treatment options are extremely varied in terms of both the paradigmatic approach and the specific substance in question. Medical-psychological approaches are expanding beyond simple detoxification and group therapy to the use of cue desensitisation techniques and even immune response sensitisation to the substance. Success is very limited and may be influenced not only by context but also by individual predispositions to substance addiction and abuse. To date the only truly effective means to avoid an individual becoming substance dependent is education and the preventative approach: that is, individuals choosing not to take the substance in the first place. The legal context of drug use is frequently in conflict with effective clinical intervention and has provoked a long-standing debate regarding the movement of illicit drug use from the forensic domain to clinical practice, as is currently the case with alcohol and tobacco.

The only certain way to prevent substance harm is early education and voluntary avoidance.
Source: Pearson Online Database.

Case study
Just a little bit for me afterwards

Billy was always 'a bit of a lad' at school and seemed to show little fear for anything or anyone. His mum thought he was a 'rough diamond' and would charm his way through life, but grew weary of apologising to neighbours when Billy lied to gain favour or 'borrow' money. His father worked nights and had little time for his troublesome son, whom he thought would amount to nothing.

Billy was naturally bright, but ended up leaving before his A-levels because he was 'bored with school when there was a real world out there for him'. After a month or so of Billy hanging around with his mates, his dad made it clear that Billy had either to get a job or leave. After short-lived jobs as a shelf-filler in a supermarket and a petrol station attendant, he found himself sleeping on his friend's settee 'just for a couple of nights', which passed into weeks as he learned to claim state benefits and steal from cars. Billy had also started drinking but tended to socialise all night with just one-half of bitter, returning home to his 'tinnies' late at night. One evening, one of Billy's innumerable acquaintances approached him and asked if he could sell them some 'gear'. He was thrown by this request, as he had never had much to do with drugs since trying dope at school, which he did not enjoy as it made him 'lose his edge and slow down'. But Billy was already considering this extension to his moneymaking ventures.

Billy's contacts for stolen goods warned him about jumping into someone's patch and dealing openly, but they gave him a safe 'wholesaler's' number and basic advice. He thrived on risk but found this cash-only culture harder to manipulate. His small-scale dealing was tolerated, as his charm and risk-taking made him a handy runner for moving 'stocks' and cash from drugs around. 'Billy, you have got to try some of this,' Billy heard from behind him one evening, to which his stock reply was 'I don't *do* gear, I

deal!' 'Billy, you have only ever had booze and dope yourself. This is different and it's time you knew what you are selling, or is it more than you can cope with?' Within minutes, Billy had discovered that cocaine was not like booze or dope; it made him into a 'better Billy', and he could out-talk and outwit anyone. When he could not skim some coke from a deal, he would steal amphetamine from his flat mate instead.

One afternoon Billy was covering so many deals, and skimming a bit from each, that he lost track of what he had taken. He felt in control but began to stammer and lose patience with customers and suppliers, whilst becoming more agitated and aggressive. Suddenly the law seemed to be on to Billy and they were everywhere, glancing from shops and peering around corners. He was visibly twitching and darting from doorway to doorway, attracting the attention of passers-by, when an elderly man at a bus-stop suddenly turned and said, 'You OK, lad?' Billy turned and pulled a gun from his pocket. One hour later, two of Billy's 'clients' were holding him down and giving him a tranquilliser, but he could only hear the hissing of blood through his head. Not much scared him, except being out of control or feeling ill, and this had been both. 'Try this, Billy,' he heard, and as he took a drag on what he thought was dope, his lips seemed numb and he felt like he was going to be ill on the carpet. 'Ha! My head is full of snow! Billy is 10 feet tall again!' he said as he passed out smiling. His fringe society friends from the twilight world between serious criminals and middle-class drug users had given him heroin. They considered that he really needed psychological help, but could not risk their way of life by taking Billy to hospital.

The following day Billy was back on the offensive. 'Look, I really owe you guys, but I haven't got anything to give you.' 'Hey, come on Billy, just get us some gear, you know.' He thought that if anything went pear-shaped again, these guys were good danger insurance and he returned that night with a fistful of wraps of 'smack' (cut heroin) as payback. Some people could take heroin and leave it, but for Billy it filled a need; it was satisfaction without lifting a finger and that suited him. It was the same scheming Billy a year later, calling on favours and dealing, who wandered into a 'party' back

CASE STUDY CONTINUED

with the friends who had saved him from street paranoia. 'You got much gear, mate?' Billy lied as always and proceeded to take all that was going for free, thinking he still had his own little stash, and this time good stuff, not cut-up trash for 'street scum'.

At about 6 a.m. a mate leaned over him and whispered, 'Billy, you sly dog, you were holding out on us.' Billy was silent and immobile. To keep his 'stash' to himself, he had held out for so long that he overdosed as everyone else left, with no one to notice that he had kept 'a little bit for later'. Whether it was heroin, greed or just being an anti-social loner that killed Billy can never be certain.

Many heroin (and other substance) users survive their habit or survive with their habit by managing their drug-taking rationally (RSA, 2007), but others die from poor living conditions or health, accidents during criminal activity

and very occasionally from an overdose. Billy was always going to be a problematic individual from childhood onwards and heroin did not cause him to be that way; his involvement with drugs merely overcomplicated an already complex life. Billy never came into contact with clinical help or advice; indeed, any information regarding his involvement with drugs came from criminal peers and other users, which is a common experience in this context. In the case of Billy, drug use was secondary to a criminal lifestyle, which is often how drugs are connected with crime (RSA, 2007). However, for many users of drugs, substance use is the only crime they commit, and for students of clinical and forensic psychology, understanding the distinction between criminals who become engaged with illicit drug use and those crime-free individuals who become users can be important in the context of any twenty-first-century debate around the issue of decriminalising all psychoactive substances.

General issues in substance-related disorders

Throughout history, the level of ignorance, hypocrisy and misinformation surrounding substance use and misuse has been very problematic, and it has been further complicated by issues of legality for over a century (see Gregory, 2003). Given the label of 'substance abuse' or 'addict', the public will usually generate the media-given image of a sensationalised, degenerate and stereotyped 'heroin addict', but be much less likely to imagine someone on a drinking binge. Thus, substance users are both demonised and portrayed to the public as a homogeneous population (RSA, 2007). It may be useful to broaden the concept of substance abuse by restating from Chapter 10 the problem of one of the most commonly abused substances, that being food, which has been amply illustrated by the recent epidemic of obesity in developed countries. Almost addictive frequencies and levels of refined sugar intake amongst children are particularly concerning (Somerset, 2003). This is not a trivial example as the three most medically damaging substances of abuse are **tobacco**, **alcohol** and **food** (Holmes, 1998), in that order, and as detailed in Chapter 10, food abuse may be on the ascent in this deadly trilogy. A further link between the disorders in this and the preceding chapter has been established for some time

by research associating eating and substance disorders (Grilo et al., 1995).

The **European Monitoring Centre for Drugs and Drug Addiction** (EMCDDA) estimates that there are around 1 billion drug users in the world, equating to one person in every seven (Vizi, 2007). Not all of these individuals will be addicted to the substance they use and not all deaths from drugs involve illicit substances. Long-established and emphasised by the RSA report in 2007, the overall deaths or serious illnesses resulting from all illicit drugs combined would seem tiny in comparison to those directly resulting from tobacco and alcohol (*without* the addition of food abuse). RSA is an abbreviation of the Royal Society for the Encouragement of Arts, Manufactures and Commerce. It is a think-tank that was founded by William Shipley in 1754 in the UK and commissioned to examine illegal drugs, communities and public policy in 2005. The RSA (2007) report further recommended making the management of illegal drugs a medical rather than criminal issue and suggested that a calm, rational approach be adopted to the problem rather than the counterproductive combination of prohibition and demonisation.

Some abused substances, clearly illustrated by the example of food, are not dangerous within the limits of normal or moderate intake, which raises the issues of **toxicity**, **purity** and **collateral damage** in relation to substance use disorders (Holmes, 1998). Our bodies are built

Food can be an addictive and harmful substance of abuse.
Source: Pearson Online Database.

to deal with reasonable levels of toxins; indeed, if we had 'purified intakes' we might become hypersensitive to impurities, in a similar manner to lacking immunity to disease. However, some substances have an unknown toxicity: for example, designer drugs that are synthesised to resemble known psychoactive substances but differ slightly in their molecular structure. In the past, this has allowed such new synthetics to evade specific legislation by being outside of the legal specification. Other substances have many impurities that cause widespread collateral damage, as in the case of smoking tobacco to obtain nicotine. Occasionally, abused substances may be so pure as to be easily overdosed, leading to rapid unconsciousness and possibly death. For example, heroin is rarely available to street users in a pure form as it is usually mixed or **cut** with some other medium, and uncut heroin given to a user will almost certainly result in an accidental overdose.

Cannabis provides a further illustration of these factors, in that it has a pronounced psychological effect but very low toxicity when eaten, and although there is some level of tolerance at high doses, there is arguably little potential for physical addiction in its natural form. However, when mixed with tobacco and smoked, it takes on all the (considerable) risks of smoking both cannabis and tobacco, as well as introducing the user to nicotine addiction. In addition, genetically modified cannabis has increased potency and potential for harm and should be distinct in its classification. Thus, as the comedian **Lenny Bruce** often asserted, albeit with more truth than sarcasm, not all drugs are the same.

Polydrug users, as the name suggests, use more than one substance. Initially intended to identify illicit drug users who show little preference for one substance and demonstrate opportunist approaches to drug use, the term must also be applied to the very common occurrence of those who both drink alcohol and smoke tobacco, who may not think of themselves as polydrug users. Multiple drug use can compound health problems and risks: for example, alcohol and tobacco can show **cross-tolerance**, thus worsening withdrawal in combination, and less well-known interactions such as that between **fluoxetine** (Prozac) and MDMA can be problematic (see Parrott et al., 2004). Research into specific drug effects in the real world is also confounded by the use of multiple drugs, as it is very rare to find a user of an illicit substance who does not also indulge in other illicit drugs, drink alcohol and smoke tobacco. Thus short- and long-term damage is difficult to attribute accurately to one of these indulgencies. Clinically and forensically, substance use disorders are a very complex area. Modern thinking in this area has adopted a more informed approach to interventions within forensic contexts, but these approaches are still far from resolving the entanglement of illegality with clinical need, often due to political constraints – an issue discussed in the next section.

Substance use and the law

Governments have the ability to pass laws, but those governments only survive as a result of their popularity with the electorate. Thus the decision as to whether to treat or imprison illegal substance users may ultimately lie with a voting population confused by tabloid images of 'crazed drug fiends leaving infected needles for children', along with sporadic and often greatly exaggerated research findings (Costello, Costello and Holmes, 1995). As a consequence, resultant laws intended to restrict drug use are at odds with clinical realities, and the responsibility for drug supply and control is largely given over to the criminal fraternity (Gregory, 2003). During the twentieth century, many people from non-criminal backgrounds found that casual 'recreational' drug use, such as smoking cannabis or taking amphetamines, introduced them to the additional risk of confronting the law enforcement agencies. Thus, it is an important issue in studying substance use that most countries designate a wide range of substances as illegal, as this exposes the user to the further complication of attracting forensic as well as clinical attention. In this dilemma, conviction tends to lead not to treatment orders, but usually to gaining a criminal record or even imprisonment, often exacerbating the problems of the individual drug user (RSA, 2007).

In England, the main drug control legislation was the Misuse of Drugs Act (1971), which divided illicit substances into **class A, B and C** drugs, with class A carrying the highest penalty (see Table 11.1 below). The **Intoxicating Substances (Supply) Act (1985)**, along with the 1999 regulations on lighter refill regulations and the **Medicines Act (1968)** (covering possession of prescription-only drugs, which included the production of ketamine or amyl nitrite), added to the original Act. However, revisions that are more recent have attracted greater publicity due to the perceived direction of the changes made, rather than as a result of the degree of change to existing law. Thus, the movement of cannabis downwards from a class B to a class C drug in 2004 attracted a lot of critical attention from the media and critics of 'softer' drug policies. This reaction was perhaps premature, as most critics failed to note that the penalty for trafficking, dealing and production (including growing) of cannabis and other class C substances was simultaneously raised from 5 to 14 years. Cannabis was reclassified to class B in 2008 as a result of political interests being under pressure and against scientific advice.

The **Drugs Act (2005)** in the UK extended police and court powers with the aim of placing more users on treatment programmes. It included police powers to test for drugs on arrest and subsequently to require those testing

Table 11.1 Drug classifications in English law

Class A drugs

Include: MDMA (ecstasy), LSD, heroin, cocaine, crack-cocaine, magic mushrooms (if prepared for use), amphetamines (if prepared for injection), methamphetamine (from January 2007).

Penalties for possession: up to 7 years in prison or an unlimited fine, or both.

Penalties for dealing: up to life in prison or an unlimited fine, or both.

Class B drugs

Include: amphetamines, methylphenidate (Ritalin), pholcodine, cannabis.

Penalties for possession: up to 5 years in prison or an unlimited fine, or both.

Penalties for dealing: up to 14 years in prison or an unlimited fine, or both.

Class C drugs

Include: tranquillisers, some painkillers, GHB (Gamma hydroxybutyrate), ketamine.

Penalties for possession: up to 2 years in prison or an unlimited fine, or both.

Penalties for dealing: up to 14 years in prison or an unlimited fine, or both.

positive to be assessed by a drugs worker, as well as various powers of entry and extended detainment when substances might have been swallowed. 'Magic mushrooms', i.e. the raw fungi containing **psilocybin** (not just those prepared for use), were also added to the 1971 Act as a class A drug on the somewhat cavalier assumption that they presented the same 'risks' as LSD. Genetically modified sources of cannabis ('skunk') with high levels of **d-Tetrahydrocannabinol** were under consideration in relation to the 2004 reclassification of cannabis, but no changes to this substance were made at that time.

Table 11.2 lists the drug-related activities that are deemed offences under English law. Similar offences are recognised in many countries around the world, with some nations having administered much harsher penalties than those in Table 11.1, including the death penalty. However, Holland has adopted a very different approach in decriminalising some aspects of drug use to manage substance use, and this has been arguably more successful than countries using prohibitive legislation. The Dutch approach will be discussed in the decriminalisation section later in this chapter.

UK drug offences in Table 11.2 also show the legal system's emphasis on the commercial aspects of illicit drug possession and supply. It is interesting to note that there is little mention of drug use, addiction or abuse in the

Table 11.2 Drug offences in English law

- Possession of a controlled substance unlawfully
- Possession of a controlled substance with intent to supply it
- Supplying or offering to supply a controlled drug (even where no charge is made for the drug)
- Allowing premises you occupy or manage to be used unlawfully for the purpose of producing or supplying controlled drugs
- Being in charge of a motor vehicle whilst unfit due to the influence of drugs or alcohol, under the Road Traffic Act 1972.

wording of these laws, which perhaps further emphasises that the law tends to focus on illicit profit and acts that can be proven in court, but not clinical harm to the individual user. McKeganey (2006) noted that the 'intent' to reduce harm in UK drug policy since the late 1980s had left a legacy of increasing harm, and that policy should shift towards prevention rather than harm, reduction via prohibition. Every country in the world, and even each state in the USA has its own drug laws and although some may have similarities (almost all outlaw drug trafficking), the many variations are beyond this text to illustrate.

Classification and categorisation of substance-related disorders

Whenever a substance enters the body it is broken down, some is absorbed and when metabolised it may affect our mental state, usually by stimulating or otherwise altering neurotransmission (see the section on neurochemistry in Chapter 3). Such substances that can pass the **blood–brain barrier** are said to be **psychoactive**. Humanity has been quick to identify the most psychoactive substances, especially if the effect is pleasant. Even if the effect is less than pleasant, it offers a change of state, which can be seen as a 'mental holiday', an escape from boredom or even a 'spiritual journey' (Leary, 1970). Moderate **substance use** is thus considered medically and socially acceptable in healthy individuals, providing the substance is legally allowed. **Intoxication** literally means 'poisoning' and is where the intake of a substance exceeds the ability of the body to eliminate it. The speed at which a specific substance is eliminated from the body is given as the **half-life**, which is the time it takes a substance to reach half its original

concentration in the blood plasma. Higher levels of intoxication have clinical and forensic consequences in the short and long term, including liver disease, driving whilst intoxicated, accident, violence and death from **overdose**.

With repetition, the body learns to **tolerate** some psychoactive substances: that is, compensate for their presence. This means that larger doses will be required to produce the same psychological effect and abstinence will leave the body still physically compensating for some time. These **withdrawal effects** can be immediately avoided by continued use (Costello, Costello and Holmes, 1995). Thus, **physical dependence** is a process of taking a sufficient amount of a substance so as to avoid withdrawal symptoms (a **maintenance dose**) and **psychological dependence** is the anticipation of the mental change or 'high' (which would require *more* than the maintenance dose at this stage) as well as anticipating and thus avoiding withdrawal. Where dependence is detrimental to an individual's ability to function at an adequate level, the label **addiction** is appropriate. The lesser disorder of **substance abuse** involves taking a repeated or large dose of a substance on one occasion (e.g. five drinks of alcohol in a short period, such as an hour) to produce substantial change in mental state. This is often referred to as **bingeing** and does not usually involve dependence, just an inability to moderate intake once started, even though medical (and social-occupational) damage may be substantial (Costello, Costello and Holmes, 1995). It is often this detrimental effect on social and occupational functioning that leads to the label of substance abuse (American Psychiatric Association, 2000).

DSM-IV-TR also lists a number of **substance-induced conditions**, where dependence on or abuse of a substance has led to other physical and mental conditions. These disorders include complications such as substance-induced delirium, dementia, amnestic disorder, psychotic disorder, mood disorder, anxiety disorder, sleep disorder and sexual dysfunction, each of which may have the onset phase of the substance disorder specified, such as 'substance-induced psychotic disorder with onset during withdrawal' (American Psychiatric Association, 2000). The manual also identifies hallucinogen persisting perception disorder, which is also referred to by the term flashbacks (see the section on hallucinogens below). These disorders can seriously complicate substance-use disorders, as the symptoms may persist long after the substance dependence or abuse has ceased. To make a clear distinction, *DSM-IV-TR* refers to such conditions that *neither* are substance-induced *nor* arise from general medical conditions as **primary mental disorders** (American Psychiatric Association, 2000).

There are many types of abused substances, both legal and illegal, and their characteristics vary vastly. These substances can be very roughly grouped by their major effects on brain neurochemistry (see Chapter 3) into the three categories below.

- **CNS depressants** such as alcohol, opiates (opium, morphine and heroin), barbiturates and benzodiazepines (e.g. valium) tend to *reduce* inhibitions, control and sophisticated thought by progressively shutting down areas of the brain, beginning with the higher functions.

- **CNS stimulants** such as amphetamine, caffeine, cocaine and nicotine can increase confidence, vigilance and activity, but can also produce paranoia and agitation.

- **Hallucinogens** such as cannabis, MDMA (ecstasy), LSD, **phencyclidine** (PCP or angel dust) and **psilocybin** (from magic mushrooms) can produce intense or distorted perceptions, hallucinations, insightful or pseudo-creative thought, and users of some hallucinogens may seem quiet and introspective, sometimes fearful. Many hallucinogens *also* have stimulant properties (e.g. cannabis and MDMA). Some, such as cannabis and PCP, have such unique properties as to be considered atypical or outside the hallucinogen group by classificatory systems (e.g. American Psychiatric Association, 2000).

Clearly, such a crude grouping can only provide a basic framework for categorising the substances covered in this chapter, and each of these drugs may share properties with substances from another category. Further drug groups based on effects would include anxiolytics and hypnotics, but other approaches use differing generic classifications such as 'recreational drugs' or placing all opiates in a category of their own. Cannabis has so many differing aspects to its effects as to be thought of as unclassifiable in this way. *DSM-IV-TR* makes reference to substance groupings but simply lists the 11 substances covered in alphabetical order within the manual (American Psychiatric Association, 2000). There are also many more psychoactive substances than are listed in this chapter, some of which are rarely found or used currently, but may find their way into future classificatory systems if they are 'discovered' by mainstream recreational drug users.

Depressants

CNS depressants inhibit neural activity generally by activating the gamma-aminobutyric acid (GABA) inhibitory neurotransmission system. Most of the public find it difficult to accept that alcohol can be classified with heroin and are often astounded that it is responsible for far more deaths, injuries and illnesses than the illicit opiate. The CNS depressant drugs in this section represent a small but familiar sample from a large number of depressant substances, most of which are prescription drugs.

Alcohol

Ethyl alcohol is the active ingredient in all alcoholic drinks, the strength of these being indicated by the percentage of alcohol content or by **proof** (approximately double the percentage by volume figure), as a legacy from sailors judging the 'proof' of strength of rum by its forming a combustible combination when mixed with gunpowder. The substance has been used for many thousands of years with some of the first Mesopotamian writings on clay tablets referring to laws on alcohol control (Parrott et al., 2004). It is a CNS depressant and has been used for relaxation and anxiety reduction, and even as a crude anaesthetic in early surgery. This inhibition in the CNS can paradoxically remove social inhibitions, leading to anti-social acts, with poor judgement and skills adding accidents to this damaging behaviour.

Because alcohol is cheap and easily available it is readily abused, with around 5 per cent of adults having a drinking problem and around a third of those under 25 consuming double the then recommended limits of 21 units for males and 14 for females at the turn of the millennium (ONS, 2000). Alcohol is easily dispersed in water-retaining organs and thus has a more potent effect on females due to their higher proportion of body fat and lower body mass, concentrating the amount taken when compared to males. The biochemistry of female digestion also leads to more alcohol being ingested. This effect is more profound in some ethnic groups (e.g. Asian and Chinese) due to a genetic trait in these populations. This trait results in less alcohol dehydrogenase, the enzyme that breaks alcohol down within the body, and these individuals are thus far more susceptible to the effects of alcohol and may often subjectively feel 'ill' rather than 'drunk' (see Crabb et al., 2004).

The effects of larger amounts of alcohol (i.e. insensitivity, disinhibited aggression, staggering and slurred speech) are very common in hospital casualty units, where violence towards the hospital staff themselves has become a major problem in the twenty-first century. High dose effects also include serious impairment of mental and physical functioning, and eventual death from choking or vital function failure. Long-term excessive use is commoner amongst some professions due to stress levels and ease of access, such as journalists, alcohol industry workers and even doctors (Brooke, Edwards and Taylor, 1991). Long-term high intake of alcohol leads to serious medical conditions such as cirrhosis, where the liver's normal recovery process is overcome by alcohol attrition, with fat and protein destroying liver cells, leading to inflammation and permanent scarring. It is an important avenue of research that some alcoholics seem to escape liver damage (Parrott et al., 2004). Alcohol is also directly associated with gout, heart failure, strokes and pancreas damage, as well as many other forms of organ failure and signs of general decline in health.

Alcoholic suppression of vitamin B complex absorption can lead to amnestic syndrome (**Wernicke's syndrome**), which may be reversible by the administration of thiamine. However, if Wernicke–Korsakov's syndrome develops, the memory loss is no longer reversible. Even small regular amounts of alcohol during pregnancy can lead to foetal alcohol syndrome. Abstinence from alcohol during pregnancy has been advised in order to avoid a significant chance of premature delivery (Sokol et al., 2007), as well as possible mental and physical problems with the child (e.g. Baroff, 1986). However, there is evidence that low-level alcohol use can reduce the risk of coronary heart disease when compared to alcohol abstinence. However, this relationship is complex and other factors, such as increased leisure time activity, may be mediators (Poikolainen et al., 2005).

Aetiological factors in alcohol use

Amongst the known factors affecting the rates of alcoholism are availability, cost and peer pressure as well as the presence of anxiety and mood disorders. More fundamentally, evidence of *genetic factors* in some alcohol disorders is fairly strong; much evidence has been around for some time, including that from twin and adoption studies (e.g. Searles, 1988). Some markers have been identified for alcoholism, such as specific P3 waves (i.e. the third positive wave) in EEG-measured event-related potentials (see Cloninger and Begleiter, 1990; also see Chapter 3). However, these P3 potentials may be markers for a broader spectrum of externalising factors with a common genetic basis (Hicks et al., 2007). Another marker has been the D2 receptor (dopamine receptor type 2), which occurs more often in alcoholic individuals (Karp, 1992).

The use of linkage analyses to detect genes involved in alcohol-related problems has been a major approach of the Collaborative Study on the Genetics of Alcoholism (see Dick et al., 2002). They have had success in identifying phenotypes of alcohol problems, which have then been used in subsequent linkage analyses implicating locations on chromosome 1 (Dick et al., 2002). Further analyses have also highlighted locations on chromosomes 1, 4, 13 and 15 (Arya et al., 2005). Alcoholism is almost certain to be heterogeneous and some genetic factors may have an indirect influence, for example, by affecting the levels of alcohol dehydrogenase or aldehyde dehydrogenase and the consequent ability to metabolise alcohol (Crabb et al., 2004).

Personality traits involving 'under-control' have been found to be mediating factors between specific genes and

Focus

Forensic aspects of alcohol use

The effects of alcohol use confound many medical conditions and psychiatric disorders, especially **antisocial personalities** (e.g. Kwapil, 1996) and depression (where it co-occurs in 50 per cent of suicides). Psychiatric patients may **self-medicate** with alcohol, which may potentiate their medication and undermine their treatment regime. Alcohol taken in combination with medication or illicit drugs, particularly barbiturates or heroin, has led to many fatalities, and combining alcohol in this way has also been a frequent means to commit suicide.

In addition, alcohol users are prone to fatal overdose (especially with spirits), as alcohol disinhibits individuals and impairs their judgement in respect of further intake, in addition to its being a fairly toxic substance. UK National Statistics show that alcohol-related deaths have risen from 6.9 per 100,000 in 1991 to 13.3 per 100,000 in 2007.

Characteristic effects of alcohol, such as impaired judgement, risk taking and disinhibition, also cause accidents (e.g. from drunk driving), homicide, violence (particularly domestic and street violence) and most other forms of crime (Shaw et al., 2006). Alcohol also creates victims because risk taking can lead to sexual disinhibition with the risk of HIV and other infections.

In many cases of drug-assisted **date rape** where the use of a drug such as Rohypnol is suspected, only alcohol is found in the victim's system on subsequent analysis.

These problems lead to a massive diversion of society's financial and other resources due to alcohol misuse alone. Paradoxically, given the adverse effects of alcohol, it is legally available in most countries of the world. This said, very moderate use of alcohol can assist some biochemical processes involving a range of endogenous substances such as lipoproteins.

alcohol dependence (Slutske et al., 2002). In this explanation, alcoholism has been associated with pre-existing personality traits such as impulsivity, aggressiveness and non-conformity (Caspi et al., 1997), and this association is then linked to the long-established finding that a substantial genetic basis exists for personality traits (see Loehlin, 1992). Perhaps emphasising the importance of prevention, or in this case even postponement of initial drinking, those who begin to drink prior to the age of 15 years are four times more likely to develop alcoholism than those who have their first drink after the age of 20 (Sartor et al., 2007). However, many of the other factors associated with the development of alcoholism also confound the age at which an individual starts drinking, this being earlier where there is alcoholism in the family, or if conduct disorder or attention-deficit hyperactivity disorder are present. Parental attitudes and interactions with their offspring have been found to influence alcohol consumption in these children in adolescence. However, again the interplay between other factors, including personality, needs to be considered before assuming that interactive aspects such as more defined parental rules and lower consumption form a simple relationship (see Wood, 2007).

Treatment of alcohol disorders

Alcoholism is difficult to treat in the long term, and although individuals can be induced to stop drinking in the short term, relapse is a major hurdle in alcohol treatment, as is the case with most substance disorders (Costello, Costello and Holmes, 1995). In the short term,

detoxification involves 2 weeks of often severe physical withdrawal (longer and more dangerous than for heroin, but less difficult than with barbiturates). Though rare, sudden withdrawal can produce delirium tremens, which in addition to delirium, feverishness and physical tremors may produce unpleasant hallucinations of creatures around and on the sufferer. These withdrawal symptoms can be reduced with **benzodiazepines** (though secondary dependence to these is possible) or other drugs. However, it is thought that side-stepping the adverse consequences may behaviourally lead to assisted detoxification being considered a routine option, in the manner of taking aspirin for a hangover. Tolerance effects such as increases in GABA receptors or their sensitivity may take some time to return to nearer normal functioning.

Following detoxification, alcohol avoidance can be maintained by the supervised administration of disulfiram, which acts by inhibiting aldehyde dehydrogenase. The net effect of this is to make the individual ill if they take alcohol, and it may even prove lethal in persistent cases due to this poisoning effect. This can act both as a physical **aversion therapy** and also as a weak form of psychological aversion therapy as a result of classical conditioned aversion (see Chapter 3). Behavioural aversion can be induced by aversion therapy where the ill response is conditioned rather than pharmacologically maintained by disulfiram. However, these can often only be short-term measures, as supervision is difficult and alcohol is socially ubiquitous. If alcoholism is comorbid with depression, pharmacological treatment of the depression can reduce alcohol use (Lawrence, 2007). The blocking of brain reward properties of alcohol by the

Alcohol consumption by younger people has changed the character of some cities at night.
Source: Pearson Online Database.

use of opiate antagonists has reduced alcohol craving, but relapse rates are high (Lawrence, 2007). Desensitisation to the cues or triggers for drinking behaviour may be a way to reduce relapse rates, as has been successful for cocaine, but cues for alcohol are many and penetrate most areas of our personal lives, and such approaches often also use opiate antagonists and disulfiram (Brewer and Streel, 2003).

Cognitive therapeutic approaches can help the individual avoid the self-deception and cues that lead to use, or even to cope with moderate consumption. Peer group support is often available in hospital alcohol treatment units under professional guidance and there are also well-established organisations such as **Alcoholics Anonymous.** This form of guided support from fellow sufferers can help maintain motivation in the case of those who stay with the group. However, many individuals drop out of these groups as hard rules such as total abstinence are seen as too restrictive and controlled consumption is thought to be more sustainable.

Norman, Bennett and Lewis (1998) have suggested changes to the drinking environment to reduce the rising trend in binge drinking among groups of young men. Amongst their suggestions is the feminisation of the drinking environment, as females are less likely to binge drink or approve of such conduct. However, binge drinking amongst females is also rising in the twenty-first century. Increasing problems of alcohol use and its treatment appear to be attracting greater research focus over the years. Sánchez-Carbonell et al. (2005) have noted the increase in publications on this topic in the European Union, as well as increasing collaboration between researchers from the different EU countries. Unfortunately, deaths from alcohol-related illness in the UK doubled in the decade up to 2004, somewhat outpacing the research into this destructive substance, and elsewhere in Europe, Luxembourg has a level of alcohol consumption more than 60 per cent greater than that of the UK (see Frances, Miller and Mack, 2005).

Opiates

Opiates are **narcotic analgesic alkaloids** extracted and refined from the opium poppy, *Papaver somniferum.* Opium poppy seeds have been found in Neolithic burial sites and opium was used by the Sumerians as well as being passed through various civilisations including the Egyptians, indicating that the use of opium stretches back many thousands of years (Parrott et al., 2004). Processing the dried extracted fluid from the opium poppy-head (raw opium) produces **morphine. Codeine** is chemically almost identical to morphine but is much weaker in its analgesic properties.

As CNS depressants, opiates produce sedation and pain relief that has been extensively utilised medically in the case of morphine and codeine. Opium has been welcomed as a cure for most ailments from Galen in ancient Greece through to nineteenth-century Europe. **Heroin** or **diacetylmorphine** was extracted from morphine in 1874. It is an example of the historical relativity in clinical and forensic science that heroin at that time was used in cough mixtures and even children's remedies for many years. Further hypocrisy over drug attitudes are illustrated by the British government sanctioning the East India Company's opium trade to problem users in places such as China in the 1830s, on the basis of revenue received from what was effectively the drug trade. The ceding of Hong Kong to Britain by China was a direct result of a specific military response to the Chinese Emperor's efforts to ban opium smoking (Vizi, 2007). Parrott et al. (2004) point out the irony that those countries supplied by the UK in history are now the *suppliers* of heroin to Europe and elsewhere.

Despite the spectre of the heroin addict created by the media, some individuals seem to use heroin sporadically, usually smoked, or develop a stable intravenous habit, which they maintain for years with few ill effects. These are usually middle-class individuals, who maintain employment and health, and avoid criminalisation and contaminated supplies or needles. Such individuals often evade treatment

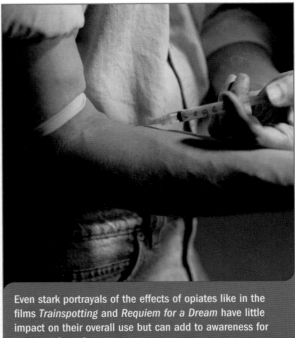

Even stark portrayals of the effects of opiates like in the films *Trainspotting* and *Requiem for a Dream* have little impact on their overall use but can add to awareness for the need for safer use.
Source: Pearson Online Database.

options such as methadone, a synthetic heroin substitute which accounts for far more annual deaths than heroin (UK Office of National Statistics figures), possibly due to the problematic profile of those given methadone. However, far more individuals fall prey to the cycle of increased need, loss of employment, crime and ill health. In the twenty-first century, heroin- and morphine-related deaths in Europe have been increasing out of proportion to other drug-related fatalities (European Monitoring Centre for Drugs and Drug Addiction, 2003). Deaths from overdose are common in situations where there is relapse from withdrawal or a change in the purity of heroin supplied. One means to reduce these deaths is to prescribe **naloxone**, which is a specific opiate antagonist with no agonist or addictive properties. Naloxone would rapidly reverse the symptoms of heroin overdose and could save many lives (Sporer and Kral, 2007).

Heroin has proved the most addictive of the opiates, as it produces an instant and sustained euphoria, a 'high', which tends to be absent with the other derivatives. Heroin also undermines the body's endogenous reward system (see the Focus box) and **pain gating systems**, adding considerably to its addictive potential. Thus heroin has a very powerful psychological hold on susceptible individuals who enter its subculture. As William Burroughs wrote, 'Junk is the ideal product, the ultimate merchandise. No sales talk necessary. The client will crawl through a sewer and beg to buy' (Burroughs, 1959: p. 9). Note, 'junk' is a slang term for all opiate derivatives. Withdrawal is brief, but psychologically painful with flu-like symptoms and jerky body movements (hence the phrase 'kicking the habit'). One unusual tool in easing the process of withdrawal is the use of **poppy seed tea**, an unpleasant infusion of legally obtainable poppy seeds containing low levels of opiates. This practice has come to attention in some countries where illicit opiates have been scarce (Bray et al., 2007).

Treatment of opiate use and dependence is a broad and increasingly complex area with many psychological and biological interventions, as well as programmes of management and treatment often designed for the prison context. Methadone was synthesised during the Second World War to be used in the absence of morphine (Parrott et al., 2004). It has been used as an oral substitute for heroin to wean addicts off the 'high' provided by heroin and the use of needles, whilst avoiding concurrent opiate withdrawal by 'methadone maintenance' (White and Lopatko, 2007). As mentioned above, methadone leads to more deaths than heroin and is addictive, as well as carrying stigma and causing drowsiness, which has led some to argue for prescription heroin for maintenance on condition of engaging in treatment. Although this creates the possibility of prescription heroin being sold on the black market, it does provide a means of removing addicts from their illicit supplier and ending a vast amount of drug-related crime (see Bennett and Holloway, 2005).

Different approaches to methadone treatment practised across Europe have also been examined, but although lessons in fatality reduction can be learned for the UK, the basic problems remain (see Zador, 2007). Other opiate substitutes have been suggested, such as the shorter-acting **dihydrocodeine**, but these are merely alternatives rather than real improvements in the substitute approach (Robertson et al., 2006). It has also been found that, for more addicted rats, alternative rewards such as food provide greater competition than they do for lesser addicted animals, which may hold promise for human interventions (Lenoir and Ahmed, 2007).

Proportionately greater amounts of crime are committed in the UK by individuals addicted to opiates in order to fund their illicit drug purchases (Bennett and Holloway, 2005). This is in the form of theft of cash or goods routinely 'fenced' to produce sufficient daily income to afford the average $\frac{1}{2}$–1 gram a day heroin habit – a bill that can be vastly inflated if co-addiction to cocaine is present (Leri, Bruneau and Stewart, 2003). This would indicate that something about drug crime policy in the UK is less effective than that in other countries with similar drug problems, including the USA. It may be that UK approaches are unduly influenced by public opinion and **media myths** surrounding opiates and crime, such as the myth that opiate dealers are irrational and a danger to their customer, which is illogical as most dealers make money (see Coomber, 2006).

Inhalants

Often seen as the bottom rung in terms of their status in the hierarchy of misused substances, inhalants are often abused by adolescents and children. In the form of volatile substances such as lighter fuel, glue, paint or petrol, most of these inhalants are readily available and legal, and although most legal guidelines try to prevent their sale directly to children, access is difficult to control effectively, if at all. Inhalant use produces a high morbidity rate, usually as a result of suffocation due to fumes displacing oxygen, airway blockage or choking on vomit (Fendrich et al., 1997). Inhalant use and its associated mortality are unfortunately common amongst schoolchildren with a peak at 14–15 years of age. Lacey and Ditzler (2007) amongst others have also found high levels of use in the US military, where inhalants were found to be the third most common substances of abuse. There was a sharp rise in the use of inhalants in the early 1990s but some decline

Focus

Drugs and the endogenous reward system

In 1954 **James Olds** (1922–1976) along with Peter Milner opened up a new psychophysiological understanding of behaviour and addictive drug action. They attached an electrode to a rat's brain to stimulate the septum (and other brain areas) when the animal pressed a lever. Not only did the animal rapidly learn to press the lever, but also it did not seem to satiate its appetite for this reinforcement. For this reward, the hungry rat would brave a shock far greater than for food, sex or any other inducement. This provides a clear animal illustration and validation of the words of Burroughs (1959) on the subject of opiate addiction.

This neurophysiological mechanism, which proved so powerfully rewarding in rats and also in humans (see Heath, 1972), depended on dopamine activity in specific regions (including those identified by Olds), such as the **nucleus accumbens**, the **ventral tegmental area** and the **prefrontal cortex** (Schultz, 2002; Berridge and Robinson, 1998). If dopamine action is prevented, the rewarding aspect of this stimulation dissipates. However, there is debate as to how this dopamine action actually changes the animal's motivation. It does seem to strongly increase the salience (noticeability) of the associated stimuli (Berridge, 2006). This system within the brain is referred to as the **endogenous reward system**, producing a significant sense of pleasure if we gain food, mate or accomplish something significant (see Foy, 2007). It is nature's way of **operantly conditioning** us to achieve, to get to the good things in life. It operates in harmony with the endogenous punishment mechanism, which helps us to avoid danger by producing fear and a 'sense of failure' via mechanisms such as the ANS and the hormone **cortisol** (see Chapter 3).

Almost all addictive substances and behaviours (e.g. compulsive gambling or shopping – see Chapter 10) act on this same endogenous reward mechanism and stimulate these brain regions, powerfully triggering the reward mechanism in the absence of the user 'achieving' anything. By reverse association, the drug user will instead attach great importance to the procedures immediately prior to feeling the rewarding effects of the drug, as this is the 'behaviour' that the brain assumes is producing the synthetic 'reward'. These behaviours, such as the rituals of preparing the substance, are typical of the junk culture (the culture surrounding opiate use) described by William Burroughs (Burroughs, 1959). Thus, the user may prefer reward system stimulating drugs to sex etc. and lack the need to be productive or accomplish, with the continued use of the drug reducing the potential reward felt for eating

or sex (Foy, 2007). In the case of cocaine, anhedonia (lack of normal pleasure-seeking behaviour) is part of the addiction to the drug's use, but in contrast to the opiates, it is also part of the withdrawal syndrome for cocaine (Parrott et al., 2004). In the case of morphine, Parrott et al. (2004) note that opioid receptor stimulation in the hypothalamus produces dependence, but that addiction due to dopamine reward stimulation may be relatively absent. Thus, morphine given for pain relief in hospital may produce dependence due to tolerance and withdrawal, but lack addiction or the compulsive desire to seek reward from the drug (Parrott et al., 2004). A further distinction in the development of addiction has been made in France by Le Moal and Koob (2007), relating early addiction to lack of impulse control and later stages to compulsive reward seeking. In more advanced stages of opiate use, addicts report that the rewarding effects of opiates reduce over time, which in animal studies seems to correspond with changes in the mesolimbic dopamine reward system (Harvey, Hope and Shaham, 2007).

Many hallucinogenic drugs lack or provide very little of this reward stimulation, which is possibly one reason why they also lack the addictiveness of drugs like cocaine or alcohol. Although the dopamine response in the reward areas for alcohol varies greatly between people, there is a clear relationship between this activity and alcohol seeking (Yoder et al., 2007). However, alcohol not only stimulates the reward system, but also inhibits the punishment mechanism in the brain, which is why drunken individuals have a lowered threshold for danger and often end up in accidents or situations where violence occurs. It has long been established (e.g. see Wise, 1987) that some drugs, especially opiates and cocaine, also stimulate the **central endogenous pain gating** system in the body, reducing pain and increasing dependence.

Thus, animal studies have provided the neural mechanisms for the addictive qualities of some drugs (and behaviours) and may continue to be employed to suggest potential therapeutic agents for use with humans (Yücel et al., 2007). Addiction to substances in humans may depend greatly on their specific reward system stimulating abilities, which may involve dopamine, opioid or other complex interactive systems, and therapeutic agents may also need to be drug specific (Foy, 2007). Therefore, the long process of unravelling the exact neurobiological mechanisms of cocaine action will be a prerequisite to providing a precise therapy for this particular addiction (Kalivas, 2007).

in the twenty-first century, although actual prevalence may be masked by the open availability of the source materials and underreporting (Neumerk, Delva and Anthony, 1998). Inhalants can be subdivided into three groups (see Williams et al., 2007).

- solvent fuels (e.g. lighter fuel) and anaesthetics (e.g. ether)

- nitrous oxide, which is intended for medical purposes but could also be found in some whipped cream aerosol cans

- alkyl nitrites such as isoamyl nitrite, butyl nitrite and isopropyl nitrite.

Many volatile substances in the first group of inhalants, such as glue, solvents (e.g. nail varnish remover), fuels (e.g. butane) and anaesthetics (e.g. ethyl chloride), are inhaled by covering the mouth and/or nose with a container. Placing a plastic bag over the head to concentrate exposure, or 'bagging', is both common and dangerous with some inhalants (Williams et al., 2007). **Nitrous oxide** is a gas that produces euphoria and light-headedness, and reduces negative feeling associated with pain. It has been nick-named 'laughing gas' and has been utilised in the past for dental surgery, as the proportion of air to gas can easily adjust the level of the effect. Nitrous oxide has appeared on the dance club scene as the gas used to inflate balloons released at events that can be subsequently burst to allow inhalation. Isoamyl nitrite or 'amyl' is an inhalant intended to keep vital bodily functions (e.g. heart rate) continuing during situations such as cyanide poisoning (used as part of the original Bentley Cyanide Kit to counteract cyanide poisoning) as well as other assaults on vital functions. It is sold as a 'club drug' under the label 'poppers', as a result of the breakable phials that are 'popped' to release the inhalant. Amyl nitrite has stimulant effects and thus sits uneasily amongst other inhalants in the depressant classification. Although there are different types of inhalant, their overall effects generally mimic those of alcohol, with some stimulation of opioid receptors producing analgesic effects and other depressant effects mediated by GABA and glutamate systems (Williams et al., 2007).

An association has been found between various forms of childhood abuse and later heavy inhalant use, though this relationship may not be causal (Fendrich et al., 1997). The treatment or, more accurately, the management of inhalant abuse is greatly hampered by underreporting, concealment and other difficulties in detection with symptoms being mistaken for other ailments, which has led to suggestions for a more aggressive approach to diagnosis by clinicians (Lacey and Ditzler, 2007). Cognitive

Some common sources of inhalants may be legitimately bought in a supermarket.
Source: Pearson Online Database.

approaches in instilling skills to reduce use are probably less effective than widely disseminated information to help potential users or their parents to avoid children engaging with inhalant use. Treating the issue as a public health problem may be effective in the long term, utilising awareness and prevention campaigns to help the public realise the extent of this relatively hidden substance use problem (Neumerk, Delva and Anthony, 1998; Gibson, 2007). Prohibition is impractical as the volatile substances are contained in products or compounds that are ubiquitous, utilitarian and largely legal (Williams et al., 2007).

Other depressants

Synthetic opiates were the first **designer drugs**, such as **alpha-methlfentanyl** or '**china white**', which was sold to heroin addicts in the early 1980s as being 200 times as strong as morphine (Leonard, 1997). Due to the fine line between attaining a high and overdose, the use of china white resulted in a high mortality rate. A further synthetic opiate, dubbed '**new heroin**', was even more destructive as one of its metabolites, MPTP, led to irreversible **Parkinsonism** (see Chapter 20), although MPTP was subsequently of value to research into Parkinson's disease (Leonard, 1997).

Prescribed medications are frequently abused (often by females or the elderly) and may be sold on the black market. First synthesised in 1846, **barbiturates** were used to produce sedation in the twentieth century as CNS depressants but are very infrequently used now, as they are *highly* addictive with *very severe* withdrawal effects, including death (Holmes, 1998). In addition, a barbiturate's effect of neurochemically acting on GABA receptors dangerously potentiates with the effects of alcohol, and the combination has resulted in many deaths, both accidental and suicide. Barbiturates have a very high level of **toxicity**, which is not moderated by tolerance. To illustrate, a heroin user may increase the dose to maintain the effect of the drug, but their physical ability to tolerate heroin also increases, so they may progress to intake levels that could produce overdose in a naïve user. However, the need to increase the dose of barbiturates is met with little increase in the ability to tolerate the toxic effects of the drug, leading to a greater possibility of a lethal overdose. Paradoxically, the hypnotic and anxiolytic effects of barbiturates occur at relatively high doses, but at very low doses the drug can produce stimulant and euphoric outcomes by acting on lower brain areas and the reticular system (see Parrott et al., 2004).

The first **benzodiazepine** synthesised was chlorodiazepoxide, marketed as Librium. Benzodiazepines are sedative hypnotics and effective anxiolytics, which were widely used for anxiety in the twentieth century as they had a very low toxicity, and replaced barbiturates in many applications such as sedation for insomnia. However, they have proven to be insidiously *addictive* in the long term due to a slow rise in anxiety on withdrawal, which has resulted in their being prescribed far less and for short periods of time only. In a twenty-first-century French sample of forged prescriptions, most were for benzodiazepines and the majority of the recipients were female (Boeuf and Lapeyre-Mestre, 2007). Former heroin addicts using methadone as a maintenance treatment often abuse benzodiazepines. Withdrawal from benzodiazepines can incur sleep disturbance, which may destabilise heroin treatment; however, **melatonin** can aid sleep in many such cases until sleep patterns return when benzodiazepine withdrawal is complete (Peles et al., 2007). It is worth noting that the selective serotonin reuptake inhibitors (SSRIs) were greeted and prescribed with similar enthusiasm to the way benzodiazapines were originally dispensed.

Rohypnol or flunitrazepam is a prescription sleep aid that has become infamous as a so-called **date-rape drug**, whereby the sedative and amnesic effects of the drug are utilised by unscrupulous individuals for sexual gratification without consent. In many cases where there is suspicion of rohypnol use, the drug has not been found in the victim's body and the true culprit, alcohol, has been concluded to be the drug most used in this form of sexual assault. Rohypnol has also become one of the club drugs associated with the dance music scene (Gahlinger, 2004). Another

sedative that has been adopted by the 'club drug' scene is Gamma-hydroxybutyrate (GHB). GHB has also gained a reputation as a date-rape drug, which at high doses can result in coma or death. Both GHB and rohypnol in moderate doses produce states of relaxation and sedation in which the user has little recall of events.

Self-test questions

- How does substance use become an addiction?
- Discuss the conflict between legal and health approaches to substance disorder.
- What is meant by the endogenous reward system?
- When have opiates been legally available?
- What are date-rape drugs?

Stimulants

Most CNS stimulants increase cortical activity or reduce inhibitory activity in various brain areas, as much cortical activity is organised by selective inhibition. Stimulants often overlap with the final category of hallucinogenic drugs, therefore many hallucinogens have stimulant properties and could be included below.

Nicotine and tobacco

Nicotine is an addictive stimulant found in the tobacco plant *Nicotiana tabacum*, which was used by the indigenous inhabitants of America before being taken elsewhere by Spanish conquistadores (Parrott et al., 2004). Tobacco can be sniffed, chewed or smoked, which combines a habitual behaviour with nicotine intake. Smoking is the most addictive and deadliest means of using tobacco, being responsible for harming virtually every organ in the human body (Tait et al., 2006). It results in massive **collateral damage** to the body, leading to cancers, cardiovascular and lung disease, permanent lung damage, and bronchial complications. Tobacco is legal in more parts of the world than alcohol, which does not truly reflect its danger to health. It is currently the most dangerous substance of abuse in the world today amongst legal and illegal substances, and there is *no* safe level of tobacco use (Holmes, 1998).

The major causes of smoking are **modelling** of the behaviour and **peer group pressure**; the fact that smoking

As a heroic explorer, Columbus' spreading of tobacco use has only been questioned in retrospect. Until relatively recently tobacco companies were allowed to advertise. Source: Pearson Online Database.

is dangerous merely *adds* to its appeal for children and adolescents, who tend to believe they will live for ever. These are the very people who have the greatest chance of avoiding the habit by not starting to smoke (Costello, Costello and Holmes, 1995). Smoking is initially very unpleasant and requires *persistence* to acquire the habit, so not starting is *easy*. Perhaps *real* cinema heroes could have been shot whilst fumbling for a cigarette or have lost fights whilst wheezing with bronchitis? Children from disadvantaged backgrounds are more likely to smoke as adults and it is thought that this relationship is at least partly mediated by susceptibility and types of media, peer and parental role model (Fergusson et al., 2007).

Giving up can be helped by **nicotine patches** or 'nicotine replacement therapy' (NRT) to remove the initial withdrawal from nicotine content, but greater determination and positive thinking are needed to conquer the smoking habit, with all too many people 'giving up giving up'.

Denicotinised cigarettes can help to break the association between smoking and nicotine-based reward (Rose, 2007). However, 'giving up' tobacco for many people is a temporary state in a similar manner to dieting, whereas both should really be permanent lifetime decisions to maintain abstinence or healthy eating. Belated moves to reduce smoking in the population by governments in the twenty-first century are probably based on health costs outweighing the revenue from tobacco sales rather than concern for the health of individual voters. Moves to make smoking less acceptable and minimise secondary smoking were achieved by banning smoking in buildings used by the public or businesses including public houses, which were the main venues for smokers in a number of European countries. Social factors, public pressure and aids such as NRT can be effective even in the case of elderly smokers, and cessation at any age brings quantifiable health benefits (Tait et al., 2006).

Caffeine

Caffeine is the most commonly used drug in the world and provides the stimulant effect in coffee, which contains around 170 mg of caffeine in a strong fresh cup (Parrott et al., 2004). Other beverages, such as tea and hot chocolate, contain less caffeine but as the same drug is in each, the net effect is cumulative. Caffeine is also added to 'soft' drinks, which are the main source of caffeine for children and may increase later use of both soft drinks and coffee (Mattioli, 2007). True **cross-tolerance** occurs between different substances with a similar neurochemical effect, where tolerance gained for one substance may be transferred to the other substance within the same user. Although the mechanisms of action may differ between caffeine and amphetamine, the search for a replacement subjective effect may link their use in these terms. This also may partly explain the increased preference for amphetamines in adolescents brought up before the promotion of decaffeinated soft drinks. Stronger sources of caffeine come in the form of 'energy drinks' such as 'Red Bull' and espresso (or even double espresso) coffee. Children may be rather vulnerable to caffeine intake as a bar of chocolate may also contain around 25 mg of the drug, besides the many 'soft' drinks that are all widely available to children (Mattioli, 2007).

Caffeine stimulates the CNS and PNS by blocking **adenosine** receptors and thus reducing the inhibitory action of adenosine (Shapiro, 2007). Withdrawal symptoms from caffeine tend to occur when a person is removed from their regular source of the drug or they stop drinking coffee because they are ill, in which case a substitute source may be used, such as 'energy' or 'convalescent' drinks like 'Lucozade' for the infirm. There is a surprising lack of public concern over the fact that sudden abstinence from as little as two cups of coffee a day can produce pronounced withdrawal symptoms, such as anxiety, headaches and loss of energy (Shapiro, 2007; Silverman et al., 1992). All too often, routine drug intake such as caffeine in coffee is neglected in the clinical field, even though there may be consequences for important therapeutic interventions (Dratcu et al., 2007).

The clinical importance of caffeine dependence is often overlooked when examining drug law and policy. Given the possibility of dependence and clearly defined withdrawal symptoms, it has been suggested that at the very least the caffeine content of all products containing it should be clearly marked on the packaging along with warnings regarding the health risks (Ogawa and Ueki, 2007).

Cocaine

The Incas in Peru chewed leaves from the South American coca plant (*Erythroxylon coca*) in ceremonies and later for increased endurance during mine working – a use that still survives in the twenty-first century (Parrott et al., 2004). Spread by the Spanish invaders, coca leaves continued to be chewed or smoked until 1855 when the alkaloid cocaine was extracted from the plant by Friedrich Gaedcke, a German chemist (Barik, 2007). Cocaine use began to rise

in the 1970s, but this became more dramatic in the 1980s as prices fell and amphetamine supplies were restricted. The rise in the use has continued into the twenty-first century, placing cocaine as the second most popular illegal recreational drug behind cannabis in many countries such as the USA and in Europe (Barik, 2007).

Chewed in its original coca leaf form, the drug is very slowly and steadily absorbed, with few reported addictive or other problems. However, when extracted as **cocaine hydrochloride** it can be metabolised in around 3 minutes via the nasal membrane when it is sniffed, or producing a more immediate effect when taken by injection (Dhawan and Wang, 2007). When cocaine is heated or freebased with ether, the resulting lumps or crack cocaine can be smoked and produce a highly addictive euphoric state in less than 10 seconds. This euphoria may only last a few minutes, followed by restlessness and discomfort. Crack cocaine is associated with high levels of addiction, crime, violence and health problems over and above those already linked to cocaine (Jones, 2004; Day and Norman, 2007). Most users are surprisingly naïve about these consequences at the point of initiation to crack cocaine, which would imply a need for drug-specific health warnings to be widely disseminated, with some targeting of those most vulnerable subcultures within society (Day and Norman, 2007). Speedball is a name given to a mix of cocaine and heroin that is usually taken orally.

Focus

Cocaine in common use

The early secret ingredients for Coca-Cola included cocaine, which was later replaced by caffeine.
Source: Pearson Online Database.

Sigmund Freud initially made a serious mistake in advocating cocaine – a decision he later reversed when observing cocaine psychosis. Freud was not alone in considering the generalised stimulant and pain relieving properties of cocaine to be a possible panacea (cure-all); Pope Leo XIII also publicly sanctioned the drug. Pain relief made cocaine common amongst treatments for toothache as a tincture, even for children during the nineteenth and early twentieth century.

In addition, cocaine was the infamous original ingredient of Coca-Cola in 1884, which also contained caffeine and along with similar beverages was promoted as a healthy teetotal alternative to alcoholic drinks (Parrott et al., 2004). Following widespread realisation of the addictive effects of cocaine, the drug was removed from the coca leaves prior to their use in Coca-Cola from 1906. Cocaine use became far more restricted for many years, although illicit supplies often continued, taken from those intended for medical purposes.

Cocaine or **benzoylmethlyecgonine** is an alkaloid with stimulant, anaesthetic and short-term euphoric effects. It is associated with producing confidence and mental stamina similar to **hypomania**, which has made it popular with media performers and other celebrities who have always been able to afford it even prior to the 1980s (see the Focus box). Cocaine produces a strong sense of reward, possibly as a result of boosting dopamine action at critical sites in the brain, which may substantially account for its addictive qualities (Hrafnkelsdottir, Valgeirsson and Gizurarson, 2005). This high level of reward can strongly reinforce learned associations with the process of taking cocaine (Kalivas et al., 1998). Breaking these associations by behavioural interventions can thus be a more effective treatment approach in the case of cocaine (see the section on treatment, pp. 341–2).

As with amphetamines, cocaine raises the availability of dopamine and noradrenaline at synapses, whilst to a lesser extent raising serotonin levels. Repeated raising of dopamine availability can lead to paranoid states, which are evident in heavy cocaine or amphetamine users (see the case study at the start of this chapter). Cocaine is thus a sympathomimetic, in that it mimics the effects of adrenaline and noradrenalin, placing strain on the cardiovascular system. This leads to very serious cardiac and cerebrovascular pathology that is a direct result of using the drug and not a consequence of a drug-associated lifestyle (Darke, Kaye and Duflou, 2006). Crack cocaine use in mothers can also lead to cardiac problems as well as learning disabilities in offspring, for which there may be a direct molecular causal link involving the methylation of an enzyme (see Barik, 2007). The seriousness of such cocaine-induced cardiovascular complications is often not fully appreciated by users, who may yet be aware of the drug's addictive qualities. Dhawan and Wang (2007) describe a case example of long-term cocaine and immediate crack cocaine use resulting in multiple amputations following gangrene of the hands and feet.

Amphetamines

In the early twentieth century, the stimulant **ephedrine** was extracted from the Chinese medicinal herb *Ephedra vulgaris*, which proved useful in the amelioration of breathing problems in asthma. Synthetic equivalents were tested and further variants developed to avoid reliance on the imported plant. **Benzedrine** had been synthesised in 1927, which not only aided breathing but also seemed to promote energy, confidence, alertness and vigilance – qualities that were promoted in the 1930s. Amphetamines were seized upon by the military in a number of countries and used during the Second World War in a variety of applications, such as keeping pilots alert on long missions (see Parrott et al., 2004). Across Europe, in the USA and in Japan, military personnel were using amphetamines regularly, and some of the problems of addiction and withdrawal began to be evident in this context and after discharge of these personnel. Following the end of the Second World War, similar military uses were maintained during the 'cold war' between the old USSR and the West, wherein amphetamines to remain alert were juxtaposed with barbiturates in order to sleep when not on duty (McKenzie, 1965). This dangerous use of pharmaceutically assisted sleeping and waking cycles became common across US high society and was problematic for many celebrities and prominent individuals in the public eye (see the Focus box on p. 339).

Until the 1960s, amphetamines such as **dexamphetamine sulphate** (Dexedrine) continued to be widely prescribed for depression or as a powerful diet aid, and others for narcolepsy or as a decongestant (see Iversen, 2006), until they were becoming regularly abused and frequently stolen from pharmacies or spuriously gained via prescription for illicit resale. They were also conclusively found to be highly addictive and no longer recommended for dieting or depression. They were then made illegal to possess without prescription, and prescribed use was limited to treating narcolepsy and in the form of **methylphenidate** (Ritalin) for children with attention-deficit hyperactivity disorder (see Chapter 9). The abuse of methylphenidate intended for medical use by adolescents has become a frequent problem in the USA where prescriptions for the drug are common (Williams et al., 2004).

Amphetamines are usually taken orally but may be injected by those who have developed a high tolerance for capsule ingestion. As CNS stimulants, they not only increase energetic activity and stamina, but also produce a subjective sense of confidence and mental acceleration, hence the street name **speed** (for drug slang terms, see Volans and Wiseman, 2008). They produce rapid tolerance and are highly addictive as well as being prone to 'weekend abuse' amongst those from the dance or clubbing cultures, who then have occupational and mood difficulties during their weekday recovery period.

Under the Smith Klein and French brand name **Methedrine**, the very powerful stimulant **methamphetamine** has in the past been injected by '**speed freaks**' in search of an extreme 'hit'. The crystalline form of methamphetamine hydrochloride, 'crystal meth' or 'ice', is probably the most addictive form of amphetamine compound. It can be swallowed, injected or sniffed but is often smoked in a similar manner to crack cocaine, although with longer-lasting effects. Methamphetamine was reclassified as a class A drug in 2007 in the UK due to its highly addictive nature, and has been found as an adulterant in cocaine and 'skunk' (see cannabis) in order to bring these users into the market for the drug. Methamphetamine abuse, particularly amongst the young, has become a global problem in the twenty-first century, somewhat exacerbated by its ease of manufacture (Iversen, 2006). Initially a growing problem in the USA, methamphetamine abuse has rapidly spread around the world, with increasing incidence in diverse regions such as Europe, South Africa and Taiwan (Rawson et al., 2007). The European Monitoring Centre for Drugs and Drug Addiction has revealed from survey that the use of methamphetamine by the 15–24-year age group of both males and females has been rising for almost two decades (Rawson et al., 2007).

Methamphetamine can enhance sexual desire and lower inhibitions – qualities that led it to be adopted by gay men as a sex aid prior to its spread into youth culture, although it also induces erectile failure, which is common to most amphetamines. In order to counter this unwanted side-effect, these early users dangerously combined Viagra (see Chapter 13) with crystal meth, which magnified health risks as both drugs raise blood pressure, as well as behaviourally increasing HIV risk (Bolding et al., 2006). As with cocaine, most amphetamines also place dangerous strain on the cardiovascular system and can lead to confused paranoid states that may mimic psychosis. These health risks are particularly high with methamphetamine, chronic use of which has been linked to persisting damage to the dopamine transport system and a reduction in hippocampal volume (Thompson et al., 2004). The production of methamphetamine is simple and cheap but it is also highly dangerous, involving volatile constituents. Many of these factors were considered in raising the legal status of methamphetamine to that of a class A drug in 2007.

Other stimulants

The leaves and shoots of the shrub *Catha edulis* from parts of Africa are sold as the herbal stimulant **khat** (or Qat), which is being assessed as a candidate substance to bring under the 1971 Misuse of Drugs Act. Although little known to most drug users, around 6 tons of khat per week are imported legally into the UK alone. The fresh plant leaves contain the alkaloid stimulants cathinone and cathine, and although khat influences the dopamine system and thus has potential for addiction, there is little sign of this in most users, who indulge about once a week on average (Advisory Council on the Misuse of Drugs, 2005a). Some have tried to align khat with amphetamine, but cathinone and particularly cathine are substantially weaker stimulants than amphetamine and much of the suspicion over it being dangerous or linked to mental illness may be a result of the cultural context of its use (Warfa et al., 2007). Khat's low cost and legal status is possibly why it has no clear association with crime or other drugs apart from tobacco. However, there are physical risks such as oral cancers from chewing it and, in common with other stimulants, cardiovascular risks (Advisory Council on the Misuse of Drugs, 2005a). **Yaba** is a synthetic amphetamine derivative originally manufactured by the Nazi military

Mod culture in the 1960s was associated with the use of amphetamines, although many young mods were naïve regarding drug use.
Source: David A. Holmes.

Table 11.3 Illicit drugs adopted by youth culture in history

Amphetamines	Early 1960s scooter riding **mod** culture, symbolised by bands such as The Who and The Small Faces, represented ongoing working-class youth rebellion that was increasingly infiltrated by middle-class counterparts. It was part of mod culture to take amphetamines in youth venues that did not have an alcohol licence, with heavier users getting 'blocked' or a in a state where coherent speech was disrupted and paranoid thinking was evident. An association between amphetamines and violence also began with mod culture and progressed through working-class antecedents such as **suede-heads**, **skinheads** and the **scally culture**. During the 1970s, **Wigan soul** firmly established the all-night dance scene in which, often aided by amphetamines, many participants literally danced till dawn. From mod culture onwards, amphetamines have accompanied dance cultures into the twenty-first century.
Cannabis and LSD	In the mid- to late 1960s, cannabis moved from the jazz music based **beatnik** movement of the 1950s into mainstream pop music, headed by the **Beatles** and **Rolling Stones** in Europe and the **Byrds** and the **Doors** in the USA. UK clubs such as the Peppermint Lounge and the entire San Francisco district of Haight Ashbury were littered with hallucinogen-using musicians and artists. In 1965 LSD appeared in the same culture, having moved from the opiate drug-influenced **Beat Generation**, who included writers **Jack Kerouac**, **Ken Kesey** and **William Burroughs** via the 'merry pranksters' formed by Kesey and the alternative music culture, and then being dramatically personified by **Jimmi Hendrix** as a global musical phenomenon. Cannabis and LSD continued as drugs with musical and artistic 'integrity' for the young until the 1980s, only to re-emerge in the 1990s dance scene as 'chill out drugs'.
MDMA (ecstasy)	Slowly emerging from the mostly gay US dance clubs in the late 1970s, MDMA or 'ecstasy' began to spread in Europe. At first it was taken in homes and bars, as with many illicit substances, but its potential for combining with electronically produced dance music to produce a sea of endlessly repetitively moving **ravers** was rapidly realised as both elements spread in a dance music revolution during the late 1980s. This mixture of young clubbers and older experienced 'hippies' danced alone but felt empathically at one with all present. Alcohol sales plummeted and large 'raves' tended to move outside the official club scene to warehouse or open-air impromptu events, often organised as hundreds of carloads of enthusiasts appeared at prearranged service stations. A second generation of 'peace and love' appeared to emerge in the 1990s with ecstasy taking the role formerly held by LSD. However, interpersonal harmony began to dissipate as criminal gangs moved in on the lucrative drug markets inside clubs such as the Hacienda in Manchester. In contrast, violence at football matches fell noticeably as ecstasy replaced alcohol for many newer football fans.

as another stimulant for use with wartime troops. It is currently spreading as a result of ease of manufacture, but although common in the Far East, it is rare in Europe. However, Yaba also has hallucinatory effects and may enter mainstream use as a **club drug**.

Self-test questions

- What youth cultures embraced the use of amphetamines?
- What are the reasons for concern over the use of methamphetamine?
- What is the basis for cocaine addiction?
- What makes tobacco the most dangerous substance of abuse?
- Is the caffeine in coffee addictive?

Hallucinogens

As a basic criterion, all the substances below produce hallucinations at some level of dosage and this tends to be the prominent feature of the drug for its users. Hallucinogens have been associated with religious ritual throughout the histories of many civilisations, as their primary effect has been compared with true spiritual experiences. This concept of the 'chemical religion' continues to be debated in the twenty-first century with labels such as **neurotheology** being applied to the science of hallucinogen-induced and neurologically based spiritual experience (see Morris, 2006).

LSD

LSD is an abbreviation of **d-lysergic acid diethylamide**. However, when first synthesised as a derivative from the ergot fungus on rye bread in 1938 by chemists Stoll and Hoffman at the Sandoz Laboratories in Basle, it was referred to as batch 25 or **LSD-25**, a name that remained in use

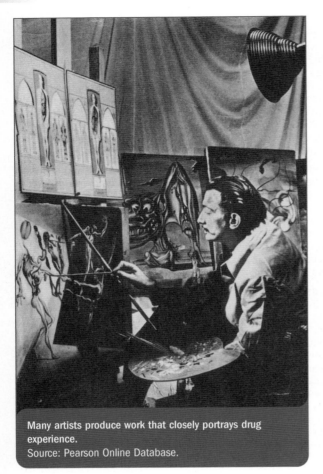

Many artists produce work that closely portrays drug experience.
Source: Pearson Online Database.

until the 1960s (Wells, 1973). One of these chemists, Albert Hoffman, accidentally ingested a trace of the substance some 5 years later. Following a profound and lengthy psychedelic experience, including an enhanced journey home on his bicycle, Hoffman concluded that the toxin responsible was LSD-25 and the quantity had to be in terms of micrograms not milligrams. He tried a controlled dose of 250 micrograms and, as a consequence of naivety and what was still a very large dose, had a 'bad trip' or adverse subjective experience. A tenth of that amount could still have produced a profound experience (Parrott et al., 2004). LSD was initially labelled a **psychotomimetic**, as it was assumed that it synthetically produced psychosis, however, there were clear distinctions from psychosis, such as hallucinations being primarily visual in contrast to the auditory hallucinations found in psychoses. Later the category names psychedelic (mind-expanding) and hallucinogen were adopted in an attempt to characterise the primary effects of the drugs (Cohen, 1967). Attempts were made to use LSD in many psychotherapeutic contexts during the 1950s and 1960s, with famous individuals such as **Cary Grant** endorsing its positive effects.

Hoffman documented the profound changes that LSD made to his mental state, as have many others in music and literature, and such accounts have led many to take the drug in search of these reported insights or the intense visual experiences of bright vivid colour and cascading complex hallucinations sustained for many hours (Wells, 1973). Cross-modality sensory experiences or synaesthesia are common, in which users report 'seeing sounds' or

Focus

Timothy Leary and LSD controversy

In 1960 at the Harvard University Center for Research in Personality in the USA, Timothy Leary and **Richard Alpert** had some poorly controlled experimental successes in reducing recidivism in prisoners by the use of the hallucinogen **psilocybin** (see below). In 1963 Leary was dismissed from the faculty when it was revealed that he had been experimenting on himself, a 'cult' of colleagues and hundreds of volunteers with psychedelics. He went on to become the 'messenger of the psychedelic movement' in the 1960s and beyond, attempting to establish LSD use as a religion to defend it against persecution by the authorities. His phrase 'turn on, tune in, drop out' (Leary, 1970: p. 287) was to be quoted in the context of promoting the 'peace and love generation' of the 1960s beyond his death and into the twenty-first century.

Despite the US authorities' opposition to Leary and others of his view, the CIA experimented with LSD to facilitate interrogations, and even 'spiked' their own agents to inoculate against possible enemy use of the same techniques. Leary's open promotion of the use of psychedelics possibly hastened the legislation banning its manufacture, sale and use, including the therapeutic applications in the 1960s that were still in their infancy. The complexities of the effects of LSD are better understood in the twenty-first century, but due to legislation, much of the work has to be on animal models (e.g. Gresch et al., 2007).

'hearing colours'. The correspondence between internal experience and external stimulation at the peak of the experience may become difficult to distinguish, with reports of closing eyelids making no difference to the visual image. Time and space distortion can produce the effect of time slipping through hours, stopping or even running backwards, and distant objects being close enough to touch or rooms having the dimensions of cathedrals. The 'cognitive boost' gives extraordinary significance to insights and concepts, many of which seem mundane after the LSD experience (for more descriptive detail, see Cohen, 1967; Wells, 1973; Parrott et al., 2004).

LSD is a very powerful **hallucinogen** that triggers a complex serotonergic reaction and, due to the difficulty in tracking such tiny biochemical changes, a reaction that is still largely unknown. LSD and other hallucinogens bind to serotonin and presynaptic serotonin-2 receptors, with greater binding to these sites corresponding to the strength of the psychedelic experience (Parrott et al., 2004). Hallucinogens such as LSD and psilocybin are **indole-alkylamines** mimicking serotonin, and act on the **locus coeruleus** (influencing noradrenalin) and **raphe nuclei** (influencing serotonin) in the reticular system, with the former site intensifying visual perception (Leonard, 1997). As little as 30 micrograms produces profound effects such as disturbance of time and sensory perception, and consciousness change lasting up to 12 hours. LSD has a half-life of around 3 hours (Leonard, 1997). Higher doses produce effects on peripheral organs such as dilation of the pupils and a longer experience (Parrott et al., 2004). The 250 microgram dose taken by Hoffman produced a 14-hour 'trip'. However, in the rare case of intravenous administration of LSD, the experience is reported as more intense and of shorter duration. Average users take the drug once or twice in a fortnight. The physical size of an average dose of LSD is invisibly small, and the medium used to carry the drug can also be tiny as in the 'microdot' pill, or relatively large and distinctive as is the case with 'blotters'. As the nature of LSD trips can vary greatly, superstitious attachment to types or logos of pills can develop.

The social and physical context the drug is taken in, prior experiences, expectations and the presence of an experienced user guide or 'ground control', who is experienced but does not take the drug, can greatly help users to have a pleasant 'trip' and an enlightening insight into their thinking and sensory mechanisms. However, if these conditions fall short of supportive or there is pre-existing anxiety or mental disturbance, the LSD experience will be affected, with rising anxiety and apprehension potentially leading to panic or paranoia; this may require reassurance or even interventions such as benzodiazepines or antipsychotics in the case of a panic attack (Costello, Costello and Holmes, 1995). Chlorpromazine may so abruptly reverse the effects of LSD that recipients often prefer the 'bad trip' to the intervention (Parrott et al., 2004). Adulterants and impurities from the manufacture of LSD, such as strychnine, tend also to affect the experience disproportionately due to the intensifying effect of the LSD. If panic and paranoia occur at the peak of an LSD experience, fears are magnified greatly and a sense of being treated as a joke and of going insane may lead many to unnecessarily reconsider their sanity after the drug has left their system. Anxious individuals and disturbed individuals, who have logically suffered somewhat disturbing experiences using LSD, may often persist in taking the drug partly in an attempt to overcome the problems that have become evident and in pursuit of the kind of 'good trip' their peers describe (Wells, 1973). Most normal individuals enjoy a profound, sometimes spiritual experience and many first-time users never feel the need to repeat what is often an exhausting experience, for which there was no precedent in their lives.

Latent mental disturbance may be precipitated with the possibility of psychotic behaviour arising during the LSD experience greatly adding to initial confusion or fear. It would seem that the profound experience of the drug might act as the stressor in the manner of the **diathesis–stress** model of mental state precipitation, and this is supported by the fact that the majority who suffer this type of reaction had identifiable pre-existing conditions (Parrott et al., 2004). As other stressors fail to produce psychosis in the absence of any predisposition, it would seem equally unlikely that any drug-induced hallucinogenic experience could produce real psychosis in any normal individual without a pre-existing condition. It would therefore seem prudent to assess individuals presenting with such hallucinogen-related reactions for underlying conditions.

Curious reported phenomena associated with hallucinogens such as LSD are **flashbacks** or **hallucinogen persisting perception disorder**, which are psychedelic experiences, usually hallucinations, that occur long after all traces of the substance have left the body (Leonard, 1997). There are no physiological, drug-related or neurological bases for flashbacks and, as these only occur in around 15 per cent of users, they may be indicators of pre-existing psychotic predispositions (Parrott et al., 2004). Flashbacks are unlikely to be related to LSD itself, as not only are all traces of the drug absent, but so are any longer-term effects of the substance. They may have a basis in the cognitive inability of some individuals to separate recalled experiences from current sensations. A further misleading avenue of inquiry regarding the use of hallucinogens and LSD in particular are third-party reports of attempts to 'fly', or other impossible endeavours such as strolling in front of speeding vehicles. Along with many others, Parrott et al. (2004) consider that those taking LSD are unlikely to be deluded into thinking they can fly, and that tragic accidents reported by others are errors based on space-time distortion, where great heights seem a step away and speeding cars very slow and distant.

The potential for physical addiction with LSD is minimal, in part due to lack of reward system stimulation by the drug. A high degree of tolerance to LSD develops rapidly, with the desensitisation of serotonin receptors occurring after around three daily doses, which renders further administration somewhat ineffective (see Leonard, 1997). There is cross-tolerance with mescaline and psilocybin but not MDMA, confirming differing actions on the serotonin system between the hallucinogens. There are no significant psychological or physical withdrawal effects from abrupt cessation of LSD, contributing to the drug's lack of addictive potential (Leonard, 1997). The use of LSD to ease the spiritual and physical pain of **terminal illness** ended along with other psychotherapeutic evaluations due to its criminalisation in the 1960s. There has been some re-emergence of interest in the positive value of LSD in clinical applications in the twenty-first century, which may include work begun in the 1960s and 1970s on children with autism (see Sigafoos et al., 2007).

Cannabis

The hemp plant *Cannabis sativa* has been used medically for 3000 years, so its long-term effects are documented. Throughout history, the use of cannabis for intellectual, medical, religious and artistic purposes has been welcomed by prominent names from **Galen** to **Baudelaire**, and it has been a component of a number of religions such as Hinduism. It has been used for almost every ailment from speech impediments to bowel disorders and contains many active ingredients, some of which are **cannabinoids** that have psychoactive properties (see Parrott et al., 2004). The primary active ingredient in cannabis is delta-9-tetrahydrocannabinol (THC), which has stimulant and hallucinogenic properties. Other cannabinoids are psychoactive and can confound the attribution of effects assigned to THC: for example, **cannabidiol** reduces the anxiety induced by THC (Williamson and Evans, 2000). However, cannabis as a whole tends to defy classification, and although it produces hallucinogenic effects, it also has analgesic, anti-convulsant and anti-inflammatory properties amongst many others (see Parrott et al., 2004).

As the most commonly used illicit substance in the world, **cannabis** comes in many forms and 'grades', partly reflecting the level of production and often characteristic of the country of origin (see Andrews and Vinkenoog, 1972). Different parts of the plant have varying concentrations of cannabinoids, with the upper leaves and flower heads being targeted for commercial use. When dried, these parts of the plant are sold as '**grass**', '**weed**' or **marijuana**, but they are unpopular with illicit dealers as marijuana is very bulky and it is difficult to prevent the distinctive smell attracting attention. Genetically modified cannabis plants have been produced by Dutch growers in Europe, and the dried plant form of this hybrid, called **skunk** due to its strong smell, has up to five times the THC content of the organic plant. When the organic plant is threshed or sifted through sieves and the residue heated and compressed into blocks, it is then sold as **hashish** or **cannabis resin**, which is much stronger than marijuana. The gauge of the sieves (usually given numerically, e.g. '00') can produce a rougher or more refined consistency of resin, as can the threshing of only flower heads (Andrews and Vinkenoog, 1972). Cannabis can be refined into the highly concentrated liquid THC or **THC-oil**, and although this can be transported efficiently, it is expensive to produce and is not always popular with regular cannabis users, for whom potency is not a major criterion.

Cannabis in all forms is usually smoked in a '**joint**' with tobacco, but it can be smoked on its own in a '**bong**' pipe, or ritualistically using hot implements to burn resin under a bottomless bottle or '**hot knives**'. It can also be eaten or drunk with coffee or other liquid infusion, in which case it is considerably less harmful in relative medical terms, but the effects can be much more unpredictably timed (1–3 hours latency) than when smoked. When smoked, the effects are shorter and more controllable, but carry the very serious health risks of smoking tobacco. Cannabis itself contains a number of carcinogens and thus still presents a serious health risk due to smoking, even when this is without tobacco.

The global effects of cannabis are dependent on the amount of the drug taken. The effects of a low dose are mild euphoria, sociability and an experience that is usually pleasant in retrospect. Moderate levels incur time and perceptual distortion, with users often tending to be quiet, detached and introspective, and there is often an increased appetite and thirst. As these effects tend to be the opposite of alcohol, naive users may often continue taking more of the drug, not noticing that they are already intoxicated. This may lead to a heavy dose, which can produce anxiety, panic and paranoia. In the first half of the twentieth century, there was a great deal of deliberate misinformation regarding the effects of cannabis (Parrott et al., 2004). Films such as *Reefer Madness* portrayed its use as instantly leading to sexual predation and violence, which were so far removed from reality that they became cult viewing by the young some half a century later. There are no long-term effects from heavy doses, with all discernible effects, including fleeting schizophreniform psychotic reactions, disappearing within days of cessation. Long-term cognitive deficits have been suggested by some studies but are absent in others. Lyketsos et al. (1999) found no differences when comparing light, heavy and non-users.

As THC and other cannabis compounds are broken down in the liver, some of the resulting metabolites are also psychoactive compounds extending the effects of the drug and reducing the need for another dose, particularly for regular users who metabolise the drug more efficiently. THC tends to collect in areas of fatty tissue, which in combination with experience and the cascading action of metabolites means that regular users tend to need less of the drug over time – a kind of reverse tolerance. These factors and other processes mean that cannabis has a complex half-life, which can be between 28 and 56 hours, and it remains detectable in the body for around 30 days (Parrott et al., 2004).

In addition to other reactions, there are two cannabinoid receptors that are specifically stimulated by THC inhibiting the enzyme that stimulates cyclic adenosine monophosphate, which changes the excitability state on the particular neuron (Hirst, Lambert and Notcutt, 1998). These receptors are normally stimulated by two natural brain substances, **2-arachidonoylglycerol** and **arachidonoylethanolamide** or anandamide, which are the endogenous forms of THC; however, in contrast to the relationship of opioids to opiates, anandamide is less potent than THC (see Smita, Kumar and Premendran, 2006). The effects of cannabis on brain regions are necessarily as complex as the substance itself, and there are also secondary effects via increased noradrenaline and dopamine as well as withdrawal affecting the serotonin system (Parrott et al., 2004).

Cannabis has potential to be psychologically addictive, particularly in individuals who have been previously poorly motivated in their lives and employment or school, leading to assumptions of an 'amotivational syndrome' for which there is little substantial evidence (McKim, 2003). However, physical addiction to the substance is also controversial with little evidence to support it. Withdrawal symptoms from cannabis use are negligible, although there is the residual alteration in dopamine, noradrenalin and serotonin systems mentioned above (Parrott et al., 2004). In recognition of the lack of withdrawal problems, *DSM-IV* has omitted withdrawal from the diagnosis of cannabis dependence (Gillespie et al., 2007). It has also been accused of being a **gateway** drug, leading users to use 'harder' drugs such as heroin. This is a claim often made in ignorance of the fact that the effects of these substances tend towards polar opposites, unlike alcohol, which is more frequently used by heroin addicts. What these substances have in common is that they are illegal and supplied by dealers who will gain more profit and be exposed to less risk from heroin than cannabis (Holmes, 1998).

Some research has produced data or rationales indicating that cannabis use may potentially lead to psychosis, either precipitated in the predisposed or arising in non-psychotic individuals (e.g. Linszen and van Amelsvoort, 2007). Survey evidence that cannabis precipitates psychosis in predisposed individuals is supported by its association with higher levels of schizotypy, which is assumed to be an indicator of psychosis proneness (Barkus et al., 2007). However, this relationship between psychosis and schizotypy may not be sufficiently substantial to extend to a third factor in this way. Polydrug use in existing users and ethics preventing the experimental allocation of substantial cannabis to eliminate those psychosis-prone individuals who are attracted to cannabis use, particularly

Focus

The medical value of cannabis

The **decriminalisation debate** has surrounded cannabis use for many years (see pp. 345–6). This has rested on two principles: that cannabis is one of the least harmful of all recreational drugs; and that cannabis has many medical and other applications. Needless to say, both of these positions have been attacked by a highly motivated movement, as has been argued above regarding the harm issue.

The medical uses of cannabis include: symptom relief for **multiple sclerosis** (Consroe et al., 1996); severe or chronic **pain relief** (Parrott et al., 2004); the reduction of intra-ocular pressure in **glaucoma** (Green, 1998); anti-nausea effects during **chemotherapy**; **asthma** symptom relief; easing alcohol and opiate withdrawal; and **migraine** relief (Williamson and Evans, 2000). Cannabis can also counter appetite loss as well as having anti-convulsant and anti-inflammatory properties (Parrott et al., 2004).

for **self-medication**, means that such research may never be conclusive (see Hall and Degenhardt, 2000). The zealous use of research suggesting a cannabis psychosis (somewhat reminiscent of 'reefer madness') to reintroduce prohibitive legislation is particularly concerning given the true clinical implications of such a suggestion being serious (Pollack and Reuter, 2007), especially in a political context that condones high-dose alcohol use. Given the considerable financial interest of the alcohol industry in maintaining its sales of the most socially damaging but legal drug, equivocal research findings regarding illicit competitors should be considered carefully.

MDMA (ecstasy)

MDMA or 3,4-methylenedioxymethamphetamine and MDA or 3,4-methylenedioxyamphetamine and the less popular MDEA or 3,4-methylenedioxyethylamphetamine are stimulants that also have pronounced hallucinogenic properties and as such could just as easily be listed under stimulants with the amphetamines. These drugs share some of their chemical structure with both mescaline and amphetamine but have unique effects of their own. MDMA was first synthesised around 1910 and patented by the Merck Company in Germany in 1914 as a possible appetite suppressant. However, after 2 years of trials it was mostly ignored in terms of clinical use or research until around 1965 when it began to be tested in psychiatry

to break through defences as an 'empathy agent' (see Parrott, 2001). MDMA began to be synthesised again by Californian pharmacologist **Alexander Shulgin** in the 1970s and by 1985 it was being produced in large quantities by illegal sources (Gahlinger, 2004).

MDMA has been referred to as an **enactogen**, as it and similar drugs seem to increase feelings of closeness, empathy and euphoria (Morgan, 2000). The drug became associated with the electronic dance culture of the 1980s and gained the nickname 'empathy'. Both MDMA and MDA are sold on the illegal drug market as **ecstasy** and MDEA as 'eve'. As a drug used regularly by young people in nightclubs, MDMA was made illegal with little recourse to empirical evidence. With its effects of hallucinations, increased empathy, high energy, sexual enhancement and obsessive repetitive movement, MDMA became inextricable from the dance environment (Gahlinger, 2004). As its association with youth dance culture became public (see Table 11.3), it attracted concern from parents, authorities and the media across the world. The publicity generated by this interest in a global drug and club culture served to popularise further the use of MDMA, and in Europe the island of Ibiza became a focal point for the gathering of young clubbers. The effects of MDMA had been far 'calmer' in the relaxed domestic setting of a Californian 'new age' home or the early therapeutic empathy-enhancing sessions in which it was initially taken (Parrott, 2001). In the twenty-first century there is still a movement to use MDMA in psychotherapeutic contexts (Sessa, 2007).

DJ culture has been associated with the use of MDMA, 'Ecstasy', in many cases erroneously. Source: David A. Holmes.

MDMA primarily acts on the serotonin system in complex ways, but also elevates dopamine, noradrenalin, acetylcholine and histamine action. There are extremely rare fatal reactions to MDMA, possibly as a result of the non-linear relationship between the dose level of the drug and the rise in blood plasma levels, which makes any one reaction to a specific dose unpredictable and disproportionately greater for some individuals (Parrott, 2001). Common complications of MDMA use involve hyperthermia and anxiety, which are exacerbated by the typical user being in the context of a hot crowded club where there are no 'chill-out' rooms and with the user dancing energetically for prolonged periods (Gahlinger, 2004). These conditions can also lead to dancers or 'ravers' feeling dehydrated, despite the fact that MDMA is an anti-diuretic. In these circumstances, many clubbing youngsters take in too much fluid, leading to hyponatraemia where the blood electrolyte levels become diluted to a perilous degree, occasionally leading to death as in the much-publicised case of Leah Betts in the UK (Parrott, 2001). Attribution of toxicity is confounded in the case of MDMA, as it is often uncertain whether MDA or MDEA may be partly or wholly involved, and the relative toxicity of each will still have to await the outcome of ongoing animal research (see Freudenmann and Spitzer, 2004).

Short-term ill effects as a result of the drug MDMA itself tend to involve hyperthermia, sometimes leading to what has been termed the serotonin syndrome with a dangerously rising core body temperature and autonomic instability (Gahlinger, 2004). Mid-term effects within a few days involve serotonin depletion, reducing the effects of further MDMA use and leading to feelings of depression (Parrott, 2001). The long-term effects are still not fully known and regular users have been acting as a large-scale and lengthy 'uncontrolled drug trial' in this respect for the last 30 years. Animal research has been used, particularly in the wake of human laboratory research on humans provoking accusations of being unethical. Potential damage to memory has been researched as well as other long-term cognitive deficits (e.g. Heffernan, Ling and Scholey, 2001). Many aspects of neurocognition have been examined and, although there is little difference with controls for some domains of cognition, evidence for deficits remains for a number of areas such as attention and concentration (Kalechstein et al., 2007). Damage to the serotonergic neurotransmitter system is a long-term consequence of MDMA use, which can also be precipitated by a single high dose, and there is evidence for damage to the dopaminergic system (Montoya et al., 2002). Ecstasy is often adulterated or entirely substituted for with amphetamine, caffeine or even codeine, and most people taking it are polydrug users, which makes an assessment of long-term

effects in the field an inexact science (Gahlinger, 2004; McCambridge et al., 2005).

The forensic aspects of MDMA possibly became more controversial than the legal issues surrounding cannabis during the 1990s. For the last 25 years, millions of young people around the world have taken MDMA as 'ecstasy' every weekend. This is a large proportion of the world's population of young people, who are being criminalised as a result of undue media focus sensationalising a tiny number of fatalities, many of which were indirectly related to MDMA use. This led to the drug being designated a class A illegal substance. Patterns of use of the drug differ from most other drugs, in that in the early 1990s the average user had only ever taken the drug on ten or fewer occasions. Although this average had increased dramatically by the twenty-first century, the pattern of use of MDMA was still sporadic, tending to be confined to once a week or once a month (Parrott, 2001). Further into the century, this trend in the use of MDMA has continued, with fewer overall users but some ongoing users increasing the amount taken per session (McCambridge et al., 2005).

Psilocybin

Psilocybin and psilocin are the active ingredients in many of the *Psilocybe* genus of fungi, also known as and commonly referred to as **magic mushrooms**. The presence of the drug is often checked by crushing the freshly picked stems, which later turn blue to indicate psilocybin. However, other fungi may produce a cyanic reaction in a similar visual way but are often dissimilar in appearance, aiding discrimination. *Psilocybe semilanceata* or **liberty cap** mushrooms are found in parks and gardens in the UK, where the knowing possession of the mushroom containing psilocybin or its means of production was made illegal as from 2005. Even the raw fungus has been somewhat over-severely designated a class A drug. This classification and the hasty way in which drug law has been applied in the case of psilocybin and LSD will do little to dispel the criticism that European and US drug legislation lacks intelligence. As illustration of the confusion that can arise when legislation is hasty, in 2005 UK Customs and Excise still believed it had the remit to collect VAT on what had actually become class A drug sales.

As with LSD, psilocybin is an **indolealkylamine** resembling serotonin and thus acting on that neurotransmitter system (Parrott et al., 2004). Effects are descriptively similar to LSD, including synaesthesia, although they are reported to manifest more gradually but are equally influenced by expectation and setting. Often claimed as a 'natural' or 'organic' alternative to LSD by users, psilocybin is a potent hallucinogen but with a greater potential for dose control by the user. One of the problems for illicit LSD use is the microscopic dose level, which when produced in crude 'home factories' can result in random-strength products. However, although the drug content of mushrooms varies between species and to a lesser extent within species, the sale of mushrooms by weight or number gives the user a fairly reliable gauge of the amount of psilocybin taken. Psilocybin has to be ingested because smoking destroys the active ingredients, and little effort is given to extraction of psilocybin for direct entry to the bloodstream as users are content with ingestion techniques.

There are variants from around the world, notably the large Mexican variety. Albert Hoffman isolated psilocybin from *Psilocybe mexicana* in 1958, but the dried mushrooms are believed to have been used for their hallucinogenic properties in earlier civilisations, such as the Mayan and Aztec cultures in their religious rituals. These 'pagan' activities involving mushrooms were suppressed by Christian invaders. Championed by Timothy Leary before he focused on LSD, psilocybin is some 50 times stronger than mescaline and one-two hundredth the strength of LSD in terms of its hallucinogenic effects (Maruyama et al., 2006). Anecdotal case-based evidence for **hallucinogen persisting perception disorder** (flashbacks) has been reported for psilocybin as well as LSD, sometimes persisting up to 5 years after cessation of the drug, but these are rarely pure psilocybin users; nor are the cases empirically free of background psychopathology (e.g. Espiard et al., 2005).

Ketamine

Ketamine is a dissociative anaesthetic primarily used in veterinary surgery, but it has been used illegally in association with other **club drugs** for its hallucinatory and dissociative properties (Curran and Morgan, 2000). However, the drug would also be appropriately located amongst the depressant drugs and it is more its use than its CNS effect that places it with hallucinogens in the thinking of many authors, along with rohypnol and GHB (e.g. Gahlinger, 2004). Reported effects of ketamine include euphoria, depersonalisation, empathy and bonding with others, distortion of tactile sensations and the subjective sense of entering the 'k-hole' (a ketamine slang term), in which users describe the sensation of 'tunnel-vision' preceding their 'going under' as the dissociative effects take hold, and even 'seeing a light' or 'out-of-body' experiences, giving the drug a mystical allure (Critchlow, 2006). Ketamine is N-methyl-D-aspartate receptor antagonist, which affects cognitive function in addition to its anaesthetic and dissociative effects (Curran and Morgan,

2000). There is mounting evidence for ketamine dependence, and severe withdrawal symptoms begin within 1 hour of cessation of prolonged use of the drug (Critchlow, 2006). The drug also produces cross-tolerance with alcohol, which may prove problematic given the nightclub context in which it is used.

Ketamine can produce dangerous states where these dissociative effects, which may last for about an hour, combine with anaesthesia to lead to accidents and self-injury. Individuals have been badly burned without being aware of the seriousness of their injuries, and in one example a girl's boyfriend removed all of her teeth whilst both were under the influence of ketamine. In some individuals, post-ketamine psychotic behaviour has also been noted, and it is well established that high doses will result in coma and death (Parrott et al., 2004). The use of ketamine has increased in the twenty-first century, somewhat paradoxically amongst a few of those individuals taking MDMA as part of the dance and club culture movement of the 1990s, possibly as a result of common suppliers and its being a **contaminant** in batches of MDMA (Curran and Morgan, 2000). The lability of such a rise in use has created anomalies in the literature, in that some leading texts have no information on the drug (e.g. Schuckit, 2006). Ketamine is a class C drug, but this may be further revised at a later date (Advisory Council on the Misuse of Drugs, 2004).

PCP

PCP is an abbreviation of **phencyclidine**, also known by the street name of 'angel dust' or 'ozone'. It is another dissociative anaesthetic that, along with ketamine, sits uneasily amongst other hallucinogens in part due to the additional effects of delusions, irrationality, reduced muscular coordination and disorientation. PCP has a much greater affinity for the N-methyl-D-aspartate receptor than ketamine, is much more exitotoxic and has a long half-life of 12 hours (Curran and Morgan, 2000). As a dissociative drug, it affects glutamate neurotransmission. As an **arylcyclohexylamine**, PCP was originally developed as an anaesthetic in the 1950s, but due to side-effects it only continued as a veterinary tranquilliser (Leonard, 1997).

It is sometimes mixed with marijuana joints and named 'crystal supergrass', but it can be sniffed and is easily soluble in water or alcohol for ingestion. Although it is highly addictive, many users do not return to PCP once they break the initial habit because of the unpleasant, destructive and anti-social or violent side-effects. Others continue as it confers feelings of invulnerability and power. High doses may result in coma, seizures or death, and prolonged use may leave persisting memory, speech and thought dysfunction (Parrott et al., 2004). Clinical forensic involvement with PCP can be specialised, as individuals on the drug taken into custody or busy clinical environments can become very violent and self-destructive.

Other hallucinogens

Mescaline is an alkaloid isolated from the growths on the *Lophophora williamsii* or peyote cactus in 1896. The plant had been used for many years by the indigenous population around the Mexico–USA border to aid religious experience in rituals. In *The Doors of Perception* (1954), Aldous Huxley documented the effects of mescaline at length, seeing the drug and other hallucinogens as gateways to greater awareness, and to this end the author took the drug on his death bed. Mescaline is less potent than LSD 888.

Another common fungus found throughout the world having known hallucinogenic content is Amanita muscaria or 'fly agaric'. It was used by Viking raiders prior to an attack for its stimulant and hallucinogenic effects (Parrott et al., 2004), and is commonly used in Siberia. Popular in traditional fairy tale illustrations as a stereotyped 'toadstool', it is a familiar red colour with white spots and gills, and was featured in the surreal movie *Performance* (Roeg and Cammell, 1970). Amanita muscaria contains **muscimol** and **ibotenic acid**, which have structural similarities to the GABA and glutamic acid neurotransmitters (Benjamin, 1995). Amanita muscaria has sufficiently low concentrations of toxins compared with more lethal fungi to be used as a hallucinogen, but it still presents some risk if used without care over dosage. One outcome of the UK legislation governing psilocybin use has been an increase in the use of Amanita muscaria. Its main effects peak around 3 hours and disappear within 12 hours (Benjamin, 1995).

Other synthetic hallucinogens have been developed, such as dimethyltryptamine or **DMT** and dimethoxymethamphetamine or STP (standing for serenity, tranquillity and peace). STP or **DOM** is an amphetamine derivative developed by Alexander Shulgin, who later re-established the synthesis of MDMA. STP is weaker than LSD and is associated with a greater incidence of less pleasant experiences (Parrott et al., 2004). The anti-tussive cold remedy **dextromethorphan** is similar in pharmacology to ketamine and phencyclidine, and has been abused for its hallucinogenic effects (Bryner et al., 2006). As with the abuse of many over-the-counter medicines, dextromethorphan abuse is difficult to detect and diagnose, and a low level of reporting leads to a lack of awareness amongst clinicians (Desai et al., 2006). There has been a recent rise in the use of the short-acting **Salvia divinorum**, a water-soluble hallucinogen, by adolescents. This appears to have some problematic longer-term effects (see Singh, 2007).

Self-test questions

- Why has MDMA use been of particular concern since the 1980s?
- In what ways do opiates and hallucinogens differ in terms of addiction?
- Why are there reports of LSD users 'trying to fly'?
- To what extent is cannabis harmful?
- In what ways are ketamine and PCP different from other hallucinogens?

Focus

The association of drugs with celebrity status

The use of both illegal and other drugs by the famous is not unique to musicians. There is some foundation to the public's view of drug indulgence being an intrinsic part of having celebrity status. This association with fame refers to prescribed, illicit and legal substances, and would seem to stretch back in history further than twenty-first-century sensationalist news stories would imply. However, in taking a historical perspective it has to be noted that, with the exception of the prohibition era in the USA, drug knowledge, legislation and public awareness were at a much lower level before 1970.

Clearly, in the time of **Alexander the Great,** the use of any substance to bolster the courage or performance of soldiers in battle would not have been considered in any way improper, even for Alexander himself. This was similarly the case for German soldiers in the Second World War, who were given **methamphetamine** in the

Focus continued

The association of celebrity with drug use is not a new phenomenon. Oscar Wilde smoked opium and cannabis in addition to drinking absinthe.
Source: Pearson Online Database.

introduced to the substance by their medical doctor for some ailment, which continued to be a common route to drug use until the 1960s. **Oscar Wilde** also drank absinthe, and in addition he smoked **opium** cigarettes and **hashish** (a form of cannabis). Wilde was warned about his alcohol consumption by his physician, but took little heed, and he was not alone in his family in this respect.

In the twentieth century, drug taking amongst those in creative professions became less hidden with the alcohol and heroin use of the musician **Charlie Parker** and the singer **Billie Holiday** contributing to their deaths. Some later heroes of the music world, such as **Lou Reed, Iggy Pop** and **Keith Richards**, were nearly as famous for surviving drug taking early in their careers as for their music, and others like **Roy Harper** were applauded for becoming 'psychedelic pioneers' in their youth with drugs such as **LSD**. Casualties have been all too frequent where musicians became involved with more addictive drugs such as cocaine or CNS depressant drugs, particularly combinations of alcohol, heroin and barbiturates. There have been many losses to the music industry, such as **Jimmy Hendrix, Frankie Lymon, Sid Vicious** and **Tim Buckley**, to name a few.

Drug use has not been confined to musicians and poets: the comedian **Lenny Bruce** died of a morphine overdose and actress **Marilyn Monroe** from barbiturates. Even US president **John F. Kennedy** took numerous amphetamines and other drugs for ailments. He would often have difficulties from interactions between these substances. The abuse and use of prescription drugs has for some time tended to label the user as a victim and less culpable than an illicit drug user. This reflects the public assumption, reinforced by the legitimacy of drug companies, that there are good drugs (legal) and bad drugs (illegal), and these judgements are then used to label the users (Degrandpre, 2006). The self-styled celebrity **Anna Nicole Smith** died from a lethal combination of prescription drugs. In the past, status has been evident even amongst illicit drugs, with cocaine being seen as the elite drug of celebrity, possibly as a result of its high cost before 1980, whilst heroin has been associated with street users and failure. The accusations levelled at UK model **Kate Moss** for cocaine use and her former musician boyfriend **Pete Doherty** for public persistence in his drug habits produced a record run of tabloid headlines in the twenty-first century. The media assume the public have an insatiable appetite for such celebrity drug stories and show little adherence to the morals they impose on the famous (Gibson, 2007; Furedi, 2004). These individual but very

form of 'Pervitin' tablets to reduce fatigue and improve aggression, and the Nazi leader **Adolf Hitler** received injections of this drug amongst others for suspected ailments.

The use of psychoactive substances by early poets and writers is well documented and perhaps hinted at in the content of their works. In the case of the Romantic poets such as **Lord Byron** and **Shelley**, the early opium-based drug laudanum was used for more than its painkilling functions. Laudanum was a mixture of spices, opium and wine, and was commonly dispensed by physicians in the nineteenth century for a variety of pain-based complaints (Parrott et al., 2004). Along with drinking the anise and herb-based alcoholic spirit absinthe, laudanum fitted well with image of the pale, love-struck poet of this era. As with many medicinally used drugs, the artistic and the famous were often public stories also contain some clearer indications of how celebrity and drugs have been linked repeatedly throughout recent history.

Celebrity involves a great deal of competitive stress and pressure on personal lives, from which drug use appears to provide some temporary respite without having to leave the workplace. For those in such positions, there are few barriers to accessing illicit drugs, as supply contacts are often inherent in musician, modelling and other celebrity fields, as well as finance being no barrier. Many performers feel they need inspiration from drug use or simply feel that they perform better with certain substances, as has been the case with comedians feeling that cocaine or amphetamine may give them an 'edge' in terms of confidence and speed of rapport. Some types of musicians may be under peer pressure to join in, but many others find that the frantic stresses of performance followed by anti-climax and endless hours or days of boredom in between leave them needing little encouragement to indulge. Film stars, models and other celebrities often endure very similar working conditions, almost always distanced from the stability and support of loved ones and a home life.

It is not just a simple matter of greater pressure to indulge in substance use, but there is a greater chance of highly publicised exposure and dogged police pursuit. The media relentlessly shadow celebrities, as ordinary events in their lives attract readers and viewers, making celebrity news a valuable commodity (Freeman, 2006). Tabloid press photographers and writers often intrude in search of stories, and will take risks and invade privacy to uncover scandal, often under the smokescreen of it being for the 'public good' (Gibson, 2007; also see Chapter 8). Some individuals in search of a saleable story may use coercive tactics that would earn the label 'entrapment' if carried out by the police. Even minor legitimate activities can be built into headline stories, such as the *Sun* newspaper in the UK sensationalising **Pete Doherty** simply purchasing two

syringes from a pharmacy (*Sun*, 28 September 2006). Thus as a celebrity you are more likely to be reported as using drugs, and being a public figure you are easily monitored by both media and law enforcement agencies. The press may also use any new incident to remind the public of previous celebrity offenders, such as the exhumation of the trial of **Mick Jagger, Keith Richards** and **Marianne Faithful** in the wake of a Pete Doherty court appearance by the *Independent on Sunday* ('Rear window: Stoned but not broken. The days of rock and roll-ups: celebrity drug busts 1960s', 12 February 2006). Many more successful celebrities have distanced themselves from such threats to their drug use and other aspects of their private lives by having remote residences, entering therapy or using some form of 'smokescreen' involvement with a religious movement or other organisation, which may provide a defence against police intrusion, but a lesser shield against the relentless media (Furedi, 2004).

As celebrity status becomes an increasingly salient influence on the young, those celebrities who adhere to traditionally wayward behaviour are increasingly under pressure to project a near-perfect image for their young fans (Giles and Maltby, 2004). These parasocial relationships with the famous have come to replace peer relationships for many youngsters across the world, isolated by parental fears of child predators. Separated from their peers for much of the time, these youngsters may also be those most susceptible to imitating the drug-taking aspects of their virtual role models. However, Hogg and Vaughan (2005) point out from social psychology that engaging in an activity as a result of liking the person influencing you produces less change in attitude to the activity, in this case drug taking, than if the activity is suggested by someone less liked, due to cognitive dissonance. Thus, being introduced to drug taking by a local dealer may be rationalised as indulging due to liking the drugs, but copying a celebrity is rationalised as using drugs because they like that celebrity.

Further issues in the aetiology and treatment of substance-related disorders

The question has to be posited as to why, if there are so many adolescents experimenting with drugs, so few become addicted or dependent in some way. The distinction between those who use drugs and those who progress in this use has tended to embed initial use within

environmental factors, and progression to heavier use or protracted substance-related problems with genetic factors (Fowler et al., 2007). Fowler et al. (2007) see the need to target interventions for the genetically predisposed, as they form the long-term clinical challenge, despite the fact that temporary users may, by virtue of their greater numbers, provide an apparent clinical and forensic challenge. Neurocognitive and neuroimaging studies are able to identify some of the neurological events, such as brain injury or early substance use, which both precede and compound chronic drug use, producing a pattern of

behavioural dysregulation commonly seen in such users (Yucel and Lubman, 2007).

In a perfect world, no one would try a drug or abuse a substance in the first instance and the behavioural cycle would not begin. However, we live in a world with rapidly increasing substance use and abuse (Vizi, 2007). Surviving the situation may be a matter of tolerance and education. Propaganda and repression may simply be amplifying the situation, as it did during the 1920s in the USA, when alcohol was prohibited. Some individuals may be at greater risk for addictive behaviour by inheriting a greater tolerance, having associated mental disorders, a high conflict environment, poor stress tolerance, greater exposure or simply being impressionable (Parrott et al., 2004). These individuals may need targeting. RSA (2007) recommendations to move drugs education into primary schools from older groups may be one attempt to move the agenda towards earlier prevention (RSA, 2007: p. 18). The differing motivations towards substances may also provide a guide to appropriate responses, with younger people tending to escape boredom and older individuals avoiding pain and fear. The latter point may account for the low level of illicit substance use in the over 60s and their also being the highest users of legitimately prescribed pain relief and tranquillisers.

It is also worth repeating the irony of medical doctors, as one of the very groups who have to deal with alcohol and drug abuse, suffering higher than average levels of these problems, many of which can be related to their access to legitimate supplies of substances (Brooke, Edwards and Taylor, 1991). Detecting those with a biological disposition to substance abuse early in life – for example, detecting abnormalities such as P3 event-related potentials for alcohol (see above) – would allow better monitoring, education and other preventative interventions. This approach has also been applied to other substances (see Brigham, Herning and Moss, 1995). With regard to risk factors such as exposure, stress and modelling, it is clear that society should *not* be putting commercial interest before the health of future generations, nor confusing the concepts of danger, glamour, crime and abuse, especially in the young (see the Focus box on p. 339).

Treatments

One controversial treatment approach that may be applied to a range of substances, though pioneered on cocaine, has been to produce a drug-specific 'vaccine' to 'inoculate' against future use of that substance. This stimulates an **immune reaction** to the substance as it enters the body, and antigens attaching to the drug molecules then prevent

it from passing the blood–brain barrier. In a way, the individual becomes 'immune' to the drug. For cocaine, a nasal application has been found as effective as a much higher-dose subcutaneous vaccine, possibly due to cocaine being hindered in entering the brain via olfactory routes by nasal mucous specific antibodies (see Hrafnkelsdottir, Valgeirsson and Gizurarson, 2005). However, the successful use of this treatment may create problems for legitimate future use of some drugs: for example, confounding the future use of opiates for pain relief. Mettens and Monteyne (2002) in Belgium use the term **life-style vaccines** in referring to the wide-ranging and increasing use of immunological techniques such as this for a growing number of conditions, including cocaine and nicotine addiction.

One behaviourally based treatment that has produced consistently good results over the last 25 years is cue exposure therapy or cue desensitisation (see Marissen et al., 2005). Here the cues that are classically conditioned to predict drug reward are presented without the final drug taking, whilst autonomic and psychological responses are monitored. By repeated exposure in this way, responses are reduced and drug cues no longer produce anticipatory 'withdrawal'-type symptoms (Marissen et al., 2005). This has been targeted on cocaine and opiate users but may be applicable to all abused substances, particularly where psychological addiction plays a large part. The effectiveness of cue exposure therapy for addiction has been good in terms of reduced relapse rates and looks to be following its valuable application in obsessive–compulsive disorder (Marissen et al., 2005).

Treatments for substance disorders usually begin with detoxification, followed by clinical guidance, education and peer group support. However, the full catalogue of diverse treatments has been tried in these numerous disorders with various claims of success (e.g. **methadone substitution treatment** or even **portable shock machines** for heroin). Opiate addiction is the main target of treatment programmes and some minor and more radical adjustments to traditional treatment approaches have resulted in evidence-based improvements in outcomes (see Fudala and Woody, 2004). Long-term studies have indicated that self-efficacy and the ability to address additional psychological problems help to sustain recovery in the case of heroin addiction (Hser, 2006). Thus, one highly successful strategy for maintaining recovery from substance disorders is the sustained determination to enjoy life without abuse on the part of the sufferer. In the analogy used by Brewer and Streel (2003), the ex-user may have to learn to understand a life without a drug, its rewards and cues, just as someone immersed in a new language has to cease to translate from their old language but must learn to 'think' in the newly adopted one.

Focus

Conditions comorbid with substance use

Some conditions are more likely than others to be confounded by comorbid substance abuse, including diagnostic groups regularly seen by clinical psychologists, such as those with **borderline personality disorder**, who are overrepresented amongst drug users by up to 30 times that of the prevalence in the general population (Darke et al., 2007). Treatment of **depression**, which is commonly associated with opiate users, may require continuous monitoring of both conditions in order to select and adjust appropriate interventions, particularly pharmacological treatments (Nunes, Sullivan and Levin, 2004).

Although most psychiatric disorders, such as **schizophrenia**, show high rates of comorbidity with substance use, conditions such as **post-traumatic stress disorder** and **attention-deficit hyperactivity disorder** interact adversely with drug use (Szobot et al., 2007; Mills et al., 2007).

Clinical issues

Dual diagnosis refers to having more than one diagnosable disorder, which most commonly includes a substance use disorder comorbid with another category of psychiatric disorder. Sobell and Sobell (2007) consider that this is an increasingly important issue in treatment programmes, that recognition of substance comorbidity should extend beyond diagnosable substance disorders and that the interactions between disorders should be part of clinical psychology training. Clinicians in practice need to expect and assess clients on the assumption that dual diagnosis is far more common in treatment settings than in the general population (Sobell and Sobell, 2007). Over the last 25 years there has been a phenomenal increase in interest in comorbidity with substance disorders, and a universal recognition that comorbidity not detected by a clinical psychologist can impact negatively on interventions (Mueser and Drake, 2007). Detection of comorbidity is not built into assessment procedures and many patients successfully keep their true diagnostic status covert, which is problematic as there is an increased risk of violence and suicide in addition to poorer clinical outcomes (Lowe and Abou-Saleh, 2004). The NHS in the UK has often struggled with the management of dual diagnosis clients, who often 'fall between the cracks' of drug services and general psychiatric provision, and this is a substantial proportion of the patient population (Lowe and Abou-Saleh, 2004).

The clinical view of substance use is still tarnished with the image of clients who have self-inflicted disorders and criminal careers. Hyman (2007) has argued for at least a partial disease model for addiction, and criticised the view of a 'moral condition' and the stigma this generates for treatment. Countering this overt prejudice in the health care and justice systems may be a key to reversing the UK's poor performance in this area. To this end, general practitioners should not be allowed to continue the current practice of 'opting out' of providing treatment for drug users (RSA, 2007). Making treatment programmes more openly available for substance users outside of the criminal justice system has been seen as a future priority for health resource delivery in the UK, as a result of the current situation where the treatment of substance use disorder is more often available for those committing offences than for those for whom drug use is their only offence (RSA, 2007).

Forensic issues

Substance use is inextricable from crime as most abused substances are illegal to use, possess, sell and traffic, and legal substances such as alcohol are strongly linked with crime; even tobacco has been a focus of police attention over sales to children and individuals abusing duty-free imports for bulk sales on the black market (see Bennett and Holloway, 2005). However, it has been argued that the link between alcohol and violence has a number of confounding variables, especially considered in a historical context (Graham, 2007). Although alcohol and heroin are used by non-offenders, alcohol abuse and heroin addiction are major factors in the bulk of street crimes of violence and theft (Boles and Miotto, 2003). Alcohol (along with some other depressants) reduces the effect of the **punishment mechanism** in the brain, which makes us feel bad in a polar opposite to the reward mechanism (see the Focus box on p. 324). This also reduces associated emotion and cognitions, in that the alcohol reduces brain activity during the affective processing of negative information (Franken et al., 2007). As a result of this, feeling ill or fearful in the presence of danger or risk is suppressed, with the obvious consequences of impulsive criminal acts of violence; this has been referred to as providing the 'courage' to offend (Bennett and Holloway, 2005). Most of us have met drunks who are 'invincible'.

Female susceptibility to the effects of alcohol is also exacerbated by a rise in testosterone, which is less noticeable in males where levels are normally higher, but in females this can lead to risky and aggressive behaviour (see Gussler-Burkhardt and Giancola, 2005). Alcohol is still the commonest **date-rape drug** and has been the only drug used in many situations where other drugs were suspected. Alcohol is also highly implicated in mutual intimate partner violence (Cunradi, 2007). Many prostitutes are also opiate users and this tautological relationship with drug dependence can be worse in the case of crack cocaine (Bennett and Holloway, 2005). Females tend towards prostitution or dealing to support drug dependency, whereas males tend towards theft (see Bennett, 1998). Amphetamines have a strong association with violence amongst men, as has cocaine, leading to a general view that with the exception of hallucinogens, substance use is as much a forensic as a clinical issue, which may not sit easily with the call to decriminalise drugs and treat them as a clinical issue (see Boles and Miotto, 2003).

Crime and substance use

Since the 1960s, a proliferation of user-dealers were generated, who began by buying drugs for their friends and progressed to subsidising their own use with modest dealing, usually in cannabis alone (Cohen, 1967). Such 'dealers' began to disappear towards the twenty-first century as penalties for dealing increased and pressure from criminal gangs wanting the business threatened real violence. Failure of a 'user-dealer' contact (who usually has little other contact with crime) may bring the user into contact with **career criminals**, for whom drugs are just another source of criminal income. Such individuals prefer to sell profitable, addictive substances (e.g. heroin or crack cocaine) and will 'convert' customers from bulky, easily detected, less profitable and arguably less addictive substances such as non-genetically modified cannabis. The user may even be drawn into other criminal activity, and is liable to blackmail if they hold a vulnerable position in society. Thus, the user's social and occupational functioning can be undermined by many factors beyond the simple drug use cycle, including possible arrest for possession and consequent **criminalisation** (see Bennett and Holloway, 2005).

Compulsory drug testing on arrest in the UK and Europe has been criticised as uneconomic and ineffectual, and it is argued that the resources would be better used for expanding specialised drug courts (RSA, 2007). This approach is an unapologetic adoption of policy from US initiatives such as the **Arrestee Drug Abuse Monitoring Program** (ADAM) in 1997, based on work dating back to 1987 (Bennett, 1998). Intentions to use information gained in this way to direct individuals to drug services have often been sidelined in favour of further charges or pressure to admit to other offences, again reflecting an attitude of diminished rights for drug users. The rationale for this punitive attitude towards drug users can be traced back to government policy (see Stevens, 2007).

Van Duyne and Levi (2005) have examined the issue of organised crime and drug trafficking from an international perspective. Issues are raised about the possible overestimation of large-scale income from drug sales and the unspecified threat this poses to legal economies. Questions are also raised about the conflict between foreign policy and domestic drug policy with specific reference to US war zones in the Middle East and elsewhere, in that the war on drugs in the USA may be at odds with trafficking 'windows of opportunity' as a by-product of US allegiances abroad (Van Duyne and Levi, 2005). These authors also use European data to question the 'drug problem' as it is universally posited. Degrandpre (2006) has also questioned how powerful drug companies arrive at their position of excessive profit by dealing in legitimate pharmaceuticals, whereas the illicit drug market is credited with all the harm resulting from drug use and for profiteering from human misery.

Drugs in prison

Drug use in prison is confounded by clinical issues of mental and physical health (Watson, Stimpson and Hostick, 2004). Health-related problems in the prison setting are considerable, particularly in the light of a growing population and overcrowded environment. **HIV, hepatitis B and C infections** are exacerbated directly by drug use within the prison environment, as well as by risky sexual behaviour, which is in turn increased by substance use and mental health problems (Watson, Stimpson and Hostick, 2004; McKeganey, 2006). There are fears that a background of increased drug use may lead to a rise in harm from such infections over time (McKeganey, 2006). These conditions clearly act against the prison aims of rehabilitation, re-education and reform. Some mental health conditions have potential drug abuse amongst the disorder criteria. Anti-social personality disorder is endemic in prison and is highly associated with alcohol and other substance abuse (Petry, 2005). **Personality disorders** are a factor in the comorbidity of substance abuse in secure forensic psychiatric units (Miles et al., 2007). The issue of comorbidity influences both relapse and reoffending rates in such contexts (Durand, Lelliott and Coyle, 2006).

The prevalence of drug use in prison has been very high due to the boredom inherent in secure confinement, and it has often been easier to maintain discipline by allowing a level of 'self-medication' among prisoners (see Maguire, Morgan and Reiner, 2002). However, measures such as **urine testing** have led to unrest in prisons and a move from easily detectable drugs such as cannabis, which may remain in the body for a month, to less detectable ones such as heroin with a much shorter half-life. Many inmates acquire drug habits whilst in prison as a result of peer contact and their alternating stressful and mundane experiences, but large numbers enter confinement (especially psychiatric secure units) with drug problems (Durand, Lelliott and Coyle, 2006). However, mandatory drug testing in prison did lead to a 25 per cent decrease in abuse in prison by 1997 (Coyle, 2005).

The UK government's 2005 '**Tough Choices**' agenda has been an effort to move to coerced rather than voluntary participation in **drug treatment programmes**. This has been reflected in similar policies throughout Europe, and in most cases, these mandatory approaches have resulted in a sustained reduction not only in drug use, but in offending and social functioning as well (McSweeney et al., 2007). A three-stage model of integrated treatment for substance use problems has been implemented in secure psychiatric institutions. This includes 12-week treatment programmes and a 'just say no' participant-led social group to maintain abstinence throughout and beyond confinement. Preliminary outcomes from evaluation studies have been promising, in that clients had more insight and felt more in control of their problem whether substance use ceased or continued (Miles et al., 2007).

The decriminalisation debate

Thus there are many arguments for **decriminalising drugs**, especially the less medically dangerous substances (Uttermark, 2004). Drugs such as cannabis are not without harm, but they carry substantially lower clinical and forensic risk than legal drugs such as alcohol and tobacco (RSA, 2007). Some recognition of the lesser harm of cannabis by the UK Home Office was demonstrated in 2002 in downgrading it from a class B to a class C drug, and again in 2005 when this decision was reaffirmed despite strong opposition (Advisory Council on the Misuse of Drugs, 2005a). Cannabis has often been accused of being a gateway drug leading users on to 'hard' drugs such as heroin. There is little evidence for this and, furthermore, the substances have such polar opposite effects as to undermine the logic of such a move for the user. In addition, the only well-established gateway drugs are alcohol and nicotine in combination, where users are 25 times more likely to use illicit drugs. One of the only true links between 'soft' and 'hard' illicit drugs is the criminal source of supply, which is often biased in favour of the 'ultimate merchandise' (Burroughs, 1959: p. 9). Thus criminal suppliers are motivated to shift users from less profitable soft drugs to hard drugs with a guaranteed market (Gregory, 2003). Decriminalisation would remove the criminal link between 'soft' and 'hard' drugs, preventing 'progression' (Levine, 2003). It would also allow consideration of drug use as a medical treatment issue, not simplistically as a criminally punishable act, drastically cutting levels of crime and its cost, and removing the drug income to organised crime in line with policies advocated by RSA (2007).

Additional impetus for decriminalisation rests with the possible medical uses of many illicit substances (see Kalant, 2001). Research programmes to verify such possibilities are hampered by access to LSD, cannabis and other drugs, even though potential for medical uses has already been established (Hirst, Lambert and Norcutt, 1998). Calls have been made for exceptions to be made in law to allow the medical use of cannabis to relieve nausea in **cancer treatment**, pressure in **glaucoma**, suffering in **multiple sclerosis**, improvement in **AIDS cases**, analgesia, anti-spasticity and many other areas that have established potential (Hirst, Lambert and Norcutt, 1998; Kalant, 2001; Green, 1998; Williamson and Evans, 2000; Salan, Zinberg and Frei, 1975). Some have suggested placing caveats in place for any such move to prevent cannabis being actually smoked to gain such benefits (Hall and Degenhardt, 2003). Researchers also raise concerns over users who consume higher doses of drugs such as cannabis, particularly in its stronger, genetically modified form, even though moderate daily doses in the specific case of cannabis (expected with medicinal use) present no dependence problems (Looby and Earleywine, 2007). Amongst a number of illicit substances, MDMA has also been examined for its contemporary use as a psychotherapeutic agent (Parrott, 2007).

International perspective

Lessons from criminalising substance use

Although shops in most countries cannot sell cannabis, they sell most associated products which can act as cues to users. However, some societies have had success in reducing drug use by removing the 'attraction of its illegality'. In this café in Amsterdam, cannabis is smoked freely by the customers.
Source: Alamy Images/ Julie Woodhouse.

Arguments against decriminalisation tend to rely on the need to punish and control users, and often play on unrealistic fears of 'the spectre of mass drug use' (Vizi, 2007). The historical lesson from the USA during **prohibition** of alcohol appears not to have had impact. Prohibition enabled an escalation in organised crime and led to many deaths due to poorly manufactured alcohol poisoning. More rational arguments against even partial decriminalisation in the Western world centre on the need for forceful control when dealing with addictive substance use, and the loss of market control and profit for the legal drug producers (i.e. medicines and alcohol). However, some see this as society shifting the blame for drug use on to the victim or end user (Gregory, 2003), whilst it is universally agreed that *any* reduction in alcohol use will reduce crime (Bennett and Holloway, 2005).

Many Middle Eastern and east Asian countries have harsh penalties for illicit substance use, although this has little impact on substance use in many of the countries. Some societies seen as liberal or enlightened, notably Canada, Switzerland and parts of the Netherlands (Amsterdam in particular), have experimented with partial decriminalisation of drugs for many years and have produced some long-term signs of success, but they are equally open about any limitations (Uttermark, 2004). In the UK, ministers have also called for 'harm minimisation' strategies in relation to drugs, such as the issuing of clean needles to addicts, but this falls far short of the Dutch **cannabis cafés**.

Critical evaluation

The hypocrisy that seems to be inherent in government approaches to substance use has been pervasive both internationally and historically (Vizi, 2007). From British government-sanctioned sales of opium in the past to current US political decisions regarding local drug markets in their occupied countries, the scale of the credibility gap overtakes even the use of doctors to sanction smoking or propaganda material such as '**Reefer madness**' in the earlier part of the twentieth century (Vizi, 2007). The drug user in the midst of this, who is facing draconian penalties for taking a substance less harmful than that openly sold and promoted in their own street, is rightly confused and appalled. In terms of research, the readiness of tobacco and alcohol industries to fund research creates fundamental ethical concerns over any limitations in the research agenda (see Adams, 2007). Despite safeguards and guidelines, the question of whether research funded by illicit drug barons would be equally acceptable tends to reopen ethical wounds.

Many authors stress the multidimensional nature of addiction. However, this should not be used as a smoke-screen for muddying the waters of understanding with an unrestrained proliferation of theories, especially with overemphasis on interpersonal explanations (see Gifford and Humphries, 2007). Literature on the subject of addiction and substance use, both as crime and disorder, can regularly border on opinion in a manner rarely published for other areas. Some research into substance-related clinical and forensic issues can also be problematic with respect to researchers or funding bodies that take either a pro-decriminalisation or prohibitionist stance, either overtly or covertly. Although much research is neutral, findings presented in a manner representing a biased agenda have found their way into the literature and are unsurprisingly seized upon as newsworthy by the press (Vizi, 2007). As with the pro/anti-medical model debate in schizophrenia, not only does such academic competition confound a clear view of the problem of drugs, but the undignified rush to claim the moral high-ground can increase public scepticism of expert advice when it may be of vital importance.

The RSA (2007) report on illicit drug use recommended sweeping reforms in the very approach to substance use disorders and their forensic context. Bringing all drugs, whether illegal or not, under a single regulatory framework has been under consideration by the UK government's National Drug Strategy review in 2008. The commission was highly critical of the current version of the Misuse of Drugs Act 1971, labelling it 'not fit for purpose' (RSA, 2007: p. 15). A new Misuse of Substances Act has been suggested to replace the 1971 Act and its ABC classification, based on the premise that drug use cannot be eliminated and that harm reduction should be the aim of legislation and health investment (Gregory, 2003). Harm to individuals should also be the criterion by which all drugs, legal and currently illegal, are regarded in terms of their relative legal and clinical attention (RSA, 2007). An 'index of substance-related harms' would be central to new legislation, which would include associated harm from individual vulnerabilities of types of user and harm from related criminal activity (RSA, 2007: p. 16). A new Act would reserve criminal sanctions for only the most harmful drugs and the most serious offences.

Modern young drug users are most frequently poly-drug users internationally as well as in the UK, and there has been a process of deindividuation of former drug subcultures in contemporary society, such that users of drugs such as MDMA (or cannabis) are increasingly indistinguishable from non-users (McCambridge et al., 2005). These trends alone would indicate that the perpetuation of a prohibitionist stance against drug use may become an embarrassment in the light of the number of crime-naive individuals being brought into the criminal justice system instead of a therapeutic system. It could be said that the scapegoating of young drug users with legal sanctions merely provides a smokescreen to hide the true causes of drug use in the form of poverty, despair and boredom. One interesting speculation would be to consider what would happen if the 'war on drugs' were a clear victory and all supplies of heroin and other substances medicating and inhibiting the boredom and frustration on our streets suddenly dried up.

Self-test questions

- What are the confounding issues in the cause and treatment of substance disorder?
- What is 'cue exposure therapy'?
- In what ways are crime and substance use related?
- Are there sufficient reasons for decriminalising cannabis?
- Is it possible to win the 'war on drugs'?

Chapter summary

Many **psychoactive** substances have been used in history, but most of these can be grouped into their major effects: **depressants, stimulants** and **hallucinogens**. The case study of Billy emphasises that many individuals with substance problems never seek professional help or information. General issues in substance use include the **hypocrisy** and prejudice regarding which substances are dangerous and which should be outlawed. The three most medically dangerous substances are **tobacco, alcohol** and **food**. Drug law in the UK was defined in 1971 but modified to account for changes in harm perception and new substances being abused. Classification of substances by **CNS effects** is useful, as is the distinction between **dependence** and abuse. The body can develop a **tolerance** to substances, leading to **withdrawal**, which motivates continued use, or **dependence**. When continuation disturbs functioning it is termed **addiction**, which is distinguished from **abuse**, or sporadic excessive use. Most substances differ in their **purity, toxicity** and the **global damage** they cause, and the issue of **legality** can confound treatment for some substances.

CNS depressants include alcohol, which has been researched for many years in relation to its history of harm and relationship to crime. **Opiates** are the drugs that are most associated with addiction, partly due to their strong relationship to the **endogenous reward system**, which reacts to **endogenous opioids** and **dopamine**. **Inhalants** are dangerous and used by children and adolescents. Other depressants mostly consist of abused prescription medications, which include **rohypnol**, a 'date-rape drug'.

CNS stimulants include **nicotine, caffeine, cocaine, amphetamine** and less well-known substances such as **khat** and **yaba**, some of which have a very high potential for addiction and abuse. Youth culture and specific drug use have been related since the 1950s; to some degree, these drugs define generations and their drug prejudices. Hallucinogens include **LSD, cannabis, MDMA, psilocybin, ketamine, PCP** and others such as **muscimol** and **STP**, which lack much of the addictiveness of the other groups of drugs.

Drugs have been associated both with **celebrity** and with the downfall of many famous individuals. Although there may be **biological predisposing factors** to substance use, treatments tend to involve behavioural, cognitive and pharmacological interventions, but success depends greatly on the will of the user. **Clinical issues** include the problem of **dual diagnosis** and the attitude towards clients confounding outcomes. **Forensic issues** in substance disorders pervade the topic and include their role as a factor in crime, drug use in prison and the debate over **decriminalisation**, particularly of cannabis. **Critical reflection** on substance use encompasses debates on the dual standards of government agencies, the **multidimensional** nature of the disorder and **radical future strategies**.

Suggested essay questions

- Discuss the issues of propaganda and misinformation in the history of substance use.
- Evaluate the relative potential for addiction amongst substances of abuse.
- Critically discuss the costs and benefits of decriminalising illicit substances.

Further reading

Overview texts

British National Formulary (2009, revised biannually) published by the British Medical Association and the Pharmaceutical Society of Great Britain.

Cohen, L. M., Collins Jr, F. L., Young, A., McChargue, D., Leffingwell, T. R., and Cook, K. (eds) (2009) *Pharmacology and treatment of substance abuse: Evidence and outcome based perspectives.* London: Routledge.

Foy, A. (2007) Circuit breakers for addiction. *Internal Medicine Journal*, 37, 320–5.

Frances, R. J., Miller, S. I., and Mack, A. H. (2005) *Clinical textbook of addictive disorders* (3rd edn). London: Guilford Press.

McKim, W. A. (2003) *Drugs and behaviour: An introduction to behavioural pharmacology.* Englewood Cliffs, NJ: Prentice Hall.

Parrott, A., Morinan, A., Moss, M., and Scholey, A. (2004) *Understanding drugs and behaviour.* London: Wiley.

Teesson, M., Degenhardt, L., and Hall, W. (2002) *Addictions.* Hove: Psychology Press.

Volans, G., and Wiseman, H. (2008) *Drugs handbook 2008.* Basingstoke: Palgrave Macmillan.

Specific and more critical texts

Bennett, T., and Holloway, K. (2005) *Understanding drugs, alcohol and crime.* Maidenhead: Open University Press.

Drummond, D. C., Tiffany, S., Glautier, S., and Remington, B. (1995) *Addictive behaviour: Cue exposure theory and practice.* London: Wiley.

Grant, M., and O'Connor, J. (2005) *Corporate social responsibility and alcohol: The need and potential for partnership.* London: Routledge.

Jarvis, T., Tebbut, J., and Mattick, R. (1995) *Treatment approaches for alcohol and drug dependence: An introductory guide.* London: Wiley.

Lala, S., and Straussner, A. (2004) *Clinical work with substance abusing clients.* London: Guilford Press.

Rosenthal, R. N. (2003) *Dual diagnosis.* London: Routledge.

Strang, J., and Gossop, M. (2004) *Heroin addiction and the British system. Volume I: Origins and evolution.* London: Routledge.

Strang, J., and Gossop, M. (2004) *Heroin addiction and the British system. Volume II: Treatment and other responses.* London: Routledge.

Visit **www.pearsoned.co.uk/davidholmes** for a range of resources to support study. Test yourself with multiple choice questions and access a bank of over 100 videos that will bring the topics to life. Video coverage for this chapter includes an interview with Chris, who suffers from alcoholism, an explanation of how cocaine affects the mind and body and an ex-drug user's experience of how her addiction evolved.

CHAPTER 12 Anxiety disorders

 Watch Bonnie discuss the impact of post traumatic stress disorder. This is one of several videos that explore issues and disorders relevant to this chapter at **www.pearsoned.co.uk/davidholmes**.

Public fear and private terror

Edvard Munch suffered from anxiety and possibly bipolar disorder, producing *The Scream* in 1893, a painting that for many represents the unbridled personal fear felt by those suffering anxiety disorders. Anxious fear at a shared event such as a rollercoaster ride quickly dissipates and, being shared with others, does not isolate or embarrass. However, the personal, overwhelming fear felt by those with anxiety disorders does estrange them from others and adds embarrassment and alienation to their suffering. How do you explain to someone who does not share such fears that you are genuinely terrified of the ordinary buttons on clothes?

Obsessive–compulsive symptoms may lead to industrious perfectionism in some of those who suffer this tendency, such as actor Woody Allen, footballer David Beckham and even evolutionary pioneer Charles Darwin. However, the full criteria for **obsessive–compulsive disorder (OCD)** include disabling symptoms that constitute one of the most intractable psychiatric disorders. The film producer Howard Hughes became almost a recluse over his obsessive fear of germs, which included bizarre compulsions such as lining his car windows with newspapers to protect him.

Many individuals experience anxiety in social situations and self-medicate with alcohol. However, those with social anxiety disorder may avoid such events entirely.
Source: Pearson Online Databse.

Overview

Earlier in the twentieth century, the disorders in this chapter were referred to as **anxiety neuroses.** *ICD-10* has retained the word 'neurotic' in the title 'neurotic, stress related and somatoform disorders', which includes anxiety disorders. On the other hand, 'neurotic' has been removed from *DSM-IV* to avoid assumptions of (psychodynamic) aetiology and to focus on objective symptom description rather than any inferred cause. However, some professionals still use these terms and often refer to the neurotic personality in describing individuals with 'trait anxiety' (Spielberger, 1972). These 'neurotic' individuals tend to have overreactive autonomic responses (see Chapter 3) and are thus assumed to be more than usually prone to anxiety-related conditions. In the category 'neurotic, stress related and somatoform disorders', *ICD-10* adds **reaction to severe stress and adjustment disorders,** but it is otherwise very similar to *DSM*'s anxiety, somatoform and dissociative disorder groupings (see Chapter 15 for the latter groupings).

Obsessive–compulsive disorder (OCD) is possibly the most serious of the anxiety disorders, as illustrated by the protracted difficulties seen in the case study of Sonja. One of the commonest types of *DSM* disorder (Michael, Zetsche and Margraf, 2007), anxiety disorders are explained in biological, behavioural and cognitive terms, with each providing aetiological bases and successful interventions. Classifications of anxiety disorders include **panic disorder,** three forms of **phobia** (specific, social and agoraphobia), OCD, **post-traumatic stress disorder** (PTSD) and **generalised anxiety disorder** (GAD). Anxiety is prominent in each disorder but is activated and expressed in a manner distinctive to each, with overlapping symptoms in panic disorder, **agoraphobia** and GAD. Some authors have mentioned forms of health anxiety alongside the *DSM* classifications (e.g. Hirsch, 2007), but this text will refer to this form of anxiety when considering **hypochondriasis** within the existing **somatoform disorders** (see Chapter 15).

Anxiety disorders have been successfully treated for over half a century by the biological and behavioural approaches. However, contemporary clinical psychology has combined this heritage with cognitive interventions to produce an effective approach in CBT, but one that has limitations with some treatment-resistant cases, particularly those involving OCD, PTSD and GAD. This said, anxiety disorders are the 'client staple diet' of clinical psychologists and as such deserve more than one chapter. Forensic psychologists frequently become aware of this disorder grouping in assessing PTSD in victims or witnesses following crimes of assault or violence for courtroom purposes. This area of work has been broadly extended, overlapping into the work of **occupational psychologists** in considering the effects on police officers and other professionals subject to trauma.

Case study

A degree of uncertainty

Sonja's mother had always put her clothes in a neat pile before dressing her as a child, and she insisted that Sonja did so when she began to dress herself. Sonja seemed to assimilate these habits and other 'rituals' that her mother carried out, including washing her hands just prior to eating and flushing water over the bathroom taps prior to touching them. Her father had an impressively large collection of compact discs and even some old vinyl records that he had no means of playing. These records, discs and other musical memorabilia seemed to be secreted in almost every available space in the family home, even under the sofa. This seemed a quite normal home environment to Sonja, who reflected some of her parents behaviour in feeling some anxiety if she did not wash her hands or moved a pile of old CDs to get into her bedroom.

As Sonja engaged with her school friends, she became aware of the interest her 'habits' generated with her friends. Occasionally she would return home somewhat resentful of the way her mother's habits had become entrained into her own behaviour. As she became older, Sonja could see her mother's behaviour and anxieties worsen, which made life very difficult. Sonja had to take on increasing amounts of housework in addition to studying for her exams. Her mother rarely went out, and washing and dressing took up most of her day. She was constantly buttoning and unbuttoning her clothes and when she finally emerged from her room, muttering to herself that she did not feel she was 'right', she would return for yet more rituals. Whilst studying, Sonja watched her mother spend over an hour turning off the light switch, clicking it again and again until she felt certain it was off. Her mother could see the light was off, but she needed to feel certain about it in order to move on to the next task.

Although her father tolerated the situation, as he had for most of their marriage, Sonja felt that things could not go on in this way. Sonja herself had begun to feel anxious about checking things had been switched off or locked safely, occasionally returning from school to make certain that the cooker was off and did not endanger her mother. When Sonja was small her father had tried to get her mother to seek help. However, through relatives Sonja found out that this attempt at getting help resulted in her mother making a suicide attempt. At that point her father resigned himself to getting by from day to day rather than confronting the problem. Sonja eventually visited her GP, who had no reservations in referring her to a clinical psychologist, but he could not agree to her and her mother being seen jointly, as this was both unethical and beyond his capacity. However, he did make a suggestion to Sonja and had a quick word with the clinical psychologist.

When Sonja suggested that her mother came along to her appointment for moral support, her mother's face became ashen. Sonja took the risk of coercing her mother with the idea that she could not face talking through her habits with a stranger alone, and eventually her mother agreed to accompany her. Her mother's checking seemed to intensify as the appointment approached, and on the day this looked like making the venture impossible. However, Sonja was determined that things should not simply deteriorate. At the appointments, her mother became a nervous and passive partner during early therapy sessions for **obsessive–compulsive disorder**. After Sonja's progress became apparent, her mother finally approached her GP for a referral in her own right.

What could be described as 'vicarious therapy desensitisation' for Sonja's mother is not an orthodox approach and nor is it officially sanctioned. However, vicarious learning in therapy has been utilised for many years, usually with the therapist demonstrating normal responses to stimuli and situations. Families can become dysfunctional in maintaining such behaviours by supporting or tolerating them, and a combination of shared genetic traits, behaviour and attitudes within a family unit can contribute to abnormal behaviours becoming common to a number of family members. Thus, in some cases there may be many years of suffering before any intervention is sought, or even seen as desirable by some individuals with anxiety.

General issues in anxiety disorders

Individuals susceptible to anxiety disorders tend to report experiencing more headaches, chest pains and palpitations, and will report apprehension up to 20 times more often than non-neurotic individuals (Marks and Lader, 1973). Collectively, anxiety conditions are fairly common, with around one in four people in Western countries being affected by an anxiety disorder at some time in their lives. Specific phobias are the more common, with around a 10 per cent prevalence, and OCD is least prevalent at 1 per cent (Michael, Zetsche and Margraf, 2007). There is a high comorbidity in this group of disorders, with 75 per cent

of anxiety sufferers having another psychiatric disorder (Michael, Zetsche and Margraf, 2007).

Anxiety disorders are associated with mood disorders and to a lesser extent substance-related disorders, disorder groups with which they share some risk factors and also the status of being amongst the commonest groups of mental disorders. However, although anxiety and depression are closely associated, there are distinctions in causes and style of cognitive processing, indicating that they should not be measured or studied in isolation (Beuke, Fischer and McDowall, 2003). Tobacco abuse is particularly pertinent to anxiety disorders as it is highly prevalent, interacts to worsen nicotine withdrawal and this substance disorder increases the risk of later developing some anxiety disorders (Morissette et al., 2007). Peak ages for developing anxiety disorders are at the younger end of the life span between the ages of 10 and 25, with females, those unemployed or on low income, and individuals with less education being more likely to be affected (Michael, Zetsche and Margraf, 2007). Much research has been carried out on this age group, leaving something of a gap in knowledge regarding anxiety disorders in the elderly. Although most older adults develop anxiety in their youth, as many as 40 per cent have onset in later years and this is not always comorbid with depression (Wetherell, Maser and van Balkom, 2005).

When we are exposed to sudden threat or a fearful situation, we experience high levels of arousal or **sympathetic autonomic nervous system responses** (see Chapter 3), which have been developed by evolution to prepare our body for 'fight or flight'. Thus there will be a rise in adrenaline release, increased heart rate, reduced digestion and a mental state of alertness that prepared our former selves perhaps to confront a wild beast, which in a contemporary context would probably be transposed into confronting someone pushing into the supermarket queue, or escaping from the path of a speeding vehicle. Fear is part of this response as in the learned **fear potentiated startle** response (see Charney, 2003) and this may switch the fight to flight if the threat is great. High levels of autonomic activity can become debilitating and result in behavioural 'freezing' as well as other symptoms in extreme circumstances.

In an anxiety disorder this response occurs in the absence of real threat and is experienced as autonomic symptoms with debilitating levels of fear, including the characteristic symptoms of apprehension, tension and physiological arousal, as well as an inability to take any action to counter this reaction. Often there is a positive feedback loop in relation to psychological and physiological interaction, whereby physical symptoms increase levels of fear, and this in turn further exacerbates the autonomic response (McManus, 2007). These consistently maladaptive responses result in a measurably poorer **quality of life** for sufferers (Olatunji, Cisler and Tolin, 2007).

Most individuals seek a currently comfortable position on a continuum between stimulation or excitement at one end and security or calm at the other. The impetus for change tends to come when security turns to boredom and excitement turns to fear. Those with anxiety disorders respond with fear at an earlier point at the excitement end of this continuum. Anxiety sufferers also experience anxious cognition in perceiving more threat in benign circumstances and by attending more to threatening stimuli than non-anxious individuals (Hirsch, 2007). They respond more rapidly to perceived threat and more readily construe menace from ambiguity, all of which can generate and maintain anxiety. The anxious imagery generated by sufferers tends to be characteristic of each specific anxiety disorder and provides material for focus during CBT interventions (Hirsch, 2007). Although clients vary in their susceptibility to this type of treatment, they usually have good **insight** into their fears and realise that they are irrational, which provides a good basis for CBT approaches. However, these clients cannot control their irrational feelings, which override their logical thinking, and such overriding feelings may need to be undermined by exposure or behavioural relearning.

As with most conditions, assessment of anxiety disorders requires some judgement of the severity, reactivity and consequences of symptoms for the client's functioning. Clinical judgement focused on these aspects may reveal some individuals to be subthreshold for a diagnosis of anxiety disorder, requiring only minor intervention. Efficient screening in the case of anxiety disorders can also be a factor in improved outcome for clients (Katon and Roy-Byrne, 2007). When using diagnostic instruments to distinguish between subtypes of anxiety disorder, the level of comorbidity within this grouping can be problematic. The extent of this has prompted past authors to argue for a 'general neurotic anxiety syndrome', with a prolonged course that varies its presentation over time (e.g. Tyrer, 1985). However, current approaches require discrete co-occurring disorders to be identified, which may require broader treatment interventions. The focus of the client's fear and anxiety, and the beliefs they hold about this gleaned at assessment, are useful when applying cognitive explanations and associated therapeutic interventions (McManus, 2007). Assessment of individual anxiety disorders requires familiarity with the classification criteria relevant to the system used, which for this text is based on *DSM-IV-TR*.

Classifications of anxiety disorders

Most anxiety disorders are characterised by the differing 'triggers' that produce anxiety in sufferers, but have little or no effect on non-anxiety-prone individuals. This is most obviously the case with the **specific phobias**, but **generalised anxiety disorder** (GAD) is characterised by the absence of a definite trigger and appears to be precipitated by autonomic lability and maladaptive thinking in the individual. There is some overlap between GAD and **major depression** in terms of aetiology, and this may underpin some of the traditional close association between anxiety and depression in the psychiatric literature (see Kendler, 2004). A number of medical conditions such as hypoglycaemia and hypothyroidism produce some anxiety-type symptoms and need to be eliminated prior to a final diagnosis. Comorbidity and large areas of overlap between anxiety disorders have been used as factors in the debate for a dimensional system rather than classificatory system of diagnosis for these as well as other conditions (see Brown and Barlow, 2005).

The individual (*DSM-IV-TR*) anxiety disorders are: panic attack; agoraphobia; panic disorder without agoraphobia; panic disorder with agoraphobia; agoraphobia without a history of panic disorder; specific phobia; social phobia; obsessive–compulsive disorder; post-traumatic stress disorder; acute stress disorder; generalised anxiety disorder; anxiety disorder due to general medical condition; substance-induced anxiety disorder; and anxiety disorder not otherwise specified. **Separation anxiety disorder** is not included here as an anxiety disorder, but it can be found in Chapter 9 as a disorder beginning in childhood. To avoid too much repetition, *DSM* anxiety disorders have been partly grouped in the following sections.

Panic disorder

Panic disorder consists of recurrent and unexpected **panic attacks**. They can occur in a number of disorders and are characterised by extreme anxiety symptoms such as derealisation (feeling that the world around is unreal), trembling, breathlessness, choking, numbness, palpitations and a fear of dying (see Table 12.1). Any four or more of these symptoms co-occurring constitutes a **full panic attack**, whereas three or less would be referred to as a **limited symptom panic attack** (American Psychiatric Association, 2000). At the time of an attack or impending attack, some sufferers have the urge to escape the situation, and most interpret the experience as a sign that they may be dying or losing control of themselves or their minds. These symptoms will often peak and fall within 10 minutes

Table 12.1 *DSM* symptoms of panic attack

Palpitations	Trembling	Sweating
Shortness of breath	Choking	Chest pain
Nausea	Dizziness	Derealisation
Chills or hot flushes	Numbing	Fear of dying
Fear of losing control		

- 4 or more of the above indicates a **full panic attack**
- 3 or fewer indicates a **limited symptom panic attack**

and disable the sufferer during this time, leaving them apprehensive with the expectation that they will recur (American Psychiatric Association, 2000).

Panic attacks occur in the absence of a consistent known cause such as substance use, a genuine threat or a medical condition. Those prone to panic attacks may find they are precipitated by elements of these factors, such as caffeine or stress. Panic attacks can be characterised by their onset into three types:

- **Unexpected attacks** arise without warning across contexts.
- **Situation-bound attacks** only seem to arise in specific circumstances and not others.
- **Situationally predisposed attacks** sometimes occur in response to certain cues or contexts but not always.

The latter two types tend to be associated with other anxiety disorders such as social or specific phobias. Most individuals who experience panic attacks – even limited symptom, situationally predisposed attacks – will usually have a history of attacks, including those of greater severity. Many of these individuals will fulfil the criteria for panic disorder.

For a *DSM* diagnosis of panic, there must be more than one full panic attack that is unexpected, and as a consequence of an attack there will be avoidance or behavioural change, fear of more attacks or worry about the consequences and causes of such attacks during the following month (American Psychiatric Association, 2000). Sufferers may avoid situations that they think will provoke an attack, or where having an attack would be embarrassing or difficult to cope with, and may engage in drastic avoidance behaviour such as leaving their job or ending a personal relationship. They may suspect that the panic attacks are indicative of a serious underlying physical or psychiatric illness, and this may exacerbate fears of future attacks. Concern over potential underlying disorders can border on to hypochondriasis (American Psychiatric Association, 2000; see Chapter 15). Avoidance and failure to carry out normal tasks can lead to self-blame, apathy and lowered self-image or confidence. Panic disorder is twice as common in females as males, with onset tending to occur most frequently in either the late teens or late 20s age groups (Carr and McNulty, 2006).

Panic disorder can be diagnosed as with or without **agoraphobia** (see below). Lifetime prevalence of panic disorder without agoraphobia is 3.7 per cent (Kessler et al., 2006). Across studies, agoraphobia is around twice as common as panic disorder (Michael, Zetsche and Margraf, 2007), although it is very rare to find a case of agoraphobia with no history of panic attacks (Carr and McNulty, 2006). Panic attacks are associated with a range of anxiety and mood disorders in youth (Goodwin and Gotlib, 2004). The use of alcohol often found in panic disorder may relate to self-medication, although Goodwin and Gotlib (2004) did not find any association between panic problems and general substance use in earlier years. However, smoking has been associated with panic disorder as well as other anxiety disorders (Morissette et al., 2007). Tobacco use is thought to play a role in both the onset and maintenance of panic-related problems (Zvolensky et al., 2005).

Personality disorders (see Chapter 14) have been found to be as prevalent as 86 per cent in those who develop panic disorder, and personality problems have also been found predictive of a poor response to interventions for panic (Marchesi et al., 2006). Personality problems will also exacerbate the self-image and self-esteem issues in panic disorder raised above. However, Carrera et al. (2006) did not find other personality variables to relate to pharmacological treatment response or to the severity of panic disorder. Combined pharmacological and cognitive behavioural treatment is recommended for those panic sufferers scoring low on the personality variable self-directedness (Marchesi et al., 2006).

Although most first-degree relatives of those with panic disorder do not have the condition, a first-degree relative of a sufferer is up to 20-fold more likely to have the disorder than a non-relative (American Psychiatric Association, 2000). This inherited trait is likely to relate to autonomic reactivity and what has been referred to as the fear network. This network of neurotransmitters and brain structures is thought to become oversensitised and progressively conditioned to be reactive to mild stimuli (Gorman et al., 2000). Panic-disordered patients have consistently been found to process unconditioned fear abnormally (Del-Ben et al., 2001).

Treatments for panic disorder were often pharmacological during most of the twentieth century, and drug interventions remain in place for many panic-prone patients, especially those with short-term panic problems. Benzodiazepines have been used effectively with panic and produce better results than MAOIs (monoamine oxydase inhibitors) or tricyclic anti-depressants, which are also used (e.g. imipramine), but benzodiazepines tend to precipitate attacks on withdrawal (Watanabe, Churchill and Furukawa, 2007). SSRIs have shown fewer side-effects for panic disorder as well as being successful for patients who can tolerate the initial effects and are responsive to this type of drug (Carr and McNulty, 2006). Other intervention approaches largely consist of cognitive behavioural treatments (CBT), which have been usefully augmented with self-management and computer-based schemes. Partner-assisted CBT and self-management of CBT have

Focus

A cognitive approach to panic attacks

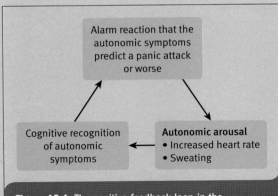

Figure 12.1 The positive feedback loop in the catastrophic misinterpretation of panic symptoms; based on Clark's (1986) cognitive explanation of panic attacks.

Clark (1986) proposed a cognitive explanation of panic attacks, in that panic-prone individuals precipitate their attacks by catastrophic misinterpretation of their anxiety symptoms. If a panic-prone individual's heart rate rises, they interpret this as an indication that they are going to have a panic attack or even a fatal heart attack. The apprehension this causes then intensifies their symptoms in the manner of a self-fulfilling prophecy, and their cognitive alarm precipitates more symptoms of panic (Carr and McNulty, 2006).

The positive feedback loop between physical symptoms and psychological alarm almost ensures that a full panic attack can arise from this cycle of expectation and autonomic reaction. CBT approaches to panic can intervene to stop this **positive feedback loop** by having the client substitute de-escalating thoughts and if necessary using physical aids to reduce autonomic arousal, thereby averting the extremes of panic.

been effective and are associated with improved relationships as well as higher psychological well-being ratings (see Barlow et al., 2005).

Although CBT is effective for panic disorder, there are treatment-refractory clients (non-responsive). Their suboptimal responding could result from factors such as non-compliance, comorbidity, secondary gain (i.e. where there is an advantage to the client in having the illness) or a poor therapeutic relationship (see Sanderson and Bruce, 2007). Client motivation and the therapist's adherence to the CBT protocols are factors that interact to improve outcome, but an absence of one factor can prove detrimental (Huppert et al., 2006). Combined drug therapy and CBT can be effective with comorbid or difficult clients (Marchesi et al., 2006). However, the evidence for combined CBT and drug therapy being superior to the individual therapies is weak and scarce, and although the combination is better than drug treatment alone, CBT alone can be more effective than combined for long-term interventions (Watanabe, Churchill and Furukawa, 2007), although there is also support for **sequential treatment**, which may be best applied with drug intervention during the acute phase followed by CBT during the withdrawal or tapering of drug dosage (Carr and McNulty, 2006). Non-scientific treatments such as psychodynamic approaches, hypnosis and mindfulness meditation have yielded no controlled evidence of effectiveness, though the latter may hold some promise for the future (Carr and McNulty, 2006).

Phobias

Phobias are described in *DSM-IV-TR* as a disruptive fear of an object or situation that is out of proportion to the danger posed (American Psychiatric Association, 2000). The grouping of phobias collectively in this text is to enable the student to organise better what is effectively a list of over nine anxiety-based disorders in *DSM-IV-TR*. These phobic disorders are as follows.

Agoraphobia (without history of panic disorder)

Agoraphobia translated from Greek literally means fear of the marketplace and is associated with a fear of being outdoors, although this is a limited definition that does not align exactly with the clinical criteria for the disorder. It is better described as a fear of being in exposed situations where escape is difficult or embarrassing (American Psychiatric Association, 2000). Agoraphobia has in the past

been considered to be a complex phobia: that is, one consisting of a number of fears, which involve fear of being alone outside of secure places, or in a situation where safe exit is difficult or help unavailable and humiliation from unexpected illness or panic may occur. Sufferers may also be anxious when alone in the home, in a crowd or in vehicles, but if it is only very few of these situations, then the possibility of a **specific phobia** diagnosis needs to be considered (American Psychiatric Association, 2000). It is made progressively worse by sufferers avoiding such situations and even not going out or into inescapable situations altogether. Avoidance behaviour in agoraphobia may also have to be distinguished from that found in **social** phobia, where avoidance is for social situations only (see below). If such situations are not avoided, they are endured with marked distress (American Psychiatric Association, 2000). Most agoraphobia sufferers are comorbid for other phobias as well as panic disorder.

For *DSM-IV-TR*-defined agoraphobia without a history of panic disorder, fear of panic attacks occurring in such situations is restricted to anticipating embarrassing, limited-symptom attacks or panic-like symptoms and there should

Agoraphobia is traditionally associated with fear of being out of doors, but is more specifically a fear of being where escape is difficult.
Source: Sarah Busby.

be no history of the full criteria for panic disorder (American Psychiatric Association, 2000). Although study data may be limited in this area, agoraphobia without a history of panic disorder would seem to be more common than panic disorder with agoraphobia (American Psychiatric Association, 2000). Heyward and Wilson (2007) have considered explanations for the development of agoraphobia in the absence of panic disorder, and although there is a place for misdiagnosis in this population, the authors consider there is a case for high **anxiety sensitivity** as a risk factor for agoraphobia in the absence of full panic attacks.

There are four times as many female agoraphobia sufferers as male, for which there have been many posited general explanations, such as female dependence and low autonomy in general (Bekker, 1996). Thus gender bias in agoraphobia may be the long-term result of the traditional dependent role of females in social situations, and also a consequence of the traditional 'female role' as homemaker increasing females' average exposure to 'safe' environments, as compared with the historical role of males as breadwinners outside the home. However, Bekker (1996) considers a broader-spectrum approach is needed to explain these gender differences in this specific disorder. Cultural factors can also operate to emphasise the dependent position of females in some ethnic groups, which can crudely mimic some aspects of agoraphobia.

Case study

Agoraphobia without history of panic disorder

The children in the neighbourhood knew Serena's sweet shop well, not for the usual assortment of sweets but for the fact that the lady who worked in the shop, Serena, had some predictable characteristics. By a process of trial and error as well as word on the grapevine, the local children knew that if they helped themselves to sweets and ran from the shop, they would not be pursued beyond the door. The inadvertent cruelty of the children failed to draw attention to the problems that Serena had in leaving the security of her shop, even when this progressed to her being reluctant to exit the room behind the shop when a customer entered. This was 1968 and mental health problems tended to be a source of gossip rather than a need for help, and Serena's family and husband considered her difficulties just part of her that had to be coped with. However, rather than Serena 'getting over it', her behaviour and fears had progressively worsened. Serena was comfortable behind the shop and at her parents' home, but she felt very anxious elsewhere, especially being at the wrong side of a lockable door that might close and leave her stranded without means of escape.

Serena's relationship with Winston, her husband, had not been perfect, but he had accepted the routine of always visiting her at her parents', and having a busy job as a salesman, he did not particularly worry about their lack of holidays or days out. Running the sweet shop had been an inspiration that Winston had in merging Serena's limitations with his plans to make them wealthy. However, he had not particularly planned on Serena's mother having to help run the shop, nor the many times he had to divert back home during his working day to resolve problems with people calling at the shop to deliver stock or even read the electric meter. Winston assumed that Serena's difficulties stemmed from 'nerves' and that if she had more confidence this would improve, but his hopes were constantly dashed in this respect. As with many relatives of anxiety disorder sufferers at this time, the routine of coping with everyday life with the additional burden that the disorder entailed left little space for gaining insight into the situation.

The trips from the shop to Serena's mother's house each Sunday afternoon had become a set ritual involving Winston following a routine that had become almost automatic. Serena would place a coat over her head in the shop, then be guided by Winston into the back seat of their four-door car parked outside. Winston would talk to Serena throughout, but pointedly not mentioning the contradiction between Serena's fear of showing her anxiety in front of the neighbours and her partaking in this cloak and dagger drama each Sunday. One Sunday, talking and guiding became complicated by Winston having parked the car facing the opposite way. His now ritualised actions led him to inadvertently collide with the rear door and Serena fell against the car in disarray. This proved so traumatic for Serena that not only was the day's trip abandoned but also Winston vowed that something had to be done to stop his wife being so distressed. The tranquillisers her GP had prescribed years before just seemed to make her sleepy and had been abandoned. This time Serena was given an appointment to see a psychiatrist, who made a provisional diagnosis and referred her to their psychological medicine outpatient unit, where Serena's entrenched symptoms of agoraphobia were successfully addressed with exposure therapy (exposing the client to their feared stimuli).

At this time, many individuals and their relatives simply endured anxiety disorders, not recognising them as symptoms of something treatable. The stigma of serious mental illness led many to suffer their 'behavioural quirks' with stoic acceptance. Winston's dedication to his wife surpassed any fear of prejudice, and Serena's resilience in facing the rigours of early behavioural interventions resulted in a turning point in their lives from which they would never look back. Serena's final return to the sweet shop counter was a source of pride for Winston and a great deal of confusion for the local children.

Panic disorder with agoraphobia

In panic disorder with agoraphobia, there is an anticipatory fear of full and unexpected panic attacks occurring in situations where escape or help is perceived to be difficult or would prove embarrassing (American Psychiatric Association, 2000). There will also be a history of the full criteria for panic disorder (see above) in addition to this anxious expectation and behavioural avoidance meeting the criteria for agoraphobia. Lifetime prevalence rates are 1.1 per cent for panic disorder with agoraphobia, but for agoraphobia with panic (not meeting the full criteria for panic disorder) the prevalence can be as low as 0.8 per cent (Kessler et al., 2006). Patients who have panic disorder with agoraphobia tend to have a disabling and chronic course of illness with little respite, in contrast to those who only suffer panic disorder alone, who follow a more relapsing course of illness (Francis et al., 2007). Low extraversion scores in clients with panic disorder tend to predict the presence of comorbid agoraphobia (Carrera et al., 2006). Francis et al. (2007) consider that factors relevant to the course of the illness should be recognised in improving treatments for this disorder.

Agoraphobia tends to be more responsive to treatment than panic disorder. However, a combination of antidepressants and behavioural exposure in vivo (i.e. exposure to the feared situation in real life – see Chapter 3) has been found to be a very effective treatment for either panic disorder or agoraphobia separately, or for panic disorder with agoraphobia in a meta-analysis (see Chapter 5) of studies (Van Balkom et al., 1997). One of the most successful aspects in the development of CBT over the last 30 years has been the application of exposure therapy to anxiety disorders, particularly in the case of panic disorder and agoraphobia (McKay et al., 2007). Disconfirmation of catastrophic cognitive beliefs in the process of exposure in

CBT can maximise clinical improvement in the case of panic disorder with agoraphobia (Salkovskis et al., 2006). In examining the factors influencing treatment choices for this disorder by psychiatrists, Starcevic et al. (2004) noted that CBT alone was chosen for anxiety-related cognitive phenomena, but with prominent panic attacks high-dose benzodiazepines were added, and combination treatments were frequently chosen for intensive treatment of panic disorder with agoraphobia, even in clinical settings where CBT was accepted as the basic treatment for this disorder.

Specific phobias

Specific phobias were (and still are by some) termed 'simple phobias', inferring a single response, in contrast to 'complex phobias' such as agoraphobia, which are assumed to involve multiple fears and responses. Specific phobias are characterised by marked persistent fears clearly pertaining to particular things or situations, such as fire (**pyrophobia**) or heights (**acrophobia**), which always provoke an immediate anxious response out of proportion to any danger posed by the stimuli. This also involves disabling anticipatory fear and avoidance of the phobic situation (see the case study on p. 361). The phobic response may include situationally bound or predisposed panic attacks along with anticipatory fears of having an attack or losing control. Sometimes the feared situation is endured with distress, precipitating a panic attack, which can be delayed (American Psychiatric Association, 2000).

Milder versions of the fears found in specific phobias are common in the population, especially children. However, these fears must be disabling to social, occupational and normal daily functioning to be diagnosed as specific phobia (American Psychiatric Association, 2000). Phobic individuals have good insight into their disorder, meaning that they

Some professions would never be an option for individuals with specific phobias.
Source: Pearson Online Database.

realise their fears are irrational, and an absence of insight may indicate that the fears could be delusional. This insight increases with age and may be absent in children with these fears (American Psychiatric Association, 2000). Some individuals have a rationalisation for their fear, which may be developed by repeated excuses for their behaviour given to others, or covert misapprehensions such as the notion that tiny spiders may deliver a dangerous bite. One client rationalised her fear of pigeons as 'not knowing what they wanted' as the birds pursued her.

The lifetime prevalence rate for specific phobias in Europe is around 7.7 per cent (Michael, Zetsche and Margraf, 2007). There may be variation between countries, with higher estimates in the USA and very low rates reported in China and Japan, possibly due to a more somatic presentation (a tendency to report physical arousal symptoms rather than fears) resulting in a different diagnosis. They are more common in females and have been found to be the most common mental disorder in women, with lifetime rates double that of men (Magee et al., 1996). Although lifetime prevalence rates in young women have been as high as 26 per cent in some studies, in a representative German sample this was placed at 12.4 per cent (Becker et al., 2007). Specific phobias usually develop in childhood and are generally evident before the age of 20 (Michael, Zetsche and Margraf, 2007).

Table 12.2 Some specific phobias and their targets

Phobia	Fear target	Phobia	Fear target
Acrophobia	Heights	Carnophobia	Meat
Anablephobia	Looking up	Chromophobia	Colours
Anuptaphobia	Being single	Dendrophobia	Trees
Arachnophobia	Spiders	Ecophobia	Home
Atelophobia	Imperfection	Genophobia	Sex
Aviatophobia	Flying	Gnosiophobia	Knowledge
Bathophobia	Depth	Koniophobia	Dust
Bibliophobia	Books	Oneirophobia	Dreams
Bunophobia	Toads	Peladophobia	Bald people
Cainophobia	Newness	Somniphobia	Sleep
Caligynephobia	Beautiful women	Xerophobia	Dryness

Note: Due to language variations, some phobias have more than one term.

DSM-IV-TR divides specific phobias into five subtypes on the basis of classifications of the target fears and these are as follows.

- **Animal subtype.** These cover a vast range of animals and insects, and are more frequently based on the alien appearance of the creature than on any inherent danger; thus tiny spiders may be more feared than very dangerous species such as sharks or tigers.

- **Natural environment subtype.** As with the animal subtype, these have onset in childhood and include heights, storms and water in various forms.

- **Blood-injection-injury subtype.** As the name suggests, these fears include many medical procedures and common injuries, and show a familial pattern and produce a strong vasovagal response in sufferers (American Psychiatric Association, 2000).

- **Situational subtype.** As opposed to the natural environment subtype these situations are often man-made, such as vehicles, bridges, lifts, tunnels and modes of flying. Here the onset age is similar to that of panic disorder in being bimodal with peaks in childhood and mid-twenties age groups (American Psychiatric Association, 2000).

- **Other subtype.** A typical *DSM* catch-all subtype for any item or situation not covered by the other categories, which in this case includes fears of choking, sound, space or newness.

The most common subtype, particularly in females, is the animal subtype of specific phobia, with a prevalence rate of around 5 per cent. This has an average age of onset around 6 years and tends to persist longer than other subtypes with an average duration of 16 years (Becker et al., 2007). The specific focus of the fear is important in differentiating specific phobia from other disorders such as social phobia, in that the latter is a more pervasive fear. Where in social phobia there would be avoidance of most social occasions such as eating in restaurants due to the fear of embarrassment, the same avoidance behaviour due to specific phobia would pertain to a fear of specific items such as choking, waiters or serviettes (American Psychiatric Association, 2000).

The aetiology of specific phobias has been accepted as a combination of classical conditioning and genetic predisposition for much of the twentieth century. Psycho-dynamic attribution of phobic fear unresolved childhood conflicts was critically and successfully contested by early behaviourist such as J. B. Watson and more definitively by the likes of Joseph Wolpe. As early as 1921, Watson and Rayner demonstrated the means by which fear is associated with a benign stimulus by **classical conditioning**

(see Chapter 3). Limitations in this apparently universal explanation led Seligman (1971) to propose genetic preparedness for such fears, which has been enhanced by Öhman in terms of a **multi-level evolutionary perspective** (see Öhman and Mineka, 2001). Kendler et al. (2001) have suggested a genetic rather than learned explanation for fears of specific stimuli, as favoured from the epidemiological pattern of specific phobia. Ontogenetic and phylogenetic explanations have been refined and enhanced by the addition of cognitive elements of phobia development and phobic reactions. Armfield (2006) has suggested that a **cognitive vulnerability model** of the aetiology of fear, incorporating the perceptual schema of feared stimuli as uncontrollable, dangerous, unpredictable and disgusting, provides a unifying explanatory theory. Specific phobias have received little research attention by comparison to other anxiety disorders, but have been the basis for very important historical advances in aetiology and treatment for clinical psychology (see Armfield, 2006, for more detail).

The biological underpinnings of conditioned fear and responses in specific phobia are becoming more explicit through neuropsychological research. The implied involvement of the **amygdala**, **hippocampus** and parts of the **prefrontal cortex** has been examined and evaluated using **magnetic resonance imaging** techniques. Rauch et al. (2004) have measured evidence of increased cortical thickness in the areas of the **cingulate cortex** and **left visual cortex** in clients with animal-type specific phobias. This work adds to growing support for involvement of the paralimbic and visual cortex in the symptoms of specific phobia. The amygdala seems to play a lesser role in specific phobia than in other anxiety disorders (Wright et al., 2003). This may indicate a comparatively greater genetic rather than learned basis for specific phobias. However, Wright et al. (2003) along with other studies have found some distinguishing response for specific phobia in the **right posterior insula** connecting to areas of the prefrontal cortex. Some prefrontal areas may be involved in reactions relating to disgust rather than fear in specific phobias, such as some phobic reactions to insects or blood-injection-injury. The role of disgust in psychopathology in specific phobias and other disorders has been revived in the twenty-first century (see Olatunji and McKay, 2007).

Treatments for specific phobias are mostly built on the highly effective exposure therapies described in Chapter 3, such as **systematic desensitisation** and **flooding**, as well as virtual reality versions of these interventions (Grös and Antony, 2007; Choy, Fyer and Lipsitz, 2007). These have often been incorporated into a broader CBT approach dealing with the anticipatory fears and addressing avoidance of the feared stimuli. Avoidance can increase the phobic response in a process referred to historically as the

Case study
Specific phobia (arachnophobia)

Rather than its inherent danger, the more alien an animal looks the more potential it has for triggering a phobic response. Exposure to the feared stimulus can be real, imagined or simulated, as with these plastic spiders. A child may instinctively pick up on a fear being modelled by a parent and associate it with the same stimulus.
Source: Pearson Online Database.

For most of Mary's life, she and her mother had shared a fear of spiders, even the smallest. As far back as Mary could remember, most situations where spiders would be encountered were avoided, and on the rare occasion when one was near Mary she had vivid recollections of her mother being rigid with fear, hurting Mary's hand with her grip. Now Mary had her own child and did not want little Amy to have the same fear. She tried not to show her anxieties, though with little success.

One day, she was giving Amy a typical child's 'extended' bath, and as this had lasted over half an hour, Mary warmed the water by turning on the hot tap. Mary suddenly fell back to the bathroom door gasping for air. A very large garden spider had fallen from the towel over the bath and was circling its edge. Amy played on oblivious and even approached the spider, but Mary was frozen with fear, she could not approach the tap *or* Amy. After a few minutes Amy's splashing turned to cries and then screams as Mary realised her child was in danger of scalding. The situation was saved by Mary's husband hearing the child's first cries by chance from outside in the garden. The trauma of the incident produced a panic attack in Mary as she relived the incident in her mind. She never found out whether she would have confronted her fear to save Amy, but she had already made her mind up to seek therapy, urgently.

Six months later, Mary spoke of her exposure therapy with a kind of pride, and kept the promise she made to herself to show spiders to little Amy in a relaxed way; well, as long as they were not too big.

neurotic paradox, in which the relief felt from avoiding the feared stimuli can operantly reinforce the avoidance response (see the review by Choy, Fyer and Lipsitz, 2007). Thus, many facets of specific phobias may be addressed successfully by CBT, and other treatment approaches such as pharmacotherapy and eye movement desensitisation have also been applied (for a review, see Grös and Antony, 2007). Straube et al. (2006) measured the neural response to CBT in clients with animal-type specific phobia. Their

data confirm the possible involvement of the **insula** (see above) in specific phobia, as the hyperactivity in this area compared with controls was selectively reduced by CBT. This physiological aspect of the CBT approach is a reminder that behavioural interventions are often effective in disorders that have a behavioural or genetic-neurological basis. Sufferers of specific phobias often require support in therapy as they are regarded as irrational or emotionally weak by the public, who do not sympathise with those fearing something harmless, and who see their anxiety as being inconsequential, lacking significance or a rational basis (see Davidson, 2005).

Social phobia

Social phobia involves a persistent and marked fear of performance or social situations in which the sufferer believes embarrassment will occur (American Psychiatric Association, 2000). Social phobia can be specific and restricted to a narrow range of social events, or generalised to most situations in which others may judge them to be weak, unstable or stupid. *DSM-IV-TR* uses the specifier '**generalised**' to emphasise this as a more debilitating form of the disorder, in that fear and avoidance become attached to a wide range of situations involving social and performance elements, such as parties, dating, giving business talks or even conversations. A clinician may need to probe to establish if the generalised specifier is appropriate, as the client may not mention problems beyond the immediate presenting symptom and may fail to report anxiety in other areas. In addition to poorer functioning due to the restriction of social and occupational activity, individuals with wider-ranging social avoidance may also lack social skills (American Psychiatric Association, 2000).

When speaking with an audience, sufferers anticipate overt signs of anxiety that will be noticed by others, such as trembling or voice stress. Avoidance of acts in public such as eating or even writing will usually lead to restricted social and occupational functioning as well as possible damage to relationships or family ties. Engaging in such acts or appearances in public always results in a range of anxiety symptoms, which may infrequently be endured with great distress (American Psychiatric Association, 2000). Many people are nervous at public speaking and shy in social situations, but for a diagnosis each must cause a significant degree of distress or interfere with occupational functioning, such as not being able to speak at meetings (American Psychiatric Association, 2000). Self-report instruments attempt to quantify the number and type of feared situations that individual clients experience, which seem to vary greatly between individuals (Hofmann, Heindrichs and Moscovitch, 2004).

Social phobia is usually found to be twice as common in females as males and is less frequent in those with higher socioeconomic status (Kessler, 2003). The prevalence of social phobia has varied over time as the criteria for the disorder and methods of measurement have changed, and studies using *DSM-IV* have produced lifetime rates of between 7 and 12 per cent (Wittchen and Fehm, 2003). Onset of social phobia rarely occurs after adolescence but

Avoiding performance situations in social phobia can be in conflict with some occupations.
Source: Pearson Online Database.

can begin in childhood. This impairment increases over the course of the sufferer's life and the disorder's impact on social roles and career progress can be cumulative (Wittchen and Fehm, 2003). The disorder is frequently comorbid with mood and substance disorders, and the fears in social phobia also introduce serious information processing and attentional biases that confound communication and compound role impairments (Kessler, 2003). The impairments in role function as a result of the disorder begin in adolescence and indicate that attempts to identify the disorder and treatment interventions should be aimed at schools (Kessler, 2003).

Anxiety and fear have both shared and distinct neurochemical and neuroanatomical pathways, which are implicated in the neurobiology of social anxiety, such as the complex interactions between **noradrenergic** and **serotonergic** systems (Marcin and Nemeroff, 2003). The generalised influence of inheritance in this disorder would point to environmental events or biological insult producing a neurobiological imbalance in these systems, leading to the more specific increased inhibition, anxiety and fear seen in social phobia (Marcin and Nemeroff, 2003). Alden and Taylor (2004) examined the role of **interpersonal processes** in the maintenance and development of social phobia and how anxiety affects the cognitive processing of social information. These interpersonal processes will not only shape and perpetuate social fears but also impact upon the process and outcome of cognitive behavioural

Focus

Differential diagnosis of social phobia

Differentiating social phobia from **avoidant personality disorder** is acknowledged as being difficult and has relied on symptoms being distinct in terms of severity (Hummelen et al., 2007). Hummerlen et al. (2007) considered that this distinction lacked specificity and in examining differentiating factors found avoidant personality disorder to entail greater dysfunction, earlier onset and a broader constellation of symptoms and personality features, whereas social phobia had a stronger association with panic disorder. From *DSM-III-R* onwards an individual can be **comorbid** for social phobia and avoidant personality disorder, with around 30 per cent of clients falling into this area of overlap (Wittchen and Fehm, 2003).

Agoraphobia with or without panic disorder tends to involve anxiety both in situations where there is scrutiny by other people and where there is not. However, in social phobia only situations involving such interpersonal or public scrutiny produce severe anxiety. The social avoidance seen in **pervasive developmental disorders** such as **autism** (see Chapter 10) and also in **schizoid personality disorder** (see Chapter 14) tends to be based on indifference to others rather than other people producing anxiety, as in social phobia. In contrast, sufferers of social phobia are interested in other people and display social skills in limited contexts, but are restrained by fear of scrutiny and humiliation (American Psychiatric Association, 2000).

interventions. These clinical implications of the bias in the way those with social phobia process social information have been considered in terms of probability judgements, cost estimates of social situations and bias in memory (see Hirsch and Clark, 2004). However, cognitive explanations of the disorder drawn from clinical cognitive approaches have been found limited in terms of their ability to reveal true causal factors (Stravynski, Bond and Amado, 2004). Rapee and Spence (2004) have provided a thorough review of the many aetiological factors in social phobia and have generated a tentative model combining genetic, developmental, social, experiential, cognitive and risk factors.

A multifactor account of the aetiology of social phobia could suggest a similarly disparate range of interventions. Exposure therapy is effective and usually combined with other aspects of CBT such as cognitive restructuring, and the combination has been compared very favourably with exposure in vivo (i.e. using real rather than imagined situations) on its own (Ponniah and Hollon, 2007). Although a number of approaches are supported by empirical evidence, there is little support for the use of social skills training for social phobia, and CBT tends to emerge overall as the treatment of choice for this disorder (Ponniah and Hollon, 2007). Bögels and Tarrier (2004) have suggested refining the designs of clinical trials within the health service context to establish the efficacy and effectiveness of currently available treatments. These authors have also suggested that future research towards an understanding of aetiological factors may usefully target the factors underlying the comorbidity of social phobia with other conditions (Bögels and Tarrier (2004)).

Self-test questions

- What is the relationship between a panic attack and panic disorder?
- How does catastrophic misinterpretation of symptoms relate to panic attacks?
- How can a specific phobia be best treated?
- What are the distinctions between specific phobias and agoraphobia?
- What differentiates the subtypes of specific phobia?
- What is the neurotic paradox?
- How does agoraphobia differ from social phobia?
- What are the cognitive explanations of social phobia?

Obsessive–compulsive disorder

Obsessive–compulsive disorder (OCD) is characterised by the presence of **obsessions** and **compulsions** that are severe enough to cause distress or impairment, or excessively consume the sufferer's time (American Psychiatric Association, 2000). These intrusive thoughts and unwarranted activities are not a result of substance use or better accounted for by another disorder. Individuals can be cautious in their behaviour and may engage in some superstitious rituals such as not stepping on cracks in the pavement, but it is only when such beliefs and behaviour are excessive and significantly interfere with functioning that a disorder may be diagnosed (American Psychiatric Association, 2000). As with other anxiety disorders, OCD sufferers usually have good insight and know that their behaviour is odd most if not all of the time, but feel compelled to continue by anxiety and a fear that 'something awful will happen'. OCD can be diagnosed as being 'with poor insight', where for most of the time the sufferer cannot recognise that their obsessions and compulsions are excessive, which is in recognition of the fact that the degree of insight can vary in OCD (American Psychiatric Association, 2000). Individuals with OCD may also avoid situations that provoke obsessions, such as sources of contamination or situations that provoke relevant doubts, and this kind of avoidance can exacerbate their symptoms (Carr and McNulty, 2006).

Obsessions are persistent thoughts, images or impulses that are ego-dystonic (not within the individual's control and unwanted), and which intrude into the sufferer's life, causing marked anxiety or distress (American Psychiatric Association, 2000). These obsessive thoughts range from what may seem to be exaggerations of normal uncertainties as to whether the person has locked the front door, to less common thoughts that the sufferer will hit passing strangers, with obvious clinical forensic implications if they were to act on this impulse in order to end the intrusive fear. Sufferers attempt to suppress these ideas and intrusions or perform some action (compulsion) to neutralise or distract their anxiety-producing effect (DeSilva and Rachman, 2004). Compulsions are repetitive behaviours such as checking, or mental acts such as praying, which are often carried out in the belief that they will provide *short-term* relief from the anxiety caused by the obsessions (American Psychiatric Association, 2000). Compulsions for the door-locking obsession may involve checking doors but to be OCD this would be done repeatedly to an unreasonable extent, or an individual would need to be so consumed by severe doubt as to drive home from a holiday in order to end the obsessive thought that the front door had been left unlocked (see DeSilva and Rachman, 2004).

In OCD an obsessive fear that has contamination by germs as its content may be thought to be reduced by compulsive hand washing. However, the level of hand washing and associated time-consuming rituals will tend to increase steadily until the sufferer's life is taken up by these activities, which may begin to involve other members of the family (see the case study at the start of this chapter). Hands may

David Beckham suffers from OCD and has admitted to obsessive and repetitive behaviour such as having to line up drinks cans in a straight line in pairs in his fridge or clearing away books and leaflets in a hotel before he can relax.
Source: Getty Images/FilmMagic.

be scrubbed until the skin is broken. Thus the compulsive behaviour serves to *increase* the sufferer's anxieties in the long term. The level of ritualistic checking and routines may consume so much of the sufferer's daily life that little else may be achieved before the routine begins again the following day (DeSilva and Rachman, 2004). This is referred to as obsessional slowness and is one of the reasons why a sufferer may attract clinical attention.

In the twentieth century, Akhtar et al. (1975) considered the different types of obsession commonly experienced as follows.

- **Fear of giving way to impulses.** This could involve fear of shouting obscenities or harming someone such as a family member.
- **Doubts.** This involves uncertainty such as whether one has locked a door or turned an appliance off.
- **Images.** The images are usually disturbing, such as the image of a dead child on the floor.

Some obsessional thoughts have been considered to be more upsetting than others. However, rather than relating to the different types of obsession listed above, the factors affecting the degree of upset were found to relate to: the obsession undermining the person's sense of self; the degree of current personal relevance of the obsession (e.g. a new parent having images of harmed babies); and the obsessions resulting when the victim is suffering stress

Focus

The distinction between knowing and feeling in OCD

There are evolutionary reasons for our obsessive fears. The reaction is there to make us avoid harmful things and this same mechanism that is extreme in OCD is built into all of us, but a lesser reaction and under our control. To understand something of the OCD sufferer's dilemma, such as knowing they have turned a light off, but continuing to switch it for hours until it feels off (as in the case study at the start of the chapter), we need to examine milder examples from our own experience.

As young schoolchildren, we may have pretended to 'wipe something' on to a friend's arm, who promptly pretended to wipe it off and on to another child's arm, and so on. Although this is only a 'game', the individual at the end of this line of ten or more children still *feels* that there is something on their arm, even though they *know* there is nothing there. Thus the obsessive individual usually *knows* their behaviour to be bizarre, but cannot control the *feelings* that produce it, and these feelings are much more compelling than our reactions to that 'wiping' as a child.

attrition (Rowa et al., 2005). Akhtar et al. (1975) also considered two types of compulsion.

- **Yielding compulsions.** This is where sufferers submit to the obsession: for example, by going to check the door is locked.
- **Controlling compulsions.** Where the sufferer attempts to prevent the obsession by exerting control over it, such as repeating a verse out loud to blot out the doubting thoughts.

Normal individuals may also engage in mild obsessive–compulsive behaviour when under great stress, and strong believers in some religious faiths have been found to have significantly higher levels of obsessive compulsive behaviours in some studies (see the Focus box on p. 366). Although intrusive thoughts are similar in form and content to obsessions, they have been considered as part of the process of obsession formation. Julien, O'Connor and Aardema (2007) considered the evidence that intrusive thoughts occurred in normal individuals and were dismissed, but that in those with dysfunctional belief systems such intrusive thoughts are appraised according to these beliefs and develop into obsessions. Some, but not all of this explanation was supported by Julien et al.'s review, and just how the sufferer's appraisals turn intrusive thoughts into obsessions remained to be clarified. **Compulsive hoarding** has been covered in Chapter 10 as an impulsive–compulsive disorder, but for many it also falls within the OCD symptom range and is a component of **obsessive–compulsive personality disorder** (see Chapter 14). In compulsive hoarding a vast amount of clutter of no real useful value is allowed to accumulate because the sufferer is unable to sort or discard any item, and they will carry out obsessive and repeated searches of waste bags for fear

of losing items of value (DeSilva and Rachman, 2004). There is overlap between OCD and obsessive–compulsive personality disorder (OCPD); however, the two disorders do have distinct criteria and 75 per cent of those with OCD do not meet the criteria for OCPD, whilst 80 per cent of those diagnosed with OCPD do not have OCD (Mancebo et al., 2005).

OCD is the rarest of the anxiety disorders with estimates of lifetime prevalence generally being under 2 per cent (Michael, Zetsche and Margraf, 2007). There are two peak ages of onset at around 13 and 21 years of age and a low onset rate above the age of 35 (Grant et al., 2007). OCD sufferers with onset after the age of 30 have similar clinical characteristics to those with early onset but have less severe obsessions, are more responsive to CBT and seek treatment earlier in the illness (Grant et al., 2007). It is found that more severe OCD symptoms are predictive of a longer course of illness, so early intervention in such cases is even more valuable (Kempe et al., 2007). Some symptom dimensions in OCD, such as those with hoarding symptoms and to a lesser extent those with sexual or religious obsessions, are less responsive to CBT intervention than other dimensions, such as cleaning or checking, where hoarding etc. was absent (Rufer et al., 2006).

The comparatively serious nature of OCD amongst the anxiety disorders is illustrated by its being one of the few psychiatric disorders for which **psychosurgery** was still used in the late twentieth century as a final resort in treatment-resistant cases. Surgery is still an option in some parts of the world and alternative **gamma knife** techniques have been used in OCD (see Chapter 3). Although neurosurgery was sought for OCD, the neurophysiological focus of the disorder is less clear, and even though psychiatric outcomes of brain injury are common, those resulting in OCD are rare (Perez-Alvarez et al., 2006). Neuroimaging studies have led to two potential neurological models for OCD. One of these is higher brain or **executive dysfunction**, in that there is failure to inhibit redundant responses, or perseveration involving brain areas such as the caudate nucleus, thalamus, striatum and dorsolateral prefrontal cortex. The other emphasises **modulatory control** of acceptable behaviour and the brain areas implicated for this are the medial prefrontal cortex, orbitofrontal cortex and cingulate gyrus. However, although there has been much support for these models, they also have limitations and lack universal agreement from multiple imaging studies (Friedlander and Desrocher, 2006).

Obsessive–compulsive behaviour has a paradoxical relationship to the generally inhibitory neurotransmitter **serotonin**. Although increased levels have been found in the disorder, treatment with **SSRIs** (selective serotonin reuptake inhibitors) such as fluoxetine (Prozac), which are serotonin agonists, can reduce obsessive symptoms and also act on any comorbid depression. The **tricyclic anti-depressant** clomipramine has also been found to be as effective as SSRIs in OCD (Eddy et al., 2004), and both of these successes perhaps relate to the clear relationship that has been found between OCD and **depression**, in that intervention for one disorder assists recovery from the other (DeSilva and Rachman, 2004). Pharmacological treatments such as SSRIs and tricyclic anti-depressants, with their non-selective serotonin reuptake effects,

produce significant symptom reduction and this improvement is enhanced by combining drug treatment with CBT (Eddy et al., 2004).

Evolutionary explanations of OCD have focused on factors within the normal repertoire of thought and action that relates to OCD behaviour. Feygin, Swain and Leckman (2006) have considered the dysregulation of the neural circuits for detecting threat and avoiding harm. Although partly based on neuroimaging evidence, this explanation relates more closely to cognitive approaches to the disorder than the neural theories above. Cognitive approaches emphasise the exaggeration of threat and danger in many anxiety disorders, and this also applies to OCD. Some cognitive approaches have also stressed that the disparity between a sufferer's desired and perceived level of control influences the tendency to engage in superstitious ritual and beliefs (Moulding and Kyrios, 2006). Other approaches have examined deficits in emotion recognition, such as the tendency in OCD to interpret neutral female faces as 'sad' (Aigner et al., 2007). These characteristics of OCD provide targets for interventions such as CBT in both adults and children (Turner, 2006). Each of the treatment approaches of CBT or behaviour therapy alone is effective in OCD (Eddy et al., 2004). OCD is a disorder that is inherently difficult to treat as both elements, reduction of obsessions and associated anxiety, as well as response prevention for compulsions have to be addressed (Carr and McNulty, 2006).

Research

Religious belief and mental disorder

The area of coherent religious belief and mental disorder brings together some very disparate and sometimes contradictory research.

A singular focused belief has anecdotally been associated with motivating the sick to health and providing solace for those in mental turmoil. It has also been a focus of clinical attention in terms of exacerbating or contributing to mental disorder, particularly the anxiety disorder OCD (Marshall, 2003). Many of the delusions and hallucinations in **schizophrenia** (Chapter 18) and some of the thinking in **bipolar disorder** (Chapter 17) are influenced by religious content, and some religious states have been diagnosed as psychiatric disorder. Having the hearing of hallucinatory voices in a religious context designated as a symptom of psychosis has

been considered misdiagnosis by some authors. The same writers also claim that the differences between such experiences as the case of Joan of Arc and actual schizophrenic symptoms are only detectable by religious leaders and, by implication, invisible to clinicians (e.g. Dein and Littlewood, 2007). Many would doubt this assertion and in the case of Dawkins (2006) consider ill-founded beliefs such as God or religion to be a dysfunctional by-product of the brain's evolutionary development. A UK YouGov opinion poll revealed that 42 per cent of the general public considered religion to be harmful (see Humphries, 2007).

Such polarised views of religion as being an aid or toxic to mental well-being undermine conclusive research on the topic, leaving each opposing camp with selective and limited substance to their arguments. In the case of anxiety disorders and religion, studies have been used to support the idea of religion as anxiolytic (anxiety reducing), but others consider it a cause of anxiety, particularly in research on OCD. In a review, Shreve-Neiger and Edelstein (2004) consider that there are proportionately very few studies of the relationship between religion and anxiety, and that what little evidence there is, is flawed by small samples and poor definitions or measures of religion. The extrinsic concept of overt religiosity is often equated with the intrinsic personal experience of spirituality. In addition, correlations are confounded with causation, as in the example of church attendance being used as a measure of religiosity when it may equally stand as a measure of **social capital** or sociability (see Shreve-Neiger and Edelstein, 2004).

Glas (2007) points to the long history of using demonic possession as an explanation of mental illness, indicating that aspects of such fears remain enshrined in culture, such as the djin or 'evil eye' (see Chapter 1). Fear-invoking concepts have also been used in religions to enforce rules and rituals, producing anxiety in those believers who disobey. Leavey and King (2007) have called for partnerships between religion and psychiatry to help end traces of demonology or exorcism as well as the concept of mental illness as a 'sin'. This has, for some, been portrayed in the film *Requiem* (Schmid, 2006). Others have gone so far as to call for the active promotion of religion in psychiatry, in the context of increasing ethnicity in the patient population (Boehnlein, 2006). Most research into the effects of religion utilises Judeo-Christian concepts in white Western populations and lacks perspectives on effects of more diverse religions (Leavey and King, 2007). D'Souza and George (2006) consider the need for ethical sensitivity to the patient as 'a whole person', which would include recognition of their diverse religious beliefs. This is particularly the case with the overlap between religious ritual and the symptoms of OCD, where cultural sensitivity is needed if rigid practices interact with such symptoms within an individual (Burt and Rudolph, 2000).

Individuals with OCD overvalue the importance of thoughts and control over thinking, which is a common feature of many religions (Veale, 2002). Other symptoms of OCD are characteristic of harsher religious practices such as: rigid repeated behaviours; intrusive thoughts and images; anxiety or guilt at failing to carry out practices; scrupulosity and cleansing rituals; and a sense that 'something bad will happen' in failing to think correctly. This occurs to the point where OCD symptom checklists are likely to register such behaviours as pathological. For example, O'Sullivan (1995) found significant correlations between OCD self-report scores and religiosity scores across a number of religions in a non-clinical sample. Freud (1907) referred to religion as the universal obsessive ritual when pointing out the similarity between methods in religion and the control of obsessive fears in OCD. However, Tek and Ulug (2001) found no significant relationship between religious behaviours and OCD, but as with many such studies this was a clinical sample. It may be that such a relationship may be more evident at subclinical levels in the general population. The relationship between strict religious upbringing and OCD has been examined for a number of years (e.g. Okasha et al., 1994), and there may be a more complex interplay between aspects of religion and OCD if the caveats of Shreve-Neiger and Edelstein (2004) are acknowledged. For example, Zohar et al. (2005) noted that those in a Jewish sample who showed more evidence of OCD became more religious than their parents and those with lower OCD symptoms became less religious.

Generally, intrinsic religiosity or personal spiritual belief is thought to relate to lower anxiety in the general population, and extrinsic religion or public religious practice to increased anxiety (Glas, 2007). Although this is partly contradicted by a finding that common mental disorders are more frequent in those who hold a spiritual life view without religious practice (King et al., 2006), it may just be that for some people inner religious faith provides a kind of ameliorative equivalent to anti-anxiety medication, and for others imposed religious practices invoke anxiety and intrusive thought. In measuring well-being based on religious influence, the common error is often made of equating 'feeling good' with symptom reduction (Favazza, 2004). Therapist and client sharing common religious beliefs, practices or concepts can also confound objective evaluation of religious effects. **Mindfulness** is an aspect of religious belief that has been applied to some alternative therapeutic settings, which tends to induce commonality between therapist and client. In this, the client engages in Buddhist meditation techniques to become aware of the source of anxieties that distract them (Moran, 2007). However, even those practising Buddhists experience worry levels that relate to the extrinsic orientation of their practices, which has been interpreted as a product of their belief in the inevitability of karma governing the outcomes of their actions or inactions (Tapanya, Nicki and Jaruswad, 1997).

Post-traumatic stress disorder

Post-traumatic stress disorder (PTSD) is an extreme response to a severe stressor, resulting in characteristic symptoms that persist long after the event has passed (American Psychiatric Association, 2000). These symptoms must persist for more than 1 month, and can be considered chronic after 3 months. Initial definitions and early classifications for this disorder have only regarded life-threatening situations to be sufficiently traumatic for PTSD, but more recent criteria recognise more diverse precipitating events. Thus, fulfilling criteria usually stem from personal experience involving death, injury or threat to the personal integrity of another person, including harm to associates or family (American Psychiatric Association, 2000). Examples of these could be experience of war, homicide, assault, a motor accident or the sometimes controversial delayed effects of childhood abuse. In cases of PTSD this produces a response of intense fear, horror and helplessness, or disorganised, agitated behaviour in the case of children (American Psychiatric Association, 2000). The extreme response can be characterised by five groups of symptoms (*DSM-IV-TR* contracts these into three groups).

- **Avoidance of reminders of the event** includes such strategies as self-distraction to avoid recurring thoughts or images. A sufferer may physically avoid the location or even the surrounding area of an attack or accident. They may also avoid other reminders, such as particular activities or people (American Psychiatric Association, 2000). There may be poor recall of aspects of the original trauma and such amnesia can seem to contrast with the overreaction seen to mnemonic stimuli below.

- **Numbing of responses** includes anhedonia, difficulty in feeling positive, alienation and lack of emotional or general interest in others. There is a diminished interest in former activities and participation may cease. Sufferers display a restricted range of emotion and blunted affect may be very evident in close personal relationships. There is a lack of investment in relationships and their own future may be viewed as limited, with a related lack of interest in building a career or having children (American Psychiatric Association, 2000).

- **Reliving the experience** occurs repeatedly in the form of nightmares and daydreams. These can occur whilst awake where the sufferer re-experiences the emotions and actions of the traumatic event, sometimes with hallucinations. Children may enact these actions in play (American Psychiatric Association, 2000). Everyday

In all major incidents involving loss of life there will be a proportion of those surviving who will develop PTSD.
Source: Pearson Online Database.

sounds, such as a car backfiring recalling gunfire, may prompt feelings of the event reoccurring and cause distress. Images of the traumatic event may also be prompted or intrude into consciousness in the absence of external stimuli. The distress is always disproportionate to the nature of the precipitating stimuli.

■ **Increased arousal** results in insomnia, difficulty in concentration, hypervigilance (constantly monitoring for danger), an exaggerated startle response (i.e. an over-reaction to change in stimuli) and increased physiological reactions to associated words or images. The latter can be usefully measured using a modified Stroop test, where related words slow the processing of print colour naming, and easily measured physiologically using heart rate (see Blanchard et al., 1996). These reactions are not evident prior to the trauma (American Psychiatric Association, 2000).

■ **Learned helplessness** can be produced by the single uncontrollable event and generalised to other situations, in which the sufferer has learned that they are helpless to control significant events and behaves ineffectually and apathetically when confronting new challenges. This can often lead to depression. The sense of helplessness may be coupled with guilt that they are in some way responsible for the outcome of the traumatic event, as they survived whilst others may have died. These symptoms can be further complicated by substance abuse and suicidal tendencies.

There may be **psychosomatic** complaints such as abdominal pains and possibly **dissociative** symptoms (see Chapter 15), which are often noticed when the source of trauma is child sexual or physical abuse. It is becoming increasingly common practice to conceptualise the adult effects of child abuse as PTSD, especially when considering treatment approaches. Psychological processes have been found to be disrupted in PSTD (see Brewin and Holmes, 2003). Memories of trauma tend to be intrusive, sometimes described as 'flashbacks', but lacking in contextual detail and error prone. Individuals with PTSD have memory deficits in recalling the trauma but also for events that are not trauma related, for which there may be neurological correlates in brain areas such as the frontal lobes, hippocampus and amygdala (Isaak, Cushway and Jones, 2006). Sufferers show bias towards threat and there are dysfunctional beliefs regarding threat to life and a generalisation of mistrust or a sense of failure to most areas of life. A PTSD sufferer's efforts to avoid thinking about distressing events and trauma-associated stimuli tends to be counterproductive and leads to worsening of symptoms (Brewin and Holmes, 2003).

PTSD affects over 1 per cent of the population at any one time, with a lifetime prevalence that varies internationally from less than 2 to over 7 per cent (Michael, Zetsche and Margraf, 2007). Prevalence may also be affected by occupational or clinical forensic factors where claims for insurance, compensation or forensic evidence are actively sought. Age of onset for PTSD varies greatly, as it is dependent on the time when the precipitating trauma occurs (Michael, Zetsche and Margraf, 2007). The proximity of onset to trauma may not always be close as, although symptoms usually occur within 3 months of the trauma, they can be delayed by years in some cases. In around half of PTSD cases, symptoms remit within 3 months, but many others suffer symptoms for more than a year (American Psychiatric Association, 2000). *DSM-IV-TR* uses the following specifiers to distinguish the differing courses the disorder takes.

■ **Acute** is used if the symptoms cease within 3 months.

■ **Chronic** refers to symptoms persisting beyond 3 months from onset.

■ **With delayed onset** is used where symptoms do not appear until 6 months or more following the trauma.

Not everyone who experiences such trauma develops the disorder, which has provided researchers with the opportunity to examine the individual differences between those who are and are not susceptible. Perceived stress differs between those with PTSD and controls, which can be measured by instruments such as the Stress Vulnerability Scale (Connor et al., 2007). It follows that some individuals may be predisposed to PTSD by certain factors both inherited and resulting from cognitive styles. For example, having an **external locus of control** by considering one's fate to be outside of personal control could contribute to a post-traumatic reaction, attributing events to external factors such as the acts of others or genetic predisposing factors. Alternatively, it may be that those who do not develop PTSD have greater social support and are more able to accept that the event is in the past. The distress produced by events is often assumed to be proportionate to the degree and directness of exposure to trauma. However, Long, Meyer and Jacobs (2007) found no significant differences between Red Cross workers with direct exposure to the disaster scenes of the terrorist attacks of 11 September 2001 and those who were not directly exposed in terms of distress.

Many of the models in the Focus box represent a great deal of accumulated research and also imply routes for interventions. Olde et al. (2006) have examined PTSD reactions following the trauma of childbirth, where prior knowledge of the event and its circumstances allows

Focus

Explanations of PTSD

In some large-scale disasters, like the 11 September 2001 terrorist attacks in New York, many of those exposed to trauma will be the members of the emergency and rescue services.
Source: Pearson Online Database.

There have been a number of explanatory models for PTSD, such as the following (see Brewin and Holmes, 2003, for more detail).

- **Stress response theory.** This early approach emphasises the opposing demands on an individual to suppress traumatic information but at the same time to try to work through the trauma experience systematically and use the information to update their view of the world.

- **Learning approaches.** Conditioning is used to explain how benign stimuli can produce a fear response due to association with the trauma and can thus be targeted for behavioural desensitisation. Affected individuals tend to be more easily conditioned to fear in general, which also leads to considering if the individual has been more readily conditioned to fear prior to the trauma as a potential vulnerability factor (Brewin and Holmes, 2003).

- **Anxious apprehension model.** This focuses on the distorted cognitive processes that occur following trauma, producing hypervigilance for cues relating to the experience in a manner similar to the cognitive explanation for panic. Thus the person is apprehensive about alarm cues and may defend themselves by numbing their responses.

- **Emotional processing theory.** Here more rigid pre-trauma views of self-competence and a safe world make an individual more prone to PTSD when these views are contradicted by the event, often followed by similarly rigid negative views of the world and self. For Foa and Rothbaum (1998), working through the trauma as a form of exposure can enable these rigid views to be challenged as well as limiting the generalisation of danger, and places the event in its true context whilst the client is not traumatised and thinking more rationally.

- **Dual representation theory.** This stems from the premise that traumatic memories are distinct from normal memory and stored in a different memory system. These dual memory systems require different means for interpretation that are not interchangeable and one of these systems may take precedence over the other. Recovery from PTSD under this model is a complex process, which includes restoring intrusive emotions and images with reduced arousal and negative affect (see Brewin and Holmes, 2003).

- **Cognitive models.** A number of information-processing and cognitive theories have been applied to PTSD, one of which is **Ehlers and Clark's cognitive model** (Ehlers and Clark, 2000). This examines the operation of faulty cognitive processing of trauma information, whereby the past trauma affects anxiety about the future. In common with other models there is focus on poor elaboration of the trauma memory and its lack of accurate context. Ehlers and Clark (2000) examine the peri-traumatic influences on the memory, such as the data-driven processing of sensory impressions that lack integration on recall, compared with conceptual processing where meaningful information is integrated into the individual's autobiographical database.

research opportunities into the disorder that permits close scrutiny of a priori and post-trauma factors. Decreased cerebral blood flow in the thalamus has been found in PTSD patients and could provide a physiological strategy for reducing re-experiencing symptoms in sufferers (Kim et al., 2007). Rather than focusing on the negative outcomes of trauma, Zoellner and Maercker (2006) have reported the increasing interest in **post-traumatic growth**, where there is focus is on positive aspects of recovery and overcoming the challenge of a traumatic event. Neuroevolutionary conceptualisations of PTSD and other species-atypical fear behaviours involve consideration of the neural fear circuitry, harm-avoidance genetics, stress-resilience and other factors, as well as comparisons between phylogenetically developed circuitry for combat in a Neolithic background and its application in a contemporary warfare context (see Bracha, 2006).

Pharmacological treatments for PTSD have come to rely on **SSRIs**, which have largely replaced the older monoamine oxidase inhibitors. However, drug treatments are best used in combination with CBT (Carr and McNulty, 2006). Most contemporary treatment approaches are based on CBT following through many of the specific errors of thinking and memory identified in the theories above. CBT has the strongest evidence-base for its efficacy and outcomes (Carr and McNulty, 2006), although some evaluations are confounded by the tendency for PTSD to remit spontaneously. CBT is often begun shortly after the point of trauma following major incidents as a preventative measure prior to the onset of symptoms; this is sometimes referred to as **stress debriefing**. Some newer interventions, such as **eye-movement desensitisation and reprocessing** (EMDR), lack good evidence-based evaluation data and may owe any reported success to the confounding factor of elements of CBT being delivered in parallel (Carr and McNulty, 2006). These practices raise ethical questions regarding clients being deprived of established effective therapy. Group treatments have been established in the treatment of PTSD for many years, and the support provided helps to counter clients' fears of being vulnerable individuals.

PTSD has been a familiar disorder to forensic psychologists for many years as a common outcome for victims of violent crimes. Victims of violence, rape and terrorism, as well as those subjected to trauma in non-criminal acts where there is attribution of blame, are increasingly being assessed for symptoms of PTSD. This assessment may then be used in court as evidence of increased injury and to increase compensation claims. Also increasing is the number of assessments of individuals thought to be malingering as PTSD for use as mitigation in court, financial return or evasion of occupational duties (Guriel and Fremouw, 2003). PTSD is also a frequent problem for frontline services such as the police, fire service, ambulance crews and active armed forces, who may be involved in traumatic events during the course of their jobs. Another target group are psychiatric patients admitted to forensic wards due to criminal behaviour, who often have a history of trauma and should be routinely screened for symptoms of PTSD that may confound their comorbid condition (Garieballa et al., 2006). PTSD is one of the few disorders that individuals, particularly in the West, are content to admit to having, which may be related to the rapidly growing 'compensation culture' (see Summerfield, 2001).

Acute stress disorder

Acute stress disorder is a less protracted reaction to a similar stressor as found in PTSD, resulting in high levels of fear, helplessness or horror (American Psychiatric Association, 2000). During or after the event, the individual will have three or more dissociative symptoms, such as subjective numbing or absence of emotional reaction, subjective distancing from the event, derealisation, depersonalisation and dissociative amnesia for aspects of the event (see Chapter 15). The symptom groupings are also similar to those of PTSD with a re-experiencing of the traumatic event by means of intrusive thoughts and images, dreams, an illusory sense of reliving the event, and distress caused by cues associated with the event (American Psychiatric Association, 2000). Sufferers also show marked avoidance for physical aspects of the event as well as associated thoughts, people, conversations and feelings. There are marked increases in anxiety and arousal, leading to insomnia, restlessness and poor concentration.

In the case of acute stress disorder, symptoms begin within 4 weeks of the trauma and last for a minimum of 2 days and a maximum of 4 weeks (American Psychiatric Association, 2000). The duration of the disorder demarcates it from PTSD, as does the dissociative symptom criterion, but due to the shorter duration there can also be other differences in the symptoms that can manifest in this time. If the duration extends beyond the 4 weeks, the diagnosis is changed to PTSD providing the criteria are met. There is little or no data on the lifetime prevalence of acute stress disorder (Michael, Zetsche and Margraf, 2007), but amongst those who have been exposed to trauma the incidence varies from 14 to 33 per cent (American Psychiatric Association, 2000). Treatments are similar to those for PTSD, as it is uncertain whether the diagnosis will change, but early intervention is desirable to reduce the possibility of the disorder developing. When dealing with victims of violent crime within the first month after trauma, Brewin, Andrews and Rose (2003) found that the high level of overlap between acute stress disorder and PTSD brought into question whether these classifications represented truly distinct diagnoses.

Generalised anxiety disorder

Generalised anxiety disorder (GAD) has been referred to as 'free-floating anxiety', as it has no specific or consistent trigger, but the symptoms of uncontrolled, excessive apprehension, worry and anxiety appear unsystematically. GAD sufferers worry disproportionately about unlikely events and show an exaggerated anxious response to routine daily tasks such as bill paying, repairs, appointments or even leisure activities. These anxiety symptoms will include at least three of the following: restlessness or being wound up; tiring easily; poor concentration; irritability; physical tension; sleep disturbances (American Psychiatric Association, 2000). As it is almost impossible to identify any one source for these anxieties and the fear is generalised across most situations, the sufferer is unable to avoid particular situations or objects that would be equivalent to the triggers in other anxiety disorders, and often adopts the strategies of avoiding the worrying thoughts or engaging in systematic worry around current life demands. Excessive worry takes place across a very wide range of events or work demands. This anxiety occurs most days for at least 6 months to meet the *DSM* criteria (American Psychiatric Association, 2000). The anxiety in GAD is distinct from the essential criteria for the other anxiety disorders: for example, it is not due to anticipation of a social event, as in social phobia. Wells (1997) divides the worry symptoms of GAD into those concerned with events (type 1 worries) and cognitive worries or 'worry about worry' (type 2 worries), a distinction that is useful when treating the disorder.

The incidence of GAD amongst clients at anxiety clinics is around 12 per cent and it occurs in 5 per cent of the general population at some point during their lifetime (Wells, 1997). However, Lieb, Becker and Altamura (2005) examined the epidemiology of GAD in Europe, and although around 2 per cent of the general population were reported as having the disorder, the research revealed discrepancies in prevalence across populations and a lack of information about the natural course of GAD in some of these populations. In an overview by Michael, Zetsche and Margraf (2007), lifetime prevalence in Europe 2.8 per cent was around half that taken from US study data at 5.7 per cent, perhaps illustrating discrepancies rather than national differences. The disorder has an earlier onset than most anxiety and mood disorders at around 21 years, with a later onset indicating that GAD is secondary to another disorder (Fisher and Durham, 2004). GAD is more common in women than men, with females regularly accounting for two-thirds of the cases in epidemiological data (Rubio and López-Ibor, 2007). GAD patients tend to consume high levels of health care resources in Europe, and this is exacerbated by the disorder not being well detected in general medical practice (Lieb, Becker and Altamura, 2005).

Risk factors for poor prognosis in GAD have been found to be: being female; poor treatment continuity; and onset of the disorder before the age of 25 (Rubio and López-Ibor, 2007). Recent studies have provided more

evidence for genetic involvement in GAD and there are genetic links with major depression (American Psychiatric Association, 2000). Kendler (2004) provided evidence that major depression and GAD are the result of the same genetic factors in females, and that the environmental risk factors that predispose individuals to GAD may differ from those increasing risk for depression. Developmental risk factors have been suggested for GAD, such as insecure early attachment, childhood trauma (including abuse), parental separation, limited social interactions, and modelling of anxiety by a relative (Fisher and Durham, 2004). The anxious apprehension model described in the previous section has also been applied to the development of GAD, wherein worry becomes a dysfunctional coping strategy for developing hypervigilance to threat (Fisher and Durham, 2004).

As above, the lack of target stimuli limits the treatment approaches for GAD, and this has in the past increased the reliance on pharmacological interventions. These greatly involved benzodiazepines until the problems of this medication were evident and a shift towards the use of **SSRIs** and tricyclic anti-depressants resulted in better management of symptoms, with SSRIs being the current preferred pharmacological treatment (Bennett, 2006). Controlled trials of **Sertraline** have shown effectiveness over both worry symptoms and problematic **somatic** symptoms in GAD, which are the physical symptoms of anxiety such as gastro-intestinal complaints or headaches (Dahl et al., 2005). Somatic symptoms of the somatization disorder type (see Chapter 15) tend to increase in the elderly as GAD symptoms remit around the age of 50 (Rubio and López-Ibor, 2007). Although the effectiveness of CBT and exposure approaches is reduced by lack of consistent target stimuli, a more recent refocusing of approaches has increased the success of CBT (see Wells, 1997). These approaches involve a focus on setting tasks for the client to develop coping skills by exposing themselves to their worry processes rather than blocking out these thoughts, restructuring their negative thoughts on a more realistic basis and introducing relaxation training (Carr and McNulty, 2006).

The **metacognitive model of GAD** has been outlined by Wells (1997), utilising the above symptom distinction between general, type 1 worry and type 2 metacognitions or worry about worry. For Wells (1997), GAD is characterised by a shift from type 1 to type 2 worrying when sufferers begin to be anxious about their own level of worrying. The therapy that follows from this approach can then target the unrealistic beliefs about the uncontrollability of their excessive worrying and remove erroneous beliefs about negative consequences of worrying for the client's functioning. In Wells' (1997) approach, the self-sustaining reliance on worry as a means of coping with problems or 'worrying through tasks', or the use of distracting activities, also needs to be replaced with true coping actions. There are other cognitive models applied to GAD that vary in their explanation, but which suggest interventions along similar lines to the metacognitive approach (see Fisher and Durham, 2004).

Self-test questions

- What is the difference between an obsession and a compulsion in OCD?
- What is the role of serotonin in OCD?
- How can dysfunctional beliefs increase OCD symptoms?
- How does intrinsic and extrinsic religiosity relate to anxiety?
- What are the main symptom areas in PTSD?
- How does acute stress disorder differ from PTSD?
- What are the forensic implications of PTSD?
- In what ways is acute stress disorder distinguished from PTSD?
- What factor makes GAD more difficult to treat without medications?
- What is the metacognitive approach to GAD?

The aetiology of anxiety disorders

The different paradigms in psychology have all laid claim to success in their various approaches to anxiety disorders. However, cognitive, behavioural and biogenic approaches appear most effective both in explaining the origins of anxiety disorders and in their treatment. From the somewhat unethical demonstrations of phobic learning using classical conditioning by Watson and Rayner (1920), through to the systematic application of this approach to treatment by Wolpe (1958), the behavioural explanation of anxiety disorders has held a primary position. This has been greatly elaborated on by more recent cognitive insights (e.g. Wells, 1997) and systematically underpinned by advancing neurophysiological research (Matiax-Cols and Phillips, 2007).

It is widely assumed that most, if not all, sufferers have some predisposing **diathesis**, as anxiety disorders have been established for many years as at least partly inherited (e.g. Carey and Gottesman, 1981). Hettima, Neale and Kendler (2001) established a significant familial aggregation for anxiety disorders in a meta-analysis of genetic epidemiology, which is mostly accounted for by genetic influence. At around 30–40 per cent, heritability is lower across the anxiety disorders than for disorders such as schizophrenia or bipolar disorder, although excluding measurement error from the data for phobias has produced figures of 50–60 per cent (Hettima, Neale and Kendler, 2001). Thus, although the level of genetic influence in anxiety disorders would not be sufficient for genetic counselling, inherited biochemical abnormalities may explain the differential effectiveness of pharmacological treatments (e.g. Lydiard, Brawman-Minzer and Ballenger, 1996).

Examples of inheritable factors that could influence anxious reactions are **autonomic overreactivity**, **gamma-amino butyric acid** levels (affecting general anxiety levels), **noradrenaline** levels (PTSD) and **serotonin** levels (obsessive–compulsive disorder). Genetic factors may also influence **cortisol** production levels (see Abelson and Curtis, 1996). Although these levels are not always tied to current anxiety symptoms, persistent anxiety problems co-occur with higher awakening and morning cortisol levels (Greaves-Lord et al., 2007). As mentioned in the previous section, in females, the same genes are thought to be responsible for both anxiety (GAD) and major depression, with symptom distinctions guided by environmental factors (Kendler, 2004). This and other common aetiological factors may partly explain the similarity of treatments for these disorders as well as the traditional association between mood and anxiety in older literature (see Goldberg, Benjamin and Creed, 1994).

Charney (2003) reviewed functional neuroimaging in anxiety disorders and revealed inconsistencies in results, which were attributed to variation in neurobiology inherent in criteria-based psychiatric diagnoses. The neuro-anatomical areas involved in fear learning involve the **amygdala** in a crucial role, which is combined with links to the **mesiotemporal cortex**, **sensory thalamus**, **orbital** and **medial prefrontal cortex** and the **hypothalamus**, amongst other structures that may be implicated in the aetiology of anxiety disorders (Charney, 2003). Arguably, the most useful applications of functional imaging methods of examining neural activity in anxiety include identifying the neural loci of treatment effects and developing the potential to predict treatment outcomes (Matiax-Cols and Phillips, 2007).

Risk factors drawn from epidemiological studies, such as being single, poor, unemployed or lacking in education, may be consequential as well as causal, but some factors in childhood have been related to the later development of anxiety disorders. Parents can act as models for inappropriate fear and anxiety, which a child may then acquire by vicarious learning. Not all **negative life events** have a clear impact on the development of later anxiety conditions, but early experience of violence has been linked in this way (Michael, Zetsche and Margraf, 2007). Some children are inhibited in approaching new situations and this **behavioural inhibition** has been linked to later anxiety disorders. This is more prominently the case with social phobia, but childhood inhibition has been associated with all of the anxiety disorders in adulthood (Michael, Zetsche and Margraf, 2007). Counter to the assumptions of some paradigmatic approaches to the factors associated with childhood anxiety, a meta-analysis of studies revealed parenting to account for very little of the variance in this anxiety. In this marginal association, parental control was more closely related to anxiety in childhood than parental rejection (McLeod, Wood and Weisz, 2007).

Cognitive explanations stem from work by Ellis (1962) in proposing that rigidly held irrational beliefs lead to illogical cognitions, or 'thinking disorder' as Beck (1976) labels this process. These irrational beliefs, or dysfunctional schemas as they are conceptualised in schema-based theory, consist of unrealistic imperatives and assumptions that require the sufferer to conform to the impossible, such as perfection in behaviour or acceptability to everyone (see Wells, 1997). In anxiety, the preoccupying thoughts centre on danger and an inability to cope. Tautologically, the ensuing anxiety increases the sense of danger and reduces the perceived ability to cope, producing yet further anxiety. Wells (1997) sees this cognitive explanation as paving a clear path for cognitive interventions challenging the underlying dysfunctional schemas (Wells, 1997: p. 2).

Armfield (2006) has drawn together a number of cognitive explanations of fear and anxiety and presented a model of the aetiology of fear based on **cognitive vulnerability**. A schema of vulnerability is generated by an anxiety sufferer's perception of a stimulus as being dangerous and unpredictable. Uncontrollable aversive events impact negatively on those with anxiety disorders and create sensitivity to perceived alarm triggers. Lohr, Olatunji and Sawchuck (2007) carried out a functional analysis on these danger signals reacted to by those with anxiety disorders, but also examined reactions in relation to safety signals that predict the termination of threat. Their analysis suggests that anxiety can be conceptualised in terms of balancing the threatening effect of danger signals against the safety precautions that can be used. Controllability and predictability of safety and danger signals could therefore be specific products of cognitive interventions, in contrast to their muting as a result of pharmacological treatments (Lohr, Olatunji and Sawchuck, 2007).

The treatment of anxiety disorders

Many anxious individuals self-medicate with **alcohol** and often greatly confound their condition as a result. Anxiolytics (e.g. benzodiazepines) and anti-depressants such as the less addictive **tricyclics** (e.g. imipramine for GAD or panic, clomipramine for OCD and amitriptyline for PTSD) have all been useful in the past (Nash and Hutt, 2007). Benzodiazepines were progressively removed during the twentieth century as a general intervention in this area and there are cautious guidelines in place for their current use in the UK. At the same time, SSRIs have become the treatment of choice for anxiety disorders and have proven effective in each case (see Nash and Hutt, 2007). However, the broad acceptance of SSRIs is not without caveats or adverse findings. In a review, Breggin (2004) considers there is common evidence that SSRIs can produce iatrogenic conditions (i.e. symptoms due to treatment), some resembling OCD that are prone to misdiagnosis, and which can in some cases progress to suicidality and violence. Adherence to medication statistics from the **2000 National Psychiatric Morbidity Survey** revealed that over one-third of patients ceased taking their medication (Cooper et al., 2007). However, the largest portion of these and the majority of

There is an association between anxiety and alcohol use, as many individuals develop a habit of self-medicating with the drug, greatly complicating their medical and psychiatric problems.
Source: Pearson Online Database.

SSRI non-compliers forgot to take their medication and only 14.2 per cent ceased because of side-effects (Cooper et al., 2007). Anxiety treatments focusing on **glutamate** transmission may have fewer side-effects than the present treatments based on serotonin, and glutamergic neuromodulation may thus be suitable for anxiety sufferers who cannot tolerate the current medications (Amiel and Mathew, 2007).

The behavioural approaches to anxiety disorders were fundamental in establishing clinical psychology as an effective profession. Reinforcement of **avoidance behaviour** by 'relief' increases fear and provides an explanation of why phobic responses worsen in the absence of the feared stimulus and why exposure to the feared stimulus tends to be an essential part of therapy (Choy, Fyer and Lipsitz, 2007; see Chapter 3). Exposure treatments (imaginal or in-vivo), such as systematic desensitisation and flooding (see Chapter 3), have long been found to produce success rates of around 80 per cent across studies from the earliest evaluations (e.g. Kazdin and Wilson, 1978). Response prevention needs to be added to these behavioural techniques when dealing with the compulsions in obsessive–compulsive disorder. This success is often maintained in the long term, and cognitive aspects of the therapy were found to be an important aspect of this sustained improvement (Kendall and Southam-Gerow, 1996).

During the history of anxiety treatment, cognitive approaches were found to combine well with these established behavioural techniques in the form of CBT and have been used effectively in this permutation by experts in this field, such as Aaron Beck, for over 30 years. Foa et al. (1996), amongst others, have shown cognitive bias to threat-related stimuli to be a mechanism in a number of anxiety disorders. As previously mentioned, disorders such as panic attacks can be greatly exacerbated by faulty cognition (Clark, 1986). In general, cognitive approaches help to restore a sense of control over the irrational thoughts that often precipitate anxiety, although focus on feared situations can occasionally result in sensitisation (e.g. Wells and Dattilio, 1992). Cognitive approaches can address the residual fear that often remains following behavioural exposure therapy (Rachman, 2004). The underlying mechanisms of successful exposure approaches in CBT have been reviewed by McNally (2007), providing a great deal of insight into potential neural, cellular, molecular and behavioural conceptual underpinnings of fear reduction, including recent developments in **emotional processing theory**.

Thus, the overall treatment of choice for anxiety disorders follows the cognitive behavioural approach in the form of CBT (Choy, Fyer and Lipsitz, 2007; Norton and Price, 2007). Although this implies a cognitive behavioural cause for the disorder, this is not necessary for the effectiveness of behaviourally based treatments as an intervention (Holmes, 1998). Fava and Ruini (2005) suggest that an optimum approach to therapy for anxiety is to incorporate pharmacotherapy in the early stages and move to CBT-based therapy in the mid- and long term. This sequential approach may need to be adjusted depending on the type of drug employed and the possibility that the client may respond well to CBT throughout without the need for initial medication. One of the important positive outcomes of CBT for anxiety is the client's retention of self-help skills to maintain their recovery. Self-management of disorders during the main treatment period has also been very useful to anxiety sufferers and warrants further research (Barlow et al., 2005). The difficult issue of refractory anxiety disorders (i.e. treatment-resistant conditions) has been evaluated by Pollack et al. (2007), who suggest novel approaches such as the next generation of SSRIs, but also point out that addressing the lack of CBT being offered currently in many cases may solve more problems than refining CBT for the cases where it *is* used at the moment.

In many anxiety disorders the mental imagery evoked by the disorder, particularly PTSD, is one of the sustaining factors for the condition and provides an important target for CBT (see Hirsch and Holmes, 2007). Exposure therapy is often carried out by the client imagining the feared stimulus rather than in vivo, which may not always be practical (Choy, Fyer and Lipsitz, 2007; Holmes, 1998). For over half a century it has been considered that imaginal exposure is not as effective as in vivo, and that real-world exposure should be used to check effective progress for the former (Wolpe, 1958; Emmelkamp, 2003). One means of bridging the gap and exposing a client to apparent 'real' stimuli conveniently in a clinic is to use computerised virtual environments for the encounter, which may vary from realistic screen graphics to total sensory immersion with computer supplied visual, auditory, tactile and motion feedback (Choy, Fyer and Lipsitz, 2007). Krijn et al. (2004) reviewed the use of **virtual reality exposure therapy** for anxiety disorders, revealing that the application of this technology is progressing with most anxiety situations, but that evidence for success lies mostly with height and flying phobias. Computers are also used in delivering the routine aspects of CBT or computer-guided cognitive behavioural therapy (CCBT), which can be accessed via the internet, DVDs and mobile phones. Peck (2007) has found this use of technology to be comparable with face-to-face alternatives, to produce high levels of satisfaction and to be the only means of delivery for some individuals.

A total of 108 alternative therapeutic approaches for anxiety conditions, including medicines, homoeopathic remedies, diet, physical activities and diet or lifestyle change, have been evaluated for evidence of efficacy by Jorm et al. (2004). They found some effectiveness for the herbal plant kava or exercise for GAD, and relaxation for GAD, panic disorder and some phobias. However, although there was weak evidence for a few other alternative approaches, there was no evidence of effectiveness for many of those tested, such as homoeopathy, prayer or hydrotherapy. Following a single controlled trial that produced evidence of psychoanalytic psychotherapy being better than relaxation for panic, McKay et al. (2007) pointed to the lack of explicit scientific basis for psychoanalytic techniques and called for more robust evaluations that may eliminate apparent effects from more reliable ones. The **National Institute for Health and Clinical Excellence** (NICE) has stated that the most effective treatments for anxiety disorders are pharmacotherapy and CBT, which may additionally be subject to the personal preferences of the client (Hirsch, 2007). However, a client with anxiety would be ill advised to venture from these effective treatments until such alternatives acquire the same evidence-based reputation.

Clinical issues

The detection of anxiety disorder symptoms has been described in the USA as 'the neglected stepchild of primary care-based mental health care' particularly in comparison to depression (Katon and Roy-Byrne, 2007: p. 390). In European clinical psychology delivery, the reverse has tended to be the case over the last 25 years with a great deal of research-driven practice development in the detection as well as treatment of anxiety disorder, particularly for PTSD. However, both sides of the Atlantic have similar shortcomings when it comes to clients adhering to treatments and sufficient access to therapy sessions (Katon and Roy-Byrne, 2007). In Europe as in the USA, there is a distinct underuse of CBT with anxiety patients, although pharmacological treatments are used frequently, suggesting a need for improved guidelines (Stein et al., 2004). The overall global burden of anxiety disorders has been assessed in a number of epidemiological surveys, although only those carried out after the advent of the standardised **Diagnostic Interview Schedule** in the 1980s have produced

Focus

The three-factor model of fear

Lang (1968) proposed a **three-factor model of fear** in identifying the cognitive, emotional and behavioural components of fear. Thus anticipation (cognitive) of an anxious situation may lead to avoidance (behavioural) or autonomic arousal (emotional) if the feared situation is confronted. Lang considered that the three factors are capable of independent change.

In separating these elements they can be individually treated by a clinician logically by cognitive, behavioural and physiological or relaxation techniques. However, evaluations of interventions often use only one of these elements as an indicator, such as a reduction in avoidance behaviour, whilst ignoring the physiological arousal or cognitive expectation. By considering all three elements for clinical assessment, treatment and outcome evaluation, better overall progress can be made in addressing anxiety problems on a sound, evidence-based foundation.

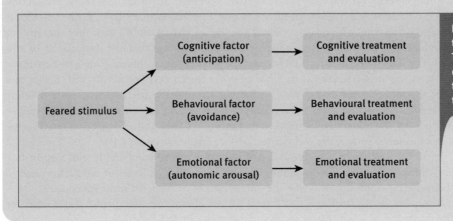

Figure 12.2 Lang's (1968) three factor model of fear. The three separable aspects of fear and anxiety all need to be addressed in treatment evaluations.

truly comparable international data such as the ESEMeD (see Kessler, 2007).

The cognitive explanation of anxiety as a thinking disorder (Beck, 1976; Beck, Emery and Greenberg, 1985) and as resting on specific irrational beliefs or **dysfunctional schemas** has become the cornerstone of contemporary clinical psychological practice in treating anxiety disorders. The current investment in cognitive therapeutic approaches to anxiety disorders has been built on a foundation of highly successful behavioural interventions relaunched by Wolpe in 1958. As mentioned above, the success of both these interventions when combined as CBT and applied to anxiety has also provided a degree of respect for psychology when compared with other professionals in the medical field, including psychiatry. The arena of anxiety disorders is thus of critical historical importance to the contemporary standing of clinical psychology (see Chapter 6). Clinical psychologists should therefore make every effort to maintain and refine the effective elements of CBT and avoid injuring this reputation by incorporating aspects of other approaches where evidence-based efficacy is absent.

Clinical assessment of anxiety symptoms may change radically if suggested **dimensional** systems replace the current categorical classifications in *DSM-V*. There are proposed plans to implement this change, which will inevitably be complex to configure (Brown and Barlow, 2005). There are advantages in configuring treatment more precisely to symptom needs revealed at assessment, which would be realised by all clinical psychologists working with anxiety clients. A dimensional system would detect comorbid disorders that are currently missed due to focus on the primary anxiety disorder. This can have positive implications in practice, as comorbid disorders can require greater resources and have other outcomes such as greater occupational absenteeism than 'pure' disorders, which is still the case for some comorbidities that should be detectable within the current *DSM* axes (Buist-Bouwman et al., 2005).

There are many issues of practice involved in bringing clinical attention to anxiety disorders (McManus, 2007). It is almost inevitable that clients will have to endure some level of discomfort in therapy during desensitisation, exposure and response prevention. It is most expedient to address the client's greatest fears first, and in graded exposure this will mean confronting fear levels as high as the client can tolerate as a preferred clinical strategy (McNally, 2007). **Incomplete exposure** in this context is a common failing of client compliance, in which the sufferer will offer a 'light touch' or incomplete imaginal, visual or tactile contact with the feared stimulus and not truly confront their fear (Carr and McNulty, 2006). This clearly reduces the effectiveness of the process but could also lead to short-term sensitisation to the stimulus, a potentially

time-consuming retrograde step. The client's belief in the controllability of their anxiety, which is part of Well's (1997) metacognitive approach, can be an indicator of the degree of engagement with the exposure process. Controllability can be rated at various points in therapy and usefully added to the data on the client's progress (Carr and McNulty, 2006).

Forensic issues

Breggin's (2004) study of the adverse effects of SSRIs, which are a common treatment for anxiety, has clear applications in forensic psychology, in that manufacturers may be involved in product liability cases, and Breggin outlines the potential implications of criminal malpractice. Anxiety disorders have often been viewed as less serious than, or even trivial by comparison to, others such as schizophrenia or medical conditions (Davidson, 2005). This has left this classification more susceptible than others to the use of less established or effective treatment approaches, which can lead to exacerbation of client problems as it has in the past in other cases (e.g. Lieberman, Yalom and Miles, 1973), as well as to potential litigation for iatrogenic conditions. This said, clearly some activities have traditionally reduced anxiety by focusing attention and distracting from concerns, such as the use by Toshihiro Nakahara and his colleagues of 'juggling therapy' for anxiety disorders (see Nakahara et al., 2007). However, whether such interventions should be given the full status and associated expectations of therapy may in itself become a legal issue in the future.

As mentioned above for PTSD, forensic and clinical psychologists frequently become involved in assessing victims or witnesses for anxiety conditions following a variety of crimes involving personal suffering or corporate negligence outcomes for the purposes of courtroom evidence (Howitt, 2009). An example of anxiety symptoms, particularly the criteria for PTSD, meeting forensic criteria was the establishment of **grievous mental harm** in 1996 to recognise the psychiatric injury inflicted by persistent **stalkers**. This form of mental injury may also be extended to witnesses or professionals involved in traumatic incidents who are also subject to mental or physical stress. Pseudo-PTSD is a troublesome factor in cases of litigation, claims for damages or extended leave from the workplace, and can have grave consequences where serious criminal charges are involved (Rosen and Taylor, 2007). *DSM-IV-TR* refers to guidelines to rule out malingering in cases of PTSD, recommending checks where profit or gain may be involved (American Psychiatric Association, 2000). Those with mental illnesses tend to be at much greater risk of crime victimisation (Teplin et al., 2005). Those with anxiety conditions will be more nervous and avoidant, and less likely to confront in a criminal encounter than those without anxiety conditions.

It is well established that offenders have higher levels of psychiatric disorders than the general population (e.g. Soderstrom et al., 2004). Surprisingly, this also includes anxiety disorders, as there is higher incidence of anti-social behaviour in those with anxiety disorders than in the general population, even when controlling for other variables (Sareen et al., 2004). This finding tends to be counterintuitive to most professionals and thus makes detection of this comorbidity of anxiety and anti-social conditions less likely (Sareen et al., 2004). One insight into this relationship is the finding that murderers with anxiety disorders are more likely to use a knife in an attack than offenders without anxiety conditions, thus inflicting greater injury (Frierson and Finkenbine, 2004). This would perhaps indicate that their anxiety levels would result in their being more likely to find greater security in the use of weapons in confrontations and therefore to face higher conviction rates. There is also an established comorbidity between substance use and anxiety, and young people with anxiety disorders are 1.3 to 3.9 times more likely to be substance

dependent (Goodwin, Fergusson and Horwood, 2004). This comorbidity is thought to stem from a common factor and not from a process of self-medication by those with anxiety (Goodwin, Fergusson and Horwood, 2004).

Self-test questions

- Which brain areas are likely to be involved in the inheritance of anxiety?
- What are the problems associated with SSRI use?
- What is 'virtual therapy'?
- Explain the applications of the three-factor model of fear.
- Explain 'incomplete exposure'.
- What does the term 'dysfunctional schema' represent?
- What is the relationship between PTSD and crime?
- Explain why anxiety can be common in both offenders and victims of crime.

Chapter summary

Anxiety disorders originate from what were termed **the neuroses**, a term that due to its association with psychodynamic aetiology was dropped by *DSM* systems. The anxiety disorders are: **panic disorder; agoraphobia; specific phobia; social phobia; obsessive–compulsive disorder; post-traumatic and acute stress disorders; and generalised anxiety disorder.** These are all characterised by anxiety that is inappropriate to the situation and that may have come about by a learning experience facilitated by biological and maladaptive thinking.

Panic disorder consists of frequent panic attacks, which are escalating levels of panic that may be a **limited-symptom attack** or become a **full panic attack** with four or more symptoms, such as choking, palpitations and numbing, as the sufferer **catastrophically misinterprets** their body signs, escalating their fears. **Phobias** include **agoraphobia** (classified with or without panic disorder), characterised by fear of being where there would be no escape in the event of illness or a panic attack. In **specific phobias** there is fear of specific objects or situations, which are anticipated, avoided or endured with distress.

Social phobia has embarrassment as its feared stimulus and places are avoided where this may occur, including **social** and **performance** situations. These phobias are best treated by **exposure therapy,** usually in the context of **cognitive behavioural therapy** (CBT).

Obsessive–compulsive disorder (OCD) is characterised by **obsessions** such as unwanted intrusive thoughts, images or impulses, and **compulsions** or repeated behaviours such as checking or cleaning that are maladaptively carried out to address the obsessions. It is the most serious of the anxiety disorders and resistant to therapy in many cases. Religious ritual has been associated with OCD but there are also assertions that faith can be therapeutic. **Post-traumatic stress disorder** (PTSD) refers to a group of symptoms, such as hypervigilance, arousal re-experiencing, avoidance and numbing of responses, which occur following a severe stressor. This response may be delayed and persist over considerable time, but only in some individuals. **Acute stress disorder** is similar to PTSD, but the symptoms remit within a month and include dissociative symptoms. **Generalised**

anxiety disorder (GAD) has no consistent feared stimulus and is characterised by anxiety that may occur across many contexts.

Anxiety disorders have potential inherited neurochemical and autonomic diatheses, but have a substantial learned behavioural and cognitive component. Overall anxiety disorders are best treated by CBT approaches with some pharmacological support from SSRIs, particularly in the early stages of intervention. Exposure therapy can be imaginal, in vivo or even virtual, and CBT can be delivered by computerised means. Clinical issues in treating anxiety involve the importance of psychology's place in this area of therapy, but the lack of availability of this therapy to many clients. Forensic issues in this area often centre on the consequences of crime-induced anxiety and its assessment for court purposes. Counter to the expectations of clinicians, anti-social behaviour is more common amongst those with anxiety disorders and thus may not be detected due to the surprisingness of this comorbidity.

Suggested essay questions

- Discuss the assumption that anxiety disorders are an extreme distortion of natural evolutionary and biological functions.
- Discuss the implications for relatives living with an individual with OCD.
- Critically compare the treatment of anxiety disorders with pharmacology versus CBT.

Further reading

Overview texts

Barlow, D. H. (2002) *Anxiety and its disorders: The nature and treatment of anxiety and panic* (2nd edn). London: Guilford Press.

Davey, G. (1997) *Phobias*. London: Wiley.

DeSilva, P., and Rachman, S. (2004) *Obsessive–compulsive disorder: The facts* (3rd edn). Oxford: Oxford University Press.

Fisher P. L., and Durham, R. C. (2004) Psychopathology of generalized anxiety disorder. *Psychiatry*, 3(4), 26–30.

Joseph, S., Yule, W., and Williams, R. (1997) *Understanding posttraumatic stress*. London: Wiley.

Rachman, S. J. (2004) *Anxiety* (2nd edn). London: Psychology Press.

Starcevic, V. (2004) *Anxiety disorders in adults: A clinical guide*. Oxford: Oxford University Press.

Specific and more critical texts

Armfield, J. M. (2006) Cognitive vulnerability: A model of the etiology of fear. *Clinical Psychology Review*, 26, 746–68.

Brewin, C., and Holmes, E. A. (2003) Psychological theories of posttraumatic stress disorder. *Clinical Psychology Review*, 23, 339–76.

Nutt, D. J., Zohar, J., and Stein, M. (2008) *Posttraumatic stress disorder*. London: Taylor and Francis.

Psychiatry, volume 6, issues 4–7, April 2007. (These issues of *Psychiatry* examine anxiety disorders, providing a thorough review of the area.)

Rapee, R. M., and Spence, S. H. (2004) The aetiology of social phobia: Empirical evidence and an initial model. *Clinical Psychology Review*, 24, 737–67.

Swinson, R. P., Antony, M. M., Rachman, S., and Richter, M. A. (2002) *Obsessive-compulsive disorder: Theory, research and treatment*. New York: Guilford Press.

Vasterling, J. J., and Brewin, C. R. (2005) *Neuropsychology of PTSD: Biological, cognitive and clinical perspectives*. New York: Guilford Press.

Wells, A. (1997) *Cognitive therapy for anxiety disorders: A practice manual and conceptual guide*. Chichester: Wiley.

Wells, A. (2009) *Metacognitive therapy for anxiety and depression*. London: Guilford Press.

Visit **www.pearsoned.co.uk/davidholmes** for a range of resources to support study. Test yourself with multiple choice questions and access a bank of over 100 videos that will bring the topics to life. Video coverage for this chapter includes an interviews with people suffering from PTSD, Panic Disorder, Obsessive Compulsive Disorder, Social Phobia and Agoraphobia.

CHAPTER 13 Sexual and gender identity disorders

Hear Jade discuss her role as a dominatrix. This is one of several videos that explore issues and disorders relevant to this chapter at **www.pearsoned.co.uk/davidholmes**.

Sexual behaviour: a very public secret

The cult TV drama, *The Year of the Sex Olympics* (Elliott, 1968) portrayed a future where a powerful media elite control the population by showing continuous pornography. However, in the real twenty-first century, sexual activity is still of the 'behind closed doors' variety depicted in the film *Eyes Wide Shut* (Kubric, 1999). Although sex has pervaded advertising, TV, film and internet, its private nature appeals to most people. The desire to keep sex personal and hidden has also served to conceal sexual problems, inhibiting assessment and treatment. This chapter will explore some of the difficulties in detecting these problems, which can have profound effects on many aspects of the lives of sufferers.

Early magazines that broached the subject of sexual problems, such as *Forum*, the more journalistic sister publication of *Penthouse*, often revealed a very wide variety of sexual concerns and activities in letters from readers. Paraphilic activity is very much hidden within society and most is not tolerated. Even films dealing lightly with the subject, such as *The Secretary* (Shainberg, 2002), or more seriously, such as *Quills* (Kaufman, 2000) and *Evilenko* (Grieco, 2004) are uncommon and 'difficult' in terms of public acceptance. Thus, as well illustrated by **Malcolm McDowell** as the paedophile Evilenko, the problem of some forensically dangerous paraphilias can remain hidden and therefore undetected. This chapter will also discuss the balance between public condemnation and the forensic need for transparency regarding paraphilic activity.

The romantic aspects of sex and attraction will often override the blemishes and shortcomings of each participant.
Source: David A. Holmes.

Ignorance and anxiety as a result of a lack of sex education, access to advice or specific health services have not just exacerbated sexual disorders but have been considered as causal factors in sexual problems (Ramage, 2006). From being the hidden preserve of religion and writers on moral values, sex and sexual problems have become far more openly addressed in the twenty-first century with explicit and useful information being published in mainstream magazines and newspapers or addressed in other media such as TV or on the internet. This progress has been a result of the pioneering work of a very few early sex researchers who made a largely embarrassed and inhibited public aware of their sexual problems. The change of public and professional attitudes towards sexuality and the study of its problems became evident in the range and specificity of disorders in the diagnostic systems. Sexual problems became organised by stages of sexual activity, and the differences between male and female problems were incorporated into these classifications. In addition, there has been more focus on how these problems interact with clients' interpersonal relationships as well as the individual sexual needs of partners or medical views of their disorders (Crowe, 2006).

There are three divisions of sexual disorders; these are dysfunctions, paraphilias and gender identity disorder. Sexual dysfunctions emanate from physiological and psychological problems that interfere with normal sexual activity. However, the definition of normal in relation to sexuality has led to less stringent criteria than for other *DSM* disorders, which has incurred criticism (Balon, Sergraves and Clayton, 2007). Paraphilias are conditions where orientation to a sexual target is beyond that which is socially or morally acceptable, and where distress may be caused to self or others. These disorders are defined and categorised by the nature of the target for sexual release (see DeSilva, 2006). Those with paraphilias tend to be seen as criminals or at the very least judged morally undesirable, and in the case of paedophilia vilified by the public and media. Gender identity disorder is applied to individuals where the distress of their natural gender assignment is dysphoric to the extent of their wishing to change their gender identity by any means possible (see Green, 2007).

The area of sexual disorders and their treatment is of necessity a broad and weakly delineated area. There are many professionals involved in both clinical and forensic spheres, such as gynaecologists, urologists, endocrinologists and police pathologists, as well as both clinical and forensic psychologists and even sociologists. Areas of concern span from the psychological implications of genital injury to societal reactions to paedophilia. Sexual dysfunction can be conceptualised as the 'hidden distress of society', in that the effects on an individual's motivation or social and occupational functioning may be profound and these difficulties may further impact on other people in their lives without any explicit explanation (Wincze and Carey, 2001). Public forums for such problems in magazines such as *Cosmopolitan* and invited audience shows such as *Tricia* can help educate, but in a sensational way, making some individuals even more embarrassed at revealing their personal problems. The importance to society of this invisible distress may be profound, given that the incidence of sexual problems as a whole has been estimated as being as high as 50 per cent in the general population by studies such as Masters and Johnson (1970). Forensic aspects of sexual disorders usually involve paraphilic behaviour but will extend to pornography and the sex worker industry.

Case study

Philip's secret

For Philip, the thought of marriage to his childhood sweetheart was everything he had hoped for. However, for Janine it was a less enchanted outcome of her deliberate celibacy during those long teenage years, during which Philip had clearly and publicly been less than celibate.

The honeymoon did not develop as Philip had hoped. Janine wanted to talk in the hope that Philip would finally stop covering up his conquests and admit the celibacy vows they had made at 11 years of age had lapsed for him. Finally, after hours of small talk and reminiscences, a rather fumbled attempt at consummation resulted in increasing frustration, bordering on anger for Philip, and anguished confusion for Janine.

On return from honeymoon, Philip's erectile problems still prevented the marriage being consummated, but he was still not about to admit that this had only happened once before, when he was drunk, in an otherwise 'successful' sexual history. Philip desperately wanted this to be his best ever sexual performance, but the more he tried the worse it became and he could really no longer blame Janine. Janine tried to relax him, only to be met with accusations that she should stop being so patronising. Philip began to be angry with himself, as both he and Janine began to anticipate his erectile difficulties and this cued expectation became habitual. Overcoming severe embarrassment, Janine finally managed to coax Philip into attending a local family planning clinic, where the staff proved very helpful in giving the couple leaflets, and also the name of a psychologist specialising in sexual problems. But they recommended first seeing their GP for a referral. Philip made it clear he was not going to the family GP and said he would pay for private consultation.

Natalie left her original profession of nursing to study psychology and eventually trained as a clinical psychologist. She then chose to work with sexual anxiety and, building on her previous training, eventually became a sex therapist. Natalie interviewed the couple and then saw each of them individually, as was her usual pattern of preliminary assessment. Natalie did not have to dig very deeply to uncover Philip's anxiety-provoking secret of having an affair, even though

he suspected that Janine knew. Natalie saw this as an area of anxious focus and, rather than confronting it, decided that her job was to treat the immediate couple interaction and see if that eased other aspects of the relationship. So she applied basic desensitisation and resensitisation in the manner of the classic **sensate focus therapy** of Masters and Johnson, banning (attempts at) sexual intercourse and giving Philip and Janine exercises to carry out together (see later in this chapter). These were designed to reintroduce the couple without the pressure of sexual expectation and to refocus on their giving pleasure to each other more personally.

This worked remarkably rapidly and within a week of successful sexual activity, Philip confessed his anxieties to Janine, who just wanted him to be honest with her. Pharmacological, educational, behavioural and cognitive behavioural therapies have resulted in a great deal of success in the treatment of sexual dysfunction and are mostly limited by the difficulties people face in presenting themselves for treatment and adhering to the intervention given. As illustrated above, the reasons for not engaging with a therapist are often based around fear, embarrassment and uncertainty about their condition.

General issues in sexual and gender identity disorders

Sexual problems have always been underreported and effective treatment has often not been sought due to embarrassment or shame, which is a situation that has progressively improved but never fully remedied. **Krafft-Ebbing** began the study of sexual disorders with his volume titled *Psychopathia sexualis* (Krafft-Ebbing, 1886). However, the history of the study of sex was largely one of ignorance, and in 1938 Alfred Kinsey found himself looking in vain for information on sexual activity to aid his teaching about marriage. Kinsey was thus motivated to produce extensive survey information on the various sexual activities of the public (Kinsey et al., 1948; 1953), who were in turn shocked by the extent of the sexual diversity revealed within Kinsey's sample. This was a time when 'normal sexual behaviour', guided by religion, was for procreation not recreation, and homosexuality was considered a disorder requiring

treatment. Around this time a man had been imprisoned in the USA for excessively demanding sex with his wife, to the extent of more than twice a week! With little idea of what was 'normal', even professionals were unsure of what constituted a disorder (Eskapa, 1989). This situation did little to reduce the reluctance of individuals with sexual difficulties to ask for help.

By the 1960s, sexual knowledge had increased and sexual liberty was seen as a *right* assisted by the arrival of oral contraception. Masters and Johnson (1966; 1970) produced observation data on sexual activity and disorder, which began to be widely read about in popular magazines and replicated by authors of self-help publications. The public became less inhibited about seeking advice and eventually felt comfortable in seeking treatment to increase sexual enjoyment (Spence, 1991). The advent of AIDS (auto-immune deficiency syndrome) and the spread of AIDS awareness in the 1980s somewhat temporarily inhibited sexual liberty, and the limited clinical resources began to restrict treatment to problems causing distress or suffering.

Alfred Kinsey could be credited for starting objective research into sexual activity and sexual disorders.
Source: Getty Images/Time and Life Pictures.

Despite the similarity of the terms, it is important to differentiate between the generic term 'sexual disorders' and the subclassification of 'sexual dysfunctions', as the former includes paraphilias as well as gender identity disorders, whereas the latter refers only to disturbances in the sexual response cycle rather than inappropriate or unwanted desires or states. The three main groupings have some overlap but remain the best means of subclassifying sexual disorders. Precise definitions are important in all mental disorder groupings, but are particularly of concern with sexual disorders where clinical judgement plays a greater role in diagnosis. Loose criteria with regard to distress levels or problem duration will produce anomalies, whereas more stringent criteria will reduce prevalence figures for these disorders (Balon, Sergraves and Clayton, 2007).

Sexual dysfunctions consist of sexual desire disorders, arousal disorders, orgasmic disorders and pain disorders, as well as dysfunction due to medical conditions, substance use and the catch-all category of 'sexual dysfunction not otherwise specified' (American Psychiatric Association, 2000). Most of these classifications are separately classified for male or female dysfunctions. The paraphilias are subclassified as exhibitionism, fetishism, frotteurism, paedophilia, sexual masochism, sexual sadism, transvestic fetishism and voyeurism, as well as paraphilia not otherwise specified. Gender identity disorder is not subclassified but does have specifiers in *DSM-IV-TR*.

Not long after its publication, Potts and Bhugra (1995) argued that the current major revision of the *DSM-IV* (as well as *ICD-10*) fails to demarcate clearly between normal and abnormal behaviour in the coverage of sexual disorders. This has eventually resulted in some salient issues to be addressed in the revisions for *DSM-V*. In addition to clarifying the cut-off between a sexual difficulty and a sexual disorder, the criteria for sexual disorders should be more specific in terms of duration and distress caused, in line with other *DSM* disorders (Balon, Sergraves and Clayton, 2007).

As with other *DSM* disorders, these criteria reduced the need to define explicitly what was normal from the vast range of sexual activities and their associated deficiencies or excesses. By the 1990s, rationality had replaced both the repression and enthusiasm of former years, but most sexually transmitted diseases (STDs) began to increase rapidly amongst younger people in the 2000s, at a time when services for STDs had been reduced in the UK.

Sexuality and sexual disorders have become a major subject of media interest as mainstream TV, radio, newspapers and magazines as well as the internet have become increasingly liberal in their pursuit of audience and readership figures. Unfortunately, the pursuit of sensationalism does not always lead to realistic representation of sexual disorders. This in itself can contribute to the perpetuation of unwarranted fears amongst sufferers, even in the twenty-first century. However, it is a climate in which individuals are more aware of such disorders, which was far from the case only a century earlier (Harvey, Wenzel and Sprecher, 2004).

Classification of sexual disorders

Sexual disorders are classified by *DSM-IV* into three main groups: **sexual dysfunctions**, **paraphilias** and **gender identity disorders** (American Psychiatric Association, 2000).

Self-test questions

- What problems existed for sex research in the 1930s?
- Why was Kinsey's research of strategic importance?
- What factors distinguish sexual disorders from other disorder classifications?
- What three main divisions are there in sexual disorders?

Sexual dysfunctions

The *DSM* and *ICD* classificatory systems are very similar for sexual dysfunctions, but the *ICD* has some additional classifications regarding 'lack of sexual enjoyment' and also a form of hyperphilia (Crowe, 2006). Most sexual dysfunctions are **hypophilias** or *less* than normal sexual activity. The term **hyperphilia** represents more than normal sexual activity and is recognised in *ICD-10* as 'excessive sex drive', but it is not represented in *DSM-IV* (Crowe, 2006). Hyperphilias tend to receive far less research interest, although they can be damaging to relationships if the partner does not enjoy the level of activity. Apart from the disorder classifications themselves, sexual dysfunctions are divided in other ways that are listed as subtypes in *DSM-IV-TR*, as follows.

- **Lifelong type** or **primary dysfunctions** have *always* affected the sufferer during their sexual history. Alternatively, **acquired type** or **secondary dysfunctions** are problems that have only developed after a period of normal functioning (American Psychiatric Association, 2000).

- A **generalised type** or **complete dysfunction** is one that occurs with all partners or forms of stimulation and in all situations. In the case of the **situational type** or **partial dysfunction**, this only pertains to *some* situations, partners or prompts, such as a man only having erectile failure when having an affair but not with his partner (American Psychiatric Association, 2000).

- Some **stages** or phases of the sexual act are used to subdivide sexual dysfunction disorders (see below).

- **Males** and **females** can both suffer common problems affecting their sexual functioning or enjoyment: for example, either gender may lack sexual desire or fail to orgasm. However, some sexual disorders have differing presentations in males or females, and the descriptors for some dysfunctions have always been sex-specific, such as 'erectile disorder'.

In addition to these, it is very important to identify dysfunctions that arise directly from the consequences of medical conditions, substance use or the natural process of ageing, before assuming other aetiologies. *DSM-IV-TR* assumes that the disorders in this section are due either to **psychological factors** alone or to **combined factors**. In the case of combined factors leading to the disorder, medical factors only partly contribute to the disorder, as if they were to primarily account for the disorder the diagnosis would be **sexual dysfunction due to a general medical condition** (American Psychiatric Association, 2000). This is a difficult area for sexual disorders, where medical conditions may not be obvious and sexual dysfunction may be the first sign of the underlying condition. Research into physiological and neurological correlates of sexual function and dysfunction have been advanced by techniques such as brain imaging during the stages of the sexual response cycle (Levin and Riley, 2006; see the Focus box).

Focus

Stages of the sexual response cycle

DSM-IV-TR divides the sexual response cycle into four stages, which are as follows.

- **Desire** is the initial phase of wanting sexual activity and may be accompanied by fantasies and expectations. Some authors consider there to be two components to the desire phase: a spontaneous or proactive form of desire and a reactive form that can be thought of as being a reaction to physiological arousal (Levin and Riley, 2006). In addition, the general urge to be sexual or 'sex-drive' has been thought of as distinct from the desire to be sexual with a particular person or sexual desire (Crowe, 2006).

- **Arousal or excitement** involves the interaction between psychological pleasure and physiological reactions such as male penile tumescence leading to erection and female vaginal lubrication and

expansion. This interaction prepares and encourages sexual intercourse between the sexual partners. The 'plateau phase' identified and thought of as distinct by Masters and Johnson (1966) is now incorporated into this stage (Levin and Riley, 2006).

- **Orgasm** is the climax of sexual pleasure where ejaculation is inevitable for males and part of the outer wall of the vagina contracts in females. This marks the release of sexual tension and is accompanied by rhythmic contractions of the perineal muscles (American Psychiatric Association, 2000).

- **Resolution** is the post-orgasmic phase, with muscular relaxation and a sense of euphoria. Females may respond further at this stage but males are usually unable to gain a further erection or to orgasm (referred to as a refractory period for arousal).

Some of the stages or phases of the sexual process in the Focus box have been used to categorise the disorders, namely the **desire**, **arousal** and **orgasm phases**, in addition to less stage-specific problems, such as **sexual pain**. Each of the sexual dysfunction disorders can have the above subtypes: lifelong versus acquired; generalised versus situational; due to psychological factors versus due to combined factors, which can be specified (American Psychiatric Association, 2000). The current specific sexual dysfunction disorders are as follows.

Sexual desire disorders

This sexual phase is the initial interest in having sex: not simply caring for a partner, but actually wanting to become erotically aroused and initiate or accept a sexual advance. Sexual satisfaction at later stages of the sexual process can act as a reinforcer for sexual desire (Levin and Riley, 2006), but it cannot reinforce if progress beyond desire dysfunction cannot be overcome. The two disorders listed for this phase must cause significant distress to be diagnosed as disorders and can apply to males and females without change in criteria. As previously mentioned, *ICD-10* has the category of **excessive sexual drive** in this context, which is not found in *DSM-IV-TR* (Crowe, 2006).

Hypoactive sexual desire disorder

The presence of this disorder indicates an absence of desire for, or very little interest in, sexual activity. There is also a lack of sexual fantasy and this lack of desire causes marked distress or interpersonal difficulty (American Psychiatric Association, 2000). It may be important to know if the lack of desire is restricted to one partner, situation or activity, or whether it is more generalised. As with most disorders, it is not diagnosed if the lack of desire is the product of drug or alcohol use or some other known medical condition. The sufferer does not initiate sexual activity but may be prompted by a partner and engage with reluctance, appearing to be more frequently active than their lack of desire would indicate (American Psychiatric Association, 2000). This interaction between a demanding partner and one with less desire necessitates both partners being assessed to explore if it is a case of one partner with hypoactive desire or the other having excessive expectations. Alternatively, it may be that both are incompatibly placed on a continuum of desire, but that neither could be described as abnormal in this respect (Crowe, 2006).

In hypoactive sexual desire cases, it is important to differentiate acquired from lifelong, and generalised from situational subtypes, as these may indicate different causal factors and treatments. The disorder can affect both males and females, and the passive absence of desire needs to be distinguished from active sexual aversion (Wylie, 2007). The prevalence in women varies considerably between 17 and 55 per cent and increases with age, but is less common in men until they are over 60 years (Lewis et al., 2004). Hypoactive desire can be related to emotional distress or the onset of depression, particularly with accompanying anhedonic symptoms (Crowe, 2006). It is also associated with relationship problems, including difficulties in initiation and maintenance as well marital disruption and dissatisfaction. Lifelong forms of the disorder begin in puberty, but the acquired form is more common with a later onset in adulthood (American Psychiatric Association, 2000).

Sexual aversion disorder

In sexual aversion disorder there is recurrent and active avoidance of sexual contact as the central characteristic. The individual has an aversion to genital contact, rather than a lack of interest in having sex. Disgust, anxiety and fear can be experienced to different degrees and may be a reaction to specific aspects of sexual contact, such as penetration or lubrication, or may be more widely focused on all aspects of intimacy, such as kissing (American Psychiatric Association, 2000). Strategies to avoid potential sexual contact, such as neglect of appearance, being over-attentive to children, sleeping early or over-involvement with other activities, may lead to relationship strain, dissatisfaction or relationship termination. Even though the criteria met for sexual aversion may qualify the reaction as a specific phobia, the latter diagnosis is not given, even though other anxiety features may be present, such as panic attacks (American Psychiatric Association, 2000).

Arousal dysfunctions

Physiological changes prepare both males and females for sexual activity, some of which are similar, as in the response of vasocongestion, and others of which are sex specific, such as vaginal lubrication. One paradox in the process of the sexual act, particularly for males, relates to the need for both arousal and relaxation based on the opposing sympathetic and parasympathetic autonomic responses. Thus, sexual arousal in the form of penile erection also requires a level of relaxation. Irrespective of the cause, failing to become aroused or maintain arousal can have severe psychological effects on esteem and may become predictive of future dysfunction as a result of anticipation (Wincze and Carey, 2001). Arousal needs to be differentiated from desire, which precedes it. Arousal can be divided into the components of subjective mental arousal and physiological arousal (Levin and Riley, 2006).

Female sexual arousal disorder

Female sexual arousal disorder involves a persistent or recurrent failure to become physically sexually aroused, indicated by blood flow to the pelvic area, vaginal lubrication and vaginal and clitoral expansion, or for this arousal to dissipate before the end of the sex act (American Psychiatric Association, 2000). Lack of female arousal, particularly lubrication, can lead to painful sexual experiences, which will impact on levels of sexual desire and lead to aversion, as well as making orgasm difficult if not impossible to attain. Subjective sexual arousal in sufferers may be diminished or absent, and all these primary and secondary effects are very likely to severely undermine the sufferer's relationship with her sexual partner (American Psychiatric Association, 2000). Female sexual arousal disorder should be clearly differentiated from arousal deficits due to medical conditions, which should always be diagnosed as **sexual dysfunction due to a general medical condition** (American Psychiatric Association, 2000).

Historically, this disorder has received little research, as it is '**non-fatal**' in that it does not prevent intercourse or procreation. Such disregard for female sexual enjoyment is disappearing and innovative evidence-based therapeutic approaches to female sexual disorders of arousal and desire are emerging worldwide (Basson et al., 2005). Subjective feelings of arousal tend to be simultaneous with physiological arousal in males, but in females genital or physical arousal may occur without notable subjective sexual arousal (Levin and Riley, 2006). This physical arousal in females is shown to diverse cues such as those that accompany long-term relationships and even to stimuli they do not like (Levin and Riley, 2006). This asymmetry in male and female arousal could be associated with the female's need for such long-term aspects to their bonding in evolutionary terms.

Male erectile disorder

Erectile disorder involves the persistent or recurrent failure to achieve or maintain a sufficiently erect penis to complete the sex act. The degree and pervasiveness of the problem needs to cause sufficient distress and interpersonal difficulties, as well as potential marital failure due to non-consummation, to warrant the diagnosis of a disorder (American Psychiatric Association, 2000). Biologically, an erection is a haemodynamic response in the two encased corpora cavernosa and the corpus spongiosum (Levin and

Riley, 2006). Sympathetic autonomic activity keeps the penis flaccid and sexual stimulation relaxes the cavernous muscle leading to engorgement, which progressively closes the blood outlets, leading to penile rigidity (see Levin and Riley, 2006). Nitric oxide stimulates the enzyme that produces cyclic guanosine monophosphate, which lowers calcium levels, producing the relaxation of the cavernous muscle and erection (Udelson, 2007).

This complex interplay of sympathetic, parasympathetic and vasoactive responses is susceptible to subversion from many sources, including psychological interference (for detail on erection function, see Udelson, 2007). Forms of erectile failure vary in that some individuals may never achieve an erection without intervention, whilst others experience masturbatory, nocturnal or morning tumescence but not for intercourse, and there are those who lose erections on penetration or with only some partners. Different degrees of dysfunction can indicate differing aetiologies, ranging from previous failure, inability to relax, guilt or substance effects to a wide range of medical conditions, all contributing to what is a common source of complaint for males. It is estimated that there are 150 million sufferers worldwide (see Jackson, Gillies and Osterloh, 2005).

Symptoms and contributory factors are greatly exacerbated by the so called 'fatal' outcome, which for many individuals can be interpreted to mean that full intercourse and procreation are prevented. Thus research into the treatment of erectile failure has historically outstripped that for female arousal disorder. However, such conditions have benefited from pharmacological advances made in the late twentieth century (Carson, 2003). The most revolutionary treatment for erectile disorder has been **Sildenafil citrate** or **Viagra**, which has been considered to be a 'magic bullet' for the condition in accurately targeting symptoms, and has been used by well in excess of 20 million sufferers and rising in over 110 countries (Carson, 2003). By inhibiting the enzyme that breaks down cyclic guanosine monophosphate, the latter remains, maintaining the erectile response and smooth muscle relaxation. Other type 5 phosphodiesterase inhibitors in similar use are tadalafil and vardenafil, marketed as Cialis and Levitra respectively (Alpert, 2005).

Viagra and its successors have almost entirely replaced a plethora of vacuum tubes, splints creams and direct penile injections, as well as displacing many non-pharmacological treatments (Jackson, Gillies and Osterloh, 2005). However, although it tends to facilitate rather than prompt the sexual response, it has still been regarded as 'mechanical' in its effects by some, but this level of argument would apply to any pharmacological intervention. Unlike previous forms of pharmacological intervention, the drug only provides an erectile response during sexual stimulation (Jackson, Gillies and Osterloh, 2005). As with most medications, however, Viagra does have side-effects such as headache, dyspepsia and abnormal vision, but these are remarkably few given the therapeutic efficacy (Carson, 2003). Many cases of the disorder that had formerly been attributed to psychological factors became 'instantly resolved' by administering the drug, thus pointing towards a reinterpretation of erectile disorder aetiology in terms of biological rather than psychological factors (Jackson, Gillies and Osterloh, 2005). However, the relative certainty of erectile function and the confidence that manifests in clients may mean that psychological fears and associations would be countered by those secondary psychological effects of the drug. Thus, regardless of the aetiology of the erectile dysfunction, whether psychological, concerning physical condition (diabetes) or psychiatric (depression), Viagra provides a uniquely successful pharmacological intervention (Jackson, Gillies and Osterloh, 2005).

Reviews of the effectiveness of these selective vasodilators drugs have gathered data from both double-blind and placebo-controlled studies. Large-scale physician surveys have provided empirical evidence that sildenafil compounds are highly effective in targeting erectile dysfunction and have a low incidence of adverse effects (Jackson, Gillies and Osterloh, 2005). Sairam et al. (2002) found a 91 per cent success rate with 80 per cent of those treated wishing to continue with Viagra, although only half of sufferers were eligible for this intervention under UK National Health Service criteria. Ineligibility may be a failure to qualify for inclusion due to severity or conditions such as diabetes, or exclusion due to cardiovascular contraindications (Sairam et al., 2002). Not only has Viagra made significant improvements in erectile dysfunction, but it has been found to impact in other areas of the sufferer's life, such as improved self-esteem and confidence (Heiman et al., 2007). A meta-analysis of ten randomised controlled trials re-affirmed the drug's consistent highly significant performance above that of placebo and its acceptability to those using it (Moore, Edwards and McQuay, 2002).

From a forensic perspective, Viagra and other similarly acting drugs have become major recreational drugs for some individuals, with Viagra possibly becoming the most commonly abused prescription drug (Alpert, 2005). The drug has become widely available through the global market provided by the internet, where it is offered without prescription. Manufacture, supply and use of these drugs in such markets will clearly lack medical supervision or regulation and can be a health threat, particularly in the context of the abuse of these peripheral vasodilators with other substances. Combined abuse of methamphetamine and Viagra amongst homosexual males has also been associated with high-risk sexual practices, and the abuse of Viagra alone has resulted in a 2 to 5.7-fold increase in unsafe sex (Swearingen and Klausner, 2005). Alpert (2005) expressed concern that such risks for sexually transmitted diseases (STDs), including HIV infection, may be reflected amongst heterosexual users and abusers of Viagra, as well as there being the potential for combined drug use to contribute to the development of more virulent strains of HIV and STDs.

Orgasm dysfunctions

A persistent or recurrent failure to achieve a sexual orgasm or an unreasonable delay in doing so following normal sexual excitement can affect both males and females. This was previously known as inhibited female/male orgasm and takes into account the age, experience and level of stimulation received (American Psychiatric Association, 2000). This failure can cause marked distress or relationship difficulties. As with arousal disorders, there has been a prioritisation of male orgasmic disorder in research as a result of the view that sex is primarily for reproduction, thus referring to the outcome that a male needs to orgasm to impregnate but failure of a female to orgasm does not prevent conception.

Female orgasmic disorder

The diagnosis of female orgasmic disorder relies on clinical judgement, which can take into account the known factors such as age and sexual experience (American Psychiatric Association, 2000). The female form of orgasmic disorder is a surprisingly common complaint and tends to persist during the lifetime. About 15 per cent of females never have orgasms and are referred to as being anorgasmic (Balon and Segraves, 2005), which also tends to become a lifelong condition (Cole, 1988). Intermittent orgasm difficulties are very common amongst females for a variety of physical, behavioural and cognitive reasons, but these occasional orgasmic problems need to be persistent and incur marked distress to reach the threshold for diagnosis of female orgasmic disorder (American Psychiatric Association, 2000). Few psychological or physiological factors are associated with this condition in females, even those that impair sexual arousal such as diabetes. However, other disorders such as major depressive disorder should be eliminated as the primary condition prior to a diagnosis of female orgasmic disorder (American Psychiatric Association, 2000).

Sexual experience tends to increase a female's ability to orgasm, and thus orgasmic disorder may be more common earlier in life (American Psychiatric Association, 2000).

Females who have achieved orgasm are unlikely to lose this ability unless trauma such as rape or a poor relationship intervene (American Psychiatric Association, 2000). Thus, education as to how to achieve orgasm may be a simple but effective intervention in this disorder. The use of vibrators has enabled many females to achieve orgasm for the first time and also provided them with an insight into the factors leading to orgasm. Female attitudes towards their sexuality and sexual needs may prevent a female from admitting to a lack of orgasmic satisfaction and inhibit her seeking treatment. Myths regarding traditional views of 'respectable females' not having overt sexual needs, as well as more liberated but still erroneous expectations of modern females having to be universally sexually competent and skilled, both undermine a sufferer's ability to seek help for their problem (Spence, 1991). Education as to realistic expectations and the prevalence of orgasmic problems amongst others may encourage females to take a more active role with regard to their orgasmic needs.

Education on the importance of the female orgasm and requirements for producing it should also be directed towards sexual partners, who not only provide sexual stimulation but also need to make an encouraging emotional environment available for orgasmic activity. Female orgasmic disorder has sometimes been linked to male premature ejaculation, which in this case may be the primary condition that makes orgasm difficult for the female. Therapeutic interventions for the sufferer focus on attitude change using **cognitive behavioural therapy** (CBT) as well as supportive education and skill training for the sufferer (Meston et al., 2004). Anxiety reduction is important in orgasmic problems and can be addressed by the **sensate focus** approach (see below). This is helped by behavioural exercises including directed masturbation as well as desensitisation exercises, particularly where the disorder is acquired and there is some aversion to touching her own genitalia (Meston et al., 2004).

Male orgasmic disorder

Male orgasmic disorder is characterised by the persistent absence of, or significant delay in, achieving orgasm (and thus ejaculation). It is most frequently the case that orgasm can be achieved through non-coital approaches such as manual or oral stimulation, and in some males prolonged stimulation of this type may allow coital orgasm (American Psychiatric Association, 2000). The extended efforts made by the sufferer often become pleasureless and 'mechanical' to the sufferer, which can also be painful to the female. This can lead to marital stress as conception may be impossible by normal means, and this interpersonal

friction can be exacerbated by orgasm being easily reached by non-vaginal means (American Psychiatric Association, 2000). Orgasm can still occur in the absence of ejaculation or full erection in males. The absence of orgasm or ejaculation, **anorgasmia** and anejaculation respectively, tends to indicate a biological failure of emission, but in some cases the process may be inhibited by psychological factors (McMahon et al., 2004).

Premature ejaculation

Premature ejaculation refers to the male sexual partner's inability to delay orgasm and ejaculation for a reasonable period on or shortly after vaginal penetration. An important issue is the concept of what constitutes too brief a period of time, as distress and interpersonal difficulty may be evident in either or both partners and expectations may differ between partners as well as across sufferers. Original surveys revealed that the majority of men ejaculated within 2 minutes of penetration, in a sample where only 6 per cent considered this to be a problem (Kinsey et al., 1948). Ultimately, what is a reasonable delay is up to the individual couple and this is dependent on subjective time and level of satisfaction rather than any artificial 'stopwatch quota' or performance competitiveness (Balon and Segraves, 2005) – situations that could be seen as less satisfactory than having premature ejaculation (Cole and Dryden, 1988). However, studies of premature ejaculation require more precise criteria to make meaningful measurements, and with latencies varying between 1 and 7 minutes in diagnosed individuals, an operational definition is elusive and consequently clinical research is scarce (McMahon et al., 2004). The condition of premature ejaculation can inhibit males without partners from seeking intimate relationships.

Age and experience tend to increase control over orgasm for many men, as they do with women, but for some the problem persists and a few acceptably functioning males then lose their ability to delay ejaculation. As with female orgasmic disorder, education and the introduction of physical techniques can help some individuals to extend their pre-ejaculatory period. The **squeeze/pause technique** consists of firmly squeezing from each side of the coronal ridge of the penis several times early in intercourse, which removes the urge to ejaculate, with some loss of erection. In order not to remove the penis during this 'pause and squeeze' process, the base of the penis can be squeezed with the female on top of the male to facilitate this. However, this is less effective than the use of topical creams and the use of **selective serotonin reuptake inhibitors** (SSRIs), particularly **paroxetine** (McMahon et al., 2005). These interventions can improve sexual control in general, but for many sufferers delaying ejaculation during masturbation is not a problem; it is coitus that induces rapid orgasm (American Psychiatric Association, 2000). McMahon et al. (2005) examined the role of Viagra in the treatment of premature ejaculation in the UK and found the increased sexual confidence and control felt by males taking the medication was accompanied by reported improvement in control over ejaculation. However, measures of ejaculatory latencies were not significantly longer during coital intercourse in this study, although post-ejaculatory refractory time (the time taken to be ready for sexual intercourse again after orgasm) was decreased, allowing for a second, more controlled ejaculation (McMahon et al., 2005; McMahon et al., 2004).

Case study
Female orgasmic disorder

Jeanette had never been inhibited when it came to chatting up young men in the office or local bars, until she met George. George was not the usual young 'bloke' with whom Jeanette was commonly seen, being older and more sophisticated. As their relationship blossomed, George became aware of the large number and rather juvenile nature of Jeanette's past relationships, but as someone who genuinely loved her, he pushed these thoughts aside and eventually stunned her with a marriage proposal. Her family had not only accepted George being older, but realised the stabilising influence this was having on Jeanette's somewhat promiscuous past behaviour.

Unlike the youths from Jeanette's past, George was experienced in giving as well as receiving sexual stimulation and satisfaction. This was something of a new experience for Jeanette. However, based on his experience, George came to the conclusion that she was sexually receptive and very attentive, but was only pretending to reach any kind of sexual climax. This concerned George deeply, as he loved her and his own pleasure was secondary, in his view of their relationship, to mutual satisfaction. George was no expert in such problems but had been aware of the fact that females did not orgasm that often and a few felt the need to feign a climax. He was sensitive but very direct in approaching the subject with Jeanette, who at first protested but then became tearful as George explained how her post-orgasm behaviour tended to give away her pretence.

The couple began to try to reapproach their sexual encounters with honesty and some communication over Jeanette's real feelings. This advanced their relationship greatly but the problem remained, prompting George to reveal his own residual naivety in thinking that all females must be able to orgasm eventually. Jeanette's fears of seeing a psychosexual therapist were swept aside by George, who was subsequently sent out of the session by experienced therapist Edwina when the problem had been made explicit. As Edwina suspected, Jeanette had never been able to orgasm whilst trying to impress the local boys or attempting to be what she thought George really wanted in a wife. Her efforts to perform and control in sex left her own needs and feelings very much in the background.

Jeanette found the 'homework' she was given somewhat embarrassing to explain to George, but was surprised how he accepted the need for her to learn about her ability to be aroused and how this differed from reaching orgasm. It was Jeanette who found trying to reach orgasm and use a vibrator on her own very inhibiting. It was after about a week that George offered to be part of this skill training, and in his company, Jeanette found non-coital stimulation less inhibiting and eventually felt herself losing control and climaxing for the first time in her life. This success was not the breakthrough both partners had assumed, however, as it was a couple of weeks before the experience was repeated and around 6 months before Jeanette climaxed during intercourse. Both accepted that Jeanette's satisfaction in this respect would be sporadic, but for both George and Jeanette the integrity of their intimacy finally matched the love and concern each had for the other.

Sexual pain disorders

These disorders are characterised by pain or severe discomfort associated with sexual intercourse, which can occur before, after or, most often, during coitus (American Psychiatric Association, 2000). This can lead to **sexual avoidance** via classical conditioning (see Chapter 3) of the discomfort to be associated with sexual activity, leading to the expectation of sexual contact producing an avoidant response. Pain can originate from physiological states or reactions, but in all cases it leads to marked distress or interpersonal difficulty and tends to follow a chronic course (American Psychiatric Association, 2000).

Dyspareunia

Dyspareunia is genital pain of variable intensity that is associated with sexual intercourse, usually during but also before or after coitus. It can affect males or females and is not exclusively due to a medical condition, substance use or **vaginismus** (see below). Pain qualities can vary over the sex act, particularly for females, but if it causes significant distress or problems between partners, dyspareunia is diagnosed (American Psychiatric Association, 2000). Most patients will report this to a medical physician and it is relatively rarely considered a mental health issue by sufferers. Dyspareunia can be comorbid with other sexual dysfunctions except vaginismus.

Vaginismus

Vaginismus is an involuntary contraction of the outer **perineal muscles** of the vagina that is persistent or recurring. This usually occurs when penetration is attempted and may prevent the insertion of objects such as tampons as well as sexual penetration including use of a finger, which may be attempted with painful results (American Psychiatric Association, 2000). This spasm can occur merely as a result of anticipated penetration, not just attempted approaches. As with erectile problems, interpersonal conflict and distress are both diagnostic criteria as well as expected outcomes, given the improbability of normal intercourse. Non-consummation of marriage due to vaginismus has led to divorce in the past and it is more common in the case of younger women, negative views of sex, and histories of sexual trauma or abuse (American Psychiatric Association, 2000). The response may be triggered by forms of contact such as medical examinations, and may be painful in its intensity.

Onset of vaginismus is usually highly correlated with first attempts at vaginal contact and tends to be self-perpetuating, becoming chronic unless there is intervention. Traumatic sexual events or medical problems may instigate a latent onset (American Psychiatric Association, 2000). Progressive insertion and acceptance of objects of increasing size whilst relaxing can help to reduce this spasm. This may be achieved by the partner progressively using fingers or more usually the use of purpose-made progressively larger dilators.

Aetiology and treatment of sexual dysfunctions

Aetiology of sexual dysfunctions

The causes of sexual disorders include faulty learning experiences but often with biological abnormalities as a catalyst. Problems that arise as a result of learning, such as the association of anxiety with sexual activity, are usually amenable to behavioural treatments in reducing the association and countering the anxiety. However, cognitive behavioural explanations of erectile failure in terms of performance anxiety (Bancroft, 1999) as well as psychodynamic hypotheses in terms of a number of oedipal conflict fears, such as those of castration or incest (Janssen, 1985), are all easily addressed by the biological treatment Viagra, bringing these psychological explanations into question (Jackson, Gillies and Osterloh, 2005). Although Kinzl, Traweger and Biebl (1995) draw attention to family dysfunction as well as sexual abuse in childhood in the aetiology of sexual disorders, these disorders are too prevalent to be explained by this factor and must commonly occur in its absence. Thus, the underlying effects of biological factors cannot be dismissed in the case of sexual dysfunctions, especially in view of the effectiveness of some biological treatments.

Biological factors

Some sexual disorders are exclusively a result of biological factors or secondary to other disorders such as **diabetes** or **depression**. In such cases, the combined factors subtype should be added to the diagnosis (American Psychiatric Association, 2000). Biological explanations of sexual dysfunctions can be complex, as they often involve diverse biological processes at many levels of analysis and differing systems within the body. Although much research has been conducted, the focus for this has often been from the perspective of commercial interest in producing pharmacological solutions. Davis et al. (2004) have identified the need for much more detailed trials of such interventions to refine endocrine treatment products for females, which is a major pharmaceutical market.

The endocrine system plays a key role in sexual functioning and therefore sexual dysfunctions in males and females (Morales et al., 2004; Davis et al., 2004). In a basic sense, testosterone raises sexual desire and oxytocin promotes bonding, whereas raised prolactin levels can lower desire, and other endocrine substances such as oestrogen, progesterone and glucocorticosteroids also influence sexual behaviour in females. Changes in the activity of these substances and their interactions with neurotransmitters throughout the central and peripheral nervous as well as vascular systems clearly influence sexual desire, arousal and performance (Morales et al., 2004; Davis et al., 2004). However, interventions based on endocrine function are limited by the interactivity of these systems, in that simple pharmacological treatments produce cascading effects that are widespread rather than targeted or localised.

Neurological correlates of sexual behaviour have been identified by examining patients with brain lesions. Key brain regions associated with specific aspects of human sexual functions include both cortical and subcortical areas, and in terms of sexual motivation the amygdala is of crucial importance and the mesial temporal lobe has a prominent role in sexual excitement (Baird et al., 2007). The hypothalamus also has a key function, which is linked to its central role in endocrine regulation. These and other key structures are thought to be sequentially coordinated through the stages of sexual behaviour (Baird et al., 2007). Thus, dysfunctions may not simply be a result of damage or failure in one or more key brain areas, but may also result from disruption of this sequencing. Although case studies of brain lesions have limited external validity (see Chapter 5), many of these findings tend to be replicated when viewed across a number of studies, although there are conflicts between some studies over which brain areas are activated or deactivated (Levin and Riley, 2006).

Psychological factors

Many sexual dysfunctions are a result of anxiety and may be treated as anxiety disorders. Sexual activity often relies on a fine balance of the opposing **sympathetic** and **parasympathetic** branches of the **autonomic nervous system**, a balance that is easily disrupted by anxiety (see Levin and Riley, 2007). The relationship between dysfunction and anxiety is bidirectional, as sexual dysfunction can also be a source of anxiety, producing a reciprocating cycle of anxiety and sexual dysfunction. Cognitive behavioural therapy is most successful here, especially when the disorder results from a 'self-fulfilling prophecy' following a previous problematic experience. Expectation of dysfunction may not just lead directly to arousal and performance problems, but will also impact on desire and sexual initiative. Thus cognitive behavioural intervention is necessary even if the origin of the dysfunction is physiological due to the secondary effects of dysfunctional thinking.

Life-cycle and evolutionary factors

Sexual dysfunctions in men increase with advancing age, which may be compounded by increasing levels of age-associated illness (Lewis et al., 2004). In women, sexual dysfunctions vary less with age and sexual pain may decrease in prevalence with advancing years, although increasing ill health will still impact on sexual function (Hayes and

Focus

Evolutionary strategies and orgasmic disorder

Evolutionary, or **ultimate,** explanations have contributed to the area of human sexuality and given insights beyond the **proximal** (e.g. genetic or biological) **explanations** above (see Cartwright, 2000). One curious evolutionary explanation of female orgasmic disorder sees it as not being a true disorder but a product of what could be described as female 'quality control' (see Cole and Dryden, 1988). Females of a number of species have the clitoral 'equipment' and can be stimulated to orgasm, but this rarely (if ever) happens during intercourse as it is usually too brief. In humans, 50 per cent of females have orgasmic problems but only a minority of females see orgasm as important in sex and often view it as secondary to intimacy or penetration.

One answer to the female orgasm falling into evolutionary disuse is that not reaching orgasm places the female in control of exactly whom she may conceive to and when she may conceive. This is an extension of the 'sperm wars' view of natural selection, which assumes that females are subconsciously seeking the best 'material' for their offspring and that males compete on many levels to impregnate. Control over coital orgasm and its delay in females has been found to regulate the number of sperm accepted and rejected from a partner (Singh et al., 1998).

Dennerstein, 2005). In females there is a decrease in sexual activity, frequency of orgasms and desire, which may not be seen as dysfunctions and thus not be reported as such (Hayes and Dennerstein, 2005). Health risk factors for sexual dysfunction in men and women include diabetes mellitus, cardiovascular disease, genitourinary disease as well as general and psychiatric health (Lewis et al., 2004).

Treatment of sexual dysfunctions

Sexual disorders demonstrate almost the complete range of therapies available; in many cases, a number of therapies are applied in treating the same disorder. Clients are usually carefully assessed first, with initial examinations to eliminate biological abnormalities or diseases as well as alcohol or drug complications, which may often be the result of **self-medication** for anxiety. Fedoroff, Kuban and Bradford (2009) has also emphasised the importance of taking a full sexual history for these and other disorders so that potentially crucial factors are not overlooked.

Most people treated for sexual dysfunctions are in a relationship, but some are not, and a therapist is presented with difficulties when dealing with an individual without a partner (Crowe, 2006). This can be approached in a somewhat controversial way by the use of **sexual surrogate partners** (see the Focus box on p. 394). Sexual dysfunctions in gay and lesbian couples have been researched little, but they tend to follow similar patterns to those of heterosexual couples, although often under greater external social pressure, and equally benefit from interventions such as that of Masters and Johnson below (Bhugra and Wright, 2007).

Physical interventions

Biomedical therapies have been steadily on the increase for a number of years (Leiblum, 1996) and include physical interventions such as surgery to correct physical abnormalities and surgical implants that can provide controllable artificial erections for erectile disorder. Mechanical devices such as **vacuum tubes** for inducing erections may seem crude, but the equally crude device the vibrator has become a sophisticated and commonplace sex-aid in the non-dysfunctional population. **Vibrators** have been very successful in aiding females with orgasmic disorder, particularly in chronic and **treatment refractory** (i.e. treatment resistant) cases. Vibrators have been incorporated into **directed masturbation**, a therapeutic approach by LoPiccolo and Libitz (1972) for females to explore their own body and learn how to produce and sustain pleasure to orgasm, prior to having a partner join in with this sexual momentum. Life-size functional adult dolls have emerged over the last decade, providing single males with a realistic if non-organic partner. However, this may be encouraging fetishism and discouraging social skill development.

Drug therapy

Pharmacological interventions for sexual dysfunctions can take the form of anxiolytics to reduce anxiety, 5 phosphodiesterase inhibitors such as **sifdenafil** (Viagra) to produce erections and the various hormone therapies for a range of dysfunctions. Even though it is known to impair libido, fluoxetine has been effective for treating premature ejaculation, but other drug types have also proven useful

Masters and Johnson were trailblazers in the area of treating sexual dysfunctions and their names have become inextricably tied to some interventions.
Source: Corbis/Bettmann.

for this disorder, such as Viagra (McMahon et al., 2005). When approved in the USA for use in 1998, Viagra (sildenafil citrate) made a great deal of impact, not only on erectile problems, but also on other sexual dysfunctions and secondarily on clients' confidence in other areas of their lives (Heiman et al., 2007; Jackson et al., 2005). There are some caveats and side-effects with sildenafil, such as cardiovascular stress, which can be of concern in the older target age group. However, sildenafil and its variants have provided a remarkably effective treatment for erectile disorder in evaluation studies (Moore, Edwards and McQuay, 2002), and in 2007 they were trialled over the counter by Boots the Chemist in Manchester, UK.

Hormones therapies such as androgen therapy to increase arousal and orgasm are less specific in their effects, but for some dysfunctions they can be applied locally, as in vaginal oestrogen cream used for dyspareunia (see Davis et al., 2004; Morales et al., 2004). The role dopamine plays in rewarding aspects of sexual behaviour is well established (Giuliano and Allard, 2001). The use of these reward systems to improve the sexual responsiveness of men, but not women, has been achieved by the use of levodopa to influence dopamine activity (Both et al., 2005). The lack of effect in females may be due to differential hormonal interractions with the dopamine changes between the genders (Both et al., 2005). In some cases, the use of pharmacological interventions can be temporary, with improved functioning being either self-sustaining or supported by psychological interventions.

Cognitive behavioural therapies

CBT developed from behaviour therapy, which has for many years formed the basis of desensitisation approaches to anxiety associated with sex (as well as aversion therapy for paraphilias; see the next section). When combined with cognitive approaches as CBT, this sound basis of behaviourism, whilst also addressing the many cognitive distortions and anticipatory fears in sexual dysfunctions, provides a powerful tool for intervention in this disorder area. CBT techniques are highly effective for some dysfunctions and form the basis of therapies that are carried out under a variety of names, often combined with other techniques.

In their conjoint therapy, Masters and Johnson (1970) dealt with couples, attempting to take their clients' attention away from their dysfunction and instead encouraging them to focus on their relationship, emphasising that even individual problems can only have shared solutions. Their **sensate focus** technique removed the anxieties producing dysfunction and refocused their attention on the giving and receiving of pleasurable sensation by the participating

couple. This involved initially banning intercourse, which had three effects: removing the fear of failure; reducing anxieties due to anticipation of problems; and making intercourse 'forbidden' and therefore attractive. The couple are then given non-genital touching exercises (i.e. whilst relaxed), which become more erotic over the sessions until they transgress the ban or progress to further stages of control being given to the female over engaging in and progress during coitus (Masters and Johnson, 1970).

During the later stages of sensate focus, couples often have to confront their specific problems, but they are usually in a much better-educated and experienced position to deal with them, backed by advice from the therapist. Engaging in the spectator role was seen by Masters and Johnson (1970) as a pervasive problem, whereby one partner will focus objectively on their performance and lose their subjective involvement in the process. Clearly, conjoint therapy is partly a form of systematic desensitisation (see Chapter 3) with added cognitive and educational instructions. Masters and Johnson's approach is still a successful technique, even if ostensibly less so than in the original studies (Segraves and Althol, 1998). However this may be due to changes in the participant samples over the years (Kring et al., 2007). The sensate focus component of conjoint therapy still forms the cornerstone of interventions for sexual dysfunctions (Wincze and Carey, 2001).

Other approaches

Sex education alone tends to reduce the effects of sexual dysfunctions and is included as a matter of course in many treatment approaches (Kring et al., 2007). Education was always seen as an important component in conjoint therapy and would be focused on the area of any known dysfunction (Masters and Johnson, 1970). Skill development and improvement can be achieved partly by education and practice; in sensate focus there was often a daytime demonstration followed by 'homework' practice in hotel rooms for their couples. Skills are often learned from instructional DVDs and repeated practice is encouraged. Sometimes a change of attitude towards sex or their partner is needed in addition to instruction (Wincze and Carey, 2001). This is often achieved by challenging erroneous or maladaptive thoughts and assumptions in the manner of **rational emotive therapy** (see Chapter 3). Non-sexual issues in a relationship, such as housing, family or child pressures, can also be addressed to help in the process of facilitating adequate sexual functioning (Kring et al., 2007). There have been combinations of cognitive and psychodynamic approaches based on modest success, such as that of Helen Kaplan in producing a number of variations and combinations of techniques.

Focus

Surrogate sexual partners

Surrogate sexual partners are a controversial but ostensibly effective means of treating individuals with sexual dysfunctions or more minor sexual problems (see Cole, 1982). As the name suggests, surrogates stand in place of sexual partners to engage in practical sexual activity in vivo as well as guiding and educating clients. Masters and Johnson (1970) coined the term 'surrogate' in the context of sexual therapy and evaluated the use of a number of surrogates to treat a larger sample of males positively, but found a high rejection rate for the surrogates. They held the opinion that sexuality cannot be learned without experiencing intimacy with a real partner. At this time, Masters and Johnson considered male surrogates to be impractical due to the 'psychosocial position of females preventing a response', a rather old-fashioned view of female sexuality. The term **sexual therapy practitioner** has also been used by Sommers and others (see Johnson and Kempton, 1981), and in evaluations of a number of such therapy sessions, almost all clients were recorded as showing a marked improvement. Cole (1982) evaluated his own use of surrogates for the more common dysfunctions, finding females to benefit more than males and less success with retarded ejaculation, but high rates of success with heterophobia (fear of heterosexual relations). These early evaluations by those administering the surrogate therapy tended to be subjective judgements. The US-based International Professional Surrogate Association (IPSA) trains surrogates and all are supervised for each therapy session by a sex therapist, who may also be medically qualified. In former years, some surrogates have been ex-patients or their partners sympathetic to the process (Cole, 1982).

Surrogates are seen as most appropriate with male or female clients who have no current partner, but they have also been effective with clients in relationships. Johnson and Kempton (1981) drew attention to the potential that surrogate partners offer for individuals who are placed at a disadvantage in learning appropriate sexual behaviour and methods of attaining gratification, such as individuals with disabilities or in institutions. This approach has thus been applied in the case of individuals with disabilities that restrict gratification in other areas of their lives, but for whom sexual gratification is intact, such as in the outcome of **traumatic brain injury** (see Aloni, Keren and Katz, 2007).

Trained surrogate therapists engage in progressive sexual skill building with clients by active learning, repetition and other techniques drawn from behavioural interventions, whilst also educating and instructing. These skills include the ability to give as well as receive pleasure and in some cases the ability to establish an intimate relationship with the surrogate. During the therapy period, sexual relations with individuals other than the surrogate are usually not allowed. As the client will normally want to please the surrogate, there will be motivation to develop social intimacy skills in addition to giving mutual pleasure. An operant conditioning approach may be needed for basic skill development with some clients, in that receiving pleasure may be made contingent on their giving an equal amount to the surrogate.

The individual client may require fundamental skill building or have fully developed sexual skills and be suffering a specific sexual dysfunction. Orthodox sexual therapy techniques, such as **sensate focus**, are incorporated with the surrogate in place of the partner in this form of conjoint therapy (see Masters and Johnson, 1970). If the dysfunction being treated is a result of partner-specific anxieties, sexual responses with a surrogate are likely to show adequate functioning. The client may also experience less performance anxiety or fear of failure with a relative stranger (see Cole, 1982). Having a trained surrogate partner with access to problems and sexual histories means the client does not have to give excuses or be embarrassed about dysfunctions (Johnson and Kempton, 1981). The client also benefits from feedback on progress, which should be jointly discussed between client, surrogate and supervising therapist (Cole, 1982).

Thomas Szasz has criticised sexual surrogacy as being little more than prostitution. However, more skilled prostitutes have often provided this therapeutic function for many years, either knowledgeably or inadvertently (see the Focus box on p. 401). Although surrogacy has had difficulties due to AIDS and sensationalist publicity during the twentieth century, it has emerged in the twenty-first century as a valuable extension of the therapy process for sexual dysfunctions, with evaluations being a routine aspect of research-based practice. Ben-Zion et al. (2007) compared surrogate use with couple therapy for vaginismus, finding that the surrogate males were at least as effective as own partners, therefore suggesting their use for female sufferers without a partner. Work with individuals for whom regular partners have not usually been an option due to disability or situation is also contributing to research evidence on the efficacy of surrogate therapy (Aloni, Keren and Katz, 2007).

The paraphilias

Paraphilia (literally 'preference for that beyond') is taken to mean intense sexual arousal and consequent desire for that which is inappropriate. Paraphilia replaced the archaic term 'sexual deviation' but still contains a similar judgement as to what is clinically, forensically or morally inappropriate sexual desire or behaviour. Although individuals with paraphilias may function in a sexually adequate manner within this context, the inappropriate nature defines the desire as abnormal and needing intervention (Wincze and Carey, 2001). 'Inappropriate' desire is usually directed at non-human objects, suffering and humiliation, or non-consenting partners such as children (American Psychiatric Association, 2000). These sexual targets are usually necessary for arousal or are the preferred targets of sexual activity, either in life or in fantasy. Preferences range from the ostensibly bizarre, such as being aroused by sneezing (King, 1990), to the unacceptable, such as the sadistic or coercive use of children. The vast range of paraphilic targets cannot be fully represented by the disorder classifications in this section, which tend to reflect traditional categories. Most prostitutes are familiar with at least some of these paraphilias and will indulge their clients within limits.

Many of these activities have been criminalised, but unfortunately this has often exacerbated the paraphilia due to the activity being hidden from others, making detection and treatment difficult. These disorders are usually detected in the wake of the behaviour being reported as a crime rather than the disorder being self-reported (American Psychiatric Association, 2000). Some of the issues surrounding covert activity by sex offenders have been discussed in Chapter 8. Further to this, people with paraphilias tend not to seek treatment, partly through embarrassment, but in many cases because they fundamentally do not wish to change their preferences or behaviour. For example, only a small percentage of sadomasochists express a desire to be rid of their problem, whilst the majority of transvestites do not seek advice, and surveys have also revealed that although 18 per cent of men report sexual fetishism, very few of these seek treatment (Gosselin and Wilson, 1980). Arousal may be gained by actual or fantasised paraphilic activity, which usually begins in adolescence (with signs in childhood) and declines with old age. Although some individuals will always indulge their paraphilic needs, others may be episodic in this behaviour with periods free from such activity or fantasy, which can create further problems when assessing paraphilias in a forensic context (Tollison and Adams, 1979).

The classification of paraphilias

DSM and ICD classificatory systems have similar categories of paraphilias, but the ICD also includes 'multiple sexual preference disorder' and also 'dual role transvestism', the latter possibly being more related to gender identity disorder (Crowe, 2006). There are many named paraphilias beyond those listed in DSM-IV-TR, such as hypoxyphilia or sexual excitement resulting from reduced oxygen intake, which has been associated with deaths due to accidental auto-asphyxiation. It may be argued that many of these diverse paraphilias relate to the major classifications, such as masochism subsuming hypoxyphilia. Although the diagnostic criteria for paraphilias include fantasies or desires causing marked distress and interpersonal impairment, some of these disorders, such as voyeurism, frotteurism, exhibitionism, sadism and paedophilia, can be diagnosed by their being acted upon (American Psychiatric Association, 2000). It is common to have comorbidity of different paraphilias (Marshall, 2007) and these are diagnosed and recorded by adding the disorders to each other in the DSM-IV-TR. The main classifications of paraphilias are as follows.

Exhibitionism

Exhibitionism involves the recurrent desire to expose or actual exposure of the genitals to a non-consenting other, almost always an unsuspecting female stranger. This is a more common paraphilia, mostly found in younger males, and is sometimes accompanied by masturbation.

A professional burlesque dancer. Exhibitionism may not be as prevalent in females as it is not labelled as such when formalised as a performance, even though some of the performers may enjoy both performance and exposure. However, in many cases, it has to be questioned whether this is in fact exhibitionism or, as in this picture, simply a professional at work. Source: © Brandi Grooms Photography.

Anonymity and the ability to shock are key factors for the exhibitionist, who will rarely pursue the interaction further, even though some have fantasies of arousing the victim (American Psychiatric Association, 2000). Although this is the least potentially harmful of all paraphilias, male exhibitionists are the most likely to be criminally prosecuted, as they are easily caught. Some have speculated that they have a desire to be caught. Although, as with most paraphilias, exhibitionists are usually male, this may be partly due to the public acceptability of female exposure in public, as female exotic dancers and similar roles greatly outnumber those featuring males. This gender bias may also relate to perceiving exposed females as less of a threat to children than males.

Fetishism

Fetishism is sexual arousal by the use of an inanimate object, or the 'fetish'. Although these are most commonly items of female underwear and stockings or shoes, particularly items made of leather or rubber, they may also range from mundane items such as food to somewhat disturbing items such as surgical apparel. *DSM* considers fetishistic arousal for areas of the human body such as the feet to be partialism rather than fetishism, although this may confound rather than clarify definitions for some (De Silva, 2006). In what would seem partialism, King (1990) describes the development of a case of sneezing as a sexual fetish, but also refers to its autoerotic origins in childhood, perhaps providing links to hypoxyphilia. Thus, the term 'fetish' is commonly used throughout the paraphilias,

somewhat confounding the boundaries of fetishism as a diagnostic category. In fetishism, a fetish object may be used during sex by getting a partner to wear it, or by rubbing and fondling it as a substitute for a sexual partner, and orgasm may not be achievable without the fetish object (American Psychiatric Association, 2000).

Fetishism overlaps with **sadomasochism** and **transvestism**, but clothing used for cross-dressing should not be considered a fetish, nor should items designed to stimulate arousal such as vibrators (American Psychiatric Association, 2000). Also many non-disordered individuals adopt the symbolic appearance associated with these disorders, but purely as a fashion statement, and this should not be confused with behavioural fetishism (Snowden, 1996). In the UK, the company Skin Two produces magazines, events and apparel for a broader fetish market amongst those in the general population with fetish traits. The organisation is more seriously associated with fetishism than organisations with a wider sexual appeal. Rubber is a very common fetish material, particularly in association with sadomasochism, and as with many other fetishes, specialist groups have formed such as the 'International Mackintosh Society' for rubber enthusiasts (not to be confused with the Charles Rennie Mackintosh Society in Glasgow).

Frotteurism

Frotteurism is the repeated desire to rub genitals against the thighs or buttocks and use hands to touch breasts or genitals of non-consenting strangers. This usually takes place in crowded places such as lifts or on public transport where escape is easier (American Psychiatric Association, 2000). Although the frotteurist may fantasise about having a relationship with their victim, anonymity is usually maintained and evading arrest kept a high priority. On rare occasions, acts of frotteurism are not always disapproved of by the victim, though as such these would fall short of the definition of the disorder. Curious observations have been made by Stern and Stern (1981) of anonymous sexual acts, including intercourse, on crowded public buses in the old Soviet Union in frotteuristic styles of contact. As above, this is a consensual act outside the definition of frotteurism, but a tacit agreement to anonymity between these participants was also reported by the authors. Peak age for acts of frotteurism is between 15 and 25, and as with other paraphilias they are mostly carried out by males (American Psychiatric Association, 2000).

Paedophilia

The term 'paedophilia' (or with the spelling 'pedophilia' in US texts, including *DSM*) covers a spectrum of behaviours. In *DSM-IV* these are given as sexual acts with a pre-pubescent child by an individual who should be 16 years old and at least 5 years older than the victim (American Psychiatric Association, 2000). However, in the case of younger individuals with paedophilia, there is flexibility in these ages to allow clinical judgement based on individual variables such as maturity. Subclassifications of paedophilia are concerned with whether the individual is attracted to children only, the preferred gender(s) of the victim, and whether the act is also one of **incest**. Although strangers are feared as paedophiles by parents, the sad fact is that children are most vulnerable to sexual predation within the family home and at the hands of family members. In addition, those with control over and access to young children, such as care workers, priests and scoutmasters, tend to be under a great deal of scrutiny in the twenty-first century due to deliberate paedophile infiltration in the past and retrospective prosecutions. Those individuals with paedophilia referred to as **exclusive types** only desire children, whereas some, the **non-exclusive type**, will occasionally desire adults. Those desiring females tend to be more common and select younger victims than those preferring males, whilst others are attracted to both genders (American Psychiatric Association, 2000). The course of the disorder tends to be chronic, especially in the case of those with a male victim preference, who tend also to have higher recidivism rates and occasionally may have onset later in life (American Psychiatric Association, 2000).

Not all individuals with paedophilia act out their desires, and those who do vary greatly in the degree of intimacy and forced contact. The blanket term covers behaviour ranging from the coercive fondling of a child, who is not disturbed by the act (at the time), to forceful, repeated intercourse, and sadistic acts, with intimidation. The latter would be better distinguished as **sexually sadistic paedophilia**, but as no child of this age can be considered to give 'consent', all cases must be assumed to be by 'force' in law and clinical assessments. The majority of paedophiles do not engage in violence and prefer coercive means, but they tend to be forensically grouped with the rarer sadistic individuals who will harm victims for gratification (Groth, Hobson and Guy, 1982). Even in cases of forceful sexual acts on children, the perpetrator will rationalise the act as somehow being initiated by the child or in some way a beneficial act towards the child. These **paedophilic myths** are often promoted by paedophile pornography and networking websites (see Bocij, 2004). These rationalisations make it unlikely that an individual with paedophilia would suffer distress or loss of function as a result of their desires or acts. Thus, marked distress or impaired functioning is not required for a diagnosis in those having acted on their paedophilic desires (American Psychiatric Association, 2000). Those who act on their desires are most likely to come to clinical attention in the wake of criminal prosecution and rarely present prior to forensic involvement. Paedophilia has been dealt with briefly as a clinical disorder here, but it is also an important area for forensic psychology and will be returned to in the section on forensic issues below (also see Chapter 8).

Sexual masochism

In sexual masochism, being subject to suffering is repeatedly sought by such means as humiliation, restraint or violence, as part of sexual gratification. The name is derived from Leopold von Sacher-Masoch (1835–1895), who wrote about sex-acts involving pain, including the book *Venus in Furs*. These fantasies may pervade and acts may be carried out during intercourse simulating acts of being held whilst raped (American Psychiatric Association, 2000). However, these fantasies may be enacted alone and can involve self-harm in cutting, electrocution or asphyxiation. As previously mentioned, the autoerotic practice of self-strangulation or suffocation, termed **hypoxyphilia**, may usefully be included in this classification, although some consider it an additional paraphilia (see De Silva, 2006). As in some tragic cases, such as that speculated of the singer **Michael Hutchence**, the solitary nature of the practice may result in death as the participant has no one to come to their rescue.

Other practices may involve bondage and humiliation, either verbal or by acts such as urination on the masochist and being forced into enactments such as cross-dressing or being treated as an animal. There may be a link between pain and orgasm for some masochistic individuals. One area of overlap between masochism and fetish is the need to be treated as a helpless infant with a dominant 'mother'. The paraphernalia for this form of infantilism can be very elaborate, hence the overlap with fetishism, with some commercial outlets producing complete adult 'nurseries' for installation in private homes. Some masochistic desires may lead to bizarre 'consensual' agreements made over the internet, which have included the extremes of homicide and cannibalism.

For example, the obsessive persistent desire to have a healthy limb amputated is controversial in its diagnosis (First, 2005) and has been associated with masochistic internet sites supporting such desires, but it may also be thought of as **body dysmorphia** (see Chapter 15) and aligned with the kind of need for surgical transformation found in **gender identity disorder** (First, 2005). Amputees are also seen as attractive by a segment of the population, which may relate to the disordered population who desire amputation (see Smith, 2006). Masochism may be detected in childhood and tends to run a chronic course, which may escalate in risk to the individual or in other cases remain stable with repeated scenarios (American Psychiatric Association, 2000).

Sexual sadism

Often seen as 'complementary' to masochism, the sexual sadist seeks to inflict suffering or humiliation on their partner or victim, and thus takes a dominant role to what would be seen as the masochist's subservient sexual role. These acts are real, not simulated, but such desires may occur as fantasies, in which case they involve total control over their terrified sexual target, which may be ego dystonic (American Psychiatric Association, 2000). The term 'sadism' in this context is derived from a writer, Donatien-Alphonse-Francois de Sade (1740–1814), who wrote about and performed acts of sexual sadism on women and children that have been portrayed in movies such as *Quills* (Kaufmann, 2000). Although sadistic acts with non-consenting partners can result in **rape** or **sexual homicide**, consenting partner activity can occasionally result in accidental tragedy, especially where restraint is involved. It is thus unwise for anyone to allow themselves to be placed in total restraint, regardless of how well the other party is known. Sado-masochistic relationships are thought to be a gross exaggeration of the dominant–subservient male–female sexual roles from human history, and the biting, pinching and slapping of sex-play may represent the acceptable elements of sado-masochistic activity. These acts run the full spectrum of punitive,

humiliating and painful acts, such as cutting, strangling, whipping, mutilating, burning, restraining or impairing the senses of victims, and it is the suffering in the target person that produces the arousal (American Psychiatric Association, 2000). As with masochism, onset of sadistic desire is detected in childhood and the prognosis once acts begin in early adulthood is normally chronic (American Psychiatric Association, 2000).

In practice, most sadistic or masochistic fantasy enactments are quite benign in nature, involving mutually respectful restraint and minimal discomfort, which may be conducted in an organised manner by paid participants. Some nightclubs may specialise in clients who pursue such fantasies with a great deal of overlap with fetishism, such as the Skin Two annual 'Rubber Ball Weekend' (Snowden, 1996). However, some sado-masochistic practices warrant more forensic attention than others, particularly if comorbid with **anti-social personality disorder**, and these fantasies may on rare occasions fuel the unusual aspects of more gruesome sexual attacks and homicides (Holmes and Holmes, 2002).

Some films attempt to portray sado-masochistic relationships in a positive or at least sympathetic light.
Source: Alamy Images/Photos 12.

Transvestic fetishism

Transvestic fetishism is where primary sexual pleasure is repeatedly gained from or during **cross-dressing**; in *DSM-IV-TR* this is exclusively males dressing, or dressing and acting as females. However, in an attempt to establish prevalence, Längstöm and Zucker (2005) found that 2.8 per cent of men and 0.4 per cent of women admitted to one episode of transvestic fetishism in a Swedish sample. Thus, although not diagnosed in women, it does occur. *DSM-IV-TR* describes autogynephilia, where the thought for males of themselves being a woman is sexually arousing (American Psychiatric Association, 2000). The males with transvestic fetishism are usually of heterosexual orientation, but there tend to be few female partners and they may have homosexual experiences on occasions (American Psychiatric Association, 2000). Homosexual experiences and higher levels of masturbation have also been found to relate to the disorder in the Swedish sample (Längstöm and Zucker, 2005). Although transvestic fetishism has often been tritely referred to in the popular media, **David Walliams** in the UK comedy series *Little Britain* (BBC1) has drawn attention to alternative motivations for cross-dressing, albeit in the somewhat cruel context of comedic pretence.

There may be attempts to imitate female genitalia, but initial diagnosis does not include **transsexualism**, or the need to change gender permanently. If the behaviour leads to a gender identity disorder (i.e. transsexual behaviour), then the subtype **with gender** dysphoria may be diagnosed. The disorder is distinct from fetishism as the items of clothing tend to be part of the aim of impersonating or feeling like a female and not an object of sexual desire in themselves due to properties of texture, etc. However, over time transvestic fetishism in some individuals may change and certain clothing items may become a focus of masturbatory activity and be incorporated into intercourse (American Psychiatric Association, 2000).

Voyeurism

Voyeurism or scoptophilia is gaining sexual pleasure from the secret watching of other people who are in states of undress or engaging in sexual acts. This is usually an anonymous activity with no contact being sought with the victim, except in fantasy, and the 'peeping tom' activity is usually accompanied or followed by masturbation (American Psychiatric Association, 2000). As with many of the paraphilias above, onset is usually around puberty; the usual course is chronic. Metzl (2004) gives a description of the history of voyeurism and makes the unavoidable link with what is considered to be a contemporary 'voyeuristic society' gaining vicarious satisfaction from international TV phenomena such as *Big Brother* and voyeuristic activity over the internet.

Case study

Fetishism

Paul's relationship with his wife Ann had become strained and Ann had convinced him to join her on a visit to a counsellor. Neither party was forthcoming about what their 'bedroom problem' was, other than that Paul preferred Ann to keep most of her clothes on, and she wanted children but Paul wanted 'something else'. On the counsellor's recommendation, Ann saw a sex therapist on her own. During the meeting Ann burst into tears, confessing her worst fears that Paul did not love her, but seemed to prefer her underwear, and that she had discovered boxes of old stockings and tights in the garage, some of which were clearly not her own.

The therapist managed to interview Paul on his own, but only after Ann had threatened to leave the marriage. At first, Paul claimed he was frightened to have children. However, when faced with the 'evidence' he confessed to only being sexually aroused by nylon stockings, preferably tights, and that this had gone back as far as he could remember to early masturbation experiences. He even remembered running around his mother's stockinged legs as a child, while she served in a shop. Paul agreed to undergo some sexual-reorientation therapy, which included talking through his difficulties, relaxing with Ann *without* underwear, and aversion therapy for tights. In time, Paul responded well to sexual relations with Ann, but he still had an uneasy relationship with underwear, occasionally crossing the road to avoid lingerie shops.

Aetiology and treatment of paraphilias

Aetiology of paraphilias

Explanations of paraphilias are diverse and include all of the paradigm approaches (see Chapter 3). James (2006) considered the hypothesis that paedophilia in offspring may relate to the progressive immunisation of mothers to male-specific antigens by each succeeding male foetus. This would increase the neurodevelopmental effects of anti-male antibodies with each succeeding male foetus, but evidence for this effect is weak (James, 2006).

Genetic and biological approaches to paraphilias have also been combined with early formative learning experiences to explain paraphilic desires. Individuals with paraphilias are also thought to have neurological abnormalities which predispose them to less discriminate early erotic attachments during infancy or childhood. It is also suggested that their earliest sexual experiences are associated, in a classical conditioning sense, to atypical or even bizarre stimuli (Gebhard, 1965). Rachmann (1966) demonstrated the creation of a 'fetish' in pairing footwear with sexually arousing material using basic classical conditioning procedures. The early precursors to paraphilic responses are then in turn reinforced by repeated erotic association and orgasmic reward (Gebhard, 1965).

Animal studies have confirmed some mechanisms that help create and sustain paraphilic responses and drives. Fetishism has been developed in the Japanese quail, which showed persistent sexual responding to a terrycloth inanimate target. This fetish behaviour was maintained by copulatory behaviour with the inanimate target and tended not to be sustained in the absence of copulation (Köksal et al., 2004). Thus the animal model supports the notion of paraphilias being sustained in humans as a result of association and orgasmic reinforcement.

The part played by association and reward in the formation of paraphilias may partly explain the reporting of increased sexual abuse in the histories of sexual offenders, particularly aggressive offenders. Early abuse may also provide a route to therapeutic intervention for such sex offenders (Dudeck et al., 2007). In a German review, Berner and Bricken (2007) consider the importance of hostility to relationships as a symptom and precursor to paraphilias, and the relationship of this factor to early attachment experiences in developing close relationships with primary caregivers. However, all such approaches tend to overlook the possibility that aberrant interactions may be inherent in the individual (and relatives), leading to both early- and later-life abusive interactions. It also has to be noted that most abused boys do not become abusers (James, 2006). Bogaerts et al. (2006) produced results that related the development of exhibitionism to recalled parental sensitivity and also to having **avoidant personality disorder**.

Treatment of paraphilias

An important aspect of assessment prior to treatment for paraphilia, particularly in offenders, is to measure differential sexual arousal to varying stimuli. This has been achieved for many years with males by using a **penile strain gauge** or **penile plethysmography**, which is highly sensitive to any change in circumference of the penis (Barlow et al., 1970). Erectile function in males tends to be an autonomic function and not under direct conscious control (though it can be indirectly influenced by controlled thoughts) and is a sensitive indicator of sexual arousal (see Udelson, 2007). Thus any change in erectile state would indicate variation in the level of sexual interest, which can be correlated with particular types of stimulus, such as pre-pubescent children or fetish objects. Treatment may then be targeted more accurately towards the particular paraphilic stimuli revealed. The response information can also be used to reveal denial or responses of those contesting criminal charges concerning related desires.

Tong (2007) has compared this reliable method of measurement with self-report measures and found a correlation with the **Abel Assessment for Sexual Interest** (Abel et al., 2001). Tong (2007) suggests that the latter provides a possible replacement for the former controversial phallometric methods. In females, both **thermisters** measuring vaginal temperature and photoplethysmography measuring vaginal opacity are indicators of blood engorgement, which is used to infer sexual arousal in women. Female measures tend to be subject to political controversy based on the low rate of female sex offenders and arguments as to whether females are susceptible to such conditions.

Aversion therapy is thought of as archaic by some, but is still considered an effective treatment for paraphilias by others, providing it is combined with skill creation and encouragement towards more acceptable sexual desires and activity. Aversion is conditioned by the carefully timed association of the paraphilic object on a computer screen with noxious stimuli (De Silva, 2006). These may be either in vivo, including electrical shock or more rarely nausea-inducing drugs and pungent smells; or cognitive, such as imagining discovery or the consequences of their actions. There are many variations on these techniques which are useful for offenders such as paedophiles, who are willing to participate. For example, in masturbatory satiation the client masturbates to orgasm with a *non-deviant* fantasy, then attempts to masturbate to their deviant fantasy, and is frustrated, unable to orgasm (Marshall, 1970). Thus, satisfaction comes to be associated with normal images and discomfort with deviance over time. In orgasmic reconditioning, masturbation takes place to paraphilic stimuli until the point of orgasmic inevitability when the fantasy is switched to a conventional acceptable stimulus (De Silva, 2006).

Chemical control of paraphilic offenders tends to be more common than would be suggested by its long-term effectiveness, as it provides a quick and economic short-term solution. The partial reduction of paraphilic drives by drugs such as the hormonal agent **medroxy-progesterone acetate** can make drives more manageable to facilitate cognitive behavioural interventions (De Silva, 2006). The drug reduces plasma testosterone levels via the induction of the liver enzyme testosterone-A-reductase. Other anti-androgen compounds, such as **leuprolide**, have been used with some success in adults and adolescent patients with a range of paraphilias, such as paedophilia, sexual sadism and frotteurism (Saleh, Neil and Fishman, 2004). The use of **SSRIs** for some sex offenders has been mentioned in Chapter 8, and further pharmacological interventions have met with success in evaluations. For example, the anti-convulsant **topiramate** has had reported success in reducing fetishism and may be of value with other paraphilias (Shia et al., 2006). Saleh and Berlin (2004) have reviewed all these pharmacological treatments and others as positively beneficial for the treatment of paraphilias.

Cognitive behavioural treatment (CBT) has become routine for paraphilias, particularly when the clients are offenders in a prison context (De Silva, 2006). These often break down the thought patterns that lead to denial, blaming others and adherence to mythical beliefs about

International perspective

Prostitution: crime, career or therapy?

Prostitution exists in all countries and is the exchange of sexual activity for remuneration, although definitions can vary depending on whether it is seen in a positive or negative light (Jesson, 1993). Those who regularly offer this service are referred to as prostitutes, whores, call girls, (female) escorts, street walkers or courtesans, amongst other colloquial terms. Their clients are variously termed 'kerb-crawlers', punters or Johns (in the USA). Male prostitutes offering this service to females can be referred to as male escorts or gigolos, and when offered to other males as rent boys or hustlers. Those managing or housing prostitutes are called **pimps** if they are male and **madams** if female. Although prostitution is generally condemned, it has served functions beyond the economic need of prostitutes or being a safety valve for sexually frustrated males. It can be seen as functioning in a similar therapeutic manner to sexual surrogates (see the Focus box on p. 394). Working in areas often overlooked by moral authoritarianism, the Danish sexologist Sten Hegeler in 1984 suggested introducing male prostitutes into old age homes for elderly females, as female prostitutes were already providing this service for elderly males at this time (see Eskapa, 1989).

Although erroneously described as the 'oldest profession', prostitution is not a new enterprise by any means and has persisted across eras, cultures and states of war, peace, affluence and poverty. Prostitutes sought sanctuary in ancient temples and were revered in Sumerian eras, as well as some achieving high status in ancient Greek society, but captive slaves and criminals were increasingly used in ancient Roman prostitution. In the Middle Ages, 'church brothels' in Europe housed working prostitutes who spent some of their time praying and performing additional chores (see Tannahill, 1980). Over 2000 years ago in China, large numbers of prostitutes were used to gain political advantage in diplomatic dealing. Sophistication of the skills of Chinese prostitutes beyond those pertaining to sex made them progressively indispensable to businessmen. In nineteenth-century Europe, prostitution and brothels proliferated and so did **sexually transmitted infections** (STIs). Prostitutes servicing troops in various armies have been referred to as 'camp followers' for millennia, and those providing this service in the middle of the nineteenth century infected entire armies. In some parts of Europe, over one-third of the general population were estimated to have STIs due to ignorance regarding these diseases, leading to the passage of the **Contagious Diseases Acts** in the UK to control the spread (Tannahill, 1980). Attempts to exclude camp followers from military campaigns failed due to low troop morale, and during the First World War they were present in all armies. German camp followers moved efficiently with the battle lines (Tannahill, 1980).

The laws governing what is seen as a perversion of sexual behaviour by some cultures and individuals vary greatly and sharply across countries and states.

International perspective continued

Legal sanction can involve the death penalty (e.g. Sudan) or even be subject to decriminalisation and state protection for licensed prostitutes (e.g. Netherlands). Anti-prostitution laws tend to exclude individuals being paid to engage in sex, such as porn actresses and those performing the same activity before a camera in mainstream film-making or stage productions. The laws on prostitution are more complex than it being simply legal or illegal. Prohibitive approaches may focus on all involved, the prostitute alone or, as in Sweden, a feminist-influenced prosecution of the client, not the prostitute. Others primarily focus on the pimps and peripheral activities, as in Canada where prostitution itself is not prosecuted. These laws can change to suit the prevailing attitudes towards the prostitute and client. Decriminalisation often involves some legal obligation in practising prostitution, such as health regulations (as applied to professions such as nursing), whereas legalisation tends only to apply other existing laws to the situation, such as those concerning tax evasion or drug offences.

Prostitutes are at high risk of being victims of physical or mental illness as well as crime including assault and homicide. In the case of homicide, sex-workers have been referred to as 'less than dead' (a term taken from the murder of poor workers on the Mexico–USA border), meaning their deaths are less noticed than those of non-prostitutes. Adolescent prostitutes are thought to have higher levels of depression and anxiety as well as unstable home histories and early sexual experience, often in the form of sexual abuse, which can lead to the acceptance of the principles of prostitution (Jesson, 1993). This is less the case with male prostitutes, who are also less fixed in their prostitution behaviour and less dependent on the income from it (Weitzer, 2005). Some approaches place the health of the sex-worker at the top of the agenda and suggest taking prostitution out of the black market, which would largely separate sex work from crime and criminals in addition to reducing health risks. The iconic red light district of Amsterdam is both a tourist attraction and a symbol of the approach that imposes health checks and attempts to separate the trade from general criminal involvement, child prostitution and sexual slavery. This **welfare approach** began in the 1980s and with hiccups has evolved in a number of countries with differing legal strategies. The UK strategy to move women out of the sex-trade has involved multi-agency regulation, with progressive governance devolving enforcement to a coordinated network. This is in line with the UK Home Office's 2006 **a Coordinated Prostitution Strategy** (ACPS), which

involves intervention in housing, drug rehabilitation and partner abuse (Scoular and O'Neill, 2007). This adopts a rather Dickensian approach in assuming lack of skills on the part of prostitutes and is still ultimately coercive, using punishment for non-compliance.

Child prostitution has a long and disturbing history, and tolerance of the activity currently varies substantially across geographic boundaries. Although legislation is difficult to enforce, some countries extend their laws to include activities by their citizens in distant countries. Child prostitution carries both the penalties of prostitution and offences against children. **Trafficking** of individuals for the purpose of enforced prostitution has increased during the twenty-first century as a gang-driven form of modern slavery. Vulnerable individuals are targeted and tempted by vacuous promises of a better life and jobs in entertainment or modelling to travel to other countries, where they are intimidated by threats to themselves and their families. The kidnap of children for trafficking is greatly feared by parents when travelling away from their own country, but some children may even be sold by their own parents into these criminal organisations, although not all are used for child prostitution or other activities such as pornography. The **Council of Europe Convention: Action against Trafficking of Human Beings**, launched in 2005, has been agreed to by over 30 countries.

In the twenty-first century there has been some reduction in the level of prostitution in sexually liberal countries. Knight (2007) has speculated in the UK *Sunday Times* that sex freely given by young girls was reducing the need for paid prostitutes, when describing the level of sexual abuse young girls voluntarily accepted when 'partying' with UK footballers in a hotel. This behaviour may possibly show similar associations to the developmental factors found in adolescent prostitutes, such as a sexualised and chaotic childhood (Jesson, 1993).

In balancing need against harm, the issue of prostitution is probably irresolvable with protectionist and libertarian views eternally in opposition to one another. One thing that is certain about prostitution is its contradictory perspectives (Jesson, 1993). Anti-prostitution political agendas and in particular the radical feminist view are distorting theoretical work on the topic by invariably assuming male domination or coercion of sex-workers (Weitzer, 2005). The use of language such as 'prostituted woman', 'survivors' and 'paid rape' assumes no free will on the part of prostitutes, and with attention-grabbing headlines such as 'all clients are expressing hatred for the female body' could be seen as setting biased agenda (Weitzer, 2005).

their behaviour. Such CBT-based sex offender treatment programmes have been considered in Chapter 8. There have been many reviews of these treatment regimes, although comparisons with behavioural approaches such as aversion are fraught with methodological problems, such as the differing evaluation criteria for effectiveness. Contemporary, more comprehensive treatment regimes tend to incorporate indirect (but effective) elements, such as anger management and social skills training, which in combination should improve recidivism rates. In a systematic review, Brooks-Gordon, Bilby and Wells (2006) did not clearly support the popularly assumed overall effectiveness of such regimes, and suggested that careful evaluation be conducted as an ongoing process with treatment programmes in this area.

Some sexual disorders are particularly difficult to treat, such as paedophilia, but are better treated than ignored in prison, where decaying social skills may worsen the individual's risk of offending on release. As mentioned earlier, some paraphilic individuals do not want treatment and may even fail to perceive that their condition is abnormal or immoral. In the absence of willing partners, such individuals may fulfil fantasies using prostitutes, images or unwilling partners (American Psychiatric Association, 2000). Commercial organisations have developed that supply materials to aid paraphilic fantasies, as well as real and online self-help groups that may be legitimate or illegal in their status. Established commercial outlets in the UK include: the 'Foot Lovers Admiration Society' for foot, shoe, leg and stocking preferences; 'Hush-a-Bye Baby Club' for adult baby supplies; 'Sh!' or female sex supplies; and 'SSSH' for focus on seamed stockings and stiletto heels.

Self-test questions

- What is the relationship between paraphilias and anonymity?
- What are the issues raised by the monitoring of paedophiles in the community?
- What is the relationship between the paraphilias and sex offenders?
- What factors compromise the treatment of the paraphilias?
- To what extent are paraphilic activities and acceptable sexual behaviour related?
- How is prostitution argued to be 'acceptable'?

Gender identity disorder

DSM and *ICD* classificatory systems both recognise gender identity disorder, but the *ICD* also includes transsexualism as a category and 'dual role transvestism' mentioned above (Crowe, 2006). Individuals of either gender with a persistent conviction that they should be of the **opposite gender** and feel significant discomfort with their assigned sex, in the *absence* of physiological factors such as **androgen insensitivity** (see below), qualify as being gender identity disordered. Adults diagnosed with gender identity disorder are around 80 per cent male wishing to be female (Green, 2007). It is a rare disorder with little epidemiological information other than the number of individuals referred for surgery, at a rate of 0.003 per cent of the population from European data (American Psychiatric Association, 2000). Gender-inappropriate behaviour is usually apparent from early childhood but excludes that encouraged as a result of 'modern sex-role modelling', in which opposite gender behaviour is encouraged. For example, the male child with early signs of gender identity disorder will consistently adopt and identify with female roles in play. Even as children, those with gender identity problems may resent their genitalia and make pretence at having that of the opposite sex. Boys may even claim they will grow up to be women (American Psychiatric Association, 2000). Females will adopt male haircuts and clothing even as children and be mistaken for boys, much to their own delight. They may even claim to have or be developing male genitalia (American Psychiatric Association, 2000).

Identification with the opposite sex tends to isolate such children from both their same-sex peers and eventually from their acquaintances gained as their adopted sex. This is more pronounced in males, who suffer greater rejection than females at least until adolescence (American Psychiatric Association, 2000). They may abscond from school due to an inability to identify, often augmented by bullying and teasing on being identified as an outcast. As the gender-dysphoric adolescent progresses to adulthood, the failure to make either peer or sexual partner relationships easily increases a sense of isolation and a consequent level of psychological problems (American Psychiatric Association, 2000). Solace may be sought in culturally fashionable groups, where their sexually uncertain manner and dress may be seen as acceptable and may even carry status, such as in the UK punk movement in the 1970s.

Although explanations of this disorder include reinforcement of sex-inappropriate behaviour in childhood, there is little empirical evidence for this and some biological disposition or imbalance may be responsible for gender identity disorder. Gender identity and associated behaviour is greatly dependent on the presence or absence of pre-natal steroid levels, especially androgen levels (male hormones). Congenital virilising adrenal hyperplasia leads to high androgen levels in genetic females, resulting in masculine traits as adults, and androgen insensitivity in genetic males will lead to female appearance and behaviour (see Green, 2007). Consistent gender differences in the size of part of the bed nucleus of the **stria terminalis** have been found to be reversed in the case of transsexuals (Zhou et al., 1995). Although this size difference develops later in life than gender identity, both may be linked by a common factor. Genetic influences on gender identity problems have been traced through families via the female line (see Green, 2007).

Initial treatment may consist of cross-sex **hormone treatment**. If the condition causes sufficient distress, the label **transsexualism** may be used and sex-reassignment surgery considered, once the required legal age is attained.

This is a drastic procedure in which the current sex genitalia are removed and those of the opposite sex fashioned within the limits of surgical technology, supplemented with hormone therapy. The final result often disappoints those who have the unrealistic expectation of becoming the opposite gender, and levels of regret can compound problems that may need subsequent treatment (Olsson and Möller, 2006). Applicants are thus rigorously tested for their conviction and realistic view of the outcome and must adopt opposite gender lifestyles for lengthy periods prior to surgery being granted. For females wanting to be male, high androgen levels produce dramatic effects in terms of publicly visible attributes without surgery, although larger breasts can promote a desire for early surgery (Green, 2007). Some individuals may mutilate their own genitalia in a desperate bid to qualify for or obtain transsexual surgery earlier than an assigned date (Baltieri and de Andrade, 2000).

Case study
Gender identity disorder

As a toddler, Andy avoided the rough and tumble of most of the boys in his nursery group, and instead sat with the nursery nurses, often with a doll across his lap. Andy's parents were not aware of this, but they had become a little disturbed by a constellation of behaviours, such as his placing a tea-towel over his head and pretending it was long hair. In 1959, having a child of dubious sexuality was a worry for fathers, though less so for mothers, and Andy's mum took a certain amount of pleasure in her son's helping with washing and cleaning, and his concentrated interest in applying make-up to her and himself.

Andy's school years were not a source of happiness for him or his family. His affiliation with the girls led him to be popular with some female students and teachers, but it provoked bullying from boys, including those local boys he (and his mum) had considered close friends. Eventually, he began to abscond from school more often than he attended, and his father

began to argue with his mother about his 'sissy' behaviour and how it would ruin any chance of earning his own keep. His mum was still protective but had been disturbed by a serious Andy saying that he would love to have his genitalia removed and was hoping that he might still grow up to be a proper woman. His father caught Andy wearing female clothing a number of times, but one day it came to a head. A violent argument ensued and Andy ran away from home for 3 days, staying at his only two (female) friends' homes.

As an adult, Andy indulged more in his thinking of himself as female with very few and mostly awkward relationships. Following a morbid drunken episode during which he made an attempt to cut off his penis, he found himself confronted by a psychiatric registrar. Having convinced her that he was neither depressed nor suicidal, Andy made it explicit what his motivation was for his self-harm. Following endless interviews and some costly consultations, Andy at the age of 40 found himself on a programme of living as a woman for the coming year. He felt comfortable in this role and often went beyond the requirements of his supervision team. It was a determined Andy who accepted hormonal therapy and eventually surgery, and a far more content Andrea who emerged years later. Andy did not expect perfection nor to be genetically transformed into a female, and this rational expectation enabled him to make the most of his second life as Andrea.

Ego-dystonic **homosexuality** (unwanted homosexuality) is a disorder in the residual category, **gender disorders not otherwise specified**. Although ego-syntonic homosexuality (i.e. homosexuality the ego is content with) is not considered a disorder, sexuality of **any orientation** that causes sufficient distress can be considered a sexual disorder. This is important in the lifetime development of gender identity disorder, as many men who show early signs of this disorder develop into bisexual or homosexual males without gender dysphoria (Green, 1987).

Forensic issues

Forensic issues are pervasive throughout sexual disorders, particularly the paraphilias, in which each disorder can provide a context for forensic interest. It is also the case that sex-offenders have very high levels of comorbid sexual dysfunctions (Bownes, 1992). Thus forensic interest is not confined to the paraphilias alone. Diagnostic accuracy is placed under greater scrutiny in the case of the paraphilias, as these judgements may carry serious forensic as well as clinical implications for the client. Although not all *DSM* classifications are clearly aligned with sexual offences, major sex crimes are intended to be accommodated within the categories: for example, rape has been assigned to the non-diagnostic category of **sexual abuse of an adult** in the chapter 'Other conditions that may be a focus of clinical attention' (see Marshall, 2007). Prominent amongst the sexual disorders in terms of forensic issues is paedophilia.

Paedophilia

It is unfortunate that paedophilia tends to receive more forensic than clinical attention. This may be a consequence of a somewhat pessimistic attitude towards changing the course of or even preventing this paraphilia in its early stages that echoes a similar fatalistic view of psychopaths being untreatable. Thus one of the forensic issues regarding paedophilia is the lack of emphasis on early assessment treatment prior to offences being committed. Research in the area of early detection is sparse and tends to rely on crimes against children being reported in retrospect, prior to assessment. However, some research pursues factors that may possibly be detected a priori. Amongst other examples, Smith and Waterman (2004) have shown that information-processing bias for salient words can distinguish paedophile responses from those of others, including the responses of individuals in other sex-offender

groups. Glasgow, Osborn and Croxen, (2003) have examined a means of measuring the degree of paedophile sexual interest shown by offenders with a learning disability using viewing time of selected images. The chronic nature of paedophilia, especially that relating to male victims, in combination with the potentially high 'hidden figure' of true prevalence, would also suggest intervention strategies at every stage be a higher priority than incarceration (see Howitt, 2006).

Other offences are usually committed in the course of pursuing paedophilic interests, some of which may be a consequence of maintaining control over and silence in the victim. Victim compliance is achieved by a variety of coercive and forceful means, particularly for abuse within a domestic context. However, around 40 per cent of incestuous abusers also report offending against children outside of the family (Studer et al., 2002). There may be intensive attention to the child in order to be trusted and liked, then capitalising on this nurtured affection (American Psychiatric Association, 2000). Guilt and shame are often encouraged in the victim to prevent reporting, in addition to more direct threats and physical intimidation. When directed at a child, threats to loved ones or pets can instil sufficient fear to maintain control over the victim.

The issues of public order in the light of the so-called 'anti-paedophile riots' in the UK during summer 2000 have been examined in Chapter 8. The apparent media-provoked public unrest at having identified paedophiles in the community had immediate implications both for the management of these offenders and for their compliance with monitoring procedures (Thomas, 2000). In the case of the **Paulsgrove riots** at this time, some of these assumptions have been challenged as media myths, with analysis revealing failures of local authority action over individual offenders. This also includes the rather disparate nature of subgroups within those whom the media collectively labelled 'vigilantes' (Williams and Thompson, 2004). Williams and Thompson (2004) consider that a realistic approach to the problems of policing paedophiles in the community would help existing police and **multi-agency public protection arrangements** to be more effective.

Other forensic issues

General sex-offender issues have been examined in Chapter 8. Some serious sex offenders are associated with comorbid paraphilias. Multiple-victim sexual homicide perpetrators have been found to have higher incidences of paraphilias as well as personality disorders and 'character sadism' (Hill et al., 2007). Some of these paraphilic desires and other drives originating in childhood have been

Focus

Internet grooming of child victims

Children have always been 'groomed' by paedophiles into accepting contact and maintaining silence. **Internet grooming** has allowed individual and organised groups of paedophiles to attract and subsequently groom children using a plausible alias, such as posing as an 8-year-old female and operating from a remote international location (see Bocij, 2004). Sophisticated technology is being used by paedophiles operating in this context to maintain anonymity, but this technical activity may in itself be detectable automatically using advanced **cyberforensic approaches** (Penna, Clark and Mohay, 2005).

The term **sexual grooming** is poorly defined and has been divided into three types: self-grooming of the offender; grooming the environment and significant others; and grooming of the child themselves. This more detailed understanding of an obvious precursor to the acts of abuse can aid the prevention of this process progressing to contact (Craven, Brown and Gilchrist, 2006). For example, police have raised the awareness of potential grooming tactics in educational visits to schools by a trained officer fooling pupils by posing as a young child online.

---

examined in terms of their contribution to sexual predation as an adult (Palermo, 2007). Although most exhibitionists do not make contact with their victims, subgroups have proven dangerous, prone to violent assault and highly recidivist. These more dangerous exhibitionists tend to be less well educated and poorer sexual functioning, and to have higher ratings of psychopathy, paedophile indices and non-exhibitionist crime records (Rabinowitz Greenberg et al., 2002).

The outcome of sex offences (including those involving paedophilia) for victims can often include sexual dysfunctions, which would imply that treatment should be available along with other support services for victims of sex crimes. Thus, effective limitation of the forensic outcomes of sex-offender activity may depend on early clinical intervention for victims and, as mentioned above, for potential perpetrators. The poor sexual skills and abilities can be addressed by the use of surrogates, and although this is likely to reduce recidivism, it is also controversial in challenging assumptions favouring the punishment of offenders at the cost of rehabilitation.

Clinical issues

Culture affects the presentation, causation, understanding and treatment as well as beliefs, attitudes and perceptions of sexual dysfunctions and disorders. Ahmed and Bhugra (2007) identify education, a flexible approach and tailored therapy as the main ways of addressing problems emanating from cultural influences in therapeutic interventions. They also report large variations in the incidence

of sexual disorders between cultures and the phenomenon of so-called culture-bound syndromes (see Chapter 21), which tend to demonstrate cultural concerns being translated into specific fears or sexual disorders. However, with the example of Dhat syndrome or the fear of loss of semen in urine, this disorder can be found in the USA as well as its traditional cultural home of India, indicating that the concept of 'faulty culture' may be erroneous (Ahmed and Bhugra, 2007). Some such cultural influences may be more problematic in less supportive contexts, such as premature ejaculation in Islamic men living in the West being related to haste during initial sexual experiences, due to culturally driven fear of discovery (Ahmed and Bhugra, 2007).

Embarrassment has already been identified as a barrier to assessment and treatment in sexual disorders. However, in the twenty-first century this may be circumvented by relatively impersonal access to information, advice and even treatment via the internet. Much information as well as the treatments supplied online lack the controls and quality checks found in terrestrial sources, and may deliberately misrepresent information for commercial gain or reasons based on belief systems. Thus, individuals too embarrassed to approach orthodox services may be disproportionately influenced by less reliable sources. Reducing the 'medicalisation' sometimes inherent in clinical sexual services and removing judgements of 'adequacy' may facilitate greater participation with orthodox services (Crowe, 2006).

Compulsive sexual behaviour (CSB) that is non-paraphilic, consensual and ego syntonic (enjoyed) may still be pathologised by society if it is very frequent, as it has consequences for the individuals concerned and society as a whole (Muench et al., 2007). CSB is likely to be included among impulsive–compulsive disorders in future classificatory systems, but it is mentioned here as a future issue for clinicians dealing with sexual disorders as something of a crossover condition containing compulsive and hypersexual elements. Measuring the consequences of CSB with the **Compulsive Sexual Behaviour Consequences Scale** can help to target areas of behaviour amenable to change and aid in planning individual treatment regimes (Muench et al., 2007).

Non-compliance with treatment in addition to denial of disorders and the challenges of assessment are forensic issues that inevitably pass to clinicians assigned to cases of paraphilias. These major clinical challenges may be greatly exacerbated by comorbid disorders, especially personality disorders, which are significantly more prevalent in sexual offenders (Dudeck et al., 2007). Treatment approaches for personality disorders are traditionally challenging and more so in the context of comorbid paraphilias; however, comprehensive treatment approaches for such cases have been proposed and documented (see Marshall, 2007). Sexual dysfunctions are also very commonly comorbid with anxiety disorders, as each may precipitate and exacerbate

the other (Corretti and Baldi, 2007). Most clinicians addressing sexual dysfunctions will be very familiar with treating anxiety disorders, but the expectation for those treating paraphilias may be less so, even though the co-occurrence of these disorders has had a high prevalence recorded in some populations (see Marshall, 2007).

Self-test questions

- What is the relationship between gender identity and the biological differentiation of gender?
- Can gender identity disorder be successfully treated?
- To what extent are forensic and clinical aims in relation to sexual offenders in accord with one another?
- What issues make paedophilia potentially the most problematic of the paraphilias to address?

Chapter summary

As a result of ignorance and embarrassment, sexual disorders have only relatively recently been openly considered for therapy, and have remained relatively hidden until well publicised work in the 1960s by **Masters and Johnson**. They are now grouped into three broad groups: **sexual dysfunctions**, **paraphilias** and **gender identity disorders**.

Sexual dysfunctions are problems in the process of intercourse that result in distress or interpersonal conflict. These may be transitory or partial, differ in males and females, and are considered in the light of the four stages of the **sexual process: desire, arousal, orgasm** and **resolution**. At the desire stage there is **hypoactive sexual desire disorder** and **sexual aversion disorder** affecting both males and females, and at the arousal stage, **female sexual arousal disorder** and **male erectile disorder**. Dysfunctions of the orgasm phase are **female and male orgasmic disorders**, and **premature ejaculation** in the male. **Dyspareunia** is sexual genital pain and **vaginismus** is a spasm of the vaginal muscles which causes pain and may prevent penetration. Treatments for these disorders

are based on known **biological** and **psychological** causes and include the highly successful drug **Viagra**. Based on CBT, **conjoint therapy** is a very effective psychosocial intervention, which includes the **sensate focus technique**. One controversial therapy is **sexual surrogacy**, which has been both criticised as immoral and praised for effectiveness.

The **paraphilias** are sexual responses to preferred but inappropriate stimuli, including **exhibitionism, fetishism, frotteurism, paedophilia, masochism, sadism, transvestism** and **voyeurism**, many of which are criminalised. Although often punished, the paraphilias may be treated with SSRIs, CBT or **aversion therapy**. **Prostitution** has been associated with meeting the needs of paraphilic individuals and is an area of continuous debate and sharply conflicting views. **Gender identity disorder** is the overriding belief that one should be of the other gender, but the adult treatment with **hormones** and **transsexual surgery** has a limited outcome.

There are many **forensic issues** when considering sexual disorders, particularly surrounding the

Chapter summary continued

paraphilias. **Paedophilia** raises issues of conflict between treatment and punishment, with newer concerns such as **internet grooming** of victims leading to public pressure towards incarceration and punishment. **Clinical issues** include the challenges of treating incarcerated individuals with paraphilias often comorbid with other disorders. **Social and cultural factors** can make detection of and intervention in sexual dysfunctions difficult.

Suggested essay questions

- Evaluate the difficulties posed by the secretive and embarrassing view of sexual dysfunctions.
- Discuss the significance of Masters and Johnson to the development of therapies for sexual dysfunction.
- Critically discuss the forensic implications of the diagnosis of paraphilias.

Further reading

Overview texts

Cole, M., and Dryden, W. (1988) *Sex therapy in Britain*. Buckingham: Open University Press.

Eskapa, R. (1989) *Bizarre sex*. London: Grafton.

Kaplan, H. (1995) *Sexual desire disorders*. New York: Brunner Mazel.

LeVay, S., and Valente, S. (2006) *Human sexuality* (2nd edn). London: Sinauer Associates.

Masters, W., Johnson, V. E., and Kolodny, K. C. (1995) *Human sexuality*. London: Allyn and Bacon.

Porst, H., and Buvat, J. (2006) *Standard practice in sexual medicine*. New York: Blackwell.

Rosen, I. (1996) *Sexual deviation* (3rd edn). Oxford: Oxford University Press.

Spence, S. (1991) *Psychosexual therapy: A cognitive-behavioural approach*. London: Chapman and Hall.

Szuchman, L. T., and Muscarella, F. (2000) *Psychological perspectives on human sexuality*. New York: Wiley.

Tomlinson, J. (2006) *ABC of sexual health* (2nd edn). London: BMJ.

Trigwell, P. (2005) *Helping people with sexual problems: A practical approach for clinicians*. London: Elsevier.

Specific and more critical texts

Balon, R., and Taylor Segraves, R. (2005) *Handbook of sexual dysfunction*. Boca Raton, FL: Taylor and Francis.

Cole, M. (1985) Sex therapy: a critical appraisal. *British Journal of Psychiatry*, 147, 337–51.

Harvey, J. H., Wenzel, A., and Sprecher, S. (2004) *The handbook of sexuality in close relationships*. Mahwah, NJ: Lawrence Erlbaum.

Howitt, D. (1995) *Paedophiles and sexual offences against children*. London: Wiley.

Leiblum, S. R. (2006) *Principles and practice of sex therapy*. London: Guilford Press.

Letherby, G., Birch, P., Cain, M., and Williams, K. (2007) *Sex as crime*. London: Willan.

Marshall, W. L. (2007) Diagnostic issues, multiple paraphilias and comorbid disorders in sexual offenders: their incidence and treatment. *Aggression and Violent Behaviour*, 12, 16–35.

Thomas, T. (2000) *Sex crime, sex offending and society*. Cullompton, Devon: Willan.

Weeks, G. D., and Gambescia, N. (2000) *Erectile dysfunction: Integrating couple therapy, sex therapy and medical treatment*. London: Norton.

Wincze, J. P., and Carey, M. P. (2001) *Sexual dysfunction: A guide for assessment and treatment*. London: Guilford Press.

Visit **www.pearsoned.co.uk/davidholmes** for a range of resources to support study. Test yourself with multiple choice questions and access a bank of over 100 videos that will bring the topics to life. Video coverage for this chapter includes an interview with Denise who suffers from Gender Identity Disorder, a discussion with Jade, a Dominatrix, and an exploration of sexual dysfunction in men.

Watch this interview with Liz who suffers from borderline personality disorder. This is one of several videos that explore issues and disorders relevant to this chapter at www.pearsoned.co.uk/davidholmes.

More than 'bad'

In the film *No Country for Old Men* (Joel and Ethan Coen, 2007), Javier Bardem plays the part of psychopathic hitman Anton Chigurh. The character's cold indifference to his own and others' mortality is symbolised by the killer's use of a captive bolt pistol (or bolt gun), normally used to stun animals prior to slaughter. The entire atmosphere of film captures the cold, ruthless but vacuous world of the psychopathic personality, in which there is no room for feelings, sentiment or empathy.

Media interpretations of 'personality disorder' have almost always assumed a psychopathic character, as in the overly glamourised but chilling portrayal of Dr Hannibal Lecter by Anthony Hopkins in the film *Hannibal* (Scott, 2001).

In this chapter we find that **psychopathy** is one of the less common personality distortions and represents only a small proportion of those with **anti-social personality disorder**. This is one of the ten *DSM* **personality disorders**, many of which have been inadvertently illustrated in film due to the 'larger than life' characterisations popular with the audience. This has been the case even from the early days of the cinema: for example, the character of Scarlett O'Hara (Vivien Leigh) in *Gone with the Wind* (Fleming, 1939) very clearly illustrates the unstable moods and extreme love–hate relationships that characterise **borderline personality disorder**. This disorder is illustrated in the case study below and detailed with the other *DSM* personality disorders in this chapter.

Being born with potential, brought up in a brutal environment, and neurologically damaged in early adulthood, perhaps formed the basis for Fred West being psychopathic and possibly one of the most brutal serial killers in history.
Source: Corbis/Matthew Polak/Sygma.

The concept and study of personality is a cornerstone of psychology and assumes that individuals have consistent ways of dealing with the world in terms of their thinking, feeling and behaviour (see Maltby, Day and Macaskill, 2007). We all think we can judge the character of others and make intuitive assumptions about how they will react, forming our individual or implicit personality theories, and we often share these concepts with others. More objective measures of personality such as the **five-factor** model and its psychometric measures (see the Research box on p. 414), produce a personality profile of scores along a number of personality trait dimensions (Costa and McCrae, 1992). In the case of personality disorders, rather than scoring along a number of dimensions, individuals are placed in a disorder category by meeting diagnostic criteria, as with other *DSM* disorders (see Chapter 4). Personality disorders are also more extreme and rigid in terms of their traits than normal personality profiles, and this leads to distress in the individual or those around them, and difficulties in occupational and social functioning. Thus, a personality disorder is a maladaptive pattern of behaviour that is pervasive and persistent throughout life.

There are three groups of personality disorders, referred to as **clusters** in *DSM-IV-TR*, which are given the labels **odd–eccentric**, **dramatic–emotional** and **anxious–fearful**. Within these clusters are a total of ten personality disorders (see Figure 14.1) that, although appearing to have fairly distinct primary features, mostly co-occur or overlap with each other. Often seen as related to **anti-social personality disorder**, the category of **psychopathy** (see Chapter 8) is not found amongst the *DSM* personality disorders, but it has been included here as an important aspect of the history of personality disorder and its forensic significance. The more contemporary category of **dangerous and severe personality disorder** (DSPD; see pp. 434–5) could be considered a relabelling and expansion of the forensic content of psychopathy, in that DSPD identifies those at risk of causing harm to others due to personality disorder.

The pervasive nature of personality disorders as well as the long-established fact that they are difficult to change or unlikely ever to be corrected by interventions (Livesley, 2001) has led to the use of the terms 'development' and 'management' in place of aetiology and treatment in this chapter. This approach also applies to psychopathy and DSPD, where intervention limitations have serious forensic implications for those diagnosed in terms of risk and incarceration. Personality disorders are an established area within forensic psychology, and professionals working in prison environments will frequently find themselves assessing such client groups for these disorders and in terms of any related elevated risk. There are many clinical challenges in working with personality-disordered clients, including their treatment refractory nature and the difficulties posed by a client's personality traits to the therapeutic process. Clinical assessment and diagnosis of personality disorders may be radically changed by any move to a **dimensional system** of measuring a profile of traits, in place of the current categorical system (see Clark, 2007). As this is a possibility within the period towards *DSM-V*, it will be examined further in the clinical issues section towards the end of this chapter.

Case study
The need for more: borderline personality disorder

Zoë had always been an impulsive child and her father often said that she picked this up from her mother. Her mother was also prone to mood swings, which frustrated Zoë's father, who blamed them for the many rows they had. When Zoë stayed with her grandmother, her parents often got drunk and argued. Her grandmother would ask her what happened in the home, but Zoë would be very sparing with the truth, using it to manipulate and extend her bedtime considerably. Zoë's emotionally chaotic home was transformed for ever when one of her mother's frequent suicide attempts proved fatal when she mistook one bottle of tablets for another.

Zoë was just 13 and reacted very badly to being kept by her father, who progressively took to drink as Zoë increasingly took to erratic and risky behaviour. Relatives assumed the situation to be inappropriate, with Zoë emulating her mother's role to some degree, and rumours of sexually inappropriate behaviour and clear evidence of violence towards her father. When Marc came into Zoë's life, she saw him as her knight in

CASE STUDY CONTINUED

shining armour to carry her away, but Marc was less impressed by a 16-year-old neurotic girl who seemed determined to keep him awake every night till 4 a.m. and disrupt every aspect of his life. She was often intensely caring, sentimental-ising every aspect of their relationship, but would seamlessly slip into recriminations and exhausting emotional outbursts to the point where he could no longer cope. He wanted to leave, but each time it was even mentioned, Zoë would violently accuse him of infidelity, cut her arms and make suicide threats.

Zoë had been severely underweight on a number of occasions and was obsessed with wearing 'size 0' clothes. She would impulsively buy on credit and pressure Marc into borrowing money from his parents. Marc began to see his life as a living hell, far from boring, but too chaotic and unstable to allow him to function normally. At that point Zoë met John, a wealthy socialite,

whose parents were accustomed to financing his excesses. Marc reacted badly to this and although he was relieved at returning to normal life, it hurt that Zoë's complete attention moved to John. Marc realised that Zoë's expectations of both John and himself were unattainable and that she might never be satisfied or settled with anyone. About a year later, he read about a socialite and his girlfriend colliding with a police car whilst arguing.

Zoë, having borderline personality disorder, had a substantial negative impact on many people's lives and as such would meet one of the criteria for treatment. Her zealous enthusiasm often covered up depressive moods, and desperate attempts to be secure and loved masked a great vacuum within her. However, Zoë could only ever see those close to her as either heroes or hated fiends, with little understanding of the reality in between.

General issues in personality disorders

Forensic origins of personality disorders

In courtrooms, being 'of good character' can have forensic implications, but this is a non-clinical judgement of personality and perhaps more specifically an implicit assumption of the presence or absence of aspects of personality disorder. The concept of 'not being of good character' could be said to mark out much of the documented history of personality disorders, which tended to emphasise their more disruptive and anti-social aspects. Early personality disorder literature along such lines was attributed to Pinel (1806) in his description of manie sans délire, or violence in the absence of delusions (Burton, 2006). In terms of identifying the dilemma posed by psychopathic behaviour, the short-lived term **moral insanity** used by Prichard (1835) was as apt as the phrase used in the later book title by Cleckley (1976), 'the mask of sanity'. This focus on those aspects that make up the psychopathic personality continued with Kraepelin, who expanded the concept to several types but kept within the confines of anti-social traits (Burton, 2006). However, the extreme traits found in current *DSM-IV-TR* personality disorders

are not all so profoundly anti-social or criminally based, but include disabling levels of dependency or perfection-ism (Emmelkamp and Kamphuis, 2007). This expansion beyond purely anti-social personality disturbances began with Schneider (1923), who provided the basis for contemporary personality disorder classifications (Burton, 2006).

DSM status of personality disorders

In *DSM-IV*, personality disorders are located on Axis II, indicating that they are relatively permanent disorders that should be considered in addition to and diagnosed separately from any other mental disorder from Axis I (see Chapter 4). Unlike the Axis I disorders, personality disorders are characterised by stable traits rather than transient symptoms or recurrent episodes. Thus, these prominent traits must be long-standing and not a reaction to specific situations or temporary mental states. Personality-disordered individuals may suffer difficulties, but it is often others around them who suffer most from their behaviour. Occasionally, specific employment or relationships may be found that are more consistent with these personality distortions. For example, an individual with **obsessive–compulsive** traits may adapt to work as an archive librarian, or the more **schizoid** personality could sustain employment as a systems analyst working in isolation. The disorder will inevitably lead to some

Research

Personality: state or trait?

Students of psychology will be familiar with the **state–trait** debate over the causes of behaviour, which has instigated a great deal of research to support each side of this very important theoretical division. Trait theorists, who believe that the fixed personality characteristics of the individual predict how they will react in any situation, disagree with **state theorists** or **situationists** such as **Walter Mischel**, who consider that people react differently depending on the situation in which they find themselves (see Carver and Scheier, 2008).

Mischel (1968) considered what he termed the **personality coefficient**, or relationship between traits and behaviour, to be a correlation of about 0.3, which would be a very weak relationship (see Chapter 5).

However, in normal individuals, the same traits are expressed by an individual across situations, although potential for change does exist if circumstances facilitate this (Maltby, Day and Macaskill, 2007). Some studies have reported personality disorders to change and become less prominent over time, such as Paris and Zweig-Frank (2001) finding reduced borderline personality symptoms over a number of years, suggesting the traits are not absolutely fixed for life.

However, personality disorder traits are very resistant to change with therapy. When these exaggerated traits enter a situation, it is the situation that tends to change in a predictable and problematic direction – a self-fulfilling prophecy of personality that follows the individual through life.

interpersonal conflict or other occupational problems, but these can be less fundamentally disruptive in more compatible contexts. Although this could be seen as stereotyping the character parts implied by each disorder, it is better viewed as damage limitation, as jobs can be changed but personality disorders tend to remain over time.

Differentiation of personality disorders

There are a number of specific categories of personality disorder, each deriving its name from the most prominent trait, which significantly disrupts the individual's occupational and social functioning. Having categories in abnormal psychology creates the illusion that they are clearly differentiated, with definite boundaries between them. However, 'carving nature at the joints' is not a simple matter and the boundaries in personality disorders, as with many other disorder subtypes, are far from clear (Holmes, 1994). Morey (1988) has demonstrated the remarkable overlap between the different personality disorders, with most sufferers qualifying for two or more personality disorder diagnoses at the same time, although more often than not these are from the same cluster (see below). More precise diagnostic criteria in *DSM-IV-TR* have brought about greater reliability in the delineation of individual personality disorders (Bennett, 2006).

Prevalence of personality disorders

Personality disorders are common, with general estimates that they affect around 10–13 per cent of the general population (Weissman, 1993). A smaller-scale UK study found that 4.4 per cent had a personality disorder with a predominance of males over females (Coid et al., 2006). However, the prevalence of personality disorders is very difficult to estimate for a number of reasons, including that many remain undiagnosed, but a reasonably reliable estimate of those having at least one personality disorder has been put at 13 per cent with data taken across a number of studies (Mattia and Zimmerman, 2001). The prevalence of personality disorders in inpatient and outpatient populations is much higher at around 50 per cent, and despite this comorbidity being separated on the separate axes of the *DSM*, it still confounds assessment and diagnosis to a significant extent (Burton, 2006). This figure is the same for the prevalence of personality disorders amongst those presenting with alcohol and substance use disorders, and it would seem to be the case that treatment approaches usefully overlap these comorbid disorders (Welch, 2007). In the general population, schizotypal, histrionic, dependent and obsessive–compulsive personality disorders are the most common, and narcissistic personality disorder is the rarest at around 0.2 per cent (Mattia and Zimmerman, 2001). Onset is almost always evident by adolescence or early adulthood (American Psychiatric Association, 2000).

Research

Psychometric instruments in the measurement of personality disorders and psychopathy

The assessment of personality traits has played a major part in the development of psychometric instruments, which are usually written tests that are used to infer inner mental processes. These have often been **self-report** questionnaires, such as the original **16PF** by Cattell (1956), the **EPQ** by Eysenck and Eysenck (1964) and the more recent **NEO-Personality Inventory-Revised** (NEO-PI-R) by Costa and McCrae (1992). Each of these instruments utilises a group of questions to rate the individual, who provides the answers on a number of dimensions of personality, such as **neuroticism, extraversion** or **agreeableness** by means of a score. These instruments have been tested for **reliability** and **validity** (see Chapter 5) and the final scores may be subject to statistical weighting depending on the population surveyed. Personality measures such as these are intended to differentiate personality types or patterns of dimensional scores in normal populations, but most have clinical criteria or score limits indicating the point at which greater scores indicate pathology. Since the 1980s, there has been development of the clinical potential for such scales as well as refining their use in non-clinical populations. In addition, instruments designed to assess personality pathology have also been used on normal individuals to enable comparisons between normal and abnormal populations (see Livesley, 2001).

The taxonomic measures for personality disorders (diagnosis) are more difficult to administer, as these usually comprise lengthy interview schedules in which clinicians make judgements on responses and observed signs. Rush, Pincus and First (2000) have edited an overview of psychiatric instruments for identifying *DSM* disorders, which include a number of diagnostic interviews for personality disorders. Here the five commonly used semi-structured interviews are explained, including the **International Personality Disorder Examination** (Loranger, 1999) and the **Diagnostic Interview for DSM-IV Personality Disorders** (Zanarini et al., 1996). These measures have to produce psychometric data for each successive edition of the *DSM* and *ICD* diagnostic manuals, as criteria for the disorders' change. However, in the initial use of new editions, reliability is often accepted on the basis of good reliability data from previous editions, which is generally above the standard cut-off of kappa 0.7 for interrater reliability (the degree of agreement between independent clinicians' ratings), in addition to good correspondence between testing on successive occasions or test–retest reliability data (Clark and Harrison, 2001).

Unlike the self-report personality inventories (questionnaires) for the normal population, interview examinations for personality disorders are usually more time consuming and range from 1 to 2 hours' administration time. However, some of these interviews can be obtained in computer-administered form and most have computer-assisted scoring. Because the nature of personality disorders includes instability, these measures tend to produce variable results over time as compared with the more stable personality traits in the normal population. Paradoxically, lower reliability figures in delayed test–retest studies may counter-intuitively make the measures seem to have good **validity**, a valid instrument being one that measures what it purports to and not something else (Livesley, 2001). These semi-structured interviews are generally scored by the client fulfilling the criteria for the presence of one feature of the disorder in a crudely graded manner. Absence of the criteria is usually scored as 0, with 1 being scored for a subclinical presence of the feature and a maximum score of 2 indicating that the full criteria are met for this aspect of the disorder. Alternative scoring scales can be used, with some interviews giving a score range of 0–6 and 4 being the clinical cut-off for the presence of disorder (see Clark and Harrison, 2001).

Personality disorder assessment interviews are aimed towards categorical diagnosis by fulfilling the criteria for *DSM* or *ICD* personality disorders. Other interviews assess pathological personality traits, but tend to be single-trait items such as the Psychopathy Check List-Revised 2nd Ed (PCL-R, Hare, 2003). Psychopathy is not a listed personality disorder in *DSM*, although it has been the major focus of personality disorder diagnosis in history. Based on the original psychopathy concept proposed by Cleckley (1976), the PCL-R is a very common instrument in forensic contexts as it is successful in estimating risk in offenders as well as the presence of psychopathic personality traits. It has high reliability and this is true when using non-clinicians specifically trained in the use of the PCL-R. This training is considered compulsory for clinicians by Hare (2003), as the criteria are too readily met without it, inflating scores and lowering both reliability and validity in administration. Although there are correlations with *DSM* anti-social personality disorder, those designated psychopathic by the PCL-R only comprise around 25 per cent of those diagnosed with anti-social personality disorder in prison (see Clark and Harrison, 2001).

In the assessment of personality disorders, the distinction has to be made between normal personality variations and the more extreme distortions that fulfil the criteria for these disorders. Thus the interviews used for this purpose tend to involve clinical ratings and judgements rather than the self-report data utilised for non-disordered personality measurement. However, with a move towards a dimensional system of personality diagnosis (see pp. 438–9), trait-based measures such as personality questionnaires may play a greater part in future assessments (Clark and Harrison, 2001).

Classification of personality disorders

Table 14.1 shows the slight differences between the equivalent *DSM-IV* and *ICD-10* personality disorders. There are more divisions in the *DSM-IV* system, although there are subtypes of emotionally unstable personality disorder in *ICD-10* (impulsive and borderline). This leaves no major *ICD-10* categories for narcissistic or schizotypal personality disorder. However, the *ICD-10* system *does* provide a category of schizotypal disorder in its section for schizophrenic disorders, and lists narcissistic under 'other specific personality disorders'.

The *DSM-IV* personality disorders are divided into three subgroupings or **clusters**. These share general features, which can also be viewed as **dimensions** of these disorders but are not measured as such (American Psychiatric Association, 2000). The clusters are as follows.

Table 14.1 *DSM-IV-TR* and *ICD-10* classifications of personality disorder (PD)

DSM-IV		ICD-10
A	Paranoid PD	Paranoid PD
	Schizoid PD	Schizoid PD
	Schizotypal PD	
B	Anti-social PD	Dissocial PD
	Borderline PD	Emotionally unstable PD
	Histrionic PD	Histrionic PD
	Narcissistic PD	
C	Avoidant PD	Anxious (avoidant) PD
	Dependent PD	Dependent PD
	Obsessive–Compulsive PD	Anancastic PD
		Also included with ICD
		Mixed PD
		Troublesome changes
		Other specific PDs
		(eccentric, 'unstable'
		type, narcissistic,
		passive-aggressive,
		psychoneurotic,
		immature)

- **Cluster A** personality disorders are characterised by odd and eccentric behaviour and possibly represent mild features of schizophrenia, such as paranoia, withdrawal and fanciful thought. However, there are no psychotic symptoms and these individuals are not schizophrenic. This cluster includes **paranoid personality disorder**, **schizoid personality disorder** and **schizotypal personality disorder**.

- **Cluster B** disorders have dramatic, attention-seeking, emotional and selfish features, with a tendency towards reckless and impulsive behaviour in some of these personality disorders. Individuals with these disorders tend to make others victims of their behaviour, although they can be destructive to themselves. **Anti-social personality disorder** is an important and controversial category here (also see Chapter 4). The more restrictive concept of **psychopathy** and the related forensic category of **DSPD** relate closely to anti-social personality disorder but belong as separate categories outside of *DSM-IV-TR* with important distinguishing features. The other disorders in this cluster are **borderline personality disorder**, **histrionic personality disorder** and **narcissistic personality disorder**.

- **Cluster C** personality disorders tend to show traits such as anxiety, apprehensiveness and fearfulness traits, and tend to be the victims of circumstance. The disorders in this cluster are **avoidant personality disorder**, **dependent personality disorder** and **obsessive–compulsive personality disorder**.

In all cases the individual traits that form the pattern of behaviour deviate from the expectations of the cultural context and are evident in at least two of the following areas:

- cognition, including the way the individual interprets others, the world and themselves
- emotion, its intensity, stability, appropriateness and scope
- interpersonal functioning
- impulse control.

To further meet *DSM-IV-TR* diagnostic criteria, the behaviour must be enduring, inflexible and pervasive across all situations, as well producing distress or impairing social and occupational functioning. The pattern tends to be stable from adolescence or early adulthood and not due to the effects of other mental or physical disorders, or the effects of substances (American Psychiatric Association, 2000). Diagnosis is usually applied after the age of 18 and may become evident via signs rather than symptoms (see Chapter 3), as symptoms tend to be **ego syntonic**, or consistent with ego integrity, as compared with the primarily **ego-dystonic** symptoms of **Axis I** disorders. However, it may be that only the long-term persistence of the extreme traits distinguishes these **Axis II** personality disorders from some **Axis I** disorders with similar symptoms (American Psychiatric Association, 2000).

The odd–eccentric cluster (A)

This cluster of three personality disorders shows mild or muted features that in more serious forms relate to disorders such as schizophrenia and possibly the autistic spectrum. Thus unreasonable suspiciousness and odd beliefs in **paranoid** and **schizotypal personality disorders** respectively can be related to **positive symptoms of schizophrenia** (see Chapter 19) specifically, paranoid ideation and delusions, whereas indifference to others and social environment found in **schizoid personality disorder** can parallel similar features found in the negative symptoms of **schizophrenia** or possibly **Asperger's syndrome** from the **autistic spectrum** (see Chapter 9). However, for the purposes of their research Gooding, Tallent and Matts (2007) considered all three disorders in this cluster to be **schizophrenia spectrum disorders**. Individuals in this cluster tend to show **inadequate coping styles** in avoiding social contacts during development (Bijttebier and Vertommen, 1999), which leaves an absence of any social support that could counter their self-isolation. There has been less research into the personality disorders in this cluster, and of the research that has been carried out, most has been directed at schizotypal personality disorder (Emmelkamp and Kamphuis, 2007). The three disorders in this cluster are as follows.

Paranoid personality disorder

As its name suggests, this personality disorder has pervasive, persistent and unjustifiable suspiciousness of others as its central feature, and sufferers anticipate being exploited and abused in the absence of any evidence that such suspiciousness is justified (American Psychiatric Association, 2000).

Such general suspiciousness can precipitate negative reactions in others and lead to friction or worse consequences requiring forensic involvement. In addition, paranoid individuals who are not in receipt of well-organised management of their disorder can undermine their treatment and other outcomes (Bateman and Tyrer, 2004b). They can be competitive with others and may emphasise areas of rehearsed expertise in order to appear superior to those they believe to be undermining them.

This determination to prove themselves right and others wrong also leads to viewing themselves as infallible, tending to look down on others or ridicule them in a sarcastic manner, and blaming others for their own mistakes. They are argumentative, complaining and competitive in a counterproductive way. Paranoid individuals may work hard to maintain a façade of superiority and the self-esteem that it justifies. This can give the impression of being cold and unemotional in interpersonal exchanges, which is exacerbated by aloofness and a need to control others (American Psychiatric Association, 2000). Although this gives the impression that paranoid individuals are insensitive, self-consciousness tends to co-occur with such paranoid traits as misinterpreting others' behaviour as threatening (Fenigstein and Vanable, 1992). This would suggest that sufferers are highly self-conscious about their public image and overly sensitive to potential attacks on it.

Those with paranoid personality disorder tend to be preoccupied with testing the loyalty and trustworthiness of other friends and work colleagues. This often leads to their feeling that there may be a conspiracy against them, or that they are the victims of discrimination or vindictive campaigns, which are remarkably similar to the ones they themselves try to orchestrate. Paranoid individuals can bear a grudge for extended periods, perpetuating resentment and vengefulness towards the other as well as being measurably lower on the trait of forgiveness (Munoz-Sastre et al., 2005). There is often hostility as a result of their interpreting the actions of others as being threatening towards them: for example, neighbours deliberately play loud music to annoy them, so they vacuum in the early hours in retaliation.

There may be a genetic relationship with schizophrenia, and paranoid behaviour often occurs as part of the prodromal syndrome or behaviour preceding the onset of schizophrenia. This association with schizophrenia is a major aspect of the hypothesised genetic aetiology of paranoid personality disorder (Gooding, Tallent and Matts, 2007). Their suspiciousness of others includes extreme jealousy in close relationships, and the relationship with schizophrenia in sufferers is such that both disorders can lead to pathological jealousy (American Psychiatric Association, 2000), with increased susceptibility to the delusional disorder, **morbid jealousy**, which includes more pronounced and specific suspiciousness in interpersonal relationships (see the case study below). This almost invariably proves highly destructive to their intimate relationships, in which they are constantly testing their partners, making unwarranted accusations with the most implausible evidence, and often engaging in complex investigative activities to obtain tenuous 'evidence' that cannot be understood by anyone but themselves. This can be devastating for loyal partners, as loyalty and kindness are usually viewed as highly suspicious (American Psychiatric Association, 2000). Ironically, the pressure put on intimates and close friends may lead to withdrawal, distrust and even infidelity in a kind of 'self-fulfilling prophecy'. This tautological cycle may spiral into anger or even violence without intervention. However, in cases where schizophrenia is the source of delusional jealousy, paranoid personality disorder should not be diagnosed, although those with a diagnosis may have brief psychotic episodes of up to a few hours in response to stressors, or may go on to develop schizophrenia subsequently (American Psychiatric Association, 2000).

Case study

Morbid jealousy

Aimee was always a suspicious but determined youngster and even considered that her parents had plotted against her 'behind her back' in having her admitted to hospital as a result of her refusing to eat during puberty. As with most teenagers, her early relationships were intense and difficult, but Aimee went further in monitoring her boyfriends and even girlfriends, checking on just who else they were friendly with and why. This lack of trust in even her closest friends led to conflict on a number of occasions and in particular when Aimee erroneously accused her boyfriend of just 2 weeks of seeing her school friend Joanne in secret. This alienated both parties from her and more or less directly led to them actually meeting up and dating for a while. For Aimee this was almost anticipated and the experience redoubled her efforts to make sure anyone she called her boyfriend would stay hers and would never stray.

Simon was a lot older than Aimee, but this reassured her in a strange way as her youth seemingly gave her the upper hand and Simon's fatherly manner evoked security and predictability. For Simon things were less straightforward, as he felt pressure to keep a running account of everything he did for Aimee, who would ring, text or even appear throughout his working day

and even during the night. Aimee was always apologetic and quick to move the conversation on to a different topic, but Simon felt mounting intrusion into every area of his life. After a few months, this became intolerable. He found Aimee looking through his mobile phone and this was followed by mounting accusations regarding the phone numbers of his female work colleagues. Papers began to disappear from his briefcase and study desk when Aimee was staying, with embarrassing consequences at work. Arguments ensued and eventually Simon began to think there would be no future for them as a couple if he wanted to retain his job and sanity.

Simon confided in a friend Janet, who was prepared to help and even have a chat to Aimee in her new professional role as marital counsellor. Simon met Janet for lunch and felt hopeful that a professional meeting of the three of them would help save the relationship. Aimee readily agreed to this, but kept referring to it in negative terms as if Janet were a voyeur laughing at their plight. At the meeting, pleasantries were dispersed by Aimee accusing Janet and Simon of having an affair and plotting to humiliate her before dashing from the room. It would be two further fraught relationships and several more years before Aimee received any professional help and even this intervention had only been precipitated by an actual assault on her then boyfriend. Whilst showing signs of morbid jealousy, Aimee demonstrated traits of paranoid, schizotypal and unusually borderline personality. As with a number of personality-disordered individuals, her general suspicion of others, including therapists, not only made her difficult to treat, but also brought her to the attention of clinicians in the first place.

Cognitive approaches to the disorder identify the erroneous assumption that others are always a threat or have malevolent intentions to be the primary error of thinking, leading to the paranoid behaviour and suspiciousness characterising paranoid personality disorder (Beck, Freeman and Davis, 2004). This attributional bias produces not only suspiciousness but also a tendency to blame others for negative events, as well as an emphatic reluctance to take the blame for such events or even the consequences of their own actions (Kinderman and Benthall, 1997). Emmelkamp and Kamphuis (2007) emphasise how those with paranoid personality disorder personalise blame for negative events that are more logically attributed to situational factors. Thus, their being impeded by a traffic jam during the rush hour will be blamed on another individual driver rather than the build-up of vehicles. Externalised paranoid beliefs such as these can engage a number of paranoid individuals who may be seen as a 'cult' of extremists in their joint blame of negative events on a target group of individuals who are usually simplistically differentiated from the paranoid personalities themselves (American Psychiatric Association, 2000).

Paranoid personality disorder may be detected during childhood in the form of eccentricity, odd communications, solitary behaviour and poor relationships (American Psychiatric Association, 2000). These traits exacerbate social problems by preventing the development of social support networks. The disorder is more common in males and has a prevalence of around 0.5–2.5 per cent in the general population (American Psychiatric Association, 2000). The disorder overlaps and co-occurs with borderline and avoidant personality disorders (Bernstein, 1993). The disorder should be differentiated from intergroup conflicts, where friction between opposing minority groups naturally produces suspicion and accusations, as opposed to the one-sided persecution that emanates from paranoid people in groups (American Psychiatric Association, 2000).

Schizoid personality disorder

The schizoid individual demonstrates a pervasive lack of engagement in social relationships, appears withdrawn and has a tendency to reject the company of others in almost all circumstances. They tend to avoid social events, which make them uncomfortable, and they have no close friends or people to share problems with apart from immediate relatives. In contrast to paranoid personality disorder, schizoid individuals seem indifferent to criticism or praise from others. Their indifference to others extends to their self-presentation, making no concessions to

fashion or taste in clothes. In a similar manner to those with Asperger's disorder, they present a 'bland face' to others, being poor at reading or expressing non-verbal information or other social cues (see Tantam, Holmes and Cordess, 1993; Holmes, 1994). They appear self-absorbed and lacking in emotional expression or gestures, and even under duress their emotions are muted (American Psychiatric Association, 2000). Both schizoid and schizotypal personalities score low on the Big Five personality traits of extraversion and agreeableness (Ross, Lutz and Bailly, 2002). However, schizoid individuals distinguish themselves from schizotypal by their lack of openness to experience in terms of the amount of variance explained in trait scores (Saulsman and Page, 2004). The social avoidance in schizoid individuals is distinct from that seen in avoidant personality disorder, in that the former is more pervasive and based on lack of interest rather than fear of embarrassment (American Psychiatric Association, 2000).

Schizoid individuals are not fearful of others but have no fundamental interest in other people, preferring solitary or impersonal object-oriented pursuits such as computing. This is usually evident from childhood when poor peer relationships may lead to their being picked on by others in school (American Psychiatric Association, 2000). They live in an unemotional world, seeming 'cold' and aloof, and have no real desire for sexual experiences, or intimacy of any kind. They are anhedonic: that is, they lack pleasure-seeking behaviour and would not understand much of the motivation for a beach holiday or joining in with a lively party crowd. Thus, they derive no pleasure from other people and do not find them rewarding for their own sake (American Psychiatric Association, 2000). This indifference includes a lack of sexual interest or interest in sharing any experience, substituting solitary activities that are often of an impersonal, mechanical nature. This lack of responsiveness also includes negative emotions, in that schizoid individuals can find expression of anger very difficult even under duress (American Psychiatric Association, 2000).

The schizoid individual's lack of social networks or socialising skills can also limit their occupational functioning (American Psychiatric Association, 2000) and even in jobs where this is not an essential component of their work, indifference to colleagues may lead to disengagement. Thus, schizoid individuals are seen as 'loners' and even in isolation do not seem to derive much pleasure from sensory experiences or activities. This clinical picture of self-isolation from social and other activities has been found more common amongst older patient groups (Engels et al., 2003). However, many of the criteria for the social withdrawal aspect of schizoid personality disorder are commonly found to increase naturally in the elderly as their social networks naturally decrease and their interest in sexual activity diminishes. Thus, some caution may need to be exercised in diagnosing the disorder in populations such as the elderly, where the baseline for these deficits may be higher.

Such general and **social anhedonia** has been linked to the later development of schizophrenia spectrum disorders (Gooding, Tallent and Matts, 2007) and provides a link to both the **autistic spectrum** and **negative symptom schizophrenia** (Holmes, 1994; Frith and Frith, 1991). Further links between schizophrenia and schizoid personality disorder can be inferred from their both being elevated by prenatal exposure to famine. Thus prenatal nutritional deficiency during the first trimester of gestation can predispose to both disorders (Hoek et al., 1996). However, the positive relationship between low body weight in children and adolescents and their having schizoid personality disorder is a correlation also shared with Asperger's disorder (Hebebrand et al., 1997). However, any interrelationship between these disorders may be on the basis that there is a great deal of overlap in the symptoms of schizoid personality disorders, Asperger's disorder and the negative syndrome in schizophrenia (Holmes, 1994). Some authors have gone so far as to question the basis for differentiating between some autistic spectrum disorders and schizoid personality disorder (see Kay and Kolvin, 1987).

Research and literature on schizoid personality disorder is both scarce and weak in empiricism, as most is based on psychodynamic case analysis, which lacks objective evaluation, and the theoretical approach no longer aligns with the current diagnostic criteria (Emmelkamp and Kamphuis, 2007). However, areas of accumulated case evidence have allowed some insights into the inner experiences of individuals with this disorder once individuals were reassured as to the purpose of these disclosures (see Emmelkamp and Kamphuis, 2007), although such insights will be subjectively coloured by the disorder itself.

Schizotypal personality disorder

Schizotypal personality disorder lies somewhere between normality and schizophrenia and has been thought of as attenuated schizophrenia, demonstrating a pervasive pattern of social and interpersonal deficits (American Psychiatric Association, 2000). Although schizotypal personality disorder often co-occurs with schizophrenia within individuals, to be diagnosed it has to be evident prodromally or outside of psychotic episodes. Schizotypal

Research

Links between schizotypy and schizophrenia

Researchers have sought to produce evidence of links between schizotypy personality disorder and schizophrenia. These links allow schizotypy, as a measurable trait, to be used in research relating these measures to selected psychological factors in the normal population. These findings are then used to make implications about schizophrenia itself on the basis that it is linked to schizotypy (see Chapters 12 and 18).

Schizotypy has genetic links with schizophrenia that have been evident in research for some time (Chang et al., 2002; Siever et al., 1990). Familial risk for schizotypy in comparison to other psychopathology has tended to confirm the suggestion that schizotypal personality disorder is a familial disorder representing a **phenotypic** (genetic) **expression** of liability to schizophrenia (Battaglia et al., 1995). Other biological similarities have been established for a number of years (e.g. Baron et al., 1984), including neuroimaging evidence of comparable brain abnormalities and a possible relationship to less severe cognitive deficits (Emmelkamp and Kamphuis, 2007).

There is much more research into schizotypal personality disorder when compared with the other disorders in cluster A and much of the research into schizotypy is biologically based as a possible consequence of its assumed genetic relationship to schizophrenia (Clark, 2007). In a further parallel to schizophrenia, the positive and negative symptom groupings have been transposed by Ross, Lutz and Bailly (2002) as positive and negative schizotypy factors thought to underpin the personality disorder. These two factors are considered to reflect the disorganised and eccentric aspects as opposed to the withdrawn, anhedonic aspects respectively. This conceptualisation of schizotypy as a multidimensional construct is perhaps recognised in *ICD-10*, where it is considered a syndrome not a personality disorder.

individuals have illusions, such as sensing an 'aura', odd beliefs, such as those surrounding the paranormal, as well as superstitious or magical thinking, such as that they have telepathic abilities. These illusory thoughts contrast by degree with the more profound hallucinations and delusions of schizophrenia. Thus schizotypal personality disorder shares features of schizophrenia but in clearly milder forms (Siever and Davis, 2004). Sufferers tend towards eccentricity and this extends to their appearance and adds to the overall 'mystical' image they adopt, which is also reminiscent of the eccentricity sometimes evident in individuals with schizophrenia when in remission. There are other mild versions of schizophrenic symptoms, such as unclear or peculiar speech, ideas of reference and some restriction or flattening of emotion (American Psychiatric Association, 2000). Tsakanikos and Reed (2005) found that individuals scoring high on **schizotypy** misperceive words more than controls, though these false perceptions fall well short of the hallucinations in schizophrenia. However, this deficit may indicate a basis for inreased levels of creativity in schizotypal individuals (e.g. Nette, 2001), providing some rationale for theories supporting an evolutionary reproductive advantage in such individuals (see Emmelkamp and Kamphuis, 2007).

A prominent feature of those with schizotypal personality disorder is their difficulty with close relationships, in which they may experience discomfort as well as displaying a diminished capacity for social contact. Schizotypal individuals have few close contacts beyond their immediate family and may not feel comfortable with people outside of these, even if very familiar with them. This alienation tends to be based on paranoid suspicions rather than negative self-judgement (American Psychiatric Association, 2000). Although sufferers express regret at their lack of friends, this is not reflected in their ongoing behaviour towards others, as they still avoid social closeness. However, there may be some compensatory behaviour, in that adolescents with schizotypal personality disorder use the internet for social interaction more than controls. This is in contrast to their consistently lower levels of real-world social interaction (Mittal, Tessner and Walker, 2007).

The prevalence of schizotypal personality disorder in the general population is around 3 per cent (American Psychiatric Association, 2000). There may be comparisons with the 'downward drift' hypothesis which is used to explain the lower socioeconomic status of schizophrenia sufferers (see Chapter 18), as the demographic characteristics of schizotypy also include lower employment, education and socioeconomic status (Emmelkamp and Kamphuis, 2007). Depressive and anxiety symptoms are common in schizotypy. As well as its relationship with schizophrenia, there are also large overlaps with other personality disorders, such as schizoid, paranoid, avoidant, narcissistic and borderline personality disorders.

Self-test questions

- What is meant by the state–trait debate?
- Are individual personality disorders clearly distinguished?
- Name a psychometric measure for each of personality, psychopathy and personality disorders.
- What distinguishes the three clusters of personality disorders?
- List two features distinguishing schizoid and schizotypal personality disorders.
- What is the relationship between cluster A disorders and schizophrenia?

The dramatic–emotional cluster (B)

This cluster contains personality disorders that have consistent implications for the involvement of forensic psychology. Some of the issues relevant to this have already been raised in Chapter 8 but will be examined here and in the later section on psychopathy from a more diagnostic and clinical perspective. Personality disorders have historically been an area that psychodynamic theorists and therapists have made their domain. Although this is no longer the case, this legacy persists, particularly with cluster B disorders such as narcissistic personality disorder (Emmelkamp and Kamphuis, 2007).

Anti-social personality disorder

Anti-social personality disorder is characterised by a pervasive and persistent disregard for the rights and feelings of others. This also includes the repeated violation of these rights and anti-social acts, as well as contravening accepted social norms by behaviour that would constitute grounds for arrest by legal authorities (American Psychiatric Association, 2000). Other acts include deceitfulness and persistent lying, including the repeated use of false aliases and using these approaches to manipulate others for personal, monetary or other benefits. They display a failure

The majority of convicted prisoners are personality disordered and the vast majority of these have anti-social personality disorder.
Source: Corbis/Dominique Aubert/Sygma.

to plan ahead, but instead a tendency to act impulsively for immediate reward and to display aggressive or assaultive behaviour towards others. There is persistent risk taking, disregarding the safety of all concerned including themselves, which is accompanied by indifference and an absence of remorse for the suffering or loss sustained by others. *DSM-IV-TR* criteria also include a lack of general responsibility in maintaining employment or fulfilling financial or other obligations (American Psychiatric Association, 2000). At least three of the above aspects of behaviour are required for a *DSM* diagnosis of the disorder.

The *DSM-IV-TR* set of criteria for anti-social personality disorder requires a diagnosis of **conduct disorder** before the age of 15 and assumes this pattern of behaviour is evident from childhood or adolescence with the average age of first symptom being 8 years (Robins, 1991). However, despite criteria reaching back into adolescence, *DSM* criteria set the minimum age for a diagnosis of anti-social

personality disorder at 18 years (American Psychiatric Association, 2000). Around 50 per cent of adolescents with conduct disorder become adults with anti-social personality disorder (Robins, 1991). If a diagnosis of childhood ADHD (see Chapter 9) is added to that of conduct disorder, the prediction of adult anti-social personality disorder increases to two-thirds of those young people (Simonoff et al., 2004). Adult behaviour parallels the truancy, theft, lying, arson, vandalism or running away found in conduct disorder in the form of the items mentioned above (e.g. irresponsibility, recklessness, lack of empathy or remorse, deceit, impulsivity, general irritability and aggression). These behavioural patterns may see expression in abusive domestic situations where a spouse or child may be assaulted and in social situations where aggression may result in fighting (American Psychiatric Association, 2000). Recklessness and risk taking can lead to their harming themselves, as in indiscriminate substance abuse, and involve others, as in dangerous driving or pranks in the workplace leading to actual bodily harm. *DSM-IV-TR* also identifies features that are very pertinent to **psychopathy**, such as superficial charm, overconfidence, a readiness to exploit and a lack of empathy that extends into their sexual and family relationships.

Dodge and Petit (2003) focused on social information biases as well as familiarity and readiness for aggressive responses in examining how developing anti-social responses in children differ from those of controls. Such children give selective attention to hostile cues and show bias in interpretation and a readiness to make aggressive responses, which they believe to be effective. This cognitive style of social information processing in children has been linked to persistent conduct problems later in life (Dodge and Petit, 2003). The development of aggressive responses and anti-social behaviour has often been blamed on what is labelled 'bad parenting' as a causal factor, which includes rejection, physical abuse, neglect and harsh inconsistent discipline. This is due to a consistent association of this parental behaviour and anti-social behaviour in the developing child (e.g. Farrington, 2005). However, as will be referred to in the later section on development, this association could also be due to parental reaction to pre-existing challenging behaviour in the developing child, or a third factor influencing both child and parental behaviour as well as the interaction of more than one of these (see Raine, 2002).

In addition to the interaction between child and parent above, if there is a genetic component for the child's anti-social responses, the trait is very likely to be present in one or both of the parents as well. Evidence for genetic involvement is supported by adoption studies, and heritability of anti-social personality disorder has been placed at 40–50 per cent by twin studies (Eley, Lichtenstein and Moffitt, 2003). Biological contributions to anti-social behaviour are now well established and have been discussed in Chapter 8 (e.g. Raine, 2002; Arseneault et al., 2000). Factors influencing development prenatally (during gestation) and perinatally (around birth) have also been found to relate to levels of aggression mediated by neurological abnormalities (Brennan, Grekin and Mednick, 1999; Moffitt and Caspi, 2001). One of these prenatal influences is maternal substance use (Moffitt and Caspi, 2001), and there is also a close association between later anti-social diagnoses and substance disorders, particularly alcohol abuse (Sutker and Adams, 2001). Substance use, anti-social personality disorder and its precursors are thought to share a common genetic influence, which may be environmentally differentiated into individual cases (Kendler et al., 2003). Thus anti-social behaviour may be thought of as a multidimensional construct with differing genetic, biological and environmental components in varying combinations for each facet.

Many of these antecedents of anti-social personalities are not easily prevented or changed, but as with other personality disorders, interventions can change the direction of their influence, limit the impact on others and moderate the resulting behaviour (see Emmelkamp and Kamphuis, 2007). Anti-social development pathways also often leave educational and skill deficits, either by associated brain area abnormalities, neglect, exclusion or behaviour disrupting the learning processes. If these deficits are addressed early in life then later anti-social behaviour can be reduced, particularly in the case of basic precursors such as language development and literacy (Snowling et al., 2000). Treatment of anti-social personality disorder is difficult but generally more successful than interventions for psychopathy. However, treatment for both disorders tends to be confounded by the element of punishment, due to intervention almost always taking place in prison.

Anti-social personality disorder is four times more common in males with a prevalence of around 4 per cent compared to 1 per cent in females. Prevalence from various studies has varied between geographic samples but has also varied as diagnostic criteria change, with a median prevalence of around 3.7 per cent in the wake of *DSM-III* (Livesley, 2001). Individuals with anti-social personality disorder more commonly meet premature deaths due to suicide, homicide, violence or accident (American Psychiatric Association, 2000). The close association of the disorder with lower socioeconomic status and living in poor areas can require some consideration during diagnosis, in that some anti-social behaviour may appear less disturbed when seen in a more hostile context. Although the disorder is one of the least amenable to therapeutic change, there is a moderating of anti-social behaviour as sufferers approach middle age (American Psychiatric Association, 2000).

The *DSM* diagnostic criteria for anti-social personality disorder tend to focus on objective anti-social and mostly criminal acts and could be said simply to redescribe a recidivist criminal. Thus, the majority of prison inmates

Focus

Clarification of terms

Anti-social personality disorder, psychopathy and sociopathy have been used interchangeably in the literature. However, the popular use of these labels breaches diagnostic boundaries and very much misrepresents each of these disorder concepts, which in some cases may be less than accidental.

The term **psychopath** is often substituted for anti-social personality disorder. However, psychopathy represents more psychological and intractable characteristics, which will be clarified later in this chapter. Similarly confounded is the more euphemistic US term **sociopath**, which has proven popular in the UK due in part to its implicit assumptions of a social rather than biological aetiology, and which could be seen as superfluous as it has similar defining features to psychopathy. The *ICD-10* classification **dissocial personality disorder** more directly parallels anti-social personality disorder in terms of criteria, but as with sociopath has been seen as a less overtly criminal label. Currently, the term **dangerous and severe personality disorder** (DSPD) has replaced psychopathy in the UK justice system, and represents any individual whose personality traits may pose a severe risk to self and others (see pp. 434–5).

Each of these terms implies behaviour that is manipulative and deceitful (American Psychiatric Association, 2000), lending credibility to their interchangeability. Perhaps as a result of this, there is obvious confusion in the minds of professionals, not to mention the media or public, over what each means. Given the forensic implications of these terms, there needs to be care and precision over their exact application.

would qualify as having anti-social personality disorder due to these overlapping definitions. In producing these objective criteria, *DSM-III* has been identified by some as having confounded the distinction between anti-social personality and criminality, in making it difficult to categorise an individual as one but not the other (Oltmanns and Emery, 2004). To some extent *DSM-III* sacrificed a degree of validity for reliability in dropping some of the more psychological criteria for objective behavioural items.

DSM-IV-TR differentiates **narcissistic personality disorder** by a lack of aggression, deceit and impulsiveness compared with anti-social individuals. **Histrionic personalities** also share many features, but tend not to engage in overtly anti-social activity and tend to exaggerate 'emotional' gestures more. Anti-social personalities rarely need nurturance from others as **borderline personalities** do, but tend to focus on material gain from manipulation (American Psychiatric Association, 2000).

Borderline personality disorder

Borderline personality disorder is characterised by unstable personal relationships, insecure self-identity, affective instability and pronounced impulsivity (American Psychiatric Association, 2000). As with other personality disorders, this unremitting and pervasive pattern of behaviour tends to persist from adolescence or early adulthood throughout life. The original name implied that these individuals were on the borderline of neurosis and psychosis but this is misleading (Kamphuis and Emmelkamp, 2000) and the disorder is better thought of as related to **mood disorder**, with which it is frequently comorbid. This close association of borderline personality disorder with mood disorders is characterised by unstable mood, with emotional swings from child-like dependence to intense and uncontrolled anger. Emotional outbursts tend not to return to a baseline of neutral mood but oscillate, so one upheaval tends to follow another (Emmelkamp and Kamphuis, 2007). Mood disturbance tends to be brief, rarely lasting more than just hours, and may involve anxiety, **dysphoria** or irritability (American Psychiatric Association, 2000). They may battle with dysphoria by constantly seeking stimulation and activity to avoid boredom and increasing awareness of a persistent and chronic sense of emptiness regarding themselves. Emotional outbursts in the form of intense anger tend to be uncontrolled and inappropriate to the situation, followed by guilt and recriminations against themselves for being inherently wicked (American Psychiatric Association, 2000).

A key characteristic of this disorder is that borderline individuals frantically avoid being alone through real or imagined abandonment, to which they react dramatically. Perceived abandonment is often interpreted as personal failure reflecting on their worth and a sense of being 'bad' as a result (American Psychiatric Association, 2000). The reaction to imminent separation is out of proportion to the perceived loss, and attempts at self-harm or even suicide indicate the desperate need to avoid the imagined pain of intolerable isolation. Abandonment may be projected on to emotionally benign situations such as unavoidable separations (e.g. business trips, changes to meetings or plans, or other people simply being late for meeting them). Paradoxically, given their need for dependable relationships, the intense but unstable relationships that borderline individuals make are under constant pressure, and as an inevitable outcome of a self-fulfilling prophesy, these relationships are usually short lived.

Borderline individuals are prone to intrusive harassing behaviour when testing the validity of relationships, which can result in **stalking** activity (Kamphuis and Emmelkamp, 2000). Individuals with borderline personality disorder very rapidly establish close binding relationships within a few meetings, often idealising the other person and demanding the same level of regard and attention from them. When the other individual inevitably falls short of these expectations, there is a dramatically rapid switch to devaluing them for not giving enough support, caring sufficiently or being totally committed to the needs of the borderline individual (American Psychiatric Association, 2000).

Their sense of self-identity is disturbed, leaving them uncertain as to what they really want in life. This unstable sense of self can be reflected in changes to their identity towards others, as in changing careers, future plans, circles of friends and other aspects of identity, even sexuality (American Psychiatric Association, 2000). There are often self-defeating elements to their behaviour, in undermining their own potential achievements, frequently just as they are about to come to fruition. For diagnosis, borderline individuals must engage in at least two areas of impulsive self-damaging behaviour, such as drug abuse (including medication), casual sex, reckless driving, binge eating, shopping sprees and gambling. Self-harm is a constant danger with borderline individuals and this includes self-mutilation, with around two-thirds of sufferers engaging in acts such as cutting or burning (Stone, 1993b).

Self-destructive behaviour also includes high levels of suicidality, resulting in impulsive acts of **parasuicide** (non-serious attempts) as well as actual suicide. The constant danger of suicide is very real, with up to 10 per cent of borderline individuals committing suicide, and this factor, combined with their being common in patient

Adolf Hitler was well known for his angry outbursts and moodiness. He is thought by many to meet the criteria for borderline personality disorder.
Source: Pearson Online Database.

populations and being a challenge to treatment attempts, makes this disorder a focus of research attention (Kring et al., 2007). Some individuals with this disorder may suffer psychotic-like or dissociative symptoms when under stress or at a point of abandonment (American Psychiatric Association, 2000). Borderline personality disorder is also associated with reported verbal, physical and sexual abuse in childhood (Ogata et al., 1990). However, the current mental state of borderline individuals is likely to distort recollections of abusive activity (Kring et al., 2007).

Impulsivity in borderline personality has been related to prefrontal cortex dysfunction, in that Soloff et al. (2003) found relative prefrontal hypometabolism in sufferers. In a female sample, Irle, Lange and Sachsse (2005) pointed to a possible neurodevelopmental deficit in the right hemisphere of borderline individuals, indicated by reduced right parietal cortex size and reduced hippocampal size, in agreement with previous studies. Irle, Lange and Sachsse (2005) relate these abnormalities to the experience of

milder psychotic symptoms and affective symptoms seen in borderline personality disorder. Some of these findings are tied to the premise that a reduction in **hippocampal** (and **amygdala**) size relates to exposure to childhood sexual and physical abuse.

In a review of neuroimaging in relation to borderline personality disorder, Lis et al. (2007) confirmed the disinhibition resulting from reduced function (and structure in some cases) of neural regions such as the amygdala, **orbito-frontal cortex** and **prefrontal cortex** as a probable cause of impulsive behaviour and emotional liability. The same review examined potential genetic contributions to these functional abnormalities, such as the **serotonin** transporter gene **5-HTT**, and posited possible roles for the genes for **dopamine** and MAOA. However, Lis et al. (2007) did identify methodological and other limitations in some of the studies in this area, as well as conflicting results across studies.

The difficulties of treating borderline personality disorder have become almost legendary in the psychiatric and psychological literature. However, although it is highly resistant to treatment, some have claimed progressive reduction of pronounced symptoms over periods of 6 years, to the extent that the majority of the sample no longer met the diagnostic criteria (Zanarini et al., 1996). Attractive borderline individuals with ability and intelligence tend to improve more easily over time, and those with poor socioeconomic status or education and with ongoing abuse are less likely to improve (Emmelkamp and Kamphuis, 2007). This said, a great deal of research and focused application of a very wide range of therapies have been applied to this disorder with limited success overall.

Dialectic behaviour therapy originated by **Marsha Linehan** has been directed at bipolar individuals, as it prioritises self-harm behaviours early in the treatment. However, empirical studies of its effectiveness are so few as to require more support before the treatment's effectiveness could be considered conclusive (Bateman and Tyrer, 2004a). Also having achieved some success with the disorder, **schema-focused therapy** utilises cognitive, behavioural and experiential techniques to address the individual's 'schemas' or beliefs and methods by which the borderline individual deals with the world, which in personality disorders are dysfunctional and resistant to change (Emmelkamp and Kamphuis, 2007; Beck et al., 2004). **Selective serotonin reuptake inhibitors** (SSRIs) have had some success in reducing impulsiveness and risk-taking behaviour in borderline individuals, as have mood-stabilisers for their affective symptoms (Tyrer and Bateman, 2004). Borderline individuals have to be medicated with caution, as they are likely to abuse their medications or even utilise them for suicide attempts.

With most personality disorders, but especially borderline personalities, reducing the extreme traits rather than a return to any form of normal functioning is the only rational goal.

The genetic liability for borderline personality disorder has been placed at 69 per cent in a large twin study (Torgerson et al., 2000), although there were some methodological limitations. The heritability of borderline features has been examined in an international sample, and additive genetic influences were found to explain a more modest 42 per cent of the variance of these features (Distel et al., 2007). Females scored higher on borderline features in this sample and have been found to have a higher prevalence than men in most studies, with females accounting for 75 per cent of the cases of borderline personality disorder (American Psychiatric Association, 2000). Although overall prevalence of borderline personality disorder is between 1 and 2 per cent in the general population, it is more common amongst patients at around 15–20 per cent of psychiatric inpatients (American Psychiatric Association, 2001).

Histrionic personality disorder

Individuals with histrionic personality disorder have a persistent and pervasive need to engage in overly dramatic, attention-seeking behaviour, and to use excessive emotionality in sustaining being the centre of attention (American Psychiatric Association, 2000). Often unable to deal with not being a focus for others, they feel awkward until they can draw attention to themselves by physical attractiveness, enthusiasm, seductiveness, dramatic over-disclosure, creating a scene or making up tales. These may be differentiated between males and females in that gender stereotypes may shape the behaviour, such as towards physical prowess in males and more feminine glamour in females. In exchanges between acquaintances, this behaviour combined with a propensity for seductiveness can seem threatening to existing relationships of those around them. Exaggerated gestures can also prove embarrassing to others, especially as these strongly expressed emotions can appear or disappear in an instant and thus seem faked. They tend to crave novelty or immediate satisfaction and may express great enthusiasm for a project or career and then let others down abruptly, having lost interest (American Psychiatric Association, 2000). As with other cluster B disorders, the effects of this disorder are mostly felt by those around the histrionic individual.

Histrionic individuals are preoccupied with attractiveness as a very important attribute and are often attractive themselves. They are disproportionately concerned with their own attractiveness and the superficial appearance of others, often making judgements based on these characteristics alone. A great deal of effort, time and financial resources are dedicated by histrionic individuals to improving their appearance, which they use to gain attention and impress others (American Psychiatric Association, 2000). They also use their appearance in a sexually seductive way and are often sexually provocative in all situations, including inappropriate social, occupational or professional circumstances, such as being a client with a legal adviser or clinician. They exaggerate the importance of passing acquaintances or transitory friendships, seeing these as more intimate and important than they are. They are also easily influenced by others, particularly authority figures and those with fame and power. Histrionic individuals are suggestible and may place their faith in trivial fashionable beliefs as well as individuals, in whom they tend to place too much trust too rapidly (American Psychiatric Association, 2000).

Theatrical displays of emotion hide the poverty of emotion actually felt by these self-centred people, who are attracted to acting and similar professions. Dramatic emotional overtures may be heaped on an acquaintance, but with little substance or detail as to why they deserve praise (American Psychiatric Association, 2000). This characteristic fits well with the phrase, 'it's not what you say but the way that you say it', in that much of the histrionic individual's dramatic and often opinionated style of speech and expression is designed to impress others but is in essence vacuous. They carry these performances into their personal lives, where they tend to *act* rather than honestly *live* their lives, and consequently have poor and short-lived relationships, often further undermined by sexual provocativeness and seductiveness, and exacerbated by impulsiveness. Histrionic individuals in relationships may play the role of the helpless victim or being ill, in almost fairy-tale-like attempts to manipulate and control partners.

The histrionic individual's concentration on the superficial and child-like attention seeking suggests some retardation of emotional development. Psychodynamic theory considers this to be a product of cold abandoning parents producing children who gain attention by creating crises or by other means recover some protective nurturing (Kuriansky, 1988). Cognitive approaches can similarly see histrionic adults assuming the role of a helpless child, seeking others to help them with their needs (Beck, Freeman and Davis, 2004). Theories of the aetiology of the disorder have survived much of the 'evolution' of histrionic personality disorder, where there have been shifts in criteria that are now attributed to borderline diagnoses (Emmelkamp and Kamphuis, 2007). However, study samples may have varied over time due to this, including those used for treatment evaluations.

Regardless of sample variations, there is still a lack of empirical research into histrionic personality disorder. As with other cluster B disorders, the use of CBT to reduce the extremes of the disorder tends to be an ongoing treatment process rather than an attainable goal (Bateman and Tyrer, 2004a). As with other cluster B personality disorders, there is the difficulty that the disorder tends to be ego syntonic, and although sufferers do seek treatment in the case of histrionic personality disorder, a good therapeutic relationship is difficult to achieve. A number of psychodynamic therapies have been applied, addressing the above proposed emotional biases emanating from childhood, but with no empirical support for this approach (Kring et al., 2007). There appears to be no specific treatment

approach for histrionic personality disorder with controlled evaluation data (Emmelkamp and Kamphuis, 2007). Medication such as SSRIs may be being taken for other comorbid disorders, but can in some cases exacerbate the 'helpless' role adopted by the histrionic client (see Gintalaite, 2007).

Although higher in clinical populations, the prevalence of this disorder in the general population is around 2–3 per cent and appears more common in females within clinical populations, though there is little current gender difference in the general population (Mattia and Zimmermann, 2001; American Psychiatric Association, 2000). Female bias in assumed prevalence may be due to the selective application of this diagnosis (Pfohl, 1995). Histrionic personality disorder overlaps with borderline personality disorder and has a high rate of comorbidity

Focus

Narcissism and living in fantasy

To what extent can personality disorders be an excuse for serious crime if insight is intact? Brian Blackwell used Narcissistic Personality Disorder to reduce culpability for killing his parents.
Source: Press Association Images (PA Photos).

The self-image of narcissistic individuals is often tinged with fantasy or what normal people would consider the material of day-dreams, such as fictional mass recognition, celebrity status, attractiveness or success, with which they are very often preoccupied. They have a need for high levels of admiration and may resort to their fantasies to create a **persona** for themselves, which can thus fulfil this need. They then enact this persona, often aided by pathological lying to gain the attention of others.

The UK teenager **Brian Blackwell** created a fantasy role as a champion tennis player, which he used to impress his girlfriend and others. He went on to use narcissistic personality disorder in a plea of diminished responsibility when charged with killing his parents, whom he had seen as preventing him from living out this fantasy. He subsequently funded a lavish holiday with their money, with little sign of guilt or remorse. This was the first time narcissistic personality disorder had been used for such a plea in a UK court. Although his plea did reduce his sentence, he is likely to have his risk to others assessed prior to his being able to be released.

with anti-social personality disorder, with which it may share some causal elements.

Narcissistic personality disorder

As the name suggests, individuals with narcissistic personality disorder are highly self-centred, having an unrealistically high opinion of themselves and their position in life. This grandiosity is pervasive and persistent from before adulthood, affecting all areas of their lives, and is not just a matter of showing off to some friends. Those with narcissistic personality disorder require constant attention and compliments, but lack genuine empathy for others and thus take advantage of those around them (Emmelkamp and Kamphuis, 2007). They may select acquaintances on the basis of utility or attentiveness, and exploit them with little concern for their feelings or welfare. Their overriding concern for themselves is not reflected in their regard for others, which tends to be non-existent and closer to disdain (American Psychiatric Association, 2000).

Narcissistic individuals also believe they can only properly relate to people with high status, which is how they see themselves, and they may ignore those they perceive as ordinary, regardless of genuine personal characteristics. They may overly rate or praise these special friends or professionals, whom they regard as being associated with them, enhancing their own status even further. However, if these select associates fail to reciprocate this affiliation or fall short of expectations, thus failing to meet the narcissistic individual's unrealistic expectations, they will be devalued and criticised (American Psychiatric Association, 2000). The lack of insight of those with this disorder means that they are often surprised when their arrival does not warrant special treatment, attention fails to be given to them, or their achievements are not praised. They will also continue to focus on the minutiae of their own concerns on the erroneous assumption that all are as infinitely interested as they are themselves (American Psychiatric Association, 2000). This self-obsession and particularly their grandiose view of themselves differentiates the narcissistic individual from other cluster B disorders (Emmelkamp and Kamphuis, 2007).

They devalue the efforts and achievements of others and inflate the importance of their own, whilst assuming that the wider audience see these distortions the way they do (American Psychiatric Association, 2000). This egocentricity, combined with their lack of empathy, leads to a lack of concern for the welfare of others and an expectancy that others will be as interested in the narcissistic individual's welfare as they are themselves. This is highly destructive to any relationships they may have, which also suffer from their jealousy and an arrogant sense that they deserve superior treatment at all times based on their self-proclaimed uniqueness (Emmelkamp and Kamphuis, 2007). Their jealousy and presumed jealousy of others for them can lead to berating or denying others' achievements and a bizarre sense of entitlement, which can lead to usurping the recognition of others or even their possessions. They are often aloof or arrogantly snobbish towards others, even supposed friends (American Psychiatric Association, 2000). However, they are also very sensitive to criticism of themselves and will react very badly to this with retaliation, rage or a false humility to protect their pride. This has been related to the paradoxical coexistence of both vulnerability and grandiosity in narcissistic individuals, which can result in a narcissistic rage when they are let down (Morf and Rhodewalt, 2001).

This disorder has been thought to be on the increase as a result of society being more selfish in general and, as with histrionic personality disorder, may reflect a failure to grow out of a childish, self-centred way of regarding others. Sperry (2003) amongst others considers overly supportive parenting to behaviourally and cognitively encourage narcissistic attitudes and behaviour in their children, often attributing them with special talents they do not possess. However, although many teenagers and children tend to be much higher on narcissism than adults, this does not necessarily lead to a diagnosis of the disorder (American Psychiatric Association, 2000). Psychodynamic theorists adopting the object relations approach, such as Kernberg and Caligor (2005), emphasise striving to be independent and self-sufficient as driving narcissism, which may indirectly relate to the higher numbers of narcissistic individuals who have lost parents when younger (Comer, 2007).

Breaking down the egocentric views of narcissistic individuals is one goal of schema-based therapy and other forms of CBT, as well as increasing their ability to empathise with others and not overreact to criticism from them (Comer, 2007). Therapists are often subject to attempts by narcissistic individuals to make them subscribe to their inflated view of themselves, and psychodynamic therapists claim that clients project their narcissism on to them. As with most personality disorders, various therapeutic approaches have produced very limited success (Comer, 2007). Narcissistic personality disorder is one of the rarest personality disorders, with a prevalence of 1 per cent in the general population (American Psychiatric Association, 2000). There is little empirical research on this personality disorder (Emmelkamp and Kamphuis, 2007).

The anxious–fearful cluster (C)

In contrast to cluster B, cluster C disorders primarily inflict suffering on those with the disorder and these personality disorders do respond better to interventions (Comer, 2007). The lives of sufferers are dominated by fears which limit their social and occupational functioning significantly and can lead to problems in other areas of their lives. Although these disorders are anxiety based, there is no clear relationship with the anxiety disorders (see Chapter 12).

Avoidant personality disorder

Avoidant personality disorder is characterised by a pervasive and persistent pattern of inadequate feelings, oversensitivity to criticism and social inhibition and avoidance (American Psychiatric Association, 2000). Avoidant individuals are very sensitive to any negative evaluation by others and are fearful of causing social embarrassment for themselves from early adulthood. This anxiety leads them to exaggerate the potential difficulties of exposing themselves to public scrutiny in order to avoid such situations. Fear of criticism often results in not engaging in any activities during school or later at work where interaction with others would potentially lead to rejection or criticism. This would include taking on senior roles or participating in societies or groups where they might be subject to greater scrutiny (American Psychiatric Association, 2000). They will avoid or cancel commitments at the last minute in anticipation of possible scrutiny or embarrassment. Such fears and avoidance, exacerbated by low self-esteem, can severely limit career progress, especially where social networking is a necessary part of the job (American Psychiatric Association, 2000).

Intimate relationships are very difficult and participating in intimacy or disclosing personal feelings is seen as taking a high risk of exposure to criticism or even devastating ridicule. Anxieties about rejection or criticism can lead those with avoidant personality disorder to avoid relationships entirely, or even avoid the attention of others unless they are certain that they will be uncritically liked and not subject to evaluation (American Psychiatric Association, 2000). They become hypersensitive to the smallest indicators of rejection and may inadvertently precipitate criticism by their sensitivity and tense apprehensive demeanour. Avoidant personalities are thought to avoid novel situations and experiencing emotions, and to have a low tolerance for emotional distress (Emmelkamp and Kamphuis, 2007). They try not to be salient in any way in situations involving others, and appear shy and inhibited in social settings. The belief that they are inferior can make avoidant individuals strive to achieve perfection, in the hope of thus gaining a predictable positive response from others. Regardless of achieving a high level of skill and control over their appearance, they alway consider themselves unattractive, socially clumsy and inferior to others. Whatever they say in public is likely to be embarrassing or subject to criticism, so they tend to be silent (American Psychiatric Association, 2000).

These characteristics can isolate avoidant individuals, making them appear as inadvertent loners to others. Their **social capital** is greatly reduced and they have few friends whom they can, or would dare to, call on if in need. In describing this disorder in 1981, **Theodore Millon** stressed that the avoidance of social relationships was a result not of indifference (as in schizoid personality disorder), but of the anxiety caused to avoidant individuals by entering into relations with very low self-esteem. Thus, it should be emphasised that avoidant individuals do desire friendships and intimacy but fear being shamed. This can lead to seeking substitute relationships in fantasy, and some may come to engage in **pseudo-intimate relationships** with unattainable people, such as distant celebrities or those no longer living (Comer, 2007).

Overprotective and sheltered parenting has been thought to prevent sensitive, potentially avoidant children from habituating to aversive stimuli as they develop, leading to avoidant personality disorder (Meyer, Ajchenbrenner and Bowles, 2005). Schema-based approaches to avoidant personality disorder have followed from this aetiological theory, as well the broader approach addressing other avoidant-based schemas (Beck, Freeman and Davis, 2004; Emmelkamp and Kamphuis, 2007). Although cluster B disorders are associated with victimisation, avoidant personality traits more frequently characterise homicides of spouses than psychopathic traits (Dutton and Kerry, 1999). Avoidant personality disorder overlaps with **borderline** and **dependent personality disorders** and is very frequently comorbid with depression (Kring et al., 2007). There is thought to be a lot of overlap between avoidant personality disorder and **social phobia**. Although they come from different disorder classifications, there is much support for the idea that they come from the same aetiological background, including a common genetic vulnerability (Reichborn-Kjennerud, 2007). It has been proposed from more than one source that the two disorders differ mostly in terms of severity of symptoms and degree of aetiological contribution (Emmelkamp and Kamphuis, 2007).

Dependent personality disorder

As its name suggests, individuals with this personality disorder are abnormally passive in all relations with other people. They find making everyday decisions very difficult and will allow others, particularly partners, to make all decisions for them. They lack confidence and suffer high degrees of anxiety if they have to request anything of others or make suggestions, and they are very unlikely to express disagreement or anger with those on whom they may be dependent (American Psychiatric Association, 2000). If they do make a decision or request, it is usually on the advice of others and with a great deal of reassurance, believing themselves to be incompetent (Emmelkamp and Kamphuis, 2007). Indecisiveness and lack of initiative can be detrimental to occupational functioning and can prohibit a number of career options. More major decisions in their lives always require others to take responsibility. Dependent individuals tend not to initiate projects, make suggestions or pass comment due to their lack of confidence in themselves and their abilities, rather than as a result of any real lack of ability or motivation (American Psychiatric Association, 2000). In a kind of self-fulfilling prophecy, this dependency prevents their learning the skills and gaining the confidence to function independently in later life.

This submissiveness is pervasive and is accompanied by an extreme fear of separation that results in clinging behaviour or neediness (Emmelkamp and Kamphuis, 2007). Dependent personalities will also cling to inappropriate relationships that they often know to be damaging to them. They will rapidly rush into a new relationship, sometimes with little discrimination, as they are desperately afraid of being left alone. This fear of abandonment has similarities to the neediness in borderline personality disorder (Emmelkamp and Kamphuis, 2007). They are anxious, helpless and uncomfortable when alone, even if this is temporary, and will join in with groups they do not like to avoid being isolated (American Psychiatric Association, 2000).

Dependent individuals will agree with decisions they know to be wrong so as not to risk conflict and potential loss of a relationship. In forensic contexts, this can lead to their being relied on for **alibis**, acting as unwilling accomplices or giving **false witness** in court. In such cases their conviction that they are incapable of functioning adequately on their own leaves them open to manipulation and exploitation by others (American Psychiatric Association, 2000). Individuals with dependent personality disorder are also frequently placed in the role of victim, with around 80 per cent being victims of violence (Cormier, LeFauveau and Loas, 2006). They will also take on unpleasant, even criminal tasks as well as enduring verbal and sexual abuse in order to perpetuate their dependent relationship, even though escape from such situations is relatively easy (American Psychiatric Association, 2000).

These dependent behaviours are directed towards eliciting care-giving behaviour from others, in the belief that they are helpless on their own. There is a reluctance to appear competent or independent to any degree, as this may lead to their being abandoned, and thus the helpless role is maintained in every area of their lives (American Psychiatric Association, 2000). This nurture-seeking behaviour may be directed at a partner but also at a parent, even as an adult, relying on them to decide where the person should live or seek employment.

Many dependent personality disordered individuals seem to have failed to detach from their childhood bonds and cling to others as substitutes for their lost parental security. Some authors (e.g. Stone, 1993b) believe the sudden disruption of the maternal bond to lead to these behaviours. This abnormal development of the parental bond may be a distortion based on similar mechanisms to **John Bowlby**'s concept of **maternal deprivation** (Bowlby, 1951). There may be some history of separation anxiety in childhood, or sometimes medical illness may precipitate a dependent set of behaviours (American Psychiatric Association, 2000). Blatt (2004) considers two clusters of personality style, self-criticism and dependency, and associates them with parental upbringing that is not consistent as well as strict and controlling.

Anxiety and depression are often comorbid with dependent personality disorder, which also co-occurs with **avoidant, borderline** and **histrionic personality disorders**. Although rates vary, prevalence of this disorder is around 2.2 per cent in the general population (Mattia and Zimmerman, 2001). The rates tend to be greater for females than males and onset tends to be detected in early adulthood, as detection during early years is confounded by dependency being a normal aspect of childhood (American Psychiatric Association, 2000).

Obsessive–compulsive personality disorder

The main traits in obsessive–compulsive personality disorder include an undue focus on detail, sticking to routines and an unnecessary adherence to rules. Obsessive individuals have a pervasive preoccupation with control over themselves and others, imposing perfectionism and orderliness (American Psychiatric Association, 2000). Such overcontrol of behaviour is usually self-imposed and counterproductive, making the individual inflexible, inefficient and lacking in openness. This overly pedantic approach to life's tasks aims constantly for perfection, but this is usually accomplished by undue focus on some minor detail and is very costly to the task as a whole. Those with the disorder are prone to repetition, particularly checking for errors or that everything is in place, to the extent that the purpose of the task may be lost or progress becomes so slow that others lose patience. Getting things in order in their minds can be more important than the real-world task, and this can prove very frustrating for those who work with them.

The attention to detail leads the obsessive individual to find great difficulty in making decisions, and although they prefer work to pleasure (especially males) and seem industrious, their overall performance is poor due to bad time management and preoccupation with less relevant detail. They impose very high standards for themselves that are unlikely ever to be met, leaving them with a sense of persistent failure. They are distressed by poor performance but have limited insight into how their obsession with detail has a part to play. This obsessive focus leads to aspects of their lives or jobs outside of it being neglected and falling into disarray (American Psychiatric Association, 2000). Obsessive individuals will spend the majority of allocated time on a trivial or preparatory job, leaving the

major task till the last second and being unable to attempt, let alone complete it. The standards set for a task usually include perfectionism at all levels, which tend to make the task unachievable, regardless of the fact that insufficient time has been allocated to it (American Psychiatric Association, 2000). For example, as a university student they may rewrite essays endlessly because each falls short of 'perfect', and as a result they may miss deadlines and perhaps never finally hand in the work.

Their lack of interpersonal warmth and serious, anhedonic approach to life makes them poor partners in relationships, though some find their reliability and predictability reassuring. Their excessive devotion to work leaves little space for more social activity, both restricting access to new friendships and severely testing existing ones. Pleasurable activity is often postponed, and in the case of holidays, this postponement is often indefinite (American Psychiatric Association, 2000). In leisure time they are often uncomfortable, feeling that valuable work time is being lost, making others feel on edge and sometimes turning leisure or even play activities into serious tasks more reminiscent of work. Their rigidity of thought and attitude is damaging to social relations of all types. Obsessive individuals tend to be inflexible about moral and ethical issues and will impose these rules on others, particularly those close to them. In some individuals, this style of righteous imposition can lead to criminal acts against those flaunting these codes of conduct, especially when in combination with cluster B disorders.

Obsessive individuals can be stubborn over a wide range of issues and rigidly oppose change or attempts to work around rules (American Psychiatric Association, 2000). Although the inefficiency and drastic slowing down of current tasks can be distressing to the obsessive individual, they tend to be unaware of the fact that this procedural slowness is frustrating and annoying to others. Despite this, they are reluctant to delegate or accept help if they see it as their duty to complete a job, as the work would not be up to their perfectionist standard, which they will specify in great detail if someone is hired for a task. The obsessive rigidity of their vision of the world will prevent them from seeing such tasks from another's point of view and can lead to their being authoritarian about the way things should be done, as well as deferring to others seen to be in higher authority. They are harsh with themselves should they make a mistake and critical of work less than perfect, often exaggerating minor imperfections (American Psychiatric Association, 2000). Rarely, this can enter the forensic domain when prolonged restrained anger or repressed anger gives way to outbursts at imperfection or disruption of routine, and can result in damage or injury.

Focus

OCPD, hoarding and the anal character

Obsessive personalities have great difficulty in discarding objects that they no longer need and may still cling to damaged items of no value or use to them whatsoever, such as used train tickets. They tend to hoard objects rather than consume them – a symptom which can become an area of disorder in itself (see Chapter 10). Hoarded items can encroach on living space to a pathological extent and represent a physical indicator of the disorder to others. If another tries to help in discarding items, however trivial, it produces great distress out of proportion to the loss. This insistence on hoarding rather than using is especially focused on money, where there is an insistence on saving for a rainy day that never comes. This can result in their being seen as miserly and mean, often overlooking domestic repairs or the need for new items to save for the future (American Psychiatric Association, 2000).

Many of the obsessive traits are those described by **Sigmund Freud** in his writings on the **anal-retentive** or **anal-regressive character** (see Chapter 3). There is much anecdotal illustration of this explanation, such as the obsessively rigid behaviour of antique dealers in their hoarding and retention of essentially ageing brown objects that are ostensibly for sale. A great deal of work has been done by Paul Klein, who studied the anal character for his PhD and produced factor analytic support for aspects of Freudian theory. However, there is little unambiguous empirical evidence to support this classic aspect of psychodynamic theory (Emmelkamp and Kamphuis, 2007).

Obsessive–compulsive personality disorder is not the same as the **anxiety disorder** obsessive–compulsive disorder (see Chapter 10); obsessions or compulsions are not criteria for the personality disorder (Kring et al., 2007). However, people with obsessive–compulsive personality disorder are also prone to episodes of **obsessive–compulsive disorder**, the latter being a much rarer condition, and explanations for the anxiety disorder have also been applied to the personality disorder (Comer, 2007). The presence of obsessive–compulsive personality disorder can reduce the treatment efficiency of pharmacological and other interventions for the obsessive–compulsive anxiety disorder (Cavedini et al., 1997). CBT interventions tend to target the rigid and dichotomous thinking seen by cognitive theorists as underlying the symptoms (Beck, Freeman and Davis, 2004). Obsessive–compulsive personality disorder is thought to be the least functionally disabling of the personality disorders, and it has been suggested that it may not qualify as a disorder and be assigned as a 'problem of living' (Emmelkamp and Kamphuis, 2007).

Prevalence of the disorder varies greatly between studies and has produced a median of 4.3 per cent (Mattia and Zimmerman, 2001); however, the *DSM-IV-TR* figure for the general population is given as 1 per cent (American Psychiatric Association, 2000). Although one of the commonest personality disorders, it has received disproportionately little empirical research attention (Emmelkamp and Kamphuis, 2007). The disorder is often comorbid with avoidant personality disorder (Kring et al., 2007).

Self-test questions

- How can avoidant personality disorder and social phobia be distinguished?
- What are the distinctions between avoidant and dependent personality disorders?
- What key characteristic do all cluster C personality disorders share?
- Which cluster C disorder could increase the chance of providing a false alibi in court for a partner?
- Which Freudian stage has been used to explain obsessive–compulsive personality disorder?
- Why are obsessive–compulsive personality disorder and obsessive–compulsive disorder different?

Psychopathy and DSPD

Psychopathy

The clinical forensic context of both psychopathy and the broader contemporary labelling of it under dangerous and severe personality disorder (DSPD) has been covered in Chapter 8. As outlined in the earlier chapter, psychopathy does not appear as a personality disorder in the *DSM*, and although it shares some superficial features with anti-social personality disorder, it is differentiated in terms of psychological symptoms, pervasiveness and implications for risk within the justice system (Hare, 1993; Blair, Mitchell and Blair, 2005). Estimates from 10 per cent to around 30 per cent of individuals with anti-social personality disorder could be labelled psychopathic using these more psychological traits (see Hare, 1986), rather than the overt behavioural acts utilised as criteria for the personality disorder (see the case study on p. 433).

In trying to describe and define psychopathy, the concept of evil is often invoked and the importance of case studies is emphasised (Blair, Mitchell and Blair, 2005). The idea that an evil person should be not just someone who carries out callous acts on others, but should actually enjoy inflicting pain, has been utilised by film-makers and writers. However, for those encountering psychopaths in the real world, being manipulated and the casual disregard for the suffering of others are more commonly seen as salient features (Hare, 1993). From Chapter 8, a checklist of features of psychopathy derived from Cleckley (1976) has been usefully refined by Hare (1986; 2003) as a screening instrument for the detection of psychopathy in the form of the **PCL-R** (2nd edition). The extended list of features that characterise psychopathy, drawn together from a number of studies, can be seen in Table 14.2.

The primary characteristics of psychopathic individuals are their pervasive propensity to exploit and manipulate others and their guiltless lack of empathy in so doing (Hare, 2006). There is a myth surrounding psychopaths, portraying them as being above average intelligence, which is perpetuated by portrayals of the psychopath as criminal

Table 14.2 Characteristics of psychopathy

Socially skilled	Inability to profit from experience
Absence of guilt/remorse	
Impulsivity	Inability to maintain relationships
Stimulus seeking	Irresponsibility
Easily bored	Parasitic lifestyle
Low frustration tolerance	Manipulation of others
Shallow affect	Emotional immaturity
Unclear objectives	Promiscuous behaviour
No realistic long-term goals	Multiple short-term affairs
Grandiose sense of self-worth	Aggression
Egocentricity	Anti-social acts
Pathological lying	Criminal versatility

genius, as in Dr Hannibal Lecter in the film *Silence of the Lambs* (Jonathan Demme, 1991). In fact, their IQ does not differ significantly from non-psychopathic criminals. Being socially skilled and having superficial charm has enabled serial killers such as **Ted Bundy** to disarm victims, but the effect of the charm tends to dissolve when those being manipulated become aware of the true motives of the psychopathic individual. Although they have adequate intelligence and seem superficially charming, psychopathic individuals are paradoxically poor at social adjustment, which is thought to relate to their deficits in **trait emotional intelligence** (Malterer, Glass and Newman, 2008).

They seem to lack any sense of moral values and show no guilt or remorse for exploiting or harming others, sometimes in extreme ways (Hare, 2006). Their impulsivity and failure to look beyond the present or plan for the future has been illustrated in laboratory experiments in which psychopathic individuals postponed inevitable punishment significantly more than controls who wished to 'get it over with' (Hare, 1970). This may find some of its explanation in studies which revealed that psychopathic individuals showed less anticipatory fear or arousal to aversive stimuli, suggesting biological differences (Lykken, 1995). This possibly extends to their real-world behaviour not being changed by punishment and their inability to profit from experience.

A low boredom threshold and stimulus-seeking behaviour often lead to drug and alcohol abuse but may also extend to other thrill seeking and risk taking, which could include manipulation or even harm to others (Cleckley, 1976). Psychopathic individuals have a low frustration tolerance and cannot delay gratification, even if to do so is profitable. This seeking of quick thrills at the expense of longer-term satisfaction also characterises their promiscuous approach to short-lived affairs and other relationships, in which they cannot give or receive emotion of any depth (Hare, 2006). They are parasitic and irresponsible in and out of relationships, where their ability to lie pathologically to feed their egocentric needs destroys the lives of those around them (Hare, 1993). Amongst the remaining criteria for psychopathy is aggression as well as anti-social or criminal acts. Factor analysis of the checklist items has tended to reveal two factors, one under the label of anti-social and impulsive traits, and a factor pertaining to interpersonal or affective items (Blair, Mitchell and Blair, 2005).

Psychopathic individuals are frequently identified among caught criminals and are six times more likely to offend than these convicted peers (Wong, 1985), but not all are found on the wrong side of the law. As pointed out in Chapter 8, those narrowly escaping criminalisation may be less aggressive, such as the homeless and feckless drifter, more creative, such as an unethical experimental scientist, or using their insensitivity to others to some advantage in business, politics or the military (Hare, 1993; Blackburn, 1993). Such views of psychopaths as being successful in military battles as cold ruthless 'terminators' may need to be tempered by the fact they also tend to take dangerous risks and to be too selfish to be heroes (Hare, 1993).

Psychopathy has not always been regarded as a form of pathology in the sense that the nervous system or behaviour is 'ill' or dysfunctional. Although damage to brain areas such as the prefrontal cortex is associated with psychopathic symptoms, there is also evidence for significantly fewer obstetric birth complications in people who become designated psychopathic, and some evidence for psychopathic behaviour being a successful evolutionary reproductive strategy (Lalumière, Harris and Rice, 2001). In common with cluster B personality disorders, it also tends to be those around the psychopath who suffer from

the symptoms rather than the psychopathic individual. This has led some to consider psychopathy as an adaptive evolutionary trait regardless of its negative consequences for others. Cartwright (2008) has drawn together some evidence for this and such a view may add substantially to the debates surrounding the uncertain place of psychopathic individuals in the justice system.

Within the constraints of checklists, psychopathy cannot be verified in individuals less than 18 years of age. However, the issue of **fledgling psychopaths** has been raised each time callous crimes have been committed by children and adolescents. Moran et al. (2008) have assessed the predictive value of the core factor of psychopathy, labelled as callous and unemotional traits, in individuals of this age, finding longitudinal effects at follow-up. The callous/unemotional and anti-social traits of children at the age of 7 years have been related to later psychopathy and demonstrate a substantial genetic risk for the disorder

Case study

Psychopathy

Andy was the younger of two brothers. Born at the start of a 1-year prison sentence for his father, Andy was raised by his mother alone for the first year. By the age of 2 his father would randomly strike Andy when drunk or annoyed with his mother, 'to make a man of him'. During his third year, his mother found herself screaming at Andy to stop hitting the tin drum his father had bought, but Andy's laughter indicated that he enjoyed his mother's shouts as much as the drum. A month later the pet budgie was found on the carpet, mortally injured, having paid the ultimate price for failing to dance to Andy's drum. As soon as he was able, Andy joined in with the neighbourhood 'gang' and, although he was the youngest, was soon leading the more disreputable faction in 'adventures'. One 'adventure' consisted of throwing burning newspaper over the rear walls of houses, which eventually led to near disaster when fire spread from a shed to the rear of a house. The other boys were terrified, but Andy revelled in the chaos and seemed

even more excited at the noise of the police and fire services arriving. Although only 7 years old, Andy lied convincingly, blaming an older boy, with no fear of reprisals. His father beat him anyway, but a week later, Andy was repeating the behaviour and included attacks on his own house.

By the time he was 11, Andy had added theft, taking and driving, and truancy to a growing list of wrongdoings, often stealing worthless items for the 'thrill of it'. Although one of the smallest boys in the neighbourhood, he was established as the local bully, never seeming to experience fear. He became interested in being a butcher when he grew up, perhaps because the local butcher was the only person who would employ him. During his delivery rounds, he would use his undeniable charm and confidence to con extra money from customers, and occasionally force his attentions on girls as young as 12 who happened to answer the door. One girl claimed that Andy had raped her, but Andy convincingly denied this.

By the age of 30, Andy had spent more time in prison than out and he was finally given a 10-year sentence for killing, then sexually assaulting a 10-year-old girl. When asked why he killed her before having sex, he smiled and replied, 'It would have been illegal otherwise, wouldn't it?' Andy was moved to a special hospital following diagnosis of psychopathy.

evident in these challenging children (Viding et al., 2005). Across many types of study, the earlier these predictive traits are found in individuals, the greater the overall chance of psychopathy as an outcome (Blair, Mitchell and Blair, 2005).

Genetic factors contribute to the impairment of emotion in psychopathic individuals (Viding et al., 2005). One way this is thought to occur is by disruption to the functioning of the **amygdala**, which leads to impaired emotional learning (Blair, Mitchell and Blair, 2005). This amygdala dysfunction weakens the autonomic response to fearful or sad facial expressions, which limits their effect of inhibiting violence and aggression. It also limits **social cognition** and weakens punishment learning, leading to poor moral socialisation with increased reliance on aggression. Dysfunction of the orbito-frontal cortex also impairs learning and can reduce the sense of revulsion felt in carrying out callous acts (Zeld and Rauch, 2006). This brain area and the frontal lobes are thought to be abnormal in psychopathy, which in the latter case will impair planning and concern for the future, lessen the inhibition of impulses and increase reactive aggression (Blair, Mitchell and Blair, 2005).

Much of the neurological research in this area is on violence and aggression rather than psychopathy per se, but many such as **Adrian Raine** have made a good case for cross-referencing these findings. Environmental factors such as birth trauma or stress due to sexual abuse have been dismissed as aetiological factors in psychopathy (Blair, Mitchell and Blair, 2005). However, the damage to frontal brain areas as a result of physical abuse during childhood and adolescence can lead to increased reactive aggression as mentioned above (Raine, Brennan and Mednick, 1997). The literature on the relationship between neurological structure and function, and aggression, and as well as that specifically focusing on psychopathy, is flourishing with greater access to brain imaging techniques (e.g. Völim et al., 2004; Raine and Yang, 2006; Raine, 2002).

Even in comparison to the personality disorders in this chapter, psychopathy is very difficult to treat and some have considered it untreatable (Cleckley, 1976). However, some success has been shown in moderating core symptoms and responses using intensive CBT and other approaches directed at these behaviours and working on their coping and functioning (Timmerman and Emmelkamp, 2005; Salekin, 2002). This said, psychopaths are notoriously adept at 'faking good' and can work out what responses may be needed to lower scores with no fundamental change in behaviour. Table 14.3 contains some of the caveats that all therapists need to be aware of when working with this client group (taken from Lion, 1978). Rice, Harris and

Table 14.3 Caveats for therapists working with psychopathic individuals

A therapist must:

- be constantly vigilant regarding manipulation
- assume the patient's account contains fabrication
- assume psychopathic clients will be pathological liars
- realise their client will have no insight and will not care about the future
- assume their client will have no concern for victims or the effects of acts
- not expect a working alliance with the psychopath
- ensure that they are in charge of reinforcement not the psychopath
- realise that most therapies fail

Source: adapted from Lion (1978).

Cormier (1992) found that treatment actually increased reoffending rates at follow-up compared with an untreated group, somewhat reaffirming the pessimistic view of therapy being a form of 'finishing school' for psychopathic offenders. Harris and Rice (2005) suggest that psychopathic offenders require a specific and different treatment to other offenders. The prevalence of psychopathy in the community has not been measured but estimates place this at just under 1 per cent (Blair, Mitchell and Blair, 2005). Little research has been carried out on gender and psychopathy, with most studies focusing on males.

Dangerous and severe personality disorder

Although the construct or concept of psychopathy as a disorder category has always been problematic, Mullen (2007) points out that the genetic, neurological and **nosological** entity labelled as psychopathy has also been the concept behind the construct of **dangerous and severe personality disorder** (DSPD; see Chapter 8). DSPD itself is seen as a challenging and ill-defined group (Dolan and Doyle, 2000), but its development would not have been possible if the **psychopathy check list** (PCL; see Hare, 2003) had not already reified the concept of psychopathy by making it measurable and identifiable. Thus, to this extent, the emergence of the concept of DSPD was dependent on the successful application of the PCL (Maden, 2007).

One early problem with the original use of psychopathy to identify and incarcerate high-risk personality-disordered criminals was the need for them to be of 'unsound mind'. This is because human rights legislation would not allow individuals of sound mind to be detained for the sole reason of preventing their future criminal behaviour, as depicted in the film *Minority Report* (Stephen Spielberg, 2002). Thus, to some extent, it is the susceptibility to treatment inherent in the DSPD concept that circumvents some of the historical problems of managing those with personality disorders who present a risk. It is suggested that the implementation of DSPD adds the involvement of a mental health context to give respectability to what was previously a more blatant form of preventative detention and indeterminate sentencing (Mullen, 2007). Wooton and Fahy (2006) describe this as warehousing problematic individuals under the guise of psychiatric treatment. Others have gone so far as to question whether the issue surrounding DSPD is really about harm from dangerous offenders or about the state becoming dangerous to its citizens as a result of a defensive penal policy and a national obsession with risk and dangerousness (Christie, 2000).

Development and management of personality disorders

Development

This is a weak area of abnormal and clinical psychology, with little certainty about the causes of personality disorders and most treatments being more limited in their effectiveness; hence the use of the terms 'development' and 'management' rather than 'aetiology' and 'treatment' in the above title. Personality disorders can begin to be evident in childhood or adolescence and become an enduring and salient trait during adulthood. Bernstein et al. (1996) have identified some of the childhood characteristics that seem to predict later personality disorders – a prediction that tended to be better for girls than boys (Cohen, 1996). These maladaptive traits become less influential as middle-age approaches, although they are highly resistant to any attempt to change them at any stage of life.

Although abnormalities in the behaviour of adults with personality disorders can be traced back to childhood and are not usually due to later 'life events', their exact onset and aetiology have not yet been made explicit in objective terms (Bernstein et al., 1996). Although this should indicate genetic predispositions for traits, traditional explanations have pointed to early disturbances of development – approaches that have been dominated by the psychodynamic school (Emmelkamp and Kamphuis, 2007). An example of psychodynamic reasoning around life events can be found in the many descriptions of **affectionless psychopathy** by **John Bowlby** based on **maternal deprivation** (see Chapter 9). Fixation at a Freudian psychosexual stage of development and overuse of defence mechanisms are proposed to account for the differing personality disorders in later life. The Freudian, 'anal character', as a result of fixation at the anal stage due to harsh toilet training, has been specifically used to explain obsessive–compulsive personality disorder (see Chapter 3).

Thus, in these psychodynamic explanations, it is generally proposed that disruptive childhood experiences can lead to later personality deficits, although there is little empirical evidence for this. Furthermore, any association between adverse childhood reactions and personality distortion could also result from parental reactions to pre-existing challenging behaviour, due to early manifestations of personality problems in the developing child. This is supported by the fact that there are often siblings who have undergone a very similar parenting experience but who do not show such profound personality distortions as adults. It also has to be stated that personality problems in childhood are likely to precipitate other difficult experiences during that period. For example, Bowlby would be unlikely to consider that his delinquents' affectionless psychopathy could have existed prior to any maternal deprivation and in some cases it may have led to this separation or rejection. Thus cause and effect in such theories can be easily confounded and need to be isolated.

The lifetime persistence of personality disorders, and the rigidity of responses made, led Beck, Freeman and Associates (1990) to presume an evolutionarily based genetic explanation for the inability of all individuals with these disorders to adapt to their current environment, even during childhood development. Thus, responses and cognitions that are adaptive strategies at some point in evolutionary history are rigidly maintained in a different context, in which they are maladaptive and may cause distress. Cartwright (2008) has proposed this for personality distortions as well as psychopathic behaviour. Even though the **ultimate explanation** (evolutionary explanation) for a personality disorder can be specified, the proximate explanation (i.e. the genetic or biosocial mechanism creating it in individuals) is still elusive.

There is evidence for inherited traits in many of the personality disorders, and some neurological explanations of how these are expressed have been attempted (see further reading). Current thinking has moved away from environmental factors producing personality disorders, towards seeing those individuals with specific genetic and neurodevelopmental outcomes seeking and creating compatible environments (see Livesley, 2001: p. ix; Ruocco and Swirsky-Sacchetti, 2007). There have also been illustrative cases of abrupt personality change, without other deficits, following neurological damage. The example of **Phineas Gage** has been detailed in Chapter 3, which illustrates such change due to neurological damage. In 1848, Phineas suffered severe damage to his frontal lobes and rapidly developed marked anti-social traits in the absence of other major impairments. Such precedents as well as the extreme nature of the traits and resistance to treatment would suggest that a part is played by abnormal neurodevelopment in personality disorder (Emmelkamp and Kamphuis, 2007). Thus, in the cases of abuse, neglect and inconsistent discipline leading to anti-social behaviour in later life, the relationship between abuse, head injury and neural damage also needs to be acknowledged. Such assumptions of neurocognitive underpinnings are not just confined to anti-social traits, but may be mediating other personality disorders (Ruocco and Swirsky-Sacchetti, 2007). However, a *DSM* diagnosis of personality disorders should eliminate adult onset such as that in the example of Phineas Gage, where the diagnosis of personality disorder is due to general medical condition, in this example brain injury (American Psychiatric Association, 2000).

Given the enduring, pervasive and classifiable nature of personality disorders, genetic and neurodevelopmental explanations such as the above tend to be more credible. There are examples of these in this chapter, such as the evidence for a genetically predisposed reduction in right parietal cortical and hippocampal size in borderline individuals and abnormal amygdala function in psychopathy (Irle, Lange and Sachsse, 2005; Blair, Mitchell and Blair, 2005). Modern studies of the aetiology of anti-social traits have become better controlled and much more specific in terms of what exactly is inherited (e.g. Viding et al., 2005). For example, Völim et al. (2004) used fMRI (see Chapter 3) to investigate impulse control in borderline and anti-social personalities, differentiating them from controls in terms of specific prefrontal cortex areas of activation during response inhibition. Some brain areas for individual traits can be specified. However, the exact combination of contributing factors in personality disorder will require much more research of this nature. The task of mapping all neurological factors for each of the individual personality disorders may take us some way into the future (Emmelkamp and Kamphuis, 2007). However, some disorders such as dependent personality disorder may involve a greater contribution from environmental factors (O'Neill and Kendler, 1998).

Management

In addition to a general difficulty in altering behaviour in personality disorders, some of these disorders are highly resistant to treatment approaches, particularly borderline, anti-social and obsessive–compulsive personality disorder, as well as psychopathy. It is difficult to set up a **therapeutic relationship** with a borderline individual, exacerbated by their tendency to change therapist and threats of suicide which often occur during mood disturbance (Isometsa et al., 1996). The nature of most of the personality disorders tends to confound the therapeutic relationship: for example, treating it as a personal relationship with all the interpersonal difficulties that entails. Failure to learn by mistakes is a common feature of anti-social personality disorder and psychopathy, and these clients will frequently manipulate the therapeutic relationship to their short-term advantage (Hare, 1993). Treatment evaluations are also confounded by the personality disorders being complex disorders with a complex treatment, necessitating a complex evaluation process.

Some specific approaches can help, such as assertion training with dependent personality disorder. Black et al. (1996) have found cognitive therapy superior to drug therapy and placebo (no treatment) in changing traits, and cognitive therapy has been found generally useful in managing the more amenable personality disorders. Given the fact that personality disorders are lifelong propensities that weaken after middle age, self-sustaining approaches (e.g. cognitive change) are preferred to more short-term remedies (e.g. drug therapy), particularly as these disorders are not episodic and medication would have to be continuous. The aim of therapy for personality disorders is not to cure or eliminate the personality distortions, as this would be an unattainable goal in the vast majority of cases. The rational aim is one of reducing the extremes of the disordered personalities or 'smoothing the rough edges' to a more socially and functionally acceptable level (Emmelkamp and Kamphuis, 2007).

Historically, there has been a pessimistic attitude towards the successful treatment of personality disorders; however, this vision of a therapeutic cul-de-sac should no longer be accepted as more recent treatment approaches, both intensive and specific, have been evaluated positively (Bateman and Tyrer, 2004a). For example, psychopathy has a long history of being considered virtually untreatable (Cleckley, 1976). However, targeting aspects of attitudes and assumptions has made progress in moderating the excesses of this challenging disorder. For example, assumptions that CBT can erode are that of psychopathic individuals 'always being right' and that their 'personal satisfaction is more important than the lives of others, who are impotent'. A further strategy with this difficult group is to appeal to their highly developed selfish interest by explaining that power, wealth and satisfaction are legal and it is only the client's method of attaining them that needs to change. Intensive programmes of CBT mixed with other approaches have made progress to date in this difficult area of intervention (Timmerman and Emmelkamp, 2005).

In terms of managing less severe personality distortions in a less challenging way, some affected individuals find certain environments more conducive to their propensities. Rather than reducing the extremes of their personalities, situations that accommodate them may also prevent their reaching clinical attention. Thus, there may be some 'clustering' of personality disorders in subsections of society, in which their traits may be less salient, such as anti-social individuals in prisons and 'criminal haunts', schizotypal personalities joining 'new age travellers' and even schizoid individuals 'gathered in isolation' within computer-based companies. However, these environments are not therapeutic communities and may come more closely to resemble psychological ghettoes.

Forensic issues

In the case of personality disorders, there are numerous long-standing forensic issues that can only be sampled here. However, one contemporary issue raised in the section on psychopathy is that of DSPD (dangerous as a result of severe personality disorder). Although there are enough issues within this ambitious diagnostic category to fill a substantial textbook, only an outline is possible within this volume. Definitions of severe personality disorder are many and the DSPD criteria consist of what has been described as an arbitrary mixture of PCL-R scores and personality disorder diagnoses (Blackburn, 2007). DSPD individuals pose a risk to others or themselves but do not display conventional psychiatric symptoms and will reject help, which leads to the ethically questionable treatment of these personality disorders in secure settings (Wootton and Fahy, 2006).

The forensic reasoning behind DSPD is that specific pathologies initiate and sustain criminal behaviour and that by treating the pathology you reduce the risk of crime, theoretically making crime treatable (Mullen, 2007). As mentioned previously, many see this as a means of incarcerating those problematic individuals who fall between the health care and criminal justice systems (Wootton and Fahy, 2006). However, the system is under way and will have to accommodate various offender groups from the previous regimes, such as discretionary life prisoners, who have been successfully managed and rehabilitated with minimal mental health input (Maden, 2007). The financial cost of the DSPD system is very high, and governments will be scrutinising and evaluating progress intensively, placing pressure on staff in these forensic settings – staff who are already under stress due to the isolating nature of work with personality disorders (Kurtz, 2007).

Most of the literature examining personality disorder in a forensic context concerns psychopathy and anti-social personality disorder, which is not surprising as the latter of these two disorders is defined in terms similar to those of a persistent offender. However, most other personality disorders place an individual at higher risk of forensic involvement. Using a **smallest space type analysis** (see Chapter 5) in a Finnish sample, Häkkänen and Laajasalo (2006) found the crime scene associations with the involvement of personality disorders to be: kicking and hitting; use of guns; and use of blunt and sharp weapons, which distinguish them marginally from other disorders in terms of their breadth and a lack of other strongly associated factors (Häkkänen and Laajasalo, 2006).

An examination of schizoid personality disorder has revealed a potential for violence both against others in the form of homicide and against the self in terms of suicide (Loza and Hanna, 2006). Borderline personality disorder has a strong relationship with physical aggression and assault due to the associated traits of impulsiveness, anger and rapid changes in mood. These traits also place borderline individuals at a high risk of suicide (Emmelkamp and Kamphuis, 2007). However, some personality disorders can predispose to being forensically involved in a less instrumental way. Cluster C personalities have been found to be at much greater risk of victimisation, especially in the case of dependent personality disorder, where there is a high risk of being a target for violence (Cormier, LeFauveau and Loas, 2006).

Borderline individuals are very prone to substance disorders and remain at a higher level of risk during the outcomes of treatment approaches for substances such as heroin (Darke et al., 2007). This comorbidity can make them even more challenging in prison contexts, where they are overrepresented. Those with anti-social personality disorder present with similar dual diagnosis problems, and as they form the majority of incarcerated offenders, this propensity can create further confounding difficulties in terms of the illicit trade in substances within penal institutions (Sutker and Adams, 2001).

Focus

Gender bias and the mad–bad debate

There are apparent gender biases among the personality disorders, with more males being diagnosed as having anti-social personality disorder and a predominance of females with borderline personality disorder. However, this bias could be seen as an extension of the '**mad–bad**' debate, with male deviance being seen as 'bad' (anti-social personality disorder is associated with criminal behaviour) and female deviance as 'mad' (borderline personality disorder involves emotional instability) (Hollin, 1989).

Such differences are thought to reflect an inherent bias in the diagnostic and classificatory process, in a similar manner to the gender bias assumed in the criminal justice system. In this, the prevalence of crime is much higher amongst males than females. Amongst the reasons given to account for this gender difference in crime statistics is an inherent bias towards males fitting the criminal stereotype. This male bias is apparent from the point of being detained by police right through to being sentenced by a court (Walklate, 1995).

A similar gender bias has been assumed in personality disorder diagnosis but seeing females as fitting the stereotype. Akhtar (1996) has refuted the notion of this female bias in borderline personality disorder. However, the study does confirm the existence of a male bias in anti-social personality disorder.

Personality disorder probably involves more input from forensic psychologists and clinical forensic psychologists than any other disorder in this textbook. The forensic issues involved would require their own volume to detail both the implications of the disorders and the many ways in which these professionals have worked with this difficult offender group throughout the penal and justice systems.

Clinical issues

The assessment of personality disorders can both confound and be confounded by their comorbidity with mood, substance, anxiety and sometimes psychotic disorders. As well as predisposing individuals to psychiatric disorders, personality disorders can obscure the presence of other disorders during assessment, and can subsequently affect the treatment responses for these comorbid disorders (Burton, 2006). Given the high prevalence of personality disorders at around 50 per cent in psychiatric patient samples, clinicians have to be keenly aware of attributing signs and symptoms correctly to identify disorders separately. Treatment evaluations are also made difficult by high levels of comorbidity, but also by lengthy periods of observation of up to a year and the fact that personality disorders are complex, with complex treatments and, consequently, complex evaluations (Bateman and Tyrer, 2004a).

Cultural backgrounds of clients can also be confused with the presence of personality disorder, particularly in cases of **acculturation** where their cultural practices and beliefs become isolated in an alien culture (American Psychiatric Association, 2000). Where there is doubt in identifying such potential indications of disorder, reference should be made to informants familiar with the specific cultural background. Informants who know the client personally should also be resorted to in assessing signs of personality disorders and verifying the stability and pervasiveness of key symptoms. Although less than 10 per cent of research on these disorders resorts to interviewing other people close to the clients (Bornstein, 2003), this useful practice can be crucial in confirming pervasiveness and consistency of behaviour (American Psychiatric Association, 2000).

There are also difficulties with the diagnosis of these disorders and some would say difficulties with the way personality disorders are conceptualised as categories. As Clark (2007) noted, Tyrer et al. (2007) put their view of the current assessment of personality disorders somewhat uncompromisingly as being 'currently inaccurate, largely unreliable, frequently wrong and in need of improvement' (Tyrer et al., 2007: p. 435). Many professionals have suggested replacing the **taxonic** system with a **dimensional system** of diagnosis and classification for personality disorder, giving a score on each of a number of personality traits such as obsessiveness (Clark, 2007). The impetus for this change is such that implementation of a dimensional approach may be seen in the forthcoming versions of the classificatory systems of *DSM* and *ICD*. This change will be accompanied by a conceptual change in viewing the structure of personality disorders as dimensional, based on the outcome of research (e.g. Trull and Durrett, 2005).

Current personality research suggests five dimensions, the so-called **five-factor model** (for an overview, see Deary and Matthews, 1993). There has already been research favourably comparing the five-factor model with current

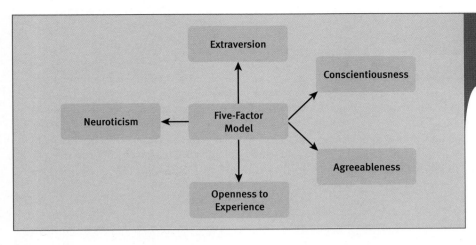

Figure 14.1 The factors measured in the five factor model in personality measurement.

personality disorders (see Saulsman and Page, 2004). Since 1991, Widiger has believed that if both dimensional and categorical methods are used, there would be more information and flexibility, and fewer arbitrary decisions involved when applying the existing categories of personality disorder. However, it has to be asked whether such changes will aid or hamper service delivery for individuals with personality disorders. Bateman and Tyrer (2004b) have examined mental health provision for personality disorder and find that most current models need more focus on: careful assessment of needs and risk; consistency of staff and approach; team coherence; and good inpatient support. A radical change in assessment and diagnostic skills may further undermine already scarce, well-established experience and skills.

A major problem for clinicians dealing with personality disorders is that the characteristics of the disorder can interact with the client–clinician relationship to distort and disrupt it. This is particularly pertinent to the case of cluster B personalities where much of the behaviour, including the symptoms presented, may be synthesised to gain attention or manipulate the clinician (American Psychiatric Association, 2000; Emmelkamp and Kamphuis, 2007). Borderline individuals may rapidly switch from regarding their therapist as saviour to seeing them as uncaring and evil with little in between, which along with their self-harming and suicidal tendencies make this patient group one of the most challenging. There is little expectation of a genuine therapeutic relationship in the case of psychopathic individuals, who will manipulate even the most astute and aware clinicians to gain advantage or simply to amuse themselves (see Hare, 1993).

There are considerable overlaps between personality disorders, to the extent that most clients are diagnosed with at least two of the categories. For example, schizoid personality disorder overlaps with paranoid, schizotypal and avoidant personality disorder. However, schizoid person-

ality disorder also overlaps considerably with **Asperger's syndrome**, to the extent that Kay and Kolvin (1987) considered the schizoid label possibly redundant. Although diagnostic distinctions exist between these disorders, as there are between avoidant personality and social phobia, the similarity of some features has led to speculation that there may be relationships between such disorders in terms of their aetiologies or severity (Emmelkamp and Kamphuis, 2007). Such blurring of boundaries can confound the clinical assessment process, where the emphasis should be on differentiation not confounding associations.

As mentioned above in relation to forensic issues, gender bias has been identified in the diagnosis of personality disorders (Widiger, 1991) and this has led to critical attacks on the criteria used. Definitions of the personality disorders in this chapter have been perceived as conforming to sex-role stereotyped behaviour. This in turn can lead to accusations of pathologising gender-specific behaviour, particularly the 'subservience of females' that could be seen in the criteria for dependent personality disorder. Although less based on overall gender bias, the labile emotional reactions pertaining to histrionic and borderline personality disorders have been seen as treating female attempts to resist imposed stereotyping or even attempts to deal with the aftermath of sexual abuse as a sign of pathology (Kaplan, 1983; Warner, 2001).

One final caveat for those clinicians, trainees and students working with personality disorders is in reference to the medical student syndrome. This is a tendency for students falsely to believe that they or their colleagues have many of the disorders they study, a kind of academic hypochondriasis. Personality disorders are very open to this kind of misidentification. However, although personality disorders are relatively common, they do represent extreme traits, and although you may be a little obsessive or jealous, it is unlikely that this debilitates you or your colleagues to the degree of qualifying as a disorder.

Self-test questions

- What is the relationship between psychopathy and DSPD?
- How does psychopathy differ from anti-social personality disorder?
- Contrast the categorical and dimensional approaches to personality disorders.
- Give an example of how to therapeutically improve personality disorder.

- Give an example of how culture can confound personality disorder diagnosis.
- Give three differences between obsessive–compulsive personality disorder and obsessive–compulsive disorder.
- Can gender bias in diagnosis explain the ratios of males to females in individual personality disorders?
- Give two reasons for the difficulty in treating personality disorders.

Chapter summary

Personality disorders are characterised by **persistent exaggerated personality traits** which can be traced to childhood or adolescence, but weaken in middle age. They are on **Axis II**, a separate dimension of the *DSM-IV-TR* to most disorders, on the assumption that they are lifelong propensities and will be diagnosed in addition to other disorders. There are forensic issues surrounding these disorders, as they are common amongst offenders and are often implicated during trials. The measurement of personality is a fundamental part of **psychometrics**, and personality disorders are a challenging part of this to the extent that the use of other systems, such as the **Big Five** structure and a dimensional as opposed to criterion based approach, have been proposed.

There are three groups or **clusters** of these disorders in *DSM-IV*. **Cluster A** personality disorders are characterised by odd and eccentric behaviour and possibly represent mild features of schizophrenia such as paranoia, withdrawal and fanciful thought. However, psychotic symptoms are not part of the criteria and these individuals are not schizophrenic but show similar features. This cluster includes **paranoid personality disorder, schizoid personality disorder** and **schizotypal personality disorder**. **Cluster B** disorders have dramatic, attention-seeking, emotional and selfish features, with a tendency towards reckless and impulsive behaviour in some of these personality disorders. Individuals with these disorders tend to make others victims of their behaviour, although they can be destructive to themselves. **Anti-social personality disorder** is an important and controversial category here, with criteria similar to that for **criminality**. The other disorders in this cluster are **borderline personality disorder, histrionic**

personality disorder and **narcissistic personality disorder**. **Cluster C** personality disorders tend to show traits such as anxiety, apprehensiveness and fearfulness traits and tend to be the victims of circumstance. The disorders in this cluster are **avoidant personality disorder, dependent personality disorder** and **obsessive–compulsive personality disorder**. In addition the disorder of **psychopathy** has more serious forensic implications and has been rationalised within the concept of **DSPD** in the UK.

The development of personality disorders seems to involve **genetic, neurodevelopmental, early attachment** and **learning** experiences, but their durability and other features make single-explanations difficult. Evidence for genetically driven neurological abnormalities is now well established. Management is troublesome, although **cognitive behavioural therapy** is useful and intensive interventions have given new optimism to an area that traditionally has poor outcomes. Forensic and clinical issues in these disorders include gender bias in diagnostic criteria and the difficulties of overlap, suggesting that a **dimensional approach** is adopted for *DSM-IV*.

Suggested essay questions

- Compare and contrast the psychological approaches to personality and the concept of personality disorders using examples.
- Discuss the distinctions between the three *DSM* clusters of personality disorders using the examples of schizotypal, anti-social and dependent personality disorders.
- Critically discuss the forensic and clinical implications of DSPD.

Further reading

Overview texts

Bernstein, D., Cohen, P., Skodol, A., Bezirganian, S. et al. (1996) Childhood antecedents of adolescent personality disorders. *American Journal of Psychiatry*, **153**, 907–13.

Blackburn, R. (1988) On moral judgements and personality disorders: The myth of psychopathic personality revisited. *British Journal of Psychiatry*, **153**, 505–12.

Lenzenweger, M., and Clarkin, J. (2004) *Major theories of personality disorder* (2nd edn). New York: Guilford Press.

Derksen, J. (1995) *Personality disorders: Clinical and social perspectives.* Chichester: Wiley.

Dowson, J., and Grounds, A. (1995) *Personality disorders: Recognition and clinical management.* Cambridge: Cambridge University Press.

Emmelkamp, P. M., and Kamphuis, J. H. (2007) *Personality disorders.* Hove: Psychology Press.

Livesley, W. J. (ed.) (2001) *Handbook of personality disorders.* New York: Guilford Press.

Paris, J. (1996) *Social factors in personality disorders.* Cambridge: Cambridge University Press.

Specific and more critical texts

Beck, A. T., Freeman, A., and Davis, D. D. (2004) *Cognitive therapy of personality disorders.* New York: Guilford Press.

Bell, J., Campbell, S., Erikson, M., Hogue, T., McLean, Z., Rust, S., and Taylor, R. (2003) An overview: DSPD programme concepts and progress. In A. Lord and L. Rayment (eds), *Dangerous and severe personality disorder (Issues in Forensic Psychology 4)*. Leicester: British Psychological Society, Division of Forensic Psychology.

Blair, J., Mitchell, D., and Blair, K. (2005) *The psychopath: Emotion and the brain.* Oxford: Blackwell.

Cleckley, H. (1976) *The Mask of Sanity.* St Louis: C. V. Mosby.

Dolan, M. C., and Park, I. (2002) The neuropsychology of antisocial personality disorder. *Psychological Medicine*, **32**(3), 417–27.

Home Office and Department of Health (1999) *Managing dangerous people with severe personality disorder: Proposals for policy development.* London: Home Office and Department of Health.

Hummelen, B., Wilberg, T., Pedersen, G., and Karterud, S. (2007) The relationship between avoidant personality disorder and social phobia. *Comprehensive Psychiatry*, **48**, 348–56.

Mancebo, M. C., Eisen, J., Grant, J., and Rasmussen, S. A. (2005) Obsessive–compulsive personality disorder and obsessive–compulsive disorder: Clinical characteristics, diagnostic difficulties and treatment. *Annals of Psychiatry*, **17**(4), 197–204.

Millon, T., and Davis, R. (1996) *Disorders of personality: DSM-IV and beyond.* New York: Wiley.

Prins, H. (2005) *Offenders, deviants or patients?* (3rd edn). London: Routledge.

Raine, A., Lencz, T., and Mednick, S. (1995) *Schizotypal personality.* Cambridge: Cambridge University Press.

Soderstrom, H., Sjodin, A-K., Carlstedt, A., and Forsman, A. (2004) Adult psychopathic personality with childhood-onset hyperactivity and conduct disorder: A central problem constellation in forensic psychiatry. *Psychiatry Research*, **121**, 271–80.

Visit **www.pearsoned.co.uk/davidholmes** for a range of resources to support study. Test yourself with multiple choice questions and access a bank of over 100 videos that will bring the topics to life. Video coverage for this chapter includes interviews with Janna and Liz who suffer from borderline personality disorder.

CHAPTER 15 Somatoform, dissociative and factitious disorders

- Overview
- Case study
- Background to somatoform and dissociative disorders
- Classifications of somatoform disorders
- Classifications of dissociative disorders
- Clinical issues in somatoform and dissociative disorders
- Forensic issues in somatoform and dissociative disorders
- Factitious disorders
- Clinical issues and forensic implications in factitious disorders
- Critical evaluation
- Chapter summary

 Watch this classic footage of 'Eve' in her three dissociative states. This is one of several videos that explore issues and disorders relevant to this chapter at www.pearsoned.co.uk/davidholmes.

Alien abductions

The basis for the highly successful 1990s TV series *The X-files* and the first newsworthy case of Betty and Barney Hill tell similar tales of visiting UFOs heralded by bright lights. These UFOs contain 'telepathic' alien beings, which abduct people from earth and perform surgical experiments on them before returning them, sometimes with amnesia for the abduction. The original Betty and Barney case was investigated by the use of hypnosis, bringing about further 'memories' of their capture. However, the clinical conclusion on the case was that there was no abduction, just an elaborate shared fantasy (Klass, 1989). For some theorists, these kinds of 'recollections' are even thought to indicate abuse in childhood (Comer, 2007).

In this chapter, strange recollections and states of mind will be explored. It is often the same individuals claiming such experiences, including contact with aliens, who also have alterations of consciousness, support unconventional beliefs and have rich fantasy lives perhaps contributing to their 'recollections' (Warner, 2004). In terms of scientific logic, alien abductions are highly improbable during the entire history of the earth, let alone in the last 70 years. This chapter will reveal that many of these and other strange 'memories' reflect the views of therapists who uncover them and frequently show improbable similarities across different clients, indicating that they are illusory and result from suggestion (Spanos, 1996).

Some individuals who claim dissociative experiences also claim to have been abducted in alien spacecraft, casting doubt over the validity of their reports and diagnosis.
Source: Pearson Online Database.

Overview

Somatoform and **dissociative disorders** have become associated with psychoanalytic history and have remained an area where such explanations and treatment approaches are still applied by some therapists despite a lack of empirical support for the effectiveness of such interventions (Shorter, 1997). In somatoform disorders, physical symptoms are presented; and in dissociative disorders, there are complaints of abnormal mental processes. The word 'somatoform' indicates a bodily origin and the suffix 'form' is often used to mean 'mimicks' or appears to be a somatic medical disorder (Rief and Sharpe, 2004). In both of these cases, known medical/somatic explanations for these complaints are absent. Individual disorders can be characterised by the location and type of symptom or sign presented: for example, pain disorder assumes reports of clinically significant pain in various locations, whereas dissociative amnesia refers to disruption of memory processes. For either case, there are no established medical explanations.

These disorders have been and remain controversial for many authors and clinicians, despite being described more objectively since *DSM-III* (American Psychiatric Association, 1980). **Dissociative amnesia** and **identity disorders** have been subject to particular criticism, as both have been implicated in contested cases of child sexual abuse and have limited empirical validity (see Spanos, 1996). Given the problems of validity associated with these dissociative disorders, interventions have also been seen in a critical context, to the extent that treating the belief that the client has the disorder, rather than addressing the disorder directly, has been suggested for *DSM* inclusion. In practice, some somatoform disorders are also difficult to distinguish with any certainty from genuine medical conditions, **malingering** or **factitious disorders**. It is also the case that clients often resist being diagnosed with somatoform disorders, as this suggests that their symptoms are not genuine medical conditions (Starcevic, 2007).

In factitious disorders there are also symptoms presented that appear to conform to a specific condition, but these symptoms are deliberately feigned or fabricated by the pseudo-patient. The signs and symptoms usually point to a medical condition and there is no motive for gain, such as avoiding standing trial or claiming insurance, as there would be in the case of **malingering**. When the symptoms are reported or created in another person to gain this kind of attention, it is termed **factitious disorder by proxy**. More severe forms of factitious disorder are referred to as **Münchausens syndrome** in the UK. Confusion over terminology has led to a move to adopt the term fabricated or induced illness (Bass and Jones, 2006).

Probably the most prolific serial killer in the UK, Harold Shipman has been viewed as a case of Münchausen's Syndrome by Adult Proxy as a result of the manner in which he killed at least 250 of his patients.
Source: Getty Images/ Chris Gleave/AFP.

Case study

Who is Jade?

Jade had a complicated childhood; she once remembered opening six tin cans to find the one containing baked beans because her father had removed all the labels from every food tin in the cupboard to 'confuse those watching'. She also knew how to avoid his coming home from work angry due to his paranoid view of a world that was against him. However, her mother Rose was not so astute and often suffered verbal and sometimes physical abuse. Rose had tried to keep the family financially stable, despite her husband's poor income and her own frequent depressions. Jade spent a lot of her time alone at home, greatly restricted in the friends she had as a result of her father's interference. He insisted that other children were just using her to spy on him for their parents and would steal from the house. However, Jade had a number of fantasy friends she would openly talk to in front of her parents, although others thought her a little strange.

Occasionally Jade would insist that she or her fantasy friends were ill and that her family should nurse them. She enjoyed the play-acting of her family as 'doctors and nurses'. Such attention was rare, as her mother was often away visiting her ill grandparents and usually took Jade's sister with her to help. Jade, being 'too young' to help out, had to remain with her father, who resented being left to look after both the house and youngest child. He would often lock his daughter in the house whilst he went out drinking, returning in the early hours ill-tempered and abusive. Jade's mother seemed indifferent to her plight and would chastise her if she complained about her father. As Jade advanced through her teenage years, she felt that the more abusive attention she received from her father was preferable to the coldness and indifference of her mother.

Jade left home at barely 16 years of age with James an older man whom she had got to know through her father. He was a friend who would sometimes bring Jade's father home when he was drunk. Jade saw him as her saviour, but their life together was chaotic, emotionally stressful and only made tolerable in the short term by mutual abuse of alcohol. James read about occult practices, which endlessly fascinated Jade. She, in turn, would tell James tales of ghosts she claimed to have seen and other strange experiences. However, the paranormal did not explain the man's shirt or whisky that James found by their bed when he returned from work. Jade's assertion that she could not remember what had happened that day only made James angrier; he could not believe the blatant nature of Jade's apparent behaviour. Further absences in Jade's memory led to James leaving her. On seeing her GP for headaches and dizziness, Jade revealed her memory problems and was referred for neurological testing.

Petra, the psychologist who carried out some testing for dissociative research after Jade's clinical examinations, had a reputation for her radical view of such absences in memory. As feedback from the results of subjective tests, she suggested that Jade see her privately, and during these sessions she asked her about her relationship with her father. Jade was evasive, not wishing to reveal how she had felt and behaved as a child. Petra suggested hypnosis, which produced results that appeared conclusive to the therapist. After only a few more sessions, Petra was convinced she was having conversations with Jade's alternate personalities, who appeared to take possession of her consciousness during the memory absences previously ascribed to alcohol. One of these 'alters' claimed the name Jimmy and was abusive. Petra found that Jimmy seemed to know many of the remarkable adventures that Jade had been involved in, including violent incestuous relations with Jade's father and his neighbour. Petra began using the names of these alters, which she claimed Jade used to defend herself against intolerable abuse in the past. She assured Jade that it was a perfectly rational reaction and began to relate to a total of nine very different personalities, including one who seemed to be someone from the eighteenth century.

Over the following months, Jade came to trust Petra and finally gave a statement to the police accusing her father and others of sexual abuse.

CASE STUDY CONTINUED

When confronted, her father became ill and had to be medicated, but his somewhat deluded and obsessive behaviour was interpreted as suspicious by the police. However, social workers insisted that his relapse was consistent with his psychiatric history. The case was finally dropped after months of enquiries when Jade's 'recollections' failed to be established by the facts of her personal history. Jade eventually retracted her accusations and became quite bitter regarding the hold that Petra seemed to have exerted over her. Petra was told by the leading officer that such accusations took resources from other genuine cases, but she insisted that her position was highly justified in exposing possible abuse of children.

In subsequent years, many of Jade's family no longer communicated with each other and her father became a recluse, having no contact with family in addition to being rejected by his few drinking friends. At the age of 28, Jade was diagnosed with a neurological condition producing seizures, blackouts and occasional hallucinations.

Although cases of **false memory syndrome** occur, clinicians are trained to take each case on its individual merits as unique and not to prejudge outcomes. They are trained to exercise caution at all stages in light of the consequences of cases such as Jade's.

Background to somatoform and dissociative disorders

Heavily influenced by the psychodynamic school, somatoform and dissociative disorders were referred to as hysterical neuroses conversion type and hysterical neuroses dissociative type respectively. The *ICD-10* has retained the word 'neurotic' in the title for these disorder groups, but it was removed, along with the term 'hysterical', from *DSM-III* in 1980 (and subsequent *DSM* editions) to avoid assumptions of psychodynamic aetiology in keeping with the objective, descriptive approach of the *DSM*. This replacement of the neuroses with a group of disorders under the somatoform label in *DSM-III* caused a great deal of acerbic argument (Hyler and Spitzer, 1978). Some professionals still adhere to these terms and often refer to the **neurotic personality** in describing individuals with 'trait anxiety', who tend to have overreactive autonomic responses (see Chapter 3), and who also may be more prone to suggestibility and fantasy (see Brenneis, 1995).

Somatoform and dissociative disorders should by definition be distinct from **malingering**, in which symptoms are deliberately feigned in order to attain some advantageous goal for the person presenting that is usually objective, such as financial gain or evading work. Similarly, the symptoms of somatoform and dissociative disorders are distinguished from those of **factitious disorder** in that symptoms of the latter are intentionally fabricated in order to gain medical attention only, and in the case of **factitious disorder by proxy**, fabricated in another

individual. All of the disorders in this chapter present a challenge for health care systems, and in the case of **factitious** (or **Münchausen's**) **disorder by proxy**, serious forensic implications. The **psychophysiological disorders** in Chapter 16 may also seem to have similarities to somatoform disorders, but in contrast, they are diagnosable as recognised medical conditions such as asthma.

Individuals prone to what have been termed 'neurotic' disorders are thought to report more headaches, chest pains and palpitations, and will report apprehension up to 20 times more often than non-neurotic individuals (Marks and Lader, 1973). This tendency to overreport symptoms they genuinely believe they have can be seen to contribute to the diagnosis of both anxiety and somatoform disorders (see Chapter 12). Unlike the disorders in Chapter 12, this assumed anxiety is not overt, but is thought by some to underlie their symptoms. In this psychodynamic explanation, anxiety in **somatoform disorders** is thought to be perceived as physical complaints by the patient. In **dissociative disorders**, the patient is thought to be psychologically 'running away' from their anxiety, dissociating themselves from the source of their fear. These traditional descriptions of somatoform and dissociative disorder groups are very much taken from the **psychoanalytic** approach, which some may think inappropriate in cases involving suggestible individuals. Much contemporary thinking would consider psychoanalytic therapy for somatoform and dissociative disorders a case of complying with the disordered process rather than addressing it (see the section on critical evaluations, pp. 470–1).

Focus

Hysteria

There are broadly three related applications of the term 'hysteria'.

- One refers to being hysterical, or so overwhelmed by overt arousal and emotion as to be out of control.
- A second refers more precisely to a form of psychological contagion or mass hysteria (for illustration, see Talbot, 2002).
- The third application used here is that of the generation of apparent physical or mental symptoms as a result of psychological disturbance.

In the past, the term and concept of hysteria in this latter application has tended to be assumed to be an integral part of the disorders in this chapter. However, the clinical validity of both the term and its application has been increasingly questioned from the mid-twentieth century (see Shorter, 1997). The history of hysteria is now seen as one not of discovery but of invention, as the concept is now regarded as a pseudo-diagnosis produced in an effort to explain clinical phenomena in the absence of a developed science of neuropsychology.

The ancient Greeks held relatively primitive beliefs to explain this type of aberrant behaviour, for which there was no obvious observable cause. They adopted the medical term **hysterikos** from **hystera** or uterus. One explanation of hysteria attributed to **Hippocrates** involved the physiological displacement of the uterus, which was thought to become too light and dry due to lack of sex and drift upwards in the body, placing pressure on heart and lungs, subsequently causing problems in this new location (Veith, 1965). Hence the symptoms and explanation were primarily associated with older unattached females. The association of female hysteria with sexual abstinence led to a somewhat bizarre 'intervention' towards the end of the nineteenth century, by clinicians holding this view, of moistening and manipulating the genitalia of the client to orgasm. This practice is closely related to the theoretical ideas put forward by Freud. However, it also relates to much earlier ideas, including the primitive concepts surviving from the ancient Greeks. The practice fortunately died out in the early twentieth century.

Pierre Briquet (1796–1881) drew on these early medical records of Hippocrates and his contemporaries in using the term 'hysteria'. In 1859, when **Sigmund Freud** was only 3 years old, Briquet described **Briquet's hysteria**, which now approximates to **somatisation disorder** (in this chapter). **Thomas Sydenham** considered hysteria to be a common and chronic condition. Briquet

influenced the thinking of **Charcot** at Salpêtrière with his **personalité hystérique**. However, Charcot did not believe in one-to-one forms of therapy for hysteria up until his death in 1893, after which his pupil **Pierre Janet** adopted the psychological treatment approach to hysterical symptoms (Janet, 1907). **Sigmund Freud** had embraced the concept of hysteria (Breuer and Freud, 1885), and as the early twentieth century unfolded, he became inextricably tied to the concept as a disorder when advancing psychoanalysis as therapy, which proved to be fashionable and highly popular at this time (Shorter, 1997). The conceptual errors passed from Charcot to Janet and Freud were perhaps understandable given the neurological naivety of this era (Shorter, 1997).

By the time Freud had popularised psychoanalysis, the concept of hysteria had become accepted, even though it was so ill-defined that there were a ridiculous number of symptoms attached to it (Biggs, 2000). Its proponents were neurologists by profession, but they were working at a time when neuroscience was merely finding empirical direction, with very little accumulated knowledge of the complex functioning of the brain or the myriad of potential neurological disorders. However, the legacy of Charcot's inability to understand neurological symptoms (see Charcot, 1889) was further confounded by Freud and others in his wake by their inventing even more explanations for symptoms for hysteria, which would now be diagnosed as resulting from neurological lesions or epilepsy. Thus, the alternative explanation used at this time for such symptoms was the catch-all term 'hysteria' (Macnalty, 1966).

There have been studies revealing some neurological abnormalities in patients presenting with symptoms of hysteria (Black et al., 2004). However, conclusions from such imaging studies require caution, as we are entering the area between neurophysiology and psychiatry, both confounded by hysteria and with additional reliance on clinical judgement (Broome, 2004). For example, some work has suggested explanations for hysterical conversion that lie in the failure of the neurological circuits when preparing to execute a movement (see Broome, 2004). Such accounts could offer some explanation as to the true origins of symptoms in the early cases of Janet and Freud. There are further consistent research findings that sufferers of **open angle glaucoma** score more highly on hysteria and hypochondriasis (Lim et al., 2007). However, these scores also vary with the number of systemic medications used, which may relate to primary effects of the medication, or the secondary effect of reminding patients of their ill-health (Lim et al., 2007).

It may also be that the label of hysteria could be serving to confound rather than explain the associated symptoms. The seizures attributed to hysteria are characteristic of brain lesions, and some symptoms of **temporal lobe epilepsy** (first identified around the time of Freud's death) resemble the **depersonalisation** or **derealisation** described in hysteria. If the patients described by Freud and others as displaying signs and symptoms of hysteria were suffering from neurological disorders, it is clear that psychoanalysis would be unlikely to cure or have much impact on their complaints. This would seem to have been the case at the time. Despite claims of catharsis marking a point of recovery, many of these patients, including Bertha Pappenheim (Anna O), continued to have symptoms long after their psychoanalysis (see Shorter, 1997). Hysteria may be providing a contrived label linking post-traumatic, neurological and factitious disorders, where the true clinical picture may be clearer without such complication. Perhaps hysteria is now better considered to be a quaint anachronism that is more appropriately considered a historical anachronism. However, it will probably still continue to add intrigue to fictional movies.

Public perceptions of dissociative disorders tend to be distorted, as these relatively *rare* disorders receive a great deal of media interest. Curiously, the **prevalence** of these disorders is increasing as media coverage has grown, which could be due to increased public awareness of the disorder, or a consequence of the media influencing suggestible and dissociation-prone individuals.

Classifications of somatoform disorders

Somatoform disorders are characterised by physical symptoms for which there is no medical or somatic basis. Although the symptoms are assumed not to be intentionally created, they are often vague, atypical of this kind of disorder, and conform to the patient's understanding of such physical complaints. For diagnosis, these symptoms must disrupt social and occupational functioning, but the distress is often less than would be expected if the patient were to have the genuine medical condition. Many contemporary clinical approaches to somatoform disorders incorporate the term **health anxiety**, which provides a less stigmatising term than hypochondriasis, as the latter is in common lay use as a derogatory term. Health anxiety also incorporates a global approach to other somatoform disorders (Carr and McNulty, 2006). Across studies, somatoform disorders have a prevalence of around 15–20 per cent of all patients and 4–5 per cent of the general population, although a more recent Japanese study revealed 5.8 per cent in a patient sample (Kuwabara et al., 2007).

There are six identifiable somatoform disorders in *DSM-IV-TR*: **somatisation disorder, undifferentiated somatoform disorder, conversion disorder, pain disorder, hypochondriasis** and **body dysmorphic disorder.**

Somatisation disorder

In 1859 **Pierre Briquet** gave his name to **Briquet's syndrome** (as well as Briquet's hysteria; see the Focus box above), although the collection of pseudomedical complaints presented by these patients had been considered together as a possible disorder for many years. A more stringent set of criteria than that applied to the disorder outlined by Briquet is currently in use but now termed 'somatisation disorder'. However, there have been discussions indicating a further revision of this and other somatoform categories for *DSM-V* (Mayou et al., 2005). Somatisation disorder is characterised by there being a sufficient number of recurring clinically significant pseudomedical complaints involving different aspects of somatic function and sensation. Clinical significance is indicated by social or occupational impairment, or some level of medical intervention, which is usually prescription medication (American Psychiatric Association, 2000). For a *DSM-IV-TR* diagnosis of somatisation disorder, these complaints must include:

- complaints of pain in at least four different sites, such as the abdomen, back or head, or during functions such as sex or menstruation

- two gastrointestinal complaints other than pain, such as abdominal bloating, food intolerance or diarrhoea, which may lead to further investigations including X-rays or surgery

- one 'conversion'-type (see section below) pseudoneurological complaint, such as seizures, paralysis, blindness, balance difficulties or amnesia

- one sexual complaint, such as erectile problems, excessive menstrual blood loss or hypoactive desire.

The most common of these complaints is pain and the least frequent are those with pseudoneurological features. These symptoms are presented in the absence of known medical conditions or are clearly in excess of that expected in the case of any medical condition suspected or found. A further criterion for diagnosis is that the complaints are not knowingly feigned by the client, though the ability of a clinician to establish this with any certainty is limited. In somatisation disorder, onset needs to be in the earlier part of adulthood (i.e. before the age of 30) and the intermittent presentation of symptoms should persist for a number of years. Where such complaints arise later in life, they are almost always due to a medical condition (American Psychiatric Association, 2000). Although the psychodynamic approach views these symptoms as anxiety converted into physical symptoms, the cognitive approach varies this by considering the symptoms to be a means of communicating emotional states such as anger in ways more comfortable to the client, which in this case is a physical symptom (Comer, 2007).

Clients often elaborate at length about their symptoms, which may be exaggerated accounts devoid of clear objective evidence for a disorder. A review of a client's treatment and attendance history can be useful in identifying the diversity and persistence comprising somatisation disorder. In common with factitious patients, multiple health professionals or authorities may be involved in this history, which may also involve treatments and procedures for comorbid conditions as well as those for somatisation complaints. Some conditions contributing to a diagnosis such as **irritable bowel syndrome** are currently without clear somatic foundation but may be excluded if their medical status is confirmed. Repeated unsuccessful interventions and hospitalisation inevitably have a seriously detrimental effect on the long-term health of somatisation patients (American Psychiatric Association, 2000).

Such a level of psychologically based problems could be said to indicate a 'neurotic personality'. In contemporary terms, these clients often have complex diagnoses with comorbid personality, mood and substance disorders, the combination of which can contribute to an unstable lifestyle and clinical ratings of ability to function (American Psychiatric Association, 2000). Individuals with somatisation disorder report more occupational, marital and interpersonal difficulties (Kring et al., 2007), although this may partly be explained by a tendency to overreport and exaggerate problems. Pharmacological treatment approaches have limited effectiveness as they can confound somatising complaints: for example, side-effects such as sexual difficulties may add to the somatising picture (see Walker and Furer, 2006). Cognitive behavioural therapy (CBT) is useful in reducing somatisation and the disorder rarely remits without intervention. However, clients do not usually ask for psychological intervention, as they tend to consider their needs to be met by medical treatment.

The disorder is fairly rare with overall estimates being around 0.2 per cent for men in the general population and up to 2 per cent for females, a ratio that can vary between cultures and consequently nations (American Psychiatric Association, 2000). In a recent study, the female to male ratio is the greatest of all the somatoform disorders at 8:1 (Kuwabara et al., 2007). In cultures that traditionally inhibit emotion, rates tend to be higher as somatic complaints provide a less emotional outlet and involve less of the perceived shame associated with mental illness. Cultural factors also play a part, in that the types of complaint vary in relation to the traditional health concerns of different cultures and need to be considered by clinicians making a diagnosis (American Psychiatric Association, 2000). It is an unfortunate feature of somatisation disorder that the majority of those with this psychiatric disorder regularly receive treatment for their 'physical symptoms' as well as somatisation. This is particularly the case in the USA, and it is fair to say this is an unnecessary cost to health care that occurs in most countries (Regier et al., 1993).

Undifferentiated somatoform disorder

Undifferentiated somatoform disorder could be viewed as a milder form of somatisation disorder with less stringent criteria regarding the number and severity of pseudomedical complaints. Diagnosis requires one or more physical complaints, such as significant fatigue, genitourinary or gastrointestinal complaints, which are sustained for 6 months or more and are not feigned (American Psychiatric Association, 2000). These complaints will also have no known medical basis or will be far in excess of those expected for any actual disorder present. As with other *DSM* disorders, these symptoms must cause clinically significant distress or impairment.

This is thought of as the 'residual category' for cases considered to be below the criteria for other somatoform disorders. Being subthreshold for the main disorders categories can mean this diagnosis is less stable, with increased potential for outcomes in which a general medical condition is found or another psychiatric condition better explains the symptoms (American Psychiatric Association, 2000). It may also be the case that, due to the inconsistencies of symptom reporting in the somatoform disorders, individuals with this disorder may subsequently be reassessed as being above threshold for having somatisation disorder when all symptoms are revealed (American Psychiatric Association, 2000).

Case study
References to follow

Janice said she could start the job as a secretary the following day and this suited her new boss Angela, reassuring her that Janice was enthusiastic and well organised. Apart from her references not having arrived, Janice settled rapidly into the job and within a week Angela wondered how she had managed without her. However, the following week Janice thought she had strained her back whilst filing, but she carried on in obvious pain until the Thursday when Angela sent her home until she had seen her GP. Eager not to lose her new-found asset, Angela insisted she did not return to work until the pain was under control. It was a further 2 weeks before Janice appeared behind her desk with pain killers, insisting that she wanted to go for tests but that her GP was unwilling to approve them.

Janice had been struggling in to work around 2 days a week for a month when Angela found it necessary to redeploy her personal assistant Tina to help with Janice's backlog. Shortly after, Janice announced that she was finally going for the tests she needed after changing her GP. The tests kept her away from work for 3 weeks, which struck Angela as excessive, even if it did involve travelling to a specialist hospital at the other side of the country. Tina mentioned to her boss that Janice had spoken about fMRI tests, which did not tie in with Angela's understanding of back pain. Over the phone Janice assured her it was because of additional headaches and numbness in her hands and should be resolved by the time she returned. However, a few days later, Tina placed a 3-month-old unopened envelope on Angela's desk, which contained the references from Janice's previous employer.

Janice had hardly been seen during her previous employment or the one prior to that, covering some 3 years. In fact, her attendance at work was insufficient for a reasonable assessment of her abilities. Tina explained how she had found the references at the back of a drawer in Janice's desk. From the wide variety of illnesses documented, Angela realised that there was a problem with her new employee, but she could not believe she was malingering as she seemed so genuine and in real pain. Angela decided to keep Janice's job open – a decision that Janice's previous six employers had also taken.

Somatisation disorder can resemble many disorders and may go undiagnosed for years unless there is some coordination of the patient's medical history across various health providers. From the client's perspective, they believe their illness to be genuine to fulfil the disorder criteria.

Conversion disorder

Conversion disorder involves pseudoneurological or pseudomedical complaints, which appear to affect voluntary motor or sensory (including visceral) functions, expressed as coughing fits, paralysis, seizures, convulsions or blindness, for which there is no complete medical explanation or cultural expectation. For a *DSM* diagnosis, psychological factors need to be associated with the emergence or worsening of these symptoms (American Psychiatric Association, 2000). Thus the initiation and severity of pseudomedical complaints can be preceded by severe stress or other psychological difficulties. *DSM-IV-TR* lists four subtypes of conversion disorder based on the type of presenting symptom:

- **with motor symptom/deficit** for initial motor-effect problems with balance or carrying out movement, speech, swallowing or micturation
- **with sensory symptom/deficit** for initial sensory-affect deficits such as blindness, deafness or lack of touch sensation
- **with seizures or convulsions**, in which there can be dysfunction of both motor and sensory aspects
- **with mixed presentation**, where a mixture of the above subtypes is presented.

As with other somatoform disorders, these symptoms are assumed not to be intentionally faked; however, they do correspond to the patient's level of **medical knowledge**. For example, a client with poor medical knowledge may present with implausible, even physiologically impossible complaints (American Psychiatric Association, 2000). One often-quoted example of how complaints do not follow anatomical pathways or known biological processes is glove anaesthesia. This is where the client presents with lack of feeling in a doll-like view of hand anatomy ending at the wrist, even though any medical damage to the affective nerves of the hand would follow the more complex innervation patterns around part of the hand and extending up the arm. There are also intact efferent connections, reflexes and normal muscle tone in cases of paralysis being presented, which contradict the normal medical picture of such losses of function (American Psychiatric Association, 2000). Symptoms presented may also be modified as a result of further knowledge gained or feedback from health care professionals. This relationship between patient knowledge and symptom accuracy tends to cast doubt on the assumption that symptoms are not intentionally feigned.

There may also be unintentional 'lapses of convenience' where a paralysed hand may be temporarily used, then become unusable again. This is more often seen when there is immediate benefit to the client, such as a paralysed arm raised above actively failing to strike them when released (American Psychiatric Association, 2000). This characteristic was visually demonstrated to the author by a very eminent psychiatrist in a lady presenting with loss of balance, who only appeared to fall over if someone was on hand to catch her. As this lady began to topple, the psychiatrist removed himself suddenly from his apparent position as security net, whereupon the patient rapidly regained balance (although unbeknown to her, this patient was in no danger of actually falling). Although anecdotal, these sudden recoveries in response to awareness of circumstances would tend to undermine the diagnostic assumption that clients lack any insight into the non-medical nature of their complaints.

There may be **secondary gain** to the individual in having the pseudomedical symptoms or the actual loss of function: in other words, the disability may be advantageous to the patient in avoiding commitments or responsibilities. In psychodynamic explanations, secondary gain is not the conscious intention of the sufferer and primary gain for the client is considered to be consequent on the cause of the symptom, such as blindness occurring as a conversion reaction to a distressing visual experience. Such explanations seem empirically weak in terms of evidence, intuitively naive and reliant on the premise that all of these processes are both unconscious and inaccessible to the client's conscious awareness (see Webster, 1995).

As symptoms worsen with psychological difficulties such as stress, there can be a causal loop set in place: disadvantageous circumstances will increase stress and consequent symptom severity, and thus increase gain to the patient in being ill. Conversion clients tend thus to adopt the **sick role** or play the part of patient and may become increasingly dependent during contact with medical professionals and treatment (American Psychiatric Association, 2000). During their relationship with health care providers, it is often noticed that the conversion client will not react to their disabilities in proportion to their severity (American Psychiatric Association, 2000). The phrase la belle indifférence has been used to refer to the client's tendency to lack the degree of concern normally associated with sudden blindness or paralysis. Despite the historical acceptance of this sign of conversion disorder, Stone et al. (2006) in a review of 11 studies

---

Focus

Historical and contemporary accounts of 'Anna O'

In **Breuer's** classic case study of **'Anna O'**, his early psychoanalytic approach claimed that her paralysed arm resulted from the 'conversion' of anxiety from a repressed childhood trauma into a physical condition. Other professionals have viewed conversion more sceptically, seeing the process as a continuation of childhood irresponsibility, when flight into sickness became a habitual escape route from responsibility, and in which the child convinces itself the illness is genuine. Around half of conversion disorder symptoms were subsequently explained by medical or neurological disorders in early studies (American Psychiatric Association, 2000), which tends to cast doubt on the psychoanalytic explanation.

This move towards specific neurological explanations has accelerated as neuroscience has advanced over the years (Bradfield, 2006). During the time when psychoanalysis was led by Freud, neurological knowledge was very primitive. Most if not all of the documented patients are from this time, including **Bertha Pappenheim** ('Anna O'), who was diagnosed by **Josef Breuer** and Freud with hysteria. She would nowadays be diagnosed as having neurological disorders such as **temporal lobe epilepsy** (Webster, 2004).

considered the evidence for its use sufficiently limited as to abandon the term until its definition and usefulness are better established. They found a greater frequency of *la belle indifférence* in organic disease than in those with conversion symptoms and considered the competing explanation that this was 'putting on a brave face' rather than indifference (Stone et al., 2006).

Long-term treatment of conversion disorder may often rely on the search for an alternative medical diagnosis. Although success for the use of primarily CBT treatments for most somatoform disorders has been found in **randomised controlled trails**, there is little evidence for the same success in the case of conversion disorder (Kroenke, 2007). The disorder is more common within families and monozygotic as opposed to dyzygotic twins. However, if these symptoms are due to genuine underlying medical causes, a similar pattern may be expected. Dimsdale and Dantzer (2007) draw attention to the fact that underlying pathology can lead to the symptoms of distress that contribute to the somatoform diagnosis, and that this process can lead to underlying pathology being overlooked in cases such as immunological problems.

Onset of conversion disorder is from late childhood to early adulthood and is rarely found to arise beyond the age of 35 years (American Psychiatric Association, 2000). The disorder is rare but estimates vary greatly from 0.01 per cent (American Psychiatric Association, 2000) to possibly around 0.5 per cent (Comer, 2007) and it is more common in females. Exact prevalence is uncertain, as somatoform disorders have rarely been included in large epidemiological studies.

Pain disorder

Pain disorder is characterised by clinically significant pain at one or more sites in the body, such as back pain. Psychological factors are invariably associated with the onset and/or degree of pain reported. Although the pain may worsen due to the patient's level of psychological stress, the pain is not intentionally feigned by them. In common with other somatoform disorders, pain disorder is only diagnosed when medical causes have been eliminated (American Psychiatric Association, 2000). In a *DSM* diagnosis, **specifiers** may be used to distinguish **acute duration** of less than 6 months from that greater than 6 months or **chronic duration**. There are two subtypes of pain disorder in *DSM-IV-TR* as follows.

- **Pain disorder associated with psychological factors** is the subtype in which psychological factors are the primary influence in the pain symptoms, with a lesser influence or absence of medical factors.

- **Pain disorder associated with both psychological factors and a general medical condition** is where both the medical and psychological sources of pain make a significant contribution to the symptom presented.

A third reference to pain disorder can be found on **Axis III** of the *DSM* for conditions where psychological factors contribute little or nothing to the condition, which is given the label **pain disorder associated with a general medical condition** and is not considered a mental disorder (American Psychiatric Association, 2000).

The differentiation of pain from a medical source from that attributed to somatoform or pure psychological sources can take time and resources, as some pain is difficult to investigate from a medical viewpoint. Thus pain disorder is thought to be common and to account for a proportion of occupational absenteeism. Based on US figures, up to 15 per cent of absenteeism is due to back pain alone, but the proportion of these cases due to pain disorder is difficult to ascertain with any accuracy (American Psychiatric Association, 2000). The secondary effects of pain disorder, such as the inability to attend the workplace, also include the chronic use of healthcare systems and medication, as well as consequent interpersonal problems and an undue focus on the pain to the exclusion of other life goals (American Psychiatric Association, 2000). Females tend to report more head pains, such as the migraine type of headache, than do males.

The usefulness of CBT and other treatments for pain disorder has not been well established in randomised controlled trails (Kroenke, 2007). However, some effectiveness with the use of pharmacotherapy in the form of **venlafaxine** has been found in such trials (Sindrup et al., 2003). Psychological interventions can also help to address secondary effects of chronic pain disorder such as social isolation.

Hypochondriasis

Hypochondriasis as a disorder is an individual's pervasive and recurrent preoccupation with thinking they have serious medical disorders based on the unintentional misinterpretation of normal bodily states and functions. These preoccupations are not delusional and are not restricted to concern over appearance, which would be classified as **body dysmorphic disorder**. There may also be preoccupation with the fear and anxiety that the conviction of having a serious illness or disorder produces (American Psychiatric Association, 2000). These individuals continue to be exceedingly worried by these fears when presented with evidence of normal health, usually in the form of a thorough examination, and subsequent formal reassurance from a medical practitioner. The distress and impairment of social and occupational functioning as a result of these concerns is significant and preoccupation persists for over 6 months. The sufferer may have a coexisting medical condition, but one which does not account for their exaggerated symptom awareness (American Psychiatric Association, 2000).

Hypochondriasis can be specified as being **with poor insight**. Individuals with poor insight into their disorder do not realise they are exaggerating or misinterpreting functions and are resistant to accepting that their concerns are excessive (American Psychiatric Association, 2000). Undue concern may be focused on heart rate, perspiration, coughs or aches, with the interpretation that these represent the onset of heart disease or tumours. Lack of insight into their unreasonable preoccupation, in addition to not accepting that their health is normal, can confound already challenged treatment approaches. There is a tendency to become obsessed with serious disorders and to be overly sensitive to minor changes in their bodies, which tend to be precipitated by overconcern and even repeated self-examination. Thus, any level of intervention may be likened to walking a 'clinical tightrope' between exacerbating the client's undue focus by drawing attention to the presented symptoms when illustrating their benign nature, and minimising any reference to avoid focus for preoccupation and consequently arousing fears in the client that their complaints are not being taken seriously. The latter approach also carries fears for the clinician that serious ethical and competence issues would ensue in the unlikely event that a genuine medical condition were subsequently found.

A client with hypochondriasis is thought to retain dysfunctional belief related to health and medical illness according to a model proposed most recently by Salkovskis and Warwick (2001), based on the catastrophic misinterpretation model applied to panic by Clark (1986). Health-anxious clients were found to be more likely to interpret bodily sensations such as headache as indicative of serious illness, and in further studies they evidenced a better memory for illness-related words or even pain-related words such as 'burning' (Pauli and Alpers, 2002). Although such studies were often on analogue populations, these triggers and automatic thinking can provide specific targets for cognitive behavioural therapy with clinical populations (Salkovskis and Warwick, 2001). However, it could be erroneous to assume that those individuals low on health anxiety are accurate in heath judgements (Marcus et al., 2007). One of the difficulties for the treatment of hypochondriasis is that it seems to be a continuous trait in the manner of personality, rather than a series of separate attitudes and reactions (Marcus et al., 2007). Health

concern can be the central component of the sufferer's self-image and may dominate their conversations and life-choices, such as career. Restrictions due to perceived illness may also provide **secondary gain** to the sufferer, further confounding treatment by rewarding the pessimistic prognosis. Medical assessment may also be confounded by the 'smokescreen' of complaints and concerns leading to real illness being overlooked (American Psychiatric Association, 2000).

The disorder may be precipitated by psychological stress, and there is a greater chance of hypochondriasis where there has been experience of serious illness or death. Paradoxically, sufferers tend to show no evidence of adopting a more preventative or healthy lifestyle than the rest of the population, such as good diet or exercising (American Psychiatric Association, 2000). Regular, medically benign contact with health professionals such as GPs can create problems and lead to suspiciousness from the health providers of factitious disorder. **Hypochondriasis by proxy** (fears of illness and over-vigilance on behalf of another, such as a child) can also be confused with the deliberate fabrication of illness in another, or **Münchausen's syndrome by proxy** (Holmes, Bee and Brannigan, 2001). In common with factitious or Münchausen's disorder, unnecessary medical procedures may be carried out, precipitated by hypochondriacal fears. These procedures may be health threatening in themselves and could lead to the self-fulfilling prophesy of the hypochondriasis sufferer having iatrogenic disabilities (American Psychiatric Association, 2000).

Hypochondriasis shows some variation in its prevalence over time, less with *ICD-10* criteria as compared with *DSM-IV-TR*, with the latter producing 3 per cent (Noyes, 2001). Onset can be at any age but the condition tends to persist once established and can also be influenced by media awareness of disorders (American Psychiatric Association, 2000) or media-driven health-scares at any one time. Personal experience of serious illness in relatives or acquaintances can have a similar impact and may prompt medical text reading to worsen the illness focus. Hypochondriasis is a term in common use outside of clinical contexts, and although its lay use is similar to the clinical definition, it is often confounded with malingering when the term 'hypochondriac' is used in a derogatory sense (see p. 464). The negative connotations of the term 'hypochondriac' are not new and date back to the first use of the term in the 1600s (Berrios, 2001). Such stigma can have implications for presentation, compliance and consequently prognosis. As mentioned above in this context, Carr and McNulty (2006) have considered the alternative labels in this area, such as **health anxiety**, particularly in the case of hypochondriasis.

Body dysmorphic disorder

Historically referred to as **dysmorphophobia**, body dysmorphic disorder involves an obsessive overconcern with some aspect of appearance. This is usually an imagined or greatly exaggerated defect, which can commonly be from amongst those most visible to others, such as facial complexion, wrinkles, scars or a perceived 'defective' feature like the nose (American Psychiatric Association, 2000). Occasionally there may be more than one area of focus, but it is usually a fairly specific complaint and can relate to almost any aspect of the body. Sufferers may be less specific about their perceived defect in communicating this to others, such as referring to themselves generally as unattractive. The patient finds the appearance of this body area unacceptable, and even if there is a slight irregularity, the degree of concern over this is clearly disproportionate. There is excessive focus on this defect in the form of general attention, monitoring and attempts to alter its appearance by physical manipulation, obscuring and using various preparations or even cosmetic surgery. Some have even attempted 'DIY' cosmetic surgery (Veale, 2000). This process and the concern over the supposed defect cause significant distress and impairment in social, occupational or other routine functioning (American Psychiatric Association, 2000).

Focus

Artificial means of addressing body dysmorphia

Many of those undergoing extreme changes to their body would deny having body dysmorphic disorder but show the same preoccupation with physical appearance. Jocelyn Wildenstein is an extreme example of this.
Source: Getty Images/Wireimage.

The example of Jocelyn Wildenstein demonstrates how body dysmorphic individuals may utilise surgery in an endless pursuit of an unattainable goal. Cosmetic product companies have expanded greatly to provide expensive products that offer remedies for suggested defects aimed at those insecure individuals at the non-clinical end of the dysmorphic spectrum. This sense of need and insecurity thrives in cultures where celebrity is revered and driven by the media, in a similar manner to the body image problems seen in eating disorders (see Chapter 12). Those in the media are also under pressure to be overconcerned with their image; **Uma Thurman** has admitted to being body dysmorphic. However, for body dysmorphia sufferers, such remedies provide a costly lure, and as these products cannot provide relief from the disorder, they can lead to a significant diversion of financial resources.

Cosmetic or plastic surgery has become more accessible and affordable in the twenty-first century, and although consultant guidelines suggest filtering out body dysmorphic sufferers, multiple operations for the same patient are not prevented. The number of women seeking cosmetic surgery who have been found to meet the criteria for body dysmorphic disorder has been high at 5–7 per cent (Altamura et al., 2001) and higher at 9 per cent in subsequent European studies (Aouizerate et al., 2003) suggesting a possible steady rise with increased opportunity. Sufferers fail to reduce their concerns by surgery. Even with multiple attempts they fail to satisfy what is a psychologically based obsession, to the extent that some patients report wanting to seek legal compensation from surgeons (Veale, 2000).

The obsessive focus on the perceived defect in body dysmorphic disorder is reminiscent of that seen in **anorexia** (see Chapter 10), so it is not surprising to find that 10 per cent of sufferers are comorbid for anorexia (Phillips, 1996). Some have considered body dysmorphic disorder to be on a continuum with eating disorders due to such similarities, even though eating problems are not generally part of body dysmorphic behaviour (see Bennett, 2006). As with anorexia, the body dysmorphic individual's focus on the supposed defect as being highly salient to others leads to many sufferers trying to hide it from view under adapted clothing or contrivances such as dark glasses. However, avoiding going out in public when not essential can be an easier option. Thus the patient's embarrassment can be extreme enough to result in their becoming a recluse in avoiding work, social or other public situations (American Psychiatric Association, 2000).

Body dysmorphic individuals tend to have abnormal relationships with mirrors or reflective surfaces. They may consume a lot of time examining the body part in any reflective surface they pass, and may have elaborate lighting and magnifying mirrors at home to enable close scrutiny. Alternatively, others may actively avoid mirrors or any reminders of their perceived problem. Many aspects of body dysmorphic behaviour are reminiscent of the obsessions and compulsions in **obsessive–compulsive disorder** (see Chapter 12) in terms of both symptom definition and effective treatments. However, there are differences, in that body dysmorphic disorder is associated with greater psychopathology, lower levels of insight and higher suicide rates than obsessive–compulsive disorder (see Bennett, 2006).

Behavioural treatments such as exposure with response prevention are effective in reducing the symptoms in body dysmorphic disorder, although maintenance sessions may be needed (Cororve and Gleaves, 2001). Selective serotonin reuptake inhibitors (SSRIs) can reduce the obsessive focus and may additionally help with any comorbid depression. An interaction between low serotonin, low self-esteem and rigidly held beliefs regarding attractiveness has been thought to be part of the aetiology of the disorder (Veale, 2000; Bennett, 2006). There are some gender differences in the body parts that come under focus in body dysmorphic disorder, with Western males exhibiting **muscle dysmorphia** in perceiving a lack of muscularity as a personal defect (Grogan, 1999). Prevalence of body dysmorphic disorder is low at less than 1 per cent of the general population (American Psychiatric Association, 2000). However, the majority of individuals of either gender in the general population express some dissatisfaction with their bodies at any one time (Grogan, 1999).

Aetiology and treatment of somatoform disorders

Biologically based medical disorders such as paralysis are specifically excluded prior to diagnosis of **somatoform disorders**. Although the presenting complaint must be in the absence of underlying medical cause, mistakes have been made in the past and could still occur in the future. However, this does not eliminate the possibility that there may also be biological factors involved in the cause of the somatoform disorder itself rather than the specific (pseudo) symptoms. Neurological factors have long been suspected in this respect. The issue of conversion symptoms being primarily on the left-hand side of the body is probably better explained in terms of this being less of a practical disadvantage to (primarily) right-handed clients than any neurological underpinning. However, parallels drawn between somatisation and phantom limb pain, where pain is felt after amputation, have provided potentially valuable insight into pain symptoms (see Melzack and Wall, 1999). Studies of genetic involvement in the aetiology of somatoform disorders have failed to find evidence of inheritance (Kring et al., 2007). Biological treatments for somatoform disorders are often in the form of antidepressants. SSRIs are particularly useful in the case of somatoform disorders that have an obsessional element, such as body dysmorphic disorder and hypochondriasis (Fallon, 2004).

Clearly the pseudophysiological nature of the symptoms would implicate psychological factors in the aetiology and treatment. Pseudosomatic or pseudoneurological symptoms are viewed by psychodynamic therapists as arising from repressed events or emotional trauma which needs to be worked though during extensive psycho-analysis (see Chapter 3). These explanations of somatoform disorder, and conversion disorder in particular, are central to psychodynamic theory and psychoanalytic practice. More recent views of this tend to struggle to explain how mechanisms of repression work in the absence of objective evidence. Support has been drawn from studies of unconscious processing. Amongst these is the existence of unconscious perceptual processing phenomena such as blindsight, or evidence of visual processing in individuals who consciously consider themselves blind, as well as the effects of variation in individual personality-based or expectation-based motivation towards loss of function (see Kring et al., 2007). However, these studies also rely on subjective assessments of what is consciously perceived and do not amount to empirical evidence of repression-producing symptoms.

In contrast, some behavioural approaches see the somatoform patient as being rewarded for consciously or subconsciously adopting the 'sick role', by gaining sympathy and attention. One-third of clients attending neurology clinics for the first time have medically unexplained symptoms (Broome, 2004), which can be viewed as a health resource problem, especially when this behaviour is repeated over many years. Thus some behavioural treatments focus on removing the reinforcers of the sick role behaviour. Cognitive approaches to somatoform disorders consider how cycles of overattention to health issues, particularly in the wake of experience of physical illness, can lead to clients developing health anxiety and attraction to the sick role (Rosen, 1995). This may be combined with negative attributions about health, particularly that relating to themselves (Allen et al., 2006). Randomised, controlled studies have found CBT to be effective in addressing somatoform disorders (e.g. Allen et al., 2006; Kroenke, 2007).

Although somatoform disorders are thought by some to be treatment resistant (Rief and Sharpe, 2004), cumulative evidence from evaluative studies has favoured CBT and anti-depressant medication, with most evidence in support of the use of CBT (Sumathipala, 2007). However, there is an absence of studies comparing medication with CBT (Sumathipala, 2007). In recognising that the validity of somatoform disorders has been questioned during their entire history as a nosological classification (Janca, 2005), there may also be a need to consider what would be a suitable treatment for a disorder with serious theoretical and practical limitations (Janca, 2005). Clearly the efficacy of treatments can only be reasonably expected to improve if current and long-standing criticisms of the concept of somatoform disorder are addressed (Mayou et al., 2005).

Self-test questions

- What is the relationship between the disorders in this chapter and psychoanalysis?
- Discuss the distinction between somatisation disorder and conversion disorder.
- What explanations are given for conversion disorder?
- What is meant by hypochondriasis by proxy?
- What are the similarities and differences between body dysmorphic disorder and anorexia?
- What are the inherent difficulties in treating somatoform disorders?

Classifications of dissociative disorders

The symptoms of dissociative disorders characteristically involve disruption in the integrity of memory, perception, identity and consciousness (American Psychiatric Association, 2000). In psychoanalytic explanations, the disorders are thought to be a reaction to an unbearable event or source of anxiety, from which the individual escapes psychologically or 'dissociates'. Thus the symptoms are of a psychological nature, such as loss of memory or identity. Dissociative symptoms are also found in **post-traumatic** and **acute stress disorders** as well as **somatisation disorder**, but they are not primary criteria for the diagnosis of these disorders. In *ICD-10* conversion disorder symptoms are considered to be dissociative, leading to the heading **dissociative (conversion) disorders**, but in *DSM-IV-TR* the two symptom types are distinct and conversion symptoms are primarily classified within somatoform disorders. *DSM-IV-TR* recognises the importance of cross-cultural awareness in assessing dissociative states and disorders. Expressed in some cultural and religious contexts, dissociative symptoms would not cause distress or dysfunction and not be seen as pathological, whereas they would in other contexts such as supposed '**spirit possession**' (American Psychiatric Association, 2000).

There is perhaps more controversy surrounding dissociative disorders than somatoform disorders, particularly dissociative amnesia and dissociative identity disorder. This has gone so far as to involve questioning the validity of these diagnoses (Piper and Merskey, 2004; Spanos, 1996). The consequences of aspects of dissociative disorders such as the issue of **recovered memories** can be devastating for those involved, again raising questions over the validity of these diagnoses (see Gudjonsson, 2001; Davies and Dalgleish, 2001). Much of the theoretical basis for psychoanalytic approaches is enshrined in these disorders, and thus criticism of dissociative disorders is often opposed by those who have invested in this paradigm to a great extent (see Shorter, 1997). See the section on critical issues below and Chapter 3 for further coverage of this issue.

The term 'dissociation' is itself imprecise, and varies in its meaning between contexts to the extent that Holmes et al. (2005) have attempted to define its clinical interpretation more precisely. For diagnostic purposes, the characteristic features of dissociation are derealisation, identity confusion and alteration, depersonalisation, and amnesia, which are rated in the **Standardized Clinical Interview for DSM-IV dissociative disorders** (SCID-D; Steinberg, 1994). Corresponding to these aspects of dissociation, *DSM-IV-TR* lists four dissociative disorders:

dissociative amnesia, dissociative fugue, depersonalisation disorder and dissociative identity disorder.

Dissociative amnesia

As the term suggests, dissociative amnesia is the failure to recall important personal information that cannot be accounted for by routine forgetfulness. The information is usually considered to be of a stressful or disturbing nature, or from a period with traumatic connotations, such as suicide attempts. This information loss tends to be for autobiographical memory or **explicit memory**, whereas memories not accessible to consciousness and cognitive abilities, termed **implicit memory**, remain intact. Dissociative amnesia has been associated with shell-shock during wartime, but the latter involves physical trauma, which is more likely to be the direct cause of the amnesia. However, dissociative amnesia may be triggered as an acute episode during periods of trauma, such as being in a war zone

(American Psychiatric Association, 2000). Dissociative amnesia is almost always for events following this assumed trauma or **anterograde amnesia**, in contrast to amnesia due to medical injury, which is most often for both events prior to trauma or retrograde amnesia and anterograde amnesia. Dissociative amnesia occurs on one or more occasions and is in the absence of other explanations for memory loss, such as head injury. The amnesia results in significant distress and disruption of normal social and occupational functioning. However, this needs to be distinguished from malingered amnesia, where secondary gain is more clearly evident (American Psychiatric Association, 2000).

Dissociative amnesia can follow patterns of failure to recall that are unusual when compared with other sources of amnesia. Sometimes the dissociative amnesia is generalised over large areas of experience, and more rarely, in what is termed generalised amnesia, it covers their entire lives. Where memory loss is ongoing, or in continuous amnesia, events from a particular time to the present are

Research

Dissociation, suggestibility and false memories

Research has often found a relationship between dissociative experiences and suggestibility (Holmes and Lax, 1999). Individuals prone to dissociative amnesia tend also to score high on measures of interrogative suggestibility, such as the **Gudjohnsson Suggestibility Scale** (Gudjonnsson, 1984). This scale has enabled research into suggestibility and measures two components of suggestion:

- the participants being influenced by leading questions (yield score) about a vignette read to them
- subsequent change to their replies (shift score) following suggestion of errors in their responses.

Suggestibility can make such individuals prone to **false memory syndrome** in respect of their reported amnesia, when this is examined during therapy or direct questioning about their periods of memory absence. In this process, suggested possible events are adopted by the sufferer to replace dissociated ones and then accepted as a 'real past'. These suggestions are usually made during therapy and sometimes under **hypnosis**, which is reliant on **hypnotic suggestibility** for its use, although this is still partly related to the effects of interrogative suggestibility (Gudjonsson, 1987). However, those diagnosed with dissociative amnesia are also found

to have high scores on **hypnotisability** measures (American Psychiatric Association, 2000).

Thus already suggestible individuals may be placed in a highly suggestible state and probed with the assumption that a traumatic event must be causing the amnesia to be 'repressed' in psychoanalytic terms. Some therapists have been criticised for suggesting that child sexual abuse had led to the amnesia and for pursuing this with clients vigorously, to the extent that the individual comes to believe this false event has taken place (Shobe and Schooler, 2001; Spanos, 1996). Despite its dubious origins, such 'recalled' evidence of abuse has resulted in prosecution of individuals, often members of the same family, with devastating outcomes (Gudjonsson, 2001; Wakefield and Underwager, 1992). This has been particularly frequent in the USA, where the **False Memory Syndrome Foundation** has assisted the examination of cases where there are such allegations (Wakefield and Underwager, 1992). A review of research on neurobiological aspects of memory and amnesia suggests that the malleable nature of memory can contribute substantially to the confounding of narrative truth (Loftus and Davies, 2006), or an individual's belief about a memory, with the actual accuracy of events or historical truth (see Zola, 1998; Spence, 1982).

not recalled. Memory loss is more frequently for a specific period in time, localised amnesia, or may even take the form of **selective amnesia**, in which only certain events from a period fail to be recalled whilst memory for others seems intact. Systematised amnesia is more complex still; here memory for only certain categories of information, such as a certain person, are not recalled (American Psychiatric Association, 2000). Where a number of 'blank periods' sequence with remembered ones, there is the possibility of this being interpreted as undiagnosed **dissociative identity disorder** (see below). Systematised, continuous and generalised amnesia are associated with subsequent diagnoses of dissociative identity disorder (American Psychiatric Association, 2000). In contrast to organically based amnesia, dissociative amnesia seems to be reversible, especially when the individual is removed from the trauma. Other aspects of dissociative amnesia do not conform to cumulative knowledge regarding memory and forgetting (see Zola, 1998). Further to this, acceptance of information recovered after the reversal of dissociative amnesia should be cautious, especially in the case of childhood memories, which tend to be unreliable (see Davies and Dalgleish, 2001).

DSM-IV-TR lists a number of diverse mental disorders and other conditions associated with dissociative amnesia, including depression, sexual dysfunction, age regression and the inability to provide answers to simple questions (American Psychiatric Association, 2000). Although the disorder is assumed to present at any age, there are many difficulties inherent in assessing and differentiating dissociative amnesia in early childhood. Prevalence appears to have increased from the latter part of the twentieth century to the current time, possibly due to public awareness of the disorder and overdiagnosis in those who are suggestible (American Psychiatric Association, 2000).

Dissociative fugue

In this disorder there is an abrupt departure from the individual's normal habitat or living area and partial or total amnesia for their previous life (American Psychiatric Association, 2000). Dissociative fugue involves greater disruption to memory than dissociative amnesia. The individual may seem to lose or become confused about their identity and sometimes adopt a new identity (identity alteration). Dissociative fugue is presumed to follow stress or trauma, which in psychodynamic terms precipitates this psychological escape. Abrupt trips can be as brief as hours or develop into months of wandering in new locations. It may be some time before the individual is 'discovered', usually due to their lack of

true identity or key memories, as they may behave quite normally in other respects. After their return, there may still be amnesia surrounding the precipitating trauma, or even amnesia for the period of the **fugue state** (American Psychiatric Association, 2000). Kopelman and Morton (2001) describe a number of fugue states where there is evidence of detached islets of past memory, or functional retrograde amnesia. Most of these cases describe a compartmentalising of memory experiences, which bears a resemblance to the memory deficits seen in **organic brain disease** (Kopelman and Morton, 2001). Evidence is growing that compartmentalisation and detachment in dissociation are separate processes and may occur independently (Holmes et al., 2005).

Individuals with dissociative fugue may even establish an entirely new identity in this new location, but this is not the same manner of identity creation reported in **dissociative identity disorder** (see pp. 458–61). However, new identities are uncommon in an already rare disorder. Where new identities are formed, they tend to be more outgoing and sociable than their former baseline personality, and will be well integrated in terms of home, community relationships and friendships. Their apparent lack of pathology in their activities and relations in the new setting contributes to their not coming to clinical attention for extended periods (American Psychiatric Association, 2000).

There have been suggestions of a close association with forms of desertion during wars, where terms such as 'battle-trauma' have previously been adopted, and it has been thought possible that some soldiers suffering from dissociative fugue may have been shot as deserters during wartime. However, hardly any reports of dissociative fugue have been reported amongst documented cases of trauma such as prisoners of war (Kring et al., 2007), nor of memory loss in those who have undergone such experiences (Zola, 1998). In addition, this trauma may also take the form of marital discord or even job difficulties, and may not even directly follow the trauma but could be delayed (Hacking, 1998).

Mood, substance-related or post-traumatic stress disorders may be comorbid with fugue. As with other dissociative disorders there is a relationship between dissociative symptoms and hypnotisability (American Psychiatric Association, 2000; Butler et al., 1996). *DSM-IV-TR* draws comparisons with some culture-bound disorders (see Chapter 20). Dissociative fugue is mostly diagnosed in adulthood following reported trauma, and recovery is rapid. There is a prevalence rate of about 2 per 1000 of the population, which can rise during times of natural disasters or war (American Psychiatric Association, 2000).

Depersonalisation disorder

This disorder involves persistent recurring periods of depersonalisation, in which the sufferer experiences a dream-like detachment or estrangement from their more familiar sense of self. This feeling of detachment has been described as being outside one's body watching one's own actions, almost as a detached observer or automaton. This detached view includes one's body or parts of the body, actions and even thoughts seen as if by a separate observer. These are feelings not beliefs, and as good contact with reality is maintained throughout, these symptoms are distinguishable from the delusions and hallucinations of **psychotic states**. These states are not a consequence of other disorders or substance use but are sufficiently persistent and salient as to cause significant distress as well as impairment in social and occupational functioning (American Psychiatric Association, 2000).

This depersonalisation is sometimes accompanied by a lack of emotional involvement or sense of control over one's actions. The sense of passivity may extend to one's thoughts, speech or sensations. This lack of integration with one's feelings and sense of personal control can border on anaesthesia and resemble an aloof indifference to one's self, as if watching someone in a movie. The depersonalised state may be likened to the **trance-like states** seen in some religious rituals or cultural practices (American Psychiatric Association, 2000). Such individuals may also experience **derealisation** and feel that the external world is unfamiliar, different or unreal – a sensation common in those with **panic disorder**. If such experiences are primarily due to diagnosed substance use disorders, a diagnosis of derealisation disorder should not be made; however, substance use within derealisation disorder will exacerbate symptoms of the disorder. There is a close correspondence with trauma and life-threatening situations, either real or perceived, in terms of both transient and prolonged attacks of depersonalisation and derealisation.

Depersonalisation disorder affects twice as many women as men and is first detected in adolescence, although it may have gone undetected in earlier years. Perhaps half of all individuals will experience these feelings at some stressful point in their lives, but this is rarely persistent or recurrent (American Psychiatric Association, 2000). The experience may be more profound in around 30 per cent of those individuals involved in life-threatening situations. There is little information on the overall prevalence of the disorder, but depersonalisation experiences are common amongst those with other mental disorders, and those diagnosed are measurably high on **hypnotisability** (American Psychiatric Association, 2000).

Dissociative identity disorder

Dissociative identity disorder is still commonly called by its former title **multiple personality disorder**. It is characterised by the individual having two or more distinct identities or personality states that recurrently and sequentially take control of the client's behaviour, and in children these are not imaginary friends (American Psychiatric Association, 2000). The different personalities or **alters** may have distinct characteristics such as being highly extravert, or insensitive and callous. They are reported to have their

Focus

Dissociation

As with hysteria, the concept of dissociation is unclear in terms of its definition, and in some applications of the term it relies on the existence of a special state of mind. Much of the acceptance of the term relies on historical precedent and the use of the concept in legal defence. It is described as the disconnection from full awareness of self, time and/or external circumstances. Dissociation exists along a continuum from normal everyday experiences to serious disorders that interfere with the individual's functioning (Braun, 1988).

States of mind where the normally integrated functions of memory and consciousness appear to be markedly disturbed are now referred to as the dissociative disorders described in this chapter. It has been argued that this pathological disconnection from full awareness of self and context needs to be differentiated from non-pathological dissociation (Spiegel, 1963). The Dissociative Experiences Scale (DES; Carlson and Putnam, 1993) is widely used to identify individuals with clinical levels of dissociative symptoms. Although designed for clinical samples, it has been successfully used for measuring non-pathological dissociation. Waller, Quinton and Watson (1995) see the disorders as taxonic and resulting from trauma, but non-pathological dissociative experiences as inheritable and on a continuum, as with personality traits. Carter (2008) considers not only normal dissociation, but normal **multiplicity** in identities, or the differing personalities that we use to cope with changing circumstances in life.

Collins and Ffrench (1998) describe 'normal dissociation' as including the features **absorption**, **imaginative involvement** and **automatism**. Absorption is described as being so engrossed in something, such as a book, as to lose sense of time or surroundings. Imaginative involvement is thought of as 'tuning out' of boring tasks into a trance-like state in which there is an altered sense of self. In automatism, skilled activity is carried out but leaving no memory of events during its commission. For example, many of us may drive a car over a routine journey, arriving with no memory of the 'automated' act and perhaps feeling a little anxious regarding what exactly may have occurred. The concept of the automaton lies close to the concept of dissociation and still has an important place as a criminal defence, in that the defendant is not consciously engaged with the criminal realities of the act. In such thinking, it would seem necessary to accept Cartesian dualism (Descartes considering the mind as non-physical and separate from the physical body) in order that the driver (mind) can leave the robot (brain and body) in a degree of dissociation, which can be accepted as both pathological and also relieving the individual of responsibility for their actions. This separation of mind and brain is at odds with current empirical views of mind and brain being perspectives of the same neural processes and not separable entities (Holmes and Lax, 1999).

The origins of the concept of dissociation as a disorder began with this division of mind from external and bodily processes, but began to be documented by early neurologists in explaining symptoms not accounted for by their limited knowledge. Charcot described **'traumatic hysteria'** in those surviving traumatic accidents, indicating that there were 'symptoms beyond the trauma'. French neurologist Pierre Janet (1889) described automatism, and at around the turn of the twentieth century it was he who put forward the classic concept of dissociation. Often associated with Freud, the term **hysterical neurosis (dissociative type)** was adopted in early classificatory systems, implying the early acceptance of an unconscious basis for dissociative states. This provided a theoretical framework for the proposed unconscious selves in **dissociative identity disorder** (see below), which was in agreement with Breuer's concept of **hypnoid states**.

However, members of the **Nancy School** in France, **Leibault and Bernheim**, considered **dissociative hysteria** to result from a form of **self-hypnosis**. Not only did they use hypnosis to treat dissociative hysteria, but they generated hysterical symptoms in suggestible individuals with hypnotic suggestion. Freud visited Bernheim at Nancy and witnessed how **'hypnotic amnesia'** could be overcome *without* rehypnotising the individual. Following this, Freud abandoned the concept of dissociation (see Shorter, 1997).

Sidis (1898) referred to the human species as 'the suggestible animal'. This would seem to be an appropriate assertion if dissociative disorders are considered to result from suggestion, as proposed by Spanos (1996). A relationship between suggestibility and dissociation has been found experimentally (Ost, Fellows and Bull, 1997; Holmes and Lax, 1999). Thus, historical as well as more recent approaches to dissociative experiences have been confounded by the susceptibility of the individuals in question to suggestion or hypnotic suggestion. Even Freud had initially used hypnosis in treating clients with what he thought of as hysterical symptoms. However, Spanos (1991) found suggestion alone as effective as hypnotic suggestion in treating such psychological conditions.

As documented elsewhere in this chapter, the historical assumption of pathological dissociation provides a challenge for the credibility of the classificatory systems by including these disorders. Furthermore, this assumption provides the basis for a criminal defence against serious offences and should be subject to critical appraisal. Spanos (1996) has been highly critical of the ready acceptance of patients' accounts of dissociative experiences, especially those of amnesia or multiple identities, believing these to be **sociocognitive constructions**. Empirical evaluation tends to support this view of patients responding to leading statements by therapists or information in the media, rather than there being a pathological disruption of consciousness. A number of points add weight to this argument as follow (see Spanos, 1996, for more detail).

- There has been no empirical documented evidence of dissociative amnesia (Pope et al., 1998).

- There is currently no empirical evidence of a 'dissociative trance' state of mind.

- Dissociation relates to hypnotisability, suggestibility and fantasy proneness.

- In dissociative disorders, symptoms may be iatrogenic, can be synthesised, may be unacceptably bizarre, lack empirical evidence and appear to be diagnosed by a small number of self-supporting therapists.

Further to this, Spanos (1996) has questioned the existence of both special hypnotic and dissociative states.

own names, history, and way of dressing or speaking that contrast with that of the **primary identity** or **host** (with the individual's name). The identities can be unaware of one another or may be in conflict, and can appear when their particular personality characteristics are the most appropriate to deal with current circumstances. **Eberhardt Gmelin** reported one of the earliest cases from Germany in 1791 of a German female who changed to being a French aristocrat with discrete memories and language.

There may be over 100 personalities in some cases, but some identities are more salient than others, although the primary identity tends to be passive and dependent amongst these, often carrying the guilt and emotional burden for the rest. More powerful and hostile identities tend to dominate the individual's consciousness and may 'organise' the other identities. There seems to be an inability to integrate these aspects of identity and memory in dissociative identity disorder individuals. These alternative identities may be unaware of each other or in antagonistic conflict, and some may intrude on the time of others or try to embarrass them. The transitions, which may be precipitated by stress, usually last seconds and are marked by changes in non-verbal characteristics, disrupted thinking or rapid blinking (American Psychiatric Association, 2000).

Early presenting symptoms of dissociative identity disorder also involve apparent amnesia for important personal information, which is more than simple forgetting and may extend beyond the disorder duration to certain childhood episodes. Memory lapses can vary between alters, with the more dominant or hostile identities having more inclusive recall (American Psychiatric Association, 2000). These lapses of memory can be accompanied by changes in the environment that cannot be accounted for, such as unusual personal items left in the home or finding cigarette ends when one does not smoke. The idea that one's other identity has left these is usually the last explanation to be accepted. Symptoms of **post-traumatic stress** as well as the impulsivity, relationship instability and self-harming behaviour of **borderline personality** can occur, sometimes leading to a concurrent diagnosis of the latter (American Psychiatric Association, 2000).

The concept of dissociative identity disorder being an escape from trauma appears to be reinforced by the very high reporting of **incestuous sexual abuse** (70 per cent) and **physical abuse** (80 per cent) in the histories of patients (Putnam, 1989). Although recognising that the research literature is relatively scarce for the disorder, many currently make a causal link between sexual abuse trauma and dissociative identity disorder (see Ross, 2007). However, these are usually self-reports and there is a weight of evidence to support the view that verifiable documented abuse is never forgotten (Zola, 1998). The fact that many of the

symptoms seem implausible and resemble mythical stories of superstition, such as possession by demons, have led some professionals to doubt the very existence of the disorder, and others to consider that the 'identities' and memories of abuse arise due to the measurably greater **dissociability**, **suggestibility** and **hypnotisability** of such patients (see Frankel, 1996; Butler et al., 1996; American Psychiatric Association, 2000). Some of the more bizarre recovered memories, such as abduction by aliens, have been interpreted as distortions of early abuse (Comer, 2007). However, individuals who claim to have been abducted by aliens also experience alterations of consciousness, support unconventional beliefs and have rich fantasy lives (Warner, 2004).

Dissociative identities always seem to emerge after therapy commences, which has led to the conclusion that the disorders are iatrogenic or a product of the therapy and social network of therapists involved. What could be described as a small number of 'believers' in the dissociative identity concept have been known to use highly intrusive and interrogative questioning with these suggestible clients. This kind of persuasive interviewing has been reported both in more recent and even in so-called classic historical cases (see Merskey, 1992). This kind of questioning has often gone beyond suggestion and in historically recorded cases the client appears to be given little alternative but to admit to symptoms of disturbed identity (Piper and Merskey, 2004). The illusive and vague nature of dissociative or somatoform disorders provides an opportunity for some to utilise this for their own advantage. Others have tried to fabricate dissociative identity disorder in an attempt to evade criminal responsibility, such as **Kenneth Bianchi**, the 'hillside strangler', in the USA (see the section on forensic issues below; Schwartz, 1981).

Spanos, Weekes and Bertrand (1985) used the same questioning that the original clinician had used on Bianchi to elicit similar responses in students during role-play, even in a group naive to what might be required. Spanos (1996) proposed this as a **sociocognitive** explanation for reported cases of dissociative identity disorder as well as other dissociative phenomena. Thus suggestible clients are led into role-playing the expectations of therapists and responding to questions probing for alters or false memories in the way they thought appropriate. To reinforce this, Spanos has carried out and reported numerous studies in which convincing false identities have been created in the 'laboratory' (see Spanos, 1996). As would be expected with suggestion-led symptoms, these identities tended to change and be influenced by the social context or further suggestion. Possibly as a further outcome of this interaction, some clients generate imaginative and implausible alters and 'recalled' experiences (see Piper and Merskey, 2004).

Focus

Dissociative identity disorder and therapeutic credibility

Most dissociative identity cases are reported by the same few therapists. These therapists are in some cases ex-patients and some recovered memories of trauma are bizarre (e.g. alien rape). Such therapists form social networks and are supportive of one another, particularly when the boundaries of credibility are breached by a patient's reported experiences. For example, such therapists have reported as many as 10,000 identities in one individual (Kluft, 1995) with alters that are lobsters or stuffed animals and abuse that has taken place on alien spacecraft or in the family back garden with zoo animals (see Piper, 1998; Piper and Merskey, 2004). The language of dissociative identity disorder is also that of the superstitious concept of **'possession'** and perhaps relates to a similar type of belief system (see Chapter 2). For example, Ferracuti, Sacco and Lazzari (1996) report on individuals undergoing **exorcism** for 'devil trance possession state', whose symptoms they interpret into a dissociative framework with features of dissociative identity disorder.

Perhaps we have the right to believe these, as we have the right to believe in demonic possession or witchcraft. However, for those interested in effective therapy for real disorders, these data are embarrassing and may represent a persistent adherence to what is considered contrived folly (Piper and Merskey, 2004). The decision of US **health insurance companies** to recognise dissociative identity disorder may have contributed to the acceptability of some of the more controversial accounts of the disorder in the past. However, from the late 1990s onwards there has been a decline in those supporting the diagnosis, the cessation of the journal **Dissociation** and increasing reluctance by US courts to accept dissociative symptoms as evidence (Piper and Merskey, 2004). This may point towards a differing approach to the disorder for *DSM-V*. This would be to consider a diagnosis of dissociative identity disorder to imply that the client is considered to be disordered because he or she *believes* that they have more than one identity, rather than because they actually *have* multiple personalities.

Critical accounts of dissociative identity disorder, including the sociocognitive model, have in turn been challenged (e.g. Gleaves, 1996) and accused of being unjust in the context of dissociative identity disorder arising from incidents of abuse. However, child abuse is relatively common but dissociative identities are comparatively very rare and do not seem to occur in documented cases of abuse (Bulik, Prescott and Kendler, 2001). No study has ever verified the claim that dissociative identity disorder sufferers have been subject to high levels of childhood maltreatment (Piper and Merskey, 2004). Thus while accounts of the disorder in relation to abuse still remain open to question, a critical approach to the concept of dissociative identity disorder remains justified (Spanos, 1996; Kihlstrom, 2005; Piper and Merskey, 2004). Some accounts perhaps illustrate the vulnerability of the dissociative concept to criticism. Although a supporter of the concept of dissociative identity disorder, Colin Ross has also reported some controversial accounts of recovered memories involving 'alien abductions' in dissociative patients.

Rates of diagnosis are many times higher and the number of alters greater in females than males (American Psychiatric Association, 2000). Prevalence rates for the disorder have also been a source of controversy. At the turn of the twentieth century, when the disorder was first being

described, a number of cases were reported, but these declined up until the 1970s. At this point in time a number of cases received widespread publicity, including feature films such as *The Three Faces of Eve* (Nunnally Johnson, 1957). This dramatically introduced the public to concepts of dissociation in an uncritical but convincing manner (Butler and Palesh, 2003), which was followed by a dramatic increase in the number of new cases reported. There was more than a 1000-fold increase in incidence that some would have considered to be of 'epidemic' proportions (Kihlstrom, 2005). Thus, the incidence of dissociative identity disorder seems to vary wildly with media publicity: for example, from 0.0001 per cent to 1.3 per cent (Ross, 1991). As mentioned above, increased public and professional awareness, the suggestibility of susceptible individuals, contagion and the increasing networks of pro-dissociative identity disorder therapists may be the competing explanations for this change.

Aetiology and treatment of dissociative disorders

Consistent empirical evidence of biological factors being involved in the aetiology of the presentation of dissociative disorders tends to be elusive, as these may confound the diagnosis. However, the dissociation of conscious and unconscious processes may be more likely in some individuals than others, irrespective of their life experiences, and there may be biological correlates for this. There are a number of biological correlates, such as smaller **hippocampal** and **amygdalar volumes** in the brains of those diagnosed with dissociative identity disorder (Vermitten et al., 2006). This has been often used as evidence of childhood trauma and to conceptualise the disorder as **childhood-onset post-traumatic developmental disorder** (Vermitten et al., 2006). Some reasonably common disorders can present with dissociative-like symptoms that worsen with psychological stress, such as a case of **acute disseminated encephalomyelitis** that was initially diagnosed as probable dissociative disorder (Corrales-Arroyo and Ortiz-Pascual, 2007). Genetic factors increasing traits such as **hypnotisability** are thought to underpin some dissociative disorder (Butler et al., 1996).

Psychodynamic explanations of dissociative disorders point to trauma as the causal factor in dissociative disorders. Although older cognitive and behavioural explanations have agreed with the presumption of trauma as part of the aetiology, more recent sociocognitive explanations have challenged this (Spanos, 1996). In addition, behavioural views have emphasised the reinforcement of illness behaviour as being part of the causal chain producing this aberrant behaviour. However, in almost all diagnosed cases of dissociative disorders there are weakly substantiated assumptions of trauma as the underlying cause of the symptoms. This is highly controversial, and not only are false memories possible (Loftus and Davis, 2006; Loftus, 1993), but also some analysts claim that dissociative disorders may be false categories of diagnosis, especially dissociative identity disorder (Piper and Merskey, 2004; Spanos, 1996). Some explanations of the resulting dissociative states have returned to the idea of self-hypnosis or **autohypnosis** (e.g. Butler et al., 1996; Bliss, 1986), which was first considered for dissociative hysteria by **Leibeault** and **Bernheim** of the **Nancy School** (see Chapter 1).

Anti-depressant and anti-psychotic medication appears to help with those presenting with dissociative disorders. Anti-psychotics such as **perospirone** may also be addressing undiagnosed schizophrenia-related illness that presents as dissociative disorder, particularly dissociative identity disorder (Spanos, 1996). Naltrexone has been used in the treatment of clients presenting with depersonalisation disorder, reducing reported symptoms by 30 per cent, which suggests that higher levels of endogenous opioids may be involved in the disorder (Simeon and Knutelska, 2005). However, treatment is thought to be mainly the preserve of individual psychological approaches. Psychoanalysts

consider the process of working through the trauma, perhaps under hypnosis, as the initial goal, with abreaction or an emotional reliving of the event as a key to confronting the distress without dissociation. Some cognitive behavioural approaches would follow a similar course, but emphasising the processes of desensitisation and cognitive restructuring as producing positive outcomes. CBT has been successfully used to address specific dissociative symptoms (Goldstein et al., 2004). Other cognitive behavioural interventions are less accepting of the dissociative symptoms and, in the absence of trauma, address the maladaptive thinking of clients.

However, most treatment approaches must first accept the validity of dissociative disorders and this acceptance usually extends to historical explanations of the disorder as escape from trauma. Thus, evaluation and detail of treatments are exclusively the preserve of those who accept disorders such as dissociative identity disorder as valid diagnoses (Spanos, 1996). Any examination of issues in the individual therapy for dissociative identity disorder tends to deal with the urgent need to uncover assumed trauma rather than questioning the existence of supposed trauma (e.g. Kluft, 2003). Thus, in dissociative identity disorder the therapeutic aim is claimed to be the reintegration, not the elimination, of the extra identities (see Putnam, 1989). Many would claim that dealing with the reasons for the client believing or enacting multiple personalities should be the real goal of therapy for this disorder (Piper and Merskey, 2004; Spanos, 1996).

Clinical issues in somatoform and dissociative disorders

There can be difficulty for the clinician in distinguishing between hypochondriasis and other somatoform disorders, as well as malingering or factitious disorder. Indeed, there may be points of overlap further confounding this situation, as some of these diagnoses may be comorbid within the individual client (e.g. Rosenberg, 2003). Many provisional diagnoses may be made at the first point of contact, usually the general practitioner, and clients may not reach more specialist attention until much later in the disorder's progress, when treatment for the assumed medical condition has failed. All of the disorders and conditions in this chapter are fraught with clinical difficulties, and as with **factitious disorders**, somatoform and dissociative disorders tend to be dealt with by self-selected clinical specialists with long experience in these areas and an assumed cumulative awareness of the complex issues involved (Spanos, 1996).

Many varied borderline medical disorders are included in the symptoms for *DSM* somatoform categories, especially undifferentiated somatoform disorder. Examples of these disorders with partial medical recognition are myalgic encephalopathy (ME; chronic fatigue syndrome) and **neurasthenia**, both of which indicate fatigue and weakness, **irritable bowel syndrome** and fibromyalgia. These borderline disorders are all considered to be euphemisms for somatoform disorders by more exactingly empirical professionals (Rief and Sharpe, 2004). In this, there may be some conflict between clinical psychologists and those self-help groups or medical professionals who would prefer these disorders to be established as somatic. It has to be recognised amidst the confusion this causes that medical recognition is not the same as having an established medical aetiology. The best interests of the client are not always served by labelling them with these 'medical' conditions, when intervention for somatoform complaints may be more helpful. It is estimated that around 20 per cent of visits to GPs are potentially for somatoform symptoms (Reif and Sharpe, 2004), which in current economic climates may be an excessive diversion of resources, especially if these disorders cannot benefit from the additional cost of medical interventions.

Dissociative disorders are rarely encountered outside of a relatively small group of therapists, who appear to diagnose a disproportionately large number of clients amongst their intake (Spanos, 1996). Although many such therapists use the language of psychoanalysis, not all are recognised within this discipline. Active iatrogenic production of symptoms via the process of therapy is evident in cases of dissociative identity disorder (Spanos, 1996). During psychoanalytic therapy for dissociative disorder, memory reconstruction appears to be an almost continuous process (Spence, 1982). Clinicians with clients presenting with dissociative symptoms should exercise caution and be aware of the forensic issues that may be involved and the scepticism over such cases shown by many professionals in psychology and psychiatry.

Forensic issues in somatoform and dissociative disorders

Given that one criterion for somatoform disorder is that the client is not deliberately feigning symptoms, there cannot be the inference of false representation or dishonest use of health resources, as would be the case in **factitious disorder** (see below). However, there are resource issues in the systematic abuse of medical resources, and in the case of some somatoform disorders these can be far beyond the levels used by those with genuine and serious medical disorders. The repeated use of increasingly complex testing equipment is almost inevitable, as a medical cause is not going to be found and conclusions are not usually arrived at until exhaustive and extensive investigations reach their limits.

Some individuals seem to be more prone to dissociation and this seems to coincide with higher levels of **suggestibility** and **hypnotisability** (Butler et al., 1996; Holmes and Lax, 1999). This needs to be considered seriously when the source of symptoms is suspected to be sexual or physical abuse, to ensure that **false memories** are not inadvertently created in suggestible individuals as a result of assessment or treatment (see Gutheil, 1993). As referred to above, false memories are created and can be acted upon in legal proceedings, with far-reaching effects for individuals, families and communities (see Davies and Dalgleish, 2001). In cases where clinical observations become forensic evidence due to recall of abuse taking place during clinical assessment or therapy, there are many points differentiating false memories and true recollections that clinicians may wish to consult (see Loftus and Davis, 2006; Davies and Dalgleish, 2001; Bennett, 2006: p. 250). Some clinical forensic professionals may be given the daunting task of assessing individuals who have already invoked proceedings on the basis of possible falsely recalled events.

The existence of dissociation as a special mental state is important in legal terms and can involve crimes as serious as murder. Acting as an **automaton** can be interpreted as not being responsible for one's actions in a forensic sense, and the concept of **automatism** is very close to that of clinical dissociation (Holmes and Lax, 1999). The US murderer **Kenneth Bianchi**, 'the hillside strangler', successfully fabricated dissociative identity disorder in an attempt to evade responsibility for multiple murder charges by convincing the clinician assessing him and not deviating from the responses expected for a diagnosis (see Schwartz, 1981). **Michael Orne** (1927–2000) utilised similar deceptive techniques to undermine Bianchi's pretence, which had already convinced attending psychiatrists owing to the offender having had psychology training in former years. Orne used **demand characteristics** (see Chapter 5) to lead Bianchi into making predicted and improbable statements, which in this case involved the production of further personalities.

The vague clinical nature of dissociative and somatoform disorders, as well as the controversy surrounding these diagnoses, can produce grey areas for evidence in courtrooms, which may be exploited by legal representatives or their clients. Until these grey areas have clearer boundaries and valid criteria, the controversial nature of these disorders may continue (Piper and Merskey, 2004; Starcevic, 2007).

Self-test questions

- In what ways are dissociative disorders controversial?
- Why should recovered memories after amnesia be treated with caution?
- What is meant by dissociative fugue?
- What are the possible explanations for dissociative identity disorder?
- Why would dissociative symptoms also be found in post-traumatic stress disorder?
- At what point do dissociative identities usually emerge?

Factitious disorders

Factitious disorder is primarily characterised by physical or psychological symptoms or signs that are intentionally fabricated by an individual purely to adopt the sick role and on occasion receive medical attention (American Psychiatric Association, 2000). Subjective symptoms may be falsely reported, such as headache or back pain, or objectively fabricated, such as the client placing a stone under their own back during an X-ray for kidney stones. Factitious patients may actively self-harm to produce false symptoms such as bleeding, or may exaggerate minor

existing conditions so as to mimic acute severe episodes. Reasons for the symptoms presented only pertain to gaining medical attention and there are no medical causes for the presentation or any form of external gain for the client (American Psychiatric Association, 2000).

Symptoms can be non-specific to known disorders and will almost always require further and extensive investigations or assessment. There may be some theatrical flair in the manner of presentation and a tendency to elaborate on a theme once established, or if they succeed in arousing concern or interest in the clinician (American Psychiatric Association, 2000). In these presentations they may evidence pseudologia fantastica, which is where a kernel of truth is used to fabricate a complex web of fantasy that can be difficult to falsify. This is usually combined with above average medical knowledge and terminology, often gained from a minor medical occupation or from textbooks (American Psychiatric Association, 2000). These characteristics, of being medically informed and practised in deception, make discovery and proof difficult in the absence of objective evidence, such as interference with assessment procedures or possession of blood, drugs or other relevant paraphernalia. When confronted with discovery, clients usually deny feigning symptoms and leave, thus evading further proceedings, but they may begin again at a different hospital.

There are three subtypes of the disorder in *DSM-IV-TR*.

- **With predominantly psychological signs and symptoms.** Although not exclusively psychological complaints, these symptoms indicate a mental disorder more often than physical illness. This is a less common subtype in which clients may feign amnesia, dissociation, schizophrenia or depression, and may take psychoactive substances to support this deception. However, in the case of these disorders, presentations may be vague

Focus

Differentiating factitious, somatoform, dissociative disorders and malingering

Factitious disorder is a separate heading in *DSM-IV-TR*, and although it has been included in this chapter, it needs to be distinguished from **somatoform** and **dissociative disorders** as well as **malingering** in terms of its defining features. Although the symptoms are similar to those of the somatoform and more rarely dissociative disorders, factitious individuals deliberately present with physical or psychological symptoms for which there is no medical basis. In contrast, it is

assumed that somatoform and dissociative symptoms are not deliberately fabricated, although this has been partly contested (Piper and Merskey, 2004).

In **malingering** there is some external incentive for the patient to present fake disorders, but in factitious disorder this incentive is absent and the only goal seems to be maintaining the role of a sick person. Thus, psychopathology is assumed when the disorder is diagnosed (American Psychiatric Association, 2000).

and not conform to specific expectations based on genuine cases, but represent the client's own idiosyncratic perception of the psychiatric disorder (American Psychiatric Association, 2000).

- **With predominantly physical signs and symptoms.** This is the more common subtype, in which one or more of a vast range of medical conditions may be imitated or select symptoms may be feigned that suggest certain disorders. Those symptoms most easily synthesised tend to be most frequent, such as bleeding, creating or infecting wounds, vomiting and rashes. These presentations may be more sophisticated and challenge the clinician's knowledge, but this is dependent on the client's own medical knowledge (American Psychiatric Association, 2000).

- **With combined psychological and physical signs and symptoms.** This is where neither psychological nor physical complaints are greater, but both are present.

Factitious disordered individuals tend to be females (American Psychiatric Association, 2000) and often have occupational or other connections with health services. It is an intermittent disorder beginning in early adulthood. The prevalence of factitious disorder is usually an underestimate as many evade detection altogether, or move health providers if there are any suspicions regarding their behaviour. Those falsifying physical symptoms of illness are far more common than individuals presenting with psychological problems (American Psychiatric Association, 2000).

Münchausen's syndrome

The term **Münchausen's syndrome** is taken by Asher (1951) from the name of Hieronymous Karl Frederick von Münchausen (1720–1797) who was supposed to have lied outlandishly about his exploits fighting for Russia against the Turks. However, these were somewhat exaggerated tales published by Rudolph Erich Raspe in 1785 of a rather fictionalised version of Baron Münchausen. Perhaps furthering the association with the syndrome, the baron's wife, Bernhardine Brun, 57 years his junior, had a son who died somewhat mysteriously at 1 year of age (see Münchausen's syndrome by proxy, pp. 465–9). Over 100 years earlier than Asher, **Gavin** first described this syndrome in 1838, followed by **Charcot** who labelled it mania operative passive in 1877. These earlier descriptions also led to the term **factitious disorder** being applied to the syndrome, as used in the *DSM* classificatory system.

Many authors use the terms **Münchausen's syndrome** and factitious disorder interchangeably, and in the UK the term 'Münchausen's syndrome' has been far more widely adopted. However, Münchausen's syndrome should be reserved for more severe forms of the disorder that are distinguished in terms of the degree, persistence and pervasiveness of their seeking medical attention and environments (Libow and Schreier, 1986). There are differing degrees of factitious disorder, from passively reporting false symptoms to gain attention, through to repeated self-harm or falsifying records to receive acute surgical intervention. At the more extreme end of this continuum, individuals tend actively to seek invasive medical treatment such as surgery by faking symptoms and signs, and are labelled as having Münchausen's syndrome (Holmes, Bee and Brannigan, 2001).

These more severe cases are often male with extensive knowledge of health services (American Psychiatric Association, 2000), and they will pit their medical knowledge competitively against that of the clinician to whom they are presenting (Holmes, Bee and Brannigan, 2001). In Münchausen's syndrome, medical attention seeking is the central focus of their lives and they will move around geographically as well as changing physicians regularly to facilitate this. This may lead to an overestimate of this disorder, as there may be multiple reports of a single Münchausen's individual from different health professionals (American Psychiatric Association, 2000). In contrast to factitious disorder, Münchausen's patients may follow a chronic course with repeated hospitalisations and interventions throughout their lifetime (American Psychiatric Association, 2000). These individuals may invite **iatrogenic damage**, which may leave clinicians with a level of guilt over causing unnecessary injury such as multiple surgical procedures.

Around 10 per cent of factitious disorder patients could be described as Münchausen's syndrome. Estimates of the costs to health care systems are difficult to obtain as detection is rare and health authorities are reluctant to admit wasting resources. However, these costs will be substantial with perhaps over 2 per cent of all patients and 1 per cent of mental health patients possibly fabricating illness (American Psychiatric Association, 2000). The more direct term **fabricated or induced illness** has come to be adopted to avoid multiple and less descriptive disorder labels such as factitious and Münchausen's (Bass and Jones, 2006).

Münchausen's syndrome (and factitious disorder) by proxy

In Münchausen's syndrome by proxy (MSBP), a carer will feign symptoms in another, normally dependent

Case study
Please, my child needs help!

When Jean was born not only were her parents delighted but the whole neighbourhood rejoiced in the fact that the couple could now get on with their lives after the death of their first child Nancy, at only 18 months. Mother Nora and father Dan doted on their newborn as they had her deceased sister, but it was an understandably tense time for the new parents. Jean seemed healthy enough, but then again so had Nancy until Nora heard her stop breathing in the night via the baby alarm. The first time this happened, Dan was away and Nora had picked her child up in panic, running into the street pleading for help. The night Nancy died, Nora was standing over her in hospital and was so distraught she had to be sedated. Nora's family had rallied around her, even her estranged and competitive sister.

Each time Nora even imagined Jean may be unwell, she would rush to her room. Following Nora's conviction that her newborn had endured an episode of apnoea, she moved into her room at night. Dan thought it would be better to move Jean into their room but Nora disagreed, as there would be too many breathing sounds to monitor with three of them. Dan also became anxious that Jean had not been moved to hospital and about why the staff had not supplied them with monitoring equipment, given what had happened to their previous child. Feeling excluded from what was happening with his child, Dan visited the family GP and was startled to discover that there were no recorded problems with Jean. However, on hearing Dan's story the GP began to make phone calls and asked Dan if he could come in with his family for a chat.

During the meeting, it transpired that Nora had taken Jean to the hospital outpatients department on two occasions, of which Dan and his GP had been unaware. Their GP was reassuring and explained how he thought it might be a good idea to admit Jean to a paediatric unit for observation, in view of what had happened to her sister. Nora seemed encouraged by this and talked freely about various problems with her child she thought relevant, surprising Dan with her detached, detailed knowledge. Two months later, Dan sat in the same office with his head in his hands trying to grasp what his doctor was telling him. Nora had been observed in hospital, as well as Jean, and CCTV footage had left no doubt that Nora had been the cause of her daughter's breathing problems by using a soft teddy bear to semi-suffocate her own infant. Although Nora would not admit it, all involved realised that she was probably responsible for the death of Jean's sister.

individual in order for the latter to receive medical attention. The term was introduced by Meadow (1977) to label this process as a form of child abuse, as in the vast majority of cases it is perpetrated by a mother on her own child. In this most frequent form, MSBP is very difficult to detect with evidence (Bass and Jones, 2006). These perpetrators often also suffer from Münchausen's syndrome (Feldman and Eisendrath, 1996). Perpetrators of MSBP are very serious in their approach to deception, will lie determinedly in feigning symptoms and convincingly to cover up evidence, and will deny any such activity when confronted over faking symptoms in the dependent individual (Holmes, Bee and Brannigan, 2001). There are features of MSBP that may combine to provide warning signs to a clinician as follows (see Feldman and Eisendrath, 1996).

- Symptoms in the child are unusual, deviate from known illness and are not explained by repeated investigations; nor do they respond to treatments.

- Medical records are missing and tests do not match the child's condition.

- Symptoms disappear when the mother has no access to the child.

- The mother thrives in hospital, befriends staff, welcomes invasive procedures, shows lack of concern about unknown illness and becomes anxious if the child improves.

- In the mother's background there is a medical connection.

- The mother tends to be the only witness to events such as seizures or breathing difficulties.

Focus

Degrees of harm in MSBP

It has been suggested that there are **degrees of harm** in Münchausen syndrome by proxy (MSBP) (Bee, 2000), and this could indicate degrees of the disorder. However, this is controversial and it has been suggested that perpetrators may move between respective activity levels and not remain at the same level, making it a less useful concept and separating this form of abuse from the normal diagnostic model, which is not yet on a continuum (Eminson and Jureidini, 2003). This said, it is useful to consider the levels of activity from sub-MSBP through to the more destructive activity as follows.

- **Hypochondriasis by proxy.** This is overconcern for the child's health with the possibility of exaggerating symptoms to gain reassurance. This lacks the indifference to the true health of the child and deliberate feigning of symptoms of MSBP.

- **Münchausen's by proxy-like behaviour.** This term has been suggested for where MSBP is suspected from the behaviour of the carer but the case has not been through the MSBP confirmation process (Lasher, 2003).

- **False reporting.** Here false symptoms are knowingly reported verbally to a physician, such as reporting vomiting, apnoea and bleeding.

- **Faking symptom evidence.** This involved producing fabricated medical evidence of illness, such as contaminating samples of bodily fluids with blood, procuring infected samples from others or interfering with medical testing equipment in a hospital. For example, one mother cut her own legs for blood, which was placed in the mouth and nappy of her child.

- **Inducing symptoms in the child.** Here direct harm or disfigurement is caused to the child, including causing rashes, infecting wounds, preventing breathing by partial suffocation or introducing toxins into the child. In one anonymous case, this activity resulted in the child having an unremitting fever for 6 years and being seen at 126 different clinics.

- **Instigating and encouraging repeated invasive procedures.** This brings about iatrogenic harm to the child, which may result in permanent harm such as gridiron abdomen (physical damage to the abdomen wall from repeated abdominal surgery).

- **Causing the child's death.** This may result from inducing symptoms, interfering with medical procedures or directly and intentionally killing the child.

In the past there has been very limited awareness of MSBP, even amongst professionals, with the consequence that some cases were not being detected (Edwards, 2003; Lasher, 2003). However, the syndrome has become more familiar to the public in the twenty-first century, mostly due to media interest, but with a disproportionate focus on the perpetrator, which has somewhat distracted from the activity being child abuse (Bass and Jones, 2006). Clearly not all abuse is MSBP but all cases of MSBP are cases of abuse (Bools, Neale and Meadow, 1994).

Professionals as well as the general public have a great deal of difficulty in accepting that a mother could harm her own child. This lack of acceptance of MSBP can be to the extent that some overzealous individuals have denied the existence of MSBP – an example being Allison and Roberts (1998). This prejudice towards the denial of long-standing abuse in favour of matriarchal integrity has inspired attacks on the evidence of professionals in this specialist area. In some cases, such attacks have involved illegal intrusions; and in others they have resulted in professionally damaging inquiries into the behaviour of the

professional concerned (Rosenberg, 2003). Such outcomes have further inhibited the already difficult investigation and prosecution of new cases (Lasher, 2003; Holmes, Bee and Brannigan, 2001; Meadow, 1999).

In contrast with the lack of evidence for dissociative identity disorder in this chapter, the evidence for MSBP is objective, graphic and overwhelming (Sheridan, 2003). CCTV footage of mothers attempting to suffocate children with pillows, tampering with life-supporting equipment or introducing toxins into the child is not contestable evidence (Holmes, Bee and Brannigan, 2001) and is in addition to statistical evidence across many cases (Sheridan, 2003). However, there are errors in implicating mothers who are innocent, just as there are errors whereby abuse goes unchecked (Lasher, 2003), and independent of these, there is the inevitable 'dark figure' of cases that never reach professional attention (Rosenberg, 2003). The criteria for legally substantial evidence in these cases are necessarily exacting (see the section on forensic issues below; Lasher, 2003).

Although they may account for the vast majority of cases, not every MSBP case involves a mother perpetrating this abuse on their child. Münchausen's syndrome by adult proxy (MSBAP) refers specifically to cases where the individual in whom illness is feigned is an adult. This can take place in the family home with a dependent elderly relative or may be inflicted in a care-home or hospital setting by a carer or medical professional (Holmes, Bee and Brannigan, 2001). Such a case was that of **Colin Norris**, a registered nurse who killed four elderly patients in his care in 2002 by injecting them with high levels of **insulin** to induce illness and death. There were clear features of MSBAP in the killing of at least 215 elderly patients by general practitioner **Harold Shipman** in the years 1975–98 by injecting morphine. There are also cases of nurses inducing illness in children, such as that of **Beverly Allitt**, a state enrolled nurse, who killed four children in 1991 by inducing cardiac arrest by the use of insulin or potassium (HMSO, 1994). News media tend to publicise incidences of nurses inducing illness in patients, as this is such a paradoxical reversal of their role as carer. As long ago as 1858, **Florence Nightingale** considered it strange but necessary to state that the first principle of hospitals should be to do no harm to patients (Peate, 2008).

In the case of MSBP health amongst professionals, the issue of reporting suspicious behaviour comes into sharp focus. Colleagues are understandably reluctant to make such disclosures for fear of legal reprisals or simply being ostracised and alienated by other professionals if they are mistaken or the case fails to be proven (Rosenberg, 2003; Meadow, 1999). In the UK, the **Public Interest Disclosure Act 1998** can be used to protect those reporting malpractice (Peate, 2008); however, many professionals will often assume that such isolated incidents are misperceptions and avoid potentially lengthy procedures in which their integrity may be tested in court, particularly if precise procedures for gathering evidence are not followed (Rosenberg, 2003; Bass and Jones, 2006).

In the case of MSBP in the mother–child relationship, disclosure is also difficult and many feel that their suspicions place them against the tide of colleague opinion in addition to having to deal with the mother (Bee, 2000). Reporting MSBP abuse will also invoke a series of costly and complex procedures, including: removing the child from the mother and family; appointing a 'gatekeeper' for the child's care; checking the welfare of siblings; and long-term therapy for both child and mother (Holmes, Bee and Brannigan, 2001). Professional involvement may mean facing up to having caused iatrogenic damage to a child as well as being involuntarily involved in MSBP. Other consequences for professionals involved with MSBP cases have been found, such as: avoidance of the perpetrator; suspicion of future patients; sense of being 'used' in abuse; fear of other staff and a need for their support; loss of

confidence; fear of legal or professional repercussions; and feeling that their 'professional childhood' had ended (Bee, 2000). Thus the impact of dealing with the aftermath of MSBP and treating those involved in the syndrome is more complex than more conventional disorders and some recommend that is where research should be focused (Eminson and Jureidini, 2003).

Research has also identified a form of MSBP inflicted on animals in the care of the perpetrator, or **Münchausen's syndrome by pet proxy** (MSPP), which is largely under-reported (Brannigan, 2001; Holmes, Bee and Brannigan, 2001; Feldman, 1997). In this form, pet animals are repeatedly brought to veterinary surgeries with falsely reported or physically fabricated symptoms (Brannigan, 2001). There are clear links between animal abuse and the abuse of young children in the form of MSPP/MSBP, as both are dependent on their carers and are unable to speak for themselves (Munro, 1996). For many individuals, pets may substitute as child surrogates in an interaction that is normally supportive. However, the abuse of animals and abuse of children has also been linked within families (Boat, 1995). It has further been considered that MSPP can be an early or concurrent indicator of child MSBP (Munro, 1998).

One case illustrates the usefulness of MSPP as a marker in this context. The first child of a family presented with severe vomiting and tragically a second child from the same family died on admission. When a third child was admitted with vomiting, there was immediate suspicion that the water supply might be contaminated, even though adults in the household seemed unaffected. However, a remark by a neighbour about a litter of puppies dying suspiciously on an earlier occasion initiated a different set of enquiries. The discovery of arsenic poisoning by the mother of the children was too late to save the third child, who subsequently died. The usefulness of raising awareness amongst veterinarians of MSPP is well established (Brannigan, 2001); however, legal definitions of animal cruelty are not as rigorous as those for children (Munro, 1998), limiting discovery. Thus, consequent warning signs for welfare agencies of animal abuse indicating children at risk are all too rare.

In **factitious disorder by proxy** there are the same patterns of behaviour as MSBP, but these are usually at the lesser end of the scale of harm. As with factitious disorder or Münchausen's syndrome, the true prevalence of these proxy variations is very difficult to ascertain due to the elusive and defensive nature of perpetrators. However, increased awareness of the disorder may be improving this limited information and in addition has perhaps changed the profile of the average perpetrator (Sheridan, 2003). Earlier estimates found the proportion of mothers to be

98 per cent of all perpetrators (Rosenberg, 1987), but later estimates find a broader profile with only 76.5 per cent being the biological mother, 6.7 per cent fathers and others including stepmothers (Sheridan, 2003).

Aetiology and treatment of factitious disorders

There are factors which tend to recur in factitious disorders. During their childhood or early adulthood, there is an increasing need for both the comfort and security of medical environments and attention. Having medical knowledge and being in medical environments also gives these individuals a sense of worth and importance, especially when successfully competing with other health professionals. In the case of MSBP, the perpetrator seeks attention and a relationship with medical professionals, and will be highly competitive regarding knowledge of the types of disorder that they feign in their victims. Factitious disorder or Münchausen's syndrome can be viewed as self-harm, and in the case of it being by proxy there is a high association with self-harm behaviours and there is a very high comorbidity with borderline as well as other personality disorders (Bass and Jones, 2006). Many factitious individuals and half of MSBP perpetrators report abuse in their childhoods, although their accounts are not reliable.

MSBP mothers do not attach to their child and may even express hatred for the victim of this abuse (Holmes, Bee and Brannigan, 2001). The fabricated illness of the child may be part of a pathological homeostasis whereby a poor marital relationship is maintained or the mother gains attention from her own parents and competes with siblings by this means (Feldman and Eisendrath, 1996). One motivation that is apparent in overt behaviour of MSBP mothers is to enact the role of 'a dedicated attentive mother', even though they treat the child as an object (Meadow, 1999). As well as personality disorders, most MSBP perpetrators suffer from somatoform disorders (Bass and Jones, 2006; Sheridan, 2003). Pharmacological treatment of comorbid disorders such as depression with SSRIs can greatly assist progress with other interventions for perpetrators (Feldman and Eisendrath, 1996).

Management involves separation of mother and child, which in high-risk cases may be long term. Both mother and child will require psychotherapy. In the case of the child this may need to be followed up for some time, especially where a pathological alliance has been formed, in which the child has grown to accept the deceit, sick role and feigned attentiveness (Feldman and Eisendrath, 1996). For the child there are parallels with the interventions in cases of child sexual abuse and there needs to be awareness that generational cycles of abuse are to be avoided. CBT may initially aim to erode denial in the perpetrator and promote insight into the behaviour. The reduction of lying and any self-harm behaviour as well as adjustment to a stable and mutually supportive lifestyle can provide a better prognosis. Unfortunately, even if the perpetrator is detected and detained and does engage with therapy, these aims are rarely achieved (Bass and Jones, 2006).

Clinical issues and forensic implications in factitious disorders

In the case of factitious disorders, clinical and forensic issues (as well as treatment issues) are inextricably entwined, particularly in the case of MSBP. For example, MSBP is regarded by many not as a diagnosis but as a criminal act of abuse (Meadow, 1997). Although the clinical and forensic aspects of factitious or Münchausen's disorder involve the detailed detection of deception and self-harm as well as large-scale fraudulent abuse of health resources, it is MSBP that requires disproportionate levels of clinical and forensic professional attention (Feldman and Eisendrath, 1996).

The clinical detection of MSBP will involve both clinical and forensic assessment approaches and can be a very pedantic process, which may include the following (see Rosenberg, 2003; Bass and Jones, 2006).

- A consenting clinical interview with the parents, including the abusive mother, which may be observed and recorded. Other relatives such as grandparents should be interviewed for corroboration, as well as service providers such as GP or social worker.

- Carefully obtained exhaustive medical and welfare records of the child and any siblings. These may involve many health providers in different districts, as might those of the carer, and searches may be confounded by confidentiality restrictions.

- Medical records and forensic history of the mother/carer.

- Searches of contexts for poisons, syringes, etc.

- Monitoring and restricting perpetrator access, with careful control over food and medication for an observation period.

Focus

The case against the expert

Specialist paediatricians and other professionals have been the targets for legal and other campaigns aiming to exonerate mothers accused in Münchausen's syndrome by proxy (MSBP) cases. This has had serious consequences, in that it both inhibits the already difficult investigation or prosecution of new cases and can potentially place children at mortal risk (Holmes, Bee and Brannigan, 2001; Meadow, 1999). This has been evident in the cases of **Roy Meadow** and **David Southall**, where previously eminent experts with long histories of working against the abuse of children have had their clearly identifiable misjudgements or overzealous conclusions used to instigate personal and professional attacks. These complaints have possibly also had implications for actual cases of suspected abuse involving multiple child deaths.

In this fractious area, attacks on the messenger because the (overstated) message is unpopular can be very dangerous and misleading to a public and judicial system with limited information. However, some professionals do become overconfident and errors of judgement can occur, threatening the liberty of potentially innocent parents. Professionals dealing with children have generally more to lose in such legal battles than perpetrators of abuse. Thus, such a legal backlash, whether justified or not, is likely to inhibit others from coming forward to report future abuse with the potential for suffering that entails. It is also incontestable, from innumerable studies and forensic observations, that the clinical and forensic reality of MSBP (also termed **fabricated or induced illness**) has been firmly established in the twenty-first century (see Lasher, 2003; Bass and Jones, 2006).

■ Current forensic evidence, such as statements or documented evidence, specimens, medical data and CCTV footage. All should be carefully stored and preserved against contamination, loss or mislabelling.

■ All findings should be carefully documented to form a cumulative body of evidence.

These inquiries may take a great deal of time to complete, and in the meantime the perpetrator may still have access to the victim or other dependants. In cases of MSBP, there is also a high probability of the perpetrator absconding with the child before legal restraint can be applied (Bass and Jones, 2006; Holmes, Bee and Brannigan, 2001). Set against these time-urgencies are the obvious caveats concerning the validity of evidence obtained, in order to avoid the very damaging outcomes of a false accusation.

There are further caveats and ethical issues regarding the detection of MSBP. The identification of the disorder and matching findings to the definitional or diagnostic criteria can be quite distinct from the criteria for legal intervention or prosecution (Rosenberg, 2003; Holmes, Bee and Brannigan, 2001; Meadow, 1999). It is inevitable, given the far-reaching consequences of legal action, that the criteria for legally significant evidence in these cases are unavoidably rigorous (Lasher, 2003). This can result in a tragic failure to provide protection for a child being abused as well as providing the suspected perpetrator with sufficient warning to flee the situation. In addition, some

of the markers and definitional features of MSBP, such as a medical background or attention seeking, are of little diagnostic value in identifying MSBP situations or distinguishing perpetrators from overly-concerned carers (Rosenberg, 2003). Some rare disorders can, of course, raise understandable but nevertheless erroneous suspicions of MSBP. Such disorders can make the already very difficult **diagnosis by exclusion** of MSBP (assuming MSBP in the absence of any other medical explanation) a high-risk strategy in approaching this kind of abuse (see Rosenberg, 2003).

Some of the caveats for detection also overlap with the issues surrounding the management or treatment of the perpetrator and victim. Concerns for the health of siblings are well founded, as reviews of cases have revealed an average of 61.3 per cent of victim siblings with similar symptoms and a sobering 25 per cent having deceased (Sheridan, 2003). Thus leaving a suspected perpetrator with access to other dependants is a serious concern and further complications, such as the perpetrator having another child, need to be considered.

Critical evaluation

For the current author, the disorders in this chapter may be more closely related than has historically been recognised. Those labelled as factitious or neurological disorders as well as malingering may differ from those labelled somatoform or dissociative only in terms of their greater self-awareness and lack of undiagnosed neurological or medical complaints. Thus, to divide somatoform and dissociative clients conceptually into those with as yet undiagnosed neuropathology and those who are little more than self-convinced factitious individuals may be a controversial but revitalising move for clinical psychology and psychiatry to rid itself of any confusion from its more naive past. The arguments over the validity of somatoform and dissociative disorders have been continuous since their inclusion in classificatory systems (Janca, 2005; Spanos, 1996).

There are indicators supporting such a re-examination of these existing diagnostic boundaries, such as the finding that 70 per cent of those with MSBP meet the diagnostic criteria for somatoform disorder (Sheridan, 2003). Bradfield (2006) has reviewed the distinction made in allocating those complaints currently diagnosed as somatoform disorders as mental rather than physical disorders, and found that there were very limited and diminishing grounds for this assumption. Further evidence would be needed from disciplines other than psychiatry for the status of these disorders to be maintained in *DSM-V* (Bradfield, 2006). This need for further evidence in order to make empirical points regarding these disorders and their status is to a great extent a reflection of the lack of such research and empirical literature in this area to date. As a consequence, the reader may become aware that sources of literature in this chapter that deal with these disorders in a conventional manner are comparatively scarce, and thus outlines for the disorders are rather conservatively drawn from *DSM-IV-TR*.

The growing wealth of literature critical of many aspects of somatoform and dissociative disorders (e.g. Piper and Mersky, 2004; Bradfield, 2006; Janca, 2005) and the diminishing number of professionals assessing and treating these classifications may be indicators of the further decline in accepting what are essentially purely psychoanalytic assertions of psychological phenomena without a neurological basis (see Chapter 3). Perhaps *DSM-V* may, as has been suggested, be a turning point in twenty-first-century psychiatry and clinical psychology in no longer maintaining what is increasingly perceived as a scientific Achilles heel (Spanos, 1996; Mayou et al., 2005). Although this may be a great loss to fiction writers and movie makers (Butler and Palesh, 2003), it could benefit those professionals coping with increasing levels of mental suffering in the real world.

Self-test questions

- Discuss the distinction between somatisation disorder and factitious disorder.
- What is the difference between factitious disorder and Münchausen's syndrome?
- Discuss whether MSBP is a disorder or child abuse.
- What are the motivations behind MSBP?
- What are the issues behind the critical view of the status of dissociative and somatoform disorders?

Chapter summary

Somatoform and **dissociative disorders** are controversial diagnoses belonging to the historical psychoanalytic paradigm, and have been challenged regarding their conceptual and practical validity. **Somatoform disorders** are characterised by physical complaints in the absence of medical conditions and comprise: **somatisation disorder; pain disorder; conversion disorder; body dysmorphic disorder;** and **hypochondriasis**. They are of psychological origin and seem to respond to cognitive behavioural therapies. These disorders are a burden on health resources that have little effect on their symptoms, which appear to be psychosomatic. The **dissociative disorders** are: **dissociative amnesia; dissociative fugue; depersonalisation disorder;** and **dissociative identity disorder**. These involve the dissociation of psychological functions, usually assumed to be a reaction to trauma. Access to the original experience is difficult, but it is seen as a treatment aim if the **psychodynamic paradigm** is adopted. There is controversy over the accuracy of events recalled by these suggestible patients. **False memory syndrome** can have far-reaching effects on individuals and communities involved.

Chapter summary continued

Factitious disorder is where symptoms of medical disorders are intentionally fabricated. **Münchausen's syndrome** is a more serious and intense form of this disorder. **Factitious disorder by proxy** and **Münchausen's syndrome by proxy** are where symptoms are faked in another, usually a child. This disorder almost always involves **forensic issues** and can lead to multiple child deaths.

Suggested essay questions

- Critically evaluate the treatment approaches to somatoform disorders.
- Critically discuss the clinical validity of dissociative identity disorder.
- Discuss the difficulties in detecting and managing Münchausen's syndrome by proxy.

Further reading

Overview texts

Bass, C., and Benjamin, S. (1993) The management of chronic somatization. *British Journal of Psychiatry*, **162**, 472–80.

Mayou, R., Bass, C., and Sharpe, M. (1995) *Treatment of functional somatic symptoms.* Oxford: Oxford University Press.

Meadow, R. (1997) *ABC of child abuse* (3rd edn). London: BMJ Publishing Group.

Michelson, L., and Ray, W. J. (1996) *Handbook of dissociation: Theoretical, empirical, and clinical perspectives* (2nd edn). New York: Plenum.

Ross, C. A., and Coons, P. M. (1996) *Dissociative identity disorder: Diagnosis, clinical features and treatment of multiple personality.* New York: Wiley.

Sheridan, M. S. (2003) The deceit continues: An updated literature review of Münchausen's syndrome by proxy. *Child Abuse and Neglect*, **27**, 431–51.

Specific and more critical texts

Bass, C., and Jones, D. P. H. (2006) Fabricated or induced illness. *Psychiatry*, **5**(2), 60–5.

Bools, C., Neale, B., and Meadow, R. (1994) Münchausen syndrome by proxy: A study of psychopathology. *Child Abuse and Neglect*, **18**, 773–88.

Bradfield, J. W. B. (2006) A pathologist's perspective of the somatoform disorders. *Journal of Psychosomatic Research*, **60**, 327–30.

Davies, G. M., and Dalgleish, T. (2001) *Recovered memories: Seeking the middle ground.* Chichester: Wiley.

Piper, A., and Merskey, D. M. (2004) The persistence of folly: A critical examination of dissociative identity disorder. Part 1: The excesses of an improbable concept. *Canadian Journal of Psychiatry*, **49**(9), 592–600.

Spanos, N. (1996) *Multiple identities and false memories: A sociocognitive perspective.* Washington: American Psychological Association.

Starcevic, V., and Lipsitt, D. R. (2001) *Hypochondriasis: Modern perspectives on an ancient malady.* Oxford: Oxford University Press.

Zola, S. M. (1998) Memory, amnesia and the issue of recovered memory: Neurobiological aspects. *Clinical Psychology Review*, **18**, 915–32.

Visit **www.pearsoned.co.uk/davidholmes** for a range of resources to support study. Test yourself with multiple choice questions and access a bank of over 100 videos that will bring the topics to life. Video coverage for this chapter includes an interviews with people suffering from hypochondriasis and chronic fatigue syndrome as well as classic footage of the original 'Eve' in her three states (Eve White, Eve Black and Jane).

DISORDERS OF ADULTHOOD AND LATER LIFE

Part 4 of this textbook will examine those disorders that tend to have their onset in later life, are primarily associated with adults or tend to persist from adulthood into old age. This has to be a generalisation as there are always exceptions, such as stress-reactive disorders like asthma starting in early life, and mood disorders, which can be evident in childhood.

In Chapter 16 the area of health psychology will be considered, in examining ways in which psychology can intervene at many levels from preventative through interventive to palliative stages, in addressing the health of individuals and communities. This will involve stress-related psychophysiological disorders as well as issues of the cost of stress in industry and the poignant health issues of those in palliative care inside and outside prison. In Chapter 17 the major area of mood disorders will cover both unipolar and bipolar subtypes of the classification, as well as the difficulties of dealing with the disorder in forensic contexts and the associated factor of suicide. Intriguing aspects of mood are also addressed to answer questions such as why mood disorder is affected by geographic longitude and is highly prevalent amongst poets and other creative individuals.

The area of schizophrenia is critically explored in Chapter 18, including attempts usefully to subgroup the syndrome, including positive and negative symptom division alongside more recent views based on neural functioning. Partly based on current aetiological views, there follows a critical review of contemporary approaches to managing the disorder during its stages and varying outcomes. Under the heading of old age psychology there will be a contemporary appraisal of the clinical problems of old age in Chapter 19 with a focus on the dementias. Broader issues in ageing will also be addressed, such as the evolutionary and biological reasons for ageing and the logical and psychological caveats facing attempts to intervene in this very process. More immediate issues of care for an ageing population will also be examined as well as implications for future psychological services. A contemporary perspective on future considerations in these fields of study forms the logical last section of the text, allowing a glimpse into the clinical and forensic issues anticipated as the twenty-first century unfolds.

Chapters in this section

16 Psychophysiological disorders and health psychology

Hear how a study of worms has uncovered genetic reasons for eating when stressed. This is one of several videos that explore issues and disorders relevant to this chapter at www.pearsoned.co.uk/davidholmes

17 Mood disorders

Follow a 'day in the life' of Feliziano who suffers from bipolar disorder. This is one of several videos that explore issues and disorders relevant to this chapter at www.pearsoned.co.uk/davidholmes

18 Schizophrenia

Hear about gene studies and schizophrenia. This is one of several videos that explore issues and disorders relevant to this chapter at www.pearsoned.co.uk/davidholmes

19 Neurological and age-related disorders

Watch this interview with Alvin Paige, an artist who suffers with Alzheimers'. This is one of several videos that explore issues and disorders relevant to this chapter at www.pearsoned.co.uk/davidholmes

CHAPTER 16 Psychophysiological disorders and health psychology

- Overview
- Case study
- Stress
- Stress and anxiety-influenced

- medical conditions
- Health psychology
- Positive psychology
- Community health psychology

- Forensic health psychology
- Clinical issues
- Chapter summary

Hear how a study of worms has uncovered genetic reasons for eating when stressed. This is one of several videos that explore issues and disorders relevant to this chapter at **www.pearsoned.co.uk/davidholmes**.

Health psychology in the news

In 2009 the Scottish government released **Abdel Baset al-Megrahi** early to travel to his home in Libya. He was jailed in 2001 for the 1988 Lockerbie airline bombing, which claimed 270 lives, but freed on compassionate grounds with terminal prostate cancer. This controversial and high-profile case, and that of the gravely ill UK 'great train robber' **Ronnie Biggs**, tend to overshadow the **forensic health** dilemma of many elderly prisoners around the world who enter palliative care in penal institutions.

The broad remit of this chapter will explore this issue in **forensic health psychology** as well as the relatively new area of **positive psychology**, which looks at what factors enable happiness and good health. In the same month as the release of Abdel Baset al-Megrahi, the British government announced that it would back a scheme to promote large-scale dancing in public places. This followed the Minister for the Olympics, Tessa Jowell's visit to Bradford to witness 2012 people enjoying dancing in Centenary Square. Such a move towards increasing good health and temperament in the population is very much in line with the aims of positive psychology.

The positive aspects of health psychology, illustrated by 2012 people enjoying dancing in Centenary Square, Bedford, UK, as part of a health initiative inspired by the 2012 London Olympics.
Source: Roger Moody.

Much of the research in the area of **health psychology** emanated from the recognition of the physical impact of **psychological stress** on individuals, especially in an occupational context (Kompier and Cooper, 1999). In the previous chapter, the effect of psychological conditions leading to the presentation of medical or psychiatric symptoms, but in the absence of an underlying medical condition, was explored. In this chapter, the influences of psychological states on existing medical conditions and their aetiology are examined: for example, **coronary heart disease**. The susceptibility of these medical problems to psychological influence leads such conditions to be referred to as **psychophysiological disorders**, amongst which are some types of **headache**, **asthma** and **hypertension**.

There are limits to how much psychological intervention can achieve in the context of some disorders, in that the progress of some illnesses is irrespective of psychological states. However, a self-reported sense of well-being and health awareness may be influenced, even though the medical condition may not (Sarafino, 2008). **Health psychology** is a relatively new field but one that is expanding in terms of both its clinical applications and its theoretical diversity. Health psychology has also made progress in the areas of improved mental and physical health in the non-disordered population. This includes the specific research areas of **positive psychology** and the **psychology of well-being**, but also extends to areas of ill-health prevention.

A further extension of health awareness is that of **community health psychology**, where wider populations are considered in terms of promoting healthier lifestyles and ill-health monitoring. Prevention and health promotion have been increasingly informed by the **psychology of advertising and marketing** and the techniques established in social and cognitive psychology of attitude change and media management. Outcomes of such raised awareness can range from the initiation of self-checking behaviours for breast or testicular cancers through to lowered interpersonal stress in the workplace.

Community health psychology also has immediate relevance to **clinical psychology** in terms of public acceptability of such schemes as **care in the community** for both psychiatric patients and offender populations. **Forensic health psychology** has developed alongside health psychology, as the consequences of stress and poor health come to be realised. In forensic terms, these can be a product of placing tradition and assumed short-term profitability above long-term health, with the resultant legal consequences (Kompier and Cooper, 1999). Forensic health psychology also contributes to the identification of **malingering**, as distinct from the disorders in Chapter 15, and to the realities of serious or terminal illness in those serving penal terms.

Case study

There is only today

Brian declared to his friends during his school years that he really wanted to get somewhere in life, but just where was never very clear. However, his determination was so strong that it unnerved his peers, although it pleased his parents. He worked hard at his studies but grew frustrated with poor marks and eventually left school early after gaining the lowest mathematics mark in his class. Despite his parents' intense disapproval and bleak predictions, Brian had his own home and small internet sales business by the time he was 25, and at 35 he earned more than any two of his old school friends put together.

Behind all the industriousness and confidence, Brian constantly fought with fears of failure and the poverty he had known in his childhood. However, his grip on success began to slip when his wife declared that she had found someone else who really cared rather than simply provided for her. Brian tried to deny what was happening and worked till late each night. At the end of a late evening business meal, Brian had a stand-up argument with a colleague in which he became very agitated. His boss intervened but found that Brian was holding his chest and wheezing. This was not the asthma that Brian had suffered for much of his life but a heart attack, and an ambulance was called.

On his second visit to his GP, Brian felt that he was facing a life of purgatory, cutting down on food, drink and work. He had always been too agitated to relax and could not enjoy life in any way other than pushing himself faster and harder. His GP felt that stress management intervention was now essential in addition to Brian's medication. Gina, the clinical psychologist, was confident that a package of measures, which included biofeedback for Brian's hypertension and deep muscle relaxation training, would bring him back from the brink of being at mortal risk. Brian was enthusiastic about the interventions and even signed up for a psychology evening course, where he met Andrea who was a calming influence on him. Brian's progress was good: his blood pressure lowered and he began to see life as more than a chance to achieve.

Physiological symptoms of stress need to be taken seriously by all concerned, particularly the client themselves. Although interventions can be successful, there is often a much better prognosis if intervention takes place sooner by monitoring for early warning signs and avoiding multiple concurrent risk factors.

Stress

The work of a **health psychologist** deals partly with psychological approaches to preventing and ameliorating medical conditions such as **coronary heart disease**. Psychological factors have been examined and utilised in managing a range of disorders from **headaches** to **AIDS** (Vitetta et al., 2005). Much of the research in these approaches has focused on the concept of **stress**, which is a term that has been applied somewhat loosely in three ways, leading to as many differing approaches.

- One approach considers the stressors in the environment, such as a threatening work colleague or an ill family member.

- Another conceptualises stress as a response to the environment, in the manner of someone feeling they are stressed by their marital problems (Sarafino, 2008). These physiological and psychological effects of stress on the individual are referred to as strain, although the term 'stress' is often used universally to refer to both source and response.

- The third approach, favoured by Lazarus (1999), focuses on stress as an interaction between environmental stressors and the reactions of the individual. Within this model, the level of stress depends on the subjective cognitive appraisal of the stress source as to whether it poses a threat or perhaps cannot be coped with.

Research

Measuring stressful events

Research into stress and health requires measures of both. The **general health questionnaire** (GHQ) provides both mental and physical measures, but stress is more difficult to quantify. Stressful events vary in their impact on the individual and not all stressful events are negative ones, such as death of a family member. Positive events can also be stressful, such as getting married or buying a home; even going on holiday can produce stress as people worry about packing, travel arrangements or the security of the property they leave behind. The Social Readjustment Rating Scale (SRRS; Holmes and Rahe, 1967) is used to rate the relative impact of life events ranked below that of the most stressful event, which Holmes and Rahe (1967) found to be the death of a spouse. The SRRS scale in Table 16.1 displays the range of events identified by Holmes and Rahe from clinical experience in ranked order, along with their ratings. Note that some events were given the same rating values. The scale shows not only examples of the many positive events rated as stressful, but also the relative impact of interpersonal events as opposed to financial or health changes. Events tend to be more stressful if they have the characteristics of being negative, uncontrollable, ambiguous, unpredictable or demanding (DiMatteo and Martin, 2002).

It is curious that some joyous events, such as a wedding, are rated as more stressful than some unpleasant ones, such as the death of a friend.
Source: Pearson Online Database.

Table 16.1 The Social Readjustment Rating Scale

Life event	Value	Life event	Value
Death of spouse	100	Son or daughter leaving home	29
Divorce	73	Trouble with in-laws	29
Marital separation	65	Outstanding personal achievement	28
Jail term	63	Wife begins or stops work	26
Death of close family member	63	Begins or ends school	26
Personal injury	53	Change in living conditions	25
Marriage	50	Revision of personal habits	24
Fired from work	47	Trouble with boss	23
Marital reconciliation	45	Change in work hours or conditions	20
Retirement	45	Change in residence	20
Change in health of family member	44	Change in schools	20
Pregnancy	40	Change in recreation	19
Sex difficulties	39	Change in church activities	19
Gain of new family member	39	Change in social activities	18
Business readjustment	39	Mortgage of less than $10,000	17
Change in financial state	38	Change in sleeping habits	16
Death of a close friend	37	Change in number of family get-togethers	15
Change to different line of work	36	Change in sleeping habits	15
Change in number of arguments with spouse	35	Vacation	13
Mortgage over $10,000 (in 1967)	31	Christmas	12
Foreclosure of mortgage or loan	30	Minor violations of the law	11
Change in responsibilities at work	29		

Source: Holmes and Rahe (1967).

In the short term, some stress may be necessary for individuals to be sufficiently aroused to perform adequately. However, as the original Yerkes–Dodson law proposed, the relationship between performance and degree of arousal follows an inverted U-shaped curve, such that once the optimum arousal level is surpassed, any further increase marks a decrease in performance (Yerkes and Dodson, 1908). Thus even in the short term, high levels of stress will result in deficits. In the longer term, **chronic stress** has been consistently associated with decline in coping ability and health (Vitetta et al., 2005; Sarafino, 2008). Selye (1956; 1985) described the **stress response** and has put forward a general adaptation syndrome (GAS) to account for the progressive effects of chronic stress. This proposes three phases of the reaction to stress over time as follows.

- Phase one is the **alarm phase**, where stress initiates the **flight or fight** response, with arousal being maintained by the hypothalamus–pituitary–adrenal axis and the net result being **adrenaline**, **noradrenaline** and **cortisol** release (Vitetta et al., 2005). This is a level of arousal that cannot be maintained over time without a fatal outcome, and it usually results in remission periods, as described in the coverage of **flooding** in Chapter 12.

- Phase two is the **stage of resistance**, wherein the body attempts to adapt to the prolonged stress that is destructive but below the lethal threshold. Selye (1956) refers to diseases of adaptation, such as hypertension and ulcers, as developing at this point.

- Selye refers to phase three as the **stage of exhaustion**, in which body resources are depleted and immune responses are lowered. This leaves the body vulnerable to more serious organ damage and eventually death.

As stress is prolonged, the individual becomes overly sensitive to new stressors and may try to avoid these further sources of arousal. Cognitive factors can play a part in prolonging stress when thought patterns focus on the stressor, sustaining its effect on arousal even in its absence. Selye (1956) assumed all stressors to be equal in their effects, leading to the same sequence as above; or in his terms, they were non-specific. However, some stressors have greater emotional impact, leading to greater hormone release and subsequent damage than others, thus undermining Selye's non-specific assumption. Stress reactions and the emotional impact of stressors can also enhance memory and thus prolong its cognitive effect (see Sarafino, 2008).

Chronic stress has been associated with psychophysiological disorders as well as other conditions, and as stated above, it can lead to death. Disorders thought to be associated with prolonged stress include hypertension (high blood pressure) and coronary heart disease, ulcers, immunodeficiency, headaches and steroid diabetes. Stress also inhibits growth hormones and other growth, leading to psychogenic dwarfism and bone decalcification (Breedlove, Rosenzweig and Watson, 2007). Individuals enduring long-term stress will become apathetic and fatigued and lose body muscle, as well as suffering sexual and reproductive problems (Sapolsky, 1994). With the suppression of the immune system and endocrine effects, chronically stressed individuals will suffer higher levels of opportunist infections, and other conditions, including tumours, may be more common (Reiche, Morimoto and Nunes, 2005).

Stress and anxiety-influenced medical conditions

Amongst others, Soreff (2007) has heralded the much wider acknowledgement of psychosocial factors impacting on biological disorder. He terms this the biopsychosocial information model and gives it the status of a 'new disease paradigm', which recognises the importance of a greater information input to dealing with disease. The rising importance of health psychology is a direct result of the increased knowledge of the *extent* of psychological influence over what were originally seen as purely medical conditions.

In *DSM-IV-TR* these medical conditions do not have their own classificatory section but come under the heading of **psychological factors affecting medical condition** in the chapter 'Other conditions that may be a focus of clinical attention'. Within this section *DSM-IV-TR* has a number of psychological variables, including 'stress-related physiological responding', listed as affecting a general medical condition (to be specified).

Examples of the more prominent stress and anxiety influenced medical conditions or **psychophysiological disorders** are described below.

Hypertension and coronary heart disease

Essential hypertension is high blood pressure resulting from psychological causes. The condition is one precursor to a heart attack and is exacerbated by **self-stressing** behaviour patterns (Friedman and Rosenman, 1974). Forms of psychological stress force blood in a central direction (to the heart and lungs), constricting peripheral capillaries (blood vessels of the fingers and toes) and increasing blood pressure. This can sometimes be reversed by giving a client **biofeedback** of their blood pressure and allowing them to reduce this by adjusting their behaviour and thinking patterns. Continuous measures of hypertension can be inferred from peripheral temperature in the fingers, and fed back to the client to give an indication of how successful their alterations in behaviour are in reducing dangerous cardiovascular loading.

In early studies, the more chronic condition of **coronary heart disease** has similarly been related to stress as well as physiological factors, the latter of which are still being added to, such as the example of bacteria from poor-condition gums entering the bloodstream.

In terms of the physiological cortisol stress response, cognitive anticipation of stress has been found to be a greater predictor than personality factors or even post-hoc judgements of stress magnitude (Gaab et al., 2005). Reviews of the effects of hostility alone on coronary heart disease have been mixed in their support of this as a factor and its use as a target for intervention (Bunker et al., 2003). Some studies have suggested that the single component approach to identifying psychological personality and stress

factors may be being superseded by more global factor approaches (Trigo, Silva and Rocha, 2005).

Other behavioural problems have been identified as contributing to this area of stress and health, such as the possible syndrome of workaholism (Spence and Robbins, 1992; see coronary heart disease section), or the tendency to be highly involved with work but have low work enjoyment (Aziz and Zickar, 2006). Workaholism may be considered as a more specifically occupational source of ill health, but may be conceptually related to the driven aspects of the type A personality; see Focus box below. The inconsistent findings in terms of type A personality and coronary heart disease have not diminished the search for individual differences in personality that may influence cardiac problems (Pendersen and Denollet, 2003). A personality type in which clients display increased negative emotions in social interactions has been termed the type D personality or distressed personality, and this has been related to coronary heart disease. The type D personality suffers physiological hyperreactivity and activation of inflammatory-promoting **cytokines**, both of which may provide links to the associated cardiac problems (Pendersen and Denollet, 2003).

Focus

Type A or coronary-prone behaviour

Prominent amongst studies of stress and coronary heart disease is that of Friedman and Rosenman (1974). In this, stress resulting from time-pressured behaviour was found greatly to increase the chances of coronary heart disease and potentially fatal heart attacks. They identified what they believed to be a coronary-prone type A personality, in which impatient behaviour was chronic. The type A personality was characterised by competitive, time-urgent and hostile behaviours, as opposed to type B personality characteristics, which include a more relaxed, non-competitive and less aggressive approach to relations with others and the workplace.

Many studies since that of Friedman and Rosenman have linked the type A behaviour pattern to coronary heart disease and other health risk factors (e.g. Ewart et al., 2002). These coronary-prone behaviours can also lead to friction both at home and in the workplace, in the form of unnecessary impatience and competitiveness. Thus levels of social support are often reduced by time-urgent behaviour and this may exacerbate the effects of stress on coronary health (Tennant, 1999).

Individuals with more extreme type A personalities have provided clinical targets for interventions based on reducing these traits and the associated behaviours. Many clients have been trained to reduce this tendency towards stress-inducing behaviour and the risk of a heart attack in the years since Friedman and Rosenman's (1974) study. In addition to modifying type A behaviour as a risk factor for coronary heart disease as part of a package of measures, the behaviour modifications have been found to have other health benefits, including improving the quality of life of the clients (Thoresen and Powell, 1992). Over the years these interventions have in themselves provided clinically derived information on the type A syndrome and its interaction with cardiac problems (Thoresen and Powell, 1992).

Since its inception, this bipolar view of type A and B has been considered simplistic and some acknowledgement of individuals having both A and B personality characteristics has been documented (Steptoe, 1993). Some later reviews of studies have concluded that the type A behaviour pattern has no empirical effect on coronary heart disease (Kuper, Marmot and Hemingway, 2002).

Asthma

Asthma is the constriction of the airways in the lungs preventing oxygen entering and carbon dioxide being expelled, accompanied by wheezing, breathlessness and even death. Mucous secretion and fluid build-up in tissue causes further respiratory problems as a result of immune reactions during asthma attacks. Three major factors are differentially involved in asthma attacks: allergies, respiratory infections and psychological or physical (e.g. exercise) stress (Sarafino, 2008). Chronic airway inflammation in asthma has a basis in accumulating inflammatory cells such as mast cells or eosinophils, which are activated in the bronchial wall and airway lumen. **Th2 cytokines** regulate this inflammatory response, and differences in this response can result from environmental stress, although the precise biochemical mechanisms involved in translating this stress are not yet clear (Okuyama et al., 2007). Some have argued that focus on the Th2 cytokines may limit understanding, and that consideration of a broader range of mechanisms, such as **glucocorticoid resistance**, that lead to asthma-type reactivity may give a better explanation of what underlies this complex reaction (Wright, Cohen and Cohen, 2005).

Atopy syndrome underpins asthma and other disorders such as **eczema**, in that there is an **allergic hypersensitivity** in parts of the body not in direct contact with an **allergen**. The biological hypersensitivity in atopy is susceptible to psychological stress via the mechanism of neuroimmunoregulation (Wright, Cohen and Cohen, 2005). This interrelationship between stress, neuroimmunoregulation and the hypersensitivity reaction can become compounded during the process of an asthma attack. During an attack, symptoms of breathlessness can lead to apprehension and fear that the attack will escalate, which becomes a self-fulfilling prophesy as the apprehension and panic exacerbate the attack. Asthma can also be precipitated by psychological tension or excitement. Addressing psychological aspects such as stress and apprehension before an attack occurs can be a useful means of preventative intervention, reducing the risk of an attack. Around a third of cases of asthma are more susceptible to psychological stress than others (Okuyama et al., 2007). In this context, psychological stress has been conceptualised as a social pollutant overlapping with the effects of physical pollutants in disrupting biological mechanisms (Wright, Cohen and Cohen, 2005).

Asthma affects around 6 per cent of the population in the USA and is more common in children than adults (Sarafino, 2008). It is more common in children from lower socioeconomic groups and this may be due to chronic stress from a prolonged sense of threat influencing biochemical mechanisms (Chen et al., 2006). De Fries and Petermann (2008) found that the identification of sufferers with little knowledge of their condition for educational intervention can be useful for the management of the disorder. Many of the processes and mechanisms involved in asthma are under specific genetic control, although it may take some years into the future for all elements in the diathesis to be identified (Malerba and Pinatti, 2005).

Headaches

Many people suffer headaches from a variety of causes and few have never had one of any type. However, some individuals suffer chronically from recurrent headaches and some estimates place this as high as a quarter of the general population and around half of adolescents, when this psychophysiological disorder usually first appears (Costello, Costello and Holmes, 1995). Recurrent headaches are associated with psychological stress and tension that may have a direct physiological effect on muscular tension and cerebrovascular state. Although headaches may be considered a unitary disorder, subtypes have been defined as **migraine, cluster** and **tension headaches** (Costello, Costello and Holmes, 1995).

Migraine headache involves the dilation of blood vessels surrounding the brain, resulting in widespread stimulation of neurons equating to pain (Comer, 2007). This dilation is preceded by a reduced flow of blood producing the characteristic warning sign for migraine sufferers of a visual distortion or **aura**, often along with some nausea. This aura is described as shimmering lines in the peripheral visual field, and gives regular sufferers some time to prepare for an attack or take medication to minimise or even avoid symptoms. Some forms of migraine are more severe, sometimes referred to as **classic migraine**, which is disabling. This involves a pulse-driven throbbing pain accompanied by neurological symptoms such as numbness and co-ordination deficits as well as vomiting and nausea (Costello, Costello and Holmes, 1995). Severe migraine attacks are very disabling and rank alongside psychosis in this respect. However, because headaches are a common complaint in their various forms, there is a tendency to demean their seriousness and even their medical status (Stovner et al., 2006). This is little comfort to the sufferers of migraine headaches, who comprise 14 per cent of the population of Europe in a 1-year period (Stovner et al., 2006).

Tension headaches are sometimes referred to as **muscle tension headaches** and, as this name suggests, seem to result from the persistent contraction of head and neck muscles, which narrows blood vessels, along with dysfunction in the central nervous system (Comer, 2007). This produces a dull, consistent pain at the front of the head or the back of the head or neck, which is accompanied by a band of muscular pressure following the muscles around the head, occurring more than once a week in recurrent cases (Sarafino, 2008). This type of headache is common but rarely reported to medical practitioners, and is more susceptible to psychological factors as well as being less severe than migraine (Costello, Costello and Holmes, 1995). However, perhaps as a result of underreporting, there are few data on the prevalence of tension headaches (Stovner et al., 2006).

Cluster headache is a term given to a rarer form of headache in which there is unilateral severe pain, resulting in somewhat desperate measures to gain immediate relief that may result in injury (Costello, Costello and Holmes, 1995). There tends to be regularity in the daily timing of attacks, which tend to come in a series with periods of remission between these clusters of attacks. Attacks tend to occur in the morning or early in sleep and show a seasonal effect (May, 2005). There appears to be a genetic component to what would seem to be a neurovascular mechanism mediated by the **hypothalamus**. Although some cases of cluster headache are treatment refractory, there has been some success in using **deep-brain stimulation** (May, 2005). Schoenen et al. (2005) have successfully used stimulation of the hypothalamus in chronic refractory cases of cluster headache.

The prevalence of adults with headaches in Europe during a 12-month period has been placed at 51 per cent, and those with chronic headache, defined as occurring on half the days in a month up to daily, at 4 per cent (Stovner et al., 2006). The impact on productivity is substantial, with 15 per cent of adults being absent from work for this reason (Stovner et al., 2006). There is a chronic overuse of **analgesics** and other pharmacological interventions by sufferers of headaches (Stovner et al., 2006). More psychologically based approaches to dealing with the pain and reducing any stress-based precipitating factors are infrequently resorted to, possibly due to sufferers requiring acute and short-term remedies.

Skin conditions

There are a number of skin conditions that are impacted on to a greater or lesser extent by psychological stress. The study of this area of psychophysiology has been termed psychodermatology or psychocutaneous medicine. Taylor, Bewley and Melidonis (2006) have identified three areas where there are interactions between psychological and dermatological factors. One is where there are psychological disorders that are expressed as skin abnormalities, such as **dermatitis artifacta** and **trichotillomania** (see Chapter 10), and another is where skin disorders produce

psychological effects such as depression, particularly in the case of disfiguring complaints. The third area concerns skin disorders such as the examples below, where psychological factors precipitate, exacerbate or, in positive psychology terms, improve the condition. Psychological stress plays a key part in the latter area and has been reviewed by Gupta and Gupta (2003).

Eczema is the inflammation of the surface layers of the skin, which may be caused by contact with an inflammatory chemical or allergen, termed contact dermatitis. As a type of dermatitis, there are many forms of this disorder and one of the commonest is **atopic eczema**. Atopic eczema tends to recur within families, suggesting a genetic component. Single **nucleotide polymorphisms** of the **IL-18 gene** might be involved in the development of the disorder, possibly by partly precipitating a functional dysregulation of the IL-18 production during the lifetime (Novak et al., 2005). Those with a family history of eczema may be prone to a rare reaction to the **vaccinia virus** found in smallpox inoculations and other forms (Kaiser, 2007). In the late twentieth century, a great deal of interest was generated by research showing that a lack of exposure to a variety of environmental substances, including allergens, seemed to be as important as the established genetic component in eczema as well as other disorders in this section (Williams, Strachan and Hay, 1994). It is treated medically with corticosteroid cream, but this may exacerbate the problem in the long term due to its effect of thinning and weakening the skin, and tends to be used only to control episodes of eczema initially. Reducing the effects of stress can assist in severe and reactive

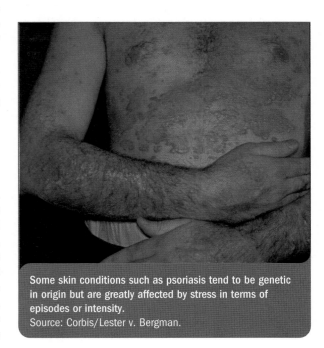

Some skin conditions such as psoriasis tend to be genetic in origin but are greatly affected by stress in terms of episodes or intensity.
Source: Corbis/Lester v. Bergman.

cases, and behavioural interventions are used to prevent habitual itching, which worsens the eczema.

Psoriasis comes in many forms such as **nail psoriasis**, but the most common type affects the skin and is referred to as **plaque psoriasis**. Normally, new skin rises through the layers of the skin and sheds in a monthly cycle, but in psoriasis this occurs rapidly every 2 or 3 days, causing itchy flaking and a burning sensation. This is distressing for the sufferer, who may consider it both uncomfortable and unsightly to the extent that it affects their socialising and even sexual activity. Affecting about 2 per cent of the population, the disorder is a polygenetic hereditary multifactorial disease that has **psychoneuroimmunological** aspects (Niemeier et al., 2005). Psoriasis seems to be a product of interaction between skin and the immune system. The link between these two has been assumed to be the cell-signalling molecule **Stat3**, which initiates perturbations in the epidermis and generates misguided T-cell responses (Pittelkow, 2005). The psychoneuroimmunological aspects seem to be mediated by stress, which may provide a means of reducing the severity of the disorder (Niemeier et al., 2005). It is a chronic lifelong condition but tends to occur in episodes, which may be precipitated by stress. As with eczema, medical treatment can involve corticosteroid creams, but also phototherapy of the skin or medication to slow skin production.

These dermatological complaints are mostly addressed by medical solutions. However, by targeting the psychological well-being and self-esteem of the client, the reduced level of skin symptoms may be more easily treated. For a number of dermatological conditions cognitive behavioural therapy (CBT) can be effective in this respect, particularly when combined with stress management interventions (see Taylor, Bewley and Melidonis, 2006). Not all studies have shown that psychological factors influence dermatological disorders; Picardi (2003) found no relationship between stressful events and the onset of **alopecia**. However, the relationship of stress to worsening skin disorders is well established across most studies (Gupta and Gupta, 2003).

Psychoneuroimmunology

Psychoneuroimmunology is the study of how behaviour and neural processing interact with the body's immune defence system. Psychological states such as **helplessness** have been considered to lower the **immune** reactions of the body to invading organisms or to weaken resistance to tumours, and psychological hardiness and a sense of **control** have been thought to help resist the progress of physical disorders. The degree of influence that psychological and neural processes have on immune reactions

and consequent health, or psychoneuroimmunological effects, have been muted a little by progress in our understanding of the precise aetiology of medical conditions. Hansell and Damour (2008) have used the example of **stomach ulcers** to illustrate this. This painful damage to the stomach wall was thought to result from stress alone, but the discovery of a bacterium in the 1980s reduced the theoretical role of stress (see Marshall and Warren, 1984). Thus, the condition is likely to begin by an unhealthy lifestyle and stress weakening the stomach's mucosal lining and lowering immune system responses. This is then followed by infection with the Helicobacter pylori bacterium (Marshall and Warren, 1984). Continued stress during and after the infection will worsen what can ultimately be a fatal condition.

Our immune system consists of a variety of cells such as **B lymphocyte**, which mediates humoral immunity, and T lymphocyte or the 'killer cell', which attacks other invading organisms such as bacteria (also simply termed **B-cells** and **T-cells**). Other immune cells such as the **T-helper cells** help to mobilise the immune defence system. The descriptors 'B' and 'T' simply refer to the initial letter of the origins of these cells, which are the bone marrow and thyroid gland respectively (Breedlove, Rosenzweig and Watson, 2007). As described above, stress activates the **sympathetic autonomic nervous system** and the release of sympathetic stress hormones such as **adrenaline** or **cortisol** and its metabolites such as **cortisone**. In the short-term case following acute stress, this results in an increase in immune cell activity, but with chronic stress there is a sustained suppression of immune cells, which hampers the ability of the individual to defend against infection (Dhabhar and McEwen, 1999).

However, Sapolsky (1994) has argued that the immediate effects of corticotrophin-releasing hormone during a very stressful event tend to suppress some immune responses. This evolutionary argument is illustrated by an animal under attack needing to suppress immune activity and thus conserve energy to escape the immediate situation, after which immunity is restored (Sapolsky, 1994). In a meta-analysis of studies into the effects of stress on the human immune system, Segerstrom and Miller (2004) found that subjective reports of stress lacked a relationship to immune function, but that the actual kind and duration of stressors were related to immune deficiencies. Brief stressors were found to affect cellular immunity but not humoral immunity, whereas chronic stressors tended to suppress both (Sergerstrom and Miller, 2004).

Persistent stress response activity is also associated with the lowering of cytotoxic T-cell and other immune responses involved in the monitoring of **tumours** and other mutations (Reiche, Morimoto and Nunes, 2005).

Focus

Immunodeficiency and AIDS

In autoimmune disease (AIDS) the human immuno-deficiency virus (HIV) invades the **CD4+ T-cells**, or **T-helper cells** (mentioned earlier), amongst other cells, and seriously damages normal immune reactions to common infections as well as the HIV. Discovered in 1983, HIV-1 produces this immunodeficiency with only nine genes, and although other agents such as **herpes** and **hepatitis** can also survive immune attack, HIV is unique in attacking and damaging the host immune system (Appay and Sauce, 2008).

The serious depletion of CD4+ T-cells tends to be the biological marker for HIV-1 and indicates the subsequent onset of AIDS. Although the human immune system is flexible and resilient, HIV-1 can push it beyond its boundaries as T-cell activation tends to propagate the virus (Appay and Sauce, 2008).

These and other immune activities may make pathological growth of tumours more likely. Behavioural strategies (see Chapter 3) to manage stress have been found beneficial for some cancer patients, as have psychopharmacological interventions for stress and depression, which also affect the immune response (Reiche, Morimoto and Nunes, 2005). Clearly stress does not cause cancer, nor can removal of stress cure it, but levels of stress can significantly alter the immune system's ability to resist and deal with tumours (Reiche, Morimoto and Nunes, 2005). Smith et al. (2005) reviewed studies of the self-administered **mindfulness-based stress reduction** given as supportive therapy in the context of cancer care. Although most reported improvements in mood, sleep and stress levels, systematic evaluations of efficacy were difficult owing to the programme being modified between studies (Smith et al., 2005).

Aetiology and treatment of stress-related conditions

Aetiology

In most cases, psychophysiological disorders are not initially caused by psychological factors, but their progress and outcomes may be significantly affected. Many of these disorders have biological causes in the form of genetic predisposition, infection, immune reactivity or inflammation, and others may originate from environmental agents or injury (see Sarafino, 2008). However, the role of anticipatory psychological factors in precipitating stress has been thought to initiate some disorders via the cortisol stress response (Gaab et al., 2005). The reasons for individual differences in stress responses, particularly the aetiology of hypersensitivity to stress, are important factors in the worsening and maintenance of psychophysiological disorders. The differences in stress responses between brief and chronic stressors may give some indication of the differing processes involved and, as mentioned earlier in this chapter, the reasons for these differing responses in terms of evolutionary survival. The distinction whereby brief stressors only suppress cellular immunity but chronic stressors suppress both cellular and humoral immunity may provide clues to the origins of dysfunctional stress responses (Segerstrom and Miller, 2004).

Some individuals develop a greater reactivity or are sensitised to stressors as a result of previous trauma (see PTSD in Chapter 12). One of the dimensions in the personality structure described by Eysenck (1970) was **neuroticism**, or having a labile **autonomic nervous system**. Thus someone scoring high on neuroticism would exhibit greater autonomic activity when the circumstances do not require this **flight or fight** reaction, resulting in accumulating stress responses and anxiety. As a personality trait, neuroticism is assumed to be a lifelong propensity with a genetic underpinning expressed via neurobiology. A stress reaction style has also been proposed as a valid personality trait or construct, distinct from others such as neuroticism, in predicting an individual's reaction to stressors (Guenole et al., 2008). Although individual reactions to stressors do tend to be affected by individual differences, most aetiological approaches tend to provide differing labels for variation in what is essentially a similar pathway for stress. In addition, although stress reactions tend to respond to the same interventions, there are many diverse treatment approaches available.

The lay concept of worry has been very much tied to physical illness as both a cause and a consequence (Brosschot, Gerin and Thayer, 2006). This aspect has been largely ignored as a contributor to stress-induced ill health, possibly as a result of worry and rumination being a routine part of non-pathological life. However, the effect of what has been termed perseverative cognition is to greatly extend the arousal and other symptoms of stress both in advance of and long after the stressful event. For example, many individuals who have been victims of stalking would have preferred the stress of direct assault to the prolonged worry and anticipation that accompany harassment (Hickey, 1998). Perseverative cognition has been found to act directly on stress-related somatic disease by increasing activation of immune, endocrine, cardiovascular and neurovisceral systems (Brosschot, Gerin and Thayer, 2006).

Treatment

There are two core approaches to treating psycho-physiological disorders. One is the direct treatment of the physiological condition, which is usually medical. Examples of this would be **bronchodilators** for asthma and **beta-blockers** for coronary-prone individuals. The other is to address the stress that is exacerbating or pre-cipitating the condition. These two approaches are usually used concurrently, although stress interventions tend to be neglected if signs of stress are not overt. Psychological stress management is more costly as an intervention, can take time to implement and in many cases cannot be relied upon to reduce symptoms on its own. As with somatoform disorders in Chapter 15, sufferers of psychophysiological disorders tend to present at the surgeries of medical practitioners and may not see a psychologist during their

Meditation training techniques have been used to teach self-stressing individuals a means of extracting themselves from time-pressured activities. Although there are many claims made for the spiritual aspect of meditation as an intervention, therapeutic effects seem to rely on the degree of relaxation and distraction from stress.
Source: Pearson Online Database.

treatment. This situation means that any stress component of the disorder presented may not receive intervention specifically aimed at stress.

Interventions for stress-related conditions can focus on the avoidance of stressors, diminution of stress reactions or reduction of stress-exacerbating behaviour, such as the type A syndrome. Interventions can be applied at three levels: **primary**, **secondary** or **tertiary** (see the section on community heath psychology below). Primary interven-tion involves measures to prevent this source of illness occurring in populations, such as the education of children and adolescents about the causes and consequences of stress and related behaviours. These interventions make much better use of health funding in averting stress problems (Thoresen and Pattillo, 1988).

Secondary interventions may target those adults particu-larly at risk for stress and be concerned with changing this existing stress-related behaviour. Examples of these would be the interventions following Friedman and Rosenman's (1974) original study specifically aimed at reducing type A behaviour, which had some limited success (Bennett and Carroll, 1990). Tertiary interventions are directed at those who are already ill with the effects of stress, and aim at reducing mortality within this population, although this is often considered to be a poor form of prevention and has been described as 'Too little, too late and too few' (Thoresen, Telch and Eagleston, 1981: p. 478). For example, tertiary psychological interventions for asthma have managed both to alleviate symptoms and to reduce 'as needed' medi-cations, although this is not significant with all clients (Yorke, Fleming and Shuldham, 2007).

The management of stress has advanced in terms of techniques and availability since the spread of health psychology in the 1970s. Many educational establishments have offered courses on stress management for a number of years now, and some professionals have this as their sole occupation with a proliferation of novel approaches dur-ing the twenty-first century. However, the stress reduction technique of progressive muscular relaxation (PMR) has been widely used in the many years since its identification by Jacobson in 1934 (McCallie, Blum and Hood, 2006).

Over the years of its application, the originally cumber-some PMR technique has been refined and a model provided by Bernstein and Borkovec (1973) has tended to be adopted as a major psychophysiological intervention for stress. The technique is carried out daily with minimal distraction from background noise, light or interruption, with the client sitting upright but in comfort. With eyes closed, the client follows pre-recorded instructions to relax and will progress through muscle groups where tension occurs, first tensing and then relaxing these muscles whilst taking a deep breath and exhaling respectively. Relaxing is a conscious action often accompanied by a verbal self-command. Eventually this may be carried out cognitively by recalling the relaxation state learned through PMR. Thus PMR is a very easily administered intervention that can be seen as a transferable skill with a wide range of potential delivery services including social work (McCallie, Blum and Hood, 2006).

PMR reduces arousal but can also improve self-confidence and a sense of control over events. Other skills can also be improved with training with the bonus effect of reducing stress, such as **time management**, assertiveness and **anger management** training. **Cognitive behavioural interventions** can also help individuals alter stress-inducing beliefs and attitudes, such as misperceptions and interpretations of the behaviour of others. Symptoms of ill health can also be managed in a way that reduces their impact, and coping with them can reduce exacerbating stress. Reducing negative self-statements and introducing coping self-statements is part of an intervention called **self-instructional training**, which has been used to improve self-perceptions of pain (Allison and Friedman, 2004). General health improvement can also impact positively on psychophysiological disorders, so developing a positive attitude towards reducing smoking and drinking as well as taking exercise can begin a cycle of improvement. Meichenbaum (1986) drew on his self-talk methods, which were added to appropriate behaviour instruction and relaxation as a practised rehearsal in preparation for future stressful events. This is known as **stress inoculation training** (Meichenbaum, 1986). **Biofeedback** can be used to educate and develop the ability to reduce health risks via control over involuntary functions such as blood pressure and involuntary types of muscle tension via electromyograph feedback (Comer, 2007).

The future of intervention strategies for stress and stress-related disorders will require some coordinating of that which has so far been upheld as making a significant contribution in empirical evaluations. However, under the general banner of health interventions a great deal of feedback between research, clinical applications and public policy is needed to produce a coherent strategy (Nicassio, Meyerowitz and Kerns, 2004). This is made more complex as a task, given the very diverse range of possible interventions and equally diverse claims and criteria for their effectiveness.

Belief-based interventions and parapsychology

Parapsychology is the psychological study of paranormal phenomena, which range from the belief in

Hot stone treatments, amongst other similar techniques, can bring physical comfort and make clients feel better but these are not magical therapies or cures.
Source: Pearson Online Database.

ghosts, unidentified flying objects or religious signs through to the belief in lucky charms, telepathic powers and, of relevance to this chapter, psychic healing and non-empirical alternative medicine (Roberts and Groome, 2001). Although parapsychology is more concerned with why people believe in such phenomena rather than with the validity of the claims made for them, claims over the value of some alternative interventions have become the focus of heated debate. It is well established that a positive mental state and anxiety can influence some psychophysiological disorders (Peters, 2001), but it is not possible simply to extend this process to a more magical mental influence on illness. It may seem unduly strict to remove hope from those who wish to try such 'belief-based interventions', and some have identified the place of 'complementary' approaches in wider future interventions (Nicassio, Meyerowitz and Kerns, 2004). However, it is equally unfair to offer false hope and dangerous to posit such 'interventions' as true alternatives to proven treatments. References to non-empirical treatments can

Research

The placebo

A **placebo** is a benign substance or procedure, which is assumed to have no medical value to the recipient. It is used in a great deal of research in a number of disciplines and is also the subject of research. Its literal meaning approximates to 'I shall please' and this can be related to the use of a placebo in medical and fringe medical history, literally to please the patient. With modern medical hindsight, virtually all medical preparations prior to the twentieth century were placebos with no real therapeutic value beyond this (Roberts and Groome, 2001). At the turn of the twenty-first century, the term **obecalp** began to appear to indicate that a preparation was a placebo to all but the patient, but as this is simply placebo written backwards, it was likely to become transparent to some recipients.

The medical use of the term was introduced by Graves (1920), but it became a popular area of study when Beecher (1955) announced the somewhat misleading statistic of 32.5 per cent of a sample having shown evidence of a **placebo effect**. Very high levels of expectation would have inflated this figure and it is unclear as to the degree of effect reported. From subsequent studies it would appear that Beecher's figure of a third represents the proportion of the population who are at all susceptible to placebos. The assumption that placebos are truly benign and have no intrinsic effects is something of a sweeping assumption, as even water given intravenously has an effect and the symbolic 'sugar pill' may not directly address specific disorders but sugar itself is not without effect.

The placebo effect, along with **spontaneous remission**, is known as a **non-specific effect**. These two non-specific effects are related in that many disorders remit over time and may even get worse, and these changes are sometimes erroneously attributed to placebos or other non-medical interventions. As explained in Chapter 5, correlation does not equate to a cause-and-effect relationship; thus, anecdotal 'evidence' of recovery following a placebo has to be taken with caution. Another weakness in reported placebo effects lies in the means of evaluating improvement. Merely asking a patient if they feel better will produce far more positive outcome results, irrespective of the actual progress of the condition, as compared with a physical examination.

A proportion of the placebo effect in patients who switch to a placebo after effective medication use can be explained by **classical conditioning**. Thus, the unconditioned initial response to the medication will produce a conditioned response to subsequent placebo use. The magnitude of a placebo response increases with the invasive nature of the administration; hence an intravenous placebo will have greater effect than oral administration. Part of the effect is what has been termed the physician effect (see Peters, 2001), producing improvement in the belief that the physician genuinely cares about the client. It is also the case that the more important or powerful the individual administering treatment, the larger the placebo effect. There is evidence from **functional magnetic resonance imaging** studies that placebos can reduce the experience of pain by expectation-reducing activity in neural pain-sensing areas such as the **thalamus, insula** and **anterior cingulated cortex** (Wager et al., 2004). Other studies have identified **endogenous opioid** activity mediating pain as a result of cognitive expectation (Zubieta et al., 2005).

A placebo is often used as a **control condition** in medical trials. For example, one randomly selected half of a sample of patients will be given a dose of the proposed treatment for a disorder and the rest a benign but similar-looking substance as a placebo. The patient and administrator will both be blind as to which substance is which, and results will be tallied by numbered records of patient and substance. This double-blind control procedure was reinforced as being necessary in such trials by the findings of Beecher (1955) on placebos. The true effectiveness of the treatment is then judged to be that beyond the placebo effect, sometimes referred to as placebo-controlled studies.

There are problems in using placebos with patient groups in clinical practice, such as the practice of giving antibiotics for viral infections, in weakening the effectiveness of such medications in subsequent use for bacterial infections. The placebo effect also tends to be temporary, eliminating its use with chronic conditions. Unethical practices have been associated with the use of placebos in general practice, such as using them to test patients for malingering practices with the twin risks of mistaking a placebo effect for malingering and failing to treat effectively where there is genuine illness. In current economic climates, the low cost of placebos in place of medications may offer a clearly unethical and ultimately false economy. These practices aside, patients responding to medically ineffective placebos or belief-based interventions can become progressively dependent on the therapist concerned, leading to potential chronic illness.

acknowledge their place as being secondary to conventional treatments, as in the term 'complementary treatments', although others place them more dangerously equal as 'alternative treatments'.

Although there is always hope that new treatment methods will be found, it is very unlikely that these will be found amongst the faith healers or those using the 'power of the mind'. Historically, such approaches as shamanism have been tried for thousands of years with no empirically measurable success despite some remarkable claims (e.g. Casson, 1997; Peters, 2001) and some rather fanciful methods such as the use of auragraphs. Yet it is only in the last few centuries that many diseases have been eradicated or controlled, and invariably by modern inoculation or pharmacological means. There are many 'alternative' treatment approaches, as healing can be a lucrative business, although money and notoriety are not the only motives for promoting psychic phenomena (Randi, 1982b). It is difficult to disprove the worth of some alternative treatments when the client may judge improvement subjectively, with this being confounded by placebo effects (see the Research box opposite). Stress is a popular target for such therapies with many variations on meditation, hypnotic suggestion and relaxation aids.

Some non-empirical interventions have apparent credibility and have even been adopted by health authorities, often due to pressure from proponents or clients eager to avoid orthodox medical approaches. For example, **homeopathy** is based on the principal of using a vastly dilute form of a substance that would normally exacerbate a condition. The substance is usually sufficiently dilute in use as to have no chemical or medical effect whatsoever. However, this approach has had royal sanction in the UK and an established base in the Royal London Homeopathic Hospital. In addition, the UK health service allowed trials of homeopathic interventions for asthma in 2006, but in 2008 most health authorities dropped the approach due to a lack of established effectiveness (*Daily Mail*, 2008).

Acupuncture is a long-standing approach based on ancient Chinese philosophy, conceptualising illness as an imbalance between the opposing forces of **yin** and **yang**, and diagnosed by analysis of the pulse and tongue. Treatment is by the insertion of needles along meridians or channels to facilitate the flow of the body's life force or **Ch'i**. There are variations on this basic belief system and each has the apparent influence on bodily function to treat all disorders and dysfunctions, although disorders as such are not named in traditional Chinese medicine. This philosophy is intriguing but has no basis in modern medical biology. Although used for thousands of years, acupuncture was banned in China in 1929. Most scientific bodies collating evaluations of acupuncture assert that there is no empirical evidence for the effectiveness of the technique, and where improvement has been reported there are methodological limitations (National Council Against Health Fraud, 1990). Some variations on acupuncture use electrical stimulation or **electro-acupuncture**, and blood oxygen level functional magnetic resonance imaging has been used to map the effects of this stimulation at acupuncture pressure points on to the brain areas concerned in order to validate the routes of action for treatment (Wang et al., 2007). Despite its apparent integration into medical establishments and the use of scientific aids in acupuncture research, it lacks official recognition in line with the lack of rigorous evaluations of it.

Masters, Spielmans and Goodson (2006) carried out a controlled study of the effects of prayer on health and illness. They carried out a meta-analysis of the effects of prayer for the health of another person and found it made no difference to their health or the conditions they were suffering from. Despite seemingly endless studies failing to find alternative health interventions effective or even having any effect beyond placebo, adherents still subscribe to what has become a vast international industry supplying palatable and exotic therapies since the 1960s. For many individuals in the twenty-first century, a trip to an alternative medicine clinic is seen as a leisure activity in a similar manner to a manicurist or hairdresser, many of which share the same premises. Although their effectiveness in tackling real disorders may be questionable, it may be overly judgemental to criticise the leisure use of these services as a possibly healthier alternative to a bar or public house.

Self-test questions

- What is the significance of the hypothalamus–pituitary–adrenal axis to the study of stress?
- What are the features of type A behaviour?
- What is meant by atopy syndrome?
- What is the significance of psychoneuroimmunology to the health effects of stress?
- What methods are applied in stress management?
- To what extent is the placebo effect dependent on the 'treatment' given?
- What evidence is there for 'alternative therapies' to be considered alongside those offered by conventionally trained professionals?

Health psychology

The above psychological approaches to medical conditions such as coronary heart disease have become part of what is now known as **health psychology**. This is a rapidly growing area of psychology and medicine, which cannot be fully represented here and which as a topic area has filled substantial texts (e.g. Sarafino, 2008). Although health psychology has been closely associated with the overlapping area of **psychological medicine** in identifying psychological factors in some medical conditions, limits have been placed on it in terms of the lack of direct impact or **primary effect** that psychology has on some disorders. However, by broadening the remit of psychology to **secondary effects**, such as promoting healthy lifestyles or adherence to treatments, health psychology makes the claim that any disease can be influenced by psychological factors (Kring et al., 2007). For example, awareness campaigns have increased self-examination for testicular cancer, which has an inevitable beneficial effect on mortality for this disorder (Munley, McGloughlin and Forster, 1999).

Health is not simply an absence of medical conditions or mental illnesses, but is better thought of as a continuum with severe illness and vulnerability at one end and high levels of fitness and immunity within a healthy lifestyle at the other (Sarafino, 2008). Health psychology plays a part at many levels in the process of moving the mean level of a given population along this continuum in the direction of better health. In the twenty-first century there has been increasing consideration of those individuals who are at the healthier end of this continuum, both in physical and in psychological terms. Thus, health psychology has become far more diverse than its application to psychophysiological disorders and has a number of specialist subdivisions such as **positive psychology**, **community health psychology** and **forensic health psychology**.

Positive psychology

Both clinical and forensic psychology have generally focused on negative aspects of behaviour, thought and emotion. However, towards the end of the twentieth century a number of psychologists such as **Martin Seligman** in the USA began to consider the features, traits and effects of positive aspects of an individual's psychology (see Seligman and Csikszentmihalyi, 2000). This has also led to the study of the state of health that such positive traits produce, or well-being psychology, a measurable state of happiness and positive adjustment (Pincus et al., 1997).

Individuals high on a scale of well-being are considered to have **disease-resistant** personalities and tend to demonstrate the specific positive factors of dispositional optimism, **hardiness**, **resilience**, **coherence** and a sense of **control** (see the Focus box).

Cognitive styles of disease-resistant individuals can reduce the ill-health effects of stress. This cognitive style includes considering stressors as temporary challenges to be overcome rather than insurmountable catastrophic threats, which greatly increases the stress reaction to an event (Matthies, Hoeger and Guski, 2000). In addition, this style of thinking does not involve the individual blaming themselves for incurring these stressors. These approaches to stress are clearly learned earlier in life, and individuals who show confidence in dealing with adversity and feel in control of events may have had parental approval and reward for progressively more difficult achievements. Such a balanced learning experience in childhood may be followed by a similar reinforcement structure during employment. This can help to build adaptive skills and attitudes towards potential sources of stress (see Sarafino, 2008).

Other positive factors that can add to the ability to cope with stress and well-being can be external to the individual, such as **social capital**. This **social network** of friends and family, on whom we can rely to a greater or lesser degree, is very important to most of us in helping us through crises as well as daily hassles. Unfortunately, those who need more social support tend to have less, such as the elderly, infirm and those surviving crises. These sections of the community tend to find it difficult to maintain social capital and often lose contact with friends or even family with time (Lepore, 1997). It is possible for such individuals to bolster their support with community support organisations and participation in community activities. Sarafino (2008) uses the beneficial effects of active engagement with religion as an example of this community support. Individuals who are demonstrating such religiousness tend to be high on well-being, are healthier and live longer (Masters, 2004). However, as mentioned above, this would appear not to be due to any spiritual effects such as prayer (Masters, Spielmans and Goodson, 2006), but a result of religion promoting healthier lifestyles and enabling a great deal of community social support (Sarafino, 2008).

Leisure activity can provide a buffer against stress-related ill health and add to a disease-resistant lifestyle. However, leisure activity can also be interpreted as passive activity such as watching TV or indulging in alcohol, which tend to produce states of boredom and poorer health (see Iwasaki and Schneider, 2003). These passive leisure pursuits are thought of as motivated by escapism, and are

Focus

Positive factors that facilitate good health

The following factors tend to be associated with disease resistance and well-being.

- **Dispositional optimism** is the belief or expectation that outcomes will be positive. Aspinwall and Taylor (1992) found that students who measured higher on optimism experienced fewer physical symptoms by the end of an academic term. Optimistic patients undergoing coronary bypass surgery were also found to heal faster than those rated as pessimistic (Scheier et al., 1989). These protective effects are partly explained by the optimist's cognitive style in directly addressing stressors by their use of challenge-oriented, problem-focused coping strategies.

- **Hardiness** refers to individuals who do not appear to suffer physical disorders as a result of stress (Ouellette and DiPlacido, 2001). Such individuals tend to consider themselves in control of their circumstances and welcome new challenges, whilst demonstrating a high level of commitment.

- **Resilience** is often taken to be synonymous with hardiness but it is based not only on the individual's ability to cope with stress and maintain health, but also on their developing cumulative protective factors against future stressful events. Thus, someone who has resilience against stress will have been confronted by stressful phenomena and dealt with it in a positive way, which they then learn as an adaptive strategy for future encounters (Luthar and Cicchetti, 2000).

- A sense of coherence implies a view that the world is comprehensible and manageable, and provides one with a sense of purpose in a meaningful environment (see Antonovsky, 1987). As a moderator between work, environment and stress, sense of coherence is considered a personality disposition protecting a high-scoring individual against stress. Thus, such individuals enjoy better general health, greater well-being and less stress than those with a low sense of coherence.

- A **sense of control** is one factor that determines the degree to which a stressor will cause a stress reaction. Events and situations that allow the individual a sense of control over the situation are less likely to produce signs of stress than those in which there is external control over the situation (Gatchel, Baum and Krantz, 1989). When individuals use lucky charms in stressful situations, they may be creating the illusion of control to reassure themselves. Rotter (1966) provided a measure of whether an individual feels that events are under their control or due to chance or external forces, which is often used in this research context. A lack of control over important events is also the basis of **learned helplessness** (Seligman, 1975; 1992). In his positive psychology approaches, Seligman (1992) advocates the training of **learned effectiveness** to combat the chronic lack of control felt in learned helplessness (see Chapter 3).

Case study

Too many cooks

Pierre's father had been a chef at a leading French restaurant in the centre of Paris but moved to run the kitchens at a large hotel in Amsterdam, as he thought the work might allow him more time with his growing family. Pierre followed in the family tradition and after working for his father for a few years he moved to be a chef in a very busy new city centre restaurant. The work was tough and very competitive, with every chef wanting to make their name there as the restaurant became increasingly famous and well reviewed. Pierre's wife became concerned when he came home early one night with a bad cut and admitted that it had been a supposed 'accident' at the hands of one of the other rising chefs. She had already lost time at her own job due to the various infections Pierre had suffered, which she blamed on the extreme changes of temperature and lack of fresh air in the basement kitchens of the restaurant.

Following more infections in the household, this time keeping their child off school, his wife

CASE STUDY CONTINUED

suggested a new career, but Pierre maintained that this was his chosen profession and 'in his blood'. Pierre began to drink at work and would arrive home later and later to avoid the confrontations with his wife. He was already in debt, and buying drinks in a restaurant bar was exacerbating these problems, which drew more criticism from his wife. Pierre visited his GP, complaining he might be run down as his childhood asthma had returned along with periodic outbreaks of eczema to add to his almost constant chest and throat infections. His GP sent Pierre for a full medical examination and found that he was showing signs of stress in the form of high blood pressure and lowered immune response, but no other serious disorders. Pierre's GP gave him a stern warning that his health was likely to decline progressively unless he changed his way of working and made an appointment with a clinical psychologist, who also worked as an occupational stress management consultant.

Pierre was naively surprised at the consultant being female and also by her having a very practical and direct approach, contradicting his preconceptions of an elderly male using complex psychological terminology. He was given some relaxation exercises and soon found himself with appointments for anger management and cognitive restructuring. After a few weeks, Pierre began to see his job differently and no longer felt it was the challenge it had once been, but a place of conflict and discontent. Pierre's wife was overjoyed when he declared that he was leaving the restaurant and intended to begin the task of training towards a career as a stress consultant.

in contrast to activities motivated by seeking, such as more active pursuits like hobbies, outings, sports or community activities. Active pursuits with intrinsic reward seeking, social networking and achievement as important components are associated with less boredom, less illness and greater well-being, and may be distinguished from populations with higher depression (Wijndaele et al., 2007). In the USA, **Buddhist philosophy** has been integrated into a positive approach to clinical psychology with claims of improved well-being, although from non-empirical sources (e.g. Wallace and Shapiro, 2006).

Community health psychology

Prevention and community forensic and clinical psychology

At the heart of community health psychology or psychiatry and community forensic psychology is the concept of prevention of ill health and criminality. As referred to in stress interventions above, this is often considered to comprise the three levels of tertiary prevention, secondary prevention and primary prevention. Each of these will be considered in more detail here, as they have become an important framework for strategies in health care and crime control services.

- **Tertiary prevention.** Closely allied to rehabilitation, this concerns the support or aftercare of those who have been suffering from ill health for some time, long-term offenders and those psychiatric patients or prisoners returned to the community. This is in order to prevent relapse, recidivism and possibly readmission. It is essential that these ex-inmates are well monitored during the early stages of adjusting to the rigours of life outside and are adequately prepared for this. The **care programme approach** provides care plans for patients who have been assessed. Patients will have a **key worker** responsible for coordinating the plan. Similarly, offenders will be supported by a probationer.

- **Secondary prevention.** This refers to the early detection of possible problems before they can develop into conditions that require hospitalisation, or prosecution in the case of offenders. It is essential that such **outreach** work does not depend on the individual actively seeking help; that problems are detected or anticipated by targeting those most at risk. In areas of the UK, a **supervision register** is kept of all the mental health patients judged to be at risk in each locality, as are registers for offenders, and this practice is replicated in other parts of Europe.

- **Primary prevention.** This involves examining whole communities rather than the needs of individuals. A primary prevention approach to the harm from stress would be to modify living and working environments to minimise stress on individuals. Primary prevention in a clinical sense will be concerned with the provision of adequate primary health care in the form of multi-disciplinary **community mental health teams** anchored by the GP, with increased use of community psychiatric nurses along with social workers, clinical psychologists and health visitors, and the addition of a variety of newer services such as **family support workers**. For potential young offenders there are many diversions from the adult penal system to avoid sustaining career offending as well as interventions in education. Primary prevention goes well beyond immediate provision into areas such as health education, educational interventions employing police and ex-inmates, environmental issues and epidemiology (examining the relative incidence of disorders or offences).

Some of the best preventative measures are those that stop disorders or offending ever occurring in the first place. Factors that are effective here are forensic and mental health education from an early age (including the importance of forensic and mental health factors), improving the general health of the population and promoting awareness of services that are available. This is especially true of services adopting a **prophylactic** (i.e. preventative) role. As mentioned, these aspects of community health have forensic counterparts, which can be seen increasingly to operate at similar levels to those above. For example, probation and resettlement at the tertiary level can be distinguished from the diversion from penal institutions and alternative interventions seen with young offenders at the secondary prevention level.

Rehabilitation and community care

As described in Chapter 1, large mental institutions, secure hospitals and prisons were built in remote locations to house an ever-increasing number of patients or offenders. Disordered offenders and psychiatric patients with psychoses could not be managed in any other way until effective drug treatments emerged in the 1950s. The institutionalisation effects (long-term effects of being in institutions) on patients and offenders were quite devastating in themselves. Even individuals who had not been very disturbed or dependent on admission were not really able to survive on their own after many years in an institution, whether this was hospital or prison. These effects were marked in the area of self-care and social skills, as so many things were done for the patients, including institutional 'social activities' for psychiatric or prison inmates. As with the institutionalised prisoners, psychiatric patients would also suffer from social stigmatisation, accentuating the difficulties of integrating into a society with which they were out of touch

and that might have changed radically during the years they had been institutionalised.

Institutionalised individuals who were not able or due to leave when appropriate pharmacological therapy became available were also increasingly suffering from the long-term effects of this medication. Seligman (1992) described **learned helplessness** in this context, which can be a consequence of the lack of personal control in institutions, leading to levels of **depression** in many long-term patients and prisoners. In **Irving Goffman**'s analysis of total institutions, he identifies other psychological effects on prisoners and inpatients, such as a lack of **personal identity**. With many longer-term prisoners, direct release back into the community was highly predictive of reconviction. This was not just a consequence of predisposition to crime or a lack of alternative skills and motivation; some institutionalised offenders deliberately gained penal convictions as a result of being unable to cope without institutional support. Various means have been tried to integrate offenders back into the community, by buffering their entry with skill training, **probationer support** and interim hostels. Community integration has met with difficulties that have been well documented in the similar case of integrating psychiatric patients into the community, the brief history of which follows.

The negative effects of institutions on offenders and psychiatric patients have been known for many years, but the issue became more immediate with the advent of drug management in the 1950s and pressure to end 'incarceration' from the global **anti-psychiatry** movement in the 1960s. At the same time, pressure to reduce the number of offenders, especially the young, entering prisons that were seen as 'schools of crime' began to see the emergence of non-custodial alternatives. In Europe and the USA, the 1960s also saw the emergence of residential **therapeutic communities**, a half-way stage between institution and independent living, and later developments such as the **Community Mental Health Centre** movement. Parallel schemes for offenders also emerged, particularly in the USA. In the 1970s, new inpatient units were attached to District General Hospitals to provide local services for the immediate population, but they were less able to cope with the severely disturbed than the large dedicated institutions. **Day hospitals** also provide interim care, but as Tantam and McGrath (1989) point out, they can also provide another route to institutionalisation. The important concepts of **rehabilitation** and **prevention** began to be seen by some professionals as *more* important than those of diagnosis and treatment.

The difficulties faced in compromising the extremes of institutionalisation and 'street patients' discussed in the international box are well represented in what Jones (1982) called '**Scull's dilemma**'. In essence, this simply restates the

International perspective

Deinstitutionalisation: the Italian experience

In Italy, **Franco Basaglia** believed strongly in the importance of rehabilitation and prevention of psychiatric disorders whilst working in Italian mental institutions in the 1960s and 1970s, founding the **Psichiatria Democratica** movement in 1974. His convictions led him to change staff attitudes within his own hospitals and to create political pressure through his writings to bring about change on a national basis. By 1978, **Law 180** had been formulated and passed in Italy, which effectively ended compulsory detention except for urgent treatment. The Italian health services began a sustained period of discharging patients (and staff!), closing institutions and putting emphasis on prevention. Jones and Poletti (1985), reporting on the Italian experience, observed that by the mid-1980s there was a strong move to reverse this achievement. Few would argue against the principles of deinstitutionalisation, community care and prevention on theoretical grounds; it is the practical and financial aspects of implementing and resourcing the process that lead to difficulties.

In Italy, the 'alternative structures' in the community spoken of by Basaglia were slow to emerge, as was the funding of any additional community provision – funding which had never been costed out in advance in any detail. However, large institutions were emptied and sold, and many psychiatrists and other health workers lost their salaries. Basaglia died in 1980 and never witnessed the limitations of deinstitutionalisation manifest themselves on the streets of the poorer areas of Italy. The police were often left to cope with 'street patients', discharged without adequate preparation or support, and the occasional tragedies that resulted from severe disturbance and inadequate care.

The unemployed professionals were quick to protest and make the most of any newsworthy failure of the process, whilst the politicians had a clear financial incentive to continue with it. The health care professionals and politicians blamed each other for the failings of deinstitutionalisation in Italy, but the process continued, albeit with diminishing political support. This practice of deinstitutionalisation to free up resources spread throughout the world, including the UK and rest of Europe.

age old problem of what to do when 'you cannot keep them in and you cannot let them out'. The answer would seem to lie in the quality of the process adopted for moving from one to the other, which varies across countries. The Netherlands and Scandinavia have shown caution in this respect.

In the UK, the deinstitutionalisation process began in the 1980s, with planned closures increasing towards the end of that decade. Professionals in Britain arrived at the conclusion that community care would be more expensive than the current use of institutions. They also discussed the difficulties and issues involved, such as rehabilitation. The same professionals were then confronted with cost cutting being at the top of the political agenda, as it had been in Italy.

Some of the many problems that needed to be addressed in deinstitutionalisation can be appreciated from the following examples.

- The **NIMBY** phenomenon, in which no one wants community care in their neighbourhood and the public education required to change this. This pressure from neighbouring public was even more pronounced for offender resettlement hostels. In community care, we cannot assume that the community actually cares and social contact is necessary for social rehabilitation (see Dilks and Shattock, 1996).

- How some **chronic and severely disabled patients or high-risk offenders** could never be adjusted to independent living and would require permanent institutional care.

- How the process of **rehabilitation** needs to begin almost as soon as a patient is admitted, to prevent institutional effects occurring, and ensuring that the difficult, expensive and often protracted transition of the patient into the community is carried out properly to prevent the waste of resources that failure brings.

- The need for adequate **support in the community**. Outreach services are needed to prevent the **revolving door** or recidivist phenomenon, in which patients or offenders oscillate between institution and inadequate support or opportunity, placing an inordinate burden on resources.

- How to avoid the **moral blackmail** that is implicit if the system relies on relatives to act as unpaid carers, in order to take some financial strain off the health care budget.

- To recognise that **emergency bed provision** is a necessity and that availability should be local. There needs to be enough 'slack' in the system to avoid the risk of 'disaster in the community'. What should clearly be prevented are cases such as that of **Ben Silcock** climbing into a lion's den for 'company' or **Christopher Clunis** stabbing to death an innocent passer-by after being refused what could arguably be described as adequate care (also see Chapter 18).

■ There still being a need for the **larger hospital**. In addition to providing for the severely disturbed, larger institutions also allow for the beds in smaller local units to be ready for emergencies and other unforeseen eventualities.

■ There is a need to avoid the use of privately run **hostels** for patients or offenders in the community (especially the elderly), where cheap accommodation for high profits produces conditions that can be worse than institutional care and far more dangerous.

The move to community-based psychiatric care seems a bleak prospect, but this need not be the case given sufficient funding and forward planning. In parallel, the secure and supportive rehabilitation of ex-offenders into the community is plagued by similar issues, less public sympathy and the difficulties of habilitation as well as rehabilitation (Abbott, 1988). The achievable aims of safe and adequate care in an understanding and supportive community and with a focus on rehabilitation and prevention of further relapse or recidivism are worthy of investment. However, these aims have been around since the time of the Greek and Roman empires but without being effectively addressed.

Forensic health psychology

There are many points where health psychology enters into forensic areas. For example, stress reactions can erode control over aggression and caring responses. A crying child can be very stressful for a parent, who will be sensitive to the child's repeated alarm raising. The repeated triggering of the **hypothalamus–pituitary–adrenal axis** response produces adrenaline and other hormones, which persist in the body long after the arousal has been initiated, can tragically weaken the inhibition of an aggressive or even violent response to a child. Under circumstances of extreme stress, such as natural disasters like the St Louis floods in the USA, individuals can become very selfish and uncaring towards others, which tends to be interpreted as self-preservation but can be the product of stress and the attrition of coping mechanisms. There are many worthy areas of forensic health psychology, such as the work of **sexual assault referral centres** (see Chapter 8) and their operational viability (McLean, 2003). However, the areas of occupational stress and health in prisons will be examined, as they have received little coverage thus far in this text.

Occupational stress

Readers may be curious as to why stress in the workplace is placed under the forensic heading. However, although related closely to the issues of stress and stress management already covered, workplace stress has become a major legal point of focus involving issues of compensation, fraudulent claims and workplace harassment (see Cooper, 2004). Issues of health and safety in the workplace and the recognition of industrial injury in terms of corporate responsibility developed during the twentieth century, as did the use of litigation to gain compensation for injured employees (Kompier and Cooper, 1999). Towards the end of the twentieth century and increasingly during this century, a wider range of conditions produced in the workplace have become the focus of legal and occupational concern, such as asbestosis and repetitive strain injury. However, industrial injury in the form of psychiatric distress and particularly that resulting from the effects of occupational stress has become an issue for both employees at risk and employers wishing to avoid large-scale compensation claims (Kompier and Cooper, 1999).

Part of the professional remit of **occupational psychologists** is involvement in the study of stress in the workplace. This area of stress research not only encompasses raising awareness of the dangers of stress effects, but also plays a part in identifying sources of stress as well as evaluating and improving interventions. Interventions for occupational stress are not just concerned with treating the individual sufferer but also try to address stressors in the work environment, which may be systemic. In the case of problems inherent throughout an organisation, preventative strategies can avert wider-scale stress-related illness, which is costly in both financial terms and in terms of personal suffering (Kompier and Cooper, 1999). Often occupational psychologists are expected to identify short-term solutions to long-term systemic problems, partly as a consequence of high staff turnover and the anticipation of longer-term consequences being passed to future management personnel. There are also resources needed to deal with individual cases where there may be corporate negligence or indifference due to prioritising financial concerns.

Occupational interventions may usefully help employees reassess their work–life balance in the long term and this may involve an attitude change as well as lifestyle adjustment (see Gatrell and Cooper, 2008). However, in the rush to achieve financial and career security, many clients can fail to implement work–life balance changes in the long term. Some individuals feel they have less choice over their stressor levels. In dual-career families, females are often found to take on the greater proportion of household responsibilities in addition to their jobs, with consequently higher stress levels (Gatrell and Cooper,

Focus

Living to work

Stress at work is exacerbated by a work- and career-centred culture, with work taking up a greater proportion of our lives. This culture undermines the **work–life balance** with 'living to work' taking priority over 'working to live'. In the twenty-first century, employees frequently work through their lunch breaks and stay late to achieve a (mythical) advantage over the following day's workloads (Cooper, 2004). In Manchester, a couch was placed in a busy shopping centre, not for tired shoppers but to encourage city workers to take 5 minutes out from work simply to do nothing partly in order to counter work-stress.

On a sterner note, **Karoshi** is a Japanese term meaning 'death from work' that has begun to appear in occupational psychology literature. This concept has been applied in the context of type A behaviour in the workplace increasing the risk of coronary heart disease, as mentioned earlier. Within-job factors such as low levels of control in an organisation have also been associated with the incidence of coronary heart disease and the possibility of cardiac arrest (Bosma et al., 1997).

2008). The recognition of the interaction of inter-familial and occupational stress has been an ongoing subject of research since the 1980s (Lero and Lewis, 2008). Although fractionally more males are willing to take a share of the housework in the twenty-first century, the number of females in equal or superior career positions is increasing at a greater rate and is indicative of important future directions in stress research (Lero and Lewis, 2008).

Porter (1996) has outlined the pathological nature and damaging consequences of the syndrome identified by Spence and Robbins (1992) of **workaholism** to individual employees (see above). Spence and Robbins (1992) derive workaholism types on the basis of either high or low scores on three scales, which are concerned with work involvement (feeling driven to work), work enjoyment and drive. Those individuals identified as workaholics in Spence and Robbins' terms are found to have lower life satisfaction and greater work–life imbalance. Thus the recognition of workaholism as a syndrome requiring intervention has been considered important in health psychology (Aziz and Zickar, 2006) and may add to the responsibilities of employers not wishing to be subject to litigation claims. However, a growing problem for employers has been health malingering or the utilisation of spurious health problems to defraud them of employee salaries and sickness benefits. Such suspicions have made some employers reluctant to engage with what are valuable schemes to reduce absenteeism (Cooper, 2004).

Health psychology in prison

A major stressor in prison is the ever-present risk of bullying combined with the generally intimidatory physical and interpersonal environment. Bullying can be extreme

enough to result in suicide and may help to propagate further bullying behaviour, as tactics and motivations are learned by victims who then may become victim-bullies (Ireland, 2002). Bullying in prisons can also be related to those intimidatory physical and social aspects of the environment such as material deprivation, population density, organisational structure, attitudes towards bullying, prisoner subculture and dominance relations (Ireland, 2002). Moving into the twenty-first century, there has been the acknowledgement of human rights for prisoners in England and Wales emanating from the **Human Rights Act (1998)**. The application of this in an environment where bullying is rife and control is intrinsic within the system is an uncertain task, especially in a prison system that has not been reformed or restructured (Okojie, 2001).

As covered in Chapter 7, **anger management** and other interventions in prison, although aimed at reducing the propensity to offend, also have health benefits in terms of stress reduction in increasing social capital. However, prison is a notoriously unhealthy environment in which a great deal of time is taken up by passive activities, with the addition of restricted diets, substance use and smoking as ill-health factors. Illness within a prison setting is treated with suspicion and self-harm more so, as medical care is inevitably a preferred environment for non-sick inmates. In 2003, UK prison populations were significantly unhealthier than the general population: more than 80 per cent were smokers; 8 per cent had **hepatitis 'B'** and 7 per cent had hepatitis 'C'; 1.2 per cent of female prisoners were HIV positive (higher than male prisoners); 20 per cent of women prisoners asked to see a doctor each day; and the overall suicide rate was higher (Crowther, Richman and Rochford, 2003).

Suicide rates within prisons are a source of concern and an increased rate of these self-inflicted deaths in UK prisons prompted a detailed review by **Her Majesty's Chief**

Inspector of Prisons, which resulted in a thorough review of Prison Service policy and practice in 2001. This helped to produce a risk-focused approach with several strategies progressively to reduce the rate of suicide in prisons. Included within this was a positive relationship with the Samaritans and the establishment of area-based forums for policy development, review of practice and the sharing of good practice (Beck, 2001). Within Manchester prison, a Samaritan-trained network of **Listeners** has been successfully used; these are volunteer prisoners who attempted initial intervention with fellow prisoners who experience problems (Coackley and Richman, 2003).

There have been attempts to improve the health of prisoners in the UK. The 'whole prison approach' was promoted by the **Prison Health Policy Unit** and **Prison Health Task Force** as strategic catalysts, but the operation of this system is problematic (Crowther, Richman and Rochford, 2003). It is inevitable that health care of long-term and elderly prisoners will develop into palliative care, but the care of dying prisoners is still contentious (Crowther, Richman and Rochford, 2001). The USA (with a prison population of over 2 million) has already faced this issue, with AIDS patients and 'life means life' inmates. Prisoners as 'buddies' have been incorporated into the palliative process, despite risks of problems such as stolen drugs (Crowther, Richman and Rochford, 2001). Crowther, Richman and Rochford (2001) have questioned whether prison, with its mechanistic rule structure and containment ethos, is an appropriate place to die. The authors have suggested a prison palliative care network, possibly with changes to rule structure to allow relatives and friends to participate in the dying trajectory with the addition of nurse support mechanisms.

Clinical issues

The wide variation of approaches to the treatment of stress and stress-related illness may be delivered by occupational psychologists, health visitors, stress management counsellors or even aromatherapists. This can place a clinician in a difficult position if specialising within this area, particularly qualified clinical psychologists, who may be requested by clients to provide an approach that is not supported by empirical evaluations, but which may be offered by an alternative clinic nearby. Needless to say, professional integrity should not allow the use of what would essentially be a placebo in the eyes of the clinician, but a certain level of professional frustration may need to be tolerated in this respect.

It has been mentioned above that the majority of patients with stress-related conditions will not be referred to a clinical specialist but may be dealt with by a GP or medical specialist entirely (Comer, 2007). Thus, it may be that clients are suffering from chronic stress by the time they are referred. The value of early interventions may need to be communicated to front-line medical professionals. Stress audits carried out in companies may provide the means for early intervention strategies, along with routine employee health checks to reveal those at risk, but of course only for employees and only those employees within health-aware companies. Clinicians also need awareness of the indirect presentations that are possible with stress-related disorders, in that a client complaining with stress symptoms may be having problems in many other potential areas: for example, they may be in need of anger management to reduce stress-provoking behaviour at work, as in the case study above. There are occasions where stressful events are inevitable, as is the case with terminal illness, chronically ill partners or simply facing a surgical procedure. There can be good preparatory work in inoculating the individual against high levels of stress emanating from fears and misconceptions. It is also useful to provide good coping skills, which may also make a material difference to post-operative survival or success.

Adherence to treatment regimes can be a problem in stress management. Most of these interventions require the client to continue with a learned cognitive behavioural activity independently, and the failure to do so is prevalent in this disorder area. However, progressive muscle relaxation can prove more immediately self-rewarding and does tend to produce better compliance than with some other interventions (see Lehrer et al., 2007). Adherence problems can have a marked effect on follow-up evaluations and as such may bias in favour of client-friendly treatments. Frequency and regularity of practice of techniques can increase treatment effectiveness as well as reducing dropout rates amongst clients (Lehrer et al., 2007).

Self-test questions

- How does positive psychology differ from conventional clinical approaches?
- What is meant by a tertiary intervention in community health psychology?
- How does the 'Italian experience' relate to mental hospital provision in the UK?
- What is meant by 'Scull's dilemma'?
- In what way is occupational stress a potential forensic issue?
- Compile critical points for a debate on the issue of human rights for prisoners.

Chapter summary

The study of stress and its effects is part of **health psychology**, which more broadly deals with psychological approaches to preventing **medical conditions** such as **coronary heart disease**. Psychological factors are evident in a range of disorders, including **hypertension, asthma, headaches** and a number of **skin conditions** such as **eczema**. **Psychoneuroimmunology** examines the ways in which stress can alter immune responses, increasing the risk or hastening the progress of a number of conditions as diverse as **ulcers, AIDS** and **cancer**. The causes of stress disorders are rarely stress, which precipitates or exacerbates conditions and is addressed with a variety of treatment approaches, such as **progressive muscle relaxation**. Some interventions have little empirical value and enter the realm of **parapsychology**, tending to be belief based. **Positive psychology** is a recent part of **health psychology** and focuses on **well-being** rather than illness.

Amongst the branches of health psychology are **community health psychology**. This is a broad area including issues of **prevention**, which is considered at three levels: **tertiary** or aftercare preventing relapse, paralleled by probation for offenders; **secondary** or the early detection of individuals developing disorders or offending; **primary** or the examination of whole communities in terms of provision, the incidence of disorders and offending as well as the factors which influence them. It also covers the effects of **institutionalisation** on patients and prisoners, and the related issue of **community care** with the historical precedent in the 'Italian experience'.

Forensic health psychology has many facets including **occupational health psychology**, with the increasing use of litigation in the area. Another issue involves the health of those in prison, including the problem of **palliative care** for inmates. There are many diverse **clinical issues** in working with stress-related disorders, some of which relate to the position of professionals in the field, where both medical professionals and **alternative therapists** may compete.

Suggested essay questions

- Critically assess the degree of influence that psychological stress has on medical conditions such as coronary heart disease.
- Critically evaluate the value of 'alternative therapeutic approaches'.
- Discuss the forensic health issues involved in *either* the workplace *or* prisons.

Further reading

Overview texts

Albery, I., and Munafo, M. (2008) *Key concepts in health psychology.* London: Sage.

Cooper, C. L. (2004) *Handbook of stress medicine and health.* Boca Raton, FL: CRC Press.

Lovallo, W. (2004) *Stress and health: Biological and psychological interactions* (2nd edn). Okia City: Sage.

Oatley, K., Keltner, D., and Jenkins, J. M. (2006) *Understanding emotions* (2nd edn). Oxford: Blackwell.

Sarafino, E. P. (2008) *Health psychology: Biopsychosocial interactions* (6th edn). New York: Wiley.

Vitetta, L., Anton, B., Cortizo, F., and Salf, A. (2005) Mind–body medicine: Stress and its inpact on overall health and longevity. *Annual New York Academy of Sciences*, **1057**, 492–505.

Specific and more critical texts

Haworth, J., and Hart, G. J. (2007) *Well-being.* London: Palgrave-Macmillan.

Kompier, M., and Cooper, C. (1999) *Preventing stress, improving productivity: European case studies in the workplace.* London: Routledge.

Lehrer, M., Woolfolk, R. L., Barlow, D. H., and Sime, W. E. (2007) *Principles and practice of stress management.* London: Guilford Press.

May, A. (2005) Cluster headache: Pathogenesis, diagnosis, and management. *The Lancet,* **366**(9488), 843–55.

Sidell, M., Jones, L., Katz, J., Peberdy, A., and Douglas, J. (2003) *Debates and dilemmas in promoting health.* London: Palgrave-Macmillan.

Van der Ploeg, E., Dorresteijn, S. M., and Kleber, R. J. (2003) Critical incidents and chronic stressors at work: Their impact on forensic doctors. *Journal of Occupational Health Psychology,* **8**(2), 157–66.

Visit **www.pearsoned.co.uk/davidholmes** for a range of resources to support study. Test yourself with multiple choice questions and access a bank of over 100 videos that will bring the topics to life. Video coverage for this chapter includes a discussion of positive psychology, an interview with Julia who suffers from Adjustment Disorder, and a study of worms which may explain stress-induced over-eating.

CHAPTER 17 Mood disorders

- Overview
- Case study
- Mood states
- Classification of mood disorders
- Unipolar or depressive disorders
- Bipolar disorders
- Specifiers for mood disorders
- Seasonal affective disorder
- Aetiology and treatment of mood disorders
- Suicide and self-harm
- Positive by-products of mood disorder
- Forensic implications
- Clinical issues
- Chapter summary

Follow a 'day in the life' of Feliziano who suffers from bipolar disorder. This is one of several videos that explore issues and disorders relevant to this chapter at **www.pearsoned.co.uk/davidholmes**.

Mood disorder, ability and celebrity

In this chapter the enigma of genius, success and mood problems will be unravelled to some degree. Anecdotal examples of this relationship abound, **Stephen Fry** being one sufferer who has spoken frankly on UK television about his and others' experiences. He has suffered the clinical highs and lows that resulted in his 'disappearances' from public life, but also seems to show the creative genius that is a possible by-product for some with mood disorders.

In addition to comedians such as Stephen Fry, many poets and writers such as **William Blake** and **Edgar Allen Poe** have clearly suffered from mood disorder. It is also common amongst musicians from **Robert Schuman** through to **Charles Mingus** and **Kurt Cobain**. All too many have suffered premature deaths that have been arguably hastened by mood problems. Painters such as **Vincent van Gough** as well as orators like **Winston Churchill** seem to struggle along the fine line between devastating mood problems and brilliance in their fields.

In this chapter we will examine why mood problems in so many who gain worldwide recognition should painfully accompany such extreme ability.

Stephen Fry is thought of as a successful, high-achieving comedian and presenter, yet he suffers from the unhappiness of mood disorder.
Source: Corbis/Rune Hellestad.

We all experience low moods following difficulties or feel elated with success, but this does not last and we would rarely wish to end it all or be at all confident about our sudden plans to save the entire world. Mood-disordered individuals experience such extreme feelings daily for long periods after related events have passed or even irrespective of life's events. Only 2 per cent of people may experience manic episodes during their lives, whereas ten times that figure, mostly females, will experience clinically significant depression, which is thus considered as 'the common cold of psychiatry' (Holmes, 1998).

Early references to low mood used the term **melancholia**, which is taken from 'melan' meaning black and 'chole' meaning bile. As implied, this early concept of depression handed down from the ancient Greeks included an aetiology based on an assumed excess of '**black bile**' in the body. In contemporary classifications, there are mood states: depression, mania, mixed mood and hypomania, which are the component parts of mood disorders. Mood disorders comprise two major divisions, reflecting the above distinction of having clinical mood problems either with manic elements (**bipolar disorder**) or without, just experiencing **unipolar depression** (see Griez et al., 2005). Thus the term 'bipolar' implies two differing states within the disorder, whereas 'unipolar' indicates just one: depression. Bipolar disorders are subdivided into a milder but chronic form or **cyclothymia**, and the presence (**bipolar I disorder**) or absence (**bipolar II**) of full mania. Unipolar depression or **major depressive disorder** also has a milder chronic form, or **dysthemia**.

The **specifiers** for mood disorders indicate notable features of the course or most recent episode of the disorder. Amongst these is 'with seasonal pattern' to indicate that onset and remission of symptoms tends to occur with changing seasons. A major issue that is salient across the mood disorders and has both clinical and forensic implications is the problem of **suicide**. Suicide rates are about 15 times higher in those with mood disorder than in the general population (Cipriani et al., 2005). As with some other mental disorders, there are some potential benefits that both come as part of the disorder symptoms and are also sometimes found with few deficits in those sharing the beneficial genes but without the disorder. One such beneficial trait associated with mood disorder is creativity (Jamison, 1992). As explained above, amongst the forensic issues involving mood disorder is suicide and particularly the scenario of the **one-sided suicide pact**, where one individual will end the lives of others, often family, as part of their suicide. Further forensic and clinical issues centre around dealing with the risk of suicide in contexts such as prison and the difficulties of balancing the medication requirements of depressive and manic episodes.

Mark had been playing in the band since he was a teenager. Five years is a long time for a teenage band to stay together. Their survival partly depended on using Mark's house as part-time rehearsal room and warehouse, but was not helped by his moody changes of enthusiasm for their success. Sometimes this was wildly ambitious, but a month or two later he would declare the band project pointless and a waste of time. During good weeks, Mark would often joke about their name, 'Redemption'.

In fact, he would joke about everything to the extent that other members suggested he did stand-up comedy rather than keyboards. However, he was an excellent musician and his songs attracted the attention of several recording company scouts. This led to something his mother repeatedly said would never happen, which was the offer of a proper contract for three studio albums and a tour of the USA. Mark's mother was certain he would end up like his father, who had taken his own life when Mark was 9. She blamed the music, as his father had done little other than collect old vinyl records in the years before his death, and in the end had even lost interest in those. In his mother's view, a proper interest and job would have been better for both father and son.

The band became excited at their new prospects, but Mark seemed to panic and began to feel that the contract might expose him as a writer of second-rate material. The band had trouble getting hold of Mark that week, and by the weekend they were worried. His mother knew well enough where Mark was. She had seen his father refuse to leave his room for days, even weeks on end. The day before the band's contract signing appointment, Mark was still 'missing' and his mother's final confirmation that he had been in his room the whole time angered the rest of the band. They had known his low moods before, but this was different, this was their big chance, which was quite the reverse of how Mark's mother viewed things, seeing the band as the cause of Mark's ills. In his room, Mark saw things very differently compared with a month ago. For him, the band was an embarrassment serving to highlight his clumsy songs, and he was letting down everyone in a pointless charade; his friends, his mother and even the memory of his father. Mark drank from a bottle of gin and contemplated taking all of his mother's migraine tablets.

Mark had lived with his changing moods for almost as long as he had been in a band and before that he was always in the shadow of

his father's depressions. As much as his GP and psychiatrist were optimistic that Mark's illness might follow a different course, his mother was not. Her hopes were raised when the news came to her doorstep that the band had lost their contract and dropped Mark as a consequence. However, his mother's somewhat naive hopes that Mark would now pull himself together and make his way in the real world were dashed when he was admitted as a psychiatric emergency following an attempt to end his life a month later. Nearer to summer, Mark's mood was becoming more manic, and at this point he failed to turn up for a cognitive behavioural treatment session with a clinical psychologist, telling his mother he was happy, confident and did not need treatment any more. He did not return home that day or ever again. Six weeks later, Mark's body was found in the reservoir below the motorway adjacent to his old school.

Not everyone with mood disorder is brilliantly creative or suicidal, but unfortunately they are more likely to have such tendencies (Jamison, 1992).

Mood states

Descriptions of mood disorders use terms such as 'mania' for **mood states** or diagnosable **episodes**, which may occur in different combinations designating different mood disorders. These states are better conceptualised as symptom complexes or the components of mood disorder classifications and not as complete disorders in themselves. This is partly because the **course** of mood states tends to change in mood disorder, and the combination and sequence of these tends to be characteristic of each disorder classification. The clinical mood states are described below.

Major depressive episode

A diagnosable episode of depression has the prefix 'major' to distinguish it quantitatively and qualitatively from commonly experienced low mood or sadness. A **major depressive episode** is primarily characterised by a profoundly depressed or irritable mood on a daily basis and/or **anhedonia**, which is a lack of pleasure gained from

any activity as well as a lack of pleasure seeking. For a diagnosable episode, this state persists for at least 2 weeks (American Psychiatric Association, 2000). In addition, an episode will also include at least four other symptoms, including sleep problems, weight change, fatigue with either agitation or lack of activity, lack of concentration, poor sense of self-worth, guilt and morbid, pessimistic or suicidal thoughts. There may also be **anxiety**, with overconcern about relatives or greatly magnified worries (Gotlib and Hammen, 1992). These symptoms are sufficient to impact negatively on occupational and social functioning as well as placing personal relationships under damaging strain (American Psychiatric Association, 2000). A number of these symptoms are prevalent in most depressive episodes and are considered in more detail below.

Sadness

Although some individuals battle against an essential depressed mood with false or 'forced jollity', the profound underlying sadness can be revealed in a diagnostic interview (American Psychiatric Association, 2000). The alternate state of irritability can emerge with outbursts of anger, which may seem at odds with the mood experienced, but is in keeping with the overall picture of major depressive episode (see Griez et al., 2005). This irritability will often stem from a sense of frustration over their uncontrollable mood, rather than a need for attention or gratification (American Psychiatric Association, 2000). Non-verbal signs of sadness, particularly facial expression, are often evident and can undermine attempts to cover up depressed mood or to report their feelings in terms of somatic complaints such as pain.

Pessimism and hopelessness

A sense of worthlessness pervades the sufferer's self-image, accompanied by a bleak view of a future in which this will continue or even worsen. There may be a tendency to ruminate over perceived actions from the past, which tend to be viewed in a negative light or interpreted as being embarrassing or pointless (American Psychiatric Association, 2000). Sufferers often see themselves as responsible for problems and will continually feel guilt for events beyond their control, sometimes even to a delusional extent. Self-recrimination and hopelessness are risk signs for **suicide** and **self-harm**, which will be dealt with in a specific section later in this chapter.

Sleep problems

Insomnia is prevalent in depression and there may be some interaction between sleep cycles and mood in terms of biochemical underpinnings (see the Focus box on pp. 517–18). Insomnia in depression can involve difficulty in falling asleep (**initial insomnia**), waking in the night (**middle insomnia**) or waking too early and not returning to sleep (**terminal insomnia**). Hypersomnia or oversleeping is less common than insomnia in depression (American Psychiatric Association, 2000). With hypersomnia, individuals may sleep on into the day and this may also disturb their **circadian rhythms** (sleep patterns). Sleep problems can often be the way depression is clinically presented by some sufferers (American Psychiatric Association, 2000).

Anhedonia

A lack of pleasure-seeking behaviour, indifference to social aspects of life and a generalised lack of interest in things or events can be profound in depressive episodes. This lack of pleasure or interest can be for activities that were long-term interests or enjoyed hobbies prior to the depression (American Psychiatric Association, 2000). The extent of anhedonia may extend to basic pleasure motivational drives such as sex or food. Such changes may be signs of withdrawal from social activity that become noticeable by relatives or friends of the depressed individual (American Psychiatric Association, 2000).

Indecision and lack of concentration

Distractibility, ambivalence and poor concentration are common features of depression (American Psychiatric Association, 2000). These aspects can impair memory and an apparent reduction of **working memory** capacity (Baddeley and Hitch, 1974) has the effect of depressed individuals not being able to carry out the mental activities they normally achieve (Williams et al., 1988), including their occupational skills or even an understanding of the problems of others around them.

Appetite and weight change

In parallel with anhedonic withdrawal, lack of pleasure from eating can reduce food intake to the point of clinically significant weight loss. Less commonly, carbohydrate craving may occur, increasing body weight and possibly precipitating a cycle of reduced activity, fatigue and weight gain, which further increases exhaustion and inactivity, exacerbating the depressed state. There may be a relationship between the sensation of warmth provided by some forms of comfort eating seen in depression and the effects of physical warmth on perceived interpersonal warmth (Williams and Bargh, 2008).

Although a major depressive episode is required to produce clinically significant effects in the above areas, there can be some variation within those meeting the criteria (American Psychiatric Association, 2000). Individuals just meeting these criteria may lose significant social and occupational functioning, but in more severe cases they may require the services of a full-time carer in order to meet basic hygiene and physical health standards. Some of these symptoms can also occur in conjunction with bereavement or serious medical conditions such as cancer, and such co-diagnoses require careful consideration before a full diagnosis of a major depressive episode can be concluded (American Psychiatric Association, 2000).

Manic episode

Mania involves persistent elation or irritability for at least a week. According to *DSM-IV-TR*, there have to be at least three additional symptoms from the following: grandiose or inappropriate levels of self-esteem; engaging in risky pleasure-seeking behaviour; decreased need for sleep; talkativeness or incessant pressured speech; distractibility; rapid changes in thinking or racing thoughts; abnormally enthusiastic for work, social or sexual activity. These symptoms need to interfere significantly with social and occupational functioning and not be due to substance use. Manic episodes can also be precipitated by some anti-depressant interventions such as **ECT** (electroconvulsive therapy), daylight replacement or anti-depressant medication. Such episodes are not included in a diagnosis of Bipolar I disorder (see below; American Psychiatric Association, 2000). *DSM-IV-TR* elaborates on the key diagnostic features of manic episodes as follows.

High self-esteem

High levels of self-esteem can be seen in the normal self-directed enthusiasm of egocentric young children, although this is often curtailed when the amusement of those around fades. However, in adult manic episodes such behaviour may be seen as initially motivating, but even more rapidly than that of a child it becomes clearly delineated from normal enthusiasm and context-appropriate behaviour. Higher levels of self-esteem may manifest as delusional beliefs that appear to challenge logic as well as belief. One example would be the case of an individual who confidently considered a 3000-mile journey on a child's tricycle to be a matter of a few hours' ride.

Risk taking

One ever-present danger in manic episodes, particularly with undiagnosed or unmedicated individuals, is the tendency to engage in risky and ill-thought-out plans or relationships. These high-risk behaviours are partly fuelled by euphoric optimism, but this is coupled with poor judgement and little or no consideration of the potential negative outcomes of these ventures (American Psychiatric Association, 2000). Risky sexual behaviour can result in infections, unwanted pregnancy and damage to personal relationships. Reckless spending binges or clearly risky business opportunities are indulged in with an optimistic abandon of all caution. Such confidence can spill out into forensic areas, with manic individuals crossing the criminal boundary into activities such as shoplifting. A heightened sense of control and optimism can lead to **stalking** behaviours or intensify existing tendencies (Mullen, Pathe and Purcell, 2000; McGuire and Wraith, 2000). Driving recklessly, interpersonal aggression and domestic conflict can lead to irreversible injury to the manic individual as well as other parties. In manic episodes, all these inappropriate behaviours persist despite their having a high probability of negative consequences (American Psychiatric Association, 2000).

There is a tendency in normal individuals to make overoptimistic, unrealistic judgements about such things as contracting terminal diseases (Healy and Moore, 2007). This may be an adaptive evolutionary mechanism in order to motivate humans to initiate and take chances in reproduction and exploration. It is perhaps this higher-mood-based distortion that is so profound in manic episodes, although curiously judgements in those who are in low mood can be more accurate than those made by individuals without mood disorder (Sanna, 1998; Abele and Hermer, 1993). These overoptimistic views in those without mood disorders tend to occur most in situations where there is greater room for subjective judgement (Armor and Sackett, 2006).

Focus

The 'Truman syndrome'

In a society where **celebrity culture** is widespread, such exaggerated enthusiasm for one's self has become more accepted, especially amongst teenagers and young adults, perhaps masking the recognition of levels of manic behaviour. Taken from the experience portrayed by **Jim Carey** in the 1998 film *The Truman Show*, Truman syndrome has been suggested to account for those individuals who, through a mixture of self-engrandiosement and paranoia, believe they are living in a TV programme, in which they are the central character.

Joel Gold from Bellevue hospital New York believes that this accounts for cases of distressed individuals who are so convinced of this delusion that they wish to have their programme terminated. Not all sufferers of manic episodes have euphoric symptoms; others experience agitation and irritation, particularly if their unreasonable plans or actions are opposed. It is common for these states of irritation and euphoria to alternate (American Psychiatric Association, 2000).

Pressured speech, distractibility and rapid changes of thought

Speech during manic episodes tends to be rapid and it may be difficult to make conversation as the pressured momentum of sufferers' monologues is hard to interrupt (Griez et al., 2005). Speech can become something of a performance and there may be elements reminiscent of the psychotic speech seen in **schizophrenia**, such as clang association, deviations, derailment and enthusiastic lapses into irrelevant topics (see Chapter 18). Thoughts may change more rapidly than speech, increasing the tendency to change topics, which in more extreme cases may result in incoherent speech (American Psychiatric Association, 2000). There is a subjective sense that their thoughts are racing too rapidly to follow. The sensory input for manic individuals seems non-selective, as if all needs to be attended to equally. This leads to their being highly distractible. Thus when speaking their attention will be drawn by noises in the room, people in the street outside, someone chewing or birds flying past the window, rather than attending to the thread of their speech (American Psychiatric Association, 2000).

Enthusiasm for work and sleeplessness

Early wakening without tiredness and an overall diminished need for sleep are salient features of manic episodes. This may become persistent, with their skipping sleep for a few nights without signs of exhaustion. Here there may be some reciprocating of effects of sleep and high mood. Reducing and changing sleep patterns has been used to counter depression and can increase the chance of mild mania. This relationship between sleep patterns and mood is examined in the Focus box on pp. 517–18.

Although high levels of goal-directed activity may be considered a sign of mental health, in mania this shows the excessive ambition and distractibility already mentioned as signs of a manic episode. A disorganised approach to multi-tasking is in evidence, with little chance of each task being completed successfully. There may be a juxtaposition of social, sexual, occupational or community activities, which are approached with a level of demand and expectation that proves distressing for others involved. *DSM-IV-TR* notes how overenthusiastic socialising can become intrusive and provide a reason for recipients to complain (American Psychiatric Association, 2000). This level of social intrusion may border on harassment or stalking, even if it only involves current friends and acquaintances (Mullen, Pathe and Purcell, 2000).

The above symptoms are often compounded by some manic individuals having little insight into their condition and believing there is nothing wrong with them, their behaviour or their judgement. When no longer manic, most express some remorse for their poorly judged actions or interactions (American Psychiatric Association, 2000).

Mixed episode

Mixed mood is when both the symptoms of mania and depression occur nearly every day over at least a week and episodes may last up to several months. The level of symptoms needs to meet all the criteria, with the exception of duration, for both manic and major depressive episodes in order to confer a diagnosis of mixed episode (American Psychiatric Association, 2000). Rapid and extreme mood change results in a significant disturbance of social and occupational functioning, and may require confinement in hospital in order to avoid their harming themselves or others (Griez et al., 2005). These mood states alternate without compensating for each other and tend to be more distressing to the sufferer than a manic episode. Those having a mixed episode tend to have more insight into their plight than with mania, and consequently a greater chance of coming to clinical attention (American Psychiatric Association, 2000).

Hypomanic episode

Hypomania means 'below mania' and includes most of the symptoms of mania but not to a disabling degree. Thus, clients will experience the rapid onset of a persistently euphoric or irritable mood for at least 4 days. In addition, there will be three (if euphoric) or four (if irritable) of the following symptoms: raised levels of self-esteem; engaging in risky pleasure-seeking behaviour; decreased need for sleep; talkativeness or pressured speech; distractibility; disruptive changes in thinking; abnormal enthusiasm for work, social or sexual activity. There are no delusions or hallucinations in hypomania and episodes may last weeks or months. The hypomanic individual shows distinct differences from normal functioning that are observable signs to those around them. They tend to remain in relatively good contact with reality and, uncharacteristically for *DSM* disorders, there is no significant decrement in their social and occupational functioning. However, some may find disruption to normal occupational or social ability, whereas others may note improved effectiveness and creative enhancement (American Psychiatric Association, 2000).

The milder nature of hypomanic episodes in comparison with episodes of mania creates many difficult boundaries with normal behaviour (Angst, 2008). Thus, the possibility of hypomanic symptoms arising from substance use or as a side-effect of therapy requires careful scrutiny (American Psychiatric Association, 2000). The hypomania needs to be a clearly distinguished state from normal behaviour and not simply a permanent personality trait characteristic of the individual, especially in the case of younger clients where the border with enthusiasm and exuberance may be fine. In addition, being more creative or efficient is not usually characteristic of illness and some hypomania sufferers may avoid treatment, particularly those creative individuals who see benefits outweighing detrimental effects (see the section on positive by-products of mood disorder, pp. 519–21). However, the more dysphoric (unwanted), irritable mood is not seen as desirable, and hypomanic episodes are often adjacent to major depressive episodes, which can also change the client's attitude to wanting treatment. The difficulties in differentiating hypomania from normal behaviour or mania are partly reflected in the *DSM* criteria.

Classification of mood disorders

Mood disorders have been recognised throughout documented history and are certainly not a product of modern life. This emphasises the distinction between mood due to environmental stress and an underlying mood diathesis (genetic cause) that has always cast suspicion over individuals with this lifelong vulnerability. Old Testament self-descriptions of David in Psalm 55 as well as parts of Ancient Egyptian papyri make clear reference to states that are symptoms of major depression (Davidson, 2006). The term **melancholia** (see above) adopted by Hippocrates was used from the Greek–Roman era through to the early twentieth century and is still retained to describe a specifier for anhedonic mood disorder in *DSM-IV-TR* (American Psychiatric Association, 2000). Hippocrates also recognised bipolar disorder and passed the term **mania** on to be used by succeeding generations of physicians. In the seventeenth century, both **Robert Burton** and **Thomas Willis** conceptualised mania and melancholia as components of the same illness, a concept that was broadened yet further by **Emile Kraepelin**, delineating all types of affective disorder as **manic-depressive insanity** (Davidson, 2006).

With mood disorders being so prevalent (Narrow et al., 2002), they tend to be comorbid with a number of other disorder categories and are particularly associated with anxiety. This association has led to some authors considering the disorders together in their publications, particularly in Europe during the twentieth century (Goldberg, Benjamin and Creed, 1994). Other associations, such as that of alcohol abuse, are a logical consequence of self-medication (Holmes, 1998) and subsequent interaction between the two conditions. Associations with disorders such as obesity have been considered as being more fundamentally related in terms of common clinical findings and associated conditions (McElroy et al., 2004).

The mood states in the preceding section are the building blocks for individual contemporary mood disorders listed in both *DSM-IV-TR* and *ICD-10*. Mood disorders have also been referred to as **affective disorders** in recognition of the distortions of emotional states listed above, as represented by the Elsevier journal title, *Journal of Affective Disorders*. This term has been used far less frequently in the twenty-first century and has given way to the global term 'mood disorder' with its many subcategories, which are outlined in the next section. These subcategories reflect the combinations of the mood states, and although presented as discrete diagnoses, these can be found to develop from one another in specific directions, with other transitions being improbable (American Psychiatric Association, 2000).

Around 10–15 per cent of mood-disordered individuals become chronic cases and 80 per cent will have more than one episode (see Griez et al., 2005). There are estimates that around 15 per cent of major depression sufferers successfully commit suicide, an ever-present danger in mood disorder (American Psychiatry Association, 2000). Mood disorders account for a very high level of disability in society, with major depressive disorder alone being responsible for a greater global burden of disability than any disorder except ischemic heart disease (Murray and Lopez, 1996). Dealing with this burden is to some degree dependent on accurate estimates of the prevalence of mood disorders, which have been discrepant across surveys, although some reasons and potential redress for this has been identified (Narrow et al., 2002).

In both *ICD* and *DSM* systems (see Chapter 4), mood disorders are broadly divided into depression without mania (**unipolar or depressive disorders**) and depression with mania (**bipolar disorders**). This is the main classificatory division for this set of disorders (Angst, 2008). Depression has in the past been described as **endogenous** or coming from within, as opposed to **reactive** or a protracted reaction to an external event. These terms have fallen into disuse as the boundary between them is usually impossible to ascertain. Mood disorders were also once described as psychotic disorders along with schizophrenia, but the term **psychotic** is now reserved for hallucinations or delusions occurring in mood disorders, and is included below as a **specifier** for these disorders. Each of the mood disorders below may include various specifiers, which are described on pp. 509–10.

As mood disorders are divided into many subtypes, by adding reference to the most recent episode as well as any additional specifiers, *DSM-IV-TR* advises a specific format for recording a diagnosis with relevant specifiers. The mood disorders listed in *DSM-IV-TR* will now be described.

Unipolar or depressive disorders

Major depressive disorder

Also referred to as unipolar depression, major depressive disorder has to be clearly distinguished from the periods of low mood or sadness in reaction to loss or upset found in most people's lives. For the diagnosis of this disorder, the criteria must be met for one or more major depressive episodes, but there must be no episodes of mania, including hypomania or mixed mood (American Psychiatric Association, 2000). It can be particularly difficult to exclude cases where the depression emanates from alcohol or medical condition as well as those at the boundaries with other disorders, such as schizoaffective disorder. As occurs in a minority of patients, episodes of mania, mixed mood or hypomania that are not a result of external factors such as medication may develop after diagnosis. In such cases, the original diagnosis of major depressive disorder is changed to that of the appropriate bipolar disorder (American Psychiatric Association, 2000).

There are three subtypings within major depressive disorder.

- The diagnosis can be the result of a **single episode** or **recurrent episodes** of depressive states. Separating episodes where there are fluctuating symptoms is not always easy, but the distinction can be important in terms of prognosis and intervention. To this end, *DSM-IV-TR* identifies a 2-month period of failing to meet the full criteria for major depressive disorder to separate episodes and this is noted in the diagnostic code for the disorder (American Psychiatric Association, 2000). Episodes may be isolated by many years in some cases.

- A further digit in this coding registers the specifier of severity of episode, but also whether or not there are **psychotic features** (hallucinations or delusions) in severe episodes.

- There is also a distinction between **partial** or **full remission** of symptoms at point of diagnosis (see the section below on specifiers). This has prognostic value, as those with partial remission tend to have further episodes (American Psychiatric Association, 2000).

Waraich et al. (2004) pooled prevalence data from 1980 to 2000, and although there was some variation between studies, the lifetime prevalence of major depressive disorder was 6.7 per cent across studies. Many estimates have arrived at a higher figure, but when more stringent criteria are applied the figure is much lower. Nevertheless, it still identifies major depressive disorder as one of the commonest mood disorders (Waraich et al., 2004). Around 10 per cent of those diagnosed with major depressive disorder will eventually develop **bipolar disorder**, leaving the majority of sufferers on a unipolar course of illness (Frank and Thase, 1999). This percentage has been increasing over the last 20 years due to better diagnosis and may be nearer 15–20 per cent (Angst, 2008). Onset of major depressive disorder is commonly during the twenties, but no age group is excluded from an initial episode.

Dysthymic disorder

Dysthymic disorder only involves unipolar depression, and although it shares the same symptoms as major depression, they are less severe. Rather than being in clear episodes, dysthymic depression tends to be less remitting. It follows a chronic course, with depression occurring for the majority of time over a period of 2 or more years, within which a period of remission of 2 months or more is sufficient to end the assumption of continuity. Onset may also be slow and start in childhood, and there is a very low rate of spontaneous remission at 10 per cent (American Psychiatric Association, 2000). It includes at least two additional symptoms from a list similar to that for a depressive episode, though less severe in each case, including sleep problems, appetite problems, fatigue or lack of energy, poor concentration or indecisiveness, poor sense of self-worth, and hopelessness. The chronic nature of dysthymic disorder often masks the salience of the onset of such criteria, as they appear constitutional. The diagnosis of dysthymic disorder is not given if the criteria for any bipolar disorder are met or if the full criteria for major depressive episode are met in the first 2 years (American Psychiatric Association, 2000).

In children, there is a higher incidence of irritability as opposed to dysphoria and criteria are set at briefer periods. Although there is no clear gender difference in child samples, adult females are three times more likely to be diagnosed with dysthymic disorder than males (American Psychiatric Association, 2000). The specifiers for dysthymic disorder mainly concern the age of onset being early or late, with the cutting point set at 21 years. *DSM-IV-TR* notes that as many as 75 per cent of clinical samples of dysthymic patients develop major depressive disorder within 5 years of original diagnosis (American Psychiatric Association, 2000). The lifetime prevalence for dysthymic disorder across studies is around 3.6 per cent (Waraich et al., 2004).

Bipolar disorders

Bipolar disorders are diagnosed following onset of mania, hypomania or mixed mood, and have a number of subtypes based on both symptom combinations and most recent episode type.

Bipolar I disorder

Bipolar I disorder is diagnosed if there is at least one manic episode or mixed episode. There is often a major depressive episode in the client's history and there may also be previous hypomanic or mixed mood episodes (Angst, 2008). Given the initial criterion, there are six subtypes of bipolar I with each being distinguished by the most recent episode type. These are shown in Table 17.1.

Specifiers for bipolar I disorder include severity and the presence or absence of psychotic features as well as catatonic, postpartum, melancholic, atypical, seasonal pattern and rapid cycling. As the criteria for one of many mood states may be met in terms of the most recent episode, all of the potential mood specifiers may apply in bipolar I disorder. Some of the specifiers for mood disorders are described in the next section. The rate of suicide in bipolar I disorder is similar to that of unipolar depression at about 15 per cent (American Psychiatric Association, 2000). Manic episodes in this disorder are particularly damaging to occupational and social functioning, as well as destructive in personal and family relations. The lifetime prevalence for bipolar I disorder has been estimated at 0.8 per cent across a number of studies (Waraich et al., 2004). Males and females tend to be equally affected, in contrast to unipolar disorders, and the average age of onset is 20 years. Late onset of a manic episode may indicate an underlying medical condition (American Psychiatric Association, 2000).

Table 17.1 Subtypes of bipolar I disorder based on most recent episode

- **Single manic episode** is diagnosed where this episode of mania is the only mood state that has been experienced.
- **Recent episode hypomanic** is diagnosed when there has been a definite manic episode in the past, but the current or most recent episode is hypomanic.
- **Recent episode manic** is diagnosed when there have been previous episodes including episodes of mania.
- **Recent episode mixed** is diagnosed when there has been a definite manic or mixed (with mania) episode in the past, but the most recent episode is mixed.
- **Recent episode depressed** is diagnosed when there has been a definite manic episode in the past, but the most recent episode is one of depression.
- **Recent episode unspecified** is diagnosed when there has been a definite manic episode in the past, but the most recent episode meets the criteria for one of the mood episodes but has not met the criterion that specifies duration.

Bipolar II disorder

Bipolar II disorder involves one or more major depressive episodes with at least one hypomanic episode. Any manic or mixed episodes would change the diagnosis to bipolar I disorder. The milder hypomanic episodes can be difficult to differentiate from high levels of normal enthusiasm or euphoria, but are still disruptive to functioning (Angst, 2008). Hypomanic episodes differ emotionally from the depressive episodes, but follow them in the majority of cases (American Psychiatric Association, 2000). Episodes tend to cycle more rapidly than for depressive disorders and may be given the rapid cycling specifier if there are four or more episodes per annum. Specifiers for the current or most recent episode can be noted at diagnosis. The lifetime prevalence for bipolar II disorder is around 0.5 per cent, with a greater prevalence amongst females than males (American Psychiatric Association, 2000).

Cyclothymic disorder

Cyclothymic disorder is the bipolar equivalent of dysthymic disorder and is diagnosed when hypomania (but no manic or mixed mood episodes) and depressive symptoms (but no major depressive episode) occur for at least 2 years in a chronic pattern. Although some patients may look forward to the hypomanic breaks from depression, social and occupational functioning is poor overall. Hypomanic symptoms may not meet the criteria for hypomanic episode, nor should the depressive periods meet the criteria for

Focus

Schizoaffective disorder

Schizoaffective disorder is not listed in *DSM-IV-TR* as mood disorder and is described in Chapter 18 of this look under the heading of schizophrenia. As stated in Chapter 18, schizoaffective disorder represents a halfway house between schizophrenia proper and bipolar disorder (Kendell, 1986), and distinctions are made between schizoaffective disorder with a bipolar component and cases where there is only depression.

It has been questioned whether schizoaffective disorder exists as a distinct diagnosis and not as an atypical form or variation of schizophrenia or mood disorder, or the simple comorbidity of these two disorders but with unclear boundaries (Maier, 2006). In conclusion of a systematic review, Cheniaux et al. (2008) considered schizoaffective disorder to be the midpoint in a continuum between schizophrenia and mood disorder.

major depressive episode, making diagnosis difficult for retrospective reports and in the presence of borderline personality. Thus, the duration criterion of 2 years is important for correct diagnosis and should not be interrupted for a period equal to or greater than 2 months (American Psychiatric Association, 2000).

Cyclothymic disorder is differentiated from rapid cycling bipolar I and II disorders by the failure to meet the full criteria for depressive, manic or mixed episodes. If these criteria are met during the 2-year duration, the diagnosis is changed (Angst, 2008). The lifetime prevalence of cyclothymic disorder is between 0.4 and 1 per cent, affecting both genders fairly equally and with a typical onset in adolescence (American Psychiatric Association, 2000).

Specifiers for mood disorders

Within each of the above disorder criteria, there may be some variation in the **severity** of the current episode or information that can be usefully added to any description of the disorder diagnosed. These further descriptions or **specifiers** that apply to most of the above mood disorders include the following.

- **Catatonic features** are severe motor disturbances, immobility or restlessness, which may occur in any of the mood states. This may be in the form of **catatonia** or **catalepsy**, the actively immobile state often referred to as 'waxy flexibility' in early cases of schizophrenia. Exhaustion and self-harm can result from **stereotypies**, or fixed-pattern, repeated, redundant movements may occur. There may also be the related symptom of **echolalia** or the purposeless repetition of speech, as seen in autism (American Psychiatric Association, 2000).

- **Melancholic features** concern the lack of interest or pleasure in almost any activity including those deemed pleasurable, which is sometimes found in depressive episodes. With this specifier, mood may not even change when in receipt of good news and these features are present at the start of the episode.

- **Atypical features** are recorded when the full criteria for the most recent episode are not met or if only specific symptoms are met for a 2-week period.

- In cases of severe episodes 'with **psychotic features**', there are delusions or hallucinations, the latter being mostly auditory. **Mood-congruent** delusions fit with the mood, such as being responsible for disasters, the world ending or bodily decay, whereas **mood-incongruent** delusions may more closely resemble the criteria for delusions in schizophrenia, such as persecutory delusions or their thoughts being open to the public (American Psychiatric Association, 2000). This is usually incorporated into the *DSM* coding with severity of symptoms and remission status.

- Postpartum onset is specified for any episode if it begins up to 4 weeks after childbirth, and it may include psychotic features. This is often a confusing time for a new mother, coping with chores and their feelings towards the child. Hormone changes at this time may relate to the onset of mood disorder (Harris, 1996; Ross, Murray and Steiner, 2005). Mood disturbance may be hidden as a result of guilt and fear, especially if the mother has negative feelings towards the child. Relatives and even clinicians may also be reluctant to acknowledge disorder at this time, thinking that it is simply a matter of the mother adjusting to her new circumstances. This type of mood disorder is also referred to as **postnatal depression** or, incorporating a slightly broader timeframe, **perinatal depression**. Risk of harm to the infant due to severe negative rumination or delusional ideation needs to be balanced against concerns for the mother's adjustment. Up to half of women who suffer this condition will have recurrences with following births and many will suffer comorbid anxiety or panic. Postpartum depression needs to be differentiated from the very common 'baby blues', with the latter only lasting a week or so and having less impact on functioning (American Psychiatric Association, 2000). There is a relationship between sleep problems and postpartum mood disorders, which requires more objective evaluation but may produce a useful intervention.

■ **Seasonal pattern** is specified when symptoms occur and remit in association with the seasons of the year. This subtype, also known as **seasonal affective disorder**, is dealt with in more detail in the next section.

Seasonal affective disorder

Seasonal affective disorder is the term applied to mood disorder listed under the *DSM-IV-TR* specifiers as 'with seasonal pattern'. This form is usually diagnosed in recurrent episodes of mood disorder if depressive episodes regularly start late in the year, as winter sets in and daylight shortens, ending in spring (Rosenthal et al., 1984). However, although less common, it can be the onset of summer which co-occurs with depressive episodes, somewhat confounding a simplistic, reactive explanation. For diagnosis, this pattern has to recur for 2 years without any intervening episodes that are 'out of season'. Seasonal pattern is mostly found in major depression and bipolar II disorders (American Psychiatric Association, 2000).

There may also be additional **hibernation**-type symptoms such as hypersomnia, carbohydrate food craving, lack of energy and weight gain. The temptation to jump to the evolutionary conclusion that the behaviour resembles a process of hibernation seen in some animals should be countered by the reversed season cases. It is more common in females and the young, and when living in the higher latitudes, although there may be other factors affecting the timing of episodes (see Barbini et al., 1995). Daylight length and intensity on awakening does appear to influence seasonally timed symptoms (Rosenthal et al., 1984). This provides a means of treatment in reversing the effective day length by the use of artificial daylight in the mornings, including the simulation of dawn at an earlier time of the natural day (Golden et al., 2005). This treatment is surprisingly effective in many cases, including some of non-seasonal depression (Golden et al., 2005; Rosenthal et al., 1984).

Most of us feel depressed by the onset of wintry weather, but for those with seasonal affective disorder this reaches clinical levels.
Source: Pearson Online Database.

Self-test questions

■ What is meant by a mixed mood episode?
■ What distinguishes cyclothymic disorder from other mood disorders?
■ What are the personal dangers of manic episodes?
■ How do unipolar and bipolar disorders differ with regard to genetics?
■ What is meant by 'seasonal affective disorder'?
■ What does the postpartum specifier imply?
■ Why might hypomania be considered desirable by some sufferers?

Case study

Bipolar I disorder

Jean's husband Ken was becoming tired and somewhat irritated with her increasing talkativeness, and they had argued more fiercely than ever before. Jean had switched channels on the TV all night, as she was checking what was happening on the other sides and at one point was following four programmes at the same time. Two days later Jean kept Ken awake till 2 a.m. with her plans for a new career in design, and at 5 a.m. Ken was woken by the sound of Jean 'spring cleaning'. Ken had never seen such enthusiasm or energy in anyone before. During the following days, Jean slept less and talked more, and Ken began to find notepaper all around the house covered with what seemed to be a cross between poetry and a shopping list. Jean claimed that these were plans for her college work, though some were to be adapted for her 'new book'. Ken was somewhat shocked at this, but was horrified to find out that their bank account had been emptied and all their savings 'invested' in two university courses, a computer, 12 new outfits and various magazine subscriptions for Jean's 'new career'.

Ken's initial fears that Jean might be too ambitious for a man like him were beginning to turn to anger. He no longer viewed Jean as the high-flying career girl, but as an overconfident adolescent creating chaos. When he confronted her, Jean gibbered wildly, pointing to the lyrics on a music CD in her hand. 'Don't you see? It's all in the Jack Durham lyrics . . . the world, we're rich . . . it will . . . I'll be worth millions . . . the Prime Minister knows all about me.' Ken's anger turned to tears as he realised that behind Jean's wide eyes was illness, and he sought emergency help from his GP. Within 2 months Jean's mood had been stabilised by medication and she returned home from hospital to Ken, who still could not believe he had ignored her symptoms for so long and felt apprehensive for their future should Jean's moods become extreme again.

Aetiology and treatment of mood disorders

Aetiology

Although there is clearly a diathesis for both unipolar and bipolar mood disorders, genetic factors are more influential in bipolar disorder (Griez et al., 2005). Thus, genetic studies are confounded by there being related but differing genetic factors contributing to bipolar and unipolar mood disorders. This is reinforced by a parent with unipolar disorder tending not to have bipolar offspring, but 'bipolar families' tend to have both disorders in their descendants with paradoxically more unipolar than bipolar offspring. Early linkage studies have implicated a dominant gene on the eleventh chromosome for bipolar disorder, but only in a specific population (see Mann, 1989). The greater genetic component for bipolar disorder also indicates that non-genetic factors have a greater part in the origin of unipolar depression, thus accounting for its greater incidence. This leaves greater scope for environmental

and cognitive behavioural factors in unipolar depression, and these influences are consequently utilised as interventions (see Griez et al., 2005).

For major depressive disorder, sufficient studies are accumulating to permit meta-analysis of data from **linkage studies** and studies identifying gene–environment interactions in the near future. Candidate items appear to be **neurotoxic** and **neuroprotective** processes in major depressive disorder (Levinson, 2006). There is genetic overlap between major depressive disorder and the personality trait of neuroticism, which may indicate some overlap in molecular processes. These investigations will add to more established connections between **polymorphisms** in the serotonin transporter promotion area linked to bipolar disorder (Levinson, 2006).

Structural neuroimaging studies have repeatedly revealed a decrease in white matter and periventricular hypersensitivities in the neurophysiology of mood disorder (Soares and Mann, 2003). In unipolar depression, consistent deficits are found in frontal lobe, cerebellar, caudate and putamen functioning (Mann, 2002). Cortical inefficiency and reduced connectivity of prefrontal regions with the limbic area have also been found in magnetic resonance imaging studies (Haldane and Frangou, 2006). These functional changes seem partly reversible following remission; however, some of these deficits remain and may be independent of the illness or treatment, perhaps indicating a causal role (Haldane and Frangou, 2006). These studies have also attempted to find differentiating factors associated with subdiagnoses such as bipolar type I and bipolar type II disorders. Abnormalities of the **anterior limbic region** may also be important in the more specific aetiology of bipolar disorder, again with a focus on the **prefrontal modulation** of these areas (Strakowski, DelBello and Adler, 2005). In seeking aetiological correlates, it is important to separate those abnormalities that predate the illness from others, such as abnormalities of the **cerebellar vermis**, that may be a consequence of the repeated episodes of the disorder (Strakowski, DelBello and Adler, 2005).

In terms of neurochemistry, **hormonal factors** clearly have a causal role in **premenstrual** and **postpartum** types of depression (Ross, Murray and Steiner, 2005), but whether the raised **cortisol** levels found in other forms of depression are a cause or consequence of the episode is difficult to resolve (see Griez et al., 2005). The same difficulty exists in determining if the levels of **dopamine**, **serotonin** and **noradrenaline**, which are raised in mania and lowered in depression, are causing the mood change, which is referred to as the monoamine hypothesis of depression, or if these raised levels are simply one consequence of another process. However, noradrenaline levels are lowered by learned helplessness and raised by treatments such as ECT (Seligman, 1992). Beyond the simple monoamine hypothesis, Alt et al. (2006) have used animal studies to identify the role of a type of **glutamate** receptor, **α-amino-3-hydroxy-5-methyl-4-isoxazoleproprionic acid** (AMPA). Potentiation of these receptors has been found to correlate with anti-depressant efficiency (Alt et al., 2006). Other animal studies have revealed that the blocking of glutamate uptake by **glia** (see Chapter 3) produces mood-related reduction of social exploration and disruption of circadian rhythms (Lee et al., 2007). This disruption has been linked to the abnormalities in glia in the postmortem brains of mood-disordered patients, to implicate glia, specifically **astrocytes**, to neuronal function in mood (Lee et al., 2007).

Early behavioural theorists such as Ferster have examined the self-reinforcing nature of depression. Inactivity leads to a lack of reinforcement for positive, or even any behaviour, which leads to a spiral of inactivity, with sufferers attempting fewer actions each day. This would, of course, lead to a progressively greater drop in reinforcement. For those such as Lewinson, Youngren and Grosscup (1979), a lack of positive social reinforcement alone can lead to

depression and, in a similar tautological relationship to that of Ferster, produces fewer behaviours that anticipate social reward. Within this learning process, sympathy given for the plight of the depressed individual is seen merely to reinforce depressive behaviour. There is thus **secondary gain** for displaying depressive behaviour. These assumptions regarding reinforcement and depression would suggest an ethically challengeable treatment in which reinforcement is given for activity not depressive behaviour.

The behavioural approach, **system dysregulation** explanation of bipolar disorder implies that, subsequent to high levels of reward or frustration, it takes longer for bipolar patients to recover to previous levels of behavioural approach system activity. This explanation has been subject to difficulties of measurement and other limitations, but has been expanded to incorporate other factors in a revised version by Urosevic et al. (2008). A further behavioural approach is that of **learned helplessness**, which has been developed into an intervention aimed at reversing the process termed **learned effectiveness** (see the Focus box).

Cognitive explanations of depression show similarities to the learned helplessness approach, in that persistent negative expectations and assumptions have self-fulfilling effects in perpetuating failure and hopelessness (Beck, 1976). The negative cognitive expectations also lead to a failure to reality-test such predictions and consequently decreased activity. There is a known cognitive bias towards negative emotional stimuli in the emotional information processing of depressed individuals. This has been verified in terms of neural activity increasing to sad face images and decreasing to happy stimuli in neuroimaging studies (Leppanen, 2006).

Environmental events such as the loss of a loved one or the success of one's sports team can precipitate significant depression or elation. However, such events do not usually account for the persistence of the extreme moods seen in mood disorders. As with schizophrenia, cumulative **life events** and **expressed emotion** (see Chapter 18) also increase the chance of episodes of mood disorder (see Vaughn and Leff, 1976a; 1976b). Geographical latitude and seasonality both determine length of daylight, which seems to influence **seasonal affective disorder**, or mood disorder with a seasonal pattern (see the previous section).

Cultural factors can influence the expression of mood symptoms. For example, Chinese individuals present more physical complaints (somatisation) and fewer emotional symptoms (dysphoria). The aetiology of mood disorder is often confounded by its comorbidity with alcoholism and personality disorders.

Focus

Learned helplessness

Martin Seligman was responsible for the important concept of learned helplessness and latterly became an exponent of positive psychology.
Source: University of Pennsylvania.

Martin Seligman (1972) considered the concept of **learned helplessness** in terms of learning contingencies or, more specifically, learning that one is unable to control significant events in one's life. In 1975, Seligman reported on a number of studies indicating that learned helplessness can produce a form of depressed state. Seligman (1975) drew on earlier studies using dogs escaping from an electric shock in a shuttle box to identify the behavioural and inferred biological mechanisms leading to helplessness. He found that if the animals underwent uncontrollable shock in a harness prior to their being placed in the shuttle box, they failed even to attempt to escape the shock by jumping over a partial barrier. Instead, the dog would adopt a defeated posture and passively accept the foot-shocks, even on subsequent trials. The animal's demeanour seemed also to suggest a depressed state. In contrast, the dogs that did not first suffer the non-contingent shock had little difficulty in learning to escape the foot-shock in the shuttle box. The experimental animals had learned something in the pre-shock stage. They had learned that they were helpless to prevent the shocks (Seligman, 1975).

Subsequent analyses of opportunist studies of humans cumulatively indicated that this lack of control over events led to higher levels of depressed mood in these populations, justifying the previous generalisation made from animal studies (e.g. Maier and Seligman, 1976). Ill health and even mortality appeared to be raised in situations where personal control over significant events was low or lost (Seligman, 1975). An example of this was the observation by Ferrari (1962) of the increased mortality amongst elderly patients placed in an overly caring institutional regime with a consequent reduction in self-care. Seligman (1975) further cites anecdotal human and experimental animal evidence of death resulting from protracted situations of helplessness resulting in hopelessness. Seligman also drew on evidence that this learning can result from single experiences such as being assaulted, and then rapidly generalised, which resulted in failure to tackle tasks, inactivity and **dysphoric** (depression and anxiety) symptoms. These consequences have already been discussed in Chapter 12 amongst the symptoms of **post-traumatic stress disorder**.

Roth and Kubal (1974) used a milder experimental analogue of inescapable punishment in the form of insoluble problems with human participants. Those receiving insoluble problems prior to soluble ones

Focus continued

made more errors and were more frustrated when attempting the latter. This experimental group also demonstrated increasing helplessness in the face of soluble tasks, which were seen as increasingly significant failures. In humans, the mere belief that an event is controllable can reduce helplessness, even if the event is not in fact under their control (Seligman, 1975). This latter finding may converge with the production of **superstitious behaviour** by **non-contingent reward**: for example, where the carrying of lucky charms leads to overly optimistic risk taking, as in a gambler's belief that he or she can beat fixed probabilities.

This form of the learned helplessness phenomenon may also account for the paradoxical levels of depression and suicide in spoilt or privileged teenagers (Seligman, 1975). These young people also have a sense that they lack control over significant events, in that they are **unconditionally rewarded** regardless of their actions. Thus, the link between meaningful effort or achievement and reward is broken, leading to higher levels of boredom, frustration and depression. A similar explanation for paradoxical dysphoria in the famous can be realised when successful celebrities are rewarded for who they are and not what they do or achieve. Further to this, those who manage to achieve their lifetime supreme goal, such as climbing Mount Everest, often feel a low mood some time later and lack the motivation to achieve in another area, feeling they have nothing left to attain.

Biological correlates of learned helplessness have been investigated in animal models of the behaviour induced by inescapable shock. Seligman (1992) refers to the **catecholamine hypothesis** for depression in assuming a lowering of the neurotransmitters **dopamine**, **noradrenaline** and **serotonin**, with the assumption that helplessness may contribute to a similar imbalance. Weiss, Glazer and Pohorecky (1974) found a reduction of noradrenaline in animals with induced helplessness. Kadamian et al. (2005) have shown that learned helplessness is reduced where there are moderate levels of **corticosterone**, and that the behaviour is more pronounced where there are high or very low levels – a U-shaped learned helplessness response to levels of the substance. Thus, manipulation of adrenal steroids can influence the learned helplessness response at least in terms of inescapable shock (Kadamian et al., 2005).

Following the verification of other aspects of learned helplessness by Maier and Seligman (1976), limitations to the model were subsequently proposed. Abramson, Seligman and Teasdale (1978) linked the attributions made to contingencies and outcomes as being significant in the development of learned helplessness. However, there has been the criticism of this reformulation that unless the exact circumstances of the attribution can be specified, the model remains tautological in its predictions (Dintzer and Wortman, 1978). Further to this, the concept of hopelessness was introduced into the model of 'depression resulting from learned helplessness' (Abramson, Metalsky and Alloy, 1989).

Interventions for depression also seem to help reduce learned helplessness. For example, Dodworth (1971) managed to reduce helplessness in experimental dogs by the use of electroconvulsive shock. Therapy for humans drawn from the learned helplessness model would be to encourage **learned effectiveness**. This can be achieved by having clients carry out achievable and preferably rewarding tasks until this success becomes self-perpetuating (see Seligman, 1992). Thus, the original learning that the client is helpless in controlling events is superseded by further learning that they are effective in this important aspect of their lives.

Treatments

Although **learned effectiveness** has already been mentioned above, the major therapies used for mood disorders are generally accepted as **pharmacological**, **electroconvulsive** (ECT) and **cognitive behavioural therapies** (CBTs) with combinations of drug and CBT producing synergistic effects (Young and Ferrier, 2006). In addition to these, **circadian rhythm** manipulation and the use of synthetic daylight have shown to be effective in many cases (Golden et al., 2005). There have also been some improvements in the methods of evaluating those **interpersonal therapy** interventions that have shown some benefits (Young and Ferrier, 2006). Treatments for unipolar and bipolar disorders differ, in probable relation to differing aetiologies, as referred to above. Depression within bipolar disorders tends to be a problematic area with regard to treatment (Young and Ferrier, 2006).

Both the main pharmaceutical treatments for depression, the **tricyclic anti-depressants** and **monoamine oxidase inhibitors**, were discovered by accident in the 1950s. One tricyclic, **chlorpromazine**, became the leading anti-psychotic, whereas **imipramine** lacked this effect but worked as an anti-depressant (Leonard, 1997). For many years, the most widely effective clinical drugs for depression have been these tricyclic anti-depressants such as **amitriptyline** (trade name Tryptizol), but numerous side-effects can make them unsuitable for some (see Griez et al., 2005). Side-effects such as dry mouth, weight gain, sexual difficulties, constipation, blurred vision and headaches can lead patients to discontinue medication prior to therapeutic effect, and others, such as hypertension and stroke likelihood, can present a real risk of mortality. **Loferpramine** is a newer tricyclic anti-depressant that lacks many of the side-effects of previous tricyclics, such as the anti-cholinergic, anti-histaminic and cardiotoxic effects, as well as being safer in overdose (Leonard, 1997).

Atypical anti-depressants such as **monoamine oxidase inhibitors** (MAOIs), such as **tranylcyonize**, can also have serious effects beyond their anti-depressive ones. Side-effects are quite severe with the MAOIs, such as dry mouth, nausea, dizziness, headaches and potentially fatal hypertension. These side-effects for first-generation MAOIs restricted their use to a few atypical cases, giving way to the tricyclics (Leonard, 1997).

Other 'second-generation' or atypical anti-depressants include the **noradrenaline reuptake inhibitors** such as **oxaprotiline,** and as with many anti-depressants they may be used or in combination or augmentation roles (Nemeroff, 2007). It is worth noting that prior to the late 1960s noradrenaline (and dopamine) uptake inhibitors in the form of amphetamines were widely used for depression and obesity. Cocaine also has its main effect via this mechanism (Leonard, 1997). Although the inhibition of amine uptake is the overt action of many anti-depressants, this may not be their clinically useful effect as the amine increase is immediate, but therapeutic effects take days or weeks. It is probable that the defective neurotransmitter transport and receptors in patients are readapted to ameliorate symptoms (Leonard, 1997).

Towards the end of the twentieth century, anti-depressants such as **fluoxetine** (branded as Prozac) were introduced. This was one of the first **selective serotonin reuptake inhibitors** (SSRIs) to be used in the context of mood disorder. Fluoxetine and other drugs from this same family, such as **fluvoxamine** and **sertraline,** have become very widely used due to their apparent lack of such obvious side-effects and low potential for overdose. However, **zimelidine** had to be withdrawn due to side-effects and there is controversy over the widespread long-term use of SSRIs (Leonard, 1997). Only some 15 years after more insidious problems emerged with the long-term use of **benzodiazepines** for anxiety, the enthusiasm for widespread SSRIs use seemed a little hasty. **Benzodiazepine**

analogues have been synthesised, such as **alprazolam**, and these are used as second-generation anti-depressants.

Side-effects for SSRIs include dry mouth, fatigue, gastrointestinal complaints, insomnia, headaches, nervousness and dizziness. A further side-effect that is controversial is suicidality, although many authors list this as a routine side-effect (e.g. Kring et al., 2007). Reports of some patients receiving SSRIs having committed suicide after commencement of therapy have been taken from anecdotal status to the point where many assume there is evidence of a general effect. Both SSRIs and tricyclics can intensify existing suicidal ideation, but their therapeutic value currently outweighs this risk and there is no other clear relationship between SSRIs and suicide (Cipriani, Barbui and Geddes, 2005). Other fears over the increasing use of SSRIs, such as a potential link with breast cancer, also seem to have been unfounded. Quite simply, there is a risk of suicide in the early phases of all pharmacological treatments due to slight edginess prior to therapeutic effect, which is why many clinicians opt for the more immediate effects of **electroconvulsive therapy** (ECT).

Where there are difficulties over pharmacological therapy, a course of ECT can often prove very effective (see Chapter 3), especially if the patient is older or, as above, if there is risk of suicide. Modern ECT is a far more controlled process than its earlier incarnations, with voltage around 100 volts and applied unilaterally to the dominant hemisphere only to the point of seizure, which is repeated for 2 to 4 weeks with two or three treatments per week (see Griez et al., 2005). ECT is considered a biological treatment with its effects assumed to be similar to some medications in altering neurotransmitter function, such as that of noradrenaline. Although via a currently unknown mechanism, the therapeutic effects of ECT can be a great relief in the cases where medication fails to have an immediate effect. It is still the most effective treatment for severe depression with psychotic features (Sackheim and Lisanby, 2001). ECT has also been considered effective, safe and much underutilised for mixed bipolar states (Valenti et al., 2008).

Transcranial magnetic stimulation and **vagus nerve stimulation** are relatively new biologically based procedures that have received research attention in recent years with a theoretical rationale for their effects (Sackheim and Lisanby, 2001; Young and Ferrier, 2006). However, transcranial nerve stimulation, vagus nerve stimulation and the older **deep-brain stimulation** have yet to be evaluated sufficiently to displace the use of ECT in such contexts (Valenti et al., 2008).

Other biological treatments have used naturally found ingredients but with identifiable ingredients or pathways. Deficits on omega-3 fatty acids have been found to contribute to mood disorders, although treatment with dietary changes or supplements needs careful evaluation. There is also a need to determine which of the fatty acids is most therapeutically beneficial, **eicosapentaenoic** or **docosahexaenoic acid** (Parker et al., 2006). **St John's wort** is a plant source for the **hypericum extract WS 5570**. This extract has been tried in major depression and its effects compared with the SSRI **paroxetine** in randomised controlled trials. St John's wort was found to be as effective as the SSRI and was better tolerated by those receiving it, which can be important in terms of compliance (Szegedi et al., 2005). **Cannabinoid** systems within the body have also been targeted in research on mood disorders, based on many years of observations on the effects of cannabis (Tzavara and Witkin, 2008). These treatments are less appropriate for bipolar disorder, although ECT is still used in both major forms of mood disorder.

Severe manic episodes may be initially treated with **neuroleptics** in the short term to reduce high levels of mania and any psychotic features. The ongoing reduction of both manic or hypomanic episodes as well as those of depression provided something of a challenge for treatment approaches (see Griez et al., 2005). It was therefore opportune that a further accidental pharmacological discovery during the mid-twentieth century was **lithium**, a salt used in beer manufacture in the past and once a major ingredient in the drink 7-Up. The recognition of its remarkable ability to slow the labile nature of emotions in bipolar disorders came quite late in its commercial use, and as a common salt it was not patented by any drug manufacturer for this purpose. With little commercial incentive to promote lithium, the spread of the treatment was slow and clinicians had to rely on peer information (Holmes, 1998). Due to its toxic nature at certain levels, lithium in the bloodstream of patients has to be monitored, which is often a problem when it is taken as maintenance medication (see Griez et al., 2005). A meta-analysis of trials has shown lithium to be clearly effective as a maintenance medication for bipolar disorders. However, the effect is more pronounced for the prevention of manic episodes and somewhat equivocal in preventing depressive episodes (Geddes et al., 2004).

Anti-convulsants such as **carbamazepine** are increasingly used to substitute for lithium, and **clozapine** may help if the others are inappropriate (Calabrese et al., 1996). Although these drugs were originally developed for **epilepsy**, anti-epileptic agents such as **valporate** or **lamotrigine** in addition to carbamazapine have proven very useful with lithium non-responders and those for whom the side-effects of lithium are problematic (Weitzer et al., 2006). Anti-epileptics are also useful, in that lithium is less effective in combating depressive episodes than manic ones, and they have been used as maintenance treatment for bipolar patients, not just to address episodes (Weitzer et al., 2006). However, in a systematic review of randomised trials, Cipriani et al. (2005) found lithium to be effective in the prevention of suicide, self-harm and all causes of death of mood disorder patients, in comparison with anti-convulsants and other mood medications. More than half of current bipolar patients receive polypharmacy with mood stabilisation via anti-epileptics and atypical anti-psychotics (Weitzer et al., 2006).

Depressive patients stabilised by physical treatments should always be considered for **cognitive behavioural therapy** (CBT) regardless of the short-term costs involved (see Chapter 2). A longer-term view tends to confirm that patients are more likely to sustain improvements if they are able to maintain the cognitive behavioural skills learned through therapy (Hawton et al., 1989). **Aaron Beck** has helped popularise these methods of reducing the negative thinking patterns that often maintain inactivity and dysphoric symptoms. CBT has been found to have a large effect size in a meta-analysis of evaluations, and has been found superior to anti-depressants in many studies (Butler et al., 2006). As mentioned above, CBT tends to impart skills to the patient that are taken forward in contrast to the more palliative effects of pharmacological treatments. It is this enduring effect, whereby risk is reduced beyond the termination of treatment, that emphasises the need for CBT to be considered at least in addition to, if not as a replacement for, drug interventions (Hollon, Stewart and Strunk, 2006).

A variant of the cognitive approach, **mindfulness training**, borrows from Eastern meditation practices and can be a component in **dialectical behaviour therapy**. Mindfulness involves bringing the client's attention to the internal and external experiences occurring in the present moment, in an objective non-judgemental way. In this a mood-disordered individual may become more aware of how negative judgements are attached to experiences and entities; however, empirical support for this approach needs expansion (see Baer, 2003). Taking a more executive and process-based view, Wells (2009) has described the importance of **metacognitive therapy** as an approach in addressing depression (and anxiety). Based on CBT, the metacognitive approach targets how thought is controlled at executive level and addresses why negative thoughts are allowed to be processed, rather than simply eliminating each negative element. Although CBT is less effective for depression in bipolar disorder, engaging bipolar patients in CBT can be essential for long-term compliance with medication and to address suicidal thinking, which may not be overtly evident during more manic phases.

It would be easy from a theoretical point of view to advocate combined therapy of CBT with pharmacological treatment in every case of mood disorder. However, this may not always be justified in terms of the extra costs, except in the case of bipolar disorder, and its value can vary depending on chronicity and type of disorder (Otto, Smits and Reese, 2006). CBT applied to mood disorders, particularly depression, has stood for some time as one of the salient successes for the application of psychology in the real world, and merits far more coverage than is possible in this text. Readers are therefore recommended to seek dedicated texts on the application of CBT to mood disorder.

Across studies, the use of **artificial daylight** in the mornings, including dawn simulation, has a significant effect not only on depressive symptoms in seasonal affective disorder but also in non-seasonal depression (Golden et al., 2005). At a sufficient intensity, this type of light therapy has a similar effect size to that of anti-depressant medication, although more rigorous studies are needed in such evaluations (Golden et al., 2005). However, training and use of light therapy has tended to be marginalised (Golden et al., 2005), perhaps because the nature of the approach resembles that of an 'alternative therapy'. Given the non-invasive aspects of this treatment and the low cost in terms of clinicians' time, more mainstream attention is needed to evaluate fully not only its efficiency, but also its further potential.

Focus

Mood and sleep

As referred to in the main text, there are aspects of **circadian rhythms** that influence mood. In Chapter 3, one of the few effects of the full moon in promoting activity was hypothesised to be due to greater light levels reducing sleep and producing a fractionally more manic mood. As a simple application of this principle, an intervention to reduce depressive symptoms and increase activity would be for the individual to miss one or more nights' sleep. This technique has significantly improved mood in studies of sleep deprivation and can now be considered a form of intervention in mood disorder (Kundermann et al., 2008).

It has further been suggested that circadian rhythm abnormalities are actually fundamental to the development of mood disorders, and this applies not just to seasonal affective disorder, but also to major depression and bipolar disorders as well (McClung, 2007). Some treatments for mood disorder are thought to operate by resetting the circadian clock. Those such as sleep deprivation, light therapy (see below) and melatonin treatments do this directly, whereas it is only hypothesised that anti-depressants or mood stabilisers are effective by this means (McClung, 2007). McClung (2007) has drawn attention to the need to

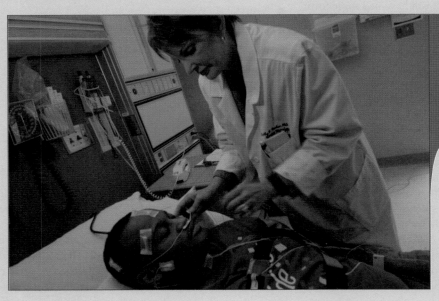

Centres for Sleep Study and other research centres are beginning to unravel the importance of sleep and its rhythms to our psychological functioning.
Source: Corbis/Karen Kasmauski.

Focus continued

coordinate recent findings at the genetic and molecular level that the genes, brain areas and neurotransmitters associated with mood regulation and circadian rhythms may be sufficiently linked as to provide further inroads into mood disorders.

One area where sleep pattern and mood have had an established relationship that has been subject to research is the case of seasonal affective disorder (Rosenthal et al., 1984). Here circadian rhythms, daylight length and daylight intensity appear to precipitate sufficient symptoms to provide the criteria for this disorder (described in a previous section). Treatments based on artificially extending daylight influence **melatonin** levels, which more globally alters the sleep cycle **circadian rhythm** for that individual (Rosenthal et al., 1984). This is effective in cases not only of seasonal affective disorder but also of other mood disorders (Golden et al., 2005; Lewy, Ahmed and Sack, 1995). Suppression of melatonin is one aim of the precise timing of intense light in this therapeutic approach. In doing this the effective photoperiod is extended, but this effect is not achieved with dim light. Research has spread to the use of this form of light therapy with other disorders such as **eating disorders** and **Alzheimer's disorder** (Golden et al., 2005).

Although sleep occurs as a routine part of our lives, this belies the dramatic effects that occur in the neurophysiology of the body in this process. Relative levels of the very neurotransmitters associated with mood disorders, dopamine, noradrenaline and serotonin, amongst others, alter in producing sleep cycles (Ross, Murray and Steiner, 2005). The various cyles within sleep stages one to four and REM are crucial for both quality of sleep and returning to wakefulness rested, and these stages are influenced by circadian factors including the timing of sleep. In depression, REM onset has a short latency, which is increased by antidepressants and other therapies (Ross, Murray and Steiner, 2005). Pregnancy also disturbs aspects of sleep, and sleep patterns during pregnancy and in the postpartum period when related mood disorders occur may be intrinsically linked to the development of these postpartum disorders. Thus, sleep-based interventions have also been applied in the case of **perinatal mood disorders** (Ross, Murray and Steiner, 2005).

Suicide and self-harm

Some 90 per cent of the 877,000 individuals known to have committed suicide in 2002 will have had some form of psychiatric disorder (Mann et al., 2005); 60 per cent of suicides will have been directly attributed to mood disorders and many others will have been indirectly attributed to mood problems (Bertolote et al., 2003). Thus, one of the ever-present and serious dangers when treating the mood-disordered patient is that they may kill themselves, and this risk needs to be considered when weighing the costs and benefits of some treatments, especially drugs and ECT. Studies in the late twentieth century revealed that men were four times more likely to commit suicide than women, who were three times more likely to *attempt* suicide (Arias et al., 2003; Holmes, 1998). Attempted or **parasuicide** can be an appeal for attention or an expression of anger, and is often revealed in terms of clues such as a phone call to enable detection. Successful suicide usually involves hopelessness and uses highly lethal methods, with no possibility of detection (Bertolote et al., 2003). Some of the main precursors and precipitating factors for suicide can be seen in Table 17.2. Paradoxically, bipolar patients

Table 17.2 Precursors and precipitating factors in suicide

Precursors for suicidal ideation
■ Stressful life events
■ Mood or other psychiatric disorder
Precipitating factors for suicide acts
■ Impulsivity
■ Hopelessness and/or pessimism
■ Access to lethal means
■ Imitation

Source: adapted from Mann (2002).

may commit suicide during more manic phases when they are more active and decisive, and perhaps able to take such drastic measures to avoid the onset of depression.

The social burden of mood disorder also includes the considerable social impact of suicide (Bertolote et al., 2003; Gotlib and Hammen, 1992). The effects of suicide on friends and family are far greater than those of sudden death by accident or illness. Many family members feel

Suicide prevention in mood disorder has often focused on preventing access to methods such as potent medicines.
Source: Pearson Online Database.

anger at the way the individual has opted out of perceived obligations to others, often after a long period of the mood-disordered individual receiving support from those close to them (Gotlib and Hammen, 1992). This resentment is then coupled with guilt both for their resentfulness and for peceived failure to prevent or avert the suicide act. Proximity to the suicide and close emotional ties can lead to acute or post-traumatic reactions.

Suicide behaviour is thought to be state dependent and avoidable when associated with mood disorder (Zoltan, 2007). Mixed mood may be a very important precursor to suicide. This is more critical in depression where bipolar disorder is not suspected and only anti-depressant monotherapy is used without prophylactic mood stabilisers. The clinical outcome may then be untempered aggressive or self-destructive behaviour as a result of an induced or undetected manic response (Zoltan, 2007). Suicide risk has a genetic component, which is evident in the increased risk in familial relatedness and twin study comparisons (Baldessarini and Hennen, 2004). In an overview, Baldessarini and Hennen (2004) report that complex interractions of environmental with inheritable risk alongside protective and vulnerability factors for psychiatric illness and suicide are suspected. However, the mechanisms of gene expression are still not entirely clear, even though many studies have investigated the genes for serotinergic neurotransmission (Baldessarini and Hennen, 2004).

Suicide is significantly reduced by maintenance use of lithium across studies (beyond placebo and other potential confounding factors) (Cipriani et al., 2005). It also serves to reduce self-harm and appears to reduce the risk of death from non-suicide causes (Cipriani et al., 2005). In a review, Mann et al. (2005) examined aspects of educating physicians in the recognition and treatment of depression that may prevent suicides. They found restricting access to lethal means of suicide to produce a significant reduction, but other aspects would need more evidence of effectiveness. For suicide prevention programmes to reduce actual rates, it is important to ascertain which components are effective in a context of limited resources (Mann et al., 2005).

Positive by-products of mood disorder

Many brilliant creators and performers throughout history have been tragically lost to suicide due to mood disorder; in fact, far more than chance would dictate. Painter **Vincent van Gough** and the writer **Sylvia Plath** both committed suicide in their thirties, each cutting short their lives overshadowed by mood disorder (Andreasen, 2008). This alternate side of mood dysfunction is the creative excess that seems to most markedly accompany some bipolar patients, especially during hypomanic states. However, many successful individuals also suffered severe bipolar disorder or even unipolar depression, with their mood disturbance allowing them, in the words of a sufferer, 'to experience life intensely as if with one layer of skin missing'. Herself a sufferer, Kay Redfield Jamison was amazed

Table 17.3 Examples of successful individuals who have suffered mood episodes

Hans C. Andersen	Vincent van Gough	John Ruskin
Honore de Balzac	Graham Greene	Robert Schumann
Ludwig von Beethoven	Tony Hancock	Mary Shelley
Winston Churchill	Ernest Hemingway	Phil Spector
John Cleese	Henrik Ibsen	Robert Lewis Stevenson
Rosemary Clooney	John Keats	Ben Stiller
Kurt Cobain	Vivien Leigh	Sting
Jean C. van Damme	Abraham Lincoln	Ilyich Tchaikovsky
Charles Darwin	Robert Lowell	Leo Tolstoy
Charles Dickens	Martin Luther	David Foster Wallace
Carrie Fisher	Florence Nightingale	Tennessee Williams
Scott Fitzgerald	Sylvia Plath	Virginia Woolf
Connie Frances	Marcel Proust	Boris Yeltsin
Sigmund Freud	Theodore Roosevelt	Emile Zola
Stephen Fry	Axl Rose	

to find the incidence of mood disorder to be many times that of the general population among famous writers and artists, and seemed to be almost obligatory among poets (Jamison, 1989; 1992). Many of the studies in this area use successful creative individuals without an equivalent control group. In a controlled study, Santosa et al. (2007) found bipolar patients from a non-successful sample to have significantly higher creativity scores than controls, but this effect was not found for unipolar depression sufferers.

Perhaps many very successful comedians such as Tony Hancock and John Cleese found a way to harness their unwanted mood problems to their advantage. A story told in Tony Hancock's honour possibly expresses this dilemma well. A depressed man visits his GP many times, finally pleading, 'Doctor, I am desperate, so depressed, I cannot go on.' The doctor, who had tried everything, paused and then began speaking excitedly. 'Go and see Grock the famous comedian; he is so funny he can make a statue laugh. Go and see him and he will lift your spirits.' The man lifted his eyes and replied, 'But doctor, I *am* Grock . . .'.

Medication can be a difficult issue for some with hypomanic episodes, as lithium can be seen as damping down their creativity as well as helping their disorder. However, Andreasen (2008) cites the case of Robert Lowell, notable American poet of the twentieth century, who had severe bipolar disorder. In this case, she points out that Lowell was more productive when medicated than he was when left to the full wrath of his disorder. A study by one of the professionals who pioneered the widespread use of lithium

Winston Churchill managed to utilise aspects of his mood disorder to be a remarkable orator.
Source: Pearson Online Database.

Focus

Why the genes for mood disorder survive

Given the damaging effects on relationships, one would think that many genetically transmitted disorders such as mood disorders would decrease in incidence across generations, as their dysfunctional traits would not be favoured by **natural selection** evolutionary terms. As this is clearly not the case, the genetics of mood must be in some way conferring reproductive advantage on those carrying these destructive genes.

The individual success of those industrious and creative hypomanic individuals may not be enough to account for this, but it does point to a solution for this enigma. In the same manner that milder cases of mood disturbance can confer some creative advantages, those who only express the genes for traits such as industriousness, leadership and innovation may have marked evolutionary advantages without any episodes of mood disorder. Yet these successful individuals may still pass on the same genes that in other combinations are debilitating. This may also be the case with the genetics of other disorders making their elimination by **genetic counselling** problematic.

treatment, found creativity to be enhanced by medication in half of the sample, and the remainder to be equally divided into those where it was detrimental and those where it made no noticeable difference (Schou, 1979).

The link between depression and creativity has often been more difficult to conceptualise than that of hypomania. Some have thought of it as an 'incubation period' with experiences registering and developing for later expression (Andreasen, 2008). Writers such as Robert Lowell have considered depression a time when the mass of creative material produced in more manic episodes is sifted and distilled to leave only the better elements. Verhaeghen, Joormann and Khan (2005) consider the link to be one of the symptoms of depression, that of self-reflective rumination. This aspect of rumination has been found to relate to self-rated creative interests and measured creative fluency, originality and elaboration (Verhaeghen, Joormann and Khan, 2005).

As referred to earlier, other observations tend to confirm that we as humans prefer optimistic views of the future, and of ourselves, even if these are unrealistic (Healy and Moore, 2007). The fact that some depressed individuals have more realistic views of their future than the normal population (Sanna, 1998; Abele and Hermer, 1993) would extend the paradoxical nature of our 'positive spin bias', in that as a population we would tend to reject negative views no matter how accurate they might be. This could account for the world recession in 2008 coming as a surprise to many financially knowledgeable individuals.

Although plagued with imprecise definitions of what is creative, the relationship of creativity to mood disorder is an important area of research. On the one hand, there is the all too frequent tragic loss of gifted individuals to suicide, and on the other, this is one of the few positive aspects of disorder that can be reported with confidence across studies (Andreasen, 2008). Much information regarding mental disorders is negative, pointing to any associated genetic inheritance being something to engineer out of population gene pools. However, evidence from mood disorders would indicate that creative elements could turn out to be the baby lost with the bathwater of disabilities if mood disturbance genes were ever to be eliminated.

Forensic implications

In 1961 suicide ceased being a crime in England and Wales, but it has continued to be a forensic issue into the twenty-first century. Kring et al. (2007) record how the bodies of victims of suicide had their hearts pierced when buried as late as the nineteenth century, emphasising that society showed anger and suspicion towards these unfortunate individuals, perhaps more so than any feelings of mourning or sympathy. Suicidal individuals are often considered dangerous in that, having no concern for their own life, they might be thought to be even less concerned with the lives of others (see the Focus box).

As noted in earlier sections, manic individuals are prone to risk taking, which can involve financial risks and spending sprees incurring high levels of debt (Prins, 2005; American Psychiatric Association, 2000). Argumentativeness and overconfidence can also lead to assault and sexual risk taking, although mood disorder is very rare in comparison to other psychiatric disorders amongst samples of offenders such as sexual murderers

Focus

Harm to others from suicide

Death and injury to others during suicides in mood disorder is a forensic issue. This is dramatically illustrated by the contemporary terrorist threat of **suicide bombers,** who may be vulnerable mood sufferers, under threat to their families, or deluded by radical religious or political propaganda, but are a very potent weapon in modern terrorism. Harm to others can be less premeditated or even quite accidental, as many falls from buildings or car crashes that involve those motivated to suicide also kill and injure innocent bystanders.

In the case of depression with psychotic features, the possibility of one-sided suicide pacts has to be a consideration in the regular assessment of those monitored for suicidal ideation. A one-sided suicide pact is a situation wherein a suicidal individual, often driven by delusional hopelessness and pessimism, may decide that their family or others would also be better off dead than face a threatening or doomed existence (Prins, 2005; Gotlib and Hammen, 1992). Such multiple deaths within a family, though tragic in themselves, can have further social and legal repercussions, and as with all cases of individual suicide, they will require extensive forensic, medical and social service investigative resources.

(Hill et al., 2007). However, Fazel et al. (2008) found higher levels of depression and lower levels of bipolar disorder amongst adolescent offenders than in other populations in a European sample. Amongst an adult Australian prison population, mood disorders were found to affect around 20 per cent of inmates (Butler et al., 2005). Mood disorder in the form of depression is often imperceptibly slow in onset and may be missed by monitoring prison staff (Prins, 2005).

There have been suspicions that the dangers of impulsive or suicidal behaviour in mood disorders may be exacerbated by SSRI medication, but in a large-scale Swedish study, no increased risk was found (Isacsson, Holmgren and Ahlner, 2005). However, anabolic androgenic steroid abuse can lead to suicide in the presence of mood problems, and can exacerbate mood symptoms, particularly in the case of irritability, leading to a patient being at risk to self and others via aggression and assault (Papazisis et al., 2007). Comorbidity of substance use and bipolar disorder has been a long-standing and frequent problem, which produces increased forensic involvement and a greatly confounded clinical picture (Sonne, Brady and Morton, 1994). The association of major depression with alcohol use disorders is long standing, and current evidence suggests this is true of some other substance use disorders (Currie et al., 2005). Substance use in major depressive disorder increases the risk of suicidal thinking (Currie et al., 2005).

Petry, Stinson and Grant (2005) found that 49.6 per cent of a sample of **compulsive gamblers** had some form of mood disorder and 73.2 per cent of that sample had alcohol problems. Such comorbidities present a difficult picture in terms of clinical forensic processing, in that complete assessment will tend to follow clinical attention via gambling debt or financial crimes. However, treatment of one disorder may simplify treatment of the comorbid conditions. Mood disorders within a prison population become more vulnerable to suicide in a forensic population where suicide levels are often seen as unacceptably high, though means of intervention have been considered in detail by international studies (e.g. Daigle et al., 2007).

Clinical issues

Those with a clinical remit share some of the forensic issues in mood disorders, including the problem of suicide. The specific procedures when suicidal intent is suspected can be quite dramatic, especially where dependants may be involved. Mood-disordered patients may be compulsorily detained if they are thought to be at high risk of suicide, which is often in the context of a suicide attempt but may follow remarks made during routine assessment or psychological treatment. Thus, care and caution are needed in following such procedures, as erring in either direction can place the clinician and patient in a difficult position or even at risk (Goldberg, Benjamin and Creed, 1994). Prediction of suicide risk is very difficult in a clinical context, but this is further confounded by the fact that the vast majority of those who attempt suicide never complete on future occasions, and almost no completed suicides have ever made a previous attempt (Angst, 2008). There is also a need for long-term evaluations of the differential efficacy of the various pharmacological treatments on suicide rates in mood disorder (Angst, 2008).

Some medical conditions can be closely associated with either depression or mania and would be designated **mood disorder due to general medical condition**. One long-standing example worthy of clinical attention is that of stroke patients where left anterior lesions of the brain tend to produce more severe depression (Robinson et al., 1984). However, those with lesions of the right anterior region were found to be more unduly cheerful, as compared with patients with right posterior lesions who were more depressed (Robinson et al., 1984). Thus, specific brain areas or neurochemistry may be more indicative than the actual medical condition.

The large overlap (up to 90 per cent) between bipolar disorder and **attention-deficit hyperactivity disorder** (ADHD) has not as yet been fully supported by longitudinal studies showing progression from ADHD in childhood to adult onset of bipolar disorder. Some have considered that a subgroup of bipolar patients with severe symptoms exists with early ADHD comorbidity (Angst, 2008). What can also confound such sequential relationships is that bipolar disorder itself is considered to be underdiagnosed. This is generally as a result of overdiagnosis of major depressive disorder, with consequences for estimating the relative financial and social burden of the different mood disorders (Angst, 2008). Improved screening tools can help in this, in addition to the early detection of high-risk individuals, such as those with rapid cycling mixed mood. More recent measures for the widest grouping of hypo-mania, such as the **Hypomania Checklist** (Angst et al., 2005) may redress the diagnostic imbalance. The HCL has recently been revised as **HCL-32 R-1** (Angst, 2008).

Treatment guidelines for mood disorders should enable research into effectiveness and standardisation of procedures during everyday clinical practice. The sequencing of monotherapy (one type of therapy) and combination therapy, and its careful evaluation, can be a more complex task in practice. Guidelines have been found to vary, and this has been exacerbated by guidelines becoming rapidly outdated. This is particularly the case with bipolar disorder, where there is a need to adopt newer recommendations more rapidly (Fountoulakis et al., 2005). A specific point within this is the use of anti-depressants for bipolar depression, and some research has sanctioned this procedure as effective in the short term. However, research that is more recent has not supported this effectiveness and there is the additional increased risk of episode switching as a result of the medication (Cipriani and Geddes, 2008). Thus, more rapid updating of guidelines needs to be accepted in clinical departments (Fountoulakis et al., 2005).

As with personality disorders, there is a move towards the use of dimensional systems for recording symptoms of depression, mania and hypomania. This would circumvent the constant need to revise the criteria for diagnostic categories that are found to have a short shelf-life in use (Angst, 2008).

Self-test questions

- What is the relationship of 'learned helplessness' to depression?
- In what ways do the treatments for unipolar and bipolar depression differ?
- Discuss the implications of suicide for treatment of mood disorder.
- How could the positive aspects of hypomanic states account for the survival of 'bipolar genes'?
- What is meant by a one-sided suicide pact?
- How might the overdiagnosis of major mood disorder be addressed?

Chapter summary

Melancholia and **mania**, now known as **mood disorders**, have a very long history and involve episodes of **major depression, mania**, a **mixed mood** and **hypomania**. Various combinations of these states differentiate the types of mood disorder. **Major (unipolar) depression** and its milder chronic form, **dysthymia**, do not involve mania. **Bipolar I** disorder always involves mania, usually cycling with other states; **bipolar II** disorder alternates hypomania with depression; and **cyclothymia** involves a milder, chronic form of this cycle without meeting the criteria for mania or major depression. **Specifiers** identify specific features of these mood disorders including: **catatonic, melancholic, postpartum** and **seasonal pattern**. The latter is also called **seasonal affective disorder** and has led to the recognition that **sleep cycles** and **daylight length** are important in forms of depression.

There is a genetic component to these disorders, which is greater for the bipolar form with its probable expression through neurotransmission. Cognitive, behavioural and environmental factors such as daylight are also implicated. **Learned helplessness** provides cognitive behavioural explanation that accounts for anomalies in health and mortality as well as depression. Treatments can be **drugs, ECT** and **cognitive therapy**, with some cases responding to **daylight levels** and 'learned effectiveness'. The knowledge base for the interrelationship of mood and **sleep cycles** may inform future treatments. **Suicide risk** is an important consideration in mood disorder and the tragic loss of very **creative** individuals in this way is sometimes a feature of mood disorder. However, industriousness can be a **positive by-product** of mood disorder inheritance. **Suicide risk** is a theme in both **forensic** and **clinical** aspects of mood disorders, as is the difficulty of managing both manic and depressive symptoms without precipitating the switching of episodes.

Suggested essay questions

- Discuss the distinctions between unipolar and bipolar disorders in terms of symptoms, aetiology and treatment.
- Evaluate the treatments for unipolar depression.
- Discuss the relationship between mood disorder and creativity.

Further reading

Overview texts

Angst, J. (2008) Bipolar disorder: Methodological problems and future perspectives. *Dialogues in Clinical Neuroscience*, 10, 251–55.

Cipriani, A., Barbui, C., and Geddes, J. R. (2005) Suicide, depression and antidepressants. *British Medical Journal*, 330(7488), 373–4.

Golden, R., Gaynes, B., Ekstrom, D., Hamer, R., Jacobsen, F., Suppes, T., Wisner, K., and Nemeroff, C. (2005) The efficacy of light therapy in the trteatment of mood disorders: A review and meta-analysis of the evidence. *American Journal of Psychiatry*, 162(4), 656–62.

Gotlib, I., and Hammen, C. (2002) *Handbook of depression*. London: Guilford Press.

Hawton, K., and van Heeringen, K. (2002) *The international handbook of suicide and attempted suicide*. Chichester: Wiley.

Moore, R., and Garland, A. (2003) *Cognitive therapy for chronic and persistent depression*. Chichester: Wiley.

Power, M. J. (2005) *Mood disorders: Handbook of science and practice*. Chichester: Wiley.

Seligman, M. (1992) *Helplessness*. New York: Freeman.

Strakowski, S. M., DelBello, M. P., and Adler, C. M. (2005) The functional neuroanatomy of bipolar disorder: A review of neuroimaging findings. *Molecular Psychiatry*, 10, 105–16.

Specific and more critical texts

Andreasen, N. C. (2008) The relationship between creativity and mood disorders. *Dialogues in Clinical Neuroscience*, 10, 251–5.

Cohen, L., and Nonacs, R. (2005) *Mood and anxiety disorders during pregnancy and postpartum.* New York: American Psychiatric Publishing.

Geddes, J., Burgess, S., Hawton, K., Jamison, K., and Goodwin, G. (2004) Long term lithium therapy for bipolar disorder: Systematic review and meta-analysis of randomised controlled trials. *American Journal of Psychiatry,* **161**, 217–22.

Griez, E. J. L., Faravelli, C., Nutt, D., and Zohar, J. (2005) *Mood disorders: Clinical management and research issues.* Chichester: Wiley.

Henden, J. (2008) *Preventing suicide: The solution-focussed approach.* Chichester: Wiley.

Wells, A. (2009) *Metacognitive therapy for anxiety and depression.* London: Guilford Press.

Visit **www.pearsoned.co.uk/davidholmes** for a range of resources to support study. Test yourself with multiple choice questions and access a bank of over 100 videos that will bring the topics to life. Video coverage for this chapter includes an interview and 'day in the life' with Feliziano who suffers from bipolar disorder, an interview with Everett who suffers from Major Depression, and a discussion about deliberate self-harm with Sarah.

CHAPTER 18 Schizophrenia

- Overview
- Case study
- The origins of the term 'schizophrenia'
- Phenomenology of schizophrenia
- Subgrouping of the syndrome
- Incidence, onset, course and outcome(s) of schizophrenia
- Aetiology of schizophrenia
- Treatment and management of schizophrenia
- Schizophrenia boundaries and other psychotic disorders
- Clinical issues
- Forensic implications
- Critical evaluation
- Chapter summary

 Hear about gene studies and schizophrenia. This is one of several videos that explore issues and disorders relevant to this chapter at **www.pearsoned.co.uk/davidholmes.**

John Forbes Nash, Jr, and schizophrenia

John Forbes Nash Jr, former Princeton professor and mathematician, received the Nobel prize in economics in 1994. He was 66 years old and had struggled with severe mental illness for at least 35 years. His life story was depicted (not entirely accurately) in the 2001 Hollywood film *A Beautiful Mind*.

His considerable intellect was recognised early on, and both his sister and mother were aware that he was an odd, isolated child with few friends and a propensity to spend many hours alone in his room conducting scientific experiments. He received his PhD in 1950 aged just 22 from Princeton and then joined the Mathematics faculty at MIT and entered a productive period of his life, writing numerous articles for scientific journals, teaching and developing his academic profile. His reputation for eccentricity also grew during this decade, and he became renowned for approaching mathematical problems from unusual and counterintuitive directions.

His mental state first noticeably deteriorated in 1959 as his first child was about to be born, when his then-wife had him admitted involuntarily to McLean Hospital (a mental institution). He received a diagnosis of paranoid schizophrenia and depression. Apart from his increasingly erratic behaviour, his main symptoms at that time seemed to involve paranoid delusions about being followed, threatened and manipulated by 'enemy forces'. He resigned his MIT post on discharge, and spent the next decade in and out of hospital, receiving numerous different treatments (including various medications and insulin coma therapy) for his mental illness, in which auditory hallucinations had become a prominent feature. His last involuntary admission occurred in 1970.

Thereafter, although still troubled by symptoms, he managed to stay out of hospital, despite refusing to take any further medications. He also returned to research and received several prestigious prizes for his work. He is now retired, and his younger son Johnny is also a mathematician, who suffers from schizophrenia.

John Forbes Nash Jnr.
Source: Corbis/Reuters.

The name 'schizophrenia' conjures up images of psychological disturbance involving split or multiple personalities, psychopathic tendencies, and bouts of delirious euphoric madness. In fact, none of these is a hallmark feature of schizophrenia, which is generally conceptualised as a severe and enduring form of functional psychosis. A psychotic disorder (a psychosis), as distinct from a neurotic one (the terms are rather old-fashioned and can be dated back to Freud's era), implies both impaired insight and recurrent or ongoing loss of contact with reality – a sort of *mental slippage* in which the individual is entirely aware neither of their immediate situation, nor of their own mental state. The prefix 'functional' is nowadays taken to indicate that the psychosis is related to functional changes in cognitive and emotional processes in the brain, as opposed to structural (organic) changes that clearly underpin, for example, Huntington's or Alzheimer's diseases.

Yet the level of insight of someone with schizophrenia will certainly vary over time, as will their degree of contact with reality (illustrated in the case of John Nash above). Equally, there can be considerable variation amongst different sufferers. One may be lucid, coherent; able to hold down a job and generally function well, albeit usually with the aid of appropriate medications. Another may be cognitively impaired, incoherent and unable to look after themselves despite a veritable *barrage* of medications. As you can see, although the hallmark features of schizophrenia have yet to be identified, the vagaries of the condition are already apparent. Add into the pot the observations that there is no single core feature of schizophrenia, nor any symptom that is entirely unique to it, and you may begin to feel that the disorder is too poorly defined to merit serious attention.

Of course, these arguments have been mustered by critics of orthodox psychiatry in support of alternative, so-called anti- or critical-psychiatry viewpoints, some of which merit closer scrutiny (e.g. Bentall, 2007) than others (e.g. Szasz, 1971). This issue is revisited later in this chapter. Nevertheless, it is probably important to realise at this stage that the majority of clinicians, researchers and psychologists take a more orthodox position regarding the nature of schizophrenia (or at least of functional psychosis), and this perspective will be reflected in the structure and organisation of the present chapter.

Case study
First episode schizophrenia

Simon was 18, and had just started his second term at college, when things began to go awry. He had always been a nervous and reserved boy with few mates, and had never had a steady girlfriend. He also professed strong religious views. He had scraped into college and seemed, for a while, to be coming out of his shell – which gave his parents a degree of encouragement that he was finally living up to their early expectations.

Unfortunately, Simon did not share his parents' optimism. He had had a strange sense of unease for several weeks, but he could not put his finger on what might be causing it. He began to think that his life was being influenced by what he called 'bad karma'. On one occasion, for instance, he thought he had been short-changed at the corner shop. But when he challenged the shopkeeper, he felt the man's reaction was totally disproportionate and even feared for his own safety.

Strange things also seemed to be happening when he was alone in his room, particularly at night. On more than one occasion, he had thought he'd seen some sort of visual apparition briefly to one side of his field of view, but it disappeared when he turned to look directly at it. It reminded him of the story of Joan of Arc, and the thought crossed his mind briefly that the vision was some sort of sign specifically for him.

One weekend when his parents had gone away and he was alone in the house, he nevertheless thought he could hear them arguing in the hall downstairs. They seemed to be discussing him, listing all his bad points and debating whether or not to 'boot' him out of the house. Next morning, having slept only fitfully the night before, he heard some other voices that seemed to be whispering to him from behind his computer monitor. He thought one might be that of the shopkeeper with whom he had had the earlier run-in. He seemed to be saying he was 'gunning for him' and would 'get him' when he least expected it. His parents would not be back until the next day, so he decided to try to make his bedroom secure against any threat by pushing heavy furniture up against the bedroom door and window. He also removed the bulb from his bedroom light and tied some rope from the bedroom door handle to the bed frame as a further precautionary measure. But later that evening he heard whispering voices again. One was that of the shopkeeper threatening to 'do him in' again. The other was his father's voice telling him he must repent all his sins if he wanted to 'survive the night'. Simon grabbed his crucifix in one hand and Bible in the other, and began chanting incoherent prayers in the pitch dark, waiting for 'the inevitable' to happen.

When his parents returned the next day, they heard his (by now) mumbled prayers as soon as they went upstairs. Simon would not open his bedroom door, and eventually, fearing that he might have taken a drug overdose (though he had not used recreational drugs at all since experiencing an adverse reaction to some cannabis on the one and only occasion he had ever used it), they broke down the door. Simon appeared to be in a trance, rocking back and forth mumbling to himself, still clutching the Bible and crucifix. He did not notice his parents entering the room.

They called out the doctor, who on seeing the state Simon was in immediately called for an ambulance, and Simon was admitted, initially as a voluntary patient, on to an acute psychiatric ward at their local hospital. Once in hospital, Simon's mood changed somewhat and he insisted on being allowed to leave in order to pay the shopkeeper a visit to beat him up in retaliation for the harm he had done to him. His doctors were sufficiently convinced of the seriousness of these threats that they decided he should be 'held' in hospital (as an involuntary patient) under a section of the Mental Health Act. Their initial assessment was that Simon had had an acute psychotic breakdown, and that his symptoms suggested schizophrenia. He was prescribed some anti-psychotic drugs to address the symptoms and some anxiolytic drugs to help him sleep.

Over the next 2 weeks, Simon's symptoms abated. He did not accept the doctor's view that he had a mental illness, interpreting everything that had happened to him as a reaction to a combination of malicious conspiracy and religious experience. Nevertheless, he was content to keep taking his medicines, which gave him confidence and boosted his 'good karma'. He was discharged from hospital into the care of a community support team, who visited him on a regular basis to check on his mental health and to confirm that he was taking his meds as prescribed. Six months later, Simon had returned to college to resume his studies. He still took his anti-psychotic medications on a regular basis, although he and his doctor had agreed to reduce the dose with a view to stopping them altogether at some point in the future.

The origins of the term 'schizophrenia'

An understanding of the current state of play may be informed by a brief look at the origins of the term, which actually takes us back to the origins of contemporary psychiatry and the work of Emil Kraepelin and Eugen Bleuler about 100 years ago. Kraepelin was renowned for his observations, descriptions and recordings of the features of illness displayed by his insane patients over extended periods of time. Longitudinal methods are taken for granted nowadays, but until Kraepelin's work, no one really had the time or interest to conduct detailed follow-ups of asylum inmates. Nevertheless, this approach gradually brought him to the realisation that three forms of insanity hitherto regarded as distinct entities shared many similarities when viewed over the long term (see Table 18.1). Catatonia involved prominent disturbances to movement and posture; hebephrenia involved disturbances to emotion and thinking with early onset; and dementia paranoides featured prominent hallucinations and delusions. All seemed to start in late adolescence or early adulthood. There was an absence of marked mood changes and, following

Table 18.1 Prominent forms of 'madness' in the late 1800s

Disorder	Age of onset	Features	Course and outcome
Hebephrenia	Late adolescence or early adulthood	Disordered thinking, flat affect, incongruity, silly bizarre behaviour	Insidious onset leading to severe deterioration over a fluctuating course.
Catatonia	Adulthood	Multiple motor and postural disturbances; stupor or excitement; stereotypy and agitation	Cyclical. Episodes may be well separated by periods of remission. Recovery possible, though deteriorating course more likely.
Dementia paranoides	Late adolescence or early adulthood	Early prodromal delusional mood, then pronounced hallucinations and delusions	Stable endpoint marked by mild to moderate deterioration. Chronic hallucinations/delusions may persist.

a lengthy period of waxing and waning symptoms, a common poor outcome which he described as mental enfeeblement (Kraepelin, 1896). He suggested that these forms of insanity were, in effect, different manifestations of the same underlying pathology, to which he gave the name dementia praecox to emphasise early onset and deteriorating course with no recovery.

Bleuler (1926) agreed with the Kraepelin's general perspective but felt that his term was inappropriate on two counts: firstly, the disorder did not always have an early onset, and secondly, the outcome was not always poor. He coined the term we now use, although in recognition of the diverse manifestations of this form of madness, he referred to 'a group of schizophrenias' rather than a single entity. Schizophrenia – literally, 'split' or 'cleaved' mind – was adopted to signify the loosening of associative threads, either between different trains of thought or between thoughts and emotions, which Bleuler regarded as fundamental to the disturbances in mental processing at the root of the illness.

Quite when (or why) the plural was dropped is a matter of debate, but it was almost certainly a mistake as clinicians have spent much time since trying to clarify the clinical picture of schizophrenia by describing its subclassifications, subtypes and subdivisions. Nevertheless, it is instructive to note that contemporary descriptions of schizophrenia still employ many of the terms that Kraepelin and Bleuler introduced or used. For example, the *DSM* classification system still carries criteria for differential diagnoses of hebephrenic, catatonic, paranoid and simple (also called undifferentiated) schizophrenia, the last being an addition of Bleuler's to encompass inexorable intellectual decline, withdrawal and asociality but only fleeting overlaid symptoms. Another contemporary subtyping of symptoms into a positive and negative profile (reviewed later) can also be traced back to Bleuler's concept of accessory and fundamental symptom clusters.

A century later, schizophrenia remains in most people's minds a devastating and enduring disorder. Most of the signs, symptoms and features described by Kraepelin and Bleuler are still seen at initial assessment, though modern medications, which many people will take for the rest of their lives having once been prescribed them, damp down some of these or even eliminate them completely. Catatonia is perhaps an exception. Early descriptions included muscular rigidity as a core feature, but this is seen rarely these days, giving rise to a view that perhaps it should not have been amalgamated into dementia praecox/schizophrenia after all, and may have a distinct organic aetiology (Northoff, 2002; Boyle, 2002). On the other hand, less exotic forms of motor disturbance are common in schizophrenia and are reviewed later.

Outcome remains variable and difficult to predict at initial onset, and some of the relevant longitudinal studies that have addressed this issue are reviewed later in this chapter. However, recent studies have shown that a relatively small proportion of patients diagnosed with schizophrenia progress down the Kraepelinian route to 'mental enfeeblement' (Harvey et al., 1999; Carpenter et al., 1999), especially if they begin treatment early and have good social support (Fenton, Blyler and Heinnsen, 1997). On the other hand, a similarly small proportion make a full recovery, despite the widespread availability of a second generation of medications intended to replace the traditional (and much maligned) original **anti-psychotics** (Lewis and Leiberman, 2008).

In the absence of a uniquely defined symptomology, specific cause or common pathology, schizophrenia does not qualify, in medical terms, as a disease. Rather, it is viewed as a **syndrome**; a constellation of signs and symptoms that wax and wane, reappearing in different combinations at different times. It is an episodic condition with periods of stability punctuated by symptomatic flare-ups, which tend to become less frequent and less intense over time (several years). Patients with full insight will often describe their recovery as good but not complete: that is, they feel they never quite get back to how they were before they became ill. Psychological assessments of such individuals tend to bear this out (Blanchard and Neale, 1994).

So in summary, the outlook for someone newly diagnosed with schizophrenia is neither as bleak as many people imagine nor indeed as it was in Kraepelin's era. However, complete recovery is also rare (Mason et al., 1994), although a combination of appropriate medication and effective social support can certainly provide a good quality of life for many patients. This may be all well and good for people in the developed world, but the same cannot be said for an individual with schizophrenia elsewhere, and it has been estimated that there are at least 10 million people in the world at any one time with untreated schizophrenia.

Phenomenology of schizophrenia

If the idea of schizophrenia as a syndrome rather than a specific disease is appropriate, there could be many (or at least several) signs and symptoms of the disorder, and it is unlikely that a single individual will experience all of them. *DSM-IV* criteria for schizophrenia stipulate that only two of a core group of symptoms need be present

(albeit for a certain period of time and at a particular intensity), in order for a diagnosis to be made (see the Focus box). Current *ICD* criteria require one absolutely clear-cut symptom from a core group of four, or at least two from a further five less specific features, which should have been present for most of the preceding month. A clinical impression of schizophrenia sufficient for treatment to be initiated may, in fact, be based on even flimsier evidence. Simple schizophrenia, as mentioned earlier, may entail none of the hallmark features listed below, but instead may be diagnosed on the basis of cognitive decline in the context of psychosis, as characterised at the start of this chapter (i.e. poor insight and loss of contact with reality).

For the time being, the most important signs and symptoms of schizophrenia will be reviewed. Initially, each will be considered individually, but it is important to realise that most patients will experience several of these in the course of their illness. Indeed, a number of studies employing factor or cluster analysis statistical techniques have shown that particular signs and symptoms tend to coalesce into groupings, and these will be considered in the subsequent section.

Schizophrenia can, in reality, impact on almost all aspects of psychological functioning. However, for descriptive purposes it is helpful to consider separately signs and symptoms related to thinking and perception, those related to volition, motivation and emotion, and those linked to movement.

Focus

Key *DSM-IV* criteria for a diagnosis of schizophrenia

Criterion A symptoms: Two (or more) of the following, each present for a significant portion of time during a 1-month period (or less if successfully treated):

1. delusions
2. hallucinations
3. disorganised speech (e.g. frequent derailment or incoherence)
4. grossly disorganised or catatonic behaviour
5. negative symptoms (i.e. affective flattening, alogia or avolition)

Note: Only one Criterion A symptom is required if delusions are bizarre or hallucinations consist of a voice keeping up a running commentary on the person's behaviour or thoughts, or two or more voices conversing with each other.

Social/occupational dysfunction: For a significant portion of the time since the onset of the disturbance, one or more major areas of functioning such as work, interpersonal relations and self-care are markedly below the level achieved prior to the onset.

Duration: Continuous signs of the disturbance persist for at least 6 months. This 6-month period must include at least 1 month of symptoms (or less if successfully treated) that meet Criterion A.

Exclusion criteria: Schizoaffective disorder and mood disorder with psychotic features have been ruled out. The disturbance is not due to the direct physiological effects of a substance (e.g. a drug of abuse, a medication) or a general medical condition.

Focus

The science (and art) of diagnosing psychotic disorders: an interview with Dr Richard Drake, senior lecturer and honorary consultant psychiatrist, University of Manchester

JS   So Richard, in an initial clinical interview, what kinds of pointers are you looking for that would lean you towards a diagnosis of psychosis?

RD   The early phase of the interview would be just asking open questions to try and find out what was going on from X's point of view, and matching this information against any other information I've been given. As the interview progresses I would be trying to pick on things that seemed important to X and that struck me as unusual or significant, and I'd ask him/her to elaborate or clarify comments suggestive of hallucinations, delusions or other unusual ideas, or thinking patterns indicative of psychosis. I'd also want to know how long things have been going on, how intensely the symptoms were experienced, and for what proportion of time in a given day or week.

JS   If, during your interview, you are beginning to form an idea that the person may have schizophrenia, are there any 'probes' that you routinely ask to try and elicit further evidence of that diagnosis?

RD   Yes, the PSE (present state examination) interview has some useful probes, so if I'm wondering if somebody has some type of psychosis then I might ask them: 'Has anything unusual been going on?' or 'if they have seen or heard any funny things'. If I'm going a bit further down that line I might ask X whether s/he thinks other people having been taking an unusual interest in them . . . and so on.

JS   I imagine some of the readers of this book will regard the *DSM* criteria as essentially artificial: I'm talking about the rule for schizophrenia being that an individual must have at least two core symptoms most of the time for the last 1-month period and have been 'ill' in some way for at least 6 months . . . I suppose the question I am trying to get to is what happens if they don't have two clear symptoms; they only have one or maybe one and a bit . . . ?

RD   Then, they don't have *DSM* schizophrenia, but they would fit somewhere else within the diagnostic framework. For example, they may have an acute psychotic disorder or an acknowledged high-risk mental state, but not meet clear criteria for a full blown functional psychosis.

JS   Are there any particular symptoms that you regard as 'first rank' (whether or not they are included in Schneider's eight or nine symptoms) for a diagnosis?

RD   Well, there is one symptom that is said to be almost pathognomonic of schizophrenia, whose presence alone would pretty much make the diagnosis for you because it doesn't seem to occur in any other illnesses. Unhelpfully, the symptom in question, delusional perception, is also fantastically rare! It involves a perfectly normal perception that suddenly comes to have an intense personal significance for the individual, leading to a delusional conclusion about it that is in no obvious way connected to it. So seeing the cupboard door ajar leads X to conclude that he is the new king of Spain . . .

As for Schneider's 'first rank' schizophrenia symptoms, they clearly have some value because they occur more frequently in schizophrenia than (for example) mania, but even so, more than 50 per cent of people with schizophrenia do not evince one during clinical interview. Additionally, extremely bizarre persistent delusions (not a 'first rank' symptom) seem to me almost always a 'marker' of schizophrenia.

Finally, although lots of people 'believe' in UFOs, repeated reference to detailed interactions with aliens and extra-terrestrials also rings alarm bells for me, and sets me thinking about possible schizophrenia rather than another psychotic condition.

JS   Anti-psychotic medications continue to play a central role in the management of schizophrenia, don't they?

RD   Yes, although there are exceptions. For example, someone with a first episode psychosis wouldn't necessarily be given medications, in order to see if the psychosis clears up. Similarly, if an individual has an acute psychotic disorder, we might simply wait for the psychosis to resolve. But if we are reasonably sure that X has a severe and enduring mental illness, anti-psychotic medications would be prescribed right away.

JS   I'm interested to know if you have ever found it difficult to evaluate culturally 'normal' (but, from your point of view, unusual) behaviour or thinking

Focus continued

in, for example, an individual from an ethnic minority grouping, and whether this has led you to misinterpret that behaviour as being so odd that it merits consideration of a psychotic feature . . .

RD   I can think of specific examples where people have described what seem to me to be unusual beliefs, but which are widespread within their culture. This would very much influence my thinking about whether a particular comment was indicative of an unusual but culturally 'normal' belief, or evidence of delusory thinking. For example, people in the UK may talk about aliens, but I would be more concerned if someone from rural Nigeria who had only recently entered this country started talking about aliens. Conversely, descriptions of witchcraft and supernatural magic processes from this individual would ring fewer alarm bells than if they had been uttered by an indigenous white UK resident. Cultural influences actually cut both ways.

JS   What about a devoutly religious individual who said that when they went to bed at night they saw the Lord dancing at the end of their bed and heard the voices of angels emanating from behind the curtains . . . ?

RD   Frankly, it would depend on what else was going on. For instance, if someone has isolated hallucinations and there appears to be no other abnormality of their mental state, I wouldn't be rushing forward to diagnose a psychosis, or at least a formal functional psychosis like schizophrenia anyway. It's more about likelihoods, context and an overall picture . . . In practice, the way one manages these things is quite nuanced by probability, so you might say X may have a psychosis but I can't be sure, so I'll manage that individual in a different way to Y, who I am more or less certain has an unambiguous psychotic disorder. Finally, remember that none of this is 'written in stone', so care plans can be revised as new information about an individual's mental state come to light. Diagnosis is an artificial thing, but it's also a helpful tool for dealing with often complex situations. It has its limitations, but it also has its strengths.

Symptoms affecting thinking and perception

Hallucinations

Hallucinations are perceptions that have no basis in external reality, but which are nevertheless perceived as real. **Auditory hallucinations**, in the form of voices, are most commonly encountered. A person may hear voices discussing them or commenting on their thoughts and actions, often in a derogatory or abusive manner. There may be more than one voice, and these may or may not be identifiable to the patient. Unsurprisingly, the sudden onset of hallucinations is often associated with great anxiety, although occasionally patients describe their voice(s) as helpful or even comforting (Romme et al., 1992). Some patients, for example, converse with or shout back at their voices, while others sit distractedly as if they are listening to them. Auditory hallucinations may also include identifiable noises such as clicks in the head or (for example) the sound of whistling.

Less commonly, hallucinations can involve other modalities, including vision, smell, touch or even taste. Visual hallucinations may take the form of apparitions (as experienced by Simon) or visual forms superimposed on an undifferentiated background, such as seeing faces in clouds or imaginary patterns on wallpaper. Somatic hallucinations may take a variety of forms: an individual may be convinced that a snake is laying eggs in their gut, or that insects are squeezing down the side of their eyeball. A relatively common olfactory hallucination is the reporting of a 'burning smell' akin to a hot electric motor.

Delusions

Delusions are fixed, false beliefs held, despite ample disconfirming evidence, with a seemingly religious zeal. For diagnostic purposes, such beliefs qualify as delusions only if they are not shared by others from the same cultural or educational background. Delusions of persecution are common; the individual might maintain that they are being pursued by secret agents from a foreign country or, as in Simon's case, that a hit-squad intended to do him harm. Delusions of power and greatness (grandiose delusions), or with a religious content, are also frequent and there is often a pronounced pseudo-philosophical theme to these. An individual may, for example, be convinced that an innocuous event (for example, a fuse in a plug 'blowing') has a specific significance for him, such as a message from God to initiate a programme of world salvation. Concerns about the need for mass re-education, or the establishment of inter-planetary government, for example, are not untypical. Often, particularly in established illness, a complex web of delusional ideas is evident, as if the individual has formed one delusion to explain others (or explain other psychotic features, such as auditory hallucinations): *'MI6 are spying on me because I can hear their agents whispering when they think I'm asleep . . .'.*

Disordered thinking

Although almost any aspect of thinking can be affected in schizophrenia, clinicians distinguish between changes to the 'content' of thinking, typically involving the experience of mental processes being interfered with in some way, and 'structural abnormalities' in the thinking process, sometimes called formal thought disorder, and almost always identified from peculiarities in an individual's use of language. Thought interference can take a variety of forms, but a common feature is the impression that one's thoughts are no longer entirely under one's own control. In the case of 'thought insertion', the individual has the sense that thoughts or ideas are, somehow, being planted in their mind. In contrast, patients with 'thought with-drawal' experience their thoughts being abruptly taken (snatched) from their minds. 'Thought block' is the term for the sudden halt to an individual's flow of thoughts: after this, they may describe a complete absence of think-ing for minutes or even hours. 'Thought broadcasting' is the experience that thoughts are radiating out from their mind and can be 'picked up' by other people. Because in each of these instances the individual senses a loss of personal control, the interference is frequently attributed to an outside agency (the secret service, radio waves, or even extra-terrestrials; see Table 18.2(a)).

Formal thought disorder is not common in acute schizophrenia, but may become more established as the illness progresses. It is apparent in a person's speech, which may be hard to follow or understand, may include 'invented words' (neologisms) and may contain grammat-ical anomalies or errors. Derailment was an early term used to describe the tendency to wander off a particular 'train of thought' in a rambling discourse. In the end, the individual may appear to have forgotten the original purpose of what they were trying to say – sometimes called loss of goal. Self-evidently, incoherence is the term for incomprehensible though sometimes grammatically correct speech. Some textbooks refer to this as schizophasia or 'word-salad'. The choice of words may seem, to all intents and purposes, random, or linked by only the flimsiest thread of meaning (see Table18.2(b)). Poverty of content of speech is a fourth characteristic of formal

thought disorder. Although replies to probe questions may be long enough, answers are vague and convey little or no information. Other instances of formal thought dis-order include circumstantiality (unnecessarily convoluted discourse), perseveration (repetition of words or phrases) and stilted speech (ornate or even pompous delivery).

Passivity phenomena (symptoms of alien control)

Some examples of passivity were encountered earlier when considering disordered thinking. The common theme of these symptoms is that one's thoughts or actions are being influenced by an external (and usually malign) force. Some patients can exercise a degree of control over such 'feelings'; others act on them, but claim that the impulse to do so had not been their own. Commonly, patients develop delusional explanations for passivity experiences, involving occult forces, hidden transmitters or telepathy. Such loss of sense of agency can have critical consequences in the forensic setting, especially if, for example, an individual declares his (aggressive) actions as being 'willed' by an external agency (see the case of the 'Yorkshire Ripper' reviewed towards the end of this chapter).

Intellectual impairment

Many people with schizophrenia have difficulties with attention, learning and working (and verbal) memory, and in their ability to plan ahead or make use of infor-mation to change their behaviour – so-called executive functions. In the most extreme cases, their performance on neuropsychological tests that address these cognitive domains is comparable to that of dementia patients (Harvey et al., 1999). Even the most basic items of personal information, such as an individual's date of birth or the names of their parents, may be lost (Crow and Mitchell, 1975). The range, nature and persistence of cognitive deficits in schizophrenia raises important questions for clinicians, as it has become apparent that for some individuals, impaired cognition may have a greater impact on 'quality of life' than the florid psychotic symptoms already listed. For example, the latter can often be controlled by medi-cations, whereas the former tend to prevail regardless of treatments (but see Bark et al., 2003, and our review of cognitive remediation therapy later). Cognitive impair-ments appear to be present for some individuals in the early stages of schizophrenia; indeed they may predate the onset of psychotic symptoms by some time (Niendam et al., 2003). Whether or not there is further deterioration over the course of the illness remains a matter of dispute, but follow-up studies have indicated that their presence early in the illness presages poor outcome.

Table 18.2 Examples of (a) disordered thinking and (b) formal thought disorder in schizophrenia

(a) Disordered thinking (thought interference)	Example
Thought withdrawal	'I used to spend lots of time just day-dreaming about the future. Now my head seems empty and I do not have a single thought worth mentioning'.
Thought block	'I was recalling last summer's holiday when my mind suddenly went completely blank, as if someone had pulled the plug out . . .'
Thought broadcasting	'I suddenly became aware that any private thoughts I might have as I was watching TV could be converted into additional TV signals and beamed around the neighbourhood . . . My thinking became public property.'
Thought insertion	'I seemed to be thinking about what to eat for supper, but these were not my own thoughts; actually I had no interest in eating. They were planted in my mind by the food ministry and the department for agriculture . . .'

(b) Formal thought disorder (changes in language structure/form)	Description/example
Derailment/tangentiality	An answer to a specific question may begin coherently, but soon wander off on other tacks that are only loosely related to the original question. Sometimes, a patient may begin their answer rather obliquely and they may never seem to get any closer to the actual appropriate response to the question.
Loss of goal	This frequently occurs in combination with derailment (above). However, 'the train of thought' is essentially abandoned and at the end of their response, the speaker may seem to have forgotten what they actually wanted to say.
Neologisms	New words or phrases are invented and freely used (as if the listener will understand their meaning). *'It's a nimby thing for cutting back weeds . . .'*
Paraphasias	Words are substituted with phonetically or semantically related words. *'Wait until I have put on my foot-covers [shoes]'*
Incoherence	Essentially, incomprehensible speech. When asked how he was doing, a patient replied, *'Can we re-amalgamate within the cone of the devil's needle to bish the do-gooders on weekend leave?'*
Poverty of content of speech	Despite being of 'normal' length, answers to probe questions are superficial and lack any relevant detail.

Symptoms affecting volition, motivation and emotion

Under this heading are a raft of signs and symptoms which, though commonly seen in schizophrenia, are regarded as having less diagnostic 'relevance' than the symptoms already listed. However, a number of these features coalesce under the heading of **negative symptoms** or, strictly speaking, **negative signs** (Frith, 1992).

Lack of insight

As mentioned earlier, level of insight can fluctuate with the course of illness, but many patients show a reduced awareness of their condition, failing to realise they are mentally unwell or in need of treatment. In extreme cases,

poor insight might lead an individual to the view that their hallucinations, delusions and other symptoms are entirely real. This state of affairs can, of course, have important implications if so-called command hallucinations instruct an individual to do harm either to themselves or to other people.

Lack of drive

Patients often show a lack of drive or initiative and a diminished interest in the outside world. The extent of this varies widely, but in extreme cases an individual may, for instance, not leave their house or even their bed for weeks on end. This feature often goes hand in hand with anhedonia (a lack of enthusiasm in pleasurable pursuits) and asociality (disinterest in engaging in normal social interactions. Lack of **volition** is usually more apparent in the later, chronic, stages of the illness, but can be present early on.

Abnormalities in the expression and understanding of emotion

Many patients with schizophrenia show a range of abnormalities in affect (the expression of emotion), but two forms predominate. On the one hand, displays of emotion may be completely unsuited to a particular situation (inappropriate affect): for example, laughing uncontrollably at someone else's misfortune. On the other, an individual may appear to be emotionally distanced or removed from others (blunted or flat affect). Their emotions seem to be 'dulled' as indicated in their speech and/or facial expression, giving the impression of aloofness or indifference to others.

Recent research has indicated that some patients with schizophrenia also struggle to understand other people's emotions. This would, for example, be apparent in terms of poor facial affect recognition skills. As with poor insight, this too can have important consequences in the forensic setting if an individual misinterprets the intentions of someone else by misreading their facial expression or tone of voice (Craig et al., (2004)).

Mood symptoms

Depressive symptoms may affect up to one-third of patients at any one time, and elation is also occasionally seen. These observations probably help to explain the ongoing and, as yet, unresolved debate about whether or not schizophrenia and **bipolar disorder** are truly distinct entities. Our sense is that the weight of opinion still favours the Kraepelinian distinction, although the boundary can certainly be blurred. As McKenna (2007) rather succinctly puts it: 'the depression and elation seen in schizophrenia does not amount to a full affective syndrome: depression is not accompanied by the biological and other accessory symptoms that define major depression; mania is stripped of its richness, and the hallmark features of distractibility, over-activity and overspending are not seen' (p. 341).

Nevertheless, about one in eight patients who meet diagnostic criteria for schizophrenia also meet the criteria for major affective disorder. The term 'schizoaffective disorder' is used to identify illnesses of this sort, and evidence suggests that people with this condition, whilst experiencing as many episodes of illness as someone diagnosed with schizophrenia, have a more favourable outcome, or are at least less likely to evince the cognitive deterioration often seen in schizophrenia (Harrow et al., 2000). One way of thinking about schizoaffective disorder is that it represents a halfway house between schizophrenia proper and bipolar disorder (Kendell, 1986).

Language abnormalities

As mentioned when reviewing types of thought disorder, the speech of people with schizophrenia may seem illogical, with abrupt or obscure shifts between one theme and the next – a feature referred to by clinicians as 'knight's move thought' (a reference to the unusual move of this chess piece). In rare cases, the speech can be so jumbled as to merit the description of 'word salad'. Patients may also sometimes use neologisms (invented words) to describe concepts of importance to them. Alogia refers to the paucity or complete absence of speech seen in some cases, in which negative symptoms are pre-eminent.

Signs and symptoms related to movement

In characterising dementia praecox, Kraepelin effectively merged the predominantly psychological disorders of hebephrenia and dementia paranoides with catatonia, which has prominent 'motor' features. Although the rigidity and waxy flexibility that characterised catatonia are relatively unusual presentations today, many other forms of motor dysfunction are seen. Indeed, according to Manschreck (1993), over 50 per cent of first episode schizophrenia cases have some identifiable form of movement disorder. Although movement-related abnormalities may be prominent, they seem unrelated to other symptoms, and their relevance to diagnosis is unclear.

Stereotypy and mannerisms

Stereotypies are repetitive but usually irrelevant or inappropriate actions: repeatedly raising and lowering an arm, or continuously seeming to grasp at an imaginary object would be two examples. Rocking, crossing and recrossing legs and rubbing hands would be three more. Stereotypies merge into mannerisms in the context of more complex behaviours: an action such as drinking from a glass might repeatedly be carried out in a theatrical and extravagant manner. An individual may engage in various forms of complex facial grimacing, or appear to have severe facial or bodily **tics**. However, in all cases, the behaviours or actions are purposeless and repetitive, and appear to be enacted with no regard for their possible effects on other people, who may find them embarrassing, intimidating or even threatening. The fact that these are seen in first episode cases is of interest because it indicates that some motor disturbances clearly predate any treatments and are therefore not caused by anti-psychotic medications. Nevertheless, it must be acknowledged that medications can exacerbate underlying motor disturbances, and tardive dyskinesia (to be discussed later) is one such instance.

More complex motor disturbances

These appear to affect volition-to-act as much as the actions themselves. Thus, in rare instances of catatonic stupor, an individual may remain motionless and silent for long periods. In catatonic rigidity, muscular tension is prominent and the person may hold a posture for a considerable period. Waxy flexibility refers to being able to 'mould' a patient into a particular (even uncomfortable) body posture, in which they will remain for several hours. In catatonic excitement an individual may appear hyperactive, engaging in multiple inappropriate and sometimes potentially dangerous activities, such as running about naked, destroying furniture or even assaulting total strangers. Rare though this last feature is, it has obvious ramifications in the forensic setting.

Neurological soft signs

These are a cluster of both motor and sensory-perceptual signs indicative of non-specific neurological dysfunction.

They are usually assessed using a comprehensive test battery such as the Neurological Evaluation Scale (NES; Buchanan and Heinrichs, 1989). Motor signs include, for example, an inability to copy hand/finger movements correctly, or the tendency to make involuntary movements when watching someone else making movements, and the inability to sustain repetitive movements (such as pronation/supination of the hand) for any length of time.

Despite more or less total ignorance regarding the origins of such signs, a series of recent investigations has established fairly convincingly their greater incidence even in first episode, never-treated schizophrenic patients than in other psychiatric and non-psychiatric groups (Scheffer, 2004). Prevalent soft signs early in someone's illness also predict poor outcome in a similar way to negative symptoms, with which they are, in fact, statistically correlated (Bombin, Arango and Buchanan, 2005).

Schneider's first rank symptoms

In the preceding sections, many of the signs and symptoms seen in the syndrome of schizophrenia have been identified and illustrated. Some are more common than others and some seem more fundamental to the disorder than others. Is it possible to identify core symptoms of schizophrenia? Schneider is credited with identifying a group of eight symptoms listed in Table 18.3, which, he believed, best

Table 18.3 Schneider's first rank symptoms

Symptom	Description/example
Audible thoughts	A patient reports hearing his own thoughts as if spoken outside his head, possibly by a third party, or at least an identifiable external source (e.g. from behind the left curtain).
Voices arguing	Two or more distinct external voices are reported, usually discussing or arguing about the patient in an uncomplimentary way.
Thought commentary	The patient describes hearing a running commentary (by an alien voice) of his or her moment-by-moment thoughts, actions or behaviour (which is often derogatory).
Somatic passivity	A patient is convinced that a physical ailment (such as a stomach pain) has been caused by X-rays that have been beamed into them by extra-terrestrials as part of an experiment into pain tolerance.
Made feelings	A patient who may seem depressed and anxious declares themselves 'inwardly well', but explains their demeanour as resulting from telepathic influences emanating from their laptop computer.
Thought insertion, withdrawal or broadcasting	See Table 18.2.
Delusional perception/ primary delusion	An innocuous event/percept suddenly seems to have particular personal significance. For example, the accidental setting of a fire alarm was understood by a patient to be a signal from God to initiate a programme of retraining of all left-handed people to use their right hands.

Source: Sims (2002).

distinguished schizophrenia from other psychotic disorders, and were therefore diagnostically most informative. This cluster of 'first rank' symptoms each represents a blurring of the boundary between self and surrounding world which, in the absence of organic brain disease, he considered a hallmark feature of schizophrenia. The presence of any one of these was deemed sufficient for a diagnosis to be made. In the 50 or more years since Schneider's work, his contributions have certainly influenced the choice of diagnostic criteria used in the various *DSMs* and latterly the *ICDs*. However, there is a consensus that not only are his first rank symptoms too restrictive (by no means all diagnosed cases evince one), but they are actually based on a false premise in that they sometimes occur in other psychotic disorders as well as in schizophrenia (Peralta and Cuesta, 1999; Nordgaard et al., 2008).

Self-test questions

Have another look at the case study of Simon.

- Identify two signs of psychological disturbance preceding the onset of 'first-rank' symptoms.
- Identify one example each of a hallucination and a delusion.
- Identify any examples of disordered thinking.

Subgrouping of the syndrome

The classic subtypes

Operational criteria for the identification of the four subtypes of schizophrenia dating back to Kraepelin and Bleuler can be found in the most recent version of the *DSM*, and it has been argued on this basis that their survival is a testament to their value in the clinical setting. Unfortunately, the diagnostic reliability of these classic subtypes is low and there is considerable symptomatic overlap between them: for example, delusions may be present in all four subtypes. Moreover, they have little to say in terms of optimal treatments or likely outcome.

Surprisingly, there has been relatively little empirical investigation of these classic subtypes. One of the most widely cited reports was by Carpenter et al. (1976), who made use of data collected in the WHO-sponsored Inter-

national Pilot Study of Schizophrenia (IPSS), the original purpose of which was to examine consistency of diagnostic practices in nine different centres around the world. Using the statistical technique of cluster analysis on 600 patients, Carpenter and his colleagues found that four clusters accounted for most patients. The first and second resembled 'paranoid' and 'hebephrenic' (disorganised) subtypes reasonably closely, but the remaining two clusters mapped on to catatonic and simple schizophrenia rather poorly. Subsequent studies have similarly provided more support for the paranoid and hebephrenic subtypes than the others, although Lykouras et al. (2001) isolated an additional group of patients with flattened affect, asociality and alogia, mannerisms and posturing, which resembled the 'simple schizophrenia' symptom profile. Thus the true value of the classic schizophrenia subtypes is in some doubt, and the current view is that, at best, they represent a description of the clinical presentation of an individual at a particular point in time.

The chronic–acute distinction

The chronic–acute distinction is an indirect descendant of Bleuler's fundamental and accessory symptom clusters (respectively) mentioned earlier. In acute schizophrenia, pronounced psychotic symptoms, particularly hallucinations, delusions and disordered thinking, might be expected. In chronic schizophrenia, these symptoms may be absent or at least much reduced, but other disabling (negative) features will predominate. Thus, someone with acute schizophrenia may be floridly psychotic, whereas someone with chronic schizophrenia may be alogic, anhedonic and probably cognitively impaired too.

This typology is arguably more useful than the classic subtypes because it is based on evidence rather than theory, and because it takes more account of current symptomology. Unfortunately, the terms themselves give rise to ambiguities and different interpretations mainly because, in the natural course of the disorder, acute features are more likely early in the illness and chronic features tend to come to the fore later, as the condition evolves; so 'acute' is sometimes taken to mean 'recent onset' and chronic may mean 'having been ill for some time'. However, schizophrenia is an episodic illness and it is well established that even people who have been ill for many years can experience sudden symptomatic flare-ups. In other words, someone with chronic schizophrenia may have an acute episode. Another problem is that negative (i.e. chronic) features can be present early in the illness but may be masked by the abundance of florid psychotic symptoms (Montague et al., 1989). Thus, on balance the chronic–acute distinction has not been particularly useful and has, to some extent, fallen out of favour.

The positive–negative dichotomy and Liddle's tripartite model

Attempts to divide schizophrenia in terms of patient groupings have not been particularly successful, and clinicians and researchers have come to realise that a more promising strategy is to group according to presenting signs and symptoms. The positive–negative dichotomy exemplifies this approach and has quickly gained widespread acceptance (albeit with certain qualifications and amendments).

The distinction between positive and negative features dates back to the work of the neurologist Hughlings-Jackson over 100 years ago. Since then precise definitions have varied, but one way of thinking about them is that a positive feature is something that is present in addition to a relatively normal repertoire of behaviour, whereas a negative feature is something that is absent from that normal repertoire (Strauss, Carpenter and Bartco, 1974). Thus someone who works, socialises with friends, and plays football, yet who hears voices and worries excessively about being assaulted, may be said to be displaying two positive symptoms (hallucinations and paranoid delusions), whereas someone who lives alone, seldom washes or speaks, and is anhedonic and cognitively impaired might be described as manifesting several negative symptoms (or as mentioned earlier, strictly speaking, negative signs).

Anticipating the potential value of this approach, a number of researchers developed assessment tools (mainly **semi-structured interviews**) to record positive and negative symptom profiles: these included Andreasen's Schedule for the Assessment of Positive Symptoms (SAPS; Andreasen, 1984) and Schedule for the Assessment of Negative Symptoms (SANS; Andreasen, 1983), and the Positive and Negative Syndrome Scale (PANSS; Kay, Opler and Fisbein, 1986), all of which remain in widespread use today. The SAPS focuses on hallucinations, delusions and disturbed thinking, whereas the SANS attempts to assess what Andreasen regarded as the five cardinal negative signs (sometime known as the 5 As), *a*ffective flattening, *a*sociality, *a*logia, *a*nhedonia, and in-*a*ttention.

The positive–negative distinction was given added impetus by Crow (1980), who suggested that the two symptom clusters (he called them type I and type II) may also be distinguished in terms of underlying aetiology. In fact, he speculated that these were linked to two distinct pathological processes in the brain: type I (positive symptom) schizophrenia could wax and wane, and responded well to medications. He suggested that this profile resulted from functional changes to **neurotransmitters (NTs)** (most likely dopamine, DA) in the brain. Type II (negative symptom) schizophrenia was enduring, did not respond favourably to medications, and was often associated with cognitive decline. This, he suggested, was a consequence of structural changes in the brain. So positive symptoms were related to a potentially reversible brain dysfunction, whereas the negative profile resulted from irreversible structural changes.

From the outset it was clear that there were problems with Crow's hypothesis. For example, it implied that chronic (type II) patients would derive little benefit from standard anti-psychotic medications, yet research in which chronic patients stopped taking medications suggested otherwise. Secondly, it implied a sort of mutual exclusivity of the two groupings, whereas in reality some patients evinced both positive and negative symptoms. Crow actually accommodated this situation by suggesting an overlapping model in which up to 25 per cent of patients met criteria for both types. Thirdly, it suggested that once negative symptoms had taken hold, recovery was unlikely. Yet instances of recovery from chronic schizophrenia, though rare, are not unheard of. Despite these specific problems, Crow's ideas, viewed within the broader positive–negative context, were generally welcomed as a significant advance and a source of several testable hypotheses.

As for the positive–negative dichotomy, a series of quantitative research studies employing the new assessment schedules was instigated to test interrelationships between and within positive and negative symptom clusters. For example, Andreasen and Olsen (1982) reported that a range of negative symptoms including (but going beyond) those assessed in the SANS showed a reasonably consistent pattern of intercorrelation. Similar associations were found for the positive symptoms of hallucinations and delusions but, somewhat counterintuitively, neither of these seemed to correlate as strongly (or at all) with formal thought disorder (Mortimer, Lund and McKenna, 1990). As for the general relationship between positive and negative symptoms, this has now been examined in more than a dozen studies and is routinely found to be non-significant (e.g. Andreasen and Olsen, 1982).

A more powerful procedure for exploring interrelationships between variables (symptoms) is **factor analysis**. Liddle (1987) used this methodology to look for latent factors in a group of 40 stable schizophrenic patients. His analysis indicated that a three-factor solution best accounted for the variance. Two of these were recognisable as positive and negative symptoms. He called the former 'reality distortion', which loaded heavily on auditory hallucinations and delusions of reference and persecution. The latter was called 'psychomotor poverty', which loaded heavily on decreased motor function, affective flattening and poverty of speech. The third factor, called 'disorganisation syndrome', loaded on disordered thinking, inappropriate affect and distractibility.

By 1992, Liddle had developed his tripartite model to include likely brain regions related to each syndrome. Using the then relatively new functional imaging procedure of positron emission tomography (PET), he and his colleagues showed that psychomotor poverty was associated with decreased blood flow in the dorsolateral and medial prefrontal cortex (especially on the left side); that disorganisation was associated with increased activity in the right anterior cingulate, coupled to decreased activity in the right ventral frontal lobe; and that reality distortion was associated with increased activity in the left medial temporal and frontal lobes (Liddle et al., 1992; and see Figures 18.1–18.3). Many functional imaging studies postdating Liddle et al. have provided additional support for these early observations.

Liddle's original work was undertaken with a small sample (arguably too small for reliable factor analysis). However, several larger multivariate studies since then have also concluded that a three- or sometimes four-factor solution best accounts for the variance in the sample data. If a fourth factor has been mooted (e.g. Lindenmayer et al., 1995), it accounts for the least variance and loads on mood fluctuations without undermining the three principal factors.

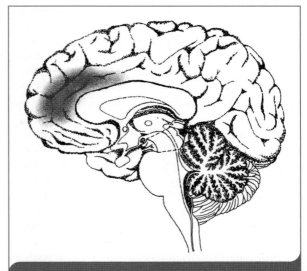

Figure 18.2 Locations of functional variations associated with Liddle's model of schizophrenia. Disorganisation: increased activity in anterior cingulate couple with reduced ventral prefrontal lobe activity (on right).

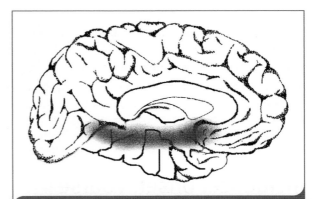

Figure 18.3 Locations of functional variations associated with Liddle's model of schizophrenia. Reality distortion: increased activity in left medial temporal lobe and left lateral frontal lobe and underactivity in posterior cingulated gyrus and adjacent parietal lobe (not shown).

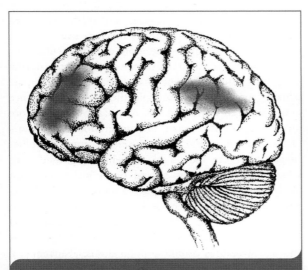

Figure 18.1 Locations of functional variations associated with Liddle's model of schizophrenia. Psychomotor poverty: reduced activity in frontal lobe(s) and left mid-parietal lobe + bilateral overactivity in caudate (not shown).

One of the most persuasive confirmatory studies was that of Grube, Bilder and Goldman (1998), who conducted a meta-analysis by pooling the data of ten independent studies in which both positive and negative symptoms had been rated on a combined total of 896 patients: factor 1 (negative syndrome) accounted for almost one-third of the variance; factor 2 (positive syndrome) accounted for an additional 20 per cent of the variance; and disorganisation accounted for 11 per cent of the variance.

Aside from the widespread empirical support that Liddle's model has received, a further advantage of it is that it overcomes the conceptual problem in the positive–negative dichotomy of where to locate formal thought disorder. The answer would appear to be: within a separate factor of disorganisation, loading on various forms of disturbed thinking, inappropriate or bizarre behaviour, and distractibility.

In summary, there would seem to be a number of ways of subdividing schizophrenia, none of which is entirely satisfactory. Yet on closer inspection, the various schemes may have more in common with each other than there appears at first glance. For example, the positive and negative syndromes overlap with paranoid and simple forms, and disorganisation shares several features with hebephrenia. For the time being, Liddle's tripartite model holds centre-stage and it will be revisited when studies of brain dysfunction in schizophrenia are reviewed later.

Self-test questions

- Identify the core features of Liddle's tripartite model.
- Summarise the anatomical basis of each.
- How well does his model 'map' on to Kraepelin's classic subtypes?

Incidence, onset, course and outcome(s) of schizophrenia

Incidence

Schizophrenia appears to affect all cultures and racial groups. For example, the IPSS indicated that schizophrenia occurs with similar frequency in all of the countries involved (though see McGrath et al., 2004, for an alternative view of this). Epidemiological studies indicate that the likelihood of a person developing schizophrenia in their lifetime is just below 1 per cent. In the developed world, the rate of occurrence of new cases (the incidence rate) is quite low, at about 2 to 4 per 10,000 population per year (Jablensky, 2000). Where higher rates are cited – for

example, in China and India – some or perhaps most of this difference appears attributable to differential diagnostic practices. It is slightly more common in males than females, and males are also likely to develop the disorder at an earlier age.

Although no tier of society is exempt, the risk of developing schizophrenia increases in more disadvantaged socioeconomic groups and there are more sufferers in deprived urban areas (Lambert and Kinsley, 2005). Initially, psychologists thought that the inner-city urban environment directly caused schizophrenia in some people. However, further analysis of the data suggested that the overrepresentation of sufferers in these locations was probably related to the effects of the illness on a patient's ability to work, involving movement of sufferers to less affluent areas where accommodation is cheaper and where there may be more opportunities for casual employment – sometimes referred to as social drift. The arguments now seem to have gone full-circle with recent renewed interest in the concept of urbanicity as a potentially 'toxic' environmental influence for young individuals with an existing (genetic?) **diathesis** to develop mental illness (Van Os et al., 2002), and this work will be reconsidered briefly later in the chapter.

A further point to note is that schizophrenia is also more commonly diagnosed in certain racial groups, particularly Afro-Caribbeans in the UK (Harrison et al., 1994) and African-Americans in the USA (Folsom, Fleisher and Depp, 2006), and less frequently in others such as UK-Asians (Thomas et al., 1993). The overrepresentation of schizophrenia in black people with African ancestry has become a pressing issue in the developed world, and many explanations for this have been mooted, ranging from selective migration of more vulnerable individuals, to increased risk of exposure to viruses during pregnancy. However, none of these explanations is particularly convincing: for example, the increased incidence of schizophrenia amongst UK Afro-Caribbeans is more marked in second- than first-generation immigrants (Thomas et al., 1993). Nevertheless, recent UK studies suggest that the likelihood of being diagnosed with schizophrenia might be several times higher amongst black people than white people – a statistic which rightly gives cause for serious concern. (Estimates vary between two and nine times, although these are difficult to be precise about in view of uncertainties about exact sizes and age structures of ethnic populations.) Currently, a multicentre UK research programme (the AESOP study) is under way to examine reasons for this overrepresentation. Incidentally, the elevated rates of psychopathology in immigrant groups are not restricted to schizophrenia, being seen in bipolar disorder (especially mania) too (Harvey et al., 1990). Nor are they restricted to Afro-Caribbeans: a study by Selten, Slaets and Kahn (1997) has reported similarly increased rates of psychopathology in Surinamese immigrants to Holland.

There are probably several reasons for the elevated rate of diagnosis of severe mental illness amongst immigrants (see Cooper, 2005). Social demographics show that such individuals are more likely to reside in decaying inner-city areas; to be unemployed and living alone; to have been separated from parents at an early age; to be exposed to the inherent dangers of city-life, including the excessive use of drugs and alcohol, criminality, etc.; and, in general terms, to be amongst the most disadvantaged in society. Each of these is a recognised 'environmental' risk factor for severe mental illness in its own right. Immigrants routinely find themselves in the unfortunate position of being exposed to a combination of these for much of their lives. Nevertheless, there remains a nagging concern that the criteria used to make a clinical diagnosis may not be entirely culture-free; and that, as a consequence, the behaviour of individuals from some ethnic minorities may mistakenly be identified as pathological (Sharpley, Hutchinson and Murray, 2001; Dein, Williams and Dein, 2007). One indisputable conclusion of these studies is that environmental factors contribute significantly to the manifestation of severe mental illness. This question is revisited later in the chapter.

Onset

The onset of schizophrenia typically occurs in late adolescence or early adulthood, although onset in later life is seen occasionally (and more so in women). Onset in childhood is very rare (but see Jardri et al. (2007) for a fascinating case study of schizophrenia in an 11-year-old child). In developed countries, the average age of people presenting for first treatment is about 24 years; somewhat earlier for men (15–24 years) than women (20–29 years) (Johnstone and Lang, 1994). The emergence of hallucinations and delusions is often preceded by a period of weeks or even months in which low mood, anxiety, bewilderment or other changes in 'affect' are seen/reported. This phase is called the prodromal period or simply prodrome, and marks the time-point when individuals may become increasingly isolated from family and friends, and may encounter difficulties in concentration and attendance at work and school. (Have another look at the case study of Simon for examples of this.) Inevitably, the gradual build-up of symptoms seen in such individuals sometimes makes it difficult to identify with any confidence precisely when their illness began.

Recently, as researchers and clinicians have begun to realise that favourable outcome may be related to early treatment, the need to identify subtle prodromal features (as opposed to the more florid symptoms seen in a first 'full-blown' episode) has become more pressing. Early intervention, either with psychotherapy (Morrison et al., 2004) or medications (Yung et al., 2003) is currently under review, but recognition of its potential benefits is already 'driving' services in some countries, notably Australia. (See Marshall and Rathbone (2006) for a critical review of this.)

Course and outcome

The Kraepelinian view of the typical course of dementia praecox was one of progressive deterioration. The expectation was that, as the illness evolved, hallucinations and delusions might become less prominent, to be replaced with deficits in intellect, drive and personality – the so-called deficit state of simple schizophrenia. In a truly monumental piece of research spanning over 20 years, Manfred Bleuler (son of Eugen) mapped the course of illness in over 200 schizophrenia patients admitted to a Swiss hospital over an 18-month period in 1942–3 (Bleuler, 1972; 1978). He described 11 patterns of course (illustrated in Figure 18.4), of which five accounted for almost three-quarters of his cohort. The most common was an undulating course involving a series of florid episodes over several years, interspersed by periods of relative stability, resolving to a residual impaired but stable state later on. He found little evidence of continuing deterioration after the first few years. On the contrary, some of his patients showed clear signs of improvement even after many years of illness. Ciompi and Muller (1976) and Harding (1988) have also completed very long-term studies plotting schizophrenia course. Exact ratios of cases evincing each trajectory differ a little, although the proportions deemed recovered or only mildly impaired (about 75 per cent) versus moderate/severely impaired (about 25 per cent) are comparable.

The later stages of each of these studies coincided with the introduction of anti-psychotic medications in the 1950s, and it is therefore difficult to disentangle genuine recovery from 'symptomatic relief' due to the therapeutic effects of the new drugs. More recent studies of the course of schizophrenia side-step the potential confounding effects of medications in so far as every patient is likely to have been prescribed them for much or all of the follow-up period. One such is the study by Shepherd, Watt and Falloon (1989) involving 107 patients followed up for 5 years, in which the following conclusions could be reached:

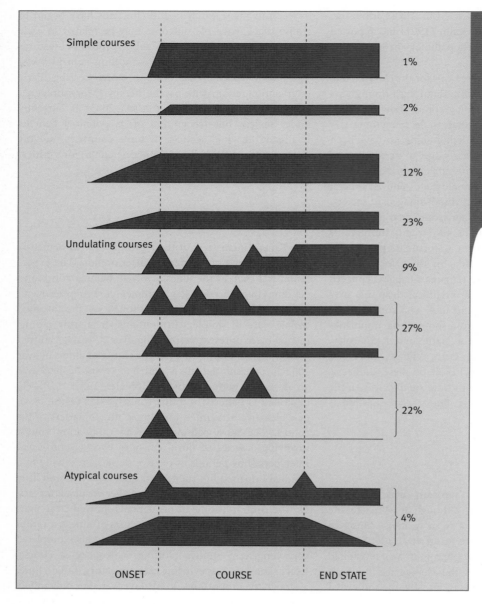

Figure 18.4 Patterns of course and outcome in schizophrenia. Bleuler (1978) identified 11 different patterns of course and outcome for schizophrenia. Five of these accounted for more than 75 per cent of all cases. Source: Bleuler, M. (1978) *The Schizophrenic Disorders: Long-term patients and family studies*. New Haven, CT: Yale University Press.

■ Approximately one in five patients will have only one acute episode, and will return close to their previous level of functioning with no (or little) lasting impairment.

■ Approximately one-third of patients will experience several acute episodes, but there will be good recovery and little lasting impairment.

■ A further one in ten patients will also have several acute episodes, with either continued symptoms or a lasting but stable level of impairment, and will not return to previous levels of functioning.

■ About one-third of patients will have several acute episodes, each of which will be associated with an increasing level of impairment and with no return to previous levels of functioning.

Turning now to outcome in schizophrenia, it is often *said* that a 'rule of thirds' seems to apply: about one in three patients recovers, one in three remains moderately impaired and a final third show a deteriorating course. In reality, these values are highly dependent on the criteria used at initial recruitment, the duration of follow-up and, critically, the criteria used to define good, moderate and poor outcome (see Liberman and Kopelowicz, 2005). Consider, for instance, a Japanese 20+ year study reported by Ogawa et al. (1987). At follow-up, 47 per cent were deemed 'self-supportive', 31 per cent were hospitalised, and the remainder hovered somewhere in between. Clinically, 31 per cent were deemed 'recovered', 46 per cent improved and 23 per cent unimproved. However, digging a little deeper, it transpires that even amongst the self-supportive cases (i.e. best outcome) over 40 per cent still experienced mild to moderate symptoms, and most were still taking anti-psychotic drugs.

A 13-year follow-up of first episode schizophrenia patients reported by Mason, Claridge and Jackson (1995) indicated a similar mixed pattern of outcomes: over half of their cohort (of 63 traceable patients) had been symptom free for the last 2 years, and a similar proportion had good/fair social functioning. However, only 17 per cent of the cohort fulfilled 'full recovery' criteria, defined as absence of symptoms without medications. These somewhat less optimistic figures were echoed in a meta-analysis of over 300 outcome studies comprising over 50,000 patients with a follow-period of more than 5 years (Hegarty et al., 1994).

In summary, course/outcome studies suggest the following: schizophrenia is an enduring condition for many, although a relatively small proportion of individuals experience the deteriorating Kraepelinian course of illness, and the majority of people show some degree of recovery in later life. However, an even smaller proportion of individuals, having once been diagnosed with schizophrenia, make a complete non-drug-assisted recovery.

Predicting outcome

In view of the mixed pattern of outcomes, there is both interest and value in trying to predict how people will fare later in the course of their illness in relation to **premorbid** or early features of psychopathology. As you can imagine, this is a notoriously imprecise science; however, being married, having a good educational and work record, and generally showing effective social competence are all predictive of better prognosis. Females have a better outcome than males. A better outcome is also associated with an acute or sudden onset of illness, particularly one following a clear stressor or precipitant, and in which positive symptoms are prominent. In addition, if the initial episode of illness is brief, lasting a month or less, and is followed by a marked symptomatic recovery (with or without continued medication), long-term outcome is better. Interestingly, as mentioned earlier, the IPSS indicated that outcome of schizophrenia may be better in developing countries than it is in the developed world. Conversely, a poor outcome

is predicted by an early insidious and progressive onset, poor premorbid social and educational adjustment, and the presence of negative symptoms and neurological signs at the start of the illness (Bombin, Arango and Buchanan, 2005; Chen et al., 2005; White et al., 2009).

Finally, there is now convincing evidence from recent research that the chances of a good long-term outcome in schizophrenia are improved if patients' symptoms are treated promptly (Agius et al., 2007). Conversely, a long delay between the onset of symptoms and the start of medication (a period of time referred to as duration of untreated psychosis or DUP) usually results in a slower recovery from the initial episode and a poorer long-term outcome (Krstev et al., 2004; Harris et al., 2005).

Self-test questions

- Is there a typical course for schizophrenia?
- What proportion of individuals make an effective recovery from schizophrenia?
- What are the best predictors of poor outcome?

Aetiology of schizophrenia

In this section, work on genetics, neurobiology of the brain (including NT dysfunctions), cognitive and neuropsychological approaches, and environmental factors, is reviewed. In the interests of clarity, these are initially presented as independent 'rival' explanations of schizophrenia causation. However, it is important to realise at the outset that these accounts are not necessarily mutually exclusive and may, in fact, share many common features. The following example, adapted from recent thinking about the aetiology of depression (Caspi et al., 2003) illustrates how all four of the approaches could combine to bring about the symptoms of schizophrenia: 'An individual carries a particular gene which affects the "efficiency" of receptors for a neurotransmitter which is itself, sensitive to the effects of experiential trauma. The neurotransmitter system is also integral to intact cognitive functioning . . .' An additional point to stress is that there *need not be* just one cause of schizophrenia: the accumulating evidence suggests that several disparate factors, acting independently or in combination, may be responsible for the condition – a point that Crow anticipated almost 30 years ago.

Genetics

An extensive literature of behavioural genetics research provides overwhelming cumulative evidence of a definite genetic component to schizophrenia. In their review of this literature, Owen, O'Donovan and Gottesman (2003) suggested that the value of H^2, the statistical measure of heritability, was approximately 80 per cent. Of course, this does not mean that four-fifths of a person's schizophrenia has a genetic basis; rather, that 80 per cent of the overall variance in a given population of people with schizophrenia may be attributed to genetic factors. (This value is higher than H^2 estimates for either coronary heart disease or type 1 diabetes.) It is equally clear from genetic research that the disorder is not purely genetic; in fact, four out of five individuals diagnosed with schizophrenia have no first-degree relatives (children, parents, siblings) with the disorder.

The evidence used to support the idea of a genetic susceptibility for schizophrenia has come from *pedigree*, *twin* and *adoption* studies. Pedigree studies (e.g. Slater and Cowie, 1971) involve the assessment of hundreds

of people from extended families in which more than one person has schizophrenia. By identifying all cases (probands) and establishing their relationship to other people in the family, conclusions can be drawn about how the illness may be inherited. Such studies show that the closer the genetic relationship to someone with schizophrenia, the greater the chance of developing the disorder. If, for example, one parent has a diagnosis of schizophrenia, the rate in any offspring is around 12 per cent; if both parents are affected (an unlikely but occasional eventuality) the figure leaps to 46 per cent (Gottesman and Bertelsen, 1989). Although early studies have been criticised on various methodological grounds (see below), a reanalysis of 11 more recent well-controlled studies by Kendler (2000) confirms the 10-fold elevated risk in first-degree relatives of an affected individual. (See Figure 18.5 for a summary of pedigree study data.)

The methodological shortcomings associated with many of the studies alluded to in the Research box included failing to use standard diagnostic criteria, not making 'blind' diagnoses, relying on self-report to establish co-relationships (including paternity and in some

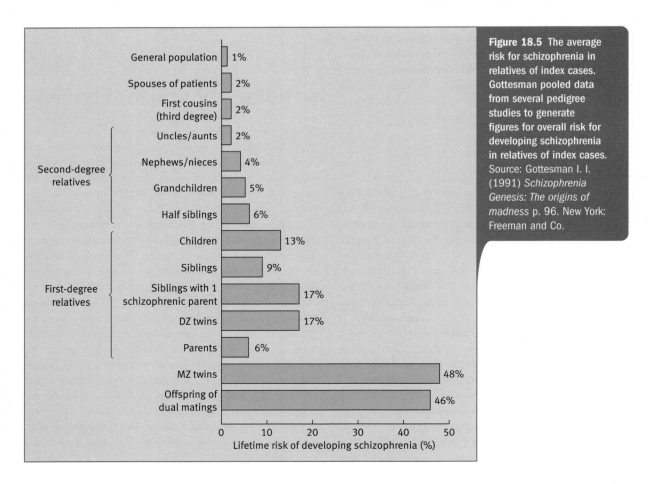

Figure 18.5 The average risk for schizophrenia in relatives of index cases. Gottesman pooled data from several pedigree studies to generate figures for overall risk for developing schizophrenia in relatives of index cases. Source: Gottesman I. I. (1991) *Schizophrenia Genesis: The origins of madness* p. 96. New York: Freeman and Co.

Research

Genetics and Schizophrenia

Twin studies

Twin studies are, in a sense, a particular form of pedigree study, in which rates amongst identical and fraternal twin pairs (where at least one has the disorder) are compared. They rely on the fact that identical twins (also known as monozygotic or MZ twins) are genetically identical, while, on average, fraternal (dizygotic, DZ, or non-identical) twins are no more genetically alike than ordinary brothers and sisters, sharing only 50 per cent of their genetic make-up. Averaging across several studies, the so-called concordance rate for monozygotic twins is about 48 per cent compared with a value of about 17 per cent for fraternal twins (Shields, 1978a).

Both pedigree and twin studies can be criticised because 'shared environment' factors such as home life, mutual friends, parenting styles, etc. are often confounded with closeness of relationship: after all, closely related people tend to live together. Little can be done about this for pedigree studies, but it can be taken into account in two ways in certain twin studies. Firstly, Fischer (1971) has shown that for MZ twins who are discordant for schizophrenia (i.e. where one twin has schizophrenia but the other does not) the rate of illness amongst offspring of the non-schizophrenic twins is almost as high (9.5 per cent) as in the children of the affected twins. Secondly, a small number of twin pairs, separated at, or shortly after birth, have been identified where at least one subsequently developed schizophrenia. Astonishingly, the incidence of illness in this small sample of co-twins is, in fact, higher (almost 70 per cent) than for MZ twins brought up together (Shields, 1978a).

Adoption studies

Adoption studies try to circumvent the potential confounding effect of common environment by examining the rate of illness in 'adopted-away' individuals known to be at increased genetic risk of schizophrenia because of an affected biological parent, compared to adoptees with no known elevated risk. Using this method, both Heston (1966) and Rosenthal (1971) have shown that there is an elevated risk of schizophrenia (and other mental illnesses) in the 'at-risk' adoptees compared with control (low-risk) adoptees. Although these studies have also been criticised on methodological grounds, a more tightly controlled study by Tienari et al. (2000) found a four-fold increased risk of narrowly defined schizophrenia in 'adopted-away' offspring of mothers with schizophrenia compared with control adoptees (8.1 per cent v. 2.3 per cent).

There have also been studies of children of healthy people who were adopted by parents who themselves had schizophrenia (e.g. Wender et al., 1974). Here, a higher than average incidence of schizophrenia in these children might be expected if the disorder was related to the conditions in the home environment. On the other hand, if genetic factors were important, then adoption by ill parents should not increase risk. Wender et al.'s data support the latter hypothesis, indicating that growing up in proximity to someone with schizophrenia is not in itself a significant risk factor for the later development of the illness.

instances even MZ-DZ status) and having very small numbers of incident-cases. Because of these problems, critics such as Lidz, Blatt and Cook (1981) continued to question the conclusions that researchers reached, particularly in relation to the strength of genetic influence. Fortunately, more recent studies in each of the three areas overcome most of these problems yet reach broadly similar conclusions. Thus, the weight of evidence from **epidemiological** studies of schizophrenia inheritance provides strong support for a substantial role of genes in its development. Researchers are now trying to establish the mechanisms by which they operate and how many there are. One rather obvious conclusion from these studies is that, whatever the eventual mechanism of schizophrenia inheritance turns out to be, it does not follow a Mendelian pattern of single dominant/recessive gene influence. Thus,

the idea of searching for *the* schizophrenia gene analogous to *the* Huntington's disease gene or *the* PKU gene is fairly pointless. Moreover, genes clearly do not cause schizophrenia; rather, they seem to make people more (or less) likely to develop it – and it is important to realise that individuals may carry so-called 'susceptibility genes' and pass them to their children yet not develop the disorder themselves. The discordant twins in Fischer's study were, in all probability, obligate carriers of such genes, since their children were as likely to develop schizophrenia as the children of the affected co-twin.

The search for susceptibility genes has thrown up many candidates, most of which fail to stand up to the rigours of replication (Tsuang and Faraone, 2000). However, this has not discouraged researchers, as schizophrenia is thought to be genetically as well as symptomatically heterogeneous, meaning that the 'diathesis' may comprise different (non-overlapping) combinations of genes in different individuals. Someone with a higher genetic risk may carry several susceptibility genes (and/or relatively few 'protective' genes, assuming these also exist), but each of these need make only a modest contribution to overall risk. Finally, it is becoming clear that particular genes may only exist or operate in specific populations or geographical locations in the world (see Tosato, Dazzan and Collier, 2005, for an illustration of this).

At time of writing (early 2009), susceptibility genes have been provisionally proposed on at least 10 of the 23 pairs of chromosomes making up the human genome. However, three are attracting particular attention: the DTNBP1 gene coding for dysbindin on chromosome 6 (Owen, Williams and O'Donovan, 2004); the NGR 1 gene coding for neuregulin on chromosome 8 (Stefansson et al., 2002) and the COMT (catchol O methyl transferase) gene on chromosome 22 (Williams, Owen and O'Donovan, 2007).

Dysbindin protein is found in the terminals of neurons that release the NT glutamate (of which more later). Its function is not known, but 11 separate studies have now reported associations between particular versions (polymorphisms) of the DTNBP coding gene and schizophrenia (Talbot et al., 2004), particularly in cases with prominent negative features and cognitive impairment (DeRosse et al., 2006). Lower levels of dysbindin have also been reported in two post-mortem studies of schizophrenia in the frontal cortex and hippocampus (Weikert et al., 2004; Talbot et al., 2004).

Neuregulin is associated with both the regulation of glutamate release and synaptic plasticity in the brain. Separate studies in Scotland, Iceland and China have reported associations between variations in this gene (so-called haplotypes) and susceptibility to schizophrenia (Tosato, Dazzan and Collier, 2005). However, it may also be associated with elevated risk for bipolar disorder (Thompson et al., 2004), making it a candidate susceptibility gene for psychosis rather than schizophrenia in particular (Li, Collier and He, 2006).

The **COMT** link is, arguably, the most interesting of all. COMT is an enzyme that breaks down NTs in the brain, notably DA. The COMT gene is located on chromosome 22 in a section which, if absent through micro-deletion, gives rise to a rare disorder known as velocardiofacial syndrome (VCFS). The intriguing point is that about one in three VCFS sufferers also meets the diagnostic criteria for schizophrenia. Several studies have shown that the so-called val-158-met polymorphism[1] of the COMT gene is associated with schizophrenia (Egan et al., 2001; Schiffman et al., 2005). Possessing one or two copies of the 'met' form confers a modest increased risk for schizophrenia coupled with impaired working memory and executive function (both frontal lobe functions). Unfortunately, more recent studies, whilst confirming the link to impaired cognition (Bearden et al., 2004), have been unable to confirm earlier findings of linkage to schizophrenia (Williams et al., 2005), so the status of COMT as a susceptibility gene is presently uncertain (Williams, Owen and O'Donoran, 2007).

Molecular genetics has largely replaced the older epidemiological approaches to exploring the genetic basis of schizophrenia. The preceding section has been deliberately selective; many other genes (or variants in genes) have been looked at, including those that code directly for the synthesis of, or receptors for, DA, serotonin, noradrenalin and even acetylcholine (all NTs that have at some stage or other been linked to schizophrenia). Even if the three candidate genes considered above are eventually confirmed as genuine susceptibility genes, their effects appear to elevate risk relatively modestly: for example, Egan et al. argued that the 'risky' COMT variant elevated risk by less than × 2. Of course, if an individual also possesses 'risky' neuregulin and dysbindin genes, their risk may double and redouble. Table 18.4 summarises our current understanding of these three susceptibility genes.

A final point to note is that each of these three candidate genes can influence either DA or glutamate neurotransmission. Some of the links between these key NT systems and schizophrenia are considered later.

Neurobiological approaches

As with genetics, a massive research effort has gone into searching for abnormalities in the brain related to schizophrenia. For convenience it makes sense to distinguish between those studies that have looked at structural differences and those that have focused on functional differences, although in reality the approaches have often overlapped.

Structural differences

Both Kraepelin and Bleuler (though with less emphasis) regarded dementia praecox/schizophrenia to have an

---

[1] This refers to a base substitution in the 158th codon of the gene giving rise to an enzyme containing either valine or methionine at this position: humans all have two copies, so they are either val-val, val-met or met-met, the latter being associated with lower levels of COMT activity and thus higher dopamine levels.

Table 18.4 Three susceptibility genes for schizophrenia/psychosis

'Gene'	Chromosome	Anatomical location	Possible effect(s)
DTNBP1 for dysbindin	6p	Brain (frontal lobes and hippocampus); in terminals that release glutamate	Regulation of glutamate release: risky variant reduces release at NMDA receptors.
NGR 1 for neuregulin	8p	Synaptic plasticity and terminals that release glutamate	Regulation of glutamate release: risky variant reduces release at NMDA receptors.
COMT (val-158-met polymorphism)	22q	Dopamine and other monoamine-mediated synapses in frontal lobes	Regulation of dopamine (and NA) metabolism at synapses. The met variant makes COMT less efficient, increasing availability of dopamine and other monoamines.

organic basis. Kraepelin's student Alzheimer spent several frustrating years examining post-mortem brains in a search for the defining lesion or abnormality, before turning his attention to a more obviously organic disorder that later took his name (Alzheimer's disease). For the next 70 or so years, analysis of post-mortem tissue remained the only viable method of searching for anomalies. Unfortunately, the procedure was confounded by the effects on brain structure of widely used but damaging treatments such as electro-convulsive shock therapy (ECT), insulin coma therapy and even certain medications, coupled with the uncertain consequences of poor diet and even basic lifestyle; so few consistent findings emerged.

However, the application of in-vivo imaging techniques over the last 30 years has completely revolutionised this field. Johnstone et al. (1976) reported one of the first studies in which groups of chronic patients and healthy controls were scanned using the then new technique of computer axial tomography (CT/CAT scanning). Results indicated that, on average, the patients with schizophrenia had significantly larger ventricles (fluid cavities in the brain) than controls – a finding which suggests loss of tissue in adjacent regions. Over the next few years, this result was replicated by several other research groups using either CT or the newer MRI scanning procedure. In a meta-analysis of MRI studies by Wright et al. (2000), in which age, sex, height and weight were all carefully controlled for, lateral ventricular volume was, on average, 26 per cent larger in patients than non-patients. Overall brain volume could also be calculated from MRI scans and this was typically about 2 per cent less amongst patients, with slightly more atrophy (shrinkage) detectable in frontal and temporal cortical regions, the hippocampus and amygdala (up to 5 per cent reduction).

For some time, it was assumed that the organic changes reported by Johnstone and others were a physical corollary

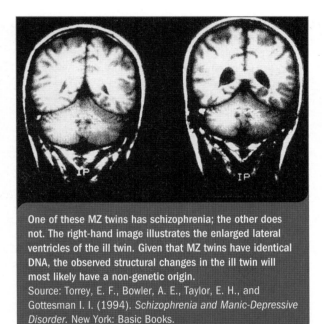

One of these MZ twins has schizophrenia; the other does not. The right-hand image illustrates the enlarged lateral ventricles of the ill twin. Given that MZ twins have identical DNA, the observed structural changes in the ill twin will most likely have a non-genetic origin.
Source: Torrey, E. F., Bowler, A. E., Taylor, E. H., and Gottesman I. I. (1994). *Schizophrenia and Manic-Depressive Disorder*. New York: Basic Books.

of the deteriorating course of the illness. After all, most of those scanned were chronic patients. However, several structural imaging studies of young or even first episode cases have shown that ventricular enlargement and brain atrophy are apparent early in the illness too (Salokangas et al., 2002). In fact, evidence of progressive tissue loss has been hard to come by (but see Lawrie et al., 2002), and researchers now think that most structural changes probably predate the onset of illness and are a sign of an abnormal neurodevelopmental process rather than a neurodegenerative one occurring post illness onset (DeLisi and Hoff, 2005).

However, to sound a note of caution, it is important to realise that results from this type of research are typically presented as group averages which can, of course, be distorted by 'outliers'. When a multiple case study approach is adopted, it becomes clear that many patients fall within the normal range. Thus, a more prudent summary of this research would be to say that *a proportion* of schizophrenia patients have enlarged ventricles or other structural anomalies, rather than implying that these are general features of 'the schizophrenic brain'. Meanwhile, the functional significance of these anomalies, even in this subgroup, remains something of a mystery. For example, a link to negative symptoms has been reported but is weak (Owens et al., 1985); Bornstein et al., 1992). More fundamentally, symptoms can wax and wane quite quickly, whereas structural anomalies show little sign of change, even in the longer term (Lawrie and Abukmeil, 1998).

As described earlier, current thinking favours a neurodevelopmental origin for the structural anomalies observed. This tallies with the realisation that structural changes probably predate illness onset, and also fits with the ideas (mentioned earlier) regarding poor premorbid adjustment in adolescence (Vourdas et al., 2003) or even childhood (Jones, Rodgers and Murray, 1994) in people who subsequently develop schizophrenia. Several potentially detrimental influences on neurodevelopment have been mooted. These include:

- perinatal obstetric complications (forceps delivery, anoxia at birth, etc.) (Cannon, Van Erp and Glahn, 2002)
- genetic influences combining with early damage to affect the rate of growth and pruning of neurons in the developing brain (McGlashan and Hoffman, 2000)
- exposure to viral infection (Kirch, 1993), which might explain the disproportionate number of schizophrenic people being born in the late winter months when the risk of complications is higher (the so-called 'season of birth effect')
- vitamin D deficiency (McGrath, 1999)
- exposure to other forms of infection (Fuller-Torrey and Yolken, 2003).

Intrinsically appealing though each of these is, no irrefutable evidence exists to support any of them, and they remain, for the time being, interesting hypotheses at best.

Functional differences

EEG has offered a means of examining brain function in schizophrenia for more than 50 years, but results from the handful of such studies were ambiguous and inconsistent. However, the introduction of in-vivo functional imaging

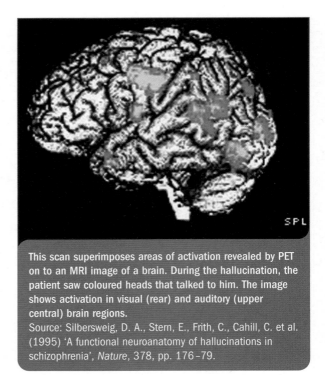

This scan superimposes areas of activation revealed by PET on to an MRI image of a brain. During the hallucination, the patient saw coloured heads that talked to him. The image shows activation in visual (rear) and auditory (upper central) brain regions.
Source: Silbersweig, D. A., Stern, E., Frith, C., Cahill, C. et al. (1995) 'A functional neuroanatomy of hallucinations in schizophrenia', *Nature*, 378, pp. 176–79.

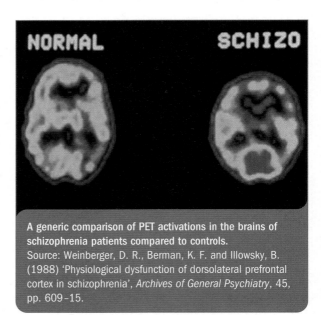

A generic comparison of PET activations in the brains of schizophrenia patients compared to controls.
Source: Weinberger, D. R., Berman, K. F. and Illowsky, B. (1988) 'Physiological dysfunction of dorsolateral prefrontal cortex in schizophrenia', *Archives of General Psychiatry*, 45, pp. 609–15.

procedures – firstly PET and subsequently fMRI – has transformed this field of research. It is now possible to observe brain functioning in real time in individuals who might, for example, be currently experiencing auditory hallucinations (Woodruff et al., 1997; Barkus et al., 2007).

Some early functional imaging studies simply compared resting levels of activity in people with schizophrenia with that seen in controls: results suggested underactivity in the former compared with the latter. Unfortunately, since anti-psychotic medications tend to reduce brain activity, this finding was hardly unexpected. More recent functional imaging studies usually employ some variant of a fairly standard procedure in which individuals are scanned 'at rest' and then again when they undertake some sort of psychological challenge, such as a working memory test (and thus serve as their own controls). By comparing activity on the two trials, it is possible to draw conclusions about what regions of the brain become active (or not) during the challenge, and whether patients show similar or distinct patterns of activity in comparison with non-patients.

Using this approach, researchers have typically reported relatively normal activations in most brain regions apart from the frontal lobes, which appear hypoactive during neuropsychological challenge (Weinberger et al., 1994). Weiss et al. (2003) employed a variant of the previous protocol in their fMRI study, deliberately selecting patients with schizophrenia who performed well (i.e. within the normal range) on a selective attention task, to compare with a matched non-patient control group. All participants were scanned whilst they completed an attention task (the **modified Stroop test**). As expected, the patient group did almost as well as the control group on the test. However, fMRI suggested that in order to achieve this level of performance, they activated more extensive cortical regions than controls, including (in particular) bilateral prefrontal areas and the anterior cingulate. Controls typically only showed left prefrontal activation. Weiss et al.'s finding suggests that, although patients can perform as well as controls, more extensive cortical activation is necessary to achieve this.

Gradually, researchers have come to realise that, given the heterogeneity of the disorder, it is fairly pointless just comparing scan data from a group of people with schizophrenia with that from a control group. Actually this was anticipated by Liddle (1987), whose PET study was described earlier. Taking a leaf from his book, more recent fMRI studies have grouped patients by subtype, or in terms of prevalent symptoms. Now a somewhat clearer pattern of results emerges: individuals with a negative symptom profile show hypofrontality under challenge, whereas those with a prevalence of positive symptoms show hyperactivation in temporal cortex and subcortical regions coupled with a disregulated pattern of activity (i.e. different but not necessarily lower activations) in their frontal lobes. These effects are usually more marked on the left side. As Liddle reported, individuals with a disorganisation syndrome show overactivity in the cingulate coupled with dysregulation in frontal regions. Even now, the picture is far from clear,

given the plethora of imaging protocols and analyses that researchers use. Nevertheless, the emerging picture is that negative features correspond to frontal hypoactivity, and that positive features correspond to dysregulated frontal activity coupled to overactivity in temporal regions (positive syndrome) or anterior cingulate (disorganisation syndrome) (see again Figures 18.1–18.3).

One conclusion from this line of enquiry is that schizophrenia is a disorder of **connectivity** rather than one of focal damage (Honey et al., 2005), and a new imaging procedure; diffusion tensor imaging (DTI; also known as tractography) is beginning to address some of the outstanding questions about altered connectivity in the brain in schizophrenia (see Minati and Aquino, 2006). This technique allows bundles of white-matter fibres (the ones that carry nerve impulses from one brain region to another, and which do not appear on conventional CT or MRI scans) to be visualised. Verma and colleagues have recently presented preliminary data from an ongoing study in which schizophrenia patients have been scanned using the DTI protocol, and their scans then 'pooled' to indicate areas of altered connectivity (Verma et al., 2008). Their data reveal reduced white matter in several cortical regions including temporal and frontal lobes, both bilaterally. The simultaneous use of DTI and fMRI offers the prospect of being able to map functional changes to specific altered connections between brain regions, and Schlosser et al. (2007) have recently described the first

A DTI image of a normal brain.
Sources: Brun, A., Knutsson, H., Park, H.-J., Shenton, M. E. and Westin, C.-F. (2004) *Cluster Fiber Traces Using Normalized Cuts: Book Series Lecture Notes in Computer Science*. Berlin: Springer.

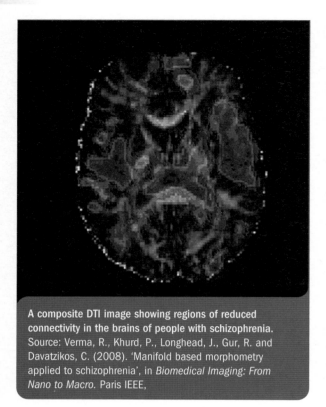

A composite DTI image showing regions of reduced connectivity in the brains of people with schizophrenia. Source: Verma, R., Khurd, P., Longhead, J., Gur, R. and Davatzikos, C. (2008). 'Manifold based morphometry applied to schizophrenia', in *Biomedical Imaging: From Nano to Macro*. Paris IEEE,

such study to be carried out on patients with schizophrenia. They found less connectivity between temporal and frontal lobes in the right hemisphere of their schizophrenia patients. This structural anomaly chimed well with a fMRI hypo-activation in the same frontal region during a working memory task.

Neurotransmitters: dopamine, (serotonin) and glutamate

Communication between brain regions is mediated by the release of NTs from the terminals of neurons, and the idea that the symptoms of schizophrenia may be related to abnormalities in one or more NT system(s) has interested researchers since the observation that chronic amphetamine use could induce psychotic-like experiences. In fact for a time, amphetamine psychosis (as it is called) was heralded as a drug model of schizophrenia. As it turned out, this was not entirely accurate. Nevertheless, there was some overlap between the features of schizophrenia and amphetamine psychosis, and it was then discovered that the principal action of amphetamine in the brain was to potentiate (boost) DA and noradrenalin (NA) neuro-transmission. This realisation coincided with two other discoveries about brain DA: firstly, that a common action of all anti-psychotics then known was to block (i.e. damp

down or inhibit) the **D2 receptor** for DA (see Seeman, 1980, for a review); and secondly, that drugs used to treat Parkinson's disease, notably a DA-boosting drug (agonist) called L-DOPA, can induce psychotic experiences in PD patients (or even healthy controls) if taken in too large a dose (Angrist, Lee and Gershon, 1974). Snyder (1976) put these three pieces of information together to propose the DA hypothesis of schizophrenia. In its simplest form, the 'DA hypothesis' proposes that symptoms arise because of overactivity within the brain-DA system.

Since Snyder's paper, many studies have examined the hypothesis experimentally. For example, researchers have used PET to measure the number of DA receptors in the brains of people with schizophrenia, when alive and after death. Although several studies have provided evidence of DA overactivity (Reynolds, 1983; 1989), some have failed to do so: the picture is complicated by the fact that anti-psychotic medicines *also* induce long-term changes to the distribution and number of DA receptors. A handful of studies have tried to get round this problem by recruiting patients who have never taken anti-psychotic medications. Wong et al. (1986), for example, examined drug-naive patients and reported a two- to three-fold increase in the number of DA receptors in the striatum (a region with major connections to both frontal and temporal lobes), but Farde et al. (1987) were unable to replicate this. However, three recent studies involving drug-naive patients (by Talvik et al., 2003; Yasuno et al., 2004; and Talvik et al., 2006) have all found anomalous DA 'binding' (i.e. receptor occupancy) in the **thalamus**. Lehrer et al. (2005) have also reported lower metabolic activity in the thalamus (and associated prefrontal regions) in a group of 'never medicated' schizophrenia patients using a combination of PET and MRI scanning. As this study shows, the thalamus, like the striatum, has multiple connections with both cortical and subcortical structures, and is regarded as a major relay station in the brain. One consequence of thalamic dysfunction would be altered selective attentional processing, a long-standing, if somewhat out-of-favour explanation for schizophrenia symptomology (Frith, 1979; Gray et al., 1991).

More recently, there has been renewed interest in the role of DA as a 'state' marker (rather than an underlying trait marker) for particular symptoms. An interesting series of studies by Laruelle and colleagues (Laruelle, 2000; Laruelle, Kegeles and Abi-Dargham, 2003) has shown that currently symptomatic patients have a more pronounced DA-stimulating response to amphetamine challenge than those whose symptoms are absent or significantly reduced. The implication of this finding is that the positive symptoms of the disorder (in particular) may be related to DA overactivity (or receptor oversensitivity).

This view chimes well with recent considerations of what, precisely, DA does, especially in relation to cognition, in the mature human brain. According to Kapur (2003) and Kapur, Mizrahi and Li (2005), one of the key non-motor roles of DA is to give 'added salience' to cognitions (thoughts, perceptions, intentions, etc.) that are important for an individual at a particular point in time. An analogy of this might be your use of a highlighter pen to identify points in a text that you want to include in an essay you are preparing. This 'tagging' process effectively directs attention towards things that are more important for the person irrespective of whether they are intrinsically rewarding or aversive. But, Kapur asks, imagine what may happen if this process goes awry and cognitions of only minor significance are wrongly tagged by DA release. Now, innocuous events may be perceived as having special significance for an individual, leading to delusion formation. In similar vein, inner speech, percepts and even random thoughts or memories may take on 'hallucinatory' qualities. According to the model, it is in this way that DA dysregulation provides the fuel for the formation of delusions and hallucinations.

Although Kapur's hypothesis only relates to positive symptoms of schizophrenia, it has attracted a lot of attention because it provides an appealing explanation for underlying cognitive changes associated with the prodromal period. It also fits well with people's accounts of the actual effects of anti-psychotics on their symptoms. Apropos the prodrome, people often describe feeling bewildered by inexplicable changes in their mood, perceptual acuity and sensitivity, all presumably related to the developing dysregulation of DA release. As for self-reports of the effects of anti-psychotics, many patients say that the drugs do not actually eradicate their symptoms, but somehow make them less prominent or intrusive and thus more manageable. Kapur's model has much in common with Myin-Germeys' work on stress sensitivity in schizophrenia, which is considered later.

Although the DA hypothesis has gained renewed support from Laruelle's and Kapur's research, it is unlikely that a disorder as varied as schizophrenia could arise from an abnormality of just one NT. Researchers are currently exploring how DA interacts with other NTs in the brain, such as serotonin (5HT) and glutamate. 5HT, for example, modifies DA release in frontal cortical regions (Kapur and Remington, 1996), and several psychedelic drugs with psychoto-mimetic effects, such as LSD, psilocin (magic mushrooms) and psilocybin, affect 5HT functioning (Roth and Meltzer, 2000). However, a problem with this line of enquiry is that the brain 5HT system is very complex, comprising at least 14 different 5HT receptor types. The NT is consequently involved in many aspects of behaviour

unrelated to psychosis, such as appetite control, sleeping, empathy and risk taking. Nevertheless, the psychoto-mimetic drugs mentioned above are all 5HT2a receptor agonists, and several of the newer anti-psychotic drugs are either (or both) 5HT2a and/or 5HT1a receptor antagonists, suggesting that these receptors may be particularly important in schizophrenia (Harrison, 1999). A current hypothesis is that 5HT-mediated control of DA release in the frontal lobes (where excitatory D1 receptors far outnumber the inhibitory D2 receptors mentioned in relation to the DA hypothesis) may be responsible for some of the cognitive impairments and negative features of schizophrenia (Meltzer, Kaneda and Ichikawa, 2003). This might explain why newer anti-psychotic drugs with 5HT as well as DA (D2) receptor blocking actions appear to reduce negative symptoms and improve cognition (although whether they are actually any more effective in relation to positive symptoms is a moot point: see below).

Glutamate has attracted particular attention for three reasons. Firstly, although widespread in the cortex, it is found in particularly high concentrations in the frontal lobes, hippocampus and amygdala, each of which has already been implicated as a putative anatomical substrate for schizophrenia symptoms. Secondly, when its presence coincides with DA, the two NTs tend to oppose one another, especially where D2 receptors are involved (Laruelle, Kegeles and Abi-Dargham, 2003). Thirdly, two recreational drugs, **ketamine** and **PCP**, which in modest quantities have psychosis-inducing effects, are glutamate NMDA receptor antagonists. Incidentally, glutamate antagonist drugs also depress cognitive function.

An emerging model (see Olney and Farber, 1995) makes glutamate neurotransmission pivotal in relation to negative and cognitive features of schizophrenia, but it must be acknowledged that the picture is, once again, incredibly complicated. For example, as with DA and serotonin, several glutamate receptor types exist; only certain of these appear to be involved in the psychoto-mimetic effects of ketamine (Deakin et al., 2008). Even then, if ketamine blocks these receptors (the NMDA type), glutamate may spill over to cause an overall increased excitation at adjacent receptors. A final complication is that glutamate-mediated frontal underactivity can induce DA overactivity in other brain regions by a process known as 'release': brain region 1 that normally inhibits another (region 2) will 'release' region 2 to become active if it (region 1) is underactive (see Lewis, Hashimoto and Volk, 2005).

Ketamine-induced psychotic-like experiences are widely regarded as the best current drug model of certain symptoms of schizophrenia. Users report dissociative, expansive and alien-control types of experience. A pointer to the significance of this line of research is that drug companies are currently very active in the development of glutamate agonists as potential treatments for the disorder.

Self-test questions

- Identify three lines of research that support the DA hypothesis of schizophrenia.
- Why, and in what way, has 5HT dysfunction been implicated in schizophrenia?
- What evidence has been mustered to implicate glutamate dysfunction in schizophrenia?
- What is the general relationship between DA and glutamate in the brain?

Neuropsychological and cognitive–neuropsychological approaches

It is impossible to do justice to the burgeoning research base emerging from these lines of enquiry and the interested reader is referred to Frith (1992) and McKenna (2007) for further detailed information. In this section just a few of the main themes currently attracting attention are summarised. To be clear about terms, the neuropsychological approach seeks to establish what domains of neurocognitive functioning are particularly impaired in schizophrenia, and which are preserved, whereas the cognitive–neuropsychological approach attempts to explain features of schizophrenia in terms of dysfunctional neurocognition.

If anything has been learned from the neuropsychological approach, it is that schizophrenia impacts on most aspects of higher mental function. So, whilst basic sensory,

motor and homeostatic mechanisms may be relatively intact, deficits have been reported in virtually all major cognitive domains including attention, memory, learning and language. A well-established finding is that people with schizophrenia typically have a reduction in IQ of about 10 points (Goldberg et al., 1990). It is therefore important to show that other deficits are not just a consequence of lower IQ or, even more fundamentally, of decreased motivation or the effects of medication. This can be done in at least two ways. A researcher may record IQ in addition to performance in other specific domains of functioning, then use IQ score as a 'covariate' in any subsequent statistical analyses. In this way the researcher can see if specific deficits remain when IQ is controlled for. A second strategy is to use a battery of tests to find specific instances of marked impairment or preservation. For example, Stirling, Hellewell and Hewitt (1997) reported a relative deficit of about one standard deviation difference in a chronic schizophrenia sample compared with controls on a battery of memory tests, but preservation of performance on one measure of long-term memory (stem completion). It is just possible that patients were highly motivated to do well on the stem completion test and not the others, but rather unlikely. Using these strategies, three domains stand out: namely, deficits in certain aspects of semantic processing (McKenna and Oh, 2005; Stirling et al., 2006), impaired working memory (Silver et al., 2002; Joyce et al., 2005) and depressed executive functioning (Kerns et al., 2008).

Turning to the cognitive–neuropsychological approach, one question might be: how do neurocognitive deficits relate to particular features of the illness? If Liddle's taxonomy of negative and disorganisation syndromes plus reality distortion is taken as a starting point, there would seem to be a clear overlap between the negative syndrome and impaired executive functioning, especially the apathetic aspects (Blumer and Benson, 1975) associated with frontal lobe damage (think of Andreasen's five As). Executive

Table 18.5 Frith's explanation of schizophrenia symptoms resulting from impaired self-monitoring

Intention	Faulty monitor	Symptom
To act	Unintended act	Delusion of control
To think	Unintended thought	Thought insertion
To think while distracted	Disrupted thought	Thought blocking/control
To switch attention	Switch elicited by external stimulus	Delusion of reference
To think subvocally	Unexpected subvocal ideas	Thought broadcast
To plan language	Unexpected verbal messages	Auditory hallucinations
To behave in context	Inappropriate behaviour	Bizarre behaviour

functions additionally include planning and strategy, goal orientation and concept formation, each of which is impaired in people with the negative syndrome. The central executive of working memory is also thought to be located in the frontal lobes (Baddeley, 2001), and impairments in working memory are regarded as one of the most prominent cognitive features of schizophrenia. However, to sound a cautionary note, working memory deficits are not *just* found in negative syndrome schizophrenics, and additionally, executive functions in general do not reside exclusively in the frontal lobes (Van den Heuvel et al., 2003).

The disorganisation syndrome is defined by disordered thinking/language and bizarre behaviour. Liddle suggested that the anterior cingulate and medial frontal lobe (and their interconnections) formed its anatomical substrate, although functional imaging studies have consistently implicated reduced temporal lobe activity during the production of thought-disordered speech (Kircher et al., 2001). However, Liddle's axis may be important in terms of behavioural inhibition to explain the 'bizarre' aspects of the syndrome; the behaviour results from a failure to inhibit inappropriate or unsuitable actions/responses. As for explanations of formal thought disorder, there is good reason to suspect that both executive (frontal) and linguistic (temporal lobe) dysfunction are involved. Patients with formal thought disorder display specific linguistic impairments in the semantic domain coupled with executive dysfunction (Stirling et al., 2006).

Frith's model of the origin of positive symptoms in schizophrenia

Liddle proposed that reality distortion was related to overactivity in the temporal lobe(s), and a raft of PET and fMRI studies since then has confirmed their involvement, especially in relation to auditory hallucinations, although changes in activation are routinely also seen in certain frontal and limbic regions, notably the hippocampus and amygdala. An influential cognitive neuropsychological explanation for some reality distortion features related to alien control was proposed by Frith (1992). He suggested that the fundamental deficit was a failure to monitor one's own intended thoughts and actions (see Table 18.5). Planned speech not recognised as being self-generated may be *explained* as thought insertion – the entirely normal experience of inner speech, if not recognised as self-generated, may be *perceived* as an auditory hallucination, and so on. Several cognitive neuropsychological studies have shown that people with alien control symptoms are impaired at identifying self-generated errors (Frith and Done, 1989), self-penned drawings (Stirling, Hellewell and

'Look at the design on the computer.'

'Now draw it on the paper under the screen.'

'Which drawing did you do?'

Figure 18.6 An illustration of a self-monitoring test similar to that used by Stirling *et al.* (1998, 2001). (a) The respondent views a geometric design for a few seconds. (b) Then s/he reproduces it without being able to see her/his actual hand movements. (c) The original drawing is then shown alongside foils (non-originals of the same design) and the respondent tries to identify their drawing.

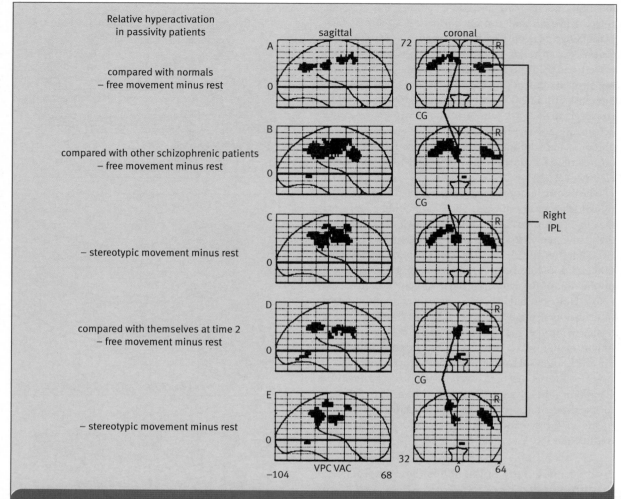

Figure 18.7 'Glass brain' images of functional changes in the brains of patients with passivity symptoms. These images show areas of increased activity in patients currently experiencing passivity phenomena (a) compared with non-patients; (b) and (c) compared to other schizophrenic patients not experiencing passivity phenomena (in two related conditions); (d) and (e) and compared to themselves when passivity phenomena had diminished (in two related conditions).
Source: Spence, S. A., Brooks, D. J., Hirsch, S. R., Liddle, P. F., Meehan, J. and Frasby, P. M. (1997) 'A PET study of voluntary movement in schizophrenic patients experiencing passivity phenomena (delusions of alien control)', *Brain*, 120, pp. 1997–2011.

Quraishi, 1998; Stirling, Hellewell and Ndlovu, 2001) their own distorted voice (Johns et al., 2001) and self-initiated movements (Bulot, Thomas and Delavoye-Turrell, 2007). Critically, in these studies, the self-monitoring impairment was independent of IQ or level of negative symptoms. Spence and colleagues (Spence et al., 1997) undertook a PET study of patients *currently* experiencing passivity symptoms and found hyperactivity in the right parietal lobe and cingulate which reduced as passivity symptoms faded (some of Spence et al.'s findings are depicted in Figure 18.6). These studies illustrate the intrinsic appeal and explanatory potential of the cognitive neuropsychological approach, especially if applied in tandem with functional imaging.

Environmental factors

People usually develop schizophrenia in early adulthood at a time in their lives when they may be facing a new range of experiential stresses without family support. So if schizophrenia results from exposure to environmental stress, higher rates of illness might be expected in individuals who are exposed to lots of it. Additionally, people with schizophrenia might be expected to report higher levels of stress or more stressful events in the period before they became ill. In fact, evidence in support of either of these contentions is hard to come by. Unlike post-traumatic stress disorder, schizophrenia is no more prevalent amongst combat troops than non-combatants, or in people with very stressful jobs such as fire-fighters and paramedics. There is patchy evidence to suggest that first episode patients report more life-events in the period just before becoming ill (Bebbington et al., 1993), although a recent large-scale study actually found lower rates in patients than in a matched control group (Horan et al., 2004). Of course, this does not preclude the possibility that some individuals may be *especially* sensitive to the effects of stress – a question to be addressed below.

An early psychodynamic account of stress-induced illness came from Fromm-Reichmann (1948) who, on the basis of a small number of case studies, declared that the root cause of schizophrenia was the manipulative aloof and cold 'schizophrenogenic' mother and the resultant dysfunctional mother–child relationship. The double-bind hypothesis (Bateson et al., 1956) and Lidz's concepts of skew and schism (Lidz et al., 1957) followed, both to be amalgamated in Wynne and Singer's model of 'communication deviance' in the family. Although the details need not concern us, the common thread in each of these theories was that the child was the innocent victim of family tensions, mixed and contradictory parental messages, and linguistic ambiguities, and gradually withdrew into a schizophrenic state almost as a form of self-protection. Each of these ideas could be tested, but only Wynne and Singer's gained any empirical support (Singer and Wynne, 1966). However, when Hirsch and Leff later replicated their study, they found that the elevated communication deviance in the parents' speech was a consequence of a rate of speech which tended to be faster in this group (Hirsch and Leff, 1971). When this was controlled for, the difference disappeared.

Despite a lack of hard evidence, the aetiological role of stress (especially family related) formed the bedrock of the subsequent 'expressed emotion' (EE) research programme (Vaughn and Leff, 1976a), which pointed the accusing finger at family tensions reflected by hostility, criticism and emotional overinvolvement expressed during a semi-structured interview with one or both parents.

International perspective

A new perspective on the relationship between stress and schizophrenia

A new perspective on stress-schizophrenia is taking shape based on international research mainly coming from Holland, France and Belgium. It strips stress of its 'psychodynamic' properties and regards it rather as an agent that can induce subtle changes in physiological processes that are linked to schizophrenia. In an ingenious study using the experience sampling method with schizophrenic patients whose symptoms were in remission, Myin-Germeys, Delespaul and Van Os (2005) recorded both recent *stressful events* (approximately ten times a day at irregular intervals for 6 days) and associated subjective changes in *current/recent psychotic-like experiences*. Patients showed subtle but continuous fluctuations in these that co-varied with the minor stresses encountered in everyday life. The authors suggested that behavioural sensitisation to experiential stress might be a (genetic?) vulnerability marker for schizophrenia, reflecting a dopaminergic hyperresponsivity to everyday stresses. Compare this statement to the hypothetical model proposed at the beginning of this section and you will see that they have much in common. Stress does not cause schizophrenia, but it can induce subtle changes in the sensitivity of NT systems, which, if already compromised due to a genetic susceptibility, might lead to the symptoms of the disorder. (See also Kapur's model of DA-induced aberrant salience reviewed earlier.)

Van Os and colleagues have argued that similar processes may contribute to the link between urban living and schizophrenia touched on earlier. Krabbendam and Van Os (2005) reported a meta-analysis of urbanicity/schizophrenia studies that showed a moderate but consistent increased risk, especially if individuals were exposed to the urban environment in early life. These researchers were unable to say what, exactly, it was about urban living that is harmful, but they were able to discount generic stress, noise and pollution. Their favoured model (which is currently being tested) is that the urban environment serves as a stressor when social buffers such as mutual trust, cooperative neighbours and sense of physical safety are absent. In their view, these factors elevate risk of subsequent psychosis in genetically predisposed individuals via a sensitisation process (Spauwen et al., 2004) akin to that proposed by Myin-Germeys and colleagues.

Although high EE is no longer regarded as a direct cause of schizophrenia (Lenior et al., 2002), family therapy, based on practical steps to reduce it, remains a potentially important psychological procedure for staving off relapse, and this is revisited in the International perspective box.

Self-test questions

Imagine you are taking part in a debate about the role of neurobiological and environmental factors in schizophrenia.

- Identify three pieces of evidence implicating 'disordered brain functioning'.
- Identify three pieces of evidence implicating experiential factors.

Treatment and management of schizophrenia

Although treating/managing schizophrenia might involve both physical and psychological procedures, it should be stressed at the outset that medications remain the fundamental (and arguably indispensable) treatment of *first* resort. The chance discovery of anti-psychotic drugs in the 1950s followed a desperate period in which a range of physical (and some psychodynamic) procedures were used with little or no success. Somatic treatment options in the era before anti-psychotics included ECT, insulin coma therapy and lobotomy. Had anyone bothered to assess the efficacy of these for schizophrenia, they would have found them ineffective, and arguably harmful.

Anti-psychotic drugs

The arrival of chlorpromazine, soon to be followed by other anti-psychotics such as haloperidol and thioridazine, rapidly transformed patient management. Not only did these medications damp down many of the positive symptoms; they also had a general calming or even soporific effect. It became possible to discharge patients from long-term wards to be treated as day- or even as outpatients. Some of these medications could be administered in the form of a depot injection (into the gluteus maximus), the effects of which could last 2–3 weeks, obviating the need

for daily tablet taking. There can be little doubt that the process of mental hospital contraction and closure and the advent of **community care** is linked to the rapid and widespread adoption of these medications into clinical practice.

Unfortunately, many first-generation anti-psychotics induced side-effects which patients found irritating at best and unbearable at worst. Most were due to the action of the drugs on the brain's motor control regions, and included tremors, unintended movements (twitches, facial grimaces), restlessness and Parkinsonism (i.e. Parkinson's disease-like features). Some of these wore off over time and others could be partially controlled by additionally giving an anti-cholinergic drug. However, a more pernicious set of side-effects known as tardive dyskinesia (TD), involving a raft of involuntary facial and limb movements, developed in a proportion of typically older patients (estimated to be as many as 20 per cent; Kane and Smith, 1982). TD did not respond to anti-cholinergics and got worse over time. Other side-effects included sleepiness, lethargy and, in women, irregularities to the menstrual cycle.

Inevitably, patients weighed the side-effects of anti-psychotics against their therapeutic benefits and often decided to stop taking them once they felt better, although standard practice was (and still is) to prescribe at least 'maintenance' levels of medication even for patients who were/are in remission. Sadly, there is good evidence to show that stopping medications was the single most likely cause of relapse. Patients themselves often came to this realisation after further episodes of illness, giving rise to a *catch-22* sense of resentment (in some) that medication kept them out of hospital but impaired their general quality of life.

As mentioned earlier, it subsequently emerged that both the therapeutic- and side-effects of anti-psychotics could be attributed to their DA receptor-blocking properties, albeit at different locations in the brain. In the late 1960s, the drug clozapine was found to have anti-psychotic properties and fewer side-effects. However, shortly after being licensed it was withdrawn due to the occurrence of a rare but potentially fatal side-effect (agranulocytosis: depletion of white blood cells) in about 1 per cent of those treated. Nevertheless, drug companies began to develop new anti-psychotics modelled (to some extent) on the pharmacological profile of clozapine; and the so-called *atypical* group of anti-psychotic drugs, including olanzapine, seroquel and aripiprazole emerged in the mid-1990s. These drugs also block DA receptors, but generally do so less completely, and they also influence various other NT/receptor systems, including serotonin, acetylcholine and histamine. Clozapine too has now been reapproved, provided that patients are given regular blood checks, and it remains, arguably, the most effective member of the group. Incidentally, the prefix *atypical* refers to a reduction or complete absence of the extra-pyramidal side-effects that marred the first generation of drugs.

Unfortunately, in addition to clozapine-induced agranulocytosis, the other atypicals also bring about various side-effects, including weight gain, diabetes and arrhythmias of the heart. However, they do genuinely have fewer extra-pyramidal side-effects (including TD; Correll, Leucht and Kane, 2004) and have become the first-line treatments of choice in much of the developed world, even though their anti-psychotic properties appear only marginally superior to first-generation drugs (Leiberman et al., 2005; Lewis et al., 2006).

Other treatments for schizophrenia currently in the pipeline include drugs that promote glutamate neuro-transmission (Patil et al., 2007), drugs that influence the cannabinoid system (notably cannabidiol; Zuardi et al., 2006) and adjuncts (add-ons) to regular anti-psychotics, such as the hormone oxytocin (Keri, Kiss and Kelemen, 2008) and the anti-convulsant lamotrigine (Deakin et al., 2008).

Psychological interventions

Family therapy

Earlier, family therapy (FT) was described as growing out of the EE research effort. The basic idea is, of course, to reduce EE, and thus the *emotional temperature of a household* (Vaughn et al., 1984). The therapy typically involves a programme of education for family members about the illness, trouble-shooting tips and stress management training (Tarrier et al., 1989; Tarrier et al., 1994). Pilling et al. (2002a) reported a meta-analysis of family therapy, which indicated a clear advantage of it over treatment as usual (TAU) in terms of relapse prevention over 1 year, but not longer periods. In their meta-analysis of FT, Pitschel-Walz et al. (2004), suggested it brought about a modest but significant reduction in relapse rate (of about 20 per cent). Unfortunately, the procedure is only applicable in family households (not for people living alone), which rules out at least half of all people with schizophrenia. A second problem is that FT studies suffer from a high drop-out rate, leaving open the possibility that only families who found the programme worthwhile stay in it. A third criticism is that it marginalises the patient by focusing on other household members. Twenty years on from these classic studies, it is difficult to know how extensively FT is now applied. Most clinicians and therapists would argue that the patient should be integral to the therapy,

and for this reason, there is much more interest in client-centred psychotherapies, which are considered in the following sections.

Social skills training

There is a reasonably long history of applying psychological theory in the therapeutic setting. For example, token economies use a form of conditioning to try to coax improvements in behaviour in patients in hospital or care home settings. Modelling (imitation?) can be used to 'teach' improved social skills and self-care. Pilling et al. (2002b) considered data from nine social skills training studies (involving 471 schizophrenic patients) published up to 2000. He concluded that they usually achieve some degree of improvement in social functioning, especially for chronic patients in care settings. It was less clear how well these behavioural improvements generalised to individuals in the community, and how long the effects last once the therapy stops.

Other psychotherapies: IPT, CBT and CRT

Three more focused psychotherapies have recently attracted attention. These are personal (or interpersonal) therapy (IPT), cognitive behavioural therapy (CBT) and cognitive remediation therapy (CRT). Hogarty et al. (1995) introduced IPT for people with schizophrenia, partly in response to earlier concerns about patient marginalisation in most FT programmes, but still in the spirit of wishing to reduce EE. Content-wise, IPT resembles FT, but is conducted one-to-one through regular meetings over a period of months or even years between the therapist and recovering patient. It is practical and educative and, in effect, a programme of taught coping and interpersonal skills conducted in an empathetic and encouraging social setting. Evaluations of IPT are thin on the ground, although Hogarty et al. (1997) reported favourable outcomes for patients in households (as opposed to patients living alone) up to 3 years post-discharge. However, two recent studies by Rosenbaum et al. (2005) and Jackson et al. (2005) cast doubt on these conclusions. The Jackson study in particular was a **randomised controlled trial** comparing IPT with treatment as usual (TAU) in 91 patients, yet there were no significant differences between groups on any of the nine outcome measures.

CBT was initially developed by Beck (1976) as a treatment for mild to moderate depression (see Chapter 17). Its manifest success in that domain has been followed by applications elsewhere, including bipolar disorder and schizophrenia. The basic idea of this form of therapy, which also usually involves regular one-to-one meetings over several months between therapist and client/patient, is to discuss in a fairly objective way how the individual's thoughts, experiences and behaviour are affecting the way they currently feel. In the schizophrenia context, the therapist encourages the client to 'test' the validity of their (often unhelpful) thoughts, to try to understand them and, eventually, to change them. CBT is practical (as well as armchair based) and thus likely to involve behaviour-related exercises (homeworks) to be completed between therapy sessions (Peters, Greenwood and Kuipers, 2005). So, a person experiencing threatening auditory hallucinations may, as a homework, be 'tasked' to see whether the voices really do carry out their threats, to record such 'tests' of the erroneous belief(s), and to think of (and test) alternative, less fanciful explanations for their presence.

Recent studies have attested to the benefits of CBT in *treatment-resistant* patients (Pilling et al., 2002a; Durham et al., 2003, Startup, Jackson and Bendix, 2004) and for patients who experience **command hallucinations** (Trower et al., 2004). Three recent UK-based studies have additionally signalled its *partial* effectiveness in first episode cases. Lewis et al. (2002) and Tarrier et al. (2004) reported an initial advantage of CBT over TAU, but benefits were short-lived with relapse and rehospitalisation rates similar in both groups within 18 months. The early onset study by Craig et al. (2004) reached similar, somewhat equivocal conclusions. A 2-year follow-up study by Startup et al. (2005) reported sustained advantages of CBT over TAU for negative symptoms and social functioning but not for positive symptoms. On the other hand, Zimmerman et al. (2005) meta-analysed 14 CBT/schizophrenia studies conducted between 1990 and 2004, involving over 1000 patients with just over half receiving CBT, and reported a modest advantage in terms of reduced levels of positive symptoms, which was more marked in acute than chronic patients.

Two CBT studies postdating Zimmerman's meta-analysis merit mention. Turkington et al. (2008) have reported a 5-year follow-up study employing a randomised controlled methodology to evaluate CBT against TAU and another non-specific intervention, befriending (essentially a blend of 'buddying' and 'mentoring'). CBT showed a more enduring effect in terms of a sustained reduction in overall symptom severity and negative symptoms than befriending or TAU. However, the CBT group did not differ from the befriending group in terms of overall symptoms of schizophrenia or, for that matter, depression. The second study by Morrison et al. (2004; 2007) used a randomised controlled methodology to compare the effects of CBT or TAU for young individuals deemed to be at high risk for psychosis because they were experiencing attenuated subclinical psychotic symptoms. The

preliminary report (2004) indicated a protective effect of the 6-month CBT programme because fewer individuals in this group *converted* to full psychosis. However, closer inspection of the data revealed that the numbers in either group who converted was very small (six versus two). The group's later paper considered outcome at 36 months. By this stage, there were seven converters in each group and the overall difference between CBT and TAU was non-significant.

Despite the amount of recent research it is, as yet, difficult to evaluate the true worth of CBT for schizophrenia, notwithstanding the almost evangelical fervour of its many supporters (Pelosi, 2003; Birchwood, 2003). Clearly, some patients seem to benefit from it in terms of symptom reduction or fewer relapses. However, it is important to remember that it is not an alternative to medication. Rather, as with most other psychological interventions, it is an adjunct procedure which, like FT (see above), may indirectly encourage stricter adherence to a medication regime. This raises the question as to whether any observed improvements are genuinely related to CBT or simply a consequence of better compliance. Research is also needed to explore the optimum delivery format of CBT. At present, a course typically involves a series of regular sessions over a relatively short period of time, but it has been suggested that a better format may be the psychological equivalent of maintenance medication: that is, a moderate amount on a regular basis. Arguably the most difficult finding for CBT proponents to address is the non-significant difference between it and 'befriending' as a means of reducing schizophrenia symptoms (Turkington et al., 2008). It is also interesting to note that, although CBT was initially 'heralded' as a procedure for reducing or even eliminating symptoms, it is nowadays presented as a therapy to ameliorate the *distress* of symptoms – a qualitatively different, though admittedly still worthy, objective.

The last of our trio of therapies, CRT, has a long and chequered history, but has attracted particular attention of late because clinicians and researchers now recognise cognitive impairment as a core feature of schizophrenia, impacting on work, social functioning and quality of life (Foster-Green, 1996; McGurk and Mueser, 2004; Nuechterlein et al., 2004). Early studies (e.g. Meichenbaum and Cameron, 1973) employed rather non-specific methods to bring about cognitive improvement. Conversely, more recent studies have used highly operationalised procedures involving, for example, 'scaffolded' incremental tasks, massed practice and errorless learning techniques, to target particular domains of impaired cognition, such as attention, memory and executive function (Delahunty et al., 2002; Wykes and Reeder, 2005). Despite the multiplicity of methods and procedures, the underlying objective in all this research is to bring about improvements in cognitive functioning, which though beneficial in itself, may additionally lead to improved social and even clinical functioning.

Three recent CRT studies provide a flavour of the technique and its effects. Bark et al. (2003) reported that ten half-hour sessions of CRT spread over a 5-week period brought about improved cognition but had only a marginal effect on psychopathology. Fiszdon et al. (2004) showed that a computer-based CRT programme led to a sustained improvement in cognitive function at 6-month follow-up, but this did not generalise to symptomatic improvement. Conversely, Reeder et al. (2004) reported the effects of a highly structured face-to-face CRT programme involving 40 sessions spread over 15 weeks, compared with two different control conditions. The CRT group showed the most pronounced cognitive improvements, and only this group recorded a significant improvement in social functioning at the conclusion of the programme.

McGurk et al. (2007) meta-analysed all CRT studies published between 1968 and 2005 meeting quite stringent methodological criteria. In fact, of the previous three, only the Reeder study was included, along with 25 other studies involving over 1100 patients. Three outcome domains were considered: cognition, social functioning and symptomology. Overall, CRT was shown to be more effective than TAU in all three domains; however, symptomatic improvement was more pronounced in patients who were also receiving concurrent psychiatric rehabilitation.

There has been one published study (by Penades et al., 2006) in which CRT has been directly compared with CBT. Forty chronic patients were randomly assigned to 4 months of either CRT or CBT (there was no TAU control group). CRT improved neurocognition and social functioning; CBT improved general psychopathology but not neurocognition; and neither procedure improved positive or negative symptom profiles.

Overall, our 'take' on CRT as an adjunct procedure for people with schizophrenia is similar to our view on CBT. It seems to have a number of moderate but helpful effects which can, but do not necessarily always, generalise beyond the specific cognitive domains being targeted. Even for these, it is presently unclear if remediation endures much beyond the completion of the CRT programme. On the other hand, CRT is widely 'liked' by patients (C. Reeder; personal communication) and the therapeutic alliance that develops between therapist and patient may encourage greater engagement with other elements of service provision, which on balance is probably a good thing.

Our overview of treatments/management of schizophrenia is now complete. As mentioned at the start, antipsychotic medication remains a fundamental component of any care-plan for schizophrenia, but the package might, and arguably should, include one or more of the psychological procedures reviewed above, each of which appears to bring some added value for the patient. One obvious conclusion from the Penades study is that some patients appear to gain benefit from CRT whilst others may get more from a programme of CBT. In other words, the therapy needs to be chosen that will best meet the individual patient's needs. At the moment it is quite hard to say with any certainty what, specifically, in either CRT or CBT, is therapeutic, and more research is needed to unpick potential confounds. Even if, as some critics have suggested, benefits are primarily linked to their encouragement of greater *social engagement* in the recovering patient, it seems to us that facilitating this by *any* means is probably to the patient's advantage.

Self-test questions

For each of the following psychological interventions for schizophrenia, indicate the 'theoretical basis' for the procedure, its basic format (schedule) and its primary intention/ambition:

- social skills training
- family therapy
- IPT
- CBT
- CRT

Schizophrenia boundaries and other psychotic disorders

So far, although the heterogeneity of schizophrenia has been extensively described, the question of its borders, either with other disorders or with 'normality', has not been addressed. On the latter point, a decision as to whether or not an individual's behaviour merits an actual diagnosis (and all that follows from that) often depends as much on practical matters as on the severity of symptoms. Access to a hospital bed, level of family support and, in some countries, money all come into the equation. In other words, individuals who may receive a diagnosis in town A or country B could slip through the net in town C or country D (see Murthy et al., 2005). For some, refuge is just as likely to be a prison or hostel for the homeless as a psychiatric clinic or ward (Lam and Rosenheck, 1999). Remember too that in most developed countries, individuals are at liberty to be mentally ill and cannot usually be forced into hospital/care unless they present some clear level of danger either to themselves or to others. Thus, it is widely accepted that level of recorded mental illness significantly underestimates the actual level of illness in the population as a whole. Although figures are notoriously difficult to gather, Kramer (1980) estimated that 3 per cent of US citizens surviving to the age of 55 had had at least one episode of schizophrenia, notwithstanding the broader definition of the condition that prevailed in the USA at that time. A stroll around most inner-city areas will provide further evidence of untreated severe mental illness in a proportion of vagrants and other street-people.

Schizotypy

In addition to undiagnosed illness in the normal population, there is a growing recognition that some features of schizophrenia described earlier are experienced in a proportion of otherwise entirely healthy individuals. Depending on how questions are framed, as many as a third of respondents acknowledge having experienced occasional hallucinatory events (Barrett and Etheridge, 1992), and about the same proportion will describe quasi-delusory experiences (Peters, Joseph and Garety, 1999). For some, the presence of symptoms in members of the general population identifies individuals at risk for developing schizophrenia in the future (e.g. Claridge, 1994; 1997). However, since the proportion of people reporting such experiences is so much higher than the incident rate of schizophrenia, a more realistic perspective might be to think of 'psychosis-proneness' or 'schizotypy' (as it is more commonly known) as a normally distributed trait with schizophrenia at an extreme end (Johns and van Os, 2001).

Today, at least a dozen self-report questionnaires are available to 'locate' an individual on the schizotypy continuum. The brief Schizotypal Personality Questionnaire (SPQ-B; Raine 1991) includes just 22 yes/no items which can be divided in positive and negative schizotypal features. The O-LIFE questionnaire has 159 items to derive scores on four subscales: unusual experiences, cognitive disorganisation, introvertive anhedonia and impulsive nonconformity. Although there is currently debate about the exact factor structure of schizotypy, there is general agreement that cognitive–perceptual distortions and interpersonal problems are distinct. Some groups include a third factor

which relates to disorganisation of thinking and behaviour (e.g. Gruzelier et al., 1995; Vollema and Hoijtink, 2000; Rossi and Daneluzzo, 2002). These authors suggest that the three factors produced by certain schizotypy scales broadly reflect the symptomology associated with Liddle's tripartite model of schizophrenia.

An absolute deluge of research papers has followed the development of schizotypy measures, and space permits only the most cursory of reviews. Nevertheless, people who score at the high end of the schizotypy continuum are at greater risk for converting to full psychosis (Miller et al., 2002); show more neuropsychological deficits (Hawkins et al., 2004); have more soft signs (Barkus et al., 2006), and evince a range of cognitive impairments in the domains of memory, attention, language and executive functioning (including **meta-cognitive** impairments; Morisson and Baker, 2000; Stirling, Barkus and Lewis, 2007) similar to, but usually less pronounced than, those seen in people with schizophrenia (Obiols et al., 1997; Niendam et al., 2006).

Other psychotic disorders

A number of unambiguously psychotic disorders border schizophrenia yet are phenomenologically sufficiently distinct to merit separate consideration. Most of these are rare in comparison with schizophrenia and consequently tend to be underresearched. *DSM-IV* identifies four disorders in addition to the routine categories of substance-induced disorder and psychotic disorder related to a general medical condition. *ICD-10* differentiates schizoaffective disorder, persistent delusional disorder, and acute transient psychotic disorder.

Schizophreniform and brief psychotic disorder

A diagnosis of schizophreniform disorder might be made for someone with classic schizophrenia symptoms that have lasted less than 6 months but more than 1 month. The term 'schizophreniform psychosis' was first introduced by Langfeldt (1937) to identify people with a good prognosis form of the illness. Since then it has undergone a series of revisions, eventually falling out of use. It reappeared in the USA as a provisional diagnosis at the same time that the authors of *DSM-III* (American Psychiatric Association, 1980) decided that a full diagnosis of schizophrenia could not be made until an individual had been ill for at least 6 months. Once again, it was characterised as a rapid-onset, short-duration condition with good prognosis. However, a recent study by Zarate, Tohen and Land (2000) casts doubt on these assumptions. Although schizophreniform cases had a better outcome at 6 months post-onset than a group with definite schizophrenia, differences disappeared at 24 months, by which time most of the schizophreniform cases had been rediagnosed with schizophrenia. Clearly, in light of such findings, the value of this diagnosis must be in doubt (also see Strakowski, 1994).

Brief psychotic disorder (which overlaps with acute transient psychotic disorder in *ICD-10*) has a duration of less than 1 month (Pillman et al., 2002). The prevalence of this rare condition is unknown, but clinicians acknowledge that it usually does indicate a better prognosis than schizophrenia. It is characterised by a sudden onset, and rapid and full recovery, typically in individuals with no prior or family history of mental illness. Of course, this raises other questions about aetiology: Was undetected substance abuse involved? Was unreported stress a precipitating factor? Recently, its value as a diagnostic entity has, like schizophreniform disorder, been questioned because follow-up studies indicate that about 50 per cent of cases will be rediagnosed to schizophrenia or schizoaffective disorder (see below) within 12 months (Jorgensen et al., 1997; Singh et al., 2004).

Schizoaffective disorder

In about 4–5 per cent of cases of psychosis, individuals present with a mixture of psychotic and affective symptoms of an intensity that might actually qualify them for a diagnosis of both schizophrenia and bipolar disorder were this possible within the diagnostic algorithm. Because it is not, the diagnosis of schizoaffective disorder would be made. Although this sounds like a 'double whammy', schizoaffective disorder actually has a more favourable prognosis than schizophrenia, with less evidence of cognitive decline and fewer enduring negative symptoms (Goodwin and Jamison, 2007).

Delusional disorder

This rare condition has been estimated to have a lifetime prevalence of 0.1 per cent. The core feature is the presence of marked delusions, typically of grandeur, jealousy or persecution, in the absence of other symptoms such as hallucinations or thought disorder (Munro, 1999). Examples include morbid jealousy and de Clérembault's syndrome. Somatic delusions may also feature.

Other rare psychotic disorders

Shared psychotic disorder (also known as *folie a deux*) may be diagnosed where an individual has a delusion which is very similar in content to that of a second person, usually a close friend, or other people involved. Its aetiology

is unknown. *Capgras syndrome* would be identified in an individual who believes that someone close to them has been replaced by an impostor pretending to be that person. It has recently been suggested that Capgras syndrome is a disconnection disorder with an organic basis (Ramachandran, 1998).

Substance-induced and psychotic disorder due to a general medical condition

Some psychoactive substances, such as amphetamine, LSD, angel dust (PCP) and ketamine can produce schizophrenia-like symptoms. These should abate in time with abstinence, which can be assessed by urine or blood analysis. In the case of amphetamine-induced psychosis, symptoms usually resolve after 10 or so days of non-use. Heavy or persistent cannabis use (to be discussed below) is known to induce transient psychotic experiences in some users (D'Souza et al., 2004). However, according to other researchers (e.g. Linszen, Dingemans and Lenoir, 1994), it may induce full episodes of schizophrenia (rather than isolated psychotic features) in individuals with a particular genetic susceptibility (Henquet et al., 2005).

A number of physical conditions, including temporal lobe epilepsy, Huntington's and Alzheimer's diseases, and tertiary syphilis, can also involve psychotic features. This may help to explain why, for example, exclusion of organic brain disease is a necessary requirement before a diagnosis of definite schizophrenia can be made. Finally, some metabolic disorders can also 'present' as psychotic disorders. These include hyperthyroidism, hypoglycemia and various disorders of electrolyte balance/function.

Cluster A personality disorders (also see Chapter 14)

As you will be aware, this trio of *DSM* axis II personality disorders (PDs) also shares common ground with schizophrenia. To complicate matters, an individual may, in fact, be comorbid for a PD and schizophrenia (or another axis I disorder). Cluster A, sometimes also known as the odd-eccentric cluster, comprises paranoid, schizoid and schizotypal PDs. Of the three, schizotypal PD has most in common with schizophrenia, being closely linked with Meehl's concept of schizotaxia (Meehl, 1962) – a sort of genetic diathesis which he believed had to be present in all cases of schizophrenia, but which might also be present in close relatives showing no *frank* features of psychosis. This matter came to the fore in some of the early epidemiological genetics studies reviewed earlier, in which, for example, researchers felt it necessary to extend, and arguably blur, diagnostic entities (e.g. borderline or latent schizophrenia, pseudoneurotic schizophrenia) to accommodate first-degree relatives of affected individuals who displayed odd or eccentric behaviours but did not meet full diagnostic criteria for schizophrenia (Heston, 1966; Kety et al., 1971). The concept gained formal recognition through inclusion in *DSM-III* (American Psychiatric Association, 1980). Features were said to include odd and eccentric thinking and beliefs, ideas of reference, cognitive and perceptual anomalies, and poor interpersonal skills.

Despite its being retained in more recent versions of the *DSM*, clinicians seem uneasy about the boundaries of schizotypal personality disorder and it remains an infrequent diagnosis as a consequence (McKenna, 2007). Others have suggested that it shares much more in common with schizophrenia than previously acknowledged. Recent studies have, for example, shown that people meeting schizotypal PD diagnostic criteria have similar cognitive dysfunctions to people with schizophrenia (Lenzenweger, 2001), similar though less marked interpersonal problems, and, perhaps most tellingly, similar though less extensive functional and structural brain anomalies to people with schizophrenia (Dickey et al., 1999; Dickey, McCarley and Shenton, 2002). An alternative take on schizotypal PD, therefore, is that it is not a PD at all, but an attenuated form of schizophrenia (Siever and Davis, 2004) that occupies some notional ground between high schizotypy and true schizophrenia.

Schizoid PD can trace its origins to the belief, widely held even in Kraepelin's and Bleuler's day, that most people who went on to develop schizophrenia-proper had unusual personalities before they became ill. Although this personality profile went by several names, recurrent descriptors included aloofness, lack of pleasure seeking, flat affect, asociality and preference for solitude. A systematic study of 24 personality features associated with schizoid PD by Tyrer (1988) indicated that people with schizophrenia had significantly higher (more pathological) scores on 19 of them. However, more than a third of patients had none of the features before becoming ill and a further significant proportion evinced only minor abnormalities. Taken together, these findings suggest that schizoid PD is not a prerequisite for subsequent schizophrenia; rather that it may or may not be present in individuals who go on to develop the disorder.

If it is a distinct entity, it is reasonable to ask: what causes schizoid PD? Psychodynamic explanations emphasise the importance of aloof hostile parental styles (the schizophrenogenic mother again?) prompting the child to develop schizoid tendencies (Kernberg and Caligor, 2005). Cognitive theorists have argued that schizoid PD stems from the acquisition in childhood of erroneous

negative beliefs (schemas) that become entrenched: examples may include the views that *'people are basically evil'* or *'people will take advantage of you if you give them the opportunity'*. Neither of these explanations has received a resounding endorsement from the handful of empirical investigations into its aetiology. A recent research approach has examined the overlap between autism (especially Asperger's syndrome) and schizoid PD (Woodbury-Smith and Volkmar, 2008). Were this link to be substantiated, it would raise the possibility of there being a biological basis to the pathological aloofness and asociality which is a hallmark feature of schizoid PD, but the jury is presently out.

As its name suggests, paranoid PD has as its core feature a pervasive, persistent and unjustifiable suspiciousness of other people (American Psychiatric Association, 2000). Such general suspiciousness inevitably precipitates negative reactions in others, which, in a vicious circle, may serve to exacerbate the paranoia felt by the PD individual. A further complication is that individuals with paranoid PD may become preoccupied with testing the loyalty and trustworthiness of acquaintances and work colleagues, leading to further resentments. Hostility towards others may be fuelled by the misinterpretation of the actions of others towards them, as threatening, overly aggressive, suspicious, etc.

The first signs of a paranoid personality disorder may be identified in childhood by instances of eccentricity, odd communications and poor interpersonal skills, leading to arguments and/or playground fights. It is more common in males and has a prevalence of around 0.5–2.5 per cent in the general population. Additionally, it frequently co-occurs with both borderline and avoidant personality disorder (Bernstein, 1993).

The overlap with schizophrenia has heuristic appeal because of the prominent position of paranoid thinking in both disorders. However, there is a qualitative distinction that should be emphasised: whereas in paranoid PD, the individual manifests a general suspiciousness of others, in paranoid schizophrenia, the suspicion is often targeted towards an individual (or organisation), imbued with bizarre fanciful explanations, and coincidental with other psychotic symptoms such as hallucinations. As with schizoid PD, more people with schizophrenia meet diagnostic criteria for paranoid PD than the prevalence rate in the general population cited above, but it remains an infrequent diagnosis even in this group. There is, additionally, some evidence to suggest that close relatives of people with schizophrenia have slightly elevated rates of paranoid PD (Kendler et al., 1993; Fogelson et al., 2007), though whether this is attributable to environmental or genetic factors has yet to be resolved.

Clinical issues

Three issues preoccupy current thinking about schizophrenia from a clinical perspective. Firstly, there is the question of how to blend treatments in order to optimise outcome. Secondly, and closely related to the first, is the question of when to commence treatments. Specifically, should treatments be directed at individuals who are at risk of psychosis but who have not yet experienced a fully fledged psychotic episode? Thirdly, on a different tack, the spectre of *self-induced* schizophrenia through excessive recreational drug use has become a pressing issue in countries where such drugs are relatively easy to acquire. The first two points have already been touched on, so arguments need not be revisited in too much detail here. The third issue, specifically the possible link between cannabis use and schizophrenia, merits more attention because cannabis use is widespread amongst individuals in the age band of greatest risk for schizophrenia, and because the chemical composition of cannabis has changed into a more potent form in recent years.

Optimal treatments

The current choice of medications for schizophrenia is wider than it has ever been, yet even the most effective offers only symptomatic relief, and is likely to induce unwanted side-effects too. Additional drugs are currently under development, either as replacements for existing anti-psychotics, or to be used as adjuncts alongside conventional drugs. This is a rapidly evolving field and there is a general sense of optimism that new drug treatments will have greater efficacy with fewer side-effects than those currently available. However, this enthusiasm must be tempered by the recent reports by Leiberman and Lewis (both cited earlier) that the second-generation atypical anti-psychotics are not much more effective than the traditional ones, so long as dosages of these are properly managed.

It should be clear from our review of psychotherapies for schizophrenia that almost any procedure (used as an adjunct) improves some aspect(s) of functioning for the recovering patient, whether it is highly operationalised (as in CRT programmes) or fairly ad hoc (as in Hogarty's IPT). However, this research raises two fundamental questions. Firstly, are the current modes of delivery of psychotherapies, which typically involve sessions with a therapist once or twice a week for a few months, optimal for a disorder that might run for many years, and possibly an entire adult life? Further research is needed to evaluate 'maintenance psychotherapy' or, alternatively, 'refresher' or 'top-up' sessions for patients whose last experience of CBT or family therapy might have been some considerable time ago. Secondly, a greater effort is required to fit the psychotherapy to the needs of the patient: those with lots of cognitive deficits are likely to get more from a course of CRT than CBT, whilst the reverse might be true for those with more intrusive positive symptoms.

Initiating treatments

As for when to start treatment, it is now widely accepted that early intervention is associated with better outcomes (Harrigan, McGorry and Krtsev, 2003). This has prompted some clinicians to advocate initiating treatment even before the first full episode of illness. As mentioned earlier, some services in Australia (Yung et al., 2003), North America (Addington et al., 2007) and the UK (Morrison et al., 2004; 2007) seek to recruit 'at-risk' individuals (typically adolescents experiencing attenuated psychotic-like phenomena) to anti-psychotic and, in one instance, CBT treatment programmes, in order to prevent or delay later psychotic breakdown. And, Morrison et al.'s CBT study excepted, initial results show an advantage in terms of lower rates of conversion to psychosis in targeted individuals than 'controls' (Larsen et al., 2007). Well-intentioned though these research efforts may be, they raise two important related questions. Firstly, is it ethically acceptable to prescribe powerful medications to individuals who are not yet mentally ill? And secondly, is it ethically acceptable to prescribe powerful medications to individuals who will *not* become ill? The latter point stems from the well-established observation that a relatively small proportion of adolescents who experience intermittent psychotic-like experiences actually go on to develop fully fledged schizophrenia within the next 24 months (Hanssen et al., 2005). Clearly, if very early treatment is to enter the mainstream, more effective means of identifying at-risk individuals (with fewer false positives) will be required.

The cannabis connection

Cannabis use has long been associated with an increase in the reporting of psychosis-like experiences for some individuals (Thomas, 1996). It also increases both the risk of relapse and severity of symptoms in people already diagnosed with schizophrenia (Linszen, Dingemans and Lenoir, 1994; Baigent, Holme and Hafner, 1995). Using complex mathematical modelling procedures, other researchers (e.g. Degenhardt and Hall, 2001; Van Os et al., 2002) have suggested that its use also increases the risk for psychosis in individuals with *no* previous history of illness. However, it is methodologically difficult to untangle cause and effect in this type of research. Are people who are prone to psychosis attracted to cannabis use (an association model), or does cannabis use truly increase the incidence of psychotic experiences (a causal model)? This question is partly answered by three recently reported studies indicating that early cannabis use, pre-dating any self-reported psychosis-like symptoms, appears to be a risk factor for later illness (Arsenault et al., 2002a; Fergusson, Horwood and Swain-Campbell, 2003; Schiffman et al., 2005).

The cannabis–psychosis link has also been examined in relation to high-schizotypy individuals (deemed at increased risk for later psychosis). Using the experience-sampling method described earlier, Verdoux et al. (2003) reported that psychosis-vulnerability and cannabis use were inde-pendently associated with unusual perceptual experiences. Henquet et al. (2005) have reported that early psychosis-like experiences increase the likelihood of subsequent psychotic states following cannabis use – an effect appar-ently mediated by genetic differences in sensitivity to the principal active ingredient, delta 9 tetrahydrocannabinol (Δ 9 THC) (Caspi et al., 2005).

Δ 9 THC binds to (occupies and stimulates) cannabinoid (CB1) receptors localised in the prefrontal cortex, basal ganglia and hippocampus (Herkenham et al., 1990) where, amongst other actions, it has general DA agonist effects (Voruganti et al., 2001). Earlier, the heightened sensitiv-ity of DA systems in acute schizophrenia was described (Laruelle, Kegeles and Abi-Dargham, 2003). Verdoux's and Henquet's data suggests that some increased sensitiv-ity may also be present along the psychosis continuum (Van Os et al., 2000) and, critically, that cannabis might increase this further.

Clearly, cannabis does not cause schizophrenia, since most casual users do not become ill. However, a small proportion do. Research findings cited above suggest that people with high schizotypy who use cannabis might be at increased risk by dint of a genetic susceptibility to the effects of THC acting on an already compromised DA system (see Barkus and Lewis, 2008). Although precise figures are notoriously hard to come by, cannabis use is currently widespread amongst young people. Recent British Crime Survey reports indicate that use has risen steadily since the early 1980s, with about 15 million people having tried it at least once, and between 2 and 5 million people using it regularly. In our survey of drug use amongst young people in the UK and Holland, over 70 per cent of our pooled sample had used cannabis at least once and most of these were regular users (Stirling et al., 2008). The problem seems to be compounded by

the fact that the cannabis available today typically contains higher concentrations of THC than that in circulation 20–30 years ago. Some clinicians have argued that excess use of stronger cannabis is the most likely explanation for the recent rise in admissions to hospital of people suffering a first episode of schizophrenia (Murray et al., 2007).

Self-test questions

- Identify the main lines of evidence in support of the view that cannabis use can lead to mental health problems.
- Why is it unlikely that cannabis actually directly causes schizophrenia or other psychoses?
- What is the significance of the findings of Henquet et al. (2005) for our understanding of vulnerability to adverse effects of cannabis?

Forensic implications

Two related issues dominate forensic aspects of schizo-phrenia: firstly, whether people with schizophrenia are inherently more violent towards themselves (than non-schizophrenics), and secondly whether they are inherently more violent towards others.

Suicide

The first question can be addressed quite easily thanks to two recently published meta-analyses of suicide in schizo-phrenia (Pinikahana, Happell and Keks, 2003; Hawton et al., 2005). Pinikahana's study, covering the 1990s, estab-lished an estimated lifetime risk of suicide for people with schizophrenia of between 9 and 13 per cent; a figure at least 20 times higher than that in the general population. Young isolated that male patients with poor or absent social support were at greatest risk. Suicide attempts were most likely relatively soon after initial diagnosis. The Hawton review sought to identify specific risk factors for suicide. It covered *all* reports of suicide in people with schizophrenia up to 2004 that met satisfactory (stringent) inclusion criteria; 29 studies from around the world span-ning the period 1964 to 2003 qualified. Risk of suicide was associated with previous depressive episodes, poor adherence to treatment and 'fear of mental disintegration'. Interestingly, presence of positive symptoms significantly reduced suicide risk. These findings suggest that greater insight might be linked to higher risk of suicide.

Violent behaviour

The question of increased levels of violence towards others arises because of rare but often well-publicised cases in which current or former patients commit acts of violence on innocent individuals. A prominent UK case was the murder of Jonathan Zito, who was repeatedly stabbed on an underground station platform by Christopher Clunis. Clunis, who had a history of paranoid schizophrenia, was ostensibly in a community care programme, but had stopped taking his medication and had, in fact, committed a series violent attacks on other people (without being apprehended) in the days before the fatal attack on Zito.

An even more controversial case was that of 'The Yorkshire Ripper', which is reviewed in the Focus box. Peter Sutcliffe (his real name) was convicted in 1981 of the murders of 13 women in the UK between 1975 and 1980.

He also pleaded guilty to seven further counts of attempted murder, and subsequently admitted to two more. At his trial, he claimed that he was acting on instructions from God who had ordered him to 'kill prostitutes.' Despite the testimony of several psychiatrists that he was probably mentally ill with paranoid schizophrenia for part or most of the period during which he carried out the attacks, his plea of 'diminished responsibility' was dismissed by the court and he was sent to prison. There, his mental health rapidly deteriorated and he was removed to a secure hospital where he still resides.

How typical are the cases of Clunis and Sutcliffe? The answer, with certain caveats, would seem to be 'not particularly'. According to a study by Wallace et al. (1998), a mere 0.3 per cent of individuals with schizophrenia will be convicted of a serious violent crime in any given year, and the probability of committing a homicide is about 1:3000 per year for men and 1:30,000 for women. Certainly, a number of other psychiatric diagnoses are significantly more closely associated with violent crime than is schizophrenia. These include bipolar disorder, substance abuse disorder and anti-social PD.

However, these statistics tell only part of the story, and careful analysis of a wealth of data examining the

---

Focus

The case of Peter Sutcliffe, 'The Yorkshire Ripper'

Sutcliffe lived an undistinguished life in West Yorkshire (UK), working in a variety of menial jobs after leaving school aged 15. He met his future wife, Czech-born Sonia Szurma, in 1967 and they married in 1974. Although there has always been some dispute about the exact number of women he attacked/murdered, the series of 13 murders of which he was eventually convicted commenced in 1975 and continued until 1980, shortly before his arrest. At his trial he also pleaded guilty to seven counts of attempted murder. A number (though not all) of his victims were prostitutes with whom he regularly visited as a young man.

When he was eventually arrested (initially because his car had false number plates), police only linked him to the Ripper case because of circumstantial evidence; his appearance matched descriptions of the Ripper; and he was with a prostitute at the time of his arrest. After 2 days of questioning, he suddenly admitted he was the Ripper and began to detail the attacks for which he was subsequently convicted.

At this time, he did not mention that his attacks were prompted by messages from God; this aspect of his defence only emerged later, nearer the time of his trial. Sutcliffe pleaded not-guilty to murder on the grounds of diminished responsibility. The 'messages-from-God' command hallucinations had now become part of his defence, and he claimed to have first heard these when he was working as a gravedigger in the early 1970s, long before his first attack. Four psychiatrists evaluated him and confirmed that he had paranoid schizophrenia. Even the prosecution were willing to accept the diminished responsibility plea, but after review, the trial judge decided that he should be tried before a jury and his plea was rejected. The trial lasted 2 weeks. New prosecution psychiatrists were found who raised doubts about the authenticity of his mental health claims, and he was found guilty on all counts.

Within weeks of starting his prison sentence, his mental health deteriorated further and he was once again diagnosed with paranoid schizophrenia. He was eventually transferred to Broadmoor Special Hospital, where he resides to this day.

association between mental health and violence leads to the conclusion that there is a small but consistent over-representation of instances of violent crime for people with a schizophrenia diagnosis. Walsh, Buchanan and Fahy (2002) have provided a comprehensive review of this research. For example, follow-up studies of cohorts of individuals with a diagnosis of schizophrenia indicate at least a doubling of the likelihood of subsequently committing a violent crime. In one 15-year follow-up study by Linqvist and Allebeck (1990), there was a four-fold increase in the rate of violent crime over this extended period. This association can also be explored by assessing the rate of mental illness in individuals who have been convicted of violent crime(s). Taylor and Gunn (1984) used this strategy to look at psychiatric morbidity in violent prisoners: 9 per cent of those convicted for a non-fatal violent crime and 11 per cent of those convicted for a fatal violent crime had schizophrenia. More recently, Wallace et al. (1998) reported that people with a schizophrenia diagnosis were four times more likely to be convicted of interpersonal violence, and ten times more likely to be convicted of homicide, than the general population. Eaton and Kessler (1985) also found a four-fold increase in violent acts in people with schizophrenia compared to non-patients. However, to put these figures in perspective, comorbidity with substance abuse increased this risk 15-fold.

Two studies postdating Walsh's review contribute to the emerging picture of the association between schizophrenia and violence. Soyka et al. (2007) analysed the subsequent criminal careers of over 1500 patients treated for schizophrenia in Germany in the early 1990s. Almost 4 per cent were convicted of violent crimes in the 7–12-year follow-up period, including five cases of homicide. Violence was predicted by lack of insight and absence of depressive features at time of discharge. Swanson et al. (2008) also tried to identify predictors of subsequent violence in schizophrenia patients. Data from almost 1500 patients confirmed earlier observations of an overall increased rate of violent criminal activity in this group, which was particularly marked in individuals with a history of childhood conduct disorder and anti-social behaviour predating their becoming ill with schizophrenia.

In sum, these data suggest that the long-standing image of individuals with schizophrenia as passive, benign and withdrawn is, in some instances, quite inaccurate. Although other conditions (particularly anti-social PD) are more likely to predict violent criminal activity, schizophrenia also carries a small but consistent elevated risk, which rises in males with a history of anti-social behaviour, and is further potentiated by comorbid substance abuse.

Critical evaluation

Thus far, we have offered an orthodox (uncritical) view of schizophrenia. Now there is a need to consider alternative perspectives and assess their standing against our more conventional 'take'. In Chapter 3, the anti-psychiatry viewpoint was introduced. In reality, there is not, nor has there ever been, a single anti-psychiatry manifesto. Instead, the term has become a rallying point for various clinicians, patient groups and academics dissatisfied with some or all aspects of orthodox psychiatric practice. In the context of this chapter, it is also important to note that although intended as a general critique of psychiatry, much of the debate has actually focused on schizophrenia.

Anti- and critical psychiatry

The original anti-psychiatry movement gathered momentum in the 1960s at a time when biological approaches to psychiatry were just beginning to gain a foot-hold after several decades in the wilderness; an era dominated in North America particularly, and Europe to a lesser extent, by psychoanalytic approaches. This context is important in helping to understand why Laing (1965) argued that schizophrenia was a sane reaction to an insane world, and Szasz (1971) argued that *the sacred symbol* of psychiatry, schizophrenia, was a myth. It is likely that they were both concerned by the potential for progress from the more scientifically rooted biological approach, and all that this meant in terms of reductionism, control (through medication) and loss of personal responsibility (for the patient), and of course, an undermining of their own positions.

Laing, an analytically oriented clinician, had been heavily influenced by some of the work reviewed earlier on family dynamics, offering various anecdotal accounts of dysfunctional parent–child discourse in support of his view that schizophrenia was, in effect, *an elective response* to repeated contradictory and ambiguous 'messages' in the social interactions of some families. As already mentioned, attempts to validate the ideas of Bateson, Lidz, Wynne and Singer were generally unsuccessful. The patterns of discourse deemed pathological by these writers were not easy to identify and, where they were observed, were certainly not unique to households in which someone went on to develop schizophrenia (e.g. Hirsch and Leff, 1971).

The central plank of Szasz's argument was (and remains) that mental illness relates to 'mind' – a hypothetical rather than physical construct. As such, the mind cannot become ill, so schizophrenia is not an illness in the sense that diabetes clearly is; rather, it is a complex behavioural and interpersonal disturbance (in Szasz's words, 'a problem of living') which, in the absence of a clear neurological lesion, should not be 'assumed' to be linked to brain dysfunction. Szasz objects to the medicalisation of psychiatry and largely ignores advances in neuroscientific research in his writing. Somewhat counterintuitively, he is happy to endorse the process of therapy as long as the patient desires it. However, he would regard treating someone against their will (as may happen under some sections of the Mental Health Act) as both unethical and immoral.

It would be hard to defend the positions of either Laing or Szasz in light of advances in our understanding of brain–behaviour relations over the last 40 years, and few clinicians adhere to these viewpoints today. Nevertheless, there are enough skeletons in psychiatry's cupboard to cause continuing concern and dissent in some quarters. For example, there are worries about the influence that pharmaceutical companies have on clinical practice (Healy, 1997). Some patient groups continue to lobby against involuntary admission to hospitals and involuntary treatment therein (MIND, 2008). There are unanswered questions about the overrepresentation of people from certain ethnic groups in care (discussed earlier). Even some clinicians express doubts about the true independence of psychiatric disorders, arguing that comorbidity is as likely as a specific diagnosis of schizophrenia or bipolar disorder (Boyle, 2007). It would probably be inaccurate to suggest that critical psychiatry is flourishing, but it certainly has a voice. To conclude this section, two current 'alternative' approaches that fit somewhere under this banner are considered.

The hearing voices network (HVN)

The HVN was formed in the UK about 20 years ago as a service-users' ('survivors') grouping. Its formation was prompted by work in Holland by Marius Romme, then an orthodox psychiatrist, who reported that the experience of hearing voices was more common than previously thought and did not inevitably imply that the person had a mental illness such as schizophrenia (Romme et al., 1992). Actually, this was not a new finding, as you will know from our earlier consideration of isolated symptoms in the normal population; but it seemed to carry greater impact because it was presented so authoritatively by Romme himself. This observation was seized upon by certain practitioners and patients as evidence that voice hearing was, in effect, a normal rather than pathological experience, and thus that hearing voices did not automatically mean an individual had a mental illness. The network, which now comprises over 180 groups in the UK

alone, organises regular local meetings offering members the opportunity to talk frankly about their experiences, and share these with other voice-hearers. It also runs training sessions for practitioners and other interested parties, such as carers.

Hearing Voices Network (2008) claims that its reputation is growing as the limitations of a solely medical approach to voices become better known (shades of Thomas Szasz here?). A recurrent theme is that its own research suggests several explanations for the origin of voices in addition to the conventional one that they are a manifestation of brain dysfunction. Details about these are patchy but appear to include the possibility that voices are a sort of *waking dream*, that they may be an overreaction to stress, or even that there may be a spiritual or other non-scientific explanation for their presence. It is a matter of conjecture as to whether or not the HVN approach to voice hearing has led to widespread recovery from schizophrenia, since no outcome research has yet been published in scientific journals. There is, additionally, an intrinsic irony in the enterprise because schizophrenia is the diagnosis that most HVN members have, *and* continue to receive treatment for, despite Romme's assertion that voices do not necessarily imply schizophrenia. Nevertheless, following the maxim that 'a problem shared is a problem halved', our view is that self-help groups of this sort deserve support.

Treating the symptoms, not the mental illness

This approach is associated with the work of Bentall and colleagues. Their argument is that the mental suffering associated with various mental illnesses is real enough and should be treated, preferably with psychological interventions, but if necessary with drugs. The point of departure from conventional thinking is that treatments should be targeted at symptoms (or 'complaints', as Bentall (2007) prefers to call them), not illnesses; and moreover, that by adopting this approach, the overarching illness itself becomes redundant as a concept. So for example, if an individual has depressive symptoms/complaints, these should be the focus of treatments irrespective of whether the individual carries a diagnosis of schizophrenia, bipolar disorder or, for that matter, post-traumatic stress disorder.

Developing this idea, Bentall argues that hallucinations result from a 'source monitoring' deficit in which the patient inappropriately identifies inner speech as having an external source (e.g. Johns et al., 2001). Delusory thinking results from a tendency to jump to premature conclusions (i.e. without a proper evaluation of the available evidence; e.g. Garety, Hemsley and Wessely, 1991). And paranoid delusions are linked to failures in a third psychological process: the ability to 'mind-read' and understand another person's thinking and motives from the subtle nuances of (mainly non-verbal) communication, known as theory of mind (ToM) (Corcoran, Cahill and Frith, 1997). Each of these psychological deficits can be addressed by CBT, and by treating the cause of the symptom/complaint, recovery should follow.

This, at least, is the ambition. At present, however, psychotherapies such as CBT and CRT lack comprehensive empirical support. It is simply not known whether long-term changes in self- or source-monitoring skills can be induced using these types of intervention, even if deficits in monitoring entirely account for the symptom/complaint in the first place. A more general problem is that this approach has so far focused on only a small subset of the many signs and symptoms of schizophrenia; the various aspects of disordered thinking, negative symptoms and cognitive features have not yet been addressed. Finally, the approach also glosses over the rather obvious point that most people with schizophrenia experience a range of signs and symptoms rather than one or two isolated ones, as anyone who has conducted a clinical interview with an acutely ill patient will know only too well.

The evidence presented earlier in this chapter has persuaded most people that the extreme positions taken by Laing and Szasz are simply untenable today. Szasz once famously argued that psychiatry was at a crossroads and had to decide whether to become 'mindless' or 'brainless' – his euphemisms for biological psychiatry, which typically eschews 'the mind', and psychotherapy, which often ignores the physical brain (Szasz, 1985). Our view is that, on the contrary, progress will most likely occur by keeping a foot in both camps. Of the two more recent counter-views

considered above, it is difficult to judge the merits or otherwise of the HVN, which, in any case, is really an advocacy and self-help organisation rather than something that can be objectively evaluated. Given the 'poverty' of the lives of many people with chronic mental illness, anything which encourages greater social engagement and interaction is probably a good thing regardless of whether the underlying motives (of the organisation) are scientifically justified. Conversely, the symptoms approach is fundamentally a scientific one, and so can be tested empirically. However, when this has been done, research findings suggest that some hallucinating patients have relatively normal source-monitoring skills (Fourneret et al., 2001); that 'jumping to conclusions' reasoning may be a general feature of psychotic illness rather than specifically related to delusion formation (Moritz, Woodward and Hausmann, 2006); and that ToM deficits are evident in people without current paranoid features (Pousa et al., 2007; Sprong et al., 2007). Intrinsically appealing though this approach is to us (as psychologists), it really is too early to say whether it will have long-term benefits.

Self-test questions

Identify the putative cognitive psychological dysfunction underpinning each of the following psychotic symptoms (according to Bentall):

- auditory hallucinations
- delusional perception/thinking
- paranoid delusions.

Chapter summary

We started this chapter with an account of how Kraepelin and Bleuler came to the view that three separate disorders, hebephrenia, catatonia and dementia paranoides, probably belonged under a common banner. Having overseen this amalgamation, clinicians have spent much of their time since arguing about how best to subdivide schizophrenia! Neither grouping by patient-profile nor grouping by symptoms is entirely satisfactory. However, Liddle's

tripartite model of reality distortion, disorganisation and psychomotor poverty has stood up well to the rigours of empirical investigation since its arrival on the scene more than 20 years ago. This model has the added advantage of a degree of aetiological validity because the three sub-syndromes rather effectively disaggregate in terms of putative underlying brain dysfunctions/cortical networks. That the symptoms of schizophrenia relate to changes in functional activity in different (mainly cortical) regions seems beyond doubt. The extent of any structural changes and whether these are static or progressive in relation to chronicity of illness is, on the other hand, currently debated, but our evaluation of the evidence is that whilst some structural changes appear to predate symptom onset, progression is not a general feature, and may in fact be quite rare.

'If schizophrenia is a myth, it is one with a heavy genetic component . . .'. So wrote Kety (1974b: p. 205), cocking a snook at Szasz's myth of mental illness. Our take on schizophrenia genetics research is that methodologically imperfect though most epidemiological genetics is (and not just in the mental health field), the collective weight of evidence strongly supports Kety's assertion. The argument has now moved on to a consideration of how many psychosis genes there are and how they operate. The answers to these related questions would seem to be respectively: probably many; and as factors which bias an individual's likelihood to develop illness, rather than directly causing it. Three susceptibility genes that are attracting particular attention at present (dysbindin, neuregulin and COMT) all effect synaptic neurotransmission where either DA or glutamate are the key players.

The DA hypothesis has held centre-stage in terms of brain functional changes linked to schizophrenia for more than 30 years. Recent work by Laruelle reinforces its pivotal role in the manifestation of positive symptoms, and this has been supplemented by the more theoretical ideas of Kapur regarding the natural functions of DA in cognition, and how positive symptoms could plausibly result from dysregulation of this 'tagging' mechanism. Treatments for schizophrenia continue to rely on drugs that antagonise DA neurotransmission. Whatever their other effects, it is this action which explains their ability to damp-down and even eliminate positive symptoms. The search is now on to develop new drugs that target the glutamate system (Patil et al., 2007) which researchers think may be dysregulated (underactive) in individuals with a predominantly negative symptom profile. This argument is supported by the observation that, in very general terms, DA and glutamate tend to antagonise one another at several cortical and sub-cortical locations.

Functional imaging studies have identified these same locations as nodes in neural networks of importance in schizophrenia.

Other therapeutic approaches have also been reviewed. Psychological treatments have enjoyed a renaissance of late, not as alternatives to medications, but as adjuncts to them. Evaluation of these studies has been difficult because of methodological problems such as high drop-out rate, small sample sizes, poor control and non-blind ratings. Nevertheless, both CBT and CRT appear to offer added value, and further research into the optimal scheduling of these interventions is urgently required. This is especially pressing because forensic research has confirmed that people with schizophrenia are both more likely to injure themselves, and more likely to commit violent acts on others, having once been discharged from hospital back into the community.

We revisited a number of anti- or critical psychiatry viewpoints. Our feeling is that the extreme polemic positions of Laing and Szasz simply do not stand up to the weight of evidence (most of it neurobiological) garnered since their work first appeared over 40 years ago. One more recent alternative approach of addressing symptoms rather than the overarching illness is intriguing because it marries together cognitive–neuropsychological models of symptom causality and tailored CBT remediation programmes, in a plausible, coherent and testable way. Unfortunately, evaluation studies are thin on the ground, and those that have been undertaken have not provided overwhelming support for it.

Suggested essay questions

- To what extent has the argument that 'schizophrenia is a neurobiological disorder of the brain' now been convincingly made?
- Evaluate treatment options for schizophrenia.
- To what extent have results of recent outcome/follow-up studies of schizophrenia challenged the Kraepelinian model of dementia praecox?
- Assess the evidence for the central role(s) of neurotransmitter dysfunction(s) in the presentation of schizophrenia.
- Is there a typical symptomatic presentation and prognosis for schizophrenia?

Further reading

Overview texts

Bleuler, M. (1978) *The schizophrenic disorders: Long-term patient and family studies.* New Haven, CT: Yale University Press.

Frith, C. D. (1992) *The cognitive neuropsychology of schizophrenia.* Hove: Lawrence Erlbaum.

Gottesman, I. I. (1991) *Schizophrenia genesis: The origins of madness.* New York: Freeman.

Jablensky, A. (2000) Epidemiology of schizophrenia: The global burden of disease and disability. *European Archives of Psychiatry and Clinical Neuroscience*, **250**, 274–85.

McKenna, P. J. (2007) *Schizophrenia and related syndromes* (2nd edn). Hove: Routledge.

McKenna, P. J., and Oh, T. (2005) *Schizophrenic speech: Making sense of bathroots and ponds that fall in doorways.* Cambridge: Cambridge University Press.

Sims, A. (2002) *Symptoms in the mind* (3rd edn). London: Saunders.

Tsuang, M. T., and Faraone, S. V. (2000) The frustrating search for schizophrenia genes. *American Journal of Medical Genetics*, **97**, 1–3.

Wykes, T., and Reeder, C. (2005) *Cognitive remediation therapy for schizophrenia: An introduction.* New York: Brunner-Routledge.

Specific and more critical texts

Caspi, A., Moffitt, E., Cannon, M., McClay, J., Murray, R., Harrington, H., Taylor, A., Arseneault, L., Williams, B., Braithwaite, A., Poulton, R., and Craig, I. W. (2005) Moderation of the effect of adolescent onset cannabis use on adult psychosis by a functional polymorphism in the catechol-O-methyltransferase gene: Longitudinal evidence of a gene–environment interaction. *Biological Psychiatry*, **57**, 1117–27.

Cooper, B. (2005) Immigration and schizophrenia: The social causation hypothesis revisited. *British Journal of Psychiatry*, **186**, 361–3.

Deakin, J. F. W., Lees, J., McKie, S., Hallack, J. E. C., Williams, S. R., and Dursan, S. M. (2008) Glutamate and the neural basis of the subjective effects of ketamine. *Archives of General Psychiatry*, **65**(2), 154–64.

DeLisi, L. E., and Hoff, A. L. (2005) Failure to find progressive temporal lobe volume decreases 10 years subsequent to a first episode of schizophrenia. *Psychiatry Research (Neuroimaging)*, **138**, 265–8.

Foster-Green, M. (1996) What are the functional consequences of neuro-cognitive deficits in schizophrenia? *American Journal of Psychiatry*, **153**(3), 321–30.

Grube, B. S., Bilder, R. M., and Goldman, R. S. (1998) Meta-analysis of symptom factors in schizophrenia. *Schizophrenia Research*, **31**, 113–20.

Hegarty, J. D., Baldessarini, R. J., Tohen, M., Waternaux, C., and Oepen, G. (1994) One hundred years of schizophrenia: a meta-analysis of the outcome literature, *American Journal of Psychiatry*, **151**(10), 1409–16.

Hogarty, G. E., Sander, M. S. W., Kornblith, J., Greenwald, D., DiBarry, A. L., Cooley, S., Ulrich, R. F., Carter, M., and Flesher, S. (1997) Three year trials of personal therapy among schizophrenic patients living with or independent of family: Description of study effects on relapse of patients. *American Journal of Psychiatry*, **154**, 1504–13.

Johns, L. C., and Van Os, J. (2001) The continuity of psychotic experiences in the general population, *Clinical Psychology Review*, **21**(8), 1125–41.

Kapur, S., Mizrahi, R., and Li, M. (2005) From dopamine to salience in psychosis – linking biology, pharmacology and phenomenology of psychosis. *Schizophrenia Research*, **79**, 59–68.

Laruelle, M., Kegeles, L. S., and Abi-Dargham, A. (2003) Glutamate, dopamine and schizophrenia from pathophysiology to treatment. *Annals of the New York Academy of Sciences*, **1003**, 138–53.

Lewis, S., and Leiberman, J. (2008) CATIE and CUtLASS: Can we handle the truth? *British Journal of Psychiatry*, **192**, 161–3.

Liddle, P. F. (1987) The symptoms of chronic schizophrenia: A re-examination of the positive–negative dichotomy. *British Journal of Psychiatry*, **151**, 145–51.

Meehl, P. E. (1962) Schizotaxia, schizotypy, schizophrenia. *American Psychologist*, **17**, 827–38.

Myin-Germeys, I., Delespaul, P., and Van Os, J. (2005) Behavioural sensitization to daily life stress in psychosis. *Psychological Medicine*, **35**, 733–41.

Romme, M. A., Honig, A., Noorthoorn, E. O., and Escher, A. D. (1992) Coping with hearing voices: An emancipatory approach. *British Journal of Psychiatry*, **161**, 99–103.

Walsh, E., Buchanan, A., and Fahy, T. (2002) Violence and schizophrenia: Examining the evidence. *British Journal of Psychiatry*, **180**, 490–5.

Williams, H. J., Owen, M. J., and O'Donovan, M. C. (2007) Is COMT a susceptibility gene for schizophrenia? *Schizophrenia Bulletin*, **33**(3), 635–41.

Visit **www.pearsoned.co.uk/davidholmes** for a range of resources to support study. Test yourself with multiple choice questions and access a bank of over 100 videos that will bring the topics to life. Video coverage for this chapter includes interviews with Georgina, Larry and Rodney who suffer from Schizophrenia and a discussion of Schizoaffective Disorder with Josh.

CHAPTER 19 Neurological and age-related disorders

- · Overview
- · Case study
- · Parkinson's disease
- · Multiple sclerosis
- · Huntington's disease
- · The dementias

- · Psychological disorders in old age
- · Management and treatment issues in neurological and age-related disorders
- · Clinical and forensic issues

- · Future considerations in abnormal, clinical and forensic psychology: what is ageing and is it necessary?
- · Chapter summary

Watch this interview with Alvin Paige, an artist who suffers with Alzheimers'. This is one of several videos that explore issues and disorders relevant to this chapter at www.pearsoned.co.uk/davidholmes.

A question of ageism

Although we accept ageing as a normal part of our lives, when examined closely in terms of life-span between species, it appears as a somewhat tragic lottery with some living centuries and others, such as some insects, living mere minutes. Later in this chapter the idea of fixed lifespans and the mechanics of longevity will be challenged, and in the process the evolutionary need for ageing and death will also be explored. Most of us have little awareness of our own ageing, as the process is gradual and our friends and family age with us. However, individuals in the public eye are often acutely aware of ageing before an audience, and many resent or refuse to accept what they feel is a process of decaying in public. For those who perceive their youthful image as essential for their success, the rather resonant lyric from The Who's 'My Generation', 'Hope I die before I get old' could be seen to be the epitaph for tragic suicides that sidestep old age. This is perhaps illustrated by the proposed '27 club', representing those

Some individuals such as Marilyn Monroe will never age due to their untimely deaths.
Source: Pearson Online Database.

famous individuals who have ended their lives at the age of 27, including Jim Morrison and Kurt Cobain. Clearly, there are many media icons who will never be seen to age due to their premature deaths, such as James Dean, Marilyn Monroe and Jimmy Hendrix.

For some the process of ageing in public has been emphasised by disorders associated with ageing. Mohammed Ali and Ronald Reagan are poignant examples of high-profile figures who have coped with disorders such as the dementias, raising public awareness of the needs of sufferers, as well as the fact that the rich and famous are not immune to these conditions. Older celebrities can also serve to dispel the ageist view that devalues the dedication, experience and skill demonstrated by the likes of David Attenborough, Clint Eastwood and Frank Sinatra. Clearly it is not how old you are that is important, but whether you let your age dictate your lifestyle.

Overview

With advancing chronological age there is some inevitable decline in physiological and mental functioning. Unfortunately, the ageing process also marks an increased risk of neurological and other age-related disorders developing, or undesirable latent genetic traits being expressed. Amongst the neurological disorders, **Parkinson's disease**, **multiple sclerosis** and **Huntington's disease** have been chosen as examples of specific types of neurodegeneration that have specific characteristic symptoms but also some common elements. The shared consequence of progressive dementia is the primary feature of the **dementias**, including **Alzheimer's disease**, **vascular** and **frontotemporal dementia**. Cell abnormalities and cell death in the brain leads to loss of normal physical function and cognitive abilities in each disorder, with characteristic features related to the areas of the brain where damage occurs. In the majority of cases these disorders are highly disabling, progressive and result in premature death.

There are other aspects of old age that are less readily classified as disorders, such as cognitive decline that is subthreshold for dementia and self-neglect, which benefit from early intervention. Elderly individuals with cognitive impairment can be vulnerable to mistreatment by relatives and others. This may not always be malicious, but it is always damaging and in extreme cases may take the form of **Münchausen's syndrome by adult proxy** (see Chapter 15). Treatment of neurological and age-related disorders has often been pharmacological, although non-medical preparations have been advocated such as **omega3 oils** and, controversially, **cannabis** preparations for multiple sclerosis (Pryce, Jackson and Baker, 2008). However, much hope for the future rests on cell replacement therapies as the research on **stem cell** use advances. This chapter will also address the issue of ageing from a future perspective and, in examining the process of ageing at the cellular level, will raise questions regarding the social, psychological and evolutionary significance of our lifespans.

Case study
To care and be cared for

David had been diagnosed with Parkinson's disease some 3 years ago, but his wife Anita had always supported his position as head of the household, even during the year when physical symptoms such as his hand tremors made retirement from work inevitable. She would deliberately resist the temptation to step in and help him with tasks in her efforts to keep up David's confidence and self-esteem. Although his physical symptoms were profound, the disorder seemed to progress very slowly and his mental functioning seemed little different from that before onset of the disorder. However, David admitted to bouts of depression and a general feeling of hopelessness about their future as a couple. Anita always countered any suggestion that her potential role as full-time carer could be in question.

During David's treatment with **levodopa**, he experienced some psychotic symptoms as a few people do, and had to receive an anti-psychotic adjunct to his medication. During his brief episodes he became paranoid and began to notice inconsistencies in what his wife told him. Even once the medication removed the paranoia, he was very much aware that Anita's recall of events was increasingly error ridden and David suspected the worst, that she might be having an affair with someone able bodied. He became very depressed at this time and distrusting of his wife. His suspicions worsened when he found that his passport had not been renewed for their holiday and most of the arrangements were in chaos. Following a motor accident when Anita was driving them both to the shops, David confronted her with his fears.

Anita failed to understand David's fears but was clearly distraught at the suggestion that she was having an affair. It was while Anita was floundering for words, as she increasingly did, that an alterative hypothesis overwhelmed David. During the following weeks and with David's firm, insistent pressure, Anita was given a battery of tests resulting in the suggestion but not confirmation that she might be in the early stages of Alzheimer's disease. Anita's mother had died of the disorder, but David hoped that if his mental faculties remained, there might be some future helping each other. Disorders of old age tend to transform relationships in many ways and for some this is tragic and devastating. However, caring relationships seem to endure and transcend even the bleakest pathology.

Neurological disorders are often associated with advancing years but can strike early in life. They invariably involve neuropathology or damage to the 'hardware' of the brain, which can have mild through to profound effects on physical and mental functioning. The major disorders of this type are:

- Parkinson's disease
- multiple sclerosis
- Huntinton's disease.

Parkinson's disease

The UK general practitioner **James Parkinson** described the 'shaking palsy' in 1817 based on five cases he observed. Later in the nineteenth century, Charcot suggested the name **Parkinson's disease**. The disease that took Parkinson's name was characterised by neuromuscular tremor, rigidity, bradykinesia and postural instability (Weintraub, Comella and Horn, 2008a). These symptoms are referred to as **parkinsonism**, and although a number of toxins and other brain insults or injuries can produce the symptoms, the usual cause is Parkinson's disease. **Idiopathic Parkinson's disease** is differentiated from Parkinson's disease from known causes, such as that induced by drug use, **post-encephalatic Parkinson's disease** and dementia pugilistica. The last of these is where the disease is thought to result from repeated blows to the head, such as that suspected in the case of **Mohammed Ali**.

Parkinson's disease is a slowly progressive degenerative disorder that shows neuronal loss and **Lewy bodies** in the **substantia nigra pars compactica** and **locus coeruleus** at autopsy (American Psychiatric Association, 2000). This neurodegeneration in the substantia nigra results in loss of **striatal dopamine**, which regulates the excitatory and inhibitory outflow of the **basal ganglia** (Weintraub, Comella and Horn, 2008a). The Lewy bodies in surviving neurons show clear evidence of α-synuclein protein accumulation, which may be an indicator of a common aetiological process in differing forms of the disorder. Lewy bodies are spherical intraneuronal cytoplasmic inclusions that can be considered the hallmark of idiopathic Parkinson's disease but are also found in the cortex in **dementia with Lewy bodies** (Goldstein and McNeil, 2004).

There is increased mortality in Parkinson's disease. It is second only to **Alzheimer's disease** in terms of being the commonest neurodegenerative disorder, placing a substantial and progressive burden on health system time as well as an economic burden on public health and personal finances (Weintraub, Comella and Horn, 2008a).

A diagnosis of Parkinson's disease can often be missed, or there may be misdiagnosis if key symptoms are overlooked. The major motor symptoms of Parkinson's disease are (from Weintraub, Comella and Horn, 2008a):

- **resting tremor** mostly in the hands but also in jaw and leg; more evident in younger cases
- **rigidity or resistance** in all muscles to being moved, usually of the intermittent type but may be continuous
- **bradykinesia**, which is slowness in movement execution and very disabling; progressively more evident in older patients
- **postural instability**, seen as postural reflexes being impaired, which may lead to injury from falls.

Motor impairments tend to begin on one side of the body but spread to the other, though often remaining asymmetrical in severity. Micrographia, or abnormally small, compacted handwriting, is one of the distortions of dominant hand function seen in the disorder (Weintraub, Comella and Horn, 2008a). Other sequelae of the disorder tend to limit social functioning, such as a mask-like face, communication difficulties, embarrassment, drooling, hopelessness, personal presentation problems and sexual limitations. These difficulties tend to compound any psychological outcomes of the disorder and its treatments.

Neuropsychiatric symptoms in Parkinson's disease very frequently include depression, which has been found in up to half of all cases (Weintraub and Stern, 2005). **Impulsive–compulsive disorders** can occur, such as gambling or compulsive buying, as well as other repetitive behaviours. Sleep disorders are also common, which may be exacerbated by medication for the disorder. Anosmia and less commonly other sensory problems are also found, as well as autonomic dysfunctions (Weintraub, Comella and Horn, 2008c). These neuropsychiatric symptoms can be more disabling than motor symptoms in many cases and require early screening for to direct patients to more specialist resources (Weintraub, Comella and Horn, 2008c).

One pathophysiological consequence of Parkinson's disease can be **dementia**, which according to *DSM-IV-TR* (American Psychiatric Association, 2000) occurs in between 20 and 60 per cent of cases, usually in older patients with a more severe form of the disorder. In a review of prevalence studies, Aarsland, Zaccai and Brayne (2005) found the prevalence of dementia in Parkinson's disease to be between 24.5 and 31.1 per cent, with the final figure being dependent on the strictness of study inclusion criteria. They concluded that around 2–4 per cent of the dementia in the general population can be attributed to Parkinson's disease. In this form of dementia, there is evidence of slowed cognitive processes, memory retrieval deficits and impaired executive functioning in addition to motor slowness. A number of individuals with Parkinson's disease are found to have comorbid Alzheimer's disease or Lewy body disease at autopsy (American Psychiatric Association, 2000).

Aetiology and treatment of Parkinson's disease

Factors in the aetiology of at least 10 per cent of neurophological Parkinson's disease clearly include genetic contributions, but environmental factors are also thought to cause symptoms of parkinsonism. Around 11 linkages with six gene mutations have been identified across studies (Weintraub, Comella and Horn, 2008a). Genetic factors alter metabolic pathways as part of a diathesis hypothesised for Parkinson's disease (Gasser, 2005). Henchcliffe et al. (2008) have reviewed the use of **multinuclear magnetic resonance spectroscopy** to provide some evidence of **mitochondrial** dysfunction in Parkinson's disease. A secondary form of parkinsonism is a common side-effect of **dopamine**-influencing medication, mainly neuroleptic anti-psychotics used in **schizophrenia**, primarily the **phenothiazines** such as **chlorpromazine**, **thioxanthenes** such as **flupenthixol**, **butyrophenones** (commonly **haloperidol**) and the **piperazines** (Leonard, 1997). For example, chlorpromazine reduces dopamine transmission by blocking receptors to the extent that Parkinson's symptoms will be likely before any therapeutic effect for schizophrenia is established (see Chapter 18).

Toxins thought of as environmental pollutants have also been linked to parkinsonism: for example, Dinis-Oliveira et al. (2006) have considered exposure to the herbicide paraquat as an etiological factor of Parkinson's disease by inducing lipid peroxidation leading to the consequent cell death of dopaminergic neurons. Another route to these characteristic symptoms is vascular parkinsonism, which is an important cause of parkinsonism in older people (Thanvi, Lo and Robinson, 2005). One drug, **1-ethyl-4-phenyl-1, 2, 3, 6-tetrahydropyridine** (MPTP), is accidentally produced and has been consumed when synthesising a chemically similar illicit heroin substitute (MPPP). This substance has proven to emulate the effects of Parkinson's disease very closely. This very specific neurotoxin damages the dopamine-producing cells in the sustantia nigra, mimicking a rapid-onset version of idiopathic Parkinson's disease, and may provide a key to its underlying biochemistry.

Although endotoxins and exotoxins are suspected as likely factors in the production of parkinsonism and, ultimately, the induction and acceleration of Parkinson's disease, some substances may also be protective factors,

Table 19.1 Nutrient effects on Parkinson's disease

Nutrient	Effect on Parkinson's disease
Calorie intake	Reduced calorie intake (1200–2200) lowers risk
Fats intake	Reduced (saturated) fat lowers risk
Carbonates	Reduced intake lowers risk
Polyphenols (tea)	Increased intake lowers risk
Coffee	Increased intake lowers risk
Dairy products	Reduced intake lowers risk
Iron and manganese	Reduced intake lowers risk
Vitamins A, C, D	Inconclusive evidence of increasing risk
Vitamins B, E	Inconclusive evidence of lowered risk
Proteins	No conclusive evidence

Source: Gaenslen, Gasser and Berg (2008).

even a few considered toxins (Gaenslen, Gasser and Berg, 2008). For example, the **polyphenols** found in **green tea** can give some protection against the development of the disorder. Tan et al. (2003) found three cups of green tea taken over 10 years to reduce the risk of Parkinson's disease by 28 per cent. Although many nutritional factors have inconclusive effects on the progress of the disorder, such an approach needs pursuing exhaustively given the growing number nutrients and toxins that have been found to significantly affect Parkinson's disease already (Gaenslen, Gasser and Berg, 2008). Table 19.1 gives a sample of nutrient effects on Parkinson's disease.

Treatments of the primary motor symptoms of Parkinson's disease are currently limited to amelioration of symptoms and reversing the effects of dopamine depletion to preserve functionality. **Levodopa** is the most effective treatment for motor symptoms, but it is associated with risk of motor fluctuations, especially with prolonged higher doses and younger patients (Weintraub, Comella and Horn, 2008b). As a result of these complications, other 'levodopa sparing agents' may be used to control motor symptoms prior to the use of levodopa, such as the dopamine agonist **pramipexole**. Pahwa et al. (2006) have reviewed the treatments for Parkinson's disease with motor fluctuations and dyskinesias. They found **amantadine** to reduce dyskinesias, but variations on levodopa to be ineffective where there are motor fluctuations. **Deep-brain stimulation** (see Chapter 3) of the **subthalamic nucleus** (but not other areas) was found to improve dyskinesias and motor function, as well as moderating the need for other medication. In this and other reviews, **rasagiline** has been recommended for general use in the case of Parkinson's, with motor fluctuations as a **monotherapy** (i.e. as the sole treatment) (Goetz et al., 2005; Pahwa et al., 2006).

One of the leading future hopes for the treatment of Parkinson's disease and other neurological disorders is the modern use of embryonic stem cells to replace those lost, damaged or deficient in the brains of sufferers (see the Focus box on p. 579). Early research in the late twentieth century seemed promising, with reduced motor problems and renewed dopamine production in Parkinson's patients. However, as further patients were followed up in double-blind studies, **dyskinesias** and abnormal movements were found as a result of the therapy (see Svendsen, 2008a; 2008b). In the original Swiss study, foetal tissue had simply been transplanted into the brains of patients, and much of the successful migration and transformation of the foetal material was by chance. Cell rejection, new cells being susceptible to the disease process, motor side-effects and other problems have somewhat dented the initial enthusiasm for this treatment. In 2005, the status of the human fetal nigral transplants was moved from 'insufficient data' to 'non-efficacious' for Parkinson's with motor fluctuations in 2005, though optimism for future advances remained high at this time (Goetz et al., 2005).

One of the challenges to the future of stem cell research is to direct the development of these cells towards the required function, which in the case of Parkinson's disease would be the formation of dopamine-producing cells. O'Keeffe et al. (2008) have managed to implement one technique in animal models with a degree of success. The researchers overexpressed one aspect (Pitx3) in neural stem cells that were then exposed to E11 developing ventral mesencephalon, which produced a significant potentiation of dopaminergic differentiation of the cells. Thus, neural stem cells can be induced to become dopaminergic neurons to differentiate into the correct nigrastriatal phenotype (O'Keeffe et al., 2008). The success and failure of what is still a technique in development has been transferred to human patients with Parkinson's disease with some success, but results have tended to raise more questions for future interventions of this type (see McKay and Kittappa, 2008).

Treatments for the neuropsychiatric symptoms such as depression and other non-motor symptoms commonly found in Parkinson's disease are also now seen as equally important interventions relative to motor dysfunction treatments (Weintraub, Comella and Horn, 2008b). As initially stated, the prognosis for those with this disorder is pessimistic and the costs of long-term care are high and growing, with estimates as high as £3.3 billion in the UK alone (Findley, 2007).

Multiple sclerosis

First described by Charcot (1868) as involving inflammatory cells in the white matter of brain and spinal cord, multiple sclerosis was seen to cause episodes of neurological dysfunction. Later studies confirmed that the inflammation occurring in these parts of the nervous system involved the destruction of the **myelin sheath** on these nerve cells (see Hafler et al., 2005). Myelin insulates nerve cell extensions to speed transmission, and its breakdown prevents or distorts these nerve signals. Sclerotic plaques build up at the sites of demyelination, further damaging nerve transmission in the affected areas. The disorder can have a very variable onset, progress and prognosis, although early onset in minors is rare. In a few late-onset cases, the disease progresses very rapidly with severe disability and even death occurring shortly after onset. In around a fifth of cases, the disease lacks progression and does not advance beyond initial symptoms (Bennett, 2006).

Symptoms can also vary, particularly in severity and location of dysfunction. The actual disabilities that ensue are dependent on which specific nerve fibres are affected by the disease. Amongst the symptoms of multiple sclerosis are the following.

- Profound fatigue is found in almost all cases. This limits motility and the ability to complete tasks, with many having to use wheelchairs or other aids.

- Muscular spasticity (uncontrolled movement) in upper limbs is common and may occur throughout motor functioning.

- Specific impairments, determined by the location of neural inflammation, could result in:
  - loss of limb functioning
  - blindness or sight difficulties from damage in and around the optic nerve
  - loss of control over micturation or defecation
  - cognitive impairments such as problem solving or memory in around 70 per cent of sufferers
  - psychological disorders such as depression, which are common in most degenerative disorders such as multiple sclerosis
  - a lowered quality of life, which can be very evident in many cases, not just those with rapid progression and extensive cell damage.

Cognitive problems including dementia are not as severe in multiple sclerosis as in Alzheimer's disease. However, psychological and neuropsychological problems such as cognitive deficits, dementia, personality change and

Focus

Immune explanations of multiple sclerosis

Genetic factors have been strongly indicated in multiple sclerosis for some time by large population-based studies (e.g. MacKay and Myrianthopoulos, 1966). Early work by Rivers, Sprunt and Berry (1933) supported the view of an autoimmune response being a possible cause of the damage in multiple sclerosis.

T-cells in the immune system seem to target healthy myelin as if it were a diseased or damaged cell. However, although models of autoimmune response inflammation are plausible, the consistent identification of a microbial agent in post-mortem analysis that may stimulate immune agent is lacking (Hafler et al., 2005). The activation of myelin-reactive T-cells in the peripheral immune system still requires precise explanation.

Increased levels of **gamma-interferon** correlate with multiple sclerosis activity and it is hypothesised that this substance in the immune system stimulates the activity of cytotoxic T-cells (Bennett, 2006). Hafler et al. (2005) have provided an extensive review of the immunopathology of multiple sclerosis, including the role of **B cells** as well as regulatory T-cells. The authors also examine work on therapeutic immunomodulation and the exploratory use of **germline DNA haplotypes, RNA expression** and **protein structures** to define the underlying molecular pathology of disorders such as multiple sclerosis.

---

emotional dysfunctions (e.g. **pathological laughing** or **pathological crying**) can have a high prevalence. The best predictor of cognitive deficits is the total number of brain lesions or total lesion score ascertained by magnetic resonance imaging data, correlated with neuropsychological testing (Béquet et al., 2003). Montel and Bungener (2007) consider mood disorders in multiple sclerosis worthy of special therapeutic attention, given their impact on quality of life.

Treatments for multiple sclerosis tend to be palliative to reduce the impact of the symptoms and also address psychological problems such as the treatment of depression. With fatigue being one of the most debilitating aspects of the disease, its treatment has received research attention. In a systematic review of the literature, Lee et al. (2008) found pharmacological and psychological interventions for fatigue to produce only modest results at best and often no evidence-based effect at all. Stress is also an interactive factor in multiple sclerosis, in that the disorder will produce stress in sufferers and, more importantly in terms of intervention, periods of stress tend to precede progression of the disease (e.g. Mohr et al., 2000). Thus stress reduction and prevention may be a consideration for intervention strategies.

Interventions to arrest or slow the progress of the disease itself tend to be pharmacological, but also include attempts to use stem cell transplantation (see the Focus box). Goodin et al. (2008) report on an evidence-based review of the use of **natalizumab** (Tysabri) for the treatment of the neural pathology of multiple sclerosis. Although there is evidence of a reduction in disease activity and severity with the drug, comparison of efficacy with others, and use in combination with interferon or in **secondary progressive multiple sclerosis** is unclear. There are also potential risks of various infections and progressive multifocal leukoencephelopathy (Goodin et al., 2008).

Immunosuppression of T-cell activity has been attempted by differing means to slow down inflammatory progress in sclerosis. Samijn et al. (2006) attempted to halt the progress of aggressive secondary multiple sclerosis by the use of an autologous bone marrow transplantation method aimed at maximum T-cell suppression. In this case, outcomes did not support this method, as progression was not arrested and side-effects were evident. However, Shevchenko et al. (2008) report some success with high-dose immunosuppressive therapy and autologous hematopoietic stem cell transplants. A lack of new lesions, non-progression of the disease and a moderation of symptoms in some of the patients indicate the viability of such approaches at some levels of disability in multiple sclerosis (Shevchenko et al., 2008). Burt et al. (2009) have also reported preliminary successes in cell replacement using bone marrow techniques.

The use of **cannabinoids** in the treatment of multiple sclerosis has been controversial due to the publicity gained by the illicit use of cannabis to ameliorate symptoms in the twentieth century. Much early enthusiasm for these substances was based on anecdotal evidence of this nature. However, a number of controlled trials have not clearly supported cannabinoids as an effective evidence-based therapy, and those that do may have had their blind status compromised (Smith, 2006). There have been concerns over possible side-effects with long term use, but these have not yet emerged in practice where cannabinoid effects have proven to be mild (Smith, 2006). Pryce, Jackson and Baker (2008) are optimistic that the evidence from clinical trials would support the recent licensing of a cannabis-based treatment for multiple sclerosis in the USA. Future limiting of adverse effects and further evidence of the potential for cannabinoids to control aspects of autoimmune and neurodegenerative processes may pave the way for their wider use as an intervention (Pryce, Jackson and Baker, 2008).

Huntington's disease

First described by general practitioner **George Huntington** in 1872 shortly after qualifying in medicine, the disorder was formerly known as **Huntington's chorea**. Huntington's disease is a serious neurodegenerative disorder that results from an autosomal dominant gene and shows degeneration in areas of the brain, particularly the **basal ganglia** (Harper, 2005). Symptoms are in three areas as follows.

- **Movement dysfunction** begins with spasmodic jerky movements of the limbs and a level of clumsiness.

- **Psychiatric syndromes** are often evident early in the disorder's onset. During onset, these may be evident in terms of change in temperament, with a tendency to make abrupt offensive remarks and rapid mood changes that may be extreme. Obsessiveness, anxiety, depression and mania may also be seen as the disease progresses. Later in the disorder there are often psychotic symptoms, including hallucinations and delusions.

- **Cognitive impairment** is evident, beginning with mild amnesia, forgetfulness and indecision, but progressing with the disorder to full dementia.

There is remarkable variation in the onset of the disorder in rare cases, even very rare onset at 12 months. However, in the majority of cases, symptoms appear around the age of 40 years with death usually occurring 15–20 years after onset (Bonelli, 2007). Being genetically based, there are areas in the world where carriers of the gene tend to live, but general prevalence is low at less than 1 in 10,000 in the UK. For example, the disorder is ten-fold less prevalent in Japan than in Europe (Harper, 2005).

The autosomal dominant gene on the short arm of chromosome 4 for Huntington's disease was the first of its type to have markers identified by **DNA polymorphic markers**, with the gene being identified some years later. Huntington's disease is one of a number of **trinucleotide repeat disorders**, which result in DNA instability. The mutation of the **interesting transcript gene 15** (IT15) is known as **huntingtin** and encodes for the **huntingtin protein** (Handley et al., 2006). The gene mutation results in neuronal inclusions specific to the protein huntingtin as well as other types of molecular aggregation associated with brain degeneration in Huntington's disease. These inclusions and aggregations are found early in the disorder, and although they could be a result of neuronal damage rather than a cause, this is unlikely (Harper, 2005). It may be a case of overproduction of the protein or generation of a new function for huntingtin, which is involved in **synaptic vesicles** (see Chapter 3) and in mutant form may alter to function of **mitochondrial respiratory chain** (Bonelli, 2007). However, much is hypothetical and there are other explanations for neurodegeneration in Huntington's disease (Bonelli, 2007). Although the precise nature of genetic expression in the disorder is not certain, some progress has been made in detecting the genes that may enable the important prediction of onset (Squitieri et al., 2006).

Pharmaceutical interventions in Huntington's disease tend to target the movement disorders and the depressive, anxious or psychotic psychiatric symptoms associated with the disorder (Bonelli and Hofmann, 2007). Standard anti-psychotic, anti-depressant and mood-stabilising medications are employed for the psychiatric symptoms, although tricyclic anti-depressants are not well tolerated by Huntington's sufferers (Handley et al., 2006; Bonelli, 2007). Hyperkinetic movement problems in the disorder are treated with dopamine-depleting drugs or anti-psychotic medication, which again reduces dopamine efficacy via receptor function. This pharmacological approach is hampered by parkinsonian symptoms and depression, amongst other side-effects (Handley et al., 2006). Alternate agents are employed to minimise side-effects, such as **amantadine**.

Dystonic symptoms (unwanted psychological symptoms) have been addressed with a range of substances, including **benzodiazepines**. Pharmacological success in arresting the progress of the disorder or the associated dementia has yet to be established, although some agents such as **minocycline** have produced preliminary neuropsychological improvements but have yet to be assessed in controlled clinical trials (Handley et al., 2006). There are reports of **omega-3 fatty acids** improving motor symptoms, and although this is not based on controlled trials, there are few problems of side-effects (Song and Zheo, 2007). However, evidence-based reviews are encouraging for traditional treatment, but provide little data to support newer interventions for movement problems (Bonelli and Wenning, 2006). Whilst useful agents are being developed, the essential ongoing conventional rehabilitation approaches to Huntington's disease should not be neglected. Directed activity such as training on tasks and other rehabilitation interventions can improve the impact of other concurrent treatments (Busse and Rosser, 2007).

As the twentieth century progressed, therapeutic approaches to Huntington's disease have moved from palliative measures and symptom suppression to the currently optimistic position of considering a cure for the disorder. Stem cell-based cell therapy for Huntington's disease offers one such approach, and clinical trials in humans will almost certainly result in renewed hope for those in the early stages of the disease (Handley et al., 2006). In a review of stem cell interventions for the disorder, Kim et al. (2007) are optimistic for neuronal replacement, alongside addressing problems such as **transcriptional dysregulation**. Again, traditional directed activity can aid successful cell implantation (Busse and Rosser, 2007).

Despite optimism for future interventions, the clearly inheritable nature of Huntington's disease combined with its disabling symptoms has made the disorder a focus of controversy. Both males and females have a 50 per cent chance of passing the disorder to offspring, and those carrying the disorder will display symptoms at some point later in life (Harper, 2005). However, as onset is usually after their child-bearing years, necessary genetic screening (accurate DNA-based predictive testing) for those at risk poses a complex moral dilemma. In order to check whether an individual is likely to pass the disorder on to their offspring, they necessarily discover if they have the disorder. In protecting future generations, individuals finding out they have Huntington's disease will live with the anticipation of its certain and bleak prognosis. Perhaps as a result of this, most individuals choose not to be tested, with only 10–20 per cent taking the test (Harper, 2005). The idea that society should intervene in this situation to protect the population from this identifiable genetic disorder tends to invoke the same critical onslaught that is directed at the **eugenic** methods of sterilisation and killing of Huntington's sufferers under the Nazi regime during the second World War. Current moves to have genetic testing for insurance purposes in the UK, and legislation in China to prevent such disorders, may see this issue revived in the twenty-first century (Harper, 2005). However, there is hopefully the potential for intelligent and humane prevention to develop over the coming years.

Self-test questions

- What are the underlying processes in Parkinson's disease?
- To what extent can nutrition help to prevent Parkinson's disease?
- Discuss the burden of care implied for the future management of Parkinson's disease.
- Describe the neural degeneration in multiple sclerosis.
- Discuss the 'right to know' in relation to prediction of future onset of disorders such as Huntington's disease.
- How are stem cells utilised in neurodegenerative disorders?

Focus

The therapeutic use of stem cells

Stem cells are the undifferentiated embryonic cells that migrate and develop into the more specific cells required in all animals, including neural cells in humans. They are classified in terms of their potential to develop into other classes of cells; thus, totipotent cells can reproduce all cell lines in an entire organism – a function which is restricted to the **zygote** and first division **blastomeres** (Jaenisch and Young, 2008). Embrionic stem cells, such as those often used experimentally from mice, are termed **pluripotent** and can subsequently form the different lineages of cells in the body. However, **multipotent** adult cells may develop into cells of one lineage only and, as the name implies, unipotent stem cells produce only one cell type (Jaenisch and Young, 2008). Although there is potential for all these cells to be used therapeutically, it is the embryonic stem cells that have been a focus of initial animal studies.

Focus continued

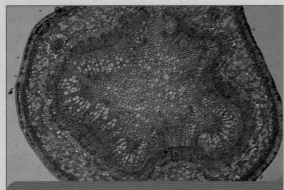

The use of embryonic stem cells has been met with similar ethical concerns to those challenging organ transplants in the mid-twentieth century.
Source: Pearson Online Database.

Recent research has focused on the use of pluripotent stem cells for the treatment of neurological disorders where the degeneration or destruction of cells occurs, such as in Parkinson's and Huntington's disease (Sveinsson, Gudjonsson and Petersen, 2008). Apart from bone marrow transplantation, stem cell treatment is still research based rather than routine practice, as well as being costly. There are still issues of matched donors to ensure cell acceptance or even the use of the patient's own cells in the absence of a match. The latter has been the case in replacing cells after chemotherapy for cancer. Methods of suppressing immune responses to cells, techniques for producing stem cells for therapy, refinement of surgical procedures and preparation of cells for implantation are all increasingly sophisticated following research, which is also increasing the knowledge base for this area (McKay and Kittappa, 2008).

The use of stem cells for neuron or oligodendrite replacement in neurological disorders is meeting with increasing success. Early research focused on Parkinson's disease, and although these were the earliest of human trials, fortunate initial successes were found from simply inserting cells. The eventual realisation of the limitations of early therapy attempts dictated a more sophisticated subsequent methodology (Braude, Minger and Warwick, 2005). This approach

has now been followed by use of stem cell therapy in Huntington's disease and successful trials in 2009 with multiple sclerosis patients. In a preliminary trial, Burt et al. (2009) found a level of reversal of multiple sclerosis degeneration in the majority of patients using haemopoletic stem cell transportation with interferon alpha immune treatment. However, some of these patients relapsed almost a year later (Burt et al., 2009). Thus, stem cell therapy is not going to produce the overnight therapeutic revolution seen with neuroleptics in the 1950s, but remains a steadily achievable goal that will bring hope to those currently living with hopelessness.

Reviews and evaluations of stem cell research are increasingly date dependent. For example, Braude, Minger and Warwick (2005) report on levels of success but are very cautionary regarding the way expectations exceed the then current state of play, especially where commercial companies inject high levels of optimism for marketing purposes. Only a few years later, Whalley's (2008) level of caution is more precisely directed at refining the methods used to prevent disease affecting the newly transplanted cells, rather than our ability to implant stem cells successfully. Thus, the detail of future research questions is growing, but the steady improvement in successful implants also grows year on year (McKay and Kittappa, 2008). Thus, in an area such as this, the reader is recommended to update by reference to information from current international conferences.

Moral objections to the use of embryonic stem cells gathered pace in the twenty-first century, which tended to view the process as using embryos to farm cells for research. However, much stem cell research does not use or require the destruction of embryos, but instead utilises the umbilical chord blood cells. In 2009, a consensus was reached that embryonic stem cells would no longer be needed for treatment research or practice for neurological disorders such as Parkinson's disease. This was partly based on the work of **Shinya Yamanaka** in inducing an embryonic pluripotent cell state by reverting normal adult skin cells. The impetus for this research was probably based in the restrictive stance of Japan in the use of embryonic cells. However, the research outcome could clearly circumvent the research-inhibiting moral dilemmas posed by the use of foetal matter (Hornyak, 2008).

The dementias

Although some of the disorders already discussed in this chapter include dementia in their symptoms, the following conditions are primarily defined by progressive dementia.

Alzheimer's disease

There are around half a million people in the UK and over 27 million worldwide suffering from Alzheimer's disease. The risk of the disease doubles every 5 years over the age of 65, and as people live longer, the population risk is inevitably rising. In its senile form (over 65) it is the fourth commonest cause of death, but rarely recognised as such (Katzman, 2008). In its sporadic form, Alzheimer's disease is the commonest form of dementia in the elderly and is unfortunately chronic, terminal and, as yet, irreversible and without cure (Tanzil and Bertram, 2005). In this form, it is the product of factors of the ageing process and the interaction of environmental and genetic influences. Bavarian **Alois Alzheimer** first described the insidious accumulation of pathological lesions as well as other characteristic deposits (Alzheimer, 1906). These other deposits consist of extracellular **beta-ameloid** and intracellular deposits of **neurofibrillary tangles**, the latter of which are composed of hyperphosphorylated tau (Tanzil and Bertram, 2005).

It has been an accepted tradition to refer to onset of dementia before the age of 65 as Alzheimer's disease and after 65 as **senile dementia**. However, there is little distinction between post-65 onset Alzheimer's disease and early onset apart from association with genetic aetiological factors, and this distinction may itself be confounded by the age grouping (Katzman, 2008). For Katzman, the pre- and post-65 distinction is arbitrary and only a single designation is needed, that of Alzheimer's disease.

Regardless of age of onset, progressive pervasive dementia is the overriding symptom, which has notable key characteristics. Amnesia is often noticed early in the disorder and there is decrement in executive mental processes such as self-organisation and planning. There is a disturbance of language (**aphasia**), an inability to recognise even familiar objects or people (**agnosia**) and difficulties in the organisation of movement (apraxia) (Thomas and Fenech, 2007). The progressive nature of Alzheimer's disease means these decrements may begin with mild forgetfulness or slightly odd or uncertain behaviour. Eventually, however, the profound unremitting dementia results in the loss of even the most personal of memories or skills, and as a result of this, relatives often cease to consider the person they knew to be present any more. Assessment for Alzheimer's disease will also include the detection of behavioural and psychiatric problems such as depression, hallucinations or delusions and misidentification of others, which are often indicators that full-time care is required (Thomas and Fenech, 2007).

Heston et al. (1981) amongst others have established a genetic component to Alzheimer's disease, which links it with **Down's syndrome** in having problems at the location of chromosome 21. **Familial Alzheimer's disease** is a rare autosomal dominant form of the disorder caused by mutations in the **ameloid precursor protein** (APP) and **presenilium** (PSEN) genes (Blennow, De Leon and Zetterberg, 2006). Amongst the genes implicated for the form of Alzheimer's associated with onset before the age of 65 is this APP gene on chromosome 21q21, and with late onset the PSEN1 on chromosome 14q24.3 (Thomas and Fenech, 2007). In Alzheimer's disease, links to the ameloid gene on chromosome 21 have established this enduring ameloid hypothesis for the disorder (Tanzil and Bertram, 2005). However, beta ameloid production is only weakly correlated with levels of dementia found in sufferers (Thomas and Fenech, 2007).

Alzheimer's disease gene susceptibility can predict risk of the development of the disorder, and disclosure of this risk to clients can greatly improve health awareness behaviour in those found susceptible (Chan et al., 2008). However, awareness of the early stages of the disorder can be detrimental in terms of the hopelessness associated with such a terminal disorder. However, accurate insight can greatly assist better planning of resources and both support the easing of future problems as well as improve the outcome of rehabilitation (Clare, 2004). There are many levels of awareness for the client and not all of these are utilised in evaluating the effects of insight for the sufferer (Clare, 2004).

Prediction and risk in Alzheimer's disease are important in terms of early intervention but, as above, they involve the moral dilemma of also bringing the damning diagnosis to the attention of the sufferer. Reliable predictors are elusive in this disease and there is no conclusive test: for example, only 8–15 per cent of those who develop **mild cognitive impairment** go on to develop Alzheimer's disease (Devanand et al., 2008). Examples of risk factors are as follows (see Thomas and Fenech, 2007).

- Age is a risk factor, particularly beyond 65.
- High blood pressure increases the risk not only of vascular dementia (see below) but also of Alzheimer's.
- Tau neurofibrillary tangles as well as Beta-ameloid and neuritic plaques are indicative biological processes that continue as the disorder is diagnosed.

- A history of depression is an independent risk factor for the later development of Alzheimer's (Ownby et al., 2006).

- The (now many) known genes associated with the disorder are obvious predictors.

- Genome damage events such as **micronuclei formation** have been associated with Alzheimer's.

- Dietary and nutritional factors such as B12 deficiency can increase risk, partly by increased DNA damage.

- Anti-oxidants such as **curcumin** can reduce damaging processes and risk for the disorder.

- High concentrations of metal such as zinc, iron and copper can increase risk via both DNA damage and plaque formation (Thomas and Fenech, 2007).

- Prescribed continuing lithium treatment appears to reduce the risk of dementia to that of the normal population, whereas a single dose may increase risk, although this evidence is based on studies of non-random data collection (Kessing et al., 2008).

Early diagnosis and the prediction of the disorder have often used a combination of age and **Mini-Mental State Examination** (MMSE) scores. Abrisqueta-Gomez et al. (2008) have found the **abbreviated neuropsychologic battery** (NEUROPSI) to be efficient at detecting the early stages of Alzheimer's disease. Devanand et al. (2008) found that a combination of five measures produced 85.2 per cent sensitivity as against less than half that sensitivity for the traditional use of age and MMSE in the prediction of Alzheimer's disease. These measures were:

- **Pfeffer Functional Activities Questionnaire** (FAQ; informant report of functioning)

- **University of Pennsylvania Smell Identification Test** (UPSIT; olfactory identification)

- **Selective Reminding Test** (SRT; immediate recall, verbal memory)

- **MRI hippocampal volume**

- **MRI entorhinal cortex volume**

Alzheimer's patients often learn to compensate for the deficits in skills and cognitive processes that result from the disorder. There may also be **compensatory neural recruitment**, whereby adjacent neural pathways take on some of the function of damaged ones, which can be assessed by the use of functional magnetic resonance imaging (FMRI) (Han, Bangen and Bondi, 2009). Without confirmation that is more careful, it is difficult to differentiate neural compensation from behavioural strategies such as using inner speech to compensate for memory deficits (Han, Bangen and Bondi, 2009).

Psychological interventions and behavioural approaches are both used to help maintain current skill and cognitive function levels by ensuring activity, reducing dependency and stimulating mental interest and motivation. This type of intervention can be beneficial to and also involve carers. Reality orientation is intended to maintain the sufferer's awareness of their place in the world and to keep their responses and thinking appropriate to things such as the seasons, mealtimes and their location and its relation to other significant places. Other aspects tend to be to educate

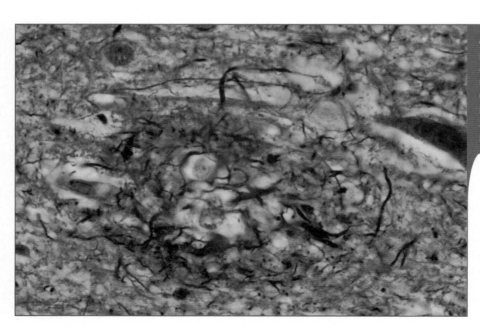

Abnormal protein production, leading to ameloid plaques and nerve cell tangles, is a characteristic neural feature in Alzheimer's disease.
Source: Pearson Online Database.

Research

Pharmacological interventions for Alzheimer's

A number of pharmacological treatments are applied in Alzheimer's disease with varying success rates, but all of these are dependent on evaluative research to be accepted as mainstream treatments. The stringent criteria for such trials mean that few interventions have met the requirements for their approval in this area.

The cholinesterase inhibitor **galantamine**, amongst others, has improved cognitive function in the disorder and significantly delayed the need for full-time care and support, with an associated reduction in costs and care burden on relatives (Kaufer et al., 2005). This reduction in relatives' care burden can be significant and have secondary gains, such as improving occupational function and thus financial independence (Kaufer et al., 2005).

However, in a review of clinical trials of cholinesterase inhibitors for Alzheimer's disease, Kaduszkiewicz et al. (2009) note that many of the findings of effectiveness for these drugs are questionable on the basis of methods used and level of clinical benefit found.

A relatively new emergent pharmacological treatment is the blocking of beta-ameloid to reduce the progress of the disorder, which has shown early signs of success (Bennett, 2006). The use of anti-oxidants in the disorder is generally supported across studies. Many agents, such as melatonin, green tea, curcumin, and vitamins C and E, have shown benefits and most without any side-effects (Frank and Gupta, 2005).

---

the sufferer and their carer as to the day-to-day realities of their disorder, medication and expectations.

Alzheimer's disease is set to increase in prevalence by three-fold in the next 30 years (Thomas and Fenech, 2007) and may present a level of burden in our ageing population beyond our current concept of what our financial commitment should be in this area. Such a lethal and debilitating epidemic will require a significant shift in allocation of resources or investment in a determined effort to enable research towards the goal of preventative interventions (Katzman, 2008; Blennow, De Leon and Zetterberg, 2006).

Vascular dementia

Formerly known as multi-infarct dementia, this form of dementia is associated with high blood pressure, retinal sclerosis, kidney failure and cardiovascular problems, which may be detected by MRI scans. As the name implies, vascular dementia is a degenerative cerebrovascular disease with progressive loss of cognitive functioning, compounded by consequent arterial blockages and strokes. Thus, neurological signs will accompany the dementia, such as weakness in a limb or language difficulties (American Psychiatric Association, 2000). Blood clots or plaque may be the cause of blockages and aneurisms (distension of weak arterial wall) which may add to the damaging effects on brain function. As this is a progressive version of the same dysfunction, symptoms may be similar to those promoted to the public for identifying when someone has had a stroke.

Kuller et al. (2005) have identified the risk factors for vascular dementia as including age, high white-matter grade, number of MRI detected infarcts, ventricular size and history of stroke(s). Early detection and treatment of these risk factors could reduce the incidence of dementia. They also point to the usefulness of MRI in identifying vascular dementia and reducing the diagnostic overlap with cases classified as Alzheimer's disease (Kuller et al., 2005). In the case of **subcortical ischemic vascular** dementia, where patients tend to suffer both ischema and microbleeds, the MRI detected microbleeds as one of the important factors in causing cognitive impairments in this disorder (Seo et al., 2007).

Treatment of vascular dementia tends to be pharmacological. **Acetylcholinesterase inhibitors** have been used, with donepezil and galantamine being found effective evidence-based treatments (Demaerschalk and Wingerchuk, 2007). Demaerschalk and Wingerchuk (2007) found the alternative drug approach with memantine for treating of vascular dementia and vascular cognitive impairment not to be universally effective, though well tolerated and safe. However, Kavirajan and Schneider (2007) did not find memantine or the cholinesterase inhibitors sufficiently effective for general use with vascular dementia.

Vascular dementia is the second commonest form of dementia following Alzheimer's disease, to which vascular problems also contribute (Alagiakrishanan, McCracken and Feldman, 2006). There is a rising prevalence of vascular disease impacting on both forms of dementia. Thus it is very important to address the risk factors for vascular disease, such as smoking, poor exercise and diet, in order to moderate expected levels and progress of dementia in the population at large (Alagiakrishanan, McCracken and Feldman, 2006).

Frontotemporal dementia

First described by **Arnold Pick** (1892), frontotemporal dementia was later described at the histological level by **Alois Alzheimer** identifying **Pick's cells** and **bodies** in what was then referred to as **Pick's disease**. The disorder is a progressive neurodegenerative syndrome with many clinical symptoms, of which changes in mood or personality and worsening non-fluent **aphasia** are the most frequent prominent features (Grossman, 2002). As the name implies, neurodegeneration in this disorder tends to be revealed as circumscribed atrophy of the frontal and temporal lobes (Neary and Snowden, 1996). There are other clinical syndromes, such as **progressive aphasia** and **semantic dementia** with degeneration, at these loci, but frontotemporal dementia is the most common when defined with broad criteria. If a narrow definition of the disorder were adopted with only the frontotemporal characteristic changes of **astrocytic gliosis** and presence of **neuronal inclusion bodies**, then the disorder would only account for a small proportion of frontal and temporal lobe atrophy (Neary and Snowden, 1996).

The age distribution of frontotemporal dementia is distributed widely around 62 years, and in contrast to many disorders in this chapter, risk does not increase with age (Grossman, 2002). The disorder is also differentiated from Alzheimer's disease by features such as early loss of social awareness, progressive reduction of speech and stereotyped or perseverative behaviour (Grossman, 2002). Huey, Putnam and Grafman (2006) reviewed the neurotransmitter changes in frontotemporal dementia with a view to identifying treatment usefulness in addressing these changes. They found no significant change in acetylecholine. Deficiencies in serotonin and dopamine suggest antidepressant treatments, which were found to improve behavioural symptoms in uncontrolled studies, but serotonergic treatments did not address cognitive symptoms (Huey, Putnam and Grafman (2006)).

Other forms of dementia

Dementia may be a consequence of a number of disorders that are listed in *DSM-IV-TR*, some of which have been described above. These include Parkinson's disease, Huntington's disease (see above), **HIV disease, Creutzfeld–Jakob disease, diffuse Lewy body disease and, head trauma,** in addition to dementia being associated with delirium or general medical conditions such as hypothyroidism, brain tumours, hydrocephalus, renal disorders and the effects of vitamin deficiency (American Psychiatric Association, 2000). In each case, aspects of the pathology of the disorder result in damage to or death of neural matter, leading to loss of cognitive function and progressive dementia.

Psychological disorders in old age

In addition to the disorders described in this chapter so far, the natural process of ageing, such as the slowing of cell replacement, physical infirmity and change in social and occupational circumstances, can impact on mental well-being. However, people over the age of 65 have the lowest prevalence of mental illness of all age groups, including psychoses and substance abuse, although, prescription medicine abuse is more likely to occur in this age group than illicit substance abuse. Depression is a problem that is both prevalent in, and compounded by, ageing and its associated factors (Karp and Reynolds, 2009). Although depression rates are lower in the over 65 group than other ages, depression is prevalent within this group. Older individuals with lower life expectancy, increasing loss of function and physical difficulties are less resilient in the face of depression. Depression is often misdiagnosed due to this plethora of confounding conditions. In the elderly, depression is associated with anxiety, sleep dysfunction and cognitive impairment, and correlates with degree of pain experienced (Karp and Reynolds, 2009). Treatment for depression in the elderly can be undermined if other factors such as pain are not also addressed.

Older individuals can be prone to anxious distress, which is often estimated using a neuroticism scale (Wilson et al., 2008). This distress proneness is associated with increased risk of dementia, including Alzheimer's disease as well as other problems (Wilson et al., 2008). Levy (1994) refers to age-associated cognitive decline, where there is memory and other cognitive function decrement, but this is subthreshold for the criteria for dementia disorders in this chapter. Higher levels of education were thought to protect against cognitive decline in old age, but recent studies have found this not to be a protective factor (Muniz-Terrera et al., 2009). Gradual age-related cognitive decline is associated with changes in the structure as well as function of brain areas. Persson et al. (2006) found reduction in the volume of the hippocampus and anterior corpus callosum that corresponded to cognitive decline.

The UK *Telegraph* reported that a severe cold spell could result in 12 pensioners dying every hour in the UK in January 2009.
Source: David A. Holmes.

Levels of functional ability in the elderly tend to decline progressively, and simultaneously many feel the need to make drastic economies as their income level falls. Older individuals tend not to access the services provided for them and will often fail to attend to personal hygiene and their general health (Pavlou and Lachs, 2006). Pavlou and Lachs (2006) reviewed evidence to consider self-neglect as a geriatric syndrome in older adults, with implications for detection and directed interventions. Perhaps as part of this syndrome, the elderly are less likely to seek medical or psychiatric services and thus many of their disorders in both domains may be underreported.

Management and treatment issues in neurological and age-related disorders

There are a number of overarching issues in the management of these disorders in the elderly, some of which overlap with clinical issues. As above, the ageing adult tends not to come forward with problems until the situation has become chronic and unmanageable, and detection and assessment can be thus important to avoid future care costs rising disproportionately. In a review of predictors for functional decline in Dutch hospitalised older adults, Hoogerduijn et al. (2007) found age, lower functional status, cognitive impairment, detectable disability,

depression and length of stay to predict functional decline, and identified three screening instruments for detecting decline. Multidimensional preventative home-visit programmes have been found to reduce the disability burden in Swiss and other populations of older adults, utilising multidimensional assessment as well as clinical examination (Huss et al., 2008). Such schemes help maintain autonomy for these adults living in the community, and consequently impact on nursing home admissions overall (Huss et al., 2008).

An issue that arises in managing the elderly, which parallels the plight of psychotic patients, is that of advocacy and decision-making capacity (Moye and Marson, 2007). This ethical and moral dilemma resides in an area of conflict between the individual's autonomy or right to self-determination, and the protection and well-being of the same individual. Decision-making capacity assessment is thus a crucial part of assessing cognitive decline, as this may impact on many areas of judgement from competence to drive a motor vehicle through to independent living and, importantly, consent to treatment (Moye and Marson, 2007). The individual's cognitive capacity in relation to their autonomy and advocacy can be decided by legal process, but often informal judgements are made by families and others: for example, denying access to a vehicle.

Pharmacological treatments for the disorders in this chapter vary, although anti-depressants and cholinesterase inhibitors recur. An area of intervention that requires some research expansion is that of diet and dietary supplements (Galli et al., 2006). Anti-oxidant-rich foods can help to ameliorate neuronal and behavioural deficits, and the reversal of dietary neglect can have a profound effect on mental and physical functioning. For example, Galli et al. (2006) found that a blueberry supplement intervention offered protection against neurodegenerative processes in an animal study. As mentioned above, dietary enhancement tends not to have side-effects and may reduce the financial burden of these disorders.

The global burden of care for the elderly with an ageing population and increasing levels of neurodegenerative disorders is set to rise significantly year on year for the foreseeable future. The implications for forward planning and an organised approach at the national level will be crucial to meet this challenge. This is one of the single most important issues in this chapter and one that cannot be dealt with simply by passing the burden to individuals, their families or private enterprise.

Clinical and forensic issues

Elderly people with failing cognitive and decision-making abilities have been recognised as being vulnerable to mistreatment and active abuse for some time (Butler, 1975). This situation is worse where Alzheimer's or other dementia reduces mental functioning to that of a child, for whom there is far greater protection in law. Public opinion tends to view abuse occurring in care homes as noted in the last section, but as with many interpersonal crimes, most elder abuse takes place in the family or marital home (Liao, 2008). Much elder mistreatment is not deliberate harm and can result from an inability to cope. However, accidental harm and trauma results in a large proportion of deaths in multiple sclerosis, and prevention would clearly save lives (Riudavets et al., 2005).

Mistreatment of the elderly can triple the number of deaths in this group and takes the form of neglect in half of all cases. With the number of unreported cases outnumbering those assessed by over five-fold, aspects of detection need to improve (Liao, 2008). This needs a multi-agency approach and development of forensic techniques beyond differentiation of accidental and intentional bruise patterns towards distinguishing sores and other problems due to neglect (Liao, 2008). A more insidious form of elderly abuse is the perpetration of **Münchausen's syndrome by adult proxy** (MSBAP). This is where illness is deliberately fabricated in an elderly individual for a variety of reasons including attention seeking, which may result in harm or even death of the target. MSBAP has been identified in the literature for many years (e.g. Sigal, Altmark and Carmel, 1986), and probably occurred in families and institutions long before that. This disorder can be found in Chapter 15.

Suicide is more common in those over 65 than in the young, and much higher in those over 75 (Butler, 2005). Mostly involving males, suicide will be the tenth most common cause of death in the elderly in 2020 (Editorial, 1997). Suicide in the elderly mostly involves males and is associated with multiple illnesses and depression (Koponen et al., 2007). Active intervention is possible in many of these cases and would be effective in changing the outcome (Koponen et al., 2007).

Focus

The elderly criminal

The elderly are less likely to commit crime or be arrested than the young across all crimes, and as a consequence there is less research on this population. However, the number of elderly arrested or in prison is growing year on year as the population ages and prison inmates grow older in jail (Lewis, Fields and Rainey, 2006).

One forensic issue for the future is going to be the increasing need to deal with older offenders in terms of processing from arrest, competence to stand trial and as prison inmates with physical ill health, alcohol problems and presence of dementias. In a US sample of those over 60 being assessed before trial, Lewis, Fields and Rainey (2006) found: 67.7 per cent were alcohol dependent; 44.4 per cent had dementia; 32.3 per cent had anti-social personality disorder; 60.6 per cent were facing charges of violence; and 80.8 per cent had been classified as recidivist offenders.

It is often assumed that personality disorders including anti-social personality disorder are ameliorated by age. However, almost half of a sample of forensic psychologists and psychiatrists considered age not to moderate anti-social personality disorder and many thought it was an idealistic view of the elderly offender (Alphen, Nijhuis and Oei, 2007). It is possible that bias in expectation and criminal processing contributes to the stereotype of the elderly as less likely to offend than younger individuals.

During the late twentieth century, the illicit use of cannabis to ameliorate the symptoms of multiple sclerosis became the subject of media attention (Smith, 2006). Irrespective of the value of the substance as a treatment (Pryce, Jackson and Baker, 2008), there was a shift in the political and therefore judicial stance taken against those both using and supplying the drug for this purpose. The cannabis was often smoked and suppliers were sometimes demographically similar to the users – elderly individuals who used the drug themselves. Initially, not wishing to be punitive towards elderly infirm individuals, there was a move towards 'sending the right message' to other users that infringement of the law on cannabis would not be tolerated, and some of these elderly individuals received custodial sentences. Chapter 11 addresses the inconsistencies created in the UK drug laws as a result of confounding good medical practice by political and legal intervention.

The tragic disorder of progeria clearly demonstrates the mechanical nature of much of the ageing process, leading us to question if it can also be reversed.
Source: Press Association Images (PA Photos).

Self-test questions

- Why is Alzheimer's disease expected to be more prevalent in the future?
- What are the neural changes associated with Alzheimer's disease?
- Are other dementias clearly distinguished from Alzheimer's disease?
- What psychological disorders are associated with older people?
- To what extent can the dementias be treated and managed?
- Suggest solutions for problem of the elderly being vulnerable to mistreatment.
- Discuss the issues raised by a growing number of elderly offenders.

Future considerations in abnormal, clinical and forensic psychology: what is ageing and is it necessary?

Ageing can be viewed as a progressive physiological, biochemical and psychological decline in optimum functioning of most species. This also combines with a finite lifespan to place cruel **ontogenetic** limits on organisms in order for **phylogenetic** progress to be made. Many have viewed this aspect of evolution as something of a lottery, with some species having lifespans of hundreds of years and others mere minutes. For centuries improved health, hygiene and medicine have improved longevity, but only at the end of the twentieth century has there been a serious attempt not only to undermine ageing in terms of longevity, but to challenge the allocated lifespans of human beings (d'Adda di Fagagna, 2008). This section will consider why such a radical approach has implications not only for the immediate change in how long we live, but also for the fundamental psychological, social, structural and even evolutionary parameters of our very existence (Holmes and Barkus, 2001).

Control over ageing processes

Rapid advances in the control of the ageing process are evident in a number of areas mentioned in this chapter, such as calorie reduction, free radical removal and the use of embryonic stem cells for organ replacement. However, some lines of biological research seem to be progressing towards the fundamental mechanisms of human ageing, and may make explicit the weaknesses of diseases such as cancer (e.g. Malkin and Knoppers, 1996). This type of research not only promises greater life expectancy, but also challenges the very notion of a fixed life span.

■ The first of these research areas is the identification of those genes and their biochemical products which are involved in the various aspects of ageing and, more importantly, those genes that may control the process.

■ The second involves the discovery that some cells in the human body, such as stem cells as well as cancer cells, have an enzyme which allows them to replicate themselves endlessly. The vast majority of cells have a limited capacity for replication, and the cessation of replication is a major factor in the ageing of the organism.

These two approaches are inevitably related, although they indicate differing points of potential intervention in the ageing process (Holmes and Barkus, 2001). There are other commonly recognised ageing factors such as oxidation, which still need to be recognised even though they are currently being addressed widely.

The Human Genome Project (e.g. Cantor and Smith, 1999) and its follow-up teams are approaching the 'genetic triggers' for the ageing process slowly, but with that sense of certainty often associated with large projects that have extensive and exhaustive aims. Having the complete genetic code for humans enables the identification of variants related to disorders, one of which will be the variant related to progeria, a profound premature ageing disorder also known as **Hutchinson–Gilford syndrome** (Bedame, 1989). This genetically based premature ageing is possible confirmation that ageing itself may have a genetic trigger (Brown, 1992). In the process of discovering the presumed genetic 'fatal bullet' or the theoretical gene(s) controlling the 'switch' from development and repair to decline and death, other genes related to more minor aspects of the ageing process have been identified. An early example of these would be information coding for high-density lipoprotein (HDL), which can protect against atherosclerosis (see Thomas, 1997).

Although many of these specific influences on ageing can only modify life expectancy by a small percentage, others more clearly indicate the future direction of such research. Rucz (2008) has reported on a handful of genes that have been identified in the twenty-first century that control ageing, and this line of enquiry may lead to change in the human lifespan. An example of radical change accomplished in animals concerns worms with mutation in four genes that outlive their normal counterparts by nearly five-fold (Thomas, 1997). This magnitude of life

Research

The importance of telomerase in age prevention

One of the most financially rewarding areas of research is that of preventing the ageing process. Unfortunately this research has few interim outcomes to help the further funding of long-term programmes of research, even though the 'elixir of youth' may be the ultimate product.

One correlate of cell ageing appears to be the relative length of telomeres or the 'ends' of chromosomes. Telomeres function to protect and stabilise chromosome ends for cell replication purposes (Bryan and Cech, 1999). They consist of tandemly repeated simple DNA sequences common to all vertebrates. In most human cells, telomeres shorten with the process of cell replication and eventually become too short to allow cell replication, and this has become a focal point for anti-ageing research.

Those few human cells that do not age in this way, such as blood cells, have their telomere lives extended by the enzyme telomerase (Bryan and Cech, 1999). This enzyme is also found in malignant cells (Sprung et al., 1999), which also replicate endlessly. In this simple model, it is clear that the problems of ageing and cancer may have related, if opposing, solutions (see Banks and Fossel, 1997). However, de Magalhaes and Toussaint (2004) have considered the anti-ageing value of telomerase to be overstated.

Researchers at the Geron Corporation have these two aims uppermost in their extensive work on the production and use of telomerase. Geron and other similar companies tend to patent each step of the processes they reveal and thus initiate a bizarre practice of 'corporate ownership' of protection against the ageing process. Specialist concerns such as Geron are supplemented by work in many cancer research laboratories that are also focusing on cellular senescence (d'Adda di Fagagna, 2008).

expectancy change is more in keeping with the immediate aims of the second line of research current in this area. In the USA, the Geron Corporation in collaboration with the University of Colorado has focused a great deal of research attention on the mechanisms of individual cell ageing (e.g. Kveiborg et al., 1999).

The Geron Corporation is not alone in this research (e.g. Stoll et al., 1994), as the rewards for success in the area of anti-ageing may be infinitely profitable, being potentially beneficial to all organisms with such cellular limitations. Although the former assertion is certainly true, the latter may be questionable.

This section primarily aims to examine the psychological and social consequences of this aspect of Geron's research successfully attaining one of its ultimate aims, the multiplication of the human lifespan. The following sections will consider the realities of such a scenario unfolding where this aspect of biotechnology is available to the general population. In this speculative eventuality, the resultant lifespan will be based on projection from current research, which produces an estimated extension by a factor of about seven-fold. This would give our current average lifespan of around 80 years a new threshold of around 500 years.

Longevity as a biological inevitability

The degree of genetic and social engineering in Huxley's *Brave New World* (1932) seemed an outrage and far from reality. Yet with the production of the first cloned animal (Trouson, 1999), fear of the potential of cloning instilled in pressure groups and subsequent demands on governing bodies led to a ban on future cloning research in many countries. Despite this ban, wealthy individuals could still use their financial power to gain personal favour in the cloning process, allowing such research to take place outside of those countries agreeing to the ban, possibly with the lack of restrictions that such 'underground' projects enjoy.

Science fiction dreams such as time travel are impossible within the current scientific paradigm. However, the substantial manipulation of biochemical processes, including extending the lives of cells and entire organisms, is uncomfortably close and well within the limits of current technology. History dictates that possibilities tend to become inevitabilities, regardless of how morally challenging they may be. If it had been possible to foresee how the motor vehicle, or something as simple as money, would grow to create systems that take priority over humanity, we could consider that their use would never have been allowed.

This is a fine theoretical ideal, but in practice, we would never be able to contain the demands of those wanting immediate speedy travel and abstract wealth.

In this way, humans are defective in their thinking, as we are adapted to having a relatively short lifespan. Thus, short-term thinking limits our consideration of consequences; in short, we as individuals are unlikely still to be here in 200 years. It has been suggested that we are overly optimistic in our predictions regarding ourselves, and thus if a new discovery has a risk then the risk will be for others and not ourselves (Armor and Sackett, 2006). We lean towards a hypomanic view of our future and shrink from less optimistic, albeit more realistic, views. Clearly, if the scales were to pit vastly extended life against a few vague complications, the latter would not receive consideration. Past scientific revelations cannot be undone, and no matter how much damage has been done to humanity, the thirst for new knowledge drives both science and society perpetually forward at a rapid pace (Dawkins, 1998).

It is worth contrasting biological innovation with its mechanical counterpart. Organic systems can be far more forgiving of the crude limitations of experimentation. The initial use of surgical techniques did not include repairing the cells and other physical details at the molecular level damaged by the process. These detailed repairs were left to the organic subsystems in the recipient of surgery (Holmes and Barkus, 2001). In the inorganic world, this would be similar to sticking some new components into a damaged car engine and expecting them to locate themselves and start to function automatically. In short, we achieve a lot by relying on nature's subprocesses, and in the case of extended life spans, we may be about to rely on these extensively.

In a hypothetical case of longer lifespans, the biotechnology has arrived with the first human tests revealing no signs of ageing or side-effects such as cancers. In this scenario, estimates of the life expectancy for the first human subjects are around 400 years and the initial media-fuelled threat of extreme biological abnormalities has begun to dissipate. If this seems implausible, it is worth placing in the context of life expectancy having almost tripled in the last 200 years without such radical intervention. However, in the suggested scenario, much of the lifespan would be spent at a biological age of about 25 due to cell regeneration, rather than the extension of life into senescence as has been achieved so far.

Initial considerations

One preliminary consideration will be the difficult decision as to who would qualify for an extended lifespan.

Moral debates will fail to defend cost limitations and a free market offering long life for the rich will parallel the growing iniquities of contemporary health care. Clearly, those who currently spend vast amounts of money marginally preserving their youth and even resorting to cryogenic solutions will certainly not accept rationing of opportunity if they can afford the technology. However, further limitations may not be negotiable, such as developmental eligibility – the possibility of older genes or cells not being easily modified. This may perhaps limit candidates to those under 16 or, as some work suggests, even limit intervention to those past their reproductive years. Other restrictions may lead to serious conflict. As with others in the field, Geron is patenting every step of its process and may thus have some legal control over distribution. This would lead to a parallel of Kohlberg's '**Heinz dilemma**' on a global scale, and given the rewards at stake and individuals' current obsession with 'cosmetic youth', the outcome would be unlikely to favour legal control.

It is also certain that some older individuals may indeed be untreatable, perhaps forming a subclass of biologically inferior human curiosities with strange wrinkly skin and squeaky voices, until their inevitable extinction as the 'new-generation humans' succeed them.

Psychological and societal implications

At first glance, the biological unknowns of extended life seem the most fear provoking, such as the unknown genetic disorders that may develop that are currently outside our lifespans, or unforeseen longer-term cellular abnormalities due to the treatment. However, a closer examination of the disruption to the normal expectations of life may place serious psychological limitations on the reality of living for 400–500 years. These limitations stretch well beyond the possibility that some of the aforementioned unknown genetic disorders are likely to have psychological symptoms.

The factors that rely on the expectations of an 80-year lifespan would provide an initial hurdle. The short-term plans on which our lives and society are based, such as the preference for quick material benefits over long-term environmental or socioeconomic prudence, will no longer be viable. The days of the motor vehicle could be drastically cut short due to excessive long-term environmental damage. In contrast to the caution this implies, we would not be saving up for our old age, as it would no longer exist as such. However, one inhibiting aspect of expecting to live half a millennium is the greatly increased loss of expected life due to premature death by accident or disease. To

die by accident at the age of 25, makes any distinction between expecting 70 or 500 years of life purely theoretical. With the relatively 'comfortable option' of dying of old age (usually in sleep) drastically reduced, we would mostly anticipate death by accident or disease. With a very long life at stake, obsessive concern over infection or danger may produce phobia epidemics or a more extreme apartheid situation than we already have, where the young and reckless are kept away from those intent on preserving their own existence.

The developmental period itself has grown with life expectancy, and with this in mind, do we anticipate a 50-year childhood? Will risk taking still be a part of youth, or will such 'children' avoid snowboarding and skydiving? It may be that 'clinging' behaviour and dependency will increase dramatically as high levels of anomie grow in a vastly increasing population. Family members will no longer need each other's support in old age, and marriages are unlikely to last such time spans. 'Till death us do part' will have little meaning with death so far in the future. Friends will be lost over such time spans, as employment will be both scarce and temporary, necessitating migration. Personality and even appearance may change over such long periods. It is worth seriously considering whether you would recognise your own mother after 300 years. We would be in uncharted time scales with regard to memory function. DNA identification (DNA-ID), probably in the form of a DNA bar code, would be an inevitable step.

In retrospect, consider if most of the people born since 1600 were still alive and wandering around the planet. Our future would be far more crowded than that, leading the way to drastically limiting births with attendant outcries of parental deprivation. A bleaker prospect as a result of population stagnation may be the precipitation of wars or opportunist disease. In a retrospective scenario, Beethoven, Einstein and even Freud may be seeking employment and accommodation, as work is increasingly scarce and their ageing skills are having to compete with the many freshly trained musicians, scientists and psychologists available. There will be too many people in senior positions and almost all professional skills are likely to be lost or dated after 300 years or more without repeated rigorous retraining. The concept of 'career' may disappear, as few professions are likely to be viable for 300 years. The world of economics may need advice from psychologists, particularly when most people will live long enough to be able to live off the proceeds of tiny early investments. Self-esteem may become a serious issue after 200 years or more in a mundane job. More difficult still may be the prospect of facing 400 years of schizophrenic illness or mood disorder. To what extent would you trust the services of a surgeon or psychiatrist who had been trained some 300 years ago?

We have evolved psychologically to fit within our lifespans; our thinking, planning and expectations are somewhat shaped by death or decline at around 80 years. The world around us has been structured in accord with this expectation (Holmes and Barkus, 2001). A forensic example, would be to consider what deterrent a 20-year jail sentence would be to a prospective murderer with a 400-year lifespan? Even sentences as brief as this are an extremely expensive burden on society; thus a proportionate sentence may not be an economic option. This may lead to a more powerful sanction, such as removal of their longevity entitlement. Could this be morally justified in the case of those with chronic illness or psychopaths? The consequences of adding to our lifespans perhaps place this scenario firmly in the territory of Huxley's novel.

The darker issue to be confronted may be to question how long humans are psychologically able to tolerate living without taking increasing risks or even becoming suicidal. Paradoxically, from being a subject that is instinctively avoided, death may become a less feared topic, perhaps even having status or becoming a media event. It may be difficult for religion to survive such change, including the loss of the fear of death. Perhaps more importantly, could the human species survive such sudden shockwaves of change? It may be worth taking time to debate some of the above points before research moves to a point that confronts us with hasty decisions.

Implications for psychologists

Dealing with the unknown is nothing new to psychologists; much of our history has been spent pushing against greater unknowns than those faced by most other sciences. Clearly, reconfiguring the way humans operate to fit a far greater lifespan is firmly within the psychological area of expertise. Psychologists are able to frame the question and could be proactive in seeking solutions. Such contingency planning should not be left to those who respond in a purely reactive manner with little psychological understanding, or to those with vested interests such as biotechnology companies, politicians and economists. Failure to have operational plans by the time the technology arrives may result in the more pessimistic outcomes suggested above. Despite the apparent speculation needed to write on the

subject, this is not science fiction; it is a highly probable outcome within 20 years. There needs to be a coherent, psychologically sound plan established, before the agenda is set by others with less psychological insight.

A new stage in evolution or a biological showdown?

At a point when the care of the elderly exceeds the resources provided by society, determinists may consider longevity to be a timely intervention. However, it would be naive not to realise that humankind's interaction with tools, including biotechnology, could challenge the stability of phylogenetic and ontogenetic processes. Such sudden change could invite rapid evolutionary leaps or precipitate dormant stabilising processes: for example, sterility is a suspected side-effect of some longevity interventions. In this area, however, most subscribe to the 'there is no revolution, only evolution' school of thought, in that the changes will not be reversible. Humankind, in a similar way to the individual ageing person, has a limited existence and is already carrying phylogenetically fatal defects, such as short-term planning and vulnerabilities that could be moderated by such radical change in its ontogeny as longevity. Ironically, longevity itself may turn out to be the ultimate limiting mechanism. It may be too attractive to resist by the individuals involved, and yet may ultimately prove fatal to the species as a whole (Holmes and Barkus, 2001).

Self-test questions

- What is the evolutionary purpose of ageing, death and a fixed lifespan?
- To what extent can ageing be prevented?
- What is the function of the enzyme telomerase?
- What are the economic considerations of extended lifespans?
- Discuss the forensic implications of longer lives.
- Discuss what psychologists can contribute to the debate over extended lifespans.

Chapter summary

Ageing is associated with risk of the neurological disorders **Parkinson's disease**, **multiple sclerosis** and **Huntington's disease**, which produce dementia. The major causes of dementia tend to be **Alzheimer's disease**, **vascular** and **frontotemporal dementia**. Each of these disorders involves neurodegeneration, is chronic and progressive, and results in increased mortality. Other clinical aspects of old age include milder cognitive decline, depression, suicide and self-neglect, which all benefit from early intervention. Elderly individuals may have the mental capacity of a child, but are not subject to such rigorous monitoring or legislation. Mistreatment by relatives and others can result from not being able to cope, but in many cases there is neglect, which may be wilful in some cases, or rarely **Münchausen's syndrome by adult proxy**.

Treatment of neurological and age-related disorders has included medicinal approaches with **cholinesterase inhibitors** and **anti-depressants**. In some cases, non-medical substances such as **omega3 oils**, **cannabis** preparations, teas and dietary changes have been beneficial. Future programmes of research on cell replacement therapies are to advance the use of **stem cells** and hope to end the hopelessness currently dominant in the above disorders. Other biotechnological advances have begun to question the fixed nature of our lifespans, but in doing so raise social, psychological and evolutionary questions.

Suggested essay questions

- Discuss the psychological impact of the early detection of neurological and age-related disorders on sufferers and their relatives.
- Critically evaluate how stem cell research has contributed to the treatment of neurodegenerative disorders.
- Critically discuss the psychological and societal implications of extended human lifespans.

Further reading

Overview texts

Candelise, L., Hughes, R., Liberati, A., Uitdehaag, B., and Warlow, C. (eds) (2007) *Evidence-based neurology: Management of neurological disorder.* London: BMJ Books.

Goldstein, L., and McNeil, J. (2004) *Clinical neuropsychology: A practical guide to assessment and management for clinicians.* Chichester: Wiley.

Lichtenberg, P., Murman, D., and Mellow, A. (eds) (2003) *Handbook of dementia: Psychological, neurological, and psychiatric perspectives.* London: Wiley.

Thomas, P., and Fenech, M. (2007) A review of genome mutation and Alzheimer's disease. *Mutagenesis,* **22**(1), 15–33.

Specific and more critical texts

Bonelli, R. M. (2007) New trends in the neuropsychiatry of Huntington's disease. *Neurologia Croatica,* **56**(5), 56–63.

Grossman, M. (2002) Frontotemporal dementia: A review. *Journal of the International Neuropsychological Society,* **8**(4), 566–83.

Hafler, D., Slavic, J., Anderson, D., O'Connor, K., De Jeger, P., and Baecher-Allan, C. (2005) Multiple sclerosis. *Immunological Reviews,* **204**, 208–32.

Weiner, L. P. (2008) *Neural stem cells: Methods and protocols* (2nd edn). New York: Springer.

Weintraub, D., Comella, C., and Horn, S. (2008a) Parkinson's disease – Part 1: Pathophysiology, symptoms, burden, diagnosis and assessment. *American Journal of Managed Care,* **14**(1), S40–S48.

Weintraub, D., Comella, C., and Horn, S. (2008b) Parkinson's disease – Part 2: Treatment of motor symptoms. *American Journal of Managed Care,* **14**(2), S49–S58.

Weintraub, D., Comella, C., and Horn, S. (2008c) Parkinson's disease – Part 3: Neuropsychiatric symptoms. *American Journal of Managed Care,* **14**(3), S59–S69.

World Health Organization (2006) *Neurological disorders: Public health challenges.* Geneva: World Health Organization.

Visit **www.pearsoned.co.uk/davidholmes** for a range of resources to support study. Test yourself with multiple choice questions and access a bank of over 100 videos that will bring the topics to life. Video coverage for this chapter includes an interview and 'day in the life' with Alvin Paige, who suffers from Alzheimer's, and a discussion of how genetics can affect ageing and lifespan.

Glossary

Abreaction A re-experiencing (reliving) of past events, usually with the emotional content. Assumed to be the process bringing about catharsis in psychoanalysis.

Absinthe The anise- and herb-based alcoholic spirit.

Acculturation Where cultural practices and beliefs become isolated in an alien culture.

Action potential A nerve impulse in a neuron that travels down the axon and causes neurotransmitters to be released into the synapse to activate the next neuron.

Actuarial role Where the probability of an event happening needs to be established and presented to a court by an expert such as a psychologist (e.g. how common are suicides in teenagers?)

Actus reus To have committed the act.

Adaptive Psychological Profiling (APP) A generic AI software program used with covert camera and microcomputer to analyse microexpressions, detecting and analysing the presence of deception.

Addiction The more serious form of substance disorder in which there is dependency on the substance for continuity of current homeostasis.

Adler, Alfred (1870–1939) Core member of the Vienna Psychoanalytic Society and also later worked in the USA and UK. He founded individual psychology, emphasising the struggle to overcome feelings of inferiority.

Adoption studies Where environmental contact between twins and parents is minimised by separation.

Adversarial legal system In use in the UK and USA where opposing defence and prosecution legal teams compete in court.

Advisory role A controversial role in which a psychologist may give an opinion of another professional's evidence in court.

AESOP study An ongoing three-centre study in London with the remit to establish the reason(s) for overrepresentation of individuals from ethnic minorities seeking help for psychological disorders.

Aetiology (etiology) The study of causes.

Affectionless psychopathy Term applied by Bowlby to those maternally deprived individuals with strong criminal inclinations and an inability to make normal emotional bonds.

Age-associated cognitive decline Where there is memory and other cognitive function decrement, but subthreshold for the criteria for dementia disorders.

Agency In psychopathology, the sense that one is responsible for one's own behaviour and psychological functioning (see also **passivity phenomena**).

Agnosia An inability to recognise even familiar objects or people.

Agonists Tend to increase the action of a substance.

AIDS (acquired immunodeficiency syndrome) A condition resulting from infection by the human immunodeficiency virus (HIV), in which immune defences are reduced to the point of simple infections having fatal results.

Alcohol dehydrogenase The enzyme that breaks alcohol down within the body.

'Alcopops generation' Very young people who regularly binge on alcohol in city centres or holiday resorts in Europe (alcopops are strong alcoholic drinks that resemble soft drinks).

All or none law A neuron fires or does not fire.

Amanita muscaria Also known as 'fly agaric', a hallucinogenic mushroom.

Ameloid hypothesis In Alzheimer's disease, dementia is thought to result from build-up of ameloid plaques.

Amenorrheic No longer menstruate.

American Psychological Association (APA) The organisation that accredits courses, clinical training and professional status in the USA.

'Anal character' A result of fixation at the anal stage due to harsh toilet training, used to explain obsessive–compulsive personality disorder.

Analogue studies Use participants who are not clinical patients, but are 'equivalent' in being given therapy for imposed situations and their abilities to cope compared with those who are not.

Anandamide The endogenous form of THC.

Androgen insensitivity Where a genetic male may develop into a normal-looking and behaving (but infertile) female.

Androgens Male hormones producing male characteristics.

Androgen therapy Hormone therapy to increase arousal and orgasm.

Anejaculation Inability to ejaculate.

Anger management Training to moderate anger responses.

Anhedonia A lack of pleasure-seeking behaviour.

Animus and anima In Jung's approach, the hidden femininity and masculinity in males and females respectively.

Anonymous missives Unwanted letters repeatedly sent by an individual who withholds their identity from a particular recipient.

Anorgasmic Describes the condition of the 15 per cent or so of females who never have orgasms.

Anosmia Lack of sense of smell.

ANOVA Analysis of variance, a statistical test of difference which is used when there are three or more groups in the analysis.

Anterograde Amnesia Loss of ability to recall.

Anti-psychotics A class of medications with the capacity to 'damp down' or even eradicate psychotic symptoms.

Anxious cognition A process whereby anxious individuals perceive more threat in benign circumstances by attending more to threatening stimuli than non-anxious individuals.

Aphasia Disturbance of language.

Apostasy Unrepentantly leaving ('turning their back on') the Islam faith; punishable by death.

Applied behaviour analysis Used when examining the way the environment reinforces problem behaviour.

Approved social workers (ASW) Have specific powers of assessing whether an individual should or should not be admitted, for which they have special training.

Apraxia Difficulties in the organisation of movement.

Archetypes From Jung, these are formless predispositions handed down through evolution, awaiting realisation.

Area psychologist England and Wales is divided into 12 areas, within which prison psychology services are coordinated by area psychologists.

Arousal or excitement phase In sexual activity, the interaction between psychological pleasure and physiological reactions such as male penile tumescence, leading to erection and female vaginal lubrication and expansion.

Artificial intelligence (AI) Computer software that is able to 'learn' and modify itself to improve effectiveness.

Association of Chief Police Officers (ACPO) Policy-making body for the British police force.

Association studies Genetic studies which compare one population or group of individuals to another to determine whether one group contains different changes in their bases on genes (or SNPs) compared to the other.

Atopy syndrome Allergic hypersensitivity in parts of the body not in direct contact with an allergen.

Attenuated schizophrenia Descripion of schizotypal personality disorder.

Attributional bias Attributing blame in a systematically biased way produces suspiciousness and a tendency to blame others for negative events, as well as an emphatic reluctance to take the blame for such events or even the consequences of their own actions.

Auditory hallucinations Auditory percepts in the absence of physical stimulation. Frequently involve one or more voices, but may also include non-verbal sounds such as whistles, clicks or music.

Autogynephilia Where males find the thought of themselves as a woman sexually arousing.

Autoimmune disease (AIDS) Chronic disorder in which the human immunodeficiency virus (HIV) invades immune cells.

Automatic thoughts In Beck's cognitive therapy, habitual negative assumptions made by depressed individuals.

Automaton Observing one's actions as a detached observer.

Autonomic nervous system (ANS) Part of the peripheral nervous system. The sympathetic division of this system responds to danger by preparing the body to fight or flee (e.g. heart rate increases), with an associated sense of fear. In the absence of threat, the parasympathetic division stimulates recuperation (e.g. digestion increases).

Autoreceptors These receptors determine the concentration of a neurotransmitter in the synapse.

Autosomal recessive inheritance A recessive gene on the 'body' or non-sex chromosomes.

Aversion therapy Associating a 'punisher' with an undesirable stimulus to reduce attraction to it in the client (e.g. alcohol).

Avoidance behaviour Key feature of anxiety disorders, which tends to maintain and increase fears.

Axon The long 'arms' of neurones through which electrochemical signals are generated and sent out to other neurones.

Bandura, Albert (1925–) Linked social learning to violence in his study, in which children were shown acts of violence and then observed in their tendency to perform them.

Barbiturates Drugs used to produce sedation in the twentieth century as central nervous system depressants, but which are very infrequently used now, as they are *highly* addictive with *very severe* withdrawal effects.

Beck, Aaron T. Major pioneer of cognitive behavioural therapy.

Beck Depression Inventory (BDI) Self-report tool for detecting depression.

'Bedlam' A pejorative term that is a contraction of 'the Priory of St Mary of Bethlehem', which was founded in 1243 and came to house a handful of mentally ill individuals over the following two centuries.

Behavioural ecology Considers the ecological and evolutionary foundations of behaviour and its adaptive value.

Behavioural genetics In the context of psychopathology, a branch of genetics research focusing on abnormal human behaviour through the use of various epidemiological methods.

Behavioural Science Unit Founded at FBI Quantico and eventually began to use psychologists in training its detectives and to assist in some investigations.

Behaviour modification Operant conditioning applied as clinical therapy.

Behaviour therapy Classical conditioning applied as a clinical therapy.

Benzodiazapines Sedative hypnotics and effective anxiolytics, which were widely used for anxiety in the twentieth century.

Berrufsverband deutscher Psychologen The organisation that accredits courses, clinical training and professional status in Germany.

Best evidence rule Where copies were deemed inferior to original evidence in court.

Bianchi, Kenneth The executed 'hillside strangler' in the USA.

Biofeedback Providing a client with information about their body's activity so they can learn to control it indirectly.

Biological positivism Focuses on only objective empirical evidence based on biological factors.

Biopsychosocial information model A model acknowledging psychosocial factors impacting on biological disorder.

Bipolar disorder A psychotic disorder characterised by wild mood swings over time, from deep depression to pronounced excitation, usually interspersed by periods of 'normality'. Previously known as manic–depressive psychosis.

Blindsight Evidence of visual processing in individuals who consciously consider themselves blind.

'Blood–brain barrier' How the brain protects itself from unknown chemicals.

Blood oxygen dependent level (BOLD) The measure of changes in oxygenated blood around regions in the brain which is used in fMRI as an indicator of activation or use of particular brain areas.

Body image The mental image we have of our bodies and ourselves.

Body-mass index (BMI) Ratio of weight to height, measured as: weight in kilograms/(height in metres)^2

Bone decalcification Physical disorder thought to be influenced by stress.

Boulder model The scientist-practitioner model was also known as this in the USA.

Bowlby, John From the psychodynamic school introduced the concept of **maternal deprivation** to explain delinquency, which also relied heavily on ethology and evolutionary psychology.

Brady, Ian Psychopathic convicted child killer, 'moors murderer'.

Breuer, Josef (1842–1925) Psychodynamic pioneer and colleague of Freud.

British Association of Behavioural and Cognitive-Behavioural Psychotherapies Organisation that oversees the use of psychological therapies in the UK.

British Crime Survey The published annual crime statistics for England and Wales.

British Psychological Society (BPS) Psychology governing body in the UK.

Britton, Paul UK clinical profiler, who has worked on many high-profile cases.

Broca's area Controls speech function, located in the left frontal lobe of the brain.

Brown, Hamish UK police stalking expert who produced a booklet giving practical guidance for police officers dealing with incidents.

Brussel, James Psychiatrist who produced one of the earliest offender profiles of Mestky, New York bomber.

Burroughs, William Acclaimed twentieth-century writer who recalled his 25 years as a morphine addict and withdrawal in *Naked Lunch*.

Canter, David Established the Centre for Investigative Psychology in 1994 at the University of Liverpool to teach and research specialist aspects of psychological investigation. Carried out the first official UK criminal profile for the 'railway rapist' case.

Career criminals Recidivist criminals for whom crime is their main occupation.

Cartesian dualism Descartes considering the mind as non-physical and separate from the physical body.

Case study Detailed information gathered about one or two individuals; usually qualitative data but not always.

Catastrophic misinterpretation (of anxiety symptoms) If a panic-prone individual's heart rate rises, they interpret this as an indication that they are going to have a panic attack or even a fatal heart attack. The apprehension this causes then intensifies their symptoms in the manner of a self-fulfilling prophecy.

Catatonia A mental disorder characterised by disturbances in movement involving muscular rigidity and loss of movement, or extreme excitement and excessive movement. One of the three disorders that Kraepelin combined under the rubric of dementia praecox.

CATCHEM (Central Analytical Team Collating Homicide Expertise Management) Derbyshire-based computerised statistical database for serious crime.

CAT scans Computerised axial tomography. Taking X-ray images at different angles enables computerised images of 'slices' through organs (e.g. the brain) to be built up.

Caudal Posterior or 'towards the tail'.

Catharsis The emotionally charged recall and reliving of an anxiety-causing early experience, usually as part of psychoanalysis.

Central nervous system (CNS) The brain and spinal cord.

Cerebellum The 'flying saucer' shaped structure at the rear of the brain that integrates information on the body's position and movement.

Cerebral cortex A 3-millimetre layer of cells on the surface of the cerebrum which controls both conscious functions and higher processes of the brain.

Chaining Using the completion of one behaviour to reinforce it and act as a prompt (discriminative stimulus) for the next action in producing a complex behaviour.

Challenging behaviour Presents a challenge for the clinician or carer.

Charcot, Jean-Martin (1825–1893) Used hypnotism following work at the Nancy school in cases of 'hysteria'.

Chartered clinical psychologist The BPS in the UK confers chartered status upon a qualified graduate clinical psychologist who has gained sufficient supervised post-qualification experience.

Children and Young Persons' Act (1969) Assumes that young criminals are victims rather than inherently 'bad' and that delinquency is a cry for help.

Chomsky, Noam His language acquisition device provided a better explanation than the behaviourist view of language acquisition as entirely learned.

Chromosome Molecules of DNA which are subdivided into 'genes', each of which codes for an individual protein.

Circadian rhythms The daily biological cycles.

Clark, David UK proponent and theorist in cognitive behavioural therapy.

Classical conditioning Also termed respondent or Pavlovian conditioning, this involves involuntary responses (reflexes) and is related in principle to sensitisation. The reinforcer precedes the response.

Client-centred therapy A therapy started by Carl Rogers, in which the object is to have the client realise their own potential and act on it. Now renamed *person*-centred therapy.

Clinical criteria Score limits identifying the point at which greater scores indicate pathology.

Clinical forensic psychology A hybrid discipline at the interface between the law and clinical psychology, involving the assessment and treatment of individuals with forensic involvement. A narrower definition would be the collection, examination and presentation of clinical evidence for judicial purposes.

Clinical governance Refers to a framework by which the National Health Service (NHS) in the UK intended to make it compulsory for NHS organisations continuously to improve the quality of their service and its delivery in all departments, and particularly at the point of contact with the client.

Clinical neuropsychology Involves the assessment and management of brain damage and dysfunction, often in older adults, usually within neurology and neuropsychiatry units.

Clinical psychology Can be interpreted literally as 'bedside psychology' (from the Greek *klinik*). It is the applied approach to studying abnormal behaviour from a psychological perspective and uses psychological techniques to change or moderate such behaviour in affected individuals, adopting the scientist-practitioner role.

Club drugs Drugs associated with the dance music scene.

Cluster headache A rarer form of headache in which there is unilateral severe pain resulting in somewhat desperate measures to gain immediate relief, which may result in injury.

CNS depressants Substances that decrease brain activity, such as heroin or alcohol.

CNS stimulants Substances that increase brain activity, such as amphetamine or nicotine.

Cognitive behavioural therapy (CBT) The combination of cognitive restructuring and behavioural therapy. The main therapeutic approach in clinical psychology.

Cognitive dissonance An uncomfortable state of holding conflicting cognitions – resolved by attitude change.

Cognitive interview Combats the inherent difficulties in recalling critical information from fallible human memories.

Cognitive remediation therapy A psychotherapy targeted at improving cognition, in the hope that this, in turn, will improve quality of life and behavioural functioning, and perhaps even lead to a reduction in symptoms.

Cognitive triad Involves a negative view of oneself, personal future and current experiences (Beck).

Coherent identity data Multiple pieces of information on a single person.

Collateral damage Indirect damage to surrounding tissue or (with drugs) to parts of the body not directly concerned with the drug effects (e.g. heart disease with alcohol).

Command hallucination A particularly problematic form of auditory hallucination in which an individual may feel compelled to follow the instructions of the 'voice(s)' for fear of something terrible happening (to them) if they ignore them. (See the case of Peter Sutcliffe in Chapter 18.)

Community care Practice initiated in the 1960s of closing long-stay mental hospitals and caring for patients in community settings such as hostels, care homes or even private accommodation.

Comorbidity Having more than one diagnosed disorder at one time.

Compulsive buying scale (CBS) Produced by Faber and O'Guinn (1992) to measure 'shopaholic' tendencies.

Compulsive hoarding Extreme tendency to hoard and not use objects, to the point where clutter is problematic.

Compulsive shopping A disorder in which individuals spend out of control. This is likely to appear in *DSM-V* with other newly defined compulsive–impulsive disorders.

Computed axial tomography (CAT scans) Produces multiple X-ray like images of the structure of the brain.

Conditioned response (CR) Occurs in response to the conditioned stimulus.

Conditioned stimulus (CS) For example, a bell, which although the animal would notice it, has no reinforcing value.

Confounding effect Something having an effect on a condition, which has not been anticipated or accounted for.

Confounding variables Variables that are not measured by the researchers, but which may influence the results of an experiment.

Congenital virilising adrenal hyperplasia Causes high androgen levels in genetic females, resulting in masculine traits as adults.

Conjoint therapy In this, Masters and Johnson (1970) dealt with couples, attempting to take their clients' attention away from their dysfunction and instead focus on their relationship.

Connectivity A term synonymous with the way we think the brain *actually* works. Given psychological functions (such as memory or attention) are not dealt with by single localised regions, but by multiple regions interacting (connecting) with each other.

Contact dermatitis A form of eczema involving contact with an allergen.

Continuous amnesia Events from a particular time to the present are not recalled.

Continuous reinforcement A reinforcing reward is delivered for each response (1:1).

Contralateral Opposite side.

Control theory Theorises that everyone could be a criminal, but some factor restrains (i.e. controls) the majority.

Coprolalia Vocal tics with obscene content.

Coronary heart disease Serious source of heart attacks related to stress as well as physiological factors.

Coronary-prone behaviour The type A personality pattern of chronic impatient behaviour.

Corpus collosum Divides the hemispheres of the brain and provides innervation linking them.

Correctional Services Accreditation Panel (CSAP) Independently accredits offender behaviour programmes.

Correlational approach Indicates the relationship between two variables, whether scores increase or decrease together, or whether one score increases as the other score decreases.

Cortisol The 'stress hormone' (also termed 'hydrocortisone'), which adapts the body's resources under stress.

Counselling Problem-focused guidance and support usually for normal clients with problems of living (a non-clinical intervention, unless given by a clinical professional or counselling psychologist rather than a counsellor).

Counselling psychologist Counselling psychologists undergo the BPS three-year Diploma in Counselling Psychology (or equivalent). They are qualified to take responsibility for clients referred to health services and provide more in-depth advice if needed. This differs from the training of counsellors, who can undergo a relatively short training period.

Crack cocaine When cocaine is heated or 'freebased' with ether, the resulting lumps can be smoked and produce a highly addictive euphoric state in less than 10 seconds.

Crime career Develops as an offender refines their behaviour over a number of repeat offences, in which they may become more confident or less liable to leave evidence.

Criminology The theoretical approach to crime and its management. Causes of criminal behaviour, the penal and justice systems of the relevant country, and more socio-logical explanations of deviant behaviour are critically analysed in this discipline.

Cross-tolerance Where tolerance to one substance produces tolerance to another.

CSI (Crime Scene Investigation) One of the popular names for forensic crime scene analysis.

Cue exposure therapy or Cue desensitisation The cues that are classically conditioned to predict drug reward are presented without the final drug taking, whilst autonomic and psychological responses are monitored.

Cultural relativism Refers to how the perception and sanctioning of behaviour can vary from culture to culture. Thus the acceptability of a particular behaviour is relative to the culture in which it occurs.

Culture-bound syndromes Tend to demonstrate cultural concerns being translated into specific fears, symptoms or sexual disorders.

Culture-free In the context of psychological and clinical assessment, a procedure not 'biased' by cultural differences between clinician and patient, or between different patients.

D2 receptor One of five receptors for the NT dopamine. D2 receptors are widespread in the brain, particularly subcortically, and appear to be predominantly inhibitory. In other words, if stimulated (by dopamine) they tend to cause neurons to become less active.

Daily life therapy (DLT) Uses routine activities that are highly structured and involve rigorous physical exercise, which combine to reduce stereotyped behaviour and mannerisms.

Dangerous and severe personality disorder (DSPD) A legal category in the UK identifying those at risk due to personality disorders, usually psychopathic, to ensure the public are protected from these offenders.

Dark Ages During AD 400–900, a period following the decline of Greek–Roman civilisations when the enlightenment of scientific knowledge began to fade as religious superstition grew across Europe and other parts of the world.

'Dark figure' Crimes not officially recorded.

Darwin, Charles (1809–1882) Published on natural selection, the initiator of the evolutionary paradigm.

Dawkins, Richard UK biologist, contemporary spokesperson on scientific rationality and contemporary evolutionary theory.

Decompensation In Freud's theory, where ego-defences break down and the personality disintegrates.

Deep-brain stimulation Stereotactically implanted electrodes positioned by MRI and powered by subcutaneous programmable generators to stimulate the brain as therapy.

Deficit state (of simple schizophrenia) An enduring symptom profile marked by many negative features and pronounced cognitive impairment, seen in about 15 per cent of chronic cases of psychosis.

Deinstitutionalisation The process of removing people from long-term institutional care and its effects.

Delirium tremens Alcohol withdrawal-induced delirium, feverishness and physical tremors, which may also produce unpleasant hallucinations of creatures around and on the sufferer.

delta-9-Tetrahydrocannabinol (THC) The main active ingredient in cannabis.

Delusions False beliefs held with unshakable conviction despite overwhelming evidence to the contrary.

Demand characteristics The effect of the experimenter alone on participants in a study.

Dementia paranoides A mental disorder characterised by marked delusions and hallucinations with a pronounced paranoid profile. One of the three disorders that Kraepelin combined under the rubric of dementia praecox.

Dementia praecox The 'umbrella' term adopted by Kraepelin to encompass catatonia, hebephrenia and dementia paranoides.

Dementia pugilistica Where the disease is thought to result from repeated blows to the head, such as that suspected in the case of Mohammed Ali.

Demographic Refers to the basic characteristics of an individual, such as age, gender, socioeconomic group, ethnicity and marital status.

Demonology The earliest explanation of psychological disorder, a belief in possession by demons.

Deoxyribonucleic acid (DNA) The double-helix structured (twin-stranded) chemical 'blueprint' carried by each gene.

Dependent variable The dependent variable is the outcome variable; it is what the researcher is expecting to change.

Descartes, Rene (1596–1650) A philosopher who thought science branched from the tree of philosophy, reflecting the superiority of philosophy. He promoted dualism in considering the mind–body (mind–brain) debate.

Designer drugs Psychoactive substances deliberately designed to mimic the effects of existing psychoactive substances, but which differ chemically to evade legislation.

Desire phase The initial phase of wanting sexual activity, which may be accompanied by fantasies and expectations.

Determinism The assumption that all events and behaviour have antecedent causes, undermining free will.

Detoxification The period of enforced abstinence from a substance, experiencing withdrawal effects.

Dhat syndrome The fear of loss of semen in urine.

Diagnostic and Statistical Manual (DSM) The US diagnostic classification system (for mental disorders) now in its fourth revision (*DSM-IV*), produced by the American Psychiatric Association.

Diathesis An underlying predisposition (to develop a psychological disorder). It may be genetic, or alternatively some pattern of behaviour or thinking acquired early in life.

Diathesis–stress An approach to causation which assumes a biological predisposition (diathesis) and an environmental stressor that precipitates the disorder.

Dichotomous variables Data which form two categories that often represent two opposites, e.g. left/right, male/female, yes/no.

Differential association theory In this, crime is learned by association with other criminally inclined people in close personal groups.

Differential diagnosis Distiguishing between two similar disorder diagnoses.

Differential reinforcement of incompatible behaviour (DRI) The reinforcement of behaviour which is incompatible with the behaviour one is trying to remove.

Differential reinforcement of other behaviour (DRO) Reinforcing *any* other behaviour in order to reduce the target behaviour.

Digital natives Those who have known the internet all their lives.

Dimensional system (of personality) Measuring a profile of traits in place of the current categorical system.

Diminished responsibility The sentence is reduced to reflect the contribution of a disorder to the criminal act.

Diogenes syndrome See **syllogomania**.

Directed masturbation A therapeutic approach for females by LoPiccolo and Libitz (1972) to explore their own body and learn how to produce and sustain pleasure to orgasm.

Disconnection disorder One of several neurological disorders in which the established or putative pathology is to the connections (pathways) between two or more intact brain regions, rather than the regions themselves. Ramachandran has proposed that Capgras syndrome results from a disconnection between the temporal lobes (where faces are recognised) and the limbic system (where emotional processing takes place).

Dispositional optimism The belief or expectation that outcomes will be positive.

Discrete variables Data which have categories of more than two which the researcher has attributed meaning to: for example, the Likert scale from a questionnaire.

Discriminative stimulus A stimulus signalling that behaviour is only reinforced when it is present.

Diseases of adaptation Stress-related responses such as hypertension or ulcers.

Disorganised crime scene Where evidence and victim may be left at the somewhat random primary scene with signs of impulsiveness and sudden violence.

Disulfiram To assist in alcohol withdrawal, acts by inhibiting aldehyde dehydrogenase, causing illness if alcohol is used.

Dizygotic twins Having two zygotes. A pair of fertilised human eggs that will develop into non-identical twins.

DNA (deoxyriboneucleic acid) A double-stranded molecule containing genetic information in its chemical structure.

DNA fingerprinting Use of DNA profile to identify a perpetrator accurately.

Dopamine Important neurotransmitter involved in control and reward, and thought to be in excess in schizophrenia.

Dorsal Towards the top of the brain.

Double-blind control procedure Where patient and administrator will both be blind as to which condition is which, and results are tallied by numbered records of patient and condition.

DSM The diagnostic and statistical manual of psychological disorders, developed and periodically updated by the American Psychological Association. *DSM-IV-TR* is the current version.

Dual diagnosis Refers to having more than one diagnosable disorder, which most commonly includes a substance use disorder comorbid with another category of psychiatric disorder.

Duration of untreated psychosis (DUP) The period of time, typically several months, between the occurrence of the first psychotic symptom and initiation of treatment.

Dyskinesias Abnormal movements.

Dysphoria Affective depressive symptoms, e.g. sadness.

Echolalia The phonologically accurate repeating of sounds, usually speech.

Eclectic approach An approach in which different therapies are employed to the extent that they are useful in the individual case.

Ecological validity The degree to which a test, experiment or measure has relevance in the real world to everyday experiences of the participants being used in a study.

ECT See **electroconvulsive therapy**.

Ectomorph Thin, frail body build.

Educational psychology Assessment and management of children within and surrounding the school or other learning context.

Effect size The properties of a test to separate out participants into their previously defined groups on the basis of their scores on either a measure or a test. Effect sizes can be small, medium or large according to the sensitivity of the measure to separate the groups (i.e. a large effect size would show a large difference between the groups).

Ego The reality component of the mind in Freud's personality theory.

Ego-dystonic 'Against the ego', something unwanted by the individual.

Ego-syntonic Something agreeable to the individual.

Electra conflict The female equivalent of the Oedipal conflict, in which the infant girl comes to identify with the mother.

Electroconvulsive therapy (ECT) The passage of an electric current through the brain to create a convulsion, which has a marked therapeutic effect in depression and catatonic states.

Electroencephalogram (EEG) Recording brain activity from electrical changes detected on the scalp.

Electromyograph feedback Monitors involuntary types of muscle tension.

Embryonic stem cells Used to replace cells lost, damaged or deficient in the brains of sufferers of degenerative disorders.

Empiricism Has come to represent the scientific approach, rejecting subjectivity in favour of objective data based on observation and experimentation. Thus, empirical observation is categorising and organising observations validated by sensory experience.

Endogenous (opioid) reward system Connections in the brain, related to pain reduction, which produce a sense of pleasure in response to achievement or successful effort.

Endogenous punishment mechanism Helps us to avoid danger by producing fear and a 'sense of failure' via mechanisms such as the autonomous nervous system and the hormone cortisol.

Endomorph A soft, rotund body shape.

Endorphins Endogenous opioids having powerful reinforcing characteristics as well as pain relief and reduction of fear response effects.

Endotoxins and **exotoxins** Damaging substances found within and external to the body respectively.

Environment of evolutionary adaptedness (EEA) The statistical composite of selection pressures that occurred during an adaptation's (e.g. erect stature) period of evolution, attempting to account for all factors responsible for developed adaptations.

Epidemiological research Large numbers of individuals, usually from the same geographical area, are included in epidemiological research. The number of individuals included has to be representative of a specific population.

Erotomania Such individuals are usually female, with the specific delusion that the victim, normally of a higher status, is in love with them and initiated the 'relationship'.

Essential hypertension High blood pressure resulting from psychological causes.

Estriadol The principal estrogen or female hormone, producing female characteristics in development.

Ethical governance The requirement to have an organised, structured approach to implementing ethical screening.

Ethology The study of animal behaviour.

Eugenics movement Assumed that 'successful' individuals should breed more and the 'unsuccessful' should breed less.

Event-related potentials (ERPs) These are electrical changes picked up from the scalp (EEG responses) in response to sensory stimuli presented to the individual.

Evidence-based practice Clinical practice that is both informed and improved by objective data from ongoing innovative research and the routine evaluation of current applications.

Evidence-based therapy Continuous empirical evaluation of therapeutic effectiveness.

Evolutionary psychology The study of how adaptive (and maladaptive) behaviour, thinking and feeling have evolved through natural selection.

Existential anxiety Anxiety provoked by the awareness of one's being and inevitable non-being.

Experience sampling An innovative research methodology in which respondents are required to report on some aspect(s) of their immediate experience or behaviour repeatedly several times each day for an extended period of a week or more. Reporting is often 'prompted' by a wrist alarm, which sounds at quasi-random intervals throughout the day.

Expert witness Expert witnesses are called upon to give opinions in court based on their area of expertise, not as individuals having witnessed criminal acts.

Expressed emotion Refers to a certain kind of interaction within a family characterised by hostility, critical comments and over-involvement, which can be detrimental to individuals with schizophrenia or depression.

Extent of the crime scene Is established following a crime and a boundary set up to keep others out.

Externalising disorders Where behaviour is outward, affecting others.

Extraneous variables Unmeasured variables that may influence the experimental situation or performance on tasks that are not under the control of the researcher. These can include demographic variables, other variables specific to the participants (such as recreational drug use) or factors that may alter the experimental situation (such as differing levels of heat or background noise).

Eye movement desensitisation and reprocessing (EMDR) Concentrating on a feared stimuli whilst engaging in eye movements. Questionable efficacy over and above the exposure.

Eyewitness testimony Concerns the factors that affect the honest, accurate acquisition, recall and presentation of eyewitness testimony, but also involves the degree of impact that statements can have on the court, especially jurors and their collective decisions.

Eysenck, Hans J. (1916–1997) Empirical personality theorist who applied his personality theory to causes of criminal behaviour.

Eysenck Personality Questionnaire (EPQ) Provides measures along three dimensions of personality described by Hans Jürgen Eysenck as extraversion, neuroticism and psychoticism.

Fabricated or induced illness A term preferred by some for Munchausen's or factitious disorder.

Factor analysis A multivariate statistical technique to identify latent factors that may best account (in a meaningful way) for variability in a multivariable data set.

False memory syndrome Where false memories (often of abuse) are 'recalled', often during suggestion under hypnosis.

Family systems approach Treats the family as an interactive unit with its own dynamics, requiring therapy as a whole.

'Fatal' and 'non-fatal' In sexual activity, whether the dysfunction does or does not prevent intercourse and procreation.

Fear network A network of neurotransmitters and brain structures thought to become oversensitised and progressively conditioned to be reactive to mild stimuli.

Federal Bureau of Investigation (FBI) The USA's centre for criminal intelligence investigation, development and training.

Field-dependence/independence A psychological trait representing the degree to which one depends on, or is distracted by, background cues.

'Fight or flight' response Prepares the body for combat or escape.

Figure–ground distinction The ability to distinguish a central 'figure' against a background or 'ground'; one of the earliest cognitive abilities to develop.

Five-Factor Inventory A current personality measure (Costa and McCrae, 1992).

Fixation In Freud's theory, getting 'stuck' at one of his stages of development.

Fixed action patterns Instinctive behaviours, which are resistant to change, species specific and need no learning.

Fixed interval schedule Here reinforcement only occurs at the end of a given time period during which at least one response must be made.

Fixed ratio schedule Reinforcement is after a specific number of responses, such as FR10 or reinforcement every 10 responses.

Fliess, Wilhelm Colleague of Freud proposing a 'nasal-genital response' explanation of disorder, which borders on fetishism.

Flooding The therapeutic enforced exposure to a feared stimulus without escape until the fear subsides.

Foetal alcohol syndrome Effects of maternal alcohol use on a gestating foetus.

Food focus Thinking about food excessively or even hoarding it.

Forensic awareness Criminals with previous contact with the justice system or police are more aware of what incriminating clues or evidence they reveal.

Forensic health psychology Has developed alongside health psychology, as the consequences of stress or poor health conditions at work have resulted in litigation, and now covers a broad field of forensic implications.

Forensic psychology Work pertaining to the law court, now including psychologists in such roles as expert witnesses, offender profilers and criminological theorists.

Formal thought disorder A particular type of psychotic symptom in which the very structure of thinking seems to have been disrupted, usually inferred from anomalous speech.

Formulation A method of integrating the comprehensive data required to treat that particular individual and predict the outcome for the case.

Free association In psychoanalysis, the patient is allowed to speak their thoughts as they come to them, without instruction or preconception.

Freebasing cocaine Purifying the psychoactive ingredient (freebase) by heating cocaine with ether.

Free will Considers that we decide what we do and are not passive in our behaviour.

Frequency coding Communication between neurons is on the basis of the frequency of the pulse (not its intensity).

Frontal lobes Brain area containing executive function areas with widely dispersed connections including that for planning behaviour. Damage, particularly to that area just behind the forehead referred to as the pre-frontal cortex results in irresponsible and even criminally reckless behaviour.

Fronto-striatal circuitry A brain area linked to behavioural disinhibition.

Functional analysis The functional purpose of the unwanted behaviour to the client is identified and can be utilised in any intervention.

Functional contextualism Explains how language is developed by learning and environmental interactions.

Functional disorder A disorder arising from function or non-biological factors.

Functionalism Based on inherited characteristics surviving to the degree that they are functional.

Functional magnetic resonance imaging (fMRI) Used to determine the blood flow changes in different areas of the brain to determine whether one brain area is active compared to surrounding areas.

Functional psychosis A psychological disorder (with no identifiable organic basis) characterised by periods of impaired insight and a blurring of the distinction between external reality and psychological state.

Functional retrograde amnesia Detached islets of past memory.

Gage, Phineas Suffered damage to the frontal lobes but survived, only to lose moral and planning abilities.

Galvanic skin response (GSR) Moistening of the skin increasing its electrical conductivity, inferring that the person is unduly aroused.

Gamma-aminobutyric acid (GABA) Inhibitory neurotransmitter system.

Gamma-hydroxybutyrate (GHB) A sedative that has been adopted as a 'club drug'. GHB has also gained a reputation as a date-rape drug.

'Gamma-knife' procedure A method introduced by Lars Leksell in 1972, which uses converging cobalt gamma rays to destroy the target cells without surgery.

Gateway drug Supposed minor drug use leading users to use 'harder' drugs such as heroin.

Gene A section of a DNA molecule (chromosome) responsible for producing a particular protein.

Gene array (DNA micro array) A recently developed genetic technique in which DNA is 'broken down' into very short strips which are 'displayed' in a two-dimensional matrix. Arrays can be compared and the technique will allow identification of different levels of expression (of genes) and subtle differences in their structure (polymorphisms).

General adaptation syndrome (GAS) Accounts for the progressive effects of chronic stress.

General Health Questionnaire (GHQ) Developed for general medical patients to fill in themselves and enables the detection of psychiatric disorders.

Generalised amnesia Memory loss covering the client's entire life.

General practitioner (GP) In England, the term for a family doctor.

Genetically modified cannabis Genetically engineered plants bred for potency.

Genetic counselling Advice when a sufferer or carrier of a genetically influenced disorder considers offspring.

Genetic engineering The altering of actual DNA sequences or genes themselves sometimes during the lifetime, or ontological genetic engineering.

Genetic preparedness Inherited fear, usually an adaptive response such as fear of snakes.

Genomics The study of an organism's entire genome. In human research this would involve all genes in a cell.

Genotype The trait information as carried by the gene.

Germ line therapy Involves pre-embryonic molecular gene treatment that can be unpredictable in terms of phenotypic outcomes.

Geron Corporation A company carrying out extensive work on the production and use of telomerase to arrest ageing.

Gestalt Concentration on the pattern of the whole rather than its component parts.

Glial cell A cell which supplies nutrients to neurones.

Glove anaesthesia Where the client presents with lack of feeling in a doll-like view of hand anatomy ending at the wrist.

Gluteus maximus The main muscle of your derrière/ 'bottom'.

Goldberg, David Eminent UK psychiatrist and retired head of the Institute of Psychiatry.

Gridiron abdomen Physical damage to the abdomen wall from repeated abdominal surgery.

Grievous mental harm In the UK this charge was established in 1996 during the well-documented harassment of Tracy Morgan by Anthony Burstow. It marked a real legal step forward in establishing that physical injury was not the only way to evidence harm to a victim.

Grooming/internet grooming/sexual grooming Coercion (over the internet) of children by paedophiles into accepting contact and maintaining silence. Over the internet this may involve posing as another child.

Gudjonsson Suggestibility Scale Assesses suggestibility in witnesses or those prone to therapist suggestion (Gudjonsson, 1984).

Guilty but insane The defendant may be thus diverted from the penal system into psychiatric care (until fit).

Hacienda Nightclub in Manchester that voluntarily closed its doors due to gang culture taking over the drug market.

Haemophilia A genetic blood disorder only expressed in males, but where females act as carriers with no phenotypical signs of the disorder.

Half-life The time it takes a substance to reach half its original concentration in the blood plasma.

Half-sibling adoption studies Genetic influence is examined without any environmental contact, including the prenatal environment, by only considering the biological father.

Hallucination A psychotic symptom in which the individual perceives something that does not exist.

Hallucinogen persisting perception disorder Also known as flashbacks, supposed psychedelic experiences, usually hallucinations that occur long after all traces of the substance have left the body.

Hallucinogens Substances that produce hallucinatory states and tend to lack reward or addictive properties, such as LSD and psilocybin.

Hardiness Refers to individuals who do not appear to suffer physical disorders as a result of stress.

Health anxiety An alternative term for **hypochondriasis**.

Health psychology The study of how psychological factors impact on physical health.

'Hearsay' evidence A legal ruling that courts will not accept evidence that is second hand.

Hebephrenia A mental disorder characterised by silly, inappropriate and/or bizarre behaviour with markedly abnormal patterns of thinking. One of the three disorders that Kraepelin combined under the rubric of dementia praecox.

Helicobacter pylori bacterium Thought to lead to ulcers following stress.

Heterogeneity Having more than one (usually genetic) cause.

Heterozygous Describes when the opposing alleles on a gene code for different forms of a trait.

Hindley, Myra One of the UK 'moors murderers' convicted of the serial killing of children.

Hippocrates (460–377 BC) 'The father of modern medicine' who believed in natural causes and the importance of physiological processes. Hippocrates was also the first to separate psychological causes (psychogenesis) from physiological ones (somatogenesis).

Historical truth Actual accuracy of events.

Hoarding The excessive collection and failure to discard poorly usable objects.

Hoffman, Albert Discovered LSD-25 in 1938.

Homeostasis Keeping variables at the optimum required.

Homogeneity of variance One of the requirements for parametric analysis. This assumption is more important when different groups of participants are being compared (e.g. males and females). It refers to the natural variation in performance or questionnaire scores which each individual expresses. The assumption requires that there is the same amount of expression of these individual differences within the two groups of participants being tested.

Homozygous Descibes when the opposing alleles on a gene code for the same form of a trait.

Hormone replacement therapy (HRT) Administering hormones to counter a naturally occurring deficiency.

Human genome A complete record of all human genetic codings, enabling comparison of the expected structure with disordered variations.

Human immunodeficiency virus (HIV) The virus invading immune cells in autoimmune disease (AIDS).

Hypersomnia Oversleeping.

Hyperthyroidism or thyrotoxicosis An excess of thyroxine, which can mimic anxiety and panic disorders.

Hypochondriasis Overconcern with normal bodily functions to the point of imagining serious illness.

Hypochondriasis by proxy Overconcern for the child's health with the possibility of exaggerating symptoms to gain reassurance.

Hypoglycaemia and hypothyroidism Conditions that produce some anxiety-type symptoms and need to be eliminated prior to a diagnosis of anxiety disorder.

Hypomania Means 'below mania' and includes most of the symptoms of mania but not to a disabling degree.

Hyponatraemia Where the blood electrolyte levels become diluted to a perilous degree, occasionally leading to death as in the much-publicised case of Leah Betts.

Hypothalamus–pituitary–adrenal axis The arousal system in the fight–flight response with adrenaline, noradrenaline and cortisol release.

Hypothesis A statement about what researchers are expecting to find in the study they are performing.

Hypothyroidism Lack of thyroid gland activity which has symptoms of lethargy and depression, and is dangerous in childhood.

Hypoxyphilia Sexual excitement resulting from reduced oxygen intake.

Hysteria An older term for disorders involving dissociation, pseudomedical symptoms or anxiety.

Iatrogenic symptoms Symptoms resulting from the effects of therapy, not the disorder.

Id The most basic of Freud's mental structures formed at birth, the source of all psychic energy and containing inherited needs and instincts.

Identity theft Three or four items of personal information are used to create a virtual economic replica identity for financial gain.

Ideographic Literally 'picture of the individual', used to imply the unique nature of one person's illness and its causes.

Ideopathic Individualistic and not generalisable.

Immunodeficiency Lowered immune response increased by stress.

Implicit personality theories When we judge the character of others and make intuitive assumptions about how they will react, forming our individual theory.

Implosion A form of flooding that uses exaggerated imagined versions of the feared stimulus in therapy.

Impulsivity The tendency to give way to impulses, e.g. eating too much or theft.

Innate releasing mechanisms Elicit reactions such as the features of a baby's face releasing protective behaviour in human adults.

Incidence The number of new cases of a disorder over a period of time (usually a year).

Inclusive fitness We protect our genes being carried by relatives to the degree of that relatedness.

Incompetent suitor (stalker) The incompetent suitor is deficient in interpersonal skills and in particular 'courtship skills' but still wants a relationship or at least some approximation to their understanding of a relationship.

Independent or between subjects design Different participants complete the conditions in an experiment.

Independent variable The independent variable defines the groups in a study. It is often something under the control of the researcher, such as the group to which a participant has been assigned in an experiment. The independent variable is thought to have some influence on the dependent variable.

Infantilism The need to be treated as a helpless infant with a dominant 'mother'.

Inquisitorial system In parts of Europe, using this system allows a wider spectrum of evidence in court (Gudjonsson and Haward, 1998). The inquisitorial legal system focuses on uncovering, analysing and considering the facts of a case.

Insight The status of having awareness of one's own psychological functioning in the context of the wider environment. The patient's ability to realise their own state of disorder.

Instinctual drift Where instinctive patterns override learned behaviour, showing species-specific preparedness.

Institute of Psychiatry London-based centre for psychiatric research in the UK.

Institutionalisation effects Long-term effects of being in institutions.

Insult to the brain Damage from toxins such as drugs.

Intelligence quotient (IQ) An estimate based on a comparison with one's age group, which can be weighted for (i.e. can account for) other factors.

International Classification of Diseases (ICD) The Geneva-based diagnostic classification system (of mental disorders) compiled by the World Health Organisation.

International Pilot Study of Schizophrenia (IPSS) A WHO sponsored multi-centre study with the original brief to compare the use and application of diagnostic criteria around the world.

International Professional Surrogate Association (IPSA) An organisation that trains sexual surrogates. All are supervised for each therapy session by a sex therapist who may also be medically qualified.

Internet addiction Substantial dependency on internet usage is found in those identified as internet addicted, with a very short period of use being required to form this addiction or dependency.

Interpersonal coherence Assumes that the offender's relationship with the victim tends to reflect the offender's relationships in the rest of their life.

Interpersonal narratives The ways in which the offender interacts with other factors, including their relationship with the victim.

Interractionism The view that events and behaviour are a result of the interaction between nature and nurture.

Interrater reliability The degree of agreement between independent clinicians' ratings.

Interrogative interviews Police or courtroom interviewing of a suspect intended to gain incriminating statements.

Interrogative suggestibility The form of suggestibility that is pertinent to police and courtroom questioning.

Interval or ratio data Data which have equal or statistically defined spaces between each number. Otherwise known as continuous data.

Intimacy seeker The intimacy seeker is often deluded or otherwise disordered, but even if pathology is not apparent, they will still engage in a one-sided fictional relationship with a particular stranger.

Investigative psychology Alternative term to forensic psychology, intended by proponent David Canter to be a more objective approach.

Investigative Support Unit The new name for the Behavioural Science Unit.

In Vivo In life. Conducting therapy in real-world situations.

Ipsilateral Indicates 'same side'.

Isoamyl nitrite 'Amyl' is an inhalant intended to keep vital bodily functions (e.g. heart rate) continuing during situations such as cyanide poisoning. It is sold as a 'club drug' under the label 'poppers'.

Italian experience Italian health services' sustained period of discharging patients (and staff), closing institutions and putting emphasis on prevention.

James Randi Educational Foundation This organisation offer a $1 million prize to anyone who can show, under proper observing conditions, evidence of any paranormal, supernatural or occult power or event, and as yet it has had no takers.

Jamison, Kay Redfield Psychiatrist and bipolar disorder sufferer found the incidence of mood disorder to be many times that of the general population among famous writers and artists.

Jung, Carl Gustav (1875–1961) was a Swiss psychiatrist who opposed Freud's emphasis on sex, giving prominence to philosophical and religious aspects in his analytical psychology.

'Junk culture' The culture surrounding opiate use.

Kegel's exercises Exercises to dilate the vaginal opening to combat vaginismus.

Ketamine A synthetic 'dissociative' anaesthetic used predominantly in veterinary medicine. In small quantities, inhaled ketamine can induce psychotic-like passivity and dissociative-like experiences in humans by blocking NMDA glutamate receptors.

'K-hole' A ketamine slang term, in which users describe the sensation of 'tunnel vision' preceding their 'going under'.

Kinsey, Alfred Produced the first extensive survey information on the various sexual activities of the public.

Klein, Melanie (1882–1960) Promoted psychoanalysis in Britain, examining early childhood relations focusing on first encounters with 'objects', the primary 'object' being the breast.

Klein, Paul Studied the anal character for his PhD at Manchester and produced factor analytic support for aspects of Freudian theory.

Kraepelin, Emil (1856–1926) Produced a biologically based coherent classificatory system, *A Textbook of Psychiatry* (Kraepelin, 1885).

Kuhn, Thomas (1922–1996) Described how paradigms change over time (Kuhn, 1996) and paradigm shifts.

La belle indifférence Has been used to refer to the client's tendency to lack the degree of concern normally associated with sudden blindness or paralysis.

Labelling refers to the effects of attaching a label such as 'schizophrenic' to an individual.

Laing, Ronald D. (1927–1989) Symbolised the anti-psychiatry movement from his initial publication in 1960 through to his worldwide cult-like status of 'psychiatrist as prophet', launching an assault on Western psychiatry.

Lanugo The development of fine downy hair on the trunk of the body.

Laudanum A mixture of spices, opium and wine, commonly dispensed by physicians in the nineteenth century for a variety of pain-based complaints.

'Law of Effect' Proposed by Thorndike, behaviour followed by punishment will decrease in frequency and behaviour followed by reward will increase in frequency.

'Lawyerese' A verbal style of questioning that may manipulate the content of an answer.

Learned effectiveness and learned optimism Seligman (1992) noted that we learn that we are effective in the world by correctly solving problems and achieving. This is used as a treatment.

Learned helplessness Learning that one is helpless to control significant events from previous experiences of lack of control.

Leary, Timothy Researcher at Harvard University Center for Research in Personality, experimented with and then promoted use of psychedelic drugs such as LSD.

'Less than dead' A term taken from the murder of poor workers on the Mexico–US border, used to mean that deaths of victims such as prostitutes are less noticed than those of middle-class or celebrity victims.

Levodopa Increases levels of dopamine in Parkinson's disease.

Libido Freud's concept of psychic energy, which had a sexual basis.

Life-events A generic term to describe significant (and usually) stressful situations or occurrences that researchers have sought to quantify (using life-event inventories) in order to relate to psychological disorders. The Homes–Rahe stress scale, which identifies (and ranks) 41 life-events such as 'moving house', 'change in financial status' and 'death of spouse' is a widely used such inventory.

Lifetime prevalence rates The percentage of a population who will develop a disorder across the lifetime.

Likert-type scale A scale based on a subjective judgement of the degree to which the given statement applies to them or is in agreement with their own attitudes selected from a row of statements (agree, very much agree, etc.).

Line of best fit Often appears on scatterplots. The line cuts through the data points on a scatterplot in such a way as to explain the largest variability in the scores possible. It therefore aims to represent as many of the data points as possible.

Linkage The tendency for genetic traits to be inherited together if they are on the same chromosome.

Linkage studies Investigate the passing of whole sections of chromosome from parent to child in large family trees.

Listeners' network A dual purpose scheme uses volunteer prisoners trained by the Samaritans to support their peers identified as high risk.

Lithium carbonate An unpatented salt that moderates mood swings in bipolar mood disorder.

Localised amnesia or selective amnesia Only certain events from a period fail to be recalled whilst memory for others seems intact.

Locus of control (Rotter, 1966) A measure from external believing factors are beyond their control to internal or putting factors down to themselves.

Loftus, Elizabeth Psychologist who brought many decades of study of eyewitness testimony into sharp focus in a series of experiments that undermined the assumptions of eyewitness validity.

Lombroso, Cesare (1835–1909) 'Father of criminology' who identified primitive 'atavistic' (i.e. belonging to remote ancestors) physical features in prisoners and related this to criminality.

Longitudinal methods A research technique in which individuals are followed up for a period of time in order to measure change (in, for example, behavioural functioning) over time.

Lorenz, Konrad (1903–1989) Observed **imprinting** behaviour in geese and considered whether this also occurred in humans.

Lovaas program A strict behavioural regime that involves controlling the child's entire environment, including the reinforcing behaviour of their parents.

LSD Lysergic acid diethylamide, a hallucinatory drug.

Lycanthropy The belief-based mythical transformation of a man into a wolf (werewolf). The belief that one has turned into a wolf is clinical lycanthropy.

Mad–bad debate Focuses on the differentiation and overlap between mental disorder and crime.

'Magic mushrooms' The raw *Psilocybe* 'liberty cap' fungus containing **psilocybin**.

Magnetic resonance imaging (MRI) A modern-day imaging technique which does not use radiation and produces high-quality images of the structure of the brain.

Magnetoencephalography (MEG) A hybrid technique that combines technologies producing high-image and temporal resolution.

Malingered amnesia Acted memory loss, where secondary gain is more clearly evident.

Malleus Maleficarum (the Witches' Hammer) A widely accepted manual published in 1428 for dealing with unnatural phenomena, giving 'signs', 'tests' and 'treatments' for witches and ungodly activity.

Mania operative passive Factitious disorder.

Manie sans délire Violence in the absence of delusions.

MANOVA Like ANOVA but allows for multiple dependent variables to be lumped together and tested for effects of the independent variable.

MAOI (monoamine-oxidase inhibitor) A drug which inhibits the action of the substance (MAO) that breaks down neurotransmitters in the synapse.

Maslow, Abraham (1908–1970) Described a 'hierarchy of needs', which all human beings strive to work through.

Mask of Sanity, The Cleckley's (1976) reference to the psychopathic personality.

Mass hysteria Psychological contagion.

Mast cells or eosinophils Accumulating inflammatory cells, which are activated in the bronchial wall and airway lumen.

Masturbatory satiation Where the client masturbates to orgasm with a non-deviant fantasy, then attempts to masturbate to their deviant fantasy, and is frustrated, unable to orgasm.

Maternal deprivation Psychological separation of a child under 6 years for more than 6 months, which was used to explain delinquency.

Medical model An approach to disorders which adopts a medical or biological view of disorder.

Medical student syndrome A tendency for students to falsely believe they or their colleagues have many of the disorders they study, a kind of academic hypochondriasis.

Melancholia An early term for depression.

Mendel, Gregor (1822–1884) Identified basic laws of genetic inheritance by empirical observation of pea plants.

Mens rea To have guilty intent as one's state of mind.

Mental Health Review Tribunal A case reviewing body consisting of a legal professional, an independent psychiatrist and a lay individual.

Mesmer, Franz Anton (1734–1815) Claimed that patients with hysteria suffered an imbalance in 'bodily magnetic fluid' to be corrected using magnetic rods used in a theatrical manner like a magician's wand. He also used 'mesmerism', producing a sleep-like suggestible state related to hypnotism.

Mesomorph An athletic and muscular body build.

Meta-analysis Usually a combined analysis of the findings from a number of studies; an analysis of a number of analyses.

Meta-cognitive therapy Literally 'above' cognition, and interpreted as a high-level monitoring of lower-level cognitive processing, as in 'thinking about what you are thinking' or 'worrying about worries'.

Methamphetamine hydrochloride 'Crystal meth' or 'ice', probably the most addictive form of amphetamine compound.

Methylphenidate (Ritalin) A central nervous system stimulant used for children with attention-deficit hyperactivity disorder.

Micro-deletion The loss of a short length of DNA during meiosis, giving rise to a chromosome that has a few genes missing.

Micrographia Abnormally small compacted handwriting.

Mind–body (mind–brain) debate Considering mental events and body/brain separate entities (dualism) or two ways of viewing the same thing (monism).

Mindfulness therapy A form of cognitive behavioural therapy which addresses a client's relationship with their thoughts.

Misuse of Drugs Act (1971) The main UK law identifying illicit drugs – modified many times.

Mitochondria Provide energy in the form of adenosine triphosphate and are believed to be an invading parasite that evolved to coexist within our cells.

Modelling An applied form of social learning theory, in which a behaviour is demonstrated to a client who has difficulty in performing it.

Modified Stroop In the standard Stroop test, the respondent has to name the colour of written colour words (such as the word RED written in blue ink) whilst ignoring the words themselves. The test can be modified in several ways. For example, in a word version of the test, distractor words may vary in 'emotional' salience or content.

Monoamine hypothesis of depression The proposal that dopamine, serotonin and noradrenaline levels are raised in mania and lowered in depression, are causing the mood change.

Monotherapy A single treatment approach is used.

Monozygotic twins Identical twins from the separation of one fertilised ovum.

'Moral insanity' Used by Pritchard (1835) to describe psychopathy.

Morbid jealousy Pathological jealousy in which paranoid and deluded beliefs are assumed as fact.

Multi-Agency Public Protection Panels (MAPPPs) Combine a number of differing professionals to assess forensic risk and restrictions.

Multiaxial Referring to the *DSM* classification system, in which clients are assessed on independent scales or 'axes' representing different aspects of the patient's functioning that contribute to a final formulation.

Multi-dimensional scaling Statistical technique producing a two-dimensional output with variables physically distanced in proportion to their relatedness.

Multi-infarct dementia This form of dementia is associated with high blood pressure, retinal sclerosis, kidney failure and cardiovascular problems.

Multiple admissibility rule Where evidence should be used for its original purpose only and not submitted for another.

Multiple case study Instead of simply reporting the average scores for different groups of respondents, a researcher may display each individual's 'score' from any given group, typically as a 'dot' on a type of scattergram. In this way, it becomes possible to see the overlap in scores between groups, and the spread of scores within each group.

Multiple sclerosis Where the body erroneously identifies myelin as an invading body and attacks it, resulting in axons becoming dysfunctional.

Multipotent stem cells May develop into cells of one lineage only.

Münchausen, Hieronymous Karl Frederick von (1720–1797) Was supposed to have lied outlandishly about his exploits fighting for Russia against the Turks.

Münchausen's syndrome by adult proxy (MSBAP) Elderly individuals who can be vulnerable to mistreatment by relatives and others in a similar manner to children in MSBP.

Munsterberg, Hugo (1863–1916) Published *On the Witness Stand* (Munsterberg, 1908). Munsterberg promoted the application of psychology to justice and courtroom, but the legal profession predictably rejected this and Wigmore (1909) even ridiculed his work.

Muscular spasticity Uncontrolled movement.

Myalgic encephalopathy (ME) Chronic fatigue syndrome.

Myelination or myelin sheath Of axons, where **oligodendroglia** in the central nervous system and **Schwann cells** in the peripheral nervous system lay myelin in segments along axons, which provides insulation against signals in other axons and speeds transmission.

Naloxone Substance that blocks the receptors for endogenous opioids and also has the potential to block the rewarding aspects of behaviour.

Narrative truth An individual's belief about a memory.

National Adult Reading Test (NART) Gives a measure of intellectual ability by the reading out loud of single words correctly (Nelson and Willison, 1991).

National Crime Faculty UK national police serious crime initiative, developing investigative intelligence.

National Crime Squad The UK-based specialist investigation unit often referred to as the British FBI, as it has similar functions.

National Health Service (NHS) The publicly funded health care provider in the UK.

National Hi-Tech Crime Unit UK specialist police unit dedicated to the detection and prosecution of computer-related crime.

National Institute for Clinical Excellence (NICE) Organisation in the UK for evaluating medical interventions.

Natural selection The evolutionary trial and error process by which useful genes and genetic mutations survive generations and others die out.

Nature–nurture (debate) Considering the effects of genetic and biological determinism versus those of environmental experience on behaviour.

Negative reinforcement In operant conditioning, the conditional removal of a punisher to increase desired behaviour.

Negative symptoms/negative signs Behavioural features marked by their absence from a normal repertoire. Strictly speaking, they are signs rather than symptoms because the individual usually does 'complain' about them.

Neodarwinism An evolutionary view that refers to inheriting genes rather than physical characteristics.

Neologisms 'New words' or words with a novel application.

Neotony A greatly extended childhood.

Neural networks Artificial neural networks mimic the human brain, with software 'neurons' having modifiable connections.

Neuroanatomy Study of the physical structure of the nervous system, including the substructures of the brain.

Neurochemistry The study of the chemical transmission of signals within and between nerve cells.

Neurodevelopment The early development of the nervous system. Deviance in this process is usually complicated as development continues and impossible to restore.

Neuroendocrinology Study of the effects of hormone activity on the nervous system.

Neuroimmunoregulation Immune triggering system sensitive to stress.

Neuroleptic A group of anti-psychotic (anti-schizophrenic) drugs, which achieve this by blocking dopamine receptors.

Neuron(e) A nerve cell.

Neuropsychology The relationship between neuroanatomy and neurochemistry (including endocrinology), and behaviour, thinking and feeling.

Neurophysiology The study of the responses of the nervous system: how signals are carried.

Neuroticism Predisposed to anxiety, having an unstable autonomic nervous system.

Neurotic paradox The apparent resistance of phobic reactions to extinction over time.

'Neurotic personality' Individuals with 'trait anxiety'. 'Neurotic' individuals tend to have overreactive autonomic responses and are thus assumed to be more than usually prone to anxiety-related conditions.

Neurotransmitters Chemical messengers which are released into synapses by neurons (when excited) usually to influence receptors on the other neurons, making them more or less likely to fire their own nerve impulses.

NIMBY 'Not In My Back Yard', a phrase often used in the context of care in the community to represent the views of those who agree with the principle, but would not like the cared-for in their neighbourhood.

Nitrous oxide A gas that produces euphoria and light-headedness, and reduces negative feeling associated with pain.

NMR Nuclear magnetic resonance imaging. Uses a magnetic field to displace hydrogen in the body's tissue, enabling computers to analyse the tiny magnetic emissions as it returns, giving good internal pictures of tissue.

Nomothetic Literally 'rule giving', used to indicate the way that disorders are classified by looking for general principles and common features that apply to all individuals with the disorder.

Non-parametric tests Distribution-free tests, which make no assumption about the spread of participants' scores or variation of scores within subgroups of participants. Examples are Chi-square, Friedman's, Kruskall Wallis and Spearman's rho.

Normal distribution Often referred to as 'the bell-shaped curve'. In a normal distribution the majority of participants score around the mean and a small number of participants score extremely high or extremely low.

Normatology The study of the distinction between normal and abnormal behaviour.

Nosology The study of classifications.

Nucleus accumbens Along with ventral tegmental area and pre-frontal cortex, the reward centres in the brain targeted by addictive substances.

Object relations Derived from Melanie Klein, this is now a therapeutic approach in its own right and examines the effects of early relationships with objects, usually beginning with the breast.

Obsessional slowness In obsessive–compulsive disorder, the slowing of daily tasks due to checking and ritual.

Occupational forensic psychology Deals with legal issues around employment and business, such as integrity in the workplace, stress compensation claims and corporate crime.

Occupational psychology The study of how abnormal behaviour affects, and is affected by, working and the workplace, with emphasis on occupational stress.

Oedipal conflict A crucial point in Freud's psychosexual stages in which the superego is formed by the boy identifying with the father, based on the dynamics of the legend of Oedipus.

Offender profiling A few forensic psychologists are contracted to work with the police to help describe or identify offenders who are often disordered.

One-sided suicide pact Where one individual will end the lives of others, often family, as part of their suicide.

Oniomania Buying mania.

Omega-3 fatty acids Deficits in these have been found to contribute to mood disorders.

Omission In operant conditioning, the conditional removal of reward to reduce undesirable behaviour.

Ontogenetic Within the lifespan.

Operant conditioning A form of associative learning in which the consequences following a behaviour serve to reinforce or reduce its recurrence, depending on the affective qualities of the consequences.

Orbitofrontal cortex Plays a role in regulating emotional responses; damage can result in a dangerous lack of restraint, leading to anti-social acts.

Organic–functional distinction This refers to whether the potential causes of a disorder are biological in origin, or a product of function (psychological).

Organised crime scene Has characteristics such as evidence of planning, control, use of restraint and removal or hiding of any evidence (including a body).

Orgasm The climax of sexual pleasure where ejaculation is inevitable for males and part of the outer wall of the vagina contracts in females.

Orgasmic reconditioning Where masturbation takes place to paraphilic stimuli until the point of orgasmic inevitability when the fantasy is switched to a conventional acceptable stimulus.

Ortgeist Going against the historical culture. Often used to refer to people or events that seem to be in opposition to their historical context.

Osteoporosis Bone mineral density loss.

Outreach work Describes services sent out into the community to aid people with disorders.

Oxytocin This hormone prepares the female for birth but also facilitates bonding with the child, which also generalises to assist bonding between male and female partners and even increases the level of trust one has in others.

Paradigm A set of assumptions guiding theory and practice. In abnormal psychology, a way of conceptualising mental disorder leading to assumptions about its aetiology and treatment.

Parametric tests Statistical tests with three requirements to be met. Examples are t-tests, ANOVA, MANOVA and regression.

Paraphilia Sexual desire of that beyond the normal.

Parapsychology How and why individuals and groups come to believe in entities, concepts and experiences beyond those of common experience and empirical evidence.

Parasocial interaction A synthetic illusory 'relationship' that is induced by interacting with the media: for example, a regular presenter on TV can be seen as a real acquaintance and the TV experience may substitute for a genuine personal relationship.

Parasympathetic See **autonomic nervous system**.

Parole system Allows for early release for 'good conduct'.

Partialism Fetishistic arousal for areas of the human body such as the feet.

Passivity phenomena A cluster of psychotic symptoms wherein the individual no longer feels in control of his or her own thoughts, motives, emotions or actions.

Pathologise To consider a particular set of behaviours to be a disorder, usually controversially.

Pavlov, Ivan (1849–1936) Discovered the laws of classical conditioning.

PCL (psychopathy checklist) Screening scale for psychopathy.

PCP A synthetic 'dissociative' anaesthetic developed for veterinary medicine but rarely used because of its side-effects. In small quantities, PCP (also known as angel dust) is used recreationally, and can induce psychotic-like passivity and dissociative-like experiences in humans by blocking NMDA glutamate (similar to ketamine) and nicotinic ACh receptors.

Pedigree studies Also known as family studies, these examine a disorder's frequency amongst different relatives within families, showing the degree of heritability.

Peripheral nervous System (PNS) Comprises the spinal nerves, cranial nerves and somatic nervous system.

Perls, Frederick (1893–1970) Developed the Gestalt approach to therapy after he disagreed with analyst colleagues over their assumptions.

Perseveration Persisting in an action or line of thought when it is no longer necessary.

Perseverative cognition A reaction extending the arousal and other symptoms of stress both in advance of and long after the stressful event.

Pervasive developmental disorder Childhood onset disorders which persist and pervade all aspects of the individual's functioning.

Phantom limb pain Where pain is felt in a limb after amputation.

Phenotype The actual trait carried by genes as expressed in the developing organism.

Pinel, Philippe (1745–1826) Represented the liberal view of treating the mentally ill and prisoners humanely; his ordering the removal of chains from patients came to symbolise the movement.

Photoplethysmography An instrument for measuring vaginal opacity as an indicator of blood engorgement, which is used to infer sexual arousal in women.

Phrenology The pseudo-science that believes that human character can be inferred from the contours of the skull.

Phylogenetic (development) Evolutionary development.

Physician effect Produces improvement in the belief that the physician genuinely cares about the client.

Pineal gland Produces melatonin in response to lack of light, aiding sleep.

Pituitary gland 'Master gland' controlling all hormone levels throughout the body.

Placebo A non-active (benign) treatment process used for comparison with an active one.

Placebo-controlled studies Where the true effectiveness of the treatment is then judged to be that beyond the placebo effect.

Plasticity The tolerance in human systems that allows some recovery from damage, especially during development.

Plethysmography (penile plethysmography/penile strain gauge) A device that is highly sensitive to any change in circumference of the penis.

Pluripotent stem cells Can form the different lineages of cells in the body.

Pneumograph Measures changes in breathing.

Police and Criminal Evidence Act (1984) (PACE) Revised the traditional priorities for interviewing witnesses in order to focus on obtaining the facts of a crime rather than on securing a prosecution.

Police National Computer (PNC) UK police database containing criminal records and links to motor vehicle records, which can be accessed by officers on patrol.

Polydrug users Use more than one substance.

Polygenetic hereditary multifactorial disease Inherited disorders, with many factors being involved both in inheritance and in the environment.

Polygraph Combines measures of blood pressure, heart rate, galvanic skin response, etc. to infer lying.

Polymerase chain reaction (PCR) Produces an adequate DNA sample for final analysis.

Polypharmacy Multiple drugs used in therapy.

Popper, Karl (1902–1996) Considered that a theory had to be capable of being falsified or tested to be scientific.

Porphyria A disorder with features of avoiding light and having pale ulcerated skin, which with other symptoms could resemble a mythical werewolf in more primitive times.

Positive feedback (loop) Where the effects of a factor serve to increase that factor.

Positive psychology Examines the origins of happiness and well-being; a progression from Martin Seligman's theories.

Positron emission tomography (PET) A means of observing brain activity in living subjects, by mapping the emissions of radioactive metabolites introduced into the brain.

Postpartum onset Specified for any episode if it begins up to 4 weeks after childbirth.

Power of a test Refers to the statistical possibility of finding a significant result in a given sample size when the difference between the groups in the analysis has been previously established in past research.

Practice-based evidence This refers to the use of clinical practice in the field for research, which is similar to the routine evaluation of current applications above but involves inductive reasoning.

Predatory stalker The predatory stalker pursues in preparation for attack, usually sexual assault or even homicide, without alerting their victim.

Pre-frontal leucotomies Primitive and damaging procedure for cutting the 'leuco' or 'white-matter' of the pre-frontal lobes with a 'tome' (knife).

Premorbid Literally, 'before illness'. In the psychosis context, the pre-morbid period may stretch back several years before onset of symptoms to encompass the prodrome and periods before this, during which developmental and/or behavioural problems were apparent.

Pre-morbid personality The client's social and personal functioning prior to the illness.

Present state examination (PSE) A commonly used psychiatric assessment tool.

Prevalence The number, proportion or percentage of a given population who have an illness at a given time point.

Primary crime scene The site of the offence or location of the victim.

Primary gain In unsupported psychoanalytic theory, this is considered to be consequent on the cause of the symptom, such as blindness occurring as a conversion reaction to a distressing visual experience.

Primary prevention Involves examining whole communities rather than the needs of individuals.

Primary process thinking In Freudian terms, how the id operates.

Probation The area of prevention and rehabilitation whereby probation officers supervise the efforts of offenders towards self-improvement and away from criminal activity.

Problem-based learning The practical training of problem-solving skills in the manner of 'discovery learning'.

Prodromal syndrome Describes the pattern of behaviour or conditions present during the **prodrome** before the onset of a disorder.

Prodrome A (variable) period of time, typically measured in months or a few years, before overt symptoms of psychosis become apparent, when an individual is nevertheless aware that their thinking and behaviour is changing (for the worse) in some way.

Progeria Premature ageing disorder. A profound form is called Hutchinson–Gilford syndrome.

Progesterone A female hormone important for maintaining the lining of the uterus and which can be antagonistic to the effects of estrogen.

Prognosis A judgement as to the future outcome for the client.

Progressive muscular relaxation (PMR) A physical stress reduction technique of tensing and relaxing muscles.

Projective tests Assume that internal conflicts will be 'projected' into benign situations and clearly are dependent on the psychodynamic approach.

Pronoun reversal Where the autistic individual will refer to himself or herself as 'he', 'she' or 'you' instead of 'I' or 'me'.

Prophylactic Preventative, e.g. maintenence medication is prophylactic.

Prophylactic detention Preventing crime by imprisoning a high-risk individual before they commit an offence.

Proximate/proximal explanations of Behaviour The immediate influences, such as genetics or biology.

Pruning of neurons Loss (or pruning) of neurons (also known as apoptosis) begins in childhood and accelerates through adolescence and adulthood. It appears to be a normal process, though certain diseases are related to excessive neuronal loss.

Pseudo-intimate relationships An example of a pseudo-intimate would be a local TV newsreader, who may appear to speak directly and personally to the viewer on a daily basis.

Pseudologia fantastica Where a kernel of truth is used to fabricate a complex web of fantasy that can be difficult to falsify.

Psychoactive In referring to drug use, those drugs which affect mental states.

Psychoanalysis Originating with Freud, an insight therapy in which a client discovers early emotional conflict by the process of free association.

Psychodermatology or psychocutaneous medicine Study of interactions between psychological and dermatological factors.

Psychodynamic The approach derived from Freud of considering mental activity as a mostly unconscious and dynamic activity.

Psychogenesis Having originated from psychological causes.

Psychogenic dwarfism Thought to result from stress, affecting growth hormones.

Psychological hardiness Thought to help resist the progress of physical disorders.

Psychological medicine Identifying psychological factors in some medical conditions.

Psychological testing A specialist area of psychology dealing with the construction, validation, correct administration and interpretation of tests.

Psychometrics The science of measuring psychological factors.

Psychoneuroimmunology Psychological neural processing effects on the immune responses.

Psychoneuropharmacology or Psychopharmacology Chemical intervention to alter thought, affect and behaviour.

Psychopath Individuals who lack empathy and offend without apparent purpose, show no remorse, are loyal to no one, and frequently indulge in perverse sexual and harmful behaviour.

Psychopathology The scientific study of abnormal behaviour, with the aim of understanding the nature and origins of this behaviour. Psychopathology tends to lie at the interface of medical and psychological science.

Psychopathy Check List–Revised 2nd Edition (*PCL-R*; Hare, 2003). Rating scale for psychopathy, based on the original psychopathy concept proposed by Cleckley (1976).

Psychosurgery Surgical procedures on the brain.

Psychotic Severely disturbed behaviour showing hallucinations, delusions or thought disorder.

Psychoto-mimetic A drug that induces psychosis-like signs and symptoms, e.g. LSD.

Quality of life A measurable evaluation of the impact of a disorder on the daily life of the sufferer.

Radical behaviourism An extreme behavioural view that accounts for all behaviour as being learned.

Randi, James Magician who has exposed mythical claims of the paranormal.

Randomised controlled trial The 'gold standard' method for establishing the effects of an intervention or treatment, in which respondents are randomly allocated to receive either the intervention or treatment as usual, and their results subsequently compared.

Rational emotive therapy (RET) The cognitive therapy of Ellis in which irrational beliefs about one's behaviour are challenged.

Raven's progressive matrices Claims to be a culture-free test of IQ as it is relatively language and symbolism free, by using only pattern matching.

Reality orientation Intended to maintain the sufferer's awareness of their place in the world and keep their responses and thinking appropriate to things such as the seasons, meal times or their location.

Real time In the context of in-vivo imaging, observing functional brain changes more or less as they happen (or within a few seconds of them happening).

Recessive–dominant genes/traits Genes have 'opposing partners' on the other chromosome of a pair. As dominant ones are expressed over recessive, it requires matching recessive traits for them to be expressed (but they may still be passed on or 'carried').

Recidivist An offender who repeatedly offends and seems undeterred by punishment, usually returning to prison on a regular basis.

Reciprocal inhibition The simple fact that some states of the autonomic nervous system, such as relaxation, are inhibitory of others, such as arousal (anxiety).

Recombinant DNA technology This uses enzymes to cut out a gene sequence from isolated DNA and insert it into the vector of a bacterium, and then replicate this gene within rapidly multiplying bacteria.

Recovered memories Retrospective recollection, usually in therapy. These may be false memories and can be devastating for those involved.

Reflex arc A 'short-circuit' in the spinal chord where a large afferent sensation (e.g. a burned hand) entering via sensory neurons automatically triggers an efferent response (hand withdrawal) via motor neurons without reference to the brain, but through interneurons in the spinal chord.

Refractory disorders Treatment-resistant conditions.

Regional Secure Units (RSU) Provide secure places in the locality and expand the provision for disturbed offenders, leaving places in the remote special hospitals free for more dangerous patients.

Rejected stalker In this type, the victim is an ex-intimate and the stalker purports to seek reconciliation.

Related or within-subjects design When the same group of participants take part in all phases or conditions in an experiment.

Reliability The ability of a measure to produce the same results from one time point to the next.

Remission A disorder is 'in remission' when its symptoms reduce and the person seems well again.

Representative Sample For a sample to be representative, it needs to be similar to the population from where it is drawn in terms of demographics (age, gender, etc.) and the variable of interest, such as cannabis use.

Resentful stalker Deliberately frightens their victims, exerting power and control by utilising more extreme tactics such as sending wreaths or some form of offensive material to their victim's address, and may involve the victim's work colleagues, family or friends.

Resolution phase The post-orgasmic phase of sexual activity with muscular relaxation and a sense of euphoria.

Ressler, Robert US criminal profiler and one of the founders of the FBI Behavioural Support Unit.

Resting potential Electrical gradient around the neuron membrane.

Restorative justice Where offenders have controlled meetings with the victims of their crimes and where possible help deal with the aftermath of the event.

Retrograde amnesia Loss of memory for past events.

Retrospective Diagnosis A diagnosis made long after the onset of a disorder based on descriptions from that time or projecting back from the current state.

Retrospectively Recalling of behaviour in the past or in general. It is often used in studies where questionnaires or interviews are the measure for recording information.

Retroviruses Used in genetic engineering to alter DNA.

Risk assessment Estimating the risk of an offender re-offending, or of a mentally disordered patient causing harm to self or others if discharged.

Risk factors The identification of variables or factors that leave individuals at risk or prone to the development of a disorder.

Rogers, Carl (1902–1987) Produced a theory of personality in 1959, which assumes humanity to be basically good and motivated towards improvement.

Rohypnol A hypnotic referred to as a 'date-rape drug'.

Rorschach ink blot test Made famous through popular fiction, this consists of interpreting a number of ambiguous 'ink blot' designs first produced by Herman Rorschach in 1912.

Rostral The anterior or 'towards the beak'.

Rotter, Julian (1916–) Established **social learning**.

Royal College of Psychiatrists The qualifying and over-seeing body for psychiatrists and their training in the UK.

RSA An abbreviation of Royal Society for the Encouragement of Arts, Manufactures and Commerce. It is a think-tank that was founded by William Shipley in 1754 in the UK.

Sacher-Masoch, Leopold von (1835–1895) Wrote about masochistic sex-acts involving pain, including the book *Venus in Furs*.

Sade, Donatien-Alphonse-François de (1740–1814) Wrote about and performed acts of sexual sadism on women and children.

Sado–masochistic relationships Considered a gross exaggeration of the dominant–subservient male–female sexual roles, these acts may include punitive, humiliating and painful acts such as cutting, strangling, whipping, mutilating, burning, restraining or impairing the senses of victims. It is the suffering in the target person that produces the arousal.

St John's wort A plant source for the hypericum extract WS 5570. This extract has been tried in major depression and found to be as effective as the SSRI and better tolerated.

Satyriasis Hypersexuality in a male, equivalent to nymphomania in a female.

Savant Refers to about 10 per cent of autistic individuals with special abilities in specific areas (mathematics, music, etc.).

Scatterplots These graphs display the relationship between two variables. Each point on the graph will represent the relationship between variable A and variable B for each participant. It is the spread and shape of these data points which will determine whether the line of best fit through the points reflects a positive or negative correlation.

Schedules of reinforcement These are economics of reinforcement in operant conditioning, which can produce more durable learning.

Schema-based theory (therapy) Challenging of unrealistic imperatives and assumptions that require the sufferer to conform to the impossible, such as perfection in behaviour or acceptability to everyone.

Schizophasia A generic term to describe instances of unusual use of language, especially in psychotic disorders.

Scientist-practitioner A practising clinician who carries out research and evaluation of this work to benefit their practice, which also informs the research.

Sclerotic plaques Growths building up at the sites of demyelination in multiple sclerosis.

Scoptophilia or **Scopophilia** Voyeurism.

Scull's dilemma Named after Andrew Scull, refers to the no-win situation in which you should not institutionalise mental patients, but cannot let them out either.

Seasonal pattern Is specified when symptoms occur and remit in association with the seasons of the year.

Secondary crime scene Other areas of forensic importance beyond the crime scene, such as the homes or possessions of suspects or victims.

Secondary gain Where there is an advantage to the client in having the illness.

Secondary labelling Where the labelled individual accepts the label and associated discrimination and begins to act in accord with these expectations.

Secondary prevention Refers to the early detection of possible problems before they can develop into conditions that require hospitalisation or prosecution in the case of offenders.

Secondary process thinking In Freudian terms, the thinking of the ego.

Secondary reinforcer A strong conditioned stimulus which is used as if it were primary reinforcer, even though it has no intrinsic value to the organism, such as money.

Secondary smoking Inhaling the damaging smoke from other people smoking.

Second-order thinking Flexible thought, such as the use of pretence, e.g. pretending a plate is a hat.

Secretin A gut hormone, which is of interest in the treatment of a certain form of autism.

Selective serotonin reuptake inhibitors (SSRIs) Controversial anti-depressant drug that prevent reuptake of serotonin, leaving more active to combat depression or obsession.

Self-actualisation In humanistic approaches, it is the aim of the therapist to have the client realise and activate their own potential.

Self-help groups A form of group therapy in which there is no professional presence, only individuals with experience of the disorder.

Self-injurious behaviour (SIB) Problem behaviour involving physical damage to the client's self, e.g. head-banging.

Self-instructional therapy or training Donald Meichenbaum noted how anxious and unsuccessful people make excuses for themselves and engage in self-defeating thoughts. Meichenbaum had his clients identify where this occurred and produce 'scripts' of positive instructions.

Self-medication The use of substances such as alcohol in place of appropriate medication.

Self-stimulatory behaviour (SSB) Problem behaviour that involves repeated rubbing or manipulation.

Semi-structured interview A loosely formatted interview schedule that includes broad areas of investigation which can be explored in greater depth by additional 'probe' questions, if deemed appropriate by the interviewer.

Sensate focus treatment Masters and Johnson formulated this desensitisation approach to sexual dysfunction.

Sense of coherence A view that the world is comprehensible and manageable, and provides one with a sense of purpose in a meaningful environment.

Serial homicide/serial killing The killing of three or more victims sequentially.

Serotonin syndrome Hypothermia induces this with a dangerously rising core body temperature and autonomic instability.

Sex-linked characteristics Characteristics due to the twenty-third pair of chromosomes that define sex typing.

Sex offender risk management approach A means of reducing risk of reoffending by practical surveillance and multi-agency intelligence exchange (see Grant, 1999).

Sex offender treatment programmes Accredited behaviour programmes delivered in prisons aimed at reducing reoffending.

Sex-reassignment surgery A drastic procedure in which the current sex genitalia are removed and those of the opposite sex are fashioned within the limits of surgical technology, supplemented with hormone therapy.

Sexual homicide The killing of a person in the context of power, sexuality and brutality.

Shaping Using operant conditioning gradually to create complex behaviours by selectively reinforcing simpler ones.

Shipman, Harold UK GP who murdered his elderly patients with pain-killing overdoses for 25 years. He went on to become one of the world's most prolific serial killers.

Shopaholic A common term when referring to individuals who enjoy bingeing on shopping behaviour.

'Sick role' Gaining sympathy and attention by presenting as ill.

Silent Talker Software program combining the information from microexpressions with AI architecture to detect and analyse the presence of deception.

Simple carbohydrates Sugar-based confectioneries such as chocolate.

Single nucleotide polymorphism A change or alteration in a base contained on a gene. It is known as functional if the change in the base alters the functioning or quality of whatever the gene codes for.

Single photon emission computed tomography (SPECT) and positron emission tomography (PET) Use low-level radioactive markers (isotopes or ligands) to high receptors, neurotransmitters or blood flow in the brain.

Situationalism Arguments that personality may change with context, proposed by state-theorists or situationalists such as Walter Mischel.

Skinner, Burrhus Frederic (1904–1990) Skinner carried the banner of behaviourism through the challenges of the twentieth century. The principles derived from the behavioural approach have been the most useful that pure psychology has offered in addressing abnormal behaviour.

Skin Two An organisation that produces magazines, events and apparel for a broad fetish market amongst those in the general population with fetish traits.

'Skunk' Genetically modified cannabis with high levels of d-Tetrahydrocannabinol.

Social capital One's network of friends and family as support.

Social comparison Theory The way we compare ourselves to others (Festinger, 1954). Relates to exposure to images in the media influencing the body image and self-esteem of an individual.

Social drift A causal model to explain why many people with severe mental health problems find themselves in the lower echelons of society, notwithstanding their own family backgrounds.

Social gaze response The inherent tendency to focus gaze on social cues and learn to follow the gaze of others.

Social learning Derived from Rotter and Bandura, concerns learning by observing the reinforcement of another's behaviour, i.e. vicarious reinforcement.

Social Readjustment Rating Scale (SRRS) Holmes and Rahe (1967) established this to rate the relative impact of life-events ranked below that of the most stressful event, which Holmes and Rahe found to be the death of a spouse.

Social stigmatisation Labelling process seen in ex-prisoners and psychiatric patients.

Sociobiology A new term coined by Wilson (1975) to replace behavioural ecology.

Sociocognitive constructions Behaviour and thinking constructed from ideas picked up socially.

SOCO Scene of crime officer.

Soft signs (neurological) Infer specific brain dysfunction from the results of psychometric tests of such abilities as cognitive, manipulation or memory function to support data from more direct assessment such as NMR scans.

Somatogenesis Originating from 'bodily' or physical causes.

Spatial patterns Refers to the areas that an offender feels safe within, usually because they are familiar. These can be seen in the pattern of the locations of linked offences.

Special hospitals Large mental hospitals with prison security.

Speciation When subgroups no longer interbreed and become separate gene pools.

Specifiers In some disorder classifications there are specified factors or parameters, e.g. 'seasonal' specifier in mood disorder.

Spectator role A pervasive problem whereby one partner will focus objectively on their performance and lose their subjective involvement in the sexual process.

Speedball A name given to a mix of cocaine and heroin that is usually taken orally.

'Sperm wars' A view of natural selection which assumes that females are subconsciously seeking the best 'material' for their offspring and that males compete on many levels to impregnate.

Spontaneous remission A non-specific effect used when disorders remit over time regardless of intervention.

Squeeze/pause technique In sexual therapy, consists of firmly squeezing from each side of the coronal ridge of the penis several times early in intercourse, which removes the urge to ejaculate.

SSRIs See **Selective Serotonin Reuptake Inhibitors**.

Stalking by proxy The use of others including the law to further the aims of the stalker.

Statistical differences A study can test whether groups within a study score significantly different from one another.

Statistical relationships A study can examine whether scores on a questionnaire or on a behaviour test vary together in a manner which suggests they are related to one another.

Stereotaxis Utilises neural reference points common across individuals by firmly clamping the skull and calculating neural targets in three-dimensional space.

Stereotypies Repetitive morbid self-stimulatory behaviour and self-injurious behaviour.

Steroid diabetes Stress-related diabetes.

STP Standing for 'serenity, tranquillity and peace', STP or DOM is an amphetamine derivative.

Strain The physiological and psychological effects of stress on the individual.

Stratification Usually refers to the groups within a study sample. This can be on the basis of demographic variables or one of the variables of interest, such as the presence of childhood adversity.

Street patients Patients discharged without adequate preparation or support.

Street users The customers of illicit drug dealers.

Stress management Intervention, usually in the workplace, to reduce the ill effects of psychological stress.

Stress reaction style Proposed as a valid personality trait or construct related to the way stress is dealt with.

Stroop test In this experimental procedure, the distraction effect of words can be measured by the delay in naming the ink colour in which target words are printed, as compared with neutral words.

Subculture Where a culture is deliberately maintained as separate from the host culture.

Substance abuse Involves taking a repeated or large dose of a substance on one occasion to produce substantial change in mental state. This is often referred to as 'bingeing' and is distinct from addiction.

SUD scale The subjective unit of discomfort scale serves two purposes: a reference scale for the client to indicate their subjective level of fear, and a series of situations for the client to work through whilst remaining calm.

Suggestibility A proneness to suggestion – a measurable trait.

Summation Where many inhibitory and excitatory signals coming into the neuron are added together. If the biochemical threshold of stimulation within the cell is reached, the neuron 'fires'.

Superego Freud's concept of a conscience and one of his mental structures formed during Oepidal or Electra conflict.

Superstitious behaviour Produced by randomly delivering a reward irrespective of the animal's behaviour, or non-contingent reinforcement.

Surrogate sexual partners A controversial but ostensibly effective means of treating individuals with sexual dysfunctions, where surrogates stand in place of sexual partners to engage in practical sexual activity in vivo as well as guiding and educating clients.

Syllogomania This consists of self-neglect and may involve the hoarding of rubbish.

Sympathetic stress hormones Those released by stress such as adrenaline or cortisol and its metabolites like cortisone.

Sympathomimetic Mimics the effects of adrenaline and noradrenalin.

Symptom substitution An unsubstantiated claim that new symptoms of anxiety will replace those removed by therapy unless the 'underlying cause' is addressed.

Synaesthesia Cross-modality sensory experiences.

Synapse The cleft between one neuron's axon terminal button and another's dendritic spine, across which pulses of neurotransmitter substances pass nerve impulses.

Synaptic plasticity A neuroscientific concept to explain functional changes in activity or sensitivity of synapses over time.

Syndrome A cluster or pool of regularly co-occurring symptoms.

Systematic desensitisation Gradually exposing a client to feared stimuli whilst they are relaxed.

Systematised amnesia Memory for only certain categories of information, such as a certain person, are not recalled.

Szasz, Thomas Professor of psychiatry, self proclaimed radical-libertarian in the USA and trained psychoanalyst, who published *The Myth of Mental Illness* (Szasz, 1960), attacking the term 'mental illness'.

Tardive dyskinesia A slowly developing movement disorder resembling, in some respects, certain features of Parkinson's disease, related to anti-psychotic use, usually in old people.

Tavistock clinic A centre for psychoanalysis in London.

Taxonomic measures Used for personality disorder diagnosis, these are difficult to administer as they usually comprise lengthy interview schedules in which clinicians make judgements on responses and observed signs.

TEACCH or TEACHC The treatment and education of autistic children and communication of handicapped children.

Telomerase An enzyme extending the life of telomeres.

Telomeres The 'ends' of chromosomes, which protect and stabilise chromosome ends for cell replication purposes.

Temporal lobe epilepsy Can result in visual hallucinations and to a lesser extent smell or taste and a disruption of experiences and memories. Sufferers of temporal lobe fits report sudden heightened comprehension or déjà vu which, combined with hallucinations, produce religious or paranormal experiences.

Terminal button The end of a neuron's axon, i.e. the output from the neuron sending chemical transmitters across the synapse to the next neuron's dendrites.

Tertiary prevention Closely allied to rehabilitation, this concerns the support or aftercare of those who have been suffering from ill-health for some time, long-term offenders and those psychiatric patients or prisoners returned to the community.

Testosterone A male hormone producing male characteristics such as muscle and beard growth, but also increasing levels of aggression.

Thalamus A major subcortical structure with massive projections to the cortex. The thalamus is therefore in the unique position of being able to influence widespread cortical activity, and has particularly important roles in visual processing and attention.

Thematic Apperception Test (TAT) Consists of a series of pictures involving people interacting in various settings for which there is no single clear interpretation.

Theory of mind This is lacking in autism, meaning that the autistic child lacks a theory as to what is in another person's mind.

Therapeutic communities Prisons and mental hospitals run with greater patient autonomy, focusing on rehabilitation not confinement.

Three systems model of fear Considers the cognitive, physiological and behavioural aspects of fear (Lang).

Tic A neurologically based abnormal muscle contraction, often involving the head or face, associated with neurological disorders such as Tourette's syndrome and Sydenham's chorea.

Tilt Review (2000) Called for increased security measures and more intensive therapeutic interventions at the same time as suppressing the counter-culture that tends to become established by the patient population.

T lymphocyte or T-cell The 'killer cell' that attacks other invading organisms such as bacteria.

Token economy A system of using tokens as secondary reinforcers to encourage inpatients to perform desirable behaviours.

Tolerance The body learns to tolerate some psychoactive substances and physically compensate for its presence.

Totipotent stem cells Cells that can reproduce all cell lines in an entire organism.

Trafficking Individuals being moved to new locations for the purpose of enforced prostitution.

'Trainspotting generation' Term coined for those whose lifestyle shows strong parallels with the film *Trainspotting* (Boyle, 1996) in terms of heroin use as a way of life.

Trait theorists Believe that the fixed personality characteristics of the individual predict how they will react in any situation.

Transcranial magnetic stimulation and vagus nerve stimulation Relatively new biologically based procedures involving specific brain area stimulation for depression and other conditions.

Transference A client projecting on to their psychoanalyst feelings originally aroused by a significant figure from their past experience.

Transgenerational transmission Non-genetic family factors that look like genetic influence.

Treatment as usual (TAU) Refers to whatever routine treatment a given patient receives. To be compared with TAU plus an additional treatment (such as a psychotherapy) to get an idea of how much added value the latter offers.

Trephination Term used to describe the cutting of a hole in the skull as far back as the Paleolithic period, which may have been to relieve pressure on the brain but was more likely intended to release 'evil spirits' from a disturbed person.

Truman syndrome Suggested to account for those individuals who, through a mixture of self-engrandiosement and paranoia, believe they are living in a TV programme, in which they are the central character.

Trycyclic anti-depressants (e.g. amitriptyline) A treatment for depression. They inhibit the reuptake of serotonin but have side-effects as they also prevent reuptake of noradrenaline.

T test A statistical test of difference used when there are two groups in the analysis.

Turing test Test to see if a computer can convince a person that it is human rather than machine.

Twin studies Compare identical or monozygotic twins (from the separation of one fertilised ovum) with non-identical or dizygotic twins (from separate ova), where one of each pair (the proband or index case) has the disorder, to apportion the relative influences of environment and genetics.

Twinkie defence argument Accused, Dan White claimed that he shot the mayor of San Francisco due to hyperglycaemia as a result of eating too many sweet confectioneries – a weak use of insanity as mitigation.

Type A personality Pattern of chronic impatient behaviour. Also known as coronary-prone behaviour.

Type B personality Behaviour pattern involving a more relaxed, non-competitive and less aggressive approach to relations with others and the workplace.

Type-D personality In this 'distressed personality' there are increased negative emotions in social interactions and this has been related to coronary heart disease.

Type one error False positive.

Type two error False negative.

Ultimate explanations of behaviour The longer-term evolutionary (ultimate) reasons for that behaviour existing in the first place.

Unconditioned response (UCR) Instinctive response to an unconditioned stimulus.

Unconditioned stimulus (UCS) A basic reinforcer that needs no conditioning to produce an instinctive response.

Unipotent stem cells Produce only one cell type.

Urbanicity A concept usually associated with the Dutch researcher/clinician Jim van Os, in which social factors linked to patterns of urban living may make some individuals more susceptible to psychotic illness.

User-dealers Drug users who buy drugs for their friends and progress to subsidising their own use with modest dealing, usually in cannabis alone.

Vaginal oestrogen cream Hormonal cream applied directly for dyspareunia.

Vaginismus An involuntary contraction of the outer perineal muscles of the vagina that is persistent or recurs.

Validity Something being or doing what it claims, e.g. a questionnaire measures what it was designed to measure and what it appears to measure.

Variable interval schedule A VI-20sec indicates that the time period in which a response has to be made is on average 20 seconds but the time varies on individual trials.

Variable ratio schedule Reward is delivered after varying numbers of responses per trial, totalling a fixed average across trials.

Variance Usually used when referring to either correlations or analysis of variance (ANOVA). Variance is the degree to which scores alter or change together.

Vasocongestion The engorging of blood vessels with blood.

Velocardiofacial syndrome A genetic abnormality associated with a micro-deletion (missing segment) of part of chromosome 22. About one in three cases also meet diagnostic criteria for schizophrenia.

Ventral The front or towards the limbic system in the brain.

Ventricle The fluid-filled spaces in the brain.

Viagra (sildenafil citrate) A revolutionary drug treatment for erectile disorder.

Vibrators Mechanical stimulating devices that have been very successful in aiding females with orgasmic disorder.

Vicarious learning Learning by watching others behave and be rewarded or punished.

Victimology The support for victims in the wake of a crime, who may also have to attend court, and factors affecting the likelihood of becoming a victim of crime.

Virtual desensitisation Using exposure therapy by the use of virtual reality.

Voice stress analysis (VSA) A means of detecting anxiety and arousal to infer deception in vocal signals. Can be applied to telephone recordings.

Volition Having initiative to engage in new actions or behaviours. Avolition is the opposite state, usually associated with negative features of psychosis.

Watson, John Broadhurst (1878–1958) Claimed that scientific psychology should stick to the observable aspects of objective experiments. Watson was a figurehead for behaviourism, even practising it in his own family. Despite much criticism, he probably made the greatest contribution to psychology of his era.

Weapon focus The effect of a weapon on witnesses, tending to lower accuracy of identification by drawing attention away from faces.

Wechsler Adult Intelligence Scale The commonest instrument for IQ and used in neurological assessments (Wechsler, 1997b).

Well-being psychology The study of the state of health in which positive traits produce a measurable state of happiness and positive adjustment.

Wernicke-Korsakov's syndrome Alcoholic memory loss that is no longer reversible.

Wernicke's area Named after Carl Wernicke, an area of the brain essential for the comprehension of speech.

Wild beast test (1724) This assumed the amoral animal reflexes of criminals to be closer to animals.

Witmer, Lightner (1867–1956) Founder of the world's first psychological clinic at the University of Pennsylvania in 1896; he also ran courses in criminal behaviour.

Wolpe, Joseph Published an influential book outlining basic procedures for behaviour therapy in 1958.

Workaholism The tendency to be highly involved with work but to have low work enjoyment.

World Health Organisation (WHO) Geneva-based international health organisation.

Yerkes–Dodson law Optimum arousal produces the best performance.

Zeitgeist Literally, spirit of the times, this is often used to refer to people and events that were in keeping with the prevailing mood of the time. Used in contrast to *Ortgeist*.

References

Aarsland, D., Zaccai, J., and Brayne, C. (2005) A systematic review of prevalence studies of dementia in Parkinson's disease. *Movement Disorders*, **20**(10), 1255–63.

Abbott, A. (1988) *The system of the professions*. London: University of Chicago Press.

Abed, R. (2000) Psychiatry and Darwinism. *British Journal of Psychiatry*, **177**, 1–3.

Abel, G., Jordan, A., Hand, C. G., Holland, L. A., and Phipps, A. (2001) Classification models of child molesters utilizing the Abel Assessment for Sexual Interest. *Child Abuse and Neglect*, **25**(5), 703–18.

Abele, A., and Hermer, P. (1993) Mood influences on health-related judgments: appraisal of own health versus appraisal of unhealthy behaviours. *European Journal of Social Psychology*, **23**, 613–25.

Abelson, J., and Curtis, G. (1996) Hypothalamic–pituitary–adrenal axis activity in panic disorder: Prediction of long-term outcome by pretreatment cortisol levels. *American Journal of Psychiatry*, **153**, 69–73.

Abramson, L. Y., Metalsky, G. I., and Alloy, L. B. (1989) Hopelessness depression: A theory-based subtype of depression. *Psychological Review*, **96**(2), 358–72.

Abramson, L. Y., Seligman, M. E., and Teasdale, J. D. (1978) Learned helplessness in humans: A critique and reformulation. *Journal of Abnormal Psychology*, **87**, 49–74.

Abrisqueta-Gomez, J., Ostrosky-Solis, F., Bertolucci, P. H., and Bueno, O. F. (2008) Applicability of the abbreviated neuropsychologic battery (NEUROPSI) in Alzheimer disease patients. *Alzheimer Disease and Associated Disorders*, **22**(1), 72–8.

Adams, P. J. (2007) Assessing whether to receive funding support from tobacco, alcohol, gambling and other dangerous consumption industries. *Addiction*, **102**, 1027–33.

Addington, J., Cadenhead, K. S., Cannon, T. D., Cornblatt, B., McGlashan, T. H., Perkins, D. O., Seidman, L. J., Tsuang, M., Walker, E. F., Woods, S. W., and Heinssen, R. (2007) North American prodrome longitudinal study: A collaborative multisite approach to prodromal schizophrenia research. *Schizophrenia Bulletin*, **33**(3), 665–72.

Addison, N. (1996) Wrong trail. *Police Review*, 16 August.

Adolphs, R., Sears, L., and Piven, J. (2001) Abnormal processing of social information from faces in autism. *Journal of Cognitive Neuroscience*, **13**, 232–40.

Advisory Council on the Misuse of Drugs (2004) *Technical committee: Report on ketamine*. London: British Home Office.

Advisory Council on the Misuse of Drugs (2005a) *Khat (qat): An assessment of risk to the individual and communities in the UK*. London: British Home Office.

Advisory Council on the Misuse of Drugs (2005b) *Further consideration of cannabis under the Misuse of Drugs Act 1971*. London: British Home Office.

Agius, M., Shah, S., Ramkisson, R., Murphy, S., and Zaman, R. (2007) Three year outcomes of an early intervention for psychosis service compared with treatment as usual for first psychotic episodes in a standard community mental health team: Preliminary results. *Psychiatria Danubina*, **19**(1–2), 2–4.

Ahmed, K., and Bhugra, D. (2007) The role of culture in sexual dysfunction. *Psychiatry*, **6**(3), 115–20.

Aichhorn, A. (1925) *Wayward youth (translated 1955)*. New York: Meridian.

Aigner, M., Sachs, G., Bruckmüller, E., Winklbaur, B., Zitterl, W., Kryspin-Exner, I., Gur, R., and Katschnig, H. (2007) Cognitive and emotion recognition deficits in obsessive–compulsive disorder. *Psychiatry Research*, **149**(1–3), 121–8.

Ainsworth, M. (1989) Attachments beyond infancy. *American Psychologist*, **44**(4), 709–16.

Ainsworth, P. B. (1998) *Psychology, law and eyewitness testimony*. Chichester: Wiley.

Ainsworth, P. B. (2000) *Psychology and crime: Myths and reality*. Harlow: Pearson.

Ainsworth, P. B. (2001) *Offender profiling and crime analysis*. Cullompton, Devon: Willan.

Aitken, C., Connolly, T., Gammerman, A., Zhang, G., and Oldfield, D. (1995) *Predicting an offender's characteristics: An evaluation of statistical modelling (paper 4)*. London: Police Research Group Special Interest Series, Home Office.

Akhtar, S. (1996) Further exploration of gender differences in personality disorders. *American Journal of Psychiatry*, **153**, 846–7.

Akhtar, S., Wig, N., Varma, V., Pershad, D., and Varma, S. (1975) A phenomenological analysis of symptoms in obsessive–compulsive neurosis. *British Journal of Psychiatry*, **127**, 342–8.

Alagiakrishanan, K., McCracken, P., and Feldman, H. (2006) Treating vascular disease risk factors and maintaining vascular health: Is this the way towards successful cognitive aging and preventing cognitive decline? *Postgraduate Medical Journal*, **82**, 101–5.

Albery, I., and Munafo, M. (2008) *Key concepts in health psychology*. London: Sage.

Alden, L. E., and Taylor, C. T. (2004) Interpersonal processes in social phobia. *Clinical Psychology Review*, **24**, 857–82.

Alder, J. R. (ed.) (2004) *Forensic psychology: Concepts, debates and practice*. Uffculme, Devon: Willan.

Alexander, F., and Healey, W. (1935) *Roots of crime*. New York: Knopf.

Alison, L. (ed.) (2005) *The forensic psychologist's casebook: Psychological profiling and criminal investigation*. Uffculme, Devon: Willan.

Allen, L., Woolfolk, R., Escobar, J., Gara, M., and Hamer, R. (2006) Cognitive-behavioural therapy for somatization disorder. *Archives of International Medicine*, **166**, 1512–18.

Allison, D. B., and Roberts, M. S. (1998) *A disordered mother or disordered diagnosis: Münchausen by proxy syndrome*. Hillsdale, NJ: Analytic Press.

Allison, K. C., and Friedman, L. S. (2004) Soothing a sensitive gut. *Newsweek*, 27 Sept, **144**(13), 71.

Allnutt, S. H., and Chaplow, D. (2000) General principles of forensic report writing. *Australian and New Zealand Journal of Psychiatry*, **34**, 980–7.

Allport, G. W., and Postman, L. (1947) The basic psychology of rumour. *Transactions of the New York Academy of Sciences*, **8**, 61–81.

Aloni, R., Keren, O., and Katz, S. (2007) Sex therapy surrogate partners for individuals with very limited functional ability following traumatic brain injury. *Sexuality and Disability*, **25**, 125–34.

Alpert, J. S. (2005) Viagra: The risks of recreational use. *American Journal of Medicine*, **118**, 569–70.

Alpert, J. E., and Spilman, M. K. (1997) Psychotherapeutic approaches to aggressive and violent patients. *Psychiatric Clinics of North America*, **20**, 453–71.

Alphen, S. P., Nijhuis, P. E., and Oei, T. (2007) Antisocial personality disorder in older adults: A qualitative study of Dutch forensic psychiatrists and forensic psychologists. *International Journal of Geriatric Psychiatry*, **22**, 813–15.

Alt, A., Nisenbaum, E. S., Bleakman, D., and Witkin, J. (2006) A role for AMPA receptors in mood disorders. *Biochemical Pharmacology*, **71**(9), 1273–88.

Altamura, C., Paluello, M. M., Mundo, E., Medda, S., and Mannu, P. (2001) Clinical and subclinical body dysmorphic disorder. *European Archives of Psychiatry and Clinical Neuroscience*, **251**, 105–8.

Alzheimer, A. (1906) Uber Einen eigenartigen schweren Erkrankung-sprozeb der Himrinde. *Neurologishes Cenrealblatt*, **23**, 1129–36.

American Psychiatric Association (1980) *Diagnostic and statistical manual of mental disorders third edition (DSM-III)*. Arlington, VA: American Psychiatric Association.

American Psychiatric Association (2000) *Diagnostic and statistical manual of mental disorders fourth revision, text revision (DSM-IV-TR)*. Arlington, VA: American Psychiatric Association.

Amiel, J. M., and Mathew, S. J. (2007) Glutamate and anxiety disorders. *Current Psychiatry Reports*, **9**(4), 278–83.

Anderson, G. (2002) Genetics of childhood disorders: XLV. Autism, Part 4: Serotonin in autism. *Journal of the American Academy of Child and Adolescent Psychiatry*, **41**(12), 1513–16.

Andreasen, N. C. (1979) Thought, language, and communication disorders 1. Clinical assessment, definition of terms, and evaluation of their reliability. *Archives of General Psychiatry*, **36**, 1315–21.

Andreasen, N. C. (1983) Scale for the Assessment of Negative Symptoms (SANS). Iowa City: University of Iowa.

Andreasen, N. C. (1984) Scale for the Assessment of Positive symptoms (SAPS). Iowa City: University of Iowa.

Andreasen, N. C. (1987) Creativity and mental illness: Prevalence rates in writers and their first-degree relatives. *American Journal of Psychiatry*, **144**, 1288–92.

Andreasen, N. C. (1989) Neural mechanisms of negative schizophrenia. *British Journal of Psychiatry*, **155**(suppl. 7), 93–8.

Andreasen, N. C. (2008) The relationship between creativity and mood disorders. *Dialogues in Clinical Neuroscience*, **10**, 251–5.

Andreasen, N. C., and Olsen, S. A. (1982) Negative and positive schizophrenia. *Archives of General Psychiatry*, **39**, 789–94.

Andréasson, S., and Allebeck, P. (1990) Cannabis and mortality among young men: a longitudinal study of Swedish conscripts. *Scandinavian Journal of Social Medicine*, **18**(1), 9–15.

Andréasson, S., Allebeck, P., Engström, A., and Rydberg, U. (1987) Cannabis and schizophrenia. A longitudinal study of Swedish conscripts. *Lancet*, **2**(8574), 1483–6.

Andrews, G., and Vinkenoog, S. (1972) *Book of grass* (rev. edn). Harmondsworth: Penguin.

Angrist, B., Lee, H. K., and Gershon, S. (1974) The antagonism of amphetamine induced symptomatology by a neuroleptic. *American Journal of Psychiatry*, **131**, 817–19.

Angrist, B., Retrosen, J., and Gershon, S. (1980) Differential effects of amphetamine and neuroleptics on negative vs. positive symptoms in schizophrenia. *Psychopharmacology*, **72**, 17–19.

Angst, J. (2008) Bipolar disorder: Methodological problems and future perspectives. *Dialogues in Clinical Neuroscience*, **10**, 251–5.

Angst, J., and Merikangas, K. R. (2001) Multi-dimensional criteria for the diagnosis of depression. *Journal of Affective Disorders*, **62**, 1–7.

Angst, J., Adolfsson, R., Benazzi, F., Gamma, A., Hantouche, E., Meyer, T., Skeppar, P., Vieta, E., and Scott, J. (2005) The HCL-32: Towards a self-assessment tool for hypomanic symptoms in outpatients. *Journal of Affective Disorders*, **88**(2), 217–33.

Annett, M. (1970). A classification of hand preference by association analysis. *British Journal of Psychology*, **61**, 303–21.

Antonovsky, A. (1987) *Unraveling the mysteries of health: How people manage stress and stay well*. San Francisco: Jossey-Bass.

Aouizerate, B., Pujol, H., Grabot, D., Faytout, M., Suire, K., Braud, C., Auriacombe, M., Martin, D., Baudet, J., and Tignol, J. (2003) Body dysmorphic disorder in a sample of cosmetic surgery applicants. *European Psychiatry*, **18**(7), 365–8.

Appay, V., and Sauce, D. (2008) Immune activation and inflammation in HIV-1 infection: Causes and consequences. *Journal of Pathology*, **214**, 231–41.

Arehart-Treichel, J. (2007) Clinical and research news: Casino's arrival sparks off gambling rise, but novelty soon wears off. *Psychiatry News*, **42**(3), 29.

Arias, E., Anderson, R. N., Kung, H. C., Murphy, S. L., and Kochaneck, K. D. (2003) Deaths: Final data for 2001. *National vital statistics reports*, **52**(3). Hyattsville, MD: National Center for Health Statistics.

Armfield, J. M. (2006) Cognitive vulnerability: A model of the etiology of fear. *Clinical Psychology Review*, **26**, 746–68.

Armor, D. A., and Sackett, A. M. (2006) Accuracy, error, and bias in predictions for real versus hypothetical events. *Journal of Personality and Social Psychology*, **91**(4), 583–600.

Arseneault, L., Tremblay, R. E., Boulerice, B., Seguin, J. R., and Saucier, J. F. (2000) Minor physical abnormalities and family adversity as risk factors for violent delinquency in adolescence. *American Journal of Psychiatry*, **157**, 917–23.

Arseneault, L., Cannon, M., Poulton, R., Murray, R., Caspi, A., and Moffit, T. E. (2002a) Cannabis use in adolescence and risk for adult psychosis: A longitudinal prospective study. *British Medical Journal*, **325**, 1212–13.

Arseneault, L., Tremblay, R. E., Boulerice, B., and Saucier, J. F. (2002b) Obstetrical complications and violent delinquency: Testing two developmental pathways. *Child Development*, **73**, 496–508.

Arya, R., Dyer, T., Warren, D., Jenkinson, C. P., Duggirala, R., and Almasy, L. (2005) Effect of genotype × alcoholism interaction on linkage analysis of an alcoholism-related quantitative phenotype. *Bio Med Central Genetics*, **6** (suppl 1), doi:10.1186/1471-2156-6-S1-S120.

Asch, S. E. (1952) *Social psychology*. Englewood Cliffs, NJ: Prentice Hall.

Aschermann, E., Mantwill, M., and Köhnken, G. (1991) An independent replication of the effectiveness of the cognitive interview. *Applied Cognitive Psychology*, **5**, 489–95.

Asher, R. (1951) Munchausen's syndrome. *The Lancet*, **1**, 339–41.

Ashmore, J., Jones, J., Jackson, A., and Smoyak, S. (2006) A survey of mental health nurses' experiences of stalking. *Journal of Psychiatric and Mental Health Nursing*, **13**, 562–9.

Asperger, H. (1944) Die 'Autistschen Psychopathen' in Kindesalter. *Archiv fur Psychiatrie und Nervenkrankheiten*, **117**, 76–136.

Asperger, H. (1979) Problems of infantile autism. *Communication*, **13**, 45–52.

Aspinwall, L. G., and Taylor, S. E. (1992) Modeling cognition adaptation: A longitudinal investigation of the impact of individual differences and coping on college adjustment and performance. *Journal of Personality and Social Psychology*, **63**, 989–1003.

Atkinson, A., and Rickel, A. (1984) Postpartum depression in promiscuous parents. *Journal of Abnormal Psychology*, **93**, 115–19.

Attia, E., and Schroeder, L. (2005) Pharmacological treatment of anorexia nervosa: Where do we go from here? *International Journal of Eating Disorders*, **37**(Supp.), 60–3.

Ayllon, T., and Azrin, N. (1968) *Token economy: A motivation system for therapy and rehabilitation*. New York: Appleton-Century-Crofts.

Aziz, S., and Zickar, M. (2006) A cluster analysis investigation of workaholism as a syndrome. *Journal of Occupational Health Psychology*, **11**(1), 52–62.

Baddeley, A. D. (1990) *Human memory: Theory and practice*. Hove: Lawrence Erlbaum.

Baddeley, A. D. (2001) The concept of episodic memory. *Philosophical Transactions of the Royal Society (B): Biological Sciences*, **356**, 1345–50.

Baddeley, A. D., and Hitch, G. (1974) Working memory. In G. H. Bower (ed.), *The psychology of learning and motivation*, Vol. 8. London: Academic Press.

Baer, R. A. (2003) Mindfulness training as a clinical intervention: A conceptual and empirical review. *Clinical Psychology: Science and Practice*, **10**, 125–43.

Baigent, M., Holme, G., and Hafner, R. J. (1995) Self reports of the interaction between substance abuse and schizophrenia. *Australian and New Zealand Journal of Psychiatry*, **29**, 69–74.

Bailey, A. (1993) The biology of autism (editorial). *Psychological Medicine*, **23**, 7–41.

Bailey, S. (1999) The interface between mental health, criminal justice and forensic mental health services for children and adolescents. *Current Opinion in Psychiatry*, **12**(4), 425–32.

Baird, A. D., Wilson, S. J., Bladin, P. F., Saling, M. M., and Reutens, D. C. (2007) Neurological control of human sexual behaviour: Insights from lesion studies. *Journal of Neurosurgery and Psychiatry*, **78**, 1042–9.

Baker, A. (ed.) (2000) *Serious shopping: Essays in psychotherapy and consumerism*. London: Free Association Books.

Baker, R. (1996) *Sperm wars: The science of sex*. New York: Basic Books.

Baldessarini, R. (1977) *Chemotherapy in psychiatry*. Cambridge, MA: Harvard University Press.

Baldessarini, R., and Hennen, J. (2004) Genetics of suicide: An overview. *Harvard Review of Psychiatry*, **12**(1), 1–13.

Balon, R., and Segraves, R. T. (2005) *Handbook of Sexual Dysfunction*. Boca Raton, FL: Taylor and Francis.

Balon, R., Sergraves, R. T., and Clayton, A. (2007) Issues for DSM-V: Sexual dysfunction, disorder, or variation along normal distribution: Toward rethinking DSM criteria of sexual disorder. *American Journal of Psychiatry*, **164**(2), 198–200.

Baltieri, D. A., and de Andrade, A. G. (2000) Transsexual self-mutilation. *American Journal of Forensic Medicine and Pathology*, **26**(3), 268–70.

Banaschewski, T., Brandeis, D., Heinrich, H., Albrecht, B., Brunner, E., and Rothenberger, A. (2003) Association of ADHD and conduct disorder: Brain electrical evidence for the existence of a distinct subtype. *Journal of Child Psychology and Psychiatry*, **44**(3), 356–76.

Bancroft, J. (1999) Central inhibition of the sexual response in the male: A theoretical perspective. *Neuroscience Behavioural Review*, **23**, 763–84.

Bandura, A. (1965) Influence of a model's reinforcement contingencies on the acquisition of imitative responses. *Journal of Personality and Social Psychology*, **11**, 589–95.

Bandura, A. (1976) Social learning analysis of aggression. In E. Ribes-Inesta and A. Bandura (eds), *Analysis of delinquency and aggression*. Hillsdale, NJ: Lawrence Erlbaum.

Bandura, A. (1986) *Social foundations of thought and action*. Englewood Cliffs, NJ: Prentice Hall.

Banister, P. A., Heskin, K. J., Bolton, N., and Smith, F. V. (1973) Psychological correlates of long-term imprisonment: I. Personality variables. *British Journal of Criminology*, **13**, 323–30.

Banks, D., and Fossel, M. (1997) Telomeres, cancer and ageing. Altering the human life span. *Journal of the American Medical Association*, **278**(16), 1345–8.

Barak, A. (1999) Psychological applications on the internet: A discipline on the threshold of a new millennium. *Applied and Preventative Psychology*, **8**, 231–46.

Baranek, G. T. (2002) Efficacy of sensory and motor interventions for children with autism. *Journal of Autism and Developmental Disorders*, **32**(5), 397–422.

Barbini, B., Di-Molfetta, D., Gasperini, M., Manfredonia, M., and Smeraldi, E. (1995) Seasonal concordance of recurrence in mood disorder patients. *European Psychiatry*, **10**, 171–4.

Barik, S. (2007) The thrill can kill: Murder by methylation. *Molecular Pharmacology*, **71**, 1203–5.

Bark, N., Revheim, N., Huq, F., Khalderov, V., Watras-Ganz, Z., and Medalia, A. (2003) The impact of cognitive remediation on psychiatric symptoms of schizophrenia. *Schizophrenia Research*, **63**, 229–35.

Barkley, R. A., Fisher, M., Smallish, L., and Fletcher, K. (2004) Young adult follow-up of hyperactive children: antisocial activities and drug use. *Journal of Child Psychology and Psychiatry*, **45**(2), 195–211.

Barkus, E., and Lewis, S. (2008) Schizotypy and psychosis-like experiences from recreational cannabis in a non-clinical sample. *Psychological Medicine*, **38**, 1–10.

Barkus, E. J., Stirling, J., Hopkins, R. S., and Lewis, S. (2006) Cannabis-induced psychotic-like experiences are associated with high schizotypy. *Psychopathology*, **39**(4), 175–8.

Barkus, E., Stirling, J., Hopkins, R., McKie, S., and Lewis, S. (2007) Cognitive and neural processes in non-clinical auditory hallucinations. *British Journal of Psychiatry*, **191**(suppl. 51), 76–81.

Barlow, D. H., Becker, H., Leitenberg, H., and Agras, W. S. (1970) A mechanical strain gauge for recording penile circumference change. *Journal of Applied Behaviour Analysis*, 3(10), 73–6.

Barlow, J. H., Ellard, D. R., Hainsworth, J. M., Jones, F. R., and Fisher, A. (2005) A review of self-management interventions for panic disorders, phobias and obsessive–compulsive disorders. *Acta Psychiatrica Scandinavica*, 111(4), 272–85.

Barlow, D. H., O'Brien, G. T., and Last, C. G. (1984) Couples treatment for agoraphobia. *Behaviour Therapy*, 15(1), 41–58.

Baroff, G. (1986) *Mental retardation: Nature, cause and management*. Washington, DC: Hemisphere Publishing.

Baron, M., Levitt, M., Gruen, R., Hunter, R. C., and Asnis, L. (1984) Platelet MAO activity and genetic vulnerability to schizophrenia. *American Journal of Psychiatry*, **141**, 836–42.

Baron-Cohen, S. (1995) *Mindblindness: An essay on autism and theory of mind*. Cambridge: Cambridge University Press.

Baron-Cohen, S. (2002) The extreme male brain theory of autism. *Trends in Cognitive Sciences*, **6**, 248–54.

Baron-Cohen, S., Bolton, P., Wheelwright, S., Scahill, V., Short, E., Mead, G., and Smith, A. (1998) Autism occurs more often in the families of physicists, engineers and mathematicians. *Autism*, 2, 296–301.

Baron-Cohen, S., Leslie, A., and Frith, U. (1985) Does the autistic child have 'a theory of mind'? *Cognition*, 21, 37–41.

Baron-Cohen, S., Ring, H., Wheelwright, S., Bullmore, E., Brammer, M., Simmons, A., and Williams, S. (1999) Social intelligence in the normal and autistic brain: an fMRI study. *European Journal of Neuroscience*, 11, 1891–8.

Barraclough, J., and Gill, D. (1996) *Hughes' outline of modern psychiatry* (4th edn). London: Wiley.

Barrett, T. R., and Etheridge, J. B. (1992) Verbal hallucinations in normals 1: people who hear voices. *Applied Cognitive Psychology*, 6, 379–87.

Barry, D. T., Grilo, C. M., and Masheb, R. M. (2002) Gender differences in patients with binge eating disorder. *International Journal of Eating Disorders*, 31, 63–70.

Barry, J. (2006) The rise of ethics fundamentalism in the UK: A warning to Europe. *Europe's Journal of Psychology*, 11 Feb., 1–6.

Bartlett, F. C. (1932) *Remembering: A study in experimental and social psychology*. Cambridge: Cambridge University Press.

Bartol, C., and Bartol, A. (2004) *Introduction to forensic psychology*. Thousand Oaks, CA: Sage.

Bartz, J. A., and Hollander, E. (2006) Is obsessive–compulsive disorder an anxiety disorder. *Progress in Neuro-Psychopharmacology and Biological Psychiatry*, **30**(3), 338–52.

Basaglia, F. (1968) *L'Istituzione Negata*. Turin: Einaudi.

Bass, C., and Jones, D. P. H. (2006) Fabricated or induced illness. *Psychiatry*, 5(2), 60–5.

Basson, R., Brotto, L. A., Laan, E., Redmond, G., and Utian, W. H. (2005) Assessment and management of women's sexual dysfunctions: Problematic desire and arousal. *Journal of Sexual Medicine*, **2**, 291–300.

Basson, R., Leiblum, S., Brotto, L. A., Derogatis, L., Fourcroy, J., Fugli-Mayer, K. S., Graziotin, A., Heirman, J., Laan. E., Meston, C., Schrover, L., van Lankveld, J., and Schultz, W. W. (2004) Revised definitions of women's sexual dysfunctions. *Journal of Sexual Medicine*, **1**(1), 40–8.

Bateman, A. W., and Tyrer, P. (2004a) Psychological treatment for personality disorders. *Advances in Psychiatric Treatment*, **10**, 378–88.

Bateman, A. W., and Tyrer, P. (2004b) Services for personality disorder: Organisation for inclusion. *Advances in Psychiatric Treatment*, **10**, 425–33.

Bateson, G., Jackson, D., Haley, J., and Weakland, J. (1956) Towards a theory of schizophrenia. *Behavioural Science*, **1**, 251–64.

Battaglia, M., Bernardeschi, L., Franchini, L., Bellodi, L., and Smeraldi, E. (1995) A family study of schizotypal disorder. *Schizophrenia Bulletin*, **21**(1), 33–45.

Baumann, M., and Kemper, T. (1985) Histo-anatomic observations of the brain in early infantile autism. *Neurology*, **35**, 866–74.

Bayne, R., and Horton, I. (2003) *Applied psychology*. London: Sage.

Bazzett, T. J. (2008) *An introduction to behaviour genetics*. Sunderland, MA: Sinaur.

BBC2 (2004) *IF*, Drama-documentary (Diverse Productions), broadcast 22 Dec.

Bearden, C. E., Jawad, A. F., Lynch, D. R., Sokol, S., Kanes, S. J., McDonald-McGinn, D. M., Saitta, S. C., Harris, S. E., Moss, E., Wang, P. P., Zackai, E., Emanuel, B. S., and Simon, T. J. (2004) Effects of a functional COMT polymorphism on pre-frontal cognitive function in patients with 22q11.2 deletion syndrome. *American Journal of Psychiatry*, **161**(9), 1700–2.

Beauchaine, T. P., Katkin, E. S., Strassberg, Z., and Snarr, J. (2001) Disinhibitory psychopathology in male adolescents: Discriminating conduct disorder from attention-deficit/hyperactivity disorder through concurrent assessment of multiple autonomic states. *Journal of Abnormal Psychology*, **110**, 610–24.

Bebbington, P., Wilkins, S., Jones, P., Foerster, A., and Murray, R. (1993) Life events and psychosis: Initial results from the Camberwell Collaborative Psychosis study. *British Journal of Psychiatry*, **162**, 72–9.

Beck, A. T. (1976) *Cognitive therapy and the emotional disorders*. New York: International Universities Press.

Beck, A. T., Emery, G., and Greenberg, R. L. (1985) *Anxiety disorders and phobias: A cognitive perspective*. New York: Basic Books.

Beck, A. T., Freeman, A., and Associates (1990) *Cognitive therapy of personality disorders*. New York: Guilford Press.

Beck, A. T., Freeman, A., and Davis, D. D. (2004) *Cognitive therapy of personality disorders*. New York: Guilford Press.

Beck, G. (2001) Suicide prevention. Paper presented at the Forensic Research Group Conference, *Forensic psychology in prisons: Current developments*. 10 Nov., Manchester Metropolitan University. Proceedings of the British Psychological Society, **10**(2), 50.

Becker, E. S., Rinck, M., Türke, V., Krause, P., Goodwin, R., Neumer, S., and Margraf, J. (2007) Epidemiology of specific phobia subtypes: Findings from the Dresden Mental Health Study. *European Psychiatry*, **22**, 69–74.

Bedame, A. (1989) Progeria. *Archives of Dermatology*, **125**, 540–4.

Bee, J. (2000) *Munchausen syndrome by proxy: The perceptions, judgements and feelings of the medical professionals involved*. Unpublished thesis, Manchester Metropolitan University.

Beecher, H. K. (1955) The powerful placebo. *Journal of the American Medical Association*, **159**, 1602–6.

Bekker, M. H. J. (1996) Agoraphobia and gender: A review. *Clinical Psychology Review*, **16**(2), 129–46.

Bell, A. (2002) *Debates in Psychology*. Hove: Routledge.

Bell, J., Campbell, S., Erikson, M., Hogue, T., McLean, Z., Rust, S., and Taylor, R. (2003) An overview: DSPD programme concepts and progress. In A. Lord and L. Rayment (eds), *Dangerous and severe personality disorder (Issues in Forensic Psychology 4)*. Leicester: British Psychological Society, Division of Forensic Psychology.

Benjamin, D. R. (1995) *Mushrooms, poisons and panaceas: A handbook for naturalists, mycologists and physicians*. London: W. H. Freeman.

Bennett, P. (2006) *Abnormal and clinical psychology* (2nd edn). Maidenhead: Open University Press.

Bennett, P., and Carroll, D. (1990) Stress management approaches to the prevention of coronary heart disease. *British Journal of Clinical Psychology*, 29, 1–12.

Bennett, T. (1998) *Drugs and crime: The results of research on drug testing and interviewing arrestees (Home Office research study 183)*. Research and Statistics Directorate Report, London: Home Office.

Bennett, T., and Holloway, K. (2005) *Understanding drugs, alcohol and crime*. Maidenhead: Open University Press.

Benson, A., and Gengler, M. (2004) Treating compulsive buying. In R. H. Coombs (ed.), *Handbook of addictive disorders: A practical guide to diagnosis and treatment*. New York: Wiley.

Bentall, R. P. (2003) *Madness explained: Psychosis and human nature*. London: Penguin.

Bentall, R. P. (2007) Researching psychotic complaints. *The Psychologist*, **20**(5), 293–5.

Ben-Zion, I., Rothschild, S., Chudakov, B., and Aloni, R. (2007) Surrogate versus couple therapy in vaginismus. *Journal of Sexual Medicine*, **4**(3), 728–33.

Béquet, D., Taillia, H., Clervoy, P., Renard, J. L., and Flocard, F. (2003) Psychological and neuropsychological problems in multiple sclerosis. *Bulletin de l'Académie Nationale de Médicine*, **187**(4), 695–7.

Berlim, M. T., Fleck, M. P., and Shorter, E. (2003) Notes on antipsychiatry. *European Archives of Psychiatry and Clinical Neuroscience*, **253**, 61–7.

Berner, W., and Bricken, P. (2007) Paraphilia, sexual preference disorders: Diagnosis etiology epidemiology, treatment and prevention. *Bundesgesundheitsblatt Gesundheitsforshung Gesundheitsschutz*, **50**(1), 33–43.

Bernstein, D. (1993) Paranoid personality disorder: A review of the literature and recommendations for DSM-IV. *Journal of Personality Disorders*, **7**, 53–62.

Bernstein, D. A., and Borkovec, T. D. (1973) *Progressive relaxation training: A manual for the helping professions*. Champaign, IL: Research Press.

Bernstein, D., Cohen, P., Skodol, A., Bezirganian, S., and Brook, J. S. (1996) Childhood antecedents of adolescent personality disorders. *American Journal of Psychiatry*, **153**, 907–13.

Berridge, K. C. (2006) The debate over dopamine's role in reward: The case for incentive salience. *Psychopharmacology*, **191**(3), 391–431.

Berridge, K. C., and Robinson, T. E. (1998) What is the role of dopamine in reward: Hedonic impact, reward learning or incentive salience? *Brain Research Review*, **28**(3), 309–69.

Berrios, G. (2001) Hypochondriasis: History of the concept. In V. Starcevic and D. R. Lipsitt (eds), *Hypochondriasis: Modern perspectives on an ancient malady*. Oxford: Oxford University Press.

Bertolote, J., Fleischmann, A., De Leo, D., and Wasserman, D. (2003) Suicide and mental disorders: Do we know enough? *British Journal of Psychiatry*, **183**, 382–3.

Bertelsen, A. (2004) Book review: Cross-walks ICD-10 – DSM-IV-TR. *Acta Psychiatrica Scandinavica*, **109**(3), 239.

Bettelheim, B. (1967) *The empty fortress*. New York: Free Press.

Beuke, C. J., Fischer, R., and McDowall, J. (2003) Anxiety and depression: Why and how to measure their separate effects. *Clinical Psychology Review*, **23**, 831–48.

Beutler, L. E., Williams, R. E., Wakefield, P. J., and Entwistle, S. R. (1995) Bridging scientist and practitioner perspectives in clinical psychology. *American Psychologist*, **50**(12), 984–94.

Bhattacharjee, C., Bradley, P., Smith, M., Scally, A., and Wilson, B. (2000) Do animals bite more during a full moon? Retrospective observational analysis. *British Medical Journal*, **321**, 1559–61.

Bhugra, D., and Wright, B. (2007) Sexual dysfunctions in gay men and lesbians. *Psychiatry*, **6**(3), 125–9.

Biederman, J., Spencer, T., and Wilens, T. (2004) Evidence-based pharmacotherapy for attention-deficit hyperactivity disorder. *International Journal of Neuropsychopharmacology*, **7**, 77–97.

Biggs, L. (2000) The race of hysteria: 'Overcivilisation' and the 'savage' woman in late nineteenth-century obstetrics and gynecology. *American Quarterly*, **52**, 246–73.

Bijttebier, P., and Vertommen, H. (1999) Coping strategies in relation to personality disorders. *Personality and Individual Differences*, **26**, 847–56.

Binet, A., and Simon, T. (1911) *The development of intelligence in children*. Paris: Coneslant.

Birchwood, M. (2003) Is early intervention for psychosis a waste of valuable resources? *British Journal of Psychiatry*, **182**, 196–8.

Birnbaum, M. H. (2004) Human research and data collection via the internet. *Annual Reviews of Psychology*, **55**, 803–32.

Blaauw, E., and Winkel, F. W. (2002) *Stopping stalking*. Manuscript submitted for publication.

Black, D. N., Seritan, M. D., Taber, K. H., and Hurley, R. A. (2004) Conversion hysteria: Lessons from functional imaging. *Journal of Neuropsychiatry and Clinical Neuroscience*, **16**, 245–51.

Black, D. W. (2007) A review of compulsive buying disorder. *World Psychiatry*, **6**, 14–18.

Black, D. W., Monahan, P., Wesner, R., Gabel, J., and Bowers, W. (1996) The effects of fluvoxamine, cognitive therapy and placebo on abnormal personality traits in 44 patients with panic disorder. *Journal of Personality Disorders*, **10**, 185–94.

Black, D. W., Repertinger, S., Gaffney, G. R., and Gabel, J. (1998) Family history and psychiatric comorbidity in persons with compulsive buying: Preliminary findings. *American Journal of Psychiatry*, **155**, 960–3.

Blackburn, R. (1993) *The psychology of criminal conduct*. Chichester: Wiley.

Blackburn, R. (1996) What is forensic psychology? *Legal and Criminological Psychology*, **1**(1) Feb., 3–16.

Blackburn, R. (2007) Personality disorder and psychopathy: Conceptual and empirical integration. *Psychology Crime and Law*, **13**(1), 7–18.

Blair, R. (1995) A cognitive developmental approach to morality: Investigating the psychopath. *Cognition*, **57**, 1–29.

Blair, J., Mitchell, D., and Blair, K. (2005) *The psychopath: Emotion and the brain*. Oxford: Blackwell.

Blake, L. (2005) Assessment and treatment of autism. *Advances in Paediatrics*, **72**(1), 45–52.

Blanchard, E., Hickling, E., Buckley, T., Taylor, A., et al. (1996) Psychophysiology of posttraumatic stress disorder related to motor vehicle accidents: Replication and extension. *Journal of Consulting and Clinical Psychology*, **64**, 742–51.

Blanchard, J., and Neale, J. (1994) The neuropsychological signature of schizophrenia: generalised or differential deficit? *American Journal of Psychiatry*, **151**, 40–8.

Blatt, S. J. (2004) *Experiences of depression: Theoretical clinical and research perspectives*. Washington, DC: American Psychological Association.

Blennow, K., De Leon, M., and Zetterberg, H. (2006) Alzheimer's disease. *Lancet*, **368**(9533), 387–403.

Bleuler, E. (1911) *Dementia praecox or the group of schizophrenias*. London: Allen and Unwin.

Bleuler, E. (1926) *Textbook of Psychiatry* (trans. A. A. Brill). London: George Allen and Unwin.

Bleuler, E. (1930) *Textbook of psychiatry*. New York: Macmillan.

Bleuler, E. (1950) *Dementia praecox or the group of schizophrenias*. International Universities Press: New York.

Bleuler, M. (1972) *Die schizophrenen Geistesstörungen im Lichte langjähriger Kranken- und Familiengeschichten*, Stuttgart: Thieme.

Bleuler, M. (1978) *The schizophrenic disorders: Long-term patient and family studies*. New Haven, CT: Yale University Press.

Bliss, E. (1986) *Multiple personality, allied disorders and hypnosis*. New York: Oxford University Press.

Blud, L., Travers, R., Nugent, F., and Thompson, D. (2003) Accreditation of offending behaviour programmes in HM Prison Service: 'What Works' in practice. *Legal and Criminological Psychology*, **8**(1), 69–81.

Blumer, D., and Benson, D. F. (1975) Personality changes with frontal and temporal lobe lesions. In D. F. Benson and D. Blumer (eds), *Psychiatric aspects of neurological disease*. New York: Grune and Stratton, pp. 151–70.

Boat, B. W. (1995) The relationship between violence to children and violence to animals: An ignored link? *Journal of Interpersonal Violence*, **10**(2), 229–35.

Bocij, P. (2004) *Cyberstalking: Harassment in the internet age and how to protect your family*. London: Praeger.

Bocij, P. (2006) *The dark side of the internet: Protecting yourself and your family from online criminals*. London: Praeger.

Bocij, P., and McFarlane, L. (2002) Online harassment: Towards a definition of cyberstalking. *Prison Service Journal*, **139**, 31–8.

Bocij, P., and McFarlane, L. (2003) Seven fallacies about cyberstalking. *Prison Service Journal*, **149**, 37–42.

Boehnlein, J. K. (2006) Religion and spirituality in psychiatric care: Looking back, looking ahead. *Transcultural Psychiatry*, **43**(4), 634–51.

Boeuf, O., and Lapeyre-Mestre, M. (2007) Survey of forged prescriptions to investigate risk of psychoactive medications abuse in France: Results of OSIAP survey. *Drug Safety*, **30**(3), 256–76.

Bogaerts, S., Vanheule, S., Leeuw, F., and Desmet, M. (2006) Recalled parental bonding and personality disorders in a sample of exhibitionists: A comparative study. *Journal of Forensic Psychiatry and Psychology*, **17**(4), 636–46.

Bögels, S. M., and Tarrier, N. (2004) Unexplored issues and future directions in social phobia research. *Clinical Psychology Review*, **24**, 731–6.

Bolding, G., Hart, G., Sherr, L., and Elford, J. (2006) Use of crystal methamphetamine among gay men in London. *Addiction*, **101**, 1622–30.

Boles, S., and Miotto, K. (2003) Substance abuse and violence: A review of the literature. *Aggression and Violent Behaviour*, **8**, 155–74.

Bombin, I., Arango, C., and Buchanan, R. W. (2005) Significance and meaning of neurological signs in schizophrenia: Two decades later. *Schizophrenia Bulletin*, **31**(4), 962–77.

Bonelli, R. M. (2007) New trends in the neuropsychiatry of Huntington's disease. *Neurologia Croatica*, **56**(5), 56–63.

Bonelli, R. M., and Hofmann, P. (2007) A systematic review of the treatment studies in Huntington's disease since 1990. *Expert Opinion on Pharmacotherapy*, **8**(2), 141–53.

Bonelli, R. M., and Wenning, G. K. (2006) Pharmacological management of Huntington's disease: An evidence-based review. *Current Pharmaceutical Design*, **12**(21), July, 2701–20.

Bools, C., Neale, B., and Meadow, R. (1994) Münchausen syndrome by proxy: A study of psychopathology. *Child Abuse and Neglect*, **18**, 773–88.

Boon, J., and Sheridan, L. (2002) *Stalking and psychosexual obsession: Psychological perspectives for prevention, policing and treatment*. Chichester: Wiley.

Bornstein, R. A., Schwarzkopf, S. B., Olson, S. C., and Nasrallah, H. A. (1992) Third ventricle enlargement and neuropsychological deficit in schizophrenia. *Biological Psychiatry*, **31**, 954–61.

Bornstein, R. E. (2003) Behaviourally reinforced experimentation and symptom validation: A paradigm for 21st century personality disorder research. *Journal of Personality Disorders*, **17**, 1–18.

Bosanac, P., Burrows, G., and Norman, T. (2004) Olanzapine in anorexia nervosa. *Australian and New Zealand Journal of Psychiatry*, **17**, 1–18.

Bosma, H., Marmot, M. G., Hemingway, H., Nicholson, A. C., Brunner, E., and Stansfeld, S. A. (1997) Low job control and risk of coronary heart disease in Whitehall II (prospective cohort) study. *British Medical Journal*, **14**, 558–65.

Both, S., Everaerd, W., Laan, E., and Gooren, L. (2005) Effect of a single dose of levodopa on sexual response in men and women. *Neuropsychopharmacology*, **30**, 173–83.

Bottoms, A., Rex, S., and Robinson, G. (2004) *Alternatives to prison: Options in an insecure society*, Uffculme, Devon: Willan.

Boulton, N. (2007) Hoarding behaviour in relation to shopping and pathological traits in the normal population. Unpublished thesis, Manchester Metropolitan University.

Bourke, C., Porter, R. J., Sullivan, P., Bulik, C. M., Carter, F. A., McIntosh, V. V., and Joyce, P. R. (2006) Neuropsychological function in bulimia with comorbid borderline personality disorder and depression. *Acta Neuropsychiatrica*, **18**(3–4), 162–7.

Bowers, L. (2002) *Dangerous and severe personality disorder: Response and role of the psychiatric team*. London: Routledge.

Bowlby, J. (1944) Forty-four juvenile thieves. *International Journal of Psychoanalysis*, **25**, 1–57.

Bowlby, J. (1951) *Maternal care and mental health*. Geneva: World Health Organisation; London: HMSO; New York: Columbia University Press.

Bowlby, J. (1980) *Attachment and loss: Sadness and depression*. London: Basic Books.

Bowling, B. (1998) *Violent racism, policing and social context*, London: Clarendon.

Bowman, E. S., and Nurnberger, J. I. (1993) Genetics of psychiatric diagnosis. In D. L. Dunner (ed.), *Current psychiatric therapy*. Philadelphia: W. B. Saunders.

Bownes, I. T. (1992) Sexual and relationship dysfunction in sexual offenders. *Sexual and Marital Therapy*, **8**, 157–65.

Boyle, M. (1993) *Schizophrenia: A scientific delusion*. London: Routledge.

Boyle, M. (2002) *Schizophrenia: A scientific delusion* (2nd edn). London: Routledge.

Boyle, M. (2007) The problem with diagnosis. *The Psychologist*, **20**(5), 290–2.

Boyle, M., and Whitely, C. (2003) Clinical psychology. In R. Bayne and I. Horton (eds), *Applied Psychology*. London: Sage.

Bracha, H. S. (2006) Human brain evolution and the 'Neuroevolutionary time-depth principle': Implications for the reclassification of fear circuitry related traits in DSM-V and for studying resilience to warzone-related posttraumatic stress disorder. *Progress in Neuro-psychopharmacology and Biological Psychiatry*, **30**, 827–53.

Bracken, P., and Thomas, P. (2001) Postpsychiatry: a new direction for mental health. *British Medical Journal*, **332**, 724–7.

Bradfield, J. W. B. (2006) A pathologist's perspective of the somatoform disorders. *Journal of Psychosomatic Research*, **60**, 327–30.

Bradshaw, C. (2007) A study of shopping behaviour in relation to personal and subject variables. Unpublished thesis, Manchester Metropolitan University.

Bradshaw, J. L. (1997) *Human evolution: A neurological perspective*. Hove: Psychology Press.

Brannigan, D. (2001) The validity and prevalence of the concept of Münchausen syndrome by pet proxy. Unpublished thesis, Manchester Metropolitan University.

Braude, P., Minger, S., and Warwick, R. (2005) Stem cell therapy: hope or hype? *British Medical Journal*, **330**, 1159–60.

Braun, B. (1988) The Bask model of dissociation. *Dissociation*, **1**, 4–23.

Bray, K., Harwood, T., Inder, R., Beasley, R., and Robinson, G. (2007) Poppy seed tea and opiate abuse in New Zealand. *Drug and Alcohol Review*, **26**, 215–19.

Breedlove, S. M., Rosenzweig, M. R., and Watson, N. V. (2007) *Biological psychology: An introduction to behavioural, cognitive and clinical neuroscience* (5th edn). Sunderland, MA: Sinauer.

Breggin, P. R. (2004) Suicidality, violence and mania caused by selective serotonin reuptake inhibitors (SSRIs): A review and analysis. *International Journal of Risk and Safety in Medicine*, **16**(1), 31–49.

Brennan, J. J. (1964) Mentally ill aggressiveness, popular delusions as reality. *American Journal of Psychiatry*, **120**, 1181–4.

Brennan, P. A., and Raine, A. (1997) Biosocial bases of antisocial behaviour: Psychophysiological, neurological and cognitive factors. *Clinical Psychology Review*, **17**(6), 589–604.

Brennan, P. A., Grekin, E. R., and Mednick, S. A. (1999) Maternal smoking during pregnancy and adult male criminal outcomes. *Archives of General Psychiatry*, **56**, 215–19.

Brennan, P. A., Mednick, S. A., and Raine, A. (1997) Biosocial interactions and violence: A focus on perinatal factors. In A. Raine, P. Brennan, D. P. Farrington and S. A. Mednick (eds), *Biosocial bases of violence*. New York: Plenum.

Brennan, P. A., Raine, A., Schulsinger, F., Kirkegaard-Sorensen, L., Knop, J., Hutchings, B., Rosenberg, R., and Mednick, S. A. (1997) Psychophysiological protective factors for male subjects at high risk for criminal behaviour. *American Journal of Psychiatry*, **154**, 853–5.

Brenneis, C. (1995) On Brenner's 'The dissociative character'. *Journal of the American Psychoanalytic Association*, **43**, 297–300.

Breuer, J. E., and Freud, S. (1885) *Studien über hysterie*. Leipzig: Deuticke.

Brewer, C., and Streel, E. (2003) Learning the language of abstinence in addiction treatment: some similarities between relapse-prevention with disulfiram, naltrexone, and other pharmacological antagonists and intensive 'Immersion' methods of foreign language teaching. *Substance Abuse*, **24**(3), 157–73.

Brewin, C. R., Andrews, B., and Rose, S. (2003) Diagnostic overlap between acute stress disorder and PTSD in victims of violent crime. *American Journal of Psychiatry*, **160**, 783–5.

Brewin, C., and Holmes, E. A. (2003) Psychological theories of posttraumatic stress disorder. *Clinical Psychology Review*, **23**, 339–76.

Brigham, J. (1999) What is forensic psychology, anyway? *Law and Human Behaviour*, **233**, 273–98.

Brigham, J., Herning, R., and Moss, H. (1995) Event related potentials and alpha synchronisation in pre-adolescent boys at risk for psychoactive substance use. *Biological Psychiatry*, **37**, 834–46.

British Psychological Society (2000) *Code of conduct, ethical principles and guidelines*. Leicester: British Psychological Society.

British Psychological Society: Division of Clinical Psychology (2001) *Core purpose and philosophy of the profession*. Leicester: British Psychological Society.

Britton, P. (1997) *The jigsaw man*. London: Bantam.

Britton, P. (2000) *Picking up the pieces*. London: Bantam.

Brooke, D., Edwards, G., and Taylor, C. (1991) Addiction as an occupational hazard: 144 doctors with drug and alcohol problems. *Addiction*, **86**(8), 1011–16.

Brooks-Gordon, B., Bilby, C., and Wells, H. (2006) A systematic review of psychological interventions for sexual offenders I: Randomised control designs. *Journal of Forensic Psychiatry and Psychology*, **17**(3), 442–66.

Broome, M. R. (2004) A neuroscience of hysteria? *Current Opinion in Psychiatry*, **17**, 465–9.

Brosschot, J. F., Gerin, W., and Thayer, J. (2006) The perseverative cognition hypothesis: A review of worry, prolonged stress-related physiological activation and health. *Journal of Psychosomatic Research*, **60**(2), 113–24.

Brown, A., Begg, M., Gravenstein, S., Schaefer, C., Wyatt, R., Bresnahan, M., Babulas, V., and Susser, E. (2005) Serologic evidence of prenatal influenza in the etiology of schizophrenia. *Obstetrical and Gynecological Survey*, **60**(2), 77–8.

Brown, G., Dubin, W., Lion, J., and Garry, L. (1996) Threats against clinicians: A preliminary descriptive classification. *Bulletin of the American Academy of Psychiatry and the Law*, **24**, 367–76.

Brown, G. W., and Harris, T. (1978) *Social origins of depression*. London: Tavistock.

Brown, J. (1998) Helping police with their enquiries. *The Psychologist*, Nov., 539–42.

Brown, J. (2004) Occupational stress and the criminal justice practitioner. In A. Needs and G. Towl (eds), *Applying psychology to forensic practice*. Oxford: Blackwell.

Brown, T. A., and Barlow, D. H. (2005) Dimensional versus categorical classification of mental disorders in the fifth edition of the Diagnostic and Statistical Manual of Mental Disorders and beyond: Comment on the special edition. *Journal of Abnormal Psychology*, **114**(4), 551–6.

Brown, W. (1992) Progeria: A human-disease model of accelerated aging. *American Journal of Clinical Nutrition*, **55**, 1222S–1224S.

Brussel, J. A. (1968) *Casebook of a crime psychiatrist*. New York: Simon and Shuster.

Bryan, T., and Cech, T. (1999) Telomerase and the maintenance of chromosome ends. *Current Opinion in Cell Biology*, **11**(3), 318–24.

Bryner, J. K., Wang, U. K., Hui, J. W., Bedodo, M., MacDougall, C., and Anderson, I. B. (2006) Dextromethorphan abuse in adolescence: An increasing trend. *Archives of Pediatric Adolescent Medicine*, **160**, 1217–22.

Buchanan, R. W., and Heinrichs, D. W. (1989) The Neurological Evaluation Scale (NES): A structured instrument for the assessment of neurological signs in schizophrenia. *Psychiatry Research*, **27**(3), 335–50.

Buchanan, T., and Smith, J. L. (1999) Using the internet for psychological research: Personality testing on the World Wide Web. *British Journal of Psychology*, **90**(1), 125–44.

Budd, T., and Mattinson, J. (2000) *The extent and nature of stalking: Findings from the 1998 British Crime Survey* (Home Office Research Study No. 210). London: HMSO.

Buffington-Vollum, J., Edens, J. F., Johnson, D. W., and Johnson, J. K. (2002) Psychopathy as a predictor of institutional misbehaviour among sex offenders: A prospective replication. *Criminal Justice and Behaviour*, **29**(5), 497–511.

Buist-Bouwman, M. A., de Graaf, R., Volleberrgh, W. A., and Ormel, J. (2005) Comorbidity of physical and mental disorders and the effect on work-loss days. *Acta Psychiatrica Scandinavica*, **111**, 436–43.

Bulik, C. M., Prescott, C. A., and Kendler, K. S. (2001) Features of childhood sexual abuse and the development of psychiatric and substance abuse disorders. *British Journal of Psychiatry*, **179**, 444–9.

Bulik, C. M., Sullivan, P. F., and Kendler, K. S. (1998) Heritability of binge eating and broadly defined bulimia nervosa. *Biological Psychiatry*, **44**, 1210–18.

Bull, R. H. C. (1982) Physical appearance and criminality. *Current Psychological Reviews*, **2**, 269–81.

Bulot, V., Thomas, P., and Delavoye-Turrell, Y. (2007) A pre-reflective indicator of an impaired sense of agency in patients with schizophrenia. *Experimental Brain Research*, **183**, 115–26.

Bunker, S. J., Colquhoun, D. M., Esler, M. D., Hickie, I. B., Hunt, D., Jelinek, V. M., Oldenburg, B. M., Peach, H. G., Ruth, D., Tennant, C. C., and Tonkin, A. M. (2003) 'Stress' and coronary heart disease: Psychosocial risk factors, National Heart Foundation of Australia position statement update. *Medical Journal of Australia*, **178**, 272–6.

Burns, A., Dening, T., and Baldwin, R. (2001) Care of older people: Mental health problems. *British Medical Journal*, **322**, 789–91.

Burroughs, W. (1959) *The naked lunch*. Paris: Olympia.

Burt, R., Loh, Y., Cohen, B., Stefosky, D., Balabanov, R., Katsamakis, R., Oyama, Y., Russell, E., Stern, J., and Muraro, P. (2009) Autologous non-myeloablative haemopoietic stem cell transplantation in relapsing–remitting multiple sclerosis: a phase I/II study. *The Lancet Neurology*, **8**(3), 244–53.

Burt, V. K., and Rudolph, M. (2000) Treating an orthodox Jewish woman with obsessive–compulsive disorder: Maintaining reproduction and psychological stability in the context of normative religious rituals. *American Journal of Psychiatry*, **157**(4), 620–4.

Burton, N. (2006) *Psychiatry*. Oxford: Blackwell.

Buss, D. (1999) *Evolutionary psychology: The new science of the mind*. Boston: Allyn and Bacon.

Busse, M. E., and Rosser, A. E. (2007) Can directed activity improve mobility in Huntington's disease? *Brain Research Bulletin*, **72**(2–3), 172–4.

Butler, A., Chapman, J., Forman, E., and Beck, A. (2006) The empirical status of cognitive-behavioural therapy: A review of meta-analyses. *Clinical Psychology Review*, **26**(1), 17–31.

Butler, L., and Palesh, O. (2003) Spellbound: Dissociation in the movies. *Journal of Trauma and Dissociation*, **5**(2), 61–87.

Butler, L., Duran, R., Jasiukaitis, P., Koopman, C., and Spiegel, D. (1996) Hypnotisability and traumatic experience: A diathesis–stress model of dissociative symptomatology. *American Journal of Psychiatry*, **153**, 42–63.

Butler, R. N. (1975) Psychiatry and the elderly: an overview. *American Journal Psychiatry*, **132**, 893–900.

Butler, T., Allnut, S., Cain, D., Owens, D., and Muller, C. (2005) Mental disorder in a New South Wales prisoner population. *Australian and New Zealand Journal of Psychiatry*, **39**(5), 25–38.

Buunk, A., Angleitner, A., Oubaid, V., and Buss, D. M. (1996) Sex differences in jealousy in evolutionary and cultural perspective: Tests from the Netherlands, Germany and the United States. *Psychological Science*, **7**, 359–63.

Byrne, P. (2000) Stigma of mental illness and ways of diminishing it. *Advances in Psychiatric Treatment*, **6**, 65–72.

C, Robert (anonymised) (2006) Managing risk from the inside looking out. *Criminal Behaviour and Mental Health*, **16**, 142–5.

Cadoret, R., Yates, W., Troughton, E., Woodsworth, G., and Stewart, M. (1995) Adoption study demonstrating two genetic pathways to drug abuse. *Archives of General Psychiatry*, **52**, 42–52.

Calabrese, J., Kimmel, S., Woyshville, M., and Rapport, D. (1996) Clozapine for treatment-refactory mania. *American Journal of Psychiatry*, **153**, 759–64.

Campbell, M., Perry, R., Small, A., McVeigh-Tesch, L., and Curren, E. (1988) Naltrexone in infantile autism. *Psychopharmacology Bulletin*, **24**, 135–9.

Cannon, T. D., and Marco, E. (1994) Structural brain abnormalities as indicators of vulnerability in schizophrenia. *Schizophrenia Bulletin*, **20**, 89–102.

Cannon, T. D., Van Erp, T. G., and Glahn, D. C. (2002) Elucidating continuities and discontinuities between schizotypy and schizophrenia in the nervous system. *Schizophrenia Research*, **54**(1–2), 151–6.

Cannon, W. B. (1927) The James–Lange theory of emotions: A critical examination and an alternative theory. *American Journal of Psychology*, **39**(1/4), 106–24.

Canter, D. (ed.) (1985) *Facet theory: Approaches to social research*. New York: Springer-Verlag.

Canter, D. (1989) Offender profiles. *Psychologist*, **2**, 12–16.

Canter, D. (1994) *Criminal shadows: Inside the mind of the serial killer*. London: HarperCollins.

Canter, D. (2003) *Mapping Murder: The secrets of geographical profiling*. London: Virgin.

Canter, D., and Allison, D. (1999a) *Interviewing and deception*. Aldershot: Dartmouth.

Canter, D., and Allison, L. (1999b) *Profiling in policy and practice*. London: Ashgate.

Canter, D., and Allison, L. (2000a) *Profiling property crimes*. London: Ashgate.

Canter, D., and Allison, L. (2000b) *The social psychology of crime*. London: Ashgate.

Canter, D., Bennell, C., Allison, L., and Reddy, S. (2003) Differentiating sex offences: A behaviourally based thematic classification of stranger rapes. *Behavioural Sciences and the Law*, **21**, 157–74.

Cantor, C. (2005) *Evolution and posttraumatic stress: Disorders of vigilance and defence*. London: Routledge.

Cantor, C., and Smith, C. L. (1999) Masters of all trades – Geronics: The science and technology behind the Human Genome Project. *Trends in Genetics*, **15**(9), 381.

Carey, G., and Gottesman, I. (1981) Twin and family studies of anxiety, phobic and obsessive disorders. In D. Klein and J. Rabkin (eds), *Anxiety: New research and changing concepts*. New York: Raven Press.

Carlbring, P., Nilsson-Ihrfelt, E., Waara, J., Kollenstam, C., Buhrman, M., Kaldo, V., Söderberg, M., Ekselius, L., and Andersson, G. (2005) Treatment of panic disorder: Live therapy vs self-help via the internet. *Behaviour Research and Therapy*, **43**, 1321–33.

Carlson, E. B., and Putnam, F. W. (1993) An update on the Dissociative Experiences Scale. *Dissociation*, **6**, 16–27.

Carlson, N. (2004) *Physiology of behaviour* (8th edn). London: Pearson.

Carlsson, M. (2001) On the role of prefrontal cortex glutamate for an antithetical phenomenology of obsessive–compulsive disorder and attention deficit hyperactivity disorder. *Progress in Neuropsychopharmacological Biological Psychiatry*, **25**(1), 5–26.

Carlsson, M., and Carlsson, A. (1990) Interactions between glutaminergic and monoaminergic systems within the basal ganglia: Implications for schizophrenia and Parkinson's disease. *Trends in Neuroscience*, **13**, 272–6.

Carpenter, W. T., and Conley, R. R. (1999) Sense and nonsense: An essay on schizophrenia research ethics. *Schizophrenia Research*, **35**(3), 219–25.

Carpenter, W. T., Arango, C., Buchanan, R. W., and Kirkpatrick, B. (1999) Deficit psychopathology and a paradigm shift in schizophrenia research. *Biological Psychiatry*, **46**, 352–60.

Carpenter, W. T., Bartko, J. J., Carpenter, C. L., and Strauss, J. L. (1976) Another view of schizophrenic sub-types. *Archives of General Psychiatry*, **33**(4), 508–16.

Carper, R., and Courchesne, E. (2000) Inverse correlation between frontal lobe and cerebellum sizes in children with autism, *Brain*, **123**, 836–44.

Carr, A., and McNulty, M. (2006) *The handbook of adult clinical psychology: An evidence-based practice approach*. Hove: Routledge.

Carrera, M., Herrán, A., Ramírez, M. L., Ayestarán, A., Sierra-Biddle, D., Hoyuela, F., Rodríguez-Cabo, B., and Vázquez-Barquero, J. L. (2006) Personality traits in early phases of panic disorder: Implications on the presence of agoraphobia, clinical severity and short-term outcome. *Acta Psychiatrica Scandinavica*, **114**(6), 417–25.

Carson, C. C., 3rd (2003) Sildenafil: A 4-year update in the treatment of 20 million erectile dysfunction patients. *Current Urology Reports*, **4**, 448–96.

Carter, J. C., and Fairburn, C. G. (1998) Cognitive-behavioural self-help for binge eating disorder: A controlled effectiveness study. *Journal of Consulting and Clinical Psychology*, **66**(4), 616–23.

Carter, R. (2008) *Multiplicity: The new science of personality*. London: Little, Brown.

Cartwright, J. (2000) *Evolution and human behaviour*. London: Macmillan.

Cartwright, J. (2008) *Evolution and human behaviour* (2nd edn). London: Macmillan.

Carver, C. S., and Scheier, M. F. (2008) *Perspectives on personality*. New York: Pearson.

Casale, S. (1995) Suicide and custody. *Aids Care*, **7**(suppl. 2), 139–43.

Caspi, A., Begg, D., Dickson, N., Harrington, H., Langley, J., Moffitt, T., and DeSilva, P. A. (1997) Personality differences predict health-risk behaviours in adulthood. *Journal of Personality and Social Psychology*, **73**, 1052–63.

Caspi, A., Moffitt, E., Cannon, M., McClay, J., Murray, R., Harrington, H., Taylor, A., Arseneault, L., Williams, B., Braithwaite, A., Poulton, R., and Craig, I. W. (2005) Moderation of the effect of adolescent onset cannabis use on adult psychosis by a functional polymorphism in the catechol-O-methyltransferase gene: Longitudinal evidence of a gene X environment interaction. *Biological Psychiatry*, **57**, 1117–27.

Caspi, A., Sugden, K., Moffitt, T. E., Craig, I. W., Harrington, H., McClay, J., Mill, J., Martin, J., Braithwaite, A., and Poulton, R. (2003) Influence of life stress on depression: Moderation by a polymorphism in the 5-htt gene. *Science*, **301**, 386–9.

Castellanos, F., Giedd, J., Marsh, W., Hamburger, S., Viatuzis, A., Dickstein, D., Sarfatti, S., Vauss, Y., Snell, J., Rajapakse, J., and Rapoport, J. (1996) Quantitative brain magnetic resonance imaging in attention deficit hyperactivity disorder. *Archives of General Psychiatry*, **53**, 607–16.

Casson, J. (1997) Therapeusis of the audience. In S. Jennings (ed.), *Dramatherapy: Theory and practice 3*, Vol. 3. London: Routledge.

Catalan, J., and Gath, D. (1985) Benzodiazepines in general practice: A time for decision. *British Medical Journal*, **290**, 1374–6.

Cattell, R. B. (1956) Validation and interpretation of the 16PF questionnaire. *Journal of Clinical Psychology*, **12**, 205–14.

Cavadino, M., and Dignan, J. (2002) *The penal system: An introduction*. London: Sage.

Cavedini, P., Erzegovesi, S., Ronchi, P., and Bellodi, L. (1997) Predictive value of obsessive compulsive personality disorder in antiobsessional pharmacological treatment. *European Neuropsychopharmacology*, **7**, 45–9.

Chabrol, H., and Peresson, G. (1997) ADHD and maternal smoking during pregnancy. *American Journal of Psychiatry*, **154**(8), 1177–8.

Chan, S., Roberts, J. S., Marteau, T. M., Silliman, R., Cupples, L. A., and Green, R. C. (2008) Health behaviour changes after genetic risk assessment for Alzheimer's disease: The REVEAL study. *Alzheimer's Disease and Associated Disorders*, **22**(1), 94–7.

Chang, C. J., Chen, W. J., Liu, S. K., Cheng, J. J., Yang, W. C., Chang, H. J., Lane, H. Y., Lin, S. K., Yang, T. W., and Hai-Gwo Hwu, H. G. (2002) Morbidity risk of psychiatric disorders among the first degree relatives of schizophrenia patients in Taiwan. *Schizophrenia Bulletin*, **28**(3), 379–92.

Chapman, S., and Morrell, S. (2000) Barking mad? Another lunatic hypothesis bites the dust. *British Medical Journal*, **321**(7276), 1561–3.

Charcot, J. M. (1868) Histologic de la sclerose en plaque. *Gaz Höp*, **41**, 554–66.

Charcot, J. M. (1889) *Clinical lectures on diseases of the nervous system*. London: New Sydenham Society.

Charlop-Christy, M. H., Carpenter, M., Le L., LeBlanc, L. A., and Kellet, K. (2002) Using the picture exchange communication system (PECS) with children with autism: Assessment of PECS acquisition, speech, social-communicative behavior, and problem behavior. *Journal of Applied Behaviour Analysis*, **35**, 213–31.

Charney, D. S. (2003) Neuroanatomical circuits modulating fear and anxiety behaviors. *Acta Psychiatrica Scandinavica*, **108**(s417), 38–50.

Chen, E., Hanson, M., Paterson, L., Griffin, M., Walker, H., and Miller, G. (2006) Socioeconomic status and inflammatory processes in childhood asthma: The role of psychological stress. *Journal of Allergy and Clinical Immunology*, **117**(5), 1014–20.

Chen, E., Hui , C., Chan, R., Dunn, E., Miao, M., Yeung, W., Wong, C., Chan, W., and Tang, W. (2005) A 3 year prospective study of neurological soft signs in first episode schizophrenia. *Schizophrenia Research*, **75**(1), 45–54.

Chen, W., Chang, H., Lin, C., Chang, C., Chiu, Y., and Soong, W. (1999) Diagnosis of zygocity by questionnaire and polymarker polymerase chain reaction in young twins. *Behaviour Genetics*, **29**, 115–23.

Cheniaux, E., Landeira-Fernandez, J., Lessa Telles, L., Lessa, J. L. M., Dias, A., Duncan, T., and Versiani, M. (2008) Does schizoaffective disorder really exist? A systematic review of the studies that compared schizoaffective disorder with schizophrenia or mood disorders. *Journal of Affective Disorders*, **106**, 209–17.

Cheshire, K., and Pilgrim, D. (2004) *A short introduction to clinical psychology*. London: Sage.

Chisholm, J. (1993) Death, hope and sex: Life-history theory and the development of reproductive strategies. *Current Anthropology*, **34**(1), 1–24.

Chiu, H. (1994) Erotomania in the elderly. *International Journal of Geriatric Psychiatry*, **9**, 673–4.

Chomsky, N. (1957) *On syntactic structure*. The Hague: Mouton.

Choy, Y., Fyer, A. J., and Lipsitz, J. D. (2007) Treatment of specific phobia in adults. *Clinical Psychology Review*, **27**, 266–86.

Christenson, G. A., Pyle, R. L., and Mitchell, J. E. (1991) Estimated lifetime prevalence of trichotillomania in college students. *Journal of Clinical Psychiatry*, **52**, 415–17.

Christian, R., Frick, P. J., Hill, N., Tyler, L. A., and Frazer, D. (1997) Psychopathy and conduct problems in children: II. Subtyping children with conduct problems based on their interpersonal and affective style. *Journal of the American Academy of Child and Adolescent Psychiatry*, **36**, 233–41.

Christiansen, K. O. (1968) Threshold of tolerance in various population groups illustrated by results from the Danish criminological twin study. In A. V. de Reuck and R. Porter (eds), *The mentally abnormal offender*. Boston: Little, Brown.

Christiansen, K. O. (1974) Seriousness of criminality and concordance among Danish twins. In R. Hood (ed.), *Crime, criminology and public policy*. London: Heinemann.

Christie, N. (2000) Dangerous states. In M. Brown and J. Pratt (eds), *Dangerous offenders: Punishment and social order*. London: Routledge.

Christmas, D., Morrison, C., Eljamel, M., and Mathews, K. (2004) Neurosurgery for mental disorder. *Advances in Psychiatric Treatment*, **10**, 189–99.

Ciompi, L., and Muller, C. (1976) *Lifestyle and age of schizophrenics: A catamnestic long-term study in to old age* (monograph). Berlin: Springer-Verlag.

Cipriani, A., and Geddes, J. R. (2008) Antidepressants for bipolar disorder: A clinical overview of efficacy and safety. *Psychiatric Times*, **25**(7), 1 June, 1–6.

Cipriani, A., Barbui, C., and Geddes, J. R. (2005) Suicide, depression and antidepressants. *British Medical Journal*, **330**(7488), 373–4.

Cipriani, A., Pretty, H., Hawton, K., and Geddes, J. R. (2005) Lithium in the prevention of suicidal behavior and all-cause mortality in patients with mood disorders: A systematic review of randomized trials. *American Journal of Psychiatry*, **162**, 1805–19.

Clare, A. (1980) *Psychiatry in dissent* (2nd edn). London: Tavistock.

Clare, L. (2004) Awareness in early-stage Alzheimer's disease: A review of methods and evidence. *British Journal of Clinical Psychology*, **43**, 177–96.

Claridge, G. (1994) Single indicator of risk for schizophrenia: Probable fact or likely myth? *Schizophrenia Bulletin*, **20**(1), 151–68.

Claridge, G. (1997) *Schizotypy: Implications for illness and health*. Oxford: Oxford University Press.

Clark, A., Mankikar, G. D., and Gray, I. (1975) Diogenes syndrome: A clinical study of neglect in old age. *Lancet*, **1**, 366–8.

Clark, D. M. (1986) A cognitive approach to panic. *Behaviour Research and Therapy*, **24**, 461–70.

Clark, D. M., and Fairburn, C. G. (eds) (1997) *Science and practice of cognitive behavioural therapy*. Oxford: Oxford University Press.

Clark, L. A. (2007) Assessment and diagnosis of personality disorder: Perennial issues and an emerging reconceptualisation. *Annual Review of Psychology*, **58**, 227–57.

Clark, L. A., and Harrison, J. A. (2001) Assessment instruments. In W. J. Livesley (ed.), *Handbook of personality disorders*. New York: Guilford Press.

Clarke, A., and Clarke, A. (eds) (1976) *Early experience: Myth and evidence*. London: Open Books.

Cleckley, H. (1941) *The mask of sanity* (4th edn). St Louis: C. V. Mosby.

Cleckley, H. (1976) *The mask of sanity* (5th edn). St Louis: C. V. Mosby.

de Clérambault, G. G. (1942) Les psychoses passionelles. *Oeuvres Psychiatriques*. Paris: Presses Universitairs de France, pp. 315–22.

Clifford, B. R. (2003) Forensic psychology. In R. Bayne and I. Horton (eds), *Applied Psychology*. London: Sage.

Clifford, B. R., and Hollin, C. (1981) Effects of type of incident and the number of perpetrators in eyewitness testimony. *Journal of Applied Psychology*, **66**, 352–9.

Cloninger, C., and Begleiter, H. (eds) (1990) *Genetics and the biology of alcoholism*. New York: Cold Spring Harbour Laboratory Press.

Cloninger, C., and Gottesman, I. (1987) Genetic and environmental factors in antisocial behaviour disorders. In N. S. Mednick, T. Moffit and S. Stack (eds), *The causes of crime: New biological approaches*. Cambridge: Cambridge University Press.

Coackley, A., and Richman, J. (2003) Suicide is a permanent solution to a temporary problem: A case study of listeners at HMP Manchester. Paper presented at the Forensic Research Group Conference, 'Forensic Health Psychology', 8 Nov., Manchester Metropolitan University. *Proceedings of the British Psychological Society*, **12**(2), 138.

Coccaro, E., Kavoussi, R., and Hauger, R. L. (1997) Serotonin function and antiaggressive response to fluoxetine: A pilot study. *Biological Psychiatry*, **42**(7), 546–52.

Coccaro, E., Kavoussi, R., Cooper, T., and Hauger, R. L. (1997) Central serotonin activity and aggression: Inverse relationship with prolactin response to d-fenfluramine, but not CSF 5-HIAA concentration, in human subjects. *American Journal of Psychiatry*, **154**(10), 1430–5.

Coghill, D. (2004) Use of stimulants for attention deficit hyperactivity disorder. *British Medical Journal*, **329**, 907–9.

Cohen, L. M., Collins Jr, F. L., Young, A., McChargue, D., Leffingwell, T. R., and Cook, K. (eds) (2009) *Pharmacology and treatment of substance abuse: Evidence and outcome based perspectives*. London: Routledge.

Cohen, P. (1996) Childhood risks for young adult symptoms of personality disorder: Method and substance. *Multivariate Behavioural Research*, **31**, 121–48.

Cohen, S. (1967) *Drugs of hallucination*. St Albans: Paladin.

Coid, J., Yang, M., Tyrer, P., Roberts, A., and Ullrich, S. (2006) Prevalence and correlates of personality disorder in Great Britain. *British Journal of Psychiatry*, **188**, 423–31.

Cole, M. (1982) Surrogates and sexual dysfunction. *British Journal of Sexual Medicine*, **9**, 13–20.

Cole, M. (1988) Normal and dysfunctional sexual behaviour: Frequencies and incidences. In M. Cole and W. Dryden (eds), *Sex therapy in Britain*. Milton Keynes: Open University Press.

Cole, M., and Dryden, W. (eds) (1988) *Sex therapy in Britain*. Milton Keynes: Open University Press.

Collins, F., and Ffrench, C. (1998) Dissociation, coping strategies and locus of control in a non-clinical population: Clinical implications. *Journal of Clinical and Experimental Hypnosis*, **26**(2), 113–26.

Comer, R. J. (2007) *Abnormal psychology* (6th edn). New York: Worth.

Compton, W., and Guze, S. (1995) The neo-Kraepelinian revolution in psychiatric diagnosis. Special issue: Emil Kraepelin and 20th century psychiatry. *European Archives of Psychiatry and Clinical Neuroscience*, **245**, 196–201.

Condon, W. (1975) Multiple response to sound in dysfunctional children. *Journal of Autism and Childhood Schizophrenia*, **5**(1), 37–56.

Condon, W. S., and Ogston, W. D. (1967). A segmentation of behaviour. *Journal of Psychiatric Research*, **5**, 221–35.

Connor, K. M., Vaishnavi, S., Davidson, J. R. T., Sheehan, D. V., and Sheehan, K. H. (2007) Perceived stress in anxiety disorders and the general population: A study of the Sheehan stress vulnerability scale. *Psychiatry Research*, **151**(3), 249–54.

Consroe, P., Musty, R., Rein, J., Tillery, W., Pertwee, R. (1997) Perceived effects of cannabis smoking on patients with multiple sclerosis. *European Neurology*, **38**, 44–8.

Consroe, P., Musty, R., Tillery, W., and Pertwee, R. G. (1996) The perceived effects of cannabis smoking on patients with multiple sclerosis. *Proceedings of the International Cannabinoid Research Society*, **7**, 67–73.

Coomber, R. (2006) *Pusher myths: Re-situating the drug dealer*. London: Free Association Books.

Coombs, R. H. (2004) *Handbook of addictive disorders: A practical guide to diagnosis and treatment*. New York: Wiley.

Cooper, B. (2005) Immigration and schizophrenia: the social causation hypothesis revisited. *British Journal of Psychiatry*, **186**, 361–3.

Cooper, C. L. (2004) *Handbook of stress medicine and health*. Boca Raton, FL: CRC Press.

Cooper, C., Bebbington, P., King, M., Brugha, T., Meltzer, H., Bhugra, D., and Jenkins, R. (2007) Why people do not take their psychotropic drugs as prescribed: Results of the 2000 National Psychiatric Morbidity Survey. *Acta Psychiatrica Scandinavica*, **116**(1), 47–53.

Cooper, D. (1967) *Psychiatry and antipsychiatry*. London: Tavistock.

Cooper, M. J., and Fairburn, C. G. (1992) Selective processing of eating, weight and shape related words in patients with eating disorders and dieters. *British Journal of Clinical Psychology*, **31**, 363–5.

Cooper, R. (2004) What is wrong with the DSM? *History of Psychiatry*, **15**(1), 5–25.

Copson, G. (1995) *Coals to Newcastle? Part 1: A study of offender profiling*. London: Police Research Group Special Interest Series, Home Office.

Copson, G., and Holloway, K. (2003) Coals to Newcastle? Pt 2: An analysis of offender profiling advice, methods and results. In G. H. Gudjonsson and G. Copson (eds), *The role of the expert in criminal investigation in offender profiling*. Chichester: Wiley.

Corcoran, R., Cahill, C., and Frith, C. D. (1997) The appreciation of visual jokes in people with schizophrenia. *Schizophrenia Research*, **24**, 319–27.

Cormier, J., LeFauveau, P., and Loas, G. (2006) Dependent personality and hetero-aggressive risks: Study of a group of 252 patients in forensic medicine. *Annales Medico-Psychologiques*, **164**, 230–6.

Cororve, M. B., and Gleaves, D. H. (2001) Body dysmorphic disorder: A review of conceptualizations, assessment and treatment strategies. *Clinical Psychology Review*, **6**, 949–70.

Corrales-Arroyo, M. J., and Ortiz-Pascual, A. (2007) Acute disseminated encephalomyelitis initially diagnosed as dissociative disorder. *Journal of Neuropsychiatry and Clinical Neuroscience*, **19**(3), 339–40.

Correll, C. U., Leucht, S., and Kane, J. M. (2004) Lower risk of tardive dykinesia associated with second generation anti-psychotics: A systematic review of 1 year studies. *American Journal of Psychiatry*, **161**, 414–25.

Corretti, G., and Baldi, I. (2007) The relationship between anxiety disorders and sexual dysfunction. *Psychiatric Times*, **24**(9), 1–4.

Cosmides, L., and Tooby, J. (1992) *The adapted mind*. Oxford: Oxford University Press.

Costa, P. T., Jr, and McCrae, R. R. (1992) *NEO-PI-R, professional manual*. Odessa, FL: Psychological Assessment Resources.

Costello, T. W., Costello, J. T., and Holmes, D. A. (adapting author) (1995) *Abnormal Psychology*. London: HarperCollins.

Coyle, A. (2005) *Understanding prisons: Key issues in policy and practice*. Maidenhead: Open University Press.

Crabb, D. W., Matsumoto, M., Chang, D., and You, M. (2004) Overview of the role of alcohol dehydrogenase and aldehyde dehydrogenase and their variants in the genesis of alcohol-related pathology. *Proceedings of the Nutrition Society*, **63**, 49–63.

Craig, J. S., Hatton, C., Craig, F. B., and Bentall, R. P. (2004) Persecutory beliefs, attributions and theory of mind: Comparison of patients with paranoid delusions Asperger's syndrome and healthy controls. *Schizophrenia Research*, **69**, 29–33.

Craig, L. A., Browne, K. D., Beech, A., and Stringer, I. (2006) Differences in personality and risk characteristics in sex, violent and general offenders. *Criminal Behaviour and Mental Health*, **16**, 183–94.

Craig, L. A., Browne, K. D., Stringer, I., and Beech, A. (2006) Sexual recidivism: A review of static, dynamic and actuarial predictors. *Journal of Sexual Aggression*, **11**(1), 65–84.

Craven, S., Brown, S., and Gilchrist, E. (2006) Sexual grooming of children: Review of the literature and theoretical considerations. *Journal of Sexual Aggression*, **12**(3), 287–99.

Critchlow, D. G. (2006) A case of ketamine dependence with discontinuation of symptoms. *Addiction*, **101**, 1212–13.

Crow, T. J. (1980) Molecular pathology of schizophrenia: More than one disease process? *British Medical Journal*, **280**, 66–8.

Crow, T. J., and Mitchell, W. S. (1975) Subjective age in chronic schizophrenia: Evidence of a sub-group of patients with a defective learning capacity. *British Journal of Psychiatry*, **126**, 360–3.

Crowe, M. (2006) Sexual problems: Introduction, description and classification. *Psychiatry*, **6**(3), 87–104.

Crowe, R. R. (1974). An adoption study of antisocial personality. *Archives of General Psychiatry*, **31**, 785–91.

Crowther, K., Richman, J., and Rochford, S. (2001) Issues of palliative care in HMP Manchester. Paper presented at the Forensic Research Group Conference, 'Forensic Psychology in Prisons: Current Developments'. 10 Nov., Manchester Metropolitan University. *Proceedings of the British Psychological Society*, **10**(2), 50.

Crowther, K., Richman, J., and Rochford, S. (2003) A critical comment on the whole prison approach to health promotion. Paper presented at the Forensic Research Group Conference, 'Forensic Health Psychology'. 10 Nov., Manchester Metropolitan University. *Proceedings of the British Psychological Society*, **12**(2), 138.

Cunradi, C. B. (2007) Drinking level, neighbourhood social disorder, and mutual intimate partner violence. *Alcoholism: Clinical and Experimental Research*, **6**, 1012–19.

Curran, H. V., and Morgan, C. (2000) Cognitive, dissociative and psychotogenic effects of ketamine in recreational users on the night of drug use and 3 days later. *Addiction*, **95**(4), 575–90.

Currie, S. R., Patten, S. B., Williams, J. V. A., Wang Jian Li, Beck, C. A., El-Guebaly, N., and Maxwell, C. (2005) Comorbidity of major depression with substance use disorders. *Canadian Journal of Psychiatry*, **50**, 660–6.

Cutting, J. (1985) *The psychology of schizophrenia*. Edinburgh: Churchill-Livingstone.

d'Adda di Fagagna, F. (2008) Cellular senescence and cellular longevity: Nearly 50 years on and still working on it. *Experimental Cell Research*, **314**, 1907–8.

Dahl, A. A., Ravindran, A., Allgulander, C., Kutcher, S. P., Austin, C., and Burt, T. (2005) Sertraline in generalized anxiety disorder: Efficacy in treating the psychic and somatic anxiety factors. *Acta Psychiatrica Scandinavica*, **111**(6), 429–35.

Daigle, M., Daniel, A., Dear, G., Frottier, P., Hayes, L., Kerkhof, A., Konrad, N., Liebling, A., and Sarchiapone, M. (2007) Preventing suicide in prisons, Part II: International comparisons of suicide prevention services in correctional facilities. *Journal of Crisis Intervention and Suicide Prevention*, **28**(3), 122–30.

Daily Mail (2008) Homeopathy treatments flounder as NHS trusts cancel contracts, 30 Jan.

Dalgaard, O., and Kringlen, E. (1976) A Norwegian twin study of criminality. *British Journal of Criminology*, **16**, 213–33.

Daly, M., and Wilson, M. (1988) *Homicide*. New York: Aldine De Gruyter.

Daly, M., and Wilson, M. (1989) Evolutionary theory and family violence. In C. Crawford, M. Smith and D. Krebs (eds), *Sociobiology and psychology*. London: Lawrence Erlbaum.

Damasio, H., Gabrowski, T., Frank, R., Galaburda, A., and Damasio, A. (1994) The return of Phineas Gage: Clues about the brain from the skull of a famous patient. *Science*, **264**, 1102–5.

Darjee, R., and Crichton, J. (2004) New mental health legislation (Editorial). *British Medical Journal*, **329**, 634–5.

Darke, S., Kaye, S., and Duflou, J. (2006) Comparative cardiac pathology among deaths due to cocaine toxicity, opioid toxicity and non-drug-related causes. *Addiction*, **101**, 1771–7.

Darke, S., Ross, J., Williamson, A., Mills, L., Havard, A., and Teeson, M. (2007) Borderline personality disorder and persistently elevated levels of risk in 36-month outcomes for the treatment of heroin dependence. *Addiction*, **102**, 1140–6.

Darwin, C. (1859) *On the origin of the species by means of natural selection*. London: John Murray.

Darwin, C. (1871) *The descent of man and selection in relation to sex*. London: John Murray.

Darwin, C. (1872) *The expression of emotion in man and animals*. London: John Murray.

David, A. S., Zammit, S., Lewis, G., Dalman, C., and Allebeck, P. (2008) Impairments in cognition across the spectrum of psychiatric disorders: Evidence from a Swedish conscript cohort. *Schizophrenia Bulletin*, **34**(6), 1035–41.

Davidson, J. (2005) Contesting stigma and contested emotions: Personal experience and public perception of specific phobias. *Social Science and Medicine*, **61**, 2155–64.

Davidson, K. (2006) Historical aspects of mood disorders. *Psychiatry*, **5**(4), 115–18.

Davies, G. M., and Dalgleish, T. (2001) *Recovered memories: Seeking the middle ground*. Chichester: Wiley.

Davies, G., Hollin, C., and Bull, R. (2008) *Forensic psychology*. Chichester: Wiley.

Davis, C., and Claridge, G. (1998) The eating disorders as addiction: A psychobiological perspective. *Addictive Behaviours*, **23**(4), 463–75.

Davis, C., Katzman, D. K., and Kirsh, M. A. (1999) Compulsive physical activity in adolescents with anorexia nervosa: A psychobehavioural spiral of pathology. *Journal of Nervous and Mental Diseases*, **187**(6), 336–42.

Davis, S. R., Guay, A., Shifren, J. L., and Mazer, N. A. (2004) Endocrine aspects of female sexual dysfunction. *Journal of Sexual Medicine*, **1**(1), 82–6.

Davis, W. (1980) *Magic and exorcism in modern Japan*. California: Stanford University Press.

Davison, G., Neale, J., and Kring, A. (2004) *Abnormal psychology* (9th edn). London: Wiley.

Dawkins, R. (1986) *The blind watchmaker*. London: Penguin.

Dawkins, R. (1989) *The selfish gene* (2nd edn). Oxford: Oxford University Press.

Dawkins, R. (1998) *Unweaving the rainbow*. London: Penguin.

Dawkins, R. (2006) *The God delusion*. London: Bantam.

Day, M., and Norman, L. R. (2007) An exploration of gender differences in the initiation of and attitudes toward crack cocaine use in the English-speaking Caribbean. *Addiction Research and Theory*, **15**(3), 285–97.

Deakin, J. F. W., Lees, J., McKie, S., Hallack, J. E. C., Williams, S. R., and Dursan, S. M. (2008) Glutamate and the neural basis of the subjective effects of ketamine. *Archives of General Psychiatry*, **65**(2), 154–64.

Dean, M. (2000) News: Tabloid campaign forces UK to reconsider sex-offence laws. *The Lancet*, **365**, 745.

Deary, I., and Mathews, G. (1993) Personality traits are alive and well. *The Psychologist*, July, 299–311.

Deaver, C. M., Miltenberger, R. G., Smyth, J., Meidinger, A., and Crosby, R. (2003) An evaluation of affect and binge eating. *Behaviour Modification*, **27**(4), 578–99.

De Fries, U., and Petermann, F. (2008) Asthma management: What impact does knowing about asthma have on the ability of patients to self-manage the disease? *Deutsche Med. Wochenschr.*, **133**(4), 139–43.

Degenhardt, L., and Hall, W. (2001) The association between psychosis and problematic drug use among Australian adults: Findings from the National Survey of Mental Health and Well-Being. *Psychological Medicine*, **31**, 659–68.

Degrandpre, R. (2006) The cult of pharmacology: How America became the world's most troubled drug culture. Durham, NC: Duke University Press.

Dein, K., Williams, P. S., and Dein, S. (2007) Ethnic bias in the application of the Mental Health Act 1983. *Advances in Psychiatric Treatment*, **13**, 350–7.

Dein, S., and Littlewood, R. (2007) The voice of God. *Anthropology and Medicine*, **14**(2), 213–28.

Delahunty, A., Reeder, C., Wykes, T., Morice, R., and Newton, E. (2002) *Revised Cognitive Remediation Therapy Manual*. London: Institute of Psychiatry.

Del-Ben, C. M., Vilela, J. A. A., Hetem, L. A. B., Guimaraes, F. S., Graeff, F. G., and Zuardi, A. W. (2001) Do panic patients process unconditioned fear vs unconditioned anxiety differently from normal subjects? *Psychiatry Research*, **104**(3), 227–37.

DeLisi, L. E., and Hoff, A. L. (2005) Failure to find progressive temporal lobe volume decreases 10 years subsequent to a first episode of schizophrenia. *Psychiatry Research (Neuroimaging)*, **138**, 265–8.

Dell'Osso, B., Altamura, A. C., Allen, A., Marazziti, D., and Hollander, E. (2006) Epidemiologic and clinical updates on impulse control disorders: A critical review. *European Archives of Psychiatry Clinical Neuroscience*, **256**, 464–75.

Demaerschalk, B. M., and Wingerchuk, D. (2007) Treatment of vascular dementia and vascular cognitive impairment. *The Neurologist*, **13**(1), 37–41.

De Magalhaes, J. P., and Toussaint, O. (2004) Telomeres and telomerase: A modern fountain of youth. *Rejuvination Research*, **7**(2), 126–33.

Department of Health (1998) *A first class service: Quality in the new NHS*. London: Department of Health.

Department of Health (2000) *Reforming the Mental Health Act 1983*. London: HMSO.

Department of Health (2001) *Treatment choice in psychological therapies and counselling*. London: HMSO.

Department of Health (2006) *Plans to amend the Mental Health Act 1983*. London: HMSO.

Department of Health and Social Security (1977) *The role of psychologists in the Health Service*. London: HMSO.

DePaulo, B. M., Lindsay, J. L., Malone, B. E., Muhlenbruck, L., Charlton, K., and Cooper, H. (2003) Cues to deception. *Psychological Bulletin*, **129**, 74–118.

DeRosse, P., Funke, B., Burdick, K. E., Lencz, T., Ekholm, J. M., Kane, J. M., Kucherlapati, R., and Malhotra, A. K. (2006) Dysbindin genotype and negative symptoms of schizophrenia. *American Journal of Psychiatry*, **163**, 532–4.

Desai, S., Aldea, D., Daneels, E., Soliman, M., Braksmajey, A. S., and Kopes-Kerr, C. P. (2006) Chronic addiction to dextromethorphan cough syrup: A case report. *Journal of Amerian Board of Family Medicine*, **19**, 320–3.

De Silva, P. (2006) Paraphilias. *Psychiatry*, **6**(3), 130–4.

De Silva, P., and Rachman, S. (2004) *Obsessive–compulsive disorder: The facts* (3rd edn). Oxford: Oxford University Press.

Devanand, D., Liu, X., Tabert, M., Pradhaban, G., Cuasay, K., Bell, K., de Leon, M., Doty, R., Stern, Y., and Pelton, G. (2008) Combining early markers strongly predicts conversion from mild cognitive impairment to Alzheimer's disease. *Biological Psychiatry*, **64**(10), 871–9.

Devereux, E. (2003) *Understanding the media*. London: Sage.

Dhabhar, F. S., and McEwen, B. S. (1999) Enhancing versus suppressive effects of stress hormones on skin immune function. *Proceedings of the National Academy of Sciences*, **96**(3), 1059–64.

Dhawan, S. S., and Wang, B. W. E. (2007) Four-extremity gangrene associated with crack cocaine abuse. *Annals of Emergency Medicine*, **49**(2), 186–9.

Dick, D. M., Nurnberger, J., Edenberg, H. J., Goate, A., Crowe, R., Rice, J., Bucholz, K. K., Kramer, J., Schuckit, M. A., Smith, T. L., Porjesz, B., Begleiter, H., Hesselbrock, V., and Foroud, T. (2002) Suggestive linkage on chromosome 1 for a quantitative alcohol-related phenotype. *Alcoholism: Clinical and Experimental Research*, **26**(10), 1453–60.

Dickens, B. M., and Cook, R. J. (2000) Law and ethics in conflict over confidentiality? *International Journal of Gynaecology and Obstetrics*, **70**(3), 385–91.

Dickey, C. C., McCarley, R. W., and Shenton, M. E. (2002) The brain in schizotypal personality disorder: a review of structural MRI and CT findings. *Harvard Review of Psychiatry*, **10**, 1–15.

Dickey, C. C., McCarley, R. W., Volgmaier, M. M., Niznikkiewicz, M. A., Seidman, L. J., Hirayasu, Y., Fischer, I., Teh, E. K., Van Rhoads, R., Jakab, M., Kikinis, R., Jolesz, F. A., and Shenton, M. E. (1999) Schizotypal personality disorder and MRI abnormalities of temporal lobe gray matter. *Biological Psychiatry*, **45**, 1393–1402.

Dickinson, A., and Boakes, R. A. (1979) *Mechanisms of learning and motivation*. Hillsdale, NJ: Lawrence Erlbaum.

Dickinson, A., and Dearing, M. F. (1979) Appetitive-aversive interactions and inhibitory processes. In A. Dickinson and R. A. Boakes (eds), *Mechanism of Learning and Motivation*, Hillsdale, NJ: Lawrence Erlbaum.

Dies, R. (1969) Electroconvulsive therapy: A social learning therapy interpretation. *Journal of Nervous and Mental Diseases*, **149**, 334.

Dietz, P. E., Mathews, D. B., Martell, D. A., Stewart, T. M., Hrouda, D. R., and Warren, J. (1991) Threatening and otherwise inappropriate letters to members of the United States Congress. *Journal of Forensic Sciences*, **36**, 1445–68.

Digby, A. (1985) *Madness, morality and medicine: A study of the York Retreat 1796–1914*. Cambridge: Cambridge University Press.

Dilks, S., and Shattock, L. (1996) Does community residence mean more community contact for people with severe, long-term psychiatric disabilities? *British Journal of Clinical Psychology*, **35**, 183–92.

DiMatteo, M. R., and Martin, L. R. (2002) *Health psychology*. London: Allyn and Bacon.

Dimsdale, J., and Dantzer, R. (2007) A biological substrate for somatoform disorders: Importance of pathophysiology. *Psychosomatic Medicine*, **69**, 850–4.

Dinglemans, A. E., Bruna, M. J., and van Furth, E. F. (2002) Binge eating disorder: A review. *International Journal of Obesity*, **26**, 299–307.

Dinis-Oliveira, R. J., Remião, F., Carmo, H., Duarte, A., Sánchez Navarro, A., Bastosa, M. L., and Carvalho, F. (2006) Paraquat exposure as an etiological factor of Parkinson's disease. *Neurotoxicology*, **27**(6), 1110–22.

Dintzer, L., and Wortman, C. B. (1978) Is an attributional analysis of the learned helplessness phenomenon viable? A critique of the Abramson-Seligman-Teasdale reformulation. *Journal of Abnormal Psychology*, **87**(1), 75–90.

Dion, K. (1972) Physical attractiveness and evaluations of children's transgressions. *Journal of Personality and Social Psychology*, **24**, 207–13.

Dion, K., Berscheid, E., and Walster, E. (1972) What is beautiful is good. *Journal of Personality and Social Psychology*, **24**, 285–90.

Distel, M. A., Trull, T. J., Derom, C. A., Thiery, E. W., Grimmer, M. A., and Martin, N. G. (2007) Heritability of borderline personality disorder feature is similar across three countries. *Psychological Medicine*, doi: 10.1017/S0033291707002024, published online by Cambridge University Press, 8 Nov.

Dittmar, H. (2005) Compulsive buying – a growing concern? An examination of gender, age, and endorsement of materialistic values as predictors. *British Journal of Psychology*, **96**, 467–91.

Division of Clinical Psychology (1995) *Professional practice guidelines*. Leicester: British Psychological Society.

Division of Criminological and Legal Psychology (1997) *Ethical guidelines on forensic psychology*. Leicester: British Psychological Society.

Dixon, A. (2003) 'At all costs let us avoid any risk of allowing our hearts to be broken again': A review of John Bowlby's forty-four juvenile thieves. *Clinical Child Psychiatry and Psychology*, **8**(2), 278–89.

Dobson, K. S., Hollon, S. D., Dimidjian, S., Schmaling, K. B., Kohlenberg, R. J., Gallop, R. J., Rizvi, S. L., Gollan, J. K., Dunner, D. L., and Jacobson, N. S. (2008) Randomized trial of behavioral activation, cognitive therapy, and antidepressant medication in the prevention of relapse and recurrence in major depression. *Journal of Consulting and Clinical Psychology*, **76**(3), 468–77.

Dodge, K. A., and Petit, G. S. (2003) A biopsychosocial model of the development of chronic conduct problems in adolescence. *Developmental Psychology*, **39**, 349–71.

Dodworth, T. R. (1971) The effect of electroconvulsive shock on 'helplessness' in dogs. Unpublished doctoral dissertation, University of Minnesota.

Dolan, M. C., and Doyle, M. (2000) Violence prediction: Clinical and actuarial measures and the role of the psychopathy checklist. *British Journal of Psychiatry*, **177**, 303–11.

Dolan M. C., and Park, I. (2002) The neuropsychology of antisocial personality disorder. *Psychological Medicine*, **32**(3), 417–27.

Dolan, M. C., Anderson, I. M., and Deakin J. F. W. (2001) Relationship between 5-HT function and impulsivity and aggression in male offenders with personality disorders. *British Journal of Psychiatry*, **178**, 352–9.

Dolan, M. C., Deakin, J. F. W., Roberts, N., and Anderson, I. M. (2002) Quantitative frontal and temporal structural MRI studies in personality-disordered offenders and control subjects. *Psychiatry Research: Neuroimaging*, **116**, 133–49.

Dollard, J., and Miller, N. (1950). *Personality and psychotherapy*. New York: McGraw-Hill.

Dougherty, D., Baer, L., Cosgrove, G., Price, B. H., Nierenberg, A. A., Jenike, M. A., and Rauch, S. L. (2002) Prospective long-term follow-up of 44 patients who received cingulotomy for treatment-refractory obsessive–compulsive disorder. *American Journal of Psychiatry*, **159**, 269–75.

Douglas, J., and Olshaker, M. (1995) *Mindhunter: Inside the FBI Elite Serial Crime Unit*. New York: Scribner.

Downes, D., and Rock, P. (1998) *Understanding deviance: A guide to the sociology of crime and rule breaking* (3rd edn). Oxford: Oxford University Press.

Dratcu, L., Grandison, A., McKay, G., Bamidele, A., and Vasudevan, V. (2007) Clozapine-resistant psychosis, smoking and caffeine: Managing the neglected effects of substances that our patients consume every day. *American Journal of Therapeutics*, **14**(3), 314–18.

D'Souza, R., and George, K. (2006) Spirituality, religion and psychiatry: Its application to clinical practice. *Australasian Psychiatry*, **14**(4), 408–12.

D'Souza, D. C., Perry, E., MacDougall, L., Ammerman, Y., Cooper, T., Wu, Y., Braley, G., Gueorguieva, R., and Krystal, J. H. (2004) The psychotomimetic effects of intravenous delta 9 tetrahydrocannabinol in healthy individuals: implications for psychosis. *Neuropsychopharmacology*, **29**, 1558–72.

Dudeck, M., Spitzer, C., Stopsack, M., Freyberger, H., and Barnow, S. (2007) Forensic inpatient male sexual offenders: The impact of personality disorder and childhood sexual abuse. *Journal of Forensic Psychiatry and Psychology*, **18**(4), 494–506.

Duncan, I. D., Goldman, S., Macklin, W., Rao, M., Weiner, L. P., and Reingold, S. (2008) Stem cell therapy in multiple sclerosis: promise and controversy. *Multiple Sclerosis*, **14**(4), 541–6.

Dunning, D., and Perretta, S. (2002) Automaticity and eyewitness accuracy: A 10–12 second rule for distinguishing accurate from inaccurate positive identifications. *Journal of Applied Psychology*, **87**, 951–62.

Durand, M. A., Lelliott, P., and Coyle, N. (2006) Availability of treatment for substance misuse in medium secure psychiatric care in England: A national survey. *Journal of Forensic Psychiatry and Psychology*, **17**(1), 611–25.

Durham, R. C., Guthrie, M., Morton, R. V., Reid, D. A., Treliving, L. R., and Fowler, D. (2003) Tayside-Fife clinical trial of cognitive behavioural therapy for medication resistant psychotic patients: Results from a 3-month follow-up. *British Journal of Psychiatry*, **182**, 303–11.

Durst, R., Katz, G., Teitelbaum, A., Zislin, J., and Dannon, P. N. (2001) Kleptomania: Diagnosis and treatment options. *CNS Drugs*, **15**(3), 185–95.

Durston, S. (2003) A review of the biological bases of ADHD: What have we learned from imaging studies? *Mental Retardation and Developmental Disabilities Research Reviews*, **9**(3), 184–95.

Dutton, D. G., and Kerry, G. (1999) Modus operandi and personality disorder in spousal killers. *International Journal of Law and Psychiatry*, **22**, 287–99.

Earll, L., and Licamele, W. L. (1995) Prediction of antisocial behaviour in ADHD. *Journal of the American Academy of Child and Adolescent Psychiatry*, **34**(4), 397.

Easton, S., and Piper, C. (2005) *Sentencing and punishment*. Oxford: Oxford University Press.

Eaton, W., and Kessler, L. (1985) The NIMH epidemiological catchment area study. *Epidemiological Field Methods in Psychiatry*. New York: Academic Press.

Ebbinghaus, H. (1897) *Grundzüge der Psychologie*. Leipzig: Veit.

Eccleston, L., and Sorbello, L. (2002) The RUSH program – real understanding of self-help: a suicide and self-harm prevention initiative within a prison setting. *Australian Psychologist*, **37**(3), 237–44.

Eckblad, M., and Chapman, L. J. (1986) Development and validation of a scale for hypomanic personality. *Journal of Abnormal Psychology*, **95**(3), 214–22.

Eddy, K. T., Dutra, L., Bradley, R., and Western, D. (2004) A multidimensional meta-analysis of psychotherapy for obsessive–compulsive disorder. *Clinical Psychology Review*, **24**, 1011–30.

Edemariam, A., and Scott, K. (2009) Choose life? Why would I do a thing like that? *Guardian*, Saturday, 15 Aug., 22–3.

Editorial (1997) From what we will die in 2020. *The Lancet*, **349**(9061), 1263.

Edwards, G., Strang, J., and Jaffe, J. (1993) *Drugs, alcohol and tobacco: Making the science and policy connections*. Oxford: Oxford University Press.

Edwards, H. (2003) Münchausen syndrome by proxy: The degree of credibility in the professionals involved. Unpublished thesis, Manchester Metropolitan University.

Edwards, P. (2002) Under new legislation. Paper presented at the Forensic Research Group Conference, *New Laws for Forensic Psychology*, 9 Nov., Manchester Metropolitan University.

Efron, D. (1941) *Gesture and environment*. New York: King's Crown.

Egan, M. F., Goldberg, T. E., Kolachana, B. S., Callicott, J. H., Mazzanti, C. M., Straube, R. E., Goldman, D., and Weinberger, D. R. (2001) Effect of COMT Val108/158Met genotype on frontal lobe function and risk for schizophrenia. *Proceedings of the National Academy of Sciences USA*, **98**, 6917–22.

Ehlers, A., and Clark, D. M. (2000) A cognitive model of posttraumatic stress disorder. *Behaviour Research and Therapy*, **38**, 319–45.

Eich, E., Macauley, D., and Ryan, L. (1994) Mood dependent memory for events of a personal past. *Journal of Experimental Psychology: General*, **123**, 201–15.

Eisen, S., Lin, N., Lyons, M. J., Scherrer, J., True, W., Goldberg, J., and Tsuang, M. T. (1998) Familial influences on gambling behaviour: An analysis of 3359 twin pairs. *Addiction*, **93**(9), 1375–84.

Ekman, P. (1992) *Telling lies: Clues to deceit in the marketplace, politics and marriage*. New York: W. W. Norton.

Ekman, P. (1997) *What the face reveals: Basic and applied studies of spontaneous expression using the facial action coding system*. New York: Oxford University Press.

Eley, T. C., Lichtenstein, F., and Moffitt, T. E. (2003) A longitudinal genetic behavioural analysis of the aetiology of aggressive and nonaggressive antisocial behaviour. *Development and Psychopathology*, **15**, 383–402.

Elliott, C., and Quinn, F. (2000) *Criminal law* (3rd edn). Harlow: Pearson.

Ellis, A. (1962) *Reason and emotion in psychotherapy*. New York: Lyle Stuart.

Eminson, D. M., and Jureidini, J. (2003) Concerns about the research and prevention strategies in Munchausen syndrome by proxy (MSBP) abuse. *Child Abuse and Neglect*, **27**, 413–20.

Eminson, D. M., and Postlethwaite, R. J. (1992) Factitious illness: Recognition and management. *Archives of Disease in Childhood*, **67**, 1510–16.

Emmelkamp, P. M. (2003) Behaviour therapy with adults. In Lambert, M. (ed.), *Handbook of psychotherapy and behaviour change* (5th edn). New York: Wiley.

Emmelkamp, P. M., and Kamphuis, J. H. (2007) *Personality disorders*. Hove: Psychology Press.

Emmelkamp, P. M., Krijn, M., Hulsbosch, A., de Vries, S., Schuemie, M. J., and van der Mast, C. A. (2002) Virtual reality treatment versus exposure in vivo: A comparative evaluation in acrophobia. *Behaviour Research and Therapy*, **40**(5), 509–16.

Engels, G. I., Duijsens, I. J., Haringsma, R., and van Putten, C. M. (2003) Personality disorders in the elderly compared with four younger age groups: A cross-sectional study of community residents and mental health patients. *Journal of Personality Disorders*, **17**, 447–59.

Epperley, T. (1993) Drugs and sport. In W. Lillegard and K. S. Rucker (eds), *Handbook of sports medicine*. Stoneham, MA: Andover.

Eskapa, R. (1989) *Bizarre sex*. London: Grafton.

Espiard, M., Lecardeur, L., Abadie, P., Halbecq, I., and Dolifus, S. (2005) Hallucinogen persisting perception disorder after psilocybin consumption: A case study. *European Psychiatry*, **5–6**, 458–60.

Ettelt, S., Ruhrmann, S., Barnow, S., Buthz, F., Hochrein, A., Meyer, K., Kraft, S., Reck, C., Pukrop, R., Klosterkötter, J., Falkai, P., Maier, M., Wagner, M., Freyberger, H. J., and Grabe, H. J. (2007) Impulsiveness in obsessive–compulsive disorder: Results from a family study. *Acta Psychiatrica Scandinavica*, **115**, 41–7.

European Monitoring Centre for Drugs and Drug Addiction (2003) *The state of the drug problem in the European Union and Norway*. Luxembourg: EMCDDA.

Evans, J., and Henson, C. (1999) Incident management. In G. J. Towl and C. McDougall (eds), *What do forensic psychologists do? Current and future directions in the prison and probation services* (Issues in Forensic Psychology, No. 1), Leicester: British Psychological Society.

Evett, I., and Weir, B. (1998) *Interpreting DNA evidence*. Sunderland, MA: Sinauer.

Ewart, C. K., Jorgenson, R. S., Suchday, S., Chen, E., and Mathews, K. A. (2002) Measuring stress, resilience and coping in vulnerable youth: The social competence interview. *Psychological Assessment*, **14**(3), 339–52.

Exner, J. E., and Erdberg, P. (2005) The rorschach: A comprehensive system, Vol. 2: Advanced interpretation (3rd edn). France: Lavoisier.

Eysenck, H. J. (1952) The effects of psychotherapy: An evaluation. *Journal of Consulting and Clinical Psychology*, **16**, 319–24.

Eysenck, H. J. (1960) *Behaviour therapy and the neuroses*. Oxford: Pergamon.

Eysenck, H. J. (1964) *Crime and personality*. London: Routledge and Kegan Paul.

Eysenck, H. J. (1970) *The structure of human personality*. London: Methuen.

Eysenck, H. J. (1985) *Decline and fall of the Freudian empire*. Harmondsworth: Penguin.

Eysenck, H. J. (1990) Biological dimensions of personality. In L. Pervin (ed.), *Handbook of personality: Theory and research*. London: Guilford.

Eysenck, H. J., and Eysenck, S. B. G. (1964) *Manual of the Eysenck Personality Inventory*. London: Routledge and Kegan Paul.

Eysenck, H. J., and Eysenck, S. B. G. (1968) A factorial study of psychoticism. *Multivariate Behavioural Research* (special edn), 15–31.

Eysenck, H. J., and Eysenck, S. B. G. (1975) *Manual of the Eysenck Personality Questionnaire*. London: Hodder and Stoughton.

Eysenck, H. J., and Gudjonsson, G. (1989) *The causes and cures of criminality*. New York: Plenum.

Eysenck, H. J., Arnold, W. J., and Meili, R. (1975) *Encyclopaedia of Psychology, Vol 2: L–Z*, Suffolk: Fontana.

Faber, R. J., Christenson, A., de Zwaan, M., and Mitchell, J. (1995) Two forms of compulsive consumption: Comorbidity of compulsive buying and binge eating. *Journal of Consumer Research*, 22(3), 296–304.

Faber, R. J., and O'Guinn, T. C. (1992) A clinical screener for compulsive buying. *Journal of Consumer Research*, 19, 459–69.

Fahy, T. A. (1988) The diagnosis of multiple personality disorder: A critical review. *British Journal of Psychiatry*, 153, 597–606.

Fahy, T. A. (1989) Lycanthropy: A review. *Journal of the Royal Society of Medicine*, 82, 37–9.

Fairburn, C. G. (1997) Eating disorders. In D. M. Clark and C. G. Fairburn (eds), *Science and practice of cognitive behavioural therapy*. Oxford: Oxford University Press.

Fairburn, C. G., and Brownell, K. D. (2001) *Eating disorders and obesity: A comprehensive handbook* (2nd edn). Hove: Guilford Press.

Fairburn, C. G., and Harrison, P. J. (2003) Eating disorders. *The Lancet*, 361, 407–16.

Fairburn, C. G., Doll, H. E., Welch, S. L., Hay, P. J., Davies, B. A., and O'Connor, M. E. (1998) Risk factors in binge eating disorder. *Archives of General Psychiatry*, 55, 425–32.

Fairburn, C. G., Shafran, R., and Cooper, Z. (1999) A cognitive behavioural theory of anorexia nervosa. *Behaviour Research and Therapy*, 37, 1–13.

Fairburn, C. G., Welch, S. L., Norman, P. A., O'Connor, M., and Doll, H. E. (1996) Bias and bulimia nervosa: How typical are clinical cases? *American Journal of Psychiatry*, 153, 386–91.

Fallon, B. A. (2004) Pharmacotherapy of somatoform disorders. *Journal of Psychosomatic Research*, 56(4), 455–60.

Falloon, I., Boyd, J., McGill, C., Williamson, M., Razani, J., Moss, H., Gilderman, A., and Simpson, G. (1985) Family management in the prevention of morbidity of schizophrenia. *Archives of General Psychiatry*, 42, 887–96.

Fals-Stewart, W., Schafer, J., Lucente, S., Rustine, T., et al. (1994) Neurobehavioural consequences of prolonged alcohol and substance abuse: A review of findings and treatment implications. *Clinical Psychology Review*, 14, 755–78.

Faraone, S., and Biederman, J. (1994) Is attention deficit hyperactivity disorder familial? *Harvard Review of Psychiatry*, 1, 271–87.

Faraone, S., Biederman, J., Jetton, J., and Tsuang, M. (1997) Attention deficit disorder and conduct disorder: Longitudinal evidence for a familial subtype. *Psychological Medicine*, 27, 291–300.

Faraone, S., Tsuang, M., and Tsuang, D. (1999) *Genetics of mental disorders*. London: Guilford Press.

Farber, S. (1990) Institutional mental health and social control: The ravages of epistemological hubris. *Journal of Mind and Behaviour*, 11, 285–300.

Farde, L., Weisel, F. A., Hall, H., Halldin, C., Stone-Elander, S., and Sedvall, G. (1987) No D2 receptor increase in PET study of schizophrenia. *Archives of General Psychiatry*, 44, 671–2.

Farrington, D. P. (1982) Longitudinal analysis of criminal violence. In M. Wolfgang and N. Weiner (eds) *Criminal violence*. Beverly Hills, CA: Sage.

Farrington, D. P. (1997) The relationship between low resting heart rate and violence. In A. Raine, P. Brennan, D. P. Farrington and S. A. Mednick (eds), *Biosocial bases of violence*. New York: Plenum.

Farrington, D. P. (2005) Family background and psychopathy. In C. J. Patrick (ed.), *Handbook of psychopathy*. New York: Guilford Press.

Farwell, L. A., and Smith, S. S. (2001) Using brain MERMER testing to detect concealed knowledge despite efforts to conceal. *Journal of Forensic Sciences*, 46(1), 1–9.

Faunce, G. J. (2002) Eating disorders and attentional bias: A review. *Eating Disorders*, 10, 125–39.

Fava, G. A., and Ruini, C. (2005) What is the optimal treatment of mood and anxiety disorders? *Clinical Psychology: Science and Practice*, 12(1), 92–6.

Favazza, R. A. (2004) *Psycho bible: Behaviour, religion and the Holy Book*. Charlottesville, VA: Pitchstone.

Fazel, M., Langstrom, N., Grann, M., and Fazel, S. (2008) Psychopathology in adolescent and young criminal offenders (15–21 years) in Sweden. *Social Psychiatry and Psychiatric Epidemiology*, 43, 319–24.

Fedoroff, J. P., Kuban, M., and Bradford, J. M. (2009) Laboratory measurement of penile response in the assessment of sexual interest. In F. M. Saleh and A. J. Grudzinskas (eds), *Sex offenders: Identification, risk assessment, treatment, and legal issues*. Oxford: Oxford University Press.

Feingold, B. (1973) *Introduction to clinical allergy*. Springfield, IL: Charles C. Thomas.

Feinstein, A. (1967) *Clinical judgement*. Baltimore: Williams and Wilkins.

Feldman, M. D. (1997) Canine variant of factitious disorder by proxy. *American Journal of Psychiatry*, **154**(9), 1316–17.

Feldman, M. D., and Eisendrath, S. J. (1996) *The spectrum of factitious disorders: Clinical practice series*. New York: American Psychiatric Press.

Feldman, M. P. (1977) *Criminal behaviour: A psychological analysis*. Chichester: Wiley.

Fendrich, M., Mackesy-Amiti, M. E., Wislar, J. S., and Goldstein, P. J. (1997) Childhood abuse and the use of inhalants: Differences by degree of use. *American Journal of Public Health*, **87**(5), 765–9.

Fenigstein, A., and Vanable, P. (1992) Paranoia and self-consciousness. *Journal of Personality and Social Psychology*, **62**, 129–38.

Fenton, W. S., Blyler, C. R., and Heinnsen, R. K. (1997) Determinants of medication compliance in schizophrenia: Empirical and clinical findings. *Schizophrenia Bulletin*, **23**(4), 637–51.

Fergusson, D., Horwood, J., Boden, J., and Jenkin, G. (2007) Childhood social disadvantage and smoking in adulthood: Results of a 25-year longitudinal study. *Addiction*, **102**, 475–82.

Fergusson, D. M., Horwood, L. J., and Swain-Campbell, N. R. (2003) Cannabis dependence and psychotic symptoms in young people. *Psychological Medicine*, **33**, 15–21.

Fernandez-Aranda, F., Jimenez-Murcia, S., Alverez-Moyo, E. M., Granero, R., Vallejo, J., and Bulik, C. M. (2006) Impulse control disorders in eating disorders: Clinical and therapeutic implications. *Comprehensive Psychiatry*, **47**, 428–88.

Ferracuti, S., Sacco, R., and Lazzari, R. (1996) Dissociative trance disorder: Clinical and Rorschach findings in ten persons reporting demon possession and treated by exorcism. *Journal of Personality Assessment*, **66**, 525–39.

Ferrari, N. A. (1962) Institutionalisation and attitude change in an aged population: A field study and dissidence theory. Unpublished doctoral dissertation, Western Reserve University.

Ferster, C. (1961) Positive reinforcement and behavioural deficits of autistic children. *Child Development*, **32**, 437–56.

Ferster, C., and Skinner, B. F. (1957) *Schedules of reinforcement*. Englewood Cliffs, NJ: Prentice Hall.

Festinger, L. (1954) A theory of social comparison processes. *Human Relations*, **7**, 117–40.

Feygin, D. L., Swain, J., and Leckman, J. F. (2006) The normalcy of neurosis: Evolutionary origins of obsessive–compulsive disorder and related behaviours. *Progress in Neuro-psychopharmacology and Biological Psychiatry*, **30**, 854–64.

Field, A. (2003) *Clinical psychology*. Exeter: Crucial Division of Learning Matters Ltd.

Finch, E. (2003) What a tangled web we weave: Identity theft and the internet. In Y. Jewkes (ed.), *Dot.cons: Crime, deviance and identity on the internet*. London: Willan.

Finch, E., and Fafinski, S. (2007) *Identity theft*. London: Willan.

Findley, L. J. (2007) The economic impact of Parkinson's disease. *Parkinsonism Related Disorders*, **13**, S8–S12.

First, M. B. (2005) Desire for amputation of a limb: Paraphilia, psychosis or a new type of identity disorder. *Psychological Medicine*, **35**, 919–28.

Fischer, M. (1971) Psychoses in the offspring of schizophrenic monozygotic twins and their normal co-twins. *British Journal of Psychiatry*, **118**, 542–3.

Fisher, M., Brennan, K. H., and McCauley, M. R. (2002) The cognitive interview method to enhance eyewitness recall. In M. Eisen, J. A. Quas and G. S. Goodman (eds), *Memory and suggestibility in the forensic interview*. Mahwah, NJ: Lawrence Erlbaum.

Fisher, P. L., and Durham, R. C. (2004) Psychopathology of generalized anxiety disorder. *Psychiatry*, **3**(4), 26–30.

Fisher, R. P., and Geiselman, R. W. (1992) *Memory enhancing techniques for investigative interviewing: The cognitive interview*. Springfield, IL: Charles C. Thomas.

Fisher, R. P., Geiselman, R. W., Raymond, D. S., Jurkevitch, L. M., and Wahrhaftig, M. L. (1987) Enhancing enhanced eyewitness memory: Refining the cognitive interview. *Journal of Police Science and Administration*, **15**, 291–7.

Fishman, D. (1999) *The case for pragmatic psychology*. New York: New York University Press.

Fiszdon, J. M., Bryson, G. J., Wexler, B. E., and Bell, M. D. (2004) Durability of cognitive remediation training in schizophrenia: Performance on two memory tasks at 6-month and 12-month follow-up. *Psychiatry Research*, **125**, 1–7.

Fitzgerald, M., Bellgrove, M., and Gill, M. (2007) *Handbook of attention deficit hyperactivity disorder.* London: Wiley.

Flannelly, K. J., Koenig, H. G., Ellison, C. G., Galek, K., and Krause, N. (2006) Belief in life after death and mental health: Findings from a national survey. *Journal of Nervous and Mental Diseases,* **194**(7), 524–9.

Foa, E. B., and Rothbaum, B. O. (1998) *Treating the trauma of rape: Cognitive-behavioural therapy for PTSD.* New York: Guilford Press.

Foa, E. B., Franklin, M., Perry, K., and Herbert, J. (1996) Cognitive biases in generalised social phobia. *Journal of Abnormal Psychology,* **105**, 433–9.

Fodor, J. (1983a) *The modularity of the mind.* Cambridge, MA: MIT Press.

Fodor, J. (1983b) *The trouble with science.* Cambridge, MA: MIT Press.

Fogelson, D., Neuchterlein, K., Asarnow, D., Payne, K., Subotnik, K., Jacobson, K., Neale, M., and Kendler, K. (2007) Avoidant personality disorder is a separable schizophrenia-spectrum personality disorder even when controlling for the presence of paranoid and schizotypal personality disorders: The UCLA family study. *Schizophrenia Research,* **91**(1–3), 192–9.

Folks, D. (1995) Münchausen's syndrome and other factitious disorders. Special issue: Malingering and conversion reactions. *Neurologic Clinics,* **13**, 267–81.

Follette, W. C., and Houts, A. C. (1996) Models of scientific progress and the role of theory in taxonomy development: A case study of the DSM. *Journal of Consulting and Clinical Psychology,* **64**(6), 1120–32.

Folsom, D. P., Fleisher, A. S., and Depp, C. A. (2006) Schizophrenia. In D. Jeste and J. H. Freidman (eds), *Psychiatry for Neurologists.* Totowa, NJ: Humana Press.

Fontenelle, L. F., and Hasler, G. (2008) The analytical epidemiology of obsessive–compulsive disorder: Risk factors and correlates. *Progress in Neuropsychopharmacology and Biological Psychiatry,* **32**(1), 1–15.

Forbes, D. (1994) *False fixes: The cultural politics of drugs, alcohol, and addictive relations.* Albany, NY: State University of New York Press

Foster-Green, M. (1996) What are the functional consequences of neuro-cognitive deficits in schizophrenia? *American Journal of Psychiatry,* **153**(3), 321–30.

Foucault, M. (1980) *Power/Knowledge* (Ed. Colin Gordon). Brighton: Harverster.

Fountain, J. (2000) Exorcists and exorcisms proliferate across the US. *New York Times,* 28 Nov.

Fountoulakis, K., Vieta, E., Sanchez-Moreno, J., Kaprinis, S., Goikolea, J., and Kaprinis, G. (2005) Treatment guidelines for bipolar disorder: A critical review. *Journal of Affective Disorders,* **86**(1), 1–10.

Fourneret, P., Franck, N., Slachevsky, A., and Jeannerod, M. (2001) Self-monitoring in schizophrenia revisited. *Neuroreport: Cognitive neuroscience and neuropsychology,* **12**(6), 1203–8.

Fowler, T., Lifford, K., Shelton, K., Rice, F., Thapar, A., Neale, M. C., McBride, A., and van den Bree, M. B. M. (2007) Exploring the relationship between genetic and environmental influences on initiation and progression of substance use. *Addiction,* **101**, 413–22.

Foy, A. (2007) Circuit breakers for addiction. *Internal Medicine Journal,* **37**, 320–5.

Frances, R. J., Miller, S. I., and Mack, A. H. (2005) *Clinical textbook of addictive disorders* (3rd edn). London: Guilford Press.

Francis, J. L., Weisberg, R. B., Dyck, I. R., Culpepper, L., Smith, K., Edelen, M. O., and Keller, M. B. (2007) Characteristics and course of panic disorder and panic disorder with agoraphobia in primary care patients. *Primary Care Companion to the Journal of Clinical Psychiatry,* **9**(3), 173–9.

Frank, B., and Gupta, S. (2005) A review of antioxidants and Alzheimer's disease. *Annals of Clinical Psychiatry,* **17**(4), 269–86.

Frank, E., and Thase, M. E. (1999) Natural history and preventative treatment of recurrent mood disorders. *Annual Review of Medicine,* **50**, 453–68.

Frank, I. (1989) Non-specific aspects of treatment: The view of a psychotherapist. In M. Shepherd and N. Sartorius (eds), *Non-specific aspects of treatment.* Toronto: Hans Huber.

Frankel, F. (1996) Dissociation: The clinical realities. *American Journal of Psychiatry,* **153**, 64–70.

Frankel, S. (1998) The Fashion of Destruction. *Guardian,* 7 Feb., 5.

Franken, I. H., Nijs, I. M., Muris, P., and Van Strien, J. W. (2007) Alcohol selectively reduces brain activity during the affective processing of negative information. *Alcoholism: Clinical and Experimental Research,* **31**(6), 919–27.

Franks, C. M. (1956) Conditioning and personality: A study of normal and neurotic subjects. *Journal of Abnormal Psychology,* **52**(2), 143–50.

Franks, C. M. (1957) Personality factors and the rate of conditioning. *British Journal of Psychology,* **48**(2), 119–26.

Freedman, D., Coon, H., Myles-Worsley, M., Orr-Utreger, A., Olincy, A., et al. (1997) Linkage of a neurophysiological deficit in schizophrenia to a chromosome 15 locus. *Proceedings of the National Academy of Science,* **94**, 587–92.

Freeman, B., and Ritvo, E. (1984) The syndrome of autism: Establishing the diagnosis and principles of management, *Pediatric Annals*, **13**, 284–305.

Freeman, H. (2006) Worn to be wild. Guardian, 10 June.

Freud, S. (1907) Obsessive actions and religious practices. In S. Freud, *The complete psychological works of Sigmund Freud, vol. IX (standard edn), pp. 115–27*. London: Hogarth Press.

Freudenmann, R. W., and Spitzer, M. (2004) The neuropsychopharmacology and toxicology of 3,4-methylenedioxy-N-ethyl-amphetamine (MDEA). *CNS Drugs Review*, **10**(2), 89–116.

Frick, P., and Ellis, M. (1999) Callous-unemotional traits and subtypes of conduct disorder. *Clinical Child and Family Psychology Review*, **2**(3), 149–68.

Friedlander, L., and Desrocher, M. (2006) Neuroimaging studies of obsessive–compulsive disorder in adults and children. *Clinical Psychology Review*, IB **26**, 32–49.

Friedman, M., and Rosenman, R. (1974) *Type A behaviour and your heart*. New York: Knopf.

Friendship, C., Blud, L., Erikson, M., Travers, R., and Thornton, D. (2003) Cognitive-behavioural treatment for imprisoned offenders: An evaluation of HM Prison Service's cognitive skills programmes. *Legal and Criminological Psychology*, **8**, 103–4.

Frierson, R. L., and Finkenbine, R. D. (2004) Psychiatric and neurological characteristics of murder defendants referred for pretrial evaluation. *Journal of Forensic Sciences*, **49**(3), 771–7.

Frisby, J. (1979) *Seeing: Illusion, brain and mind*. Oxford: Oxford University Press.

Frith, C. D. (1979) Consciousness, information processing and schizophrenia. *British Journal of Psychiatry*, **134**, 225–35.

Frith, C. D. (1992) *The cognitive neuropsychology of schizophrenia*. Hove: Lawrence Erlbaum.

Frith, C. D., and Done, D. J. (1989) Experiences of alien control in schizophrenia reflect a disorder in the central monitoring of action. *Psychological Medicine*, **19**, 359–63.

Frith, C., and Frith, U. (1991) Elective affinities in schizophrenia and childhood autism. In P. Bebbington (ed.), *Social psychiatry: Theory, methodology and practice*. New Brunswick, NJ: Transaction.

Frith, U. (ed.) (1991) *Autism and Asperger syndrome*. Cambridge: Cambridge University Press.

Frith, U. (2003) *Autism: Explaining the enigma* (2nd edn). Oxford: Blackwell.

Frith, U., Morton, J., and Leslie, A. (1991) The cognitive basis of a biological disorder: Autism. *Trends in Neuroscience*, **14**, 433–8.

Fritzon, K., Canter, D., and Wilton, Z. (2001) The application of an action system model to destructive behaviour: The examples of arson and terrorism. *Behavioural Sciences and the Law*, **19**(5–6), 657–90.

Fromm-Reichmann, F. (1948) Notes on the development of treatment of schizophrenics by psychoanalytic psychotherapy. *Psychiatry*, **11**, 63–273.

Frost, R. O., and Hartl, T. L. (1996) A cognitive-behavioural model of compulsive hoarding. *Behaviour, Research and Therapy*, **34**, 341–50.

Fudala, P. J., and Woody, G. W. (2004) Recent advances in the treatment of opiate addiction. *Current Psychiatry Reports*, **6**, 339–46.

Fuller-Torrey, E., and Yolken, R. H. (2003) Toxoplasma gondii and schizophrenia. *Emerging Infections Diseases*, **9**(11), 1375–80.

Furedi, F. (2004) *Therapy culture: Cultivating vulnerability in an uncertain age*. London: Routledge.

Gaab, J., Rohleder, N., Nater, U. M., and Ehlert, U. (2005) Psychological determinants of the cortisol stress response: The role of anticipatory cognitive appraisal. *Psychoneuroendocrinology*, **30**(6), 599–610.

Gabbay, M., Keimle, G., and Maguire, C. (1999) Clinical supervision for psychologists: Existing provision and unmet needs (Practitioner report). *Clinical Psychology and Psychotherapy*, **6**, 404–12.

Gaenslen, A., Gasser, T., and Berg, D. (2008) Nutrition and the risk for Parkinson's disease: Review of the literature. *Journal of Neural Transmission*, **115**, 703–13.

Gahlinger, P. M. (2004) Club drugs: MDMA, Gamma-hydroxybuterate (GHB), rohypnol and ketamine. *American Family Physician*, **69**, 2619–27.

Gallagher, C. D., Wilson, D. B., Hirschfield, P., Coggleshall, M. B., and MacKenzie, D. L. (1999) A quantitave review of the effects of sexual offender treatment on sexual reoffending. *Corrections Management Quarterly*, **3**, 19–29.

Gallagher, R. (2001) *I'll be watching you: True stories of stalkers and their victims*. London: Virgin.

Galli, R., Bielinski, D., Szprengiel, A., Shukitt-Hale, B., and Joseph, J. (2006) Blueberry supplemented diet reverses age-related decline in hippocampal HSP70 neuroprotection. *Neurobiology of Aging*, **27**, 344–50.

Garety, P. A., Hemsley, D. R., and Wessely, S. (1991) Reasoning in deluded schizophrenic and paranoid patients: Biases in performance on a probabilistic inference task. *Journal of Nervous and Mental Disease*, **179**, 194–201.

Garieballa, S. S., Schauer, M., Neuner, F., Saleptsi, E., Kluttig, T., Ebert, T., Hoffmann, K., and Rockstroh, B. S. (2006) Traumatic events, PTSD, and psychiatric comorbidity in forensic patients – assessed by questionnaires and diagnostic interview. *Clinical Practice and Epidemiology in Mental Health*, **2**, 88–95.

Garland, D. (2002) Of crimes and criminals: Development of criminology in Britain. In M. Maguire, R. Morgan and R. Reiner (eds), *The Oxford handbook of criminology* (3rd edn). Oxford: Oxford University Press.

Gasser, T. (2005) Genetics of Parkinson's disease. *Current Opinion in Nuerology*, **18**, 363–9.

Gatchel, R. J., Baum, A., and Krantz, D. S. (1989) *An Introduction to Health Psychology* (2nd edn). New York: Newbery Awards Records.

Gatrell, C. J., and Cooper, C. L. (2008) Work–life balance: Working for whom? *European Journal of International Management*, **2**(1), 71–86.

Geberth, V. J. (1996) *Practical homicide investigation: Tactics, procedures and forensic techniques*. Boston, MA: CRC Press.

Gebhard, P. (1965) Situational factors affecting human sexual behaviour. In F. Beach (ed.), *Sex and behaviour*. New York: Wiley.

Geddes, J., Burgess, S., Hawton, K., Jamison, K., and Goodwin, G. (2004) Long term lithium therapy for bipolar disorder: Systematic review and meta-analysis of randomised controlled trials. *American Journal of Psychiatry*, **161**, 217–22.

Geiselman, R. E. (1987) The cognitive interview technique for interviewing victims and witnesses of crime. *National Sheriff*, Oct.–Nov., 54–6.

Geiselman, R. E., and Fisher, R. P. (1985) Interviewing victims and witnesses of crime. *The National Institute of Justice: Research in brief*. Dec., 1–4.

Geiselman, R. E., Fisher, R. P., Firstenberg, I., Hutton, L. A., Sullivan, S. J., Avetissian, I. V., and Prosk, A. L. (1984) Enhancement of eyewitness memory: An empirical evaluation of the cognitive interview. *Journal of Police Science and Administration*, **12**, 74–80.

Geraerts, E., Schooler, J. W., Merckelbach, H., Jelicic, M., Hauer, B. J. A., and Ambadar, Z. (2007) The reality of recovered memories: Corroborating continuous and discontinuous memories of childhood sexual abuse. *Psychological Science*, **18**, 564–8.

Ghiandoni, G., Secli, R., Rocchi, M., and Ugolini, G. (1998) Does lunar position influence the time of delivery? A statistical analysis. *European Journal of Obstetric, Gynecological and Reproductive Biology*, **77**, 47–50.

Gibson, G. (1999) Developmental evolution: Going beyond the 'just so'. *Current Biology*, **9**, 942–5.

Gibson, T. A. (2007) Warning – The existing media system may be toxic to your health: Health communication and the politics of media reform. *Journal of Applied Communication Research*, **35**(2), 125–32.

Gifford, E., and Humphries, K. (2007) The psychological science of addiction. *Addiction*, **102**, 352–61.

Gilbert, P. (1989) *Human nature and suffering*. London: Lawrence Erlbaum.

Gilbertson (1999) Ethical review of research. *British Journal of Anaesthesia*, **82**(1), 6–7.

Giles, D. C., and Maltby, J. (2004) The role of media figures in adolescent development: Relations between autonomy, attachment and interest in celebrities. *Personality and Individual Differences*, **36**, 813–22.

Gill, D. (2007) *Hughes' outline of modern psychiatry* (5th edn). London: Wiley.

Gillberg C. (1988) The role of endogenous opioids in autism and the possible relationships to clinical features. In L. Wing (ed.) *Aspects of Autism: Biological Research*. London: Gaskell.

Gillberg, C. (2000) Typical neuroleptics in child and adolescent psychiatry. *European Child and Adolescent Psychiatry*, **9**(1), 2–8.

Gillberg, C., and Gillberg, J. (1983) Infantile autism: A total population study of reduced optimality in the pre-, peri-, and neonatal period. *Journal of Autism and Developmental Disorders*, **13**, 153–66.

Gillespie, N., Neale, M., Prescott, C., Aggen, S., and Kendler, K. (2007) Factor and item-response analysis DSM-IV criteria for abuse of and dependence on cannabis, cocaine, hallucinogens, sedatives, stimulants and opioids. *Addiction*, **102**, 920–30.

Gilligan, C. (1982) *In a different voice*. Cambridge, MA: Harvard University Press.

Gintalaite, K. (2007) A case report: Medical helplessness in the treatment of histrionic personality (abstract for poster session). *European Psychiatry*, **22**, S174.

Giuliano, F., and Allard, J. (2001) Dopamine and sexual function. *International Journal of Impotence Research*, **13**, S18–S28.

Glas, G. (2007) Anxiety, anxiety disorders and spirituality. *Southern Medical Journal*, **100**(6), 621–5.

Glasgow, D., Osborn, A., and Croxen, J. (2003) An assessment tool for investigating paedophile sexual interest using viewing time: An application of a single case methodology. *British Journal of Learning Disabilities*, **31**, 96–102.

Gleaves, D. H. (1996) The sociocognitive model of dissociative identity disorder: A reexamination of the evidence. *Psychological Bulletin*, **120**(1), 42–59.

Glueck, S., and Glueck, E. (1950) *Unravelling juvenile delinquency*. New York: Commonwealth Fund.

Glueck, S., and Glueck, E. (1956) *Physique and delinquency*. New York: Harper and Row.

Goetz, C., Poewe, W., Rascol, O., and Sampaio, C. (2005) Evidence-based medical review update: Pharmacological and surgical treatments of Parkinson's disease: 2001 to 2004. *Movement Disorders*, **20**(5), 523–39.

Goffman, E. (1968) *Asylums: Essay on the social situation of mental patients and other inmates*. Harmondsworth: Penguin.

Goldberg, D. (1996) A dimensional model for common mental disorders. *British Journal of Psychiatry*, Supplement **30**, 44–9.

Goldberg, D. (2000) Plato versus Aristotle: Categorical and dimensional models for common mental disorders. *Comprehensive Psychiatry*, **41**(2) Supplement 1, 8–13.

Goldberg, D., and Goodyer, I. (2005) *The origins of common mental disorders: Vulnerability, destabilisation and restitution*. London: Routledge.

Goldberg, D. P., and Huxley, P. (1980) *Mental illness in the community: The pathway to psychiatric care*. London: Tavistock.

Goldberg, D. P., Benjamin, S., and Creed, F. (1994) *Psychiatry in Medical Practice* (2nd edn). London: Routledge.

Goldberg, L. R. (1990) An alternative 'description of personality': The big-five factor structure. *Journal of Personality and Social Psychology*, **59**, 1216–29.

Goldberg, L. R., Johnson, J. A., Eber, H. W., Hogan, R., Ashton, M. C., Cloninger, C. R., and Gough, H. G. (2006) The international personality item pool and the future of public-domain personality measures. *Journal of Research in Personality*, **40**(1), 84–96.

Goldberg, T. E., Ragland, J. D., Gold, J. M., Bigelow, L. B., Torrey, E. F., and Weinberger, D. R. (1990) Neuropsychological assessment of monozygotic twins discordant for schizophrenia. *Archives of General Psychiatry*, **47**, 1066–72.

Golden, R., Gaynes, B., Ekstrom, D., Hamer, R., Jacobsen, F., Suppes, T., Wisner, K., and Nemeroff, C. (2005) The efficacy of light therapy in the treatment of mood disorders: A review and meta-analysis of the evidence. *American Journal of Psychiatry*, **162**(4), 656–62.

Goldman, H. H. (1992) *Review of general psychiatry* (3rd edn). London: Prentice Hall.

Goldstein, E. C., and Farmer, K. (1992) *Confabulations*. Boca Raton, FL: SIRS.

Goldstein, L., and McNeil, J. (2004) *Clinical neuropsychology: A practical guide to assessment and management for clinicians*. Chichester: Wiley.

Goldstein, L., Deale, A., O'Malley, S. J., Toone, B. K., and Mellers, J. (2004) An evaluation of cognitive behavioural therapy as a treatment for dissociative seizures: A pilot study. *Cognitive and Behavioural Neurology*, **17**(1), 41–9.

Goncalves, M. (1998) *Windows Nt 4.0 Server Security Guide*. New York: Prentice Hall.

Goodey, J. (2005) *Victims and Victimology: Research, policy and practice*. Harlow: Pearson.

Goodin, D. S., Cohen, B. A., O'Connor, P., Kappos, L., and Stevens, J. C. (2008) Assessment: The use of natalizumab (Tysabri) for the treatment of multiple sclerosis (an evidence-based review): Report of the Therapeutics and Technology Assessment Subcommittee of the American Academy of Neurology. *Neurology*, **71**, 766–73.

Gooding, D. C., Tallent, K. A., and Matts, C. W. (2007) Rates of avoidant, schizotypal, schizoid and paranoid personality disorders in psychometric high-risk groups at 5 year follow-up. *Schizophrenia Research*, **94**, 373–4.

Goodwin, K. F., and Jamison, K. R. (2007) *Manic-depressive illness: Bipolar disorders and recurrent depression* (2nd edn). New York: Oxford University Press.

Goodwin, R. D., and Gotlib, I. H. (2004) Panic attacks and psychopathology among youth. *Acta Psychiatrica Scandinavica*, **109**(3), 216–21.

Goodwin, R. D., Fergusson, D. M., and Horwood, L. J. (2004) Association between anxiety disorders and substance use disorders among young persons: Results of a 21-year longitudinal study. *Journal of Psychiatric Research*, **38**, 295–304.

Gordon, R. A. (1990) *Anorexia and bulimia: Anatomy of a social epidemic*. Oxford: Blackwell.

Goring, C. (1913) *The English convict: A statistical study*. London: HMSO.

Gorman, J., Kent, J. M., Sullivan, G. M., and Coplan, J. D. (2000) Neuroanatomical hypothesis of panic disorder: Revised. *American Journal of Psychiatry*, **157**, 493–505.

Gosselin, C., and Wilson. G. (1980) *Sexual variations*. London: Faber and Faber.

Gotlib, I. H., and Hammen, C. L. (1992) *Psychological aspects of depression: Towards a cognitive-interpersonal integration*. Chichester: Wiley.

Gottesman, I. I. (1991) *Schizophrenia genesis: The origins of madness*. New York: Freeman.

Gottesman, I. I., and Bertelsen, A. (1989) Dual mating studies in psychiatry: Offspring of inpatients with examples from reactive (psychogenic) psychoses. *International Review of Psychiatry*, **1**, 286–96.

Gottfredson, L. S. (1998) The general intelligence factor. *Scientific American presents: Exploring intelligence*, **9**(4), 24–9.

Graham, K. (2007) Using the historical context to identify confounders, mechanisms and modifiers in aggregate level studies of the relationship between alcohol consumption and violent crime. *Addiction*, **102**, 348–9.

Granhag, P. A., Andersson, L. O. Stromwall, L. A., and Hartwig, M. (2004) Imprisoned knowledge: Criminals' beliefs about deception. *Legal and Criminological Psychology*, **9**, 103–19.

Grant, D. (1999) Multi-agency risk management of mentally disordered sex offenders. In D. Webb and R. Harris (eds), *Mentally disordered offenders: Managing people nobody owns*. London: Routledge.

Grant, J. E. (2006) Understanding and treating kleptomania: New models and new treatments. *Israeli Journal of Psychiatry Related Science*, **43**(2), 81–7.

Grant, J. E., and Kim, S. W. (2005) Quality of life in kleptomania and pathological gambling. *Comprehensive Psychiatry*, **46**, 34–7.

Grant, J. E., Kim, S. W., and McCabe, J. S. (2006) A Structured Clinical Interview for Kleptomania (SCI-K): Preliminary validity and reliability testing. *International Journal of Methods in Psychiatric Research*, **15**(2), 83–94.

Grant, J. E., Mancebo, M. C., Pinto, A., Williams, K. A., Eisen, J. L., and Rasmussen, S. A. (2007) Late-onset obsessive compulsive disorder: Clinical characteristics and psychiatric comorbidity. *Psychiatry Research*, **152**(1), 21–7.

Grant, J. E., Odlaug, B. L., and Wozniak, J. R. (2007) Neurological functioning in kleptomania. *Behavioural Research Theory*, **45**(7), 1663–70.

Grant, M., and O'Connor, J. (2005) *Corporate social responsibility and alcohol: The need and potential for partnership*. London: Routledge.

Graubner, B., and Brenner, G. (1999) German adaptations of ICD-10. Paper presented for proceedings from *MIE 1999*, Ljubljana, Slovenia, 22 Aug.

Graves, T. C. (1920) Commentary on a case of hyteroepilepsy with delayed puberty: Treated with testicular extract. *The Lancet*, **196**(5075), 1134–5.

Gray, J. A. (1992) *The neuropsychology of anxiety: An enquiry into the functions of the sept-hippocampal system*. Oxford: Oxford University Press.

Gray, J. A., Rawlins, J. N. P., Hemsley, D. R., and Smith, A. D. (1991) The neuropsychology of schizophrenia. *Behavioural and Brain Sciences*, **14**, 1–84.

Greaves-Lord, K., Ferdinand, R. F., Oldehinkel, A. J., Sondeijker, F. E. P. L., Ormel, J., and Verhulst, F. C. (2007) Higher cortisol awakening response in young adolescents with persistent anxiety problems. *Acta Psychiatrica Scandinavica*, **116**(2), 137–44.

Green, K. (1998) Marijuana smoking vs cannabinoids for glaucoma therapy. *Archives of Opthalmology*, **116**, 1433–7.

Green, R. (1987) *The 'sissy boy syndrome' and the development of homosexuality*. New Haven, CT: Yale University Press.

Green, R. (2007) Gender development and reassignment. *Psychiatry*, **6**(3), 121–6.

Gregory, R. J. (2003) Reflections on the drug scene. *Drugs: Education, Prevention and Policy*, **10**(1), 1–5.

Gregory, R. J. (2004) *Psychological testing: History, principles and applications*. New York: Pearson.

Gregory, R. L., and Coleman, A. M. (1995) *Sensation and perception*. Harlow: Longman.

Gresch, P. J., Barrett, R. J., Sanders-Bush, E., and Smith, R. L. (2007) 5-hydroxytriptamine (serotonin)-2A receptors in rat anterior cingulated cortex mediate the discriminative stimulus properties of d-lysergic acid diethylamide. *Journal of Pharmacology and Experimental Therapeutics*, **320**(2), 662–9.

Grice, D. E., Halmi, K. A., Fichter, M., Strober, M., Woodside, D. B., Treasure, J. T., Kaplan, A. S., Magistretti, P. J., Goldman, D., Kaye, W. H., and Berrettini, W. H. (2002) Evidence for a susceptibility gene for anorexia nervosa on chromosome 1. *American Journal of Human Genetics*, **70**, 787–92.

Griesinger, W. (1845) *Pathologie und Therapie der psychischen Krankheiten*. London: New Sydenham Society.

Griez, E. J. L., Faravelli, C., Nutt, D., and Zohar, J. (2005) *Mood disorders: Clinical management and research issues*. Chichester: Wiley.

Grilo, C. M. (2006) *Eating and weight disorders*. Hove: Psychology Press.

Grilo, C., Levy, K., Becker, D., Edell, W., and McGlashan, T. H. (1995) Eating disorders in female inpatients with versus without substance use disorders. *Addictive Behaviours*, **20**, 255–60.

Grogan, S. (1999) *Body image: Understanding body dissatisfaction in men, women and children*. London: Routledge.

Grös, D. F., and Antony, M. M. (2007) The assessment and treatment of specific phobias: A review. *Current Psychiatry Reports*, **8**(4), 298–303.

Grossman, M. (2002) Frontotemporal dementia: A review. *Journal of the International Neuropsychological Society*, **8**(4), 566–83.

Groth, A. N., Burgess, A. W., and Holmstrom, L. L. (1977) Rape, power, anger and sexuality. *American Journal of Psychiatry*, **134**, 1239–48.

Groth, A. N., Hobson, W. F., and Guy, T. S. (1982) The child molester: Clinical observations. In J. Conte and D. A. Shore (eds), *Social work and child sexual abuse*. New York: Haworth.

Grover, C., and Soothill, K. (1996) Press reporting and its aftermath: The Rachel Nickell case. *Police Journal*, **LXIX**, 330–8.

Grube, B. S., Bilder, R. M., and Goldman, R. S. (1998) Meta-analysis of symptom factors in schizophrenia. *Schizophrenia Research*, **31**, 113–20.

Grunberg, F., Klinger, B. I., and Grumet, B. (1977) Homicide and deinstitutionalisation of the mentally ill. *American Journal of Psychiatry*, **134**, 685–7.

Grunebaum, H. (1986) Harmful psychotherapy experience. *American Journal of Psychotherapy*, **40**(2), 165–76.

Gruzelier, J., Burgess, A., Stygall, J., Irving, G., and Raine, A. (1995) Patterns of cognitive asymmetry and syndromes of schizotypal personality. *Psychiatric Research*, **56**, 71–9.

Grylli, V., Hafferl-Gattermayer, A., Wagner, G., Schober, E., and Karwautz, A. (2005) Eating disorders and eating problems among adolescents with type 1 diabetes: Exploring relationships with temperament and character. *Journal of Paediatric Psychology*, **30**(2), 197–206.

Gudjonsson, G. (1984) A new scale of interrogative suggestibility. *Personality and Individual Differences*, **5**, 303–14.

Gudjonsson, G. (1987) Historical background to suggestibility: How interrogative suggestibility differs from other types of suggestibility. *Personality and Individual Differences*, **8**, 347–55.

Gudjonsson, G. (1992) *The psychology of interrogations, confessions and testimony*. Chichester: Wiley.

Gudjonsson, G. (1996) Psychological evidence in court: Results from the 1995 survey. *The Psychologist*, **5**, 213–17.

Gudjonsson, G. (2001) Recovered memories effects upon the family and community. In G. Davies and T. Dalgleish (eds), *Recovered memories: Seeking the middle ground*. Chichester: Wiley.

Gudjonsson, G. (2003) *The psychology of interrogations and confessions: A handbook*. Chichester: Wiley.

Gudjonsson, G., and Clark, R. (1986) Suggestibility in police interrogations: A social psychological model. *Social Behaviour*, **1**, 83–104.

Gudjonsson, G. H., and Copson, G. (1997) The role of the expert in criminal investigation. In J. L. Jackson and D. A. Bekerian (eds), *Offender profiling: Theory, research and practice*. Chichester: Wiley.

Gudjonsson, G., and Haward, L. R. (1998) *Forensic psychology: A guide to practice*. London: Routledge.

Guenole, N., Chernyshenko, S., Stark, S., McGregor, K., and Ganesh, S. (2008) Measuring stress reaction style: A construct validity investigation. *Personality and Individual Differences*, **44**, 250–62.

Guldberg, P., Rey, F., Zschocke, J., Romano, V., Francios, B., Michiels, L., Ullrich, K., Hoffmann, G., Burgard, P., Schmidt, H., Meli, C., Riva, E., Dianzani, I.,

Ponzone, A., Rey, J., and Guttler, F. (1998) A European multicentre study of phenylanaline hydroxylase deficiency: Classification of 105 mutations and general system for genotype-based prediction of metabolic phenotype. *American Journal of Human Genetics*, **63**, 71–9.

Gull, W. W. (1874) Anorexia nervosa. *Transactions of the Clinical Society (London)*, **7**, 22–8.

Gunn, J. (1996) The management and discharge of violent patients. In N. Walker (ed.), *Dangerous people*. London: Blackstone.

Gunn, J. (2000) Future directions for treatment in forensic psychiatry. *British Journal of Psychiatry*, **176**, 332–8.

Gunn, J., Grounds, A., Mullen, P., and Taylor, P. J. (1993) Secure institutions: Their characteristics and problems. In J. Gunn and P. Taylor (eds), *Forensic psychiatry: Clinical, legal and ethical issues*. Oxford: Butterworth-Heinemann.

Gupta, M. A., and Gupta, A. K. (2003) Psychiatric and psychological comorbidity in patients with deratological disorders. *American Journal of Clinical Dermatology*, **4**, 833–42.

Guriel, J., and Fremouw, W. (2003) Assessing malingering posttraumatic disorder: A critical review. *Clinical Psychology Review*, **23**, 881–904.

Gussler-Burkhardt, N. L., and Giancola, P. R. (2005) A further examination of gender differences in alcohol-related aggression. *Journal for the Study of Alcohol*, **66**, 413–22.

Gutheil, T. (1993) True or false memories of sexual abuse? A forensic psychiatric view. *Psychiatric Annals*, **23**, 527–31.

Guthrie, E. R. (1942) Conditioning: A theory of learning in terms of stimulus, response and association. In N. B. Henry (ed.), *The forty-first yearbook of the National Society for the Study of Education, Part II: The psychology of learning*. Chicago: University of Chicago Press.

Haberstick, B. C., Schmitz, S., Young, S. E., and Hewitt, J. K. (2006) Genes and developmental stability of aggressive behavior problems at home and school in a community sample of twins aged 7–12. *Behavioural Genetics*, **36**(6), 809–19.

Hacking, I. (1998) *Mad travellers: Reflections on the reality of transient mental illness*. Charlottesville, VA: University Press of Virginia.

Hadcroft, W. (2005) *The feeling's unmutual: Growing up with Asperger syndrome (undiagnosed)*. London: Jessica Kingsley.

Hafler, D., Slavic, J., Anderson, D., O'Connor, K., De Jeger, P., and Baecher-Allan, C. (2005) Multiple sclerosis. *Immunological Reviews*, **204**, 208–32.

Häkkänen, H., and Laajasalo, T. (2006) Homicide crime scene actions in a Finnish sample of mentally ill offenders. *Homicide Studies*, **10**, 33–54.

Haldane, M., and Frangou, S. (2006) Functional neuro-imaging studies in mood disorders. *Acta Neuropsychiatrica*, **18**, 88–99.

Hall, W., and Degenhardt, L. (2000) Cannabis use and psychosis: A review of the clinical and epidemiological evidence. *Australian and New Zealand Journal of Psychiatry*, **34**, 26–34.

Hall, W., and Degenhardt, L. (2003) Medical marijuana initiatives: Are they justified? How successful are they likely to be? *CNS Drugs*, **17**(10), 689–97.

Hamilton, W. D. (1964) The genetical evolution of social behaviour. I and II. *Journal of Theoretical Biology*, **7**, 1–52.

Han, D., Bangen, K., and Bondi, M. (2009) Functional magnetic resonance imaging of compensatory neural recruitment in aging and risk for Alzheimer's disease: Review and recommendations. *Dementia and Geriatric Cognitive Disorders*, **27**(1), 1–10.

Handley, O., Naji, J., Dunnett, S., and Rosser, A. (2006) Pharmaceutical, cellular and genetic therapies for Huntington's disease. *Clinical Science*, **110**, 73–88.

Hansell, J., and Damour, L. (2008) *Abnormal psychology* (2nd edn). Hoboken, NJ: Wiley.

Hanson, R. K. (2000) *The effectiveness of treatment for sexual offenders: Report for the Association of Sexual Abusers Collaborative Data Research Committee*. Presentation at the Association for the Treatment of Sexual Abuser 19th Annual Research and Treatment conference, San Diego, CA.

Hanssen, M., Bak, M., Bijl, R., Vollebergh W., and Van Os, J. (2005) The incidence and outcome of subclinical psychotic experiences in the general population. *British Journal of Clinical Psychology*, **44**(2), 181–91.

Harding, C. (1988) Course types in schizophrenia: An analysis of European and American studies. *Schizophrenia Bulletin*, **14**, 633–44.

Hare, R. D. (1970) *Psychopathy: Theory and research*. New York: Wiley.

Hare, R. D. (1986) Twenty years experience with the Cleckley psychopath. In W. Reid, D. Dore, J. Walker and J. Bonner (eds), *Unmasking the psychopath: Antisocial personality and related syndromes*. New York: W. W. Norton.

Hare, R. D. (1993) *Without a conscience: The disturbing world of the psychopaths among us*. New York: Pocket.

Hare, R. D. (2003) *The Hare Psychopathy Checklist – Revised (PCL-R)* (2nd edn). Toronto: Multi-Health Systems.

Hare, R. D. (2006) Psychopathy: A clinical and forensic overview. *Psychiatric Clinics of North America*, **29**(3), 709–24.

Harlow, H. E. (1959) Love in infant monkeys. *Scientific American*, **200**, 68–74.

Harper, P. S. (2005) Huntington disease. In *Encyclopedia of Life Sciences*. London: Wiley.

Harrelson, L. H. (1998) *Lie test: Deception, truth and the polygraph*. Indiana: Jonas.

Harrigan, S. M., McGorry, P. D., and Krtsev, H. (2003) Does treatment delay in first episode psychosis really matter? *Psychological Medicine*, **33**, 97–110.

Harrington, M. (2006) *The design of experiments in neuroscience*. Belmont, CA: Thompson Wadsworth.

Harris, B. (1996) Hormonal aspects of postnatal depression. *International Review of Psychiatry*, **8**, 27–36.

Harris, G. T., and Rice M. E. (2005) Treatment of psychopathy: A review of empirical findings. In C. J. Patrick (ed.), *Handbook of psychopathy*. New York: Guilford Press.

Harris, J. (2000) *An evaluation of the use and effectiveness of the Protection from Harassment Act 1997* (Home Office Research Study No. 203). London: HMSO.

Harris, M. G., Henry, L. P., Harrigan, S. M., Purcell, R., Schwartz, O., Farrelly, S., Prosser, A., Jackson, H., and McGorry, P. (2005) The relationship between duration of untreated psychosis and outcome: An eight year prospective study. *Schizophrenia Research*, **79**, 85–93.

Harrison, G., Mason, P., Glazebrook, C., Medley, I., Croudace, T., and Docherty, S. (1994) Residence of incident cohort of psychotic patients after 13 years follow up. *British Medical Journal*, **308**, 813–16.

Harrison, K., and Cantor, J. (1997) The relationship between media consumption and eating disorders. *Journal of Communication*, **47**, 40–66.

Harrison, P. J. (1999) The neuropathology of schizophrenia: A critical review of the data and their interpretation. *Brain*, **122**, 593–624.

Harrow, M., Grossman, L. S., Herbener, E. S., and Davies, E. W. (2000) Ten year outcome: Patients with schizoaffective disorders, schizophrenia, affective disorders and mood-incongruent psychotic symptoms. *British Journal of Psychiatry*, **177**, 421–6.

Hart, S. D., Cox, D. N., and Hare, R. D. (1995) *Manual for the Hare Psychopathy Checklist – Revised: Screening Version (PCL: SV)*. Toronto: Multi-Health Systems.

Hartston, H. J., and Koran, L. M. (2002) Impulsive behaviour in a consumer culture. *International Journal of Psychiatry in Clinical Practice*, **6**, 65–8.

Harvey, B. K., Hope, B. T., and Shaham, Y. (2007) Tolerance to opiate reward: Role of midbrain IRS2-Akt pathway. *Nature Neuroscience*, **10**, 9–10.

Harvey, J. H., Wenzel, A., and Sprecher, S. (2004) *The handbook of sexuality in close relationships*. Mahwah, NJ: Lawrence Erlbaum.

Harvey, P. D., Keefe, R. S. E., Moskowitz, J., Putnam, K. M., Mohs. R. C., and Davis, K. L. (1990) Attentional markers of vulnerability to schizophrenia: Performance of medicated and unmedicated patients and normals. *Psychiatry Research*, **33**, 179–88.

Harvey, P. D., Silverman, J. M., Mohs, R. C., Parrella, M., White, L., Powchik, P., Davidson, M., and Davis, K. L. (1999) Cognitive decline in late-life schizophrenia: A longitudinal study of geriatric chronically hospitalised patients. *Biological Psychiatry*, **45**, 32–40.

Hausenblas, H. A., Janelle, C. M., Gardner, R. E., and Hagan, A. L. (2002) Effects of exposure to physique slides on the emotional responses of men and women. *Sex Roles*, **47**(11–12), 569–75.

Haward, L. R. C. (1981) *Forensic psychology*. London: Batsford.

Hawkins, K. A., Addington, J., Keefe, R. S., Christensen, B., Perkins, D. O., Zipursky, R., Woods, S. W., Miller, T. J., Marquez, E., Breier, A., and McGlashan, T. H. (2004) Neuropsychological status of subjects at high risk for a first episode of psychosis. *Schizophrenia Research*, **67**(2–3), 115–22.

Haworth, J., and Hart, G. J. (2007) *Well-being*. London: Palgrave-Macmillan.

Hawton, K., Salkovskis, P. M., Kirk, J., and Clark, D. M. (1989) *Cognitive behaviour therapy for psychiatric problems*. Oxford: Oxford University Press.

Hawton, K., Sutton, L., Haw, C., Sinclair, J., and Deeks, J. J. (2005) Schizophrenia and suicide: Systematic review of risk factors. *British Journal of Psychiatry*, **187**, 9–20.

Hayden, D. (2003) *Pox: Genius, madness and the mysteries of syphilis*. London: Perseus.

Hayes, N. (1994) *Principles of comparative psychology*. Hove: Psychology Press.

Hayes, R., and Dennerstein, L. (2005) The impact of aging on sexual function and sexual dysfunction in women: A review of population-based studies. *Journal of Sexual Medicine*, **2**, 317–30.

Hayes, S. C., Barnes-Holmes, D., and Roche, B. (2001) *Relational frame theory: A post-Skinnerian account of human language and cognition*. New York: Plenum.

Hazelwood, R. R. (1987) Analysing rape and profiling the offender. In R. R. Hazelwood and A. W. Burgess (eds), *Practical aspects of rape investigation: A multidisciplinary approach*. New York: Elsevier.

Healy, D. (1997) *The anti-depressant era*. Cambridge, MA: Harvard University Press.

Healy, P. J., and Moore, D. A. (2007) The trouble with overconfidence (22 May). Available at SSRN: http://ssrn.com/abstract=1001821.

Hearing Voices Network (2008) http://www.hearing-voices.org/information.htm.

Hearnshaw, H. (2004) Comparison of requirements of RECs in 11 European countries for a non-invasive interventional study. *British Medical Journal*, **328**, 140–1.

Heath, R. G. (1972) Pleasure and brain activity in man. *Journal of Nervous and Mental Diseases*, **154**, 3–18.

Hebebrand, J., Henninghausen, K., Nau, S., Himmelmann, G. W., Schulz, E., Schäfer, H., and Remschmidt, H. (1997) Low body weight in male children and adolescents with schizoid personality disorder or Asperger's disorder. *Acta Psychiatrica Scandinavica*, **96**(1), 64–7.

Hedley, A. A., Ogden, C. L., Carroll, M. D. Curtin, L. R., and Flegal, K. M. (2004) Prevalence of overweight and obesity among US children, adolescents and adults 1999–2002. *Journal of the American Medical Association*, **291**, 2847–50.

Heffernan, T. M., Ling, J., and Scholey, A. B. (2001) Subjective ratings of prospective memory deficits in MDMA (ecstasy) users. *Human Psychopharmacological Clinical Experimentation*, **16**, 607–13.

Hegarty, J. D., Baldessarini, R. J., Tohen, M., Waternaux, C., and Oepen, G. (1994) One hundred years of schizophrenia: A meta-analysis of the outcome literature. *American Journal of Psychiatry*, **151**(10), 1409–16.

Heilbrun, K., and Griffin, P. A. (1998) Community-based forensic treatment. In R. M. Wettstein (ed), *Treatment of offenders with mental disorders*. New York: Guilford Press.

Heiman, J. R., Talley, D. R., Bailen, J. L., Oskin, T. A., Rosenberg, S. J., Pace, C. R., Creanga, D. L., and Bavendam, T. (2007) Sexual function and satisfaction in heterosexual couples when men are administered sildenafil citrate (Viagra ®) for erectile dysfunction: A multicentre, randomised, double-blind, placebo-controlled trial. *Obstetrical and Gynnecological Survey*, **62**(11), 712–13.

Henchcliffe, C., Shungu, D., Mao, X., Huang, C., Nirenberg, M., Jenkins, B., and Beal, M. F. (2008) Multinuclear magnetic resonance spectroscopy for *in vivo* assessment of mitochondrial dysfunction in Parkinson's disease. *Annals of the New York Academy of Sciences: Mitochondria and Oxidative Stress in Neurodegenerative Disorders*, **1147**, 206–20.

Henquet, C., Krabbendam, L., Spauwen, J., Kaplan, C., Leib, R., Wittchen, H. U., and Van Os, J. (2005) Prospective cohort study of cannabis use, predisposition for psychosis and psychotic symptoms in young people. *British Medical Journal*, **332**, 172–5.

Herbert, M. (1998) *Clinical child psychology: Social learning, development and behaviour* (2nd edn). Chichester: Wiley.

Hergenhahn, B. (2005) *An introduction to the history of psychology* (5th edn). Belmont: Wadsworth Thompson.

Hergenhahn, B., and Olsen, M. (1993) *An introduction to theories of learning*. Englewood Cliffs, NJ: Prentice Hall.

Herkenham, M., Lynn, A. B., Little, M. D., Ross-Johnson, M., Melvin, L. S., De Costa, B. R., and Rice, K. C. (1990) Cannabinoid receptor localization in the brain. *Proceedings of the National Academy of Sciences USA*, **87**, 1932–36.

Hertel, G., Naumann, S., Konradt, U., and Batinic, B. (2002) Personality assessment via internet: Comparing online and paper-and-pencil questionnaires. In B. Batinic, U-D. Reips and M. Bosnjak (eds), *Online Social Sciences*. Göttingen: Hogrefe and Huber.

Heston, L. L. (1966) Psychiatric disorders in foster home reared children of schizophrenic mothers. *British Journal of Psychiatry*, **122**, 819–25.

Heston, L. L., Mastri, A. R., Anderson, V. E., and White, J. (1981) Dementia of the Alzheimer's type: Clinical genetics, natural history and associated conditions. *Archives of General Psychiatry*, **38**, 1085–90.

Hettima, J. M., Neale, M. C., and Kendler, K. S. (2001) A review and meta-analysis of the genetic epidemiology of anxiety disorders. *American Journal of Psychiatry*, **158**(10), 1568–78.

Heyward, C., and Wilson, K. A. (2007) Anxiety sensitivity: A missing piece to the agoraphobia-without-panic puzzle. *Behaviour Modification*, **31**(2), 162–73.

Hickey, E. W. (1991) *Serial Murderers and Their Victims*. Pacific Grove, CA: Brooks/Cole.

Hickey, E. W. (1998) Profiling stalkers and their victims: Assessing the utility of psychology in cases of violent crime. Paper presented at The 5th International Investigative Psychology Conference, University of Liverpool, 14–16 Sept.

Hicks, B., Bernat, E., Malone, S., Iacono, W., Patrick, C., Krueger, R., and McGue, M. (2007) Genes mediate the association between P3 amplitude and externalizing disorders. *Psychophysiology*, **44**(1), 98–105.

Hill, A. J. (2007) Obesity and eating disorders. *Obesity Review*, **8** (suppl. 1), 151–5.

Hill, A., Habermann, N., Berner, W., and Briken, P. (2007) Psychiatric disorders in single and multiple sexual murderers. *Psychopathology*, **40**, 22–8.

Hinde, R. (1982) *Ethology*. Oxford: Oxford University Press.

Hirsch, C. R. (2007) Anxiety disorders, Part 1: Introduction. *Psychiatry*, **6**(4), 135.

Hirsch, C. R., and Clark, D. M. (2004) Information-processing bias in social phobia. *Clinical Psychology Review*, **24**, 799–825.

Hirsch, C. R., and Holmes, E. A. (2007) Mental imagery in anxiety disorders. *Psychiatry*, **6**(4), 161–5.

Hirsch, S. R., and Leff, J. P. (1971) Parental abnormalities of verbal communication in the transmission of schizophrenia. *Psychological Medicine*, **1**, 118–27.

Hirsch, S., and Leff, J. (1975) *Abnormalities in parents of schizophrenics*. Maudsley Monograph No. 22, Oxford: Oxford University Press.

Hirst, R. A., Lambert, D. G., and Notcutt, W. G. (1998) Pharmacology and potential therapeutic uses of cannabis. *British Journal of Anaesthesia*, **81**, 77–84.

HMSO (1994) *The Allitt Inquiry: Independent inquiry relating to deaths and injuries on the children's ward at Grantham and Kesteven General Hospital during the period February to April 1991*. London: HMSO.

Hobson, R. (1986) The autistic child's concept of people. *Communication*, **20**, 12–17.

Hobson, R. (1990) On acquiring knowledge about people and the capacity to pretend: Response to Leslie (1987). *Psychological Review*, **97**, 114–21.

Hodgins, S., and Müller-Ishberner, R. (eds) (2000) *Violence crime and mentally disordered offenders: Concepts and methods for effective treatment*. Chichester: Wiley.

Hodgson, R. J., and Rachman, S. J. (1977) Obsessional–compulsive complaints. *Behaviour Research and Therapy*, **15**, 389–95.

Hoek, H. W., and van Hoeken, D. (2003) Review of the prevalence and incidence of eating disorders. *International Journal of Eating Disorders*, **34**, 383–96.

Hoek, H. W., Susser, E., Buck, K. A., Lumey, L. H., Lin, S. P., and Gorman, J. M. (1996) Schizoid personality disorder after prenatal exposure to famine. *American Journal of Psychiatry*, **153**(12), 1637–9.

Hofmann, S., Heindrichs, N., and Moscovitch, D. (2004) The nature and expression of social phobia: Towards a new classification. *Clinical Psychology Review*, **24**, 769–97.

Hogarty, G. E., Kornblith, S. J., Greenwald, D., DiBarry, A. L., Cooley, S., Flesher, S., Reiss, D., Carter, M., and Ulrich, R. (1995) Personal therapy: A disorder-relevant psychotherapy for schizophrenia. *Schizophrenia Bulletin*, **21**, 379–93.

Hogarty, G. E., Sander, M. S. W., Kornblith, J., Greenwald, D., DiBarry, A. L., Cooley, S., Ulrich, R. F., Carter, M., and Flesher, S. (1997) Three year trials of personal therapy among schizophrenic patients living with or independent of family: Description of study and effects on relapse of patients. *American Journal of Psychiatry*, **154**, 1504–13.

Hogg, M. A., and Vaughan, G. M. (2005) *Social Psychology* (4th edn). London: Pearson-Prentice Hall.

Hoghughi, M. S., and Forest, A. R. (1970) Eysenck's theory of criminology: An examination of approved school boys. *British Journal of Criminology*, **10**, 240.

Holden, C. (2001) Behavioural addictions: Do they exist? *Science*, **294**, 980–2.

Holland, T., Clare, I. C. H., and Mukhopadhyay, T. (2002) Prevalence of 'criminal offending' by men and women with intellectual disability and the characteristics of 'offenders': Implications for research and service development, *Journal of Intellectual Disability Research*, **46**(1), 6–20.

Hollander, E., and Allen, A. (2006) Is compulsive buying a real disorder, and is it really compulsive? *American Journal of Psychiatry*, **163**(10), 1670–2.

Hollin, C. R. (1989) *Psychology and Crime: An introduction to criminological psychology*. London: Routledge.

Hollin, C. R. (2002) An overview of offender rehabilitation: Something old, something borrowed, something new. *Australian Psychologist*, **37**(3), 1–6.

Hollin, C. R., and Howells, K. (1991) *Clinical approaches to sex offenders and their victims*. Chichester: Wiley.

Hollon, S., Stewart, M., and Strunk, D. (2006) Enduring effects for cognitive behaviour therapy in the treatment of depression and anxiety. *Annual Review of Psychology*, **57**, 285–315.

Holmes, D. A. (1994) Nonverbal behaviour in autism and schizophrenia. Unpublished PhD thesis: Manchester Metropolitan University. British Library copy held.

Holmes, D. A. (1998) *The essence of abnormal psychology*. London: Prentice Hall.

Holmes, D. A. (2002) Forensic psychology in prisons. *Forensic Update*, **69**, Apr., 29–30.

Holmes, D. A. (2003a) New laws for forensic psychology. *Forensic Update*, **73**, Apr., 49–51.

Holmes, D. A. (2003b) Quotation from: Software can investigate suspicious deaths. *New Scientist*, 7 July, 2.

Holmes, D. A. (2004) Forensic health psychology. *Forensic Update*, **77**, Apr., 25–7.

Holmes, D. A., and Barkus, E. (2001) The psychological and social consequences of extended human life-spans. Paper presented at the British Psychological Society's '200 years of Psychology' Conference, Hulme Hall, Manchester, 6 Oct.

Holmes, D. A., and Gross, D. H. (2004) Cyberforensics. *Forensic Update*, **76**, Jan., 19–23.

Holmes, D. A., and Lax, A. (1999) Dissociative experiences, interrogative suggestibility and trait anxiety. Paper presented at BPS supported 'Current Developments in Clinical Psychology' conference, 27 Nov., Didsbury Campus, Manchester Metropolitan University.

Holmes, D. A., and McFarlane, L. (2006) Cyberstalking. Paper presented at the Forensic Research Group Conference 'Technology and Crime', 4 Feb., Manchester Metropolitan University.

Holmes, D. A., Bee, J., and Brannigan, D. (2001) Münchausen syndrome by proxy: Child professional and animal abuse. Paper presented at the Forensic Research Group Conference, 11 Nov., Manchester Metropolitan University. *Proceedings of the British Psychological Society*, **9**(2), 33.

Holmes, D. A., Taylor, M., and Saeed, A. (2000) Stalking and the therapeutic relationship: Ongoing research. *Forensic Update*, **60**, Jan., 31–5.

Holmes, E., Brown, R., Mansell, W., Fearon, R., Hunter, E., Frasquilho, F., and Oakley, D. (2005) Are there two qualitatively distinct forms of dissociation? A review and some clinical implications. *Clinical Psychology Review*, **25**, 1–23.

Holmes, R. M., and Holmes, S. T. (2002) *Profiling violent crimes: An investigative tool* (3rd edn). Newbury Park, CA: Sage.

Holmes, T. H., and Rahe, R. H. (1967) The social readjustment rating scale. *Journal of Psychosomatic Research*, **11**, 213–18.

Holt, R. I. G. (2005) Obesity – an epidemic of the twenty-first century: An update for psychiatrists. *Journal of Psychopharmacology*, **19**(6) Supplement, 6–15.

Home Office and Department of Health (1999) *Managing dangerous people with severe personality disorder: Proposals for policy development*. London: Home Office and Department of Health.

Honey, G. D., Pomarol-Clotet, E., Corlett, P. R., Honey, R. A. E., McKenna, P. J., Bullmore, E. T., and Fletcher, P. C. (2005) Functional dysconnectivity in schizophrenia associated with attentional modulation of motor function. *Brain*, **128**(11), 2597–611.

Hoogerduijn, J., Schuurmans, M., Duijnstee, M., de Rooij, S., and Grypdonck, M. (2007) A systematic review of predictors and screening instruments to identify older hospitalised patients at risk for functional decline. *Journal of Clinical Nursing*, **16**(1), 46–57.

Hooton, E. (1939) *The American criminal*. Cambridge, MA: Harvard University Press.

Horan, W. P., Ventura, J., Nuechterlein, K. H., Subotnik, K. L., Hwang, S. S., Mintz, J. (2004) Stressful life events in recent onset schizophrenia: Reduced frequencies and altered subjective appraisals. *Schizophrenia Research*, **75**, 363–74.

Hornyak, T. (2008) Turning back the cellular clock: A farewell to embryonic stem cells? *Scientific American Magazine*, 2 Dec.

Horselenberg, R., Merckelbach, H., and Josephs, S. (2003) Individual differences and false confessions: A conceptual replication of Kassin and Kiechel (1996). *Psychology, Crime and Law*, **9**, 1–8.

Howard, R. C., and Menkes, D. B. (2007) Brief report: Changes in brain function during acute cannabis intoxication: Preliminary findings suggest a mechanism for cannabis-induced violence. *Criminal Behaviour and Mental Health*, **17**(2), 113–17.

Howitt, D. (2009) *Introduction to forensic and criminal psychology* (2nd edn). Harlow: Pearson.

Howlin, P. (1997a) *Autism: Preparing for adulthood*. London: Routledge.

Howlin, P. (1997b) Prognosis in autism: Do specialist treatments affect long-term outcome? *European Child and Adolescent Psychiatry (Historical Archive)*, **6**, 55–72.

Howlin, P., and Rutter, M. (1989) *Treatment of autistic children*. London: Wiley.

Hrafnkelsdottir, K., Valgeirsson, J., and Gizurarson, S. (2005) Induction of protective and specific antibodies against cocaine by intranasal immunisation using a glyceride adjuvant. *Biological and Pharmaceutical Bulletin*, **28**(6), 1038.

Hser, Y. (2006) Predicting long-term stable recovery from heroin addiction: Findings from a 33-year follow-up study. *Journal of Addictive Diseases*, **26**(1), 51–60.

Hsu, L. K., Mulliken, B., McDonagh, B., Krupa Das, S., Rand, W., Fairburn, C. G., Rolls, B., McCory, M. A., Saltzman, E., Shikora, S., Dwyer, J., and Roberts, S. (2002) Binge eating in extreme obesity. *International Journal of Obesity*, **26**, 1398–1403.

Hudziak (2001) Latent class analysis of ADHD and comorbid symptoms in a population sample of adolescent female twins. *Journal of Child Psychology and Psychiatry and Allied Disciplines*, **42**, 933–42.

Huey, D. (2001) The potential utility of problem-based learning in the education of clinical psychologists and others. *Education for Health*, **14**(1), 11–19.

Huey, D., and Britton, P. (2002) A portrait of clinical psychology. *Journal of Interprofessional Care*, **16**(1), 69–78.

Huey, E. D., Putnam, K., and Grafman, J. (2006) A systematic review of neurotransmitter deficits and treatments in frontotemporal dementia. *Neurology*, **66**, 17–22.

Huff, C. R. (2002) *Gangs in America III*. London: Sage.

Hugdahl, K. (1981) The three systems model of fear: A critical examination. *Behaviour Research and Therapy*, **19**, 75–85.

Hummelen, B., Wilberg, T., Pedersen, G., and Karterud, S. (2007) The relationship between avoidant personality disorder and social phobia. *Comprehensive Psychiatry*, **48**, 348–56.

Humphries, J. (2007) *In God we doubt*. London: Hodder and Stoughton.

Hunter, R. (1973) Psychiatry and neurology: Psychosyndrome or brain disease. *Proceedings of the Royal Society of Medicine*, **66**, 17–22.

Huppert, J. D., Barlow, D. H., Gorman, J. M., Shear, M. K., and Woods, S. W. (2006) The interaction of motivation and therapist adherence predicts outcome in cognitive behavioral therapy for panic disorder: Preliminary findings. *Cognitive and Behavioral Practice*, **13**(3), 198–204.

Hurst, T. E., and Hurst, M. M. (1997) Gender differences in mediation of severe occupational stress in correctional officers. *American Journal of Criminal Justice*, **22**, 121–37.

Huss, A., Stuck, A., Rubenstein, L., Egger, M., and Clough-Gorr, K. (2008) Multidimensional preventative home visit programs for community-dwelling older adults: A systematic review and meta-analysis of randomised controlled trials. *Journal of Gerontology*, **63**(3), 298–307.

Hutchings, B., and Mednick, S. A. (1974) Registered criminality in the adoptive and biological parents of registered male adoptees. In S. A. Mednick, F. Schulsinger, J. Higgins and B. Bell (eds), *Environment and Psychopathology*. New York: Elsevier North-Holland Inc.

Huxley, A. (1932) *Brave new world*. London: Flamingo.

Hyler, S. E., and Spitzer, R. L. (1978) Hysteria split asunder. *American Journal of Psychiatry*, **135**, 1500–4.

Hyman, S. E. (2007) The neurobiology of addiction: Implications for voluntary control. *American Journal of Bioethics*, **7**(1), 8–11.

Inch, H., Rowlands, P., and Solomon, A. (1995) Deliberate self-harm in a young offenders institution. *Journal of Forensic Psychiatry*, **6**, 161–71.

Ireland, J. L. (1998) Direct and Indirect Prisoner Behaviour Checklist (DIPC). Unpublished report, University of Central Lancashire, Preston.

Ireland, J. L. (2002) *Bullying among prisoners: Evidence research and intervention strategies*. Hove: Brunner-Routledge.

Irle, E., Lange, C., and Sachsse, U. (2005) Reduced size and abnormal asymmetry of parietal cortex in women with borderline personality disorder. *Biological Psychiatry*, **57**, 173–82.

Isaak, C. L., Cushway, D., and Jones, G. V. (2006) Is post-traumatic stress disorder associated with specific deficits in episodic memory? *Clinical Psychology Review*, **26**, 939–55.

Isacsson, G., Holmgren, P., and Ahlner, J. (2005) Selective serotonin reuptake inhibitor antidepressants and the risk of suicide: A controlled forensic database study of 14 857 suicides. *Acta Psychiatrica Scandinavica*, **111**, 286–390.

Isometsa, E., Henriksson, M., Heikkinen, M., Aro, H., Marttunen, M., Kuoppasalmi, J., and Lonnqvist, J. (1996) Suicide among subjects with personality disorders. *American Journal of Psychiatry*, **153**, 667–73.

Iversen, L. (2006) *Speed, ecstasy, Ritalin: The science of amphetamines*. Oxford: Oxford University Press.

Iwasaki, Y., and Schneider, I. E. (2003) Leisure, stress, and coping: An evolving area of inquiry. *Leisure Sciences*, **25**(2–3), 107–13.

Izumoto, Y., Inoue, S., and Yasuda, N. (1999) Schizophrenia and the influenza epidemics of 1957 in Japan. *Biological Psychiatry*, **46**(1), 119–24.

Jablensky, A. (1995) Schizophrenia: The epidemiological horizon. In S. Hirsch and D. Weinberger (eds), *Schizophrenia*. Oxford: Blackwell.

Jablensky, A. (2000) Epidemiology of schizophrenia: The global burden of disease and disability. *European Archives of Psychiatry and Clinical Neuroscience*, **250**, 274–85.

Jablensky, A. (2005) Boundaries of mental disorders. *Current Opinion in Psychiatry*, **18**(6), 652–8.

Jackson, G., Gillies, H., and Osterloh, I. (2005) Past, present, and future: A 7-year update of Viagra (sildenafil citrate). *International Journal of Clinical Practice*, **59**(6), 680–91.

Jackson, H., McGorry, P., Edwards, J., Hulbert, C., Henry, L., Harrigan, S., Dudgeon, P., Francey, S., Maude, D., Cocks, J., Killackey, E., and Power, P. (2005) A controlled trial of cognitively oriented psychotherapy for early psychosis (COPE) with four year follow-up readmission data. *Psychological Medicine*, **35**(9), 1295–1306.

Jackson, J. L., and Bekerian, D. A. (1997) *Offender Profiling: Theory, research and practice*. Chichester: Wiley.

Jackson, J. L., van Koppen, P. J., and Herbrink, J. C. M. (1993) *Does the service meet the needs?* Leiden: NSCR (Nederlands Studiecentrum Criminaliteit en Rechshandhaving).

Jacobs, P. A., Brunton, M., and Melville, M. M. (1965) Aggressive behaviour, mental subnormality and the XYY male. *Nature*, **208**, 1351.

Jacobsen, C., Wolfe, J., and Jackson, T. (1935) An experimental analysis of the functions of the frontal association areas in primates. *Journal of Nervous and Mental Disorders*, **82**, 1–14.

Jacobsen, R., Le Couteur, A., Howlin, P., and Rutter, M. (1988) Selective subcortical abnormalities in autism. *Psychological Medicine*, **18**, 39–48.

Jaenisch, R., and Young, R. (2008) Stem cells, the molecular circuitry of pluripotency and nuclear reprogramming. *Cell*, **132**(4), 567–82.

James, O. (2005) Think again: New research on schizophrenia suggests that the drugs won't always work. *Guardian*, Saturday, 22 Oct., 27–8.

James, P. T., Rigby, N., and Leach, R. (2004) The obesity epidemic, metabolic syndrome and future prevention strategies. *European Journal of Cardiovascular Prevention and Rehabilitation*, **11**, 3–8.

James, S. H., and Nordby, J. J. (2005) *Forensic science: An introduction to scientific and investigative techniques*. New York: Taylor and Francis.

James, W. H. (2006) Two hypotheses on the causes of male homosexuality and paedophilia. *Journal of Biological Science*, **38**, 745–61.

Jamison, K. R. (1989) Mood disorders and patterns of creativity in British writers and artists. *Psychiatry*, **52**, 125–34.

Jamison, K. R. (1992) *Touched with fire: Manic depressive illness and the artistic temperament*. New York: Free Press.

Janca, A. (2005) Rethinking somatoform disorders, personality disorders and neurosis. *Current Opinion in Psychiatry*, **18**(1), 65–71.

Janet, P. (1889) *L'automatisme psychologique*. Paris: Centre National de la Recherche Scientifique.

Janet, P. (1901) *The mental state of hystericals*. New York: Putnams.

Janet, P. (1907) *The major symptoms of hysteria*. London: Macmillan.

Janssen, P. L. (1985) Psychodynamic study of male potency disorders: An overview. *Psychotherapy and Psychosomatics*, **44**, 6–17.

Jardri, R., Lucas, B., Delevoye-Turrell, Y., Delmaire, C., Delion, P., Thomas, P., and Goeb, J. L. (2007) An 11 year old boy with drug resistant schizophrenia treated with temporo-parietal rTMS. *Molecular Psychiatry*, **12**, 320–3.

Jarvic, L. F., Klodin, V., and Matsuyama, S. S. (1973) Human aggression and the extra Y chromosome. *American Psychologist*, **28**, 674–82.

Jaspers, K. (1959) *General psychopathology* (7th edn). Manchester: Manchester University Press.

Jeffrey, C. R. (1965) Criminal behaviour and learning theory. *Journal of Criminal Law, Criminology and Police Science*, **56**, 294–300.

Jesson, J. (1993) Understanding adolescent female prostitution: A literature review. *British Journal of Social Work*, **23**, 517–30.

Jewkes, Y. (2003) *Dot.cons: Crime, deviance and identity on the internet*. London: Willan.

Jewkes, Y. (2004) *Media and Crime*. London: Sage.

Jewkes, Y. (2007) *Handbook on prisons*. London: Willan.

Johns, L. C., and van Os, J. (2001) The continuity of psychotic experiences in the general population, *Clinical Psychology Review*, **21**(8), 1125–41.

Johns, L. C., Rossell, S., Frith, C. D., Ahmad, F., Hemsley, D., Kuipers, E., and McGuire, P. K. (2001) Verbal self-monitoring and auditory verbal hallucinations in patients with schizophrenia. *Psychological Medicine*, **31**, 705–15.

Johnson, A. M., and Szurek, S. A. (1952) The genesis of antisocial acting out in children and adults. *Psychoanalytic Quarterly*, **21**, 323–43.

Johnson, W., and Kempton, W. (1981) *Sexual education and counselling of special groups*. Springfield, IL: Charles C. Thomas.

Johnstone, E. C., and Lang, F. H. (1994) The course and outcome of schizophrenia. *Current Opinion in Psychiatry*, **7**, 56–60.

Johnstone, E. C., Crow, T. J., Frith, C. D., Husband, J., and Kreel, L. (1976) Cerebral ventricular size and cognitive impairment in chronic schizophrenia. *The Lancet*, **2**(7992), 924–6.

Johnstone, S., and Halstead, S. (2000) Forensic issues in intellectual disability. *Current Opinion in Psychiatry*, **13**(5), 475–80.

Jones, C., Cormac, I., Silveira da Mota Neto, J. I., and Campbell, C. (2004) Cognitive behaviour therapy for schizophrenia. *The Cochrane Database of Systematic Reviews*, Issue 4. Art. No.: CD000524.pub2. DOI: 10.1002/14651858.CD000524.pub2.

Jones, D. (2004) HIV risk reduction strategies for substance abusers: Effecting behaviour change. *Journal of Black Psychology*, **30**, 59–77.

Jones, K. (1982) Scull's dilemma. *British Journal of Psychiatry*, **141**, 221–6.

Jones, K., and Poletti, A. (1985) Understanding the Italian experience. *British Journal of Psychiatry*, **146**, 341–7.

Jones, M. C. (1924) The elimination of children's fears. *Journal of Experimental Psychology*, **7**, 383–90.

Jones, P., Rodgers, B., and Murray, R. (1994) Childhood development risk factors for adult schizophrenia in the British 1946 birth cohort. *The Lancet*, **344**, 1398–1402.

Jones, S. (2006) *Criminology* (3rd edn). Oxford: Oxford University Press.

Jorgensen, J. P., Bennedsen, B., Christensen, J., and Hyllested, A. (1997) Acute and transient psychotic disorder: A 1 year follow-up study. *Acta Psychiatrica Scandinavica*, **96**, 150–4.

Jorm, A. F. (2000) Mental health literacy: Public knowledge and beliefs about mental disorders. *British Journal of Psychiatry*, **177**, 396–401.

Jorm, A. F., Christensen, H., Griffiths, K. M., Parslow, R. A., Rodgers, B., and Blewitt, K. (2004) Effectiveness of complementary and self-help treatments for anxiety disorders. *Medical Journal of Australia*, **181**(7), 29–46.

Joyce, E. M., Hutton, S. B., Mutsatsa, S. H., and Barnes, T. R. E. (2005) Cognitive heterogeneity in first-episode schizophrenia. *British Journal of Psychiatry*, **185**, 516–22.

Juby, H., and Farrington, D. (2001) Disentangling the link between disrupted families and delinquency. *British Journal of Criminology*, **41**, 22–40.

Julien, D., O'Connor, K. P., and Aardema, F. (2007) Intrusive thoughts, obsessions, and appraisals in obsessive–compulsive disorder: A critical review. *Clinical Psychology Review*, **27**, 366–83.

Jung, C. G. (1921) *Psychological types*. London: Kegan Paul.

Jung, C. G. (1933) *Modern man in search of soul*. London: Kegan Paul.

Kadamian, S., Bignante, A., Lardone, P., McEwan, B., and Volosin, M. (2005) Biphasic effects of adrenal steroids on learned helplessness behaviour induced by inescapable shock. *Neuropsychopharmacology*, **30**(1), 58–66.

Kaduszkiewicz, H., Zimmermann, T., Beck-Bornholdt, H-P., and van den Bussche, H. (2009) Cholinesterase inhibitors for patients with Alzheimer's disease: Systematic review of randomised clinical trials. *British Medical Journal*, **331**, 321–7.

Kaiser, J. (2007) Smallpox vaccine. A tame virus runs amok. *Science*, **316**(5830), 1418–19.

Kalant, H. (2001) Medicinal uses of cannabis: History and current status. *Pain Research and Management*, **6**(2), 80–91.

Kalechstein, A., De La Garza, R., Mahoney, J., Fantegrossi, W., and Newton, T. (2007) MDMA use and neurocognition: A meta-analytic review. *Psychopharmacology*, **189**, 531–7.

Kalivas, P. W. (2007) Neurobiology of cocaine addiction: Implications for new pharmacotherapy. *American Journal on Addictions*, **16**(2), 71–8.

Kalivas, P. W., Pierce, R. C., Cornish, J., and Sorg, B. (1998) The role for sensitisation in craving and relapse in cocaine addiction. *Journal of Psychopharmacology*, **12**(1), 49–53.

Kamin, L., Rose, S., and Lewontin, R. C. (1984) *Not in our genes: Biology, ideology and human nature*. Harmondsworth: Penguin.

Kamińska, B., Czaja, M., Kozielska, E., Mazur, E., and Korzon, M. (2002) Use of secretin in the treatment of childhood autism. *Medical Science Monitor*, **8**(1), 22–6.

Kamphuis, J. H., and Emmelkamp, P. M. G. (2000) Stalking: A contemporary challenge for forensic and clinical psychiatry. *British Journal of Psychiatry*, **176**, 206–9.

Kandel, E., Schwartz, J., and Jessell, T. (1995) *Essentials of neural science and behaviour*. London: Prentice Hall.

Kane, J. M., and Smith, J. M. (1982) Tardive dyskinesia: Prevalence and risk factors 1959–79. *Archives of General Psychiatry*, **39**, 473–81.

Kanner, L. (1943) Autistic disturbances of affective contact. *Nervous Child*, **2**, 217.

Kanner, L. (1948) Problems of nosology and psychodynamics in early infantile autism. *American Journal of Ortho-psychiatry*, **19**, 416–26.

Kaplan, M. (1983) A woman's view of DSM-III. *American Psychologist*, **39**, 786–92.

Kapur, S. (2003) Psychosis as a state of aberrant salience: A framework linking biology, phenomenology, and pharmacology in schizophrenia. *American Journal of Psychiatry*, **160**(1), 13–23.

Kapur, S., Mizrahi, R., and Li, M. (2005) From dopamine to salience to psychosis – linking biology, pharmacology and phenomenology of psychosis. *Schizophrenia Research*, **79**, 59–68.

Kapur, S., and Remington, G. (1996) Serotonin–dopamine interaction and its relevance to schizophrenia. *American Journal of Psychiatry*, **153**, 466–76.

Karp, J., and Reynolds, C. (2009) Depression, pain and aging. *Focus*, **7**, 17–27.

Karp, R. W. (1992) D2 or not D2. *Alcoholism: Clinical and experimental research*, **16**, 786–7.

Kasanin, J. (1933) The acute schizoaffective psychoses. *American Journal of Psychiatry*, **90**, 97–126.

Katon, W., and Roy-Byrne, P. (2007) Anxiety disorders: Efficient screening is the first step in improving outcomes. *Annals of Internal Medicine*, **146**(5), 390–2.

Katzman, R. (2008) The prevalence and malignancy of Alzheimer's disease. *Alzheimer's and Dementia*, **4**, 378–80.

Kavirajan, H., and Schneider, L. (2007) Efficacy and adverse effects of cholinesterase inhibitors and memantine in vascular dementia: A meta-analysis of randomised controlled trials. *The Lancet Neurology*, **6**(9), 782–92.

Kaufer, D., Borson, S., Kershaw, P., and Sadik, K. (2005) Reduction of caregiver burden in Alzheimer's disease by treatment with galantamine. *CNS Spectrum*, **10**(6), 481–8.

Kay, P., and Kolvin, I. (1987) Childhood psychoses and their borderlands. *British Medical Bulletin*, **43**, 570–86.

Kay, S. (2005) *No more clutter: How to clear your space and free your life*. London: Hodder and Stoughton.

Kay, S. R., Opler, L. A., and Fisbein, A. (1986) *Positive and Negative Syndrome Scale (Manual)*. North Tonawanda, NY: Multi-Health Systems.

Kaye, W., and Strober, M. (1999) The neurobiology of eating disorders. In D. S. Charney, E. J. Nestler and B. S. Bunney (eds), *The neurobiology of mental illness*. New York: Oxford University Press.

Kazdin, A. E. (1998) *Research design in clinical psychology* (3rd edn). Needham Heights, MA: Allyn and Bacon.

Kazdin, A. E. (1999) The meanings and measurement of clinical significance. *Journal of Consulting and Clinical Psychology*, **67**(3), 332–9.

Kazdin, A. E., and Wilson, G. T. (1978) Criteria for evaluating psychotherapy. *Archives of General Psychiatry*, **35**, 407–16.

Kearns, A. (2001) Forensic services and people with learning disability: In the shadow of the Reed Report. *Journal of Forensic Psychiatry*, **12**(1), 8–12.

Kebbell, M. R., and Giles, D. C. (2000) Lawyer's questions and witness confidence: Some experimental influences of complicated lawyer's questions on witness confidence and accuracy. *Journal of Psychology*, **134**(2), 129–39.

Kebbell, M. R., and Milne, R. (1998) Police officers' perceptions of eyewitness factors in forensic investigations: A survey. *Journal of Social Psychology*, **138**, 323–30.

Keeler, L. (1933) Scientific methods for criminal detection with the polygraph. *Kansas Bar Association*, **2**, 22–31.

Keeling, J. A., Rose, J. L., and Beech, A. R. (2006) An investigation into the effectiveness of custody-based cognitive behavioural treatment for special needs sexual offenders. *Journal of Forensic Psychiatry and Psychology*, **17**(3), 372–92.

Kelly, D. (1985) Neurosurgical treatment of psychiatric disorders. In K. Granville-Grossman (ed.), *Recent advances in clinical psychiatry*. Edinburgh: Churchill Livingstone.

Kempe, P., van Oppen, P., de Haan, E., Twisk, J. W., Sluis, A., Smit, J. H., van Dyck, R., and van Balkom, A. J. (2007) Predictors of course in obsessive–compulsive disorder: Logistic regression versus Cox regression for concurrent events. *Acta Psychiatrica Scandinavica*, **116**, 201–10.

Kendall, P. (2000) *Childhood disorders*. Hove: Psychology Press.

Kendall, P., and Southam-Gerow, M. (1996) Long-term follow-up of a cognitive–behavioural therapy for anxiety-disordered youth. *Journal of Consulting and Clinical Psychology*, **64**, 724–30.

Kendell, R. E. (1986) The relationship of schizo-affective illness to schizophrenic and affective disorders. In A. Marneros and MT Tsuang (eds), *Schizoaffective Psychoses*, Berlin: Springer.

Kendell, R. E. (2001) The distinction between mental and physical illness. *British Journal of Psychiatry*, **178**, 490–3.

Kendler, K. S. (2000) Schizophrenia genetics. In B. J. Sadock and V. A. Sadock (eds), *Kaplan and Sadock's comprehensive textbook of psychiatry*, vol. 1, Philadelphia: Lipincott, Williams and Wilkins.

Kendler, K. S. (2004) Major depression and generalised anxiety disorder: Same genes, (partly) different environments revisited. *Focus*, **2**, 416–25.

Kendler, K. S., McGuire, M., Gruenberg, A. M., O'Hare, A., Spellman, M., and Walsh, D. (1993) The Roscommon family study I. Methods, diagnosis of probands and risk of schizophrenia in relatives. *Archives of General Psychiatry*, **50**, 527–40.

Kendler, K. S., Myers, J., Prescott, C. A., and Neale, M. C. (2001) The genetic epidemiology of irrational fears and phobias in men. *Archives of General Psychiatry*, **58**, 257–67.

Kendler, K. S., Prescott, C. A., Myers, J., and Neale, M. C. (2003) The structure of genetic and environmental risk factors for common psychiatric and substance use disorders. *Archives of General Psychiatry*, **60**, 929–37.

Kennedy, J., Giuffra, L., Moisis, H., Cavalli-Sforza, L., Pakstis, A., Kidd, J., Castigleone, C., Sjorsen, B., Wetterberg, L., and Kidd, K. (1988) Evidence against linkage to markers on chromosome 5 in a northern Swedish pedigree. *Nature*, **336**, 167–70.

Keppens, J., and Schafer, B. (2006) Knowledge based crime scenario modelling. *Expert Systems with Applications*, **30**, 203–22.

Keppens, J., and Zeleznikow, J. (2003) A model based reasoning approach for generating plausible crime scenarios from evidence. *Proceedings of the 9th International Conference on Artificial Intelligence and Law: Evidence Session*, Scotland, 51–9.

Keri, S., Kiss, I., and Kelemen, O. (2008) Sharing secrets: Oxytocin and trust in schizophrenia. *Social Neuroscience*, Aug., 1–7.

Kernberg, O. F., and Caligor, E. (2005) A psychoanalytic theory of personality disorders. In M. F. Lenzenweger and J. F. Clarkin (eds), *Major theories of personality disorder* (2nd edn). New York: Guilford Press.

Kerns, J., Nuechterlein, K., Braver, T., and Barch, D. (2008) Executive functioning component mechanisms and schizophrenia. *Biological Psychiatry*, **64**(1), 26–33.

Kesey, K. (1962) *One flew over the cuckoo's nest*. New York: Viking.

Kessing, L., Sondergard, L., Forman, J., and Andersen, P. K. (2008) Lithium treatment and risk of dementia. *Archives of General Psychiatry*, **65**(11), 1331–5.

Kessler, R. C. (2003) The impairments caused by social phobia in the general population: Implications for intervention. *Acta Psychiatrica Scandinavica*, **108**(s417), 19–27.

Kessler, R. C. (2007) The global burden of anxiety and mood disorders: Putting ESEMeD findings into perspective. *Journal of Clinical Psychiatry*, **68**(suppl. 2), 10–19.

Kessler, R. C., Chiu, W. T., Jin, R., Ruscio, A. M., Shear, K., and Walters, E. E. (2006) The epidemiology of panic attacks, panic disorder, and agoraphobia in the National Comorbidity Survey Replication. *Archives of General Psychiatry*, **63**, 415–24.

Kety, S. S. (1974a) From rationalisation to reason. *American Journal of Psychiatry*, **131**, 957–63.

Kety, S. S. (1974b) Problems in biological research in psychiatry. In J. Mendels (ed.), *Biological psychiatry*. New York: Wiley.

Kety, S. S., Rosenthal, D., Wender, P. H., and Schulsinger, F. (1971) Mental illness in the biological and adoptive families of adopted schizophrenics. *American Journal of Psychiatry*, **128**, 302–6.

Kety, S. S., Rosenthal, D., Wender, P., Schulsinger, F., and Jacobson, B. (1975) In R. Fieve, D. Rosenthal and H. Brill (eds), *Genetic research in psychiatry*. Baltimore: Johns Hopkins University Press.

Kety, S. S., Rosenthal, D., Wender, P., Schulsinger, F., and Jacobsen, B. (1976) Mental illness in the biological and adoptive families of adopted individuals who have become schizophrenic. *Behavioural Genetics*, **6**, 219–25.

Kiernan, C., and Bailey, C. (1999) Issues in research in forensic learning disability. Paper presented at the Forensic Research Group Conference, 'Current Developments in Forensic Psychology in the North-West', 1 May, Manchester Metropolitan University.

Kiesler, S., and Sproull, L. S. (1986) Response effects in the electronic survey. *Public Opinion Quarterly*, **50**, 402–13.

Kihlstrom, J. F. (2005) Dissociative disorders. *Annual Review of Clinical Psychology*, **1**, 227–53.

Kim, J. H., and Lennon, S. J. (2007) Mass media and self-esteem, body image and eating disorder tendencies. *Clothing and Textiles Research Journal*, **25**(1), 3–23.

Kim, M., Lee, S-T., Chu, K., and Kim, S. (2007) Stem cell-based cell therapy for Huntington disease: A review. *Neuropathology*, **28**(1), 1–9.

Kim, S. J., Lyoo, I. K., Lee, Y. S., Kim, J., Sim, M. E., Bae, S. J., Kim, H. J., Lee, J-Y., and Jeong, D-U. (2007) Decreased cerebral blood flow of thalamus in PTSD patients as a strategy to reduce re-experience symptoms. *Acta Psychiatrica Scandinavica*, **116**(2), 145–53.

Kincaid, J. R. (1998) *Erotic innocence: The culture of child molesting*. Durham, NC: Duke University Press.

Kinderman, P. (2002) Reforming the Mental Health Act: The role of the clinical psychologist. Paper presented at the Forensic Research Group Conference, *New Laws for Forensic Psychology*, 9 Nov., Manchester Metropolitan University.

Kinderman, P., and Benthall, R. P. (1997) Causal attributions in paranoia and depression: Internal, personal and situational attributions for negative events. *Journal of Abnormal Psychology*, **106**, 341–5.

King, M. (1990) Sneezing as a fetishistic stimulus. *Sexual and Marital Therapy*, **5**, 69–72.

King, M., Weich, S., Nazroo, J., and Blizard, R. (2006) Religion, mental health and ethnicity: EMPIRIC – A national survey of England. *Joural of Mental Health*, **15**(2), 153–62.

Kinkade, P., Burns, R., and Fuentes, A. I. (2005) Criminalizing attractions: Perceptions of stalking and the stalker. *Crime and Delinquency*, **51**, 3–25.

Kinsey, A., Pomeroy, W., Martin, C., and Gebhard, P. (1948) *Sexual behaviour in the human male*. London: W. B. Saunders.

Kinsey, A., Pomeroy, W., Martin, C., and Gebhard, P. (1953) *Sexual behaviour in the human female*. London: W. B. Saunders.

Kinzl, J., Traweger, C., and Biebl, W. (1995) Sexual dysfunctions: Relationships to childhood sexual abuse and early family experiences in a nonclinical sample. *Child Abuse and Neglect*, **19**, 785–92.

Kirch, D. G. (1993) Infection and autoimmunity as aetiologic factors in schizophrenia: A review and reappraisal. *Schizophrenia Bulletin*, **19**, 355–70.

Kircher, T. T. J., Liddle, P. F., Brammer, M. J., Williams S. C. R., Murray, R. M., and McGuire, P. K. (2001) Neural correlates of formal thought disorder in schizophrenia: Preliminary findings from a functional magnetic resonance imaging study. *Archives of General Psychiatry*, **58**, 769–74.

Kirley, A., Hawi, Z., Daly, G., McCarron, M., Mullins, C., Millar, N., Waldman, I., Fitzgerald, M., and Gil, M. (2002) Dopaminergic system genes in ADHD: Toward a biological hypothesis. *Neuropsychopharmacology*, **27**(4), 607–19.

Klass, P. J. (1989) *UFO abductions: A dangerous game*. Buffalo, NY: Prometheus.

Klin, A., Volkmar, F., Sparrow, S., Cicchetti, D., et al. (1995) Validity and neuropsychological characterisation of Asperger syndrome: Convergence with nonverbal learning disabilities syndrome. *Journal of Child Psychology and Psychiatry and Allied Disciplines*, **36**, 1127–40.

Kluft, R. (1995) Current controversies surrounding dissociative identity disorder. In L. Cohen, J. Berzoff and M. Elin (eds), *Dissociative identity disorders: Current theoretical and treatment controversies*. Hillsdale, NJ: Jason Aronson.

Kluft, R. (2003) Current issues in dissociative identity disorder. *Bridging Eastern and Western Psychiatry*, **1**(1), 71–87.

Knight, A. (2002) *How to become a clinical psychologist: Getting a foot in the door*. Hove: Brunner-Routledge.

Knight, I. (2007) A new profession: free prostitutes. *Sunday Times*, 23 Dec.

Knutson, B., Rick, S., Wimmer, G. E., Prelec, D., and Loewenstein, G. (2007) Neural predictors of purchases. *Neuron*, **53**(1), 147–56.

Kocsis, R., Cooksey, R., and Irwin, H. (2002) Psychological profiling of offender characteristics from crime behaviours in serial rape offences. *International Journal of Offender Therapy and Comparative Criminology*, **46**, 144–69.

Kocsis, R. N., Hayes, A. F., and Irwin, H. J. (2002) Investigative experience and accuracy in psychological profiling of a violent crime. *Journal of Interpersonal Violence*, **17**, 811–23.

Kocsis, R. N., Irwin, H. J., Hayes, A. F., and Nunn, R. (2000) Expertise in psychological profiling: A comparative assessment. *Journal of Interpersonal Violence*, **15**, 311–31.

Kohlberg, L. (1964) Development of moral character and moral ideology. In M. L. Hoffman and L. V. Hoffman (eds), *Review of child development research*, Vol. 1. New York: Russell Sage Foundation.

Köhnken, G., Malpass, R. S., and Wogalter, M. S. (1996) Forensic applications of line-up research. In N. S. Sporer, R. S. Malpass and G. Köhnken (eds), *Psychological issues in eyewitness identification*. Mahwah, NJ: Erlbaum.

Köksal, F., Domjan, M., Kurt, A., Sertel, O., Örüng, S., Bowers, R., and Kumru, G. (2004) An animal model of fetishism. *Behaviour Research and Therapy*, **42**(12), 1421–34.

Koller, K. M., and Castanos, J. N. (1970) Family background in prison groups: A comparative study of parental deprivation. *British Journal of Psychiatry*, **117**(539), 371–80.

Kompier, M., and Cooper, C. (1999) *Preventing stress, improving productivity: European case studies in the workplace*. London: Routledge.

Kopelman, M., and Morton, J. (2001) Psychogenic amnesias: Functional memory loss. In G. Davies and T. Dalgleish (eds), *Recovered memories: Seeking the middle ground*. Chichester: Wiley.

Koponen, H., Viilo, K., Hakko, H., Timonen, M., Meyer-Rochow, V. B., Sarkioja, T., and Rasanen, P. (2007) Rates and previous disease history in suicide. *International Journal of Geriatric Psychiatry*, **22**, 38–46.

Koran, L. M. (1999) *Obsessive–compulsive and related disorders in adults: A comprehensive clinical guide*. Cambridge: Cambridge University Press.

Koran, L. M., Faber, R. J., Aboujaoude, E., Large, M. D., and Serpe, R. T. (2006) Estimated prevalence of compulsive buying behaviour in the United States. *American Journal of Psychiatry*, **163**(10), 1806–12.

Kotowicz, Z. (1997) *R. D. Laing and paths of anti-psychiatry*. London: Routledge.

Krabbendam, L., and Van Os, J. (2005) Schizophrenia and urbanicity: A major environmental influence-conditional on genetic risk. *Schizophrenia Bulletin*, **31**(4), 795–9.

Kraepelin, E. (1885) *A textbook of psychiatry*. Leipzig: Ambr. Abel.

Kraepelin, E. (1893) *Psychiatrie: Ein kurzes Lehrbuch fur Studirende und Arzle*. Leipzig: Ambr. Abel.

Kraepelin, E. (1896) Dementia praecox. Trans. in J. Cutting and M. Shepherd (eds), *The clinical roots of the schizophrenia concept*. Cambridge: Cambridge University Press, 1987.

Kraepelin, E. (1915) *Psychiatrie* (8th edn). Leipzig: Barth.

Kraepelin, E. (1919) *Dementia praecox and paraphrenia*. Edinburgh: E. and S. Livingstone.

Krafft-Ebbing, R. von (1886) *Psychopathia sexualis*. Reprinted, Burbank, CA: Bloat Books, 1999.

Kramer, M. (1980) The rising pandemic of mental disorders and associated chronic diseases and disabilities. *Acta Psychiatrica Scandinavica*, **62**, 382–97.

Krebs, D. L. (2000) The evolution of moral dispositions in the human species. *Annals of the New York Academy of Sciences*, **907**, 132–48.

Kretschmere (1921) *Physique and character* (2nd edn). Translated and reprinted, New York: Cooper Square Publishers, 1936.

Krijn, M., Emmelkamp, P. M. G., Olafsson, R. P., and Biemond, R. (2004) Virtual reality exposure therapy of anxiety disorders: A review. *Clinical Psychology Review*, **24**, 259–81.

Kring, A. M., Davison, G. C., Neale, J. M., and Johnson, S. L. (2007) *Abnormal Psychology* (10th edn). New York: Wiley.

Kroenke, K. (2007) Efficacy of treatment for somatoform disorders: A review of randomised controlled trials. *Psychosomatic Medicine*, **69**, 881–8.

Krstev, H., Carbone, S., Harrigan, S. M., Curry, C., Elkins, K., and McGorry, P. D. (2004) Early intervention in first episode psychosis. *Social Psychiatry and Psychiatric Epidemiology*, **39**, 711–19.

Krueger, R. F., Caspi, A., Moffitt, T. E., and Silva, P. A. (1998) The structure and stability of common mental disorders (DSM-III-R): A longitudinal-epidemiological study. *Journal of Abnormal Psychology*, **107**(2), 216–27.

Kuhn, T. S. (1996) *The structure of scientific revolutions* (3rd edn). Chicago: University of Chicago Press.

Kuile, M. M., van Lankveld, J. J., de Groot, E., Melles, R., Neffs, J., and Zandbergen, M. (2007) Cognitive behavioural therapy for women with lifelong vaginismus: Process and prognostic factors. *Behaviour Research and Therapy*, **45**(2), 359–73.

Kuller, L., Lopez, O., Jagust, W., Becker, J., DeKosty, S., Lyketsos, C., Kawas, C., Breitner, J., Fitzpatrick, A., and Dulberg, C. (2005) Determinants of vascular dementia in the Cardiovascular Health Cognition Study. *Neurology*, **16**, 1548–52.

Kundermann, B., Hemmeter-Spernal, J., Huber, M., Krieg, J., and Lautenbacher, S. (2008) Effects of total sleep deprivation in major depression: Overnight improvement of mood is accompanied by increased pain sensitivity and augmented pain complaints. *Psychosomatic Medicine*, **70**(1), 92–101.

Kuntsi, J., Eley, T., Taylor, A., Hughes, C., Asherson, P., Caspi, A., and Moffitt, T. (2004) Co-occurrence of ADHD and low IQ has genetic origins. *American Journal of Medical Genetics*, **124**, 41–7.

Kuper, H., Marmot, M., and Hemingway, H. (2002) Systematic review of prospective cohort studies of psychosocial factors in the aetiology and prognosis of coronary heart disease. *Seminars in Vascular Medicine*, **2**, 267–314.

Kupfermann, L., Castellucci, V., Pinsker, H., and Kandel, E. (1970) Neuronal correlates of habituation and dishabituation of the gill withdrawal response in Aplysia. *Science*, **167**, 1743–5.

Kuriansky, J. B. (1988) Personality style and sexuality. In R. A. Brown and J. R. Fields (eds), *Treatment of sexual problems in individual and couples therapy*. Costa Mesa, CA: PMA Publishing.

Kurtz, A. (2007) An exploratory study of the needs of staff who are for offenders with a diagnosis of personality disorder. *Psychology and Psychotherapy: Theory Research and Practice*, **80**(3), 421–35.

Kuwabara, H. Y., Otsuka, M., Shindo, M., Ono, S., Shoiri, T., and Someya, T. (2007) Diagnostic classification and demographic features in 283 patients with somatoform disorder. *Psychiatry and Clinical Neurosciences*, **61**, 283–9.

Kveiborg, M., Kassem, M., Langdahl, B., Eriksen, E., Clark, B., and Rattan, S. (1999) Telomere shortening during ageing of human osteoblasts in vitro and leukocytes in vivo: Lack of excessive telomere loss in osteopathic patients. *Mechanisms of Aging and Development*, **106**(3), 261–71.

Kwapil, T. (1996) A longitudinal study of drug and alcohol use by psychosis-prone and impulsive non-conforming individuals. *Journal of Abnormal Psychology*, **105**, 114–23.

Lacey, B. W., and Ditzler, T. F. (2007) Inhalant abuse in the military: An unrecognised threat. *Military Medicine*, **172**(4), 388–92.

Lacey, J. H. (1993) Self-damaging and addictive behaviour in bulimia nervosa: A catchment area study. *British Journal of Psychiatry*, **163**, 190–4.

Ladd, C., Owens, M., and Nemeroff, C. (1996) Persistent changes in corticotrophin-releasing factor neuronal systems induced by maternal deprivation. *Endocrinology*, **137**, 1212–18.

Ladouceur, R., Sylvian, C., Boutin, C., and Doucet, C. (2002) *Understanding and treating the pathological gambler*. Ontario: Wiley.

Laing, R. D. (1960) *The divided self*. London: Tavistock.

Laing, R. D. (1965) *The divided self: A study of sanity and madness*. Harmondsworth: Penguin.

Lala, S., and Straussner, A. (2004) *Clinical work with substance abusing clients*. London: Guilford Press.

Lalumière, M. L., Harris, G. T., and Rice, M. E. (2001) Psychopathy and developmental instability. *Evolution and Human Behaviour*, **22**, 75–92.

Lam, J. A., and Rosenheck, R. (1999) Street outreach for homeless persons with serious mental illness: Is it effective? *Medical care*, **37**(9), 894–907.

Lambert, K. G., and Kinsley, C. H. (2005) *Clinical neuroscience: The neurobiological foundations of mental health*. New York: Worth Publishers.

Lang, P. (1968) Fear reduction and fear behaviour: Problems in treating a construct. In M. Shilen (ed.), *Research in psychotherapy*, Vol. III. Washington, DC: American Psychological Association.

Lange, J. (1929) *Verbrechen als Schicksal: Studien an kriminellen Zwillingen*. Trans. 1930. New York: Charles Boni.

Langfeldt, G. (1937) The prognosis of schizophrenia and the factors influencing the course of the disease. *Acta Psychiatrica et Neurologica Scandinavica*, suppl. 13, 7–228.

Längstöm, N., and Zucker, K. J. (2005) Transvestic fetishism in the general population: Prevalence and correlates. *Journal of Sexual and Marital Therapy*, **31**(2), 87–95.

Larsen, T. K., Melle, I., Friis, S., Roa, I., Johannessen, J. O., Opjordsmoen, S., Simonsen, E., Vaglum, P., and McGlashan, T. H. (2007) One year effect of changing duration of untreated psychosis in a single catchment area. *British Journal of Psychiatry*, **191**(suppl.), 128–32.

Larson, E. J. (1989) *Trial and Error: The American Controversy over Creation and Evolution*. Oxford: Oxford University Press.

Larson, J. A. (1932) *Lying and its Detection*. Chicago: University of Chicago Press.

Laruelle, M. (2000) The role of endogenous sensitization in the pathophysiology of schizophrenia: Implications from recent brain imaging studies. *Brain Research Review*, **31**, 371–84.

Laruelle, M., Kegeles, L. S., Abi-Dargham, A. (2003) Glutamate, dopamine and schizophrenia from pathophysiology to treatment. *Annals of the New York Academy of Sciences*, **1003**, 138–53.

Lasher, L. J. (2003) Munchausen by proxy (MBP) maltreatment: An international educational challenge. *Child Abuse and Neglect*, **27**, 409–11.

Last, C., Barlow, D., and O'Brien, G. (1984) Cognitive changes during in vivo exposure in an agoraphobic. *Behaviour Modification*, **8**, 93–113.

Law, S. (1986) The regulation of menstrual cycle and its relationship to the moon. *Acta Ostetrica Gynocologica Scandinavica*, **65**, 45–8.

Lawrence, A. J. (2007) Therapeutics for alcoholism: What's the future? *Drug and Alcohol Review*, **26**, 3–8.

Lawrie, S. M., and Abukmeil, S. S. (1998) Brain abnormality in schizophrenia: A systematic and quantitative review of volumetric magnetic resonance imaging studies. *British Journal of Psychiatry*, **172**, 110–20.

Lawrie, S. M., Whalley, H. C., Abukmeil, S. S., Kestelman, J. N., Donnelly, L., Miller, P., Best, J. K., Owens, D. G., and Johnstone, E. C. (2002) Temporal lobe volume changes in people at high risk of schizophrenia with psychotic symptoms. *British Journal of Psychiatry*, **181**, 138–43.

Lazarus, A. (1984) Multimodal therapy. In R. Corsini (ed.), *Current psychotherapies*. Itaska, IL: Peacock.

Lazarus, R. S. (1999) *Stress and emotion: New synthesis*. New York: Springer.

Lea, M., and Spears, R. (1991) Computer-mediated communication, de-individuation and group decision-making. *International Journal of Man-Machine Studies*, **39**, 283–301.

Leary, T. (1970) The politics of ecstasy. London: Granada.

Leavey, G., and King, M. (2007) The devil is in the detail: Partnerships between psychiatry and faith-based organisations. *British Journal of Psychiatry*, **191**, 97–8.

Lee, D., Newell, R., Zeigler, L., and Topping, A. (2008) Treatment of fatigue in multiple sclerosis: A systematic review of the literature. *International Journal of Nursing Practice*, **14**(2), 81–93.

Lee, J. K. P., Pattison, P., Jackson, H., and Ward, T. (2001) The general, common and specific features of psychopathology for different types of paraphilias. *Criminal Justice and Behaviour*, **28**(2), 227–56.

Lee, M. I., and Miltenberger, R. G. (1997) Functional assessment and binge eating. *Behaviour modification*, **21**(2), 159–71.

Lee, S., and Mysyk, A. (2004) The medicalisation of compulsive buying. *Social Science and Medicine*, **58**, 1709–18.

Lee, Y., Gaswkins, D., Anand, A., and Shekhar, A. (2007) Gia mechanisms in mood regulation: A novel model of mood disorders. *Psychopharmachology*, **191**, 55–65.

Legg, C., and Booth, D. (1994) *Appetite: Neural and behavioural bases*. Oxford: Oxford University Press.

Lehmann, C. (2004) Health panel urges government to adopt ICD-10 for coding. *Psychiatric News*, **39**(1), 5.

Lehrer, D. S., Christian, B. T., Mantil, J., Murray, A. C., Buchsbaum, B. R., Oakes, T. R., Byrne, W., Kemether, E. M., Buchsbaum, M. S. (2005) Thalamic and prefrontal FDG uptake in never-medicated patients with schizophrenia. *American Journal of Psychiatry*, **162**(5), 931–8.

Lehrer, M., Woolfolk, R. L., Barlow, D. H., and Sime, W. E. (2007) *Principles and practice of stress management*. London: Guilford Press.

Leiberman, J. A., Stroup, S., McEvoy, J. P., Swartz, M. S., Rosenheck, R. A., Perkins, D. O., Keefe, R. S. E., Davis, S. M., Davis, C. E., Lebowitz, B. D., Severe, J., and Hsiao, J. K. (2005) Effectiveness of antipsychotic drugs in patients with chronic schizophrenia. *New England Medical Journal*, **353**, 1209–23.

Leiblum, S. R. (2006) *Principles and practice of sex therapy*. London: Guilford Press.

Leifer, R. (1970) The medical model as ideology. *International Journal of Psychiatry*, **9**, 13–19.

Leippe, M. G. (1994) the appraisal of eyewitness testimony. In D. F. Ross, J. D. Read and M. P. Toglia (eds), *Adult eyewitness testimony: Current trends and developments*. New York: Cambridge University Press.

Lejoyeux, M., Feuche, N., Loi, S., Solomon, J., and Ades, J. (1999) Study of impulse-control disorders among alcohol dependent patients. *Journal of Clinical Psychiatry*, **60**(5), 302–5.

Le Moal, M., and Koob, G. F. (2007) Drug addiction: Pathways to the disease and pathophysiological perspectives. *European Neuropsychopharmacology*, **17**, 377–93.

Lenoir, M., and Ahmed, S. H. (2007) Supply of a non-drug substitute reduces escalated heroin consumption. *Neuropsychopharmacology*, Advance Online Publication. http://dx.doi.org/10.1038/sj.npp.1301602.

Lenoir, M. E., Dingemans, P. M., Schene, A. H., Hart, A. A., and Linszen, D. H. (2002) The course of parental expressed emotion and psychotic episodes after family intervention in recent onset schizophrenia: A longitudinal study. *Schizophrenia Research*, **57**, 183–90.

Lenzenweger, M. F. (2001) Reaction time slowing during high-load, sustained attention task performance in relation to psychometrically identified schizotypy. *Journal of Abnormal Psychology*, **110**, 290–6.

Lenzenweger, M., and Clarkin, J. (2004) *Major theories of personality disorder* (2nd edn). US: Guilford Press.

Leonard, B. (1997) *Fundamentals of psychopharmacology* (2nd edn). Chichester: Wiley.

Lepore, S. J. (1997) Social-environmental influences on the chronic stress process. In B. H. Gottleib (ed.), *Coping with chronic stress*. New York: Plenum.

Leppanen, J. M. (2006) Emotional information processing in mood disorders: A review of behavioural and neuroimaging findings. *Current Opinion in Psychiatry*, **19**(1), 34–9.

Leri, F., Bruneau, J., and Stewart, J. (2003) Understanding polydrug use: Review of heroin and cocaine use. *Addiction*, **98**(1), 7–22.

Lero, D. S., and Lewis, S. (2008) Assumptions, research gaps and emerging issues: Implications for research, policy and practice. In K. Korabik, D. S. Lero and D. L. Whitehead (eds), *Handbook of work-family integration: Research, theory, and best practices*. London: Academic Press.

Leslie, A. (1990) Pretence, autism and the basis of 'theory of mind'. *The Psychologist*, **3**, 120–3.

Leslie, J. (2002) *Essential behaviour analysis*. London: Arnold.

Letherby, G., Birch, P., Cain, M., and Williams, K. (2007) *Sex as crime*. London: Willan.

Leudar, I., and Thomas, P. (2000) *Voices of reason, voices of insanity: Studies of verbal hallucinations*. London: Brunner-Routledge.

Levin, R., and Riley, A. (2006) The physiology of human sexual dysfunction. *Psychiatry*, **6**(3), 90–4.

Levine, H. (2003) Global drug prohibition: Its uses and crises. *International Journal of Drug Policy*, **14**, 145–53.

Levine, N. (2006) Crime mapping and the Crimestat program. *Geographical Analysis*, **38**, 41–56.

Levinson, D. F. (2006) The genetics of depression: A review. *Biological Psychiatry*, **60**(2), 84–92.

Levy, R. (1994) Aging-associated cognitive decline. *International Psychogeriatrics*, **6**(1), 63–8.

Lewinson, P. M., Youngren, M. A., and Grosscup, S. J. (1979) Reinforcement and depression. In A. Depue (ed.), *The psychology of the depressive disorders*. New York: Academic Press.

Lewis, C., Fields, C., and Rainey, E. (2006) A study of geriatric forensic evaluees: Who are the violent elderly? *Journal of the American Academy of Psychiatry and Law*, **34**, 324–32.

Lewis, D. A., Hashimoto, T., and Volk, D. W. (2005) Cortical inhibitory neurons and schizophrenia. *Nature Reviews: Neuroscience*, **6**, 312–18.

Lewis, R. W., Fugli-Mayer, K. S., Bosch, R., Fugi-Mayer, A. R., Laumann, E. O., Lizza, E., and Martin-Morales, A. (2004) Epidemiology/risk factors of sexual dysfunction. *Journal of Sexual Medicine*, **1**(1), 35–9.

Lewis, S. (1994) 'ICD-10: A neuropsychiatrist's nightmare?' *British Journal of Psychiatry*, **164**, 157–8.

Lewis, S., and Leiberman, J. (2008) CATIE and CUtLASS: Can we handle the truth? *British Journal of Psychiatry*, **192**, 161–3.

Lewis, S., Tarrier, N., Haddock, G., Bentall, R., Kinderman, P., and Kingdon, D. (2002) Randomised controlled trial of cognitive-behavioural therapy in early schizophrenia: Acute phase outcomes. *British Journal of Psychiatry*, **181** (suppl. 43), 91–7.

Lewis, S. W., Barnes, T. R. E., Davies, L., Murray, R. M., Dunn, G., Hayhurst, K. P., Markwick, A., Lloyd, H., and Jones, P. B. (2006) Randomised control trial of effect of prescription of clazapine versus other second generation anti-psychotic drugs in resistant schizophrenia. *Schizophrenia Bulletin*, **32**, 715–23.

Lewy, A., Ahmed, S., and Sack, R. (1995) Phase shifting the human circadian clock using melatonin. *Behavioural Brain Research*, **73**, 131–4.

Li, D., Collier, D. A., and He, L. (2006) Meta-analysis shows strong positive association of the neuregulin 1 (NRG1) gene with schizophrenia. *Human Molecular Genetics*, **15**, 1995–2002.

Liao, S. (2008) Preventing and detecting elder abuse. *Virtual Mentor*, **10**(6), 389–92.

Liberman, R. P., and Kopelowicz, A. (2005) Recovery from schizophrenia: A concept in search of research. *Psychiatric Services*, **56**, 735–42.

Libow, J. A., and Schreier, H. A. (1986) Three forms of factitious illness in children: When is it Münchausen syndrome by proxy? *American Journal of Orthopsychiatry*, **56**, 602–11.

Lidberg, L., Belfrage, H., Bertilsson, L., Evenden, M., and Asberg, M. (2000) Suicide attempts and impulse control disorder are related to low cerebrospinal fluid 5-HIAA in mentally disordered violent offenders. *Acta Psychiatrica Scandinavica*, **101**(5), 395–402.

Liddle, P. (1987) The symptoms of chronic schizophrenia: A re-examination of the positive–negative dichotomy. *British Journal of Psychiatry*, **151**, 145–51.

Liddle, P. F., Friston, K. J., Frith, C. D., and Frackoviak, R. S. J. (1992) Cerebral blood flow and mental processes in schizophrenia. *Journal of the Royal Society of Medicine*, **85**, 224–7.

Lidz, T., Blatt, S., and Cook, B. (1981) Critique of the Danish–American studies of the adopted-away offspring of schizophrenic parents. *American Journal of Psychiatry*, **138**, 1063–8.

Lidz, T., Cornelison, A., Fleck, S., and Terry, D. (1957) The intrafamilial environment of schizophrenic patients II. Marital schism and marital skew. *American Journal of Psychiatry*, **114**, 241–8.

Lidz, T., Cornelison, A., Terry, D., and Fleck, S. (1958) Intrafamilial environment of the schizophrenic patient, VI: The transmission of irrationality. *Archives of Neurology and Psychiatry*, **79**, 305–16.

Lieb, R., Becker, E., and Altamura, C. (2005) The epidemiology of generalised anxiety disorder in Europe. *European Neuropsychopharmacology*, **15**(4), 445–52.

Lieber, A. (1978) Human aggression and the lunar synodic cycle. *Journal of Clinical Psychiatry*, May, 385–92.

Lieberman, M., Yalom, J., and Miles, M. (1973) *Encounter groups: First facts*. New York: Basic Books.

Liebert, M. A. (2003) Flow-based model of computer hacker's motivation. *CyberPsychology and Behaviour*, **6**(2), 171–80.

Lim, M. C., Shiba, D. R., Clark, I. J., Kim, D. Y., Styles, D. E., Brandt, J. D., Watnik, M. R., and Barthelow, I. J. (2007) Personality type of the glaucoma patient. *Journal of Glaucoma*, **16**(8), 649–54.

Lindenmayer, J. P., Bernstein-Hyman, R., Grochowski, S., and Bark, N. (1995) Psychopathology of schizophrenia: Initial validation of a five-factor model. *Psychopathology*, **28**, 22–31.

Lindsay, W. R., Olley, S., Jack, C., Morrison, F., and Smith, A. H. W. (1998) The treatment of two stalkers with intellectual disabilities using a cognitive approach. *Journal of Applied Research in Intellectual Disabilities*, **11**, 333–44.

Linqvist, P., and Allebeck, P. (1990) Schizophrenia and crime: A longitudinal follow-up of 644 schizophrenics in Stockholm. *British Journal of Psychiatry*, **157**, 345–50.

Linszen, D., and van Amelsvoort, T. (2007) Cannabis and psychosis: An update on course and biological plausible mechanisms. *Current Opinion in Psychiatry*, **20**(2), 116–20.

Linszen, D. H., Dingemans, P. M., and Lenoir, M. E. (1994) Cannabis abuse and the course of recent onset schizophrenia disorders. *Archives of General Psychiatry*, **51**, 273–79.

Lion, J. R. (1978) Outpatient treatment of psychopaths. In W. Reid (ed.), *The psychopath: A comprehensive study of antisocial disorders and behaviours*. New York: Brunner-Mazel.

Lis, E., Greenfield, B., Henry, M., Guile, J. M., and Dougherty, G. (2007) Neuroimaging and genetics of borderline personality disorder: A review. *Journal of Psychiatry Neuroscience*, **32**(3), 162–73.

Little, A. (1965) Parental deprivation, separation and crime: A test on adolescent recidivists. *British Journal of Criminology*, **5**, 419–30.

Livesley, W. J. (ed.) (2001) *Handbook of personality disorders*. New York: Guilford Press.

Llewelyn, S. (2003) Clinical psychology: New directions in applied psychology. In R. Bayne and I. Horton (eds), *Applied psychology*. London: Sage.

Lloyd, E. (1999) Evolutionary psychology: The burdens of proof. *Biology and Philosophy*, **14**, 211–33.

Lloyd-Bostock, S. (1996) The jury in the United Kingdom: Juries and jury research in context. In G. Davies, S. Lloyd-Bostock, M. McMurren and C. Wilson (eds), *Psychology, law and criminal justice: International developments in research and practice*. Berlin: de Gruyter.

Lochner, C., Seedat, S., Du Toit, P. L., Nel, D. G., Niehaus, D., Sandler, R., and Stein, D. (2005) Obsessive–compulsive disorder and trichotillomania: A phenomenological comparison. *BioMed Central Psychiatry*, **5**(2), www.biomedcentral.com/1471-244X/5/2.

Loehlin, J. C. (1992) *Genes and environment in personality development*. Newbury Park, CA: Sage.

Loftus, E. F. (1979) *Eyewitness testimony*. Cambridge, MA: Harvard University Press.

Loftus, E. F. (1993) The reality of repressed memories. *American Psychologist*, **48**, 518–37.

Loftus, E. F. (1997) Creating false memories. *Scientific American*, **227**, 51–5.

Loftus, E. F., and Davis, D. (2006) Recovered memories. *Annual Review of Clinical Psychology*, **2**, 469–98.

Loftus, E. F., and Palmer, J. C. (1974) Reconstructions of automobile destruction: An example of the interaction between language and memory. *Juornal of Verbal Learning and Verbal Behaviour*, **13**, 585–9.

Lohr, J. M., Olatunji, B. O., and Sawchuck, C. N. (2007) A functional analysis of danger and safety signals in anxiety disorders. *Clinical Psychology Review*, **27**, 114–26.

Lombroso, C. (1876) *L'Uomo delinquente*. Turin: Fratelli Bocca.

Lombroso, C. (1906) *Crime: Causes et remèdes* (2nd edn). Paris: Alcan.

Long, M., Meyer, D., and Jacobs, G. (2007) Psychological distress among American Red Cross disaster workers responding to terrorist attacks of September 11, 2001. *Psychiatry Research*, **149**(103), 303–8.

Looby, A., and Earleywine, M. (2007) Negative consequences associated with dependence in daily cannabis users. *Substance Abuse Treatment, Prevention and Policy*, **2**(3), 27–31.

LoPiccolo, J., and Libitz, W. C. (1972) The role of masturbation in the treatment of orgasmic dysfunction. *Archives of Sexual Behaviour*, **2**, 163–71.

Loranger, A. W. (1999) *International personality disorder examination manual: DSM-IV module*. Washington, DC: American Psychiatric Press.

Lorenz, K. (1957) The nature of instinct: The conception of instinctive behaviour. In C. H. Schiller (ed.), *Instinctive behaviour: The development of a modern concept*. New York: International Universities Press.

Lorenz, K. (1966) *On aggression*. London: Methuen.

Lovaas, O. (1987) Behavioural treatment and normal educatonal and intellectual functioning in young autistic children. *Journal of Consulting and Clinical Psychology*, **55**, 3–9.

Lowe, A. L., and Abou-Saleh, M. T. (2004) The British experience of dual diagnosis in the National Health Service. *Acta Neuropsychiatrica*, **18**, 41–6.

Lowenstein, L. (2006) Aspects of young sex abusers: A review of the literature concerning young sex abusers (1996–2004). *Clinical Psychology and Psychotherapy*, **13**, 47–55.

Loza, W., and Hanna, S. (2006) Is schizoid personality a forerunner of homicidal or suicidal behaviour? *International Journal of Offender Therapy and Comparative Criminology*, **50**(1), 338–43.

Lundt, I. (1998) History and emerging trends in education and training for clinical psychologists in the European

Union. In A. S. Bellack and M. Hersen (eds), *Comprehensive clinical psychology*, vol. 2. Amsterdam: Elsevier Science.

Luthar, S. S., and Cicchetti, D. (2000) The construct of resilience: Implications for interventions and social policies. *Development and Psychopathology*, **12**, 857–85.

Lydiard, R., Brawman-Minzer, O., and Ballenger, J. (1996) Recent developments in the psychopharmacology of anxiety disorders. *Journal of Consulting and Clinical Psychology*, **64**, 660–8.

Lyketsos, C. G., Garrett, E., Liang, K. Y., and Anthony, M. (1999) Cannabis use and cognitive decline in persons under 65 years of age. *American Journal of Epidemiology*, **149**, 794–800.

Lykken, D. T. (1995) *The antisocial personalities*. Hillsdale, NJ: Lawrence Erlbaum.

Lykken, D. T. (1998) *A tremor in the blood: Uses and abuses of the lie detector* (2nd edn). New York: Plenum.

Lykouras, L., Oulis, P., Daskapoulou, E., Psarros, K., and Christodolou, G. N. (2001) Clinical sub-types of schizophrenic disorders: a cluster analytic study. *Psychopathology*, **34**, 23–8.

Maass, A., and Köhnken, G. (1989) Eyewitness identification: Simulating the weapon effect. *Law and Human Behaviour*, **13**, 397–408.

McCallie, M. S., Blum, C. M., and Hood, C. J. (2006) Progressive muscle relaxation. *Journal of Human Behaviour in the Social Environment*, **13**(3), 51–66.

McCambridge, J., Mitchelson, L., Winstock, A., and Hunt, N. (2005) Five-year trends in patterns of drug use among people who use stimulants in dance contexts in the United Kingdom. *Addiction*, **100**, 1140–9.

McCauley, J., Chun Li, C., Jiang, L., Olson, L., Crockett, G., Gainer, K., Folstein, S., Haines, J., and Sutcliffe, J. (2005) Genome-wide and ordered-subset linkage analyses provide support for autism loci on 17q and 19p with evidence of phenotypic and interlocus genetic correlates. *BMC Medical Genetics*, **6**(1), 1–11 (assigned).

McClung, C. A. (2007) Circadian genes, rhythms and the biology of mood disorders. *Pharmacology and Therapeutics*, **114**(2), 222–32.

McConaghy, N. (1999) Unresolved issues in scientific sexology. *Archives of Sexual Behaviour*, **28**, 285–318.

McCrae, R. R., and Costa, P. T., Jr (1999) A five-factor theory of personality. In L. A. Pervin and O. P. John (eds), *Handbook of personality: Theory and research*. New York: Guilford Press.

MacCulloch, M. J., Snowden, P. R., Wood, P. J., and Mills, H. E. (1983) Sadistic fantasy, sadistic behaviours and offending. *British Journal of Psychiatry*, **143**, 20–9.

McEachlin, J., Smith, T., and Lovaas, O. (1993) Long-term outcome for children with autism who received early intensive behavioural treatment. *American Journal on Mental Retardation*, **97**, 359–72.

McElroy, S., Kotwal, R., Malhotra, S., Nelson, E., Keck, P., Jr and Nemaroff, C. (2004) Are mood disorders and obesity related? A review for the mental health professional. *Journal of Clinical Psychiatry*, **65**(5), 634–51.

McFarlane, J. M., Campbell, J. C., Wilt, S., Sachs, C. J., Ulrich, Y., and Xu, X. (1999) Stalking and intimate partner femicide. *Homicide Studies*, **3**, 300–16.

McFarlane, L., and Bocij, P. (2003) Cyberstalking: Defining the invasion of cyberspace. *Forensic Update*, **72**, 18–22.

McG. Kelley, D. (1942) Mania and the moon. *Psychoanalytic Review*, **9**, 406–26.

McGlashan, T. H., and Hoffman, R. E. (2000) Schizophrenia as a disorder of developmentally reduced synaptic connectivity. *Archives of General Psychiatry*, **57**, 637–48.

McGrath, J. (1999) Hypothesis: Is low prenatal vitamin D a risk-modifying factor for schizophrenia? *Schizophrenia Research*, **40**(3), 173–7.

McGrath, J., Saha, S., Welham, J., Saadi, O. E., MacCauley, C., and Chant, D. (2004) A systematic review of the incidence of schizophrenia: The distribution of rates and the influence of sex, urbanicity, migrant status and methodology. *BMC Medicine*, **2**, 13–35.

McGuire, B. E. (1999) Clinical psychology in Australia. *Clinical Psychology Forum*, **127**, 24–7.

McGuire, B., and Wraith, A. (2000) Legal and psychological aspects of stalking: A review. *Journal of Forensic Psychiatry*, **11**(2), 316–27.

McGuire, J. (1996) Forensic psychology: Contrasting practices. *European Federation of Professional Psychologists Associations Newsletter*, **10**, 3–6.

McGuire, M., and Troisi, A. (1997) *Darwinian psychiatry*. Oxford: Oxford University Press.

McGuire, M., Fawzy, F., Spar, J., Weigel, R., and Troisi, A. (1994) Altruism and mental disorders. *Ethology and Sociology*, **15**, 299–321.

McGurk, S. R., and Mueser, K. T. (2004) Cognitive functioning, symptoms and work in supported employment: A review and heuristic model. *Schizophrenia Research*, **70**, 147–73.

McGurk, S. R., Twamley, E. W., Sitzer, D. I., McHugo, G. J., and Mueser, K. T. (2007) A meta-analysis of cognitive remediation in schizophrenia. *American Journal of Psychiatry*, **164**, 1791–1802.

McKay, D., Abramowitz, J., Taylor, S., and Deacon, B. (2007) Evolving treatments for panic disorder. *American Journal of Psychiatry*, **164**(6), 976–7.

McKay, R., and Kittappa, R. (2008) Will stem cell biology generate new therapies for Parkinson's disease? *Neuron*, **58**(5), 659–61.

MacKay, R. P., and Myrianthopoulos, N. C. (1966) Multiple sclerosis in twins and their relatives. *Archives of Neurology*, **15**, 449–62.

McKeganey, N. (2006) The lure and the loss of harm-reduction in UK drug policy and practice. *Addiction Research and Theory*, **14**(6), 557–88.

McKenna, P. J. (1997) *Schizophrenia and related syndromes*. Hove: Psychology Press.

McKenna, P. J. (2007) *Schizophrenia and related syndromes* (2nd edn). Hove: Routledge.

McKenna, P., and Oh, T. (2005) *Schizophrenic speech: Making sense of bathroots and ponds that fall in doorways*. Cambridge: Cambridge University Press.

McKenzie, E. (1965) Amphetamine and barbiturate use in aircrew. *Aerospace Medicine*, **36**, 774.

McKim, W. A. (2003) *Drugs and behaviour: An introduction to behavioural pharmacology*. Englewood Cliffs, NJ: Prentice Hall.

Mackintosh, N. J. (1983) *Conditioning and associative learning*. Oxford: Oxford University Press.

Mackintosh, N. J. (1995) Classical and operant conditioning. In N. J. Mackintosh and A. Coleman (eds), *Learning and skills*. London: Longman.

McLean, I. (2003) St Mary's Centre: Services for people in Greater Manchester who have been raped or sexually assaulted. Paper presented at the Forensic Research Group Conference, 'Forensic Health Psychology', 8 Nov., Manchester Metropolitan University. *Proceedings of the British Psychological Society*, **12**(2), 2004, 138.

McLeod, B. D., Wood, J. J., and Weisz, J. R. (2007) Examining the association between parenting and childhood anxiety: A meta-analysis. *Clinical Psychology Review*, **27**, 155–72.

McMahon, C., Abdo, C., Incrocci, L., Perelman, M., Rowland, D., Waldiger, M., and Xin, Z. C. (2004) Disorders of orgasm and ejaculation in men. *Journal of Sexual Medicine*, **1**(1), 58–65.

McMahon, C., Stuckey, B., Andersen, M., Purvis, K., Koppiker, N., Haughie, S., and Boolell, M. (2005) Efficacy of sildenafil citrate (Viagra) in men with premature ejaculation. *Journal of Sexual Medicine*, **2**, 368–75.

McManus, F. V. (2007) Assessment of anxiety. *Psychiatry*, **6**(4), 149–55.

McMurran, M. (1994) *The psychology of addiction*. London: Taylor and Francis.

McMurren, M., and Shapland, P. (1989) What do prison psychologists do? *The Psychologist*, **12**(7), 287–9.

McNally, R. J. (2007) Mechanisms of exposure therapy: How neuroscience can improve psychological treatments for anxiety disorders. *Clinical Psychology Review*, **27**, 750–9.

Macnalty, A. S. (1966) A history of hysteria. *Nature*, **210**, 66–7.

McPherson, F. (1992) Clinical psychology training in Europe. *British Journal of Clinical Psychology*, **31**(4), 419–28.

McSweeney, T., Stevens, A., Hunt, N., and Turnbull, P. J. (2007) Twisting arms or a helping hand? Assessing the impact of 'coerced' and comparable 'voluntary' drug treatment options. *British Journal of Criminology*, **47**, 470–90.

Maden, A. (2007) Dangerous and severe personality disorder: Antecedents and origins. *British Journal of Psychiatry*, **198**(supp. 49), s8–s11.

Madsen, L., Parsons, S., and Grubin, D. (2004) A preliminary study of the contribution of periodic polygraph testing to the treatment and supervision of sex offenders. *Journal of Forensic Psychiatry and Psychology*, **15**(4), 682–95.

Magee, W., Eaton, W., Wittchen, H., McGonagle, K., and Kessler, R. (1996) Agoraphobia, simple phobia and social phobia in the notional comorbidity survey. *Archives of General Psychiatry*, **53**, 159–68.

Maguire, M. (1997) Crime statistics, patterns and trends: Changing perspectives and their implications. In M. Maguire, R. Morgan and R. Reiner (eds), *The Oxford handbook of criminology* (2nd edn). Oxford: Oxford University Press.

Maguire, M. (2002) Crime statistics: The data explosion and its implications. In M. Maguire, R. Morgan and R. Reiner (eds), *The Oxford handbook of criminology* (3rd edn). Oxford: Oxford University Press.

Maguire, M., Morgan, R., and Reiner, R. (2002) *The Oxford handbook of criminology* (3rd edn). Oxford: Oxford University Press.

Maguire, M., Morgan, R., and Reiner, R. (2007) *The Oxford handbook of criminology* (4th edn). Oxford: Oxford University Press.

Maier, S. F., and Seligman, M. E. P. (1976) Learned helplessness: Theory and evidence. *Journal of Experimental Psychology*, **105**(1), 3–46.

Maier, T. (2004) On phenomenology and classification of hoarding: A review. *Acta Psychiatrica Scandinavica*, **110**(5), 323–37.

Maier, W. (2006) Do schizoaffective disorders exist at all? *Acta Psychiatrica Scandinavica*, **113**, 369–71.

Maio, G. R., Haddock, G. G., and Jarman, H. L. (2007) Social and psychological factors in tackling obesity. *Obesity Reviews*, **8** (suppl. 1), 123–5.

Malerba, G., and Pinatti, P. F. (2005) A review of asthma genetics: Gene expression studies and recent candidates. *Journal of Applied Genetics*, **46**(1), 93–104.

Malkin, D., and Knoppers, B. (1996) Genetic predisposition to cancer: Issues to consider. *Seminars in Cancer Biology*, **7**(1), 49–53.

Maltby, J., Day, E., and Macaskill, A. (2007) *Personality, individual differences and intelligence*. London: Pearson.

Malterer, M. B., Glass, S. J., and Newman, J. P. (2008) Psychopathy and trait emotional intelligence. *Personality and Individual Differences*, **44**, 735–45.

Management Advisory Service (2003) *The development of the role of assistant clinical psychologists: A feasibility study*. Cheltenham: MAS.

Mancebo, M. C., Eisen, J., Grant, J., and Rasmussen, S. A. (2005) Obsessive–compulsive personality disorder and obsessive–compulsive disorder: Clinical characteristics, diagnostic difficulties and treatment. *Annals of Psychiatry*, **17**(4), 197–204.

Mann, J. J. (ed.) (1989) *Models of depressive disorders: Psychological, biological and genetic perspectives*. New York: Plenum.

Mann, J. J. (2002) A current perspective of suicide and attempted suicide. *Annals of International Medicine*, **136**, 302–11.

Mann, J. J., Apter, A., Bertolote, J., Beautraise, A., Currier, D., Haas, A., Hegerl, U., Lonnqvist, J., Malone, K., Marusic, A., Mehlum, L., Patton, G., Phillips, M., Rutz, W., Rihmer, Z., Schmidtke, A., Shaffer, D., Silverman, M., Takahashi, Y., Varnic, A., Wassermen, D., Yip, P., and Hendin, H. (2005) Suicide prevention strategies: A systematic review. *Journal of the American Medical Association*, **294**(16), 2064–74.

Mann, R. E. (2004) Innovations in sex offender treatment. *Journal of Sexual Medicine*, **10**(2), 141–52.

Manning, J. T. (2002) *Digit ratio: A pointer to fertility, behaviour and health*. Piscataway, NJ: Rutgers University Press.

Manschreck, T. (1993) Psychomotor abnormalities. In C. G. Costello (ed.), *Symptoms of schizophrenia*. New York: Wiley.

Marchesi, C., Cantoni, A., Fontò, S., Giannelli, M. R., and Maggini, C. (2006) The effect of temperament and character on response to selective serotonin reuptake inhibitors in panic disorder. *Acta Psychiatrica Scandinavica*, **114**(3), 203–10.

Marcin, M. S., and Nemeroff, C. B. (2003) The neurobiology of social anxiety disorder: The relevance of fear and anxiety. *Acta Psychiatrica Scandinavica*, **108**(s417), 51–64.

Marcus, D. K., Gurley, J. R., Marchi, M. M., and Bauer, C. (2007) Cognitive and perceptual variables in hypochondriasis and health anxiety: A systematic review. *Clinical Psychology Review*, **27**, 127–39.

Marissen, M., Franken, I., Blanken, P., van den Brink, W., and Hendriks, V. (2005) Cue exposure therapy for opiate dependent clients. *Journal of Substance Use*, **10**(2–3), 97–105.

Marks, I. M., and Lader, M. (1973) Anxiety sates (anxiety neurosis): A review. *Journal of Nervous and Mental Disease*, **156**, 3–18.

Marrazzi, M. A., and Luby, E. D. (1986) Auto-addiction model of chronic anorexia nervosa. *International Journal of Addiction*, **5**(2), 191–208.

Marshall, B. J., and Warren, J. R. (1984) Unidentified curved bacilli in the stomach of patients with gastritis and peptic ulceration. *The Lancet*, **1**(8390), 1311–15.

Marshall, M., and Rathbone, J. (2006) Early intervention for psychosis. *Cochrane Database of Systematic Reviews*, **4**, CD004718.

Marshall, R. J. (1983) A psychoanalytic perspective on the diagnosis and development of juvenile delinquents. In W. S. Laufer and J. M. Day (eds), *Personality theory, moral development and criminal behaviour*. Lexington, MA: Lexington Books.

Marshall, W. L. (1970) Satiation therapy: A procedure for reducing deviant sexual arousal. *Journal of Applied Behaviour Analysis*, **12**, 10–22.

Marshall, W. L. (1996) Assessment, treatment and theorising about sex offenders: Developments during the past 20 years and future directions. *Criminal Justice and Behaviour*, **23**(1), 162–99.

Marshall, W. L. (2007) Diagnostic issues, multiple paraphilias and comorbid disorders in sexual offenders: Their incidence and treatment. *Aggression and Violent Behaviour*, **12**, 16–35.

Marshall, Y. (2003) A study into the possible links between obsessive–compulsive disorder, neuroticism and the practice of Judaism in a non-clinical sample. Unpublished thesis, Manchester Metropolitan University.

Marston W. M. (1917) Systolic blood pressure symptoms of deception. *Journal of Experimental Psychology*, **2**, 117–63.

Martinson, R. (1974) What works? Questions and answers about prison reform. *The Public Interest*, **35**, 22–54.

Maruyama, T., Kawahara, N., Yokoyama, K., Makino, Y., Fukiharu, T., and Goda, Y. (2006) Phylogenetic relationship of psychoactive fungi based on rRNA gene for a large subunit and their identification using the TaqMan assay (II). *Forensic Science International*, **163**(1–2), 51–8.

Marzillier, J., and Hall, J. (1999) *What is clinical psychology?* (3rd edn). Oxford: Oxford University Press.

Maslow, A. H. (1943) A theory of human motivation. *Psychological Review*, **50**, 370–96.

Mason, C. A., Cauce, A. M., Gonzales, N., and Hiraga, Y. (1994) Adolescent problem behavior: The effect of peers and the moderating roles of father absence and the mother–child relationship. *American Journal of Community Psychology*, **22**, 723–43.

Mason, O., Claridge, G., and Jackson, M. (1995) New scales for the assessment of schizotypy. *Personal and Individual Differences*, **18**(1), 7–13.

Mason, T., and Mercer, D. (1999) *A sociology of the mentally disordered offender*. Edinburgh: Pearson.

Masson, J. (1985) *The complete letters of Sigmund Freud to Wilhelm Fliess, 1887–1904*. Cambridge, MA: Havard University Press.

Masters, K. S. (2004) Religion and health. In A. J. Christiansen, R. Martin and J. M. Smyth (eds), *Encyclopedia of health psychology*. New York: Kluwer.

Masters, K. S., Spielmans, G. J., and Goodson, J. T. (2006) Are there demonstrable effects of distant intercessory prayer? A meta-analytic review. *Annals of Behavioural Medicine*, **32**, 21–6.

Masters, R. (2001) Biology and politics: Linking nature and nurture. *Annual Review of Political Science*, **4**, 345–69.

Masters, W., and Johnson, V. (1966) *Human sexual response*. London: J. A. Churchill.

Masters, W., and Johnson, V. (1970) *Human sexual inadequacy*. London: J. A. Churchill.

Masters, W., Johnson, V., and Kolodny, R. (1986) *Masters and Johnson on sex and human loving*. London: Macmillan.

Masters, W., Johnson, V. E., and Kolodny, K. C. (1995) *Human sexuality*. London: Allyn and Bacon.

Matheson, K., and Zanna, M. P. (1988) The impact of computer-mediated communication of self-awareness. *Computers in Human Behavior*, **4**, 221–33.

Mathias, P. (2003) Force for change. *The Psychologist*, **16**(2), 82–3.

Matiax-Cols, D., and Phillips, M. L. (2007) Psychophysiological and functional neuroimaging techniques in the study of anxiety disorders. *Psychiatry*, **6**(4), 156–60.

Matthies, E., Hoeger, R., and Guski, R. (2000) Living on polluted soil: Determinants of stress symptoms. *Environment and Behaviour*, **32**, 270–86.

Mattia, J. I., and Zimmerman, M. (2001) Epidemiology. In W. J. Livesley (ed.), *Handbook of personality disorders: Theory, research and treatment*. New York: Guilford Press.

Mattioli, A. V. (2007) Effects of caffeine and coffee consumption on cardiovascular disease and risk factors. *Future Cardiology*, **3**(2), 203–12.

Matza, D. (1964) *Delinquency and drift*. New York: Wiley.

Mawson, D., Grounds, A., and Tantam, D. (1985) Violence and Asperger's syndrome: A case study. *British Journal of Psychiatry*, **147**, 566–9.

May, A. (2005) Cluster headache: Pathogenesis, diagnosis, and management. *The Lancet*, **366**(9488), 843–55.

May, R. (1983) *The discovery of being: Writings in existential psychology*. New York: Norton.

Mayer-Gross, W., Slater, E., and Roth, M. (1969) *Clinical psychiatry*. London: Bailliere, Tindall and Cox.

Mayford, M., and Kandel, E. R. (1999) Genetic approaches to memory storage. *Trends in Genetics*, **15**, 463–70.

Mayou, R., Kirmayer, L., Simon, G., Kroenke, K., and Sharpe, M. (2005) Somatoform disorders: Time for a new approach in DSM-V. *American Journal of Psychiatry*, **162**, 847–55.

Meadow, R. (1977) Münchausen syndrome by proxy: The hinterland of child abuse. *The Lancet*, **2**, 343–5.

Meadow, R. (1985) Management of Münchausen syndrome by proxy. *Archives of Disease in Childhood*, **60**, 385–93.

Meadow, R. (1997) *ABC of child abuse* (3rd edn). London: BMJ Publishing Group.

Meadow, R. (1999) Unnatural sudden infant death. *Arcvhives of Disease in Childhood*, **80**(1), 7–14.

Mealey, L. (1995) The sociobiology of psychopathy: An integrated evolutionary model. *Behavioural and Brain Sciences*, **18**, 523–99.

Mechanic, M. B., Weaver, T. L., and Resick, P. A. (2000) Intimate partner violence and stalking behaviour: Exploration of patterns and correlates in a sample of acutely battered women. *Violence and Victims*, **15**, 55–72.

Mednick, N. S., Moffit, T., and Stack, S. (1987) *The causes of crime: New biological approaches*. Cambridge: Cambridge University Press.

Mednick, S. A., Gabrielli, W., and Hutchings, B. (1984) Genetic influences on criminal convictions: Evidence from an adoption cohort. *Science*, **224**, 891.

Meehl, P. (1950) On the circularity of the law of effect. *Psychological Bulletin*, **47**, 52–75.

Meehl, P. E. (1962) Schizotaxia, schizotypia, schizophrenia. *American Psychologist*, **17**, 827–38.

Meehl, P. E. (1999) Clarifications about taxometric method. *Applied and Preventive Psychology*, **8**, 165–74.

Meichenbaum, D. (1986) *Stress inoculation training*. New York: Pergamon.

Meichenbaum, D., and Cameron, R. (1973) Training schizophrenics to talk to themselves: A means of developing attentional controls. *Behaviour Therapy*, **4**, 515–34.

Meloy, J. R., and Gothard, S. (1995) A demographic and clinical comparison of obsessional followers and offenders with mental disorders. *American Journal of Psychiatry*, **152**, 258–63.

Meloy, J. R. (1998) *The psychology of stalking: Clinical and forensic perspectives*. San Diego, CA: Academic Press.

Meloy, J. R. (1999) Stalking: An old behaviour but a new crime. *Psychiatric Clinics of North America*, **22**, 85–99.

Meltzer, H. Y., Li, Z., Kaneda, Y., and Ichikawa, J. (2003) Serotonin receptors: Their key role in drugs to treat schizophrenia. *Progress in Neuropsychopharmacology and Biological Psychiatry*, **27**(7), 1159–72.

Melzack, R., and Wall, P. D. (1999) *Textbook of pain* (4th edn). New York: Churchill Livingstone.

Memon, A., Hope, L., Bartlett, J., and Bull, R. (2002) Eyewitness recognition errors: The effects of mugshot viewing and choosing in young and old adults. *Memory and Cognition*, **30**, 1219–27.

Memon, A., Vrij, A., and Bull, R. (2003) *Psychology and law* (2nd edn). London: Wiley.

Mendle, J., Harden, K. P., Turkheimer, E., Van Hulle, C. A., D'Onofrio, B. M., Brooks-Gunn, J., Rodgers, J. L., Emery, R. E., and Lahey, B. B. (2009) Associations between father absence and age of first sexual intercourse. *Child Development*, **80**(5), 1463–80.

Merckelbach, H., de-Jong, P., Muris, P., and van den Hout, M. (1996) The aetiology of specific phobias: A review. *Clinical Psychology Review*, **16**, 337–61.

Merskey, H. (1992) The manufacture of personalities: The production of multiple personality disorder. *British Journal of Psychiatry*, **160**, 327–40.

Meston, C., Hull, E., Levin, R. J., and Sipski, M. (2004) Disorders of orgasm in women. *Journal of Sexual Medicine*, **1**(1), 66–8.

Mettens, P., and Monteyne, P. (2002) Life-style vaccines. *British Medical Bulletin*, **62**, 175–86.

Metzl, J. M. (2004) From scopophilia to survivor, a brief history of voyeurism. *Textual Practice*, **18**(3), 415–34.

Meyer, B., Ajchenbrenner, M., and Bowles, D. P. (2005) Sensory sensitivity, attachment experiences and rejection responses among adults with borderline and avoidant features. *Journal of Personality Disorders*, **19**, 641–58.

Meyer, J., and Quenzer, L. (2005) *Psychopharmacology*. Sunderland, MA: Sinauer.

Michael, T., Zetsche, U., and Margraf, J. (2007) Epidemiology of anxiety disorders. *Psychiatry*, **6**(4), 136–42.

Miles, H., Dutheil, L., Welsby, I., and Haider, D. (2007) 'Just say no': A preliminary evaluation of a three-stage model of integrated treatment for substance use problems in conditions of maximum security. *Journal of Forensic Psychiatry and Psychology*, **18**(2), 141–59.

Miles, J. (2000) Darwin's final message: We have no honour. *Children and Society*, **14**, 110–20.

Milgram, S. (1963) Behavioural study of obedience. *Journal of Abnormal and Social Psychology*, **67**, 371–8.

Miller, F. G., Pickar, D., and Rosenstein, D. L. (1999) Addressing ethical issues in the psychiatric research literature. *Archives of General Psychiatry*, **56**(8), 763–4.

Miller, J., McGlashan, T. H., Rosen, J. L., Somjee, L., Markovich, P. J., Stein, K., and Woods, S. W. (2002) Prospective diagnosis of the initial prodrome for schizophrenia based on the Structured Interview for Prodromal Syndromes: Preliminary evidence of interrater reliability and predictive validity, *American Journal of Psychiatry*, **159**, 863–5.

Millon, T. (1981) *Disorders of Personality: DSM-III, Axis II*. New York: Wiley.

Mills., J. F., and Kroner, D. G. (2003) Antisocial constructs in predicting institutional violence among violent offenders and molesters. *International Journal of Offender Therapy and Comparative Criminology*, **47**(3), 324–34.

Mills, K., Teesson, M., Ross, J., and Darke, S. (2007) The impact of post-traumatic stress disorder on treatment outcomes for heroin dependence. *Addiction*, **102**(3), 447–54.

Milne, R., and Bull, R. (1999) *Investigative interviewing: Psychology and practice*. Chichester: Wiley.

Minati, L., and Aquino, D. (2006) Probing neural connectivity through diffusion tensor imaging. *Cybernetics and Systems*, **37**, 263–8.

MIND (2008) Healthcare Commission reveals the extent to which acute mental health wards are failing patients. http://www.mind.org.uk/News+policy+and+campaigns/Press/Healthcare+commission+acute+wards+July+2008.htm.

Mischel, W. (1968) *Personality and assessment*. New York: Wiley.

Mitchell, J. E., Agras, S., and Wonderlich, S. (2007) Treatment of bulimia nervosa: Where are we and where are we going? *International Journal of Eating Disorders*, **40**(2), 95–101.

Mittal, V. A., Tessner, K. D., and Walker, E. F. (2007) Elevated social internet use and schizotypal personality disorder in adolescents. *Schizophrenia Research*, **90**, 50–7.

Moffitt, T. E., and Caspi, A. (2001) Childhood predictors differentiate life-course persistent and adolescence-limited antisocial pathways among males and females. *Developmental Psychology*, **13**, 355–75.

Mohan, R., and Fahy, T. (2006) Is there a need for community forensic mental health services? *Journal of Forensic Psychiatry and Psychology*, **17**(3), 365–71.

Mohandie, K., Meloy, J. R., McGowan, M. G., and Williams, J. (2006) The RECON typology of stalking: Reliability and validity based upon a large sample of North American stalkers. *Journal of Forensic Sciences*, **51**(1), 147–55.

Mohr, D. (1995) Negative outcome in psychotherapy: A critical review. *Clinical Psychology*, **2**, 1–27.

Mohr, D. C., Goodkin, D. E., Bacchetti, P., Boudewyn, A. C., Huang, L., Marrietta, P., Cheuk, W., and Dee, B. (2000) Psychological stress and the subsequent appearance of new brain MRI lesions in MS. *Neurology*, **55**, 55–61.

Montague, L. R., Tantam, D., Newby, D., Thomas, P., and Ring, N. (1989) The incidence of negative symptoms in early schizophrenia, mania and other psychoses. *Acta Psychiatrica Scandinavica*, **79**, 613–18.

Montel, S., and Bungener, C. (2007) Mood and emotional disorders in multiple sclerosis: A literature review. *Review of Neurology (Paris)*, **163**(1), 27–37.

Montoya, A., Sorrentino, R., Lukas, S., and Price, B. (2002) Long-term neuropsychiatric consequences of 'ecstasy' (MDMA): A review. *Harvard Review of Psychiatry*, **10**, 212–20.

Moore, R. A., Edwards, J. E., and McQuay, H. J. (2002) Sildenafil (Viagra) for male erectile dysfunctions: A meta-analysis of clinical trial reports. *BioMed Central Urology*, **2**, 6; available at www.biomedcentral.com/1471-2490/2/6.

Morales, A., Buvat, J., Gooren, L. J., Guay, A. T., Kaufman, J., Tan, H. M., and Torres, L. O. (2004) Endocrine aspects of sexual dysfunction in men. *Journal of Sexual Medicine*, **1**(1), 69–81.

Moran, M. (2007) Their religion may differ, but goals are the same. *Psychiatry News*, **42**(6), 10.

Moran, P., Ford, T., Butler, G., and Goodman, R. (2008) Callous and unemotional traits in children and adolescents living in Great Britain. *British Journal of Psychiatry*, **192**, 65–6.

Moran, R. (1981) *Knowing right from wrong: The insanity defence of Daniel McNaughten*. New York: Wiley.

Morel, B. A. (1852). *Traité des maladies mentales*. Paris: Masson.

Morey, L. (1988) Personality disorders in DSM-III and DSM-IIIR: Convergence, coverage and internal consistency. *American Journal of Psychiatry*, **145**, 573–7.

Morf, C. C., and Rhodewalt, F. (2001) Unravelling the paradoxes of narcissism: A dynamic self-regulatory processing model of narcissism. *Psychological Inquiry*, **12**, 177–96.

Morgan, E. (1997) *The aquatic ape hypothesis*. London: Souvenir.

Morgan, L. (1894) *An introduction to comparative psychology*. London: Walter Scott.

Morgan, M. J. (2000) Ecstasy (MDMA): A review of its possible persistent psychological effects. *Psychopharmacology*, **152**, 230–48.

Morissette, S. B., Tull, M. T., Gulliver, S. B., Kamholz, B. W., and Zimering, R. T. (2007) Anxiety, anxiety disorders, tobacco use and nicotine: A critical review of interrelationships. *Psychological Bulletin*, **133**(2), 245–72.

Moritz, S., Woodward, T. S., and Hausmann, D. (2006) Incautious reasoning as a pathogenetic factor for the development of psychotic symptoms in schizophrenia. *Schizophrenia Bulletin*, **32**, 327–31.

Morris, D. (1969) *The human zoo*. London: Jonathan Cape.

Morris, D. (1977) *Manwatching*. London: Jonathan Cape.

Morris, D. (1990) *Animal watching: A field guide to animal behaviour*. London: Jonathan Cape.

Morris, K. (2006) Hallucinogen research inspires 'neurotheology'. *The Lancet*, **5**, 732.

Morrison, A. P. (ed.) (2002) *A casebook of cognitive therapy for psychosis*. Hove: Brunner-Routledge.

Morrison, A. P., and Baker, C. A. (2000) Intrusive thoughts and auditory hallucinations: A comparative study of intrusive in psychosis. *Behavioural Research and Therapy*, **38**, 1097–1106.

Morrison, A. P., French, P., Parker, S., Roberts, M., Stevens, H., Bentall, R. P., and Lewis, S. (2007) Three year follow-up of a randomised controlled trial of cognitive therapy for the prevention of psychosis in people at ultra-high risk. *Schizophrenia Bulletin*, **33**(3), 682–7.

Morrison, A. P., French, P., Walford, L., Lewis, S. W., Kilcommons, A., Green, J., Parker, S., and Bentall, R. P. (2004) A randomised controlled trial of early detection and cognitive therapy for the prevention of psychosis in people at ultra-high risk, *British Journal of Psychiatry*, **185**, 291–7.

Mortimer, A. M., Lund, C. E., and McKenna, P. J. (1990) The positive:negative dichotomy in schizophrenia. *British Journal of Psychiatry*, **157**, 41–9.

Moulding, R., and Kyrios, M. (2006) Anxiety disorders and control related beliefs: The exemplar of obsessive–compulsive disorder (OCD). *Clinical Psychology Review*, **26**, 573–83.

Moye, J., and Marson, D. (2007) Assessment of decision-making capacity in older adults: An emerging area of practice and research. *Journal of Gerontology*, **62**(1), P3–P11.

MPAG (Manpower Advisory Group) (1990) *Clinical psychology: Full report*. London: Department of Health.

MTA Cooperative Group (1999) A 14-month randomised clinical trial of treatment strategies for attention-deficit hyperactivity disorder. MTA Cooperative Group Multimodal Treatment Study for Children with ADHD. *Archives of General Psychiatry*, **56**, 1073–86.

Mueller, J. H., Jacobsen, D. M., and Schwarzer, R. (2000) What are computing experiences good for: A case study in on-line research. In M. H. Birnbaum (ed.), *Psychological experiments on the internet*. San Diego, CA: Academic Press.

Muench, F., Morgenstein, J., Hollander, E., Irwin, T., O'Leary, A., Parsons, J. T., Wainberg, M. L., and Lai, B. (2007) The consequences of compulsive sexual behaviour: The preliminary reliability and validity of the Compulsive Sexual Behaviour Consequences Scale. *Sexual Addiction and Compulsivity*, **14**(3), 207–20.

Mueser, K. T., and Drake, R. E. (2007) Comorbidity: What have we learned and where are we going? *Clinical Psychology: Science and Practice*, **14**, 64–9.

Mullen, P. E. (1997) Disorders of passion. In D. Bhugra and A. Munro (eds), *Troublesome disguises: Under-diagnosed psychiatric syndromes*. Oxford: Blackwell Science.

Mullen, P. E. (2007) Dangerous and severe personality disorder and in need of treatment. *British Journal of Psychiatry*, **190** (supp. 49), s3–s7.

Mullen, P. E., Pathe, M., and Purcell, R. (2000) *Stalkers and their victims*. Cambridge: Cambridge University Press.

Mullen, P. E., Pathe, M., and Purcell, R. (2001) The management of stalkers. *Advances in Psychiatric Treatment*, **7**, 335–42.

Mullen, P. E., Pathe, M., Purcell, R., and Stuart, G. W. (1999) A study of stalkers. *American Journal of Psychiatry*, **156**, 1244–9.

Müller-Ishberner, R., and Hodgins, S. (2000) Evidence-based treatment for mentally disordered offenders. In S. Hodgins and R. Müller-Ishberner, R. (eds), *Violence crime and mentally disordered offenders: Concepts and methods for effective treatment*. Chichester: Wiley.

Muniz-Terrera, G., Mathews, F., Dening, T., Huppert, F., and Brayne, C. (2009) Education and trajectories of cognitive decline over 9 years in very old people: Methods and risk analysis. *Age and Ageing*, **10**, 1–6.

Munley, G., McGloughlin, A., and Forster, J. (1999) Gender differences in health-check attendance and intention in young adults: An application of the health belief model. *Behaviour Change*, **16**(4), 237–45.

Munoz-Sastre, M. T., Vinsonneau, G., Chabrol, H., and Mullett, E. (2005) Forgiveness and the paranoid personality style. *Personality and Individual Differences*, **38**, 765–72.

Munro, A. (1999) *Delusional disorder: Paranoia and related illnesses*. Cambridge: Cambridge University Press.

Munro, H. (1996) Battered pets. *Irish Veterinary Journal*, **49**, 712–13.

Munro, H. (1998) The battered pet syndrome. In P. Olson (ed.), *Recognising and reporting animal abuse: A veterinarian's guide*. American Humane Association.

Munro, H., and Thrusfield, M. V. (2001) 'Battered pets': Munchausen syndrome by proxy (factitious illness by proxy). *Journal of Small Animal Practice*, **42**(8), 385–9.

Munsterberg, H. (1908) *On the witness stand*. New York: McClure.

Munsterberg, H. (1909) *Psychotherapy*. New York: Moffat, Yard.

Murali, V., and George, S. (2007) Lost online: An overview of internet addiction. *Advances in Psychiatric Treatment*, **13**, 24–30.

Murray, C. J. L., and Lopez, A. D. (1996) *The global burden of disease*. Geneva: World Health Organisation.

Murray, J., Fell-Rayner, H., Fine, H., Karia, N., and Sweetingham, R. (2004) What do NHS staff think and know about clinical governance? *Clinical Governance: An International Journal*, **9**(3), 172–80.

Murray, R. M., Morrison, P. D., Henquet, C., and Di Forti, M. (2007) Cannabis, the mind and society: The hash realities. *Nature Reviews Neuroscience*, **8**, 885–95.

Murrie, D., Warren, J., Kristiansson, M., and Dietz, P. (2002) Asperger's syndrome in forensic settings. *International Journal of Forensic Mental Health*, **1**(1), 59–70.

Murta, S. G., Sanderson, K., and Oldenburg, B. (2007) Process evaluation in occupational stress management programs: A systematic review. *American Journal of Health Promotion*, **21**(4), 248–54.

Murthy, R., Srinivasa, I., Kumar, K. V., Kishore, I., Chisholm, D., Thomas, T., Sekar, K., and Chandrashekar, C. R. (2005) Community outreach for untreated schizophrenia in rural India: A follow-up study of symptoms, disability, family burden and costs. *Psychological Medicine*, **35**(3), 341–51.

Muscatell, K. A., Slavich, G. M., Monroe, S. M., and Gotlib, I. H. (2009) Stressful life events, chronic difficulties, and the symptoms of clinical depression. *Journal of Nervous and Mental Disease*, **197**(3), 154–60.

Myers, D. (1995) Gravitational effects of the period of high tides and the new moon on lunacy. *Journal of Emergency Medicine*, **13**(4), 529–32.

Myin-Germeys, I., Delespaul, P., and Van Os, J. (2005) Behavioural sensitization to daily life stress in psychosis. *Psychological Medicine*, **35**, 733–41.

Nace, E. (1995) *Achievement and addiction*. New York: Brunner Mazel.

Nagata, T., Kawarada, Y., Ohshima, J., Iketani, T., and Kiriike, N. (2002) Drug use disorders in Japanese eating disorder patients. *Psychiatry Research*, **109**, 181–91.

Nagin, D. S., and Farrington, D. P. (1992) The stability of criminal potential from childhood to adulthood. *Criminology*, **30**, 235–60.

Nakahara, T., Nakahara, K., Uehara, M., Koyama, K., Li, K., Harada, T., Yasuhara, D., Taguchi, H., Kojima, S., Sagiyama, K., and Inui, A. (2007) Effect of juggling therapy on anxiety disorders in female patients. *Biosocial Medicine*, **1**(10), 92–6.

Narrow, W., Rae, D., Robins, L., and Regier, D. (2002) Revised prevalence estimates of mental disorders in the United States: Using a clinical significance criterion to reconcile 2 survey estimates. *Archives of General Psychiatry*, **59**, 115–23.

Nash, J., and Hutt, D. (2007) Psychopharmacology of anxiety. *Psychiatry*, **64**, 143–8.

National Council Against Health Fraud (1990) NCAHF position paper on acupuncture. Loma Linda, CA: NCAHF.

Neary, D., and Snowden, J. (1996) Fronto-temporal dementia: Nosology, neuropsychology and neuropathology. *Brain and Cognition*, **31**, 176–87.

Needs, A., and Towl, G. (2004) *Applying psychology to forensic practice*. Oxford: Blackwell.

Neilsen, S. (2001) Epidemiology and mortality of eating disorders. *Psychiatric Clinics of North America*, **24**, 201–14.

Neisser, U. (1967) *Cognitive psychology*. New York: Appleton Century Crofts.

Neisser, U. (1982) *Memory observed: Remembering in natural contexts*. San Francisco: W. H. Freeman.

Neitzel, M. (1979) *Crime and its modification: A social learning perspective*. New York: Pergamon.

Nelson, H., and Willison, J. (1991) *National Adult Reading Test manual* (2nd edn). Windsor: NFER-Nelson.

Nemeroff, C. B. (2007) The burden of severe depression: A review of the diagnostic challenges and treatment alternatives. *Journal of Psychiatric Research*, **41**(3–4), 189–206.

Nette, D. (2001) *Strong imagination: Madness, creativity and human nature*. Oxford: Oxford University Press.

Neumark-Sztainer, D. (2005) Can we simultaneously work toward the prevention of obesity and eating disorders in children and adolescence? *International Journal of Eating Disorders*, **38**, 220–7.

Neumerk, Y. D., Delva, J., and Anthony, J. C. (1998) The epidemiology of adolescent drug involvement. *Archives of Paediatric and Adolescent Medicine*, **152**, 781–6.

Newman, D. W., Kellett, S., and Beail, N. (2003) From research and development to practice-based evidence: Clinical governance initiatives in a service for adults with mild intellectual disability and mental health needs. *Journal of Intellectual Disability Research*, **47**(1), 68–74.

Newman, G., and Clarke, R. (2003) *Superhighway robbery: Preventing e-commerce crime*. Cullompton: Willan.

Nicassio, P. M., Meyerowitz, B. E., and Kerns, R. D. (2004) The future of health psychology interventions. *Health Psychology*, **23**(2), 132–7.

Nielsen, J., and Wohlert, M. (1991) Chromosome abnormalities found among 34,910 newborn children: Results from a 13-year incidence study in Arhus, Denmark. *Human Genetics*, **87**(1), 81–3.

Niemeier, V., Klein, H., Gieler, U., Schill, W. B., and Kupfer, J. (2005) Stress and psoriasis: A psychoneuro-immunological study. *Psychotherapy Psychosomatic Medicine and Psychology*, **55**(1), 20–8.

Niendam, T. A., Bearden, C. E., Rosso, I. M., Sanchesz, L. E., Hadley, T., Nuechterlein, K. H., and Cannon, T. D. (2003) A prospective study of childhood neurocognitive functioning in schizophrenic patients and their siblings. *American Journal of Psychiatry*, **160**(11), 2060–2.

Niendam, T., Bearden, C., Johnson, J., McKinley, M., Loewy, R., O'Brien, M., Neuchterlein, K., Green, M., and Cannon, T. (2006) Neurocognitive performance and functional disability in the psychosis prodrome. *Schizophrenia Research*, **84**(1), 100–11.

Nietzel, M. T., Bernstein, D. A., and Mirlich, R. (1998) *Introduction to clinical psychology* (5th edn). Englewood Cliffs, NJ: Prentice Hall.

Nilsson, P. M., Nyberg, P., and Ostergren, P. O. (2001) Increased susceptibility to stress at a psychological assessment of stress tolerance is associated with impaired fetal growth. *International Journal of Epidemiology*, **30**(1), 75–80.

Nolan, P., and Hopper, B. (1997) Mental health nursing in the 50s and 60s revisited. *Journal of Psychiatric and Mental Health Nursing*, **4**, 333–8.

Nordgaard, J., Arnfred, S. M., Handest, P., and Parnas, J. (2008) The diagnostic status of first-rank symptoms. *Schizophrenia Bulletin*, **34**(1), 137–54.

Nordin, C., and Nylander, P. O. (2007) Temperament and character in pathological gambling. *Journal of Gambling Studies*, **23**(2), 113–20.

Norman, P., Bennett, P., and Lewis, H. (1998) Understanding binge drinking among young people: An application of the theory of planned behaviour. *Health Education Research*, **13**(2), 163–9.

Northoff, G. (2002) What catatonia can tell us about top-down modulation: A neuropsychiatric hypothesis. *Behavioural and Brain Sciences*, **25**, 555–604.

Norton, P. J., and Price, E. C. (2007) A meta-analytic review of adult cognitive-behavioural treatment outcome across the anxiety disorders. *Journal of Nervous and Mental Disease*, **195**(6), 521–31.

Novaco, R. W. (1994) Anger as a risk factor for violence among the mentally disordered. In J. Monahan and H. Steadman (eds), *Violence and mental disorder: Developments in risk assessment*. Chicago: Chicago University Press.

Novaco, R. W. (1997) Remediating anger and aggression with violent offenders. *Legal and Criminological Psychology*, **2**, 77–88.

Novak, N., Kruse, S., Potreck, J., Maintz, L., Jenneck, C., Weidinger, S., Fimmers, R., and Bieber, T. (2005) Single nucleotide polymorphisms of the gene are associated with atopic eczema. *Journal of Allergy and Clinical Immunology*, **115**(4), 828–33.

Noyes, R., Jr (2001) Epidemiology of hypochondriasis. In V. Starcevic and D. R. Lipsitt (eds), *Hypochondriasis: Modern perspectives on an ancient malady*. Oxford: Oxford University Press.

Nuechterlein, K. H., Barch, D. M., Gold, J. M., Goldberg, T. E., Green, M. F., and Heaton, R. K. (2004) Identification of separable cognitive factors in schizophrenia. *Schizophrenia Research*, **72**(1), 29–39.

Nunes, E. V., Sullivan, M. A., and Levin, F. R. (2004) Treatment of depression in patients with opiate dependence. *Biological Psychiatry*, **15**, 793–802.

Oatley, G. C., and Ewart, B. W. (2003) Crimes analysis software: 'Pins in maps', clustering and Bayes net prediction. *Expert Systems with Applications*, **25**(4), 569–88.

Obiols, J. E., Serrano, F., Barrantes, N., Garcia-Marimon, M., Gras, S., Bosch, E., Caparros, B., and Carandell, F. (1997) Frontal dysfunction and psychosis proneness in CPT-linked vulnerable adolescents. *Personality and Individual Differences*, **23**(4), 677–83.

O'Connor, T., Rutter, M., Anderson-Wood, L., Beckett, C., Castle, J., Dunn, J., Groothues, C., Ehrich, K., Harborne, A., Hay, D., Jewitt, J., Keaveney, L., Kreppner, J., Messer, J., Quinton, D., and White, A. (2000) Attachment disorder behaviour following early severe deprivation: Extension and longitudinal follow-up. *Journal of the American Academy of Child and Adolescent Psychiatry*, **39**(6), 703–12.

O'Craven, K. M., and Kanwisher, N. K. (2000) Mental imagery of faces and places activates corresponding stimulus-specific brain regions. *Journal of Cognitive Neuroscience* **12**(6), 1013–23.

O'Dea, J. A., and Abraham, S. (2000) Improving the body image, eating attitudes and behaviours of young male and female adolescents: A new educational approach that focuses on self-esteem. *International Journal of Eating Disorders*, **28**(1), 43–57.

Offer, D., and Sabshin, M. (1991) *The diversity of normal behaviour*. New York: HarperCollins.

Office of Public Service Reform (2002) *Reforming our Public Services*. London: Cabinet Office.

Ogata, S., Silk, K., Goodrich, S., Lohr, N. E., Westen, D., and Hill, E. M. (1990) Childhood sexual and physical abuse in adult patients with borderline personality disorder. *American Journal of Psychiatry*, **147**, 1008–13.

Ogawa, K., Miya, M., Watarei, A., Nakazawa, M., Yuasa, S., and Utena, H. (1987) A long-term follow-up study of schizophrenia in Japan with special reference to the course of social adjustment. *British Journal of Psychiatry*, **151**, 758–65.

Ogawa, N., and Ueki, H. (2007) Clinical importance of caffeine dependence and abuse. *Psychiatry and Clinical Neurosciences*, **61**, 263–8.

O'Hara, M., Rehm, L., and Campbell, S. (1982) Predicting depressive symptomatology: Cognitive-behavioural models and postpartum depression. *Journal of Abnormal Psychology*, **91**, 457–61.

Öhman, A., and Mineka, S. (2001) Fears, phobias, and preparedness: Toward an evolved module of fear and fear learning. *Psychological Review*, **108**, 483–522.

O'Kane, A., Fawcett, D., and Blackburn, R. (1996) Psychopathy and moral reasoning: Comparison of two classifications. *Personality and Individual Differences*, **20**, 505–14.

Okasha, A., Saad, A., Khalil, A., el Dawla, A. S., and Yehia, N. (1994) Phenomenology of obsessive–compulsive disorder: A transcultural study. *Comprehensive Psychiatry*, **35**(3), 191–7.

O'Keeffe, F. E., Scott, S. A., Tyers, P., O'Keeffe, G. W., Dalley, J. W., Zufferey, R., and Caldwell, M. A. (2008) Induction of A9 dopaminergic neurons from neural stem cells improves motor function in an animal model of Parkinson's disease. *Brain*, **131**(3), 630–41.

Okojie, P. (2001) Human rights in prisons. Paper presented at the Forensic Research Group Conference, 'Forensic Psychology in Prisons: Current Developments'. 10 Nov., Manchester Metropolitan University. *Proceedings of the British Psychological Society*, **10**(2), 50.

Okuyama, K., Ohwada, K., Sakurada, S., Sato, N., Sora, I., Tamura, G., Takayanagi, M., and Ohno, I. (2007) The distinctive effects of acute and chronic psychological stress on airway inflammation in a murine model of allergic asthma. *Allergology International*, **56**(1), 29–35.

Olatunji, B. O., and McKay, D. (2007) Disgust and psychiatric illness: Have we remembered? *British Journal of Psychiatry*, **190**, 457–9.

Olatunji, B. O., Cisler, J. M., and Tolin, D. F. (2007) Quality of life in the anxiety disorders: A meta-analytic review. *Clinical Psychology Review*, **27**, 572–81.

Olde, E., van der Hart, O., Kleber, R., and van Son, M. (2006) Posttraumatic stress following childbirth: A review. *Clinical Psychology Review*, **26**, 1–6.

Olds, J., and Milner, P. (1954) Positive reinforcement produced by electrical stimulation of septal area and other regions of the rat brain. *Journal of Comparative and Physiological Psychology*, **47**, 419–27.

Olney, J. W., and Farber, N. (1995) Glutamate receptor dysfunction and schizophrenia. *Archives of General Psychiatry*, **52**(12), 998–1007.

Olsson, S-G., and Möller, A. (2006) Regret after sex reassignment surgery in a male-to-female transsexual: A long-term follow-up. *Archives of Sexual Behaviour*, **35**(4), 501–6.

Oltmanns, T. F., and Emery, R. E. (2004) *Abnormal psychology* (4th edn). Englewood Cliffs, NJ: Pearson. Publishing.

Olvera, R. L. (2002) Intermittent explosive disorder: Epidemiology, diagnosis and management. Therapy in practice. *CNS Drugs*, **16**(8), 517–26.

O'Mahoney, G., and Lucey, J. (1998) *Understanding psychiatric treatment: Therapy for serious mental disorder in adults*. Chichester: Wiley.

O'Neill, F. A., and Kendler, K. S. (1998) Longitudunal study of interpersonal dependency in female twins. *British Journal of Psychiatry*, **172**, 154–8.

ONS (Office of National Statistics) (2000) *Living in Great Britain: Results from the 1998 General House Survey*. London: HMSO.

Opitz, J. M., Smith, J. F., and Santoro, L. (2008) The FG syndromes: Perspective in 2008. *Advances in Pediatrics*, **55**, 123–70.

Orians, G. (1986) An ecological and evolutionary approach to landscape aesthetics. In E. Penning-Rowsell and D. Lowenthal (eds), *Landscape meaning and values*. London: Allen and Unwin.

Orleans, C. T., and Slade, J. (1994) *Nicotine addiction: Principles and management*. Oxford: Oxford University Press.

Ormerod, D. (1999) Criminal profiling: Trial by judge and jury not by criminal psychologist. In D. Canter and L. Alison (eds), *Interviewing and deception*. Aldershot: Dartmouth.

Orne, M. T. (1979) The use and misuse of hypnosis in court. *International Journal of Clinical and Experimental Hypnosis*, **27**, 311–41.

Ornstein, R. (1975) *The psychology of consciousness*. London: Jonathan Cape.

Ost, J., Fellows, B., and Bull, R. (1997) Individual differences and the suggestibility of human memory, *Contemporary Hypnosis*, **14**(2), 132–7.

O'Sullivan, T. (1995) Degrees of obsessive–compulsive behaviour in relation to religiosity in ritualistic religions (Catholicism, Judaism and Islam): A non-clinical representation. Unpublished dissertation, Manchester Metropolitan University.

Otto, M., Smits, J., and Reese, H. (2006) Combined psychotherapy and pharmacotherapy for mood and anxiety disorders in adults: Review and analysis. *Clinical Psychology: Science and Practice*, **12**(1), 72–86.

Ouellette, S. C., and DiPlacido, J. (2001) Personality's role in the protection and enhancement of health: Where research has begun, where it is stuck and how it might move. In A. Baum, T. A. Revenson and J. E. Singer (eds), *Handbook of health psychology*. Mahwah, NJ: Erlbaum.

Owen, C., Tarantello, C., Jones, M., and Tennant, C. (1998) Lunar cycles and violent behavior, *Australia and New Zealand Journal of Psychiatry*, **32**, 496–9.

Owen, D. R. (1972) The XYY male: A review. *Psychological Bulletin*, **78**, 209–33.

Owen, F., and Cross, A. J. (1989) Schizophrenia. In R. A. Webster and C. C. Jordan (eds), *Neurotransmitter, drugs and disease*. Blackwell: Oxford.

Owen, M. J., O'Donovan, M., and Gottesman, I. I. (2003) *Psychiatric genetics and genomics*. Oxford: Oxford University Press.

Owen, M. J., Williams, N. M., and O'Donovan, M. C. (2004) The molecular genetics of schizophrenia: New findings promise new insights. *Molecular Psychiatry*, **9**, 14–27.

Owens, D. G., Johnstone, E. C., Crow, T. J., Frith, C. D., Jagoe J. R., and Kreel, L. (1985) Lateral ventricular size in schizophrenia: Relationship to the disease process and its clinical manifestations. *Psychological Medicine*, **15**, 27–41.

Owley, T., Steele, E., Corsello, C., Risi, S., McKaig, K., Lord, C., Leventhal, B., and Cook, E. H. (1999) A double-blind, placebo-controlled trial of secretin for the treatment of autistic disorder. *Med General Medicine*, **6**, 2.

Ownby, R., Crocco, E., Acedevo, A., John, V., and Loewenstein, D. (2006) Depression and risk for Alzheimer's disease. *Archives of General Psychiatry*, **63**, 530–8.

Ozonoff, S., and Cathcart, K. (1998) Effectiveness of a home program intervention for young children with autism. *Journal of Autism and Developmental Disorders*, **28**, 25–32.

Pace, G., Ivancic, M. T., Edwards, G. L., Iwata, B. A., and Page, T. J. (1985) Assessment of stimulus preference and reinforcer value with profoundly retarded individuals. *Journal of Applied Behaviour Analysis*, **18**(3), 249–55.

Pahwa, R., Factor, S., Lyons, K., Ondo, W., Gronseth, G., Bronte-Stewart, H., Hallett, M., Miyasaki, J., Stevens, J., and Weiner, W. (2006) Practice parameter: Treatment of Parkinson disease with motor fluctuations and dyskinesia (an evidence-based review). *Neurology*, **66**, 983–95.

Palermo, G. B. (2007) The mind of a sexual predator. *Current Opinion in Psychiatry*, **20**(5), 497–500.

Palermo, G. B., and Kocsis, R. N. (2005) *An introduction to the sociopsychological analysis of violent crime*. Springfield: Charles C. Thomas.

Palermo, M. (2004) Pervasive developmental disorders, psychiatric comorbidities and the law. *International Journal of Offender Therapy and Comparative Criminology*, **48**(1), 40–8.

Palmer, R. (2006) Come the revolution: Revisiting the management of anorexia. *Advances in Psychiatric Treatment*, **12**, 5–12.

Pankratz, L. (2003) More hazards: Hypnosis, airplanes and strongly held beliefs. *The Skeptical Enquirer*, May, 31–9.

Panksepp, J. (1978) A neurochemical theory of autism. *Trends in Neuroscience*, **2**, 174–7.

Papazisis, G., Kouvelas, D., Mastrogianni, A., and Karastergiou, A. (2007) Anabolic androgenic steroid abuse and mood disorder: A case report. *International Journal of Neuropsychopharmacology*, **10**, 291–3.

Paris, J., and Zweig-Frank, H. (2001) A 27 year follow-up of patients with borderline personality disorder. *Comprehensive Psychiatry*, **42**, 482–7.

Park, J. H., and Lennon, S. J. (2004) Television apparel shopping: Impulse buying and parasocial interaction. *Clothing and Textile Research Journal*, **22**(3), 135–44.

Parker, G., Gibson, N., Brotchie, H., Heruc, G., Rees, A-M., and Hadzi-Pavlovic, D. (2006) Omega-3 fatty acids and mood disorders. *American Journal of Psychiatry*, **163**(3), 969–78.

Parker, I. (ed.) (1999) *Deconstructing psychotherapy*. London: Sage.

Parker, I., Georgaca, E., Harper, D., McLaughlin, T., and Stowell-Smith, M. (1995) *Deconstructing psychopathology*. London: Sage.

Parks, G. A., and Bard, D. E. (2006) Risk factors for adolescent sex offender recidivism: Evaluation of predictive factors and comparison of three groups based upon victim type. *Sex Abuse*, **18**(4), 319–42.

Parliamentary Office of Science and Technology (2005) Ethical scrutiny of research. *Postnote*, **243**, July.

Parrott, A. C. (2001) Human psychopharmacology of ecstasy (MDMA): A review of 15 years of empirical research. *Human Psychopharmacology Clinical Experimentation*, **16**, 557–77.

Parrott, A. C. (2007) The psychotherapeutic potential of MDMA (3,4-methylenedioxymethamphetamine): An evidence based review. *Psychopharmacology*, **191**(2), 181–93.

Parrott, A. C., Morinan, A., Moss, M., and Scholey, A. (2004) *Understanding drugs and behaviour*. Chichester: Wiley.

Parry, G., Cape, J., and Pilling, S. (2003) Clinical practice guidelines in clinical psychology and psychotherapy. *Clinical Psychology and Psychotherapy*, **10**, 337–51.

Parsons, S., Beardon, L., Neale, H., Reynard, G., Eastgate, R., Wilson, J. Cobb, S. V., Benford, S. Mitchell, P., and Hopkins, E. (2000) Development of social skills amongst adults with Asperger's syndrome using virtual environments: The 'AS Interactive' project. Proceedings of 3rd International Conference, '*Disability, Virtual Reality and Associated Technology*', Alghero, Italy.

Passamanick, B., Dinitz, S., and Lefton, M. (1959) Psychiatric orientation and its relation to diagnosis and treatment in mental hospital. *American Journal of Psychiatry*, **116**, 127–32.

Pathé, M. (2002) *Surviving stalking*. Cambridge: Cambridge University Press.

Pathé, M., and Mullen, P. (1997) The impact of stalkers on their victims. *British Journal of Psychiatry*, **170**, 12–17.

Pathé, M., Mullen, P., and Purcell, R. (2001) Management of victims of stalking. *Advances in Psychiatric Treatment*, **7**, 399–406.

Pathé, M., Mullen, P., and Purcell, R. (2002) Patients who stalk their doctors: Their motives and management. *Medical Journal of Australia*, **36**, 114–20.

Patil, S. T., Zhang, L., Martenyi, F., Lowe, S. L, Jackson, K. A., Andreev, B. V., Avedisova, A. S., Bardenstein, L. M., Gurovich, I. Y., Morozova, M. A., Mosolov, S. N., Neznamov, N. G., Reznik, A. M., Smulevich, A. B., Tochilov, V. A., Johnson, B. G., Monn, J. A., and Schoepp, D. D. (2007) Activation of mGLU2/3 receptors as a new approach to treat schizophrenia: A randomised phase 2 clinical trial. *Nature Medicine*, **13**, 1102–7.

Patrick, C. J., and Iacono, W. G. (1991) A comparison of field and laboratory polygraphs in the detection of deception. *Psychophysiology*, **28**, 632–8.

Pauli, P., and Alpers, G. W. (2002) Memory bias in patients with hypochondriasis and somatoform pain disorder. *Journal of Psychosomatic Research*, **52**, 45–53.

Pavlidis, J., Eberhardt, N. J., and Levine, J. A. (2002) Seeing through the face of deception. *Nature*, 415–35.

Pavlou, M., and Lachs, M. (2006) Could self-neglect in older adults be a geriatric syndrome? *Journal of the American Geriatrics Society*, **54**(5), 831–42.

Pawson, R. (2002) Evidence and policy and naming and shaming. *Policy Studies*, **23**(3), 211–30.

Pearce, J., and Gudjonsson, G. H. (1999) Measuring influential police interviewing tactics: A factor analytic approach. *Legal and Criminological Psychology*, **4**, 221–38.

Pease, A. (1994) *Body language: How to read others' thoughts by their gestures*. London: Sheldon Press.

Peate, I. (2008) Do them no harm. *British Journal of Healthcare Assistants*, **2**(3), 109.

Peck, D. (2007) Computer-guided cognitive behavioural therapy for anxiety states. *Psychiatry*, **6**(4), 166–9.

Peck, D., and Shapiro, C. (1990) *Measuring human problems: A practical guide*. Chichester: Wiley.

Peles, E., Bar-Hamburger, R., Hetzroni, T., Schreiber, S., and Adelson, M. (2007) Melatonin effect on sleep during benzodiazepine withdrawal: A double bind clinical trial. *European Psychiatry*, **22** (Suppl. 1), 285.

Pelosi, A. (2003) Is early intervention for psychosis a waste of valuable resources? *British Journal of Psychiatry*, **182**, 196–8.

Penades, R., Catalan, R., Salamero, M., Boget, T., Puig, O., Guarch, J., and Gasto, C. (2006) Cognitive remediation therapy for outpatients with chronic schizophrenia: A controlled and randomised study. *Schizophrenia Research*, **87**, 323–31.

Pendersen, S. S., and Denollet, J. (2003) Type-D personality, cardiac events and impaired quality of life: A review. *European Journal of Cardiovascular Prevention and Rehabiltation*, **10**(4), 241–8.

Penke, L., Denissen, J., and Miller, G. (2007) The evolutionary genetics of personality. *European Journal of Personality*, **21**, 549–87.

Penna, L., Clark, A., and Mohay, G. (2005) Challenges of automating the detection of paedophile activity on the internet. Paper presented in First International Workshop on Systematic Approaches to Digital Forensic Engineering.

Pennisi, E. (2005) Talking about a revolution: Hidden RNA may fix mutant genes. *Science*, 25 Mar., 1852–3.

Peralta, V., and Cuesta, M. J. (1999) Dimensional structure of psychotic symptoms: An item level analysis of SAPS and SANS symptoms in psychotic disorders. *Schizophrenia Research*, **38**(1), 13–26.

Perelle, I., and Granville, D. (1991) Assessment of the effectiveness of a pet facilitated therapy program in a nursing home setting. *Society and Animals Journal of Human–Animal Studies*, **1**(1), 1–8.

Perez-Alvarez, F., Peñas, A., Bergadà, A., and Mayol, L. I. (2006) Obsessive–compulsive disorder and acute traumatic brain injury. *Acta Psychiatrica Scandinavica*, **114**(4), 295.

Persaud, R., Crossley, D., and Freeman, C. (2003) Should neurosurgery for mental disorders be allowed to die out? *British Journal of Psychiatry*, **183**, 195–6.

Persson, J., Nyberg, L., Lind, J., Larsson, A., Nilsson, L-G., Ingvar, M., and Buckner, R. (2006) Structure-function correlates of cognitive decline in ageing. *Cerebral Cortex*, **16**(7), 907–15.

Petch, E. (2002) Anti-stalking laws and the Protection from Harassment Act 1997. *Journal of Forensic Psychiatry*, **13**(1), 19–34.

Peters, D. (2001) *Understanding the placebo effect in complementary medicine: Theory, practice and research*. London: Elsevier Health Sciences.

Peters, E., Greenwood, K., and Kuipers, E. (2005) Cognitive behaviour therapy: It's good to talk. *Your Voice*, Autumn, 7–9.

Peters, E. R., Joseph, S. A., and Garety, P. A. (1999) Measurement of delusional ideation in the normal population: Introducing the PDI (Peters et al. delusions inventory). *Schizophrenia Bulletin*, **25**(3), 553–76.

Petry, N. M. (2001) Substance abuse, pathological gambling and impulsiveness. *Drug and Alcohol Dependence*, **63**(1), 29–38.

Petry, N. M. (2005) Antisocial personality disorder is associated with increased severity of gambling, medical, drug and psychiatric problems among treatment-seeking pathological gamblers. *Addiction*, **100**(8), 1183–93.

Petry, N. M., Stinson, F. S., and Grant, B. F. (2005) Comorbidity of DSM-IV pathological gambling and other psychiatric disorders: results from the National Epidemiologic Survey on Alcohol and Related Conditions. *Journal of Clinical Psychiatry*, **66**(5), 564–74.

Pettit, F. A. (2002) A comparison of World-Wide Web and paper-and-pencil personality questionnaires. *Behaviour Research Methods Instruments and Computers*, **34**(1), 50–4.

Pfeifer, S. (1994) Belief in demons and exorcism in psychiatric patients in Switzerland. *British Journal of Psychiatry*, **165**(3), 386–8.

Pfohl, B. (1995) Histrionic personality disorder. In W. J. Livesley (ed.), *The DSM-IV personality disorders*. New York: Guilford Press.

Phillips, C., and Bowling, B. (2002) Racism, ethnicity, crime and criminal justice. In M. Maguire, R. Morgan and R. Reiner (eds), *The Oxford handbook of criminology* (3rd edn). Oxford: Oxford University Press.

Phillips, K. A. (1996) *The broken mirror*. Oxford: Oxford University Press.

Phillips, S. M. (2002) Free to speak: Clarifying the legacy of the witch hunts. *Journal of Psychology and Christianity*, **21**, 29–41.

Picardi, A. (2003) Psychosomatic factors in first onset alopecia acreata. *Psychosomatics*, **44**, 374–81.

Pick, A. (1892) Über die Beziehungen der senilen Hirnatrophie zue Aphasie. *Prager Medicinischer Wochenschrift*, **17**, 165–7.

Pickel, K. (1999) The influence of 'context' on the weapon focus effect. *Law and Human Behaviour*, **23**, 299–313.

Pilgrim, D., and Eisenberg, N. (1985) Should special hospitals be phased out? *Bulletin of the British Psychological Society*, **38**, 281–4.

Pilgrim, D., and Rodgers, A. (1993) *A sociology of mental health and illness*. Buckingham: Open University Press.

Pilgrim, D., and Treacher, A. (1992) *Clinical psychology observed*. London: Tavistock/Routledge.

Pilling, S. (1991) *Rehabilitation and community care*. London: Routledge.

Pilling, S., Bebbington, P., Kuipers, E., Garety, P., Geddes, J., Orbach, G., and Morgan, C. (2002a) Psychological treatment in schizophrenia, I: Meta-analysis of family intervention and cognitive behaviour therapy, *Psychological Medicine*, **32**, 763–82.

Pilling, S., Bebbington, P., Kuipers, E., Garety, P., Geddes, J., Martindale, B., Orbach, G., and Morgan, C. (2002b) Psychological treatment in schizophrenia, II: Meta-analyses of randomised controlled trials of social skills training and cognitive remediation. *Psychological Medicine*, **32**, 783–91.

Pillman, F., Harding, A., Balzuweit, S., Bloink, R., and Marneros, A. (2002) The concordance of ICD-10 acute and transient psychosis and DSM-4 brief psychotic disorder. *Psychological Medicine*, **32**(3), 525–33.

Pincus, T., Griffiths, J., Isenberg, D., and Pearce, S. (1997) The Well-being Questionnaire: Testing the structure in groups with rheumatoid arthritis. *British Journal of Health Psychology*, **2**, 167–74.

Pinel, P. H. (1806) *A treatise on insanity*. New York: Hafner.

Pinikahana, J., Happell, B., and Keks, N. A. (2003) Suicide and schizophrenia: A review of literature for the decade 1990–1999 and implications for mental health nursing. *Issues in Mental Health Nursing*, **25**(1), 5–7.

Pinizzotto, A. J., and Finkel, N. J. (1990) Criminal personality profiling: An outcome and process study. *Law and Human Behavior*, **14**, 215–33.

Piper, A. (1997) *Hoax and reality: The bizarre world of multiple personality disorder*. Northvale, NJ: Jason Aronson.

Piper, A. (1998) Multiple personality disorder: Witchcraft survives in the twentieth century. *Sceptical Enquirer*, May/June.

Piper, A., and Merskey, D. M. (2004) The persistence of folly: A critical examination of dissociative identity disorder, Part 1: The excesses of an improbable concept. *Canadian Journal of Psychiatry*, **49**(9), 592–600.

Piper, C. D. (2000) Historical conceptions of childhood innocence: Removing sexuality. In E. Heinze (ed.), *Of innocence and autonomy: Children, sex and human rights*, Aldershot: Dartmouth Publishing.

Pitschel-Walz, G., Leucht, S., Bauml, J., Kissling, W., and Engel, R. R. (2004) The effect of family interventions on relapse and rehospitalisation in schizophrenia: a meta-analysis. *Focus*, **2**, 78–94.

Pittelkow, M. R. (2005) Psoriasis: More than skin deep. *Nature Medicine*, **11**, 17–18.

Plomin, R., DeFries, J., McLearn, G., and McGuffin, P. (2001) *Behavioural genetics*. New York: Worth Publishers.

Poikolainen, K., Vahtera, J., Linna, A., and Kivimaki, M. (2005) Alcohol and coronary heart disease risk – is there an unknown confounder? *Addiction*, **100**(8), 1150–7.

Pollack, H. A., and Reuter, P. (2007) The implications of recent findings on the link between cannabis and psychosis. *Addiction*, **102**, 173–6.

Pollack, M. H., Otto, M. W., Roy-Byrne, P. P., Coplan, J. D., Rothbaum, B. O., Simon, N. M., and Gorman, J. M. (2007) Novel treatment approaches for refractory anxiety disorders. *Depression and Anxiety*, **25**, 467–76.

Polyn, S. M., Natu, V. S., Cohen, J. D., and Norman, K. A. (2005) Category-specific cortical activity precedes retrieval during memory search. *Science*, **310**, 1963–6.

Ponniah, K., and Hollon, S. (2007) Empirically supported psychological interventions for social phobia in adults: A qualitative review of randomised controlled trials. *Psychological Medicine*, **37**, 1–12.

Pope, H., Hudson, J., Bodkin, A., and Oliva, P. (1998) Questionable validity of 'dissociative amnesia' in trauma victims. *British Journal of Psychiatry*, **172**, 210–15.

Popper, K. (2002) *Conjectures and refutations: The growth of scientific knowledge*. New York: Routledge (first published 1935).

Porst, H., and Buvat, J. (2006) *Standard practice in sexual medicine*. New York: Blackwell.

Porter, G. (1996) Organizational impact of workaholism: Suggestions for researching the negative outcomes of excessive work. *Journal of Occupational Health Psychology*, **1**(1), 70–84.

Potenza, M. N., Xian, H., Shah, K., Scherrer, J. F., and Eisen, S. (2005) Shared genetic contributions to pathological gambling and major depression. *Archives of General Psychiatry*, **62**(9), 1015–21.

Potts, S., and Bhugra, D. (1995) Classification of sexual disorders. *International Review of Psychiatry*, **7**, 167–74.

Pousa, E., Duno, R., Brebion, G., David, A. S., Ruiz, A. I., and Obiols, J. E. (2007) Theory of mind deficits in chronic schizophrenia: Evidence for state dependence. *Psychiatry Research*, **158**(1), 1–10.

Povinelli, D., and Preuss, T. (1995) Theory of mind: Evolutionary history of a cognitive specialisation. *Trends in Neuroscience*, **18**, 418–24.

Prentice-Dunn, S., and Rogers, R. W. (1982) Effects of public and private self-awareness on deindividuation and aggression. *Journal of Personality and Social Psychology*, **43**, 503–13.

Preskorn, S. (1995) Beyond DSM-IV: What is the cart and what is the horse? *Psychiatric Annals*, **25**, 53–62.

Prichard, J. (1835) *Treatise on insanity*. London: Gilbert and Piper.

Prins, H. (1990) *Bizarre behaviour: Boundaries of psychiatric disorder*. London: Routledge.

Prins, H. (1999) *Will they do it again? Risk assessment and management in criminal justice and psychiatry*. London: Routledge.

Prins, H. (2005) *Offenders, deviants or patients* (3rd edn). London: Routledge.

Prior, M. R. (1987) Biological and neuropsychological approaches to childhood autism. *British Journal of Psychiatry*, **150**, 8–17.

Pritchard, J. (1835) *A treatise on insanity*. London: Sherwood, Gilbert and Piper.

Proudfoot, J., Ryden, C., Everitt, B., Shapiro, D. A., Goldberg, D., Mann, A., Tylee, A., Marks, I., and Gray, J. (2004) Clinical efficacy of computerised cognitive-behavioural therapy for anxiety and depression in primary care: Randomised controlled trial. *British Journal of Psychiatry*, **185**, 46–54.

Pryce, G., Jackson, S. J., and Baker, D. (2008) Cannabinoids for the control of multiple sclerosis. In A. Köfalvi (ed.), *Cannabinoids and the brain*. New York: Springer.

Putnam, F. (1989) *Diagnosis and treatment of multiple personality disorder*. New York: Guilford Press.

Quill, K., Gurry, S., and Larkin, A. (1989) Daily life therapy: A Japanese model for educating children with autism. *Journal of Autism and Developmental Disorders*, **19**(4), 625–35.

Quinsey, V. L. (2002) Evolutionary theory and criminal behaviour. *Legal and Criminological Psychology*, **7**(1), 1–13.

Quinsey, V. L., Harris, G. T., Rice, M. E., and Lalumiere, M. L. (1993) Assessing treatment efficacy in outcome studies of sex offenders. *Journal of Interpersonal Violence*, **8**, 512–13.

Quiroga, R. Q., Reddy, L., Kreiman, G., Koch, C., and Fried, I. (2005) Invariant visual representation by single neurons in the human brain. *Nature*, **435**, 1102–7.

Rabinowitz Greenberg, S. R., Firestone, P., Bradford, J. M., and Greenberg, D. M. (2002) Prediction of recidivism in exhibitionists: Psychological, phallometric and offence factors. *Sexual Abuse: A Journal of Research and Treatment*, **14**(4), 329–47.

Rachman, S. J. (2004) *Anxiety* (2nd edn). London: Psychology Press.

Rachmann, S. (1966) Sexual fetishism: An experimental analogue. *Psychological Record*, **16**, 293–8.

Rada, R. T., Laws, D., Kellner, R., Stivastave, L., and Peak, G. (1983) Plasma androgens in violent and non violent sex-offenders. *American Academy of Psychiatry and the Law*, **11**, 149–58.

Raine, A. (1991) The SPQ: A scale for the assessment of schizotypal personality based on DSM-III-R criteria, *Schizophrenia Bulletin*, **17**, 555–64.

Raine, A. (1993) *The psychopathology of crime: Criminal behaviour as a clinical disorder*. San Diego, CA: Academic Press.

Raine, A. (1997) Antisocial behaviour and psychophysiology: A biosocial perspective and a prefrontal dysfunction hypothesis. In D. Stoff, J. Breiling and J. D. Maser (eds), *Handbook of antisocial behaviour*. New York: Wiley.

Raine, A. (2002) Biosocial studies of antisocial and violent behaviour in children and adults: A review. *Journal of Abnormal Child Psychology*, **30**(4), 311–26.

Raine, A., and Venables, P. (1981) Classical conditioning and socialisation: A biosocial interaction. *Personality and Individual Differences*, **2**, 273–83.

Raine, A., and Yang, Y. (2006) Neural foundations to moral reasoning and antisocial behaviour. *Social, Cognitive and Affective Neuroscience*, published online, 20 Oct.: http://scan.oxfordjournals.org.

Raine, A., Brennan, P., Farrington, D. P., and Mednick, S. A. (eds) (1997) *Biosocial bases of violence*. New York: Plenum.

Raine, A., Brennan, P., and Mednick, S. A. (1997) Interaction between birth complications and early maternal rejection in predisposing individuals to adult violence: Specificity to serious early-onset violence. *American Journal of Psychiatry*, **154**, 1265–71.

Raine, A., Brennan, P., Mednick, B., and Mednick, S. A. (1996) High rates of violence, crime, academic problems, and behavioral problems in males with both early neuromotor deficits and unstable family environments. *Archives of General Psychiatry*, **53**, 544–9.

Raine, A., Buchsbaum, M. S., and La Casse, L. (1997) Brain abnormalities in murderers indicated by positron emission tomography. *Biological Psychiatry*, **42**, 495–508.

Raine, A., Lencz, T., Bihrle, S., Lacasse, L., and Colletti, P. (2000) Reduced prefrontal gray matter volume and reduced autonomic activity in antisocial personality disorder. *Archives of General Psychiatry*, **57**, 119–27.

Raine, A., Lencz, T., and Scerbo, A. (1995) Antisocial personality: Neuroimaging, neuropsychology, neurochemistry, and psychophysiology. In J. H. Ratey (ed.), *Neuropsychiatry of behavior disorders*. Oxford: Blackwell.

Raine, A., Park, S., Lencz, T., Bihrle, S., LaCasse, L., Widom, C. S., Al-Dayeh, L., and Singh, M. (2001) Reduced right hemisphere activation in severely abused violent offenders during a working memory task: An fMRI study. *Aggressive Behaviour*, **27**, 111–29.

Raine, A., Reynolds, C., Venables, P., Mednick, S., and Farrington, D. (1998) Fearlessness, stimulation-seeking and large body size at age 3 years as early pre-dispositions to childhood aggression at age 11 years. *Archives of General Psychiatry*, **55**, 745–51.

Rajendran, G., and Mitchell, P. (2000) Computer mediated interaction in Asperger's syndrome: The bubble dialogue program. *Computers and Education*, **35**(3), 189–207.

Rajna, P., and Veres, J. (1993) Correlations between night sleep duration and seizure frequency in temporal lobe epilepsy. *Epilepsia*, **34**, 574–9.

Ramachandran, V. S. (1998) Consciousness and body image: Lessons from phantom limbs, Capgras syndrome and pain asymbolia. *Philosophical Transactions of the Royal Society (London)*, **353**, 1851–9.

Ramage, M. (2006) Female sexual dysfunction. *Psychiatry*, **6**(3), 105–10.

Randi, J. (1982a) Atlanta child murderer: Psychics' failed visions. *Skeptical Inquirer*, **7**, 12–13.

Randi, J. (1982b) *Flim-flam*. New York: Prometheus.

Randi, J. (1995) *An encyclopedia of claims, frauds and hoaxes of the occult and supernatural*. New York: Griffen.

Rapee, R. M., and Spence, S. H. (2004) The aetiology of social phobia: Empirical evidence and an initial model. *Clinical Psychology Review*, **24**, 737–67.

Rauch, S. L., Wright, C. I., Martis, B., Busa, E., McMullin, K. G., Shin, L. M., Dale, A. M., and Fischl, B. (2004) A magnetic resonance imaging study of cortical thickness in animal phobia. *Biological Psychiatry*, **55**, 946–52.

Rawson, R., Gonzales, R., McCann, M., and Ling, W. (2007) Use of methamphetamine by young people: Is there a reason for concern? *Addiction*, **102**, 1021–2.

Reeder, C., Newton, E., Frangou, S., and Wykes, T. (2004) Which executive skills should we target to affect social functioning and symptom change? A study of a cognitive remediation therapy program. *Schizophrenia Bulletin*, **30**(1), 87–100.

Rees, J. T. (1995) A history of police psychological services. In M. J. Kirke and E. M. Scrivner (eds), *Police psychology into the 21st century*. Hillsdale, NJ: Lawrence Erlbaum.

Regier, D. A., Narrow, W. E., Rae, D. S., Manderscheid, R. W., Locke, B. Z., and Goodwin, E. K. (1993) The de-facto US Mental and Addictive Disorders Service System prospective one-year prevalence rate of disorders in services. *Archives of General Psychiatry*, **50**, 85–94.

Reichborn-Kjennerud, T. (2007) The relationship between avoidant personality disorder and social phobia: A population-based twin study. *American Journal of Psychiatry*, **164**(11), 1722–8.

Reiche, E. M. V., Morimoto, H. K., and Nunes, S. M. V. (2005) Stress and depression-induced immune dysfunction: Implications for the development and progression of cancer. *International Review of Psychiatry*, **17**(6), 515–27.

Reichelt, K., Knivsberg, A., Nodland, M., and Lind, G. (1994) Nature and consequences of hyperpeptiduruia and bovine casomorphins found in autistic syndrome. *Developmental Brain Dysfunction*, **7**, 71–85.

Reisman, J. M. (1966) *The development of clinical psychology*. New York: Appleton-Century-Crofts.

Repp, A. C., and Horner, R. (1999) *Functional analysis of problem behaviour*. Belmont, CA: Wadsworth.

Ressler, R. K., and Schachtman, T. (1992) *Whoever fights monsters*. New York: Pocket Books.

Ressler, R. K., Burgess, A. W., and Douglas, J. E. (1985a) Classifying sexual homicide crime scenes: Interrater reliability. *FBI Law Enforcement Bulletin*, **54**(8), 13–16.

Ressler, R. K., Burgess, A. W., and Douglas, J. E. (1985b) Crime scene and profile characteristics of organized and disorganized murderers. *FBI Law Enforcement Bulletin*, **54**, 18–25.

Ressler, R. K., Burgess, A. W., and Douglas, J. E. (1988) *Sexual homicide: Patterns and motives*. Lexington, MA: Lexington Books.

Ressler, R. K., Douglas, J. E., Burgess, A. W., and Burgess, A. G. (1992) *Crime classification manual*. New York: Simon and Schuster.

Reynolds, G. P. (1983) Increased concentrations and lateral asymmetries of amygdale dopamine in schizophrenia. *Nature*, **305**, 527–9.

Reynolds, G. P. (1989) Beyond the dopamine hypothesis. *British Journal of Psychiatry*, **155**, 305–16.

Reynolds, J. (1855) *The diagnosis of diseases of the brain, spinal chord and their appendages*. London: Churchill.

Rhee, S., and Waldman, I. (2002) Genetic and environmental influences on antisocial behaviour: A meta-analysis of twin and adoption studies. *Psychological Bulletin*, **128**, 490–529.

Rice, M. E., Harris, G., and Cormier, C. (1992) An evaluation of a maximum security therapeutic community for psychopaths and other mental disordered patients. *Law and Human Behaviour*, **116**, 399–412.

Richdale, A., and Prior, M. (1995) The sleep/wake rhythm in children with autism. *European Child and Adolescent Psychiatry*, **4**(3), 175–86.

Richman, J., Raskin, V., and Gaines, C. (1991) Gender roles, social support and post-partum depressive symptomatology: The benefits of caring. *Journal of Nervous and Mental Diseases*, **179**(3), 139–47.

Ricks, D. (1972) The beginning of vocal communication in infants and autistic children. Unpublished doctoral dissertation, University of London.

Rief, W., and Sharpe, M. (2004) Somatoform disorders: New approaches to classification, conceptualisation and treatment. *Journal of Psychosomatic Research*, **56**, 387–90.

Rimland, B. (1998) Critique of 'Efficacy of vitamin B6 and magnesium in the treatment of autism'. *Journal of Autism and Developmental Disorders*, **28**(6), 580–1.

Risinger, D. M., and Loop, J. L. (2002) Three card Monte, Monty Hall, modus operandi and 'offender profiling': Some lessons of modern cognitive science for the law of evidence. *Cardozo Law Review*, **23**, 193.

Riudavets, M. A., Colegial, C., Rubio, A., Fowler, D., Pardo, C., and Troncoso, J. (2005) Causes of unexpected death in patients with multiple sclerosis: A forensic study of 50 cases. *American Journal of Forensic Medicine and Pathology*, **28**(3), 244–8.

Rivers, T., Sprunt, D., and Berry, G. (1933) Observations on attempts to produce acute disseminated encephalomyelitis in monkeys. *Journal of Experimental Medicine*, **58**, 39–53.

Roback, H. (2000) Adverse outcomes in group psychotherapy: Risk factors, prevention, and research directions. *Journal of Psychotherapy Practice and Research*, **9**, 113–22.

Roberts, G. W. (1990) Schizophrenia: The cellular biology of a functional psychosis. *Trends in Neuroscience*, **6**, 207–11.

Roberts, K. A. (2005) Women's experience of violence during stalking by former romantic partners: Factors predictive of stalking violence. *Violence Against Women*, **11**(1), 89–114.

Roberts, L. W. (1999) Ethical dimensions of psychiatric research: A constructive, criterion-based approach to protocol preparation: The Research Protocol Ethics Assessment Tool (RePEAT). *Biological Psychiatry*, **46**, 1106–19.

Roberts, L. W., and Roberts, B. (1999) Psychiatric research ethics: An overview of evolving guidelines and current ethical dilemmas in the study of mental illness. *Biological Psychiatry*, **46**(8), 1025–38.

Roberts, R., and Groome, D. (2001) *Parapsychology: The science of unusual experience*. London: Arnold.

Robertson, G. (1992) Objections to the present system. *Criminal Behaviour and Mental Health*, **2**, 114–23.

Robertson, J., Raab, G., Bruce, M., McKenzie, J., Storkey, H., and Slater, A. (2006) Addressing the efficacy of dihydrocodeine versus methadone as an alternative maintenance treatment for opiate dependence: A randomised controlled trial. *Addiction*, **102**, 1752–9.

Robins, L. N. (1991) Conduct disorder. *Journal of Child Psychology and Psychiatry*, **32**(1), 193–212.

Robins Wahlin, T. (2006) To know or not to know: A review of behaviour and suicidal ideation in preclinical Huntington and aposs disease. *Patient Education and Counseling*, **65**(3), 279–87.

Robinson, R., Kubos, K., Starr, L., Rao, K., and Price, T. (1984) Mood disorders in stroke patients. *Brain*, **107**, 81–93.

Rogers, C. R. (1951) *Client-centered Therapy*. Boston, MA: Houghton-Mifflin.

Rogers, S. (1998) Empirically supported comprehensive treatments for young people with autism. *Journal of Clinical Child Psychology*, **27**(2), 168–79.

Rojas, D., Smith, J. A., Blenkers, B., Camou, B., Reite, M., and Rogers, S. (2004) Hippocampus and amygdale volumes in parents of children with autistic disorder. *American Journal of Psychiatry*, **161**, 2038–44.

Romans, J., Hays, J., and White, T. (1996) Stalking and related behaviours experienced by counselling centre staff members from current or former clients. *Professional Psychology, Research and Practice*, **27**, 595–9.

Romme, M. A., Honig, A., Noorthoorn, E. O., and Escher, A. D. (1992) Coping with hearing voices: An emancipatory approach. *British Journal of Psychiatry*, **161**, 99–103.

Rosack, J. (2006) Professional news: Patient charged with murder of schizophrenia expert. *Psychiatry News*, **41**(19), 1–4.

Rose, J. (2007) Denicotinized cigarettes: A new tool to combat cigarette addiction? *Addiction*, **102**, 181–2.

Rose, S., Kamin, L., and Lewontin, R. C. (1984) *Not in our genes: Biology, ideology, and human nature.* Harmondsworth: Penguin.

Rosen, G. M., and Taylor, S. (2007) Pseudo-PTSD. *Journal of Anxiety Disorders*, **21**, 201–10.

Rosen, J. C. (1995) The nature of body dysmorphic disorder and treatment with cognitive-behaviour therapy. *Cognitive and Behavioural Practice*, **2**(1), 143–66.

Rosenbaum, B., Valbak, K., Harder, S., Knudsen, P., Koster, A., Lajer, M., Lindhardt, A., Winther, G., Petersen, L., Jorgensen, P., Nordentoft, M., and Andreasen, A. H. (2005) The Danish national schizophrenia project: Prospective, comparative longitudinal treatment study of first episode psychosis. *British Journal of Psychiatry*, **186**, 394–9.

Rosenberg, D. A. (1987) The web of deceit: A literature review of Münchausen syndrome by proxy. *Child Abuse and Neglect*, **11**, 547–63.

Rosenberg, D. A. (2003) Münchausen syndrome by proxy: Medical diagnostic criteria. *Child Abuse and Neglect*, **27**, 412–30.

Rosenfeld, B. (2004) Violence risk factors in stalking and obsessional harassment: A review and preliminary meta-analysis. *Criminal Justice and Behaviour*, **31**(1), 9–36.

Rosenhan, D. (1973) On being sane in insane places. *Science*, **179**, 250–8.

Rosenthal, D. (1971) Two adoption studies of heredity in the schizophrenic disorders. In M. Bleuler and J. Angst (eds), *The Origins of Schizophrenia.* Bern: Huber.

Rosenthal, N., Sack, D., Gillin, J., Lewy, A., Goodwin, F., Davenport, Y., Mueller, P., Newsome, D., and Wehr, T. (1984) Seasonal affective disorder: A description of the syndrome and preliminary findings with light therapy. *Archives of General Psychiatry*, **41**, 72–80.

Rosenthal, R. (2002) Suggestibility, reliability and the legal process. *Developmental Review*, **22**, 334–69.

Rosenthal, R. N. (2003) *Dual diagnosis.* London: Routledge.

Ross, C. (1991) Epidemiology of multiple personality disorder and dissociation. *Psychiatric Clinics of North America*, **14**, 503–17.

Ross, C. (2007) Dissociative identity disorder. *Current Psychosis and Therapeutics Reports*, **4**(3), 1545–83.

Ross, L., Murray, B., and Steiner, M. (2005) Sleep and perinatal mood disorders: A critical review. *Journal of Psychiatry and Neuroscience*, **30**(4), 247–56.

Ross, R. R., and Fabiano, E. A. (1985) *Time to think: A cognitive model of delinquency prevention and offender rehabilitation.* Johnson City, TN: Institute of Social Sciences and Arts.

Ross, S. R., Lutz, C. J., and Bailly, S. E. (2002) Positive and negative symptoms of schizotypy and the five-factor model: A domain and facet level analysis. *Journal of Personality Assessment*, **79**, 53–72.

Rossi, A., and Daneluzzo, E. (2002) Schizotypy dimensions in normals and schizophrenic patients: A comparison with other clinical samples. *Schizophrenia Research*, **54**, 67–75.

Rossmo, D. K. (2000) *Geographical profiling.* Boca Raton, FL: CRC Press.

Rossow, I., and Romelsjö, A. (2006) The extent of the 'prevention paradox' in alcohol problems as a function of population drinking patterns. *Addiction*, **101**(1), 84–90.

Roth, B. L., and Meltzer, H. Y. (2000) The role of serotonin in schizophrenia. In: *Psychopharmacology: The 4th generation of progress.* Nashville: American College of Neuropsychopharmacology. http://www.acnp.org.

Roth, M. (1973) Psychiatry and its critics. *British Journal of Psychiatry*, **122**, 174–6.

Roth, S., and Kubal, L. (1974) Effects of noncontingent reinforcement on tasks of differing importance: Facilitation and learned helplessness effects. *Journal of Personality and Social Psychology*, **32**, 680–91.

Rothwell, J., Bandar, Z., O'Shea, J., and McLean, D. (2006) Silent talker: A new computer-based system for the analysis of facial cues to deception. *Applied Cognitive Psychology*, **20**, 757–77.

Rotter, J. B. (1954) *Social learning and clinical psychology.* New York: Prentice Hall.

Rotter, J. (1966) Generalised expectancies for internal versus external control of reinforcement. *Psychological Monographs*, **30**(1), 1–26.

Rotton, J., and Kelly, I. W. (1985) Much ado about the full moon: A meta-analysis of lunar-lunacy research. *Psychological Bulletin*, **97**, 286–306.

Rowa, K., Purdon, C., Summerfeld, L. J., and Antony, M. M. (2005) Why are some obsessions more upsetting than others? *Behaviour Research and Therapy*, **43**(11), 1453–65.

Rowe, A., Bullock, P., Polkey, C., and Morris, R. (2001) 'Theory of mind' impairments and their relationship to executive functioning following frontal lobe excisions. *Brain*, **124**(3), 600–16.

Rowe, D. C. (1990) Inherited dispositions towards learning delinquent and criminal behaviour: New evidence. In L. Ellis and H. Hoffman (eds), *Crime in biological, social and moral contexts*. New York: Praeger.

Rowe, D. C. (2001) *Biology and crime*. Los Angeles: Roxbury.

Royal College of Psychiatrists (2000) *Neurosurgery for mental disorder: Report from the neurosurgery working group of the Royal College of Psychiatrists*. London: Royal College of Psychiatrists.

RSA (2007) *Drugs – Facing the facts: The report of the RSA Commission on Illegal Drugs, Communities and Public Policy*. London: Royal Society for the Encouragement of Arts, Manufactures and Commerce.

Rubio, G., and López-Ibor, J. J. (2007) Generalized anxiety disorder: A 40-year follow-up study. *Acta Psychiatrica Scandinavica*, **115**(5), 372–9.

Rucz, K. (2008) Longevity genes. *Hungarian Medical Journal*, **2**(4), 499–507.

Rufer, M., Fricke, S., Moritz, S., Kloss, M., and Hand, I. (2006) Symptom dimensions in obsessive-compulsive disorder: Prediction of cognitive-behaviour therapy outcome. *Acta Psychiatrica Scandinavica*, **113**, 440–6.

Ruocco, A. C., and Swirsky-Sacchetti, T. (2007) Personality disorder symptomatology and neuropsychological functioning in closed-head injury. *Journal of Neuropsychiatry and Clinincal Neurosciences*, **19**, 27–35.

Rush, A. J., Pincus, H. A., and First, M. B. (2000) *Handbook of psychiatric measures*. Washington, DC: American Psychiatric Press.

Russell, G. (1979) Bulimia nervosa: An ominous variant of anorexia nervosa. *Psychological Medicine*, **9**, 429–48.

Rutter, M. (1972) *Maternal deprivation reassessed*. Harmondsworth: Penguin.

Rutter, M. (1974) The development of infantile autism. *Psychological Bulletin*, **4**, 147–63.

Rutter, M. (1979) Maternal deprivation, 1972–1978: New findings, new concepts, new approaches. *Child Development*, **50**, 283–305.

Rutter, M. (1983) Cognitive deficits in the pathogenesis of autism. *Journal of Child Psychology and Psychiatry*, **24**, 513–31.

Rutter, M. (1991) A fresh look at 'maternal deprivation'. In P. Bateson (ed.), *The development and integration of behaviour*. Cambridge: Cambridge University Press.

Rutter, M. L. (1997) Nature–nurture integration: The example of antisocial behaviour. *American Psychologist*, **52**, 390–8.

Rutter, M. (1999) Resilience concepts and findings: Implications for family therapy. *Journal of Family Therapy*, **21**(2), 119.

Rutter, M., and Giller, H. (1983) *Juvenile delinquency: Trends and perspectives*. Harmondsworth: Penguin.

Ryle, A., and Kerr, I. (2002) *Introducing cognitive analytic therapy*. Chichester: Wiley.

Sachdev, P. (2004) Debate on neurosurgery. *British Journal of Psychiatry*, **184**, 85.

Sackheim, H. A., and Lisanby, S. A. (2001) Physical treatments in psychiatry: Advances in electroconvulsive therapy, transcranial magnetic stimulation and vegus nerve stimulation. In M. Weissman (ed.), *Treatment of depression: Bridging the 21st century*. Washington, DC: American Psychiatric Publishing.

Sairam, K., Kulinskaya, E., Hanbury, D., Boustead, G., and McNicholas, T. (2002) Oral sildenafil (Viagra®) in male erectile dysfunction: Use, efficacy and safety profile in an unselected cohort presenting to a British district general hospital. *BioMed Central Urology*, **2**(4), available from www.biomedcentral.com/1471-2490/2/4.

Salan, S., Zinberg, N., and Frei, E. (1975) Antiemetic effects of delta-9-THC in patients receiving cancer chemotherapy. *New England Journal of Medicine*, **293**, 795–7.

Saleh, F. M., and Berlin, F. S. (2004) Sex hormones, neurotransmitters and psychopharmacological treatments in men with paraphilic disorders. *Journal of Child Sexual Abuse*, **12**(3/4), 233–53.

Saleh, F. M., Neil, T., and Fishman, M. J. (2004) Treatment of paraphilia in young adults with leuprolide: A preliminary case report series. *Journal of Forensic Sciences*, **49**(6), 224–30.

Salekin, R. T. (2002) Psychopathy and therapeutic pessimism: Clinical lore or clinical reality? *Clinical Psychology Review*, **22**, 97–112.

Salkovskis, P. M., Hackmann, A., Wells, A., Gelder, M. G., and Clark, D. M. (2006) Belief disconfirmation versus habituation approaches to situational exposure in panic disorder with agoraphobia: A pilot study. *Behaviour Research and Therapy*, **45**, 877–85.

Salkovskis, P. M., and Warwick, H. C. (2001) Meaning misinterpretations and medicine: A cognitive-behavioural approach to understanding health anxiety and hypochondriasis. In V. Starcevic and D. R. Lipsitt (eds), *Hypochondriasis: Modern perspectives on an ancient malady*. Oxford: Oxford University Press.

Salokangas, R. K., Cannon, T., Van Erp, T., Ilonen, T., Taiminen, T., and Karlsson, H., et al. (2002) Structural magnetic resonance imaging in patients with first episode schizophrenia, psychotic and severe non-psychotic depression and healthy controls. *British Journal of Psychiatry*, 181(suppl. 43), 58–65.

Samenow, S. E. (1984) *Inside the criminal mind*. New York: Time Books.

Sameroff, A., and Emde, R. (1989) *Relationship disturbances in early childhood*. New York: Basic Books.

Samijn, P., te Boekhorst, P., Mondria, T., van Doorn, P., Flach, H., van der Meché, F., Cornelissen, J., Hop, W., Löwenberg, B., and Hintzen, R. (2006) Intense T cell depletion followed by autologous bone marrow transplantation for severe multiple sclerosis. *Journal of Neurology, Neurosurgery, and Psychiatry*, 77, 46–50.

Sánchez-Carbonell, X., Guardiola, E., Bellés, A., Beranuy, M. (2005) European Union scientific production on alcohol and drug misuse (1976–2000). *Addiction*, 100, 1166–74.

Sandberg, A. A., Koepf, G. F., Ishiara, T., and Hauschka, T. S. (1961) An XYY human male. *The Lancet*, 262, 488–9.

Sanderson, W. C., and Bruce, T. J. (2007) Causes and management of treatment-resistant panic disorder and agoraphobia: A survey of expert therapists. *Cognitive and Behavioural Practice*, 14, 26–35.

Sanna, L. J. (1998) Defensive pessimism and optimism: The bitter-sweet influence of mood on performance and prefactual and counterfactual thinking. *Cognition and Emotion*, 12(5), 635–65.

Santosa, C., Strong, C., Nowakowska, C., Wang, P., Rennicke, C., and Ketter, T. (2007) Enhanced creativity in bipolar disorder patients: A controlled study. *Journal of Affective Disorders*, 100(1–3), 31–9.

Sapolsky, R. M. (1994) *Why zebras don't get ulcers*. New York: Freeman.

Sarafino, E. P. (2008) *Health psychology: Biopsychosocial interactions* (6th edn). New York: Wiley.

Sareen, J., Stein, M., Cox, B., and Hassard, S. (2004) Understanding comorbidity of anxiety disorders with antisocial behaviour: Findings from two large community surveys. *Journal of Nervous and Mental Disease*, 192(3), 178–86.

Sartor, C. E., Lynskey, M. T., Heath, A. C., Jacob, T., and True, W. (2007) The role of childhood risk factors in initiation of alcohol use and progression to alcohol dependence. *Addiction*, 102, 216–25.

Sartor, C. E., Scherrer, J. F., Shah, K. R., Xian, H., Volberg, R., and Eisen, S. A. (2007) Course of pathological gambling symptoms and reliability of the Lifetime Gambling History measure. *Psychiatry Research*, 152(1), 55–61.

Sartorius, N., Ustin, T., Korten, A., Cooper, J., et al. (1995) Progress toward achieving a common language in psychiatry, II: Results from the international field trials of the ICD-10 Diagnostic Criteria for Research for mental and behavioural disorders. *American Journal of Psychiatry*, 152, 1427–37.

Satterfield, J. H., Hoppe, C. M., and Schell, A. M. (1982) A prospective study of delinquency in 110 adolescent boys with attention deficit disorder and 88 normal adolescent boys. *American Journal of Psychiatry*, 138, 795–8.

Satterfield, J. H., Satterfield, B. T., and Cantwell, D. P. (1981) A 3-year multimodal study of 100 hyperactive boys. *Journal of Paediatrics*, 98, 650–5.

Satterfield, J. H., Schell, A. M., Nicholas, T., and Backs, R. W. (1988) Topographic study of auditory event-related potentials in normal boys and boys with attention deficit disorder with hyperactivity. *Psychophysiology*, 25(5), 591–606.

Satterfield, J. H., Swanson, J., Schell, A. M., and Lee, F. (1994) Prediction of antisocial behaviour in attention-deficit hyperactivity disorder boys from aggression/defiant scores. *Journal of the American Academy of Child and Adolescent Psychiatry*, 33, 185–90.

Saulsman, L. M., and Page, A. C. (2004) The five-factor model and personality disorder empirical literature: A meta-analytic review. *Clinical Psychology Review*, 23, 1055–85.

Schaufeli, W. B., and Peeters, M. C. (2000) Job stress and burnout among correctional officers: A literature review. *International Journal of Stress Management*, 7, 19–47.

Scheffer, R. E. (2004) Abnormal neurological signs at the onset of psychosis. *Schizophrenia Research*, 70, 19–26.

Scheier, M. F., Matthews, K. A., Owens, J. F., Magovern, G. J., Lefebvre, R. C., Abbott, R. A., and Carver, C. S. (1989) Dispositional optimism and recovery from coronary artery bypass surgery: The beneficial effects on physical and psychological well-being. *Journal of Personality and Social Psychology*, 57, 1024–40.

Schiffman, J., Nakamura, B., Earleywine M., and LaBrie, J. (2005) Symptoms of schizotypy precede cannabis use. *Psychiatry Research*, 134, 37–42.

Schilder, P. (1950) *The image and appearance of the human body*. New York: International Universities Press.

Schlaadt, R., and Shannon, P. (1994) *Drugs* (4th edn). Englewood Cliffs, NJ: Prentice Hall.

Schlosser, R. G., Nenadic, I., Wagner, G., Gullmar, D., Von Consbruch, K., Kohler, S., Schultz, C. C., Koch, K., Fitzek, C., Matthews, P. M., Reichenbach, J. R., and Sauer, H. (2007) White matter abnormalities and brain activation in schizophrenia: A combined DTI and fMRI study. *Schizophrenia Research*, **89**, 1–11.

Schneider, K. (1923) Die psychopathischen Persönlichkeiten. Vienna: Deuticke.

Schneider, K. (1959) *Clinical psychopathology* (trans. by M. W. Hamilton). New York: Grune and Stratton.

Schoenen, J., Di Clemente, L. Vandenheede, M., Fumal, A., De Pasqua, V., Mouchamps, M., Remacle, J., and de Noordhout, A. M. (2005) Hypothalamic stimulation in chronic cluster headache: A pilot study of efficacy and mode of action. *Brain*, **128**(4), 940–7.

Schön, D. A. (1983) *The reflective practitioner: How professionals think in action*. New York: Basic Books.

Schou, M. (1979) Artistic productivity and lithium prophylaxis in manic-depressive illness. *British Journal of Psychiatry*, **135**, 56–65.

Schröck, E., du Manoir, S., Veldman, T., Schoell, B., Wienberg, J., Ferguson-Smith, M., Ning, Y., Ledbetter, D., Bar-Am, I., Soenksen, D., Garini, Y., and Ried, T. (1996) Multicolor spectral karyotyping of human chromosomes. *Science*, 26 July, **273**, 494 (reports).

Schuckit, M. A. (2006) *Drug and alcohol abuse: A clinical guide to diagnosis and treatment*. New York: Springer.

Schultz, W. (2002) Getting formal with dopamine and reward. *Neuron*, **36**, 241–9.

Schultz, W., Basson, R., Binik, Y., Eschenbach, D., Wesselmann, U., and van Lankveld, J. (2005) Women's sexual pain and its management. *Journal of Sexual Medicine*, **2**, 301–16.

Schumaker, J. F. (1991) *Human suggestibility: Advances in theory, research and application*. New York: Routledge.

Schwartz, M. W., Woods, S. C., Porte, D., Jr, Seeley, R. J., and Baskin, D. G. (2000) Central nervous system control of food intake. *Nature*, **404**, 661–71.

Schwartz, T. (1981) *The hillside strangler: A murderer's mind*. New York: New American Library.

Scott, E. (1997) Antievolution and creationism in the United States. *Annual Review of Anthropology*, **26**, 263–89.

Scott, J. (2009) *Behavioural and cognitive psychotherapy*. Cambridge: Cambridge University Press.

Scoular, J., and O'Neill, M. (2007) Regulating prostitution: Social inclusion, responsibilization and the politics of prostitution reform. *British Journal of Criminology*, **47**, 764–78.

Scull, A. (1999) A quarter of a century of the history of psychiatry. *Journal of the History of the Behavioural Sciences*, **35**(3), 239–46.

Searles, J. S. (1988) The role of genetics in the pathogenesis of alcoholism. *Journal of Abnormal Psychology*, **97**, 153–67.

Seeman, P. (1980) Dopamine receptors and the dopamine hypothesis of schizophrenia. *Pharmacological Reviews*, **32**, 229–313.

Segerstrom, S. C., and Miller, G. (2004) Psychological stress and the human immune system: A meta-analytic study of 30 years of inquiry. *Psychological Bulletin*, **130**(4), 601–30.

Segraves, R. T., and Althol, S. (1998) Psychotherapy and pharmacotherapy of sexual dysfunctions. In P. E. Nathan and J. M. Gorman (eds), *A guide to treatments that work*. New York: Oxford.

Seigert, R., and Ward, T. (2002) Evolutionary psychology: Origins and criticisms. *Australian Psychologist*, **37**, 20–9.

Seligman, M. E. P. (1971) Phobias and preparedness. *Behaviour Therapy*, **2**, 307–20.

Seligman, M. E. P. (1972) Helplessness. *Annual Review of Medicine*, **23**, 407–12.

Seligman, M. E. P. (1975) *Helplessness*. New York: Freeman.

Seligman, M. E. P. (1992) *Helplessness* (revised edn). New York: Freeman.

Seligman, M. E., and Csikszentmihalyi, M. (2000) Positive psychology: An introduction. *American Psychologist*, **55**, 5–14.

Selten, J. P., Slaets, J. P., and Kahn, R. S. (1997) Schizophrenia in Surinamese and Dutch Antillean immigrants to the Netherlands: Evidence of increased incidence. *Psychological Medicine*, **27**, 807–11.

Selye, H. (1956) *The stress of life*. New York: McGraw-Hill.

Selye, H. (1985) History and present status of the stress concept. In A. Monat and R. S. Lazarus (eds), *Stress and coping: An anthology* (2nd edn). New York: Columbia University Press.

Seo, S. W., Lee, B. H., Kim, E-J., Chin, J., Cho, Y. S., Yoon, U., and Na, D. L. (2007) Clinical significance of microbleeds in subcortical vascular dementia. *Stroke*, **38**, 1949–51.

Sessa, B. (2007) Is there a case for MDMA assisted psychotherapy in the UK? *Journal of Psychopharmacology*, **21**(2), 220–4.

Shah, A., and Frith, U. (1983) An islet of ability in autism: A research note. *Journal of Child Psychology and Psychiatry*, **24**, 613–20.

Shapiro, D., and Firth, J. (1987). Prescriptive v. exploratory psychotherapy: Outcomes of the Sheffield Psychotherapy Project. *British Journal of Psychiatry*, **151**, 790–9.

Shapiro, D. A., and Shapiro, D. (1982) Meta-analysis of comparative therapy outcome studies: A replication and refinement. *Psychological Bulletin*, **92**, 581–604.

Shapiro, P. N., and Penrod, S. (1986) Meta-analysis of facial identification studies. *Psychological Bulletin*, **100**, 139–56.

Shapiro, R. E. (2007) Caffeine and headaches. *Neurological Sciences*, **28**(2), 179–83.

Sharpley, M. S., Hutchinson, G., and Murray R. M. (2001) Understanding the excess of psychosis among the African-Caribbean population of England. *British Journal of Psychiatry*, **178**(suppl.), 60–8.

Shaw, J., Amos, T., Hunt, I. M., Flynn, S., Turnbull, P., Kapur, N., and Appleby, L. (2004) Mental illness in people who kill strangers: Longitudinal study and national clinical survey. *British Medical Journal*, **328**, 27 Mar., 734–7.

Shaw, J., Hunt, I. M., Flynn, S., Amos, T., Meehan, J., Robinson, J., Bickley, H., Parsons, R., McCann, K., Burns, J., Kapur, N., and Appleby, L. (2006) The role of alcohol and drugs in homicides in England and Wales. *Addiction*. **101**(8), 1117–24.

Sheldon, W. (1942) *The varieties of temperament: A psychology of constitutional differences*. New York: Harper.

Sheldon, W. (1949) *Varieties of delinquent youth*. New York and London: Harper.

Shepherd, M., Watt, D., and Falloon, I. (1989) The natural history of schizophrenia: A five year follow-up study of outcome and prediction in a representative sample of schizophrenics. *Psychological Medicine Monograph Supplement*, **15**, 1–46.

Sheridan, L., and Davies, G. (2001) Stalking: The elusive crime. *Legal and Criminological Psychology*, **6**, 133–47.

Sheridan, L., and Davies, G. (2004) Stalking. In J. R. Alder (ed.), *Forensic psychology: Concepts, debates and practice*. Collumpton: Willan.

Sheridan, L., Blaauw, E., and Davies, G. (2003) Stalking: Knowns and unknowns. *Trauma, Violence and Abuse*, **4**(2), 148–62.

Sheridan, L., Davies, G., and Boon, J. C. W. (2001) Stalking: Perceptions and prevalence. *Journal of Interpersonal Violence*, **16**, 151–67.

Sheridan, L., Gillett, R., and Davies, G. (2002). Perceptions and prevalence of stalking in a male sample. *Psychology, Crime and Law*, **8**, 289–310.

Sheridan, M. S. (2003) The deceit continues: An updated literature review of Münchausen's syndrome by proxy. *Child Abuse and Neglect*, **27**, 431–51.

Sherrington, R., Brynjolfsson, J., Peutrsson, H., Potter, M., Duddleston, K., Barraclough, B., Wasmuth, J., Dobbs, M., and Gurling, H. (1988). The localisation of a susceptibility locus for schizophrenia on chromosome 5. *Nature*, **336**, 164–7.

Shevchenko, Y., Novik, A., Kuznetsov, A., Afanasiev, B., Lisukov, I., Kozlov, V., Rykavicin, O., Ionova, T., Melnichenko, V., and Fedorenko, D. (2008) High-dose immunosuppressive therapy with autologous hematopoietic stem cell transplantation as a treatment option in multiple sclerosis. *Experimental Hematology*, **36**(8), 922–8.

Shia, I. S., Chao, C. Y., Mao, W. C., and Chuang, Y. J. (2006) Treatment of paraphilic sexual disorder: The use of topiramante in fetishism. *International Journal of Clinical Psychopharmacology*, **21**(4), 241–3.

Shields, J. (1978) MZA twins: Their use and abuse. In W. E. Nance (ed.), *Twin research: Psychology and methodology*. New York: Alan R. Liss.

Shields, J. (1978) Genetics. In J. K. Wing (ed.), *Schizophrenia: Towards a new synthesis*. London: Academic Press.

Shifman, S., Bronstein, M., Sternfeld, M., Pisante-Shalom, A., Lev-Lehman, E., and Weizman, A., et al. (2002) A highly significant association between a COMT haplotype and schizophrenia. *American Journal of Human Genetics*, **71**(6), 1296–1302.

Shobe, K. K., and Schooler, J. W. (2001) Discovering fact and fiction: Case-based analyses of authentic and fabricated discovered memories of abuse. In G. Davies and T. Dalgleish (eds), *Recovered memories: Seeking the middle ground*. Chichester: Wiley.

Short, J. F. (1968) *Gang delinquency and delinquent subcultures*. New York: Harper and Row.

Shorter, E. (1997) *A history of psychiatry: From the era of the asylum to the age of prozac*. Chichester: Wiley.

Shreve-Neiger, A. K., and Edelstein, B. A. (2004) Religion and anxiety: A critical review of the literature. *Clinical Psychology Review*, **24**, 379–97.

Sidis, B. (1898) The psychology of suggestion. Cited in J. F. Schumaker (1991) *Human suggestibility: Advances in theory, research and Application*. New York: Routledge.

Siever, L., and Davis, K. L. (2004) The pathophysiology of schizophrenia disorders: Perspectives from the spectrum. *American Journal of Psychiatry*, **161**, 398–413.

Siever, L., Silverman, J., Horvath, T., Klar, E., Coccaro, E., Keefe, R. S., Pinkham, L., Rinaldi, P., Mohs, R. C., and Davis, K. L. (1990) Increased morbid risk for schizophrenia-related disorders in relatives of schizotypal personality disordered patients. *Archives of General Psychiatry*, **47**, 634–40.

Sigafoos, J., Green, V. A., Edrisinha, C., and Lancioni, G. E. (2007) Flashback to the 1960s: LSD in the treatment of autism. *Developmental Neurorehabilitation*, **10**(1), 75–81.

Sigal, M. D., Altmark, D., and Carmel, I. (1986) Münchausen syndrome by adult proxy: A perpetrator abusing two adults. *Journal of Nervous and Mental Disease*, **174**, 696–8.

Silva, C. E., and Kirsch, I. (1992) Interpretive sets, expectancy, fantasy proneness, and dissociation as predictors of hypnotic response. *Journal of Personality and Social Psychology*, **63**(5), 847–56.

Silva, J. A., Ferrari, M., and Leong, G. (2000) The case of Jeffrey Dahmer: Sexual serial homicide from a neuro-psychiatric developmental perspective. *Journal of Forensic Science*, **47**(6), 1–13.

Silver, H., Feldman, P., Bilker, W., and Gur, R. C. (2002) Working memory deficit as a core neuropsychological dysfunction in schizophrenia. *American Journal of* Psychiatry, **160**(10), 1809–16.

Silverman, K., Evans, S. M., Strain, E. C., and Griffiths, R. R. (1992) Withdrawal syndrome after the double-blind cessation of caffeine consumption. *New England Journal of Medicine*, **327**, 1109–14.

Silverstein, B., Peterson, B., and Perdue, L. (1986) Some correlates of the thin standard of physical attractiveness of women. *International Journal of Eating Disorders*, **5**, 898–905.

Simeon, D., and Knutelska, M. (2005) An open trial of naltrexone in the treatment of depersonalisation disorder. *Journal of Clinical Psychopharmacology*, **25**(3), 267–70.

Simonoff, E., Elander, J., Holmshaw, J. M., Pickles, A., Murray, R., and Rutter, M. (2004) Predictors of antisocial personality: Continuities from childhood to adult life. *British Journal of Psychiatry*, **184**, 118–27.

Simpson, M. A. (1989) Correspondence 'multiple personality disorder.' *British Journal of Psychiatry*, **155**, 565.

Sims, A. (2002) *Symptoms in the Mind* (3rd edn). London: Saunders.

Sindrup, S., Bach, F., Madsen, C., Gram, L., and Jensen, T. (2003) Venlafaxine versus imipramine in painful polyneuropathy: A randomised controlled trail. *Neurology*, **60**, 1284–9.

Singer, M. T., and Wynne, L. C. (1966) Principles for scoring communication defects and deviances in parents of schizophrenics, *Psychiatry*, **29**, 260–8.

Singh, D., Meyer, W., Zambarano, R. J., and Hurlbert, D. F. (1998) Frequency and timing of coital orgasm in women desirous of becoming pregnant. *Archives of Sexual Behaviour*, **21**(1), 15–29.

Singh, S. (2007) Adolescent salvia substance abuse. *Addiction*, **102**(5), 823–5.

Singh, S. P., Burns, T., Amin, S., Jones, P. B., and Harrison, G. (2004) Acute and transient psychotic disorders: Precursors, epidemiology, course and outcome. *British Journal of Psychiatry*, **185**, 452–9.

Skinner, B. F. (1938) *The behaviour of organisms*. New York: Appleton Century Crofts.

Skinner, B. F. (1953) *Science and human behaviour*. New York: Macmillan.

Skinner, B. F. (1974) *About behaviourism*. London: Cape.

Skinner, B. F. (1986) What is wrong with daily life in the Western world? *American Psychologist*, **41**, 568–74.

Slater, E., and Cowie, V. (1971) *The genetics of mental disorders*. London: Oxford University Press.

Slater, E., and Roth, M. (1969) *Clinical psychiatry*. Bailliere, Tindall and Cassell.

Slutske, W. S., Heath, A. C., Madden, P. A., Bucholz, K. K., Statham, D. J., and Martin, N. G. (2002) Personality and the genetic risk for alcohol dependence. *Journal of Abnormal Psychology*, **111**, 124–33.

Smalley, S. (1991) Genetic influences in autism. *Psychiatric Clinics of North America*, **14**, 125–39.

Smita, K., Kumar, V. S., and Premendran, J. S. (2006) Anandamide: An update. *Fundamental and Clinical Pharmacology*, **21**, 1–8.

Smith, A., and Rogers, V. (2000) Ethics-related responses to specific situation vignettes: Evidence of gender-based differences and occupational socialization. *Journal of Business Ethics*, **28**(1), 73–85.

Smith, B. A., and Leigh, B. (1997) Virtual subjects: Using the internet as an alternative source of subjects and research environment. *Behaviour Research: Methods, Instruments and Computers*, **29**, 496–505.

Smith, G. (2003) *Anorexia and bulimia in the family: One parent's practical guide to recovery*. London: Wiley.

Smith, J. E., Richardson, J., Hoffman, C., and Pilkington, K. (2005) Mindfulness-based stress reduction as supportive therapy in cancer care: Systematic review. *Journal of Advanced Nursing*, **52**(3), 315–27.

Smith, M. (1994) Selfhood at risk: Postmodernism perils and the perils of postmodernism. *American Psychologist*, **49**, 405–11.

Smith, S. J. (1984) Crime in the news. *British Journal of Criminology*, **24**(3), 289–95.

Smith, P. (2006) The safety of cannabinoids in the treatment of multiple sclerosis. *Expert Opinion on Drug Safety*, **4**(3), 443–56.

Smith, P., and Waterman, M. (2004) Processing bias for sexual material: The emotional Stroop and sexual offenders. *Sexual Abuse: A Journal of Research and Treatment*, **16**(2), 163–71.

Smith, R. C. (2006) Amputee identity disorder and related paraphilias. *Psychiatry*, **3**(8), 27–30.

Snook, B., Wright, M., House, J. C., and Alison, L. J. (2006) Searching for a needle in a needle stack: Combining criminal careers and journey-to-crime research for criminal suspect prioritisation. *Police, Practice and Research*, **7**(3), 217–30.

Snowden, D. (1996) Spiritual and sexual attitudes: Special issue, masochism as a product of a strict religious upbringing. Unpublished thesis, Manchester Metropolitan University.

Snowling, M. J., Adams, J. W., Bowyer-Crane, C., and Tobin, V. (2000) Levels of literacy among juvenile offenders: The incidence of specific reading difficulties. *Criminal Behaviour and Mental Health*, **10**, 229–41.

Snyder, S. H. (1976) The dopamine hypothesis of schizophrenia: Focus on the dopamine receptor. *American Journal of Psychiatry*, **133**(2), 197–202.

Snyder, S. H. (1996) *Drugs and the Brain*. New York: W. H. Freeman.

Soares, J., and Mann, J. (2003) The anatomy of mood disorders. *Biological Psychiatry*, **41**(1), 86–106.

Sobell, M. B., and Sobell, L. C. (2007) Substance use and mental health. *Clinical Psychology: Science and Practice*, **14**, 1–5.

Södersten, P., and Bergh, C. (2004) Antidepressants use in anorexic girls. *Science*, **305**, 1401.

Soderstrom, H., Sjodin, A-K., Carlstedt, A., and Forsman, A. (2004) Adult psychopathic personality with childhood-onset hyperactivity and conduct disorder: A central problem constellation in forensic psychiatry. *Psychiatry Research*, **121**, 271–80.

Sohn, E. F. (1994) Antistalking statutes: Do they actually protect victims? *Criminal Law Bulletin*, **30**, 203–41.

Sokol, D., and Edwards-Brown, M. (2004) Neuroimaging in autistic spectrum disorder (ASD). *Journal of Neuroimaging*, **14**, 8–15.

Sokol, R. J., Janisse, J. J., Louis, J. M., Bailey, B. N., Ager, J., Jacobson, S. W., and Jacobson, J. L. (2007) Extreme prematurity: An alcohol-related birth effect. *Alcoholism: Clinical and Experimental Research*, **31**(6), 1031–7.

Soloff, P. H., Meltzer, C. C., Becker, C., Greer, P. J., Kelly, T. M., and Constantine, D. (2003) Impulsivity and prefrontal hypermetabolism in borderline personality disorder. *Psychiatry Research*, **123**, 153–63.

Somerset, S. M. (2003) Refined sugar intake in Australian children. *Public Health Nutrition*, **6**(8), 809–13.

Song, C., and Zheo, S. (2007) Omega-3 fatty acid elcosapentaenoic acid: A new treatment for psychiatric and neurodegenerative diseases: A review of clinical investigations. *Expert Opinion on Investigational Drugs*, **16**(10), 1627–38.

Sonne, S., Brady, K., and Morton, A. (1994) Substance abuse and bipolar affective disorder. *Journal of Nervous and Mental Disease*, **182**(6), 349–52.

Soreff, S. (2007) The biopsychosocial information model: The new disease paradigm. *Medscape General Medicine*, **9**(1), 37.

Southam-Gerow, M., and Kendall, P. (1997) Parent-focussed and cognitive-behavioural treatments of antisocial youth. In D. Stoff, J. Breiling and J. Maser (eds), *Handbook of antisocial behaviour*. New York: Wiley.

Soyka, M., Graz, C., Bottlender, R., Dirschedl, P., and Schoech, H. (2007) Clinical correlates of later violence and criminal offences in schizophrenia. *Schizophrenia Research*, **94**, 89–98.

Spanos, N. P. (1991) A sociocognitive approach to hypnosis. In S. J. Lynn and J. W. Rhue (eds), *Theories of hypnosis: Current models and perspectives*. New York: Guilford Press.

Spanos, N. P. (1996) *Multiple identities and false memories: A sociocognitive perspective*. Washington, DC: American Psychological Association.

Spanos, N. P., Weekes, J. R., and Bertrand, L. D. (1985) Multiple personality: A social psychological perspective. *Journal of Abnormal Psychology*, **94**, 362–76.

Spauwen, J., Krabbendam, L., Lieb, R., Wittchen, H. U., and Van Os, J. (2004) Does urbanicity shift the population expression of psychosis? *Journal of Psychiatric Research*, **38**(6), 613–18.

Spearman, C. (1904) General intelligence, objectively determined and measured. *American Journal of Psychology*, **15**, 201–93.

Spellman, D., and Ross, J. (1987) A bridge for the scientist-practitioner gap? *Clinical Psychology Forum*, **11**, 19–20.

Spence, A. (2001) The genetics of autism. *Current Opinion in Paediatrics*, **13**(6), 561–5.

Spence, D. (1982) *Narrative truth and historical truth*. New York: Norton.

Spence, J. T., and Robbins, A. S. (1992) Workaholism: Definition, measurement and preliminary results. *Journal of Personality Assessment*, **58**, 160–78.

Spence, S. (1991) *Psychosexual therapy: A cognitive-behavioural approach*. London: Chapman and Hall.

Spence, S. A., Brooks, D. J., Hirsch, S. R., Liddle, P. F., Meehan, J., and Grasby, P. M. (1997) A PET study of voluntary movement in schizophrenic patients experiencing passivity phenomena (delusions of alien control). *Brain*, **120**, 1997–2001.

Spence-Diehl, E. (2004) Intensive case management for victims of stalking: A pilot test evaluation. *Brief Treatment and Crisis Intervention*, **4**(4), 323–41.

Sperry, L. (2003) *Handbook of diagnosis and treatment of DSM-IV-TR personality disorders* (2nd edn). New York: Brunner-Routledge.

Sperry, R. (1982). Some effects of disconnecting the cerebral hemispheres. *Science*, **217** (4566), 1223–6.

Spiegel, H. (1963) The dissociation–association continuum. *Journal of Nervous and Mental Diseases*, **136**, 374–8.

Spielberger, C. D. (1972) Anxiety as an emotional state. In C. D. Spielberger, (ed.), *Anxiety: Current trends in theory and research*, Vol. 1. New York: Academic Press.

Spitzberg, B. H. (2002) The tactical topography of stalking victimisation and management. *Trauma, Violence and Abuse*, **3**(4), 261–88.

Spitzer, R., Endicott, J., and Robins, E. (1978) Research diagnostic criteria: Rationale and reliability. *Archives of General Psychiatry*, **38**, 773–82.

Sporer, K., and Kral, A. H. (2007) Prescription naloxone: A novel approach to heroin overdose prevention. *Annals of Emergency Medicine*, **49**(2), 172–7.

Springer, S., and Deutsch, G. (1997) *Left brain, right brain* (5th edn). New York: W. H. Freeman.

Sprong, M., Schothorst, P., Vos, E., Hox, J., and Van Engeland, H. (2007) Theory of mind in schizophrenia: Meta-analysis. *British Journal of Psychiatry*, **191**, 5–13.

Sprung, C., Afshar, G., Chavez, G., Lansdorp, P., Sabatier, L., and Murnane, J. (1999) Telomere instability in human cancer cell line. *Mutation Research*, **429**(2), 209–23.

Squitieri, F., Ciarmiello, A., Di Donato, S., and Frati, L. (2006) The search for cerebral biomarkers of Huntington's disease: A review of genetic models of age at onset prediction. *European Journal of Neurology*, **13**(4), 408–15.

Staats, A. W. (1981) Paradigmatic behaviourism, unified theory, unified theory construction methods, and the Zeitgeist of separatism. *American Psychologist*, **36**, 239–56.

Starcevic, V. (2007) Omatoform disorders and DSM-V: Conceptual and political issues in the debate. *Psychosomatics*, **47**(4), 277–81.

Starcevic, V., Linden, M., Uhlenhuth, E. H., Kolar, D., and Latas, M. (2004) Treatment of panic disorder with agoraphobia in an anxiety disorders clinic: Factors influencing psychiatrists' treatment choices. *Psychiatry Research*, **125**(1), 41–52.

Startup, M., Jackson, M. C., and Bendix, S. (2004) North Wales randomised controlled trial of cognitive behavioural therapy for acute schizophrenia spectrum disorders: Outcome at 6 and 12 months. *Psychological Medicine*, **34**(3), 413–22.

Startup, M., Jackson, M. C., Evans, K. E., and Bendix, S. (2005) North Wales randomised controlled trial of cognitive behavioural therapy for acute schizophrenia spectrum disorders: Two-year follow-up and economic evaluation. *Psychological Medicine*, **35**(9), 1307–16.

Stefansson, H., Petursson, H., Sigurdsson, E., Steinhorsdottir, V., Bjornsdottir, S., and Sigmundsson, T., et al. (2002) Neureglin 1 and susceptibility to schizophrenia. *American Journal of Human Genetics*, **71**, 877–92.

Steffenberg, S., Gillberg, C., Hellgren, L., Andersson, L., Gillberg I., Jakobsson, G., and Bohman, M. (1989) A twin study of autism in Denmark, Finland, Iceland, Norway and Sweden. *Journal of Child Psychology and Psychiatry and Allied Disciplines*, **30**, 405–16.

Stein, A., Wooley, H., and McPherson, K. (1999) Conflict between mothers with eating disorders and their infants during mealtimes. *British Journal of Psychiatry*, **175**, 455–61.

Stein, G. (1992) Drug treatments of the personality disorders. *British Journal of Psychiatry*, **161**, 167–84.

Stein, M., Sherbourne, C., Craske, M., Means-Christensen, A., Bystritsky, A., Katon, W., Sullivan, G., and Roy-Byrne, P. (2004) Quality of care for primary care patients with anxiety disorders. *American Journal of Psychiatry*, **161**(12), 2230–7.

Steinberg, M. (1994) *Stuctured Clinical Interview for DSM-IV dissociative disorders (SCID-D), revised*. Washington, DC: American Psychiatric Association.

Steinhausen, H. (2002) The outcome of anorexia in the 20th century. *American Journal of Psychiatry*, **159**, 1284–93.

Steptoe, A. (1993) Stress and the cardiovascular system: A psychosocial perspective. In S. C. Stanford and P. Salmon (eds), *Stress: From synapse to syndrome*. London: Academic Press.

Stern, L. W. (1903) *Contributions to the psychology of testimony*. Leipzig: Verlag Barth.

Stern, M., and Stern, A. (1981) *Sex in the Soviet Union*. London: W. H. Allen.

Stevens, A. (2007) When two dark figures collide: Evidence and discourse on drug-related crime. *Critical Social Policy*, **27**(1), 77–99.

Stevens, A., and Price, J. (1996) *Evolutionary psychiatry: A new beginning*. London: Routledge.

Stevens, J. A. (1997) Standard investigatory tools and offender profiling. In J. Jackson and D. Bekerian (eds), *Offender profiling: Theory, research and practice*. Chichester: Wiley.

Stirling, J., and Hellewell, J. (1999) *Psychopathology*. London: Routledge.

Stirling, J., Barkus, E., and Lewis, S. (2007) Hallucination proneness, schizotypy and meta-cognition. *Behaviour Research and Therapy*, **45**, 1401–8.

Stirling, J., Barkus, E. J., Nabosi, L., Irshad, S., Roemer, G., Schreudergoidheijt, B., and Lewis, S. (2008) Cannabis-induced psychotic-like experiences are predicted by high schizotypy: confirmation of preliminary results in a large cohort. *Psychopathology*, **41**, 371–8.

Stirling, J., Hellewell, J., Blakey, A., and Deakin, W. (2006) Thought disorder in schizophrenia is associated with both executive dysfunction and circumscribed impairments in semantic function. *Psychological Medicine*, **36**, 1–10.

Stirling, J. D., Hellewell, J. S. E., and Hewitt, J. (1997) Verbal memory impairment in schizophrenia: No sparing of short term recall. *Schizophrenia Research*, **25**, 85–95.

Stirling, J., Hellewell, J. S. E., and Ndlovu, D. (2001) Self-monitoring dysfunction and the positive symptoms of schizophrenia. *Psychopathology*, **34**, 198–202.

Stirling, J. D., Hellewell, J. S., and Quraishi, N. (1998) Self-monitoring dysfunction and the schizophrenic symptoms of alien control. *Psychological Medicine*, **28**, 675–83.

Stirling, J., Hopkins, R., White, C., and Lewis, S. (2007) Predictors of deficit syndrome schizophrenia. *Schizophrenia Bulletin*, **33**(2), 247.

Stirling, J., Tantam, D., Thomas, P., Newby, D., Montague, L., Ring, N., and Rowe, S. (1993) Expressed emotion and schizophrenia: The ontogeny of EE during and 18 month follow up. *Psychological Medicine*, **23**, 771–8.

Stoll, S., Hafner, U., Pohl, O., and Muller, W. (1994) Age related memory decline and longevity under treatment with selegiline. *Life Sciences*, **55**, 2155–63.

Stone, J., Smyth, R., Carson, A., Warlow, C., and Sharpe, M. (2006) La belle indifference in conversion symptoms and hysteria. *British Journal of Psychiatry*, **188**, 204–9.

Stone, M. (1993a) Cluster C personality disorders. In D. Dunner (ed.), *Current psychiatric therapy*. Philadelphia: W. B. Saunders.

Stone, M. H. (1993b) *Abnormalities of personality within and beyond the realm of treatment*. New York: Norton.

Stone, T., and Young, A. (1997) Delusions and brain injury: The philosophy and psychology of belief. *Mind and Language*, **12**, 327–64.

Stovner, L., Zwart, J., Hagen, K., Terwindt, G., and Pascual, J. (2006) Epidemiology of headache in Europe. *European Journal of Neurology*, **13**, 333–45.

Strakowski, S. M. (1994) Diagnostic validity of schizophreniform disorder. *American Journal of Psychiatry*, **151**, 815–24.

Strakowski, S. M., DelBello, M. P., and Adler, C. M. (2005) The functional neuroanatomy of bipolar disorder: A review of neuroimaging findings. *Molecular Psychiatry*, **10**, 105–16.

Strang, J., and Gossop, M. (1994) *Heroin addiction and drug policy: The British system*. Oxford: Oxford University Press.

Strang, J., and Gossop, M. (2004a) *Heroin addiction and the British system, Vol. I: Origins and evolution*. London: Routledge.

Strang, J., and Gossop, M. (2004b) *Heroin addiction and the British system. Vol. II: Treatment and other responses*. London: Routledge.

Straube, T., Glauer, M., Dilger, S., Mentzel, H-J., and Miltner, W. H. R. (2006) Effects of cognitive-behavioural therapy on brain activation in specific phobia. *NeuroImage*, **29**, 125–35.

Strauss, J. S., Carpenter, W. T., and Bartco, J. J. (1974) The diagnosis and understanding of schizophrenia, III: Speculations on the processes that underlie schizophrenic symptoms and signs. *Schizophrenia Bulletin*, **1**, 61–9.

Strauss, M. (1993) Relations of symptoms to cognitive deficits in schizophrenia. *Schizophrenia Bulletin*, **19**, 215–33.

Stravynski, A., Bond, S., and Amado, D. (2004) Cognitive causes of social phobia: A critical appraisal. *Clinical Psychology Review*, **24**, 421–40.

Strober, M., Freeman, R., Lampert, C., Diamond, J., and Kaye, W. (2000) A controlled family study of anorexia nervosa and bulimia nervosa: Evidence for shared liability and transmission of partial syndromes. *American Journal of Psychiatry*, **157**, 393–401.

Strobl, R., Klemm, J., and Würtz, S. (2005) Preventing hate crimes: Experiences from two East-German towns. *British Journal of Criminology*, **45**, 634–46.

Studer, L. H., Aylwin, A. S., Clelland, S. R., Reddon, J. R., and Frenzel, R. R. (2002) Primary erotic preference in a group of child molesters. *International Journal of Law and Psychiatry*, **25**, 173–80.

Stunkard, A. J., Grace, W. J., and Wolff, H. G. (1955) The night-eating syndrome: A pattern of food intake among certain obese patients. *American Journal of Medicine*, **19**, 78–86.

Suchowersky, O., Gronseth, G., Perlmutter, J., Reich, S., Zesiewicz, T., and Weiner, W. J. (2006) Practice parameter: Neuroprotective strategies and alternative therapies for Parkinson disease (an evidence-based review). Report of the Quality Standards Subcommittee of the American Academy of Neurology. *Neurology*, **66**, 976–82.

Sumathipala, A. (2007) What is the evidence for the efficacy of treatments for somatoform disorders? A critical review of previous intervention studies. *Psychosomatic Medicine*, **69**, 889–900.

Summerfield, D. (2001) The invention of post-traumatic stress disorder and the social usefulness of a psychiatric category. *British Medical Journal*, **322**, 95–8.

Susman, E. J., and Finkelstein, J. W. (2001) Biology, development and dangerousness. In G. F. Pinard and L. Pagani (eds), *Clinical assessment of dangerousness: Empirical contributions*. New York: Cambridge University Press.

Sutherland, E. H. (1939) *The professional thief*. Chicago: Chicago University Press.

Sutherland, E. H., and Cressey, D. (1960) *Principles of criminology* (6th edn). Philadelphia: Lippincott.

Sutherland, E. H., and Cressey, D. (1970) *Criminology* (8th edn). Philadelphia: Lippincott.

Sutker, P. B., and Adams, H. E. (2001) *Compehensive handbook of psychopathology* (3rd edn). New York: Kluwer Academic-Plenum.

Sveinsson, O. A., Gudjonsson, T., and Petersen, P. H. (2008) The application of stem cells for research and treatment of neurological disorders. *Laeknabladid*, **94**(2), 117–22.

Svendsen, C. (2008a) Stem cells and Parkinson's disease: Toward a treatment, not a cure. *Cell Stem Cell*, **2**(5), 412–13.

Svendsen, C. (2008b) Combining stem cell and gene therapy for neurological disorders. Paper presented at 'NIH Symposium: Challenges and Promise of Cell-Based Therapies', Natcher Conference Center, NIH Main Campus, Bethesda, Maryland, 6 May.

Swanson, J. M., Flodman, P., Kennedy, J., Spence, A., Moyzis, R., Schuck, S., Murias, M., Moriarity, J., Barr, C., Smith, M., and Posner, M. (2000) Dopamine genes and ADHD. *Neuroscience and Behavioural Reviews*, **24**, 21–5.

Swanson, J., Sergeant, J., Taylor, E., Sonuga-Barke, E. J., Jensen, P., and Cantwell, D. (1998) Attention deficit disorder and hyperkinetic disorder. *The Lancet*, **351**, 429–33.

Swanson, J. W., Van Dorn, R. A., Swartz, M. S., Smith, A., Elbogen, E. B., Monahan, J. (2008) Alternative pathways to violence in persons with schizophrenia: The role of childhood antisocial behaviour problems. *Law and Human Behaviour*, **32**(3), 228–40.

Swearingen, S., and Klausner, J. D. (2005) Sildenafil use, sexual risk behaviour and risk for sexually transmitted diseases, including HIV infection. *American Journal of Medicine*, **118**, 571–7.

Szasz, T. (1960) The myth of mental illness. *American Psychologist*, **15**, 113–18.

Szasz, T. (1971) *The manufacture of madness*. London: Routledge and Kegan Paul.

Szasz, T. (1985) Psychiatry: rhetoric and reality. *The Lancet*, Sept., 711–12.

Szasz, T. (1987) *Insanity: The idea and its consequences*. New York: Wiley.

Szasz, T. (1993) Curing, coercing and claims making: A reply to critics. *British Journal of Psychiatry*, **162**, 797–800.

Szasz, T. (2001) Mental illness: Psychiatry's phlogiston. *Journal of Medical Ethics*, **27**, 297–301.

Szatmari, P. (1992) The validity of autistic spectrum disorders: A literature review. *Journal of Autism and Developmental Disorders*, **22**, 583–600.

Szegedi, A., Kohnen, R., Dienel, A., and Kieser, M. (2005) Acute treatment of moderate to severe depression with hypericum extract WS 5570 (St John's wort): Randomised controlled double-blind non-inferiority trial versus paroxetine. *British Medical Journal*, **330**(7490), 330.

Szobot, C., Rohde, L., Bukenstein, O., Molina, B., Martins, C., Ruaro, P., and Perchansky, F. (2007) Is attention-deficit hyperactivity disorder associated with illicit substance use disorders in male adolescents? A community based case-control study. *Addiction*, **102**, 1122–30.

Szuchman, L. T., and Muscarella, F. (2000) *Psychological perspectives on human sexuality*. New York: Wiley.

Tait, R., Hulse, G., Waterreus, A., Flicker, L., Lautenschlager, N., Jamrozik, K., and Almeida, O. (2006) Effectiveness of a smoking cessation intervention in older adults. *Addiction*, **102**, 148–55.

Talbot, K., Eidem, W. L., Tinsley, C. L., Benson, M. A., Thomson, E. W., Smith, R. J., Hahn, C. G., Seigel, S. J., Trojanowski, J. Q., Gur, R. E., Blake, D. J., and Arnold, S. E. (2004) Dysbindin 1 is reduced in intrinsic glatamatergic terminals of the hippocampal formation in schizophrenia. *Journal of Clinical Investigation*, **113**, 1353–63.

Talbot, M. (2002) The H-word. *Guardian*, 31 Aug.

Talvik, M., Nordstrom, A. L., Okubo, Y., Olsson, H., Borg, J., Halldin, C., and Farde, L. (2006) Dopamine D2 receptor binding in drug-naive patients with schizophrenia examined by raclopride-C11 and positron emission tomography. *Psychiatry Research: Neuroimaging*, **148**(1–2), 165–73.

Talvik, M., Nordstrom, A. L., Olsson, H., Halldin, C., and Farde, L. (2003) Decreased thalamic D2/D3 receptor binding in drug naïve patients with schizophrenia: A PET study with [C11] FLB 457. *International Journal of Neuropsychopharmacology*, **6**, 361–70.

Tan, E. K., Tan, C., Fook-Chong, S. M., Lum, S. Y., Chai, A., Chung, H., et al. (2003) Dose-dependent protective effect of coffee, tea, and smoking in Parkison's disease: A study in ethnic Chinese. *Journal of Neurological Science*, **216**, 163–7.

Tannahill, R. (1980) *Sex in history*. London: Hamilton.

Tannock, R. (1998) Attention deficit hyperactivity disorder: Advances in cognitive, neurobiological and genetic research. *Journal of Child Psychology and Psychiatry*, **39**(1), 65–99.

Tanofsky-Kraff, M., and Yanvski, S. Z. (2004) Eating disorders or disordered eating? Non-normative eating patterns in obese individuals. *Obesity Research*, **12**, 1361–6.

Tantam, D. (1988) *A mind of one's own: A guide to the special difficulties and needs of the more able autistic person, for parents, professional and autistic people*. London: National Autistic Society.

Tantam, D. (1991) The antipsychiatry movement. In G. E. Berrios and H. Freeman (eds), *150 years of British psychiatry 1841–1991*. London: Gaskell.

Tantam, D. (1992) Characterising the fundamental social handicap in autism. *Acta Paedopsychiatrica*, **55**, 83–91.

Tantam, D. (2000) Adolescence and adulthood of individuals with Asperger's syndrome. In A. Klin, F. Volkmar and S. Sparrow (eds), *Asperger's syndrome*. New York: Guilford Press.

Tantam, D. (2009) *Can the world afford autistic spectrum disorder?* London: Jessica Kingsley.

Tantam, D., and McGrath, G. (1989) Psychiatric day hospitals – another route to institutionalisation? *Social Psychiatry and Psychiatric Epidemiology*, **24**, 96–101.

Tantam, D., Holmes, D., and Cordess, C. (1993) Nonverbal expression in autism of Asperger's type. *Journal of Autism and Developmental Disorders*, **23**, 111–33.

Tantam, D., Stirling, J., Monaghan, L., and Nicholson, H. (1989) Autistic children's ability to interpret faces: A research note. *Journal of Child Psychology and Psychiatry*, **39**, 623–30.

Tanzil, R. E., and Bertram, L. (2005) Twenty years of the Alzheimer's disease amyloid hypothesis: A genetic perspective. *Cell*, **120**, 545–55.

Tapanya, S., Nicki, R., and Jaruswad, O. (1997) Worry and intrinsic/extrinsic religious orientation among Buddhist (Thai) and Christian (Canadian) elderly persons. *Aging and Human Development*, **44**, 75–83.

Tarrier, N., Barrowclough, C., Porceddu, K., and Fitzpatrick, E. (1994) The Salford family intervention project: Relapse rates of schizophrenia at five and eight years. *British Journal of Psychiatry*, **165**, 829–32.

Tarrier, N., Barrowclough, C., Vaughn, C., Bamrah, J. S., Porceddu, K., Watts, S., and Freeman, H. (1989) Community management of schizophrenia: A two-year follow-up of a behavioural intervention with families. *British Journal of Psychiatry*, **154**, 625–8.

Tarrier, N., Lewis, S., Haddock, G., Bentall, R., Drake, R., Kinderman, P., Kingdon, D., Siddle, R., Everitt, J., Leadley, K., Benn, A., Grazenbrook, K., Haley, C., Akhtar, S., Davies, L., Palmer, S., and Dunn, G. (2004) Cognitive behaviour therapy in first episode and early schizophrenia: 18 month follow-up of a randomised controlled trial. *British Journal of Psychiatry*, **184**, 231–9.

Taylor, P. J., and Gunn, J. (1984) Violence and psychosis, 1: Risk of violence amongst psychotic men. *British Medical Journal*, **288**, 1945–9.

Taylor, B., Miller, E., Farrington, C., Petropoulos, M. C., Favot-Mayaud, I., Li, J., and Waight, P. A. (1999) MMR vaccine and autism: No epidemiological evidence of a causal association. *The Lancet*, **353**, 2026–9.

Taylor, I., Walton, P., and Young, J. (1973) *The new criminology*. London: Routledge and Kegan Paul.

Taylor, R. E., Bewley, A., and Melidonis, N. (2006) Psychodermatology. *Psychiatry*, **5**(3), 81–4.

Teesson, M., Degenhardt, L., and Hall, W. (2002) *Addictions*. Hove: Psychology Press.

Teitelbaum, P., Teitelbaum, O., Nye, J., Fryman, J., and Maurer, R. (1998) Movement analysis in infancy may be useful for early diagnosis of autism. *Proceedings of the National Academy of Sciences USA*, **95**(23), 13982–7.

Tek, C., and Ulug, B. (2001) Religiosity and religious obsessions in obsessive–compulsive disorder. *Psychiatry Research*, **104**(2), 99–108.

Temrin, H., Buchmayer, S., and Enquist, M. (2000) Step-parents and infanticide: New data contradict evolutionary predictions. *Proceedings of the Royal Society: Biological Sciences*, **267**, 943–5.

Tennant, C. (1999) Life stress, social support and coronary heart disease. *Australia and New Zealand Journal of Psychiatry*, **33**, 636–41.

Teplin, L. A., McLelland, G. M., Abram, K. M., and Weiner, D. A. (2005) Crime victimisation in adults with severe mental illness. *Archives of General Psychiatry*, **62**, 911–21.

Terman, L. M., and Merrill, M. A. (1937) *Measuring intelligence*. Boston: Houghton-Mifflin.

Tewksbury, R. (2006) Sex offender registers as a tool for public safety: Views from registered offenders. *Western Criminology Review*, **7**(1), 1–8.

Thakur, C., and Sharma, D. (1984) Full moon and crime. *British Medical Journal (Clinical Research Edition)*, **289**(6460), 1789–91.

Thanvi, B., Lo, N., and Robinson, T. (2005) Vascular parkinsonism: An important cause of parkinsonism in older people. *Age and Ageing*, **34**(2), 114–19.

Thomas, C. S., Stone, K., Osborn, M., Thomas, P., and Fisher, M. (1993) Psychiatric morbidity and compulsory admission among UK-born Europeans, Afro-Caribbeans and Asians in central Manchester. *British Journal of Psychiatry*, **163**, 91–9.

Thomas, D., and Loader, B. (2000) *Cybercrime: Law enforcement, security and surveillance in the information age*. London and New York: Routledge.

Thomas, H. (1996) A community survey of adverse effects of cannabis use. *Drug and Alcohol Dependence*, **42**, 201–7.

Thomas, P., and Fenech, M. (2007) A review of genome mutation and Alzheimer's disease. *Mutagenesis*, **22**(1), 15–33.

Thomas, R. (1997) Biology isn't destiny – but it's part of it. *Harvard Health Letter*, **22**(6), 1.

Thomas, T. (2000) *Sex crime, sex offending and society*. Cullompton: Willan.

Thomson, P. A., Christoforou, A., Morris, S. W., Adie, E., Pickard, B. S., Porteus, D. J., Muir, W. J., Blackwood, D. H., and Evans, K. L. (2007) Association of neuregulin 1 with schizophrenia and bipolar disorder in a second cohort from the Scottish population. *Molecular Psychiatry*, **12**(1), 94–104.

Thompson, P. M., Hayashi, H. M., Simon, S. L., Geaga, J. A., Hong, M. S., Sui, Y., Lee, J. Y., Toga, A. W., Ling, W., and London, E. D. (2004) Structural abnormalities in the brains of human subjects who use methamphetamine. *Journal of Neuroscience*, **24**, 6028–36.

Thoresen, C. E., and Pattillo, J. R. (1988) Exploring the Type A behavior pattern in children and adolescents. In B. K. Houston and C. R. Snyder (eds), *Type A behavior pattern: Research, theory, and intervention*. New York: Wiley.

Thoresen, C. E., and Powell, L. H. (1992) Type A behavior: New perspectives on theory, assessment, and intervention. *Journal of Consulting and Clinical Psychology*, **60**(4), 595–604.

Thoresen, C. E., Telch, M. J., and Eagleston, J. R. (1981) Approaches to altering the Type A behavior pattern. *Psychosomatics*, **22**(6), 472–80.

Tienari, P., Wynne, L. C., Moring, J., Laksy, K., Nieminen, P., and Sorri, A. (2000) Finnish adoptive family study: Sample selection and adoptee DSM III R diagnoses. *Acta Psychiatrica Scandinavica*, **101**, 433–43.

Tiggemann, M., and Rothblum, E. (1988) Gender differences and social consequences of perceived overweight in the United States and Australia. *Sex Roles*, **18**, 75–86.

Timmerman, G. M. (2006) Restaurant eating in non-purge binge eating women. *Western Journal of Nursing Research*, **28**(7), 811–24.

Timmerman, I. G. H., and Emmelkamp, P. M. G. (2005) The effects of cognitive-behavioural treatment for forensic inpatients. *Internatioinal Journal of Offender Therapy and Comparative Criminology*, **49**, 590–606.

Timmi, S., and Taylor, E. (2004) ADHD is best understood as a cultural construct. *British Journal of Psychiatry*, **184**, 8–9.

Tinbergen, N. (1951) *The study of instinct*. London: Oxford University Press.

Tjaden, P., and Thoennes, N. (1998) *Stalking in America: Findings from the National Violence Against Women Survey (NCJ 169592)*. Washington, DC: National Institute of Justice and Centers for Disease Control and Prevention.

Tollison, C. D., and Adams, H. E. (1979) *Sexual disorders: Treatment, theory, and research*. New York: Gardner Press.

Tong, D. (2007) The penile plethysmograph, Abel Assessment for Sexual Interest and MSI-II: Are they speaking the same language? *American Journal of Family Therapy*, **35**, 187–202.

Tooby, J., and Cosmides, L. (1992) Psychological foundations of culture. In J. Barkow, L. Cosmides and J. Tooby (eds), *The adapted mind*. Oxford: Oxford University Press.

Torgerson, S., Lygren, S., Oien, P. A., Skre, I., Onstad, S., Edvardsen, J., Tambs, K., and Kringlen, E. (2000) A twin study of personality disorders. *Comprehensive Psychiatry*, **41**, 416–25.

Tosato, S., Dazzan, P., and Collier, D. (2005) Association between the neuregulin 1 gene and schizophrenia: A systematic review. *Schizophrenia Bulletin*, **31**(3), 613–17.

Towl, G. J. (2002) Psychological services in HM Prison Service and the National Probation Service: Working towards an effective partnership. *British Journal of Forensic Practice*, **4**(3), 2–10.

Towl, G. J., and Crighton, D. A. (1996) *The handbook of psychology for forensic practitioners*. London: Routledge.

Treasure, J., and Holland, A. (1989) Genetic vulnerability to eating disorders: Evidence from twin and family studies. In H. Remschmidt and M. H. Schmidt (eds), *Child and youth psychiatry: European perspectives*. New York: Hogrefe and Huber.

Trevor-Roper, H. (1967) *The European witch craze of the 16th and 17th centuries*. Harmondsworth: Penguin.

Trigo, M., Silva, D., and Rocha, E. (2005) Psychosocial risk factors in coronary heart disease: Beyond type A behavior. *Review of Portugese Cardiology*, 24(2), 261–81.

Trower, P., Birchwood, M., Meaden, A., Byrne, S., Nelson, A., and Ross, K. (2004) Cognitive therapy for command hallucinations: Randomised controlled trial. *British Journal of Psychiatry*, 184, 312–20.

Trull, T. J., and Durrett, C. A. (2005) Categorical and dimensional models of personality disorder. *Annual Review of Clinical Psychology*, 1, 355–80.

Trull, T. J., and Phares, E. J. (2001) *Clinical psychology*. Belmont, CA: Wadsworth.

Trouson, A. (1999) Hello again Dolly: Human cloning. *Molecular Medicine Today*, 5(10), 423.

Tryon, W. W. (2005) Possible mechanisms for why desensitisation and exposure therapy work. *Clinical Psychology Review*, 25, 67–95.

Tsakanikos, E., and Reed, P. (2005) Positive schizotypal symptoms predict false perceptual experiences in non-clinical populations? *Journal of Nervous and Mental Disease*, 193, 809–12.

Tseng, W. S. (2003) *Clinician's guide to cultural psychiatry*. San Diego, CA: Academic Press.

Tsuang, M. T., and Farone, S. V. (2000) The frustrating search for schizophrenia genes. *American Journal of Medical Genetics*, 97, 1–3.

Tulving, E. (1974) Cue dependent forgetting. *American Scientist*, 62, 74–8.

Turkington, D., Sensky, T., Scott, J., Barnes, T. R., Nur, U., Siddle, R., Hammond, K., Samarasekara, N., and Kingdon, D. (2008) A randomised controlled trial of cognitive behaviour therapy for persisitent symptoms in schizophrenia: A five year follow-up. *Schizophrenia Research*, 98, 1–7.

Turmanis, S. A., and Brown, R. I. (2006) The Stalking and Harassment Behaviour Scale: Measuring the incidence, nature, and severity of stalking and relational harassment and their psychological effects. *Psychology and Psychotherapy: Theory, Research and Practice*, 79, 183–98.

Turner, C. (2006) Cognitive-behavioural theory and therapy for obsessive–compulsive disorder in children and adolescence: Current status and future directions. *Clinical Psychology Review*, 26(7), 912–38.

Tyler, A., Ball, D., and Crawford, D. (1992) Pre-symptomatic testing for Huntington's disease in the UK. *British Medical Journal*, 304, 1593–6.

Tyrer, P. (1985) Classification of anxiety. *British Journal of Psychiatry*, 144, 78–83.

Tyrer, P. (1988) *Personality disorders: Diagnosis, management and course*. London: Wright.

Tyrer, P., and Bateman, A. W. (2004) Drug treatment for personality disorders. *Advances in Psychiatric Treatment*, 10, 389–98.

Tyrer, P., Coombs, N., Ibrahimi, F., Mathilakath, A., Bajaj, P., Ranger, M., and Din, R. (2007) Critical developments in the assessment of personality disorder. *British Journal of Psychiatry*, 190, S51–S59.

Tzavara, E., and Witkin, J. J. (2008) *Cannabinoids and the brain*. New York: Springer.

Udelson, D. (2007) Biomechanics of male erectile function. *Journal of the Royal Society Interface*, 4, 1031–47.

Undeutsch, U. (1992) Highlights of the history of forensic psychology in Germany. In F. Losel, D. Bender and T. Bliesener (eds), *Psychology and law: International perspectives*. Berlin: Walter de Gruyter.

Urosevic, S., Abramson, L. Y., Harmon-Jones, E., and Alloy, L. B. (2008) Dysregulation of the behavioural approach system (*BAS) in bipolar spectrum disorders: Review of theory and evidence. *Clinical Psychology Review*, 28(7), 1188–205.

Uttermark, J. (2004) The Dutch approach towards drugs. *Journal of Drug Issues*, 34, 511–32.

Valenti, M., Benabarre, A., Garcia-Amado, M., Molina, O., Bernardo, M., and Vieta, E. (2008) Electroconvulsive therapy in the treatment of mixed states in bipolar disorder. *European Psychiatry*, 23(1), 53–6.

Van Balkom, A. J. L. M., Bakker, A., Spinhoven, P., Blaauw, B. M. J. W., Smeenk, S., and Ruesink, B. (1997) A meta-analysis of the treatment of panic disorder with or without agoraphobia: A comparison of psychopharmacological, cognitive-behavioral, and combination treatments. *Journal of Nervous and Mental Disease*, 185(8), 510–16.

Van den Heuvel, O. A., Groenewegen, H. J., Barkhof, F., Lazeron, R. H., van Dyck, R., and Veltman, D. J. (2003) Frontostriatal system in planning complexity: A parametric functional magnetic resonance version of Tower of London task. *Neuroimage*, 18, 367–74.

Van Duyne, P. C., and Levi, M. (2005) *Drugs and money: Managing the drugs trade and crime money in Europe*. London: Routledge.

Van Koppen, P. J., and Lochun, S. K. (1997) Portraying perpetrators: The validity of offender descriptions by witnesses. *Law and Human Behaviour*, 21(6), 661–85.

Van Os, J., Bak, M., Hanssen, M., Bijl, R. V., de Graaf, R., and Verdoux, H. (2002) Cannabis use and psychosis: A longitudinal population-based study. *American Journal of Epidemiology*, **156**(4), 319–27.

Van Os, J., Hanssen, M., Bijl, R. V., and Ravelli, A. (2000) Strauss (1969) revisited: A psychosis continuum in the general population? *Schizophrenia Research*, **45**, 11–20.

Vaughn, C., and Leff, J. (1976a) The measurement of expressed emotion in the families of psychiatric patients. *British Journal of Social and Clinical Psychology*, **15**, 157–65.

Vaughn, C. E., and Leff, J. P. (1976b) The influence of family and social factors on the course of psychiatric illness. *British Journal of Psychiatry*, **129**, 125–37.

Vaughn, C. E., Snyder, K. S., Jones, S., Freeman, W. B., and Falloon, I. R. (1984) Family factors in schizophrenic relapse: Replication in California of British research on expressed emotion. *Archives of General Psychiatry*, **41**, 1169–77.

Veale, D. (2000) Outcome of cosmetic surgery and 'DIY' surgery in patients with body dysmorphic disorder. *Psychiatric Bulletin*, **24**, 218–21.

Veale, D. (2002) Over-valued ideas: A conceptual analysis. *Behaviour Research and Therapy*, **40**, 383–400.

Veith, I. (1965) *Hysteria: The history of a disease*. Chicago: University of Chicago Press.

Velastin, S. A., Lo, B., and Sun, J. (2004) A flexible communications protocol for a distributed surveillance system. *Journal of Network and Computer Applications*, **27**(4), 221–53.

Vennard, J., and Hedderman, C. (1998) Effective treatment with offenders. In P. Goldblatt and C. Lewis (eds), *Reducing offending: An assessment of research evidence on ways of dealing with offending behaviour*. Home Office Research Study No. 171, London: Home Office.

Verdoux, H., Gindre, C., Sorbara, F., Tournier, M., and Swendsen, J. D. (2003) Effects of cannabis and psychosis vulnerability in daily life: An experience sampling test study. *Psychological Medicine*, **33**, 23–32.

Verhaeghen, P., Joormann, J., and Khan, R. (2005) Why we sing the blues: The relation between self-reflective rumination, mood and creativity. *Emotion*, **5**(2), 226–32.

Verma, R., Khurd, P., Longhead, J., Gur, R., Davatzikos, C. (2008) Manifold based morphometry applied to schizophrenia. *Biomedical imaging: From nano to macro*, 704–7, Paris: IEEE.

Vermitten, E., Schmahl, C., Lindener, S., Loewenstein, R. J., and Bremner, J. D. (2006) Hippocampal and amygdalar volumes in dissociative identity disorder. *American Journal of Psychiatry*, **163**(4), 1–8.

Viding, E., Blair, J. R., Moffitt, T., and Plomin, R. (2005) Evidence for substantial genetic risk for psychopathy in 7-year-olds. *Journal of Child Psychology and Psychiatry*, **46**(6), 592–7.

Vitetta, L., Anton, B., Cortizo, F., and Salf, A. (2005) Mind–body medicine: Stress and its inpact on overall health and longevity. *Annual New York Academy of Sciences*, **1057**, 492–505.

Vizi, E. S. (2007) Drugs of abuse: The myth of creativity and the reality of destruction. *European Review*, **15**(2), 241–56.

Vogeley, K., Bussfeld, P., Newen, A., Herrmann, S., Happé, F., Falkai, P., Maier, W., Shah, N., Fink, G. R., and Zilles, K. (2001) Mind reading: Neural mechanisms of theory of mind and self-perspective. *Neurological Imaging*, **14**, 170–81.

Volans, G., and Wiseman, H. (2008) *Drugs handbook 2008*. Basingstoke: Palgrave Macmillan.

Völim, B., Richardson, P., Stirling, J., Elliott, R., Dolan, M., Chaudhry, D. B., Mclier, S., Anderson, I., and Deakin, J. F. W. (2004) Neurobiological substrates of antisocial and borderline personality disorder: Preliminary results of a functional fMRI study. *Criminal Behaviour and Mental Health*, **14**(1), 39–54.

Volkmar, F., and Klin, A. (2000) Diagnostic issues in Asperger's syndrome. In A. Klin, F. Volkmar and S. Sparrow (eds), *Asperger's syndrome*. New York: Guilford Press.

Volkmar, F., Szatmari, P., and Sparrow, S. (1993) Sex differences in pervasive developmental disorders. *Journal of Autism and Developmental Disorders*, **23**, 579–91.

Vollema, M. G., and Hoijtink, H. (2000) The multidimensionality of self report schizotypy in a psychiatric population. *Schizophrenia Bulletin*, **26**(3), 565–75.

Voruganti, L. N., Slomka, P., Zabel, P., Mattar, A., and Awad, A. G. (2001) Cannabis-induced dopamine release: An in vivo SPECT study. *Psychiatry Research*, **107**, 173–7.

Vourdas, A., Pipe, R., Corrigall, R., and Frangou, S. (2003) Increased developmental deviance and premorbid dysfunction in early onset schizophrenia. *Schizophrenia Research*, **62**(1–2), 13–22.

Vrij, A. (2000) *Detecting Lies and Deceit: The psychology of lying and its implications for professional practice*. Chichester: Wiley.

Vrij, A. (2004) Why professionals fail to catch liars and how they can improve. *Legal and Criminological Psychology*, **9**, 159–81.

Vrij, A., and Mann, S. (2001) Who killed my relative? Police officers' ability to detect real-life high stake lies. *Psychology, Crime and Law*, **7**, 119–32.

Vrij, A., Mann, S., Robbins, E., and Robinson, M. (2006) Police officer's ability to detect deception in high stakes situations and in repeated lie detection tests. *Applied Cognitive Psychology*, **20**, 741–55.

Wadden, T. A., and Stunkard, A. J. (2002) *Handbook of obesity treatment*. Hove: Guilford Press.

Waddington, C. (1957) *Strategies of genes: A discussion of some aspects of theoretical biology*. London: Allen and Unwin.

Wager, T. D., Rilling, J. K., Smith, E. E., Sokolik, A., Casey, K. L., Davidson, R. J., Kosslyn, S. M., Rose, R. M., and Cohen, J. D. (2004) Placebo-induced changes in fMRI in the anticipation and experience of pain. *Science*, **303**(5661), 1162–7.

Wagstaff, G. F. (1993) What expert witnesses can tell courts about hypnosis: A review of the association between hypnosis and the law. *Expert Evidence*, **2**, 3–12.

Wakefield, H., and Underwager, R. (1992) Recovered memories of alleged sexual abuse: Lawsuits against parents. *Behavioural Sciences and the Law*, **10**, 483–507.

Wakefield, J. (1999) Philosophy of science and the progressiveness of DSM's theory neutral nosology: Response to Follette and Houts Pt1. *Behaviour Research and Therapy*, **37**, 963–9.

Walker, J., and Furer, P. (2006) Health anxiety: Hypochondriasis and somatisation. In A. Carr and M. McNulty (eds), *The handbook of adult clinical psychology: An evidence-based practice approach*. Hove: Routledge.

Walker, N. (1996) *Dangerous people*. London: Blackstone.

Walklate, S. (1989) *Victimology: The victim and the criminal justice process*. London: Unwin and Hyman.

Walklate, S. (1995) *Gender and crime*. London: Prentice Hall.

Walklate, S. (1998) *Understanding criminology*. Buckingham: Open University Press.

Wallace, A. (1858) On the tendency of varieties to depart from the original type. *Journal of the Proceedings of the Linnean Society*, **3**, 53–62.

Wallace, B. A., and Shapiro, S. L. (2006) Mental balance and well-being: Building bridges between Buddhism and Western psychology. *American Psychologist*, **61**(7), 690–701.

Wallace, C., Mullen, P. E., Burgess, P., Palmer, S., Ruschena, D., and Browne, C. (1998) Serious criminal offending and mental disorder: Case linkage study. *British Journal of Psychiatry*, **172**, 477–84.

Waller, G., Quinton, S., and Watson, D. (1995) Dissociation and the processing of threat-related information. *Dissociation*, **8**, 84–90.

Walsh, B. T., and Devlin, M. J. (1998) Eating disorders: Progress and problems. *Science*, **280**, 1387–90.

Walsh, E., Buchanan, A., and Fahy, T. (2002) Violence and schizophrenia: Examining the evidence. *British Journal of Psychiatry*, **180**, 490–5.

Walters, G. D. (1992) A meta-analysis of the gene-crime relationship. *Criminology*, **30**, 595.

Wang, G-J., Volkow, J. L., Logan, J., Pappas, N. R., Wong, C. T., Zhu, W., Netusil, N., and Fowler, J. S. (2001) Brain dopamine and obesity. *The Lancet*, **357**, 354–7.

Wang, W., Lui, L., Zhi, X., Huang, J. B., Lui, D. X., Wang, H., Kong, X. Q., and Xu, H. B. (2007) Study on the regulatory effect of electrodermal-acupuncture on hegu point (L14) in cerebral response with functional resonance imaging. *Chinese Journal of Integrated Medicine*, **13**(1), 10–16.

Waraich, P., Goldner, E. M., Somers, J. M., and Lorena Hsu, L. (2004) Prevalence and incidence studies of mood disorders: A systematic review of the literature, **49**, 124–38.

Ward, D., Scott, J., and Lacey, M. (2002) *Probation: Working for justice*. Oxford: Oxford University Press.

Warden, J. (1999) Ashworth report confirms problems with special hospitals. *British Medical Journal*, **318**, 211.

Wardle, J. (2007) Eating behaviour and obesity. *Obesity Review*, **8** (suppl. 1), 73–5.

Warfa, N., Klein, A., Bhui, K., Leavey, G., Craig, T., and Stansfield, A. (2007) Khat use and mental illness: A critical review. *Social Sciences and Medicine*, **65**, 309–18.

Warner, J. (2004) Alien abduction tales offer clues on memory: Study: Distress doesn't necessarily validate traumatic memories. *WebMD Health*, 25 June.

Warner, S. (2001) Women patients, child sexual abuse, and high security mental hospitals: Making sense of 'effects'. Paper presented at the Forensic Research Group Conference, 11 Nov. 2000, Manchester Metropolitan University. *Proceedings of the British Psychological Society*, **9**(2), 33.

Watanabe, N., Churchill, R., and Furukawa, T. A. (2007) Combination of psychotherapy and benzodiazepines versus either therapy alone for panic disorder: A systematic review. *BioMed CentralPsychiatry*, **7**, 18–30.

Watson, D., and Wu, K. D. (2005) Development and validation of the Schedule of Compulsions, Obsessions and Pathological Impulses (SCOPI). *Assessment*, **12**(1), 50–65.

Watson, J. B., and Rayner, R. (1920) Conditioned emotional reactions. *Journal of Experimental Psychology*, **3**, 1–14.

Watson, R., Stimpson, A., and Hostick, T. (2004) Prison health care: A review of the literature. *International Journal of Nursing Studies*, **41**(2), 119–28.

Webb, D., and Harris, R. (1999) *Mentally disordered offenders: Managing people nobody owns*. London: Routledge.

Webster, R. (1995) *Why Freud was wrong: Of sin science and psychoanalysis*. London: HarperCollins.

Webster, R. (2004) Freud, Charcot and hysteria: Lost in the labyrinth. Retrieved on 6 Aug. 2008 from www. richardwebster.net/freudandcharcot.html.

Wechsler, D. (1997a) *WAIS-III: Administration and scoring manual*. San Antonio: Psychological Corporation.

Wechsler, D. (1997b) *Wechsler Adult Intelligence Scales – Third edition (WAIS-III)*. San Antonio: Psychological Corporation.

Weertman, A., Arntz, A., Schouten, E., and Dreessen, L. (2006) Dependent personality traits and information processing: Assessing the interpretation of ambiguous information using the Thematic Apperception Test. *British Journal of Clinical Psychology*, **45**, 273–8.

Weikert, C. S., Straub, R. E., McClintock, B. W., Matsumoto, M., Hashimoto, R., Hydoe, T. M., Herman, M. M., Weinberger, D. R., and Kleinman, J. E. (2004) Human dysbindin (DTNBP1) gene expression in normal brain and in schizophrenic prefrontal cortex and mid-brain. *Archives of General Psychiatry*, **61**, 544–55.

Weinberger, D. R., Aloia, M. S., Goldberg, T. E., and Berman, K. F. (1994) The frontal lobes and schizophrenia. *Journal of Neuropsychiatry*, **6**(4), 419–27.

Weintraub, D., and Stern, M. B. (2005) Psychiatric complications in Parkinson's disease. *American Journal of Geriatric Psychiatry*, **13**, 844–51.

Weintraub, D., Comella, C., and Horn, S. (2008a) Parkinson's disease, Part 1: Pathophysiology, symptoms, burden, diagnosis and assessment. *American Journal of Managed Care*, **14**(1), S40–S48.

Weintraub, D., Comella, C., and Horn, S. (2008b) Parkinson's disease, Part 2: Treatment of motor symptoms. *American Journal of Managed Care*, **14**(2), S49–S58.

Weintraub, D., Comella, C., and Horn, S. (2008c) Parkinson's disease, Part 3: Neuropsychiatric symptoms. *American Journal of Managed Care*, **14**(3), S59–S69.

Weiss, E. M., Golaszewski, S., Mottaghy, F. M., Hofer, A., Hausmann, A., Kemmler, G., Kresmer, C., Brinkhoff, C., Felber, S. R., and Fleischhacker, W. W. (2003) Brain activation patterns during a selective attention tests: A functional MRI study of healthy volunteers and patients with schizophrenia. *Psychiatry Research (Neuro-imaging)*, **123**, 1–15.

Weiss, J. M., Glazer, H., and Pohorecky, L. (1974) Coping behaviour and neurochemical change in rats. Paper presented at The Kittay Scientific Foundation Conference, New York, Mar.

Weiss Cohen, S., Dugan, L. M., McLaughlin, R. H., and Soucar, E. (1995) Dr Satterfield replies. *Journal of the American Academy of Child and Adolescent Psychiatry*, **34**(4), 398–9.

Weissman, M. (1993) The epidemiology of personality disorders: A 1990 update. *Journal of Personality Disorders*, Spring Supplement, 44–62.

Weitzer, R. (2005) New directions in research on prostitution. *Crime, Law and Social Change*, **43**, 211–35.

Weitzer, R., Cutler, A., Ballenger, J., Post, R., and Ketter, T. (2006) The use of antiepileptic drugs in bipolar disorders: A review based on evidence from controlled trials. *CNS Spectr*, **11**(10), 788–99.

Welch, M. (1989) Towards prevention of developmental disorders. *Pre and Peri Natal Psychology Journal*, **3**, 319–28.

Welch, S. (2007) Substance use and personality disorders. *Psychiatry*, **6**(1), 27–9.

Wellman, H., Baron-Cohen, S., Caswell, R., Gomez, J., Swettenham, J., Toye, E., and Lagattuta, K. (2002) Thought bubbles help children with autism acquire an alternative to a theory of mind. *Autism*, **6**(4), 343–63.

Wells, A. (1997) *Cognitive therapy for anxiety disorders: A practice manual and conceptual guide*. Chichester: Wiley.

Wells, A. (2009) *Metacognitive therapy for anxiety and depression*. London: Guilford Press.

Wells, A., and Dattilio, F. (1992) Negative outcomes in cognitive behavioural therapy: A case study. *Behavioural Psychotherapy*, **20**, 291–4.

Wells, B. (1973) *Psychedelic drugs: Psychological medical and social issues*. Harmondsworth: Penguin.

Welch, S. (2007) Substance use and personality disorders. *Psychiatry*, **6**(1), 27–9.

Welsh Assembly Government (2004) *Stronger in partnership*. Cardiff: Welsh Assembly Government.

Welte, J., Barnes, G., and Wieczorek, Q., Tidwell, M. C., and Parker, J. (2001) Alcohol and gambling pathology amongst US adults: Prevalence, demographic patterns and comorbidity. *Journal of Studies of Alcohol*, **62**, 706–12.

Wender, P. H., Rosenthal, D., Kety, S. S., Schlusinger, F., and Welner, J. (1974) Crossfostering: A research strategy for clarifying the role of genetic and experimental factors in the aetiology of schizophrenia. *Archives of General Psychiatry*, **31**, 121–8.

Wender, P., Wolf, L., and Wasserman, J. (2001) Adults with ADHD: An overview. *Annals of the New York Academy of Science*, **931**, 1–16.

West, D. J. (2000) The sex crime situation: Deterioration more apparent than real? *European Journal on Criminal Policy and Research*, **8**, 399–422.

Westen, D., Novotny, C., and Thompson-Brenner, H. (2004) The empirical status of empirically supported therapies: Assumptions, methods and findings. *Psychological Bulletin*, **130**, 631–63.

Westphal, J. R. (2007) Are the effects of gambling treatment overestimated? *International Journal of Mental Health and Addiction*, **5**(1), 65–79.

Wetherell, J. L., Maser, J. D., and van Balkom, A. (2005) Anxiety disorders in the elderly: Outdated beliefs and a research agenda. *Acta Psychiatrica Scandinavica*, **111**(6), 401–2.

Wettstein, R. (1998) *Treatment of offenders with mental disorders*. New York: Guilford Press.

Whalley, K. (2008) Neurodegenerative disease: Taking stock of grafts. *Nature Reviews Neuroscience*, **9**, 412–13.

Wheatcroft, J. M., Wagstaff, G. F., and Kebbell, M. R. (2004) The influence of courtroom questioning style on actual and perceived eyewitness confidence and accuracy. *Legal and Criminological Psychology*, **9**, 83–101.

Wheen, F. (2004) *How Mumbo-Jumbo Conquered the World*. New York: Perennial Press.

White, C., Stirling, J., Hopkins, R., Morris, J., Montague, L., Tantam, D., and Lewis, S. (2009) Predictors of ten year outcome of first episode psychosis, *Psychological Medicine*, **39**, 1–10.

White, J., and Lopatko, O. (2007) Opioid maintenance: A comparative review of pharmacological strategies. *Expert Opinion on Pharmacotherapy*, **8**(1), 1–11.

White, M. J., Spengler, P. M., Maugherman, A. S., Anderson, L. A., Cook, R. S., Nichols, C. N., Lampropoulus, G. K., Walker, B. S., Cohen, G., and Rush, J. D. (2006) The meta-analysis of clinical judgement project: Fifty-six years of accumulated research on clinical versus statistical prediction. *Counselling Psychologist*, **34**(3), 341–82.

White, W. (1914) Moon myth in medicine. *Psychoanalytic Review*, **3**, 241–56.

Whiteley, P., Rodgers, J., Savery, D., and Shattock, P. (1999) A gluten-free diet as an intervention for autism and associated spectrum disorders: Preliminary findings. *Autism*, **3**, 45–65.

Whitwell, F., and Barker, M. (1980) 'Possession' in psychiatric patients in Britain. *British Journal of Medical Psychology*, **53**(4), 287–95.

Widiger, T. (1991) Personality dimensional models proposed for the DSM-IV. *Journal of Personality Disorders*, **5**, 386–98.

Wigmore, J. (1909) Professor Munsterberg and the psychology of testimony. *Illinois Law Review*, **3**, 399–434.

Wijndaele, K., Matton, L., Duvigneaud, N., Lefevre, J., Bourdeaudhuij, I. D., Duquet, W., Thomis, M., and Philippaerts, R. M. (2007) Association between leisure time physical activity and stress, social support and coping: A cluster-analytical approach. *Psychology of Sport and Exercise*, **8**(4), 425–40.

Wilding, J. P. H. (2007) Treatment strategies for obesity. *Obesity Review*, **8** (suppl. 1), 137–44.

Wilie, K. R. (2006) Male sexual dysfunction. *Psychiatry*, **6**(3), 99–104.

Wilkinson, R. G. (2005) *The impact of inequality: How to make sick societies healthier*. London: Routledge.

Williams, A., and Thompson, W. (2004) Vigilance or vigilantes: The Paulsgrove riots and policing paedophiles in the community, Part II: The lessons of Paulsgrove. *Police Journal*, **77**, 193–205.

Williams, G., Power, K. G., Millar, H. R., Freeman, C. P., Yellowlees, A., Dowds, T., Walker, M., Campsie, L., Macpherson, F., and Jackson, M. A. (1993) Comparison of eating disorders and other dietary/weight groups on measures of perceived control, assertiveness, self-esteem and self-directed hostility. *International Journal of Eating Disorders*, **4**, 7–32.

Williams, H. C., Strachan, D. P., and Hay, R. J. (1994) Childhood eczema: Disease of the advantaged? *British Medical Journal*, **308**, 1132–5.

Williams, H. J., Glaser, B., Williams, N. M., Norton, N., Zammit, S., MacGregor, S., Kirov, G. K., Owen, M. J., and O'Donovan, M. C. (2005) No association between schizophrenia and polymorphisms in COMT in two large samples. *American Journal of Psychiatry*, **162**(9), 1736–8.

Williams, H. J., Owen, M. J., and O'Donovan, M. C. (2007) Is COMT a susceptibility gene for schizophrenia? *Schizophrenia Bulletin*, **33**(3), 635–41.

Williams, J. F., Storck, M., Committee on Substance Abuse and Committee on Native American Child Health (2007) Inhalant abuse. *Pediatrics*, **119**, 1009–17.

Williams, J. M., Watts, F. N., MacLeod, C., and Mathews, A. (1988) *Cognitive psychology and emotional disorders*. Chichester: Wiley.

Williams, K. S. (2001) *Textbook on criminology* (4th edn). Oxford: Oxford University Press.

Williams, L. E., and Bargh, J. A. (2008) Experiencing physical warmth promotes interpersonal warmth. *Science*, **322**, 606.

Williams, R. J., Goodale, L. A., Shay-Fiddler, M. A., Gloster, S. P., and Chang, S. Y. (2004) Methylphenidate and dextroamphetamine abuse in substance-abusing adolescents. *American Journal on Addictions*, **13**(4), 381–9.

Williamson, E. M., and Evans, F. J. (2000) Cannabinoids in clinical practice. *Drugs*, **60**(6), 1303–14.

Williamson, T. (1996) Police investigations – separating the false and genuine. *Medicine Science and the Law*, **36**, 135–40.

Wilson, E. O. (1975) *Sociobiology: The new synthesis*. Cambridge, MA: Harvard University Press.

Wilson, G. T., and Shafran, R. (2005) Eating disorder guidelines from NICE. *The Lancet*, **365**, 79–81.

Wilson, J. Q., and Herrnstein, R. S. (1985) *Crime and human nature*. New York: Simon and Schuster.

Wilson, J., and Tobacyk, J. (1990) Lunar phases and crisis centre telephone calls. *Journal of Social Psychology*, **130**, 47–51.

Wilson, R., Arnold, S., Schneider, J., Kelly, J., Tang, Y., and Bennett, D. (2008) Chronic distress and risk of Alzheimer's disease in old age. *Neuro-epidemiology*, **27**(3), 143–53.

Wimmer, H., and Perner, J. (1983) Beliefs about beliefs: Representations and constraining function of wrong beliefs in young children's understanding of deception. *Cognition*, **13**, 103–28.

Wincze, J. P., and Carey, M. P. (2001) *Sexual dysfunction: A guide for assessment and treatment*. London: Guilford Press.

Wing, L. (1981) Asperger's syndrome: A clinical account. *Psychological Medicine*, **11**, 115–29.

Wing, L. (1996) Autistic spectrum disorders: No evidence for or against increase in prevalence. *British Medical Journal*, **312**, 327–28.

Wing, L., and Gould, J. (1979) Severe impairments of social interaction and associated abnormalities in children: Epidemiology and classification. *Journal of Autism and Developmental Disorders*, **9**, 11–29.

Wing, L., and Potter, D. (2002) The epidemiology of autistic spectrum disorders: Is the prevalence rising? *Mental Retardation and Developmental Disabilities Research Reviews*, **8**, 151–61.

Wing, L., and Shah, A. (2000) Catatonia in autistic spectrum disorders. *British Journal of Psychiatry*, **176**, 357–62.

Wise, R. (1987) The neurobiology of craving: Implications for the understanding and treatment of addictions. *Journal of Abnormal Psychology*, **97**, 118–32.

Wiseman, R., West. D., and Stemman, R. (1996) An experimental test of psychic detection. *Journal of the Society for Psychical Research*, **61**, 34–45.

Witkin, H. A., Mednick, S. A., Schulsinger, F., Bakkstrøm, E., Chritiansen, K. O., Goodenough, D. R., Hirschorne, K., Lunsteen, C., Owen, D. R., Philip, J., Rubin, D. B., and Stocking, M. (1976) Criminality in XYY and XY men. *Science*, **193**, 547–55.

Witmer, L. (1907) Clinical psychology. *Psychological Clinic*, 1, 1–9.

Wittchen, H-U., and Fehm, L. (2003) Epidemiology and natural course of social fears and social phobia. *Acta Psychiatrica Scandinavica*, **108**(s417), 4–18.

Wolf-Schein, E. (1996) The autistic spectrum disorder: A current review. *Developmental Disabilities Bulletin*, **24**, 33–55.

Wolpe, J. (1958) *Psychotherapy by reciprocal inhibition*. Stanford, CA: Stanford University Press.

Wolpe, J. (1982) *The practice of behaviour therapy* (3rd edn). New York: Pergamon.

Wong, D. F., Wagner, H. N. Jr, Tune, L. E., Dannals, R. F., Pearlson, G. D., Links, J. M., Tamminga, C. A., Broussolle, E. P., Ravert, H. T., Wilson, A. A., Toung, J. K., Malat, J., Williams, J. A., O'Tuama, L. A., Snyder, S. H., Kuhar, M. J., and Gjedde, A. (1986) Positron emission tomography reveals elevated D_2 dopamine receptors in drug-naive schizophrenics. *Science*, **234**, 1558–62.

Wong, S. (1985) *Criminal and institutional behaviours of psychopaths*. Ottowa, Ontario: Programs Branch Users Report, Ministry of the Solicitor General of Canada.

Wong, S. (2000) Psychopathic offenders. In S. Hodgins and R. Müller-Ishberner, R. (eds), *Violence, crime and mentally disordered offenders: Concepts and methods for effective treatment*. Chichester: Wiley.

Wood, J. (1993) Reform of the Mental Health Act 1983: An effective tribunal system. *British Journal of Psychiatry*, **162**, 14–22.

Wood, J. (2006) Profiling high-risk offenders: A review of 136 cases. *Howard Journal*, **45**(3), 307–20.

Wood, M. (2007) Parenting practices and adolescent alcohol use. *Addiction*, **102**, 1019–20.

Woodbury-Smith, M. R., and Volkmar, F. R. (2008) Asperger syndrome. *European Child and Adolescent Psychiatry*, 18 June, [Epub ahead of print].

Woodruff, P. W., Wright, I. C., Bullmore, E. T., Brammer, M., Howard, R. J., Williams, S. C., Sharpleske, J., Rossell, S., David, A. S., McGuire, P. K., and Murray, R. M. (1997) Auditory hallucinations and the temporal cortical response to speech in schizophrenia: A functional magnetic resonance imaging study. *American Journal of Psychiatry*, **154**, 1676–82.

Wootton, B. (1959) *Social science and social pathology*. London: Allen and Unwin.

Wootton, B. (1962) A social scientist's approach to maternal deprivation. *Public Health Papers*, **14**, 63–73.

Wooton, L., and Fahy, T. (2006) Dangerous severe personality disorder: Beyond the ethical boundary of psychiatry? *Psychiatry*, **6**(2), 52–5.

World Health Organisation (1973) *The international pilot study of schizophrenia*. Geneva: WHO.

World Health Organisation (1992) *Tenth revision of the International Classification of Diseases*. Geneva: WHO.

World Health Organisation (1997). *Obesity: Preventing and managing the global epidemic*. Geneva: WHO.

World Health Organisation (2005) *Preventable suicide*. Geneva: WHO.

Wrangham, R. W., and Wilson, M. L. (2004) Collective violence: Comparisons between youths and chimpanzees. *Annals of the New York Academy of Science*, **1036**, 233–56.

Wright, C., Martis, B., McMullin, K., Shin, L., M., and Rauch, S. L. (2003) Amygdala and insular responses to emotionally valenced human faces in small animal specific phobia. *Biological Psychiatry*, **54**, 1067–76.

Wright, I. C., Rabe-Hesketh, S., Woodruff, P. W., David, A. S., and Murray, R. M. (2000) Meta-analysis of regional brain volumes in schizophrenia. *American Journal of Psychiatry*, **157**, 16–25.

Wright, J. (1993) Mania following sleep deprivation. *British Journal of Psychiatry*, **196**, 679–80.

Wright, R. J., Cohen, R. T., and Cohen, S. (2005) The impact of stress on the development and expression of atopy. *Current Opinion in Allergy and Clinical Immunology*, **5**(1), 23–9.

Wrightsman, L. (2001) *Forensic psychology*. Toronto: Wadsworth.

Wyatt, R. C. (2004) Thomas Szasz: Liberty and the practice of psychotherapy. *Journal of Humanistic Psychology*, **44**, 71–85.

Wykes, T., and Reeder, C. (2005) *Cognitive remediation therapy for schizophrenia: An introduction*. New York: Brunner-Routledge.

Wylie, K. (2007) Assessment and management of sexual problems in women. *Journal of the Royal Society of Medicine*, **100**, 547–50.

Yang, J., He, H. S., Shifley, S. R., and Gustafson, E. J. (2007) Spatial patterns of modern period human-caused fire occurrence in the Missouri Ozark Highlands. *Forest Science*, **53**(1), 1–15.

Yasuno, F., Suhara, T., Okubo, Y., Sudo, Y., Inoue, M., Ichimiya, T., Takano, A., Nakayama, K., Halldin, C., and Farde, L. (2004) Low dopamine D2 receptor binding in subregions of the thalamus in schizophrenia. *American Journal of Psychiatry*, **161**, 1016–22.

Yerkes, R. M., and Dodson, J. D. (1908) The relation of strength of stimulus to rapidity of habit-formation. *Journal of Comparative Neurology and Psychology*, **18**, 459–82.

Yochelson, S., and Samenow, S. E. (1976) *The criminal personality, Vol. 1: A profile for change*. New York: Jason Aronsen.

Yoder, K., Constantinescu, C. C., Kareken, D. A., Normandin, M. D., Cheng, T-E., O'Connor, S. J., and Morris, E. D. (2007) Heterogeneous effects of alcohol on dopamine release in the striatum: A PET Study. *Alcoholism: Clinical and Experimental Research*, **31**(6), 965–73.

Yorke, J., Fleming, S., and Shuldham, C. (2007) Psychological interventions for adults with asthma: A systematic review. *Respiritory Medicine*, **101**(1), 1–14.

Young, A., and Ferrier, I. N. (2006) Overview of treatment for mood disorders. *Psychiatry*, **5**(6), 183–4.

Young, K. S. (1996) Internet addiction: The emergence of a new clinical disorder. *CyberPsychology and Behaviour*, **1**(3), 237–44.

Young, S. (2007) Forensic aspects of ADHD. In M. Fitzgerald, M. Bellgrove and M. Gill (eds), *Handbook of attention deficit hyperactivity disorder*. London: Wiley.

Yücel, M., and Lubman, D. I. (2007) Neurocognitive and neuroimaging evidence of behavioural dysregulation in human drug addiction: Implications for diagnosis, treatment and prevention. *Drug and Alcohol Review*, **26**, 33–9.

Yücel, M., Lubman, D. I., Solowij, N., and Brewer, W. J. (2007) Understanding drug addiction: A neuropsychological perspective. *Australian and New Zealand Journal of Psychiatry*, **41**(12), 957–68.

Yuille, J., and Cutshall, J. (1986) A case study of eyewitness memory of a crime. *Journal of Applied Psychology*, **71**(2), 291–301.

Yung, A. R., Phillips, L. J., Yuen, H. P., Francey, S. M., McFarlane, C. A., Hallgren, M., and McGorry, P. D. (2003) Psychosis prediction: 12-month follow up of a high-risk ('prodromal') group, *Schizophrenia Research*, **60**(1), 21–3.

Zador, D. (2007) Methadone maintenance: Making it better. *Addiction*, **102**, 350–1.

Zammit, S., Allebeck, P., Andreasson, S., Lundberg, I., and Lewis, G. (2002) Self reported cannabis use as a risk factor for schizophrenia in Swedish conscripts of 1969: Historical cohort study. *British Medical Journal*, **325**(7374), 1199.

Zanarini, M., Frankenburg, F. R., Sickel, A. E., and Yong, L. (1996) *Diagnostic Interview for DSM-IV Personality Disorders*. Laboratory for the Study of Adult Development, McClean Hospital and the Department of Psychiatry, Harvard University.

Zarate, C. A., Tohen, M., and Land, M. L. (2000) First episode schizophreniform disorder: Comparisons with first-episode schizophrenia. *Schizophrenia Research*, **46**, 31–43.

Zeanah, C. (2000) Disturbances of attachment in young children adopted from institutions. *Journal of Developmental Behavioural Pediatrics*, **21**(3), 230–6.

Zeld, D., and Rauch, S. (2006) The orbitofrontal cortex. Oxford: Oxford University Press.

Zhou, J. N., Hofman, M. A., Gooren, L. J., and Swaab, D. F. (1995) Sex differences in the human brain and its relation to transsexuality. *Nature*, **378**, 68–70.

Zigman, J. M., and Elmquist, J. K. (2003) Minireview: From anorexia to obesity – the yin and yang of body weight control. *Endocrinology*, **144**(9), 3749–58.

Zigmond, T. (2004) New Mental Health Act for England and Wales. *Advances in Psychiatric Treatment*, **10**, 161–3.

Zilboorg, G., and Henry, G. (1941) *A history of medical psychology*. New York: Norton Press.

Zimmerman, G., Favrod, J., Trieu, V. H., and Pomini, V. (2005) The effect of cognitive behavioural treatment on the positive symptoms of schizophrenia spectrum disorders: A meta-analysis. *Schizophrenia Research*, **77**, 1–9.

Zipfel, S., Seibel, M., Lowe, B., Beumont, P., Kasperk, C., and Herzog, W. (2001) Osteoporosis in eating disorders: A follow-up study of patients with anorexia and bulimia nervosa. *Journal of Endocrinology and Metabolism*, **86**(11), 5227–33.

Zoellner, T., and Maercker, A. (2006) Posttraumatic growth in clinical psychology: A critical review and introduction to a two component model. *Clinical Psychology Review*, **26**, 626–53.

Zohar, A. H., Goldman, E., Calamary, R., and Mashiah, M. (2005) Religiosity and obsessive-compulsive behaviour in Israeli Jews. *Behaviour Research and Therapy*, **43**, 857–68.

Zola, S. M. (1998) Memory, amnesia and the issue of recovered memory: Neurobiological aspects. *Clinical Psychology Review*, **18**, 915–32.

Zoltan, R. (2007) Suicide risk in mood disorders. *Current Opinion in Psychiatry*, **20**(1), 17–22.

Zona, M., Lane, J., and Palaria, R. (1997) The psychodynamics of stalking. Paper presented at the Seventh Annual Threat Management Conference, Aug. Los Angeles, CA.

Zona, M., Sharma, K., and Lane, J. (1993) A comparative study of erotomanic and obsessional subjects in a forensic sample. *Journal of Forensic Sciences*, **38**, 894–903.

Zuardi, A. W., Crippa, J. A., Hallack, J. E., Moreira, F. A., and Guimares, F. S. (2006) Cannabidiol, a cannabis sativa constituent as an antipsychotic drug. *Brazilian Journal of Medical and Biological Research*, **39**(4), 421–9.

Zubieta, J. K., Bueller, J. A., Jackson, L. R., Scott, D. J., Xu, Y., Koeppe, R. A., Nichols, T. E., and Stohler, C. S. (2005) Placebo effects mediated by endogenous opioid activity on mu-opioid receptors. *Journal of Neuroscience*, **25**(34), 7754–62.

Zvolensky, M. J., Feldner, M. T., Leen-Feldner, E. W., and McLeish, A. C. (2005) Smoking and panic attacks, panic disorder and agoraphobia: A review of the empirical literature. *Clinical Psychology Review*, **25**, 761–89.

Index